# T H E
# GREEN
# Encyclopedia

# THE
# GREEN
# Encyclopedia

## Irene Franck and David Brownstone

Prentice Hall General Reference

New York    London    Toronto    Sydney    Tokyo    Singapore

PRENTICE HALL GENERAL REFERENCE
15 Columbus Circle
New York, New York 10023

Library of Congress Cataloging-in-Publication Data

Franck, Irene M.
    The green encyclopedia / Irene Franck and David
Brownstone.
        p.    cm.
    Includes bibliographical references.
    ISBN 0-13-365685-3 : ISBN 0-13-365677-2 (pbk)
    1. Environmental protection—Encyclopedias. 2. Nature
conservation—Encyclopedias. 3. Environmental law—
Encyclopedias.
    4. Environmental protection—Directories. 5. Nature conser-
vation—Directories. I. Brownstone, David M. II. Title.
TD9.F73   1992
363.7'003—dc20                          92-12240
                                            CIP

Designed by Richard Oriolo
Manufactured in the United States of America

First Edition

10  9  8  7  6  5  4  3  2  1

# Preface

As the modern environmental movement has grown, so has the need for a comprehensive guide to the issues, dangers, endangered species and endangered places, environmental disasters, people, philosophies, works, laws, and treaties that most concern environmentally-minded people—issues from *acid rain* and *air pollution* to *zebras* and *zoos*. This book aims to fill that need, by combining a clear, balanced entry outlining what is known, conjectured, and at issue regarding each matter discussed, with a good deal of additional material on sources of information and means of taking further action, if desired.

As the "green" movement has increasingly taken up many of the most pressing issues facing humanity today, concerned people have formed groups of every shape, size, and orientation on a host of environmental issues, to study, research, inform, educate, influence, persuade, mobilize, and take direct action on areas of shared concern. Of significant interest also are many government agencies charged with providing information and carrying through public policy and legislation. Because these private organizations and public agencies are so important to the environmental movement, we have chosen to focus as heavily on them as on the substantive matters discussed in this book, with many organizations and agencies being treated as major "subjects" in the A-Z encyclopedia and others being directly appended to key topics.

Note that, for many entries, sources of information and action appear directly following the entry, but for the most major concerns they are presented in separately boxed *Information and Action Guides*. The organizations are se-

lected from among those that have signaled their interest in the topic by their programs and publications. Indeed, publications from environmental organizations provide some of the best popular sources of information and action on green issues, but are often extremely hard to find, since many such works do not appear in the normal library or books-in-print sources. *The Green Encyclopedia* includes only a selection of the most recent materials available on these topics; these organizations have far more publications than appear here, and libraries will also have many other books on each such topic. Readers who are planning to join one or more groups on issues that concern them will find that descriptions of a group's publications and programs can help them find which organizations are most congenial to their own ideas and approaches. Also note that the list of organizations is necessarily selective; many other organizations, including many with a highly restricted or regional focus, can be found in general environmental directories such as those listed in the Green Bookshelf on page 480.

For ease of use, *The Green Encyclopedia* has a network of internal cross-references, with small capital letters—such as ACID RAIN—being used to indicate that a stand-alone entry exists on that topic. These guide readers to entries and other special information on topics of related interest. For some references, page numbers are provided, as to boxed material (including organizations that appear only in boxed *Information and Action Guides*) and material in the book's Special Information Section. This section, an index for which is given on page 361, includes a list of endangered wildlife and plants; lists of toxic chemicals and hazardous substances, and their known health effects; a list of Superfund sites; lists of internationally important wetlands, biosphere reserves, and world natural heritage sites; an environmental alphabet (a guide to the acronyms and abbreviations of the environmental movement); and a Green Bookshelf, including general environmental works and also a selection of recent environmentally oriented books for children.

The result is, we think, a unique book. We mean it to be useful for a wide spectrum of readers, from those just beginning their involvement with environmental concerns to seasoned and sophisticated environmentalists.

Many people from organizations and agencies around the world were enormously helpful and generous in answering our questions and sending us information about their activities and publications. Our thanks go to all of them. Though we do not have the space to mention them all by name, we would be remiss if we did not acknowledge the special help of Dale Adams of the Environmental Law Institute, Thomas Hawkins of the National Institute of Environmental Health Sciences, Joan Poling of the Johns Hopkins Center for Alternatives to Animal Testing, Carol Beale of the Center for Environmental Information, Sandy Marsh of the Morrison Institute for Population and Resources Studies, Thomas Bigford of the Coastal Society, Claudie Grout of the Environmental Hazards Management Institute, Al Utton of the International Transboundary Resources Center, Dave Cheney of the Sustainable Agriculture Program at the University of California at Davis, Lyra Halperin of the Agroecology Program of the University of California at Santa Cruz, Yvonne Spaltoff of the Elm Research Institute, Tom Hall of the U.S. Department of Energy's Office of Conservation and Renewable Energy, Carol McDonnell of the Bureau of Land Management, Linda Bennett of the Center for Marine Conservation, Patty Yoxall of Ducks Unlimited, Elliot Gruber of the National Parks and Conservation Association, Cindy Whittaker of The Nature Conservancy, Deborah Gangloff of the American Forestry Association, Linda Shotwell of the Friends of the United Nations Environment Programme, Elizabeth Kelpinski of the Rails-to-Trails Conservancy, Marge Barnacle of the Rodale Institute, John Victor of Sanctuary Travel Services, Bill Whittington of the SARA/Title III and Emergency Planning and Community Right-to-Know Hotline, Lucy Peets of the Scientists' Institute for Public Information, Cindy Clark of the Scripps Institute, Susan Jacobsen of the Society for Conservation Biology, Connie Bland of the Society of American Foresters, Sonya Varley of the Tropical Resources Institute, Diane O'Connor of the U.S. Department of Agriculture, David Blanton of Voyagers International, Noreen Kennedy of the World Environment Center, Anne Browne of the World Forestry Center, and Jeffrey Jones of the World Wildlife Fund—U.S.

Thanks also to our editor Kate Kelly and her assistant Susan Lauzau for their interest and support. And special thanks, as always, to the librarians who help us gain access to vital sources of information, especially the many who are involved in the interlibrary loan system and those who work at the Chappaqua Library, including director Mark Hasskarl; the expert reference staff, including Martha Alcott, Teresa Cullen, Carolyn Jones, Paula Peyraud, Mary Platt, and Alice Smith; and Marilyn Coleman, Lois Siwicki, Jane McKean, and the rest of the circulation staff.

IRENE FRANCK
DAVID BROWNSTONE
CHAPPAQUA, NEW YORK

# THE
# GREEN
# Encyclopedia

# A

**Abbey, Edward** (1927–1989), U.S. radical environmentalist and author, whose work provided an anarchist-oriented basis for people eager to take direct, often illegal action in pursuit of environmentalist goals. His thinking considerably influenced Dave FOREMAN and other leaders of EARTH FIRST!, among others. Their MONKEYWRENCHING techniques were inspired by Abbey's best-known novel, *The Monkey Wrench Gang* (1975), which tells the story of a group of direct action environmentalists who plan to blow up the highly controversial GLEN CANYON DAM. Abbey's sequel to that book was the posthumously published *Hayduke Lives!* (1990).

**acaricides,** a type of compound used for killing members of the *Acarina* and *Arachnidae* family, such as mites, ticks, and spiders (see PESTICIDES).

**acceptable daily intake (ADI),** the maximum amount of a subtance that—in the judgment of those setting the standards—humans can take daily without lifetime risk; an amount set by government or government-sponsored testing organizations, often the subject of considerable controversy by those alleging that the levels are too high for human safety (see TOLERANCE LEVEL).

**acid rain,** atmospheric water that has picked up acidic particles from the air, reacted with them to form acids, then fallen to earth as rain, snow, or other precipitation; in more precise chemical terms, rain that has a pH below 5.6. The result, sometimes as acidic as lemon juice or vinegar, is harmful to both living and nonliving things, the most obvious effects being dead or crippled lakes,

withered and dying FORESTS (what the Germans call *Waldsterben*, or tree death), and sharply increased weathering of monuments and other buildings.

Acid rain is not a new phenomenon, nor does it result solely from industrial pollution. Acid particles are released into the air from natural processes, such as volcanic eruptions and forest fires, and from other nonindustrial activities, such as burning forests to clear the land in Africa or South America. But the industrial explosion of the last century and a half has dwarfed other contributions to the problem.

The main culprits are emissions of SULFUR DIOXIDE, largely from the industrial burning of FOSSIL FUELS, such as COAL and OIL, and nitrogen oxide, formed mostly from automobile emissions, which is readily transformed into NITROGEN DIOXIDE. These mix with water in the atmosphere to form sulfuric acid and nitric acid. Industrial and natural processes also produce smaller amounts of other acids. In the northeastern United States, for example, about 65 percent of the acid in rain is sulfuric acid, about 30 percent nitric acid, and 5 percent hydrocholoric acid. Carried aloft on air currents, acid rain is sometimes deposited as much as 2,500 miles away from the source of the particles.

Earth's ECOSYSTEMS can deal with a certain amount of acid through natural "buffers," alkaline substances in soil or rocks that neutralize acid. Areas with highly alkaline soil, such as the American Midwest, or those laid on beds of limestone or sandstone, as in southern England, have some natural protection. However, areas with thin soil and those laid on granite rock have little ability to neutralize

MEASURING ACIDITY--pH SCALE

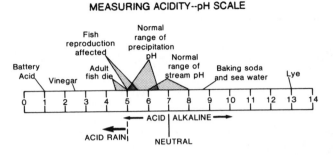

**Source:** "Water Fact Sheet." U.S. Geological Survey, Department of the Interior, 1987.

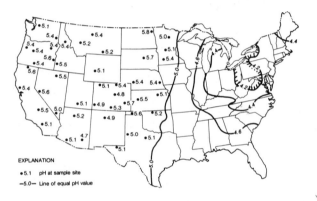

EXPLANATION
- 5.1   pH at sample site
- —5.0— Line of equal pH value

**Source:** "Water Fact Sheet." U.S. Geological Survey, Department of the Interior, 1987.

the acid rain. Unfortunately, many such areas are in the direct path of the heaviest concentrations of acid rain and therefore are among the world's worst affected areas, including the northeastern United States and Canada, Scandinavia, Scotland, and much of Central Europe. Acid can be especially destructive when concentrated, as during spring runoff, when both animals and plants are starting a new life cycle, or after a massive volcanic eruption or seasonal forest-burning.

The damage done by acid rain is varied and complex, and scientists continue to study precisely how living beings are damaged and killed. In LAKES, the smaller organisms often die off first, leaving the larger animals to starve to death. Sometimes the larger animals, such as fish, are killed directly; as lake water becomes more acidic, it dissolves HEAVY METALS such as MERCURY, MANGANESE, LEAD, zinc, and especially ALUMINUM, leading to concentrations at toxic and often lethal levels. Loss of life in

lakes also disrupts the system of life on the land and in the air around them.

Forests and crops, too, are affected in complex ways. Acid rain leaches vital nutrients, such as potassium, calcium, and magnesium, directly out of the leaves and needles of trees, as well as from the roots. As in lakes, metals become concentrated in the soil, sometimes to levels toxic to beneficial microbes in the soil, disrupting the processes by which fungi and bacteria break down organic matter so that the trees can gain necessary nutrients (see BIOGEO-CHEMICAL CYCLES). These and other destructive effects weaken trees and make them more susceptible to disease and damage from cold.

Effects on humans and other land life have been identified even less precisely, but widespread and varied negative effects can clearly be expected from breathing air containing acidic moisture, drinking groundwater contaminated by acid and high levels of dissolved heavy metals, and being at the end of a FOOD CHAIN, reaping the concentrated effects of acid rain on both plants and animals used for food (see BIOACCUMULATION). Some of the effects on humans may also be surmised from the increased weathering of buildings and other monuments, from Greece's Parthenon to the tombstones at Gettysburg, and from the rapid corrosion of water pipes and cooking utensils in areas with highly acidic groundwater. In southwest Sweden, blonde hair has sometimes even been turned green from excess dissolved COPPER in the water. The NATIONAL ACID PRECIPITATION ASSESSMENT PROGRAM (NAPAP), begun in 1980, is researching the effects that have so far been experienced by the lakes, rivers, and forests in the United States.

Despite publicly expressed concern, actual attempts to deal with the problem of acid rain have been minimal, at best. Some countries, notably Sweden, but also elsewhere in Europe, have tried spreading lime (an alkaline subtance) on lakes and forests, to bolster their buffering ability. And German scientists have found that at least some damaged trees can be helped by using fertilizer containing some of the vital metals lost through leaching.

But the only long-term solution is to limit the amount of acidic particles sent into the atmosphere. Sulfur dioxide emissions can be reduced in a variety of ways:

- **Switch from coal or oil to natural gas.** Natural gas contains very little sulfur; however, new furnaces are a substantial expense, and all these fuels are declining resources.
- **Switch to low-sulfur coal or oil.** These require no new furnaces, but cost considerably more and are also declining resources.

- **Add SCRUBBERS or CATALYTIC CONVERTERS to smokestacks.** These devices remove much of the sulfur dioxide or convert emissions into harmless substances, but are expensive and require careful installation and maintenance to work properly.
- **Conserve energy.** This both reduces emissions and saves declining resources, and savings may cover the cost for other modifications, but conservation alone cannot solve the problem.
- **Use ALTERNATIVE ENERGY sources.** This is, of course, the best long-term solution, but developing new energy sources (such as SOLAR ENERGY) requires money, which both government and industry have been reluctant to provide, and some alternatives (such as NUCLEAR ENERGY) carry major environmental problems of their own.

The problem of sulfur dioxide is complicated by the fact that emissions cross international boundaries and are deposited as acid rain in other countries. International cooperation is required, but so far little has been forthcoming. In 1979, various European countries signed the CONVENTION ON LONG-RANGE TRANSBOUNDARY AIR POLLUTION (LRTAP), ratified in 1983 and stating intentions only. Chafing at the slow pace, Norway, Sweden, Canada, and several other countries, mostly victims of acid rain, formed the 30 Per Cent Club, whose members pledged to reduce sulfur dioxide emissions by 30 percent in 1993. Some major producers of acid rain, including the United States and the United Kingdom, were not members of the club, but its target was adopted by the LRTAP in 1985. In 1991, the United States and Canada signed an agreement to reduce sulfur dioxide and nitrogen oxide emissions.

Nitrogen oxide emissions, which come mostly from automobile exhaust, can also be reduced by using catalytic converters and alternative fuels or energy sources. But, as in any area of industry, such changes cost money, which reduces profits and makes firms less competitive. Because of this, modifications generally occur only when required by government or when products are so widely recognized as environmentally sound that consumers will pay higher prices for them. Though alternative fuel sources have had little public support, U.S., Japanese, and some German carmakers now build catalytic converters into new cars. Few other countries, industrialized or not, have so far followed suit, but members of the European Community (EC) have pledged to do so by 1995. (See ACID RAIN INFORMATION AND ACTION GUIDE on page 4; see also AIR POLLUTION).

**Acid Rain Foundation** (1410 Varsity Drive, Raleigh, NC 27606; 919-828-9443; Harriett S. Stubbs, Executive Director), an international organization founded in 1981 to promote awareness, understanding, education, and research in relation to ACID RAIN, AIR POLLUTION, and other problems affecting air quality. The Foundation maintains a speakers bureau, expert referral services, a library, and a computerized information retrieval system. It also publishes *Acid Rain Resources Directory*, and other directories, bibliographies, information packets, references lists, and curriculum materials on acid rain.

**active ingredient (AI),** the specific part of a mixture that leads to the desired result; in a PESTICIDE, for example, the compound that actually kills an unwanted insect, as opposed to the other presumably inert ingredients (such as water) that are used to facilitate delivery or to stabilize the mixture.

**Adamson, Joy Gessner** (1910–80) and **George Adamson** (1906–89), Kenya-based naturalists, whose work with Kenyan wildlife attracted worldwide attention. Austrian-born Joy Gessner, then primarily a painter, went to Kenya in 1937. She and Kenyan game warden George Adamson married in 1944. In 1956 they adopted a female lion cub they named Elsa, which they sent back into the wild hundreds of miles away in 1958. They found Elsa unable to survive well and moved her closer to their camp, where she continued to live in the wild and had cubs of her own, often visiting the camp with the offspring.

Joy Adamson wrote three tremendously popular books about Elsa and her cubs: *Born Free* (1960) and *Living Free* (1961), which were made into films, and *Forever Free* (1963). Virginia McKenna and Bill Travers played the Adamsons in the popular 1966 film of *Born Free;* Susan Hampshire and Nigel Davenport portrayed the Adamsons in the 1972 film version of *Living Free*. The Adamsons continued to raise cubs and free them in the wild. One was a cheetah cub they named Pippa, the subject of two books by Joy Adamson: *The Spotted Sphinx* (1970) and *Pippa's Challenge* (1972). Through their work, the Adamsons made a substantial contribution to the worldwide campaign to save threatened and ENDANGERED SPECIES that was beginning to take hold in the 1960s. The ELSA WILD ANIMAL APPEAL was directly inspired by their work.

Some critics of the Adamsons' approach felt that predatory animals raised in captivity and then freed would become hunters of humans, and one lion raised in captivity, which the Adamsons named Boy, did later attack humans. The Kenyan government withdrew its support of the Adamsons' work in 1980.

Joy Adamson was murdered in 1980, during a dispute with an employee about wages. George Adamson, who

## Acid Rain Information and Action Guide

**For more information and action on acid rain:**

ACID RAIN FOUNDATION, (919-828-9443). Publishes numerous directories, bibliographies, information packets, reference lists, curriculum materials on acid rain, and brochures, including "Air Pollution and Forest Decline: Is There a Link?" (1990) and "The Air Around Us: An Air Pollution Primer" (1989).

AIR AND WASTE MANAGEMENT ASSOCIATION (A&WMA), (412-232-3444).

AMERICAN COUNCIL FOR AN ENERGY EFFICIENT ECONOMY (ACEEE), (202-429-8873). Publishes *Acid Rain and Electricity Conservation.*

AMERICAN PLANNING ASSOCIATION (APA), (202-872-0611). Publishes *Acid Rain: Industrial Pollution* (1988).

CENTER FOR ENVIRONMENTAL INFORMATION (CEI), (716-546-3796). Publishes the monthly *Acid Precipitation Digest* and numerous proceedings, study guides, and bibliographies.

ENVIRONMENTAL DEFENSE FUND (EDF), (212-505-2100). Publishes $CO_2$ *and* $SO_2$: *Consistent Policy Making in a Greenhouse* (D. Dudek et al., 1990) and *Polluted Coastal Waters: The Role of Acid Rain* (D. Fisher et al., 1988).

ENVIRONMENTAL PROTECTION AGENCY (EPA), (202-260-7751 or 202-260-2080).

INFORM, INC., (212-689-4040).

KIDS FOR SAVING EARTH™ (KSE), (612-525-0002 or 800-800-8800.)

NATIONAL AUDUBON SOCIETY, (212-832-3200; Audubon Action Line, 202-547-9017). Maintains the Citizens Acid Rain Monitoring Network and Audubon Activist Network.

NATIONAL PARKS AND CONSERVATION ASSOCIATION (NPCA), (202-944-8530).

NATURAL RESOURCES AND ENERGY DIVISION (NRED), UNITED NATIONS, (212-963-6205).

SIERRA CLUB, (415-776-2211 or 202-547-1141; legislative hotline, 202-547-5550). Recent campaigns include the Clean Air Act Authorization. Publishes *A Killing Rain, Acid Rain Policy,* and *Toxic Air Pollutants Policy.*

SOIL AND WATER CONSERVATION SOCIETY OF AMERICA (SWCS), (515-289-2331 or 800-THE-SOIL [843-7645]).

U.S. PUBLIC INTEREST RESEARCH GROUP (PIRG), (202-564-9707).

WILDLIFE MANAGEMENT INSTITUTE (WMI), (202-371-1808).

WORLD RESOURCES INSTITUTE (WRI), (202-638-6300).

**Other references:** *Acid Rain.* Mary Turck. Macmillan, 1990. *Acid Rain.* Gail Stewart. Lucent, 1990. *Air Pollution, Acid Rain and the Environment.* K. Mellanby, ed. Elsevier, 1989. *Air Pollution and Acid Rain: The Biological Impact.* Alan Wellburn. Wiley, 1988.

---

had retired as a game warden in 1963, lived until 1989, when he and two of his assistants were murdered by bandits.

**Addo Elephant National Park,** an ELEPHANT preserve in South Africa's Cape Province; its 111,000 acres (173 square miles) are the home of over 100 cape elephants, an ENDANGERED SPECIES decimated and nearly destroyed by 19th-century ivory hunters. Also in the fenced-in preserve are cape buffalo and several kinds of antelopes, smaller animals, and a wide range of plants. (See WILDLIFE REFUGE.)

**Adriatic Sea,** a 500-mile-long, shallow arm of the MEDITERRANEAN SEA, averaging only approximately 100 miles in width (varying from 60 to 140 miles wide). Bordered by Italy to the west and Yugoslavia and Albania to the east, the Adriatic is plagued by the same toxic and nontoxic waste problems that have in recent decades made the Mediterranean so inhospitable to life. But the narrow Adriatic, a virtually closed system that takes the heavy, polluted flow of the Po River, is even more vulnerable than the Mediterranean to the kinds of nontoxic algal

blooms that struck it in the summers of 1988 and 1989, leaving the sea near Venice and for hundreds of miles south of Trieste with greatly inadequate oxygen supplies and seriously threatening the remaining fish and shellfish populations. (See OCEANS.)

**Advance Technology Alert System (ATAS),** an arm of the United Nation's CENTER FOR SCIENCE AND TECHNOLOGY FOR DEVELOPMENT (CSTD), designed to "provide third world nations with technology assessment and forecasting services in fields ranging from biotechnology to satellite communications."

**African Wildlife Foundation (AWF)** (1717 Massachusetts Avenue NW, Washington, DC; 202-265-8393 or 800-344-TUSK [8875]; Paul D. Schindler, Director; field office: P.O. Box 48177, Nairobi, Kenya 23235), an international organization, founded in 1961, working to save Africa's natural resources. The AWF has founded two colleges of wildlife management in Africa, training professional rangers and wardens for African parks and reserves and also aiding them with equipment, such as radios and vehicles, needed to work against poaching. The organization gives special attention to saving the ELEPHANT, black RHINOCEROS and mountain GORILLA. It also carries out conservation education through youth hostels, education centers, and wildlife clubs, and through its quarterly *Wildlife News*, as well as conducting African safaris.

**afterburner,** a device to rid air of pollutants by incinerating them. The device is placed after an existing INCINERATION device, to burn off remaining products of incomplete combustion, such as ORGANIC COMPOUNDS. (See AIR POLLUTION.)

**Agent Orange,** a type of PESTICIDE; a chemical compound used as a defoliant, most notoriously during the Vietnam War, when it was sprayed to reduce jungle cover that might shelter North Vietnamese troops. It was formed by a 50–50 mixture of 2,4,5-T and 2,4-D, both *phenoxy herbicides* long thought to be nontoxic to humans. While 2,4-D is still widely used (though its safety is now more widely questioned), 2,4,5-T was banned in the United States in 1985, since it was found to cause cancer and birth defects and to be toxic to unborn babies. It also was commonly contaminated with DIOXIN. Though the scientific evidence as to the toxicity of Agent Orange was sufficient to have the ENVIRONMENTAL PROTECTION AGENCY (EPA) in 1979 withdraw it from the market in the United States, many soldiers who were exposed to Agent Orange and experienced the above problems (as well as *chloracne*, the disfiguring skin condition associated with dioxin) were for years denied recompense. U.S. veterans had protracted lawsuits against their government and the chemical's manufacturers, only in the mid-1980s winning an out-of-court settlement establishing a compensation fund, but with companies admitting no liability. In Australia, Vietnam veterans were denied even that, as a Royal Commission ruled that Agent Orange did not cause adverse health effects among the claimants. (See PESTICIDES.)

**agroecology,** an interdisciplinary field of study focusing on applying ecological principles—such as BIOGEOCHEMICAL CYCLES, energy conservation, and BIOLOGICAL DIVERSITY—to the design and management of agricultural systems and on their interrelationships with the biological, economic, political, and social systems of the wider world. Research in agroecology is key to INTEGRATED PEST MANAGEMENT, in developing ways to reduce reliance on PESTICIDES by applying methods suited to the environment as a whole, and to SUSTAINABLE AGRICULTURE, which can be carried on over the long term without undue reliance on pesticides and fertilizers. (See SUSTAINABLE AGRICULTURE.)

**agroforestry,** the use of techniques from both agriculture and forestry to increase the total productivity of an area. In an approach that combines traditional practice with modern scientific knowledge, woody plants—both trees and shrubs—are cultivated in areas also used for agricultural purposes Trees are used to provide shade; to shelter natural enemies of crop pests; to reduce EROSION; to help retain water; to lessen ENVIRONMENTAL DEGRADATION as through DEFORESTATION and OVERGRAZING; to provide fuelwood (see BIOMASS) and wood for construction and fences; to provide food for humans, such as fruits and nuts; to provide food for livestock; to provide products such as fibers and materials for dyes, medicines, and cosmetics; and to provide vital nutrients, notably nitrogen, for the land.

Trees and crops may be grown together, in the *agro-silvicultural* approach. The trees themselves may be the prime crop, with livestock pastured in the area, in the *silvo-pastoral* approach; often specifically selected crops are grown between rows of trees, in a practice called *intercropping*. Sometimes trees, crops, and livestock are all raised on the same plot, in the *agro-silvo-pastoral* approach. In some parts of the world, poor farmers often have the short-term right to grow crops in FOREST plantations, meanwhile helping to tend the tree seedlings, until the trees are tall enough to shade out the crops; this practice is called *taungya* in Burma and appears in other countries under different names.

Widely used in the Third World, agroforestry is an alternative to the slash-and-burn approach of *swidden agriculture* or *shifting cultivation* in which forests are cleared, dried, and burned; used for crops for several years; and then abandoned to rejuvenate as forest. This ancient swidden approach has been responsible for much of the world's recent deforestation, as a rapidly rising POPULATION has sought new lands to clear and as farmers have been driven to reclear forests before they have fully rejuvenated. Many international agencies have therefore been funding agroforestry and community forestry projects, especially in heavily populated areas with soil and rainfall suitable for tree-growing. Agroforestry is used primarily where farmers have rights to the land and are not just tenants, and so have incentive for long-term protection of trees.

**For more information and action:**

- NITROGEN FIXING TREE ASSOCIATION (NFTA), (808-956-7985).
- TROPICAL RESOURCES INSTITUTE, (203-432-5116).
- WINROCK INTERNATIONAL INSTITUTE FOR AGRICULTURAL DEVELOPMENT, (501-727-5435).
- WORLD BANK, (202-477-1234).

(See also FORESTS; EDGE EFFECT; BIOFUEL; BIOLOGICAL CONTROL.)

## Air and Waste Management Association (A&WMA)

(H3W Gateway Building, Pittsburgh, PA 15222; 412-232-3444; mailing address: P.O. Box 2861, Pittsburgh, PA 15230; Martin E. Rivers, Executive Vice President), an international membership organization for environment management professionals in over 50 countries, though primarily in North America. It was founded in 1907 as the International Association for the Prevention of Smoke, changing its name several times to reflect changes in its members' interests, most recently (before 1988) known as (the Air Pollution Control Association (APCA). The A&WMA aims to provide "a neutral forum where all viewpoints of an environmental management issue (technical, scientific, economic, social, political and public health) receive equal consideration." Its main areas of concern are air pollution control, environmental management, and waste processing and control; its board is set up to have an equal number of members from industry, government agencies, and academic, research, or consulting organizations, so "that no one segment dominates the Association's programs and activites."

The Association holds an annual meeting and exhibition, as well as numerous specialty conferences, workshops, seminars, section and chapter meetings, and continuing education courses throughout the year. It also publishes numerous materials, including the peer-reviewed scientific monthly, *Journal of the Air & Waste Management Association*, the bimonthly newsletter, *News & Views, A Dictionary of Air Pollution Terms*, the annual *Directory and Resource Book*, and the annual *Government Agencies Directory*; books such as *Combustion Processes and the Quality of the Indoor Environment* (1989), *Environmental Challenges in Energy Utilization During the 1990s* (1989), and *Managing Asbestos in Schools, Public, Commercial and Retail Buildings* (1989); and numerous training manuals, videotapes, technical papers, and reprints.

**air pollution,** a concentration of substances in the atmosphere that may interfere with environmental health. "Pure" air consists of a little under 21 percent oxygen, a little over 78 percent nitrogen, and small amounts of CARBON DIOXIDE, argon, and other elements; water vapor is also present to some degree. Everything else is considered a contaminant. Almost any substance is capable of polluting the air if it is light enough—and in the case of solids, in small enough pieces—to be airborne.

Air pollutants may be gases, liquid droplets, solid particles (see PARTICULATE MATTER), or a combination of these. Many of these come from *point sources*, or *stationary sources*, identifiable and immovable sites such as industrial plants, municipal plants, or mines, but a very large proportion comes from *nonpoint sources*, also called *mobile sources*, meaning that the sources are many, various, movable, and often individually small, such as automobile EMISSIONS, aerosol cans, smoke from wood fires, or dust blown from eroding fields. Among the most problematic of air pollutants are OZONE, particulate matter, CARBON MONOXIDE, SULFUR DIOXIDE, LEAD, NITROGEN DIOXIDE—in the United States all called *criteria air pollutants*—and hazardous air pollutants such as ASBESTOS, beryllium, MERCURY, VINYL CHLORIDE, arsenic, radionuclides, benzene, and coke oven emissions. In the United States, all of these are regulated under the CLEAN AIR ACT (CAA), and regulation of many more is scheduled to be phased in during the 1990s, under the 1990 amendments to the Act. (For a list of those air pollutants covered, see TOXIC CHEMICALS AND HAZARDOUS SUBSTANCES on page 407.) Other common air pollutants include CHLORINATED HYDROCARBONS, ORGANOPHOSPHATES, fluorides, and HYDROCHLOROFLUOROCARBONS.

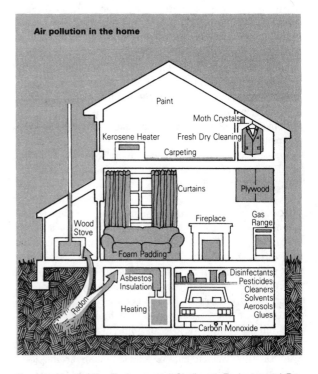

**Source:** *Meeting the Environmental Challenge.* Environmental Protection Agency, 1990.

## Do You Have Indoor Air Pollution?

If you think you have a problem with indoor air pollution, you should first consult a physician. Then you may want to monitor the air inside your home to determine the source. The Federal Government recommends that all residents measure the levels of radon in their homes. Researchers have developed techniques to monitor levels of indoor pollution, but most are expensive and sophisticated. There are, however, a few passive devices for monitoring levels in homes that are inexpensive and easy to use.

Passive monitors are available for radon, formaldehyde, nitrogen dioxide, and water vapor. You can install one of these devices and leave it in your home to detect certain pollutants. Over time, you will need to send the device to a laboratory to be analyzed. Monitors for each pollutant, with laboratory analysis, cost between $15 and $50. Organizations such as the American Society of Heating, Refrigerating, and Air Conditioning Engineers (ASHRAE, 191 Tullie Circle NE, Atlanta, GA 30329), the World Health Organization (WHO, Publications Center, 49 Sheridan Avenue, Albany, NY 12210), and the American Council of Govermental and Industrial Hygienists (6500 Glenway Avenue, Building D-7, Cincinnati, OH 45211) can offer guidance as to what levels of indoor air pollution may be harmful to your health.

**Source:** "Residential Indoor Air Pollution." Conservation and Renewable Energy Inquiry and Referral Service, U.S. Department of Energy, 1989.

---

Some air pollutants react together chemically, the best-known interaction being the *photochemical reaction* that takes place when nitrogen oxide (mostly from automobile exhaust), HYDROCARBONS and other ORGANIC COMPOUNDS mix in the air in the presence of sunshine, which triggers the creation of toxic nitrogen dioxide and ozone. It is this reaction that is at the heart of the formation of SMOG, the notoriously murky, irritating, and sometimes immediately dangerous form of air pollution.

Because it affects the very air we breathe, air POLLUTION is the concern of everyone, not simply those who think of themselves as environmentalists. The damage done by air pollution is increasingly well documented. In humans, the effects generally center on the eyes and respiratory tract, though airborne toxic substances all have their own particular effects, with some causing cancer, birth defects, danger to unborn babies, and other serious problems. (For more information, see HEALTH EFFECTS OF THE REGULATED AIR POLLUTANTS on page 8; see also the tables associated with UNFINISHED BUSINESS: A COMPARATIVE ASSESSMENT OF ENVIRONMENTAL PROBLEMS, which ranks 31 environmental problem areas, including criteria air pollutants, hazardous air pollutants, indoor air pollution, and radon). Other life—both plants and animals—is also affected, directly from breathing polluted air and also indirectly from contact with the ACID RAIN that forms when compounds in the air react with water to form acids that then rain down on the whole environment. In plants, leaves—and therefore the ability to carry on PHOTOSYNTHESIS—are damaged, especially mature leaves in moist conditions.

Not all air pollution stems from industrial activity. The slash-and-burn approach to clearing FORESTS in Third World countries contributes significantly, as do natural events such as volcanic eruptions. The trend back to wood-burning stoves, after the energy crisis of the 1970s, also brought with it a surprising amount of air pollution, both indoors and out. Nature has other air pollutants, too, in the form of pollens, spores, fungi, and dust, all of which can prove exceedingly irritating. And a 1991 study found that a significant amount of air pollution—especially of particulate matter small enough to be inhaled, and also PESTICIDES and other hazardous substances—comes from the surprising source of broiling meat, both by restaurants and on backyard barbecues.

Whatever the source, the combination of air pollutants produces a haze that circles the globe, significantly reducing visibility in places such as the Arctic and the Great Smoky Mountains, far from industrial centers. In industrial centers, or areas immediately downwind, the haze is consistently so heavy that many people no longer recognize it as such—though they may routinely have 40 percent less visibility than was once normal. Haze also has the capacity to lower temperature noticeably for a time, as has happened in the wake of some extremely large earthquakes, such as Krakatoa or (to a lesser extent) Mt. St. Helen's, or more locally in Kuwait during the PERSIAN GULF WAR ENVIRONMENTAL DISASTERS.

Concentration of pollutants also varies widely. Some areas tend to trap layers of pollution-laden air (see INVERSION); others are primary pollutant-producing areas. Many communities around the world measure levels of the major local pollutants and, by comparing them with the desired levels, come up with an *Air Pollution Index*. In the United

## Health Effects of the Regulated Air Pollutants

| Criteria Pollutants | Health Concerns | Hazardous Air Pollutants | Health Concerns |
|---|---|---|---|
| Ozone | Respiratory tract problems such as difficult breathing and reduced lung function. Asthma, eye irritation, nasal congestion, reduced resistance to infection, and possibly premature aging of lung tissue. | Asbestos | A variety of lung diseases, particularly lung cancer. |
| | | Beryllium | Primarily lung disease, although also affects liver, spleen, kidneys, and lymph glands. |
| Particulate matter | Eye and throat irritation, bronchitis, lung damage, and impaired visibility. | Mercury | Several areas of the brain as well as the kidneys and bowels affected. |
| Carbon monoxide | Ability of blood to carry oxygen impaired; cardiovascular, nervous, and pulmonary systems affected. | Vinyl chloride | Lung and liver cancer. |
| | | Arsenic | Cancer. |
| | | Radionuclides | Cancer. |
| Sulfur dioxide | Respiratory tract problems; permanent harm to lung tissue. | Benzene | Leukemia. |
| | | Coke oven emissions | Respiratory cancer. |
| Lead | Retardation and brain damage, especially in children. | | |
| Nitrogen dioxide | Respiratory illness and lung damage. | | |

**Source:** *Environmental Progress and Challenges: EPA's Update.* Environmental Protection Agency, 1988.

States, under the Clean Air Act, the ENVIRONMENTAL PROTECTION AGENGY(EPA) defines NATIONAL AMBIENT AIR QUALITY STANDARDS (NAAQSs) for criteria air pollutants in the outside (ambient) air and NATIONAL EMISSIONS STANDARDS FOR HAZARDOUS AIR POLLUTANTS (NESHAPs), indicating the acceptable amount of pollutants in the area. The U.S. model has been widely followed in other countries as well.

Generally, local measurements are compared with national standards, to give a *Pollutant Standards Index* (PSI). This air quality index is often reported daily to the media, and on days when the index exceeds acceptable levels, the public—especially people with respiratory illnesses—is warned to exercise caution in outside activities. Localities that meet air quality standards for a given pollutant are called *attainment areas*, while those that do not are called *non-attainment areas*. Similarly, an industrial facility that meets set emissions standards is said to be in *compliance*, while one that does not is in *noncompliance*. A locality or industry may meet standards for one pollutant but not for another. Standards are far from being met in many areas; in 1988 the United States had 90 urban areas that fell short of the standard for ozone or smog and 40 for carbon monoxide.

In analyzing the amount of air pollution that is within the control of a particular locality, researchers often separate out *background air pollution*, which includes the level of pollutants in the air from natural sources and from else-

where upwind, such as a factory two states away (see BACKGROUND LEVEL). The EPA also reviews potential new sources of pollutants, to block unchecked pollution increases in areas with relatively clean air, the aim being *prevention of significant deterioration* (PSD).

Numerous national and international programs focus on air pollution. The NATIONAL ACID PRECIPITATION ASSESSMENT PROGRAM (NAPAP), begun in 1980, is researching the effects that have so far been experienced from acid rain by the LAKES, RIVERS, and FORESTS in the United States. The UNITED NATIONS ENVIRONMENT PROGRAMME (UNEP) operates the GLOBAL ENVIRONMENT MONITORING SYSTEMS (GEMS), which gathers air pollution and other environmental data from around the world.

Several approaches have been used to reduce air pollution. CATALYTIC CONVERTERS are used (as on automobiles) to remove nitrogen oxides from exhaust; SCRUBBERS are used to remove pollutants from EMISSIONS before release into the environment; ELECTROSTATIC PRECIPITATION is used to clean dust out of polluted air; and AFTERBURNERS are used to remove burnable organic pollutants by incinerating them. Particulate matter may also be filtered out by having polluted air forced through a large filter bag (*baghouse*) of fiberglass, polyester, nylon, or cotton, or swirled in a centrifuge, with the heavy particles being thrown to the outside by the centrifugal force. As temporary or supplemental aids to reaching ambient air quality levels, *dispersion* may be used—simply diluting the amount of the

## Air Pollution Information and Action Guide

**For more information and action on air pollution:**
ACID RAIN FOUNDATION, (919-828-9443). Publishes *The Air Around Us* and *Air Pollutants' Effects on Forest Ecoystems.*
AIR AND WASTE MANAGEMENT ASSOCIATION (A&WMA), (412-232-3444). Publishes *A Dictionary of Air Pollution Terms*; books such as *Visibility and Fine Particles* (1990) and *Effects of Air Pollution on Western Forests* (1989), training manuals, videotapes, and numerous technical papers.
Alternative Farming Systems Information Center, (301-344-3724 or 344-3559). Provides Quick Bibliography *Air Pollution Effects on Crops and Forests.* (See ORGANIC FARMING AND SUSTAINABLE AGRICULTURE INFORMATION AND ACTION GUIDE on page 226.)
AMERICAN COUNCIL FOR AN ENERGY EFFICIENT ECONOMY (ACEEE), (202-429-8873). Publishes *Residential Indoor Air Quality and Energy Efficiency.*
American Forestry Association (AFA), (202-667-3300). Publishes *Forest Effects of Air Pollution.* (See FORESTS INFORMATION AND ACTION GUIDE on page 369.)
CENTER FOR ENVIRONMENTAL INFORMATION (CEI), (716-546-3796). Publishes the monthly *Acid Precipitation Digest* and numerous proceedings, study guides, and bibliographies; operates the *Air Resources Information Clearinghouse (ARIC).*
CONSERVATION AND RENEWABLE ENERGY INQUIRY AND REFERRAL SERVICE (CAREIRS), (800-523-2929; for AK and HI, 800-233-3071). Publishes *Residential Indoor Air Pollution.*
ENVIRONMENTAL AND ENERGY STUDY INSTITUTE (EESI), (202-628-1400). Publishes policy reports, such as *Clean Air Legislation and Issues: An Information Guide* (1990).
ENVIRONMENTAL DEFENSE FUND (EDF), (212-505-2100).
ENVIRONMENTAL PROTECTION AGENCY (EPA), (202-475-7751 or 202-382-2080). Publishes *The Inside Story: A Guide to Indoor Air Quality* (1988).
GREENPEACE (202-462-1177). Runs the *Atmosphere and Energy Campaign.* Publishes *Citizens Waste Audit Manual.*
HUMAN ECOLOGY ACTION LEAGUE (HEAL), (404-248-1898). Publishes information sheets on indoor air pollution.
INFORM, INC. (212-689-4040). Publishes *Toxics in Our Air, Drive for Clean Air: Natural Gas and Methanol Vehicles,* and *Air Pollution and Alternative Fuel Vehicles.*
KIDS FOR SAVING EARTH™ (KSE), (612-525-0002 or 800-800-8800).
NATIONAL AUDUBON SOCIETY, (212-832-3200; *Audubon Action Line,* 202-547-9017).
NATIONAL ENVIRONMENTAL HEALTH ORGANIZATION (NEHA), (303-756-9090). Publishes *Air Quality.*
NATURAL RESOURCES DEFENSE COUNCIL (NRDC), (212-727-2700). Publishes *A Who's Who of American Toxic Air Pollut-*
*ers: A Guide to More Than 1500 Factories in 46 States Emitting Cancer Causing Chemicals* (D. Sheiman, 1989).
RENEW AMERICA, (202-232-2252). Publishes *Indoor Pollution Control* (1988).
RESOURCES FOR THE FUTURE (RFF), (202-328-5000).
SIERRA CLUB, (415-776-2211 or 202-547-1141; legislative hotline, 202-547-5550). Recent campaigns include the Clean Air Act Authorization. Publishes *Clean Air, Toxic Air Pollutants Policy, and Indoor Air Pollution Policy.*
STUDENT ENVIRONMENTAL ACTION COALITION (SEAC), (919-967-4600).
UNITED NATIONS ENVIRONMENT PROGRAMME (UNEP), (212-963-8138 or -8098).
U.S. PUBLIC INTEREST RESEARCH GROUP (PIRG), (202-546-9707). Publishes *Genuine GM Pollution: A Report on the Expenditures of General Motors to Block Clean Air Legislation* (1990), and *Exhausting Our Future: An Eighty-Two City Study of Smog in the 80's* (1989) and *Clean Air PAC Study* (1990).
WATER ENVIRONMENT FEDERATION (WEF), (703-684-2400 or 800-666-0206).
WORLD RESOURCES INSTITUTE, (202-638-6300). Publishes *Breathing Easier, Taking Action on Climate Change, Air Pollution, and Energy Insecurity, Ill Winds: Airborne Pollution's Toll on Trees and Crops,* and a series of *World Resources* annual or biannual reviews.

**Other references:**
*Global Air Pollution: Problems for the 1990s.* Howard Bridgman. Columbia University Press, 1991. *Air Pollution.* Kathlyn Gay. Watts, 1991. *Environmental Awareness: Air Pollution.* M.E. Snodgrass. BSP Publisher, 1991. *Air Pollution.* Darlene Stille. Children's, 1990. *Air Pollution's Toll on Forests.* James J. Mackenzie. Yale University Press, 1990. *Environmental Hazards: Air Pollution.* E. Willard Miller and Ruby M. Miller. ABC Clio, 1989. *Air Pollution and Conservation: Safeguarding Our Architectural Heritage.* J. Rosvall and E. Aleby, eds. Elsevier, 1989. *Air Pollution and Forests,* 2nd ed. W. H. Smith. Springer-Verlag, 1989. *Air Pollution, the Automobile, and Public Health.* Donald Kennedy and Richard R. Bates, eds. National Academy Press, 1988. *Air Pollution and Acid Rain: The Biological Impact.* Alan Wellburn. Wiley, 1988.

**On indoor air pollution:** *Indoor Air Pollution: A Source Guide.* Gordon, 1991. *Indoor Air Pollution: Radon, Bioaerosols, and VOCs.* Jack G. Kay et al. Lewis, 1991. *Indoor Air Pollution: A Health Perspective.* Jonathan M. Samet and John D. Spengler. Johns Hopkins, 1991.

(See also ACID RAIN, TOXIC CHEMICALS; HAZARDOUS WASTE; RADON; ASBESTOS.)

pollutant with other, less polluted air. In addition, many technical processes have been redesigned, or the materials being used pretreated, to reduce the amounts of pollution produced. Those devices or changes in process that are readily available, reasonably priced, and effective at minimizing air pollution are generally termed *reasonably available control technology* (RACT). In many cases, new technology is being required in new plants or those undergoing major modifications, but sometimes installation of pollution control technology is being required on existing plants, as part of a *retrofit* program. This has been especially true in Germany, as the dimensions of acid rain damage to its forests have become clear.

The fight against air pollution will continue, but it can have only limited success as long as industry and daily life, especially transportation, continues to rely on high-polluting FOSSIL FUELS. Treatment of air pollution is itself costly, not just in terms of money but also of energy—for which even more fuel must be used. It is for these reasons that so many people have sought alternative sources of power (see ALTERNATIVE ENERGY). Some think they have found it in NUCLEAR ENERGY, but many others fear that nuclear energy simply adds greater pollutants to the mix and carries other massive hazards, as well.

While atmospheric air pollution has been the focus of enormous attention in recent years—if only because you can smell it, see it, and taste it—scientists recently have found that for many people *indoor* air pollution is an even greater problem. In its 1991 report *Environmental Stewardship: EPA's First Two Years in the Bush Administration*, the EPA put it bluntly: "Growing scientific evidence indicates that air within homes and other buildings can be more seriously polluted than outdoor air, even in the largest and most industrialized cities." In addition to the general pollution of outdoor air, indoor air in a building, vehicle, or other enclosed space has special exposures, including

- the colorless, naturally occurring, radioactive gas RADON;
- additional EMISSIONS of carbon monoxide and nitrogen dioxide from improperly functioning or vented heating systems;
- formaldehyde from furnishings and construction materials, most notably insulation;
- environmental tobacco smoke (ETS) from smokers, also affecting *passive smokers* who simply breathe the air;
- TOXIC CHEMICALS found in household products, such as pesticides, aerosol sprays, cleaning agents, synthetic materials, paints, and wood stains;
- bacteria, fungi, and viruses, whose growth is often encouraged by humidifiers, air conditioners, and the presence of humans and animals.

Many sources of indoor pollution are tracked into houses on shoes, since the dirt around houses is often full of pollutants, such as LEAD (especially from pre-1950 homes, which tended to use heavily leaded paints), wood preservatives from treated decks and porches, and pesticides. One 1990 study of a home that received quarterly pest-control treatments outdoors found 16 pesticides in the dust on the living room carpet, eight of which (along with two others) were found in samples of the room's air. Some researchers suggest that such toxic "reservoirs" can be lessened by changing shoes on entering the home and by more efficient cleaning, aided by selecting low-pile carpets and using vacuum cleaners with powered carpet beaters. Some studies suggest that houseplants can help filter out indoor air pollutants, though critics point out that the plants will themselves become sick and that the main approach should be to eliminate the pollutants. For information on identifying indoor air pollution, see DO YOU HAVE INDOOR AIR POLLUTION? on page 7; and for help on how to handle the problem, see HOW CAN YOU IMPROVE INDOOR AIR QUALITY? on page 77 and RADON REDUCTION METHODS on page 451.

Nor is indoor air pollution confined to homes. Many other structures, including factories and office buildings, have built up potentially damaging air pollution. This is especially true of modern buildings with windows that do not open, have numerous SYNTHETIC ORGANIC COMPOUNDS in their construction and furnishings, and depend on a system of ducts to circulate—often simply recirculate—the air. Some such new or newly renovated buildings have proved so toxic to the people living and working in them that the illness they produce was given the name *sick building syndrome*, the main symptoms being respiratory complaints and fatigue, but with some reactions being markedly more severe and disabling (see ENVIRONMENTAL ILLNESS). The problem has only been magnified by the tendency to make houses "tighter" to conserve heat and save energy. (See AIR POLLUTION INFORMATION AND ACTION GUIDE on page 9.)

**Alar (daminozide),** a PESTICIDE used on fruit, primarily red apples, to keep them firm and colorful. Questions about Alar's safety were raised as far back as 1973, but the ENVIRONMENTAL PROTECTION AGENCY (EPA) felt a study indicating that it caused tumors in mice was scientifically flawed and did not justify a ban. After additional studies, the EPA announced in early 1989 that it was banning Alar but that the health threat was not immediate, so growers could continue to use the pesticide for 18 months. At the same time, the NATURAL RESOURCES DEFENSE COUNCIL published a report, *Intolerable Risk*, based on existing studies, concluding that Alar could cause cancer in thousands of children, since they eat a disproportionately large number of apples; the conclusion was widely publicized on CBS's "60 Minutes." Sales of apples and apple products plummeted, despite EPA assurances that apples were safe to eat. Government estimates were that Alar was never used by more than 15 percent of the apple growers, down to 5 percent in 1988, but all suffered in the apple crash. In quick response, apple growers announced a voluntary ban on the use of Alar, but the damage was done, and some family farms ended up in bankruptcy.

The nature and extent of the actual risk is still unclear. While the NRDC and CBS assert that their reports were "well researched and well documented," some critics charge that the danger was minuscule and that the findings were irresponsibly distorted and oversimplified. Such questions will undoubtedly be aired as part of a lawsuit filed in 1991 by Washington State apple growers against the NRDC, their public relations firm, and CBS.

**For more information and action:**

NATURAL RESOURCES DEFENSE COUNCIL (NRDC), (212-727-2700).
• **Northwest Coalition for Alternatives to Pesticides (NCAP),** (503-344-5044). Publishes *Pesticides in Our Food: From Alar and Apples to Alternative Agriculture.* (See PESTICIDES INFORMATION AND ACTION GUIDE on page 238.)

**aldicarb,** a type of CARBAMATE, a family of chemical compounds containing carbon and nitrogen, many of them used as PESTICIDES.

**aldrin,** a highly toxic PESTICIDE (see CYCLODIENES).

**alligator, Florida,** see CROCODILE, AMERICAN.

**alternative energy,** an umbrella term for types of ENERGY RESOURCES that produce little or no environmental damage—or at least less than FOSSIL FUELS—and generally are RENEWABLE RESOURCES, rather than those that disappear with use; the term is also applied to sources that are more efficient than modern fossil-fuel-based technologies. Among the alternative energy sources and approaches discussed separately in this book are BIOFUEL, BIOMASS, GEOTHERMAL ENERGY, HEAT PUMP, HYDROPOWER, SOLAR ENERGY, SYNTHETIC FUELS, WAVE POWER, and WIND POWER. (See also ENERGY RESOURCES.)

**alternative farming systems,** a general term for farming practices that are—to a greater or lesser extent—backing away from heavy use of PESTICIDES, chemical fertilizers, and other off-farm purchases, which characterize most current farming. The term may apply to systems that only slightly reduce dependence on such inputs, as through better use of soil tests and INTEGRATED PEST MANAGEMENT, to those that avoid them altogether, such as ORGANIC FARMING relying on BIOLOGICAL CONTROL and other methods. (See SUSTAINABLE AGRICULTURE.)

**aluminum (Al),** a type of HEAVY METAL that is toxic to living organisms in all but the smallest amounts; called *aluminium* in Canada and some other countries. Aluminum is widespread in rocks, except limestone and sandstone, forming 7 to 8 percent of the earth's crust, its most abundant metal. Because it is so corrosion resistant, aluminum is heavily used in food containers and packaging, such as beer and soda cans, and in processing equipment for food and chemicals. Cans that are all aluminum—with no labels, caps, tops, or sides of other materials—do not need to be separated from other containers and can readily be melted down and reused. This made aluminum a main early focus of RECYCLING efforts—over half of all aluminum cans are now recycled—and a considerable environmental success story, paving the way for wider recycling efforts.

The benefits of these efforts are enormous. Aluminum is found only in combination with other metals, so it is expensive to mine; it is generally extracted from bauxite ore found on the surface in tropical rain FOREST areas, so recycling aluminum cans helps save the rain forest. In addition, once in the environment as a pollutant, as when dissolved by ACID RAIN and then flowing into groundwater, aluminum is highly toxic to living beings, causing central nervous system disorders and also being implicated in Alzheimer's and Parkinson's diseases. (See HEAVY METALS.)

***Alvenus* oil spill,** leakage of an estimated 1.8 million gallons (approximately 6,000 tons) of heavy crude oil from the British tanker *Alvenus* into the Gulf of Mexico off Lake Charles, Louisiana, as the ship tore open after grounding while moving into the port of Lake Charles, on July 30, 1984. The oil spill in the Gulf caused considerable environmental damage when much of it washed ashore on the coasts of Louisiana and south Texas. (See OIL.)

**Amazon rain forest,** one of the last of the world's great tropical rain FORESTS, covering much of the 2.7-million-square-mile (7-million-square-kilometer) Amazon basin, the huge drainage area of South America's Amazon River. The river, flowing from the Andes to the Atlantic, is the second longest in the world, after the Nile, and by far the largest in terms of its ultimate flow into the sea. Half of its basin is in Brazil, the rest in Peru, Colombia, Bolivia, Ecuador, Guyana, Surinam, and French Guiana. The basin harbors an enormous range of flora and fauna, some estimates running to several hundred thousand different species in all (one estimate is as high as one million), and including at least 1,000 species of trees, 2,000 of fish, 2,000 of birds, and 8,000 of insects. This is one of the most prolific places on earth, the land of the huge castanheiro and silk-cotton tree, the piranha and giant catfish, the boa constrictor and anaconda, the toucan and parrot, and armies of ants and enormous numbers of butterflies.

In the Brazilian portion of the rain forest, the 1960s saw the beginning of a powerful government effort to spur the settlement and economic development of the Amazon basin, with tax incentives to encourage such industries as MINING, cement manufacture, and OIL refining, and also to encourage slash-and-burn agriculture, with land ceded to settlers from other parts of the country after they had cleared it. A very important motor force was the rapid growth of the Brazilian POPULATION, which grew approximately 350 percent from 1940 to 1990, from 45 million to over 150 million.

The result was a severe attack on some parts of the Brazilian portion of the Amazon rain forest and on its rich variety of life. With it came an attack on the local Native American populations (see INDIGENOUS PEOPLES), who numbered no more than 100,000 in the early 1960s and had little ability to resist direct attack or the diseases of "civilization."

The largest area of destruction was in the Brazilian area of Rondonia, where government incentives encouraged tens of thousands of settlers to move in and clear the land, much as had North American settlers going west by the millions in the century following the American Revolution. Rondonia was also made accessible by the large government-financed Polonoroeste project, which built roads into the Amazon. There was a vast difference from the North American experience, however; much of the land cleared in the Amazon proved only barely suitable for farming, and some of it was abandoned soon after being slashed down and burned.

Considerable deforestation also occurred in the eastern Amazon, as tax-subsidized ranchers attacked local Native American populations, cleared rain-forest lands, and turned these lands into cattle ranches, although the unsuitability of the land for ranching later caused many of the ranches to be abandoned. In one very notable incident that attracted worldwide attention, local ranchers in December 1988 murdered Chico Mendes (Francisco Mendes Filho), president of the Brazilian rubber tappers union, outside his home in Acre. Three ranchers were later convicted of the murder.

Deforestation is also anticipated by such mining and industrial activities as the Grande Carajas mining complex in northeastern Brazil, where plans call for the generation of charcoal for pig-iron smelters from the burning of rain-forest trees. On a somewhat smaller, but still quite significant scale, a recent gold rush by thousands of miners into the northeastern Amazon brought sharp attacks on the local Native American populations.

Some environmentalists have also pointed out that the burning of parts of the Amazon rain forest also makes a significant addition to the CARBON DIOXIDE content of the world's air, adding to the GREENHOUSE EFFECT, though considerably less than do the year-after-year carbon dioxide emissions of the United States or Europe.

During the 1980s, the worldwide environmental movement acted to try to save the Amazon and other tropical rain forests of the world, all of them seriously threatened. That attempt continues, though with uneven results around the world. In Brazil, however, there has been some substantial success, largely due to Brazilian government intervention. The homesteading techniques that encouraged settlers to clear the land wastefully have mostly been discontinued, and local Native American populations have been somewhat protected against the formerly routine attacks of ranchers and goldminers. DEBT-FOR-NATURE SWAPS have been encouraged in Brazil as in many parts of the world, with some international loans forgiven in return for the setting aside of nature preserves. Tree "farming" has been encouraged, with replanting aimed at replacing destroyed trees, although such farming has drawn criticism from some environmentalists, concerned about any plan that condones or fosters any destruction in the rain forest. The destruction of the Amazon rain forest has been considerably slowed, and before much of the forest has been lost. Estimates as to the extent of that destruction vary, but most indicate that 5 to 7 percent of the Brazilian portion of the forest has been lost, with much smaller losses in the other countries sharing the Amazon basin, so that probably 3 to 5 percent of the whole Amazon rain forest has been destroyed.

Yet there continues to be valid worldwide concern for the future of the Amazon rain forest, for current trends can mean destruction of the forest in only a few decades—and once gone, the forest will not return. The countries of the Amazon basin are all poor, all carrying huge, draining international debts that cannot possibly be repaid. All are experiencing enormous population increases that cannot possibly be handled, with tens of millions of their people gathering in wholly unsanitary shantytowns around their major cities and with epidemic diseases such as cholera, once thought almost eradicated, again taking tens of thousands of lives. Given these circumstances, the enormous mineral and forest wealth of the Amazon basin can prove irresistible to hard-pressed governments and people, as is so clearly indicated by 1990 and 1991 Amazon basin oil exploration and drilling agreements between several international oil companies and the governments of Peru, Bolivia, and Ecuador. In Peru and Ecuador, rain-forest areas threatened by drilling and access road plans included Ecuador's Yasuni National Park and Peru's Pacaya-Samiria Reserve.

If the long struggle to save the Amazon rain forest is to succeed beyond the preservation of a few park and preserve areas, the main population, economic, and social problems of the countries of the basin will have to be addressed far more successfully than has so far been the case.

### For more information and action:

- CULTURAL SURVIVAL (CS), (617-495-2562). Publishes studies on Brazil.
- INSTITUTE FOR FOOD AND DEVELOPMENT POLICY (IFDP), popularly called *Food First* (415-864-8555). Publishes *Brazil's Debt and Deforestation—A Global Warning.*
- SIERRA CLUB, (415-776-2211 or 202-547-1141; legislative hotline, 202-547-5550). Publishes *The Rivers Amazon.*
- WORLD BANK, (202-477-1234).
- WORLD WILDLIFE FUND (WWF), (202-293-4800). Publishes *Government Policies and Deforestation in Brazil's Amazon Region.*

**Other references:** *The Decade of Destruction: The Crusade to Save the Amazon Rain Forest.* Adrian Cowell. Holt, 1990. *The Burning Season: The Murder of Chico Mendes and the Fight for the Amazon Rain Forest.* Andrew Revkin. Houghton Mifflin, 1990. *The World Is Burning.* Alex Shoumatoff. Little, Brown, 1990. *Explorers of the Amazon.* Anthony Smith. Viking Penguin, 1990. *The Fate of the Forest: Developers, Destroyers, and Defenders of the Amazon.* Susanna B. Hecht. Verso, 1989. (See also FORESTS; DEVELOPMENT; POPULATION.)

**ambient air,** the air outside, unconfined by structures, as opposed to the air within a home or office. Standards for AIR POLLUTION normally refer to ambient air, though government and other agencies also monitor air in the work-place and have become increasingly concerned about indoor air, as in homes and schools.

**Amboseli National Park,** Kenyan WILDLIFE REFUGE, 25 miles south of Mount Kilimanjaro, Africa's highest mountain, at 19,340 feet. The 145-square-mile park is named after what is for most of each year the dry, salt lake bed of Lake Amboseli. The park is 130 miles south of Nairobi and very much part of every tourist's visit to Kenya, as it is world-famous for its large animals and its constantly changing views of the great mountain. On view here—and uncaged, though scarcely in the wild—are ELEPHANTS, LIONS, CHEETAHS, black RHINOCEROSES (still coming back after widescale poaching), ZEBRAS, elk, giraffes, buffalo, lands, gnus (wildebeests), impalas, MONKEYS, baboons, hyenas, antelopes, foxes, LEOPARDS, and other African mammals, many of them fast disappearing elsewhere as Africa's POPULATION soars and DESERTIFICATION, recurrent wars, disease, and FAMINE AND FOOD INSECURITY threaten many peoples and governments. Also here are hundreds of bird species, including many varieties of herons, storks, plovers, ducks, vultures, eagles, doves, cuckoos, larks, flycatchers, warblers, orioles, tits, weavers, sparrows, finches, and waxbills.

As elephant poaching took a turn for the worse in the 1970s and early 1980s, more and more elephants sought protection at Amboseli; their grazing patterns had considerable impact on the park's foliage. But the chief adverse impact on the seriously threatened park comes from tourists—200,000 a year in the early 1990s—whose vehicles, off-road driving, and sheer numbers have driven animals from the park and desolated the areas around the park's waterholes, where the sought-after animals tend to be found. In the early 1990s, Kenya's National Wildlife Service, headed by Dr. Richard E. Leakey, was beginning the process of reclamation, much impeded by the fact that the park provided needed hard currency income for the Kenyan government. (See WILDLIFE REFUGE; ECOTOURISM.)

**American Association of Botanical Gardens and Arboreta (AABGA)** (786 Church Road, Wayne, PA 19087; 215-688-1120; Susan H. Lathrop, Executive Director), a membership organization founded in 1940 for public garden professionals and volunteers, and institutional members, in the United States and Canada. The AABGA acts as a professional forum, resource center, network, and job clearinghouse; it also provides consulting services, in-service training, and public advocacy, and publishes various materials, including the quarterly *The Public Garden,* the monthly *AABGA Newsletter,* a membership directory, mini-surveys and resource packets, and books.

**American Association of Zoo Keepers (AAZK)** (Administrative Offices, 635 SW Gage Boulevard, Topeka, KS 66606; 913-272-5821, ext. 31; Barbara Manspeaker, Administrative Secretary), an international membership organization founded in 1967 for animal keepers—zoo keepers, aquarium keepers, lab attendants, or anyone caring for animals in a zoo or aquarium—and other persons "interested in quality animal care and in promoting animal keeping as a profession," seeking to "foster a professional attitude in animal keepers by encouraging them to become active members of the professional teams at today's zoos and aquariums." The AAZK encourages zoo keepers to "communicate and discuss new methods of care, and observations on behavior, working conditions, and other vital information through conferences, chapter activities, and publications, including the monthly *Animal Keepers' Forum*, and the *Conservation, Preservation & Restoration Committee Bulletin*, and books and brochures on zookeeping.

**American Association of Zoological Parks and Aquariums (AAZPA)** (Oglebay Park, Wheeling, WV 26003; 304-242-2160; Robert O. Wagner, Executive Director), a membership organization founded in 1924 to promote the health of ZOOS, aquariums, scientific centers, and conservation agencies and their role as educational, cultural, and recreational resources. The AAZPA strongly supports efforts to protect and conserve the earth's endangered and rare species. It maintains the *International Species Inventory System (ISIS)*, a computerized inventory of living zoo animals for use in selective breeding programs, and oversees the *Species Survival Plan (SSP)*, supporting captive breeding programs for endangered species. The AAZPA publishes various materials, including the monthly *Communique*, brochures, such as *Conservation: Protecting the Present to Protect the Future, The New Ark, Wild Animals Do Not Make Good Pets, The Purposes of Zoos and Aquariums,* and *Zoo and Aquarium Career;* and professional publications.

**American Canal Society** (809 Rathton Road, York, PA 17403; 717-843-4035; William E. Trout III, President), a membership organization founded in 1972 "to promote the wise use of America's many historic canal resources through research, preservation, restoration, recreation, and parks." A national clearinghouse of information on canals, the Society works with other groups and individuals to help save threatened canals and related sites, identify canal resources, and carry out related activities, including a projected national inventory of U.S. canals. It publishes various materials, including the quarterly *American Canals*

and various historical works on canals and travel-related topics.

**American Cetacean Society (ACS)** (P.O. Box 2369, San Pedro, CA 90731; 213-548-6279; Patricia Warhol, Executive Direction), a volunteer organization founded in 1967, focusing on protection of marine mammals, especially WHALES and DOLPHINS. The ACS supports research; gathers and disseminates research information; has chapters around the United States; runs conferences and special tours; monitors new legislation, works with other like-minded organizations to educate the public and legislators; maintains a research library; and trains boat skippers and "whalewatch docents." It also publishes various materials, including the newsletter *Whale News*, quarterly journal *Whalewatcher*, educational tools, audiocassettes, videocassettes, posters, bumper stickers, and books. (See DOLPHINS; OTTERS; SEALS AND SEA LIONS; and WHALES.)

**American Council for an Energy Efficient Economy (ACEEE)** (1001 Connecticut Avenue NW, Suite 535, Washington, DC 20036; 202-429-8873; Robert Socolow, Chairman), a nonmembership organization funded by foundations, government agencies, utilities, and private corporations, "dedicated to advancing energy-conserving technologies and policies." Staff and other professionals carry out research and analysis, disseminate information, and act as energy-conservation advocates, in areas such as energy efficiency and the environment, in developed and developing countries; utilities; transportation; buildings; appliances, lighting, and equipment; and conservation research and development. The ACEEE publishes numerous books, research reports, and consumer guides (See ENERGY RESOURCES; AIR POLLUTION; ASBESTOS; RADON).

**American Fisheries Society (AFS)** (5410 Grosvenor Lane, Suite 110, Bethesda, MD 20814; 301-897-8616; Carl R. Sullivan, Executive Director), an international membership organization, functioning since 1870, for people interested in "fisheries science and education and the conservation and management of fisheries resources." The AFS has various geographic divisions and chapters, as well as special discipline sections in the areas of bioengineering, computer use, early life history, education, fish culture, fish genetics, fish health, fisheries administration, fisheries management, international concerns, introduced fish, marine fisheries, socioeconomics, and water quality. The AFS also seeks to influence public policy, as in legislation and education, and works with the FOREST SERVICE on fisheries policy for U.S. FOREST land. It offers symposia and workshops, provides professional certification and awards for achievement and service, gives discounts on a wide range of professional books from other publishers, and publishes various materials, including the *Directory of North American Fisheries and Aquatic Scientists* and the *AFS Membership Directory*, numerous textbooks, manuals, and conference proceedings; and five peer-reviewed journals.

**American Hiking Society (AHS)** (1015 31st Street NW, Washington, DC 20007; 703-385-3252; Susan Henley, Executive Director), a membership organization founded in 1977 in support of hiking, encouraging preservation of existing footpaths, often through legislative lobbying, and volunteer trailbuilding and maintenance, often through volunteer vacations (see ECOTOURISM). The AHS maintains an information service for hikers and other interested people and publishes various materials, including the *American Hiker Newsletter*, the quarterly magazine *American Hiker*, the quarterly newsletter *Pathways Across America*, *Helping Out in the Outdoors* (a directory of volunteer projects on public lands), *AHS Directory of Technical Assistance* (on trail development), *Trail Development: Opportunities, Obstacles, and Issues* (1990), *Report on the Status of Trails on Federal Public Lands* (1990), brochures, and periodic legislative alerts.

**American Nature Study Society (ANSS)** (5881 Cold Brook Road, Homer, NY 13077; 607-749-3655; John A. Gustafson, Treasurer), a membership organization founded by naturalist Liberty Hyde Bailey in 1908, "devoted to the appreciation and understanding of our natural world." In addition to naturalists and educators, members include anyone interested in natural science and environmental education. ANSS holds various meetings and workshops, often accompanied by field trips to unique environments, "domestic or exotic," led by experienced interpreters. It also offers awards to outstanding environmental educators and interpreters, and publishes various materials, notably a theme-oriented journal *Nature Study* and the quarterly *ANSS Newsletter*.

**American Oceans Campaign (AOC)** (725 Arizona Avenue, Suite 102, Santa Monica, CA 90401; 213-576-6162; Robert H. Sulnick, Executive Director), an organization founded in 1987 by actor Ted Danson and his wife, Casey Danson, dedicated to the restoration and preservation of America's OCEANS and protection of COASTS. AOC seeks to influence national policy, educate the public about what they can do, and assist local groups and communities. It focuses especially on coastal POLLUTION, OFFSHORE DRILLING, and DRIFTNETS, seeking to mobilize a coalition of business and entertainment interests, including celebrity participation; it also runs the citizen action program, the

*American Oceans Conservation Committee (AOCC)*. The AOC publishes the quarterly newsletter *Making Waves*, and it helps produce environmental videos and television series.

**American Ornithologists' Union (AOU)** (c/o Division of Ornithology, National Museum of Natural History, Smithsonian Institution, Washington, DC 20560; 202-357-1970; Brina Kessel, President), a membership organization founded in 1883 for the scientific study of birds. Though primarily a professional organization, it also includes many amateur ornithologists. The AOU supports research, undertakes conservation projects, holds annual meetings often linked with field trips, provides awards for excellence in research, and publishes various materials, including the quarterly journal *The Auk*, a bimonthly newsletter, and numerous specialized monographs and other special publications.

**American Planning Association (APA)** (Headquarters: 1776 Massachusetts Avenue NW, Washington, DC 20036; 202-872-0611; Membership and Subscriptions: 1313 East 60th Street, Chicago, IL 60637; 312-955-9100; Israel Stollman, Executive Director), a membership organization for planning professionals and others concerned with city and regional planning problems, founded in 1909 as the National Conference on City Planning. The APA provides a nationwide network giving members current information on planning practice and techniques, and acts as an advocate of planning on the federal, state, and local levels.

While the APA itself represents the planning community as a whole, various APA divisions focus on special interests: City Planning and Management; Economic Development; Environment, Natural Resources, and Energy; Federal Installation Planning; Housing and Human Services; Information Technology; Intergovernmental Affairs; International Planning and Law; Planning and the Black Community; Planning and Women; Private Practice Division; Resorts and Tourism; Small Town and Rural Planning; Transportation Planning; and Urban Design and Preservation. Each division publishes its own newsletters and often other special publications, holds its own annual meeting, and has its own sessions at APA national conferences; however, divisions cooperate with each other and with local APA chapters, act as liaisons with related organizations, and supply technical assistance to the APA's overall policy and lobbying activities, as in preparing guidelines for government programs and giving testimony before legislative and policymaking groups. APA members may be active in more than one division.

In addition to establishing general planning policy and

lobbying activities, the APA seeks to educate the public on planning and its importance. It also operates the *Planning Advisory Service (PAS)*, a research and information service for communities, agencies, and other organizations and consultants, providing an answer service, ordinance searches, general planning advice, loan services, and several publications, including *PAS Reports*, the monthly newsletter *PAS Memo*, and the quarterly *Public Investment*, and various PAS reports, such as *Preserving Rural Character* (1990) and *A Survey of Zoning Definitions* (1989).

Another arm of the APA is the *American Institute of Certified Planners (AICP)*, which is active in accreditation of planning education and provides the only national certification program for planners. In addition, it offers the Planners Training Service, with continuing education programs on specific topics at workshops and special conferences, such as the annual Zoning Institute. The AICP also has established the AICP Code of Ethics and Professional Conduct for planners and runs a Historical Planning Landmarks Program, recognizing the major influences of plans, projects, and pioneer planners.

The APA operates a JobMart and Planners Referral Service for planning professionals. It also offers insurance programs and discounts on materials promoted in the mail-order Planners Bookstore, which stocks more than 700 books, technical reports, and bibliographies from various publishers and organizations.

Also available through the APA is a series of bibliographies on various topics (24 a year) from *Council of Planning Librarians (CPL)*. The APA itself publishes the monthly magazine *Planning*, the quarterly *Journal of the American Planning Association (JAPA)*; various brochures; videotapes of workshops and conferences; periodicals, and over 150 books including *Everyone Wins! A Citizen's Guide to Development* (Richard D. Klein, 1990), *Planning Small Town America* (Kristina Ford et al., 1990), *Neighborhood Planning* (Bernie Jones, 1990), *Zoning and the American Dream* (Charles M. Haar and Jerold S. Kayden, eds., 1989), *Land Use and the Constitution* (Brian W. Blaesser and Alan C. Weinstein, eds., 1989), *The Small Town Planning Handbook* (Thomas L. Daniels et al., 1988), *Strategic Planning* (John M. Bryson and Robert C. Einsweiler, eds., 1988), and *The Practice of Local Government Planning* (2nd edition, Frank S. So and Judith Getzels, eds., with ICMA, 1988). (See also DEVELOPMENT; ENVIRONMENTAL PLANNING; WASTE DISPOSAL; LAND USE).

**Americans for the Environment (AFE)** (1400 16th Street NW, Washington, DC 20036; 202-797-6665; Roy B. Morgan, President), a national educational institute

founded in 1980 to provide the U.S. environmental community with training in electoral skills to maximize their impact at the polls. AFE is non-partisan and does not take positions on specific environmental issues, nor does it have membership or a newsletter. Rather it offers national and regional workshops and special publications to environmental groups and individual activists on how political campaigns work and how to get effectively involved in them, including ''voter contact, volunteer organization, media, targeting, get-out-the-vote, fundraising, organizational management, and planning''; technical assistance, as on conducting voter research, targeting campaign resources, and developing campaign strategies and messages; and advanced training for environmental professionals. Among its publications are *The Power of the Green Vote, Taking the Initiative,* and *The Rising Tide: Public Opinion, Policy and Politics.*

**American Society for Environmental History (ASEH)** (Center for Technology Studies, New Jersey Institute of Technology, Newark, NJ 07102; 201-596-3270; John Opie, Editor), an international organization founded in 1977 to ''promote the interdisciplinary study of past environmental change,'' including natural changes in climate, vegetation, disease, and the rest of the natural world, and also those resulting from human manipulation of nature. Seeking to foster serious scholarly research, the ASEH sponsors a biennial conference for its membership, drawn from various intellectual backgrounds, including history, geography, ecology, anthropology, natural resource management, landscape architecture, and literature. It also publishes the quarterly scholarly journal *Environmental History Review* and the *Environmental History Newsletter.*

**American Society of Zoologists (ASZ)** (104 Sirius Circle, Thousand Oaks, CA 91360; 805-492-3585; Mary Adams-Wiley, Executive Officer), a membership organization for professional zoologists and student-in-training (SIT) members, for ''presentation, discussion, and public dissemination of new or important facts and concepts in the area of animal biology'' and the advancement of the zoological sciences. The ASZ holds regional conferences; maintains several committees, including the Public Affairs Committee and Education Committee; and publishes various materials, including the journal *American Zoologists*, a booklet *Careers in Animal Biology*, and periodical newsletters. Members also receive discounts on subscriptions for numerous other journals in the field.

**American Water Resources Association (AWRA)** (5410 Grosvenor Lane, Suite 220, Bethesda, MD 20814;

301-493-8600; Kenneth D. Reid, Executive Director), a professional scientific and educational membership association founded in 1964 by and for professionals, "dedicated to the advancement of interdisciplinary water resources research, planning, management, development and education." The AWRA provides a forum for "the collection, organization, and dissemination of ideas and information in the physical, biological, economic, social, political, legal, and engineering aspects of water related problems." Within AWRA are state sections and student chapters, various committees, and technical working groups for special interests, including Limnology/Aquatic Biology, Agricultural Hydrology, Surface Hydrology, Ground Water, Hydrometerorology, Modeling/Statistics, Remote Sensing, Water Policy and Management, Water Law, Water Quality, Wetlands, and Wildland Hydrology/Watershed Management.

AWRA holds annual regional conferences and symposia, often built around a broad theme, and publishes numerous materials, including the bimonthly newsletter *Hydata-News & Views*, the bimonthly peer-reviewed journal *Water Resources Bulletin*, a membership directory, conference proceedings, monographs, and other works such as *Redefining National Water Policy: New Roles and Directions* (Stephen M. Born, ed., 1989), *Water Management in the 21st Century* (A. Ivan Johnson and Warren Viessman, Jr., eds., 1989), *Indian Water Rights and Water Resources Management* (William B. Lord and Mary G. Wallace, eds., 1989), *Wetlands: Concerns and Successes* (David W. Fisk, ed., 1989), *Water: Laws and Management* (Frederick E. David, ed., 1989), and *Water-Use Data for Water Resources Management* (Marvin Waterstone and R. John Burt, eds., 1988).

---

We do not inherit the Earth from our Ancestors; we borrow it from our Children.

Quotation from American Wildlands Alliance.

---

**American Wildlands Alliance (AWL)** (7500 East Arapahoe Road, Suite 295, Englewood, CO 80112; 303-771-0380; Sally A. Ranney, President), a membership organization founded in 1977, formerly called the *American Wilderness Alliance (AWA)*, whose mission is "to insure through its programs and activities the responsible management and protection of forests, wildlife, wilderness, wetlands, watersheds, rivers and fisheries." Among AWL's main concerns are BIOLOGICAL DIVERSITY, ENDANGERED SPECIES, and the quality of life and "perhaps even the sustainability of humankind." It works through "pub-

lic education, research, litigation, policy dialogue, coalition building, films, lobbying, and hands-on experience" to educate the public and policy-makers. Its major activities include the *Timber Management Policy Reform Program (TMPRP)*, involving a "forest watch network"; *Wildlands Conservation Program (WCP)*, to mobilize and coordinate citizen action on public land policy, involving the *River Defense Fund* to protect RIVERS in the National Wild and Scenic River System; *Wildland Economic Research Program*, involving studies of the "economic benefits of wilderness, rivers and watersheds"; *Ancient Forests of the Interior West*, involving inventories and management protection strategies of remnants of ancient FORESTS; and *Watershed and Riparian Rehabilitation*, working with private and public land owners and managers to protect these resources. American Wildlands also works with other international individuals and organizations on wildlife and resource issues; operates the *Eco-Adventure Connection*, offering "wild country experiences" in natural areas of the world, focusing on the "people, flora, fauna, geology, history, and conservation issues" of the area; and publishes the quarterly journal *On the Wild Side* and alerts on key issues.

**America the Beautiful Fund (ABF)** (219 Shoreham Building, Washington, DC 20005; 202-638-1649; Paul Bruce Dowling, Executive Director), an organization founded in 1965 aiming to "preserve our national heritage by assisting community-level programs and projects to save the natural and man-made environment and improve the quality of life." The Fund not only offers support and direction, but also operates as a clearinghouse of ideas for community projects and a catalyst for new ones, with special concern for neglected areas such as rural communities, bypassed cities, small towns, and depleted neighborhoods. ABF has three major programs: *Operation Green Plant*, which distributes surplus seeds donated by seed companies (for everything except trees) free to thousands of community action committees, hunger relief projects, community gardens, and environmental projects; *American Landscapes*, which helps preserve areas such as seashores, streams, WETLANDS, farmscapes, and unique or historic neighborhoods and villages; and *Rediscover America*, which focuses on preserving and revitalizing local heritage, cultural, and historical sites.

***Amoco Cadiz* oil spill,** the loss of the entire 226,000-ton crude OIL cargo of the supertanker *Amoco Cadiz* into the Atlantic Ocean, on March 17, 1978, off Portsall, Brittany. The accident occurred during a storm: the ship lost its steering ability, ran aground on rocks while a tug was trying to tow it out of trouble, and broke up. The huge oil slick from this very large spill (about eight times the size of the 1989 *EXXON VALDEZ* spill off Alaska) caused an environmental disaster, as the oil fouled coastal waters and 200 miles of the French COAST. Although the ship was registered as Liberian, a federal judge in Chicago after years of litigation ultimately found Standard Oil of Indiana guilty of several counts of negligence and failure to train the ship's crew. In 1988, Amoco was ordered to pay over $85 million in damages to a wide range of French claimants. (See OIL.)

**animal rights movement,** a broad and diverse movement, an umbrella name for a wide spectrum of organizations and views, united primarily by the idea that humans need to reassess their relationship with animals, and in particular to acknowledge that animals have their own intrinsic value and right to exist, as individuals and as species, and should not be seen only in terms of their usefulness or attractiveness to humans.

For much of history, animals have been seen primarily in their relationship to humans, providing food, as through ranching, dairy farming, HUNTING, and FISHING; providing working help and companionship, as dogs, cats, and horses have done for thousands of years; offering sport, as through hunting, fishing, and racing; and being used to test the possible harmfulness of a substance or situation, from the use of canaries in mines as "early warning systems" of possible toxic gases to the laboratory testing of modern medicines and cosmetics on animals (see ANIMAL TESTING).

Aside from a few times and places, such as among Buddhists and Hindus of India, humans have not generally questioned their right to use animals as they saw fit. Indeed, in the Judeo-Christian tradition, the Bible is often cited as giving humans domination over all other animals, though many Christians interpret the Bible quite otherwise. In the 19th century, a small but vocal group of antivivisectionists began to publicly question the use of animals in testing, often inspired by the thinking of philosophers such as the Englishman Jeremy Bentham, who wrote about animals: "The question is not, can they reason? nor, can they talk? but, can they suffer?" From the late 19th century, a somewhat larger group of people focused on obtaining humane treatment for animals, working through groups such as the American Society for the Prevention of Cruelty to Animals (see ANIMAL RIGHTS AND WELFARE INFORMATION AND ACTION GUIDE on page 361).

But it was not until the late 1960s that concern for animal rights and welfare became a mass movement. Much of the new concern for animals was—and continues to be—focused on questions of animal testing and on the development and promotion of alternatives to animal use in scientific research. But a much wider groundswell began to build around more general questions of human–animal relationships, as exemplified in the work of Australian animal rights guru Peter Singer, notably his *Animal Liberation* (1975). It was Singer who made popular the concept of *speciesism*, which he defined as "a prejudice or attitude of bias toward the interests of members of one's own species and against those of members of other species." Others, notably Tom Regan in *The Case for Animal Rights* (1983), have stressed the inherent value of all animals, meaning that "all have an equal right to be treated in ways that do not reduce them to the status of things, as if they existed as resources for others."

In reevaluating society's traditional views of the human–animal relationship, people in the animal rights movement have come to a wide variety of positions. At one end of the animal rights spectrum are those who believe that people should treat animals humanely but do not seek to ban all human use of animals. They often stress that humans have a sense of moral values and an obligation to look after the welfare of domesticated animals and those in natural environments affected by human activities. In relation to animal testing, for example, they believe that animal research should be allowed, but only when no alternatives are available and when all possible means are used to eliminate pain and suffering. At the other end of the spectrum are animal rights activists who oppose human use of animals altogether. They do not focus on humane treatment of animals in FACTORY FARMING, for example, since they oppose the eating of animals altogether (see VEGETARIANISM).

Between these two poles are many people who have a general sympathy and kinship for animals, not necessarily based on a particular philosophical or logical position, and who have made up much of the vocal and active opposition to cruel and wanton treatment of animals. Much of their attention is focused on those animals with whom humans have a close kinship or relationship, such as dogs, cats, rabbits, and primates. Despite discussions of speciesism, insects and other less "attractive" species receive little support—there are few protests against fruit fly experiments, for example.

The animal rights movement has also been strengthened by its overlapping with more general environmental issues, including ENDANGERED SPECIES, BIOLOGICAL DIVERSITY, WILDLIFE TRADE, and the importance of protecting and restoring, where possible, WILDLIFE REFUGES and WILDERNESS areas threatened or damaged by human activities.

Many in the scientific community still accept the human right to use animals, but even they have been affected by animal rights views. As the National Research Council of the National Academy of Sciences put it, in a 1988 report on animal research use, ''we have the option to decide to dominate animals, but we also have a mandate to make choices responsible to comply with the obligations of stewardship.''

Animal rights supporters have used a variety of methods to press their cause. Many have focused on legislation, such as passage and enforcement of the ANIMAL WELFARE ACT, the MARINE MAMMAL PROTECTION ACT, the CONVENTION ON INTERNATIONAL TRADE IN ENDANGERED SPECIES OF WILD FAUNA AND FLORA (CITES), and numerous other laws and local ordinances. Many others have effectively used publicity campaigns, boycotts, and other types of nonviolent protests to press organizations into changing their stance on animal activities. Some radical animal rights activists use confrontation and direct actions that can range all the way to bombings and other destructive actions, akin to MONKEYWRENCHING techniques employed for wider environmental issues; among these are the Animal Liberation Front (labeled a ''terrorist organization'' by the FBI). These activities are directed variously at organizations that perform animal testing, especially those using painful procedures for unnecessary products; individuals, particularly those who wear fur coats; and also against aquariums and ZOOS, where animals are placed on display. One of the most successful campaigns has been that directed against humans wearing fur coats; it has included throwing red paint on baby harp seals (see SEALS AND SEA LIONS) to ruin their fur, and so save their lives; numerous overlapping publicity campaigns, often with celebrity support, attempting to deglamorize the wearing of fur coats; and sometimes direct attacks (as with knives or paint) on fur coats being worn in public.

The campaign against zoos and aquariums is a difficult and complicated one. Many animal rights supporters are fighting to improve conditions in zoos, circuses, and aquariums, especially old-style zoos where animals are penned in small, often unkempt cages. Many modern zoos and aquariums are designed and kept quite differently, but some animal rights activists feel that no zoos or aquariums should be allowed to exist and that all animals should be freed into the wild. Others—including many zoo- and aquarium-keepers—respond that the natural environment has been so compromised by human activities, and so many species are endangered, that the knowledge and experience developed in modern zoos and aquariums is vital to the continuance of species and to helping animals meet the threats posed by the polluted natural environments in which we live (see BIOLOGICAL DIVERSITY). In late 1991, several aquariums even took the unusual step of going to

court, charging that three animals rights groups had falsely portrayed their activities in attempting to rescue stranded WHALES and DOLPHINS. They also stress the importance of zoos and aquariums in educating new generations about wildlife and natural environments.

Many animal rights groups are also concerned about overpopulation among animals, advising spaying or neutering of companion animals; about BIOTECHNOLOGY and GENETIC ENGINEERING, especially questioning human rights to patent animals; about cruel practices used in hunting or fishing, especially the leghold traps and DRIFTNETS; and about bullfighting and sports pitting animals against each other in deadly combat. (See ANIMAL RIGHTS AND WELFARE INFORMATION AND ACTION GUIDE on page 361; also ANIMAL TESTING; BIOLOGICAL DIVERSITY; ENDANGERED SPECIES; FACTORY FARMING; VEGETARIANISM; ZOOS; also specific laws mentioned in article.)

**animal testing,** the use of animals in scientific experiments; a subject of continuing and growing controversy in recent decades. In past decades, at least since the 19th century, some voices have been raised against painful experiments performed on live animals, generally as part of the *antivivisectionist movement*. But only in recent decades, with the rise of the ANIMAL RIGHTS MOVEMENT, has a wider portion of the population begun to question the use of animals in testing.

Concern over animal testing focuses on two overlapping areas: welfare, or the humane treatment of animals in testing situations, and animal rights, or questions about humans rights to use animals for testing purposes. There is wide agreement on welfare issues—the conditions under which the animals are housed and the amount of pain they are forced to endure. In fact, from the mid-1970s animal rights groups have received enormous publicity, and many new members, from exposing terrible conditions. In some cases, researchers have lost their funding and companies have discontinued certain testing practices because of public outcry over conditions exposed by animal rights researchers. Protests have focused particularly on animal tests in the cosmetic industry, such as the DRAIZE EYE-IRRITANCY TEST and the $LD_{50}$ TEST.

There is less agreement on the use of animal testing in more vital areas, such as assessing the DOSAGE LEVELS of new drugs or possible toxicity of new drugs or other new chemicals, as is often required by law. At one end, scientists and legislators point out that testing of drugs and TOXIC CHEMICALS helps save both human lives and environmental health, by allowing scientists to identify problems before substances are used by humans or in the environment. At the other end are some animal rights activists who argue that no animal should be caged, hurt, or sacrificed to save human lives, and that in any case scientists should stop producing so many new substances hazardous to the environment.

In between are people with a spectrum of views, attempting in various ways to balance concerns about animal rights and welfare against those for human health and safety. Among them, is process of curbing unrestrained, indiscriminate use and abuse of animals in the laboratory, making many more researchers accountable to changing public standards.

Beyond that, many have been working hard to develop alternatives to animal testing. A main focus of alternatives is *in vitro* testing—meaning "in glass"—in which substances are tested on tissue cultures and analyzed in other ways, often using computer modeling. It may take years to develop specific alternative tests—to be sure, for example, that a chicken egg membrane can in fact be used to give information formerly provided by the rabbit's eye in the Draize test. Even then, however, *in vitro* testing cannot fully match the kind of data produced by whole-animal testing, which offers what is so far an unduplicatable opportunity to observe biological and behavioral effects on an entire organism, including the interaction of cells and tissues, the changes in and recovery of damaged tissues, and the excretion of the substance from the body. Scientists point out that the historical data built up through animal testing also provides a way of comparing results, to assess the relative toxicity of different chemicals. Other observers point out, however, that animal testing requires too much time, labor, and money to keep up with the sheer number of new chemicals being developed, thus producing additional pressure for alternative tests to be developed.

Some amount of animal testing will likely continue, though under increasing supervision and guidelines, such as that put forth by the European Economic Community (EEC) in the mid-1980s: "Where an experiment has to be performed, the choice of species shall be carefully considered and, where necessary, explained to the authority. In a choice between experiments, those which use the minimum number of animals, involve animals with the lowest degree of neurophysiological sensitivity, cause the least pain, suffering, distress or lasting harm, and which are most likely to provide satisfactory results, shall be selected." In their *The Principles of Humane Experimental Technique*, W. Russell and R. Burch as early as 1959 put it more simply, in defining the "three R's" of alternatives for animal testing: reducing the number of animals used in a test; refining tests to decrease pain; and replacing animal tests with non-animal tests.

Animal rights supporters have also sought alternatives to the use of animals for educational purposes in high schools and colleges, many of which are animals taken from pounds and some of which have been stolen from their homes. Various simulations, often involving computers, are being developed and made available for use in classrooms, such as an electronic animal dummy for use in learning cardiac pulmonary resuscitation (CPR). Several animal rights groups offer help to students who wish to resist standard animal dissections (see ANIMAL RIGHTS AND WELFARE INFORMATION AND ACTION GUIDE on page 361).

Hard data on the use of animals is not readily available. Estimates of the number of animals used in experiments each year in the United States range from 10 to 100 million; the U.S. Congress's Office of Technology Assessment estimated 22 million in 1986. Under the ANIMAL WELFARE ACT, reports must be filed with the Animal and Plant Health Inspection Service (see DEPARTMENT OF AGRICULTURE) on experimental use of certain kinds of animals—notably dogs, cats, rabbits, primates, guinea pigs, hamsters, and wild animals, though mice and rats are also sometimes included—with information in three categories: nonpainful procedures, painful procedures in which animals receive anesthesia, and painful procedures with no anesthesia given. In the INVESTOR RESPONSIBILITY RESEARCH CENTER report *Animal Testing and Consumer Products*, Heidi J. Welsh reported that in 1986–88, about 6 percent of all animal use was reported as painful, about 35 percent as painful though with some form of anesthesia, and the remaining 59 percent not painful. Guinea pigs and rabbits were the most widely used animals, in both commercial and noncommercial testing, with cats, dogs, and primates used less often, presumably at least in part because they are more likely to evoke protest. Various animal rights groups monitor animal use in testing and publicize both those companies with unacceptable testing policies and those that are "cruelty-free." (See ANIMAL RIGHTS AND WELFARE INFORMATION AND ACTION GUIDE on page 361; also ANIMAL RIGHTS MOVEMENT: DRAIZE EYE-IRRITANCY TEST; and LD$_{50}$ TEST.)

**Animal Welfare Act (AWA),** a U.S. federal law passed in 1966 and amended several times, most notably in 1970 and 1976. The original law authorized the DEPARTMENT OF AGRICULTURE (DOA) to "regulate the transportation, sale, and handling of dogs, cats, and certain other animals intended to be used for purposes of research or experimentation, and for other purposes," requiring that dealers must be licensed; research facilities must be registered and comply with DOA regulations; all dogs and cats transported or sold must be identified according to DOA specifications;

and humane standards must be employed, with violations determined by inspection. Violating dealers could be suspended or have their licenses revoked, and research facilities could be fined. The 1970 amendments included exhibitors as well and expanded humane treatment standards to include handling, care, treatment, and transportation of animals, with minimum requirements cited for feeding, watering, sanitation, and veterinary care. DOA inspectors were authorized to "destroy" any animal they deemed to be suffering. Amendments in 1976 extended the law to cover intermediate handlers and carriers; required that animals could not be transported or delivered under a designated age and without a veterinarian's certificate of health; and prohibited animal fighting. When there is "probable cause to believe the Act has been violated," the AWA allows district judges to issue warrants for search and seizure of animals. Enforcement has been variable, but the Act provides a basis for suits by numerous organizations. (See also ANIMAL RIGHTS MOVEMENT.)

**Antarctica,** the fifth-largest and by far the coldest continent, its land mass approximately 5,500,000 square miles (14,200,000 square kilometers), most of it covered by an ice pack averaging 6,500 feet deep. There is little plant or animal life beyond lichens, mosses, mites, and lice on the ice sheet covering Antarctica but a great deal of life in the seas surrounding the continent. The chain of life in the sea includes plankton, on which feed enormous numbers of tiny, shrimplike KRILL, which in turn are the primary food of WHALES, DOLPHINS, seals (see SEALS AND SEA LIONS), and other sea creatures, some of which are themselves the primary food of the enormous numbers of sea birds so characteristic of the continent, from the millions of nonflying penguins to such world-traveling birds as petrels and skuas.

The continent probably contains substantial deposits of COAL and extractable metals and minerals, as well as offshore OIL pools, but into the early 1990s the cold, ice, powerful prevailing winds, and rough seas have made it difficult even to find commercially feasible resources, much less to exploit them. Offshore oil drilling, however, is thought by some environmentalists to be a real possibility and a potential major threat to this environmentally fragile area. MINING is also thought to pose a possible future threat to the Antarctic environment.

Historically, it has been the life of the Antarctic seas that has been attacked, if only because the natural resources of the continent have been so difficult to find and exploit. From the early 1780s through the 1820s, an enormous slaughter of millions of fur seals in southern seas

### Krill: The Linchpin to the Antarctic Foodweb

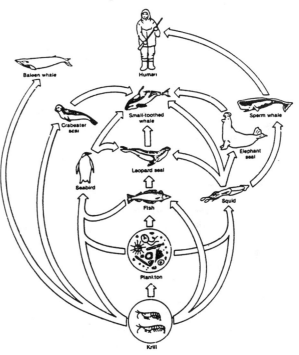

**Source:** *Technologies to Maintain Biological Diversity.* U.S. Office of Technology Assessment, 1987.

nearly destroyed the species, only a few surviving to make a modest comeback in this period. From the 1920s through the 1960s, several whale species were decimated, the huge blue whales and humpback whales becoming seriously threatened. An international moratorium prohibiting whaling in the region began in 1985, with Japanese and Soviet whalers in the late 1980s being last to observe it. Japanese Antarctic whalers still hunted the smaller and so far not endangered Mincke whales, however, allegedly for research purposes, and Soviet hunters killed several thousand seals in the late 1980s, also allegedly for this reason. Cod and several other species were overfished through the early 1970s, leading to depletion of once-abundant populations. But the greatest modern danger to the entire life of the sea around Antarctica lies in the huge krill take, which if unchecked can threaten the entire FOOD CHAIN. Less important but real environmental threats stem from tourism, which is growing, and from WASTE DISPOSAL, notably from tourist ships and permanent research stations.

A new threat to the Antarctic environment was widely recognized in the early 1980s as part of the worldwide threat created by a hole in the OZONE LAYER, in all probability caused by the presence of chlorine released from

CHLOROFLUOROCARBONS (CFCs), widely used as a coolant and in several other commercial applications. Some environmentalists believed that loss of the protective ozone might destroy the krill population, causing immense damage to the food chain and therefore to the life of the southern ocean.

Since the late 1950s, Antarctica has been the scene of a unique experiment in international cooperation and environmental preservation. The great worldwide cooperative success of the 1957–58 International Geophysical Year generated the 12-nation Antarctic Treaty of December 1959, which went into effect in 1961, signed by the United States, the Soviet Union, Great Britain, France, Japan, Argentina, Chile, Australia, New Zealand, South Africa, Norway, and Belgium; they were later joined by 27 more countries, for a total of 39. The treaty, which was to be reviewed in 1991, provided that the entire area south of 60 degrees latitude was to become a nuclear test–free, waste-free demilitarized peace zone; deferred all territorial claims until after the treaty period, with all 12 nations to be treated as equals in the region; and preserved the status of Antarctica as a huge cooperative multinational laboratory. Further agreements included the 1972 Convention for the Conservation of Antarctic Seals and the 1980 Convention on the Conservation of Antarctic Living Resources.

The original Antarctic Treaty did not explicitly cover MINING and drilling, provisionally dealt with under the 1988 Convention on the Regulation of Antarctic Mineral Resource Activities (CRAMRA), also called the Wellington Convention, covering mineral resource extraction. Many environmentalist organizations protested vigorously against any mining or drilling, some working together in an *Alliance for Antarctica*, with Jacques COUSTEAU being notably influential. As a result, ratification of this treaty was sidetracked in 1990, when France, Australia, and New Zealand declared themselves opposed to some of its provisions. These countries were not, however, in favor of the Wilderness Park proposal favored by several environmental organizations, which would designate Antarctica as a permanent, continent-wide wilderness park. An April 1991 multinational compromise proposal that would have declared a 50-year moratorium on Antarctic mineral extraction was supported by 38 countries, including Great Britain, which dropped its support of the 1988 Convention; the compromise was initially opposed by the United States, which in July 1991 reversed its position to support the moratorium on mineral extraction.

**For more information and action:**

- **Antarctica Project, The** (218 D Street SE, Washington, DC 20003; 202-544-2600; Jim Barnes, Executive Direc-

tor), an organization founded in 1982 to "protect Antarctica by monitoring, informing, and lobbying in both domestic and international forums." Its activities are implemented globally through the Antarctic and Southern Ocean Coalition (ASOC), with 200 member organizations in 35 countries, which publishes the international newspaper *ECO*. Under ASOC, the Project publishes critiques, tracks documents and strategies developed "behind closed doors," conducts policy research and legal analysis, presents ecologically sound alternatives for management of the region, and lobbies internationally, as against any oil or mineral development of the Antarctic. It also prepares articles, books, slide shows, videos, and posters for educational and advocacy purposes.

- **ARCTIC INSTITUTE OF NORTH AMERICA (AINA) OF THE UNIVERSITY OF CALGARY,** (403-220-7515).
- **ENVIRONMENTAL DEFENSE FUND (EDF),** (212-505-2100). Publishes *Paradise Lost: The Need for Environmental Regulation of Tourism in Antarctica, Ominous Future Under the Ozone Hole: Assessing Biological Impacts in Antarctica,* and *On Thin Ice.*
- **GREENPEACE,** (202-462-1177), Greenpeace Action runs the *Ocean Ecology Campaign*, and publishes the Action Factsheet "Antarctica."
- **KIDS FOR SAVING EARTH™ (KSE),** (612-525-0002 or 800-800-8800).
- **RESOURCES FOR THE FUTURE (RFF),** (202-328-5000). Publishes *The Seventh Continent: Antarctica in a Resource Age.*
- **SIERRA CLUB,** (415-776-2211 or 202-547-1141; legislative hotline, 202-547-5550). Publishes "Antarctica Policy."
- **WILDERNESS SOCIETY, THE** (202-833-2300). Publishes fact sheet "Antarctica."

**Other references:**

*Antarctica: Private Property or Public Heritage?* Keith D. Suter. Humanities, 1991. *Our Endangered Planet: Antarctica.* Suzanne Winckler and Mary M. Rodgers. Lerner, 1991. *Antarctica.* Gail B. Stewart. Macmillan, 1991. *The Future of Antarctica: Exploitation versus Preservation* Grahame Cook, ed. St. Martin's, 1990. *Antarctica: An Encyclopedia,* 2 vols. John Stewart. McFarland & Co., 1990. *The Greenpeace Book of Antarctica: A Near View of the Seventh Continent.* John May. Doubleday, 1989. *The Arctic and Antarctica: Roof and Floor of the World.* Alice Gilbreath. Macmillan, 1988. *Antarctica.* Roland Seth. Chelsea House, 1988.

**Appalachian Mountain Club (AMC),** (5 Joy Street, Boston, MA 02108; 617-523-0636; Andrew J. Falender,

Executive Director), a membership organization founded in 1986 by a group of New England professors, seeking to "encourage responsible care and use of wilderness lands, to provide information about the region, and to represent recreationists in conservation issues." The AMC pioneered in the building of trails and huts for hikers, and helped spur the formation of various other organizations, most notably the APPALACHIAN TRAIL CONFERENCE, and the passage of laws protecting the mountain regions. With the FOREST SERVICE, the AMC conducts formal training programs in mountain leadership, including the *Youth Opportunities Program* for youth program leaders; it also teaches safety skills, mountain-climbing techniques, and mountain ecology, and carries out search-and-rescue operations. Regional chapters have excursions, workshops, educational programs, and volunteer projects, as in building and maintaining trails. The AMC publishes the *Appalachia Bulletin* and various books and guides.

**Appalachian Trail Conference (ATC),** (Washington and Jackson Street, P.O. Box 807, Harpers Ferry, WV 25425; 304-535-6331; David N. Startzell, Executive Director), a membership organization founded in 1925 by individuals and organizations, public and private, seeking to develop the Appalachian Trail—including Benton MacKaye, who originally proposed it. Since the trail's completion in 1937, the ATC has supplied much of the coordination, technical assistance, training, and guidelines for the many volunteers and associated trail organizations that maintain, promote, and protect the trail and nearby lands, as through its *Trust for Appalachian Trail Lands*, which purchases or protects threatened associated properties. It publishes the *Appalachian Trailway News*, a handbook on ATC history and its programs, and guidebooks, maps, and other materials; it also maintains Trail and Conference archives and a visitors' center at its Harpers Ferry headquarters.

**Appropriate Technology Transfer for Rural Areas (ATTRA)** (P.O. Box 3657, Fayetteville, AR 72702; 501-442-9824 or 800-346-9140; Jim Lukens, Program Manager), an information service funded by the FISH AND WILDLIFE SERVICE and managed by the NATIONAL CENTER FOR APPROPRIATE TECHNOLOGY (NCAT), offering "cost free information and technical assistance to farmers, county Extension agents, agricultural support groups, and agribusiness," serving as a "bridge between rapidly changing farming technologies and farmers on the land," focusing primarily on "low input and sustainable agriculture practices." Requests received in writing or by phone are referred to a technical specialist, who reviews the literature, and consults relevant field specialists and databases,

spending no more than three to four hours per query; responses (generally within three to four weeks) often include an "ATTRA information brief, reprints from periodicals and books, bibliographies, database search results and source lists for experts who can provide additional information." ATTRA also publishes various materials, including the quarterly *ATTRA News* and information packages (IPs) on various topics.

**aquaculture,** the cultivation of fish, shellfish, and other aquatic organisms in sites such as small ponds, paddy fields, and canals. Fish farming, as it is also called, has been done for centuries on the local level in some parts of the world, notably Southeast Asia, where soil conditions are appropriate and a ready supply of uncontaminated water is available. Given the world's rising POPULATION and dwindling FISHING stocks, however, many people have looked to aquaculture to help solve the world's food supply problems, and many DEVELOPMENT grants have been made to establish fish farms. Late in the 20th century, aquaculture was estimated to account for about 10 percent of the world's fish production. However, it is not a panacea, for it brings problems of its own. The land used for aquaculture, if already cleared, is likely to be more productively used for agriculture. If not cleared, then establishing fish farms involves destruction of natural HABITATS, such as MANGROVES or other types of WETLANDS. Aquaculture may be most productive if carried on alongside other food-producing activities, as where fish are reared in irrigation canals alongside farm fields. (See FISHING; DEVELOPMENT.)

**aquifer,** an underground geological formation that temporarily stores water, such as porous rock, gravel, cavernous limestone, or rock with faults or fractures. Aquifers differ greatly in their size, thickness, and water-holding ability, but some can be several hundred feet thick and stretch horizontally for hundreds of miles. Among the most useful as water sources are those in areas with extensive sand and gravel, as from glacial deposits (common in North America and Europe); cavernous limestone areas; and some volcanic rocks. Aquifers supply water to wells and when the water table—the level of ground saturation—is high, they may also yield some of their water directly to the surface into springs or marshy grounds. In dry periods, water seeping out from aquifers supplies increasing amounts of the flow in streams and rivers.

Aquifers under pressure, as when the water-bearing rock is confined top and bottom by impenetrable rock, are called *artesian systems*. When the water table is higher than the top of the artesian system, a well drilled into it will generally yield water at the surface, without the need for pumping. In the days before heavy use of aquifers in the mid-United States, some would spurt water to the surface with sufficient force to supply a modicum of electricity. However, in heavily populated areas, aquifers are increasingly drawn on for domestic, industrial, and agricultural use, so many aquifers are much depleted and few Artesian systems have any useful pressure, virtually all needing to be pumped.

Like LAKES, which store water on the surface, aquifers are vulnerable to pollutants since, unlike RIVERS, they are not so readily "flushed out" by running water. Artesian systems are somewhat protected from POLLUTION by the confining rock layers, but those same layers also confine any pollutants that do reach the area. The POLLUTION problem is increased by ACID RAIN, which causes the stored water to dissolve even more of the minerals (see LEACHING) in the aquifer rocks than usual, sometimes causing toxic levels of HEAVY METALS and other potentially harmful substances. One of the main objections to using underground CAVES or wells for storing HAZARDOUS WASTE is

the concern that aquifers and their vital water supplies will be contaminated.

SEA LEVEL RISE is also a problem for aquifers, since as the OCEANS rise, salt water tends to sweep further inland and penetrate aquifers. Many coastal areas already have to restrict pumping from their aquifers, giving them time to be "recharged" with fresh water. If they pump out too much fresh water too quickly, they will soon find themselves pumping out salt water, and the aquifers may be permanently lost for freshwater storage.

In the United States, the SAFE DRINKING WATER ACT includes programs for protecting special groundwater areas, designated as a *Sole Source Aquifer (SSA), Critical Aquifer Protection Area (CAPA),* or *Wellhead Protection Area (WPA).* However, these programs have been severely underfunded, and sometimes totally unfunded, with no final rules to be met, though they may serve as models for state and local governments.

**For more information and action:**

- **AMERICAN WATER RESOURCES ASSOCIATION (AWRA),** (301-493-8600). Publishes a series of *Regional Aquifer System Analysis (RASA)* Program Studies with the U.S. Geological Survey.
- **INTERNATIONAL CENTER FOR ARID AND SEMIARID LAND STUDIES (ICASALS),** (806-742-2218). Publishes reports on the Ogallala aquifer.

**Aral Sea,** a large inland sea in Central Asia, shared by the Kazakh and Uzbek Republics, and until the early 1960s the world's fourth largest inland sea, receiving the flow of the rivers Amu Darya and Syr Darya. Beginning in 1959, far too much water was systematically diverted from the Aral Sea through the Karakum Canal, and then through other canals and major irrigation projects, in pursuit of Soviet Central Asian agricultural policy. The net result has been the shrinkage of the sea to approximately one third its original size; the destruction of much of the life of the sea and surrounding basin, as the sea became highly salinized; the creation of a salt desert where once the sea had been; and much destruction in the Amu Darya and Syr Darya deltas. Once a major fishing area, the Aral Sea has not supported fishing since 1983. In the late 1980s, the Soviet government recognized the damage caused by its previous agricultural policy, and began to attempt to stabilize the sea at present or at even lower levels, in a damage limitation effort. Farmers in nearby areas continued to use the waters of the two rivers for irrigation purposes, having no reasonable alternatives now that the situation had been created. In 1991, a British Royal Geographical Society study group visiting the area

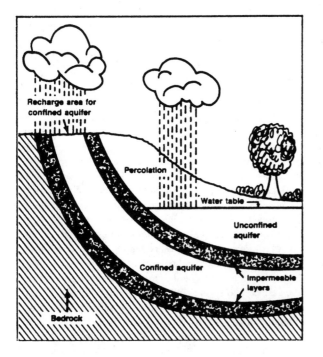

**Source:** *Maryland's Ground Water Resource.* Richard A. Weismiller, and William L. Magette. University of Maryland Cooperative Extension Service, 1987–88.

described the ecological disaster as even worse than had previously been thought, with PESTICIDE and other chemical residues left on the dried portion of the seabed causing widespread serious illness in the Aral Sea area, including massive increases in early childhood deaths, cancer, and tuberculosis. (See also LAKES; SALINIZATION.)

**Arctic Institute of North America (AINA) of the University of Calgary** (University Library Tower, 2500 University Drive NW, Calgary, Alberta, Canada T2N 1N4; 403-220-7515; Michael Robinson, Executive Director), a research and education organization founded in 1945, affiliated with the University of Calgary since 1979. Its purposes are "to assist and cooperate in the orderly development of the North through the sponsoring of research and acquisition and dissemination of information," with interests that extend also to Antarctica and to alpine environments. It sponsors research projects; offers scholarships; operates the computerized database *Arctic Science and Technology Information System (ASTIS)*, from which results a bimonthly bulletin and annual bibliography. The AINA also publishes various materials, including the peer-reviewed quarterly journal, *Arctic*; the quarterly newsletter, *Information North*; books; reports; and technical papers.

**Arctic National Wildlife Refuge (ANWR),** a very large portion of the American natural heritage—almost 19 million acres of WILDLIFE REFUGE in northeastern Alaska, its northern boundary the Arctic Ocean, its eastern the Canadian border, and containing part of the spectacular Brooks Range. This is the northernmost of the American wildlife refuges, so far north that in deep winter there is no daylight, while in summer it is the land of the midnight sun.

This north country refuge—sometimes called America's Serengeti—is a wholly protected place for a herd of 120,000 CARIBOU (some estimates run as high as 250,000); the caribou summer and calve here, and then winter in Canada. There are Dall sheep in the mountains, and the whole range of northern animals—polar BEARS, moose, WOLVES, lynx, fox, seals (see SEALS AND SEA LIONS), and more. In summer, there are birds by the million summering on the Arctic shore, such as snow geese, eider, old-squaw, whistling swans, teal, and widgeon, while inland are found such species as eagles, loons, plovers, ptarmigans, Arctic warblers, rosy finches, and wagtails. In spring and summer come the fields of Arctic flowers, among them rhododendrons, Arctic poppies, and lupines.

In May 1991, the U.S. Senate Energy Committee sent to the Senate a proposed national energy bill that included a very serious attack on the refuge, which would be opened to OIL and NATURAL GAS drilling. Conservationists promised a major campaign against this provision of the bill, should it be taken up by the full Senate.

**For more information and action:**

- **NATIONAL WILDLIFE FEDERATION (NWF),** (202-797-6808 or 800-245-5484). Publishes *The Arctic Refuge and Oil and Gas Development*.
- **NATURAL RESOURCES DEFENSE COUNCIL (NRDC),** (212-727-2700). Publishes *Tracking Arctic Oil: The Environmental Price of Drilling in the Arctic National Wildlife Refuge* (1991).
- **SIERRA CLUB,** (415-776-2211 or 202-547-1141; legislative hotline, 202-547-5550). Publishes *Midnight Wilderness: Journeys in Alaska's Arctic National Wildlife Refuge* (Debbie S. Miller, 1990).
- **WILDERNESS SOCIETY, THE,** (202-833-2300). Publishes fact sheet *Arctic National Wildlife Refuge: America's Serengeti*.

(See also TUNDRA; WILDLIFE REFUGE.)

***Argo Merchant* oil spill,** leakage of 7.5 million gallons (approximately 25,000 tons) of fuel OIL into the sea off Nantucket, after the tanker *Argo Merchant* ran aground on December 15, 1976. The ship broke apart in a storm December 21–22, and its entire cargo formed a huge oil slick approximately 120 miles long, which greatly damaged the life of the sea off New England, and with it the New England fishing industry (See OIL).

**artesian system,** a type of water-bearing rock under pressure (see AQUIFER).

**asbestos,** a class of naturally occurring minerals, fibrous silicates that have long been known and used for their insulating properties, as around water pipes and electrical devices, also being widely used in building materials and in many other ways, especially from the 19th century. Asbestos comes in three forms: white (chrysotile), blue (crocidolite), and brown (amosite). Unfortunately, it has become clear in recent decades that all forms of asbestos are extremely hazardous to health, causing a severe lung disorder called *asbestosis* and various forms of cancer, especially lung cancer and cancer of the chest lining, called *mesothelioma* (see HEALTH EFFECTS OF THE REGULATED AIR POLLUTANTS on page 8; KNOWN HEALTH EFFECTS OF TOXIC CHEMICALS on page 416). By then, however, asbestos was part and parcel of a very large percentage of the homes, offices, schools, and factories of the industrialized countries, and widely used elsewhere as well.

## General Guidelines for Handling Products Containing Asbestos

If you think that a material contains asbestos, and the material must be banged, rubbed, handled, or taken apart, you should hire a trained asbestos contractor, or obtain proper training yourself, before taking any action. Even if you are properly trained, you should not attempt anything more than minor repairs (approximately the size of your hand).

Special precautions should be taken during removal of exposed or damaged asbestos-containing material. Removal of the material is usually the last alternative.

In order to determine the experience and skill of a prospective asbestos-removal contractor, ask the contractor these questions:

- Are you certified? (Ask to see the certificate.)
- Have you and your workers been trained?
- Do you have experience removing asbestos from homes?
- Will you provide a list of references of people for whom you have worked with asbestos?
- Will you provide a list of places where you have worked with asbestos?
- Will you use the "wet method" (water and detergent)?
- Will you use polyethylene plastic barriers to contain dust?
- Will you use a HEPA (high efficiency particulate air) filter vacuum cleaner?
- Will your workers wear approved respirators?
- Will you properly dispose of the asbestos and leave the site free of asbestos dust and debris?
- Will the contractor provide a written contract specifying these procedures?

Make sure the trained asbestos contractor follows these procedures:

1. The contractor should seal off the work area from the rest of the residence and close off the heating/air conditioning system. Plastic sheeting and duct tape may be used. For some repairs (such as pipe insulation removal) plastic glove bags may be used which can be carefully sealed with tape when work is complete. The contractor should take great care not to track asbestos dust into other areas of the residence.
2. The work site should be clearly marked as a hazard area. Only workers wearing disposable protective clothing should have access. Household members and their pets should not enter the area until work is completed and inspected.
3. During the removal of asbestos-containing material, workers should wear approved respirators appropriate for the specific asbestos activity. Workers should also wear gloves, hats, and other protective clothing. The contractor

should properly dispose of all of this equipment (along with the asbestos material) immediately after using it.
4. The contractor should wet the asbestos-containing material with a hand sprayer. The sprayer should provide a fine mist, and the material should be thoroughly dampened, but not dripping wet. Wet fibers do not float in the air as readily as dry fibers and will be easier to clean up. The contractor should add a small amount of a low-sudsing dish or laundry detergent to improve the penetration of the water into the material and reduce the amount of water needed.
5. The contractor should assure that if asbestos-containing material must be drilled or cut, the drilling or cutting is done outside or in a special containment room, with the material wetted first.
6. The contractor should assure that, if the material must be removed, it is not broken into small pieces. While it is easier to remove and handle small pieces, asbestos fibers are more likely to be released if the contractor breaks the material into small pieces. Pipe insulation is usually installed in preformed blocks and should be removed in complete pieces.
7. The contractor should place any material that is removed and any debris from the work in sealed, leak-proof, properly-labeled, plastic bags (6 ml thick) and should dispose of them in a proper landfill. The contractor should comply with health department instructions about how to dispose of asbestos-containing material.
8. The contractor should assure that after removal of the asbestos-containing material, the area is thoroughly cleaned with wet mops, wet rags, or sponges. The cleaning procedure should be repeated a second time. Wetting will help reduce the chance that the fibers get spread around. No asbestos material should be tracked into other areas. The contractor should dispose of the mop heads, rags, and sponges in the sealed plastic bags with the removed materials.

Source: *Asbestos in the Home*. U.S. Consumer Product Safety Commission and U.S. Environmental Protection Agency, 1989.

Caution: Do not dust, sweep, or vacuum particles suspected of containing asbestos. This will disturb tiny asbestos fibers and may make them airborne. The fibers are so small that they cannot be seen and can pass through normal vacuum cleaner filters and get back into the air. The dust should be removed by a wet-mopping procedure or by specially-designed "HEPA" vacuum cleaners used by trained asbestos contractors.

Asbestos is one of the air pollutants for which the ENVIRONMENTAL PROTECTION AGENCY (EPA) sets NATIONAL EMISSIONS STANDARDS FOR HAZARDOUS AIR POLLUTANTS (NESHAPs), under the CLEAN AIR ACT; and asbestos compounds are regulated under numerous other laws (see TOXIC CHEMICALS AND HAZARDOUS SUBSTANCES on page 407). In 1989, the EPA announced a ban, to be phased in over six years, of almost all uses of asbestos (an estimated 94%), including new product manufacture, imports, and processing. Many countries in Europe have introduced partial bans as well. However, asbestos continues to be sold to and widely used in other parts of the world where regulations are less strict.

Meanwhile the problem remains of what to do with the asbestos that is now in place all around us, with special concern focusing on schools and homes, since children are especially at risk. The United States federal laws such as the Asbestos School Hazard Act, authorizing loans and grants to schools in financial need of help in controlling asbestos hazards, and the Asbestos Hazard Emergency Response Act, setting up a comprehensive regulatory framework for controlling asbestos hazards in schools. Under such laws, the EPA has been providing funds—in 1989–90 totaling $88 million—to help primary and secondary schools ''abate'' serious asbestos hazards. Precisely how to do this remains a serious question, however. From the 1970s, the recommended approach has been to actually remove the asbestos, wearing proper protective clothing, including special filter masks. Some recent studies suggest, though, that unless the asbestos is actually exposed and breaking apart, it might better be sealed with tape or sheeting but otherwise left alone, since removing asbestos further disperses the fibers into the air. Critics of this approach maintain that it simply postpones dealing with the problem. (See GENERAL GUIDELINES FOR HANDLING PRODUCTS CONTAINING ASBESTOS on page 26.)

**For more information and action:**

- **AIR AND WASTE MANAGEMENT ASSOCIATION (A&WMA),** (412-232-3444). Publishes *Managing Asbestos in Schools, Public, Commercial and Retail Buildings* (1989).
- **CONSUMER PRODUCT SAFETY COMMISSION (CPSC),** (Public Affairs, 301-492-6580; Hotline, 800-638-CPSC [2772]).
- **ENVIRONMENTAL PROTECTION AGENCY (EPA),** (202-260-7751 or 202-260-2080). Publishes *Asbestos in the Home*.

**Other references:**
*Asbestos: A Source Guide*. Gordon Press, 1991. *Facts on Radon and Asbestos*. Ron Taylor Watts, 1990. *Asbestos—the Unseen Peril*. Plymouth Press, 1990. *Asbestos Abatement: Asbestos Removal*. University of Florida, TREEO Staff. Kendall-Hunt, 1989.
(See also TOXIC CHEMICAL AND HAZARDOUS WASTE INFORMATION AND ACTION GUIDE on page 302.)

**Ashland Oil spill,** the January 2, 1988, collapse of an Ashland Oil storage tank on the Monongahela River, which spilled 700,000 to 750,000 gallons (approximately 2,400–2,500 tons) of diesel fuel into the river, only 20 miles north of Pittsburgh, Pennsylvania. The spill created an oil slick that was ultimately over 100 miles long along the Monongahela and Ohio rivers and caused a massive water supply emergency in the heavily populated area. Steubenville, Ohio; Pittsburgh; Wheeling, West Virginia; and scores of smaller towns and cities were forced to shut off their water supplies. Pittsburgh drew much of its drinking water from other sources, but Steubenville was particularly hard hit, as frigid temperatures froze the flowing oil in that stretch of the river, stopping all water supply to the city. The spill killed considerable numbers of birds and fish along the rivers. In April 1989, Ashland was fined $2.25 million, after pleading no contest to environmental law violations charges. In February 1990, a group of lawsuits against Ashland were settled for approximately $30 million. (See OIL; RIVERS; WATER POLLUTION.)

***Atlantic Empress-Agean Captain* oil spill,** a collision between the two OIL tankers off Tobago in the CARIBBEAN SEA on July 19, 1979, which cost 27 lives and spilled an estimated 370,000 tons of oil into the sea, making it the largest shipping spill in history, exceeded only by the 1979 *IXTOC I* OIL WELL BLOWOUT in the Gulf of Mexico and the 1983 oil well blowout at the Nowruz oil field in the Persian Gulf (see IRAN–IRAQ WAR OIL SPILL). Although the spill was large, the environmental damage done to adjacent islands was small, the spill moving out to sea. The *Atlantic Empress* sank off Barbados on August 2, while being towed. (See OIL.)

**atomic energy,** an alternate name for NUCLEAR ENERGY.

**attainment areas,** localities that meet federal or other pollution control standards for a specific pollutant; as opposed to *non-attainment areas*, which do not (see AIR POLLUTION).

**Audubon Action Line** (202-547-9017), a legislative hotline for taped information on current environmental bills before the U.S. Congress, a project of the NATIONAL AUDUBON SOCIETY.

**Auyuittuq,** a 5,300,000-acre (8,300-square-mile) Canadian national park on Baffin Island, which includes the

2,300-square-mile Penny Ice Cap. In Inuit Eskimo, *Auyuittuq* means ''The place that does not melt.'' Much of the park is on or north of the Arctic Circle; the fragile northern ECOSYSTEM preserved at Auyuittuq is part of Canada's natural heritage. As at Alaska's GLACIER BAY, the glaciers on Baffin Island continue the long melting and retreat of the last several hundred years, since the end of the Little Ice Age. As the ice recedes, plant life returns, here in such forms as mosses, lichens, Arctic poppies, saxifrages, creeping willows, and dwarf birches. On land, lemmings are plentiful, and there are polar BEARS, CARIBOU, Arctic foxes, arctic hares, WOLVES, and wolverines, as well as such sea dwellers as Atlantic white WHALES, narwhals, WALRUSES, seals (see SEALS AND SEA LIONS), and Arctic chars. The more than 40 species of birds include Canada geese, snowy owls, ducks, gulls, whistling swans, falcons, and ravens. (See TUNDRA; WILDLIFE REFUGE.)

**avicide,** a type of chemical compound used for killing birds (see PESTICIDES).

**background level,** the amount of a substance that occurs naturally in the environment, before human intervention, such as the average amount of ultraviolet RADIATION reaching earth before the depletion of the OZONE LAYER, or the amount of nitrogen normally present in an ECOSYSTEM before the addition of nitrogen-rich fertilizers. The term sometimes refers to the level beyond the control of an immediate area, discounting not just pollutants from natural sources but also those from far away, such as ACID RAIN from another country (see AIR POLLUTION).

**bactericides,** a type of chemical compound used for killing unwanted bacteria (see PESTICIDES).

**Baikal, Lake,** a deep crescent-shaped LAKE in southern Siberia, 395 miles long, as much as 40 miles wide, and over a mile deep. It is the deepest freshwater lake in the world, holding one-fifth of all the world's fresh water. Long a treasured natural place in Central Asia, it is home to approximately 1,800 animal and plant species and in 1990 was discovered to possess vents in the lake bottom that provide nutrients for many previously unsuspected deepwater species. It is fed by hundreds of rivers and streams, the most important being the Selenga River.

Baikal's abundant life is seriously endangered now. It has for several decades been under severe attack from the pulp and paper mills that pour huge masses of industrial waste into its waters, as well as from a cellulose plant and other industrial plants and mines nearby and from the industrial wastes, sewage, and agricultural chemicals pouring into the streams that feed the lake. The Russian and other governments have expressed concern about the pollution of Baikal, as have environmentalists all over the world; whether those concerns will be translated into effective action to save the life of the lake remains an open question. (See also LAKE; WATER POLLUTION.)

**Baltic Sea,** one of the most heavily polluted major bodies of water in the world, its life being under sustained and increasingly severe attack since the mid-20th century, as the populations surrounding it and the wastes generated and poured into the sea have grown. The Baltic receives the industrial and general waste of much of heavily industrialized northern Europe, from Leningrad through the Baltic Republics, Poland, northern Germany, Denmark, Sweden, and Finland. It is approximately 1,000 miles long, an average of 120 miles wide, and relatively shallow, its 160,000 square miles (420,000 square kilometers) almost landlocked. The enormous amounts of waste it receives, some of it toxic and all of it destructive of live-giving oxygen, have succeeded in making an estimated 40,000 square miles (105,000 square kilometers) into an almost literally dead sea, with only a few small organisms surviving.

International efforts to reduce toxic waste discharges, OIL pollution, and untreated wastes have been underway since the 1960s and were formalized in the Helsinki agreements of 1973, which went into full effect in 1980. Some progress has been made in reducing toxic wastes, especially MERCURY and DDT, as part of a considerable list of prohibited toxic wastes. Some progress has also been made on oil POLLUTION of the sea. But beyond studies and agreements, little progress has been made as to the enormous flow into the sea of life-destroying waste substances, many of them still toxic, spurring intensification of international efforts to reclaim the Baltic. (See OCEAN; WATER POLLUTION.)

**Banff National Park,** a great place in world conservation history, and part of a massive Canadian natural preservation area. On November 25, 1885, the Canadian government set aside a 10-square-mile area around the hot springs at Banff that had been discovered by railroad construction crews in 1883, during the building of the Canadian transcontinental railroad. In 1887, the area became the nucleus of Banff National Park, the first of what would become Canada's massive system of national parks and other nature and wildlife preserves. Banff is now part of a Canadian Rockies national park group that includes Yoho, Kootenay, and Jasper national parks, Lake Louise, and the Columbia Icefield, in all preserving an area of over 7,800 square miles and protecting a wide range of animals, including grizzly BEARS, Rocky Mountain sheep and goats, moose, elk, and deer, as well as a considerable range of fish and birds. Together, the four parks make up the Rocky Mountain World Heritage Site.

Enormously popular Banff, more than the other parks in the group, faces some difficult crowding problems, as do other very popular natural heritage places throughout the world. Very notably, though, this and the entire Canadian park and preserve system have opted for full-scale natural preservation, while attempting to ensure that as many people as possible can enjoy Canada's natural areas. There are also very difficult OIL, NATURAL GAS, and MINING questions throughout western and northern Canada,

but Banff and the other Canadian national parks so far continue to be held safely for future generations. (See WILDLIFE REFUGE; WILDERNESS; ECOTOURISM.)

**Bangladesh disasters,** a series of major flood disasters in the delta of the combined GANGES and Brahmaputra RIVERS. Flowing down to the sea the rivers flood yearly, often killing thousands and making millions homeless. The cyclones out of the Bay of Bengal have killed well over one million people during the 20th century and left tens of millions homeless. In the past half-century, there were major cyclone-caused disasters in 1942, 1960, 1963, 1965, 1970, 1977, 1987, and 1991. The 1970 disaster alone killed an estimated 300,000 to 500,000 people, and the 1991 disaster killed an estimated 150,000 to 200,000.

But these disasters are far from being purely acts of God. Only the cyclones are entirely natural forces; much of the rest results from the triple impact of overpopulation, deforestation, and poverty. In 1961, the estimated POPULATION of the area that is now Bangladesh was 50 million; by 1991 it had climbed to an estimated 120 million, an increase of 140 percent. Most of the population of the country resides on the Ganges-Brahmaputra delta, with hundreds of thousands of people on the *islands* just offshore, many of them created very recently by the deposit of enormous quantities of sediment as the combined rivers flow into the Bay of Bengal. More new islands are created every year and existing islands expand, all thickly settled as quickly as possible by the farmers of this very poor country, eager to take advantage of the new and very fertile soil deposited on their doorsteps. The sediment deposit is the largest such in the world, an estimated 3 billion tons a year (in contrast, the Mississippi desposits approximately 210 million tons of sediment into its delta yearly, only 7 percent the amount of the Bay of Bengal deposit).

The size of the sediment deposits in the rivers results largely from DEFORESTATION and mountainside cultivation in the Himalayas, the newly raw mountain hillsides eroding and depositing massive amounts of topsoil into the streams that ultimately become the rivers flowing into the Bay of Bengal. Moderate overflow and new top soil from the sediment-laden rivers help rice cultivation, while area farmers live in slightly elevated, flimsily built homes. The Bangladesh government resists any lessened flow in the rivers; a long argument began when the Indian government diverted Ganges water upstream at Farrakha Barrage (dam), with the Bangladesh government maintaining that the reduced flow caused more silting in the rivers and so enhanced the possibility of river flooding, while also providing less resistance to salt water incursions from the sea during the dry season.

The net result is that the many millions who live on the delta and its islands are always at tremendous life-threatening risk, for the cyclones, with their 150-mile-per-hour winds and 25-foot-high storm surges, are sure to come again and again. To save hundreds of thousands and perhaps millions of lives in the decades ahead, massive worldwide financing of a huge regional flood control and resettlement effort will be needed, coupled with a successful population control program. (See RIVERS; SEDIMENTATION; POPULATION.)

**bats,** small flying mammals found worldwide, except in the Arctic and Antarctic and in some high or remote mountain and island locations; the worldwide bat population numbers in the tens of billions, occurring in 950 species, one quarter of all the mammal species on earth.

For many centuries, humans have mounted a sustained attack on bat populations, partly because these night-dwellers are legendary creatures in many Western cultures, deeply associated with devil-myths and with tales of bloodsucking vampire bats. Major attacks have also come from hunters, as in the near-extinction of the Rodrigues flying fox on Rodrigues Island in the Indian Ocean, and from loss of HABITAT to ever-expanding human POPULATIONS. Vampire bats are one of 19 bat families, that take minor quantities of blood from animals, mostly livestock, and pose no substantial threat to humans. There are also hundreds of other bat species that are vitally important to humans and to the balance of life on earth, playing major roles in such matters as insect control and reseeding and pollination of rain forests.

In many countries, bat populations have become protected by law; but many bat species have already become extinct, with scores and perhaps hundreds of other species now threatened. Of the 13 bat species listed as endangered by the FISH AND WILDLIFE SERVICE, those found in the United States are: the gray bat, the Hawaiian hoary bat, the Indiana bat, the Mexican long-nosed bat, the Ozark big-eared bat, Sanborn's long-nosed bat, and the Virginia big-eared bat.

### For more information and action:

• **Bat Conservation International (BCI)** (P.O. Box 162603, Austin, TX 78716; 512-327-9721; Merlin D. Tuttle, Founder and Executive Director), an international member-supported organization, founded in 1982, of people concerned with the future of endangered bats and with preserving the overall biological diversity of earth. BCI seeks to educate the public, offers field trips and workshops, conducts research, and supports bat conservation projects worldwide; it publishes various materials, including the quarterly magazine *Bats*; booklets, *Bats, Pesticide and Politics* and *Bats and Public Health*; and audiovisual programs.

• **WILDLIFE PRESERVATION TRUST INTERNATIONAL (WPTI),** (215-222-3636).

### Other references:
*America's Neighborhood Bats.* Merlin D. Tuttle. University of Texas Press, 1988. *The Conservation of European Bats.* R.E. Stebbings et al. Helm (Bromley, U.K.) 1988. (See also CAVES; ENDANGERED SPECIES; also ENDANGERED AND THREATENED WILDLIFE AND PLANTS on page 372.)

**bears,** large omnivorous mammals at increasing risk throughout the world, as all seven species are hunted to provide Japanese, Korean, and other East Asian consumers with such supposedly medicinal preparations as bear claw soup and a powder made from bear gallbladders. These small bear parts are a very lucrative part of the large illegal trade in endangered and threatened species, and poachers with modern weapons and search technology find it easy to locate and kill even the otherwise elusive polar bear in their search for profits that can very easily be realized as affluent Japan resists limiting importation of bear parts.

In the longer term, bears are threatened by loss of HABITAT to expanding human POPULATIONS, a problem that can be solved only by careful attention to the preservation of bear populations in large enough areas to allow them to survive in the wild. But in some instances such preservation areas have made it even easier for illegal poachers, by concentrating their quarry, and it has become very clear that strong enforcement of bear protection laws is absolutely essential.

The *grizzly* or *brown bear* was once found from the Rockies to the Pacific and from Alaska to central Mexico, in populations estimated as high as 100,000. In North America, a substantial population survives only in Alaska and the Canadian northwest, with less than 1,000 surviving in the lower 48 states, about two-thirds in the Montana Rockies and most of the balance in and near YELLOWSTONE NATIONAL PARK, with a few more in Idaho and the state of Washington. The grizzly, which was also widespread in Europe and northern Asia, is almost extinct in Europe but survives in northern Russia, though how many there still are is uncertain; some estimates go as high as the tens of thousands. In spite of the small number of grizzlies left in the lower 48 states, some sport hunting of them has been allowed by the state of Montana, generating a dispute between state and federal governments and a legal challenge by environmentalists.

The *polar bear*, the world's largest carnivore, is found throughout the Arctic. It has been an internationally protected species since the 1973 multinational Agreement on Conservation of Polar Bears, which restricted polar bear hunting to stated national limits, banned the use of large boats and airplanes in such hunts, and confined the hunt mainly to the Eskimo peoples who had traditionally hunted polar bears and for whom they were economically essential.

With increasing OIL and NATURAL GAS exploration and other economic exploitation of the fragile Arctic ECOSYS- TEMS, U.S. and Canadian environmentalists and govern- ment organizations are expressing growing alarm about the future of polar bears and other Arctic animals, such as the WALRUS and the sea OTTER. Concern was sharply increased by the 1989 EXXON VALDEZ oil spill off Alaska and current efforts to invade Alaskan WILDLIFE REFUGES with intensi- fied oil and gas exploration and drilling.

Of all the world's bear species, the American *black bear* has so far survived most successfully, although illegal hunting and considerable loss of habitat to expanding human populations have reduced bear populations. But the four species of smaller bears—the *Asian black bear*, the *spectacled bear* of the Andes, the southeast Asian *sun bear*, and the Indian *sloth bear*—are all being widely hunted for sale of their body parts and all are increasingly endangered, whether or not yet so listed.

### For information and action:

- **Boone and Crockett Club,** (703-221-1888). Publishes *The Black Bear in Modern North America.* (See HUNTING.)
- **EARTH FIRST! (E.F.!),** (Direct Action Fund, 415-376- 7329). Has a *Grizzly Bear Task Force*, and publishes an *EF! Grizzly Bear Tabloid.*
- **Greater Yellowstone Coalition (GYC),** (406-586-1593). (See YELLOWSTONE NATIONAL PARK.)
- **NATIONAL WILDLIFE FEDERATION (NWF),** (202-797- 6800 or 800-245-5484). Publishes *Owner of the Earth: Grizzly Bear.*
- **SIERRA CLUB,** (415-776-2211 or 202-547-1141; legisla- tive hotline, 202-547-5550). Publishes *Track of the Griz- zly* and *Grizzly Bears.*
- **WILDLIFE INFORMATION CENTER,** (215-434-1637). Pub- lishes *Selected Bear References.*

### Other references:

*Great American Bear.* Lynn Rogers. Northword, 1990. *The Grizzly Bear.* Thomas McNamee. Viking Penguin, 1990. *Polar Bears.* Ian Stirling. University of Michigan Press, 1990. *Black Bear.* Daniel J. Cox. Chronicle Books, 1990. (See also ENDANGERED SPECIES; ENDANGERED AND THREATENED WILDLIFE AND PLANTS on page 372.)

**Bhopal,** a city in central India, the site of a Union Car- bide PESTICIDE-producing plant, located in a densely popu- lated city area. On December 3, 1984, water leaked through a faulty valve into a tank containing 15 tons of highly toxic liquid methyl isocyanate, causing a heat-pro- ducing chemical reaction and high pressure in the tank as the liquid chemical vaporized. A series of safety devices all failed or were inoperative at the time of occurrence, including a pressure gauge, a cooling unit, and a vent gas scrubber; the latter, a major safety device, had been turned off months before. Ultimately, a highly toxic cloud of methyl isocyanate was discharged into the air above the totally unprepared city of Bhopal, which at the time had a population of 800,000. The people of the city, the city government, and public health authorities had not been informed as to the toxicity of some of the chemicals in the Union Carbide plant. There were no emergency plans or procedures in place and no knowledge of how to cope with the poison cloud. An alarm was sounded by the plant an hour after the toxic cloud had vented, when much of the damage had already been done.

The result was that more than 2,000 people died imme- diately following the release of the toxic cloud; nearly 2,000 more have died in the years since then, with the deaths continuing. Some estimates of Bhopal-related deaths run as high as 10,000. An estimated 200,000 more were injured; some estimates run as high as 500,000 injur- ies, corresponding to the number of compensation claims filed following the disaster.

A long series of court battles followed the disaster, with the Indian government ultimately taking over all claims and filing $3.3 billion in claims against Union Carbide. In November 1988 murder charges against Union Carbide top managers were filed in Bhopal, and arrest warrants were issued. In February 1989 the Indian Supreme Court agreed to a settlement payment of $470 million by Union Carbide for Bhopal survivors; $5 million had already been paid, and $465 million more was paid to the Indian government in February 1989, with payments to survivors beginning in May. But in January 1990 the previous settlement was repu- diated by the new Indian government of Vishwanath Pratap Singh, which announced that it would pursue the original multibillion-dollar damage suit and the criminal charges.

Largely because of the Bhopal disaster, Union Carbide's U.S. operations came under close scrutiny, in particular the Institute, West Virginia pesticide-producing plant, which also handles methyl isocyanate, along with several other dangerous chemicals. Especially notable was the Au- gust 11, 1985 toxic leak at the Institute plant, which in- jured six at the plant and hospitalized 134 in the areas around it.

**For more information:**
*The Bhopal Chemical Leak.* Arthur Diamond. Lucent, 1990. *A Killing Wind: Inside the Bhopal Catastrophe.* Dan Kurzman. McGraw, 1987.
(See also PESTICIDES; TOXIC CHEMICALS.)

**big four,** a nickname for four key international agreements: the CONVENTION ON WETLANDS OF INTERNATIONAL IMPORTANCE ESPECIALLY AS WATERFOWL HABITAT (Ramsar Convention; 1971), the CONVENTION CONCERNING THE PROTECTION OF THE WORLD CULTURAL AND NATURAL HERITAGE (1972), the CONVENTION ON INTERNATIONAL TRADE IN ENDANGERED SPECIES OF WILD FAUNA AND FLORA (CITES; 1973), and the CONVENTION ON THE CONSERVATION OF MIGRATORY SPECIES OF WILD ANIMALS (Bonn Convention; 1979). (See ENVIRONMENTAL LAW.)

**Bikini and Eniwetok atolls,** two groups of islands in the Marshall Island group, in the South Pacific. From 1946 to 1948, after removing the atoll populations, the United States military conducted approximately 70 atmospheric atomic weapons tests on the atolls, beginning with two atomic bombs exploded in the Bikini lagoon on July 1 and 25, 1946, in the tests code-named Operation Crossroads, in which 42,000 Americans then in military service were involved. Many of those involved suffered seemingly short-term radiation sickness at the time of exposure and such radiation-related illnesses as leukemia and thyroid cancer later in their lives. The hydrogen bomb was exploded at Bikini on March 1, 1954, in the test code-named Castle-Bravo; its FALLOUT severely contaminated the island of Rongelap, 100 miles away, and several other islands in the Marshalls, as well, causing much radiation sickness and severe long-term leukemia, cancer, and other radiation-related illnesses. Rongelap was evacuated, after most of the damage to the islanders had been done; its people returned home in 1957, but their islands were still contaminated, and they left again in 1984. Some people returned to Bikini in 1968, but many left again in the late 1970s after tests showed the islands and its FOOD CHAIN to still be contaminated. The U.S. Congress voted funds to attempt to decontaminate Bikini in the late 1980s and early 1990s. (See NUCLEAR TESTING.)

**bioaccumulation,** the absorption and storage of a substance by plants and animals in an environment. Some types of substances, such as ORGANOPHOSPHATES, tend to break down relatively quickly; others, such as CHLORINATED HYDROCARBONS, do not, but instead are stored in the tissues of living organisms, as DDT tends to accumulate in fatty tissues. At each level in the FOOD CHAIN, more of the substance accumulates, a phenomenon also sometimes termed *bioconcentration* or *biomagnification*.

**biocentric,** life-centered; a term used by proponents of DEEP ECOLOGY to indicate that all species have intrinsic value and a right to exist, not just because of their possible usefulness or attractiveness to human beings, the opposing view being termed *anthropocentric*.

**biochemical oxygen demand (BOD),** a standard measure of WATER POLLUTION (see OXYGEN CYCLE).

**biocides,** an alternative term for PESTICIDES.

**biodegradable,** able to be broken down by normal biological processes in the environment, especially by bacteria and microbes as part of the great recycling of matter in the BIOGEOCHEMICAL CYCLES. Many modern synthetic compounds are not biodegradable, but persist in the environment, often damaging or disrupting natural life processes, as nonbiodegradable PLASTICS can entangle or be swallowed by animals, or PESTICIDES such as DDT and other CHLORINATED HYDROCARBONS build up in the environment, especially in animal tissue, causing long-term damage and death. A major focus of environmental action in recent years has been to replace nonbiodegradable with biodegradable materials wherever possible, as in packaging. Success has so far been modest. Though some plastics are now billed as ''biodegradable,'' many environmentalists are quick to point out that such materials are often actually *photodegradable*—that is, they break down gradually in the presence of light—of little or no benefit in garbage that ends up in landfills. (See WASTE DISPOSAL.)

**biodynamic agriculture,** a form of ORGANIC FARMING.

**biofuel,** organic matter that is used as a source of energy, either being burned directly, as for heating and cooking, or converted into other forms, such as charcoal or liquid or gas fuels. Biofuels are generally derived from recently living matter, such as trees, seaweed, peat, crop waste, and animal dung. COAL, OIL, and NATURAL GAS, all formed from once-living matter from millions of years ago, are generally known as FOSSIL FUELS.

Biofuels have the great advantage that, unlike fossil fuels, they are available everywhere plants can grow and humans can live; if not overused, they are RENEWABLE RESOURCES. They are, in fact, the traditional fuels used by all humans. In the 19th century, industrialized countries experienced a form of energy crisis, as wood sources were depleted, and they switched primarily to fossil fuels. But in developing countries and in rural areas of industrialized countries (especially after the 1970s energy crisis), many people still rely heavily on traditional biofuels. Rising POPULATIONS can lead to enormous enviornmental problems, including DEFORESTATION, resulting EROSION and DESERTIFICATION, and other kinds of ENVIRONMENTAL DEGRADATION. Bringing the use of such biofuels into balance with the environment's ability to supply them is a major concern of SUSTAINABLE AGRICULTURE and AGROFORESTRY.

In recent decades, the term *biofuels* has also come to mean a far more sophisticated use of organic matter. Especially in industrialized countries with massive WASTE DISPOSAL problems, researchers have been exploring ways to convert waste into energy, from sources such as:

- **forest products industry,** including sawdust, bark, paper pulp, wood shavings, scrap lumber, wood dust, and paper;
- **agricultural and food processing industries,** including fruit pits, nut shells, rice hulls, corn cobs, manure, and sugarcane residue (*bagasse*);
- **municipal waste,** including sewage and solid wastes;
- **forest residues,** including noncommercial timber, diseased trees, and wood material remaining after a forest has been cut, called *slash*; and
- **farm residues,** including corn stalks and straw from rice, wheat, barley, oats, and other grains.

In addition, some fast-growing, high-yield, high-energy crops can be grown on *energy farms* specially for use as biofuels, including sugar cane, sugar beets, sweet sorghum, various grains (fuel for alcohol), and fast-growing trees such as eucalyptus, willow, and sweet gum. Organic matter from WETLANDS and coastal waters, such as algae, duckweed, and water hyacinth, can also be used as biofuels, as can plants from arid or semiarid areas, especially oil-bearing plants and those with high HYDROCARBON content, some of which produce a liquid similar to diesel fuel.

There are two main ways of releasing the energy locked in biofuels: **thermochemical conversion,** using heat to transform the matter, or **biochemical conversion,** using living microorganisms to the same end. Thermochemical conversion may be done in various ways:

- **direct combustion,** the traditional burning of BIOMASS, which can also be carried on in fireplaces or wood stoves, or as a large-scale process to produce electricity by driving turbines. Municipalities, for example, may burn forest or farm waste, or the community's solid waste, once inorganic and potentially toxic materials have been removed. (See INCINERATION.)
- **pyrolysis,** breaking down organic matter by heating it with little or no oxygen available; a process also sometimes called **gasification** or **direct liquefaction.** The

products include a liquid similar to crude oil that needs refining; gases such as CARBON MONOXIDE, CARBON DIOXIDE, hydrogen, and METHANE and other HYDROCARBONS; and solids such as carbon and ash.
- **liquefaction,** heating biofuels at moderate temperatures with carbon monoxide, hydrogen or steam, and a catalyst. The resulting crude oil contains much oxygen and needs extensive refining, except for direct combustion.

Both pyrolysis and liquefaction produce what are sometimes called SYNTHETIC FUELS or *synfuels*.

There are two main biochemical conversion techniques used today to produce either liquid or gaseous fuels:

- **anaerobic digestion,** controlled decay of organic matter in the absence of oxygen; a managed version of the decomposition phase of earth's natural BIOGEOCHEMICAL CYCLES. The result is methane gas, sometimes called *biogas*, which can be directly burned for energy, as well as liquids and solids, some of which can be used as fertilizer. Used on many small farms for centuries to treat manure and agricultural waste, the anaerobic approach is increasingly being used to treat municipal solid waste from sewage treatment plants and waste from food processing plants.
- **fermentation,** breaking down of matter by yeasts; another natural process, involving the decomposition of carbohydrates such as starches and sugars into ethyl alcohol (ethanol) and carbon dioxide. Automobiles and other internal combustion engines can run without modification on a mixture of 10 percent ethanol and 90 percent gasoline; in fact, the alcohol increases the octane, and so does what LEAD once did. Many distilleries today produce ethanol. Other kinds of fuels, such as methanol (methyl alcohol), are also being tested for use in vehicles but have so far not proved economical (see ALTERNATIVE ENERGY).

Using such approaches, organic matter that would have been wasted is instead used for its energy. This is especially useful where the matter would otherwise have been released in amounts large enough to foul the environment. A growing number of industries and communities use solid waste to generate heat and electricity, often in COGENERATION systems, reducing their reliance on other fuels.

But as an approach to small-scale waste, as on a farm, the benefits of biofuels need to be weighed against the value of allowing the matter to return its nutrients to the earth naturally. This is a special concern for those committed to ORGANIC FARMING. Environmentalists are also concerned about diverting CROPLANDS needed for food production into biomass production and about the loss of natural ECOSYSTEMS such as wetlands to energy farming.

Biofuels are far cleaner than fossil fuels, since they do not release sulfur and some other contaminants into the environment, and cause less ACID RAIN, AIR POLLUTION, and SMOG, though they may release into the air HEAVY METALS and other toxic substances that plants have taken up from the environment. Biofuels do produce CARBON DIOXIDE, but in lesser amounts than fossil fuels, especially coal and petroleum. And, if biomass is produced at a sustainable rate, rather than depleted as a DECLINING RESOURCE, and is used in the same general area, the carbon dioxide is used up by the plants during PHOTOSYNTHESIS and so does not contribute to the GREENHOUSE EFFECT and GLOBAL WARMING.

However, biofuels have a lower energy content, so larger amounts are needed to produce the same energy as fossil fuels. This means that storage, handling, and transportation costs are greater. Also, biofuels must generally be used near where they were produced, in small-scale, less-efficient sites, except in industries where large amounts of organic waste are readily available, such as sugar factories and alcohol distilleries. At present, biofuels are not economically competitive with fossil fuel sources, but in the future, as these supplies dwindle and prices rise, they may prove an attractive alternative, especially for light-duty vehicles and power generation.

### For more information and action:

- **CONSERVATION AND RENEWABLE ENERGY INQUIRY AND REFERRAL SERVICE (CAREIRS),** (800-523-2929, U.S. except AK and HI; for AK and HI, 800-233-3071). Publishes *Biofuels as a Source of Energy.*
- **DEPARTMENT OF ENERGY (DOE),** (202-357-8300). Publishes biweekly abstracts on energy from biomass.
- **NATIONAL CENTER FOR APPROPRIATE TECHNOLOGY (NCAT),** (406-494-4572).
- **NATURAL RESOURCES AND ENERGY DIVISION (NRED),** (212-963-6205).
- **WORLD RESOURCES INSTITUTE (WRI),** (202-638-6300).

**biogeochemical cycles (nutrient cycles),** the series of biochemical pathways by which the earth's elements are made available for use by living organisms, find their way into the FOOD CHAIN, and are later broken down to begin the cycle again. These cycles tie together the whole BIOSPHERE—the global system consisting of the totality of life and its interaction with the nonliving environment (the GEOSPHERE). The elements involved are themselves nonliving (*inorganic*) but are essential to life sometimes if too

little of an element, such as nitrogen, is in circulation, growth in the whole ECOSYSTEM will be limited.

Fundamental to most of the cycles—and the most important set of biochemical reactions in the biosphere—is *photosynthesis*, the complex process by which green plants use their chlorophyll molecules and the sun's energy received through RADIATION to join together water and CARBON DIOXIDE, eventually converting them into oxygen (released into the atmosphere) and carbohydrates—the basic source of food energy and the fuel of life.

Within the total biosphere, as within each ecosystem, organisms are categorized by their role in these biogeochemical cycles—that is, by how they get their energy:

- *primary producers,* organisms, mostly green plants, that draw on the sun's energy to make the fuel for others to use;
- *consumers,* beings who eat the food produced by plants, starting with plant-eating (HERBIVOROUS) organisms and extending into a chain of larger, animal-eating (CARNIVOROUS) organisms (see FOOD CHAIN); or
- *decomposers,* microorganisms that break down the remains of dead plants and animals for eventual recycling within the biosphere.

Though little acknowledged in daily life, the activities of decomposers are fundamental to RECYCLING the relatively few elements vital to life, most notably carbon, hydrogen, nitrogen, oxygen, phosphorus, and sulfur, all necessary to form the internal structures and energy storehouses of living matter. While the amounts of these and other key elements on earth are fixed, the amounts actually available for use by living organisms varies; they are generally obtained for use in the form of compounds, such as water ($H_2O$), carbon dioxide ($CO_2$), nitrate ($NO_2$), ammonia ($NH_3$), sulfate ($SO_4$), and hydrogen sulfide ($H_2S$). To form usable compounds such as these, decomposers break down plant and animal matter, generally returning the elements to the simpler forms in which they existed before they were "fixed" by photosynthesis, gradually completing the cycle.

Several key biogeochemical cycles are *gaseous cycles,* in which the air acts as a major "reservoir" for elements during part of the cycle. These are discussed in separate entries, under CARBON CYCLE, OXYGEN CYCLE, NITROGEN CYCLE, SULFUR CYCLE, and WATER CYCLE. In addition to these major cycles, many essential elements are made available through the *sedimentary cycle,* including calcium, potassium, silicon, magnesium, iron, manganese, sodium, phosphorous (of special importance in forming energy-storage compounds in living organisms), and trace elements such as vanadium, cobalt, nickel, and molybdenum. Picked up by green plants from soil and soil water, and then converted into plant cells, these elements find their way into the food chain, supplying the needs of various life forms along the way, before being returned to sediment to begin the cycle again (see SEDIMENTATION).

It is these vital biogeochemical cycles that can so easily be disrupted by POLLUTION of any kind, including AIR POLLUTION, WATER POLLUTION, TOXIC CHEMICALS, HAZARDOUS WASTE, PESTICIDES, and ACID RAIN, and by other related imbalances, such as CLIMATE CHANGE and EUTROPHICATION, which can result from overenrichment of lakes and waterways, as with too much phosphorus, nitrogen, and carbons. It is also through these biogeochemical cycles that some radioactive elements from FALLOUT find their way into living things, sometimes by "mimicking" the behavior of other more common elements, as radioactive strontium imitates calcium and concentrates in bones. With sedimentary cycles, imbalance may cause future shortages, when more of the elements are taken out for use immediately than are being circulated back into use, so larger proportions of some elements (such as phosphorous) may become inaccessible in "sinks" on the ocean bottom and may eventually need to be mined.

### For more information and action:

- **NATIONAL CENTER FOR ATMOSPHERIC RESEARCH (NCAR),** (303-497-1000; Information Services, 303-497-8600).
- **UNITED NATIONS ENVIRONMENT PROGRAMME (UNEP),** (212-963-8138).

**biogeographical region,** see REALM.

**biological control (BC),** the use of various natural means, rather than PESTICIDES, to minimize damage from insect pests and weeds. In undisturbed environments, the balance of nature—that is, the equilibrium established by the various plants and animals in an ECOSYSTEM—is maintained by the relationships in the complex FOOD CHAIN, in which predators eat prey, with the populations of each being keep in check by the presence (or absence) of the other. When the environment is disturbed, this complex set of relationships is unbalanced; in many situations, human activities deliberately unbalance the ecosystems and substitute new ones, such as CROPLANDS and lawns. Then various means are employed to free the environment from unwanted plants and animals, especially insects. In recent years, that has meant increasing use of pesticides; however, these not only harm the environment, but also tend to lead to pesticide-resistant plants and insects. As a result, many people are now turning back to natural means of control.

There are various types of biological control. One approach enlists natural enemies to control weeds and pests, not attempting to rid the environment completely of the unwanted organisms but to hold them in check with the introduced organisms. Among these natural enemies, considered *beneficial agents* when used for this purpose, are:

- **predators,** hunters that feed on and kill many of the target pest. Ladybugs, for example, may be used to kill aphids, or plant lice.
- **parasites,** organisms that feed on, and sometimes kill, unwanted organisms, often on a one-to-one basis. A parasitic fly is used to help control knapweed, for example, by reducing the amount of seed it produces.
- **pathogens,** disease-causing organisms that attack target weeds and insect pests, weakening or killing them. A fungus from France, for example, has been used to help control skeletonweed in Australia.

Another form of biological control focuses on disrupting the reproductive cycle of pests. Many insects release chemicals called *pheromones* to attract mates. Using synthesized versions of these pheromones, insects are attracted and either killed directly or sterilized (chemically or by RADIATION). In a classic example, males of the target population were captured and sterilized, then released into the environment, where they mated unproductively with females. Plans can go awry, however; in one case in California, the sterilization of medflies was ineffective, and the result was a medfly epidemic.

In a wider sense, biological control also includes introduction of more BIOLOGICAL DIVERSITY into the area. Windbreaks planted to minimize EROSION may also house birds and animals that are natural enemies of pests in the area (see EDGE EFFECT), or certain types of plants toxic to target insects may be introduced. Grazing animals may be used to keep down the level of plant growth, as in a field or right-of-way. In addition, some types of plants produce natural toxins that tend to inhibit growth of other kinds of plants nearby and can be planted to keep down unwanted growth. Legumes planted in rows interspersed with wheat help keep down weeds, while also adding valuable nitrogen to the soil. One additional benefit of biological control is that once pesticide use has been stopped, natural enemies of pests often return to the area.

The biological control technique is widely used in ORGANIC FARMING and SUSTAINABLE AGRICULTURE and is a key part of INTEGRATED PEST MANAGEMENT (IPM), as one of an array of techniques to deal with pests in managed environments, including croplands, lawns, and FORESTS. In the United States, various arms of the DEPARTMENT OF AGRICULTURE have been actively exploring the identi-

## Biological Control (BC) and Integrated Pest Management (IPM) Information and Action Guide

**For more information and action on biological control (BC) and integrated pest management (IPM):**
**Alternative Farming Systems Information Center,** (301-344-3724 or 344-3559). Provides Quick Bibliographies on the use of IPM and Biological Control on field crops, horticultural crops, and weeds. (See Organic Farming and Sustainable Agriculture Information and Action Guide on page 226.)
**Bio-Integral Resource Center (BIRC),** (P.O. Box 7414, Berkeley, CA 94707; 415-524-2567 ; Sheila Daar, Executive Director), a membership organization for professionals and the general public, formed in 1978 "to provide practical information on least-toxic methods for managing pests." BIRC does research; gathers and disseminates information; maintains a library and computer database of natural enemies of shade tree pests, including *Ecolists* of pests, host plants, natural enemies, and literature about their relationships; designs pest-control programs and customized data base–derived reports; provides advice by telephone or mail; offers lectures and training courses; and publishes the newsletter, *The IPM Practitioner*, and a wide range of print and audiovisual materials on handling specific pests, from ants to yellowjackets.
**CAB International (CABI),** (602-621-7897 or 800-528-4841). Operates the *CAB International Institute of Biological Control (CIBC).*

**Committee for Sustainable Agriculture (CSA),** (916-346-2777). Publishes quarterly journals *Organic Food Matters* and *Organic Marketing News and Information Service (OMNIS).* (See Organic Farming and Sustainable Agriculture Information and Action Guide on page 226.)
**Northwest Coalition for Alternatives to Pesticides (NCAP),** (503-344-5044). Publishes *Teaching Ideas: Pesticide Awareness and the Concept of Integrated Pest Management* and *Taking the 'Pesticide' Out of Your Pest Management.* (See Pesticides.)
**Sierra Club,** (415-776-2211 or 202-547-1141; legislative hotline, 202-547-5550). Publishes *Pest Management Policy.*
**World Bank,** (202-477-1234). Publishes *Opportunities for Biological Control of Agricultural Pests in Developing Countries.*
**World Resources Institute (WRI),** (202-638-6300).
**Other references:**
*Biological Control of Insects: A Source Guide.* Gordon Press, 1991. *Biological Control by Natural Enemies*, 2nd ed. Paul DeBach and David Rosen. Cambridge University Press, 1991. *New Directions in Biological Control: Alternatives for Suppressing Agricultural Pests and Diseases.* Ralph R. Baker and Peter Dunn. Wiley, 1990.
(See also Organic Farming and Sustainable Agriculture Information and Action Guide on page 226.)

fication and use of natural enemies for biological control. Much international work along the same lines is conducted by the various centers of the Consultative Group on International Agricultural Research. (See also integrated pest management; organic farming; sustainable agriculture.)

**biological diversity,** the variety and variability of living organisms and the biological communities in which they live. Biological diversity, or biodiversity, exists at several levels:

- **Ecosystem diversity** refers to the different types of landscapes that act as home to living organisms; a landscape that includes grasslands, croplands, and forests, for example, has more diversity than one of croplands alone.
- **Species diversity** refers to the different types of species in an ecosystem; a meadow full of wildflowers, birds, insects, and small animals is far more diverse than heavily grazed rangeland that supports primarily a few hardy grasses and livestock.
- **Genetic diversity** refers to the range of characteristics coded in the DNA carried in the genes of the plants and

animals of a species; wild strains of plants and animals exhibit many more varied characteristics, for example, than do strains cultivated for certain known qualities. The greater the variety the more readily they can adapt to environmental change.

Many people focus primarily on questions of endangered species and their possible extinction—understandably so, since biodiversity is a wonder of nature and part of the world heritage. As biologist Edward O. Wilson put it: "Every species extinction diminishes humanity." But long before the question of extinction is raised, reduction of diversity has wide and serious implications, as Wilson continued: "species diversity—the world's available gene pool—is one of our planet's most important and irreplaceable resources." As biological diversity is lost, so we also lose the possibility of tapping as-yet-unknown resources for agricultural, industrial, and medical development. A classic example is the rosy periwinkle (*Catharantus roseus*), a tropical flower from Madagascar, used in making medicines to treat cancers such as Hodgkin's disease and childhood leukemia. Who knows what other so-far-unknown medicines exist? Though biotechnology has made enormous strides, scientists cannot themselves create genes through GENETIC ENGINEERING; they can only work with the genes provided in nature. Some pharmaceutical researchers are concerned that they may find in the laboratory a promising medicine, as from a tropical rain forest, only to find that the plant has become endangered or even extinct in the wild during their years of research.

Loss of diversity also means vulnerability. Where millions of acres are planted with a single variety of grain, all may be at risk from pest or disease, especially since many of them were bred for high yields at the expense of pest or disease resistance. Genes from wild plants can offer hardier strains and possible disease protection—a gene from an Ethiopian plant, for example, was used to help protect California's barley crop from a damaging virus—so efforts are being made to preserve wild strains.

Biological diversity is being lost at an increasingly rapid rate, largely because of changes resulting from human activity, often stemming from DEVELOPMENT and POPULATION pressure. Losses may be direct, as when humans strip trees and shrubs for fuelwood, kill ELEPHANTS for their ivory tusks, clear forests or grasslands for agriculture or settlements, or deliberately narrow the genetic variability of crops and livestock through breeding techniques designed to enhance certain characteristics. Losses can also be indirect, as when ACID RAIN, AIR POLLUTION, WATER POLLUTION, and CLIMATE CHANGE kill off many plants or animals in an ecosystem. Direct or indirect, biological diversity—once lost—can never be regained. As a result, local and international organizations have been making considerable efforts to maintain this diversity.

The best way to do that is to maintain plants, animals, and microbes in their natural ecosystems. That is the aim of the whole system of large-scale national parks, marine sanctuaries, and research natural areas. If the ecosystem has been significantly disturbed, conservationists still may be able to maintain the diversity of species in a series of WILDLIFE REFUGES, BIOSPHERE RESERVES, and game parks, often with working conservation biologists on site using the techniques of biotechnology to maintain gene banks and of CONSERVATION BIOLOGY to manage and protect the reserves. Where life forms are actually endangered, many conservation biologists also work in a series of ZOOS, botanical gardens, and other research areas, often crossing wild plants with domesticated ones to maintain the gene pool and doing likewise with animals in captive breeding programs. They sometimes use techniques developed for use in human or agricultural settings, such as artificial incubation, artificial insemination, and embryo transfer, in which an embryo from an endangered species is implanted in a ''surrogate mother'' from a more common related variety. Some animals have been brought back from the brink of extinction through such techniques and reintroduced into places where they once lived wild, such as the whooping CRANE. For critically endangered species, germ plasm is stored in seed and pollen banks; semen, ova, and embryo banks; and tissue culture collections. Microbes and bacteria are also carefully preserved because of their vital role in the BIOGEOCHEMICAL CYCLES that maintain life, as well as for other directly economic benefits, such as breaking down OIL after spills (see BIOREMEDIATION).

Such techniques are used only on a relatively few species, however. Conservation programs have limited resources, most of which go toward saving the most highly visible endangered species, such as the California CONDOR. And even with the best will and resources in the world, humans are limited in what they can do. We have not even discovered all the life forms that exist; the lion tamarin MONKEY, for example, was discovered on a relatively populated island off Brazil as recently as 1990. That is why the maintenance of the ecosystems themselves is such a high priority, especially in the tropical forests, where over half of the known species exist. Another important priority is sustainable development, which would encourage human use of natural resources in a protected area in such a way as to not damage the ecosystem in general (see LAND USE).

Biodiversity is under the greatest pressure in areas that are isolated. In the past that has meant islands or LAKES, but now with the rapid pace of development, land ecosystems are increasingly circumscribed, in what are called HABITAT islands (such as a patch of tropical forest surrounded by croplands), and the variety of life in them threatened. Given the high DEFORESTATION rate, Wilson estimates that as many as 4,000 to 6,000 species are being lost in rain forests alone each year. The smaller the island, the more rapid the loss. In areas where the habitat is highly fragmented, the loss of species is markedly accelerated. Loss of diversity often also sparks a downward spiral, as the weakening of one or more plants or animals in an ecosystem—especially a *keystone species* (see SPECIES)—leads to malfunctioning of the biological community as a whole.

CLIMATE CHANGE—in this period GLOBAL WARMING, but in the past also global cooling, as in ice ages—also puts great pressure on biodiversity. Many species exist only in a relatively narrow temperature range. As the climate shifts, some plants and animals are able to migrate to new areas or to adapt to changing conditions; but those unable to adapt, to migrate fast enough, or to migrate at all (such as those trapped on islands or surrounded by cities) would be extinguished. Previous narrowing of genetic diversity also makes species less ''fit'' for selection (natural or artificial).

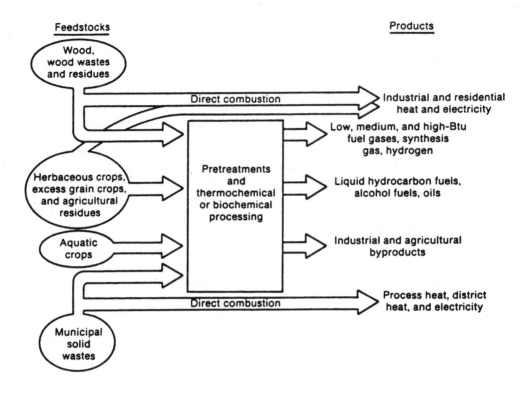

**Biomass Utilization for Energy**

**Source:** "Biofuels as a Source of Energy." Conservation and Renewable Energy Inquiry and Referral Service (CAREIRS), Department of Energy, 1987.

Biological diversity is also threatened in many areas by *introduced* or *exotic* (nonnative) species, especially where they have no natural predators and are more aggressive than the native species. Among the many "introduced species" are farm crops that, because they tend to be *monocultures*, or single crops, are significant threats to biodiversity.

Considerable international attention is being focused on biological diversity. It was made a key part of the 1980 WORLD CONSERVATION STRATEGY. The WORLD CONSERVATION MONITORING CENTRE (WCMC) is the main international organization gathering and assessing information about the world's species and developing action plans to save those threatened. The *International Board for Plant Genetic Resources (IBPGR)* (see CONSULTATIVE GROUP ON INTERNATIONAL AGRICULTURAL RESEARCH) spearheads a global network of gene banks housing plant samples and germ plasm; in the United States, a key organization is the Center for Plant Conservation (see ENDANGERED SPE-

CIES AND BIOLOGICAL DIVERSITY INFORMATION AND ACTION GUIDE on page 104) with its National Collection of Endangered Plants. The Man and the Biosphere (MAB) program is designed to protect biodiversity by establishing a network of key biosphere reserves. A National Biological Diversity Conservation and Environmental Research Act proposed in the U.S. House of Representatives would focus on saving rich and threatened ecosystems in the United States, to prevent endangerment, rather than trying later to save species one by one.

For many species, however, help may arrive too late. The Center for Plant Conservation, in their 1988 Endangerment Survey, found that of over 25,000 species, subspecies, and varieties of plants native to the United States, over 10 percent—some 3,000—are threatened by extinction in their wild habitats; of these, the CPC estimates that perhaps 680 plants may become extinct before the year 2000. Nearly 75 percent of these are in Hawaii, California, Texas, Florida, and Puerto Rico, which are therefore labeled ''Priority Regions.'' (See ENDANGERED SPECIES AND BIOLOGICAL DIVERSITY INFORMATION AND ACTION GUIDE on page 104; also ENDANGERED SPECIES; EXTINCTION.)

**biomass,** the total amount of living matter—plants and animals—available in an area at any given time. It is a measure of the amount of the sun's energy, in the form of nutrients, that the lowest levels of a FOOD CHAIN, such as green plants, are able to ''fix'' and make available to higher levels. Sometimes biomass is limited by a shortage of one or more essential ingredients, such as water or nitrogen. The use of biomass as fuel adds to some kinds of environmental problems, however, since burning produces CARBON DIOXIDE, which contributes to the GREENHOUSE EFFECT, and probable GLOBAL WARMING—except when biomass is grown on a sustainable basis, with as much grown as burned, so that plants use up the carbon dioxide in their process of PHOTOSYNTHESIS. Burning biomass also contributes to AIR POLLUTION, releasing into the atmosphere pollutants of various kinds, such as PARTICULATE MATTER, including some toxic substances taken up from the environment, such as HEAVY METALS and (a recent study has shown) even radioactive substances. (See also BIOFUEL.)

**biome,** a mature, stable biological community, in which the plants and animals have reached the fully mature, or *climax*, stage of their development, in ecological terms (see ECOLOGICAL SUCCESSION). More widely and more commonly, a *biome* is a general term for the main kinds of land-based ecological communities, distinguished by their climatic conditions, characteristic types of flora and fauna, and underlying geological features, including water; in Europe the equivalent name is *major life zone*. Among the main types of land biomes are DESERT, TUNDRA, GRASS-LAND, SAVANNA, chaparral, woodland, coniferous FOREST, deciduous forest, tropical forest, CORAL REEF, and rocky shore (see COASTS), with OCEAN included where it impinges on one of the other biomes. Within each biome are numerous ECOSYSTEMS, HABITATS, and microhabitats.

**biomonitoring,** use of plants and animals as reference points in assessing the health of an ECOSYSTEM. Field biologists look at selected *indicator species* (see SPECIES) for

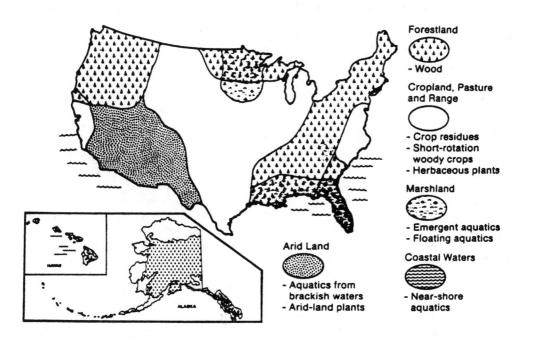

Forestland
- Wood

Cropland, Pasture and Range
- Crop residues
- Short-rotation woody crops
- Herbaceous plants

Marshland
- Emergent aquatics
- Floating aquatics

Coastal Waters
- Near-shore aquatics

Arid Land
- Aquatics from brackish waters
- Arid-land plants

**Biomass Resource Areas in the United States**

**Source:** ''Biofuels as a Source of Energy.'' Conservation and Renewable Energy Inquiry and Referral Service (CAREIRS), Department of Energy, 1987.

early warning about changes that may affect other species or perhaps the whole ecosystem. Unlike chemical monitoring in the laboratory, biomonitoring allows researchers to assess the cumulative and interactive effects of multiple sources of POLLUTION, TOXIC CHEMICALS, or other stresses. Some such testing is now being built into laws and regulations; the CLEAN WATER ACT, for example, calls for specific biological testing in screening for environmental hazards.

**bioregionalism,** an environmental approach—even more, a philosophy of living—that stresses living simply on the land, in harmony and close touch with the plants and animals of the area, raising one's own food, relying on the sun and other RENEWABLE RESOURCES, RECYCLING, and in general cutting loose from reliance on the industrialized portion of society. Bioregionalism has close ties with DEEP ECOLOGY, which stresses a BIOCENTRIC (all-life-centered) approach, as opposed to the *anthropocentric* (human-centered) approach thought to characterize many traditional environmentalists (see SOCIAL ECOLOGY). Bioregionalists stress the importance of local self-reliance, of withdrawing support for the industrialized, high-tech world, and of making a difference in an area that can be affected directly; they often express disgust for the political lobbying of more traditional environmental activists. Critics of strict bioregionalism, however, point out that the world's problems are too severe and urgent for such small-scale, individual approaches alone and urge the need for international concerted activism on issues such as GLOBAL WARMING and depletion of the OZONE LAYER.

**For more information:**
*Home!: A Bioregional Reader.* Van Andruss et al, eds. New Society, 1990. *What Happened to Ecology.* Stephanie Mills. Sierra Club Books, 1989.

**bioremediation,** the use of microorganisms to detoxify the environment. Tiny, naturally occurring microbes have been used in several situations, in the United States and abroad, to break down, or *degrade*, pollutants such as OIL and TOXIC CHEMICALS in HAZARDOUS WASTE sites, including CHLORINATED HYDROCARBONS, phenols, cyanides, and some PESTICIDES such as ORGANOPHOSPHATES. While it is no cure-all, microbial treatment has accelerated the breakdown of contaminants in research and in the field, including the *EXXON VALDEZ* OIL SPILL site. Using the techniques of GENETIC ENGINEERING, BIOTECHNOLOGY has also come into play, as some microorganisms are specifically crafted to do certain cleanup jobs. The first genetically engineered living organism to receive a patent, in the *Diamond vs. Chakrabarty* case, was in fact a genetically engineered bacterium to help clean up OIL spills. Such bacteria have been used successfully in the field, for the first time in 1990 in the GALVESTON BAY OIL SPILL and then in the MEGA BORG OIL SPILL. A July 1990 report from the Texas Water Commission said that in a 12-hour test, the microorganisms destroyed about 70 percent of the oil on the surface, and that "virtually no oil" was found between that surface water and the ocean floor; this was in contrast to chemical dispersants, which often cause surface oil to sink and contaminate the aquatic environment. In 1988, the ENVIRONMENTAL PROTECTION AGENCY (EPA) established a Biosystems Technology Development program to explore cleanup methods for groundwater and oil spills; the SUPERFUND Innovative Technology Evaluation (SITE) program explores methods applicable to Superfund hazardous waste sites. In 1990 the EPA established a Bioremediation Action Committee to 'remove barriers to and stimulate opportunities for uses of bioremediation.'' (See BIOTECHNOLOGY.)

**biosphere,** the zone of the globe that contains all life; more specifically, the region in which all living organisms interact with each other and with the GEOSPHERE—the nonliving ball of rock, soil, water, and air that we call earth; also the totality of all life and its interactions with the nonliving world. In ecological terms, the biosphere is seen as a single system in which living organisms draw on solar energy and on vital elements in the soil, water, and air to reproduce themselves and in the process continuously recycle matter, in a series of complex biochemical reactions called BIOGEOCHEMICAL CYCLES or *nutrient cycles*. Although these cycles and ecological interaction within the whole biosphere can be disrupted, traditional theory has it that the global ECOSYSTEM tends to reestablish a new equilibrium after a disturbance. Some ecologists have seen this tendency toward equilibrium as indicating that the biosphere has a "creative" nature and responds like a single living system, which James Lovelock has termed GAIA. More recently, some ecologists have questioned the equilibrium theory, suggesting that ecosystems instead respond to change more continuously and fluidly.

All matter in a biosphere exists in a hierarchy, from inorganic (nonliving) atoms and molecules to the increasingly complex units of cells, tissues and organs, organisms, SPECIES populations, biological communities, and ECOSYSTEMS. Seeing the living earth as a biosphere implies seeing humans as just one part of an interdependent system and highlights the need for human actions to be fit into the total web of life, playing a proper role in, rather than disrupting, the cycles that support it. This view has inspired more unified regional and international approaches to environmental problems, such as ACID RAIN or CLIMATE CHANGE, and also attempts to preserve unique and rare kinds of ecosystems around the world, as in the Man and the Biosphere program, which sets up a series of BIO-SPHERE RESERVES around the world to protect ENDANGERED SPECIES and HABITATS.

### For more information and action:

- **Ecological Society of America (ESA),** (301-530-7005). Publishes *The Sustainable Biosphere Initiative: An Ecological Research Agenda* (1991).

**biosphere reserve,** a type of protected area set aside under the United Nations' Man and the Biosphere (MAB) program, an area "dedicated to solving problems associated with the effects of human impacts, over time, upon natural ecosystems," the ultimate aim being to improve the relationship between humans and their environment. In the ideal biosphere reserve, the core of the reserve is a natural or relatively undisturbed area, often chosen as an example of a particular type of land or marine ECOSYSTEM, especially where it offers a unique habitat to ENDANGERED SPECIES. This core area is set aside and activities limited (under the laws of participating countries) to those that will not adversely affect natural processes and wildlife; these are often strictly protected WILDERNESS areas or nature preserves within national parks. Surrounding the core area is a buffer zone (or managed use zone) for research, management, monitoring, and education, including exploration of possibilities for sustainable DEVELOPMENT; this often corresponds to the balance of the national park in a multiple-use area. Beyond that is an undefined transition area, in which researchers apply conservation knowledge and management skills in areas that may contain settlements, CROPLANDS, managed FORESTS, intensive recreation areas, or other developed areas. As of 1990, there were 286 biosphere reserves in 72 countries; these are listed on page 401. The biosphere reserve concept and the protection afforded to core areas is only as strong as the laws of the individual country and its will to enforce them—an open question in many countries, especially in times of economic hardship and civil strife—but the program has the substantial benefit of focusing scientific and public attention on areas deserving of protection. (See also BIO-SPHERE; BIOLOGICAL DIVERSITY.)

**biotechnology,** an umbrella term for a wide range of techniques used to modify living organisms, sometimes in the process creating new ones, drawing on specialized sciences, such as microbiology, biochemistry, and chemical engineering. Among the techniques used on the frontiers of biotechnology are GENETIC ENGINEERING, which involves manipulation of the basic genetic codes in DNA to create new life forms; cell and tissue cultures; and fusion of protoplasm. These allow scientists to speed up the normally time-consuming processes of breeding plants, animals, and microorganisms.

Much attention and public concern has been focused on genetic engineering. Though still in relatively early stages, it has been used successfully in the development of animal vaccines and human medicines. Some genetically engineered microorganisms have proved to be helpful in cleaning up the environment, breaking down harmful substances such as PCBs and OIL (see BIOREMEDIATION). Genetic engineering also shows considerable promise in the diagnosis and control of diseases, the development of new growth hormones, and genetic improvement of breeds. Because the introduction of new SPECIES into an environment can have disastrous consequences, genetic engineering work has been conducted largely under stringent regulations, though these have been somewhat relaxed in recent years.

But many other forms of biotechnology are less fearsome, and some are highly beneficial and have been widely used for years, sometimes centuries. A notable example is cross-breeding, used in developing the new high-yielding varieties (HYVs) at the heart of the GREEN REVOLUTION. Biotechnology also may have a significant role to play in the turn toward lower-input forms of farming, such as BIOLOGICAL CONTROL and INTEGRATED PEST MANAGEMENT, as in identifying and developing natural enemies of weeds and insect pests. Many techniques of biotechnology are also proving important in the fight to save ENDANGERED SPECIES, notably reproductive technology to save threatened animals in captive breeding programs and various tissue culture techniques to preserve and improve on plant varieties.

In fact, much of the criticism of biotechnology is directed not at the scientific techniques themselves but at their application, and especially at a short-sighted focus that fails to take into account wider questions and the need for long-term SUSTAINABILITY and environmental safety. Environmentalists continue to express concern that the public is inadequately protected, partly because regulation of biotechnology is too inefficient and haphazard. In the United States, for example, regulations stem from over a dozen different statutes. Assessment and regulation of the risks of biotechnology, especially introduction of microorganisms into the environment, is primarily the responsibility of the ENVIRONMENTAL PROTECTION AGENCY (EPA), under the FEDERAL INSECTICIDE, FUNGICIDE, AND RODENTICIDE (FIFRA) and the TOXIC SUBSTANCES CONTROL ACT (TSCA). Biotechnology was one of the 31 environmental problem areas considered and ranked in seriousness in the

1987 EPA report UNFINISHED BUSINESS: A COMPARATIVE ASSESSMENT OF ENVIRONMENTAL PROBLEMS. (See BIOTECHNOLOGY AND GENETIC ENGINEERING INFORMATION AND ACTION GUIDE on page 43; also GENETIC ENGINEERING; BIOREMEDIATION; GREEN REVOLUTION.)

**black list,** nickname for the HAZARDOUS SUBSTANCES listed in Annex 1 of the CONVENTION ON THE PREVENTION OF MARINE POLLUTION BY DUMPING OF WASTE AND OTHER MATTER (LONDON DUMPING CONVENTION OR LDC), for which ocean dumping is absolutely prohibited, except in cases of *force majeure* or extreme emergency.

***Blueprint for the Environment: A Plan for Federal Action,*** a set of recommendations described as "advice to the President from America's environmental community," published by Howe Brothers (Salt Lake City) in 1989, edited by T. Allan Comp. It was developed through a landmark cooperative effort by many people and organizations in the environmental movement, including DEFENDERS OF WILDLIFE, Environmental Action, FRIENDS OF THE EARTH (and its now affiliates, the Environmental Policy Institute and Oceanic Society) GLOBAL TOMORROW COALITION, IZAAK WALTON LEAGUE OF AMERICA, NATIONAL AUDUBON SOCIETY, NATIONAL PARKS AND CONSERVATION ASSOCIATION, NATIONAL WILDLIFE FEDERATION, Natural Resources Council of America, NATURAL RESOURCES DEFENSE COUNCIL, RENEW AMERICA, SIERRA CLUB, TROUT UNLIMITED, UNION OF CONCERNED SCIENTISTS, WILDERNESS SOCIETY, and ZERO POPULATION GROWTH, though the work clearly notes that not all organizations endorse every recommendation. Involved are over 750 detailed recommendations, organized by the cabinet department or agency involved, the aim being to coordinate federal efforts to address environmental problems.

**Bonn Convention,** see CONVENTION ON THE CONSERVATION OF MIGRATORY SPECIES OF WILD ANIMALS.

**Bontebok National Park,** a South Africa's bontebok antelope preserve in Cape Province; its 7,400 acres (12 square miles) are the home of over 300 survivors of this endangered, though once widespread antelope species, which was nearly extinct by the early 1930s. Several other antelope species also live in the fenced-in preserve. (See WILDLIFE REFUGE.)

**Boone and Crockett Club,** (P.O. Box 547, 241 South Fraley Boulevard, Dumfries, VA 22026; 703-221-1888; W. Harold Nesbitt, Executive Director), an organization founded in 1887 by a group of "hunting rifleman," including Theodore Roosevelt and George Bird Grinnell (later founder of the NATIONAL AUDUBON SOCIETY); Club membership is limited under by-laws to 150, but an associates program was founded in 1986. Members and associates share "a love of big-game hunting and a demonstrated concern for wildlife and its necessary habitat." The Club notes that the term "conservation" was coined by member Gifford Pinchot, the first head of the FOREST SERVICE and that the "father of wildlife management," Aldo Leopold, was also a member. From the start the group has sought to educate the public and influence legislators on the importance of preserving wild animal life, especially big game, work that led to the passage of landmark laws protecting game and migratory birds from commercial exploitation, and establishing the system of national parks, FORESTS, and WILDLIFE REFUGES, such as YELLOWSTONE and DENALI. Since the 1950s it has also offered grants for research in wildlife natural history and management, as of grizzly BEAR in Yellowstone; has fought projects that would harm wildlife, such as the proposed damming of the upper Yukon River in the 1960s; and helped fund the establishment of the National Key Deer Refuge in the Florida Keys, until it became part of the FISH AND WILDLIFE SERVICE. It publishes the quarterly *Boone and Crockett Club Associates Newsletters*, "Rules of Fair Chase" for hunters, the club history *An American Crusade for Wildlife*, and reference works such as *The Black Bear in Modern North America, The Wild Sheep in Modern North America*, and big game records books.

**Borlaug, Norman Ernest** (1914– ), a plant pathologist and agricultural scientist, whose work in creating hardy, versatile, high-yielding new grains that would flourish in many climates was the basis of the GREEN REVOLUTION, which has made it possible to feed billions of people who might otherwise have experienced famine and its accompanying diseases.

Borlaug was a graduate forester, who worked with the United States FOREST SERVICE and as a college-level teacher in the late 1930s and as a plant pathologist in industry. From 1944 to 1960, working in Mexico with the Rockefeller Foundation and the Mexican government, he developed hybrid strains of wheat and other grains that from the 1960s were introduced with great success throughout the world, and especially in the less developed countries. He received the Nobel Peace Prize in 1970.

Borlaug did considerably more than introduce new grains; his work also included the introduction of new agricultural technology and methods, heavily dependent on irrigation, machines, and PESTICIDES. Although the immediate and very pressing food problems of many less developed countries were solved, Borlaug's early version of the green revolution has also created some new difficulties in

## Biotechnology and Genetic Engineering Information and Action Guide

For more information and action on biotechnology and genetic engineering:

**American Anti-Vivisection Society (AA-VS),** (215-887-0816). Publishes brochures *Halt Animal Patents* and *Don't Tread On Our Genes.* (See ANIMAL RIGHTS AND WELFARE INFORMATION AND ACTION GUIDE on page 361.)

**American Bar Association (ABA), Natural Resources, Energy, and Environmental Law Section,** (312-988-5602 or 312-988-5000). Publishes *Biotechnology and the Environment: The Regulation of Genetically Altered Organisms Used in the Environment* (1990). (See ENVIRONMENTAL LAW INFORMATION AND ACTION GUIDE on page 116.)

**American Humane Association (AHA), Animal Protection Division** (303-792-9900). Publishes *Genetic Engineering.* (See ANIMAL RIGHTS AND WELFARE INFORMATION AND ACTION GUIDE on page 361.)

**Animal Welfare Information Center (AWIC),** (301-344-3212; Public Services Desk, 301-344-3755). Distributes *Biotechnology: Methodologies Involved in the Production of Transgenic Animals* (revised, 1991), *Biotechnology: Patenting Issues* (1990), and *Biotechnology: Gene Transfer in Animal Systems* (1989). (See ANIMAL RIGHTS AND WELFARE INFORMATION AND ACTION GUIDE on page 361.)

**CAB INTERNATIONAL (CABI),** (602-621-7897 or 800-528-4841). Publishes *Agricultural Biotechnology: Opportunities for International Development,* 2nd ed.

**Center for Animals and Public Policy (CAPP),** (508-839-5302, ext. 4750). (See ANIMAL RIGHTS AND WELFARE INFORMATION AND ACTION GUIDE on page 361.)

**CENTRE FOR SCIENCE AND TECHNOLOGY FOR DEVELOPMENT (CSTD), United Nations,** (212-963-8435).

**ECOLOGICAL SOCIETY OF AMERICA (ESA),** (301-530-7005).

**ENVIRONMENTAL DEFENSE FUND (EDF),** (212-505-2100). Publishes *Biotechnology's Bitter Harvest: Herbicide-Tolerant Crops and the Threat to Sustainable Agriculture* (R.A. Gold

burg et al. 1990) and *Public Perceptions of Biotechnology: Green Revolution or Green Monster?* (R.A. Goldburg and R.A. Denison, 1990.)

**ENVIRONIMENTAL PROTECTION AGENCY (EPA),** (202-260-7751 or 202-260-2080).

**FOOD AND DRUG ADMINISTRATION (FDA),** (301-443-1544 or 301-443-3170).

**FRIENDS OF THE EARTH (FOE),** (202-544-2600).

**HUMANE SOCIETY OF THE UNITED STATES (HSUS),** (202-452-1100). Publishes *Silent World: Genetic Engineering Biotechnology.* (See ANIMAL RIGHTS AND WELFARE INFORMATION AND ACTION GUIDE on page 361.)

**NATIONAL AUDUBON SOCIETY,** (212-832-3200; Audubon Action Line, 202-547-9017.)

**WORLD RESOURCES INSTITUTE (WRI)** (202-638-6300).

**Other references:**

*Genetic Engineering.* Nigel Hawkes. Watts, 1991. *Risk Assessment in Genetic Engineering; Environmental Release of Organisms.* Morris A. Levin and H.S. Strauss. McGraw, 1991. *Agricultural Biotechnology: The Next "Green Revolution"?* World Bank, 1991. *Gene Dreams: Wall Street, Academia and the Rise of Biotechnology.* Robert Teitelman. Basic, 1991. *Biotechnology: A Resource Guide.* Gordon Press, 1991. *Agriculture: The Fourth Resource.* Henk Hobbelink. Humanities, 1991. *Biotechnology. Changing the Way Nature Works.* John Hodgson. Sterling, 1990. *The Gene Hunters: Biotechnology and the Scramble for Seeds.* Calestous Juma. Princeton University Press, 1990. *Agricultural Biotechnology: Prospects for the Third World.* John Farrington, ed. Westview, 1990. *Genetic Engineering: Opposing Viewpoints.* William Dudley, ed. Greenhaven, 1990. *The Bio-Revolution: Genetic Engineering and Farming.* Peter Wheale and Ruth McNally, eds. Paul & Co. Publishers, 1990, *Gene Technology: Confronting the Issues.* Christopher Lampton. Watts, 1990. *Genetic Engineering,* rev. ed. Eve Stwertka and Albert Stwertka. Watts, 1989.

---

many areas; for example, the pesticides have been pollution sources, as in the GANGES and many other waterways and coastal areas, and the irrigation projects have in many instances endangered animal and plant species. Borlaug himself was also keenly aware that his work needed to be accompanied by POPULATION control and that the world's ability to produce food, though greatly enhanced by his work, was far from infinite. (See also BIOTECHNOLOGY.)

**Born Free,** a work by Joy and George ADAMSON.

**Brower, David Ross** (1912– ), one of the world's leading conservationists since the early 1950s, who became an environmental activist as a member of the SIERRA CLUB

in 1935 and for over five decades has played a key role in developing what has become a worldwide green movement. He became an editor of the University of California Press in 1941, the same year he joined the Board of Directors of the Sierra Club. He was executive director of the Sierra Club from 1952 to 1969, leaving in disagreement on several issues, but later became an honorary vice-president of that organization. He founded FRIENDS OF THE EARTH in 1969 and was its first president, a position he held until 1979. In 1982, he founded the EARTH ISLAND INSTITUTE.

Brower has also been a leading editor and writer on environmental matters. He played a major role in the creation of the large Sierra Club and Friends of the Earth publication programs and has contributed many articles and several books on ecological matters. His books include *Only a Little Planet* (1975) and *For Earth's Sake: The Life and Times of David Brower* (1990).

**Brundtland Report,** an alternate name for OUR COMMON FUTURE.

**buffalo, North American,** large mammals in two subspecies—the *plains bison*, which once roamed North America in herds totaling an estimated 50 to 60 million, and the less numerous, darker, and larger *wood bison*, in northern Canada. In one of the most destructive hunting sprees in recent history, the buffalo herds were destroyed and both species nearly exterminated in a few late- 19th-century decades. Very late, buffalo hunting was banned. The surviving buffalo were protected from hunters in carefully regulated preserves, where the plains bison are no longer a directly ENDANGERED SPECIES, although there is considerable danger of potentially species-destroying disease. The wood bison are still endangered, largely because their small numbers have become smaller due to interbreeding with plains bison and through the pickup of their diseases.

In 1922, North America's last remaining herd of wood bison was protected by the creation of Canada's WOOD BUFFALO NATIONAL PARK, in northern Alberta and the Northwest Territories; at 17,300 square miles it is Canada's largest national park and offers safe haven for an interbred wood bison and plains bison herd that now numbers over 12,000. A few hundred wood bison also survive in the park, as a separate species. (See ENDANGERED SPECIES; ENDANGERED AND THREATENED WILDLIFE AND PLANTS on page 372.)

**building-related illness (BRI),** a type of ENVIRONMENTAL ILLNESS.

**Bureau of Land Management (BLM)** (Department of the Interior, Washington, DC 20240; 202-208-5717; Delos [Cy] Jamison, Director), a U.S. federal agency under the Department of Interior charged with managing and protecting over 270 million acres of public land and the resources on them, including timber, minerals, livestock forage, historical artifacts, and wild horses; it also manages the minerals on another 572 million acres, over half administered by other agencies or owned privately. Most of these lands lie in the western states and Alaska. The BLM is the successor to the General Land Office, which from 1812 administered lands in the public domain, and the U.S. Grazing Service, established in 1934 to provide range management for public lands. The BLM's special agents and rangers are responsible for enforcing laws relating to public lands, such as the Federal Land Policy and Management Act of 1976, the Wild Free-Roaming Horse and Burro Act of 1971, and the Archeological Resources Protection Act of 1979. In addition, rangers provide information to visitors, seek to eliminate hazards, investigate accidents, conduct search-and-rescue operations, and aid stranded visitors, especially in the many recreational areas, national trails, wild and scenic RIVERS, sport fishing streams, LAKES, and areas under its administration.

The BLM also handles issuance of leases, rights-of-way, and use permits for such public lands, for uses such as power lines, OIL pipelines, filming, and recreational events. Its stated philosophy is that management is "based on the principles of multiple use and sustained yield— a combination of uses that balances the needs of future generations for renewable and nonrenewable resources." It is over such questions, as well as its management of uses for FORESTS, WILDERNESS, and rangelands (for which it issues grazing permits), that controversy exists, for many individuals and commercial organizations seek fuller exploitation of the natural resources on these lands—which cover more than one-eighth of the nation—while many environmentalists seek less development of natural resources, in favor of keeping more areas in a natural state.

In response to increasing interest in the fish and wildlife resources on BLM lands, the Bureau has joined with the DEFENDERS OF WILDLIFE in sponsoring a *Watchable Wildlife Program*, "identifying and enhancing those areas where the opportunity to view animals is greatest." The BLM publishes various materials about its activities, including *Fish and Wildlife 2000: A Plan for the Future* and *State of the Public Rangelands 1990.*

**For more information and action:**

- **DEFENDERS OF WILDLIFE,** (202-659-9510).
- **RESOURCES FOR THE FUTURE (RFF),** (202-328-5000).
- **SIERRA CLUB,** (415-776-2211 or 202-547-1141; legislative hotline, 202-547-5550).

# C

**CAB International (CABI)** (Wallingford OX 10 8DE, United Kingdom; 44 491 0491 32111; North American office, 845 North Park Avenue, Tucson, AZ 85719; 602-621-7897 or 800-528-4841), an organization founded in 1928 as the Commonwealth Agricultural Bureaux, with 29 member countries. CABI is a key source of bibliographic information in agriculture and related fields such as forestry, irrigation, DEVELOPMENT, and tourism. It operates various service bureaus and four institutes, the *CAB International Institute of Biological Control (CIBC)*, focusing on integrated pest management programs; the *CAB International Institute of Entomology (CIE);* the *CAB International Mycological Institute;* and the *CAB International Institute of Parasitology*. CABI publishes various materials, including the monthly *Soil and Fertilizers*, the quarterly *Biocontrol News and Information, CAB Abstracts,* and specialized books, reports, and annotated bibliographies, many of them available in computer databases.

**cadmium (Cd),** a type of HEAVY METAL, generally found in the earth's crust associated with zinc. Cadmium is used in electroplating steel against corrosion, in PESTICIDES, in batteries, and in alloys, especially for hardness. Since its toxicity became clear, however, its uses have been limited. If inhaled, cadmium-laden fumes and dust can cause circulatory failure and death; low-level chronic cadmium exposure can damage the heart and kidneys and lead to extremely brittle bones from calcium loss; it may also be a CARCINOGEN. In the environment, cadmium is especially toxic to shellfish. Because of its toxicity, many countries routinely monitor levels of cadmium in the air and water, and some have banned certain uses, such as in pesticides or in plating of food utensils. (See PRIMARY DRINKING WATER STANDARDS on page 274; TOXIC CHEMICALS AND HAZARDOUS SUBSTANCES on page 407, KNOWN HEALTH EFFECTS OF TOXIC CHEMICALS on page 416; RANKING OF ENVIRONMENTAL PROBLEM AREAS BY POPULATION CANCER RISK on page 312.)

**carbamates,** chemical compounds containing carbon and nitrogen, many of them used as PESTICIDES, notably from the 1960s; also called *organic nitrogen compounds*. Among the best known of the carbamates are carbaryl (Sevin®), aldicarb (Temik®), carbofuran (Furadan®), and propoxur (Baygon®). Carbamates are often used as fungicides and insecticides; however, they are especially damaging to the environment because they are *wide-spectrum* compounds, which readily kill nontarget organisms. Like ORGANOPHOSPHATES, they are CHOLINESTERASE-INHIBITORS, blocking the action of enzymes necessary to the nervous system.

**carbaryl,** a type of CARBAMATE, a family of chemical compounds containing carbon and nitrogen, many of them used as PESTICIDES.

**carbofuran,** a type of CARBAMATE, a family of chemical compounds containing carbon and nitrogen, many of them used as PESTICIDES.

**carbon cycle,** the process by which living beings obtain the carbon that is essential to life (see BIOGEOCHEMICAL CYCLES). Carbon exists in massive amounts on earth,

## US Carbon Dioxide Emissions

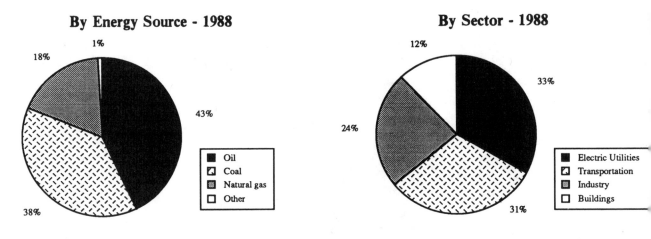

**By Energy Source - 1988**

1%
18%
43%
38%

Oil
Coal
Natural gas
Other

**By Sector - 1988**

12%
33%
24%
31%

Electric Utilities
Transportation
Industry
Buildings

**Source:** Oak Ridge National Laboratory, The Carbon Dioxide Information Analysis Center, *Trends '90: A Compendium of Data on Global Change,* (August 1990).

much of it in inorganic (nonliving) carbon compounds in rocks or dissolved in oceans; some in organic (living or once-living) deposits such as COAL, OIL, and NATURAL GAS (the FOSSIL FUELS); some in living organisms, as carbohydrates and other ORGANIC COMPOUNDS; and some in the atmosphere in the form of CARBON DIOXIDE, CARBON MONOXIDE, or METHANE. In a process called *carbon fixation*, carbon enters the life cycle through the set of biochemical reactions called *photosynthesis*, by which green plants take carbon dioxide from the air, in the presence of water and chlorophyll, and use the sun's energy to form oxygen and carbohydrates, compounds that are storehouses of energy for living beings. The carbon-containing compounds are passed up the FOOD CHAIN, with some carbon eventually being buried as dead matter in the soil, to form fossil fuel deposits (a kind of "carbon sink"). Some others are broken down and dissolved in water, often then being deposited as limestone or CORAL REEFS; and some are released into the air as carbon dioxide, ready to begin the whole process again.

The previously rather balanced carbon cycle has been disrupted in recent centuries by human activities, notably the burning of fossil fuels and widespread slash-and-burn clearing of land, both of which release large additional amounts of carbon dioxide into the air. The result has been to inadvertently "fertilize" both land and water, producing higher-than-normal plant growth. In some bodies

of water, this leads to so much increased growth of plants, such as algae, that oxygen is depleted and fish killed, in a process called EUTROPHICATION. Carbon dioxide in the atmosphere also contributes to GLOBAL WARMING (see CLIMATE CHANGE), which some environmentalists hope to counteract through tree-planting and AGROFORESTRY, since trees take carbon dioxide from the atmosphere and use it to produce new matter, or BIOMASS.

**carbon dioxide (CO$_2$),** an odorless, colorless gas, present in air and dissolved in water, where is it vital to the essential life-sustaining processes of PHOTOSYNTHESIS. During this energy-fixing process, plants release carbon dioxide's oxygen atoms but incorporate the carbon atoms into carbohydrates, the basic food energy for life. The various carbon-containing compounds make up all living things, called ORGANIC COMPOUNDS, a term that also applies to things that were once alive, including FOSSIL FUELS, such as OIL, COAL, and NATURAL GAS. When these fuels are burned, carbon atoms combine with oxygen and are released into the air as carbon dioxide; something of the same thing happens in the human body, as we inhale oxygen-laden air and exhale carbon dioxide. This CARBON CYCLE is one of the most basic of nature's BIOGEOCHEMICAL CYCLES. Carbon dioxide also performs another useful function for living beings: some amounts of it rise into the atmosphere and have throughout earth's history trapped some of the sun's heat (see GREENHOUSE EFFECT), helping to keep the globe within a relatively stable temperature range.

Unfortunately, human activities have tipped the balance of these natural functions. Excessive burning of fossil fuels has resulted in abnormally high amounts of carbon dioxide being released into the air. With other air pollutants, it seems to have increased the heat-trapping functions of the atmosphere, to the point where many scientists believe that the temperature of the earth's atmosphere and surface are rising (see GLOBAL WARMING). Excess carbon dioxide in the air also has a highly corrosive effect, since in the presence of moisture it forms carbonic acid; this then eats away at building stones, especially limestone, as well as some structural metals, notably magnesium. The precise nature and extent of effects in the long term are still being explored. However, in a 1987 report the ENVIRONMENTAL PROTECTION AGENCY (EPA) ranked carbon dioxide as tied for worst in a ranking of 31 environmental problems presenting ecological risks and fifth among those presenting WELFARE EFFECTS. (See UNFINISHED BUSINESS: A COMPARATIVE ASSESSMENT OF ENVIRONMENTAL PROBLEMS; also RANKING OF ENVIRONMENT PROBLEM AREAS BY ECOLOGICAL RISKS on page 311, and RANKING OF ENVIRONMENTAL PROBLEM AREAS BY WELFARE EFFECTS on page 317.)

### For more information and action:

- ENVIRONMENTAL DEFENSE FUND (EDF), (212-505-2100). Publishes *CO₂ and SO₂: Consistent Policy Making in a Greenhouse* and *Offsetting New CO₂ Emissions: A First Rational Greenhouse Policy Step*.
- ENVIRONMENTAL PROTECTION AGENCY (EPA), (202-260-7751 or 202-260-2080).

### Other references:

*Carbon Dioxide.* A.S. Young. Pergamon, 1991. *Impact of Carbon Dioxide, Trace Gases, and Climate Change on Global Agriculture.* B.A. Kimball, ed. American Society of Agromony, 1990. *Carbon Dioxide and Other Greenhouse Gases: Climatic and Associated Impacts.* R. Fantechi and A. Ghazi, eds. Kluwer Academic, 1989. *Carbon Dioxide and Global Change: Earth in Transition.* Sherwood B. Idso. IBR Press, 1989.
(See also CARBON CYCLE; CLIMATE CHANGE; EMISSIONS; FOSSIL FUELS; GREENHOUSE EFFECT; GLOBAL WARMING.)

**carbon monoxide (CO),** a colorless, odorless, tasteless, highly toxic gas that is a common product of incomplete fuel combustion. In the body, carbon monoxide is extremely dangerous because it has a powerful affinity for hemoglobin, the blood substance that ferries oxygen

throughout the body; when significant amounts of carbon monoxide are present, body tissues do not get enough oxygen. Early signs of carbon monoxide poisoning are dizziness, headache, disorientation, weakness, and fatigue, symptoms sometimes confused with flu or food poisoning. In unusual concentrations, as from a malfunctioning or improperly vented furnace or automobile exhaust system, carbon monoxide can cause unconsciousness and death. Less concentrated, its effects are not as lethal but more insidious, because undetected; people with anemia or cardiorespiratory disease are especially at risk, as are smokers, who already have carbon monoxide in their blood. Many people are exposed to varying levels of carbon monoxide at work, notably in factories involving combustion processes, and the gas is a notable contributor to AIR POLLUTION. As such, it is one of the CRITERIA AIR POLLUTANTS for which the ENVIRONMENTAL PROTECTION AGENCY (EPA) sets NATIONAL AMBIENT AIR QUALITY STANDARDS (NAAQS), under the CLEAN AIR ACT. These standards are often not met; 40 urban areas in the United States had unacceptably high carbon monoxide levels in 1988, for example. The EPA proposed new auto EMISSIONS standards in 1990 to reduce by 29 percent carbon monoxide emissions from automobiles in cold temperatures. Virtually every major urban area in the world is afflicted with carbon monoxide pollution. (See AIR POLLUTION.)

**carcinogen,** a substance that causes abnormal, uncontrolled growth of cells—a cancer (see RISK ASSESSMENT). (See also HEALTH EFFECTS OF REGULATED AIR POLLUTANTS on page 8; KNOWN HEALTH EFFECTS OF TOXIC CHEMICALS on page 416; and RANKING OF ENVIRONMENTAL PROBLEM AREAS BY POPULATION CANCER RISK page 312.)

**Caribbean Conservation Corporation (CCC)** (P.O. Box 2866, Gainesville, FL 32602; 904-373-6441 or 800-678-7853 for contributions or the Adopt-A-Turtle program; David Carr, Executive Director), a membership organization founded in 1959 to focus on conservation of Caribbean marine turtles, inspired by the 1956 book *The Windward Road*, by the late Florida zoologist Archie Carr, long CCC's Research Director. The CCC operates the Green Turtle Research Station on the Costa Rican coast and supports other investigations of green turtle ecology, seeking to increase international cooperation in the cause of sea turtles and to enlist public support, as through their *Adopt-A-Turtle Program*. It publishes the quarterly newsletter *Velador* and sponsors volunteer research programs in Costa Rica.

**Caribbean Sea,** the large sea off the Atlantic, in the curve of North and South America; far less polluted than some much smaller bodies of water such as the Black Sea and BALTIC SEA, the 1,020,000-square-mile and as much as 25,000-feet-deep Caribbean is continually refreshed by the huge circulation system of the Atlantic. Yet the countries surrounding and on the islands of the sea face major and increasing POLLUTION problems. There is a great deal of OIL in the sea, much of it discharged from tankers and oil drillings and some of it from much more highly publicized (though in aggregate far less damaging) oil spills. There are also pollution problems caused by the largely untreated flow of industrial waste and sewage generated by the growing POPULATIONS of the area, with resort beaches from the South American mainland shore in Venezuela north to Grand Bahama and Nassau seriously affected. EROSION washes much soil into the sea off Central America, while damaging PESTICIDES wash into the sea from all the countries of the area.

Some international conservation efforts are underway in the area, notably the 1976 Caribbean Enrivonmental Program, the 1981 22-nation Caribbean Plan, and the 1983 15-country Convention for the Protection and Development of the Marine Environment of the Wider Caribbean Region, but most efforts to date have been educational, while pollution worsens.

### For more information and action:

- **American Littoral Society,** (201-291-0055). (See COASTS INFORMATION AND ACTION GUIDE on page 62.)
- **CARIBBEAN CONSERVATION CORPORATION (CCC),** (904-373-6441).
- **GREENPEACE,** (202-462-177). Publishes *An Evaluation of International Protection Offered to Caribbean Reefs and Associated Ecosystems* (1989).
- **INTERNATIONAL COUNCIL FOR BIRD PRESERVATION (ICBP),** (United Kingdom: 0223–277318; U.S. Headquarters, c/o World Wildlife Fund–US; 202–293–4800). Publishes *Biodiversity and Conservation in the Caribbean: Profiles of Selected Islands.*
- **United Nations Environment Programme (UNEP),** (212)-963-8139). Publishes *Regional Overview of Environmental Problems and Priorities Affecting the Coastal and Marine Resources of the Wider Caribbean* (1990).

(See also OCEANS; WATER POLLUTION; COASTS.)

**caribou,** North American reindeer; three species live in northern Canada and Alaska, and one—the woodland caribou—in central Canada and the northern United States. The northern species number an estimated 1 to 1.1 million; hundreds of thousands of these are protected in such large U.S. and Canadian wildlife preserves as Alaska's ARCTIC NATIONAL WILDLIFE REFUGE, GATES OF THE ARCTIC NATIONAL PARK AND PRESERVE, NOATAK NATIONAL PRESERVE, KATMAI NATIONAL PARK AND PRESERVE, and WRANGEL-ST. ELIAS NATIONAL PARK AND PRESERVE, the largest national park area in the United States, which abuts on Canada's KLUANE NATIONAL PARK. Gates of the Arctic alone protects a herd of 120,000 to 250,000 caribou. OIL, NATURAL GAS, and mineral exploration and such massive intrusions as the Alaska Pipeline pose environmental threats to these northern caribou, but they are as yet not listed as threatened or endangered. The woodland caribou, however, which once ranged from ocean to ocean in Canada and the northern United States, is now nearly extinct in the United States, with less than 100 surviving in the Selkirk Mountains of Idaho and Washington. With some changes in local logging practices, and a transfusion of additional caribou from Canada, the FISH AND WILDLIFE SERVICE hopes to replenish this small caribou population in the United States. (See also ENDANGERED SPECIES; WILDLIFE REFUGE.)

**carnivorous,** flesh-eating; a term describing animals that eat other animals, including fish, putting them high on the FOOD CHAIN, rather than eating plants, as do *herbivores*, or eating both plants and animals, as do *omnivores*. A carnivorous diet makes less efficient use of the food energy in natural resources. In modern times, animals higher on the food chain—such as birds, large fish, and humans—are also prone to accumulate persistent TOXIC CHEMICALS, such as PESTICIDES, in their bodies (see BIOACCUMULATION).

**carrying capacity,** the total number of plants and animals that can be supported by a particular ECOSYSTEM, without reducing the environment's long-term ability to sustain life at the desired level and quality. Carrying capacity varies with the type of soil, its inherent productivity, the climate, the usable products that grow well there, and—in the case of cultivated land—the methods used to produce them. Where the POPULATION is growing too fast for the environment to handle, or where a wildlife HABITAT is shrinking faster than the plant and wildlife population dependent on it, the resulting strain leads to continued lessening of the land's capacity to support life. This process is called ENVIRONMENTAL DEGRADATION, which results from such problems as OVERGRAZING, DESERTIFICATION, EROSION, DEFORESTATION, SALINIZATION, and SEDIMENTATION. Though science and technology have given humans many ways to expand carrying capacity, these techniques are often short-term and fail to take into account longer-term, unintentionally adverse effects on the environment. In any case these are often not available to much of the developing world, where population pressure is a particular problem. The aim of SUSTAINABILITY in general is to use resources more wisely, appropriately, and efficiently, and to keep population and demand in line with the environment's life-supporting ability. Sustainability can be only a pious dream, however, where the land's carrying capacity has already been exceeded. Carrying capacity is also a key concept in the management of rangelands, referring specifically to the number of animals that can graze in a particular area, while allowing the environment to maintain or improve itself. The phrase *carrying capacity* is also applied to the global ecosystem, called the BIOSPHERE; it is a major concern relating to FAMINE AND FOOD INSECURITY and a particular focus of the 1991 update to the WORLD CONSERVATION STRATEGY.

**Carson, Rachel Louise** (1907–64), a biologist, ecologist, teacher, and writer, whose fourth and final book, *Silent Spring* (1962), was one of the most important works of what was to be become the worldwide green movement. That landmark work made her one of the early leaders of the fight to save the natural world and its lifeforms, including humanity, from the multiple attacks that have come with industrial civilization. Her particular focus was on the extraordinary damage then being caused throughout the chain of life by the nearly universal use of such deadly PESTICIDES as DDT, which was then being found to concentrate in the environment's FOOD CHAINS and in concentrated form to be toxic to a wide range of life forms. Scores of pesticides and herbicides were deadly, but DDT especially so, for it thinned the eggshells of many birds—those of such predators as golden eagles and peregrine FALCONS being most vulnerable—and so endangered whole species. Many species were close to EXTINCTION by 1972, when DDT was outlawed in the United States and then in many other countries; some species have just begun to come back, because the poisons take a long time to leave the chain of life. Carson's great contribution to all life on earth was to become one of the first to inform, alert, and persuade large numbers of people in many countries and speaking many languages that their common natural heritage was in grave danger and that massive worldwide action was needed.

Carson was a biologist, who taught at the college level from 1931 to 1936, and was an aquatic biologist with the U.S. Bureau of Fisheries (later the FISH AND WILDLIFE SERVICE) from 1936 to 1952. Her first book was *Under the Sea Wind* (1941), her second the tremendously popular *The Sea Around Us* (1951), and her third *The Edge of the Sea* (1955).

**Castillo de Bellver fire,** a fire aboard the supertanker *Castillo de Bellver* on August 6, 1983, which ultimately caused the breakup and sinking of the ship, the death of three crew members, and the development of a huge OIL slick off Cape Town, South Africa; as the vessel's 250,000 tons of crude oil spilled into the sea. The slick missed Cape Town, as offshore currents carried the oil away from land, while the broken ship was pulled out to sea and sank. (See OIL.)

**catalytic converter,** a device attached to an engine-powered machine, such as an automobile, to reduce AIR POLLUTION. More specifically, exhaust from the machine is passed through the converter, which speeds up chemical reactions—that is, acts as a *catalyst*—to convert certain pollutants into less harmful ones before the mixture is released into the environment. In the United States, under the CLEAN AIR ACT of 1970, catalytic converters have been installed on all new cars starting with the 1973 model year (1974 for Japanese cars). These convert CARBON MONOXIDE and HYDROCARBONS into water and CARBON DIOXIDE, which is less immediately polluting but unfortunately contributes to GLOBAL WARMING. Since the 1981 model year, a three-way converter has been mandated, which also reduces the amounts of nitrogen oxides (see NITROGEN DIOXIDE). Other industrialized countries have been slower to require catalytic converters, though they are increasingly being employed in Europe. (See AIR POLLUTION; ACID RAIN.)

**caves,** naturally occurring recesses or openings within the earth, often an elaborate system of interconnecting passages underground. The most common types are *solution caves*, formed when groundwater dissolves rock such as limestone, dolomite, and gypsum; sometimes the surface collapses into the cave forming a *sinkhole*. The two other main kinds of caves are *lava tubes*, remnants of old volcanic eruptions, and *shoreline caves*, formed by wave action on the steep shorelines of seas or LAKES (see COASTS). In North America the most famous regions dominated by caves and sinkholes (*karstland*) are in Kentucky and Tennessee, including Mammoth Cave, but notable caves are also found elsewhere in the Appalachian Mountains and also in the Ozarks and parts of the Midwest and Southwest. Karstland is also found widely in Eurasia, most notably in northern Italy, Yugoslavia, southern France, eastern Belgium, western Germany, the Ural and Caucasus mountains, and southeast Asia, as well as in Africa and Australia.

Because caves have little or no light, a year-round average temperature of 50 to 55°F, and humidity at or near 100 percent, they form a unique environment. Caves offer permanent shelter to inhabitants adapted to its special conditions, including eyeless fish, blind salamanders, blind beetles, eyeless white flatworms, white crayfish, amphipods (side swimmers or scuds), and isopods (water slaters). Many of these are so rare and scarce as to be ENDANGERED SPECIES, whether or not officially listed as such. Lacking the main food source from green plants and PHOTOSYNTHESIS, cave creatures depend on food washed, dropped, or blown into the cave, or brought or deposited into it by animals traveling back and forth. The best-known of these cave commuters are BATS, but among the others are pack rats, cave crickets,

## Cave Information and Action Guide

**For more information and action on caves:**

**American Cave Conservation Association (ACCA),** (Main and Cave Streets, P.O. Box 409, Horse Cave, KY 42749; 502-786-1466; David G. Foster, Executive Director), a membership organization founded in 1977 "for the purpose of protecting and preserving caves, karstlands, and groundwater." The ACCA acts as a national clearinghouse for information about cave and karst resources; develops educational and training programs for schoolchildren, the general public, and professional land managers, including cave management training seminars; and supports research, preservation, and protection projects. A major current project is establishment of a national cave and karst museum. The ACCA publishes various materials, including a newsletter, the quarterly *American Caves*, and brochures.

**Cave Research Foundation (CRF),** (4074 West Redwing Street, Tucson, AZ 85741; 602-744-2243; Rondal R. Bridgemon, President), an organization founded in 1957 "to support and promote research, interpretation, and conservation activities in caves and karst areas," in the United States and abroad. The Foundation supports research projects with volunteers and funds, including fellowship and grant programs, and maintains Field Research Stations at Mammoth Cave and at Carlsbad, Guadalupe, Sequoia, and Kings Canyon National Parks, as well as a Cartography Center. The CRF acts as an information resource for both professionals

and the general public, and seeks to assure that cave and karst areas are properly considered during environmental planning, including watershed management and agricultural practices. Books and other works about caves are made available through the Foundation's Cave Books.

**National Speleological Society (NSS),** (Cave Avenue, Huntsville, AL 35810; 205-852-1300; John Scheltens, President), a membership organization founded in 1941 by people who "love . . . caves and desire to protect the underground wilderness for future generations." The Society serves as a communication network for cavers, through local chapters ("grottos"), regional organizations, and annual meetings; maintains a library of materials on caves, including photographs and equipment of historical interest; seeks to educate the public and influence legislation and policy; evaluates new equipment and helps train cavers about how to use it and about caving safety in general; supports reasearch in the scientific study of caves; and allows members to borrow equipment for projects and to use cave properties owned by the Society. The NSS also acts as a source of cave rescue experts in emergencies, through its *National Cave Rescue Commission*, (800–851–3051). The Society publishes various materials, including the monthly *NSS News* on caving activities, semiannual *NSS Bulletin* on scientific studies relating to caves, the annual *Speleo Digest*, and various reports, manuals, and papers. It also operates a discount bookstore of books and other materials about caves.

---

and eyed salamanders. Humans, too, have traditionally found shelter in caves; some of the oldest evidence of human existence and culture comes from caves in Africa and Eurasia, and in North America, too, undisturbed caves provide an irreplaceable record for archaeologists and historians. Modern cave explorers, or *spelunkers*, are also greatly attracted to the vast and largely unexplored "underground wilderness."

But too many human visitors—even where they are not vandalizing cave deposits—can change the environment and therefore threaten the caves and cave life. Caves and sinkholes are sometimes also seen as convenient dumping places, not just for casual, local piles of mattresses and old tires, but as major "solutions" to the WASTE DISPOSAL problem, including HAZARDOUS WASTE. Environmentalists warn that just the opposite is true, since pollution can travel very far and fast—and with enormous damage—in a cave drainage system (see WATER RESOURCES). Both the groundwater and the life dependent on it are extremely sensitive to changes in the environment brought in from the outside,

such as PESTICIDES, ACID RAIN, and other kinds of WATER POLLUTION.

In an effort to protect caves, the water systems that formed them, and the life within them, various groups have formed (see CAVE INFORMATION AND ACTION GUIDE above), urging measures such as the establishment of cave preserves, with entrance gates as appropriate; restoration of damaged or despoiled caves; a ban on the sale of cave formations (*speleothems*); assistance and training in cave management for cave owners (private, commercial, and public), especially in striking a balance between recreational visiting and overuse of caves; and better education for the public, for whom the American Cave Conservation Association has simple advice: "Take nothing but pictures. Leave nothing but footprints. Kill nothing but time." In the United States, the Federal Cave Resources Protection Act (FCRPA) of 1989 provides some protection for "significant caves" on federal lands, although only about 10 percent of the 400 federal caves are covered, and even these are not protected from indirect effects, as of pollution from nearby MINING or change in water drainage after clearcutting of FORESTS on surface lands.

## Center for Environmental Information (CEI) (99 Court Street, Rochester, NY 14604; 716-546-3796; Elizabeth Thorndike, President), a private, independent membership organization, funded by membership dues, fees, contracts, grants, and contributions, open to individuals and organizations who believe that a "non-partisan information service removes communication barriers and helps individuals, public officials, business and organizations to be more effective in finding constructive solutions to difficult environmental problems." CEI maintains a library and computer data bases, with information specialists available to answer questions; sponsors educational programs on environmental issues; and publishes various materials, including the newsletter *CEI Sphere*; monthies *Acid Precipitation Digest*, and *Global Climate Change Digest; Directory of Environmental Agencies and Organizations*; and numerous reports, study guides, and bibliographies on topics such as acid rain, pesticides, energy, and biotechnology. CEI also operates the *Air Resources Information Clearinghouse (ARIC)*, including global climate change.

## Center for Marine Conservation (CMC), (1725 DeSales Street, NW, Washington, DC 20036; 202-429-5609; Roger E. McManus, President), an environmental membership organization founded in 1972 and "dedicated to the protection of endangered marine wildlife and their habitats, and to conserving coastal and ocean resources." Formerly called the *Center for Environmental Education*, the CMC conducts policy-oriented research, promotes public awareness through education, seeks to involve citizens in public policy decisions, and supports domestic and international conservation programs for marine species and their habitats. Through its *Marine Habitat Program* it works to support existing marine sanctuaries, including one for humpbacked WHALES in the CARIBBEAN, and to establish new ones; through its *Marine Debris and Entanglement Program*, it seeks to cut down on harmful use of DRIFT-NETS and also PLASTIC debris in general, harmful to both sea animals and sea birds, and promotes Turtle Excluder Devices (TEDs) to help protect sea TURTLES from drowning in shrimp nets; and through its *Species Recovery Program* it seeks to conserve endangered seals (see SEALS AND SEA LIONS) around the world. Among its other recent activities have been coordination of large-scale volunteer cleanups of beaches fouled with marine debris; seeking to control artificial light on Florida beaches that interferes with sea turtles nesting; participation in the EXXON VALDEZ cleanup, urging Exxon to step up rescue and rehabilitation of sea OTTERS; and campaigns for the whaling

moratorium. CMC publishes the quarterly newsletters *Marine Conservation News* and *Sanctuary Currents;* the biannual newsletter *Coastal Connection*; books such as *A Nation of Oceans* and *Citizen's Guide to Plastic in the Ocean*; reports such as *Marine Wildlife Entanglement in North America*; slide shows; and fact sheets.

## Center for Science in the Public Interest (CSPI) (1501 16th Street NW, Washington, DC 20036; 202-332-9110; Michael F. Jacobson, Executive Director and Co-Founder), a consumer advocacy organization founded in 1971, focusing on health and nutrition issues, such as "deceptive marketing practices, dangerous food additives or contaminants, conflicts of interest in the academic community, and flawed science propagated by industries concerned solely with their profits." CSPI maintains an office of legal affairs and special projects such as *Americans for Safe Food (ASF)*, seeking contaminant-free foods; the *Nutrition Project*; and the *Alcohol Policies Project*. It also publishes various materials, including a *Nutrition Action Healthletter*, brochures such as *Guess What's Coming to Dinner: Contaminants in Our Food*; reports, such as *Organic Agriculture: What the States Are Doing* (Dan Howell, 1989), books; posters; computer software; and a directory of mail-order sources of organically grown foods.

## Centre for Science and Technology for Development (CSTD), United Nations (One U.N. Plaza, New York, NY 10017; 212-963-8435; Sergio C. Trindade, Executive Director), one of the two main arms of the United Nations Department of Technical Cooperation for Development (UNDTCD), established by the 1979 UN Conference on Science and Technology for Development, with a mandate to "harmonize the development approaches of the UN system and its specialized agencies in the field of S&T [science and technology] for development; help developing nations sift S&T issues and options for development; [and] help developing nations respond to the opportunities offered by those new and emerging sciences and technologies which are most appropriate for their development." The CSTD sponsors a series of national dialogues bringing into direct contact with each other business leaders, bankers, scientists, universities, research institutes, public groups, and government policy-makers, aiming to find a common ground within which science and technology can be used to advantage. Main areas of concern include drought and DESERTIFICATION, CLIMATE CHANGE, ALTERNATIVE ENERGY, appropriate technology, BIOTECHNOLOGY, and ocean dumping (including PLASTICS and HAZARDOUS WASTE).

The CSTD also has an *Advance Technology Alert Sys-*

*tem (ATAS)*, to "provide Third World nations with technology assessment and forecasting services in fields ranging from biotechnology to satellite communications," and a related *Technology Alert Network (TAN)*, with information often shared through international conferences and seminars, and through publications such as the quarterly newsletter *Update*, the technology alert supplement *ATAS News*, a directory of UN information sources, a directory of research and development institutes in developing countries, an inventory of research in program, and specialized *ATAS Alert Bulletins* on new and emerging science and technology.

**cesium 137,** a radioactive form of the metal cesium, commonly found in FALLOUT from nuclear explosions, but also sometimes used in cancer research and therapy. It has a half-life (see RADIATION) of about 33 years and tends to accumulate in bones, sometimes replacing phosphorus.

**Cetacean Society International (CSI),** (P.O. Box 290145, Wethersfield, CT 06109; 203-563-6444; Robbins Barstow, Executive Director), a membership organization, founded in 1974 as the *Connecticut Cetacean Society*, of people concerned with conservation and protection of cetaceans, such as WHALES, DOLPHINS, and PORPOISES. The CSI sends observers to International Whaling Commission (see WHALE INFORMATION AND ACTION GUIDE on page 343) meetings, attends other international meetings, and acts as part of an informal international "Global Cetacean Coalition." It also supports research; actively promotes "dolphin-safe" tuna; keeps members up-to-date on local, national, and international developments concerning cetaceans; holds monthly meetings, usually in Connecticut, with international whaling experts; arranges whalewatching trips; and publishes the bimonthly newsletter *The Connecticut Whale* and other materials.

**cheetahs,** the big cats that are the fastest of all the land animals; they once roamed all of Africa and much of South Asia, including the Indian subcontinent. Small numbers are still to be found in southwest Asia, and a population estimated at 20,000 to 25,000 in central and east Africa. Despite their numbers, they are a seriously ENDANGERED SPECIES, threatened in the long term by loss of HABITAT to explosively expanding African human POPULATIONS, and in the short term by hunters. Although they are a protected species, and although worldwide campaigns have sharply cut the demand for cheetah and other fur coats in many countries, a very lucrative market for cheetah skins continues to exist in Japan and several other Asian countries, guaranteeing continued illegal killing of cheetahs and an illegal trade in their skins. Continuing political instabil-

ity in many African countries makes it relatively easy for cheetah poachers; only closing the cheetah skin market at the consuming end will in the short run save the cheetahs. In the long run, the loss of habitat question remains, and is likely to be solved only by careful protection in such magnificent African wildlife preserves as the SERENGETI, KRUGER, AMBOSELI, and MASAI MARA. (See also ENDANGERED SPECIES; also ENDANGERED AND THREATENED WILDLIFE AND PLANTS on page 372.)

**Chelyabinsk,** the Soviet nuclear complex in the Urals, about 10 miles from the town of Kyshtym, largely engaged in producing plutonium for atomic weapons. It was the site of the massive Chelyabinsk-40 nuclear waste explosion of either December 1957 or January 1958, kept secret by the Soviets at the time, but revealed by Soviet dissident Zhores Medvedev in 1976, although without hard data on the disaster. That the disaster occurred was ultimately fully confirmed by Soviet scientists in 1988, and made public after the 1991 revolution in the Soviet Union, but its scope is still unclear. The evidence seems to indicate that there were thousands of radiation sickness casualties, followed later by large numbers of radiation-related serious illnesses, and that an area of several hundred square miles with a population of an estimated 200,000 was contaminated, with at least 10,000 people evacuated. Some contaminated towns and villages have probably been left permanently deserted. Radioactive waste dumping at the nuclear complex has also contaminated the air, ground, and water of surrounding areas, including the creation of a highly toxic body of water at Lake Karachy, which contains extremely high concentrations of radioactive waste. (See also NUCLEAR WEAPONS ESTABLISHMENT.)

**Chernobyl meltdown,** the worst nuclear disaster since the World War II atomic bombing of Hiroshima and Nagasaki, and by far the worst single event in the history of the world's nuclear power industry. On April 25 and 26, 1986, a series of human errors during a test of safety systems caused the number 4 nuclear reactor at the Chernobyl nuclear power station, on the Priapat River, approximately 130 kilometers (80 miles) north of Kiev in the Ukraine, to become unstable and go out of control. At 1:23 A.M. on April 26, an extremely powerful steam explosion caused by vaporizing water inside the reactor blasted aside the 1,000-ton metal lid, breached the thick concrete containment shell, and generated a graphite core fire and huge hydrogen explosion that created an immense and extremely toxic radioactive cloud that in the next several days severely contaminated much of the eastern Soviet Union, eastern and southern Europe, and then western and northern Europe, with the cloud eventually reaching many northern hemisphere countries. Climatic conditions caused especially heavy and damaging FALLOUT in Sweden, Finnish Lapland, Great Britain, and Ireland.

The Soviet government was at first silent as to the disaster, but on April 28 Swedish and other Scandinavian sources recorded huge amounts of radioactive fallout, and the magnitude of the disaster began to become apparent; then the Soviet government announced that an accident had taken place, and within a few weeks agreed that a major disaster had occurred, even asking for foreign help for the first time since World War II. The Soviets announced that 31 people died in and soon following the accident and that several hundred more were hospitalized, less than 150 suffering from severe radiation sickness; they evacuated approximately 130,000 people from a 30-square-kilometer zone around the atomic plant.

However, the Soviet government continued to hide the full scope of the disaster from the Soviet people, then and for years afterward. By mid-1990, it had become clear that the immediate death toll was in the hundreds, rather than 31, that thousands of people had been seriously damaged by radiation, and that much larger areas, especially to the north, in Byelorussia, had been severely contaminated. Later Soviet studies showed hundreds of thousands of people probably suffering from the effects of nuclear fallout, and millions living and farming on fallout-contaminated land. Estimates of future cancer deaths resulting from the Chernobyl disaster ranged from the Soviet government's early estimates of several thousands to a possible million additional deaths estimated by some observers, with many medical observers estimating ultimate additional cancer deaths of 40,000 to 50,000. In April 1990 the Soviet parliament voted an additional $25 billion for Chernobyl-related aid, while a Soviet telethon raised tens of millions of dollars from individual contributions to aid Chernobyl victims, many of them children. One especially notable victim was Soviet helicopter pilot and national hero Anatoly Grishchenko, who flew into the nuclear fire five times, dumping sand and concrete in a finally successful attempt to put it out; he contracted radiation sickness and then leukemia, and received a bone marrow transplant in the United States in April 1990, but died in a Seattle hospital in July of that year. In the years that followed, as understanding of the scope of the disaster grew, 200,000 people were evacuated from areas downwind of the blast. In the spring of 1991, the Soviet government announced that an additional 120,000 would be evacuated from even wider areas.

**For more information:**

*The Truth about Chernobyl*. Grigori Medvedev. Basic, 1991. *Chernobyl: Insight from the Inside*. V.M. Cher-

nousenko. Springer-Verlag, 1991. *Legacy of Chernobyl*. Zhores A. Medvedev. Norton, 1990. *Fire in the Rain: The Democratic Consequences of Chernobyl*. Peter Gould. Johns Hopkins, 1990. *The Aftermath of Chernobyl: History's Worst Nuclear Power Reactor Accident*, Charles C. Bailey. Kendall-Hunt, 1990. Chernobyl: A Documentary Story. Iurii Scherbak. St. Martin, 1989. *Chernobyl*. Don Nardo. Lucent Books, 1990. *Chernobyl: The Long Shadow*. Chris Park, Routledge, 1989. *Final Warning: The Legacy of Chernobyl*. Robert P. Gale and Thomas Hauser. Warner, 1989.

(See also NUCLEAR ISSUES INFORMATION AND ACTION GUIDE on page 215.)

**Chesapeake Bay,** the ''Great Shellfish Bay,'' as it was long ago named by Native Americans; a shallow, 180-mile-long, 4-to-30-mile-wide estuary off the Maryland and Virginia coastline. It is one of the world's most productive fisheries, famous for its huge blue crab, soft-shelled crab, and oyster catches; for the striped bass, Atlantic shad, and sturgeon that spawn and are harvested in the bay; and for the bluefish and other ocean dwellers that shelter and are fished in the bay. The Chesapeake Bay has over 200 species of fish and shellfish, is a wintering place for many thousands of waterfowl, and in all has almost 3,000 animal and plant species.

The bay is also a fragile set of ECOSYSTEMS that have since mid-century been under increasingly serious attack, as POPULATIONS have increased, residential and commercial DEVELOPMENTS have filled in thousands of acres of vitally important WETLANDS, and an ever-increasing flow of industrial and municipal wastes, along with fertilizer-carrying silt, have polluted the bay. By the early 1980s, the Maryland striped bass and shad harvests had been suspended, while oyster and clam catches were severely cut.

A 1983 ENVIRONMENTAL PROTECTION AGENCY report triggered emergency moves by the federal and Maryland, Virginia, Pennsylvania, and District of Columbia governments, and a good deal of action aimed at cleaning up the bay was generated, especially as regarded toxic wastes generated by industrial polluters. But the enormous total flow of waste into the bay did not diminish, but instead increased, with population growth and further development. Although very active citizens' conservationist groups have been fighting with some success to clean up the bay, the basic waste POLLUTION problem had not, as of the early 1990s, been seriously addressed. With no real choice except to build enormously expensive treatment facilities, but without the political will to find and spend the money to do so, there seemed no place for the ever-growing flow of waste to go but into the bay.

**For more information and action:**

• **American Littoral Society,** (201-291-0055). Publishes brochure on life in the Chesapeake Bay. (See COASTS INFORMATION AND ACTION GUIDE on page 62.)
• **Chesapeake Bay Foundation (CBF),** (162 Prince George Street, Annapolis, MD 21401; 301-268-8816; William C. Baker, President), a conservation organization founded in 1967 to save the Chesapeake Bay, through three major programs: environmental defense, to represent the best interests of the bay; environmental education, working out of 17 educational centers around the bay; and land management, of 3,500 acres of land around the bay. It publishes the quarterly *CBF News,* the *Bay Book,* and various brochures.
• CLEAN WATER ACTION (CWA), (202-457-1286).
• IZAAK WALTON LEAGUE OF AMERICA (IWLA), (703-528-1818).
• WILDFOWL TRUST OF NORTH AMERICA (WTNA), (301-827-6694).
(See also COASTS.)

**chestnut, American,** one of the key native deciduous trees in the FORESTS of eastern North America, making up perhaps 25 percent of the forest where mixed with other trees, but also making up pure stands, in old-growth forests sometimes up to 600 years old. The tree was a major food source, for wildlife as well as humans, and its straight, tall trunks, often branch-free for 50 feet and easily worked, were favored by loggers and woodworkers. The tree was also coveted as a main source of tannin, used in tanning. The American chestnuts fell victim to a fungus inadvertently imported on Chinese chestnut trees in 1904, before the passage of plant quarantine laws. Even more deadly than the Dutch elm disease (see ELM, AMERICAN), the chestnut blight killed virtually all chestnut trees; of the few chestnuts that survive in the wild, most are shrubs. Research has focused on development of disease-resistant strains of American chestnut trees and of new forms of BIOLOGICAL CONTROL of the fungus; new techniques of GENETIC ENGINEERING and work in plant pathology bring hope that the American chestnut can be revived.

**For more information and action:**

• **American Chestnut Foundation** (College of Agriculture and Forestry, 401 Brooks Hall, P.O. Box 6057, West Virginia University, Morgantown, WV 26506; 304-293-0111; Philip A. Rutter, President), a membership organization founded in 1983, dedicated to supporting and coordinating independent research aimed at restoration of the American chestnut. It maintains a research farm in Virginia, the focus of its breeding program; sponsors

annual meetings on chestnut research; and publishes the *Journal of The American Chestnut Foundation.*

**chimpanzees,** with GORILLAS and ORANGUTANS one of the three groups of mammals comprising the great apes, of all the animal species the most closely related to humans. The chimpanzee is one of the most intelligent animals on earth; once far more widespread, the surviving chimpanzees now live in central and west Africa, the *common chimpanzee* from Tanzania to Zaire north of the Zaire River and the *pygmy chimpanzee* or *bonobo* in Zaire south of the Zaire river, between the Zaire and the Kasai. Although an estimated 100,000 to 200,000 chimpanzees remain, both species are endangered, partly because they are hunted for their meat but far more because of loss of FOREST and SAVANNA HABITAT to explosively expanding African human POPULATIONS. Relatively few are protected in national wildlife preserves and parks; as human populations continue to destroy necessary chimpanzee habitats, the question of adequate protected areas becomes far more urgent. (See also ENDANGERED SPECIES; also ENDANGERED AND THREATENED WILDLIFE AND PLANTS on page 372.)

***China Syndrome, The,*** a fiction film directed by James Bridges, and starring Jack Lemmon, Jane Fonda, and Michael Douglas, about a nearly disastrous nuclear accident at a United States nuclear plant, in which a core meltdown and massive nuclear catastrophe are narrowly averted, as Lemmon and Fonda triumph over incompetent, self-protective plant management. The film achieved enormous worldwide impact for very special timing reasons: made in mid-1978, it was released just after the THREE MILE ISLAND nuclear accident, its fictional series of equipment failures and human errors coming very close to what actually happened at Three Mile Island.

**chlordane,** a highly toxic PESTICIDE (see CYCLODIENES).

**chlorinated hydrocarbons (organochlorines),** a group of highly persistent PESTICIDES, compounds of various structures, but all containing primarily hydrogen and carbon, with chlorine added. Among them are DDT; benzene; CYCLODIENES such as chlordane, dieldrin, heptachlor, and aldrin; and other compounds such as hexachlorobenzene (HCB), lindane (Y-hexachlorocyclohexane), endrin, mirex, hexachloride, and toxaphene, all manufactured commercially under a variety of names. Not readily BIODEGRADABLE, chlorinated hydrocarbons are carried around the world by wind and water, from the poles to the equator. They readily dissolve in fats and accumulate in fatty tissues, and have been found in trace amounts in the tissues of almost all living organisms, including humans. These persist in the FOOD CHAIN, accumulating to sometimes damaging or lethal doses in larger animals at the end of the chain, in a process called BIOACCUMULA- TION. Concentration in humans and other animals can cause wasting, liver problems, tumors, birth defects, and failure to reproduce; in PLANKTON, the basis of the ocean's food chains, it can inhibit PHOTOSYNTHESIS and movement. If burned, chlorinated compounds produce dangerous DIOXIN.

Many of the most dangerous chlorinated hydrocarbons have been banned in Europe and North America, starting with DDT in 1972, resulting in a gradual lessening of con- centrations in the environment and some recovery of dam- aged populations, especially birds such as the bald EAGLE, the California CONDOR, peregrine FALCON, OSPREYS, and brown PELICANS, whose egg shells had been thinned by the pesticide, hindering reproduction. But chlorinated hy- drocarbons are still widely used in parts of the Third World, such as India, Latin America, and west and central Africa; when traces of them return to industrialized coun- tries on imported food, they are completing what some call the CIRCLE OF POISON.

Many chlorinated hydrocarbons are in solvent form, and because they vaporize easily are also described as VOLA- TILE ORGANIC COMPOUNDS (VOCs). Among these are dry- cleaning liquids such as perchlorethylene and trichlorethy- lene, chloroform, carbon tetrachloride, and paint removers such as methylene chloride; fumes from these and other chlorinated solvents are certainly damaging and in suffi- cient concentration (especially in closed spaces) can be deadly, as some glue-sniffers have discovered. Like other chlorinated hydrocarbons, chlorinated solvents persist in the environment; if improperly handled, they may perco- late into the water system, or evaporate, helping to deplete the OZONE LAYER. Disposal is also a problem. Chlorinated solvents may be recycled or burned in special high-temper- ature incinerators, but if burned at too low a temperature, they can cause even more dangerous by-products, such as phosgene gas (a chemical weapon used in World War I) or dioxin. (See also PESTICIDES; TOXIC CHEMICALS; HAZ- ARDOUS WASTE; INCINERATION; and specific compounds such as DDT and CYCLODIENES.)

**chlorination,** the addition of chlorine to a compound, as in CHLORINATED HYDROCARBONS; also the use of chlo- rine as a disinfectant. Chlorination of water or waste can have some adverse side effects; chlorine reacts with some other substances in the water or waste to form other chlori- nated chemicals, such as CHLORINATED HYDROCARBONS, some of which are CARCINOGENS and persist in the envi- ronment. Chlorine gas is also highly toxic (used in World War I) and leaks can be dangerous, so storage can be

hazardous. Even so, chlorination is widely used, notably in drinking water, swimming pools, and in waste treatment programs, though alternatives such as OZONE and ultravio- let RADIATION are used in some settings and are being further explored. ENVIRONMENTAL PROTECTION AGENCY (EPA) guidelines suggest that drinking water should con- tain no more than 250 mg/l of chloride (see SECONDARY DRINKING WATER STANDARDS on page 276).

The chemical *chlorine* is one of the highly reactive HALOGENS, which form many PESTICIDES and other TOXIC CHEMICALS. These are extremely difficult to handle in HAZ- ARDOUS WASTE, but the main approaches to detoxifying or destroying chlorinated compounds all involve attempts at *dechlorination*, or removal of chlorine atoms, generally replacing them with other atoms, such as hydrogen.

**For more information and action:**

- **Water Environment Federation (WEF),** (703-684-2400 or 800–666–0206). Distributes videos concerning chlorine.
- **World Environment Center (WEC),** (212-683-4700). Publishes booklet *Chlorine Safety Pays*.

**chlorofluorocarbons (CFCs),** a family of chemical compounds composed of carbon, chlorine, and fluorine atoms, heavily implicated in the destruction of the earth's protective OZONE LAYER; a family of SYNTHETIC ORGANIC COMPOUNDS (SOCs), also called *Freons* or *chlorofluoro- methanes* (CFMs). CFCs and other chlorine-based chemi- cals readily trigger chemical reactions and, in the upper atmosphere, tend to break apart OZONE, the three-atom form of oxygen ($O_3$) into the two-atom form ($O_2$) more common in the air we breathe. Unfortunately, the ozone in the upper atmosphere partly shields earth's life from destructive ultraviolet RADIATION, while $O_2$ does not.

CFCs were once thought of as wonder chemicals. Be- cause they do not burn, are relatively easy to manufacture, and are highly stable and nontoxic, they were used in a wide variety of areas, notably in refrigerators, as foaming agents in plastic and rubber insulators (including coffee cups and fast-food packaging), as solvents in the electron- ics industry, and as propellants for all sorts of products, including hair spray, deodorant, and insecticides. Their very stability is what now causes the problem. Unlike many other compounds, which break down naturally, in days, weeks, or months, chlorofluorocarbons can survive for up to a century. Only when they drift into the upper atmosphere (stratosphere) and encounter the sun's radia- tion are they broken apart; at that point chlorine atoms are released, which in turn break down the ozone molecules. Because the ozone layer is so important for all life, over

90 nations have now agreed to ban production of five key chlorofluorocarbons (CFCs 11, 12, 113, 114, and 115) by the year 2000 (see MONTREAL PROTOCOL ON SUBSTANCES THAT DEPLETE THE OZONE LAYER). Some countries had already banned CFCs for many uses, as for aerosol propellants. Even so, the CFCs already in the environment will continue to wreak destruction on the ozone layer for decades to come, unless researchers are able to develop ways to hinder or halt those upper-atmosphere chemical reactions. Chlorofluorocarbons also trap radiating solar heat, and so contribute to the GREENHOUSE EFFECT and the likelihood of GLOBAL WARMING.

The search for substitutes for CFCs may prove long and difficult. Many potential substitutes are more costly and far less efficient, and so will use more energy—one study estimates that electricity use in the United States would increase by 3 percent, and consumer costs with it. The increased energy use and some substitutes will also contribute to global warming. Some are also dangerous; before CFCs, for example, some refrigerants (like ammonia) were poisonous, while others (like propane) were explosive. Some substitutes also attack the ozone layer, though less actively, notably hydrochlorofluorocarbons (HCFCs, made of hydrogen, chlorine, fluorine, and carbon atoms). Some environmental groups, such as GREENPEACE, have objected to the 1990 agreement because it recommended only that HCFCs be phased out by 2040; parties to the agreement note that to ban them more quickly would force some developing nations to revert to using CFCs. For some uses, no substitutes of CFCs have yet been developed. Overall, the cost of developing effective substitutes for CFCs is likely to be extremely large.

**For more information and action:**

- ENVIRONMENTAL DEFENSE FUND (EDF), (212-505-2100). Publishes *Cutting the Costs of Environmental Policy: Lessons from Business Response to CFC Regulation* (1990).
- ENVIRONMENTAL HAZARDS MANAGEMENT INSTITUTE (EHMI), (603-868-1496).
- ENVIRONMENTAL PROTECTION AGENCY (EPA), (202-260-7751 or 202-260-2980).
- INVESTOR RESPONSIBILITY RESEARCH CENTER (IRRC), (202-234-7500). Publishes *Stones in a Glass House: CFCs and the Ozone Depletion Controversy* (1988).
- RESOURCES FOR THE FUTURE (RFF), (202-328-5000).
- U.S. PUBLIC INTEREST RESEARCH GROUP (PIRG), (202-546-9707). Publishes *Dupont Fiddles While the World Burns* (1989).
- WORLD RESOURCES INSTITUTE (WRI), (202-638-6300). Publishes *Protecting the Ozone Shield: Strategies for*

*Phasing Out CFCs During the 1990s* (Irving M. Mintzer et al., 1989).
(See also OZONE LAYER.)

**cholinesterase-inhibitor,** a term describing substances that disrupt the nervous system by blocking the action of the enzyme *acetylcholinesterase*, among them PESTICIDES such as ORGANOPHOSPHATES and CARBAMATES.

**chromium (Cr),** a type of HEAVY METAL used primarily in manufacturing alloys and electroplating other metals. Chromium occurs naturally in the environment, but abnormal amounts can poison or kill fish, PLANKTON, and a variety of other animals, especially accumulating in fish and shellfish (see BIOACCUMULATION). Among humans it can cause pulmonary disorders and is a probable CARCINOGEN. (See PRIMARY DRINKING WATER STANDARDS on page 274; TOXIC CHEMICALS AND HAZARDOUS SUBSTANCES on page 407; KNOWN HEALTH EFFECTS OF TOXIC CHEMICALS on page 416.)

**circle of poison,** the worldwide circular trade in PESTICIDES, in which pesticides banned in industrialized countries are sold in developing countries, and then return on imported foods; a termed coined by U.S. researchers David Weir and Mark Shapiro. In general, pesticides are developed in industrialized countries and are at first used there; if found to be sufficiently toxic in the environment, some pesticides may be banned in the home country. But chemical firms are not barred from selling—critics call it *dumping*—dangerous pesticides abroad. So it is that many highly toxic compounds, such as DDT and PCBs, banned for years in North America and Europe, are still used in increasing amounts by Third World regions, notably Latin America and India. The pesticides then continue to poison both humans and other life in the environment, with the circle of poison completed as pesticide-contaminated foods are brought back to the richer countries. The extent of the problem is not fully known because no country—including the United States—checks more than a tiny fraction of imported food for pesticides, or tests for only a small number of pesticides.

**For more information and action:**

- GREENPEACE, (202-462-1177). Runs *Toxics Campaign*; publishes *Exporting Banned Pesticides: Fueling the Circle of Poison* (1989).
- INSTITUTE FOR FOOD AND DEVELOPMENT POLICY (IFDP), popularly called *Food First*, (415-864-8555). Publishes *Circle of Poison: Pesticides and People in a Hungry World*.

**CITES,** see CONVENTION ON INTERNATIONAL TRADE IN ENDANGERED SPECIES OF WILD FAUNA AND FLORA.

**Clean Air Act (CAA),** a U.S. federal law passed and then much amended to reduce AIR POLLUTION and protect air quality. The Clean Air Act of 1963 authorized the U.S. Public Health Service to study air POLLUTION and provided grants and training to state and local agencies for controlling it. Amendments in 1970 centered air quality control activities on the ENVIRONMENTAL PROTECTION AGENCY (EPA), charging it with "conducting research and development programs, setting national standards and regulations, providing technical and financial assistance to the states, and where necessary, supplementing state implementation programs." Under the 1970 Act, the EPA was required to set National Ambient Air Quality Standards (NAAQSs) for EMISSIONS of substances posing a general threat to air quality; for these *criteria pollutants*, they set primary standards relating to human health and secondary standards for WELFARE EFFECTS, as to crops, livestock, buildings, and visibility. The EPA also set emissions standards for specific hazardous air pollutants and for industries, called National Emissions Standards for Hazardous Pollutants (NESHAPs). (For information on both NAAQSs and NESHAPs, see HEALTH EFFECTS OF THE REGULATED AIR POLLUTANTS on page 8.) They also set New Source Performance Standards (NSPSs), minimum national emissions standards for new sources of pollution in specified categories.

The 1990 Clean Air Amendments brought wide-ranging reforms, dealing with all kinds of pollution, from large or small, mobile or stationary sources, including routine and toxic emissions, ranging from power plants to consumer products. It took particular aim at several areas:

- **ACID RAIN,** targeting reductions by half of SULFUR DIOXIDE and nitrogen oxides (see NITROGEN DIOXIDE), with specific targets to be met as cuts were phased in through the 1990s.
- **urban SMOG,** establishing five categories for cities that do not meet limits on OZONE (a key ingredient in smog); these *non-attainment areas* would be classed as either *marginal, moderate, serious, severe,* or *extreme* (the latter category including only Los Angeles at the bill's passage). Specific phased-in targets for ozone reductions are set for each category.
- **automobile emissions,** setting specific targets for reducing tailpipe emissions of HYDROCARBONS and nitrogen oxides; requiring longer-lasting pollution control equipment on cars and cleaner kinds of gasoline such as gasohol (see BIOFUEL; SYNTHETIC FUELS) in cities with the worst CARBON MONOXIDE problems; and mandating development of automobiles meeting even stricter standards for extreme non-attainment areas—notably, southern California.
- **toxic air pollutants,** expanding the number of regulated toxic air pollutants from 7 to 189 (for a list, see TOXIC CHEMICALS AND HAZARDOUS SUBSTANCES on page 407; see also KNOWN HEALTH EFFECTS OF TOXIC CHEMICALS on page 416); requiring the EPA to establish some 250 categories of hazardous pollutants, and to set new safety standards for residents living near polluters and for plants where the largest amounts of TOXIC CHEMICALS are used; requiring polluters to install the best available pollution control equipment, the aim being to reduce toxic emissions by 90 percent by 2003 and to prepare formal safety reviews to be made available to the public; and establishing an independent *Chemical Safety Board,* to investigate chemical accidents.
- **depletion of the OZONE LAYER,** phasing out destruction of ozone-destroying chemicals through the 1990s, including CHLOROFLUOROCARBONS, HYDROFLUOROCARBONS, METHYL CHLOROFORM, and carbon tetrachloride, and establishing new rules for the RECYCLING and disposal of such chemicals.

The Clean Air Act also includes a program to provide compensation for workers displaced as businesses conform to the new law. (See AIR POLLUTION; ACID RAIN; OZONE; OZONE LAYER; ENVIRONMENTAL LAW.)

**clean fuel,** an alternative name for BIOFUELS or SYNTHETIC FUELS that are less polluting than FOSSIL FUELS.

**Clean Water Act (CWA),** popular name for a U.S. federal law that is a keystone of ENVIRONMENTAL LAW and is credited with significantly cutting the amount of municipal and industrial pollution fed into the nation's waterways. More formally known as the Federal Water Pollution Control Act Amendments, passed in 1972, it stems originally from a much-amended 1948 law aiding communities in building sewage treatment plants and has itself been much amended, most notably in 1977 and 1987.

Through the 1970s and 1980s, the Clean Water Act provided for coordination of WATER POLLUTION control programs, the aim being to make national waters fishable and swimmable. (Drinking water, though of course a concern, is primarily covered by the SAFE DRINKING WATER ACT.) More precisely, it sought to eliminate discharge of untreated municipal and industrial waste water into waterways, providing billions of dollars to finance building of sewage treatment facilities.

In the 1987 amendments, the Act focused more heavily on updating standards for dealing with TOXIC CHEMICALS, since much of the toxic pollution still fouling the nation's LAKES, RIVERS, and estuaries came from companies that had installed 1970s-era pollution control technologies. It also attempted to deal with water pollution stemming from non-point sources such as CROPLANDS and city streets, requiring states to identify waters that do not meet quality standards and developing programs to deal with the problem. The 1987 Act also provided for increased efforts to improve water quality in lakes, especially the GREAT LAKES and those lakes damaged by ACID RAIN. The CWA authorizes the ENVIRONMENTAL PROTECTION AGENCY (EPA) to establish a list of toxic chemicals involved in water pollution and to set standards for them.

Environmentalists have long charged that the EPA has sometimes been slow to write regulations required by the Act and that the Justice Department has been insufficiently aggressive in pursuing violators. In recent years, however, the CWA has spawned some substantial criminal and civil cases. In two criminal firsts, 1990 saw one individual sentenced $2 million for filling in WETLANDS without a permit and a company president given a $400,000 fine, 26 months' imprisonment, and two years' probation under CWA's "Knowing Endangerment" section, for exposing his employees to toxic pollutants through illegal disposal practices. Substantial civil penalties include $2.1 million against a pulp and paper company for pretreatment and permit violations and $1.5 million against Philadelphia for illegal discharges from a wastewater treatment plant.

The CWA is up for review and reauthorization in the early 1990s. Revisions of the law are expected to focus particularly on pollution from farms and cities, seeking to reduce the amount of pollution—notably from PESTICIDES, fertilizers, and soil particles (see EROSION; SEDIMENTATION)—entering waterways from the nation's fields, lawns, and streets.

**For more information and action:**

- **Environmental Law Institute (ELI),** (202-328-5150; publications office: 202-939-3844). Publishes *Clean Water Deskbook* (rev. ed., 1991). (See ENVIRONMENTAL LAW INFORMATION AND ACTION GUIDE on page 116.)
- **ENVIRONMENTAL PROTECTION AGENCY (EPA),** (202-260-7751 or 202-260-2080).
- **WATER ENVIRONMENT FEDERATION (WEF),** (703-684-2400 or 800-666-0206). (See also PESTICIDES; TOXIC CHEMICALS; SAFE DRINKING WATER ACT; WATER POLLUTION; WASTE DISPOSAL.)

**Clean Water Action (CWA),** (National Office, 1320 18th Street NW, Washington, DC 20036; 202-457-1286; David Zwick, Executive Director), a membership organi-

zation founded in 1971, dedicated to "lobbying, research, education and action on important water, toxics and public works issues on a national and local level," seeking to advance and gain "environmental protections, including the control of toxic chemicals, the protection of wetlands, surface waters, coastal areas, groundwater and other critical resources, safe solid waste management practices, and public health and environmental safety of all citizens." Working through its national and regional offices, Clean Water Action carries out various projects, such as the national *War on Waste* campaign. It also publishes the quarterly *Clean Water Action News*, as well as various monthly updates and action alerts.

**Cleveland natural gas explosion,** the explosion of a highly combustible liquefied NATURAL GAS storage tank in Cleveland, Ohio, on October 20, 1944; the explosion and resulting massive fire killed an estimated 125 people and injured hundreds, destroyed 50 city blocks and an estimated 300 buildings.

**climate change,** variations in the earth's climate, including temperature, which have profound effects on all life. At present, most attention is focused on the possibility of GLOBAL WARMING, but in the past GLOBAL COOLING—of the type that produced the great Ice Ages—has also occurred, and is expected to occur again. Though at opposite extremes, global warming and cooling may produce similar types of stresses on the life of the planet. Among the major effects of massive climate change are:

- **change in the sea level.** With global warming, the result is SEA LEVEL RISE, which may swamp islands and COASTS, placing large stretches of land underwater and fouling much other land and WATER RESOURCES with salt water. The earth's rising POPULATION would have far less land—especially fertile delta land—on which to live and grow food. FORESTS could be cleared to supply new land, but the deforestation and change in LAND USE might only intensify the GREENHOUSE EFFECT. It would also make remaining coastal areas more vulnerable to hurricanes and storm surges. With global cooling, the result would be a fall in the sea level, with coastal habitations, including ports and industries relying on water, being left high and dry.
- **change in climate patterns.** Neither global warming nor global cooling implies uniform change, but only an average rise or fall. In either case, the climate changes in ways we cannot predict, causing rain in what is usually DESERT and drought in normally rainy areas, with consequences such as floods and forest fires. A short-term analogy might be the occasional El Niño, a weather pat-

tern of the southern Pacific, which causes just this type of disruption. These will affect the health of ECOSYSTEMS, including CROPLANDS; the availability of water resources, for drinking, agriculture, industry, and other community uses; and the overall living patterns—even livability—of some regions.

- **change in the habitable ranges of plants and animals.** There is, in fact, some evidence that this is happening already, with the northern range of plants and animals being extended farther north in recent years. Plants have always been especially affected by climate change—whether warmer or cooler—since they are less able to migrate to areas that provide the requirements they need for life. In some cases, the type of ecosystem may change altogether; a forest may become permanent GRASSLAND, for example. In the past, though climate change has caused severe stress, animals have been able to adapt somewhat more easily, because they are so mobile. However, especially in recent decades, humans have sharply restricted the areas free for animals, so some may be blocked from moving to more hospitable territories. Many communities are attempting to establish GREENWAYS that might serve as MIGRATION corridors, if needed, and various countries are party to international agreements concerning migration across borders. Even so, whole ecosystems will be disrupted, and some animals that are physically able to migrate may still perish because their regular food sources are unavailable; this is especially true of fish dependent on coastal ecosystems or WETLANDS, which are highly sensitive to temperature changes. ENDANGERED SPECIES are especially at risk, but in a wider sense, most flora and fauna have been weakened by a general loss of BIOLOGICAL DIVERSITY. Farmers—and therefore the world's food supply—will also be affected, since crops grown successfully in previous times may fail in changed settings, and the transition to new crops may be difficult and, in some cases, impossible.

It is because changes such as these are so widespread and so devastating that scientists, environmentalists, and other citizens are so concerned with stabilizing the earth's climate.

Of course, not all changes would be negative in all places. Just as humans and many other forms of life found a more hospitable environment after the last Ice Age, so the warmer temperatures and changes in climate patterns might encourage growth in some parts of the world, even while others perish for lack of water. Reports by the *Intergovernmental Panel on Climate Change* (sponsored by the UNITED NATIONS ENVIRONMENT PROGRAMME and the World Meteorological Organization) suggest that a warmer climate might favor food production in northern Eurasia and northern North America, while threatening it in other areas, including southern Europe, southern North America, eastern South America, northern and southern Africa, western Australia, and Southeast Asia. This is of particular concern because global warming might create large numbers of ENVIRONMENTAL REFUGEES, some of whom may be blocked from migrating to other lands by political borders. (See GLOBAL WARMING AND CLIMATE CHANGE INFORMATION AND ACTION GUIDE on page 144.)

**coal,** black or brown burnable rock, largely formed of carbon; a major source of energy and, as one of the FOSSIL FUELS, of environmental POLLUTION as well. Coal is formed from beds of peat—accumulations of matted and partly decomposed plant matter from ancient WETLANDS—which was gradually buried under other rocks and, over geological time, through heat and pressure, converted to rock, in a process called *metamorphosis*. Coal is not a uniform substance, but varies by the kinds of plants in the original peat; the degree of alteration; and the amount and type of impurities, such as sulfur. It can be classified in various ways, but the main types are:

- **anthracite (hard coal),** black coal that is hard to ignite but burns without smoke; it is the most changed (metamorphosed) and has the highest carbon content, in the best quality up to 98 percent, and the fewest impurities.
- **bituminous (soft coal),** dark-brown-to-black coal that burns with a smoky flame; it is the most abundant source of coal, less fully converted to rock, with a lower carbon content and more impurities.
- **lignite,** brownish-black coal that is partway between peat and coal, with 30 to 40 percent water; it burns far less efficiently and with more impurities.

Coal has been used as an ENERGY RESOURCE for centuries. Its use somewhat declined in the mid-20th century, with the rise of OIL, but rose again after the energy crisis of the 1970s and still provides a major portion of the electrical power in many countries. In the United States, for example, about 55 percent of the electrical power derives from coal (up from 46 percent in the mid-1970s, with the shift from oil following the energy crisis). No longer regarded as efficient enough for its traditional uses in heating homes or directly powering transportation vehicles, most coal today—in the United States about 84 percent of the annual coal production—is used to produce electricity. Coal reserves are estimated to last at least 1,500 years at current production levels, but in the long term coal is a DECLINING RESOURCE, being used up faster than it is being resupplied by natural geological processes.

Coal must be prepared before use, to produce *feedstocks* of relatively uniform size, quality, and properties. At coal preparation plants, the rock is broken apart, crushed, sorted, and washed in water and chemical solutions to remove some impurities; has refuse removed (generally 13 to 21 percent); and is pulverized, dried, and stored for shipping. Especially since the rise of environmental concerns, much attention has also been focused on various ways to treat or "purify" coal by removing contaminants such as sulfur before burning, to produce so-called *clean coal*, but most coal is still untreated and in any case still releases CARBON DIOXIDE into the air.

Coal is expensive to transport and is mostly carried by railroad, but in some settings a coal SLURRY—bits of coal in a watery mixture—may be transported by pipeline. Since the 1970s energy crisis, researchers have explored the possibility of converting coal into gas or liquid forms, for efficiency of use and transport, in a process called *coal gasification* or *coal conversion* (see SYNTHETIC FUELS). Actual extraction of the coal from the ground causes enormous environmental problems (see MINING).

The main use of coal today is in power plants, where coal is burned in a boiler, used to turn water into steam, which drives the blades of a turbine; the mechanical energy so produced is, through a generator, converted to electricity. Only about a third of the coal's energy results in electricity; the rest is used to run the plant itself or is lost as heat, except in COGENERATION plants. The waste gases not consumed, including SULFUR DIOXIDE, nitrogen oxides (see NITROGEN DIOXIDE), and CARBON DIOXIDE, are released through stack, some with SCRUBBERS to reduce EMISSIONS, but many without, such as the one that has been fouling the air of the GRAND CANYON.

Considerable research effort is being focused on developing more efficient and less polluting coal-based technologies. An alternative to the conventional steam boiler is the *atmospheric fluidized-bed combustor* (AFBC), in which pulverized coal is mixed with limestone or dolomite, which absorb sulfur. The resulting mixture—the *fluidized bed*—is burned while suspended by jets of air, driving steam turbines at such high efficiency that temperatures can be lower, reducing formation of nitrogen oxides. In the *pressurized fluidized-bed combustor* (PFBC), burning takes place under increased pressure (as in a home

pressure cooker), making it far more efficient; pressurized hot gases power gas-driven turbines.

**For more information and action:**

- **DEPARTMENT OF ENERGY (DOE),** (202-357-8300). Publishes annual review of prospects for world coal trade.
- **FRIENDS OF THE EARTH (FOE),** (202-544-2600). Publishes *The Strip Mining Handbook* (1990).
- **INFORM, INC.** (212-689-4040).
- **NATURAL RESOURCES AND ENERGY DIVISION (NRED),** (212-963-6205). Publishes *Small-Scale Coal Mining in Developing Countries* (1989).
- **RESOURCES FOR THE FUTURE (RFF),** (202-328-5000).
- **SIERRA CLUB,** (415-776-2211 or 202-547-1141; legislative hotline, 202-547-5550). Publishes *Coal Mining Policy*.

(See also FOSSIL FUELS; MINING; ENERGY RESOURCES; also MINING INFORMATION AND ACTION GUIDE on page 196).

**Coalition for Environmentally Responsible Economies (CERES),** (711 Atlantic Avenue, 5th Floor Boston, MA 02111; 617-451-0927; Gordon Davidson, Executive Director), a project of the SOCIAL INVESTMENT FORUM, in collaboration with environmental groups, churches, labor unions, and other concerned private and public organizations, which in 1989 propounded the VALDEZ PRINCIPLES a set of guidelines for corporate responsibility. CERES publishes various materials, including a newsletter, a directory, and reports.

**coasts,** the meeting places of land and sea, the shores that hold many of the most heavily populated areas in the world and are also the site of enormous biological productivity. The fate of coasts is intertwined with that of the OCEANS. Many of the animals that live in off-shore waters breed on or near the coastlines. They inevitably come into conflict with humans, who find coastlines among the most attractive places in the world, for their beauty as well as their economic potential, as the sites of cities, trade and transport centers, industries, agriculture, AQUACULTURE, recreation areas, and a host of other activities. In addition, whatever pollutes the oceans will—sooner or later—wash back onto the shore. WATER POLLUTION, OFFSHORE DRILLING, OIL spills, MINING, HAZARDOUS WASTE, TOXIC CHEMICALS, WASTE DISPOSAL in general—whatever affects the oceans also affects the coasts. In fact, it was the large-scale fouling of American beaches with waste washing in from the sea, that in the 1980s brought home to many people the seriousness of the threats to the environment.

Apart from those coastlines that emerge out of the sea, notably volcanic structures, coasts are in general either the result of sediment deposit (see SEDIMENTATION) or EROSION of earlier coastal forms. Those formed by deposits generally have a beach—the area between the lowest and the highest points normally reached by waves. Beyond the beach is normally an inner boundary, such as a sea cliff or row of sand dunes, which tends to migrate unless fixed by grasses. Waves breaking on the shore transport eroded material, some of it from the sea floor, and drop part of it as they retreat, often concentrated in spaced triangle-shaped deposits on land, sand bars separated by troughs underwater, and also spits that curve out from the shoreline. Over time some of these deposit-formed features may form a whole range of offshore barriers, such as the Outer Banks off North Carolina.

Where RIVERS meet the sea, and both river and tidal currents operate—areas called *estuaries*—sand bars and deltas often form. With sufficient deposits, these break the surface and form new, and often quite fertile, land. Such areas have been extremely attractive places for human habitation and cultivation for thousands of years. In modern times, with sharp increases in erosion and sedimentation, some of these sand bars and deltas have silted up so much that they weigh down the local area, causing *subsidence*—in effect, a local SEA LEVEL RISE. In such areas, rivers are also made unnavigable, without large-scale dredging.

By contrast, erosional coasts are formed as waves and storms from the sea cut back the coastline into often enormously scenic cliffs, rock coasts, and beaches. Wave action and weathering by alternative drying and wetting are most effective at sea level, gradually scouring away the base of the cliff. This often forms CAVES and grottoes at the base of the cliff; if the base is sufficiently undermined and the overlying rock weakened, the cliff will collapse, and the rock fall will gradually be broken up by the waves. Not all coastal rock is equally susceptible to attack, the rate of erosion depending on local factors such as the type of rock, the climate, and the amount of water introduced to the cliff from the land above.

History abounds with tales of once-prosperous towns that fell into the sea. Whether deposition balances erosion on sea coasts is unclear; but some studies seem to indicate that more is gained than lost. The problem is that what is gained is often low, marshy land; though useful and even highly productive in some areas, such as Bangladesh, it is in many areas often considered less economically productive and attractive to humans than what is lost. As a result much human effort is expended on halting change along coasts. Massive structures are built to reinforce the base of eroding cliffs. On low coasts, piers, breakwaters, sea walls, jetties, groins, and other defenses are built as defenses against the sea's attack. Modern structures are often built in irregular shapes, to more successfully blunt the power of the waves. In general these are temporary measures, however, and often actually accelerate erosion elsewhere. Eroding beaches are maintained only by substantial replenishing efforts seasonally and after severe storms. In some areas, governments have decided that the cost of trying to halt erosion is too great, and are allowing nature to take its course.

Coasts serve as HABITATS for many and varied plant and animal life, often different from other forms of marine life (see OCEANS). The coastal zone, or *littoral zone*, generally extends from the upper wave limit on the beach out to sea as far as rooted seaweeds or reefs extend, the distance depending partly on how much light reaches the sea floor, and therefore on the clearness of the water. Unlike open ocean areas, where upper layers are sometimes short of the nutrients and oxygen needed for the life-sustaining process of PHOTOSYNTHESIS, coastal waters have plenty of both, continually renewed from the depths by the waves crashing on the shore, and so are enormously productive.

Many of the animals inhabiting this coastal zone are mud-dwellers, such as clams, winkles, sand dollars, barnacles, starfish, marine worms, and limpets. Inshore are found crabs, a variety of coastal birds and insects, and salt-tolerant plants, with algae flourishing in sheltered areas. In estuaries, marshes, swamps, bogs, MANGROVES, and other coastal WETLANDS, many birds, fish, and marine animals come to breed. These flora and fauna form a host of small, complex ECOSYSTEMS, their characteristics often depending on the nature of the bottom particles—such as coarse sand, fine sand, sediment, or mud—and the temperature or salinity, which may vary markedly in tide pools, lagoons, salt marshes, and the like.

As in all FOOD CHAINS, coastal animals are dependent on the small and large plants, from algae to huge kelp, for their nutrition, with the smaller animals then forming food for the larger ones, such as seabirds. Being adapted for particular conditions, coastal life is especially susceptible to water pollution, and to the BIOACCUMULATION of persistent toxic chemicals, such as PESTICIDES and HEAVY METALS. By the same token, they are at risk from sea level rise, which may be accelerating due to GLOBAL WARMING or local conditions, or from sea level drop, which can occur in some areas where (for various geological reasons) the coast is rising.

But the greatest danger to coastal life comes with human beings and the DEVELOPMENT that they bring, which often

## Coasts Information and Action Guide

**For more information and action on coasts:**

**American Littoral Society (ALS),** (Sandy Hook, Highlands, NJ 07732; 201-291-0055; D. W. Bennett, Executive Director), a membership organization founded in 1961 by professional and amateur naturalists concerned with the "shore and adjacent wetlands, bays and rivers—the littoral zone," especially its future health and its wildlife habitat. The Society has members with widely diversified interests, and it maintains regional offices along the Atlantic Coast and in Olympia, Washington. Among the society's activities are local and national field trips, an annual film symposium, a Fish Tag Program, and a Diver's Section. The Society seeks to educate the public and influence policy and legislation, often working with other environmental groups. It publishes various materials, including the quarterly magazine, *Underwater Naturalist*, a national newsletter *Coastal Reporter*, chapter newsletters, books, brochures, and bulletins on topics such as coral reef ecology, barrier islands and dunes, coastal birds, Florida's Everglades, life in the Chesapeake Bay, and the rise in sea level.

**American Oceans Campaign (AOC),** (213-576-6162).

**American Planning Association (APA),** (202-872-0611). Publishes a bibliography from the **Council of Planning Librarians (CPL).**

**Center for Marine Conservation (CMC),** (202-429-5609). Coordinates large-scale volunteer cleanups of beaches fouled with marine debris. Publishes the biannual newsletter *Coastal Connection.*

**Coastal Society, The (TCS),** (P.O. Box 2081, Gloucester, MA 01930; 508-281-9209, Thomas Bigford, Executive Director) an international organization, formed in 1975, "dedicated to promoting the understanding and wise use of coastal environments including the shoreline, coastal waters, and adja-

cent land areas," consistent with their dynamic natural processes. TCS fosters increased understanding through conferences, workshops, international consultation, congressional testimony, and publications, among them the quarterly *TCS Bulletin* and proceedings of biennial conferences.

**IUCN—The World Conservation Union** (202-797-5454).

**National Institute for Urban Wildlife,** (301-596-3311 or 301-995-1119). Publishes the *Wildlife Habitat Conservation Teacher's Pac* series, covering *Estuaries and Tidal Marshes* and *Wetlands Conservation and Use.*

**Natural Resources Defense Council (NRDC),** (212-727-2700). Publishes *Coastal Alert: Ecosystems, Energy, and Offshore Oil Drilling* (Dwight Holing, 1990), *No Safe Harbor: Tanker Safety in America's Ports* (1990), and *Ebb Tide for Pollution: Actions for Cleaning Up Coastal Waters* (1989).

**Resources for the Future (RFF),** (202-328-5000).

**Scripps Institutional of Oceanography,** (619-534-3624). Operates a research division, Center for Coastal Studies (CCS).

**Sierra Club** (415-776-2211; or 202-547-1141; legislative hotline, 202-547-5550). Publishes *What You Can Do to Help Protect Our Coasts from Offshore Oil Development* and *Offshore Oil and Gas Policy.*

**Woods Hole Oceanographic Institution (WHOI),** (508-548-1400; Associates Office 508-457-2000, ext. 2392). Operates the *Coastal Research Center (CRC).*

**Other references:**

*A Moveable Shore: The Fate of the Connecticut Coast.* Peter C. Patton and James M. Kent. Duke University Press, 1992. *Living with the Shore* series, Orrin H. Pilkey, Jr., and William J. Neal, series eds., sponsored by the National Audubon Society, published by Duke University Press.

---

destroys the very environment they seek to use and enjoy, and with it the habitats vital to coastal life. If development includes filling in wetlands, as it often does, the coast is made even more vulnerable to storms, flood, and erosion. In many areas, local communities are leading fights against sale of coastal lands for development and controlling uses of such lands through ZONING. However, in many parts of the world, especially in areas where POPULATION pressure is great, humans are attempting to harness the productivity of the coastal areas to ease shortages of food, in a classic and continuing conflict of interest. (See COASTS INFORMATION AND ACTION GUIDE above; also OCEANS; WETLANDS; OUTER CONTINENTAL SHELF LANDS ACT; CHESAPEAKE BAY.)

**cogeneration,** the practice of using not just the power but also the heat produced by power-producing processes; also called *combined heat and power* (CHP). In conventional power plants, fuels are burned to turn water into steam to drive turbines, which are then used to produce electricity; the heat produced during this process is released into the environment as waste. But in cogeneration, such heat is collected and directed to local use, such as heating water or building spaces. Cogeneration means that fuels are used far more efficiently and so less expensively; electricity demand is also cut, as less is needed to heat local buildings. The approach is especially well-suited to municipal use, as in several large cities in Europe and elsewhere. (See ENERGY RESOURCES.)

**Committee of International Development Institutions on the Environment (CIDIE),** (CIDIE Secretariat, P.O. Box 30552, Nairobi, Kenya; 333930 or 520699; William H. Mansfield III, Deputy Executive Director), an organization formed in 1980 "to integrate environmental considerations into economic development activities," whose members sign and agree to adhere to a *Declaration of Environmental Policies and Procedures Relating to Economic Development*, meeting annually to review progress. Members exchange information with one another and with other interested public and private environmental and DEVELOPMENT organizations and agencies. Making up CIDIE are the UNITED NATIONS ENVIRONMENT PROGRAMME (UNEP) and 15 major intergovernmental development funding organizations, including the African Development Bank (ADB), Arab Bank for Economic Development in Africa (BADEA), Asian Development Bank (ADB), Caribbean Development Bank (CDB), Central American Bank for Economic Integration (CABEI), Commission of the European Communities (CEC), European Investment Bank (EIB), Inter-American Development Bank (IDB), International Fund for Agricultural Development (IFAD), Nordic Investment Bank (NIB), Organization of American States (OAS), UNITED NATIONS DEVELOPMENT PROGRAMME (UNDP), United Nations Food and Agricultural Organization (FAO), United Nations Fund for Population Activities (UNFPA), and the WORLD BANK.

**Commoner, Barry** (1917– ), a biologist best known in his field for his work with free radicals—short-lived, highly reactive chemicals that readily set up destructive chain reactions, such as CHLOROFLUOROCARBONS involved in depletion of the OZONE LAYER. Commoner taught at Washington University in St. Louis from 1947 to 1980, was botany department chairman from 1965 to 1980, and acted as director of its Center of the Biology of Natural Systems from 1966 to 1980. He emerged as a leading ecologist in the late 1950s, during the campaign to end the atmospheric testing of NUCLEAR WEAPONS, and then focused on a wide range of environmental concerns, including POLLUTION, ALTERNATIVE ENERGY sources, and POPULATION. He became a national figure in the late 1960s, then making a major contribution to the growing green movement with scores of articles and speeches, and with such books as *Science and Survival* (1967), *The Closing Circle* (1971), *Energy and Human Welfare* (1975), *The Poverty of Power* (1976), and *The Politics of Energy* (1979). In 1980, he ran for president as the candidate of the Citizen's Party, in a quickly failed attempt to develop a directly political base that joined green and Socialist

issues. He remained a major green advocate, restating his view that major emphasis had to be placed on preventive antipollution measures, such as the use of cleaner alternative energy sources, rather than a cleanup after the creation of pollutants. His book *Making Peace With the Planet* was published in 1990.

**community supported agriculture (CSA),** an approach in which farmers and consumers join together in cooperative ventures, with the consumers easing the usual pressure of farm financing while gaining a ready supply of vegetables from a known source, often produced by ORGANIC FARMING techniques. The mechanics of a CSA venture vary. In the prototype American Community Supported Agriculture (ACSA) project begun in South Egremont, Massachusetts, in 1985 by Robyn Van En and Jan VanderTuin and inspired by European models, members of the cooperative group pay in advance for their vegetable supply. Farmers then have financing during the lean winter and are freed from the vagaries of the marketplace, while group members share in the risks of the harvest, receiving more or less, depending on the season, and have assurances of the quality and safety of the locally grown produce. In 1990, for example, ACSA shareholders paid $340 in advance for a full 43 weeks of vegetables, or alternatively could pay $240 for the summer harvest only or $100 for the winter crops only, the average coming to about $8 a week. The price of each share is determined by the size and productivity of the particular farm site, the out-of-pocket costs such as seed and machinery, and the farmer's fair wage, divided by the number of families the farm is considered able to supply. A less formal approach involves the sale of bills or coupons at a reduced rate during the winter, which can then be redeemed during the summer and fall; so a bill purchased for $9 in December might purchase $10 worth of produce in July, giving the customer a discount and the farmer some cash when it is most needed.

**For more information and action:**

- **Bio-Dynamic Farming Association,** (Kimberton, PA; 215-935-7797; Rod Shouldice, Director).
- **National Coalition Against Misuse of Pesticides (NCAMP),** (202-543-5450). (See PESTICIDES INFORMATION AND ACTION GUIDE on page 238.)

**compliance,** the condition of having met set standards, such as having less than specified acceptable levels of a pollutant in EMISSIONS; localities or industries not meeting the standards are described as being in *noncompliance* (see AIR POLLUTION).

**composting,** a kind of biological RECYCLING in which organic materials—matter that is or once was alive—are exposed to air, water, and bacteria, so that they may be broken down. It is a way of deliberately accelerating the process by which all organic matter is broken down in the environment, to release vital elements that can then be used by other living things (see BIOGEOCHEMICAL CYCLES).

Small-scale composting is widely used in gardening and ORGANIC FARMING, as a way to nourish the soil. Bacteria, fungi, and other microorganisms ingest and excrete organic matter, such as plant wastes, animal manure, and other farm and garden by-products. In the process, heat is given off, which accumulates and raises the temperature of the compost pile. This kills off disease-causing organisms (*pathogens*) and any remaining seeds and breaks down some PESTICIDE residues but encourages growth of other microorganisms, especially bacteria, that actually break down the matter into simpler form; these are helped to some extent by the action of insects and earthworms. CARBON DIOXIDE and water are also given off in the process. The resulting compost, called *humus*, is rich in elements vital to plant growth, especially nitrogen, phosphorus, and potassium, and is therefore valuable in soil-building (see SOIL CONSERVATION).

A wide variety of materials can be used in a compost pile—indeed, variety is considered important to the composting process, with manure as a major ingredient. Also important are materials high in cellulose, such as straw, cotton-gin waste, wood chips, and sawdust, to maintain microbial action. The pile is built up in layers of varying materials and needs to receive adequate air and moisture but be able to drain off excess, with the surface area maximized for penetration by microorgamisms. The pile needs to be turned regularly to improve air circulation and ensure even composting, and temperatures must be maintained (sometimes difficult during northern winters); the ENVIRONMENTAL PROTECTION AGENCY (EPA) guidelines call for composting at over 131°F for three days. The more often a compost pile is turned, the faster it will decompose; the process can take anywhere from two to six weeks, depending on the temperature and how often it is turned. After "cooking," the pile cools down to the general air temperature, and the dark, moist mixture is ready to spread on farm fields or gardens.

One approach to the modern WASTE DISPOSAL crisis is to use composting to reduce organic trash and waste to manageable and useful form. Yard waste such as grass clippings and leaves makes up a large proportion of all waste—in the United States, 18 percent. Many environmentalists recommend that homeowners develop compost piles, and use the result to nourish lawns instead of using chemical fertilizers and contributing to the pileup of garbage.

Composting is also being used on a wider scale in waste management. As of 1991, sewage sludge—the concentrated solid wastes removed from sewage during wastewater treatment—is being composted in over 150 plants in the United States. In addition, some plants have been opened and many others are planned to transform other organic household waste into nutrient-rich soil-like materials by composting. Some companies are proposing that composting is a reasonable way to dispose of diapers, paper packaging, food waste, and other organic materials, to reduce the sheer volume of trash. Many environmentalists and some waste disposal firms are concerned that the inadequate screening processes would lead to compost contaminated with HEAVY METALS, PLASTIC, glass, and other physical contaminants, as from plastic in disposable diapers. Proponents say that even if the compost is of lesser quality, it could be used for nonagricultural applications, such as covering landfills, rebuilding degraded roadsides, or on golf courses; opponents counter that some of the inferior compost would undoubtedly be misused, especially as there are presently no regulations for composting in most areas. One regulated state, Massachusetts, has established a two-tier system for compost: Class I compost, usable on fields growing food for humans, must have less than two parts per million (ppm) of CADMIUM and 10 ppm of MERCURY; Class II compost, which can have up to 25 ppm of cadmium, is barred from such fields but can be used in landscaping. (See RECYCLING AND COMPOSTING INFORMATION AND ACTION GUIDE on page 262; also WASTE DISPOSAL; RECYCLING; ORGANIC FARMING; SOIL CONSERVATION.)

**Comprehensive Environmental Response, Compensation, and Liability Act (CERCLA),** a U.S. federal law passed in 1980 to deal with release of hazardous substances in spills and from inactive and abandoned disposal sites; sometimes called the *Superfund law* because it set up large funds to pay for cleanup of abandoned dumpsites, such as LOVE CANAL. CERCLA requires the EPA to designate hazardous substances, such as PESTICIDES and other TOXIC CHEMICALS, that can present substantial danger (for a full list, see TOXIC CHEMICALS AND HAZARDOUS SUBSTANCES on page 407; also KNOWN HEALTH EFFECTS OF TOXIC CHEMICALS on page 416). CERCLA also assures financial responsibility for the long-term maintenance, containment, and cleanup of sites contaminated with such substances, and allows the EPA to recover cleanup costs from a *potentially responsible party* (PRP). By contrast, the RESOURCE CONSERVATION AND RECOVERY

ACT (RCRA) deals with day-to-day management practices in the hazardous waste industry, and with municipal solid waste, in general.

CERCLA was later expanded under the Superfund Amendments and Reauthorization Act of 1986 (SARA, or Title III), as part of the EMERGENCY PLANNING AND COMMUNITY RIGHT-TO-KNOW ACT (EPCRA), increasing the amount in the fund from $1.6 to $8.5 billion over five years. To minimize lengthy litigation, it also introduced revised procedures designed to encourage voluntary settlements from PRPs, and added an ''innocent landowner'' defense to liability, for people who had no reason to know that their land contained hazardous substances, though that has yet to be tested, and may hinge on purchasers and lenders exercising ''due diligence'' and ''all appropriate inquiry.'' (See also SUPERFUND.)

**CONCERN, Inc.** (1794 Columbia Road NW, Washington, DC 20009; 202-328-8160; Susan F. Boyd, Executive Director), an organization funded by contributions and grants, founded in 1970 to ''provide environmental information to community groups, public officials, educational institutions, private individuals, and many others involved in public education and policy development.'' Its primary activity is development, publication, and distribution of community action guides, booklets on major environmental concerns; each one outlines the key issues involved, reviews relevant legislation, describes successful regional state, and local initiatives, provides resource information, and offers specific guidelines for action. Among the topics covered are household waste, waste, groundwater, drinking water, farmland, PESTICIDES, and GLOBAL WARMING and energy choices. CONCERN estimates that 29 percent of their publications are used by federal, state, or local government; about 46 percent by environmental, public interest, or education organizations; about 12 percent by business and communications media; and 13 percent by individuals.

**condor, California,** with the Andean condor the largest of the New World vultures, with a nine-foot wingspan and a top air speed of 60 miles per hour. Once numerous throughout western North America, the California condor population was sharply attacked by hunters, by poisoned bait intended for other animals, and possibly by PESTICIDE poisoning, and sharply declined during the 20th century. Sustained efforts to save the condors in the wild began in the 1930s, but all failed. Today, there are no California condors living in the wild, but approximately 35 condors are alive in captivity, while efforts continue to preserve the species from total EXTINCTION. (See also ENDANGERED

SPECIES; also ENDANGERNED AND THREATENED WILDLIFE AND PLANTS on page 372)

***Conqueror, The,*** a 1956 fiction film directed by Dick Powell, starring John Wayne as Genghis Khan, in a cast that included Susan Hayward, Pedro Armendariz, Agnes Moorhead, and William Conrad. As a film, the work was wholly unmemorable, but its filming and aftermath provided a shocking nuclear age story. The work was filmed in 1954 near St. George, Utah, in a heavily radiation-contaminated area ''downwind'' of the NEVADA TEST SITE, with a cast and crew of over 200. By the mid-1960s, the incidence of cancer among those involved in the filming had become unusually high, though connection to the film made at the atomic test site had not yet been made. The realization came later, as the children of some of the survivors determined that by the mid-1980s almost a quarter of the cast and crew had died of cancer, probably enhanced or caused by their three-month-long radiation exposure while shooting the film. (See NUCLEAR TESTING.)

**Conservation and Renewable Energy Inquiry and Referral Service (CAREIRS),** (c/o Renewable Energy Information, P.O. Box 8900, Silver Spring, MD 20907; 800-523-2929, U.S. except AK and HI; for AK and HI, 800-233-3071), a service operated by Advanced Sciences, Inc. for the U.S. DEPARTMENT OF ENERGY (DOE), formed in 1981 from the earlier *National Solar Heating and Cooling Information Center (NDHCIC)*. CAREIRS provides information on the whole range of renewable energy technologies and energy conservation techniques for residential and commercial needs, working in concert with the *Solar Energy Research Institute's Technical Information Service*, the Department of Energy's *Office of Scientific and Technical Information*, and the *National Appropriate Technology Assistance Service*. CAREIRS publishes and distributes free fact sheets, brochures, and bibliographies, and other publications, on a range of energy-related topics, such as SOLAR ENERGY, BIOFUELS and BIOMASS conversion, wood heating, active and passive solar heating, solar thermal electric, WIND POWER, small-scale hydroelectric power systems, earth-sheltered houses, energy efficiency, photovoltaics, alcohol fuels, ocean energy, geothermal energy, municipal waste, renewable energy, residential indoor AIR POLLUTION, RECYCLING, and home energy audits. It also responds to requests for information on other related topics, sometimes with publications not otherwise listed, and makes referrals to federal agencies, trade associations, researchers, special interest groups, professional associations, and state and local groups, including those that specialize in highly technical or regionally oriented information.

**conservation biology,** a relatively new specialty, focusing on developing the information, skills, and techniques necessary to anticipate, forestall, lessen, and repair ecological damage, with particular attention to practical approaches for use in areas requiring protection, management, or restoration, such as WILDLIFE REFUGES and BIOSPHERE RESERVES. Developed in response to increasing threats to BIOLOGICAL DIVERSITY, conservation biology is a crisis discipline, dealing with problems of great urgency in ECOSYSTEMS that, if once completely destroyed, can never be restored. Among the many concerns of conservation biologists are identifying the *minimum viable population* (MVP) for an ENDANGERED SPECIES and the effects of inbreeding, CLIMATE CHANGE, POLLUTION, MIGRATION, EDGE EFFECTS, HABITAT fragmentation, and other processes in healthy and disturbed ecosystems. They stress the need for more knowledge about critical regions, especially how systems actually work in nature; the importance of proper training for resource managers; and the need to keep strong ties between research and practice. Conservation biology is an interdisciplinary study, involving areas such as ecology, population genetics, wildlife biology, resource management, economics, ethics, and anthropology.

**For more information and action:**

- **Center for Conservation Biology (CCB),** (Department of Biological Sciences, Stanford University, Stanford, CA 94305; 415-723-5924; Paul R. Ehrlich, President), an independent organization affiliated with Stanford, founded in 1984 "to help stem the accelerating loss of biological diversity by facilitating the development of conservation biology and its application to critical environmental problems," its main activities being basic and applied research, education, and the application of conservation biology principles to genetic resources, species, populations, habitats, and ecosystems. CCB provides consultation and technical assistance both nationally and internationally, especially in California and Latin America, often in collaboration with other private or governmental organizations, and publishes the biannual newsletter *Update.*
- MORRISON INSTITUTE FOR POPULATION AND RESOURCE STUDIES, (415-723-7518). Publishes *Population Biology, Conservation Biology, and the Future of Humanity* (Paul R. Ehrlich).
- **Society for Conservation Biology (SCB),** (c/o Dr. Stan Temple, Department of Wildlife Ecology, University of Wisconsin, Madison, WI 53706; 608-262-2671; for membership information: Blackwell Scientific Publications, 3 Cambridge Center, Cambridge, MA 02142), a membership organization, founded in 1985, that seeks to develop "the scientific and technical means for the protection, maintenance, and restoration of life on this planet—its species, its ecological and evolutionary processes, and its particular and total environment." The SCB promotes research and dissemination of knowledge, especially communication between biologists and people in other disciplines working on conservation and natural resource issues. It also publishes the journal *Conservation Biology* and *Research Priorities for Conservation Biology* (Michael E. Soulé and Kathryn A. Kohm, eds., 1989).

**conservation compliance provisions,** a part of the 1985 Food Security Act (Farm Bill) aimed at protecting soil from EROSION, under which farmers would risk losing commodity price supports and other federal farm aid if they produce destructive crops on highly erodible fields.

**conservation easement,** legal restrictions on specific LAND USES, such as DEVELOPMENT, logging, altering an historical building, or restricting public access, with the type of restriction being tailored to the individual situation; a key modern tool for protecting critical wildlife HABITAT and fragile WETLANDS, as well as scenic and historic areas, while still allowing private ownership and economic uses that are compatible with the area being protected. Easements are sometimes labeled by the type of restriction involved, such as a *scenic easement* or an *historic easement.*

Easement agreements may be voluntarily adopted, as a kind of donation, or may be purchased, often by an environmental group or government agency that would like to protect land but could not afford to purchase it, as under a LAND TRUST, or feels more land can be protected for less money with easements. Easements can last for a specified period of time, such as 10 or 20 years, but more often last forever, binding the original owner and all later owners, sometimes with the owners paying a contribution to the monitoring of the easement. The owner generally receives some tax benefit, since the assessed value of land for real estate taxes and estate taxes is decreased by an easement; these provide substantial incentives for easement donations, since without such deductions some families could not afford to keep the property undeveloped. Though the community collects less tax revenues, this is often balanced by less environmental POLLUTION and increased recreational opportunities in the area, for public access is generally included in the agreement. While there have been some violations on both sides, including abuses of landowners' rights and failure of landowners to comply with restrictions, in general the conservation easement approach seems to work well.

Federal and state governments also sometimes protect land under leases or land use agreements, as well as conservation easements; during 1990, the FISH AND WILDLIFE SERVICE held nearly 3 million acres in these ways, with 1.2 million of those in the Waterfowl Production Area Program, protecting prime nesting habitat for migratory waterfowl (see MIGRATION) and other wildlife, especially in the prairie pothole region of the Midwest. Much of this land is on national WILDLIFE REFUGE lands, but some is on farms, which often include important habitats. (See LAND TRUST and CONSERVATION EASEMENT INFORMATION AND ACTION GUIDE on page 178.)

**Conservation Fund, The** (1800 North Kent Street, Suite 1120, Arlington, VA 22209, 703-525-6300; Patrick F. Noonan, President), an organization founded in 1985 that works with ''private and public partners to protect land and water resources,'' its main objectives being to ''conserve open space, parkland, water resources; wetlands, wildlife and waterfowl habitat in cooperation with others; demonstrate that ecologically sound land use and economic return can be compatible and complementary; strengthen leadership and management of nonprofit conservation organizations; increase understanding that conservation is essential to the economic and environmental health of the nation; [and] develop new sources of capital and increased funding, both public and private, for land and water conservation.'' Among the Fund's projects are *American Greenways*, a network of open-space corridors, often bordering waterways and WETLANDS (see GREENWAYS); *American Land Conservation Program*, seeking protection of 100 key areas; *Public Conservation Partnerships*, focused on helping agencies expand public open space, as around parks, refuges, or wildlife areas; *Civil War Battlefield Campaign*, seeking protection of ''hallowed ground''; *Spring and Groundwater Resources Institute*, exploring new methods of protecting groundwater; and *Land Advisory Service*, focusing on cost-effective approaches to LAND USE, combining environmental planning with economic return. The Fund trains conservation leaders, raises funds for conservation, offers the Alexander Calder Conservation Award, honoring cooperation between business and conservation, and publishes various materials, including *Land Letter* and *Common Ground*

**Conservation International (CI)** (1015 18th Street NW, Suite 1000, Washington, DC 20006; 202-429-5660; Russell A. Mittermeier, President), a private membership organization founded in 1987 that aims to save ''endangered rain forests and other ecosystems worldwide and the millions of plants and animals that rely on these habitats for survival.'' CI provides and funds technical support to build sustainable economies in local communities, ''balancing conservation goals with local economic needs,'' and carries out a wide range of projects, including *Rapid Assessment Program* to quickly identify WILDERNESS areas at highest risk; *Bi-National Peace Parks*, cross-border international parks providing joint management of reserves between previously conflicting countries: *Plant Conservation and Ethnobotany*, supporting research, inventory and recovery programs for endangered plant species, especially those with ''medicinal and religious uses by indigenous peoples''; *Species Recovery Programs*, identification and recovery programs for endangered animal species; and *Ecotourism*, sponsoring small-scale travel to special environments, to benefit both conservation and local communities (see ECOTOURISM). CI has also played a key role in establishing BIOSPHERE RESERVES in rain FOREST countries; sponsored the first DEBT-FOR-NATURE SWAP; and outlined the *Rain Forest Imperative*, a 1990's action plan for saving the rain forests. It offers special travel opportunities for members and publishes a quarterly newsletter *Tropicus*.

**Conservation Reserve Program (CRP),** a program established under the U.S. Food Security Act (Farm Bill) of 1985, in which landowners may receive rental payments and other aid for taking highly erodible CROPLAND out of crop rotation and planting permanent grass and tree cover, to lessen EROSION, improve water quality, and improve wildlife HABITAT.

**Consultative Group on International Agricultural Research (CGIAR or CG)** (Mailing address: 1818 H Street NW, Washington, DC 20433; Office location: 801 19th Street, NW; 202-473-8951; Wilfried P. Thalwitz, Chairman), an organization formed in 1971 as an ''informal consortium of governments, international and regional organizations, and private foundations . . . to nurture agricultural research to improve the quantity and quality of food production in the developing countries,'' both inspired by and a main contributor to the world's GREEN REVOLUTION. With its origins in the agricultural research program funded by the Rockefeller Foundation in Mexico from 1942—its first four centers were established with Rockefeller and Ford Foundation funding—CGIAR early stated that its aim was to increase the world's ''pile of food,'' especially by increasing the potential yield for key crops, narrowing the gap between potential and actual yields, providing more stable yields, and slowing loss of yields to attacks from pests and disease. Sponsored jointly from the beginning by the WORLD BANK, Food and AgriCulture Organization (FAO), and UNITED NATIONS DEVELOPMENT PROGRAMME (UNDP), and based at the World Bank, which also supplies its chairperson and secretariat, CGIAR supports research to improve agricultural production, in 13 specialized international agricultural research centers (IARCs), each with its own research and publishing program:

- **Centro Internacional de Agricultura Tropical (CIAT, or International Center for Tropical Agriculture)** (Apartado Aereo 6713, Cali, Colombia), founded in 1967, which is concerned with "production of food staples of the tropics of the western hemisphere, particularly beans, cassava, rice, and beef."
- **Centro Internacional de Mejoamiento de Maiz y Trigo (CIMMYT, or International Center for Improvement of Corn and Wheat)** (Apartado 66 41, Mexico D.F. 06600, Mexico), founded in 1964, which supports "research around the world on maize and wheat as well as other major cereals such as barley and triticale."
- **Centro Internacional de la Papa (CIP, or International Potato Center)** (Apartado 5969, Lima, Peru), founded in 1971, which aims to "improve the solanum potato and to develop varieties suitable for growing in many parts of the developing world."
- **International Board for Plant Genetic Resources (IBPGR)** (c/o Food and Agriculture Organization of the United Nations, Via delle Sette Chiese 142, 00145 Rome, Italy), founded in 1974, which "supports and promotes a network of international and national genetic resource centres to collect and preserve plant germ plasm."
- **International Center for Agricultural Research in the Dry Areas (ICARDA)** (P.O. Box 5466, Aleppo, Syria), founded in 1976, which "concentrates on rainfed agriculture in semi-arid regions of North Africa and West Asia, with emphasis on durum wheat, barley, faba beans, and lentils."
- **International Crops Research Institute for the Semi-Arid Tropics (ICRISAT)** (ICRISAT Patancheru P.O. 502-324, Andhra Pradesh, India), founded in 1972, which is "concerned with improving the quantity and reliability of food production in semi-arid regions of Africa, Asia, Latin America, and the Middle East, with emphasis on sorghum, pearl millet, groundnuts, chick-peas, and pigeon peas."
- **International Food Policy Research Institute (IFPRI)** (1776 Massachusetts Avenue NW, Washington, DC 20036), founded in 1975, which "focuses on the sensitive economic and political issues surrounding food production, food distribution, and the international food trade."
- **International Institute of Tropical Agricultural (IITA)** (P.O. Box 5320, Ibadan, Nigeria), founded in 1967, which concentrates on "lowland tropical agricultural worldwide, with emphasis on roots and tubers, cereals, and grain legumes, as well as the improvement of traditional farming systems."
- **International Livestock Center for Africa (ILCA)** (P.O. Box 5689, Addis Ababa, Ethiopia), founded in 1974, which "carries out research and development on improved livestock production and marketing systems for tropical Africa."
- **International Laboratory for Research on Animal Diseases (ILRAD)** (P.O. Box 30709, Nairobi, Kenya), founded in 1974, which "seeks controls for two major livestock diseases, trypanosomiasis and theileriosis, that limit livestock production in huge areas of Africa, Asia, Latin America, and the Middle East."
- **International Rice Research Institute (IRRI)** (P.O. Box 933, Manila, Philippines), the first of the international centers, founded in 1960, which "continues to work on the improvement of tropical rice and rice based cropping systems and related technologies."
- **International Service for National Agricultural Research (ISNAR)** (P.O. Box 93375, 22509 AJ The Hague, Netherlands), the youngest of the centers, founded in 1979, which "responds to requests from developing countries for assistance in strengthening their national agricultural research programs."
- **West Africa Rice Development Association (WARDA)** (01 B.P. 2551, Bouake 01, Côte d'Ivoire), founded in 1971, which "aims to promote self-sufficiency in rice for a 15-country region where rice is a staple food and where there is great potential for increased production."

CGIAR was conceived as and remains "nonorganizational," acting to assist and advise the IARCs and the members of the Group, not to direct them, and acting with no formal governing charter, but on consensus decisions resulting from semiannual meetings, and with advice from a Technical Advisory Committee (TAC). Its members include any country or organization, public or private, that shares CGIAR's objectives; they are required only to "provide regular, substantial grants to support the international agricultural research system," usually at least $500,000 annually.

CGIAR also collaborates closely with a number of other international centers, supported by many of the same donors, though not formally part of the system, including:

- **Asian Vegetable Research and Development Center (AVRDC)** (Tainan, Taiwan), which promotes production, marketing, and use of vegetables in humid and sub-humid tropics, emphasizing Asia.
- **International Board for Soil Research and Management (IBSRAM)** (Bangkok, Thailand), which uses soil management technology to increase sustainable food production in developing countries.

- **International Centre for Insect Physiology and Ecology (ICIPE)** (Nairobi, Kenya), which studies methods of controlling major crop and livestock pests.
- **International Center for Living Aquatic Resources Management (ICLARM)** (Metro Manila, Philippines), which researches all aspects of fisheries and other living aquatic resources, including AQUACULTURE.
- **International Council for Research in Agroforestry (ICARF)** (Nairobi, Kenya), which is concerned with development of appropriate AGROFORESTRY systems and technologies, seeking to "identify and remove agronomic, technological and economic constraints to fertilizer use."
- **International Fertilizer Development Center (IFDC)** (Muscle Shoals, Alabama), which is concerned with research, development, and transfer of appropriate fertilizer technology.
- **International Irrigation Management Institute (IIMI)** (Digana via Kandy, Sri Lanka), which is concerned with improving irrigation systems through development and dissemination of management innovations.
- **International Network for the Improvement of Banana and Plantain (INIBAP)** (Montpellier, France), which coordinates and stimulates research on improvement of bananas and plantains.
- **International Trypanotolerance Center (ITC)** (Banjul, The Gambia), which seeks to understand and use the natural resistance of West African livestock breeds to trypanosomiasis infection.
- **International Union of Forestry Research Organizations (IUFRO)** (Vienna, Austria), which promotes international cooperation in scientific studies of forestry research, including standardization of systems of measurement.

However various the mandates and independent the operation, CGIAR centers in general share a commitment of "genetic resource conservation and classification; biological research to increase yields by genetic improvement and greater resistance to pests and disease; farming systems studies to better understand farm-level constraints and improve traditional practices; and training and other activities to strengthen national research systems." In addition to publications by specific centers, CGIAR itself publishes various materials, including the newsletter *CGIAR Highlights*, and annual reports.

**For more information and action:**

- **WORLD BANK,** (202-477-5678). Publishes *Science and Food: The CGIAR and Its Partners* (Jock R. Anderson et al., 1988).

**Consumer Product Safety Commission (CPSC),** (Washington, DC 20207; Public Affairs, 301-504-0580; Hotline 800-638-CPSC [2772]; TTY Hotline 800-492-8104; Jacqueline Jones-Smith, Chairman), a U.S. federal agency created by Congress in 1973, to "issue and enforce safety standards prescribing performance requirements, warnings, or instructions for use of consumer products." In the process, the CPSC took over various programs pioneered by other agencies, such as the FOOD AND DRUG ADMINISTRATION, under laws such as the Federal Hazardous Substances Act and the Poison Prevention Packaging Act. The agency operates by "working with industry to develop voluntary safety standards; issuing and enforcing mandatory standards, where appropriate; banning products for which no feasible standard would adequately protect the public; obtaining the recall or repair of products that fail to comply with mandatory standards or that present substantial hazards or imminent hazards to consumers; conducting research on potential hazards; and conducting information and education programs. The CPSC has the authority to ban a substance if its use poses an "unreasonable" risk, but it has rarely done so, though one example is carbon tetrachloride (see CHLORINATED HYDROCARBON). The Commission's four main programs are Hazard Identification and Analysis; Hazard Assessment and Reduction; Compliance and Enforcement; and Public Information. The CPSC maintains a hotline for obtaining information and publications on consumer products, or for reporting a product-related injury or a hazardous product. It also operates an *Injury Information Clearinghouse* on product-related injuries, gathering reports from the hospital-based nationwide network called the *National Electronic Injury Surveillance System*. It also publishes numerous reports and consumer materials, on topics such as electrical and fire safety, hazardous substances, ASBESTOS, home heating equipment, home insulation, and poison prevention.

**Convention Concerning the Protection of the World Cultural and Natural Heritage,** an international agreement signed in Paris in 1972 aimed at promoting global cooperation in safeguarding cultural or natural areas of "outstanding universal value," in which member nations agree to protect listed properties, in their own or other countries; one of the so-called BIG FOUR international conventions. The Convention established a network of protected areas and a framework for identifying, administering, and conserving them, including a World Heritage fund, from fees or contributions from member countries, intended primarily to assist developing countries. Though the Convention written strongly, effective legal strength and its members willingness and long-term ability to follow it—given substantial POPULATION and political pressures—remain to be tested. (See WORLD NATURAL

HERITAGE SITES; also the list of WORLD NATURAL HERITAGE SITES on page 406.)

**Convention on International Trade in Endangered Species of Wild Fauna and Flora (CITES),** an international agreement adopted in 1973 in Washington, DC, to control global trade in wild species of plants and animals designated in the convention's appendixes as endangered or threatened, its terms covering listed animals and plants whether dead or alive, and any "recognizable parts or derivatives thereof." One of the so-called BIG FOUR international conventions, it employs a system of import/export permits to protect named species from over-exploitation. ENDANGERED SPECIES, for which trade is tightly controlled, are listed in Appendix I of the Convention; Appendix II covers species that may become endangered if trade is not regulated; Appendix III covers "species that any party wishes to regulate and requires international co-operation to control trade." The convention, which went into force in 1975, and was amended in 1979 and 1983, has been called the most successful wildlife conservation treaty ever, with over 100 participants by 1991, each of which files annual reports on wildlife import/export trade with the CITES secretariat. Conservation organizations around the world have found CITES a useful tool for wildlife protection, and monitor wildlife trade to be sure that their government's annual reports accurately reflect reality. Many countries have developed their own legislation working in conjunction with CITES. The United States, for example, has its own ENDANGERED SPECIES ACT, and in 1981 also passed amendments to the 1900 Lacey Act barring import or export of wildlife in violation of another country's laws. CITES scientific and technical staff also work with government in various countries, especially in developing areas, to help assess whether or not trade is harmful to a particular species. (See ENDANGERED SPECIES; ENVIRONMENTAL LAW; WILDLIFE TRADE; TRAFFIC; also ANIMAL RIGHTS AND WELFARE INFORMATION AND ACTION GUIDE on page 361.)

**Convention on Long-Range Transboundary Air Pollution (LRTAP),** an international agreement adopted in 1979 by various countries, mostly European or North American, in attempts to combat ACID RAIN and AIR POLLUTION. The original convention called for cooperation in exchange of information, research, monitoring, and development of new technologies. It did not actually go into force until 1983. The following year a protocol funded the Cooperative Programme for Monitoring and Evaluating of the Long-Range Transmission of Air Pollutants in Europe (EMEP). In 1985, a further protocol called for member parties to reduce their "annual sulphur emissions of transboundary fluxes" by 30 percent below 1980 levels by 1993. This was sparked by the earlier efforts of the 30 PER CENT CLUB.

**Convention on the Conservation of Migratory Species of Wild Animals (Bonn Convention or Migratory Species Convention),** an international agreement adopted in Bonn, Germany, in 1979 and coming into force in 1983, that aims to protect those SPECIES of wild animals that "cyclically and predictably" migrate across or outside national boundaries (see MIGRATION). The Convention obliges parties to protect migratory ENDANGERED SPECIES, which are listed separately from other migratory species, and to conclude international agreements on conservation and management of those whose status is considered "unfavorable," with advice offered by a scientific council working with a Convention secretariat. Though it is considered one of the BIG FOUR international agreements, the Convention has far fewer participants than the others—only 34 as of 1991—most of them in Europe, Africa, and southern Asia, and not including the United States, Canada, or the Soviet Union. (See ENVIRONMENTAL LAW; also ANIMAL RIGHTS AND WELFARE INFORMATION AND ACTION GUIDE on page 361.)

**Convention on the Law of the Sea, or Law of the Sea Convention (LOSC),** a United Nations treaty adopted at Montego Bay in 1982, sometimes called a "constitution for the oceans," being a "comprehensive legal régime governing all ocean uses and the exploitation of all ocean resources," and covering "the whole range of marine affairs—fisheries, non-living resources, marine environment, marine science and technology, [and] settlement of disputes"; the result of years of work, from the first United Nations Law of the Sea Conference in 1958. The convention was not scheduled to go into full force until the 1990s, and the United States was not among the many early signatories, instead maintaining observer status in the startup years. Even so, the Convention was signed by many other countries and was quickly influential in providing a framework for international agreements regarding marine matters, such as OCEAN DUMPING, EXCLUSIVE ECONOMIC ZONES (EEZs), and the UNITED NATIONS ENVIRONMENT PROGRAMME (UNEP's) Regional Seas Programme. The Convention defines those areas under national jurisdiction, including the continental shelf and islands; confirms coastal nation's rights to explore, exploit, conserve, and manage natural resources, while establishing other rights and duties, as to protect and preserve the marine environment, including conserving and managing living resources; confirms rights of access for landlocked states; provides for international use of straits; defines freedom of the high seas, comprising "freedom of navigation, of overflight, of laying submarine cables and pipelines, of constructing artificial islands, and of fishing and scientific research," subject to specific provisions; outlines the necessity of developing international laws for preventing, reducing, and controlling POLLUTION of the marine environment, and for enforcement, responsibility, and liability; and establishes the sea bed, OCEAN floor, and subsoil beyond national jurisdiction as part of the "common heritage of mankind," with resources to be developed, organized, controlled, and administered under the Convention.

Many activities related to the Convention are coordinated by the *Office for Ocean Affairs and the Law of the Sea (OALOS)* (see below), working with other UN branches, with the overall aims being to "facilitate international co-operation, and to promote the peaceful use of the seas and oceans, the equitable and efficient utilization of ocean resources, the conservation of its living resources, the study, protection, and preservation of the marine environment, and the peaceful resolution of disputes concerning the sea and its uses." The Convention provides for the establishment during the 1990s of an *International Sea-Bed Authority (ISA)*, to oversee MINING of seabed resources beyond national jurisdictions; an *International Tribunal for the Law of the Sea*, to settle disputes regarding the Convention's interpretation or application; and a *Commission on the Limits of the Continental Shelf*, advising states on "the delimitation of each State's continental shelf." The future of the Convention is somewhat uncertain, since it has not received the 60 ratifications needed to come into full force. The Soviet Union, for example, had (before its breakup) signed but not ratified, while the United States has done neither, largely because of concerns about seabed mining rights, as to highly limited manganese resources. In BLUEPRINT FOR THE ENVIRONMENT, environmentalists urge ratification, arguing that the substantial benefits far outweigh any "real or theoretical disadvantages." The Convention may yet be amended before being widely ratified and coming into full force.

## For more information and action:

- **Office for Ocean Affairs and the Law of the Sea (OALOS)** (United Nations DC 2-0450, New York, NY 10017; 212-963-6424), an arm of the United Nations, established "to provide advice, assistance and information to States on all matters related to ocean affairs and the law of the sea, and to promote the widespread acceptance of the Convention, its rational and consistent application and the fullest realization of the benefits accruing to States under it," working within the UN system. It is also often asked to help develop policies and programs

for maritime areas under national jurisdiction. OALOS maintains a reference library and various computerized databases, including the Law of the Sea Information System (LOSIS), the country marine profile database (MARPRO), and a minerals database (MINDAT). It also publishes various materials, including the *Law of the Sea Bulletin*, an annual review of ocean affairs, and various reports such as *The Law of the Sea: A Select Bibliography* (1989), *The Law of the Sea: Current Developments in State Practice* (1989), and *National Legislation on the Continental Shelf* (1989).

(See also OCEANS.)

### Convention on the Prevention of Marine Pollution by Dumping of Waste and Other Matter (London Dumping Convention or LDC),

an international agreement that was adopted in London in 1972 and came into force in 1975, aimed at controlling pollution of the sea by dumping. The Convention covers all deliberate disposal of wastes other than that incidental to the normal operation of ships, aircraft, and other vessels, and in all seas. Various kinds of HAZARDOUS WASTES and TOXIC CHEMICALS are covered. For those listed in Annex I, the so-called *black list*, dumping is absolutely prohibited, except in cases of *force majeure* or extreme emergency; among these are high-level RADIOACTIVE WASTE and some other radioactive materials; highly persistent synthetic compounds such as PLASTICS; HALOGEN-containing ORGANIC COMPOUNDS; substances of or containing MERCURY or CADMIUM; materials produced for chemical or biological warfare; and OIL of various types if taken aboard for the purpose of dumping, rather than being incidental to the running of the craft. Annex II, the so-called gray list, contains substances that can be dumped only by special permit; these include PESTICIDES and related by-products; arsenic; HEAVY METALS, such as LEAD, COPPER, and zinc; silicon-containing organic compounds; cyanides; and fluorides. Other types of waste, covered in Annex III, are allowed only under general permits.

In addition to enforcing anti-dumping measures, parties to the Convention agree to establish authorities to issue permits; monitor and keep records on the condition of the sea; collaborate on training personnel, supplying equipment for research and monitoring, and disposing of and treating wastes; and promote anti-pollution measures regarding HYDROCARBONS, other not-for-dumping transported matter, waste from ships' operation, radioactive pollutants, and debris from exploration and MINING of the seabed. The Convention also calls on the parties—over 65 of them by the early 1990s—to establish regional antimarine-pollution agreements. Amendments were made in

1978 and 1980, but these have (in the early 1990s) not yet come into force. Two notable areas of disagreement among the participants are the permissibility of INCINERA-TION at sea and of the dumping of radioactive wastes, with some countries seeking a total ban, but others seeking to retain the dumping right, if the material is deemed suitable by the International Atomic Energy Agency. (See WATER POLLUTION; OCEANS; ENVIRONMENTAL LAW.)

### Convention on Wetlands of International Importance, Especially as Waterfowl Habitat (Ramsar Convention or Wetlands Convention),

an international agreement that was adopted in Ramsar, Iran, in 1971 and went into force in 1975, establishing a WETLANDS network, promoting the wise use of all wetlands, and providing special protection for those listed as being of special importance, especially for migratory waterfowl; one of the so-called BIG FOUR international conventions. Its overall objective is "to stem the progressive encroachment on and loss of wetlands now and in the future, recognizing the fundamental ecological functions of wetlands and their economic, cultural, scientific, and recreational value." By the early 1990s, over 50 member countries had joined the convention, each of whom agreed to designate at least one national wetland for coverage (for a full list of over 500 sites, see WETLANDS OF INTERNATIONAL IMPORTANCE on page 395), to "consider their international responsibilities for conservation, management, and wise use of migratory stocks of wildfowl," and to "establish wetland nature reserves, cooperation in the exchange of information, and train personnel for wetland management." In the short term, the Ramsar Convention has helped spare some key wetlands around the world, and has served as an ideal toward which to strive. Its long-term impact has yet to be seen, however, as POPULATION and DEVELOPMENT pressures continue to increase. Numerous environmentalists have expressed concern that the Convention does not provide criteria for selecting wetlands, state clear guidelines and legal obligations for management, adequately safeguard a wetland from delisting, and pay sufficient attention to the fisheries resources of wetlands. (See WETLANDS; ENVIRONMENTAL LAW.)

### Coordination in Development (CODEL)

(475 Riverside Drive, Room 1842, New York, NY 10114; 212-870-3000; Sister Mary Ann Smith, Contact), a "consortium of Christian organizations whose goal is to assist development activities among disadvantaged peoples overseas," founded in 1979. CODEL supports indigenous projects in community DEVELOPMENT, through consultative services, networks, and pooling of resources for planning, implementation, and evaluation, stressing "self-help initiatives" in an "ecumenical style," in the context of long-term, sustainable development and environmentally wise use of natural resources, the ultimate aim being "to participate with the poor and marginated peoples in the transformation of their lives." It conducts workshops and training programs in the United States and overseas, often through indigenous voluntary agencies; it also publishes various books on water, forestry, energy, livestock and small-scale agriculture projects (some also in Spanish and French).

**copper (CU),** a type of HEAVY METAL with many attractive characteristics—it is workable, corrosion resistant, a good electrical conductor, nonmagnetic, and nonsparking, so it has a wide range of uses, though replaced by cheaper metals in some uses. Copper is expensive partly because of the enormous waste incurred in MINING—an estimated 500 tons of waste for just one ton of copper, plus untallied amounts of AIR POLLUTION. Like other heavy metals, copper is a significant contaminant in the water system, some dissolved by ACID RAIN, some simply dissolved in water; a 1980 study estimated that water LEACHING from copper mines had contaminated one-third of the United States water system, and copper is a major contaminant in urban runoff. In the United States, it is treated as a TOXIC CHEMICAL and HAZARDOUS SUBSTANCE. (See TOXIC CHEMICALS AND HAZARDOUS SUBSTANCES on page 407; KNOWN HEALTH EFFECTS OF TOXIC CHEMICALS on page 416.)

Copper is required by many living beings; it is vital to the process of PHOTOSYNTHESIS and humans require 2 mg of copper per day, the average adult human body containing 100 to 150 mg. But excess copper can cause significant health problems, in humans accumulating especially in the liver. Common household sources of copper include unlined copper pots and alcohol distilled with copper tubing. In the environment copper is especially toxic to algae, sea plants, and invertebrates; less so for mammals. Copper is a major candidate for RECYCLING, for enormous amounts are thrown away each year, often in electronics products.

**coral reef,** a mass of coral colonies; the corals, also called *polyps*, are sea creatures, their hard bodies joined together into a living surface on the outside of the mass of coral skeletons composing the atoll. Close to shore this is termed a *fringe reef;* further from shore a *barrier reef.* Coral reefs are found worldwide, developing best in a low-nutrient environment in tropical or subtropical shallow, clear water, which allows vital sunlight to reach the reef; coral reefs are extremely vulnerable to such substances as sewage or excess silt, which cloud their water.

Coral reefs play host to a wide range of other sea creatures, often developing tremendously complex environments. For example, Australia's Great Barrier Reef, the world's largest, which runs 1,250 miles along the Australian northeast coast and contains over 400 different coral species in a series of reefs and islands, has created an environment that includes over 1,500 fish species, 240 bird species, and 4,000 mollusc species. Part of the Australian and world natural heritage, and long a magnet for tourists, it was by mid-century seriously threatened by OIL and mineral extraction, as well as by damaging FISHING practices. The reef became a protected place in 1975, and has since then grown into the GREAT BARRIER REEF MARINE PARK, the world's largest marine reserve, consisting of 2,500 coral reefs and 71 coral cays, covering over 85 million acres (133,000 square miles) on the continental shelf, and stretching across the whole northeastern Australian coast, off Queensland.

Many of the world's coral reefs are threatened by overfishing, the use of dynamite in fishing operations, the wear and tear created by large numbers of tourists, and a considerable range of excess nutrient and POLLUTION problems, and require careful conservation efforts if they are to survive. In the late 1980s, it also became apparent that many were seriously affected by bleaching, and accompanying weakening of underlying structures. Some environmentalists suggest that bleaching may be caused by the warming of the oceans, possibly due to GLOBAL WARMING, but many others studying the world's coral reefs and climate felt that much more study was needed before any conclusions could be reached.

**For more information and action:**

• GREENPEACE, (202-462-1177). Greenpeace Action runs the *Ocean Ecology Campaign*, publishes materials such as *An Evaluation of International Protection Offered to Caribbean Reefs and Associated Ecosystems* (1989).
• THRESHOLD INTERNATIONAL CENTER FOR ENVIRONMENTAL RENEWAL, (602-432-7353). Operates the *Coral Reef Project*.
• WORLD WILDLIFE FUND (WWF), (202-293-4800). Publishes *Coral Reef Teacher's Kit*.
(See also COASTS; OCEANS; ECOTOURISM.)

**Council on Environmental Quality (CEQ),** (722 Jackson Place, NW, Washington, DC 20503; 202-395-5750; Michael R. Deland, Chairman), a board in the U.S. Executive Branch established under the NATIONAL ENVIRONMENTAL POLICY ACT (NEPA) in 1970 "to formulate and recommend national policies to promote the improvement of the quality of the environment," its chairman is ap-

pointed by the president with the Senate's advice and consent. CEQ's main responsibilities are to advise the president on national and international environmental policies, to coordinate the positions of cabinet departments and independent agencies on environmental issues, and to administer the provisions of NEPA, setting regulations for matters covered by NEPA, such as ENVIRONMENTAL IMPACT STATEMENTS (EISs). It also "assists and advises" the president in preparing an annual *Environmental Quality Report*. While pleased that an environmental advisor is present in the White House, some environmentalists have expressed concern that the council itself is inadequately funded and inefficiently organized, as well as having little influence except when the president in office supports environmental concerns; for example, the CEQ had a staff of over 60 in the 1970s, under President Carter, but that was cut by President Reagan to 13. The cuts have been partly restored under President Bush.

In 1991 President Bush also established an additional two-year *President's Commission on Environmental Quality (PCEQ)*, at the same address and chaired by the CEQ chairman, to "develop and promote an action agenda to improve the environment in a way that integrates environmental, economic, and quality of life goals and emphasizes innovative private sector initiatives," focusing on the areas of pollution prevention and environmental quality management, natural resource management, international cooperation, and education and communication.

**Cousteau, Jacques-Yves** (1910– ), one of the leading marine explorers and inventors of the 20th century, has for a half century, been a key and extraordinarily active figure in the worldwide environmental movement. He led the worldwide fight to block and reverse the 1988 Wellington Convention, a multinational agreement that would have allowed OIL drilling and MINING in ANTARCTICA. He lobbied tirelessly against the Convention and for a proposal to recognize Antarctica and the seas around it as an inviolate international nature preserve—and seems to have won, at least for some years. France reversed its earlier support of the agreement, Australia and New Zealand expressed grave new reservations, and Cousteau's lobbying efforts brought strong support for his position in the U.S. Congress, the result being a major victory in the long, continuing battle between those who wish to exploit Antarctica and those who wish to preserve it as a world heritage area.

Jacques Cousteau became a naval officer and aviator in the early 1930s. In the late 1930s, he began developing undersea diving equipment; although his work was interrupted by the war, he was in 1943 one of the inventors of the Aqualung, now called scuba gear. During the early postwar period, he pioneered in the development of the bathysphere, for deepsea exploration. He became a world figure with his enormously popular coauthored book *The Silent World* (1952), and reached even wider audiences with the 1956 Oscar-winning documentary film based on the book. *The Living Sea* (1962) and *World Without Sun* (1965) continued a writing career that was to span four decades.

Cousteau has been extraordinarily successful in developing modern, environmentalist attitudes toward the preservation of the life of the sea, especially in such television documentary series as *The World of Jacques Cousteau* (1966–68) and *the Underwater World of Jacques Cousteau* (1968–76). In 1973 he founded the COUSTEAU SOCIETY.

**Cousteau Society** (930 West 21st Street, Norfolk, VA 23517; 804-627-1144; Jean-Michel Cousteau, Executive Vice President), a member-supported organization founded in 1973 by Jacques-Yves COUSTEAU to fund marine research, especially underwater exploration and filmmaking from specialized craft like the *Calypso* and *Alcyone*. Among the Society's recent projects are the *Marine Mammal Stranding Program*, studying strandings of WHALES and DOLPHINS, with the National Marine Fisheries Service (see NATIONAL OCEANIC AND ATMOSPHERIC ADMINISTRATION); the *Marine Mammal Events Program*, gathering stranding reports from around the world into a centralized database, for use in research; and a round-the-globe "Rediscovery of the World" focusing on current environmental changes. Other projects include a "health report" on the MEDITERRANEAN SEA (in conjunction with the International Commission for the Scientific Exploration of the Mediterranean [ICSEM]) (see MEDITERRANEAN SEA), a 20-month exploration of the Amazon Basin, and use of information from NASA satellites to measure OCEAN productivity and POLLUTION. The Cousteau Society offers first-hand, staff-guided field study programs in *Project Ocean Search*, and has established *Cousteau Centers* for public education, using films, computerized games, models, and exhibits. In addition to the widely shown films, it publishes the bimonthly periodicals *Calypso Log* (for adults) and *Dolphin Log* (for ages 7–15), filmstrips and teacher's guides for educational use, numerous scientific and technological papers, and many popular books.

**cranes,** a worldwide set of 15 species and many subspecies, among them the world's tallest birds, some standing over six feet. Such factors as HUNTING, loss of HABITAT, power line collisions, and TOXIC CHEMICALS, notably PESTICIDES, have made eight kinds of cranes endangered species. These include the *whooping crane, Mississippi* and *Cuba sandhill cranes, Siberian white crane, Japanese*

crane, Mongolian white-naped crane, Tibetan black-necked crane, and the *hooded crane*.

The whooping crane, once numerous from the northern midwest to the Canadian Rockies, and present throughout much of North America from central Mexico to the sub-Arctic, was seriously threatened by the 1870s, and by the early 1940s was thought to be almost extinct, until a small breeding population was found in 1954 at northwest Canada's WOOD BUFFALO NATIONAL PARK. From the late 1960s, with a strong Canadian–U.S. cooperative effort that included breeding whooping cranes in captivity and returning them to the wild, the whooping cranes have been saved, or at least reprieved, with a total of over 200 birds in several locations, and with good prospects for continuing success—as long as they are very carefully nurtured and guarded.

The Mississippi sandhill crane subspecies, though receiving equally careful conservationist attention, including breeding in captivity for return to the wild, has not fared as well, though it too has been reprieved, with a small breeding flock in captivity and a flock of approximately 50 at the Mississippi Sandhill Crane Wildlife Refuge. Several other kinds of sandhill cranes, however, have come back from near-extinction, most notably the flock of approximately 500,000 cranes, most of them lesser sandhill cranes, that gather on the Platte River every spring. Loss of that essential HABITAT would most probably once again threaten the now-recovered species of sandhill cranes, a major argument against building the TWO FORKS DAM.

**For more information and action:**

- DUCKS UNLIMITED (DU), (708-438-4300).
- ELSA WILD ANIMAL APPEAL (EWAA), (818-761-8387).
- **International Crane Foundation (ICF),** (EE-11376, Shady Lane Road, Baraboo, WI 53913; 608-356-9462; George Archibald, Director), a "world center for the study and preservation of cranes," founded in 1971. The ICF pioneered in the large-scale captive breeding of cranes; is active in crane habitat preservation around the world; offers workshops; organizes crane counts; educates the public, as through tours of the ICF site and films; and publishes *The ICF Bugle*.

(See also ENDANGERED SPECIES; also ENDANGERED AND THREATENED WILDLIFE AND PLANTS on page 372.)

**criteria air pollutants,** those air pollutants posing a general threat to air quality as listed under the CLEAN AIR ACT, for which the ENVIRONMENTAL PROTECTION AGENCY (EPA) is required to set NATIONAL AMBIENT AIR QUALITY STANDARDS (NAAQS). Criteria air pollutants include OZONE, PARTICULATE MATTER, CARBON MONOXIDE, SULFUR DIOXIDE, LEAD, and NITROGEN DIOXIDE. They are among the 31 environmental problem areas ranked in the EPA's report UNFINISHED BUSINESS: A COMPARATIVE ASSESSMENT OF ENVIRONMENTAL PROBLEMS (see tables associated with that entry on pages 309–315). (See also AIR POLLUTION; CLEAN AIR ACT; HEALTH EFFECTS OF THE REGULATED AIR POLLUTANTS on page 8.)

**crocodile, American,** one of the world's 14 endangered crocodile species; the famed *Nile Crocodile* is also an ENDANGERED SPECIES. The American crocodile lives in the WETLANDS of the Atlantic and Pacific coasts of the Americas, from southern Florida south to Guatemala on the Atlantic and Ecuador on the Pacific. Once numerous in southern Florida, unrestrained HUNTING and loss of wetland HABITAT to equally unrestrained DEVELOPMENT came close to destroying the Florida crocodile population, which was down to 50 to 100 in the early 1970s. Since then, a strongly enforced hunting ban and establishment of the Crocodile Lake National Wildlife refuge in the Florida Keys have allowed a substantial recovery, with the Florida crocodile population estimated in the 500-600 range in the early 1990s.

The Florida *alligator* population, similarly endangered, and especially by hunters supplying the hide products industry, has made an even stronger comeback, and is now listed as threatened, rather than endangered—though Florida alligators and crocodiles continue to be at great risk, and in need of careful preservation efforts. (See also ENDANGERED SPECIES; also ENDANGERED AND THREATENED WILDLFE AND PLANTS on page 372.)

**croplands,** highly specialized ECOSYSTEMS, managed to maximize production of useful products (primarily food) planted and harvested by humans. Some croplands may be devoted to a single crop, called *monoculture;* others may be planted in various ways, including alternating strips of different kinds of crops, or crops interspersed with trees, as in AGROFORESTRY or SOIL CONSERVATION.

Croplands are not natural environments. All are the product of the human development of agriculture, and were created from areas that were formerly different kinds of environments, such as GRASSLANDS, SAVANNAS, FORESTS, or WETLANDS. Conversion of such areas to croplands often leads to less overall productivity—in ecological terms, it is a kind of ENVIRONMENTAL DEGRADATION—but the resulting productivity is of a type more desired by humans. Unlike natural ecosystems, croplands also require input from humans. In the traditional low-input form of agricultures, this means basically planting, watering, weeding, and harvesting (see ORGANIC FARMING). On modern high-input farms, however, substantial amounts of chemicals, including PESTICIDES and fertilizers, may also

**Number of farms in the United States, by farm size, 1900–1987.**

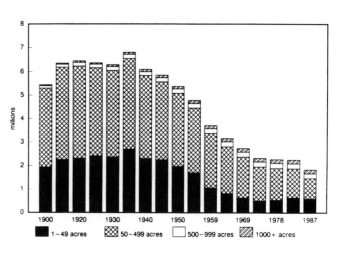

Source: *Environmental Quality.* The 21st Annual Report of the Council on Environmental Quality, 1991.

be required, often supplemented by substantial irrigation systems, along with the use of machinery for tilling, weeding, and harvesting.

Humans have been converting other types of ecosystems to croplands—clearing forests, filling in wetlands, and plowing grasslands—for thousands of years. In the process, over thousands of years, they destroyed many natural environments. However, the world's rapidly increasing POPULATION has created significant pressure to convert ever more land to croplands. As a result, many areas have become deforested, including many that are actually marginal as croplands and highly susceptible to EROSION, which can cause loss of valuable soil, and the need to create still more croplands. In many developing countries, this all takes place in a context of constantly threatening FAMINE AND FOOD INSECURITY.

In developed countries, croplands are under different kinds of pressures. With the rise of modern mechanized farming, small family farms have become less economical, and many are being swallowed up into massive, corporate-owned farms called *agribusinesses*. In addition, many previously untilled areas on such farms, such as wetlands, are being filled in to make the farms more efficient to work with modern machinery. On the other hand, near cities, croplands are disappearing at a rapid rate; these already cleared lands are often excellent sites for DEVELOPMENT, for homes to meet the rising urban population. In the United States, the result is that the amount of croplands is still much as it has been, but it is in quite different places and in different types of farms. It is this complex set of changes, involving the decline of the small family farm and creation of more uniformly filled-in land, that has been called the *cropland crisis*.

## For more information and action:

- **Alternative Farming Systems Information Center,** (301-344-3724 or 344-3559). Provides Quick Bibliography *Farmland Preservation*. (See ORGANIC FARMING AND SUSTAINABLE AGRICULTURE INFORMATION AND ACTION GUIDE on page 226.)
- **AMERICAN PLANNING ASSOCIATION (APA),** (202-872-0611). Publishes *Preserving Rural Character* (1990).
- **Institute for Food and Development Policy (IFDP),** (415–864–8555) Publishes *Family Farming*: A New Economic Vision and Action Alert pamphlet *Family Farming*: Faded Memory or Future Hope.
- **NATURAL RESOURCES DEFENSE COUNCIL (NRDC),** (212-727-2700). Publishes *Taxing the Rural Landscape: Improving State and Federal Policies for Prime Farmland* (J. Ward, 1988).
- **Population-Environment Balance,** (202-879-3000). Publishes *Balance Data* sheet ''Population Growth and Farmland Loss.'' (See POPULATION INFORMATION AND ACTION GUIDE on page 248.)
- **RESOURCES FOR THE FUTURE (RFF),** (202-328-5000) Publishes *Agricultural Protectionism in the Industrialized World* (Fred H. Sanderson, ed., 1990) and *Agricultural Productivity: Measurement and Explanation* (Susan M. Capalbo and John M. Antle, 1988).
- **SIERRA CLUB,** (415-776-2211 or 202-547-1141; legislative hotline, 202-547-5550). Publishes *Agriculture Policy*.

## Other references:

*Broken Heartland: The Rise of America's Rural Ghetto*. Osha Gray Davidson. Free Press, 1990. *Farm Policy Analysis*. Luther Tweeten. Westview, 1989. (See also ORGANIC FARMING; SUSTAINABLE AGRICULTURE; PESTICIDES; EROSION; SOIL CONSERVATION.)

**Cubatao pipeline fire,** disaster that resulted when a gasoline pipeline leak caught fire and ultimately consumed almost 1,000 slum homes at Cubatao, Brazil, on February 25, 1984. Of the 81 dead and hundreds injured, many were workers at the Petrobras oil refinery complex or other industrial or chemical plants in the highly contaminated city, long regarded as an environmental disaster area. (See OIL.)

**Cultural Survival (CS),** (53A Church Street, Cambridge, MA 02138; 617-495-2562; Jason Clay, Director), a membership organization founded in 1972 by people concerned with the rights of INDIGENOUS PEOPLES and ethnic minorities around the world, with special focus on forest tribes in tropical rain FORESTS. CS supports programs to guarantee their rights to the land and its resources, to strengthen their own grassroots organizations, and to foster sustainable DEVELOPMENT. In addition to providing direct assistance and advocacy, CS sponsors research on related issues, seeks to educate the public, conducts fund-raising projects selling rain-forest products with profits returned to the forest peoples, and publishes various materials, including the *Cultural Survival Quarterly (CSQ)*, *Indigenous Peoples and Tropical Forests: Models of Land Use and Management from Latin America* (Jason Clay, 1988), *Land Rights and Indigenous Peoples: The Role of the Inter-American Commission on Human Rights* (Shelton Davis, 1988), and numerous CS reports.

**curlew, Eskimo** (prairie pigeon or doughbird), a member of the sandpiper family, a bird last seen in quantity during the late 19th century, its range from Alaska and western Canada south to Argentina. Thought by many to be extinct, it was seen again in Texas and on the Platte River during the 1980s, and a breeding population of 100 to 150 was found in northern Canada in 1987, spurring attempts to recover this almost-lost species. (See also ENDANGERED SPECIES; also ENDANGERED AND THREATENED WILDLIFE AND PLANTS on page 372.)

**cyclodienes,** a group of chlorine-based PESTICIDES, including chlordane, dieldrin, heptachlor, and aldrin, manufactured under a variety of trade names; one in a family of persistent compounds called CHLORINATED HYDROCARBONS. Some of the earliest pesticides, used from the late 1940s, cyclodienes were later found to be damaging to humans, with long-term effects on the liver and central nervous system, and to cause tumors in laboratory animals, and so are probable human CARCINOGENS. In at least one case, a man died after having a 25 percent chlordane solution applied to his skin; and two others are known to have died after ingesting 2 to 4 grams of chlordane. As a result, the ENVIRONMENTAL PROTECTION AGENCY (EPA) canceled nearly all uses by the early 1980s, except for carefully controlled underground uses as termiticides; many European countries have also restricted or banned cyclodienes, though they are still used in some Third World countries.

Even where banned, however, tests showed that cyclodienes persisted, causing toxic indoor AIR POLLUTION, especially if improperly applied in indoor spaces (rather than

## How Can You Improve Indoor Air Quality?

There are several ways to minimize your exposure to the cyclodienes and other air pollutants:

- Increase the circulation of clean air in your house. When weather permits, periodically open windows and doors, and use fans to mix the air. In crawl spaces, clear or add vents and install a fan to constantly vent crawl space air to the outside.
- Seal those areas that directly contact treated soil, using grout, caulk, or sealant. Fill cracks in basement and ground floors and walls, joints between floors and walls, and openings around pipes, drains, and sumps. Periodically check these areas for signs of new cracks or broken seals since houses settle over time.
- Install a system that supplies outside air to appliances like clothes dryers and furnaces that now draw air from inside the house. Appliances that use indoor air may actually help draw chemical vapors from the soil into the house through walls, floors, and basements.

- Check the condition of ducts in your crawl space or basement. Use duct tape to seal openings and joints.
- For homes with high airborne levels of cyclodiene residues resulting from misapplications, building modifications may be worthwhile. They should be designed on a case-by-case basis but may include replacing or relocating air ducts, replacing furnaces or ventilation systems with air exchangers, and/or sealing crawl space soil with a layer of concrete.
- In cases where the cyclodienes have been improperly applied, household items may be contaminated. In these cases, clean or replace contaminated household items (such as carpets, carpet pads, and curtains).
- Some authorities have suggested washing contaminated items several times with ordinary household detergents. However, information on the effectiveness of cleaning with detergents is not available.

**Source:** *Termiticides.* Environmental Protection Agency, 1988. (See also RADON REDUCTION METHODS on page 451.)

---

into the ground); they frequently last in the soil for a dozen years, and in some instances traces of cyclodienes have been found in the soil 30 years or more after use. The EPA suggests that homeowners who suspect contamination with cyclodienes should have the air-concentration levels in the house tested. Names of laboratories can be obtained from the *National Pesticide Telecommunications Network* (see PESTICIDES INFORMATION AND ACTION GUIDE on page 238.) The NPTN also provides information about cleanup after heavy contamination, as from a chemical spill; about proper disposal; and about trade names the pesticides have been sold under. (See HOW CAN YOU IMPROVE INDOOR AIR QUALITY? above.)

# D

**dams,** natural or artificial structures that block or hinder the flow of water in an otherwise openly flowing RIVER, creating instead a reservoir or LAKE with controlled outflow. Dams sometimes develop naturally in an ECOSYSTEM, as when sand deposits build up and block outflow of water, or when beavers build a log dam. But the dams that exercise environmentalists are the structures built for human needs, including energy production (see HYDROPOWER), water diversion, raising water level for shipping, flood control, river regulation, and storage for later use, as in municipal systems, industries, and irrigation.

Earlier in the 20th century, dams were hailed as marvels of human ingenuity and a boon to the public. Even in the late 20th century, while some environmentalists are turning away from dams altogether, some others are touting small hydropower dams as proper small-scale energy producers. Dams and other water control structures have also freed many areas from deadly floods, and have allowed farmers to turn many DESERT areas into productive farmlands.

This has nowhere been more true than in the United States. Many developing countries, especially those with enormous POPULATION pressure, wish to have the same benefits and are, often with international DEVELOPMENT funds, building massive dams of their own, such as the NARMADA VALLEY DAM PROJECT and the THREE GORGES DAM. Their impulses are understandable, given the widespread poverty, destructive floods, and still-rising population. However, while they are reaching for what they hope will give them a better life, many others in these decades are decrying what they see as waste and the wanton destruction of irreplaceable natural resources—often threatening prime WILDERNESS areas and ENDANGERED SPECIES, as well as recreation areas—by building dams to power yet more development, such as the once-planned GRAND CANYON and TWO FORKS Dams, and the GLEN CANYON DAM actually built.

Another concern with dams is that local inhabitants (see INDIGENOUS PEOPLES) will be pushed from their lands and homes to benefit other people and interests. As population pressure keeps rising around the world, so the conflict between the human benefits of dams and the environmental costs will only intensify. To try to minimize damage from dams, some environmental groups have put forth guidelines to be followed in planning a dam (see SAN FRANCISCO DECLARATION OF THE INTERNATIONAL RIVERS NETWORK on page 79).

Another potential danger to the environment is dam failure, allowing a deadly wall of water to sweep down the river course. All dams must be inspected regularly and systematically for any sign of failure, and designs should be periodically reviewed in the light of experience at similar dams. The greatest danger comes from the many old and primitive earthen dams around the world, embankments built from varying mixtures of loose rock, gravel, sand, silt, and clay, rather than concrete. (See RIVER.)

**DDT (dichloro-diphenol-trichloroethane),** an extremely toxic PESTICIDE that is (like other CHLORINATED HYDROCARBONS) also highly persistent, readily dissolving in body fats, being stored in body tissues, and accumulating in the FOOD CHAIN (see BIOACCUMULATION). A classic

## The San Francisco Declaration of the International Rivers Network: The Position of Citizens' Organizations on Large Dams and Water Resource Management

- The specific goals of the dam project must be clearly stated, providing a clear basis for measuring the future success or failure of the project.
- During project planning, all alternatives to the project goals, both structural and nonstructural, must be clearly analyzed.
- Any governmental or international agency that funds big dam projects must allow free access to information on the project to citizens of both lending and recipient countries.
- A full assessment of the short- and long-term environmental, social, and economic effects of the project must be carried out, and an adequate opportunity provided for review and critique by independent experts.
- All people affected by the dam, both in the reservoir area and downstream, must be notified of the probable effect on their livelihood, must be consulted in the planning process, and must have effective political means for vetoing the project.
- All people who lose homes, land, or livelihood by a dam project must be fully compensated by accountable agencies.
- The threat to public safety due to potential collapse of the dam must be investigated and the analysis be made freely available to anyone living in the area potentially affected by the flood wave.
- Any irrigation project associated with a large dam must have as its primary goal the production of food crops for local consumption rather than cash crops for export.
- Any irrigation project associated with a large dam must include a fully integrated program to prevent waterlogging and salinization in order to allow the sustainable use of irrigated land.
- The dam project must be demonstrated to have no significant adverse impact (such as those caused by loss of nutrients and soil salinization) on the food supply or livelihood of people dependent on floodplain agriculture downstream.
- The dam project must be demonstrated to pose no threat to the water quality and water supplies of those living downstream.
- The project must improve public health, and must not threaten to increase the incidence of waterborne disease.
- The environmental impacts of industrial users dependent on electricity generated by the dam must be included in the project planning.
- The dam project must be demonstrated to have no significant adverse effect on downstream riverine, estuarine, or coastal fisheries.
- An adequate program for reforesting or erosion control in the reservoir watershed must be fully integrated into the project design.
- The plan for the dam project must identify whether or not the project is sustainable. It should specifically address reservoir sedimentation, soil salinization, and changes in reservoir inflow due to watershed degradation. If the project is not sustainable a restoration program should be included as part of the project design.
- Projected economic costs must include all the economic costs of environmental damage, and all the costs associated with construction, preparation, maintenance, and decommissioning.
- The economic analysis for a dam project must identify the range of uncertainty in the estimates of costs and benefits.
- Projected economic benefits and costs of the dam project must be based on demonstrated benefits and costs of prior projects.
- Plans for hydroelectric dams must present an analysis of the relative benefit and costs of alternative means of electricity generation and energy conservation.
- There must be an effective means to ensure that the operation and maintenance of the dam and associated facilities will actually be carried out to achieve the promised benefits.

A declaration resulting from a June 1988 conference sponsored by the International Rivers Network (see RIVERS) for international citizens organizations concerned with protecting rivers and water resources, especially from "their most immediate threat—construction of large dams." The position statement was adopted by the conference, and the last six points added later.

---

modern tale, DDT was by far the most widely used pesticide in the world, from the discovery of its biocidal properties in 1939. It was found to be highly toxic to fish and even more deadly for birds, since it thinned their egg shells and caused reproduction to fail, so it directly brought many to the brink of EXTINCTION (see ENDANGERED SPECIES). DDT was banned in the United States in 1972 and in many parts of Europe later in the 1970s. In some of those areas, the levels of DDT in the environment is slowly declining (since it has a half-life of 15 years), and some bird species are reviving, among them the bald EAGLE, peregrine FALCON, OSPREY, and brown PELICAN. But in the developing world, especially in Latin America, use of DDT has not only continued but increased into the 1990s, with incalculable effects on the environment (see CIRCLE OF POISON). (See PESTICIDES.)

**debt-for-nature swap,** a technique using forgiveness of international debt as a means of encouraging debtor governments to foster conservation efforts. As the ENVIRONMENTAL PROTECTION AGENCY (EPA) has described it: "Debt-for-nature swaps involve converting—at a discounted rate—official or commercial debt payable in foreign currency into local currency obligations and dedicating the resulting local currency proceeds to environmental projects. Swaps can involve projects such as acquisition or management of land for parks or nature reserves to protect fragile, valuable, or endangered ecosystems. They also may be used to fund pollution prevention or cleanup."

In one notable instance, the United States government in 1989 made a $1 million grant, to be used by the WORLD WILDLIFE FUND to buy over $2 million of MADAGASCAR's international debt, which was to be forgiven in return for a commitment by Madagascar to several kinds of conservation efforts, including reforestation projects and the training of additional national park rangers. A year later, CONSERVATION INTERNATIONAL concluded a similar arrangement, expanding the swap to include trade debt, and purchasing $5 million of Madagascar's debt. Debt-for-nature swaps have been made in several other countries, including Brazil, the Philippines, and Bolivia, and have been proposed in the United States, as well, in an attempt to save a threatened Humboldt County, California, redwood forest.

The EPA estimated that by mid-1991 U.S. NON-GOVERNMENTAL ORGANIZATIONS had successfully negotiated 15 swaps "involving commercial debt with a face value of nearly $100 million" in eight countries in Latin America, Africa, Asia, and Eastern Europe. Where such swaps require debtor governments to spend additional money in return for debt forgiveness, they can encounter problems, as the debts being forgiven may not have been seriously scheduled for repayment in any event. But at the very least they can serve to help set aside vitally important world natural heritage land, as in the threatened AMAZON RAIN FOREST, shared by eight Southern American debtor nations.

**For more information and action:**

- CONSERVATION INTERNATIONAL (CI), (202-429-5660).
- ENVIRONMENTAL PROTECTION AGENCY (EPA), (202-260-7751 or 202-260-2080).
- GREENPEACE, (202-462-1177).
- NATURE CONSERVANCY, THE, (703-841-5300).
- WORLD WILDLIFE FUND (WWF), (202-293-4800).

**Declaration of the Conference on the Human Environment (Stockholm Declaration),** a document resulting from the 1972 United Nations Conference on the Human Environment, held in Stockholm, Sweden; a notable example of "soft" ENVIRONMENTAL LAW, expressing ideals and intentions, rather than legally binding obligations. It was intended as a guide to international efforts to protect the environment, stressing that natural resources of all kinds, "especially representative samples of natural ecosystems," should be "safeguarded for the benefit of present and future generations through careful planning or management as appropriate."

**declining resources,** a supply of resources that diminishes with use, such as OIL and COAL, also called *nonrenewable resources,* as opposed to RENEWABLE RESOURCES, which occur naturally and cannot be used up, such as SOLAR ENERGY, WATER RESOURCES, or WAVE POWER, and plant and animal life in general.

**deep ecology,** a philosophical view focusing on exploration of the radical separation between human beings and nature, and other fundamental questions relating to humans and their world; a name coined in 1972 by Norwegian philosopher Arne Naess, who wrote that "the essence of deep ecology is to ask deeper questions. . . . We ask which society, which education, which form of religion is beneficial for all life on the planet as a whole." Many deep ecologists feel that traditional environmental approaches only apply "Band-aids" to a wounded world, and that what is necessary are an affirmation of the value of other species (apart from their usefulness or attractiveness to humans), a voluntary simplicity (replacing modern consumerism), and fundamental changes in humans' attitudes toward the world and the other beings in it. Deep ecologists often describe themselves as BIOCENTRIC (all-life–centered), and sometimes find themselves in opposite corners from environmental activists focusing on social issues (see SOCIAL ECOLOGY), whom they see as *anthropocentric,* or human-centered. Some environmentalists disparage deep ecology as too much talk, too little action—or, as one put it, "eco-la-la." Despite the divergence of thrust, deep ecology has been strongly associated with the green movement from its beginning, and in recent years the spiritual views of deep ecology have also often been linked with ECOFEMINISM, which holds that the separation between humans and nature results from a masculine, rather than feminine, consciousness; with

BIOREGIONALISM, stressing a return to a simple life on the land; and with direct-action environmental organizations, such as EARTH FIRST!, whose literature describes deep ecology as opposing "industrial civilization [which is] anti-Earth, anti-woman, and anti-liberty."

## For more information:

*The Journey of the Hero: Personal Growth, Deep Ecology and the Quest for the Grail.* Friedmann Wieland. Prism/Avery, 1991. *Thinking Like a Mountain.* John Seed et al. New Society (Santa Cruz, CA), 1991. *Practicing Deep Ecology.* Bill Devall. Peregrine Smith, 1989. *How Deep Is Deep Ecology? With an Essay-Review on Woman's Freedom.* George Bradford. Times Change, 1989. *Simple in Means, Rich in Ends: Practicing Deep Ecology.* Bill Devall. Peregrine Smith. 1988.
(See also ANIMAL RIGHTS MOVEMENT.)

**deer, Florida Key,** a small, white-tailed deer subspecies found only in the Florida Keys; the key deer was hunted very close to EXTINCTION by the late 1930s, and was saved only by a ban on HUNTING. After establishment of the National Key Deer Refuge in 1957, the key deer population rose from a low of between 30 and 40 to approximately 400 in the late 1970s, but since then has declined between 200 and 300, as massive DEVELOPMENT of the Florida Keys has destroyed deer habitat and brought increased automobile kills of key deer. Unfortunately, those who feed the popular deer draw them closer to roads and attacking dogs; when feeding was banned and speed limits enforced, considerably more deer survived than before, and the population slowly began to increase again, although loss of HABITAT remains a major long-term threat. In the early 1990s, the FISH AND WILDLIFE SERVICE listed 25 other threatened deer species around the world, mainly due to HABITAT loss to expanding human populations and hunting.

## For more information and action:

- NATURE CONSERVANCY, THE, (703-841-5300).
- **Trust for Public Land (TPL),** (415-495-4014). (See LAND TRUST AND CONSERVATION EASEMENT INFORMATION AND ACTION GUIDE on p. 178).
(See also ENDANGERED SPECIES; also ENDANGERED AND THREATENED WILDLIFE AND PLANTS on page 372.)

**Defenders of Wildlife** (1244 19th Street NW, Washington, DC 20036; 202-659-9510; M. Rupert Cutler, President), a contribution-supported membership organization founded in 1947 that focuses on "protection and restoration of all species of wild animals and plants in their natural communities." Defenders of Wildlife seeks to in-

fluence government legislators and agencies through wildlife advocacy at all levels; encourages grassroots citizen action, as through its *Defenders' Activist Network*; seeks to educate children and encourage their interest in animals and wildlife; and works with other concerned groups in coalitions such as the *Entanglement Network Coalition*, concerned with entanglement of marine life in nets and PLASTIC. Among its special emphases in recent years have been campaigns to strengthen protection for ENDANGERED SPECIES; to protect endangered wildlife abroad, as by banning import of wildlife to the United States and acting against ivory poaching; to reduce POLLUTION from plastics; to encourage live guard dogs instead of predator poisoning; to stop sport HUNTING and trapping of threatened animals such as WOLVES; to preserve and expand WILDLIFE REFUGES; to encourage federally funded surveys of plant and animals communities in every state, and to identify those needing protection through LAND USE planning. A special emphasis for the 1990s is to maintain BIOLOGICAL DIVERSITY, as by seeking passage of a National Biological Diversity Conservation and Research Act and an American Heritage Trust Fund to acquire species-rich habitats. The organization publishes various materials, including the bimonthly magazine *Defenders, In Defense of Wildlife: Preserving Communities and Corridors, The Biodiversity Challenge,* state-by-state wildlife viewing guides (see *Watchable Wildlife Program* under BUREAU OF LAND MANAGEMENT); educational newsletters; reports on endangered species; and action alerts.

**deforestation,** the clearing of trees from land, generally for the timber they contain, or for the land itself, as for CROPLANDS, DEVELOPMENT, or reservoirs (see DAMS). It is a major environmental concern, because FORESTS are so important in so many ways, among them sheltering wildlife and other plants, storing water, filtering the air, moderating the climate, and conserving the soil. (See FORESTS.)

**Delaware River oil spill,** leakage of an estimated 300,000 gallons (approximately 1,000 tons) of heating OIL into the Delaware River, after the *Presidente Rivera*, a Uruguayan ship, struck a rock in the river on June 24, 1989. Some environmental damage resulted, but the main result of the spill was to further focus public attention on the growing oil spill problem, as it occurred the day after major oil spills in NARRAGANSETT BAY and the HOUSTON SHIP CHANNEL, and only three months after the EXXON VALDEZ disaster. (See OIL; RIVERS.)

**Denali National Park and Preserve,** a southern Alaskan park, until 1980 named Mt. McKinley National Park;

"Denali" in Athapascan means "The Big One." At the center of the park is Mt. McKinley, at 20,320 feet, the tallest mountain in North America, and a magnet for hundreds of thousands of visitors every summer. The 6-million-acre (9,600-square-mile) park is also a major wildlife preserve, and since 1974 has been designated by the United Nations as an international BIOSPHERE PRESERVE. It is a refuge for such animals as the huge Alaska moose, grizzly BEAR, red fox, the white Dall sheep, lynx, loons, hoary marmot, snowshoe hare, WOLF, wolverine, ermine, marten, and CARIBOU, as well as many bird species, including the golden eagle, willow ptarmigan, and great horned owl, and such summer visitors as the Arctic tern, which journeys from Antarctica, warblers, snow buntings, and plovers.

Although automobile use is limited in the park, today's hundreds of thousands of visitors, who will probably in the next century become millions, inevitably bring some damage to the fragile northern ECOSYSTEM. But at least as much damage is done by the gold and other metal miners who operate—so far on a relatively small scale—in the northern regions of the park. POPULATION and commercial pressures are growing at Denali, one of the most accessible of the Alaskan parks, while environmentalists campaign to preserve this portion of the world's natural heritage.

### For more information and action:

- NATIONAL PARKS AND CONSERVATION ASSOCIATION (NPCA), (202-944-8530).
- Trust for Public Land (TPL), (415-495-4014). (See LAND TRUST AND CONSERVATION EASEMENT INFORMATION AND ACTION GUIDE on p. 178.)

(See also WILDLIFE REFUGE; WILDERNESS.)

### Department of Agriculture (USDA or DOA),

(14th Street and Independence Avenue, SW, Washington, DC 20250; Information, 202-720-2791; Edward Madigan, Secretary of Agriculture), a U.S. federal department established in 1862 to carry out research and disseminate information about agriculture, work much enhanced after the 1914 passage of the Smith-Lever Agricultural Extension Act, establishing what is now the *Extension Service (ES)*, (202-447-3029). The ES was designed originally to bring research information to farmers through a network of land-grant universities and local offices, but now provides a wider range of programs for rural communities, on topics such as more efficient production and marketing of agricultural products, natural resource management, nutrition, family living, 4-H youth programs, and community and rural DEVELOPMENT.

From the USDA's research functions sprang its now-widespread regulatory functions, including from 1884 inspections and control of livestock to control spread of disease, strengthened under the Meat Inspection Act and the Food and Drug Act, both in 1906. The Food and Drug Act has since 1940 been monitored under the separate FOOD AND DRUG ADMINISTRATION, but inspection remains a prime function of the USDA, today carried on under various branches, including:

- **Agricultural Marketing Service (AMS)** (202-720-8998), which develops quality grade standards and provides "voluntary grading services for meat, poultry, eggs, dairy products, fruits and vegetables, cotton, tobacco, and livestock," as well as overseeing marketing research and regulation, and USDA's transportation policies, especially as applied to rural areas.
- **Animal and Plant Health Inspection Service (APHIS)** (202-720-2511), which administers programs to help control or eradicate animal and plant pests and diseases; enforces the ANIMAL WELFARE ACT and the Horse Protection Act; and licenses and monitors veterinary biological products.
- **Federal Grain Inspection Service (FGIS)** (202-720-5091), which inspects and maintains standards for grain and commodities, and monitors grain inspection agencies.
- **Food Safety and Inspection Service (FSIS)** (202-720-7943), which administers the Federal Meat Inspection Act and the Poultry Products Inspection Act, including provision of uniform federal and state standards for inspection "to assure safety, wholesomeness, and truthful labeling of these products," including "harmful bacteria and residues in meat and poultry products." FSIS is charged with giving advance approval of construction and equipment of plants operating in interstate commerce; "inspection of animals and birds before, during, and after slaughter; continuous inspection of all processing operations; giving advance approval of labels of meat and poultry products;" and monitoring of foreign plants handling meat or poultry for export to the United States. The FSIS also conducts food safety consumer education programs.
- **Packers and Stockyards Administration (P&SA)** (202-382-9528), which enforces the Packers and Stockyards Act, monitoring practices in the marketing of livestock, meat, and poultry.

Meanwhile the USDA's research and information dissemination function has continued and widened, under such other branches as the:

- **Agricultural Research Service (ARS)** (301-344-2264), the USDA's main research arm, which "conducts research on production of animals and plants; protection of animals and plants from diseases, use and improvement of soil, water, and air resources; processing, storage, and safety of food; and human nutrition.''

- **Cooperative State Research Service (CSRS)** (202-401-4268), which coordinates and administers federal funds for agricultural and forestry research and maintains the *Current Research Information Service (CRIS)* of state and federal research records for publicly supported agricultural and forestry research. Research focuses on high-priority areas related to food production and human nutrition, including PHOTOSYNTHESIS, nitrogen fixation, GENETIC ENGINEERING, and biological stress.
- **Economic Research Service (ERS)** (202-219-0515), which conducts research, analyzes, and reports data on economic aspects of domestic and foreign agricultural production.
- **National Agricultural Library (NAL)** (301-344-3778; Library Services, 301-344-3755), which provides technical information on agricultural research and related subjects to scientists, educators, farmers, and other libraries, acting as the prime U.S. center for international agricultural information.
- **National Agricultural Statistics Service** (202-219-0504), which prepares official USDA data, summarized in periodic reports to the public.
- **Office of Public Affairs (OPA)** (202-720-4623; or 202-720-2798), which provides information and seeks to educate the public about USDA programs and policies.

The USDA also administers food and consumer services, such as:

- **Food and Nutrition Services (FNS)** (703-756-3039); or 703–756–3276), which administers federal food assistance programs.
- **Human Nutrition Information Service (HNIS)** (301-436-8617), which gathers and disseminates information on nutrition and food safety, including standard reference tables on the nutritive values of foods, and on the population's food consumption and dietary levels.
- **Office of the Consumer Advisor (OCA)** (202-720-3975), which coordinates USDA actions on problems and issues of importance to consumers.

USDA programs on the international front include:

- **Foreign Agricultural Service (FAS)** (202-720-7115), which gathers and disseminates information on world crops, policies, and markets; and administers agricultural import and export programs.
- **Office of International Cooperation and Development (OICD)** (202-245-5801), which coordinates USDA's in-

ternational training and technical assistance programs, including development work overseas and work with international food and agricultural organizations.
- **World Agricultural Outlook Board (WAOB)** (202-720-5447), which coordinates the USDA's forecasts of worldwide commodity supply and use, and its analyses of the agricultural situation and outlook, including the impact of weather and climate, coordinating the annual Outlook Conference.

In addition to administrative branches, other special programs under the USDA include:

- **Agricultural Stabilization and Conservation Service (ASCS)** (202-720-5237), which ''administers commodity production adjustment and support programs; natural disaster assistance to agricultural producers through payments and cost-sharing; and certain national emergency preparedness activities;'' as well as the *Conservation Reserve Program*; and conservation cost-sharing with farmers and ranchers, as on expenses for programs to prevent soil loss from wind and water erosion, solve water quality and water conservation problems, control pollution from animal waste, preserve FOREST resources, and encourage energy conservation.
- **Farmers Home Administration (FHA)** (202-720-6903), which provides loans to those who cannot obtain credit from banks or other lending institutions, including small communities to fund facilities such as wastewater treatment or water quality control programs.
- **Federal Crop Insurance Corporation (FCIC)** (202-720-3287), which insures farmers against crop losses due to natural disasters, such as hail, fire and drought.
- **Office of Agricultural Biotechnology** (202-720-4419), which coordinates USDA programs and activities regarding BIOTECHNOLOGY, including environmental safety of proposed field tests involving genetically engineered organisms; it also supports the *Agricultural Biotechnology Research Advisory Committee* and the *Biotechnology Council*.
- **Office of Energy (OE)** (202-720-2634), which coordinates the USDA's energy policy, including all issues relating to agricultural uses of energy and agricultural impacts of energy development and use.
- **Rural Electrification Administration (REA)** (202-382-1007), which makes and guarantees loans to rural electric and information systems, to provide service at affordable cost, and makes no-interest loans available for rural economic development and job creation.

Two other major programs under the Department of Agriculture are treated in separate entries: the FOREST SERVICE (FS) and the SOIL CONSERVATION SERVICE (SCS).

**Department of Energy (DOE),** (Forrestal Building, 1000 Independence Avenue, SW, Washington, DC 20585; 202-586-5000; James D. Watkins, Secretary), a U.S. federal agency established in 1977 to consolidate various energy research, development, administration, marketing, and commission functions, many formerly under the Department of the Interior. The DOE oversees major energy policy and planning issues, acting as key adviser to the President, including NUCLEAR ENERGY, conservation and renewable energy, FOSSIL FUELS, and related environmental, safety, and health programs, such as RADIOACTIVE WASTE management. Among the key programs of the DOE are:

- **Energy Research** (301-353-4944), which sponsors basic and applied research and development programs, including high energy physics and nuclear fusion, and also environmental, health, and safety aspects of various energy technologies.
- **Fossil Energy** (301-353-2617), which oversees research and development on energy from COAL, OIL, and NATURAL GAS, including new technologies such as cleaner coal or liquefied fuels.
- **Conservation and Renewable Energy** (202-586-6768), overseeing programs to increase production and use of renewable energy sources such as SOLAR ENERGY, BIOFUELS, WIND ENERGY, and GEOTHERMAL ENERGY; for consumers, it operates the CONSERVATION AND RENEWABLE ENERGY INQUIRY AND REFERRAL SERVICE (CAREIRS).
- **Nuclear Safety** (202-586-2407), which develops and implements safety policies and standards for nuclear facilities.
- **Nuclear Energy,** overseeing programs producing energy from nuclear fission, including civilian and naval reactor development, uranium enrichment, the nuclear fuel cycle, and space nuclear applications.
- **Civilian Radioactive Waste Management** (202-586-9116), managing federal programs for recommending, constructing, and operating disposal facilities for high-level radioactive waste and spent nuclear fuel.
- **New Production Reactors** (202-586-6456), overseeing acquisition and construction of new production reactors.
- **Environmental Restoration and Waste Management** (202-586-2661), which focuses on waste management, researches permanent disposal solutions, and manages assessment and clean-up of inactive waste sites and facilities.
- **International Affairs and Energy Emergencies** (202-586-5924), relating to international aspects of overall energy policy, and coordinating energy emergency preparedness plans and programs.

- **Intelligence** (202-586-5111), providing vital energy intelligence to the Department of State and other appropriate policymaking arms.
- **Defense** (202-586-2295), directing research, development, testing, production, and surveillance programs relating to NUCLEAR WEAPONS, as well as production of nuclear materials and management of nuclear waste.
- **Federal Energy Regulatory Commission (FERC)** (825 North Capitol Street NE, Washington, DC 20426; 202-208-0200) George L.B. Pratt, Executive Director, a quasi-independent five-member commission within the DOE, overseeing rates and charges for transportation and sale of various energy sources.
- **Economic Regulatory Administration** (202-586-4241), operating any regulatory programs not assigned to FERC.
- **Energy Information Administration** (202-586-1181), gathering, processing, and publishing data on energy resources, production, consumption, distribution, and technology; a clearinghouse on energy, working closely with DOE's Technical Information Center.

In addition, the DOE has numerous field operations overseeing major federal energy programs, such as the Bonneville Power Administration in the Pacific Northwest or the Western Area Power Administration, which operates a network of generating plants, including the coal-fired Navajo plant that has so contributed to AIR POLLUTION around the GRAND CANYON. (See also NUCLEAR ENERGY; NUCLEAR WEAPONS ESTABLISHMENT, U.S.)

**Department of the Interior (DOI),** (Interior Building, 1849 C Street, NW, Washington, DC 20240; 202-208-1100; Manuel Lujan, Jr., Secretary of the Interior), an arm of the federal government which has responsibility for many of the country's public lands. These are administrated under various agencies, several of them considered separately in this book, including the BUREAU OF LAND MANAGEMENT, BUREAU OF MINES, NATIONAL PARK SERVICE, and FISH AND WILDLIFE SERVICE. The DOI and its agencies have been at the center of a long and continuing battle pitting environmental interests against short-term commercial interests.

**desalinization (desalination),** removal of dissolved or suspended solids from water, often seawater but also salty water in desert or coastal areas (see SALINIZATION). Being a nearly universal solvent, water has dissolved in it varying quantities of minerals. The level of total dissolved solids (TDS) generally considered acceptable for human drinking water is 500 parts per million (ppm) TDS, though 1,000 may be considered acceptable for short periods.

Brackish water (such as that in tidal areas or MANGROVES) has 1,000 to 10,000 ppm TDS, while seawater has 10,000 to 36,000 ppm TDS (see OCEANS). Anything above 36,000 ppm TDS—such as highly concentrated wastewater from desalinization or MINING activities—is called *brine*. In areas where freshwater is plentiful, desalinization is rarely needed, except perhaps for "water softeners" in areas having "hard" water, meaning relatively more dissolved minerals than "soft" water. But in areas where freshwater is in short supply, desalinization holds out the possibility of making saline rivers and lakes drinkable and usable for irrigation, and of tapping the practically limitless water of the ocean, where over 97 percent of the earth's water is stored.

Three main methods are used for desalinization:

- **distillation,** in which the brackish or salty water is boiled, and the vapor collected, then cooled, to produce freshwater, leaving the salts behind. The most common approach, distillation has been used in laboratories since Roman times, and is especially good for extremely salty water, since the amount of energy needed is the same as for low-salt solutions. However, it is very energy-consuming, and so is not economical for large-scale environmental use. Another "change of phase" approach, which uses freezing, has the same drawbacks; also, although the resulting ice crystals are salt-free, salt water remains trapped between the crystals.
- **selective transport across membranes,** using the ability of certain materials (*semipermeable membranes*) to allow selected materials (charged particles called *ions*) to pass through them. In *electrodialysis*, electricity is used to attract positively or negatively charged salts to one side of the membrane, leaving freshened water on the other side. This approach is economical only for brackish water, and does nothing about bacteria, ORGANIC COMPOUNDS, and colloidal matter, extremely small suspended particles that do not settle or are not readily filtered. Far superior is another membrane approach, *reverse osmosis*, in which pressure is exerted on one side of the membrane to force water from the salty solution across the membrane into the freshwater side, leaving the salts behind. This is a relatively low-energy approach, which rejects bacteria, organic compounds, and colloids to produce not just acceptable but "ultrapure" water, such as that needed for boilers and rinsing material for electronics equipment. However, it is at present still too costly for large-scale environmental use.
- **ion exchange,** in which the salty solution is sent through various materials of a specific chemical makeup designed to capture salts selectively from the solution, leaving

fresh water behind. This is the main approach used in home water softeners and in many industries. However, because its costs increase with the concentration of the salty water, it is generally practical for use only on water with TDS of under 1,000 ppm.

Whatever method is used, in general salty water is fed into a pretreatment area, where settleable solids are removed, and then moved on to the desalting area. There water is separated from the concentrated brine, which is then also removed, causing some WASTE DISPOSAL problems; the desalinated water is sent on for post-treatment, such as CHLORINATION.

At present desalinization is used sparingly and in special situations, by those countries and industries with sufficient need and resources to accept the cost. Large-scale desalinization plants have been built in many parts of the world, notably in Kuwait and Saudi Arabia, supplying water where that commodity seems scarcer than gold, as well as in parts of the American Southwest and in Mexico. Costs are somewhat reduced by combining desalinization plants with electricity-generating plants. If inexpensive, renewable energy sources are developed, such as practical solar power, desalinization has the potential to transform many environmental areas now suffering from shortage of usable freshwater. (See SALINIZATION; OCEANS; WATER RESOURCES.)

**desert,** a region of little precipitation and sparse, widely spaced vegetation, with the density and diversity of plants increasing primarily with the amount of moisture available and with warmer temperatures, and being especially abundant around occasional oases where the water table is near the surface, or underlying AQUIFERS can be tapped. Desert plants are often deep-rooted, seeking underground moisture; some lie dormant for long periods, beginning their life cycles or coming into leaf only when water is available, and many store water, most notably succulents like the cactus.

Contrary to popular impression, deserts are not all hot places with huge sand dunes. Many are not at all sandy, but rather hard-packed or salt-encrusted earth or rocky wastelands, and they are characterized by extremes of temperature, between the seasons and also between day and night. Nor are deserts necessarily barren; where water is available, as around oases or through irrigation, many desert soils are extremely fertile. Among agricultural scientists, considerable attention is being paid to making use of the characteristic desert plants, and developing appropriate crops to be grown in irrigated desert lands. Water use must be carefully managed, however, to avoid accumulation of salt in the soil (see SALINIZATION). Many desert areas,

## Desert and Desertification Information and Action Guide

For more information and action on desert and desertification:

**Association of Arid Lands Studies (AALS)** (Box 4620, Texas Tech University, Lubbock, TX 79409; 806-742-2218), a professional organization of scholars studying arid and semiarid lands of the world, founded in 1977; headquartered at the INTERNATIONAL CENTER FOR ARID AND SEMIARID LAND STUDIES (ICASALS). It publishes the *AALS Newsletter* and other materials.

**CENTRE FOR SCIENCE AND TECHNOLOGY FOR DEVELOPMENT (CSTD), United Nations,** (212-963-8435).

**CONSULTATIVE GROUP ON INTERNATIONAL AGRICULTURAL RESEARCH (CGIAR),** (202-473-8951). Has research centers on desert and semiarid areas.

**INTERNATIONAL CENTER FOR ARID AND SEMIARID LAND STUDIES (ICASALS),** (806-742-2218). Publishes *Arid and Semi-Arid Lands—A Preview.*

**NATIONAL WILDLIFE FEDERATION (NWF),** (202-797-6800 or 800-245-5484). Publishes *Discovering Deserts* (1991).

**NATURAL RESOURCES AND ENERGY DIVISION (NRED), United Nations,** (212-963-6205).

**Office of Arid Lands Studies (OALS),** (University of Arizona, College of Agriculture, 845 North Park Avenue, Tucson, AZ 85719; 602-621-1955), a multidisciplinary research and information center that focuses on problems of understanding and managing the world's arid lands, on the local, state, national, and international levels. OALS researchers seek to adapt existing technologies and develop new methods of alleviating desertification and associated damage to fragile natural resources, their work organized into five programs: *Arid Lands Information Center (ALIC)*, handling research support, cataloging, libraries and computer databases, preparation of publications, housing of collections, and assistance to documentation centers in developing countries; *Bioresources Research Facility (BRF)*, developing new low–water-using crops adapted to arid lands, with potential industrial, agricultural, or fuel value; *Desert Research Unit (DRU)*, conducting "policy studies, environmental impact assessments, mine reclamation studies, and research on economically viable arid lands plants and water conservation;" *Arizona Remote Sensing Center (ARSC)*, using aircraft or satellite images to learn more about agricultural and natural resource problems in arid regions; and *Economic Development Program (EDP)*, to provide marketing and economic studies to foster development in arid areas, especially in Arizona. OALS publishes the *Arid Lands Newsletter* and technical reports, notably on arid-adapted products such as guayule and jojoba.

**SIERRA CLUB,** (415-776-2211 or 202-547-1141; legislative hotline, 202-547-5550). Recent campaigns include BLM Wilderness/Desert National Parks. Publishes BLM/Desert, and *The Changing Desert.*

**WORLD BANK,** (202-477-1234).

Other references:

*The Ecology of Desert Communities.* Gary A. Polis, ed. University of Arizona Press, 1991. *The Desert.* John C. Van Dyke. Gibbs Smith, 1991. *The Desert Reader.* Peter Wild, ed. University of Utah Press, 1991. *Deserts as Dumps: The Disposal of Hazardous Materials in Arid Ecosystems.* Charles C. Reith and Bruce M. Thomson, eds. University of New Mexico Press, 1991. *Drylands: The Deserts of North America.* David Hyde. Crown, 1990. *The Threatening Desert: Controlling Desertification.* Alan Grainger. InBook, 1990.

---

particularly cooler "semidesert" regions such as North America's Great Basin, also provide good grazing country for domesticated animals. However, desert vegetation is fragile and can easily be destroyed by OVERGRAZING, and some kinds of activities, such as off-road vehicles.

Desert is one of the world's major life zones, or BIOMES. Some areas are naturally desert, where climate and terrain conspire to limit rainfall (to under 10 inches a year) and therefore possible plant growth. But other areas are made desert by overuse and abuse of the land, especially by OVERGRAZING, DEFORESTATION, agricultural practices leading to EROSION, and improper irrigation techniques leading to accumulation of salts in the soil. The resulting process of DESERTIFICATION is causing desert areas to expand in many parts of the world, especially in areas of rising POPU-LATION, where people under threat of FAMINE AND FOOD INSECURITY are unable to allow land to regenerate between agricultural or pasture uses, or are forced to move into already marginal lands. (See DESERTIFICATION; also DESERT AND DESERTIFICATION INFORMATION AND ACTION GUIDE above.)

**desertification,** the progressive reduction in an area's ability to capture and store water, and therefore to support plant and animal life. Though many regions of the world are naturally DESERT, many other areas—once GRASSLANDS, CROPLANDS, or even FORESTS—are being turned into desert, largely by human actions, especially by overuse and abuses of the land, such as OVERGRAZING, DEFORESTATION, agricultural practices leading to soil loss (see

## What Is Sustainable Development?

Development is . . . the modification of the biosphere and the application of human, financial, living and nonliving resources to satisfy human needs and improve the quality of human life. For development to be sustainable it must take account of social and ecological factors, as well as economic ones; of the living and non-living resource base; and of the long-term as well as the short-term advantages and disadvantages of alternative actions.

**Source:** World Conservation Strategy: Living Resource Conservation for Sustainable Development, International Union for Conservation of Nature and Natural Resources (IUCN), with the UNITED NATIONS ENVIRONMENT PROGRAMME (UNEP) and the WORLD WILDLIFE FUND (WWF), 1980.

---

EROSION), and improper irrigation leading to salty soil (see SALINIZATION). Desertification is a cumulative process: as plant cover is reduced, or as salts accumulate in the soil, the land becomes dryer and harder-packed, and less able to hold water; the dry soil is readily eroded by wind and water (as in the American DUST BOWL); at each stage of this ENVIRONMENTAL DEGRADATION the land's CARRYING CAPACITY is reduced. (See DESERT; also DESERT AND DESERTIFICATION INFORMATION AND ACTION GUIDE on page 86.)

**development,** in an environmental context, the use of natural and human resources so as to improve the quality of life—a double-edged concept, since it leaves open to question whose life is improved and at what cost. In poor and rural communities all over the past, today as throughout history, there are millions of people who lack basic food, fuel, shelter, and other necessities, and their numbers are growing with the modern POPULATION explosion. By comparison, most people in so-called *developed countries*, at least in urban or suburban areas, have these basic necessities provided for—and a great deal more. Development has been the basis for the economic growth in these affluent countries, and for the comfortable-to-luxurious life lived by many of their inhabitants. It is this life that many people from poorer *undeveloped countries* wish to emulate. However, while they attempt to improve their lot in life, many people in affluent countries have begun to recognize the environmental costs of unrestrained development. Indeed, for many environmentally inclined people ''development'' is almost a dirty word, calling to mind wanton destruction of natural places for the building of ever more luxury residences and factories. For many environmentalists, the challenge of the future is to encourage planned, sustainable development in poorer areas, while containing development in already affluent areas, attempting in the process to meet human needs (though

not excessive desires) without undue strain on the environment, and recognizing the value of other forms of life.

In the second half of the 20th century, billions of dollars in aid and loans have been poured into poor and rural areas to aid in development, often through international organizations such as the WORLD BANK and other *multilateral development banks* (MBDs). Much of these funds have gone into large-scale projects like DAMS, which can supply both HYDROPOWER and irrigation for farmers, or into the creation and improvement of HIGH-YIELDING VARIETIES (HYVs), as through BIOTECHNOLOGY, in what has been called the GREEN REVOLUTION. However, such approaches have in more recent years been found to be costly to the environment, and also to the culture of INDIGENOUS PEOPLES, and often either short-lived or even counterproductive in the long run. Today, emphasis is increasingly placed on smaller-scale projects designed to produce sustainable development within a community. With SOIL CONSERVATION and other land management techniques, for example, farmers may halt EROSION and prevent the progressive environmental damage caused by OVERGRAZING, which would otherwise destroy the ECOSYSTEM, as through DEFORESTATION, DESERTIFICATION, and using up of DECLINING RESOURCES. Modern aid focuses increasingly on provision of health, educational, technical, and other services in an integrated way, to improve not just human life but the whole environment. This is an ideal, however, and environmentalists still rightly criticize much international aid as being ill-conceived and short-sighted approaches that ''throw money at the problem,'' rather than attempting to look at communities and their resources in a rational, long-term way.

In the developed countries, the problems are somewhat different. It is not simply that ENVIRONMENTAL DEGRADATION is more often driven by greed, not need—which may well be true—but that environmental concerns have until

## Development Information and Action Guide

**For more information and action on development:**

AMERICAN PLANNING ASSOCIATION (APA) (202-872-0611). Publishes or distributes books and reports such as *Everyone Wins! A Citizen's Guide to Development* (Richard D. Klein, 1990), *Project Infrastructure Development Handbook* (Donna Hanousek et al., Urban Land Institute, 1989), *A Salute to Imaginative Economic Development Programs* (National Council for Urban Economic Development, 1989), *Design Manual for Conservation and Development* (Robert D. Yaro et al., Lincoln Institute of Land Policy/Environmental Law Foundation, 1988), and bibliographies from the *Council of Planning Librarians (CPL)*, such as *Telecommunications and Regional Development* (1989) and *Urban Development Issues: What Is Controversial in Urban Sprawl?* (1989).

APPROPRIATE TECHNOLOGY TRANSFER FOR RURAL AREAS (ATTRA), (501-442-9824 or 800-346-9140).

**Bank Information Center (BIC)** (2000 P. Street NW, Suite 515, Washington, DC 20036; 202-822-6630), a "clearinghouse for environmental information on MDB [multilateral development bank] funded projects," founded in 1987 by environmental nongovernmental organizations from 14 countries, focusing especially on WETLANDS protection and rain FOREST conservation, attempting to see that MDB, notably WORLD BANK, projects are "environmentally sound and developmentally sustainable." BIC publishes recommended reforms, as well as reports, such as *Financing Ecological and Social Destruction: The World Bank and International Monetary Fund.*

CABI INTERNATIONAL (CABI), (602-621-7897 or 800-528-4841).

CENTRE FOR SCIENCE AND TECHNOLOGY FOR DEVELOPMENT (CSTD), UNITED NATIONS, (212-963-8435).

COORDINATION IN DEVELOPMENT (CODEL), (212-870-3000).

CULTURAL SURVIVAL (CS) (617-495-2562).

**Development Group for Alternative Policies (Development GAP)** (1400 I Street NW, Suite 520, Washington, DC 20005; 202-898-1566; Stephen Hellinger, Douglas Hellinger, and Fred O'Regan, Co–Directors), an international policy and resource organization founded in 1977 "not simply for the purpose of analyzing U.S. and multilateral aid policy and related foreign policy issues, but also to demonstrate practically how poor communities and popular organizations can exercise greater control over the policies, programs, and projects that affect them." The Development GAP has provided model policies for international development organizations as well as the U.S. government, working with "a coalition of development, environmental, church, and human and labor rights organizations in the United States focused on the reform of the U.S. foreign aid program" and on a range of other multilateral aid and trade issues. It publishes various materials, such as *Aid for Just Development: Report on the Future of Foreign Assistance* (1988).

---

recently not been considered at all in development. In real estate law, for example, the "highest and best use of the land" is the use that will make the land most valuable for resale—an office tower is, in these terms, "higher and better" than a home or small shop, much less "unimproved" land. Only in recent years have environmentalists brought to wide attention the idea that humans are not the only living beings to be considered in any action affecting the environment, and that even in economic terms natural resources have a value that has not generally been considered in development decisions. That has given rise to the approach of NATURAL RESOURCE ACCOUNTING, which attempts to give a truer, long-term view of the value of an area, once plants, animals, and a whole, self-sustaining ECOSYSTEM are seen to have real value. Communities are increasingly using ENVIRONMENTAL PLANNING and techniques such as ZONING to control the placement and the type of development, whether that is the siting of a new factory or the building of a new complex of homes. (See DEVELOPMENT INFORMATION AND ACTION GUIDE above.)

**Diamond v. Chakrabarty,** a 1980 Supreme Court case asserting that genetically altered life forms could be patented (see GENETIC ENGINEERING.)

**dieldrin,** a highly toxic PESTICIDE (see CYCLODIENES).

**dilution and dispersal,** a general approach to POLLUTION, which involves dilution of pollutants by adding to the original mix more of a less polluted medium—air, water, or soil—and then dispersing it. An everyday example is "airing a place out" when something has burned in the kitchen. Often the immediate aim is to meet pollution standards (see AIR POLLUTION; WATER POLLUTION), but the underlying principle is that, if properly diluted, natural processes can work more effectively to break down the offending pollutants, the catch-phrase being "dilution is the solution to pollution." Unfortunately, many modern pollution problems are so serious and persistent that this approach is ineffective; and many environmentalists stress the need to instead reduce the amount of pollution created.

EARTH FIRST! (E.F.!), (Direct Action Fund, 415-376-7329).

EARTH ISLAND INSTITUTE, (415-788-3666).

GREENPEACE, (202-462-1177).

INSTITUTE FOR FOOD AND DEVELOPMENT POLICY (IFDP), popularly called Food First, (415-864-8555). Publishes Development Reports, such as *Help or Hindrance? United States Economic Aid in Central America* and *A Fate Worse Than Debt: The World Financial Crisis and the Poor.*

IUCN—THE WORLD CONSERVATION UNION, (202-797-5454). Publishes *Common Property Resources: Ecology of Community-Based Sustainable Development* (Fikret Berkes, ed., 1989).

LEGACY INTERNATIONAL, (703-549-3630).

NATURAL RESOURCES DEFENSE COUNCIL (NRDC), (212-727-2700).

PACIFIC INSTITUTE FOR STUDIES IN DEVELOPMENT, ENVIRONMENT, AND SECURITY, (415-843-9550).

RENEW AMERICA, (202-232-2252). Publishes *Growth and the Environment* (1989).

RESOURCES FOR THE FUTURE (RFF), (202-328-5000).

SIERRA CLUB, (415-776-2211 or 202-547-1141; legislative hotline, 202–5550.) Publishes *International Development Lending Reform.*

UNITED NATIONS DEVELOPMENT PROGRAMME (UNDP), (212-906-5000).

WINROCK INTERNATIONAL INSTITUTE FOR AGRICUTURAL DEVELOPMENT (501-727-5435 or 703-525-9403).

WORLD BANK, (202-477-1234). Publishes *Environmental Accounting for Sustainable Development* (Yusuf J. Ahmad et al., 1989) and *World Development Report (1988).*

World Environment Center (WEC), (212-683-4700). Operates *International Environment and Development Service (IEDS).*

WORLD RESOURCES INSTITUTE (WRI), (202-638-6300). Publishes *Natural Endowments: Financing Resource Conservation for Development* (International Conservation Financing Project Report, 1989) and *The Shrinking Planet: U.S. Information Technology and Sustainable Development* (John Elkington and Jonathan Shopley, 1988).

WORLD WILDLIFE FUND (WWF), (202-293-4800).

Zero Population Growth (ZPG), (202-332-2200). Publishes *The Urbanization of Suburbia, Voting to Slow Growth,* and *Urban Stress Test.* (See POPULATION INFORMATION AND ACTION GUIDE on page 248.)

**Other references:**

*Ethics of Environment and Development: Global Challenge, International Response.* J. Ronald Engel and Joan Gibb Engel, eds. University of Arizona Press, 1990. *In the U.S. Interest: Resources, Growth, and Security in the Developing World,* Janet Welsh Brown, ed. Westview Press, 1990. *Downtown Inc.: How America Rebuilds Cities.* Bernard J. Freiden and Lynne B. Sagalyn. MIT Press, 1989. *The Complete Manual of Land Planning and Development.* William E. Brewer and Charles P. Alter. Prentice Hall, 1988. *Managing Economic Development* Jeffrey S. Luke et al. Jossey-Bass, 1988.

---

**dioxin,** a family of chemical compounds that contain some of the most powerfully TOXIC CHEMICALS ever known, the best known and most toxic of which is 2, 3, 7, 8-tetrachlorodi-benzo-*p*-dioxin (TCDD), often called just dioxin. The lethal dose for half the test population ($LD_{50}$) of rats has at some times been placed at only $22 \times 10^{-6}$, an amount so minute that some researchers have estimated it to be a million times more toxic than PCBs. Dioxin is in fact often associated with PCB, AGENT ORANGE (and its two components, 2,4,5-T and 2,4,-D), other CHLORINATED HYDROCARBONS, and other *halogenated* compounds (see HALOGENS), dioxin is not deliberately manufactured, but instead is a byproduct or contaminant formed during production of such other chemicals or when other chemicals are burned or heated, as in accidents or INCINERATION in HAZARDOUS WASTE sites. Large amounts of dioxin were formed in the SEVESO chemical explosion and it played a central role in the chemical disasters at LOVE CANAL and TIMES BEACH.

Dioxin is rightly feared. In 1984 the ENVIRONMENTAL PROTECTION AGENCY (EPA) reported that TCDD was the "most potent animal carcinogen" the agency had ever evaluated, though in 1991 government officials involved in the Times Beach case questioned whether, after all, dioxin was as dangerous as once feared, except at high concentrations. Beyond that, the precise effects of dioxin are not clearly known, and vary widely from species to species, but include suppression of the immune system, birth defects, damage to the liver and thymus, and a wide range of other health effects, including a severe, sometimes disfiguring skin condition called *chloracne.*

**dispersal,** see DILUTION AND DISPERSAL.

**Dissection Hotline,** (800-922-FROG [3764]), a project of the Animal Legal Defense Fund (see ANIMAL RIGHTS AND WELFARE INFORMATION AND ACTION GUIDE on page 361).

**DNA (deoxyribonucleic acid),** molecules that make up the genes carrying basic hereditary information for the characteristics of all living organisms. The genes themselves are paired strands of molecules in a twisting, ladderlike form called a *double helix*; the chemical codes they embody are passed on as instructions to RNA (*ribonucleic acid*), which reproduces itself by duplicating the paired strands. It is these chemical codes that can be damaged by some TOXIC CHEMICALS, such as certain PESTICIDES, and that are "cut and pasted" in GENETIC ENGINEERING, the result being called recombinant DNA (rDNA).

**dodo,** an extinct bird that became a symbol of stupidity and inability to change, in the phrase "dead as a dodo," but that in the late 20th century has become instead a symbol of the stupidity and savagery of the humans who destroyed it. The dodo lived only on the Indian Ocean island of Mauritius, east of MADAGASCAR. The island was well known to Indian Ocean sailors and traders, but was not known to Europeans until the Portuguese came in 1510. There they found a gray-white bird with a black-and-red bill; it was a little larger than a turkey, could not fly, and had no natural enemies and no means of self defense. The island was settled by the Dutch in 1598; they soon began the long killing that destroyed the last of the species within a century. By 1700, the dodos were gone. (See EXTINCTION; ENDANGERED SPECIES.)

**dolphins,** various marine mammals, like WHALES part of the Cetacean order; there are 37 different dolphin SPECIES, including several that are named as whales, such as the *killer whale* and *pilot whale*. Intelligent and gregarious, several kinds of dolphins have made the entire species enormously popular; to tens of millions of television viewers, dolphins are "Flipper," star of the early TV series. Many dolphins in captivity are the stars of aquarium shows and swim-with-dolphin programs, are objects of communications research, and have even been used as underwater guards by the U.S. Navy. The multiple uses of captive dolphins have also alerted environmentalists, animal defenders, and dolphin lovers to potential abuses, and have generated several campaigns and court cases. In the United States, dolphins are protected under the MARINE MAMMAL PROTECTION ACT, administered by the MARINE MAMMAL COMMISSION.

What has generated enormous worldwide attention and a massive save-the-dolphins campaign is the "incidental" kill of millions of Pacific Ocean dolphins in 10-to-30-mile-long, 40-foot-deep purse-seine DRIFTNETS, the same kinds of nets that have since the 1950s also casually killed millions of seabirds, sea TURTLES, and fish that were not their targets. In the eastern tropical Pacific, from the late 1960s through the late 1980s, at least 3 million and possibly as many as 6 million dolphins were "incidentally" killed in the driftnets of tuna boats, taking advantage of the tendency of schools of dolphins to swim just above schools of sought-after yellow finned tuna. The nets were inten-

tionally dropped above the dolphins to get at the tuna; in the process, dolphins and many other species were killed.

The United States antidriftnet campaign of the 1970s resulted mostly in the transfer of U.S. ships to foreign registry and the entry of more of the tuna boats of other nations into the southeastern Pacific. But the campaign continued, with tuna boycotts playing an important role; in April 1990, the major U.S. tuna canners renounced the use of tuna caught by nets set on dolphins, and then the incidental dolphin and other species kills declined very sharply. But the problem was not solved entirely, as the boats of other countries continued to set driftnets on dolphins in the South Pacific, and to sell their catch to some canners abroad. The use of driftnets by the fishing vessels of all countries continued to be widespread throughout the world, although multinational monitoring and restrictions on their use began to come into effect in 1988, with a series of agreements involving the United States, Canada, Japan, South Korea, Taiwan, and other Pacific Rim nations. The United Nations in 1990 called for a worldwide moratorium on driftnet use, to begin in 1992. Bills proposed before the U.S. House of Representatives would require that tuna products be labeled to indicate whether methods used to catch the tuna also killed dolphins, so consumers could identify "dolphin-safe" tuna.

Of all the dolphin species, the *river dolphins* are currently most seriously threatened, as their HABITAT is destroyed by DEVELOPMENT, toxic wastes poison their environments, and OIL spills occur. The *Chinese river dolphin (Yangtze or whitefin)* is listed as endangered by the FISH AND WILDLIFE SERVICE, while the *La Plata, Amazon, Ganges*, and *Indus River dolphins* are also very seriously threatened.

Some of the coast-dwelling dolphin species are also threatened for the same reasons; for example, great concern developed in the 1980s and early 1990s over the mass strandings of pilot whales on both North American seacoasts, and the mass kill of seacoast dolphins in several locations, possibly due to toxic waste exposure. In one recent instance, on the northern Mediterranean COAST, hundreds of dolphins were killed by a marine virus in the summer of 1990; when analyzed, they proved to be carrying extremely high levels of PCBs and other pollutants, probably reducing their resistance to the virus. (See DOLPHIN AND PORPOISE INFORMATION AND ACTION GUIDE on page 91.)

**dosage level,** the amount of a substance that a person can be exposed to daily, with various effects, according to given studies; also the amount of a substance required to gain a desired effect, such as killing fleas. Questions of dosage levels are often raised in testing of PESTICIDES

## Dolphin and Porpoise Information and Action Guide:

**For more information and action on dolphins and porpoises:**
AMERICAN CETACEAN SOCIETY (ACS), (213-548-6279). Publishes *Dolphin Fact Pack,* the audiocassette *Sound Communication by the Bottlenose Dolphin,* and books such as *Falling for a Dolphin, The Bottlenose Dolphin in the Wild,* and *World of the Bottlenose Dolphin.*
CETACEAN SOCIETY INTERNATIONAL (CSI), (203-563-6444). Publishes *Introduction to Whales and Other Cetaceans.*
COUSTEAU SOCIETY, (804-627-1144). Publishes the periodical *Dolphin Log* (for ages 7–15).
EARTH ISLAND INSTITUTE, (415-788-3666). Sponsors the *Dolphin Project* and the *International Marine Mammal Project,* including fundraising phone line 1-900-USA-DOLPHIN ($5 for first minute; 50¢ for each additional minute) with information on dolphin-related issues.
ELSA WILD ANIMAL APPEAL (EWAA), (818-761-8387). Publishes *Marine Mammals of the World.*
ENVIRONMENTAL INVESTIGATION AGENCY (EIA), (202-483-6621). Publishes various materials, including *The Global War Against Small Cetaceans, A Second Report* (1991).
GREENPEACE, (202-462-1177). Runs the *Ocean Ecology Campaign;* publishes *Greenpeace Book of Dolphins* (John May) and Action Factsheet Tuna/Dolphins.
**Humane Society of the United States (HSUS)**, (202-452-1100). Publishes *Dolphin Death: Thousands Drown in Tuna Net.* (See ANIMAL RIGHTS AND WELFARE INFORMATION AND ACTION GUIDE, on page 361.)
**International Society for Animal Rights (ISAR)**, (717-586-2200). Publishes fact sheets on dolphins. (See ANIMAL RIGHTS AND WELFARE INFORMATION AND ACTION GUIDE on page 361.)

**International Wildlife Coalition (IWC)**, (508-564-9980).
IUCN—THE WORLD CONSERVATION UNION, (202-797-5454). Publishes *Dolphins, Porpoises and Whales of the World: The IUCN Red Data Book* (Margaret Klinowska, 1990), *Biology and Conservation of the River Dolphins* (W.F. Perrins et al., eds., 1989), and *Dolphins, Porpoises, and Whales: An Action Plan for the Conservation of Biological Diversity: 1988–1992* (W.F. Perrin, comp., 1988).
OCEAN ALLIANCE, (415-441-5970).
PACIFIC WHALE FOUNDATION (PWF), (808-879-8860; for orders 800-WHALE-1-[942-5311]). Offers experiential learning programs aboard its two ocean-going vessels *Whale One* and *Whale II.* Publishes *Discovering Marine Mammals.*
SEA WORLD RESEARCH INSTITUTE (SWRI), (619-226-3870).
SIERRA CLUB, (415-776-2211 or 202-547-1141; legislative hotline, 202-547-5550). Publishes *Sierra Club Handbook of Whales and Dolphins.*

**Other references:**

*In Search of Whales and Dolphins.* Hiroya Minakuchi. Holt, 1991. *Camelot World: The Secrets of the Dolphins.* Diana Reiss. Avon, 1991. *Illustrated Encyclopedia of Whales and Dolphins.* Tony Martin. Crown, 1990. *Save the Dolphins.* Michael Donoghue and Annie Wheeler. Sheridan, 1990. *Dolphins and Porpoises,* Richard Ellis. Knopf, 1989. *Encounters with Whales and Dolphins.* Wade Doak. Sheridan, 1989. *The Dolphin Reader,* 2nd ed. Houghton Mifflin, 1989.
(See also ENDANGERED SPECIES; MARINE MAMMAL COMMISSION; MARINE MAMMAL PROTECTION ACT; also ENDANGERED AND THREATENED WILDLIFE AND PLANTS on page 372.)

---

and other chemicals for toxicity, and in estimating acceptable amounts of RADIATION exposure. In general, the relative strength of a chemical is called its *potency.* Much testing is done on animals other than humans (see ANIMAL TESTING), and the dosages are then adjusted to produce a similar effect in humans, the resulting amount being called the *human equivalent dose.*

In analyzing the toxicity of a substance—that is, its capacity to damage a living organism or to cause any adverse effects—the dose required to bring about the desired effect is called the *effective dose;* for 50 percent of the test subjects, that is often abbreviated $ED_{50}$. Those dosage levels that first trigger any effects are termed *lowest effect level* (LEL), *lowest observed effect level* (LOEL), or *lowest observed adverse effect level* (LOAEL). The lowest dose to produce measurable effects is called the THRESHOLD, while any dose that triggers signs of toxicity is called a *toxic*

*dose.* The concentration or amount required to kill 50 percent of the tested organisms is described either as *lethal concentration* ($LC_{50}$) or *lethal dose* ($LD_{50}$, see $LD_{50}$ TEST), while the smallest dose to kill a single test animal is called the *minimum lethal dose* (MLD).

On the other hand, the maximum dose to produce no observable effect on test animals' life or health is called the *maximum tolerated dose* (MTD). Below the MTD, the dose is considered to be at the *no effect level* (NEL), the *no observed effect level* (NOEL), or the *no observed adverse effect level* (NOAEL), although effects may occur undetected, or might occur under somewhat different conditions. If a substance seems to trigger no adverse responses, it is described as having *suggested no adverse response level* (SNARL). The dose may then be described as a *virtually safe dose* (VSD).

Information on dosage levels is provided by manufacturers to government agencies such as the ENVIRONMENTAL PROTECTION AGENCY (EPA) or FOOD AND DRUG ADMINISTRATION (FDA), which use the data to develop TOLERANCE LEVELS for use of the chemical product.

**Dr. Strangelove, or: How I Learned to Stop Worrying and Love the Bomb,** a 1964 fiction film, directed by Stanley Kubrick and starring Peter Sellers in three roles, including Strangelove, in a cast that included George C. Scott, Sterling Hayden, Slim Pickens, Keenan Wynn, Peter Bull, and James Earl Jones. A classic antinuclear war film satire, it is a very funny, very frightening black comedy, ending—as so many then were afraid it would all end—with the destruction of humanity in a nuclear war that nobody wanted. (See NUCLEAR WEAPONS.)

**Draize eye-irritancy test,** a procedure involving placing a test substance in the eye of an animal, often an albino rabbit; the changes then induced in the eye are compared with the condition of the other untouched eye (the *control*) and scored on an established system. Developed in 1944, the Draize test is widely used to assess the possible eye irritation triggered by pharmaceutical substances for use on eyes, cosmetics and toiletries (such as make-up, shampoo, or soap), consumer products (such as household detergents and chemicals), and industrial chemicals, including TOXIC CHEMICALS to which workers may be exposed.

Proponents of the Draize test point out that the test enables chemicals to be tested on a whole organ and in a whole animal; allows for observation of the recovery and healing process; produces a readily interpretable score; gives a conservative assessment of possible human eye irritation; and is also required by several federal laws. Critics argue that results of the Draize test are not reproducible between laboratories, because of subjective scoring and lack of fine discrimination of different responses; that it is not applicable, human and rabbit eyes being physiologically so different; and most basic of all, that the test is ethically unacceptable. Although some researchers have attempted to modify the Draize test to reduce the pain inflicted or the number of animals used, others seek alternatives, as in the area of testing cells in culture (*in vitro*, literally "in glass"). (See ANIMAL TESTING; also ANIMAL RIGHTS AND WELFARE INFORMATION AND ACTION GUIDE on page 361.)

**driftnets,** enormous open-sea fishing nets, of the purse-seine type, which are usually 10–30 miles long and extend as much as 40 feet below the surface of the sea. Made of very thin monofilament netting, they have aptly been described as "curtains of death." Driftnets began to be used by U.S. boats of the eastern tropical Pacific FISHING fleet in the 1950s and came into general use in the 1970s;

they have taken an enormous toll, endangering many of the open-sea (*pelagic*) species that are their targets. They have also killed millions of marine mammals, seabirds, sea TURTLES, and fish that were not their targets, in huge "incidental" kills, often further damaging already threatened species. Several PORPOISE and DOLPHIN species, fur seals (see SEALS AND SEA LIONS), several great WHALE species, and salmon have been among the open sea incidental kill victims of driftnets; abandoned driftnets, sometimes called "ghostnets," floating closer to COASTS have claimed such greatly endangered species as MANATEES and sea turtles.

The most notable of the incidental kills was that of dolphins in the eastern tropical Pacific from the late 1960s through the late 1980s. It stemmed from the propensity of dolphins in that part of the Pacific to swim in large schools over schools of yellow-finned tuna; vessels out after tuna would locate the tuna by spotting the dolphins, and would then sweep up tuna, dolphins, and many other species in their driftnets, "incidentally" catching and killing the dolphins and other species along with the tuna. At least 400,000 dolphins were killed in that way in 1972, the year of passage of the MARINE MAMMAL PROTECTION ACT. At least 3 million dolphins have been killed in driftnets, and some estimates of the total incidental dolphin kill to date run as high as 6 million.

A worldwide campaign against the use of driftnets developed during the 1970s, and by the late 1970s U.S. laws and regulations made it far more difficult for American-registered tuna boats to continue their past driftnet practices. Some left the southern Pacific tuna fisheries, but others merely transferred to foreign registries; meanwhile, the tuna boats of other countries stepped up their fishing in the area, and with it their incidental kills. In April 1990, however, the major U.S. tuna canners announced that they would no longer use tuna caught by nets set on dolphins, and the incidental kill of dolphins and other species declined sharply.

But the boats of other countries continued to set driftnets on dolphins in the South Pacific, and to sell their catch to some canners in other countries. They also continued to use driftnets all over the world; the northern Pacific is the world's largest driftnet fishery, with Japanese, South Korean, and Taiwanese boats all using huge driftnets. Beginning in 1988, a series of international negotiations and agreements began to limit driftnet use, with monitoring and enforcement agreements involving the United States, Canada, Japan, South Korea, Taiwan, and other Pacific Rim nations providing for monitoring and driftnet use limitation. However, enforcement, at least in the early years, has been far less than ineffective. For example, a large trade immediately began in salmon illegally caught in driftnets by a substantial fleet of Taiwan-based fishing boats, with driftnet-caught salmon spawned on the U.S. Pacific Coast caught in the Pacific, shipped to Chile as a "laundering" device to disguise their origin, and then illegally reshipped to U.S. fish brokers. In 1990, the United Nations called for a moratorium on driftnet use, to begin in 1992.

## For more information and action:

- **American Oceans Campaign (AOC),** (213-576-6162).
- **Center for Marine Conservation (CMC),** (202-429-5609). Has *Marine Debris and Entanglement Program*, including a slide show.
- **Environmental Investigation Agency (EIA),** (202-483-6621). Publishes *The Global War Against Small Cetaceans, A Second Report* (1991).
- **Greenpeace,** (202-462-1177). Greenpeace Action runs the *Ocean Ecology Campaign*.
- **National Coalition for Marine Conservation (NCMC),** (912-234-8062).
- **Ocean Alliance,** (415-441-5970).

(See also DOLPHINS, MARINE MAMMAL PROTECTION ACT; also ANIMAL RIGHTS AND WELFARE INFORMATION AND ACTION GUIDE on page 361.)

**Dubos, René Jules** (1901–82), one of the world's leading microbiologists, who for over five decades successfully pursued the idea that microbes—and other lifeforms—are best studied under natural conditions. His approach is now described as "holistic"; this view of the natural world and its lifeforms became a central tenet of 20th-century ecology, and Dubos became one of the leading ecologists of his time. Long associated with Rockefeller University (1927–43; 1945–71), Dubos was one of the first to seek and find naturally occurring antibiotics in the soil. He discovered tyrothricin in 1939; it became the first commercially produced antibiotic. He was also a leading tuberculosis researcher from the mid-1940s, with his second wife, microbiologist Jean Porter Dubos. His first wife had died of tuberculosis in 1942. Jean and Réne Dubos wrote *White Plague: Tuberculosis, Man, and Society,* published in 1952. But it was as an ecologist and prolific writer on ecological matters that he became a world figure, especially for his work on the relationship between disease and such environmental changes as chemical POLLUTION and RADIATION. His best-known ecological works include *Man Adapting* (1965); his Pulitzer Prize-winning *So Human An Animal* (1968); *Reason Awake: Science For Man* (1970); and *Only One Earth: The Care and Management of a Small Planet* (1972; with Barbara Ward), written for the 1972 United Nations Conference on the Environment.

**Ducks Unlimited (DU)** (One Waterfowl Way, Long Grove, IL 60047; 708–438–4300; Matthew B. Connolly, Jr., Executive Vice President), a private, international membership organization, founded by conservation-minded sportsmen and sportswomen in 1937, for people concerned with preservation and protection of North America's waterfowl. DU focuses on restoring and maintaining vital WETLANDS, especially critical Canadian breeding grounds and, through *Ducks Unlimited de Mexico (DUMAC)*, founded in 1974, also wintering grounds south of the U.S.–Mexico border, as well as key HABITATS in the United States, especially along MIGRATION flyways. It has conducted nearly 6,000 habitat projects covering over 5 million acres, using NASA's Landsat satellites for wetlands evaluation, in the process benefiting not simply ducks and geese, but other wildlife as well, including numerous endangered plants and animals, such as the whooping CRANE, bald EAGLE, and peregrine FALCON. DU sponsors the *North American Waterfowl Management Plan*; runs the *MARSH (Matching Aid to Restore States Habitat)* program to aid state fish and wildlife departments in acquiring, restoring, and enhancing crucial wetlands in the U.S.; offers advice on practical projects, such as building nesting boxes; and operates a special *Greenwing* program for young people under age 17. It also publishes the bimonthly magazine *Ducks Unlimited* and various brochures.

**dugongs,** see MANATEES.

**Dust Bowl,** the portions of Oklahoma, west Texas, Arkansas, and several other states that suffered DESERTIFICATION during the Great Depression of the 1930s, for some of the same reasons that farmers in other parts of world are losing their land to the desert today. The land had been successfully farmed before the Depression, mostly for grain. But the early 1930s brought terribly hard times for American farmers, with multiple mortgage foreclosures and, for those that remained, often not enough money to buy seed. On top of economic problems, the early and mid-1930s brought a series of drought years. Without seed or water, much of the topsoil of several states just blew away, in the series of great dust storms that were so notably portrayed in John Ford's film of John Steinbeck's *The Grapes of Wrath*, and the displaced farm families of the region became the wandering "Okies" of the Great Depression. The land came back in the early 1940s, with war-induced prosperity, mass reseeding, and rain. Most of the people did not, staying on after their great migration to California and the American industrial heartland cities. (See EROSION.)

# E

**eagle, bald,** the U.S. national bird, a large bird of prey that ranges throughout the lower 48 United States, western Canada, and Alaska, and as far south as northern Mexico. Although suffering some population decline as HABITAT was taken by growing human populations and hunting took its toll, bald eagles became seriously threatened in the lower 48 states only in the 1950s, when DDT and other PESTICIDES built up in the FOOD CHAIN, causing calcium deficiencies that thinned the eggshells of bald eagles and many other species, all but destroying their ability to reproduce. The Alaskan and Canadian bald eagle populations were not as severely damaged. After the ENVIRONMENTAL PROTECTION AGENCY's 1972 ban on DDT, the amount of DDT in the food chain began to diminish, and the ability to reproduce slowly began to return, although many other toxic hazards continued to threaten the eagles. A strong federal effort supplemented by private efforts has helped the eagles to recover; it includes successful relocation of young eagle chicks to former nesting grounds in many states. Several other eagle species are also listed as endangered, including the *Greenland white-tailed, harpy, Philippine*, and *Spanish imperial eagles*.

### For more information and action:

- **DUCKS UNLIMITED (DU),** (708-438-4300).
- **ELSA WILD ANIMAL APPEAL (EWAA),** (818-761-8387).
- **NATIONAL WILDLIFE FEDERATION (NWF),** (202-797-6800 or 800-245-5484).
- **WILDLIFE INFORMATION CENTER,** (215-434-1637). Publishes *Bald Eagle*.

(See also ENDANGERED SPECIES; also ENDANGERED AND THREATENED WILDLIFE AND PLANTS on page 372.)

**Earth Day,** an annual grassroots celebration of the Earth, held in late April, that calls upon humans to "nurture nature." The first Earth Day, in 1970, was a relatively modest affair, but is credited with sparking the growth of the modern environmental movement. By its 20th anniversary, Earth Day organizers estimated that 200 million people in 140 nations took part in the day's events, which involved rallies, environmentally oriented fairs, RECYCLING and energy-saving exhibits, workshops on ENDANGERED SPECIES and wildlife, and activities such as tree-planting, litter-cleaning, and protests of POLLUTION. Major environmental organizations, such as SIERRA CLUB, NATURAL RESOURCES DEFENSE COUNCIL, and GREENPEACE, joined with other international groups to orchestrate the activities. Certainly Earth Day has played a key role in raising the "environmental consciousness" of the world's humans. It remains to be seen whether Earth Day will continue to be an environmental focus, and to what extent these changed attitudes will in the long term translate into direct political action (see GREEN POLITICS).

**Earth First! (E.F.!)** (P.O. Box 5176, Missoula, MT 59806), a radical environmental group, founded in 1980 by Dave FOREMAN, Mike Roselle, and several others, which stresses that it has no paid professional staff, organizational structure, or formal leadership, and prefers to be called a movement. EF! members are diverse and individualistic, and wedded to no "particular religious or political philosophy," but in general agree:

- on the desirability of direct action against property and machinery—an environmental sabotage technique called MONKEYWRENCHING—though EF! states that it does "not engage in monkeywrenching as a group or necessarily advocate it";
- on the intrinsic value of "Earth above all else," "wilderness for its own sake," BIOCENTRIC views, and DEEP ECOLOGY, as opposed to "Industrial Civilization" and some human-centered environmental groups, which EF! members see as "anti-Earth, anti-woman, and anti-liberty"; and
- on the futility of working within "the system," seeing governments and organizations (including many environmental groups) as inherently flawed and those who maintain them as inevitably corrupted.

Earth First! supports preservation of all remaining WILDERNESS and recreation of previous areas of wilderness in key areas, by closing roads, removing DEVELOPMENT, and reintroducing wildlife; opposes construction of new DAMS and supports destruction of many others, such as GLEN CANYON; uses "confrontation, guerrilla theater, direct action, and civil disobedience to fight for wild places and life processes." The movement's slogan is "No Compromise in the Defense of Mother Earth!" and its symbol a clenched green fist.

Within the Earth First! movement are various "autonomous but cooperating" local groups, listed in each issue of the *Earth First! Journal*: the *Earth First! Foundation* (P.O. Box 1683, Corvallis, OR 97339), supporting research and the education projects; the *Earth First! Direct Action Fund* (DAF, P.O. Box 210, Canyon, CA 94516; 415-376-7329; Mike Roselle, Coordinator), supporting and coordinating "nonviolent campaigns to protect endangered wildlife habitat," sometimes working with other groups, such as GREENPEACE and the SEA SHEPHERD CONSERVATION SOCIETY; and various task forces on national or international issues. These include the *Rainforest Action Group*, which works closely with the *Rainforest Action Network* (see FORESTS INFORMATION AND ACTION GUIDE on page 369), as in opposition to DEVELOPMENT funded by the WORLD BANK; *Grizzly Bear Task Force*, seeking preservation and reintroduction in the West, as in YELLOWSTONE, and publishes the *EF! Grizzly Bear Tabloid*; *Biodiversity Project*, attempting to use the ENDANGERED SPECIES ACT to protect not only large mammals ("charismatic megafauna") but the whole range of species, including unattractive or unknown plants ("enigmatic microflora"); *Overgrazing Task Force*, which publishes the tabloid *Save Our Public Lands!*; *Preserving Appalachian Wilderness (PAW)*, which supports establishment of wilderness and wilderness recovery areas, including reintroduction of species, in the eastern United States; *Wolf Action Network*, opposing extermination in northern North America and supporting reintroduction in the United States; and *ORV Task Force*, opposing the use of off-road vehicles in wild lands.

Tying together EF!'s activities is an eight-times-a-year tabloid *Earth First! The Radical Environmental Journal*; subscription informally constitutes EF! membership, with the group noting that the "subscription list is kept entirely confidential (our list is not sold or loaned to anyone) and aliases are welcomed." EF! also holds an annual "tribal gathering" called the *Round River Rendezvous (RRR)*, including various workshops, in addition to state and regional gatherings; organizes road shows (involving musicians, poets, and speakers) to universities or local communities (Bob Kaspar, Contact, 305 North 6th Street, Madison, WI 53704; 608-241-9426); and supplies audiovisual materials.

EF's approach is inspired, at least partly, by Edward ABBEY's 1975 *The Monkey Wrench Gang*, in which some environmentalists plot to blow up the GLEN CANYON DAM. In fact, the group's first public action in 1981 was to unfurl a long black plastic streamer—which from a distance looked like a crack—down the front of the dam. EF! members often compare themselves with World War II Resistance fighters, regarding environmental damage as equivalent to the Holocaust, and comparing clear-cutting an old-growth FOREST to bombing a city. Numerous members have been arrested for various types of protest actions.

**For more information:**
*Green Rage: Radical Environmentalism and the Unmaking of Civilization*. Christopher Manes. Little, Brown, 1991. (See also MONKEYWRENCHING; Dave FOREMAN.)

**Earth Island Institute** (300 Broadway, Suite 28, San Francisco, CA 94133; 415-788-3666; David R. Brower, Chairman), a membership organization founded in 1982 to encourage and spread ideas on "cutting edge conservation issues," especially giving the Earth "CPR"—Conserve, Preserve, and Restore—and encouraging "international environment networking." The Institute operates *Earth Island Centers* around the United States and some abroad; an affiliated nonprofit (but not tax-deductible) group seeks to influence legislation and public policy. The Institute also maintains the *Brower Fund* to provide short-term aid to innovative environmental programs, and sponsors many projects, including *Conferences on the Fate and Hope of the Earth, Environmental Project on Central America (EPOCA), International Marine Mammal Project, Interna-

*tional Rivers Network, Friends of the Ancient Forest, GAIA—Green Alternative Information for Action, Sea Turtle Restoration Project, Urban Habitat Program, US/ USSR Environmental Exchange, Ben Linder Memorial Fund for Appropriate Technology, Climate Protection Institute, Dolphin Project, Environmental Litigation Fund, Green Education and Development Fund, Information for the Public Trust, Japan Environmental Exchange*, and *Rainforest Health Alliance*. (The previously affiliated *Rainforest Action Network* is now independent; see FORESTS INFORMATION AND ACTION GUIDE on page 369.). The Institute also produces audiovisual materials, including films on environmental issues in the American West, environmentally oriented videos, slide presentations, environmental radio programs, and various print materials.

**Earth Summit,** popular name for the UNITED NATIONS CONFERENCE ON ENVIRONMENT AND DEVELOPMENT.

**Earthwatch,** a three-pronged program of the UNITED NATIONS ENVIRONMENT PROGRAMME (UNEP), designed to monitor and measure environmental problems in a uniform way, the aim being to produce global information that can be used for assessment and decision-making. The three parts of the Earthwatch program are the GLOBAL ENVIRONMENT MONITORING SYSTEM (GEMS); the global information system INFOTERRA; and the INTERNATIONAL REGISTER OF POTENTIALLY TOXIC CHEMICALS (IRPTC). *Earthwatch* is also the name of a group organizing volunteer work in scientific research (see ECOTOURISM INFORMATION AND ACTION GUIDE on page 366).

**East African Wild Life Society (EAWLS)** (Caltex House, 1st Floor, Koinange Street, P.O. Box 20110, Nairobi, Kenya; 27047/337422; Mwamba H.A. Shete, Assistant Director; David Blanton, North American representative, 607-257-3091 [see *Voyagers International* in the ECOTOURISM INFORMATION AND ACTION GUIDE on page 366]), a membership organization originally founded in 1956 as two separate organizations, the Kenya Wild Life Society and the Wild Life Society of Kenya, which merged in 1961, joined then by Ugandan conservationists, concerned about the "uncontrolled hunting and poaching of various animal species." Though originally focusing on larger game species, the Society now seeks "to safeguard wildlife and its habitat in all its forms, as a national and international resource," often working in cooperation with other conservation organizations. Its main activities are in the areas of conversation education, support for antipoaching units (as by providing vehicles and communication equipment), research, animal rescue (moving threatened animals to safer locations), and specific projects, such as

current appeals for protection measures for the black RHINOCEROS and the African ELEPHANT. The EAWLS publishes a bimonthly magazine *Swara* (Swahili for "antelope") and the *African Journal of Ecology*.

**ecofeminism,** a view linking the exploitation of the earth with the subordination of women. Among the assumptions generally made in ecofeminist theory are that masculine consciousness and a patriarchal view of society have been largely responsible for the devaluation of the natural world; that the dominance of culture over nature and technology over life is intertwined with that of men over women, and that myths and legends of Mother Earth and early goddesses speak of a more nature-oriented matriarchal culture. The corollary drawn is that a feminine consciousness and a more egalitarian—or perhaps female-dominated—society are basic to a revaluation of and reunification with nature in all its biological and cultural diversity. For many ecofeminists, this offers the only hope of saving the planet from disaster. *Ecofeminism* is also sometimes used as a general term encompassing the range of efforts made by women to save the earth.

**For more information:**

• SIERRA CLUB, (415-776-2211 or 202-547-1141; legislative hotline, 202-547-5550). Publishes *Women and Wilderness*.

**Other references:**
*Reweaving the World: The Emergence of Ecofeminism.* Irene Diamond and Gloria Feman Orenstein, eds. Sierra Club Books, 1990. *Healing the Wounds: The Promise of Ecofeminism.* Judith Plant, ed. New Society, 1989.

**ecological equivalent,** two organisms that occupy the same NICHES at different sites.

**ecological illness,** an alternative term for ENVIRONMENTAL ILLNESS.

**Ecological Society of America (ESA)** (Public Affairs Office, 9650 Rockville Pike, Suite 2503, Bethesda, MD 20814; 301-530-7005; Marjorie M. Holland, Director), an international professional membership organization, founded in 1915, "to encourage the scientific study of the interrelations of organisms and their environments." Through its Public Affairs Office, the ESA seeks "to provide an ecological perspective on public policy issues," the aim being "to promote policies that protect the environment, promote the welfare of ecology and ecologists, and make available the expertise of professional scientists to society on matters of ecological concern." The Public Affairs Office maintains the *Ecological Information Net-*

*work*, a computerized data bank on members who can provide expert scientific information to education, industry, government, and conservation organizations on issues affecting domestic and international environmental quality, designed "to provide rapid answers to questions about effects of human activities on animals, plants, and microorganisms in both natural and managed ecosystems," such as about BIOTECHNOLOGY, PESTICIDES, OIL spills, or RADIATION. The ESA also organizes various workshops, symposia, and conferences, on topics such as BIOLOGICAL DIVERSITY, land management, and national parks; and publishes various materials, including the bimonthly *Ecology*, the quarterlies *Ecological Monographs* and *Bulletin of the Ecological Society of America*, and reports such as *The Sustainable Biosphere Initiative, An Ecological Research Agenda* (1991).

**ecological succession,** the orderly sequence by which an ECOSYSTEM progresses from bare ground (as after a fire or the abandonment of farm land) by stages to its mature form. First come the pioneer SPECIES, such as weeds and wildflowers, rapidly colonizing the new area; these gradually give way to shrubs, then trees, which are slowly replaced by different trees that form the basis of the last stage, *climax community*. Changes in plant life are the key to ecological succession; wildlife returns only as the vegetation changes, with different types of animals and microorganisms being characteristic at various stages, called *seral stages*.

In general, early stages of ecological succession show rapid growth, high production, and small size of organisms, often with considerable instability. By contrast, the climax community generally is characterized by larger organisms, stability, and protection of production, often through stressing quality over quantity. Once reached, the climax community is considered to be stable, self-perpetuating, and in equilibrium with its environment, barring major changes in the conditions of the region. Sometimes an ecosystem is kept from its normal ecological succession, as by successive fires or OVERGRAZING; but the community that would presumably become established in the absence of outside interference—based upon study and experience in similar settings—is called the *potential natural community* (PNC).

The classical assumption of equilibrium in ecological succession—and the corollary inferences about the climax community—have been criticized in various scientific quarters, but the actual progression of stages is clearly observable and is much used by ecologists and resource managers in the field. Managers of public lands must weigh the needs of the ecosystem against human needs and desires; to the extent that multiple use is allowed, the mature community may be weakened (see LAND USE).

**ecology,** in general, the study of the relationships between living things and their environment; also called *environmental biology*. Originally referring to primarily descriptive natural history, the name was gradually applied to the scientific study of organisms in their natural environment. With the rise of environmentalism in the 1960s, the terms *ecology* and *ecological* came into wider use, not in a strict scientific context, but as stressing the interrelationships among the inhabitants of the earth and the necessity of understanding and appreciating the functioning of ECOSYSTEMS and of the BIOSPHERE as a whole. In the process, some of the classical concepts of ecology, such as HABITAT, ecosystem, and ECOLOGICAL SUCCESSION, came into popular use. As the ecological movement grew out of the older, more traditional conservation and preservation movements, two general "wings" in the environmental spectrum came to be called DEEP ECOLOGY and SOCIAL ECOLOGY.

Within the scientific world, several sub-specialties developed. Study of individual members of a species or individual species in their environments is termed *autoecology*, while *synecology* focuses on organisms as they operate in communities in their environment. Study of human communities in their habitats is termed *human ecology*, which overlaps with other life, health, and social sciences. Mathematically based explorations of the relationships in the environments, such as quantitative analysis of energy flow in an ecosystem, comes under the heading of *systems ecology*. Focus on the structure and function of interacting organisms (as opposed to simple description of individual species) is called *functional ecology*, while study of population growth, birth–death ratios, and predator–prey relationships is *population ecology*. Specialties may also be distinguished by the kind of environment or habitat studied, in general *marine ecology, freshwater ecology*, and *terrestrial ecology*, but also even more specialized concerns, such as *estuarine ecology* or *grassland ecology*. The study of the growth of organisms and their BIOGEOCHEMICAL CYCLES, especially how certain plants or animals are able to survive in a specific environment, is called *physiological ecology*. *Applied ecology* is the use of ecological principles in managing natural resources, as in agriculture, range management, wildlife management, fisheries management, water-resources management, and management of POLLUTION. A newer specialty, RESTORATION ECOLOGY, focuses on repairing damage already done.

## On Ecology

I think that ecology is first of all a spiritual movement. . . . Ecology to me is the contemporary religion. It is only on the basis of ecology that spiritual integration of the whole global community is possible.

Sergei Tsvetko, Soviet geologist

Source: *The Journal of Sustainable Agriculture*, Spring 1990.

**ecosystem,** a stable interacting gathering of living organisms in their nonliving environment, which is unified by a circular flow of energy and nutrients. *Ecosystem* is a broad term with no size limitation, which may refer to something as small as the life in and around a fallen log to a huge LAKE or FOREST, even to the whole BIOSPHERE, depending on the focus of the observer. Each ecosystem is bound together by the BIOGEOCHEMICAL CYCLES through which living organisms use energy from the sun to obtain or ''fix'' nonliving (*inorganic*) elements such as carbon, oxygen, and hydrogen from the environment, and transform them into vital food, which is then used and recycled. An ecosystem's living organisms are characterized by where they stand in that circulatory process—that is, by how they get the elements and energy they need for life:

- *primary producers* are organisms, mostly green plants, that draw on the sun's energy to make the fuel for others to use;
- *consumers* are beings who eat the food produced by plants, starting with plant-eating organisms (*herbivores*) and extending into a chain of larger, animal-eating organisms (*carnivores*);
- *decomposers* are microorganisms that break down the remains of dead plants and animals for eventual recycling (see FOOD CHAIN).

Ecosystems are neither permanent nor unchanging. The number of organisms in a mature ecosystem and their rate of growth and ''life-style'' depend on the availability of energy and key elements, some of which may be in short supply and therefore be *limiting factors*, such as nitrogen (see NITROGEN CYCLE). Changes in the amounts of energy and elements available, as well as outside influences such as WATER POLLUTION or DEVELOPMENT, can readily disturb the established cycles. Then the organisms normally make various adjustments to try to maintain the ecosystem's equilibrium, or to find a new one; but if the damage is too great, they may be unable to adjust quickly enough or

at all, and the ecosystem may be permanently changed or even destroyed. It is fear of permanent damage and loss in ecosystems that underlies the concern about such matters as CLIMATE CHANGE and ACID RAIN, and the resulting loss of BIOLOGICAL DIVERSITY. The attempt to help ecosystems survive damage and regain their natural state has given rise to the new specialty of RESTORATION ECOLOGY.

Ecosystems do not spring full-blown, but develop in stages (see ECOLOGICAL SUCCESSION), varying by the altitude, climate, terrain, and mix of plants and animals, so wide variations exist between a FOREST ecosystem and a DESERT ecosystem, between different types of forest ecosystems, and between ecosystems in various regions of the world (see REALMS). Evironmentalists concerned with the destruction of natural areas around the world often classify threatened areas by the type of ecosystem and the realm or life zone in which it occurs, so that they can focus their efforts on saving those types that are most rare and in the greatest danger. In establishing BIOSPHERE RESERVES, members of the Man and the Biosphere program are asked to try to protect examples of each of the major types of ecosystems in their country. (See ECOSYSTEM DIVERSITY on page 99.)

**ecotage,** sabotage for environmental ends, often of machines that alter the landscape (see MONKEYWRENCHING).

**ecoterrorism,** a critic's term for radical environmental actions called MONKEYWRENCHING.

**ecotourism,** a combination of personal vacation and environmental concern; also called several other names, such as *nature tourism, green travel*, or *environmental vacations*. The terms actually refer to a wide range of activities, having in common the fact that individuals are visiting a place because of its environmental characteristics, such as ENDANGERED SPECIES or a rain FOREST. At its widest, ecotourists are those who travel to experience and enjoy natural wonders, touring independently or through a regular travel agency. But many environmentalists prefer to travel through agencies that specialize in nature tours. Among these are some non-profit agencies, or for-profit agencies that funnel some portion of their profits to the host country, either as a direct percentage, as a flat contribution, or through the funding of specific projects. Various environmental organizations also offer specialized tours and outdoor experiences. Some organizations and agencies offer more active kinds of environmental vacations, in which the tourist is a paying volunteer working on an environmentally oriented science project, often under rough conditions.

The key problem with ecotourism is the damage that

## Ecosystem Diversity

Several ways exist to classify the many scales of ecosystem diversity. An example using the Pacific Northwest to illustrate four levels of ecosystems is shown below. Animal species characteristic of each level are noted.

1. **Biome:** temperate coniferous forest
   - Rufous hummingbird
   - Mountain beaver
2. **Zone:** western hemlock
   - Coho salmon
   - Oregon slender salamander
3. **Habitat:** old growth forest
   - Vaux's swift
   - Spotted owl
4. **Microhabitat:** fallen tree
   - Clouded salamander
   - California red-backed vole

The fallen tree component of old growth and mature forests illustrates the contribution of ecosystem diversity to ecological processes. Fallen trees provide a rooting medium for western hemlock and other plants that is moist enough for growth to continue during the summer drought, a reserve of nitrogen and other nutrients, and a source of food and shelter for animals and micro-organisms that play key roles in redistributing and returning the nutrients to the regenerating forest. For example, the rotten wood provides habitat for truffles, and the truffles are eaten by the California red-backed vole, which spreads the truffle spores, so helping the growth of Douglas fir trees, which require mycorrhizal fungi (such as truffles) for uptake of nutrients.

**Source:** *Technologies to Maintain Biological Diversity.* Office of Technology Assessment. Washington, DC: 1987.

---

can be done by travel. Some places have become so popular that the sheer numbers of visitors have had a severely adverse impact on the environment; in 1990, for example, over 50,000 tourists visited the GALAPAGOS ISLANDS, twice the annual limit of 25,000 set in vain by the government in 1982. The damage is especially great where luxury resorts have been developed to cater to affluent nature travelers, destroying the very environments that drew tourists there in the first place; some, like Edward ABBEY, call this *industrial tourism*.

The alternative is variously called *environmentally sensitive travel, alternative travel, low-impact travel*, or *soft-path travel*, the aim being to minimize such damage while encouraging the host countries to preserve natural environments and cultures. Many ecotourism agencies are careful to use local people and resources (rather than relying solely on outsiders brought in for the tour); this not only gives travelers the benefits of local expertise but also infuses additional capital into the area. This is extremely important, because money from tourism is needed to bolster the economy of poor countries, making up for their not tapping WILDLIFE REFUGES for their animal, plant, and mineral resources.

Many environmentalists stress the importance of ecotourists understanding the culture and natural history of the environment, and of taking special care not to alter either the natural environment or the local culture. Members of the *Ecotourism Society* point out: "If conservation and local welfare are not both enhanced by tourist presence, then ecotourism becomes nothing more than a fancy word for selling nature." In many areas, tourism management is being made a key part of plans for wildlife refuges and other preservation efforts. (For a sampling of organizations offering ecotourism, see ECOTOURISM INFORMATION AND ACTION GUIDE on page 366.)

**edge effect,** the influence of transitional zones on the plant communities on either side, such as a hedge or shrubby border between FOREST and pasture; also the attraction of such an area for animals. By offering cover for feeding, escape, and breeding, and a variety of fruits, berries, nuts, seeds, and insects, such zones can be extremely valuable, increasing the diversity and abundance of wildlife species and contributing strongly to the health of both HABITATS and to BIOLOGICAL DIVERSITY in general. The transitional zones themselves are generally called *ecotones*. In farming country, hedges between GRASSLANDS and CROPLANDS have often been removed to promote more efficient plowing; but many people argue that hedgerows perform more important functions, including lessening EROSION, reducing runoff, offering shelter for livestock, and housing natural enemies of farm pests, including birds, and allies of the farmer, including bees that pollinate flowering crops.

The edge effect must be considered when an area is to be cleared, except for a WILDLIFE REFUGE since the edges of the preserve have different characteristics from the central natural areas, and plants and animals that survive in the center may not flourish on the edges. Butterflies accustomed to deep forest, for example, may depart from the edges; as a result the effective size of the refuge may be smaller than anticipated.

**Ehrlich, Paul Ralph** (1932–    ), U.S. biologist and POPULATION researcher, who emerged as a leading ecologist in the 1960s, attracting worldwide attention with his extraordinarily pessimistic predictions of imminent famine and societal breakdown, if current population trends were not controlled. The main body of his predictions did not come true; yet the urgency of the overpopulation problem then developing was brought home so sharply that many of his then-radical ideas and approaches to population control became mainstream tenets in the decades that followed. He became a world figure in 1968, after publication of *The Population Bomb*, coauthored with his wife, biologist **Anne Howland Ehrlich**. Some of their best known works are *The End of Affluence* (1975), *Extinction: The Causes and Consequences of the Disappearance of Species* (1981), and *The Population Explosion* (1991). Paul Ehrlich is president of Stanford University's Center for Conservation Biology (see CONSERVATION BIOLOGY), and founder and president of the organization *Zero Population Growth* (see POPULATION INFORMATION AND ACTION GUIDE on page 248).

**Ekofisk oil well blowout,** leakage of 8 million gallons (approximately 27,000 tons) of crude oil into the North Sea, from the April 22, 1977, blowout of the Bravo 14 well in the Ekofisk oil field, roughly midway between Norway and Great Britain. Although no substantial damage was done to adjacent FISHING grounds, the Norwegian government temporarily suspended operations at the Ekofisk field, responding to widespread popular concern over the potential environmental damage that might result from OFFSHORE DRILLING. (See OIL.)

**electromagnetic radiation,** radiation emitted from power lines and electrical devices, a subject of growing concern and controversy (see RADIATION).

**electrostatic precipitation (ESP),** a device that uses electrical charges to remove pollutants from the air. Polluted air is forced into an electrically charged space between a set of electrodes; dust particles (see PARTICULATE MATTER) become charged and are then attracted to one of the electrodes. The remaining air passes out of the space, to go through other cleaning or recovery processes, or to be released into the environment. The dust remains behind, and is removed for disposal or in some cases, reuse. (See AIR POLLUTION.)

**elephants,** massive HERBIVOROUS mammals that once numbered in the millions in Africa south of the Sahara,

perhaps as high as 10 million. The *Asian elephant*, somewhat less numerous but even more widespread, was found from the Middle East to the Pacific in southern Asia and even in northern China. Both are now greatly ENDANGERED SPECIES.

The *African bush or savannah elephant* is down to less than 400,000 to 600,000 in all, and that number is dropping precipitously every year, as poachers continue to kill elephants for ivory, though in somewhat smaller numbers because of recent international sanctions against the ivory trade. At the same time, the *African forest* or *Cape elephant* has been hunted to near EXTINCTION, though for the moment extinction seems to have been postponed, with a herd of approximately 100 Cape elephants surviving at South Africa's ADDO ELEPHANT NATIONAL PARK. The number of Asian elephants is down to an estimated 40,000 to 50,000 in the wild, the Indian, Ceylon, Sumatran, and Malaysian subspecies surviving in isolated pockets on the Indian subcontinent, southeast Asia, and southern China.

These enormous land animals, weighing up to 11 tons, have been the object of a massive, sustained attack by ivory hunters, which peaked early in the 20th century, but has continued ever since, with poachers in recent years able to hunt with the kinds of powerful and sophisticated weapons used in the civil and international wars that have wrecked so much of Africa in recent decades. At the same time, elephants have suffered from accelerating loss of HABITAT, as sub-Sahara and south Asian human POPULATIONS have increased explosively. From 1979 to 1989 alone, the African elephant population was cut by more than half, from an estimated 1.3 million to a little over 600,000. In 1989, in a very late attempt to save the African elephant, the CONVENTION ON INTERNATIONAL TRADE IN ENDANGERED SPECIES (CITES) voted a worldwide ban on the ivory trade, while the United States and the European Community banned imports of both raw or worked ivory. Bills put before the U.S. House of Representatives also called for revoking "most favored nation" status for countries trading in ivory. Yet several African countries continued to export ivory; countries such as Hong Kong, China, Japan, and Singapore continued to import ivory; and a worldwide illegal trade in ivory soon flourished. Despite increasing worldwide efforts to save the elephants, their future remains very much in doubt. (See ELEPHANT INFORMATION AND ACTION GUIDE on page 101.)

**elm, American,** a tall, graceful, vase-shaped shade tree once common in much of North America, as witnessed by the many Elm streets in American cities and towns. From the 1930s, it was attacked by a fungus, *Ceratocystis ulmi*, more popularly known as Dutch elm disease (DED) or the

## Elephant Information and Action Guide

**For more information and action on elephants:**

AFRICAN WILDLIFE FOUNDATION (AWF), (202-265-8393 or 800-344-TUSK [8875]).

ANIMAL PROTECTION INSTITUTE, (916-731-5521). (See ANIMAL RIGHTS AND WELFARE INFORMATION AND ACTION GUIDE, on page 361.)

EAST AFRICAN WILD LIFE SOCIETY (EAWLS), (Nairobi, Kenya: 27047/337422).

ENVIRONMENTAL INVESTIGATION AGENCY (EIA), (202-483-6621). Publishes *To Save an Elephant* (Allan Thornton and Dave Currey, 1991) and *A System of Extinction, The African Elephant Disaster* (1989).

Humane Society of the United States (HSUS), (202-452-1100). Publishes *Remember the Elephants . . . Forget Ivory.* (See ANIMAL RIGHTS AND WELFARE INFORMATION AND ACTION GUIDE, on page 361.)

INTERNATIONAL WILDLIFE COALITION (IWC), (508-564-9980).

IUCN—THE WORLD CONSERVATION UNION, (202-797-5454). Publishes *The Asian Elephant: An Action Plan for its Conservation* (Charles Santiapillai and Peter Jackson, comps., 1990) and *African Elephants and Rhinos: Status Survey and Conservation Action Plan* (D.H.M. Cummings et al., comps., 1990).

SIERRA CLUB, (415-776-2211; or 202-547-1141). Publishes *Elephants: The Deciding Decade* (Ronald Orenstein, 1991).

TRAFFIC (TRADE RECORDS ANALYSIS OF FLORA AND FAUNA), (202-293-4800). Publishes *Elephant Ivory Trade.*

WILDLIFE CONSERVATION INTERNATIONAL (WCI), (212-220-5100).

WILDLIFE INFORMATION CENTER (215-434-1637). Publishes *African Elephant.*

WORLD WILDLIFE FUND (WWF), (202-293-4800). Publishes the periodical *Pachyderm.*

**Other references:**

*The African Elephant: Twilight in Eden.* National Audubon Society Staff. Wiley, 1991. *The African Elephant: Last Days of Eden.* Boyd Norton. Voyageur, 1991. *Elephants, Economics, and Ivory.* David Pearce, ed. InBook, 1991. *Elephants.* Marcus Schneck. Crown, 1991. *Elephants.* Reinhard Kunkel. Abrams, 1990. *The Asian Elephant: Ecology and Management.* R. Sukamar. Cambridge University Press, 1990. *Elephants of Africa.* Paul Bosman, Safari Press, 1989.
(See also ENDANGERED SPECIES; also ENDANGERED AND THREATENED WILDLIFE AND PLANTS on page 372.)

---

"cancer" of elm trees. Carried by elm bark beetles, the fungus moved into the fluid-conducting vessels of the tree, soon clogging the flow of water and nutrients and killing the tree. Many communities tried unsuccessfully to halt the spread of the disease through "cut-and-burn" campaigns; once-shady tree-lined streets became bare, as elms—some dating back to the 1700s—fell to the fungus. Not until 1975 was an elm fungicide approved by the EPA for use on healthy trees. In the 1980s, a disease-resistant form of the American elm, called the American Liberty elm (*Ulmus americana libertas*), was developed and began to be planted around the country (see below). This is a stronger, larger elm tree than the Asian or European hybrids sometimes planted in recent decades, and has the classic shape of the American elm.

**For more information and action:**

• **Elm Research Institute (ERI)** (Harrisville, NH 03450; 603-827-3048 or 800-FOR ELMS [367-3567]; John P. Hansel, Founder and Executive Director), a membership organization, founded in 1967, dedicated to preserving and restoring the American elm tree, supporting and coordinating independent research on Dutch elm disease. Its efforts helped lead to development of an elm fungi-

cide and to the disease-resistant American Liberty elm. ERI sponsors *Conscientious Injector* project, by which communities inject their healthy elms with fungicide, and the *Johnny Elmseed Community Service Project*, under which tens of thousands of Liberty elm trees are given free to member organizations—communities and organizations such as the Boy Scouts—the objective being the replanting of America with elms. ERI also publishes the quarterly newsletter *News Briefs*.

**Elsa Wild Animal Appeal (EWAA)** (P.O. Box 4572, North Hollywood, CA 91617; 818-761-8387; A. Peter Rasmussen, Jr., General Manager), an international organization originally founded by *Born Free* author Joy ADAMSON and her husband George Adamson. Chartered in the United States in 1969, its main purposes are the "conservation of all wildlife, protection of endangered species and the natural environment, working to secure humane treatment of all animals everywhere, assisting however possible in the establishment of sanctuaries and preserves for wildlife . . . and the support of educational projects to benefit the natural world." The group urges people not to buy wild animals, products made from them, or products made by any firm that abuses animals, and to treat any wild animals encountered with respect and care. The EWAA encourages research; gathers and disseminates informational materials to help educate the public, especially children; seeks to influence policymakers on all levels; and advises government agencies on laws and enforcement, to "ensure that protection of wildlife and habitat is effectively carried out." It publishes various materials, notably its *Wildlife Education Kits* of projects, games, and group activities for elementary school children, including *North American Predators, Marine Mammals of the World, America's Endangered Wildlife*, and *Predators of the World*.

**Emergency Planning and Community Right-to-Know Act (EPCRA),** a U.S. federal law passed in 1986, in the wake of the BHOPAL tragedy and the widespread fears it raised. Its four main provisions involve planning for chemical emergencies; emergency notification of chemical accidents and releases; reporting of hazardous chemical inventories; and reporting of TOXIC CHEMICAL releases.

EPCRA requires states—working with both the ENVIRONMENTAL PROTECTION AGENCY (EPA) and industries—to develop emergency plans and notification procedures for responding to release of HAZARDOUS SUBSTANCES, working through *State (or Tribal) Emergency Response Commissions* (SERCs) and *Local Emergency Planning Committees* (LEPCs) (see REQUIRED ELEMENTS OF A LOCAL EMERGENCY PLAN on page 103). The EPA is charged with providing assistance in preparation of documents and plans, information management techniques, training programs, and enforcement policies, as through its National Response Team's (NRT's) *Hazardous Materials Emergency Planning Guide* and through providing other emergency planning and hazards analysis materials from other agencies, such as the Federal Emergency Management Agency (FEMA) and Department of Transportation (DOT). In its first five years, the EPA estimates, over 50,000 people have been involved in EPCRA citizen committees.

EPCRA requires industries to report on the presence and release of specified hazardous substances (for a list, see TOXIC CHEMICALS AND HAZARDOUS SUBSTANCES on page 407; for an overview of health effects, see KNOWN HEALTH EFFECTS OF TOXIC CHEMICALS on page 416). Specifically they must file a *material safety data sheet* (MSDS) on each hazardous chemical, and also an annual inventory of the amounts of such chemicals made, used, and stored. Facilities can claim that chemical identity information is a trade secret, but must substantiate that claim, which can be challenged by citizen petition; in any case, trade secret information may be disclosed to health professionals for diagnostic, treatment, and prevention

purposes. Violators of the reporting provisions are subject to penalties of up to $10,000 a day for MSDS filings and $25,000 per violation for failure to comply with annual reporting requirements.

In addition, manufacturers of any of over 300 TOXIC CHEMICALS, designated as Extremely Hazardous Substances, must report to the EPA and to state agencies any routine releases of these chemicals, with failure to file subject to civil penalties of up to $25,000 a day for each chemical involved. This information is gathered in a *Toxic Releases Inventory (TRI)*, made available to the public, and used as a basis for further investigation or action. Overall, civil and administrative infractions of EPCRA can run up to $75,000 a day, while criminal penalties of up to $50,000 or five years in prison may be applied to "anyone who knowingly and willfully fails to provide emergency release notification." Section 313 of EPCRA is also known as the Superfund Amendments and Reauthorization Act of 1986, Title III (SARA) (see SUPERFUND), expanding the 1980 COMPREHENSIVE ENVIRONMENTAL RESPONSE, COMPENSATION, AND LIABILITY ACT.

**For more information and action:**

- **Environmental Law Institute (ELI),** (202-328-5150; publications office, 202-939-3844). Publishes *Community Right-to-Know Deskbook* (1988).

(See ENVIRONMENTAL LAW INFORMATION AND ACTION GUIDE on page 116.)

**emission control device,** any device that is placed in a system, especially an exhaust system in industry or an automobile, to reduce the amount of pollutants released into the environment (see EMISSIONS; AIR POLLUTION).

**emissions,** pollutants released into the air, water, or soil of an area, as from an industry, an automobile, or a municipal waste treatment plant; the term may also apply to noise (see NOISE POLLUTION) and electromagnetic or radioactive emissions (see RADIATION). Products of incomplete combustion, emitted pollutants are often full of substances hazardous to human health and to the environment. These include not only emissions from routine sources, as from a car's exhaust or a factory's smoke-stacks, but also *fugitive emissions* that escape during transportation, processing, or storage, as from leaking pipes, contaminants on dirt roads, or piles of supplies such as coal or gravel. Governments have increasingly been monitoring the level of pollutants in the environment and setting levels that should not be exceeded. In the 1990 CLEAN AIR ACT, the United States pioneered in a market-oriented approach to SULFUR DIOXIDE, nitrogen oxides (see NITROGEN DIOXIDE), and other

## Required Elements of a Local Emergency Plan

An emergency plan must:

- use the information provided by industry to *identify the facilities and transportation routes* where hazardous substances are present.
- establish *emergency response procedures, including evacuation plans*, for dealing with accidental chemical releases.
- set up *notification procedures* for those who will respond to an emergency.
- establish methods for *determining the occurrence and severity of a release* and the areas and populations likely to be affected.
- establish ways to *notify the public* of a release.

- identify the *emergency equipment* available in the community, including equipment at facilities.
- contain a program and schedules for *training local emergency response and medical workers* to respond to chemical emergencies.
- establish methods and schedules for conducting *"exercises"* (simulations) to test elements of the emergency response plan.
- designate a *community coordinator and facility coordinators* to carry out the plan.

**Source:** *Chemicals in Your Community: A Guide to the Emergency Planning and Community Right-to-Know Act.* Environmental Protection Agency, 1988.

---

air pollutants linked to ACID RAIN. Industries are given "allowances" for specified levels of emissions; those with emissions significantly lower than allowed can trade their unused allowances to other companies, who were unable to meet stricter AIR POLLUTION standards. Markets for these allowances were just being established in mid-1991. Some environmental organizations, such as the NATURAL RESOURCES DEFENSE COUNCIL charge that the system has too many loopholes and will not significantly cut pollution. It remains to be seen how this *emissions trading* approach will work in the long run.

### For more information and action:

- **AIR AND WASTE MANAGEMENT ASSOCIATION (A&WMA)**, (412-232-3444). Publishes *Continuous Emissions Monitoring: Present and Future Applications* (1990) and training materials.
- **ENVIRONMENTAL DEFENSE FUND (EDF)**, (212-505-2100). Publishes *Emissions Trading: Environmental Perestroika or Flimflam?* (D. Dudek, 1989).
- **MORRISON INSTITUTE FOR POPULATION AND RESOURCE STUDIES**, (415-723-7518). Publishes *International Carbon Emission Offsets: A Tradeable Currency for Climate Protection Services* (Joel N. Swicher and Gilbert M. Masters).
- **RESOURCES FOR THE FUTURE (RFF)**, (202-328-5000).
- **WORLD WILDLIFE FUND (WWF)**, (202-293-4800). Publishes *Carbon Emissions Control Strategies: Case Studies in International Cooperation* (William U. Chandler, 1990).

(See also ACID RAIN; AIR POLLUTION; SMOG.)

**endangered species,** flora and fauna whose continued health and existence are at significant risk. *Note: a list of endangered animals and plants begins on page 372, and specific articles on key endangered species are found throughout this book.*

EXTINCTIONS occurred long before humans arrived on the scene (witness the dinosaurs) and when humans were still in a "state of nature" (witness the mammoths). Massive extinctions occurred in several geological periods, most notably the Permian, 240 million years ago, in which over 75 percent, perhaps 95 percent, of all sea SPECIES perished. But industrialization, economic DEVELOPMENT, and POPULATION pressure have in the past two centuries combined to cause a sharp loss of BIOLOGICAL DIVERSITY and an increase in the number of species disappearing from the face of the earth.

How many SPECIES of living organisms exist is unknown. The authors of *Technologies to Maintain Biological Diversity* note that approximately 1.7 million species had been identified by 1987, but that millions more have yet to be discovered; some researchers have estimated that there may be 30 million species of tropical insects alone. Of the known species, over half (55 percent) are of insects; 14 percent of flowering plants; 9 percent of algae, fungi, and ferns; 8 percent of noninsect arthropods; 8 percent of other invertebrates; 2 percent bacteria and protozoa; and only 3 percent vertebrates, including humans and all other mammals (figures are rounded to the nearest whole number). Conservation biologists note that most public concern focuses on the large vertebrates—which some have termed *charismatic megavertebates*—such as ELEPHANTS and WHALES, while many other species decline and disappear

## Endangered Species and Biological Diversity Information and Action Guide

**For more information and action about endangered species and biological diversity:**

AFRICAN WILDLIFE FOUNDATION, (202-265-8393 or 800-344-TUSK [8875]).

AMERICAN ASSOCIATION OF BOTANICAL GARDENS AND ARBORETA (AABGA), (215-688-1120). Publishes *The Plant Collections Directory: Canada and the United States* (Jean Schumacher, 1988).

AMERICAN ASSOCIATION OF ZOO KEEPERS (AAZK), (913-272-5821, ext. 31). Publishes *Conservation, Preservation & Restoration Committee Bulletin*.

AMERICAN ASSOCIATION OF ZOOLOGICAL PARKS AND AQUARIUMS (AAZPA), (304-242-2160). Promotes the *International Species Inventory System (ISIS)*, a computerized inventory of living zoo animals for use in selective breeding programs, and the *Species Survival Plan (SSP)*, supporting captive breeding programs for endangered species. Publishes brochures *Conversation: Protecting the Present to Protect the Future*, *The New Ark*, and *Wild Animals Do Not Make Good Pets*.

AMERICAN ORNITHOLOGISTS' UNION (AOU), (202-357-1970).

AMERICAN WILDLIFE ALLIANCE (AWL), (303-771-0380).

ANIMAL PROTECTION INSTITUTE, (916-731-5521). Publishes *Endangered Species* and *Animal Activist's Handbook*. (See ANIMAL RIGHTS AND WELFARE INFORMATION AND ACTION GUIDE, on page 361.)

CENTER FOR PLANT CONSERVATION (CPC) (c/o Missouri Botanical Garden, P.O. Box 299, St. Louis, MO 63166; 314-577-5100; Donald A. Falk, Executive Director), an organization "dedicated to the conservation and study of all endangered plants native to the United States," coordinating with, providing support services for, and working within existing regional gardens, such as the Missouri Botanical Garden where it is headquartered, with each garden conserving plants native to its own region. Founded in 1984, it is funded by private donations, grants, contracts, and service fees, with some donors "sponsoring" a particular endangered species. The CPC maintains the *National Collection of Endangered Plants*, a living collection of 20 regional conservator gardens;

a cryogenic seedbank, part of the DEPARTMENT OF AGRICULTURE's *National Plant Germplasm System*; and a database on endangered plants. The CPC also works on projects to conserve endangered plants in the wild; to develop public education programs; and to undertake research on endangered plants. It publishes various materials, including the periodical *Plant Conservation*, the brochure "Making Plant Extinction a Rare Thing," and the *CPC Endangerment Survey*.

CONSERVATION INTERNATIONAL (CI), (202-429-5660). Carries out a wide range of projects, including *Rapid Assessment Program*, *Bi-National Peace Parks*, *Plant Conservation and Ethnobotany*, and *Species Recovery Programs*.

CONSULTATIVE GROUP ON INTERNATIONAL AGRICULTURAL RESEARCH (CGIAR or CG), (202-473-8951). Sponsors the International Board for Plant Genetic Resources (IBPGR).

DEFENDERS OF WILDLIFE, (202-659-9510). Publishes *In Defense of Wildlife: Preserving Communities and Corridors*, *The Biodiversity Challenge*, reports on endangered species, and action alerts.

EARTH FIRST! (E.F.!), (Direct Action Fund, 415-376-7329). Has *Biodiversity Project*.

ECOLOGICAL SOCIETY OF AMERICA (ESA), (301-530-7005).

ENVIRONMENTAL DEFENSE FUND (EDF), (212-505-2100).

ENVIRONMENTAL INVESTIGATION AGENCY (EIA), (202-483-6621). Investigates environmental abuse, as of the international ivory trade and illegal or "'pirate" commercial whaling. Publishes various reports.

FISH AND WILDLIFE SERVICE (FWS), (202-208-4717; for publications, 703-358-1711; *Federal Wildlife Reference Service*, 301-492-6403 or 800-582-3421). Key U.S. federal agency dealing with endangered species. Publishes *Endangered Species Technical Bulletin*, full lists of endangered plants and wildlife (see ENDANGERED AND THREATENED WILDLIFE AND PLANTS on page 372), and numerous other materials, including many on specific species.

INTERNATIONAL COUNCIL FOR BIRD PRESERVATION (ICBP) (United Kingdom; 0223-277318; U.S. Headquarters, c/o World Wildlife Fund—U.S.; 202-293-4800). Maintains a computerized

---

with little fanfare, sometimes before they were even known to exist. Since human activities are so crucial in the survival stakes, a species has a competitive advantage if it is seen to be of possible use to humans, or if it is seen as beautiful, with species often perceived as "ugly" or "sinister," such as BATS, at a disadvantage.

The actual definitions used by conservationists in talking about endangered species differ markedly. Within the United States, the definitions stem from the ENDANGERED SPECIES ACT of 1973:

- **endangered species**—a species in danger of extinction throughout all or a significant part of its range.
- **threatened species**—a species likely to become endangered within the foreseeable future throughout all or a significant portion of its range.
- **critical habitats**—areas vital for the conservation of endangered or threatened species, referring to HABITAT areas, wider surrounding areas, or even areas outside the species' current range.

Under this U.S. act, *extinction* is taken to mean that no

data bank about endangered birds, from which it generates reports; develops and carries out priority projects in their *Conservation Programme*; publishes books on threatened birds.

**IUCN—THE WORLD CONSERVATION UNION,** (202-797-5454). Operates the WORLD CONSERVATION MONITORING CENTRE. Publishes *Red Data Books* and other key works on threatened life such as *The 1990 IUCN Red List of Threatened Animals, Conserving the World's Biological Diversity* (Jeffrey A. McNeely et al., 1990), *Wild Plant Conservation and the Law*, (C. de Klemm, 1989), *Economics and Biological Diversity: Developing and Using Economic Incentives to Conserve Biological Resources* (Jeffrey A. McNeely, 1988), and *Threatened Primates of Africa: The IUCN Red Data Book* (Phyllis C. Lee et al., 1988).

**KIDS FOR SAVING EARTH™ (KSE),** (612-525-0002 or 800-800-8800).

**NATIONAL WILDLIFE FEDERATION (NWF),** (202-797-6800 or 800-245-5484). Publishes the bimonthlies *National Wildlife* and *International Wildlife*, which include the *Wildlife Digest Newsletter*; and *Endangered Species: Wild & Rare* as part of its *NatureScope® Series*, an education activity series for use with children in grades K-8.

**NATURAL RESOURCES DEFENSE COUNCIL (NRDC),** (212-727-2700). Publishes *Extinction in the Enchanted Isle: Protecting Our Puerto Rican Species* (Suzette Degado-Mendoza et al., 1990) and *Extinction in Paradise: Protecting Our Hawaiian Species* (Laura King et al., 1989).

**NITROGEN FIXING TREE ASSOCIATION (NFTA),** (800-956-7985).

**RARE CENTER FOR TROPICAL BIRD CONSERVATION,** (215-568-0420).

**SEA SHEPHERD CONSERVATION SOCIETY,** (213-373-6979).

**SIERRA CLUB,** (415-776-2211 or 202-547-1141; legislative hotline, 202-547-5550). Publishes *Extinction Crisis, Do Not Disturb*, and *Animals in Their Place*.

**TRAFFIC (TRADE RECORDS ANALYSIS OF FLORA AND FAUNA IN COMMERCE),** (202-293-4800). Monitors global trade in wildlife and wildlife products; publishes "Buyer Beware!" and fact sheets.

**WILDERNESS SOCIETY, THE,** (202-833-2300).

**WILDLIFE CONSERVATION INTERNATIONAL (WCI),** (212-220-5100). Publishes the bimonthly magazine *Wildlife Conservation*.

**WILDLIFE HABITAT ENHANCEMENT COUNCIL (WHEC),** (301-588-8994).

**WILDLIFE INFORMATION CENTER,** (215-434-1637). Publishes *Selected Endangered Species References* and *Wildlife Extinction*.

**WILDLIFE PRESERVATION TRUST INTERNATIONAL (WPTI),** (215-222-3636). Operates a specialized zoo for breeding in captivity animals facing extinction in the wild. Publishes *Travels in Search of Endangered Species* (Jeremy J.C. Mallinson).

**WILDLIFE SOCIETY, THE,** (301-897-9770).

**WORLD BANK** (202-477-1234). Publishes *Conserving the World's Biological Diversity, Plant Genetic Resources: The Impact of the International Research Centers,* and *Plant Quarantine and the International Transfer of Germplasm*.

**WORLD RESOURCES INSTITUTE,** (202-638-6300). Conducts *Program in Forests and Biodiversity*. Publishes *Keeping Options Alive: The Scientific Basics for the Conservation of Biodiversity* (Walter V.C. Reid and Kenton R. Miller, 1989).

**WORLD SOCIETY FOR THE PROTECTION OF ANIMALS (WSPA),** (617-522-7000).

**WORLD WILDLIFE FUND (WWF),** (202-293-4800). Publishes *Reconciling Conflicts Under the Endangered Species Act: The Habitat Conservation Planning Experience* (Micharl J. Bean et al, 1991) and *Managing Private Lands to Conserve Biodiversity* (Michael A.O'Connell et al, 1991).

**WORLDWATCH INSTITUTE,** (202-452-1999).

**Zero Population Growth (ZPG),** (202-332-2200). Publishes *Loss of Wildlife*. (See POPULATION INFORMATION AND ACTION GUIDE on page 248.)

**Other references:**

*Consequences of the Greenhouse Effect for Biological Diversity*. Robert L. Peters II, ed. Yale University Press, 1991. *Balancing on the Brink of Extinction: The Endangered Species Act and Lessons for the Future*. Kathryn A. Kohm, ed. Island Press, 1990. *The Expendable Future: U.S. Politics and the Protection of Biological Diversity*. Richard Tobin. Duke University Press, 1990. *Shattering: Food, Politics, and the Loss of Genetic Diversity*. Cary Fowler and Pat Mooney University of Arizona Press, 1990.

---

members of the species survive in the area in question, or anywhere in the world.

By contrast, the IUCN—THE WORLD CONSERVATION UNION definitions used in the rest of the world focus not only on species but also on distinct subspecies (*taxa*), as well as defining extinction differently:

• **extinct** *taxa*—species or distinct subspecies that no longer exist *in the wild* as indicated by repeated searches of known or likely localities. Under this definition, an animal existing only in captivity, such as the California CONDOR or black-footed FERRET, would be termed extinct.

• **endangered** *taxa*—those in danger of extinction, whose survival is unlikely if factors are unchanged that are causing their decline or vulnerability.

• **vulnerable** *taxa*—those in decline and likely to become endangered, without intervention.

• **rare** *taxa*—those so rare that they could be easily eliminated, but living in relatively stable populations under no immediate threat.

• **intermediate** *taxa*—those belonging in one of the above categories, but about whom too little is known to determine which one.

The Endangered Species Act of 1973 requires that a Recovery Plan be developed for each plant and animal listed as endangered or threatened, which is the responsibility of the FISH AND WILDLIFE SERVICE (FWS). To protect a species and maintain or expand its HABITAT, the FWS can bar activities threatening the species, as by halting the building of a road or DAM, forbidding the HUNTING or taking of an endangered species, or barring sale of such species or their parts, such as ivory from elephants or shells from sea TURTLES. Penalties can include stiff fines and even jail terms for people caught stealing, injuring, or killing listed species.

The Endangered Species Act (somewhat strengthened in 1988) has led to some recoveries, such as the American ALLIGATOR and eastern brown PELICAN. But critics charge that too few species are listed, and that many of these lack any recovery plan. Over 1,000 species are currently on the U.S. list, about half native to the United States and half from other countries, but many other species are also endangered or threatened—in the U.S. alone some 4,000 or more species are candidates for listing—some of which have become extinct before ever being listed. Because most attention focuses on "attractive" or "popular" species, some have suggested that what is needed is not an Endangered Species Act, but an endangered ECOSYSTEMS act. GONE TOMORROW? on page 107 is a description of what some biologists regard as the 16 most endangered plants in the United States. For a full list of the plants and animals listed by the FWS as of mid-1990, see ENDANGERED AND THREATENED WILDLIFE AND PLANTS on page 372; note that a concluding section indicates those species that are no longer listed, because of recovery, extinction, or mistake in the original data. Many private organizations also work to protect species in the wild; for those focusing on animals, see below. Efforts to save endangered species and help them recover have given rise to some new specialties, notably CONSERVATION BIOLOGY and RESTORATION ECOLOGY.

On the international front, efforts to protect endangered species are coordinated by the IUCN, working closely with the INTERNATIONAL COUNCIL FOR BIRD PRESERVATION (ICBP). These organizations publish a series of "Red Data Books" that are the bibles in the field, providing vital information about endangered species, as well as plans to protect them and help them recover. These and many other organizations also work to save endangered species by regulating or halting animal trafficking. (See ENDANGERED SPECIES AND BIOLOGICAL DIVERSITY INFORMATION AND ACTION GUIDE on page 104; ANIMAL RIGHTS AND WELFARE INFORMATION AND ACTION GUIDE on page 361 also BIOLOGICAL DIVERSITY; CONVENTION ON INTERNATIONAL TRADE IN ENDANGERED SPECIES OF WILD FAUNA AND FLORA [CITES]; WILDLIFE TRADE.)

**Endangered Species Act,** a U.S. federal law passed in 1973 and amended in 1988, "to provide a means whereby the ecosystems upon which endangered species and threatened species depend may be conserved, to provide a program for the conservation of such endangered species and threatened species." The Endangered Species Act is primarily administered by the Department of the Interior (DOI) through the FISH AND WILDLIFE SERVICE (FWS), except that export and import of land plants is under the DEPARTMENT OF AGRICULTURE (USDA), and marine mammals and fish are under the Department of Commerce (DOC), or more precisely the National Marine Fisheries Service (NMFS) (see NATIONAL OCEANOGRAPHIC AND ATMOSPHERIC ADMINISTRATION), with the MARINE MAMMAL PROTECTION ACT specifically taking precedence. The FWS is charged with designating those animals and plants to be listed, removed, or their status changed (as from endangered to threatened); maintaining the official list of those plants and animals protected under the Act, both native and foreign (see the list of ENDANGERED AND THREATENED WILDLIFE AND PLANTS on page 372); overseeing protection of listed species, including setting aside critical HABITAT and initiating plans for recovery, working with the states, especially to make programs consistent and to monitor the progress of species that have been sufficiently helped to be removed from the list; and reviewing the status of listed species every five years.

Species that cannot be readily distinguished from listed species are also protected, and funds may be appropriated from the LAND AND WATER CONSERVATION FUND to acquire critical habitats of listed species. The Act also requires other federal agencies to see that they do not take actions that could threaten listed species, except by special exemption and with annual reports submitted to the COUNCIL ON ENVIRONMENTAL QUALITY, and allows foreign currency reserves (if appropriate) to be used to assist foreign conservation efforts, including programs and training.

Under the Act, the Fish and Wildlife Service is also designated to oversee implementation of various international treaties and conventions the United States has signed regarding conservation of fish, wildlife, and plants, such as the Convention on Nature Protection and Wildlife Preservation in the Western Hemisphere (1940); CONVENTION ON INTERNATIONAL TRADE IN ENDANGERED SPECIES OF

## Gone Tomorrow?

Perhaps 3,000 of the types of plants native to the United States—over 10 percent of the approximately 25,000 species, subspecies, and varieties—are imminently threatened with extinction in the wild. According to the Center for Plant Conservation's 1988 Endangerment Survery, about 680 of these are thought likely to disappear in the wild by the year 2000. Among these are:

*Amsinckia grandiflora* (large-flowered *amsinckia* or fiddle-neck), an annual plant with bright yellow-orange flowers, known from only one wildly fluctuating population on a U.S. Army base in California.

*Apioa priceana* (Price's potato-bean), a groundnut, whose tubers are large and edible and have been classified as an underutilized food source, probably eaten by Native Americans. It is found in about 10 widely scattered wooded locations, from Alabama and South Carolina north to Illinois.

*Astragalus robbinsii* var. *jesupii* (Jesup's milk-vetch), a small perennial herb with delicate pea-like violet flowers, found only in New Hampshire and Vermont, on the banks of the Connecticut River, threatened by recreational uses and a proposed hydropower project.

*Banara vanderbiltii* (Palo de Ramon), a small tropical tree, growing only to about 30 feet, with yellow flowers and fleshy fruit. Only about six of these trees survive in the wild, all in Puerto Rico.

*Dicerandra immaculata* (Lakela's mint), a scrub balm of the mint family, seen as having horticultural potential, with delicate foliage and pale flowers, found only in central Florida, in highly disturbed sand scrub regions.

*Dudleya brevifolia*, a tiny succulent "live-forever" that mimics the soil in its native habitats, today remaining in only a few isolated locations in California, one a mountain top scheduled for development.

*Hedeoma todsenii* (Todsen's pennyroyal), a perennial herb of the mint family, growing to about 8 inches, with 2-inch-long orange-red flowers. First discovered only in 1978, it is known from only two populations, on fragile, steep gravelly habitat on a federal missile range in New Mexico.

*Hedyotis parvula*, a small shrub of the *madder* family, with shiny dark green leaves and clusters of small white waxy flowers with pink or purple tips. Only one plant is known to survive, in a Hawaiian forest preserve; none is known in cultivation.

*Iliamna corei* (Peter's Mountain mallow), a perennial shrub with striking pink flowers, known from only four plants in its native Virginia habitat. Through cultivation, conservationists hope to reestablish a population in the wild.

*Kokia cookei* (Cook's kokia), a small tree with striking red flowers, already extinct in its native Hawaiian volcanic slopes and today known only from a few plants in a botanical garden collection.

*Lesquerella pallida*, bladderpod with delicate white flowers, with potential as a crop for seed oil extraction. Not seen for 100 years and once thought extinct, it now is known to exist in four very small Texas populations.

*Opuntia spinosisima*, a semiphore prickly pear cactus with bright red flowers, known in the United States from only six plants on one small island of the Florida Keys, near a mangrove forest, though also found on Jamaica and the Cayman Islands.

*Penstemon penlandii* (Penland beardtongue), a herbaceous perennial with tightly clustered blue-and-violet flowers, with horticultural possibilities. About 5,000 plants are known in the wild, all in a single Colorado location, at risk from grazing deer and off-road vehicles.

*Phacelia argillacea* (clay *phacelia*), a winter annual with blue-to-violet flowers, known from only one Utah location, on shale slopes where the remaining 19 plants (as of 1988) were threatened by grazing and disturbance by sheep.

*Stephanomeria malheurensis* (*Malheur* wire-lettuce), an annual plant from the mustard family, which became extinct in the wild in 1984, its only known site being in central Oregon, where 100 cultivated plants were reintroduced experimentally in 1988.

*Thymophylla tephroleuca* (ashy dogweed), a bushy grey-green plant with yellow, daisy-like flowers, known from only one roadside population in southern Texas, and at risk from herbicides, agriculture, oil and gas exploration, and other threats.

**Note:** A longer, though necessarily less detailed list of at-risk species is given in ENDANGERED AND THREATENED WILDLIFE AND PLANTS on page 372.

---

WILD FAUNA AND FLORA (CITES) (1973); various international agreements, on migratory birds (see MIGRATION) as with Canada, Mexico, and Japan, and on FISHING and whaling (see WHALES).

Specifically, the Act prohibits the import, export, taking, possession, or sale of endangered species, or violation of regulations regarding endangered or threatened species (see ENDANGERED SPECIES for definitions). Import or export of African ELEPHANT ivory, raw or worked, is also prohibited, as is selling of animals protected under the CITES treaty, or importing or exporting fish or wildlife without a proper permit or at a nondesignated port, with importers and exporters required to keep records and reports of their activities (see WILDLIFE TRADE). Exceptions granted under permit include taking prohibited species for scientific purposes or to aid in their reproduction or survival; also taking that is incidental to some other lawful activities, available on application of a conservation plan outlining the anticipated impact of the activities on the species, indicating what alternatives might ease adverse impact, describing alternatives and reasons for not adopting them, and other information as required. INDIGENOUS PEOPLES in Alaska are allowed exemptions for subsistence taking and sale of handicrafts, except where survival of the species is involved, and for material predating the law (such as scrimshaw). Civil penalties run up to $12,000 per violation, while criminal violations run up to $50,000 and up to a year in prison, per violation; both the endangered species and the property used in taking them may also be confiscated. Rewards may be paid to informers (other than public officials). Environmentalists often criticize the government for being too lax in protecting species listed under the Endangered Species Act, and some bring suits against violators (including government agencies), as provided under the Act. That applies only to listed species, however, and they note that numerous species are actually endangered, threatened, and even become extinct, without ever having even been listed as in jeopardy. (See also ENDANGERED SPECIES; BIOLOGICAL DIVERSITY; ENVIRONMENTAL LAW; ANIMAL RIGHTS; WILDLIFE TRADE.)

**endrin,** a type of PESTICIDE (see CHLORINATED HYDROCARBONS; also brown PELICAN).

**energy resources,** all the possible forms of power that can be harnessed for human ends. Most of the energy available on earth derives from the sun, directly or indirectly. It is the sun's RADIATION converted into chemical energy during the process of PHOTOSYNTHESIS, that makes possible all plant and animal life. BIOMASS (all living matter), BIOFUELS (fuels made from biomass), and FOSSIL FUELS (fossilized biomass, such as COAL, OIL, and NATURAL GAS)—all result from photosynthesis; together they supply approximately 85 percent of all the world's current energy needs. The sun also provides the necessary energy for WIND POWER; for fueling the WATER CYCLE, tapped through HYDROPOWER; and, of course, for various forms of SOLAR ENERGY, so far negligible in global terms but having great promise for the future. Much smaller amounts of the world's energy are derived from tides responding to the action of the moon (see WAVE POWER); from the

earth's core (see GEOTHERMAL ENERGY); and from cosmic sources older than the sun (see NUCLEAR ENERGY).

Before the 18th century, humans relied mostly on traditional energy sources—wind, water, and biomass, such as fuelwood, agricultural waste, animal dung, and peat—for cooking, heating, and small-scale production purposes. In developing countries, and in rural areas everywhere, these are still primary sources, though biomass is often no longer being used in a sustainable way, because of the pressure of increasing POPULATION. But elsewhere, by the mid-19th century industrializing countries had begun the major shift to coal and then also to oil and natural gas. These were used directly for heating and various manufacturing processes and to some extent still are, but at the end of the 19th century the rise of electrical power brought a further shift in energy use and distribution.

Some fuels are still used directly, particularly the fossil fuels that power home and factory furnaces and motor vehicles of various kinds, all of which have been designed specifically for these fuels. But increasingly large amounts of fuel have come to be used in power plants to produce electricity; in the United States, 85 percent of all coal used is in power plants. Electricity is extremely versatile, being usable for myriad purposes without conversion, and can readily be made available to anyone within range of transmission lines. It was partly this ready source of power that fueled the growth of the developed world, and its accessibility led to the general abandonment of traditional energy sources.

But this shift brought with it numerous problems. It meant that increasingly large numbers of humans were relying on DECLINING RESOURCES, instead of the traditional RENEWABLE RESOURCES, so that growth was at the expense of the world's environmental balance. It also meant that humans began to heavily foul their earth. Where previously the natural environment could process in a natural way the substances produced by the burning of biomass, now the amounts of pollutants being spewed into the air can overwhelm the system's natural self-cleansing processes. The result has been increasing ACID RAIN, AIR POLLUTION, and WATER POLLUTION. In addition, since they were no longer relying on local resources for energy, humans found that they were becoming reliant on unevenly distributed fossil fuel sources far beyond their borders and their control.

This point was brought home to many people with a shock in the 1970s energy crisis, highlighted by the 1973 oil embargo, when the oil-producing nations of the Middle East sharply curtailed production. This shock triggered many governments into funding research and development of ALTERNATIVE ENERGY, energy conservation, and energy

## US Energy Sources and Consumption, 1989

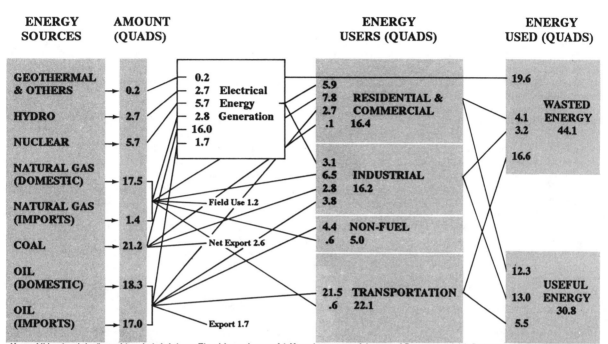

| ENERGY SOURCES | AMOUNT (QUADS) | | ENERGY USERS (QUADS) | ENERGY USED (QUADS) |

Note: additional statistics (in quads) not included above - Electricity: net imports, 0.1; Natural gas: storage, 0.4, exports, 0.7, unaccounted, 0.1; Coal: stocks, 0.3; Oil: refinery gains, 0.2, strategic reserve, 0.1, unaccounted crude, 0.5.

Energy: one quad = one quadrillion BTUs or approximately 171 million barrels of crude oil, or 1 trillion cubic feet of natural gas, or about 45 million short tons of coal. Source: Government Accounting Office.

In the US, almost 50% more energy is lost or wasted through conversion or inefficiency than is used productively. For each unit of energy used, one and one-half units are wasted.

**Source:** Lawrence Livermore National Laboratory, Livermore, California.

efficient sources and approaches, among them biofuels, geothermal energy, hydropower, solar energy, synthetic fuels, wave power, and wind power. As the oil flowed once more, and the shortage became a worldwide glut of oil, many people felt that the energy crisis had eased, and funding of and interest in alternative energy sources tailed off.

In fact, as many environmentalists have been making clear, the energy crisis is still with us—only it is a wider, deeper crisis than that of the 1970s. At the current rate of usage, environmental economists estimate, coal, natural gas, and oil are expected to last 1,500, 120, and 60 years, respectively, though improved technologies for production and use could lengthen the life of the resources. Even if they do, however, decreasing supply will lead to increasing prices. Not only that, but the current rates of usage are expected to increase significantly, despite conservation measures, because of rising POPULATION, especially in the

Third World, where traditional fuels are increasingly being replaced by commercial fuels. All this is quite apart from the questions of environmental pollution, which are growing ever more serious.

Environmentalists are concerned because no overall, coherent energy policy exists that takes into account the true costs—including those to the environment—of the various energy sources, nationally and globally. In addition, they have numerous specific complaints about current fragmented energy policies. Prime among them is that a system of taxes and subsidies encourages the use of fossil fuels over various alternative energy sources. They urge that either these be eliminated or a similar set of taxes and subsidies be put in place to foster further development of alternatives, noting that much of California's progress in developing cost-effective wind and solar-thermal power was due to that state's favorable tax policies and its

## Energy Resources Information and Action Guide

For more information and action about energy resources:

**AMERICAN COUNCIL FOR AN ENERGY EFFICIENT ECONOMY (ACEEE)**, (202-429-8873). Publishes consumer guides such as *Oil and Gas Heating Systems: Maintenance and Improvement* (1990) and *The Most Energy-Efficient Appliances* (1989), as well as professional publications, conference proceedings, research reports, and the professionally oriented magazine *Home Energy*.

**CENTRE FOR SCIENCE AND TECHNOLOGY FOR DEVELOPMENT (CSTD), UNITED NATIONS**, (212-963-8435).

**CONSERVATION AND RENEWABLE ENERGY INQUIRY AND REFERRAL SERVICE (CAREIRS)**, (800-523-2929, U.S. except AK and HI; for AK and HI, 800-233-3071). Provides information on a range of energy-related topics.

**COORDINATION IN DEVELOPMENT (CODEL)**, (212-870-3000).

**DEPARTMENT OF ENERGY (DOE)**, (202-586-5000). Publishes an annual energy review and other material on energy policy and trends, such as *International Energy Outlook 1989, Projections to 2000.* (1989) and *Energy Conservation Trends* (1989).

**ENVIRONMENTAL AND ENERGY STUDY INSTITUTE (EESI)**, (202-628-1400). Publishes policy reports such as *The Future of Electric Vehicles: Their Role in Meeting Environmental and Energy Needs* (1990).

**ENVIRONMENTAL DEFENSE FUND (EDF)**, (212-505-2100).

**GREENPEACE**, (202-462-1177). Runs the *Atmosphere and Energy Campaign*. Publishes *Changing the Utility Mission* (1990) and the action factsheet *Energy*.

**INFORM, INC.**, 212-689-4040). Publishes reports such as *Drive for Clean Air: Natural Gas and Methanol Vehicles* (James S. Cannon, 1989) and fact sheets such as *Air Pollution and Alternative Fuel Vehicles*.

**INSTITUTE FOR LOCAL SELF-RELIANCE (ILSR)**, 202-232-4108). Publishes various materials, such as *Self-Reliant Cities: Energy and the Transformation of Urban America*.

**INTERNATIONAL INSTITUTE FOR ENERGY CONSERVATION (IIEC)** (750 First Street, NE, Suite 940, Washington, DC 20002; 202-842-3388; Deborah Lynn Bleviss, Executive Director; Asian Regional Office, 10/4 Soi 49/7 Sukhumvit, Bangkok 10110, Thailand; 662-392-3936), an organization founded in 1984 "to expedite the implementation of energy efficiency throughout the developing world," acting as a "'broker' or facilitator between those institutions with experience in energy efficiency technologies and policies and those institutions in developing countries" that need such experience. The IIEC's main activities are disseminating information (as through workshops, conferences, and seminars), demonstrations of efficiency strategies, and development of local energy conservation business. It publishes various reports on energy conservation activities around the world and descriptions of current projects.

**INVESTOR RESPONSIBILITY RESEARCH CENTER (IRRC)**, (202-234-7500). Publishes *Power Plays: Profiles of America's Leading Renewable Electricity Developers* (1989).

**KIDS FOR SAVING EARTH™ (KSE)**. (612-525-0002 or 800-800-8800).

**NATIONAL AUDUBON SOCIETY**, (212-832-3200; *Audubon Action Line* 202-547-9017.)

**NATIONAL CENTER FOR APPROPRIATE TECHNOLOGY (NCAT)**, (406-494-4572).

**NATIONAL WILDLIFE FEDERATION (NWF)**, (202-797-6800 or 800-245-5484). Publishes Fact Sheet *Energy Security and the Arctic Refuge*.

**NATURAL RESOURCES AND ENERGY DIVISION (NRED), UNITED NATIONS**, (212-963-6205). Coordinates UN programs for devel

---

agreement to purchase excess power produced by these methods. Some have proposed a "carbon fee," a tax based on the carbon content of each fuel, to discourage fossil fuel use.

Environmentalists also note that the costs of energy production and use do not properly take into account the wider costs from air pollution, radiation and long-term cleanup costs from nuclear energy, and the global effects of the GREENHOUSE EFFECT, GLOBAL WARMING, and CLIMATE CHANGE. Some suggest that government, industry, environmental groups, and other citizens' organizations need to work together to develop from among alternative energy sources specialized *niche* products that will have particular appeal to potential users, paving

the way for their wider use. They stress that the utility industry needs to prepare for a gradual, long-term transition from a highly centralized fossil-fuel–based electrical supply system to a future decentralized solar energy system. Long-term planning is needed because most of the world's power plants, factories, furnaces, automobiles, and other power-using machines and devices (except for those running directly on electricity or other alternative energy sources) will have to be modified or replaced as fossil fuels are replaced.

Meanwhile, much effort is being placed on energy conservation (using less energy, as through cutting waste) and energy efficiency (using it more effectively, as through new technology), the overall aim being to to limit pollu-

oping countries in the areas of energy. Publishes or distributes the *Energy Newsletter* and reports such as *Energy Issues and Options for Developing Countries* (1989) and *Energy Conservation in the Power Sector* (1989).

RENEW AMERICA, (202-232-2252). Publishes *Sustainable Energy* (1989) and Focus Paper *Energy Pollution Control* (1988).

RESOURCES FOR THE FUTURE (RFF), (202-328-5000). Includes research arm, *Energy and Natural Resources Division*. Publishes materials on energy development, such as *Technology Options for Electricity Generation: Economic and Environmental Factors* (Hadi Dowlatabadi and Michael A. Toman, 1991).

ROCKY MOUNTAIN INSTITUTE (RMI), (303-927-3851). Offers the Competitek Subscription Service for consultation on use and misuse of electricity; publishes *Practical Home Energy Savings, Resource-Efficient Housing: An Annotated Bibliography,* and *Energy Unbound: A Fable for America's Future.*

SIERRA CLUB, (415-776-2211 or 202-547-1141; legislative hotline, 202-547-5550). Publishes *Electric Utility Rate Structures Policy, Energy and Energy Economics Policy, Energy Conservation and Renewables Policy, Suncell, Home Energy Decision Book, Geothermal Energy Policy, Nuclear Power Policy,* and *Decommissioning Nuclear Reactors Policy.*

STUDENT ENVIRONMENTAL ACTION COALITION (SEAC), (919-967-4600). Campaigns for National Energy Strategy.

UNION OF CONCERNED SCIENTISTS (UCS), (617-547-5552; or 202-332-0900). Publishes the quarterly newsletter *Nucleus;* books and reports, such as *Cool Energy: The Renewable Solution to Global Warming* (Michael Brower, 1990); and brochures such as *Cool Energy: The Renewable Solution to Global Warming, The Heat Is On: Global Warming, The Greenhouse Effect* and *Energy Solutions, How You Can Influence Government Energy Policy, Solar Power: Energy for Today and Tomorrow,* and *Nuclear Power: Past and Future.*

U.S. PUBLIC INTEREST RESEARCH GROUP (PIRG), (202-546-9707). Publishes *Fuel Efficiency PAC Study* (1991).

WORLD BANK (202-477-1234). Publishes numerous materials on traditional and alternative energy sources.

WORLD RESOURCES INSTITUTE (WRI), (202-638-6300). Publishes *Driving Forces: Motor Vehicle Trends and Their Implications for Global Warming, Energy Strategies, and Transportation Planning* (James J. MacKenzie and Michael P. Walsh, 1990), *Why We Need a National Energy Policy* (James J. MacKenzie, 1990), *Solar Hydrogen: Moving Beyond the Fossil Fuels* (Joan M. Ogden and Robert H. Williams, 1989), and *Breathing Easier: Taking Action on Climate Change, Air Pollution, and Energy Insecurity* (James J. MacKenzie, 1988).

WORLDWATCH INSTITUTE, (202-452-1999). Publishes *Renewable Energy: Today's Contribution, Tomorrow's Promise* (Cynthia Pollock Shea, 1988).

WORLD WILDLIFE FUND (WWF), (202-293-4800). Publishes *Power of Spare: The World Bank and Electricity Conservation* (Julie VanDomelen, 1988).

**Other references:**

*Energy: Production, Consumption, and Consequences.* John L. Helm, ed. National Academy Press, 1990. *Energy and Security in the Industrializing World.* Raju G.C. Thomas and Bennett Ramberg, eds. University Press of Kentucky, 1990. *Electricity: Efficient End-Use and New Generation Technologies and Their Planning Implications.* Thomas B. Johansson et al., eds. Lund University Press (Lund, Sweden), 1989. *The New Oil Crisis and Fuel Economy Technologies: Preparing the Light Transportation Industry for the 1990s.* Deborah L. Bleviss. Quorum Books/Greenwood, 1988.

---

tion and dependence on declining resources. Among the efficiency and conservation approaches new in recent decades are COGENERATION, making use of otherwise wasted heat from fuel or waste burning, and the HEAT PUMP, a reversible air conditioner using differences between indoor and outdoor temperature to achieve heating and cooling efficiencies. Many leaks have been plugged—insulation, caulking, duct tape, and the like are all more widely used—though ironically the tighter the house or office building, the greater the indoor air pollution. Today's cars run more efficiently, traveling further and more cleanly on less fuel. Large amounts of energy are simply wasted in the process of transmission or conversion. Two of the great potential advantages of decentralized solar energy are the ability to have small power plants near users, cutting transmission loss, or to use the sun's radiation to create

hydrogen fuel, which can be easily transmitted with little or no loss.

Environmentalists point out that major savings can be achieved by people being willing to settle for less—shorter, cooler showers, fewer or dimmer lights, warmer beer or soda, and the like. In the United States, lighting accounts for about a quarter of electrical use—20 percent directly and another 5 percent to counteract the heat emitted by the lights—while electrical motors consume about 50 percent of all electricity generated and about 65 to 70 percent of all electricity used in industry. Improvements in these areas could have a massive impact on overall energy consumption. The industrialized countries draw a disproportionately large amount of energy, and so are the main places where savings can be made. (For a current overview of United States energy use, see

U.S. ENERGY SOURCES AND CONSUMPTION, 1989, on page 109.)

Advanced technologies and approaches are also contributing to energy savings, among them:

- **compact fluorescent lamps,** which require 75 to 85 percent less electricity than traditional incandescent ones and last considerably longer, more than recovering the higher cost over each lamp's lifetime. Some utilities are providing bulbs free or at low cost to promote transition.
- **adjustable-speed drives and high-efficiency motors,** varying speed to more efficiently meet power needs and reducing losses, as to resistance, and improving the effectiveness of motors.
- **superwindows,** specially treated windows used as insulators, to hold heat inside buildings and save on central heating.
- **thermal storage,** capturing "free heat"—that generated by people, lights, incoming sunlight, and office equipment—through building insulation and superwindows, to heat buildings. During the summer the inside air is *precooled*—cooled off during the night, when the outside air is coolest and electricity cheapest. In "superinsulated" or "optimum" homes, hot-water heaters sometimes can double as furnaces.
- **smart buildings,** integrated control systems (for houses, generally called automated control systems) used to automatically control heating, air conditioning, lighting, and security for each room. Temperature and humidity levels can be set by screen for any room, and appliances or equipment can be programmed to run during the night, when electricity cost and demand are low.

Many efficient technologies exist that are not yet widely used, partly because customers do not know about or ask for them and partly because distribution channels have not been developed. Both of these aspects of delivery need to be considered in overall energy policy planning. Some governments encourage energy savings through setting standards for buildings, automobile use, plantings, and the like. California, for example, requires that residential and commercial properties be upgraded to meet certain minimum standards before title can be transferred, under *residential conservation ordinances* (RECOs) or *commercial building conservation ordinances* (CECOs). Some utilities and occasionally even home builders are offering a *Home Energy Rating Systems* (HERS), which indicates the efficiency level of the house and its specific energy-conserving features. Considerable energy savings can also be realized by cutting down on use of materials that require

energy for processing, especially by RECYCLING used materials. (See ENERGY RESOURCES INFORMATION AND ACTION GUIDE on page 110); also OIL; COAL; NATURAL GAS; and various specific forms of ALTERNATIVE ENERGY.)

## Environmental and Energy Study Institute (EESI)

(122 C Street, Washington, DC 20001; 202-628-1400; Ken Murphy, Executive Director), an organization established in 1984 by leaders of the *Congressional Environmental and Energy Study Conference (EESC)*, a legislative service organization, "to produce better informed debate on environmental and energy issues and dedicated to generating innovative policies for substantial development." EESI produces "pro-active educational briefings; short, timely issue and policy reports; consensus-building policy workshops; blue-ribbon task force recommendations; regional and national conferences; and Congressional testimony and provision of information and technical assistance," also helping people and organizations at the state and local level participate in development of national policy. Recent projects and programs focus on areas such as global CLIMATE CHANGE, energy efficiency and renewable energy, groundwater protection, agriculture, waste management, water efficiency, and natural resource management in the Third World. EESI publishes the Congressional Conference's *Weekly Bulletin* and *Special Reports*, and many reports of its own, such as *Clean Air Legislation and Issues; an Information Guide* (1990), *Environmental, Energy and Natural Resources Status Report for the 101st Congress* (1990), *Public Opinion Trends on Environmental and Energy Issues* (1990), *The Economics of Sustainable Agriculture* (1990), and *Environmental Sustainability Begins At Home* (1990).

## Environmental Defense Fund (EDF)

(257 Park Avenue South, New York, NY 10010; 212-505-2100; Fred Krupp, Executive Director), a national membership organization founded in 1967 that uses "an aggressive partnership of science, economics, and law to develop lasting solutions to environmental problems," its slogan being "The Power of Positive Solutions." EDF works through its offices in New York and seven other sites around the country to develop economically attractive alternatives to environmentally harmful practices; to develop stronger laws and regulations to protect the environment; and to block harmful activities through enforcement of existing environmental laws. Among its recent activities have been work to end McDonald's use of the polystyrene foam sandwich container; to pass the CLEAN AIR ACT Amendments of 1990; to block the TWO

FORKS DAM; to protect the GRAND CANYON, as from the effects of the GLEN CANYON DAM; to bar further use of HEAVY METALS and dangerous PESTICIDES; to protect coastal ECOSYSTEMS, including CORAL REEFS; and to support making ANTARCTICA a world park, along with activities on a wide range of other issues, including water conservation, energy choices, POLLUTION, global CLIMATE CHANGE, waste reduction, and RECYCLING issues. The EDF publishes many materials, including the bimonthly *EDF Letter*, and reports such as *The Global Environmental Agenda for the United States and Japan* (R.M. Fujita, 1990) and *Polluted Coastal Waters: The Role of Acid Rain* (D. Fisher et al., 1988).

**environmental degradation,** deterioration in the land's ability to sustain life; a general term for various processes that reduce the CARRYING CAPACITY of an environment, including DEFORESTATION, DESERTIFICATION, EROSION, SALINIZATION, and SEDIMENTATION, and other problems, such as those that result from ACID RAIN, AIR POLLUTION, HAZARDOUS WASTE, OVERGRAZING, WATER POLLUTION, and nonsustainable agricultural practices that overuse and sap the nutrients in the soil (see SUSTAINABLE AGRICULTURE). Environmental degradation can also refer to an environment's change from a natural to a developed state, where the assumption is that any such change is negative (see DEVELOPMENT).

**Environmental Hazards Management Institute (EHMI)** (10 Newmarket Road, P.O. Box 932, Durham, NH 03824; 603-868-1496; Alan John Borner, Executive Director), an independent organization founded in 1978 "to train public, industry and agency officials in the safe handling and management of hazardous materials and hazardous wastes." EHMI supplies training on a contract basis, some with standardized programs such as *The First 12 Hours, Planning for Compliance*, or *Chemistry for the Non-Chemist*, but also customized programs as appropriate. It also produces training films, maintains an extensive computerized information system, holds "HazMat" conferences and public outreach programs, performs confidential environmental audits (as of people in a lawsuit or concerned about compliance with relevant environmental laws), and advises firms on contaminated site management, acting "as the company's strategist, negotiator, investigation and/or remediation manager." The Institute also publishes various materials, including the monthly magazine *HAZMAT World*, and the biweekly newsletters *Environmental Manager's Compliance Advisor* (EMCA) and *OSHA Compliance Advisor* (OCA), as well as the handy *EHMI Environmental Education Wheels* for the general public, providing summaries of information on topics such as household HAZARDOUS WASTE, water sense, and RECYCLING.

**environmental illness (EI),** a term for a general and chronic medical condition resulting from exposure to chemicals, including low levels of those generally considered "safe"; also called *ecological illness*. Chemicals are all around us, in the air we breathe, the water we drink, food we eat, the clothes we wear, the furniture we use, the houses we live in, the offices and factories we work in—in short, everywhere. Some of these are clearly identified as TOXIC CHEMICALS, including PESTICIDES; the government regulates the amount and concentration that is "acceptable" in human settings. However, the possible toxic effects of many chemicals are unknown, especially when they combine with each other (see SYNERGY). And many are in unexpected places, such as in art supplies or perfumes. Reactions may be subtle and appear only after some time, or they may be immediate and severe, with symptoms as wide as the medical lexicon, affecting the central nervous system, skin, gastrointestinal system, musculoskeletal system, cardiovascular system, respiratory system, and the very vulnerable eyes, ears, nose, and throat. Environmental illnesses are often puzzling, partly because doctors are not normally trained to recognize diseases caused by environmental exposure, though that is now changing. In many cases, illnesses result from indoor AIR POLLUTION, and can be at least partly eased by reducing its level (see DO YOU HAVE INDOOR AIR POLLUTION? on page 7; and HOW CAN YOU IMPROVE INDOOR AIR QUALITY? on page 77). Some buildings are so permeated with chemicals that they cause what is called *sick building syndrome* (SBS) or *building-related illness* (BRI). New or recently renovated structures, especially completely closed office buildings constructed with synthetic materials or homes with formaldehyde insulation, are particularly affected. These may need to be reconstructed, reventilated, and in some cases partly ripped apart and rebuilt before becoming habitable places.

People vary greatly in their response to chemical exposures, at what testing agencies consider "safe" levels for the general population (see DOSAGE LEVELS). Among those groups especially vulnerable are children, older people, women and their unborn babies, and people with chronic illnesses, such as allergies. In addition, some people are unusually sensitive to chemicals and become ill from exposure to chemicals even in minute doses. In extreme cases, such people are so sensitive that—to relieve their symptoms—they must take themselves out of communities and live in isolation, with only natural materials around them. Such people are sometimes said to have *multiple chemical sensitivities* (MCS), *total allergy syndrome*, or *20th-century illness*.

**For more information and action:**

• HUMAN ECOLOGY ACTION LEAGUE (HEAL), (404-248-1898). Publishes the quarterly magazine *The Human Ecologist*, resource and reading lists, and information sheets on chemical sensitivities.

(See also TOXIC CHEMICALS; HAZARDOUS WASTE; PESTICIDES.)

**environmental impact statement (EIS),** a report analyzing the probable environmental effects, both positive and negative, of a proposed project, and suggesting ways to mitigate adverse effects, including alternatives to the project or other ways of handling parts of it. This approach was introduced in the United States in 1970, under the NATIONAL ENVIRONMENTAL POLICY ACT (NEPA), but has since been widely adopted internationally. In the U.S., NEPA regulations, under the COUNCIL OF ENVIRONMENTAL QUALITY (CEQ), require that an EIS be submitted for proposed legislation or for any major construction project involving federal funds. Various agencies may be involved; for example, the MARINE MAMMAL COMMISSION may prepare an EIS regarding the impact on marine mammals of proposed OFFSHORE DRILLING. NEPA itself does not actually require that an agency avoid actions predicted in an EIS to cause environmental harm or take steps to limit that harm (though other laws may). A 1989 Supreme Court decision, *U.S. Forest Service v. Methow Valley Citizens Council,* noted that: "If the adverse environmental effects of the proposed action are adequately identified and evaluated, the agency is not constrained by NEPA from deciding that other values outweigh the environmental costs." Before a 1986 change in regulations, agencies were required to also analyse a "worst-case scenario," but in the same 1989 case the Court upheld CEQ's decision allowing agencies to forego that if information required for evaluation were unavailable or too expensive to obtain; instead the CEQ requires "a summary of existing credible scientific information which is relevant to evaluating the reasonably foreseeable significant adverse impacts on the human environment . . ." with these including "catastrophic consequences, even if their probability of occurrence is low, provided that the analysis of the impacts is supported by credible scientific evidence, is not based on pure conjecture, and is within the rule of reason." Nor are EISs uniformly applied. In BLUEPRINT FOR THE ENVIRONMENT, various environmentalists point out that the EIS process has never been applied to the DEPARTMENT OF AGRICULTURE's (DOA's) commodity support program, and there-fore may impede farmers from switching to low-input SUSTAINABLE AGRICULTURE.

**For more information and action:**

• AMERICAN WATER RESOURCES ASSOCIATION (AWRA), (301-493-8600).
• IUCN—THE WORLD CONSERVATION UNION, (202-797-5454).
• NATIONAL INSTITUTE FOR URBAN WILDLIFE, (301-596-3311 or 301-995-1119).
• NATURAL RESOURCES AND ENERGY DIVISION (NRED), UNITED NATIONS, (212-963-6205).
• **Northwest Coalition for Alternatives to Pesticides (NCAP),** (503-344-5044). (See PESTICIDES INFORMATION AND ACTION GUIDE on page 238.)

**Environmental Investigation Agency (EIA)** (208-209 Upper Street, Londons N1 1RL, England; 4471-704-9441; or 1506 19th Street NW, #4, Washington, DC 20036; 202-483-6621; Kristina Harper, Jennifer Lonsdale, Allan Thornton, Directors), an organization founded in 1984 to investigate environmental abuse, conducting research from its Washington and London offices, and using the results of its investigations to formulate effective solutions to the environmental abuse, then publicizing the results and working with other public and private groups to effect change. Working as "eco-detectives," EIA has produced documentary evidence on campaigns such as the international ivory trade, the Faroese pilot WHALE and DOLPHIN hunt, illegal or "pirate" commercial whaling, and the trade and transport conditions of live-caught wildlife, including birds and primates. EIA publishes various materials, including the quarterly *Environmental Investigation Agency News*; the book *To Save an Elephant* (Allan Thornton and Dave Currey, 1991); and reports such as *The Global War Against Small Cetaceans, A Second Report* (1991), *Wild Bird Imports for Pet Trade, An EEC Overview* (1990), and *A System of Extinction,* and *The African Elephant Disaster* (1989).

**environmental investing,** an alternative form of SOCIALLY RESPONSIBLE INVESTING.

**environmental law,** a body of statutes, regulations, treaties, agreements, declarations, and resolutions relating to the environment, its present and future. Such legal instruments vary widely, but can be categorized very generally as either *hard law* or *soft law*. Soft law has little or no legally binding force, though it may still be useful in defining the "ideal" approach or situation envisioned and serving as a guide toward policy and future hard agreements. By contrast, hard law refers to those treaties or laws that are binding obligations under national or international law, under which governments that normally have complete authority over the natural resources in their areas agree to restrict some of their rights and assume certain obligations. However, even though hard law may be legally binding, its actual effectiveness varies considerably, depending on the amount of financial support, operational implementation, and enforcement given. So a ''hard'' international law may be applied very differently in various nations, sometimes because of differing views on the ends in question, but often because of varying levels of financial and technical capability, especially limited in developing countries.

Like other areas of the law, environmental law is a patchwork affair. Laws passed by different bodies at different times cover this or that aspect of a problem, but often gaps and overlaps exist, sometimes as priorities change (as the earlier focus on protecting large mammals and birds has more recently given way to protection of plants and animals on-site in their natural HABITATS and ECOSYSTEMS). These discontinuities are of particular concern because environmental problems are increasingly seen as regional, continental, and global in nature. Environmentalists today are making considerable efforts to fill in the gaps in environmental law, nationally and internationally and are trying to ensure relatively uniform enforcement.

On the international level, efforts at uniform enforcement often take the form of global or regional international treaties or conventions. Relating to the protection of species, among the most important ''hard laws'' are the CONVENTION ON WETLANDS OF INTERNATIONAL IMPORTANCE ESPECIALLY AS WATERFOWL HABITAT (Ramsar Convention; 1971), the CONVENTION CONCERNING THE PROTECTION OF THE WORLD CULTURAL AND NATURAL HERITAGE (1972), the CONVENTION ON INTERNATIONAL TRADE IN ENDANGERED SPECIES OF WILD FAUNA AND FLORA (CITES; 1973), the CONVENTION ON THE CONSERVATION OF MIGRATORY SPECIES OF WILD ANIMALS (Bonn Convention; 1979)—these known as the ''big four''—and the CONVENTION ON THE LAW OF THE SEA (1982). In addition, numerous regional conventions are in force; among those treated separately in this book are the CONVENTION ON THE PREVENTION OF MARINE POLLUTION BY DUMPING OF WASTE AND OTHER MATTER (LONDON DUMPING CONVENTION or LDC), the MONTREAL PROTOCOL ON SUBSTANCES THAT DEPLETE THE OZONE LAYER, and the CONVENTION ON LONG-RANGE TRANSBOUNDARY AIR POLLUTION (LRTAP).

Several key ''soft law'' declarations and resolutions have also been influential on the international level. Among these are the DECLARATION OF THE CONFERENCE ON THE HUMAN ENVIRONMENT (Stockholm Declaration),

the WORLD CONSERVATION STRATEGY (WCS), the WORLD CHARTER FOR NATURE, and the Man and the Biosphere (MAB) program (see BIOSPHERE RESERVE.) Into this category might also fall the Brundtland Report, OUR COMMON FUTURE.

On the national level, many countries already have or are planning a general conservation strategy, to give a unified approach to problems treated indifferently or at least in various ways on the state and local levels, as well as by different federal agencies. Efforts to develop such a strategy are, of course, hampered by widespread disagreements on priorities and on the nature of different groups' visions for the future. In the United States, numerous environmental organizations joined together in 1989 to publish their BLUEPRINT FOR THE ENVIRONMENT: A PLAN FOR FEDERAL ACTION, a landmark attempt to outline actions for each branch and main agency of the federal government to achieve an overall strategy for the environment. Meanwhile, the ENVIRONMENTAL PROTECTION AGENCY (EPA) published two key overview documents about environmental risks, needs, and priorities, UNFINISHED BUSINESS: A COMPARATIVE ASSESSMENT OF ENVIRONMENTAL PROBLEMS (1987) and REDUCING RISKS: SETTING PRIORITIES AND STRATEGIES FOR ENVIRONMENTAL PROTECTION (1990). Many environmentalist organizations have also published overviews of the kinds of legal protection they see as necessary for environmental protection; some of these works are listed under individual organizations throughout this book, while others appear in the GREEN BOOKSHELF on page 480.

While these and other such documents may serve as guidelines for the future—with goals around which numerous environmental action groups may mobilize—most countries are left with piecemeal environmental law. Some of the most important United States environmental-related laws are treated separately in this book, such as the CLEAN AIR ACT, CLEAN WATER ACT, EMERGENCY PLANNING AND COMMUNITY RIGHT-TO-KNOW ACT (EPCRA), the related superfund Amendments and Reauthorization Act (SARA, or Title III; see SUPERFUND), ENDANGERED SPECIES ACT, FEDERAL INSECTICIDE, FUNGICIDE, AND RODENTICIDE ACT (FIFRA), NATIONAL ENVIRONMENTAL EDUCATION ACT, NATIONAL ENVIRONMENTAL POLICY ACT (NEPA), RESOURCE CONSERVATION AND RECOVERY ACT (RCRA), SAFE DRINKING WATER ACT (SDWA), and TOXIC SUBSTANCES CONTROL ACT (TSCA or TOSCA). (See also ENVIRONMENTAL LAW INFORMATION AND ACTION GUIDE on page 116.)

**environmentally friendly,** a phrase describing products and processes that do not harm the earth and its inhabit-

## Environmental Law Information and Action Guide

**For more information and action on environmental law:** AMERICAN BAR ASSOCIATION (ABA), NATURAL RESOURCES, ENERGY, AND ENVIRONMENTAL LAW SECTION (750 North Lake Shore Drive, Chicago, Il 60611; Richard G. Stoll, Section Chair; section number 312-988-5602; main ABA number, 312-988-5000), a section of the lawyers' professional association focusing on environmental issues. It provides special educational programs and teleconferences on current environmental topics, such as developments in water law, and publishes various materials, including the quarterly journal *Natural Resources & Environment* (NR&E), quarterly *Natural Resources Law Newsletter*, an annual summary of legal developments at the state and federal levels, and practice-oriented monographs.

**Animal Legal Defense Fund (ALDF),** (415-459-0885; *Dissection Hotline* 800-922-FROG [3764]). Publishes the quarterly newsletter *The Animals' Advocate* and *ALDF Updates*. (See ANIMAL RIGHTS AND WELFARE INFORMATION AND ACTION GUIDE on page 361.)

**DEFENDERS OF WILDLIFE,** (202-659-9510).

**EARTH ISLAND INSTITUTE,** (415-788-3666).

**ENVIRONMENTAL LAW INSTITUTE (ELI)** (1616 P Street, NW, Suite 200, Washington, DC 20036; 202-328-5150; publications office: 202-939-3844; J. William Futrell, President), an organization founded in 1969 by practicing attorneys, environmental advocates, and law school professors, as a centralized source of analysis and reliable, objective information about "the growing volume of legal, legislative, and regulatory developments in the environmental field," dedicated to "open, candid debate of environmental issues," rather than "rhetoric and adversarial positions." As its mission expanded, ELI expanded into multidisciplinary research and policy analysis, increasingly for an international constituency, and educational activities such as specialized workshops, seminars, and national conferences. ELI's legal, scientific, and economic research teams work in many areas; in 1989, for example, they addressed "management of hazardous, medical, and solid waste, state and local management of natural resources issues, including groundwater, surface mining, wetlands protection, and public lands; control of atmospheric and indoor air pollution; and better energy efficiency." ELI maintains a library, open to the public weekdays; provides telephone reference assistance to environmental professionals in the United States and abroad; and has an active international program, including a visiting scholars program, often focused on branches such as its *Global Policy Research Center, Center for East European Environmental Programs,* and *Inter-American Environmental Policy Center,* co-established in 1989 with the Buenos Aires–based organization Foundacion Ambiente y Recursos Naturales. ELI also publishes the *Environmental Law Reporter*; periodicals such as the bimonthlies *The Environmen-*

---

ants, notably those that are BIODEGRADABLE and appropriate for RECYCLING, do not contribute to GLOBAL WARMING, and are not wasteful of energy (see ENERGY RESOURCES). Some countries, such as Germany, Japan, and Canada, have instituted a program in which an independent "Environmental Jury" reviews products and awards its seal to those that meet established criteria. Companies can then use the "environmentally friendly" seal in their advertising, and consumers can use it as a guide in shopping (see GREEN CONSUMERISM).

## Environmental Monitoring and Assessment Program (EMAP), a U.S. federal project established in 1990 to create a "comprehensive, continually updated survey of the status of ecological resources in the United States, linking monitoring data from the ENVIRONMENTAL PROTECTION AGENCY (EPA), DEPARTMENT OF AGRICULTURE (DOA), FISH AND WILDLIFE SERVICE (FWS), and NATIONAL OCEANIC AND ATMOSPHERIC ADMINISTRATION (NOAA). Ideally it will make it possible to study changes in specific ecosystems and determine if they result from "human-induced stress."

**environmental planning,** the process of making deliberate choices about if, how, when, where, and to what extent an area is to be developed, based on an understanding of the special nature of the area and an overall vision of its long-term figure. Though some modest amount of planning has always been involved in the DEVELOPMENT of land areas, historically cities and LAND USE patterns have developed in unplanned, hodge-podge ways, depending on general cultural and national styles, and much influenced by local figures and conditions.

Only in the 20th century has planning become widely accepted as a special and necessary discipline. Such planning has traditionally focused on populated areas, whether on the neighborhood, city, metropolitan area, state, regional, or national levels. It generally involves making a master plan for the area, setting out how each area is to be used or developed, with general guidelines to be fol-

tal Forum and *National Wetlands Newsletter*; the annual *Law of Environmental Protection;* deskbooks on key environmental laws; and policy and research reports such as *The Greenhouse Effect: Formulating a Convention* (William A Notze, 1990); *Practical Guide to Environmental Management* (Frank B. Friedman, 1990 ed.); and *Fundamentals of Negotiation: A Guide for Environmental Professionals* (Jeffrey G. Miller and Thomas R. Colosi, 1989).

**Land Trust Alliance (LTA),** (202-785-1410). Operates the *Land Conservation Law Institute.* Publishes the newsletter *The Back Forty,* bimonthly legislative updates, and books.

**National Alliance for Animal Legislation (NAAL),** (703-684-0654). (See ANIMAL RIGHTS AND WELFARE INFORMATION AND ACTION GUIDE on page 361.)

**NATIONAL AUDUBON SOCIETY,** (212-832-3200; *Audubon Action Line* 202-547-9017.)

**NATURAL RESOURCES DEFENSE COUNCIL (NRDC),** (212-727-2700).

**NATIONAL WILDLIFE FEDERATION (NWF),** (202-797-6800 or 800-245-5484). Maintains natural resource law and science centers; sponsors Washington Action Workshops, on lobbying; and publishes the quarterly *Legislative Update,* the triweekly newsmagazine *Enviroaction,* the *Citizens Action Guide,* and *The NWF Activist Kit.*

**RAILS-TO-TRAILS CONSERVANCY (RTC),** (202-797-5400).

**SIERRA CLUB,** (415-776-2211 or 202-547-1141; legislative hotline, 202-547-5550, for taped information on current environmental bills before Congress). Affiliated programs include *Sierra Club Legal Defense Fund* (415-567-6100; Frederic Sutherland, Executive Director). Publishes biweekly *National News Report* focusing on environmental legislation, and brochures such as *Sierra Club Political Committee, League of Conservation Voters Voting Chart, Platform for the Environment, The Right to Write, Federal Government Offices.*

**Society for Animal Protective Legislation (SAPL),** (202-337-2334). (See *Animal Welfare Institute* in the ANIMAL RIGHTS AND WELFARE INFORMATION AND ACTION GUIDE on page 361.)

**STUDENT ENVIRONMENTAL ACTION COALITION (SEAC),** (919-967-4600). Lobbies for legislative and policy changes; publishes *SEAC Organizing Guide* and *SEAC Student Environmental Action Guide* (published by Earthworks).

**U.S. Public Interest Research Group (PIRG),** (202-546-9707).

**Other references:**

*U.S. Environmental Laws,* rev. ed. Wallis E. McClain, Jr. Bureau of National Affairs, 1991. *Environmental Law: The Law and Policy Relating to the Protection of the Environment.* Simon Ball and Stuart Bell, eds. State Mutual Books, 1991. *The Limits of the Law: The Public Regulation of Private Pollution.* Peter C. Yeager. Cambridge University Press, 1991. *Regulating the Environment: An Overview of Federal Environmental Laws.* Neil Stoloff. Oceana, 1991. *Environmental Law for Non-Lawyers.* David B. Firestone and Frank C. Reed. SoRo Press, 1990. *International Environmental Policy: Emergence and Dimensions,* 2nd ed. Lynton K. Caldwell. Duke University Press, 1990.

---

lowed by the various agencies or departments serving the area. Plans for local areas are ideally coordinated with those of neighboring communities into wider regional plans. These may include separate plans for central business districts, residential neighborhoods, suburban subdivisions, or special complexes such as medical centers, universities, or industrial parks.

Urban planning concerns itself with numerous aspects of the community, among them:

- the size, style, and placement of specific types of development, such as housing, factories, and commercial districts.
- the provision of appropriate services, such as fire, water and other utilities, sanitation, education, health, police, recreation, and transportation, including highways and mass transportation—all coming under the heading of *infrastructure.*
- the renovation and preservation of older districts, activites often coming under the heading of *urban renewal* or *historic preservation.*

- the provision of green space and separation of traffic from residential areas—both relatively recent concerns in most parts of the world.

Within populated areas, various tools are used to carry out master plans. These include ZONING, building codes, transportation regulations such as speed limits and parking restrictions, formation of districts with special rules such as historic preservation districts or economic enterprise zones, economic incentives such as rent subsidies, mortgage or other financing programs, or tax relief, and other local, state, or national laws and regulations.

Planning starts with analyses of current land use, POPULATION distribution, anticipated population growth, economic conditions, social attitudes, and environmental quality, whether in a negative sense of possible danger (as of a nuclear power plant in a heavily populated area) or in a positive sense, as in the desirability of establishing GREENWAYS and other natural spaces within a community. In truth, some kinds of environmental concerns–especially

## Environmental Planning Information and Action Guide

**For more information and action:**

**American Planning Association (APA),** (202-872-0611). Publishes the monthly magazine *Planning*; the quarterly *Journal of the American Planning Association* (JAPA); Planning Advisory Service (PAS) reports, such as *A Survey of Zoning Definitions* (1989), *Designing Urban Corridors* (1989), *Zoning Bonuses in Central Cities* (1988), and *Enforcing Zoning and Land-Use Controls* (1988); and distributes bibliographies from the *Council of Planning Librarians (CPL)*, including *Urban Planning: A Guide to the References Sources* (1989), *Telecommunications and Regional Development* (1989), *Urban Development Issues: What Is Controversial in Urban Sprawl?* (1989), *Educational Materials in Planning for Use in Elementary and Secondary Schools* (1989), and *Citizen Participation in Planning* (1988). The APA also publishes various brochures; videotapes of workshops and conferences; periodicals such as *Land Use Law & Zoning Digest* and *Zoning News*; and over 150 books, including *Planning Small Town America* (Kristina Ford et al., 1990), *Neighborhood Planning* (Bernie Jones, 1990), *Zoning and the American Dream* (Charles M. Haar and Jerold S. Kayden, eds., 1989), and *The Small Town Planning Handbook* (Thomas L. Daniels et al., 1988).

**National Institute for Urban Wildlife,** (301-596-3311 or 301-995-1119). Publishes *Planning for Urban Fishing and Waterfront Recreation, Wildlife Reserves and Corridors in the Urban Environment: A Guide to Ecological Landscape Planning and Resource Conservation,* and *Integrating Man and Nature in the Metropolitan Environment.*

**Natural Resources Defense Council (NRDC),** (212-727-2700).

**WORLD BANK (202-477-1234).** Publishes *Monitoring and Evaluating Urban Development Programs, Urban Edge, Urban Land Policy: Issues and Opportunities,* and *Glossary of Urban Infrastructure Maintenance.*

**Other references:**

*Environmental Disputes: Community Involvement in Conflict Resolution.* James E. Crowfoot and Julia M. Wondolleck. Island Press, 1990. *People Places: Design Guidelines for Urban Open Space.* Clare Cooper Marcus and Carolyn Francis. Van Nostrand Reinhold, 1990. *Design for Mountain Communities.* Sherry Dorward. Van Nostrand Reinhold, 1990. *Creating Successful Communities: A Guidebook to Growth Management Strategies* and *Creating Successful Communities: Resource Guide for Creating Successful Communities.* Michael A Mantrell et al. Island Press, 1989. *The Politics of Urban Planning.* William C. Johnson. Paragon, 1989. *Mastering the Politics of Planning.* Guy Benveniste. Jossey-Bass, 1989. *Rural Planning and Development in the U.S.* Mark B. Lapping et al. Guilford, 1989. *Regional Planning.* Melville C. Branch. Praeger, 1988. *Vacationscape: Designing Tourist Regions,* 2nd ed. Clare A. Gunn. Van Nostrand Reinhold, 1988. *The Complete Manual of Land Planning and Development.* William E. Brewer and Charles P. Alter. Prentice Hall, 1988. *Cities of Tomorrow: An Intellectual History of Urban Planning and Design in the Twentieth Century.* Peter Hall. Basil Blackwell, 1988. *Site Planning: Environment, Process, and Development.* R. Gene Broosk. Prentice Hall, 1988.

(See also DEVELOPMENT; CROPLANDS; LAND USE.)

---

wasteful use of natural resources, and dangers from air, water, and land POLLUTION—have come to play a major role in planning only in recent decades. In the United States, a turning point was the 1970 passage of the NATIONAL ENVIRONMENTAL POLICY ACT and the resulting establishing of the ENVIRONMENTAL PROTECTION AGENCY. This required that for federal legislation and major planning proposals involving federal funds, ENVIRONMENTAL IMPACT STATEMENTS must be prepared, mandating consideration of the long-term environmental consequences of planning decisions. Similar emphasis on environmental considerations has become part of planning in other countries as well, notably in Europe, but in many parts of the world environmental planning is simply a far-distant ideal. Many of the world's cities are almost totally unplanned, often being surrounded by a densely inhabited shantytown, with little or nothing in the way of water, sanitation, or

other necessary services. Increasingly, however, environmental planning is focusing on saving natural spaces in WILDLIFE REFUGES and WILDERNESS areas.

Environmentalists like those who outlined the WORLD CONSERVATION STRATEGY, which seeks to integrate conservation with sustainable development, stress the important of starting the environmental planning process with *ecosystem evaluation* (EE). Under this approach, planners:

- evaluate each ECOSYSTEM in an area (including both land and water areas, such as WETLANDS, LAKES, and OCEANS) to assess its suitability for specific kinds of uses.

- compare the anticipated output with the amount of input required for each different kind of use.

- assess the SUSTAINABILITY of the different kinds of uses, taking into account such matters as DECLINING RE-

SOURCES and ENVIRONMENT DEGRADATION, such as ERO-SION or loss of BIOLOGICAL DIVERSITY.
- compare potential uses with existing uses.
- assess the environmental effects of proposed uses (see ENVIRONMENTAL IMPACT STATEMENT).
- allocate land and water uses so as to make optimum use of available living resources.
- review tentatively allocated uses for conflicts, which can be dealt with by such means as ZONING and scheduling, and compatibilities, which can highlight possibilities for multiple uses. Where an ecosystem is unique or irre-placeable, as when it is the critical HABITAT of an EN-DANGERED SPECIES, management to protect the habitat takes priority over other uses.
- make the planning process and land use allocations openly available, to educate the public and benefit from public input.
- review and revise land use allocations on a rolling basis, taking into account current and projected demand pat-terns, including demand for ENERGY RESOURCES, need for roads, buildings, and other infrastructure, patterns of settlement, and new knowledge about environmental consequences.

Such evaluation processes draw on understandings from multidisciplinary sciences, including ECOLOGY, related nat-ural sciences, agriculture, forestry, fisheries, economics, and sociology. (See ENVIRONMENTAL PLANNING INFORMA-TION AND ACTION GUIDE on page 118; also LAND USE; ZONING.)

## Environmental Protection Agency (EPA) (Public In-formation Center, 401 M Street, SW, Washington, DC 20460; 202-260-7751 or 202-260-2080; Office of Public Affairs, 202-260-4361; Office of Policy and Planning, 202-260-4331; William K. Reilly, Administrator), the key U.S. federal agency in the environmental arena, its de-clared mission being to preserve and improve "the quality of the environment, both national and global . . . to pro-tect human health and the productivity of natural resources on which all human activity depends." More specifically, its stated commitment is to ensure that:

- federal environmental laws are implemented and en-forced effectively;
- U.S. policy, both foreign and domestic, fosters the inte-gration of economic DEVELOPMENT and environmental protection so that economic growth can be sustained over the long term;
- public and private decisions affecting energy, transporta-tion, agriculture, industry, international trade, and nat-

ural resources fully integrate considerations of environmental quality;
- national efforts to reduce environmental risk are based on the best available scientific information communi-cated clearly to the public;
- everyone in our society recognizes the value of pre-venting POLLUTION before it is created;
- people have the information and incentives they need to make environmentally responsible choices in their daily lives; and
- schools and community institutions promote environ-mental stewardships as a national ethic.

The EPA conducts and encourages research on health and ecological risks; gathers and analyzes data on environ-mental risks and trends; promotes and supports innovative technological solutions to environmental problems; and communicates its measurements, solutions, and evalua-tions to individuals and institutions within the United States and abroad. It seeks to:

- target environmental protection resources at the problems and the geographical areas posing the greatest risks;
- develop programs that control the movement of pollut-ants across environmental media;
- apply market mechanisms and economic incentives when they are appropriate and effective;
- ensure that other government agencies consider the envi-ronmental implications of their actions;
- involve other agencies, public interest groups, the regu-lated community, and the general public in achieving national and global environmental goals.

The EPA also seeks to work with other nations to iden-tify and solve transboundary pollution problems and to ensure that "environmental concerns are integrated into U.S. foreign policy, including trade, economic develop-ment, and other policies," as well as to provide "technical assistance, new technology, and scientific expertise to other nations."

The agency's activities are authorized under numerous laws (discussed in separate entries), including the CLEAN AIR ACT (CAA); CLEAN WATER ACT (CWA); COMPRE-HENSIVE ENVIRONMENTAL RESPONSE, COMPENSATION AND LIABILITY ACT (CERCLA); EMERGENCY PLANNING AND COMMUNITY RIGHT-TO-KNOW ACT (EPCRA) (see also SU-PERFUND); FEDERAL INSECTICIDE, FUNGICIDE, AND RO-DENTICIDE (FIFRA); RESOURCE CONSERVATION AND RECOVERY ACT (RCRA); SAFE DRINKING WATER ACT (SDWA); and TOXIC SUBSTANCES CONTROL ACT (TSCA or TOSCA).

The EPA's overall assessment of current environmental

risks and plans for dealing with the problems have been laid out in recent years in two notable documents, UNFINISHED BUSINESS: A COMPARATIVE ASSESSMENT OF ENVIRONMENTAL PROBLEMS (1987) and REDUCING RISKS: SETTING PRIORITIES AND STRATEGIES FOR ENVIRONMENTAL PROTECTION (1990). Among its other recent general summaries of activities and plans are *Environmental Progress and Challenges: EPA's Update* (1988), *Meeting the Environmental Challenge: EPA's Review of Progress and New Directions in Environmental Protection* (1990), and *Environmental Stewardship: EPA's First Two Years in the Bush Administration* (1991). The EPA also publishes numerous other materials, technical reports for the scientific and political communities as well as works for the general public (some titles are mentioned under various topics throughout this book). In addition, it operates numerous special telephone lines to provide information to the public and to the regulated community on various topics.

Many environmentalists, such as those who prepared the BLUEPRINT FOR THE ENVIRONMENT, have urged the EPA to act more vigorously in crucial, often international areas such as ACID RAIN, AIR POLLUTION, WATER POLLUTION, dumping and cleanup of HAZARDOUS WASTE, depletion of the OZONE LAYER, GLOBAL WARMING and CLIMATE CHANGE, support of SUSTAINABLE AGRICULTURE globally, more stringent controls on PESTICIDES and other TOXIC CHEMICALS, better protection for ENDANGERED SPECIES, and stronger enforcement of ENVIRONMENTAL LAWS, such as those above. American environmentalists were generally pleased by the appointment of William K. Reilly, former president of the WORLD WILDLIFE FUND and before that the CONSERVATION FUND, to lead the EPA. Reilly was, among other things, a key figure in the decision against the TWO FORKS DAM and in committing public resources to the cleanup after the EXXON VALDEZ OIL SPILL. In its post-Reilly annual reports, the EPA points to significant new legislation and regulatory decisions and stronger enforcement, stressing that in 1990 it collected a record $91 million in fines, one-fourth of all the fines ever collected. All of this, however, took place within a context of considerable resistance to environmental concerns elsewhere in the federal administration.

***Environmental Quality Report,*** an annual report on the status of the U.S. environment, published yearly by the COUNCIL ON ENVIRONMENTAL QUALITY.

**environmental racism,** popular term for racial discrimination in the siting of high-pollution industrial works and HAZARDOUS WASTE sites in or near minority communities. In truth, such siting has historically been more a question of socioeconomic class than of race; the poor, whatever

their race, have traditionally lived "on the other side of the tracks," along with industrial plants. To some extent it is a chicken-and-egg question of which came first. Certainly, the poor have generally lived in the least desirable, and therefore least expensive areas, such as near industry; and new industrial plants and disposal sites have often been sited in areas inhabited by the poor, because the land is cheaper and the local inhabitants do not have the political power to bar construction, as more affluent citizens do, as through ENVIRONMENTAL PLANNING. But whether it is a question of race or class, local minority groups are increasingly making environmental racism an issue, and fighting for fairness and equality in the siting of new and potentially toxic plants and disposal sites.

Not many environmental organizations have directly taken up questions of environmental racism in their own countries, though some have focused on the threat to INDIGENOUS PEOPLES in unpopulated or developing countries. Indeed, some environmental organizations have been criticized for forming largely a White, middle-and-upper class movement, and some have even been accused in racism in their hiring practices. Such organizations counter that, and until recently, people from minority groups had expressed little interest in environmental issues and in working with such organizations.

**For more information and action:**

- **NATIONAL WILDLIFE FEDERATION (NWF),** (202-797-6800 or 800-245-5484).
- **STUDENT ENVIRONMENTAL ACTION COALITION (SEAC),** (919-967-4600).

**environmental refugees,** people forced to leave their homes and land by ENVIRONMENTAL DEGRADATION, any of various processes that reduce the land's CARRYING CAPACITY—that is, its ability to sustain its population—or by natural disasters, such as floods, which are often linked with such degradation. Both problems are often exacerbated by POPULATION pressure. On the immediate, personal level, it is generally FAMINE AND FOOD INSECURITY that spurs people to wander in search of literally greener pastures. Many such refugees flee to nearby cities, part of a long-term trend, or attempt to find haven elsewhere in their own or other countries, but too often find that their presence overwhelms the life-support systems in their new environments. The UNITED NATIONS ENVIRONMENT PROGRAMME (UNEP) has noted: "Throughout the Third World, land degradation has been the main factor in the migration of subsistence farmers into the slums and shantytowns of major cities, producing desperate populations vulnerable to disease and natural disasters . . .", with the mass exodus worsening "already dire urban problems," while hampering efforts to rehabilitate rural areas, from lack of people, will, and resources. From the Okies of the 1930s DUST BOWL to the starving families of lands such as Ethiopia and Bangladesh, the plight of these refugees has produced some of the most poignant stories of the 20th century. Also called environmental refugees are people displaced or dispossessed by large development schemes, such as DAMS, or by industrial accidents that foul the environment, such as BHOPAL, CHERNOBYL, or LOVE CANAL.

**environmental restoration,** the attempt to restore an environment to its presumed natural state, before it was damaged, polluted, or otherwise spoiled (see RESTORATION ECOLOGY).

**erosion,** the gradual wearing down of the land, especially by wind and water, involving the breaking down of rock and other underlying structures of the earth, the transport of the loose material, and the deposition of the material elsewhere. Erosion is a fundamental geological process, quite beyond human control. It is also vital to the health of the environment, for it creates soil and makes available for living organisms the vital minerals otherwise locked away in rock. It is these actions or erosion—and the resulting SEDIMENTATION, or deposit of nutrient-rich soil particles—that make river valleys and deltas so very fertile. But human actions can accelerate the processes of erosion, which can cause loss of both soil and vital nutrients from upland ECOSYSTEMS, including CROPLANDS, on which humans and wildlife depend for food.

There are two main kinds of erosion: chemical and mechanical. *Chemical erosion* involves attacks by water and air, which dissolve or react chemically with substances in rock and soil, LEACHING them away. Through this process underground CAVES are formed and ACID RAIN eats away at living and nonliving things. *Mechanical erosion* works by grinding, pounding, breaking apart, picking up, and transporting. This is the process by which waves attack coastal cliffs and sweep away beaches, to deposit them elsewhere; glaciers grind down rock, carry it a distance, and then drop the rubble; and wind picks up bits of soil and blows them away.

The two prime agents of erosion are wind and water. *Wind erosion* is the most visible and dramatic kind of erosion, because it can be seen in the air near affected areas, as in the 1930s DUST BOWL. Small particles of soil—clay and organic matter—are lifted into the air. The lightest of them are carried high into the air and in strong winds may be transported hundreds of miles. Most particles, however, remain within a foot of the ground, rising briefly into the air, bouncing on the ground, and then

spinning forward again, in a continuous process called *saltation*. Larger, sand-sized particles—many dislodged during saltation—never leave the ground, but instead creep along, moved both by wind action and by collisions with bouncing particles.

*Water erosion*, though less visible, is responsible for more soil loss than wind erosion, in the United States causing about two-thirds of the loss of agricultural land. Using both chemical and mechanical action, water erosion occurs in several ways:

- **splash erosion:** Rain drops (or sprinkle irrigation) break the natural physical and chemical bonds between soil particles, moving them a short distance and making them more vulnerable to surface water flow.
- **sheet erosion:** When rain falls faster than the ground can absorb it, water collects and flows over the surface, carrying with it particles detached by splash erosion. The same occurs during periods of heavy snowmelt and irrigation.
- **rill erosion:** Surface flow forms small, eroding channels called rills, detaching increasing amounts of soil from the sides and bottoms, and enlarging and joining with other rills as they move downslope.
- **concentrated flow erosion:** Slightly larger water channels, from large rills to small gullies, that tend to appear in the same location each year, unlike small rills that tend to disappear when a field is tilled.
- **gully erosion:** large, rapidly eroding water channels, with heavily scoured bottoms and deeply cut sides. Gullies tend to move rapidly upslope, since their uphill end, or *headcut*, is nearly vertical, making the gushing water entering it additionally erosive.
- **mass erosion** or **slumping:** When a hillside becomes saturated with water, large areas of soil can slide or creep downhill, often leading to the formation of gullies.

On farmland, most erosion is sheet and rill erosion, but in unprotected areas—those with no FORESTS or other vegetation covering the ground, including areas degraded by OVERGRAZING, land bulldozed for DEVELOPMENT, and poorly designed logging roads—other more severe types of erosion may soon take over. Depending on the type and amount of rainfall, the length and steepness of the slope, the erodability of the soil, and the management of the land, erosion can move tons of soil per acre during a single storm, or less than a ton per acre over several decades, and it may move it a few feet downslope or carry it thousands of miles to the sea. Ground cover makes soil less vulnerable to erosion, and some types of soil are more resistant than others, so the wide variety of techniques that come under

## Erosion and Soil Conservation Information and Action Guide

**For information and action on erosion and soil conservation:**

**American Farmland Trust (AFT).** (202-659-5170).
**AMERICAN PLANNING ASSOCIATION (APA).** (202-872-0611).
**CAB INTERNATIONAL (CABI),** (602-621-7897 or 800-528-4841). Publishes the monthly *Soil and Fertilizers.*
**Chesapeake Bay Foundation (CBF),** (301-268-8816). Publishes *Soil Conservation Around Your Home.* (See CHESAPEAKE BAY.)
**CONSULTATIVE GROUP ON INTERNATIONAL AGRICULTURAL RESEARCH (CGIAR or CG),** (202-473-8951).
**International Erosion Control Association (IECA),** (P.O. Box 4904, Steamboat Springs, CO 80477; 303-879-3010; Ben Northcutt, Executive Director), a professional organization founded in 1972 as the *National Erosion Control Association* by contractors, consultants, and suppliers in the erosion control industry, and gradually expanding to a wider international membership of people concerned with erosion. The IECA serves as a means of communication and exchange of information on erosion. It sponsors an annual conference, including a trade show; offers professional development courses and a training bureau; sponsors field trips and tours around the world; offers scholarships and grants; and publishes various materials, including the quarterly newsletter *ICEA Report*, an annual membership directory, a products and services directory, and conference proceedings, such as *Erosion Control—A Global Perspective* (1991), *Erosion Control—Technology in Transition* (1990), *Erosion Control Knows No Boundaries* (1989), and *Soil Erosion and Its Control* (1989).
**NITROGEN FIXING TREE ASSOCIATION (NFTA),** (808-956-7895).
**RESOURCES FOR THE FUTURE (RFF),** (202-328-5000).
**SOIL AND WATER CONSERVATION SOCIETY OF AMERICA (SWCS),** (515-289- 2331 or 800-THE-SOIL [843-7645]). Publishes the bimonthly multidisciplinary *Journal of Soil and Water Conservation (JSWC)*; the bimonthly "Conservogram," a computer program, cartoon-style booklets, guides oriented toward school-age children; and books, including *Land Husbandry: A Framework for Soil and Water Conservation* (T.F. Shaxson et al., 1989), *Soil Erosion Research Methods* (Rattan Lal, ed., 1988), and *Conservation Farming on Steep Lands* (W.C. Moldenhauer and N.W. Hudson, eds., 1988).
**WINROCK INTERNATIONAL INSTITUTE FOR AGRICULTURAL DEVELOPMENT,** (501-727-5435 or 703-525-9430).
**WORLD ASSOCIATION OF SOIL AND WATER CONSERVATION (WASWC),** (605-627-9309; May-October 218-864-8506).
**WORLD BANK,** (202-477-1234). Publishes *Soil Conservation in Developing Countries: Project and Policy Intervention.*
**WORLD WILDLIFE FUND (WWF),** (202-293-4800). Publishes *New Vegetative Approaches to Soil and Water Conservation* (Montague Yudelman et al, 1990).

---

the heading of SOIL CONSERVATION focus on management of ground cover and manipulation of soil characteristics.

In addition to the loss of nutrients in soil and organic matter, erosion damage effects croplands in various ways. With loss of topsoil, land is less able to hold and store water for use by plants and so is more vulnerable to drought and DESERTIFICATION. Uncontrolled runoff and sedimentation can damage seedlings and their seedbeds. As topsoil is lost, less productive lower layers of soil are exposed; these generally have less organic matter, more clay, and less phosphorous and may limit root growth, especially as bedrock is nearer to the surface. This is especially important because the general rule of thumb is that it takes about 30 years to form one inch of topsoil from subsoil (which is formed even more slowly from bedrock). Since an inch of soil from one acre weighs about 150 tons, if soil erosion exceeds about five tons per acre per year, the land may be losing topsoil faster than it is being created. In analyzing land, the SOIL CONSERVATION SERVICE uses established *soil loss tolerance levels*, or *T levels*, to indicate the maximum annual erosion rate that is consistent with long-term sustainable productivity.

In addition, fields with rills and other erosion are variable, meaning that they are harder to till and to fertilize and irrigate evenly. Areas near gullies are useless for either crops or livestock grazing and may be difficult or impossible to farm with modern equipment.

Erosion is also a major contributor to WATER POLLUTION, carrying into the world's RIVERS, LAKES, and WETLANDS large amounts of fertilizers and PESTICIDES, along the sediments. Bodies of water in heavily eroded areas often have diminished productivity because the sediment fouls the water, hampering the processes of PHOTOSYNTHESIS; fertilizer in runoff may lead to excess growth, or EUTROPHICATION; and meanwhile pesticides and other chemical pollutants can damage water life. In all these ways, erosion acts to disrupt natural life cycles. Heavy erosion also shortens the life of DAMS and irrigation projects and fills in canals and harbors.

Erosion is a worldwide problem, occurring in all the major agricultural regions of the world. But it is a particular problem in developing countries with rapidly rising POPULATIONS, since there FOREST and vegetative cover is often reduced by human use; improper irrigation leads to

SALINIZATION, often accelerating erosion; and many highly erodible, steep, marginal lands are pressed into production. As a result, many international projects focus on problems with erosion.

In developed countries, too, erosion is a focus of concern; in the United States, the 1985 Farm Act (Food Security Act) contained a *sodbuster provision* and *conservation compliance provisions*, under which farmers risk losing commodity price supports and other federal farm aid if they produce soil-destructive crops on highly erodible fields. The same act also established a CONSERVATION RESERVE PROGRAM (CRP) aimed at establishment of soil-saving grass and tree cover on severely eroding croplands. (See EROSION AND SOIL CONSERVATION INFORMATION AND ACTION GUIDE on page 122; also CROPLANDS; DESERTIFICATION; ENVIRONMENTAL DEGRADATION; SOIL CONSERVATION.)

**eutrophication,** increasing concentration of nutrients such as phosporus and nitrogen in an aquatic ECOSYSTEM. Eutrophication is a natural process, as when in the late stages of ECOLOGICAL SUCCESSION a LAKE becomes nutrient-rich, as plants fill in the ever-shallower area and more organic material falls to the bottom; an aged lake is, in fact, termed a *eutrophic lake*. But many human activities speed up the process, in what is called *cultural eutrophication*. Untreated human waste, nitrates (as from fertilizer), and phosphates (as from detergents) are all—in productivity terms—too much of a good thing. Plants grow to excess, providing the fuel for population explosions, or *blooms*, of tiny animals called *zooplankton* (see PLANKTON), which use considerable oxygen and generally foul the water, making it unfit for drinking without filtering and treatment. Plant remains settle to the bottom, where they are broken down by bacteria and other microorganisms, also using oxygen. In extreme cases, these processes so deplete water of oxygen that fish and other oxygen-dependent aquatic animals may die. One standard measure of WATER POLLUTION is, in fact, *biochemical oxygen demand (BOD)*, or the amount of oxygen that will be required for the biological processes of breaking down the polluting matter, assuming it is BIODEGRADABLE. Eutrophication can be controlled by limiting EROSION of fertilized soil, treating or diverting sewage, and harvesting excess aquatic crops. Action must be taken quickly in lakes, because nutrients once introduced are largely trapped there and recycled. (See WATER POLLUTION; LAKE; RIVER.)

**Everglades,** a 4,000-square-mile area of swamps and periodically flooded prairie in southern Florida, dominated by 10-foot-high sawgrass, with islands and MANGROVE, cypress, pines, palms, and other trees among the sluggish waterways. The Everglades are home to abundant wildlife, including such rare and threatened species as salt-water CROCODILES, MANATEES, anhinga, OSPREYS, bald EAGLES, brown pelicans, and Florida PANTHERS. In addition to the year-round population, the Everglades is a major stop for birds on the Atlantic Flyway (see MIGRATION). About 1,560 square miles of the area have, since 1947, been the Everglades National Park.

The Everglades receives its water largely from the Kissimmee River by way of Lake Okeechobee, but the urban and agricultural DEVELOPMENT of southern Florida in the past few decades has severely lessened the flow of water into the lake and swamp, through both drainage and water use, and has unbalanced the delicate ECOSYSTEM of the region. Some areas of peat have completely dried out, elsewhere artificial pumping must be used to keep the water moving in parts of the swamp, and salt water has moved into areas once covered by freshwater, changing long-established breeding patterns for wildlife and reducing habitable areas for many. However, environmental advocates have had considerable success in reversing this trend in recent years, first halting a proposed airport near the Big Cypress Swamp, in the northwest Everglades, and then convincing the Army Corps of Engineers to assure a basic water supply to the Everglades. A signal success occurred in 1989, when the Army Corps of Engineers agreed to fill in a straight canal they had built bypassing the Kissimmee River, restoring that slowly meandering waterway, and with it the breeding places and HABITATS used by much wildlife in the region. Additional filtering marshes are planned south of Lake Okeechobee, through conversion of farmland—a step forward, although some environmental groups feel that the planned marshes are too small. The federal government is also planning to purchase 107,000 acres of WETLANDS, to be added to the Everglades National Park, and to divert water from an existing canal into the new park area.

The Everglades are also threatened by decline in water quality, from PESTICIDES and nutrient-rich pollutants that drain into its waters from farms and communities, on one hand poisoning wildlife, on the other transforming the ecological balance, causing some species to flourish abnormally, crowding out or asphyxiating other species, as through EUTROPHICATION.

**For more information and action:**

• **Wilderness Society, The,** (202-833-2300). Publishes *''The Everglades.''*
(See also WILDLIFE; WETLANDS.)

**exclusive economic zones (EEZs),** an area extending from a nation's COAST out into the OCEANS for 200 nautical miles. Most coastal nations have declared EEZs, and they are increasingly recognized and accepted in international law. As provided for under the 1982 CONVENTION ON THE LAW OF THE SEA, coastal nations have sovereign rights to explore, exploit, conserve, and manage the natural resources in their exclusive economic zones, within a broad context of rights and duties established by the Convention. Although the Convention has yet to come into force, the concept of EEZs has become so widely accepted in recent decades that areas regarded as "international waters" have shrunk by about 30 percent, the WORLD RESOURCES INSTITUTE estimates. Among the immediate consequences have been a decline in the amount of FISHING in the North Atlantic by fleets from beyond the region and the virtual barring of long-distance fleets from around South Pacific islands, some of whom have begun to sell annual fishing licenses to other countries. Related to the EEZ is the concept of a 200-mile Fishery Conservation Zone within which nations are responsible for managing fish stocks, as through regulating fishing activities; called for under the Convention, the aim is SUSTAINABILITY rather than over-exploitation.

**For information and action:**

- **NATURAL RESOURCES AND ENERGY DIVISION (NRED), UNITED NATIONS**, (212-963-6205).
- **Office for Ocean Affairs and the Law of the Sea (OALOS)**, (212-963-6424). Maintains computerizes Law of the Sea Information System (LOSIS) and the country marine profile data base (MARPRO); publishes *National Legislation on the Continental Shelf* (1989). (See CONVENTION ON THE LAW OF THE SEA.)

**export of pollution**, see POLLUTION.

**extinction**, in general and under the U.S. ENDANGERED SPECIES ACT, the situation in which no members of a particular species survive in a given area, or in the world as a whole. Under the IUCN—THE WORLD CONSERVATION UNION definition used in the rest of the world, however, the term *extinction* may also be used to refer to species or distinct subspecies that no longer exist *in the wild*, as confirmed by repeated searches of the species' known or likely HABITATS. So a species that survives only in ZOOS or special research and preservation facilities, but not in nature, is termed extinct under IUCN definitions. Extinctions have occurred for various reasons in the past, but are increasing rapidly today, primarily due to human actions (for full discussion, see ENDANGERED SPECIES; BIOLOGICAL DIVERSITY). The term "extinction" can also apply to the process by which a type of ECOSYSTEM changes itself out of existence, as a LAKE eventually "dies" and becomes a swamp or bog. (See endangered species; biological diversity.)

***Exxon Valdez* oil spill,** the worst oil spill in American history. On March 24, 1989, at four minutes past midnight, the supertanker *Exxon Valdez* grounded on Bligh Reef, 25 miles off Valdez, Alaska, terminus for the Alyeska Pipeline; it quickly spilled over 11 million gallons (approximately 37,000 tons) of OIL into Prince William Sound.

Although the oil industry supposedly had emergency plans for such an event, and had previously promised that any spill would be contained within five hours, Exxon's initial response was totally ineffective, apart from pumping the remaining million barrels of oil into other vessels for removal. In the first two days, when the weather was relatively calm, little was done to attempt to contain the oil slick or to treat it chemically. On the third day, 70-mile-per-hour winds broke apart those containment booms that had been put out and whipped the oil slick out of control; by March 28th, Alaskan officials were asserting that they had lost the opportunity to skim oil from the surface. In the end only about 6,000 barrels (less than 2.5 percent) were recovered.

By March 29th, in desperation, Alaskan officials and local citizens took over the cleanup effort, with Exxon footing the bill. Using containment booms, they were able to save some vital salmon hatcheries, but the slick eventually extended over 50 miles and reached as far as KATMAI NATIONAL PARK, 150 miles away from the crash site, contaminating hundreds of miles of Alaskan shoreline, many of them prime wildlife breeding grounds. By September 15, when large-scale cleanup efforts were halted for the winter, Exxon claimed that 1,100 miles of affected shoreline were clean. But Alaskan officials sharply protested the claim, noting that even many areas claimed as being washed or chemically treated were hardly "clean," but often had surface oil sludge, some from reoiling as remaining oil slicks washed ashore, and deeper deposits of oil that had soaked into the ground. The ENVIRONMENTAL PROTECTION AGENCY and U.S. Coast Guard, which were monitoring, though not controlling, cleanup efforts, gave assurances that either Exxon would complete the cleanup or the government would do so, presenting the bill to Exxon. As a practical matter, however, it soon became clear that nothing approaching a full cleanup could possibly be achieved.

The short-term damage to the environment and to human lives was massive, disrupting local FISHING communities and killing at least 50,000 birds (perhaps 10 percent of the area's bird population), uncounted numbers of fish, and hundreds of other animals, including otters and seals (see SEALS AND SEA LIONS); the long-term damage is incalculable. Meanwhile, only four days after the spill, oil tankers once again began to ship out of Valdez, with no assurance that the same thing could not happen again.

On February 27, 1990, a federal grand jury indicted Exxon and its shipping company on five criminal counts, while on March 22, 1990, a jury convicted *Exxon Valdez* captain Joseph Hazelwood on one misdemeanor count, acquitting him of other felony and misdemeanor charges stemming from the accident. On March 13, 1991, Exxon, the U.S. government, and the state of Alaska settled all federal and state criminal and civil cases, with Exxon pleading guilty to four misdemeanor counts and paying $100 million in criminal fines, and from $900 million to $1 billion more in tax-deductible environmental damage payments spread over the next 10 years. But many environmentalists sharply criticized the settlement, calling it inadequate, and in April the federal courts rejected the criminal plea settlement, effectively reopening the case. In May, the entire settlement collapsed, with Exxon and the state of Alaska withdrawing from the previous agreement. Over 300 civil suits against Exxon also remained open.

In April 1991 a comprehensive NATIONAL OCEANIC AND ATMOSPHERIC ADMINISTRATION study reported that the wildlife and other environmental damage caused by the oil spill was even more massive than had previously been reported, and that the pressurized hot sea water cleaning of the oil-polluted beaches had probably been more destructive than the oil spill itself. By the spring of 1992, it was clear that environmental damage was even worse than had earlier been reported.

### For more information and action:

- **CENTER FOR MARINE CONSERVATION (CMC),** (202-429-5609). Publishes *The Exxon Valdez Oil Spill: A Management Analysis*.
- **GREENPEACE** (202-462-1177).
- **NATIONAL WILDLIFE FEDERATION (NWF),** (202-797-6800 or 800-245-5484). Publishes Fact Sheet *Exxon Valdez Oil Spill and Wildlife*.
- **SIERRA CLUB,** (415-776-2211 or 202-547-1141; legislative hotline, 202-547-5550). Publishes *In the Wake of the Exxon Valdez: The Devastating Impact of the Alaska Oil Spill*.

### Other references:

*Out of the Channel: The Exxon Valdez Oil Spill in Prince William Sound*. John Keeble. HarperCollins, 1991. *Exxon Valdez Oil Spill*. Sue Hamilton. Abdo & Daughters, 1990.

# F

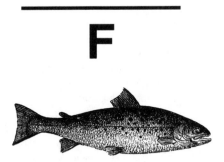

**factory farming,** the practice of raising animals for meat, dairy, and other products in an intensely overcrowded confinement. In traditional ranching and dairy farming, animals are able to move about freely in open yards or fields with only natural shelter—conditions described as *free-range* or *extensive*—or housed with some enclosures in *semi-intensive* conditions. But in recent years, livestock have been raised in increasingly *intensive* conditions, in ever smaller spaces. Animals in modern factory farms are raised in *total confinement*; they are often shackled or penned into tiny spaces—such as feedlot corrals or barns—for the whole of their lives, with no opportunity to escape or change their conditions, often unable to even change their position.

On factory farms, animals are totally dependent on humans for all the necessities of life. Food and water are often provided in assembly-line fashion; heat, ventilation, and sprinklers for cooling or firefighting are externally controlled; and excrement is flushed away or allowed to drop through the bottom of cages or slatted floors into pits and removed wholesale. In addition, animals are often "altered," so that they will not be able to injure themselves and others, as often happens in stressful confinement, with chronic boredom and understimulation. Young chicks, for example, are often "debeaked" with a searing-hot knife; chickens have combs and wattles removed; cattle have their horns removed; bulls are castrated; pigs have their teeth removed; and the like, often without any anesthesia.

Such conditions breed pain, suffering, and disease. The health of animals is readily affected by deficiencies or imbalances in diets; a breakdown in environmental controls; or contaminated food or water, as when bacteria or viruses readily sweep through a livestock shed. Partly to counteract disease and also to promote growth, animals on factory farms are often fed antibiotics and other substances, which often accumulate in the animals and are passed on to humans in meat and dairy products. Considerable concern has also focused on the conditions of transport and slaughter of factory-raised animals, including overcrowding, inadequate ventilation and heat control, lack of food and water, rough handling (as with shock devices, whips, and prods), and painful slaughter.

The practice of factory farming has risen only in recent decades, the main reason for its spread being that farmers can raise hundreds and even thousands of animals year round in huge buildings with little or no help and without large amounts of land, producing steadier incomes. Ironically, farmers themselves seem to be at risk from factory farming, from dangerous indoor AIR POLLUTION. Potentially toxic gases such as ammonia, CARBON DIOXIDE, CARBON MONOXIDE, METHANE, and hydrogen sulfide collect in the confined spaces, along with animal dander and particles of feed and dry manure. Farmers in factory-type settings have been found to have a high incidence of respiratory ailments, ranging from coughs to lung scarring to pneumonia, sometimes called *organic toxic dust syndrome*. In the 1980s, 19 farmers in the United States even died from inhaling concentrations of hydrogen sulfide (as toxic as gases used in prison executions), produced from decomposing hog waste, which collects in poorly ventilated sheds. In many cases, farmers wear filtering masks and some buildings have sophisticated ventilation systems, including walls that can be partly opened during good weather. But the animals remain confined and with no protection from the POLLUTION, from which they suffer as well; lung-scarring and pneumonia have been found among slaughtered factory-raised pigs, for example.

The conditions of factory farming have caused widespread protest and concern, bringing many people into the ANIMAL RIGHTS MOVEMENT, often seeking to pass new laws

(such as amendments to the ANIMAL WELFARE ACT) to protect animals from such treatment and to enforce the laws on the books, as well as directly pressuring retail organizations that buy their animal products from factory farms. Knowledge of factory farming practices, both in the treatment of the animals and the use of drugs, have also led many people to seek out suppliers of free-range meat and poultry or to turn to VEGETARIANISM.

**For more information and action:**

- **Animal Protection Institute (API),** (916-731-5521). Publishes "Factory Farming." (See ANIMAL RIGHTS AND WELFARE INFORMATION AND ACTION GUIDE on page 361.)
- **Humane Society of the United States (HSUS),** (202-452-1100). Publishes fact sheets on factory farming, farm animal abuses during transportation, and farm animal abuses at public stockyards, and reports such as *Factory Farming*. (See ANIMAL RIGHTS AND WELFARE INFORMATION AND ACTION GUIDE on page 361.)

*Fail Safe,* a 1964 fiction film, directed by Sidney Lumet, and starring Henry Fonda as the American president facing nuclear war, in a cast that included Walter Matthau, Larry Hagman, Dan O'Herlihy, Fritz Weaver, Sorrell Brooke, Frank Overton, and Edward Binns. At the time, with the Cuban missile crisis and the John F. Kennedy assassination in the very recent past and the war in Vietnam beginning to heat up, the film was a powerful and frightening portrayal of how humanity-destroying nuclear war might come.

**falcon, peregrine,** a bird of prey that ranges throughout the world, as do many other falcon species. The *American peregrine falcon* summers in North America as far north as central Alaska and winters in South America. It was a greatly ENDANGERED SPECIES by the late 1960s, and was very nearly extinct in eastern North America by the late 1960s, due to the poisoning of the FOOD CHAIN by DDT and other PESTICIDES. From the early 1950s, as DDT concentrations built up in the food chain, it caused calcium deficiencies to thin the eggshells of falcons and many other species, all but destroying their ability to reproduce. After the 1972 ban on DDT by the ENVIRONMENTAL PROTECTION AGENCY, the amount of DDT in the food chain began to diminish, and the ability to reproduce gradually began to return, although many other toxic hazards continued to threaten the falcons. In eastern North America a strong captive breeding and release into the wild program, much of it generated by the Peregrine Fund, a private organization, is helping to restore the peregrine falcon population.

The *Eurasian peregrine* is also listed as an endangered

species by the FISH AND WILDLIFE SERVICE, while the *Arctic peregrine* and the *peregrine* worldwide are listed as threatened species.

**For more information and action:**

- **WILDLIFE INFORMATION CENTER** (215-434-1637). Publishes *Peregrine Falcon.*
- **NATIONAL WILDLIFE FEDERATION (NWF),** (202-797-6800 or 800-245-5484).

(See ENDANGERED SPECIES; also ENDANGERED AND THREATENED WILDLIFE AND PLANTS on page 372.)

**fallout,** solid matter caught in a nuclear explosion, as from an atomic or hydrogen bomb, a nuclear reactor, or natural sources, crushed into highly radioactive dust, and thrown up into the atmosphere. Some fallout drops to the ground quickly; but some drifts in wind currents for hundreds and even thousands of miles. Fallout particles such as STRONTIUM 90, potassium 40, carbon 14, plutonium 239 and IODINE 131 lose their radioactivity slowly over time, but some may remain radioactive for many years, like CESIUM 137, which has a half-life of 33 years, meaning that it takes over three decades to lose half of its radioactivity. Such particles concentrate in the environment, and through the process of BIOACCUMULATION become especially damaging to animals at the ends of FOOD CHAINS, such as fish and CARNIVOROUS mammals and birds. Some tend to accumulate in particular parts of the body, where they remain, continuing to emit RADIATION into the body. Iodine 131 concentrates in the thyroid gland, uranium in the kidneys, and many others, including strontium 90 and cesium 137, in the bones, partly because they are chemically similar to the bone-making substances, calcium and potassium, respectively.

Radioactive fallout has already taken thousands and probably tens of thousands of lives; fallout from the NEVADA TEST SITE explosions of the 1950s contaminated areas hundreds of miles away, as did fallout from the BIKINI hydrogen bomb tests, the British bomb tests at the Australian MARALINGA test range, and the Soviet and Chinese Siberian and Central Asian tests. The 1963 Soviet-American-British Nuclear Test Ban Treaty banned atmospheric, underwater, or outer space testing for those three nations, but fallout from the air and water tests of other nations and nuclear accidents continued to be a danger. An enormous amount of highly radioactive fallout resulted from the 1986 CHERNOBYL nuclear accident, with many areas in the eastern Soviet Union and as far away as Scandinavia and Scotland still adversely affected five years

later. (See also RADIATION;) also NUCLEAR ISSUES INFORMATION AND ACTION GUIDE on page 215.)

**farmland,** an alternative name for CROPLAND.

**famine and food insecurity,** actual shortage of food or uncertainty as to its availability in the necessary types and amounts when and where needed. Ever since the beginnings of agriculture, humans have been faced with the possibility of crop failures, and consequent inability to provide a population with adequate nutrition. But in the 20th century, rapidly rising population has meant both larger numbers of hungry people and also increasing pressure on the land. As people find themselves unable to let land lie fallow occasionally to regenerate after use as CROPLANDS and pasture for livestock, and as they also move into already marginal lands, they trigger gradual ENVIRONMENTAL DEGRADATION—through such processes as OVERGRAZING, DEFORESTATION, DESERTIFICATION, and SALINIZATION—and further reduce the land's CARRYING CAPACITY. The result is a downward spiral, in which they are less and less able to provide for their food needs, and do more and more damage to the environment in the process of trying to do so.

Recognizing that, with rapidly rising population, famine and food insecurity were major world problems, various scientists in the mid–20th century turned to BIOTECHNOLOGY to increase the amount of food that farmers could produce, as through use of HIGH-YIELDING VARIETIES. The resulting GREEN REVOLUTION was highly successful in that it allowed enough food to be produced to feed the world's population as it grew. That famine and food insecurity still existed, however, made it clear that the problems were political and social, not simply agricultural, and that any solution to the problem would have to involve ways to ensure that food reached the poor and starving people who needed it. More than that, many programs involving biotechnology and DEVELOPMENT did not take into account the environmental effects of the projects, such as use of PESTICIDES or the building of DAMS. In recent years, some international development agencies, such as the WORLD BANK, have been focusing less on massive works projects and more on smaller, more environmentally conscious projects (see SUSTAINABLE AGRICULTURE)—though many environmentalists charge that the changes are too small and come too late. On a very practical level, many projects also focus on ways to reduce massive post-harvest losses, due to pests and spoilage.

But beyond the obvious centers of famine internationally, many environmentalists are also concerned about the clear possibility that, as population keeps rising, it will outrun the earth's ability to provide food enough for all.

For many, that is a call for a rethinking of diet, such as the various forms of VEGETARIANISM, to make better use of the food energy produced by the earth.

**For more information and action:**

- APPROPRIATE TECHNOLOGY TRANSFER FOR RURAL AREAS (ATTRA), (501-442-9824 or 800-346-9140).
- CONSULTATIVE GROUP IN INTERNATIONAL AGRICULTURAL RESEARCH (CGIAR OR CG), (202-473-8951). Sponsors the *International Food Policy Research Institute (IFPRI)*. Publishes *An Act of Faith: Research Helps Feed the Hungry* (1989).
- INSTITUTE FOR FOOD AND DEVELOPMENT POLICY (IFDP), popularly called *Food First*, (415-864-8555). Publishes *Food First News, Hunger Myths and Facts, Food First Curriculum, Exploding the Hunger Myth: A High School Curriculum, Food First: Beyond the Myth of Scarcity, Myths of African Hunger*, and audiovisual materials.
- MORRISON INSTITUTE FOR POPULATION AND RESOURCE STUDIES (415-723-7518). Publishes policy papers *How the Rich Can Save the Poor and Themselves, Environmental Ethics: Converging Views on a Small Planet*, and *Global Change and Carrying Capacity: Implications for Life on Earth*.
- WINROCK INTERNATIONAL INSTITUTE FOR AGRICULTURAL DEVELOPMENT, (501-727-5435 or 703-525-9430). Publishes *Food, Hunger, and Agricultural Issues* (Deborah Clubb and Polly C. Ligon, ed., 1989).
- WORLD BANK, (202-477-1234). Publishes *Poverty and Hunger: Issues and Options for Food Security in Developing Countries, Food Policy: Integrating Supply, Distribution, and Consumption. Food Policy Analysis, Household Food Security and the Role of Women, Malnutrition: What Can Be Done? Lessons From the World Bank Experience*, and *Malnutrition and Poverty Magnitude and Policy Options*.
- ZERO POPULATION GROWTH (ZPG), (202-332-2200). Publishes *World Hunger*. (See POPULATION INFORMATION AND ACTION GUIDE on page 248.)

**Other references:**

*Shattering: Food, Politics, and the Loss of Genetic Diversity*. Cary Fowler and Pat Mooney. University of Arizona Press, 1990. *Completing the Food Chain: Strategies for Combating Hunger and Malnutrition*. Paula M. Hirschoff and Neil G. Kitler, eds. Smithsonian, 1989. *World Agriculture: Toward 2000*. Nikos Alexandratos. Belhaven Press (London, U.K.), 1988.
(See also GREEN REVOLUTION; BIOTECHNOLOGY: DEVELOPMENT; SUSTAINABLE AGRICULTURE; VEGETARIANISM.)

**Farrakha Barrage,** a huge and controversial DAM project on the GANGES RIVER.

**Federal Hazardous Substances Act,** a U.S. federal law passed in 1960 which established requirements for labeling consumer products containing hazardous substances. Front labels of such products must include a warning and describe the hazard, telling how to avoid the hazard and use the product safely; the manufacturer is responsible for the accuracy of the information, and is subject to criminal penalties for false information. However, many environmentalists warn that labeling rules are vague, making safe use and first aid instructions inadequate, so many labels are misleading and dangerous. Manufacturers are also not required to include disposal instructions. Unless covered otherwise under the FOOD AND DRUG ADMINISTRATION (FDA) or ENVIRONMENTAL PROTECTION AGENCY (EPA), products come under the CONSUMER PRODUCTS SAFETY COMMISSION (CPSC). (See TOXIC CHEMICALS; HAZARDOUS WASTE.)

**Federal Insecticide, Fungicide, and Rodenticide Act (FIFRA),** a U.S. federal law enacted in 1947 that governs PESTICIDES, administered at first by the DEPARTMENT OF AGRICULTURE (DOA) but since 1970 by the ENVIRONMENTAL PROTECTION AGENCY (EPA), requiring that each pesticide be approved by the EPA for specific uses, and given a unique registration number. Using pesticides in ways and for purposes not consistent with the registration and product label is unlawful.

Originally aimed at protecting consumers from fraudulent pesticide products, FIFRA was in 1972 amended to focus more on monitoring health and environmental consequences of the pesticides. The manufacturer files a registration application for any new pesticide, including results of tests on possible risk of cancer, birth defects, and other unwanted adverse effects to humans and wildlife. Under the FIFRA registration process, the EPA is charged with weighing possible risks against the benefits of use; it can restrict some pesticides to use in specific ways and places by certified professionals, and can remove from the marketplace those pesticides deemed too dangerous for any use, such as DDT and several other CHLORINATED HYDROCARBONS. Unregistered new pesticides may be used in certain emergency situations by state or federal agencies.

EPA's authority covers over 50,000 pesticides, many introduced before the 1972 amendments, which require that existing pesticides—those already on the market before 1972—be reevaluated and reregistered. The result of these Final Registration Standards and Tolerance Reassessments are specifications of appropriate restrictions, warnings, or changes in formulation for all existing and future products containing the ACTIVE INGREDIENT involved (see TOLERANCE LEVEL). If data indicates a possible safety problem, the EPA may undertake a *special review*, an intensive emergency assessment of the pesticide's risks and benefits, after which the EPA may either continue current use, restrict some or all uses, or permanently ban use of the pesticide.

If the EPA cancels a pesticide's registration, manufacturers and users can appeal a decision, with the pesticide continuing to be marketed during the appeal process, sometimes two or more years. In an enormous loophole, however, FIFRA allows U.S. manufacturers to export banned, restricted, or even unregistered pesticides abroad, requiring only that the importing countries be informed of the substances' status; many such pesticides return to the U.S. on imported food, completing what is called the CIRCLE OF POISON.

FIFRA also directs the EPA to work with the Department of Agriculture "to develop and improve the safe use and effectiveness of chemical, biological, and alternative methods to combat and control pests that reduce the quality and economical production and distribution of agricultural products." Critics charge that the agency has not sufficiently emphasized alternative approaches, such as BIOLOGICAL CONTROL and INTEGRATED PEST MANAGEMENT (IPM), and Best Management Practices to minimize risk of pesticide use. Environmentalists are also concerned that the process of registering (or re-registering) all pesticides is going too slowly; and that the setting of tolerance levels does not take into account increased susceptibility among children and pregnant women, and the elderly.

Along with the TOXIC SUBSTANCES CONTROL ACT, FIFRA also gives EPA responsibility for regulating products of BIOTECHNOLOGY. (See PESTICIDES.)

**Fernald nuclear plant,** see NUCLEAR WEAPONS ESTABLISHMENT, U.S.

**ferret, black-foot,** a Great Plains-dwelling North American weasel, which historically lived largely on prairie dogs, and once ranged from western Canada to the U.S. Southwest. As the prairie dog population diminished, so did that of the ferrets. The FISH AND WILDLIFE SERVICE attempted to transfer some of the ferrets to wildlife preserves that still had substantial prairie dog populations, but the effort failed, and the ferrets became extinct in the wild. They were almost extinct in captivity, as well, until the captive ferret breeding program at Wyoming's Sybille Wildlife Research Institute began to take hold in the late 1980s, with results that seemed to make it possible to look forward to introduction of ferrets into the wild again in the early 1990s.

**For more information and action:**

- **ELSA WILD ANIMAL APPEAL (EWAA),** (818-761-8387). Publishes *North American Predators*.
- **WILDLIFE PRESERVATION TRUST INTERNATIONAL (WPTI),** (215-222-3636). Publishes *Conservation and Biology of the Black-footed Ferret* (Tim Clark) and *Black-footed Ferrets* (Denise Casey).

(See also ENDANGERED SPECIES; also ENDANGERED AND THREATENED WILDLIFE AND PLANTS on page 372.)

**Fish and Wildlife Service (FWS)** (Department of the Interior, Washington, DC 20240; 202-208-4717; John F. Turner, Director; publications unit: Room 130, Arlington Square, 1849 C Street, NW Washington, DC 20240; 703-358-2156; for publications, 703-358-1711; Federal Wildlife Reference Service, 5430 Grosvenor Lane, Suite 110, Bethesda, MD 20814; 301-492-6403 or 800-582-3421), the key U.S. federal agency involved in efforts to preserve ENDANGERED SPECIES, as well as other threatened animals, fish, and birds. It acts under a variety of federal laws, including the Migratory Bird Treaty Act, the MARINE MAMMAL PROTECTION ACT, the Lacey Act, and Endangered Species Act, under which it maintains a list of ENDANGERED AND THREATENED WILDLIFE AND PLANTS (see page 372), as well as coordinating U.S. actions under various international conventions on wildlife conservation.

The Service coordinates its activities with state governments; provides technical assistance at home and abroad; and is a prime source of information about fish and wildlife resources, supplying numerous materials for the public and also for scientific professionals, notably through *Federal Wildlife Reference Service (FWRS)*. The FWRS searches databases; provides copies of technical reports, the Fish and Wildlife Thesaurus (listing index terms used in the FWRS database), and indexes of fish and wildlife research from the states; publishes a quarterly newsletter; and refers researchers to additional resources, as necessary. The Fish and Wildlife Service also conducts the *National Wetlands Inventory*, and publishes from it the *National Wetlands Trends Analysis, Wetlands of the United States: Current Status and Recent Trends*, and numerous wetland maps (maps can be purchased by calling 800-USA-MAPS).

**fishery conservation zone,** see EXCLUSIVE ECONOMIC ZONES (EEZs).

**fishing,** the catching and generally killing of fish, shellfish, and other aquatic organisms from the world's OCEANS, RIVERS, LAKES, and other bodies of water, for food, sport, or various commercial purposes. Fishing has been a vital activity throughout human history, supplying an important and long thought inexhaustible supply of protein. Even today it provides the livelihood for millions of people, and fish are estimated to supply 20-25 percent of the world's protein supply (with about one-tenth of that from fish cultivation, or AQUACULTURE).

However, many aspects of modern life have adversely affected fishing. Modern technology culminating in modern "factory ships," plus the development of worldwide commercial markets and rapidly rising world POPULATION, all have combined to create the conditions under which many of the world's prime fishing areas have been overfished, to the point where the fish populations have collapsed, and some SPECIES have been brought near to EXTINCTION. The conversion of coastal WETLANDS, such as MANGROVES, to residential or commercial use has had the unconsidered effect of destroying the breeding areas of many aquatic organisms. Inland, fish stocks have also been damaged by DAMS and other obstructions along streams and rivers, as by destroying their HABITAT or blocking access to breeding pools. In all areas touched by human activities, fish have been damaged by WATER POLLUTION, with some areas becoming almost totally devoid of marine life. In addition, CLIMATE CHANGE, whether GLOBAL WARMING or GLOBAL COOLING, may be increasingly damaging to the world's fish stocks.

The severity of the problems has prompted worldwide efforts to halt pollution, loss of vital habitat, and overfishing. Numerous national and international groups have hammered out ENVIRONMENTAL LAWS to try to limit both the amount of fishing in an area and other types of damage to marine habitat. In local areas, too, groups have formed to try to reclaim areas, such as CHESAPEAKE BAY, the MEDITERRANEAN SEA, or the GREAT LAKES.

Most environmentalists accept fishing as a natural and normal human activity, both for food supply and as an occupation. However, many have strongly protested the wanton destruction of other species in the process, most notably the "incidental killing" of DOLPHINS and PORPOISES in the course of fishing for tuna with DRIFTNETS. A relatively small group of people believe that no animals, including fish, should be killed and used by humans (see VEGETARIANISM). Some people in the environmental movement also are opposed to fishing for sport, rather than for food or employment (see ANIMAL RIGHTS MOVEMENT).

**For more information and action:**

- **AMERICAN FISHERIES SOCIETY (AFS),** (301-897-8616) Publishes *Directory of North American Fisheries and Aquatic Scientists*; five journals: *Transactions of the American Fisheries Society*, *The Progressive Fish-Culturist*, *North American Journal of Fisheries Manage-*

*ment*, *Fisheries: A Bulletin of the American Fisheries Society*, and *Journal of Aquatic Animal Health*; a directory; numerous textbooks; manuals; and conference proceedings.

- **CONSULTATIVE GROUP ON INTERNATIONAL AGRICULTURAL RESEARCH (CGIAR or CG),** (202-473-8951), Works closely with the *International Center for Living Aquatic Resources Management (ICLARM)*.
- **ENVIRONMENTAL DEFENSE FUND (EDF),** (212-505-2100).
- **FISH AND WILDLIFE SERVICE (FWS),** (202-208-4717; *Federal Wildlife Reference Service*, 301-492-6403 or 800-582-3421). Publishes numerous materials.
- **NATIONAL COALITION FOR MARINE CONSERVATION (NCMC),** (912-234-8062). Publishes the periodicals *Marine Bulletin*, *Currents*, and *Ocean View*, and a series of Marine Recreational Fisheries books.
- **INTERNATIONAL COUNCIL FOR THE EXPLORATION OF THE SEA OR CONSEIL INTERNATIONAL POUR L'EXPLORATION DE LA MER (ICES or CIEM),** (Copenhagen, K, Denmark: 33 15 42 25). Maintains an international fisheries data bank; publishes numerous scientific reports and papers.
- **IZAAK WALTON LEAGUE OF AMERICA,** (703-528-1818).
- **NATIONAL OCEANIC AND ATMOSPHERIC ADMINISTRATION (NOAA),** (301-443-8910 or 202-377-8090). Publishes *Fisheries of the United States*.
- **TROUT UNLIMITED,** (703-281-1100). Publishes the magazine *Trout* and newsletter *Action Line*.

(See also WHALES; HUNTING; ENDANGERED SPECIES; COASTS; WATER POLLUTION.)

**Food and Drug Administration (FDA)** (5600 Fishers Lane, Rockville, MD 20857; 301-443-1544; Public Affairs 301-443-3170; David Kessler, Commissioner), a U.S. federal regulatory agency founded in 1927 as the Food, Drug, and Insecticide Administration, since 1968 as part of the Public Health Service; one of the nation's oldest consumer protection agencies, charged with enforcing the Federal Food, Drug, and Cosmetic Act and several related public health laws, working through over 1000 investigators and inspectors, and more than twice as many laboratory scientists. The FDA is charged with seeing that products are "made right and labeled truthfully," in accordance with the appropriate laws; where laws are violated, the FDA seeks voluntary correction or recall, but if that fails can sue in court to stop sales of the product and to have existing stocks seized and destroyed, sometimes with criminal penalties applied to manufacturers and distributors. Unacceptable foreign goods may be detained at the port of entry.

The FDA is responsible for assessing risks to public health in areas such as foods, drugs, medical devices, the blood supply, cosmetics, and biologicals, which are medications made from living organisms and their products, such as insulin and vaccines. The FDA tests food samples for contaminants, such as PESTICIDE residues, in unacceptable amounts; sets labeling standards for foods; and also monitors public health effects of drugs given to animals raised for food. The FDA does not itself research drugs, but (in a practice drawing increasing criticism) evaluates research done by manufacturers, to determine if new drugs do what they are supposed to do, without causing side effects of sufficient severity to outweigh its benefits.

Since 1971 the FDA has included the *Bureau of Radiological Health*, which was formed to protect "against unnecessary human exposure to radiation from electronic products in the home, industry, and the healing arts." The FDA also operates the National Center for Toxicological Research, which investigates the biological effects of widely used chemicals, and the Engineering and Analytical Center, which tests medical devices, radiation-emitting products, and radioactive drugs. In addition, the FDA must also review and approve (or reject) chemicals used as dyes used in foods, drugs, or cosmetics, and has the power to remove those considered unsafe. It also gathers and analyzes reports on various substances and devices previously approved, and if adverse effects are sufficiently widespread or severe, may withdraw products from the market.

The FDA is one of several federal organizations overseeing the safety of BIOTECHNOLOGY. As part of its public health education function, the FDA publishes various materials, including the general magazine *FDA Consumer* and *FDA Drug Bulletin* for health professionals.

**food chain,** the sequence of stages by which food is used by the organisms in an ECOSYSTEM. The food itself is created from nonliving (*inorganic*) elements by plants using the sun's energy in the process of PHOTOSYNTHESIS. These food-creators, called *autotrophs*, occupy the lowest level in the food chain; they are generally green plants on land and PLANKTON in the sea. They are eaten by plant-eating animals, or *herbivores*, who come next in the chain. In a *predator chain*, the most common type, the next level is occupied by meat-eating animals, first the *primary carnivores*, then the *secondary carnivores*, such as humans. A simple food chain would be grasses, eaten by field mice, eaten by foxes. The foxes later die and are decomposed, with nutrients being returned to the soil, completing the BIOGEOCHEMICAL CYCLES that unite the beings in an ecosystem. Two other kinds of food chain are the *parasite*

*chain*, in which a series of parasites live on a host organism, and the *saprophytic chain*, in which *decomposers* such as microorganisms break down dead tissues, the end result being the return of inorganic elements to the soil, air, or water, so that they may once again be used in food creation.

In one sense the food chain might better be called a pyramid, for the lowest levels are occupied by large numbers of small organisms, while at each higher level the number of organisms gets smaller and their size gets larger. And, because much energy is lost at each stage, more food is required to satisfy the needs of organisms at each level. As a result, food chains rarely extend beyond more than four or five stages (called *trophic levels*). The shorter the food chain, the more energy is available to consumers. For people concerned with conserving natural resources, that is a strong argument for VEGETARIANISM, since far more nutritional energy is available if humans eat grains than if they eat animals who ate grains. In areas of FAMINE AND FOOD INSECURITY, the shortage of food quite naturally leads to a largely grain-based diet.

The pyramidal nature of the food chain has other effects as well. Many unwanted substances, such as HEAVY METALS, PESTICIDES, and other TOXIC CHEMICALS, enter the food chain at the lowest levels, and become increasingly concentrated at each stage, magnifying the danger for those large animals at the end of the food chain, including birds of prey and humans (see BIOACCUMULATION).

In another sense, the food chain might better be called a food web, for it is less a linear set of steps than a complex, interconnecting set of exchanges. Animals occupy different levels, depending on where they are during their life cycles and on the conditions within the ecosystem, notably how much food is available. Like humans, many animals can be either herbivores or carnivores. And because of the close interrelationships between plants and animals in a food web, damage to any one can disturb or even destroy the others. For example, many observers are concerned that POLLUTION or overharvesting of KRILL off ANTARCTICA will mean loss of food supply for the many animals in the food web, such as seals (see SEALS AND SEA LIONS), squid, penguins, WHALES, other fish and seabirds, and a collapse of the food chain.

**Food First,** popular name for the INSTITUTE FOR FOOD AND DEVELOPMENT POLICY.

**Foreman, Dave** (1947–    ), a founder and leading member of the radical environmentalist movement EARTH FIRST!, whose advocacy of a wide range of actions in pursuit of environmentalist aims, some of them violent to the point of being life-threatening, began to draw a great deal of media attention in the late 1980s.

While still in college, Foreman was a conservative Young Americans for Freedom activist. He moved from there into environmental activism during the 1970s, at first as a WILDERNESS SOCIETY lobbyist, and then in 1978 as a founder of Earth First!, which openly advocated sabotage and other terrorist acts, for which the group adopted the term MONKEYWRENCHING, from Edward ABBEY's 1975 novel *The Monkey Wrench Gang*. The best known of their recommended acts of "ecotage" (environmental sabotage) is the driving of spikes into trees to make them useless for logging, which also has the effect of making such trees extremely dangerous to chain saw down. The group has been accused, but not convicted of many far more serious actions. Foreman's books include *Ecodefense: A Field Guide to Monkeywrenching* (1985) and *Confessions of an Eco-Warrior* (1991). In 1991, Foreman broke with Earth First!, reportedly over what he felt was an increasing emphasis on left-oriented political and social issues; he remained committed to radical action for conservation.

**forest,** an ECOSYSTEM dominated by trees, which with the soil, water, light, air, temperature, and topography (especially altitude) of the region, combine to form a dis-

tinctive home for animals and other plants; a type of BIOME or *major life zone*. Forest communities are not static, but develop over long periods of time. The precise course of development varies with the type of forest, but it succeeds in stages (see ECOLOGICAL SUCCESSION), with the biological community at each stage having different characteristics, until it reaches the final stable, or *climax*, community. A long-standing, fully mature forest—such as some areas in the Pacific Northwest that are hundreds or even thousands of years old—is sometimes called an *old-growth forest*. Several kinds of events, among them fire and OVERGRAZING, can prevent the succession from reaching its natural climax stage.

Several main types of forest exist:

- *coniferous forest,* land dominated by needle-leaved trees, generally evergreens such as pine and spruce. The most common type, called *taiga forest*, is found in high-altitude sub-Arctic regions, with long winters, six months of average maximum temperature under 32°F (0°C), a growing season of one to three months, and annual precipitation of 10–20 inches. Heavily logged from the mid-19th century, taiga forests are found only in the Northern Hemisphere, notably in much of Canada, parts of the United States, and a wide swath of northern Eurasia,

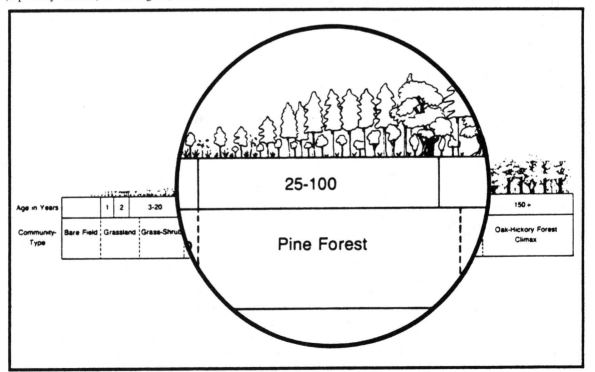

**Source:** *State of the Public Rangelands 1990.* Bureau of Land Management, Department of the Interior.

from Scandinavia to the Bering Sea. Coniferous forests are highly flammable, and large-scale destruction can easily result from human carelessness or natural causes. A different type of coniferous forest is found in the much more humid, temperate conditions of the Pacific Northwest coast, from northern California to Alaska. This type is dominated by spruce, cedar, hemlock, fir, and most notably the redwoods (*Sequoia*), massive trees that are a wonder of the world—and an enormous lure to loggers. In the United States alone, approximately 60,000 acres of old-growth coniferous forest are being cut down each year, especially in the Pacific Northwest and Alaska. Reforestation is possible, but the trees would need over 100 years or more of growth to reach maturity, with no assurance that the whole ecosystem could be revived, especially if the area is completed cleared, in what is called *clear-cutting.*

• *deciduous forest,* land dominated by broad-leaved trees that shed their leaves seasonally, notably beech, birch, aspen, oak, elm, maple, basswood, hickory, and chestnut. These forests are typical of the eastern United States, southeastern Canada, the British Isles, southern Scandinavia, and a broad swatch of land from northern Spain and the Netherlands east to the Caucasus, as well as parts of China, Japan, and Korea. Where regular fires or grazing block progress to the climax stage, the community may remain in earlier stages of succession, as in the "pine barrens" of the southeastern United States. In cooler temperate seaboard regions, as in the Southern Hemisphere in New Zealand and Chile, broad-leaved forests may be evergreen; these are highly susceptible to overgrazing, and may fail to recover from damage, turning instead into grassy turf.

• *tropical forest,* tree-covered areas in warmer regions of the world, where the rainfall is over 200 centimeters a year. The best known type of tropical forest is the continuously warm and humid *tropical rain forest* or *jungle,* such as those in South America, in the Amazon and Orinoco river basins (see AMAZON RAIN FOREST); Central Africa, especially around the Congo, Niger, and Zambezi river basins; MADAGASCAR; and the East Indies, as well as in parts of Central America, India, southeastern Australia, and southeast Asia. In these rain forests, the broad-leaved trees—notably ebony, mahogany, and teak—are green all year, with no seasonal breaks. Though coniferous and in temperate zones, the Pacific Northwest forests are a type of rain forest. Some tropical forests are marked by dry and rainy periods, with leaves falling seasonally; these are called *winter forests.* Tree-dominated communities may also snake their way into neighboring GRASSLANDS or SAVANNAS,

following RIVERS and streams; these are called *gallery forests.*

These three general types of forest—coniferous, deciduous, and tropical—differ considerably in complexity. At maturity, the coniferous is the simplest, with trees roughly of even height, little or no shrub layer, and ground plant and herbaceous layers close to the forest floor. The deciduous forest is more complex, with flourishing ground plant and herbaceous layers, the addition of a shrub layer, and trees of varying heights and shapes. By far the most complex is the rain forest, in which the trees rise considerably higher. Mature rain forests tend to sort themselves out into several horizontal layers, each with its own set of flora and fauna. The crowns of the tallest trees form the top layer, a canopy sometimes (as in the Pacific Northwest) 250 feet or more from the ground, which blocks sunlight and so hinders undergrowth, leaving the ground often relatively clear for walking, though dotted with occasional richly varied "islands" of herbaceous plants.

Tropical forests—especially the rain forests—hold over half of the known species of plants and animals, so they are the focus of widespread attempts to maintain BIOLOGICAL DIVERSITY, though they today make up only about 6 percent of the world's land. Researchers estimate that less than half of the world's tropical rain forests remain, with the amount now lost annually totaling more than the area of the Netherlands and Switzerland together—and with them perhaps 4,000–6,000 species a year (see ENDANGERED SPECIES) are lost forever. Ironically, some researchers estimate that harvesting natural products from the forest may be economically more profitable than cutting down the forests and converting them to CROPLANDS or rangelands, in both the short-term and the long-term—especially since the nutrient-poor land often supports these farming and ranching activities for only two or three years after clearing. This does not even take into account the attractions of rain forests for ECOTOURISM.

On the edges of the main types of forests exist transitional woodlands, sometimes called *forest ecotones.* Among these are *woodland* (*sclerophyllous woodlands*) regions dominated by dwarfed trees, often broad-leaved evergreens, such as oak in the Northern Hemisphere, especially around the Mediterranean, and eucalyptus in Australia. These are found where the climate is generally warm and dry, with winter rains. Closely related is *chaparral* or *thorn forest,* brushland with dwarfed evergreen trees and thickets of shrubs and thorny bushes. Regions of chaparral and woodland are found around the Mediterranean, in central and southeastern Mexico, and in the United States Southwest, especially southern California, where chaparral poses severe fire threats in the dry season. *Woodland* is also a more general term for land on which trees and shrubs are grown, including not just what is commonly called "forest," but also hedgerows, windbreaks, and tree plantations. Other common transition areas, often themselves under considerable threat, are savannas and MANGROVES.

Forests in general are enormously productive. The trees absorb sunlight, draw water and nutrients from the soil and CARBON DIOXIDE from the air, and through PHOTOSYNTHESIS (see BIOGEOCHEMICAL CYCLES) use them to produce and store organic matter, or BIOMASS. In the process they also stabilize the soil, inhibiting EROSION; prevent excess runoff of water (see WATER RESOURCES); and remove potentially destructive carbon dioxide from the air, in the process helping to lower the atmospheric temperature (see GLOBAL WARMING). Meanwhile, on the forest floor, layers of organic matter mix with the underlying mineral soil to form a natural humus, which worms, fungi, and various microorganisms work to decompose, releasing nutrients into the soil, while other flora and fauna take their part higher in the FOOD CHAIN.

The resulting diversity of life is under severe threat. Indirect threats include AIR POLLUTION, WATER POLLUTION, ACID RAIN, TOXIC CHEMICALS, and HAZARDOUS WASTE. More direct threats include overgrazing, stripping of the forest for FUELWOOD, clearing of land for cropland or rangeland, and indiscriminate logging, especially clearcutting, in which the forest is completely cut down, rather than having trees selectively culled from the still-thriving forest community.

Considerable concern has focused on the loss of the forests, and on ways to balance economic DEVELOPMENT, in both industrialized and developing countries, against the long-term survival of the forests and the unique homes they provide. Much environmentalist action has focused on halting or at least slowing logging in general and especially imports of tropical timbers; on developing commercial uses and markets for forest products other than timber; on reducing waste and incidental destruction in logging; and on boycotting imported cheap beef from cattle fed in pastures created from rain forests. Environmental priorities also include developing forest plantations in formerly cleared areas, to meet future timber needs, and blocking the conversion of forests to croplands and rangelands, especially in areas of special genetic diversity. In developing countries such conversion is often done with aid from multilateral development banks (MDBs) and to the detriment of INDIGENOUS PEOPLES in the region; some environmental groups are attempting DEBT-FOR-NATURE swaps to halt the conversion process. However, in some countries, espe-

cially those under extreme POPULATION pressure, such as Brazil, much of the land is being cleared by settlers seeking homesteads; when criticized by environmentalists, these modern-day pioneers point out that they are only seeking the better life found in America and other developed countries—which were once forest-covered.

And those who make their living from cutting down or MINING in the forests are threatened with loss of their livelihood, when forests are set aside untouched, and so need to be considered in overall programs regarding the forests. In the Pacific Northwest, for example, cutback of logging would pose a major economic hardship for loggers, and some groups have proposed help for displaced loggers as part of an overall solution. In general, the aim has been to foster sustainable DEVELOPMENT in forest areas, which would focus on planned, multipurpose commercial use of forest products without, in the process, destroying the forest. (See FORESTS INFORMATION AND ACTION GUIDE on page 369; also AMAZON RAIN FOREST; AGROFORESTY; BIOLOGICAL DIVERSITY; CHESTNUT, AMERICAN; ELM, AMERICAN; ENDANGERED SPECIES.)

**Forest Service (FS)** (P.O. Box 96090, Washington, DC 20013; 202-447-3957; F. Dale Robertson, Chief; Director, Public Affairs Office, 202-447-3760), the largest agency in the United States DEPARTMENT OF AGRICULTURE, overseeing management, protection, and use of national FORESTS, rangelands, and GRASSLANDS—almost two-thirds of all federally owned lands—working closely with state and local government as well as private owners in forest management and maintenance of wildlife resources. The agency is dedicated to "multiple-use management of these lands for sustained yields of renewable resources such as water, forage, wildlife, wood, and recreation," also carrying out forestry research and long-range planning, especially focusing on timber, watersheds, forage, wildlife HABITAT, and recreation.

The National Forest System (NFS) is made up of 156 National Forests, 19 National Grasslands, and 16 Land Utilization Projects, located in 44 states, Puerto Rico, and the U.S. Virgin Islands. Included in this are 191 million acres of National Forests, with some 86.5 million acres classified as commercial forests; 3.8 million acres of National Grasslands, on many of which grazing privileges are granted to private ranchers and farmers; 1.8 million acres of LAKES; 83,000 miles of forest streams; and WILDERNESS areas for over 32 million acres. Together these total less than 1/12 of the total area of the country, but they are home to approximately half of the nation's large game animals.

The Forest Service works with state fish and game departments to protect fish and wildlife habitats, especially those of ENDANGERED SPECIES, with projects such as developing spawning beds for fish, stabilizing stream channels, making potholes for waterfowl, erecting fencing, and developing new fishing lakes. It also works closely with the states on wildland fire management and forest pest management, and oversees considerable engineering activities, as in building and maintaining necessary structures, watersheds, water systems, WASTE DISPOSAL systems for recreational and administrative sites, and an extensive system of roads (over 343,000 miles) and trails (nearly 100,000 miles).

The Forest Service shares with the BUREAU OF LAND MANAGEMENT responsibility for protecting wild horses and burros on public rangelands, and with the Department of the Interior the regulation and management of MINING and energy activities on National Forest System lands, with special responsibility for surface operations, though strip mining is generally prohibited. The leasing of grazing, logging, mining, and other such rights is clearly authorized by law but is controversial nonetheless. Many business interests press for widening of commercial exploitation of such rights, citing the need to keep up with heavy public demand for energy, minerals, lumber, and other resources, and the importance of such activities for the economy. Many environmentalists, however, decry the damage done by these activities to the supposedly protected National Forest System, with special attention focused on the irretrievable loss of old-growth FORESTS of the Pacific Northwest, and the POLLUTION and other damage caused by heavy commercial, recreational, and other uses. Some organizations, such as EARTH FIRST!, use direct action (see MONKEYWRENCHING) to halt use of public forest lands forest Service employees counter that they are trying to hold the line against strong commercial and government pressure to open the forests still more.

**Fossey, Dian** (1932–85), U.S. primatologist, whose pioneering work with the endangered mountain GORILLAS of eastern central Africa focused international attention on conservation of the gorillas, and so contributed to the development of the worldwide late-20th-century movement to save ENDANGERED SPECIES. An occupational therapist from 1954–66, Fossey first visited Africa in 1963, and there met Louis and Mary Leakey, who encouraged her to pursue her study of the mountain gorilla. She began her long study in Zaire in 1967, and in September 1967 established the Karisoke Research Centre in Rwanda's Parc des Volcans, and spent much of the next 18 years there, with brief periods away for study and teaching in Britain and America. In 1978, she began her highly publicized fight against poachers, who were killing and kidnapping some of the small numbers of remaining gorillas in

the preserve, and also began her campaign to keep local cattleherders from grazing their herds in the park area. Her 1983 book *Gorillas in the Mist* was well received and widely distributed. She was murdered at Karisoke in 1985, probably by poachers. Her work at Karisoke was continued by the african wildlife foundation, which had developed the Mountain Gorilla Project in 1979. The Fund reversed Fossey's policy of barring tourists from Karisoke, and helped to secure Rwandan government support for the mountain gorilla conservation project by generating hard cash for that government. The Rwandan government took over and continued the project in 1990. (See also ENDANGERED SPECIES; also ENDANGERED AND THREATENED WILDLIFE AND PLANTS on page 372)

**fossil fuels,** a general term for fuels that were formed as decomposed plant matter became altered by chemical reactions, heat, and pressure under layers of soil and rock over millions of years. Extracted from reservoirs or "traps" under the ground, fossil fuels are made up primarily of HYDROCARBONS, molecules of hydrogen and carbon. Those that occur in solid form are called COAL; those in liquid form are OIL or petroleum; those in gaseous form are NATURAL GAS. Each type varies widely, depending on the amount and type of original plant matter; the amount of chemical and geological change that has been produced; and the amount and type of other substances it contains, such as sulfur and HEAVY METALS.

Fossil fuels from the basis of modern life in industrialized countries, worldwide providing about 88 percent of all energy purchased (as opposed to BIOMASS such as fuelwood or dung, which is gathered). These fuels, and especially oil, have become so dominant in the last two centuries because they are relatively accessible, efficient, clean, and portable; the oxygen needed to release their considerable chemical energy in combustion is ever present in the air; they are readily converted into forms easy for industrial and smaller-scale use; and they work efficiently in controlled combustion devices, such as automobile engines, furnaces, and turbines that produce electricity. In fact, they work so well that most such devices are tailored for use with fossil fuels; as a result, changing to alternative fuels (see BIOFUELS; SYNTHETIC FUELS) would be extremely difficult, because it would require replacement or modification (*retrofitting*) of those devices.

Unfortunately, fossil fuels are DECLINING RESOURCES, with estimated reserves of about 60, 120, and 1,500 years for oil, natural gas, and coal, respectively, at current rates of use; new technologies in production, transmission, use, and energy efficiency could double or even triple those estimates. More seriously, these fuels are major sources of POLLUTION, contributing to ACID RAIN, SMOG, AIR POL-

LUTION, and WATER POLLUTION in general, especially through releases of SULFUR DIOXIDE and nitrogen oxides (see NITROGEN DIOXIDE). Over half the sulfur dioxide and 30 percent of the nitrogen oxides are produced by the burning of coal alone, much of it in electricity-producing plants. Fossil fuels are also widely held responsible for accelerating the GREENHOUSE EFFECT and probably GLOBAL WARMING by releases of *greenhouse gases* such as CARBON DIOXIDE and METHANE.

In the long run, humans will have to switch to nonfossil fuels for their main energy sources. For a time, some thought that NUCLEAR ENERGY would provide the main alternative; many other alternatives are still being explored (see ENERGY RESOURCES). But until these are practical and economical possibilities, the main focus will be on reducing the impact of fossil fuels by the following methods:

- exploiting them more efficiently, as by creating from them cleaner fuels;
- using the cleanest forms of fossil fuels;
- removing substances such as sulfur before burning;
- reducing carbon dioxide emissions.

Some have suggested capturing the carbon dioxide before it is released into the air and storing it in underground reservoirs or injecting it deep into the ocean, though it is not clear how long it would stay there or what its long-term environmental impact would be. Others have suggested planting FORESTS to use and to absorb the carbon dioxide in the process of PHOTOSYNTHESIS, though to absorb all the carbon dioxide produced in the United States would require, by one estimate, planting a million square miles of new forests, covering roughly 25 percent of the land. The problems are considerable, since burning one ton of carbon produces over three-and-a-half tons of carbon dioxide.

### For more information and action:

- **NATURAL RESOURCES AND ENERGY DIVISION (NRED),** (212-963-6205).
- **RESOURCES FOR THE FUTURE (RFF),** (202-328-5000). (See also COAL; OIL; NATURAL GAS; CARBON DIOXIDE; GREENHOUSE EFFECT; GLOBAL WARMING; ACID RAIN; AIR POLLUTION.)

**Freshwater Foundation** (725 County Road 6, Wayzata, MN 55391; 612-449-0092; H. Martin Jessen, President), an international membership organization founded in 1968 to seek "protection of freshwater resources through educational programs, resource management, demonstration projects," and research. It seeks to educate the public and influence policy- and decision-makers, by providing a freshwater information and key personnel network, "to exchange available ideas, experts and information on freshwater problems and solutions," and sponsoring freshwater educational programs. The Foundation supports a *National Water Policy Project*, "to address the myriad of policies affecting our nation's freshwater resources"; the *Lake and Wetlands Project*; and the *Metro Area Wetlands Forum*, seeking to preserve and restore urban WETLANDS. It also has a "cooperative relationship" with the *Gray Freshwater Biological Institute*, originally established by the Foundation in 1968, but managed by the University of Minnesota since 1976. It publishes the periodicals *Freshwater Journal*, and various booklets and brochures.

**Friends of the Earth (FOE)** (218 D Street, SE, Washington, DC 20003; 202-544-2600; Michael S. Clark, Executive Director; International Headquarters, 3 Endsleigh Street, London WC1H ODD, England; 278-9686), a membership organization founded by David BROWER in 1970 to act as a global advocate for the earth and its resources, which in 1990 was strengthened by its merger with the *Environmental Policy Institute* and *Oceanic Society*. Following the slogan "the Earth needs all the friends it can get," Friends of the Earth is active in a wide variety of areas including "saving the ozone layer, ending tropical deforestation, fighting global warming, improving east-west relations, tackling the waste crisis, protecting the oceans, encouraging corporate accountability in the environment, ending nuclear weapons production, preventing groundwater and drinking water contamination, protecting coastal waters, preserving marine biodiversity, enforcing national coal policy, preventing chemical emergencies, supporting sustainable agriculture, challenging biotechnology's direction, understanding environmental problems in Central America, reforming international lending policies, and redirecting tax dollars to the environment." FOE publishes fact sheets on all of those issues, as well as the newsmagazine *Not Man Apart* and other periodicals, such as the *Atmospheric Ozone Newsletter, Community Plume Chemical Safety Newsletter*, and *Groundwater Newsletter*; flyers about FOE's activities; and other works, such as *The Strip Mining Handbook* (Mark Squillace, 1990), *Bottled Water: Sparkling Hype at a Premium Price* (Sandra Marquardt, 1989). Through Oceanic Society Expeditions, the environmental travel arm of the Oceanic Society, FOE also offered ecotours. (see ECOTOURISM INFORMATION AND ACTION GUIDE on page 366.)

**Friends of the River (FOR)** (Friends of the River Foundation, Building C, Fort Mason Center, San Francisco, CA 94123; 415-771-0400; David Bolling, Executive Director), a California-based organization founded in 1973, working ''to protect and restore rivers throughout the West and to shape new water policies which will provide a rational balance between development and preservation,'' its stated purpose being ''to conduct research, public education, and litigation on an agenda of river and water policy issues.'' Among FOR's current projects are the *100 Rivers Campaign*, seeking protection as ''Wild and Scenic'' for over 100 river and stream segments on public land in California; *Water Policy Reform*, to promote new policies focusing on better water management and alternatives to building more DAMS; the *Grand Canyon*, seeking to stop ''radically fluctuating water releases at GLEN CANYON Dam which are scouring away the heart of the river corridor inside the GRAND CANYON; *American River and Auburn Dam*, seeking to stop the proposed dam on the North and Middle Forks of California's American River, which would destroy the river canyons as tourist sites and wildlife habitats; *Hydromania and Watershed Protection*, seeking to halt logging on steep riverbank slopes and building of HYDROPOWER plants that ''dewater and destroy long sections of river.'' FOR oversees the *Friends of the River Fund*; holds an annual three-day River Conference; offers rafting trips and publishes various materials, including the bimonthly newsmagazine *Headwaters* and updates on pending river legislation and current programs.

**fuelwood,** trees and woody plants being used for energy, especially heating and cooking; a kind of BIOFUEL. (See also AGROFORESTRY; FORESTS.)

**fungicide,** a type of chemical compound used for killing fungus (see PESTICIDES).

# G

**Gaia,** the global ECOSYSTEM seen as a single living, creative system, the name being that of the Greek goddess of the earth. British atmospheric scientist James Lovelock and American microbiologist Lynn Margulis developed the theory that the earth is a living organism in the late 1960s, and the controversial idea was much discussed—and criticized—within the scientific community, then coming before the general public in Lovelock's 1979 book *Gaia: A New Look at Life on Earth*. The Gaia hypothesis is, as Lawrence Joseph put it, ''the first comprehensive scientific expression of the profoundly ancient belief that the planet Earth is a living creature.'' Basic to the idea of Gaia is the traditional ecological notion that the earth and the systems in and on it tend to reestablish equilibrium, no matter how much disturbed, a theory itself under attack in some quarters in recent years.

Supporters of the Gaia hypothesis believe that the proper study of the earth is not traditional geology and earth science, but *geophysiology*, the study of the earth as a ''superorganism'' that adjusts and regulates itself. They warn that, if their theory is true, some parts of the earth may be the equivalent of vital organs, notably key regions such as tropical rain FORESTS and OCEANS. Certainly some environmentalists have found it useful in practice to take a ''geophysiological'' view, in examining the interactions of vast ECOSYSTEMS in the earth. Many find the view attractive as a metaphor, but have difficulty with it as a scientific theory.

One key sticking point revolves around the question ''What is life?'' Detractors of the theory note that Gaia does not fit the usual definitions of life, including the ability to reproduce oneself. Supporters note that definitions of life are extremely tricky (and often skated over), as in cases of artificial intelligence. Lovelock himself, citing the lack of a clear distinction between living and nonliving matter on earth, notes that even a "living" redwood tree is 97 percent dead, and also suggests (perhaps partly with tongue in cheek) that perhaps Gaia has simply not reproduced *yet*. Lawrence Joseph summed up the basic question a little differently: "Lovelock, Margulis, and the others participating in the Gaia discussion are not trying so much to determine whether the Earth is alive as whether the planet is ultimately more subject to the generative forces of biology than the automatic processes of geology."

**For more information:**
*Gaia: The Growth of an Idea*. Lawrence E. Joseph. St. Martin's, 1990. *A Guide to Gaia: A Survey of the New Science of Our Living Earth*, by Michael Allaby. Penguin, 1989. *The Ages of Gaia: A Biography of Our Living Earth*. James Lovelock. Norton, 1988; Bantam, 1990.
(See also BIOSPHERE; BIOGEOCHEMICAL CYCLES.)

**Galapagos Islands,** a group of 13 islands and many smaller islets and rocks, in the Pacific Ocean 600 miles west of the South American coast. As the Archipelago of Colón, they are a territory of Ecuador. The islands are an unusual ECOSYSTEM, for many of their life forms, although descended from mainland forms, evolved on their own for many thousands of years, and are now separate species. The islands also occupy a notable place in human history; study of their uniquely developed lifeforms helped Charles Darwin, who visited the islands on the *H.M.S. Beagle* in 1835, to formulate his theory of evolution.

Since Darwin, humans have had great impact on the unique Galapagos ecosystem. The Giant Galapagos turtle (tortoise) has been hunted almost to EXTINCTION, and goats, pigs, and various other animals have replaced much of the earlier flora and fauna. Much now-illegal FISHING also continues to assault the marine life of the islands. At the same time, the islands have become a magnet for tourists (see ECOTOURISM), for their subtropical marine environment combines such mid-Pacific and Antarctic wildlife as seals (see SEALS AND SEA LIONS), frigatebirds, penguins, flamingos, and albatrosses. These delight tourists from all over the world, who arrive by the thousands throughout the year, by air and boat, their sheer numbers further attacking the fragile ecosystem they have come to admire and share. Their presence signals an enormous worldwide interest in saving earth's natural heritage—yet also signals one of the greatest problems to be faced by all such refuges in the century ahead.

**For more information:**
*World of Nature: Galapagos*. Smithmark, 1991. *Galapagos Islands*. Phyllis Root and Maxine McCormick. Macmillan, 1989. *Galapagos: Discovery on Darwin's Islands*. David W. Steadman and Steven Zousmer. Smithsonian, 1988.
(See ECOTOURISM.)

**Galveston Bay oil spill,** leakage of an estimated 500,000 gallons (approximately 1,700 tons) of heavy crude OIL into Galveston Bay, near Texas City, Texas, caused by the collision of two Apex Towing Company barges with the Greek tanker *Shinoussa* on July 28, 1990. Both barges leaked heavy crude oil into the bay after the collision, though leakage from the larger barge was mainly stopped by divers after it had sunk. The tanker was damaged, but did not leak oil through its double hull. The sinking and salvage work closed the Houston Ship Channel from July 29 to July 31. Some environmental damage resulted, though how much was difficult to determine, as cleanup crews were uncertain as to whether much of the spill had dissipated or sunk into the bay. An experimental and controversial use of genetically engineered oil-eating bacteria was part of the environmental cleanup of the bay area; the bacteria had also been used experimentally after the massive June *Mega Borg* spill off the same coast. (See OIL; BIOREMEDIATION.)

**Ganges River (Ganga),** the holiest river of the Hindus, running 1,600 miles from its origins in the Himalayas to the sea. It rises in the mountains of Nepal and of the Indian state of Uttar Pradesh, flows through the North Indian plain, and joins the Brahmaputra River in Bangladesh. The joined rivers then flow a further 200 miles into the Bay of Bengal. The river flows through one of the most densely populated areas on earth, the home of an estimated 325 million people, with over a score of major cities on the way. The delta of the joint rivers holds most of the population of Bangladesh, and as Himalayan mountainsides have been deforested sharply increased EROSION has contributed much to the recurrent BANGLADESH DISASTERS that have killed over one million people and made tens of millions homeless in the last several decades.

On the other hand, the highly controversial Indian dam at Farrakha Barrage, on the Indian side of the India-Bangladesh border, has since the early 1970s diverted Ganges water toward Calcutta, causing the Bangladesh government to complain that in the dry season saltwater from the Bay of Bengal invades freshwater wells in that country. Ganges water has also increasingly been used for irrigation and dammed for hydroelectric projects for much of its course in India, further reducing the flow of the river, though apparently not the enormous ultimate flow of rich topsoil-bearing sediment into the Bay of Bengal, which has been estimated at 3 billion tons annually, by far the largest such flow in the world.

The Ganges River basin has been intensively cultivated for many centuries. But in the 20th century, and particularly from mid-century, that cultivation has been accompanied by the use of chemical fertilizers, causing a new pollution problem as their often-toxic residue washes into the river. The enormous POPULATION growth of the area, and of its many cities, has also meant the deposit of tremendous amounts of sewage into the river, most of it entirely untreated. And the growth of modern industry along the river has meant the deposit of often-toxic industrial wastes into the river, as well. The net result is that the life of the Ganges—and of the hundreds of millions of people who depend on it in many ways—is severely threatened by an increasingly contaminated FOOD CHAIN and by unsanitary drinking water. From the mid-1980s, the Indian government has responded with a substantial Ganges clean-up program, but the underlying population, sewage treatment, and antipollution enforcement problems require a massive national response that has so far not been forthcoming. (See DAMS; RIVERS.)

**Gates of the Arctic National Park and Preserve,** an 8,500,000-acre (13,300-square-mile) portion of the Brooks Range in northern Alaska; abutting the preserve to the west is the 6,500,000 acre (10,100-square-mile) NOATAK NATIONAL PRESERVE. Both are international BIOSPHERE RESERVES. Together, they are a huge northern WILDERNESS area that will become an increasingly important world heritage treasure as the next century unfolds. The Gates of the Arctic area does not support very large quantities of Arctic life; this far north, much area is needed to sustain animal life. In summer, though, the Arctic tundra blooms with a wide range of shallowly-rooted flowers, miniature trees, and mosses, and a considerable variety of animals and birds are to be found, including thousands of CARIBOU, WOLVES, foxes, grizzly BEARS, and large numbers of lemmings. (See TUNDRA; WILDLIFE REFUGES.)

**genetic diversity,** one of several kinds of BIOLOGICAL DIVERSITY, referring to the range of characteristics coded in the DNA carried in the genes of the plants and animals of a species. (See BIOLOGICAL DIVERSITY.)

**genetic engineering,** deliberate manipulation of DNA, the molecules that form the chemical codes for hereditary material in genes. Since 1973, when researchers first learned how to "cut and paste" DNA, genetic engineers have been deliberately manipulating DNA for scientific purposes, such as attempting to repair a genetic defect passed on from parent to child, or to create an altered life form. Mindful of the havoc wrought by introduced SPECIES in recent centuries—and of 20th-century science fiction horror stories—the public quickly showed great concern about the possible release or escape of genetically altered forms into the environment. Largely as a result, stringent guidelines for genetic engineering research were introduced from 1974; though these were somewhat relaxed after 1980, several experiments were stopped, where researchers had failed to follow the guidelines and obtain proper clearance.

Commercial genetic engineering firms have operated since 1976. The legal status of genetically altered life forms was originally unclear, but in 1980 the U.S. Supreme Court ruled that these new forms could be patented, in *Diamond* v. *Chakrabarty*, a case involving genetically engineered bacteria intended to break down crude OIL (see BIOREMEDIATION). In 1987, the U.S. Patent and Trademark Office ruled that such patents also applied to all genetically engineered animals; the first vertebrate—a mouse—was patented in 1988. Valuable commercial products have emerged through genetic engineering, including bacteria-produced human insulin, a vaccine for hoof-and-mouth disease, and bacteria for cleaning up oil spills, used for the first time in 1990 in the GALVESTON BAY OIL SPILL and the *MEGA BORG OIL SPILL*. But widespread concern still exists about the potential danger of environmental release of genetically altered forms, and about the wisdom of allowing any living beings to be patented, with proposed laws calling for a moratorium or ban on such patenting. However, the U.S. federal government in 1992 announced that it would allow the sale of genetically altered foods. (See BIOTECHNOLOGY AND GENETIC ENGINEERING INFORMATION AND ACTION GUIDE on page 43.)

**geosphere,** the inorganic, or nonliving, portions of earth, which are home to all the globe's organic, or living, matter. The geosphere itself is divided into three spheres:

- **lithosphere,** the rocks and soil that make up the ball of matter we call earth;
- **hydrosphere,** the water, including OCEANS, LAKES, RIVERS, underground AQUIFERS, and all other forms;
- **atmosphere,** the air around us; often subdivided into several layers, including the *troposphere* (lowest layer), *stratosphere* (including the OZONE LAYER), *mesosphere*, and *ionosphere*.

Though themselves inorganic, the three main spheres are vital to life, the atmosphere and hydrosphere providing the air we breathe and the water we drink, and the lithosphere being the ultimate storehouse of minerals necessary to all life. All living organisms, from the simplest to the most complex, make their home on the "skin" of the geosphere; they and their zone of life are together called the BIOSPHERE.

**geothermal energy,** use of the earth's natural heat for human purposes; a form of ALTERNATIVE ENERGY that is potentially massive but hard to tap. Geothermal energy usually involves tapping into natural reservoirs of steam and hot water and drawing them up to the surface for heating or use in electricity generation; at present, these can be tapped only if they are within about 3,000 meters (900 feet) of the surface, though as technology advances, deeper sources will become accessible. Researchers are also exploring ways to make use of the lower-temperature water that is abundant near the surface, to produce electricity.

Several problems exist with geothermal energy. Usable hot water sources are found only in special geological settings, often along the active earthquake-and-volcano belt, as in Italy, California, New Zealand, and Iceland. Location of likely sites is hampered by lack of surveys of "thermal potential"; exploratory drilling, using techniques similar to those used in OIL exploration, is expensive and cumbersome. In addition, though cleaner than FOSSIL FUELS, this kind of geothermal energy can pollute ground and surface waters with nontoxic but unwanted compounds such as chlorides, carbonates, and sulfates from the deeper waters. Environmentalists are also concerned that DEVELOPMENT of geothermal plants may further threaten some already endangered environments, such as tropical rain FORESTS in Hawaii.

A relatively new form of geothermal energy is the *hot dry rock* system, which involves pumping water into an area of fractured, naturally hot rocks; once heated, the water is pumped up from a second well to the surface, where it is used to provide heat or produce electricity. This is a promising approach, especially as it is nonpolluting, but it is only in the early stages of development and involves significant engineering challenges to create the necessary "closed loop" for the water to travel in.

## For more information and action:

- NATURAL RESOURCES AND ENERGY DIVISION (NRED), (212-963-6205).
- SIERRA CLUB, (415-776-2211 or 202-547-1141; legislative hotline, 202-547-5550). Publishes *Geothermal Energy Policy.*

(See also ENERGY RESOURCES; ALTERNATIVE ENERGY.)

**gibbons,** the tree-dwelling family of lesser apes (the great apes are the GORILLAS, CHIMPANZEES, and ORANGUTANS); all nine species of gibbons live in southeast Asia, from eastern India to South China and Indonesia. Because they are tree-dwellers living in a set of tropical rain FOREST habitats, all the gibbons are now greatly ENDANGERED SPECIES; as southeast Asian human POPULATIONS continue to expand explosively, massive rain forest clearance proceeds. The gibbon population, estimated at approximately 4 million in the mid-1970s, is estimated at 500,000 to 1 million in the early 1990s, and is dropping fast. HUNTING also threatens the gibbons in some areas, but it is loss of HABITAT that most directly threatens gibbon survival. The countries in which gibbons live have made some progress in rain forest conservation, but far from enough to create effectively protected rain forest wildlife preserves, while they still face the needs of some of the fastest growing populations on earth. Realistically, much of the future of the gibbons and many other endangered southeast Asian species depends on the will of governments to establish and carefully hold threatened rain forest areas as wildlife preserves, perhaps helped by hard currency from ECOTOURISM, and by private and public international conservation organizations. (See also ENDANGERED SPECIES; also ENDANGERED AND THREATENED WILDLIFE AND PLANTS on page 372.)

**Glacier Bay National Park and Preserve,** A 3,200,000-acre (5,000-square-mile) southeastern Alaska park, on the spectacularly beautiful Gulf of Alaska; site of the Muir Glacier, named after naturalist John MUIR, who first visited it in 1879. It is an area of great glacial activity, with the Muir and other glaciers breaking off huge chunks of ice, some of them hundreds of feet high, as they continue the long melting and retreat of the last several hundred years, since the end of the Little Ice Age. The Muir Glacier has retreated over 100 miles since John Muir first visited it over a century ago.

The Park is also an outdoor laboratory, for as the ice recedes, plant life returns; since Muir, scientists from all over the world have come to study the successive steps and layers of life, as the massive ice sheet has receded and a northern spruce and hemlock FOREST has emerged.

Glacier Bay is also quite notable for its humpbacked WHALES and thousands of harbor seals (see SEALS AND SEA LIONS); the whales have attracted a great deal of tourist attention, so much so that by the early 1980s the tourists in cruise ships observing the whales had very nearly driven the whales away. After the ships were forced to observe from further away, the whales began to return; once again, those managing parks like Glacier Bay must balance the great and growing mass hunger to participate in the natural world against the needs of the creatures of that world. (See WILDLIFE REFUGES; ECOTOURISM.)

**Glen Canyon Dam,** a highly controversial dam on the Colorado River, 16 miles upstream of the GRAND CANYON National Park. The dam was completed in 1963, creating a 180-mile-long reservoir which was not fully filled until 1980. Since then, operation of the dam has played havoc with the fragile ecology of the Grand Canyon. During periods of heavy spring rain, with flood releases occurring an average of every four years, large quantities of water are released, which pour through the canyon, causing massive and irreversible EROSION of the banks of the river. In addition, varying power needs cause widely varying seasonal and even daily water use in the dam to create hydroelectric power, causing continual 10-to-15-foot tide surges in the river that severely damage the riverbanks and the life of the canyon. From the human point of view, one striking early casualty has been the impact on the spectacular journey on the Colorado through the floor of the canyon, likened by so many to a voyage through hundreds of millions of years of earth history.

**For more information and action:**

- **EARTH FIRST! (E.F.!),** (Direct Action Fund, 415-376-7329). Circulates movie *The Cracking of the Glen Canyon Dam* about EF!'s 1981 guerrilla theater tactic of unfurling a long black streamer, which looked from a distance like a crack on the dam face.
- **FRIENDS OF THE RIVER (FOR),** (415-771-0400). Has a Grand Canyon campaign.
- **NATIONAL PARKS AND CONSERVATION ASSOCIATION (NPCA),** (202-944-8530).

(See also DAMS; RIVERS; GRAND CANYON.)

**global commons,** those parts of the Earth that are beyond national jurisdiction—for example, beyond EXCLUSIVE ECONOMIC ZONES—or are otherwise held in common. These include the atmosphere, the open ocean, and the resources found there. The only land area considered part of the global commons is ANTARCTICA, which is under international control, though some countries have claimed parts of the continent.

**global cooling,** a long-term drop in the average temperature of the earth. Such cooling has happened at various times in the earth's history, most notably in a series of major ice ages, when massive glaciers formed in high latitudes and elevations and spread over large areas of land. Before GLOBAL WARMING became such a widespread concern, global cooling was a common fear, generally expressed as the fear that we might be heading toward another ice age. The causes of these changes are unclear (see GLOBAL WARMING for a discussion of likely triggers

for global warming or cooling), but the effects are massive, dramatically changing ECOSYSTEMS and causing a great deal of local and some worldwide EXTINCTION (for a fuller discussion, see CLIMATE CHANGE). In fact, in a 1991 report projecting a 2- to 9-degree rise in average temperature (assuming the global warming theory is correct), the National Academy of Sciences noted that global cooling of the same amount "would crush the upper Midwestern United States under ice." (See CLIMATE CHANGE; GLOBAL WARMING; also GLOBAL WARMING AND CLIMATE CHANGE INFORMATION AND ACTION GUIDE on page 144.)

**Global Environment Monitoring Systems (GEMS),** a wide-ranging project of the UNITED NATIONS ENVIRONMENT PROGRAMME (UNEP) launched in 1975 to gather data on the environment—more precisely, to monitor variations in climate, soils, plants, animals, and human impacts over time. Rather than trying to replace existing systems, GEMS seeks to link existing environmental monitoring systems and to "catalyze new stations and networks to fill any gaps," the aim being to produce global information on environmental problems and trends, monitored and measured in a uniform way, that can be used for assessment and decision-making. Uniformity of procedures are coordinated by UNEP's London-based *Monitoring and Assessment Research Centre (MARC)*, which publishes UNEP's biennial *Environmental Data Report* of global environmental statistics. Some 25 major monitoring networks, each with an associated data base, are part of GEMS, which has activities in some 142 countries, the five main areas of concern being the climate, especially CLIMATE CHANGE; transboundary POLLUTION; renewable natural resources on land; general pollution of the environment; and the OCEANS.

Two of the main networks involved in gathering data about climate change are the *Background Air Pollution Monitoring Network* (BAPMoN), run by the World Meteorological Organization (WMO), and the *World Glacier Monitoring Service* (run jointly with UNESCO and the Swiss Federal Institute of Techology), which gathers data from over 750 glacier stations in 21 countries and publishes *The World Glacier Inventory*. Regarding the OZONE LAWYER, BAPMoN and the WMO's *Global Ozone Observing System* are the key networks, monitoring changes in the ozone layer, greenhouse gases, and other air pollutants.

Information on environmental pollution in general comes from a wide range of sources, generally maintained by the World Health Organization (WHO). Regarding AIR POLLUTION, for example, GEMS measures SULFUR DIOXIDE, PARTICULATE MATTER, and other EMISSIONS in urban air from monitoring stations in over 30 cities in about 50 countries. Water quality is measured in over 340 stations in 41 countries, while food contamination is monitored by WHO and the Food and Agriculture Organization (FAO). Another network, *Human Exposure Assessment Location (HEAL)*, focuses on the actual exposure of humans to total pollutants from all sources.

Information on renewable natural resources—vegetation and animals—comes from satellite and airplane pictures, refined by fieldworkers on the ground. UNEP and FAO in 1982 produced the first full assessment of the world's tropical FOREST resources, which is being refined by even more sensitive satellites.

To make GEMS information available to decision-makers, UNEP in 1985 established the *Global Resource Information Database (GRID)*, which uses "a geographic information system (GIS) and satellite image processing technology to present environmental data and analyses as easily-understood maps and print-outs." It has been used, for example, to provide more accurate estimates of ELEPHANTS in Africa and data for DEVELOPMENT planning in the SAHEL.

Also associated with GEMS is the *World Conservation Monitoring Centre (WCMC)*, jointly operated with the WORLD WILDLIFE FUND (WWF, or the World Wide Fund for Nature) and IUCN—THE WORLD CONSERVATION UNION, which maintains data bases on ENDANGERED SPECIES and their HABITATS, from which they publish their key references, the Red Data Books.

## Global Tomorrow Coalition (GTC) (1325 G Street NW, Suite 915, Washington, DC 20005; 202-628-4016; Donald R. Lesh, President), an alliance of individuals and organizations—including environmental groups, business firms, foundations, community groups, and other concerned organizations—"committed to acting today to assure a more sustainable, equitable global tomorrow." Founded in 1981, the GTC acts as an information clearinghouse, gathering research, policy, and other material (especially relating to sustainable DEVELOPMENT) from member groups and making it available to communities throughout the United States, often through helping to create community-level *Global Issues Resource Centers* and holding *Globescope* assemblies and forums, the aim being to build community leadership on key issues, while also acting as liaison between U.S. and Third World nongovernmental organizations, and working with United Nations and other international commissions to reach wider audiences for such reports as OUR COMMON FUTURE.

In addition to other teaching tools and teacher training workshops, the Coalition publishes various materials, including the *Global Issues Education Set*, teaching materials for elementary and secondary school levels on sustainable development, BIOLOGICAL DIVERSITY, global awakening, marine and coastal resources, POPULATION, and tropical FORESTS. It also publishes more general materials including the newsletter *Interaction*; books such as *The Global Ecology Handbook: What You Can Do About the Environmental Crisis* (1990), *Sustainable Development: A Guide to Our Common Future*, *A Citizens' Guide to Global Issues*, and *U.S. Citizens' Response to Sustainable Development*; and videos such as *The World Commission on Environment and Development* and *Sustainable Development: Shaping a U.S. Response.*

**global warming,** a long-term rise in the average temperature of the earth. Whether or not global warming is actually occurring is one of the major questions facing all humans today, a matter of enormous importance to all life on earth and a subject of intense debate in the scientific community. If it is, the questions further multiply, including: Why is it doing so? How can we tell for sure? What will be the effects? What can we do about it? None of these questions can be answered for certain now, and we may not know the answers until the process has proceeded so far that it is beyond the power of humans to affect it. But, as many scientists and environmentalists have pointed out, the consequences are so serious that it is prudent to take cautionary action while there is still time to do so, noting that the longer action is delayed, the greater the CLIMATE CHANGE and the harder and more expensive it will be to deal with.

Put very simply, the theory of global warming is that the GREENHOUSE EFFECT, which provides necessary warmth for life, has been distorted by human activities, so that the upper atmosphere traps increasing amounts of heat, gradually increasing the temperature of the whole earth. In particular, activities such as burning of FOSSIL FUELS, DEFORESTATION, and use of certain aerosols and refrigerants have increased the so-called *greenhouse gases* including CARBON DIOXIDE, METHANE, CHLOROFLUOROCARBONS (CFCs), surface OZONE, nitrous oxide (see NITROGEN DIOXIDE), and water vapor; once in the upper atmosphere these trap more heat than normal.

On the level of day-to-day experience, many people note that the last decade has been the warmest since measurements began in the late 19th century and that the more general rise in temperature in the last century has coincided with heavy industrialization and use of fossil fuels. They also point to stories of receding ice and snow cover in the Arctic and ANTARCTICA. But scientists who look at temperature variations over a longer term—over thousands or even millions of years—cannot be sure that these are not simply short-term variations. The earth's temperature does vary widely, growing cold with ice ages and then warming again. Some evidence indicates that the global temperatures 5,000 to 6,000 years ago were 2 to 5 degrees warmer than the *benchmark levels* of the late 19th century, when recordkeeping began. One study in Sweden indicates that the average summer temperature has varied by almost 7 degrees over the last 1,400 years. On a longer term, in a warm period of about 125,000 years ago, temperatures are estimated to have been 3.5 to 14 degrees warmer, and some 3.3 to 4.3 million years ago they were 3.5 to 35 degrees warmer, depending on the season and location. Some scientists also point out that though the 1980s saw six of the twelve warmest known years worldwide—1987, 1988, 1983, 1980, and 1989, in descending order—that same decade also saw three of the coolest years: 1984, 1985, and 1986. Though seemingly on target to be the warmest year on record, 1991 dropped behind 1990 after the eruption of Mt. Pinatubo caused temporary global cooling.

In addition, if we are indeed seeing long-term global warming, scientists cannot be sure what is causing it. It is possible that global warming now may simply be part of a much longer trend of warming since the last ice age. Though much has been learned in the past two centuries of science, little is actually known about the causes of the worldwide GLOBAL COOLING and warming that have sent the earth through a succession of major ice ages and smaller ones, such as the Little Ice Age that started in the 14th century and reached its coolest temperatures in the 16th and 17th centuries. Among the factors believed to be involved in long-term global warming and cooling are:

- changes in the earth's position in relation to the sun, more precisely the earth's orbit around the sun, with higher temperatures when the two are closer together and lower when further apart.
- changes in the amount of RADIATION emitted by the sun, with somewhat cyclical rises and falls and occasional flares.
- major catastrophes, such as meteor impacts or massive volcanic eruptions, which throw pollutants into the atmosphere that can block out solar radiation (see NUCLEAR WINTER).
- changes in the reflectivity of the earth's surface, that is, the amount of solar radiation that is radiated *back* toward space (see GREENHOUSE EFFECT) rather than absorbed. Snow-covered ground is, for example, more reflective, and so enhances the cold by bouncing more radiation out to space, while open ground absorbs more of it.

- changes in the shape and relationship of the land and oceans, brought about by movement of the earth's crustal plates; the rise of mountain ranges and changes in the patterns of OCEAN circulation are thought to play an especially important role in shaping climate patterns.
- changes in the composition of the atmosphere, especially in the concentration of carbon dioxide and methane. These may be brought about by naturally occurring processes, such as volcanic eruptions or accelerated decay of vegetation (as during a post–ice age thaw).

It is the last possibility, of course, that is at the heart of present concern: Have human activities had a cumulative impact large enough to affect the total temperature and climate of the earth?

Numerous scientists are trying to establish ways to test whether or not greenhouse-induced global warming is occurring, looking for signs that are collectively called a greenhouse "fingerprint." If it is occurring, eventually it will be obvious to everyone. The challenge is to decipher from the mass of scientific evidence those signs that give us clear advance warning. These are currently believed to include changes in:

- **global temperature patterns,** with continents being warmer than oceans; lands near the Arctic warming more than the tropics; and the lower atmosphere warming, while the higher stratosphere becomes cooler.
- **atmospheric water vapor,** with increasing amounts of water evaporating into the air as a result of the warming, more in the tropics than in the higher latitudes. Since water vapor is a "greenhouse gas," this would intensify the warming process.
- **sea surface temperature,** with a fairly uniform rise in the temperature of oceans at their surface and an increase in the temperature differences among oceans around the globe.
- **seasonality,** with changes in the relative intensity of the seasons, with the warming effects especially noticeable during the winter and in higher latitudes.

These signs give a general overview of some of the changes that would be expected to occur with global warming, in a measured scientific way. But from the viewpoint of life on earth, the changes resulting from long-term global warming would far more serious and dramatic. Perhaps the most drastic would be SEA LEVEL RISE, which would swamp many islands and COASTS. The ranges of animals and plants would shift, in many cases threatening the existence of already ENDANGERED SPECIES. and lessening overall BIOLOGICAL DIVERSITY. Food production and

## Global Warming and Climate Change Information and Action Guide

For more information and action on global warming and climate change:

AIR AND WASTE MANAGEMENT ASSOCIATION (A&WMA), (412-232-3444). Publishes *Global Climate Change: Processes, Linkages* and *Health Issues Associated with Global Environmental Modifications.*

Alternative Farming Systems Information Center (301-344-3724 or 344-3559). Provides Quick Bibliography *Global Warming and the Greenhouse Effect* (J. MacLean, 1990). (See ORGANIC FARMING AND SUSTAINABLE AGRICULTURE INFORMATION AND ACTION GUIDE on page 226.)

AMERICAN SOCIETY FOR ENVIRONMENTAL HISTORY (ASEH), (201-596-3270).

CENTER FOR ENVIRONMENTAL INFORMATION (CEI), (716-546-3796). Publishes the monthly *Global Climate Change Digest*; operates the *Air Resources Information Clearinghouse (ARIC)*, including global climate change.

CENTRE FOR SCIENCE AND TECHNOLOGY FOR DEVELOPMENT (CSTD), UNITED NATIONS, (212-963-8435).

Climate Institute (CI) (316 Pennsylvania Avenue, SE, Suite 403, Washington, DC 20003; 202-547-0104; John C. Topping, Jr., President), a membership organization incorporated in 1986 as an international link between climate effects scholars, decision makers, and concerned citizens, its overall aim being to protect the "precious balance between climate and life on Earth," focusing especially on "developing intelligent responses to the twin challenges of greenhouse effect-induced global warming and stratospheric ozone depletion." The Institute holds international conferences, sponsors internship programs and research projects, gathers and disseminates information on climate change effects, seeks to develop laws and mechanisms to "facilitate a cooperative international response to climate change," and publishes various materials, including the quarterly newsletter *Climate Alert* and reports such as *The Arctic and Global Change* (1990), *Coping With Climate Change* (1989), and *Preparing for Climate Change* (1988), as well as slides and a talking script (available in many languages) on the greenhouse effect.

CONCERN, INC., (202-328-8160). Publishes *Global Warming and Energy Choices.*

EARTH ISLAND INSTITUTE, (415-788-3666). Sponsors the *Climate Protection Institute*, which publishes the *Greenhouse Gas-ette.*

ECOLOGICAL SOCIETY OF AMERICA (ESA), (301-530-7005). Maintains an *Ecological Information Network.*

ENVIRONMENTAL AND ENERGY STUDY INSTITUTE (EESI), (202-628-1400). Publishes *Update on the Intergovernmental Panel on Climate Change* (1990) and *Eastern and Western European Strategies to Address Global Warming* (1990).

ENVIRONMENTAL DEFENSE FUND (EDF), (212-505-2100). Publishes *Dead Heat: The Race Against the Greenhouse Effect* (1990), *Offsetting New $CO_2$ Emmissions: A First Rational Greenhouse Policy Step* (D. Dudek and A. LeBlanc, 1990), and *Developing Policies for Responding to Climatic Change* (1988).

Environmental Law Institute (ELI), (202-328-5150; publications office: 202-939-3844). Publishes *The Greenhouse Effect: Formulating a Convention* (William A. Notze, 1990). (See ENVIRONMENTAL LAW INFORMATION AND ACTION GUIDE on page 116.)

ENVIRONMENTAL PROTECTION AGENCY (EPA), (202-260-7751 or 202-260-2080). Publishes *Policy Options for Stabilizing Global Climate* (Daniel A. Lashof and Dennis A. Tripak, eds., 1989) and *The Potential Effects of Global Climate Change on the United States* (Joel B. Smith and Dennis A. Tirpak, eds., 1988).

FRIENDS OF THE EARTH (FOE), (202-544-2600).

GREENPEACE, (202-462-1177). Runs the *Atmosphere and Energy Campaign*. Publishes *Global Warming: The Greenpeace Report* (available through Oxford University Press) and Action Factsheet *The Greenhouse Effect.*

INVESTOR RESPONSIBILITY RESEARCH CENTER (IRRC), (202-234-7500). Publishes *The Greenhouse Effect: Investment Implications and Opportunities* (1990).

KIDS FOR SAVING EARTH™ (KSE), (612-525-0002 or 800-800-8800).

MORRISON INSTITUTE FOR POPULATION AND RESOURCE STUDIES (415-723-7518). Publishes *An Exploratory Model of the Impact of Rapid Climate Change on the World Food Situation* (Gretchen C. Daily and Paul R. Ehrlich) and *Global Change and Carrying Capacity: Implications for Life on Earth* (Paul R. Ehrlich et al.)

NATIONAL AUDUBON SOCIETY, (212-832-3200; *Audubon Action Line*, 202-547-9017.) Publishes *Global Climate Change and What You Can Do About It.*

---

industry would alike be affected by changes in the availability of WATER RESOURCES. (For a fuller discussion of likely effects, see CLIMATE CHANGE.)

As the description of the greenhouse signs indictes, changes would not be uniform, but would be part of a worldwide process so complicated that we cannot accurately predict how any one area or aspect of life would be affected. Among the unanswered questions are: To what extent will ocean circulation tend to stabilize the earth's atmospheric temperature. What role will cloud formations

NATIONAL CENTER FOR ATMOSPHERIC RESEARCH (NCAR), (303-497-1000; Information Services, 303-497-8600). Has *Climate and Global Dynamics Division (CGD)*.

NATIONAL WILDLIFE FEDERATION (NWF), (202-797-6800 or 800-245-5484). Publishes *Global Warming: A Personal Guide to Action*.

NATURAL RESOURCES AND ENERGY DIVISION (NRED), United Nations, (212-963-6205).

NATURAL RESOURCES DEFENSE COUNCIL (NRDC), (212-727-2700). Publishes *The Rising Tide: Global Warming and Sea Level Rise* (Lynne Edgerton, 1991), *The Statehouse Effect: State Policies to Cool the Greenhouse* (Daniel A. Lashof and Eric A. Washburn, 1990), *Cooling the Greenhouse: Vital First Steps to Combat Global Warming* (1989), *Global Change and Our Common Future* (1989), and *Farming in the Greenhouse: What Global Warming Means for American Agriculture* (J. Ward et al., 1989).

PACIFIC INSTITUTE FOR STUDIES IN DEVELOPMENT, ENVIRONMENT, AND SECURITY, (415-843-9550). Sponsors *Program on Global Environment*.

POPULATION-ENVIRONMENT BALANCE, (202-879-3000). Publishes *Global Warming and Population Growth*. (See POPULATION INFORMATION AND ACTION GUIDE on page 248.)

RENEW AMERICA, (202-232-2252). Publishes *Reducing the Rate of Global Warming: The States' Role* (1988).

RESOURCES FOR THE FUTURE (RFF), (202-328-5000). Includes research arm, *Energy and Natural Resources Division*. Publishes *Greenhouse Warming: Abatement and Adaptation* (Norman J. Rosenberg et al., eds., 1989).

ROCKY MOUNTAIN INSTITUTE (RMI), (303-927-3851). Publishes *Global Warming—A Reader* (1990).

SIERRA CLUB, (415-776-2211 or 202-547-1141; legislative hotline, 202-547-5550). Recent campaigns include Global Warming/Greenhouse Effect. Publishes *Global Warming, Global Warming, 21 Ways to Help Stop Global Warming, Global Warming Local Action Kit, Doing Something About the Weather*, and *Global Warming Policy*.

UNION OF CONCERNED SCIENTISTS (UCS), (617-547-5552 or 202-332-0900). Publishes a briefing paper, *The Greenhouse Effect*; brochures, such as *Cool Energy: The Renewable Solution to Global Warming, How You Can Fight Global Warming: An Action Guide, The Heat is On: Global Warming, the Greenhouse Effect & Energy Solutions, The Global Warming Debate: Answers to Controversial Questions*, and *Motor-Vehicle Fuel Efficiency and Global Warming*; The Book

*Global Warming: Are We Entering the Greenhouse Century?* (Stephen H. Schneider, 1989) and the videocassette *Greenhouse Crisis: The American Response* (1989).

UNITED NATIONS ENVIRONMENT PROGRAMME (UNEP), (212-963-8139). Publishes *The Full Range of Responses to Anticipated Climate Change* (1989).

WILDERNESS SOCIETY, THE, (202-833-2300). Publishes the fact sheet *Global Warming*.

WILDLIFE INFORMATION CENTER (215-434-1637). Publishes the fact sheet *Global Warming, (Greenhouse Effect)*.

WOODS HOLE OCEANOGRAPHIC INSTITUTION (WHOI), (508-548-1400; Associates Office 508-457-2000, ext. 2392). Operates the *Marine Policy Center (MPC)*, and the *Coastal Research Center (CRC)*.

WORLD BANK, (202-477-1234). Publishes *Greenhouse Effect: Implications for Economic Development*.

WORLD RESOURCES INSTITUTE (WRI), (202-638-6300). Publishes *Driving Forces: Motor Vehicle Trends and Their Implications for Global Warming, Energy Strategies, and Transportation Planning* (James J. MacKenzie and Michael P. Walsh, 1990), *Escaping the Heat Trap: Probing the Prospects for Stable Environment* (Irving Mintzer and William R. Moomaw, 1990), *Reforesting America: Combatting Global Warming?* (Mark C. Trexler and William R. Moomaw, 1990), and *Breathing Easier: Taking Action on Climate Change, Air Pollution, and Energy Insecurity* (James J. MacKenzie, 1988).

ZERO POPULATION GROWTH (ZPG), (202-332-2200). Publishes *Population and the Greenhouse Effect* and *Global Warming: A Primer*. (See POPULATION INFORMATION AND ACTION GUIDE on page 248.)

**Other references.**

*The Changing Atmosphere: A Global Challenge.* John Firor. Yale University Press, 1990. *Hothouse Earth: The Greenhouse Effect and Gaia.* John Gribbin. Grove Weidenfeld, 1990. *The Greenhouse Trap: What We're Doing to the Atmosphere and How We Can Slow Global Warming.* Francesca Lyman et al. Beacon Press, 1990. *Greenhouse Glasnost: The Crisis of Global Warming.* Terrell J. Minger, ed. Ecco/Norton, 1990. *Climate Change: The IPCC Scientific Assessment.* J.T. Houghton et al, eds.; Intergovernmental Panel on Climate Change. Cambridge University Press, 1990. *Greenhouse: Planning for Climatic Change.* Graham I. Pearman, ed. E.J. Brill (Leiden, The Netherlands), 1988.

---

play in the working out or blunting of changes. Will the changes occur gradually or as the result of an abrupt shift to a new state, in which they may "snowball."

Despite the uncertainties, even many scientists who understand that the global warming theory has not been

proved believe that humans around the world should act to reduce those activities that contribute to accelerating the greenhouse effect. This is, after all, unexplored climatic territory, and by the time the theory is proved, it may be too late to act. Expensive as actions may be, the costs of *not* taking them may be even greater in the long run. And many scientists privately believe the global warming theory to be true even if not yet provable. While knowing how much they do *not* know about the complex interactions of the world's climate, they have developed numerous elaborate computer models of what might result from global warming. Based on such models, the National Academy of Sciences in 1991 estimated that if production of greenhouse gases continued at the present rate, the average global temperature would rise by 2 to 9 degrees in the next century, and it concluded that the threat is "sufficient to justify action now." Writing in the September 1990 *Scientific American*, William Fulkerson et al. put it this way: "The problem of global warming is difficult to resolve, in part because there is disagreement over how real and dangerous the threat is and, consequently, how much money and effort should be devoted to coping with it. Still we think uncertainty should not be an excuse for inaction. . . . It seems prudent to manage fossil fuels as if a dangerous greenhouse warming were probable."

The main kinds of actions that have been suggested to reduce greenhouse gas production and global warming are:

- using energy more efficiently (see ENERGY RESOURCES).
- using less energy (though savings per person may be outweighed by the total energy needs of a rising POPULATION).
- in the short term, changing from COAL and OIL to the relatively cleaner NATURAL GAS (though recent studies suggest that, because of leaks in transmission, natural gas may contribute disproportionately to the greenhouse effect).
- in the medium-term, changing from fossil fuels to less polluting RENEWABLE RESOURCES, such as SOLAR ENERGY and other kinds of ALTERNATIVE ENERGY sources. (Use of NUCLEAR ENERGY, recommended by some, causes other environnmental problems.)
- reforesting the land, to take carbon dioxide out of the atmosphere, and also protecting threatened FORESTS around the world.
- halting slash-and-burn approaches to farming, which release greenhouse pollutants into the air as well as causing deforestation.
- adopting SUSTAINABLE AGRICULTURE techniques, such as avoiding excessive use of nitrogen fertilizers, which release nitrous oxide and hinder bacteria from absorbing methane into the soil, and of synthetic chemical PESTICIDES and oil-based fertilizers, which involve releases of carbon dioxide in their manufacture and transport.
- adopting SOIL CONSERVATION techniques that reduce the amount of tilling, and therefore the release of greenhouse gases.
- adopting practices in rice cultivation that reduce methane emissions from rice paddies.
- establishing comprehensive LAND USE planning, as in the planning of growth, transportation, and energy use, to protect resources threatened by DEVELOPMENT, which will be further degraded by the effects of global warming.
- reducing population—vital if any of the other efforts is to succeed, since demands for food, energy, and other necessities will inevitably increase greenhouse gases.

Above all, the need is for international cooperation if effects of global warming are to be blocked or minimized. Much international scientific consideration of global warming has been undertaken by the *Intergovernmental Panel on Climate Change*, sponsored by the UNITED NATIONS ENVIRONMENT PROGRAMME and the World Meteorological Organization. As of 1992, international conferences were being held aiming toward a worldwide treaty to limit EMISSIONS of carbon dioxide and other heat-trapping gases. (Some, such as chlorofluorocarbons, are already scheduled for phasing out under an international treaty to preserve the OZONE LAYER.) The major point of contention is whether to adopt a "centralized, top-down" approach, with concrete targets and timetables, as the European Community and Japan proposed, or a "decentralized, bottom-up" approach concentrating on more general efficiencies and reductions such as those in the CLEAN AIR ACT and other laws, as the United States prefers. Developing countries and China have urged development of a fund to aid poorer nations in making the transition to new technologies. (See GLOBAL WARMING AND CLIMATE CHANGE INFORMATION AND ACTION GUIDE on page 144; also CLIMATE CHANGE; GLOBAL COOLING.)

**Goodall, Jane** (1934–   ), British ethologist, who became one of the world's leading primatologists for her 30-year study of CHIMPANZEE behavior at the Gombe Stream Game Preserve in Tanzania. In her early 20s, she worked in Kenya with Louis Leakey, who encouraged her to set out on her own to study chimpanzee behavior, and suggested the Gombe Perserve. She began her study in 1960, and was joined in 1962 by Dutch photographer Hugo Van Lawick, who later became her first husband, and whose work did much to make her a world figure.

Goodall's long study quite early established that chimpanzees were not vegetarians, as had previously been thought. It also established that humans were not the only toolmakers in the animal world; so were chimpanzees—and the fact of toolmaking, coupled with the complex so-

## Greenhouse gas contributions to global warming - 1980's

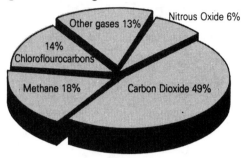

Nitrous Oxide 6%

Other gases 13%

14% Chloroflourocarbons

Methane 18%

Carbon Dioxide 49%

## Regional contributions to global warming

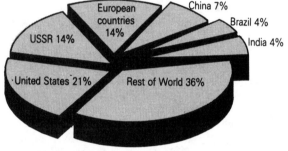

China 7%

European countries 14%

Brazil 4%

USSR 14%

India 4%

United States 21%

Rest of World 36%

**Source:** *Meeting The Environmental Challenge.* Environmental Protection Agency, 1990.

cial behavior Goodall recorded, helped build a new estimate of chimpanzee intelligence, and of acceptable human behavior toward them. Because both kinds of chimpanzees—the common and the pygmy—are ENDANGERED SPECIES, and also for humanitarian reasons, Goodall is sharply opposed to the use of chimpanzees for medical and other scientific research, and also opposes their use in entertainment or other commerical ways. Goodall has been the subject of several documentary films, and is the editor of a popular children's book series. Some of her best known books are *Through a Window: My Thirty Years With the Chimpanzees of Gombe* (1980), *In the Shadow of Man* (1983), *The Chimpanzees of Gombe* (1986), and *My Life with Chimpanzees* (1988).

**gorillas,** with CHIMPANZEES and ORANGUTANS, one of the three SPECIES comprising the great apes. Of all the animal species, the gorilla is most closely related to humanity, and is one of the most intelligent animals on earth. Gorillas are the largest of the primates, the males weighing up to 400 pounds; their remaining, greatly threatened HABITATS are in central and west Africa. The *western lowland*

*gorilla*, probably numbering 7,000 to 9,000, is found in West Africa, and the *eastern lowland gorilla*, probably numbering 3,000 to 4,000, lives mainly in Zaire.

A small *mountain gorilla* population, probably numbering 350–400, lives in a mountain area shared by Rwanda, Uganda, and Zaire, most of them in three contiguous nature preserves: Uganda's Kigezi Gorilla Sanctuary, Zaire's Parc National des Virungas, and Rwanda's Parc National des Volcans. In 1967, primatologist Dian FOSSEY established the Karisoke Research Centre at the Rwanda preserve, ultimately gaining worldwide attention for her work with publication of her 1983 book *Gorillas in the Mist.* She was murdered in 1985, probably by some of the poachers she had been resisting for 18 years. Her work has been continued by the Mountain Gorilla Project, organized in 1979 by the AFRICAN WILDLIFE FOUNDATION, and transferred to the Rwandan government in 1990.

All of Africa's gorillas are seriously endangered by loss of habitat to explosively expanding human POPULATIONS; even the national park protected areas have suffered loss of land, as governments sought new farmland. One partial solution has been to encourage ECOTOURISM in several African countries; that has occurred quite notably at the Parc des Volcans, where thousands come every year to see the mountain gorillas, supplying hard currency to the Rwandan government, and encouraging further habitat protection—although the presence of too many tourists can also threaten the environment.

All three kinds of gorillas are protected by law, but all three are also threatened by inadequate enforcement, as poachers sell gorillas for food, gorillas parts to tourists as souvenirs, and young gorillas to ZOOS. Nor can governments that face huge political and economic problems be counted on in the long run to provide protection to save species.

### For more information and action:

• **AFRICAN WILDLIFE FOUNDATION (AWF),** (202-265-8393 or 800-344-TUSK [8875]).
• **IUCN—THE WORLD CONSERVATION UNION,** (202-797-5454). Publishes the periodical *Primate Conservation* and *Threatened Primates of Africa: The IUCN Red Data Book* (Phyllis C. Lee et al, 1988).
• **WORLD WILDLIFE FUND (WWF),** (202-293-4800).

### Other references:

*The Magnificent Gorilla: The Life History of a Great Ape.* Don Cousins. State Mutual Books, 1990. *The Mountain Gorilla.* Boyd Norton. Voyageur Press, 1990. *The Year of the Gorilla.* George B. Schaller. University of Chicago Press, 1988. *The Mountain Gorilla: Ecology and Behav-*

*ior*. George B. Schaller. University of Chicago Press, 1988.

(See also ENDANGERED SPECIES; also ENDANGERED AND THREATENED WILDLIFE AND PLANTS on page 372.)

**Grand Canyon,** the extraordinarily beautiful mile-deep valley cut by the Colorado River into the high tableland of northern Arizona. First protected as a national monument in 1908, then made a national park in 1919, it is one of the world's most famous natural wonders, and a magnet for well over a million visitors every year, drawn from all over the planet. The canyon runs 217 miles; those who travel through it on the river journey traverse 277 miles, through 2 billion years of earth history and over 4,000 years of human history. The Anasazi (Old Ones) lived in the canyon 40 centuries ago; Hopi guides led the Spanish to the canyon in 1540. It is a place of red rock and desert; yet the interior of the canyon is a protected place for otters, blue herons, beavers, ducks, golden eagles, hummingbirds, OSPREYS, blackbirds, and many other animals and birds. By its nature the ECOLOGY of the canyon is fragile, and in recent decades much of what has made the canyon an irreplaceable American and world heritage treasure has become threatened.

Ironically, the greatest threat has come indirectly because of an environmentalist victory: the 1960s defeat of a proposal to build two electricity-generating dams on the Colorado to provide the power to pump water to the Central Arizona Project. Instead, the 2,250 megawatt coal-burning Navajo Generating Plant was built northeast of the canyon—without the anti-pollution scrubbers and other equipment that were to become standard later in the century. The result was a major addition to the haze of AIR POLLUTION over the Grand Canyon, with the Navajo plant in winter contributing an average of 40 to 50 percent of the haze, and on some days much more. In summer, the plant emissions are joined by polluting haze coming from Los Angeles and Mexico. Adding to the irony, the Navajo plant is 25 percent owned by the federal government and 20 percent by the city of Los Angeles. After many years of bitter dispute, the ENVIRONMENTAL PROTECTION AGENCY in 1991 ordered the Navajo plant to reduce its emissions by 70 percent, a step back from its original intention to order a 90 percent reduction. In the spring of 1991, the process of agency review of the order was proceeding, and an end to even some of the POLLUTION caused by the plant was years away.

A second major attack on the Grand Canyon came from the GLEN CANYON DAM, built 16 miles upstream of the Grand Canyon National Park in 1963. Since the final filling in 1980 of the 180-mile-long reservoir created by the

## ON THE GRAND CANYON

Do nothing to mar its grandeur. Keep it for your children, and your children's children, and all who come after you, as the one great sight which every American should see.
—Theodore Roosevelt (1903)

dam, it has been releasing water into the canyon when full, without regard for the effects of the release. During heavy spring rains, large quantities of water are released, and there is flood water release as well, on average every four years. These heavy releases pour through the canyon, causing massive riverbank EROSION. The dam's varying power needs, seasonally and sometimes even daily causes 10-to-15-foot tide surges in the river, further damaging the riverbanks and the wildlife HABITAT of the canyon.

Other problems facing the Canyon are pressure for increasing DEVELOPMENT, especially on the relatively untouched North Rim; tourist flights over the canyon, which disturb the wildlife and the general atmosphere; uranium MINING nearby; and heavy use of the Colorado's water for irrigation, leading to increasing SALINIZATION, a matter of some dispute between the United States and Mexican governments, who share the lower river.

**For more information and action:**

- FRIENDS OF THE RIVER (FOR), (415-771-0400). Campaigns to stop water releases at Glen Canyon Dam that damage the Grand Canyon.
- INTERNATIONAL TRANSBOUNDARY RESOURCES CENTER (CIRT), (505-277-6424).
- NATIONAL PARKS AND CONSERVATION ASSOCIATION (NPCA), (202-944-8530).
- WILDERNESS SOCIETY, THE (202-833-2300). Publishes *The Grand Canyon.*
- RESOURCES FOR THE FUTURE (RFF), (202-328-5000).

**Other references:**
*The Colorado River Through Grand Canyon: Natural History and Human Change.* Steven W. Carothers et al. University of Arizona Press, 1991.

(See also GLEN CANYON DAM, RIVERS; DAMS; SALINIZATION.)

**Grand Eagle** oil spill, leakage of an estimated 450,000 gallons (approximately 1,500 tons) of crude OIL from the Panamanian supertanker *Grand Eagle* into the Delaware River, after it ran aground on September 28, 1985. It was

Delaware's largest oil spill to date, and did considerable environmental damage. (See OIL.)

**grasslands,** regions dominated by grasses or grasslike plants, with few trees, and those mostly near streams and ponds. Grassland is one of the world's major life zones, or BIOMES, occupying the large middle ground between DESERT and FOREST. The classic grasslands are found in large continental temperate zones, such as the *prairies* and *plains* of North America, the *steppes* of Eurasia, the *puszta* of Hungary, and the *pampas* and *campos* of South America. In general, short grasses dominate in the dryest areas, such as those bordering on deserts, while taller and higher grasses grow where more moisture is available; many different types of grasses may be found in a region, but in each small area just a few types will predominate. A special type of grassland, common in warm areas, as in Africa, South America, and Australia, is the SAVANNA, with characteristic widely spaced trees; the TUNDRA is a special type of cold-climate grassland.

An estimated 30–40 percent of the world's land surface is naturally grassland, grasses being the normal climax of the area's ECOLOGICAL SUCCESSION. Why trees do not naturally dominate in such areas is unclear; factors involved may include frequent long droughts that trees can ill survive and naturally occurring fires from which grasses regenerate more quickly, as well as lower overall amounts of precipitation, saltier soil (see SALINIZATION), and poor drainage. However, large areas of the earth's surface have been converted to seminatural grasslands, most notably in the Americas and Eurasia where forests were cleared and kept from regenerating. Many of these are used as CROPLANDS, and include some of the richest farming land in the world, while others are employed as rangelands, providing pasture for livestock and (though from the farmer's point of view inadvertently) for wildlife.

Natural grasslands can support enormously diverse ECOSYSTEMS, with large numbers of animals; the prairies of North America, for example, once supported huge herds of grazing animals, with the size of the buffalo population alone estimated at tens of millions. These herds grazed in an area and then moved on, often in a regular pattern of MIGRATION, to new pastures, allowing the browsed ground to regenerate. The hazard with either natural or created grasslands is that, if mismanaged, they may easily be turned into desert. The process of DESERTIFICATION often results from overuse of grasses, most notably by OVERGRAZING. With loss of plant cover, the area is susceptible to EROSION and becomes less able to capture and hold vital moisture, and so less able to support plant and animal life. This is a major concern in parts of the world where

POPULATION pressure places increased strain on grasslands, and in WILDLIFE REFUGES where range managers attempt to balance use by domesticated herds with the needs of wildlife.

**For more information and action:**

- **EARTH FIRST! (E.F.!),** (Direct Action Fund, 415-376-7329). Has *Overgrazing Task Force* and a slide show on overgrazing.
- **NATURE CONSERVANCY, THE,** (703-841-5300).
- **SIERRA CLUB,** (415-776-2211 or 202-547-1141; legislative hotline, 202-547-5550). Publishes *Public Range Policy.*
- **SOCIETY FOR RANGE MANAGEMENT** (303-355-7070). Publishes *Journal of Range Management* and *Rangelands.*
- **WILDERNESS SOCIETY, THE,** (202-833-2300) Publishes *Grazing on Public Lands.*

(See also CROPLANDS; OVERGRAZING; DESERT; DESERTIFICATION.)

**Great Barrier Reef Marine Park,** the world's largest marine reserve, a huge aggregation of 2,500 CORAL REEFS and 71 coral cays, covering over 85 million acres (133,000 square miles) on the continental shelf, and stretching across the whole northeastern Australian coast, off Queensland. This is one of the world's great natural heritage preserves, holding over 400 coral species, over 1,500 fish species, over 240 bird species, and over 4,000 mollusc species, and is a magnet for tourists from all over the world. (See CORAL REEFS; ECOTOURISM; WILDLIFE REFUGES.)

**Great Dismal Swamp,** a U.S. National Wildlife Refuge in southeastern Virginia, immediately south of Norfolk on the North Carolina border. Its 100 square miles of swampland, set aside as a refuge in 1973, supply safe haven for black BEARS, white-tailed deer, otters, and gray foxes, and to well over 100 bird species, many of them numerous. The swamp in winter shelters an estimated 1 million robins; a few of its other birds are pileated woodpeckers, orioles, woodcocks, pine siskins, and more than a dozen kinds of warblers. (See WILDLIFE REFUGE; WETLANDS.)

**Great Lakes,** the five large lakes shared by Canada and the United States—Superior, Michigan, Huron, Erie, and Ontario—which contain an estimated 18 percent of the world's fresh water. For the first two-thirds of the 20th century, the life of the lakes and the people around them were under sustained and growing attack, as huge cities and a massive American heartland industrial empire grew. The cities deposited enormous amounts of sewage into the lakes, much of it untreated, while steel, chemical,

## Great Lakes Information and Action Guide

**For more information and action on the Great Lakes:**
AMERICAN PLANNING ASSOCIATION **(APA)**, (202-872-0611).
AMERICAN WATER RESOURCES ASSOCIATION **(AWRA)**, (301-493-8600). Publishes *The Great Lakes: Living with North America's Inland Waters* (David H. Hickcox, ed., 1988).
**The Center for the Great Lakes (La Fondation des Grands Lacs)** (435 North Michigan Avenue, Suite 1408, Chicago, IL 60611; 312-645-0901; or 320½ Floor Street West, Toronto, Ontario M5S 1W5, Canada; 416-921-7662; William J. Brah, President), a binational policy research institute, founded in 1983, committed to protecting and developing the Great Lakes-St. Lawrence River system as a unique natural resource. The Center promotes regional cooperation among political, business, and environmental leaders; spurred development of the Great Lakes Protection Fund; identifies key natural resource and economic issues, relating to areas such as waterfront development and revitalization, shoreline management, water resources policy, hazardous waste management, pollution prevention, wetlands, and the regional economy; analyses these issues to provide information for decision-makers; and promotes public education. The Center operates the Great Lakes Information Service for reference and referrals; conducts workshops and conferences; and maintains the Great Lakes Information Library. It also publishes a bimonthly newsletter *Great Lakes Reporter*, reports on key issues, fact sheets with remedial action plans (RAPs) on specific areas of concern (AOCs), such as the Cuyahoga River or heavy metals, and books such as *Clear Water, Clean Water: Current Programs and Future Strategies for Managing Great Lakes Water Quality*, *The Great Lakes Directory of Natural Resource Agencies and Organizations*, and *Great Lakes Water Quality Laws and Programs, A Binational Inventory*.
**Great Lakes United (GLU)** (State University College at Buffalo, Cassety Hall, 1300 Elmwood Avenue, Buffalo, NY 14222; 716-886-0142; Philip E. Weller, Executive Director; in Canada: P.O. Box 548, Station A, Windsor, Ontario, Canada N9A 6M6), an international coalition founded in 1982 by individuals, environmental groups, and other organizations in the United States and Canada concerned with the Great Lakes-St. Lawrence Basin. GLU seeks to give citizens a stronger voice in policies and programs affecting the Great Lakes, especially relating to contamination and degradation of the ecosystem, as by toxic chemicals. It holds workshops and conferences, and publishes various materials, including the quarterly newsletter *The Great Lakes United*, reports

such as *Human Health Effects from Toxic Chemicals in the Great Lakes* (1990), and numerous remedial action plans and citizens' guides.
GREENPEACE, (202-462-1177). Publishes *Water for Life: The Tour of the Great Lakes* (1989), *Great Lakes: An Abused Ecosystem* (1988), and *Great Lakes/St. Lawrence Campaign*.
**International Joint Commission (IJC or Commission Mixte internationale)** (Canadian Section: 100 Metcalfe Street, 18th Floor, Ottawa, Ontario K1P 5M1; 613-995-2984; Great Lakes Regional Office, Canada: 100 Ouellette Avenue, 8th Floor, Windsor, Ontario, N9A 6T3; 519-356-7821; United States Section: 2001 "S" Street, NW, 2nd Floor, Washington, DC 20440; 202-673-6238; Great Lakes Regional Office, U.S.: P.O. Box 32869, Detroit, MI 48232; 313-226-2170), a binational organization established by the Boundary Waters Treaty of 1909, under which the United States and Canada agree to help prevent and resolve disputes, especially those concerning water quantity and quality along the borderlines. Areas covered include the Columbia River Basin, St. Mary-Milk Rivers Basin, Souris-Red Rivers Basin, Lake of the Woods Basin, St. Croix River Basin, and Great Lakes-St. Lawrence River Basin, which has been the subject of some recent additional agreements, notably the 1972 and 1978 Great Lakes Water Quality Agreements (amended in 1983 and 1987), under which the countries expressed the commitment "to restore and maintain the chemical, physical and biological integrity of the Great Lakes Basin Ecosystem," activities under the *Great Lakes Water Quality Board*. The IJC and its subsidiary commission publish various materials, including the bimonthly newsletter *Focus on International Joint Commission Activities*, reports, and brochures such as *The Great Lakes: A Vital Resource Worth Protecting* and *The International Joint Commission: What It Is • How It Works*.
NATIONAL OCEANIC AND ATMOSPHERE ADMINISTRATION **(NOAA)**, (202-377-8090). Publishes *Lake Ontario: A Great Lake in Transition*.
NORTH AMERICAN LAKE MANAGEMENT SOCIETY **(NALMS)**, (202-466-8550).
WORLD WILDLIFE FUND **(WWF)**, (202-293-4800). Publishes *Great Lakes Great Legacy?*, 1990.

**Other references:**

*Fresh Water Seas*. Phil Weller. Between the Lines, 1990.
*Great Lakes*. Kathy Henderson. Childrens, 1989.

automobile, metal MINING, and other major industries dumped industrial waste, much of it highly toxic. By 1960, Lake Erie was widely described as "dead," and Lakes Ontario and Michigan were in little better condition.

From the late 1960s, however, joint Canadian-American federal, state, and provincial action, spurred by effective citizens' groups, has done a great deal to bring the lakes back to life. In some significant respects, the lakes are a considerable environmental success story, though major and continuing threats to the life of the lakes remain. The main agreements involved were the 1972 and 1978 Great Lakes Water Quality Agreements, the first focusing on the huge sewage discharges that were depriving the lakes of life-giving oxygen, and the second on controlling toxic pollutants, mainly from industrial waste discharges. The first generated quite effective action on sewage discharge, but the second proved far harder to enforce. But in the mid-1980s, several further agreements brought stronger enforcement, and in 1985 all OIL drilling was banned on the lakes.

What lies ahead is a long series of actions in Canadian and American courts, aimed at continuing prosecution of polluters and at cleanup of existing toxic waste sites. What also lies ahead is the continuing battle to eliminate ACID RAIN, which still attacks the life of the lakes and requires the kind of fully effective United States action that has not yet come, though the 1990 CLEAN AIR ACT is a step in the right direction. The lakes are also under attack from an invading "exotic" SPECIES—the zebra mussel, flushed into the lakes from international ships—which is growing unchecked in the absence of predators, and so is damaging the natural life of the environment. (See GREAT LAKES INFORMATION AND ACTION GUIDE on page 150; also LAKES.)

**green consumerism,** the practice of making all buying decisions–personal, business, or leisure; necessary, discretionary, or utterly luxurious–with environmental considerations in mind; sometimes called *environmental consumerism.* For some environmentalists, green consumerism can be summed up in one word: *less.* For them, the only way to truly care for the environment is to adopt an extremely simple, self-sufficient lifestyle, with minimal dependence on external purchases. But many other environmentalists believe that, even in affluent societies oriented toward convenience and consumption, widespread changes in individual buying decisions can have a significant effect on the health of the environment.

Basically, a green consumer seeks products that:

• are not in themselves dangerous to human or environmental health.

• are made by manufacturing processes that are not directly dangerous to human or environmental health, and do not consume excessive amounts of energy or other resources.

• are not needlessly wasteful, either because of a too-short useful life, excessive packaging, or disproportionate requirements of energy or other resources for disposal.

• can readily be reused or recycled, applying both to the product and to its packaging.

• do not involve unnecessary use of or cruelty to animals.

• are not made of materials deriving from ENDANGERED SPECIES or threatened environments.

Because of consumer interest, many firms now produce specifically "green" products, such as organic foods, naturally derived cleansers, and recycled paper, and often market them under terms such as ENVIRONMENTALLY FRIENDLY or BIODEGRADABLE. Green consumers need to be aware, however, that such labels are not generally controlled, and so have no precisely determined legal meaning (see ORGANIC FARMING for a discussion of various terminology); they will therefore have to exercise some skepticism and judgment in assessing advertising claims for allegedly "green" products. Environmentalists generally urge consumers do make an ENVIRONMENTAL AUDIT of their homes, offices, schools, and communities to identify those products that are harmful to the environment, and replace them with others that are not.

**For more information and action:**

• **SIERRA CLUB,** (415-776-2211 or 202-547-1141; legislative hotline, 202-547-5550) Publishes *Shopping for a Better World.*

**Other references:**

*Green Earth Resource Guide: A Comprehensive Guide about Environmentally-Friendly Services and Products.* Cheryl Gorder. Blue Bird, 1991. *The Green Consumer: A Guide for the Environmentally Aware.* John Elkington, Julia Hailes, and Joel Makower. Penguin, 1990. *Green Pages: Your Everyday Shopping Guide to Environmentally Safe Products.* Steven J. Bennett. Random, 1990. *Consumers' Guide to Ecology.* Lawrence Tasaday. Meadowbrook, 1990. *Preserving Our World: A Consumer's Guide to the Brundtland Report.* Warner Troyer. Firefly Books, 1990. *Going Green: A Kid's Handbook to Saving the Planet.* John Elkington et al. Viking, 1990; Puffin Books, 1990. *Shopping for a Better World.* Rosemary Will. Council on Economic Priorities, 1989.

(See also ANIMAL WELFARE AND ANIMAL RIGHTS INFORMATION AND ACTION GUIDE on page 361; GREEN BOOKSHELF on page 480.)

**greenhouse effect,** the warming that results when heat is retained near the earth, rather than radiating out into space. In a greenhouse, the glass walls and ceilings are largely transparent to shortwave RADIATION coming in from the sun, which is absorbed by the surfaces and objects inside the structure. Once absorbed, the radiation is transformed into longwave (*infrared*) radiation, or heat, which is radiated back from the interior of the greenhouse. But the glass does not allow the longwave radiation to escape, instead absorbing the warm rays. With the heat trapped inside, the interior of the greenhouse becomes much warmer than the air outside.

Much the same thing happens with the earth and its atmosphere. The shortwave and visible radiation that reaches earth is absorbed by the surface as heat. The long heat waves are then radiated back out toward space, but the atmosphere instead absorbs many of them. This is a natural and balanced process, and indeed is essential to life as we know it on earth. The problem comes when changes in the atmosphere radically change the amount of absorption, and therefore the amount of heat retained. That may have been happening in recent decades, as various AIR POLLUTANTS have caused the atmosphere to absorb more heat (see GLOBAL WARMING for a fuller discussion). Certainly that happens on a local level, with air pollution causing "heat islands" in and around major urban areas. The main contributors to this effect are CARBON DIOXIDE, CARBON MONOXIDE, METHANE, VOLATILE ORGANIC COMPOUNDS (VOCs), nitrogen oxides (see NITROGEN DIOXIDE), CHLOROFLUOROCARBONS (CFCs), and surface OZONE; collectively they are known as *greenhouse gases*. Scientists are not entirely sure or in agreement about whether the recently perceived worldwide warming trend is due to the greenhouse gases or to some other cause, or is simply a wider variation than normal. But if it continues unchecked, the process may lead to significant global warming, with profound—and for some types of life—perhaps catastrophic effects. (See GLOBAL WARMING; CLIMATE CHANGE; also GLOBAL WARMING AND CLIMATE CHANGE INFORMATION AND ACTION GUIDE on page 144.)

**Greenpeace** (Greenpeace USA 1436 U Street NW, Washington, DC 20009; 202-462-1177; Peter Bahouth, Executive Director; International Headquarters, Temple House, 25-26 High Street, Lewes, East Sussex BN7 2LU, England; 273-478787), an international organization founded in 1971 dedicated to "positive, non-violent action to preserve our environment and to protect the creatures that share our planet." In the United States, the organization has two arms (both at the above address), *Greenpeace USA* and *Greenpeace Action*, established in 1987 to "di-

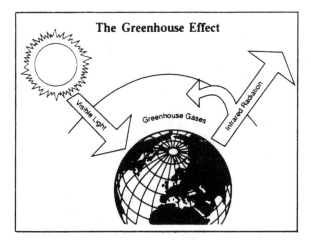

**The Greenhouse Effect**

Visible Light · Greenhouse Gases · Infrared Radiation

**Source:** *Global Warming: Emission Reductions Possible as Scientific Uncertainties Are Resolved.* Government Accounting Office, 1990.

rect actions, research and public education," pursuing "change by mobilizing grassroots pressure on the legislative process." Greenpeace Action runs various campaigns, some operating primarily out of one of Greenpeace Action's several subsidiary offices around the country and often publishing their own materials.

- The **Ocean Ecology Campaign** focuses on strengthening protection for marine mammals and their habitats; maintaining the moratorium on whaling; setting aside ANTARCTICA as a World Park; banning of DRIFTNETS; promoting "environmentally sound practices" in the management of U.S. fisheries; protecting endangered sea TURTLES from "poachers, destructive fishing techniques and degradation of their habitats"; and permanently protecting the U.S. coast from OIL and gas development. It publishes materials such as *An Evaluation of International Protection Offered to Caribbean Reefs and Associated Ecosystems* (1989).
- The **Toxics Campaign** focuses on lobbying on toxics legislation at the federal, state, and local levels, stressing not POLLUTION control but pollution prevention; achieving reduction of industrial hazardous waste generation through use of clean materials, safe technologies, and waste prevention, rather than "incineration and other polluting methods"; and seeking waste reduction by advocating bans on PLASTICS (including styrofoam) and other toxic or hard-to-recycle materials, encouraging RECYCLING, and developing markets for recycled materials and products. It publishes materials such as *The International Trade in Waste: A Greenpeace Inventory* (1990), *A Citizen's Toxic Waste Audit Manual* (1990), *Breaking Down the Degradable Plastics Scam* (1990), and

*Exporting Banned Pesticides: Fueling the Circle of Poison* (1989).

- The **Nuclear Campaign** focuses on ridding the sea of nuclear weapons and nuclear reactors; canceling the Trident 2 missile program; stopping the arms race at its source by ending production of plutonium, uranium, and tritium, and transferring resources to "environmental restoration of the polluted bomb factory areas"; pressing for a comprehensive nuclear test ban treaty, "through lobbying, public education and direct action at nuclear weapons testing sites worldwide"; and campaigning against "attempted revival of the nuclear power industry." (See NUCLEAR ISSUES INFORMATION AND ACTION GUIDE on page 215.)
- The **Atmosphere and Energy Campaign** seeks changes necessary to protect the global atmosphere and the world's human POPULATIONS and ECOSYSTEMS at risk from the GREENHOUSE EFFECT and destruction of the OZONE LAYER, focusing on halting production and use of CHLOROFLUOROCARBONS (CFCs); substituting safe, non-toxic alternatives for CFCs and other ozone-destroying chemicals; decreasing pollution and greenhouse gas EMISSIONS, including auto and industrial emissions; reducing pollution and energy waste from cars by "increasing fuel economy and changing the U.S. transportation system," and by increasing fuel economy standards; promoting more efficient energy use in lighting, heating, and cooling; switching from FOSSIL FUELS to renewable ENERGY RESOURCES; and changing global aid, trade, and investment patterns to assist in developing "efficient and renewable energy resources." It publishes *Changing the Utility Mission* (1990).
- The **Tropical Forests Campaign** focuses on developing positive alternatives to DEFORESTATION (such as establishment of "extractive reserves," for sustainable use of FOREST products); halting "destructive logging of primary forests"; opposing "foreign investments and imports that damage tropical forests;" supporting INDIGENOUS PEOPLES movements; encouraging DEBT-FOR-NATURE SWAPS; setting aside key areas as national parks or BIOSPHERE RESERVES; and pressing "institutions like the World Bank to stop funding environmentally unsound projects." It integrates its work with other Greenpeace campaigns on specific related issues.

Among Greenpeace's other activities are the *Sea Turtle Beach Patrol*, seeking to protect 150 miles of Florida coastal nesting area for the turtles; *Garbage Prevention Plan*, which supports RECYCLING and COMPOSTING, including developing a market for recycled materials, and seeks a ban on INCINERATION; *Below Regulatory Concern (BRC)* *Project*, seeking to have the Nuclear Regulatory Commission reclassify low-level RADIOACTIVE WASTE, which as presently classified can be used in consumer and industrial products, placed in landfills, or even poured down the drain; and the *Waste Project*, which seeks to halve the worldwide trade in toxic waste.

Greenpeace's first major action was in 1971, with a successful protest of underground nuclear weapons tests on the Alaskan island of Amchitka, later turned into a bird sanctuary. The organization came to world attention in 1985 when, during a protest of French atmospheric nuclear weapons tests on the Pacific atoll of Moruroa, French secret agents bombed and sank Greenpeace's *Rainbow Warrior*, killing a crew member, a Greenpeace photographer. A new *Rainbow Warrior* has since been put into service, so-named for the Native American prophecy that "when the Earth is sick and dying, all over the world, people will rise up as Warriors of the Rainbow to save the planet"; it serves alongside six other Greenpeace ships.

The main Greenpeace organization also publishes various materials, including the bimonthly magazine *Greenpeace*; books such as *Greenpeace Book of Antarctica*, *Greenpeace Book of Dolphins*, *The Greenpeace Story*, *Global Warming: The Greenpeace Report*, *Greenpeace Book of the Nuclear Age*, and *Greenpeace Coloring Book*; Action Factsheets, such as *Antarctica, Sea Turtles, Japanese Whaling, Tuna/Dolphins, Great Lakes/St. Lawrence Campaign, Pesticides, Plastics: An Environmental Menace, Energy, The Greenhouse Effect, Tropical Rainforests, Disarmament, Campaign for a Comprehensive Test Ban Treaty, Campaign to End Nuclear Weapons Production, Nuclear Power*, and *Toxics: Stepping Lightly on the Earth: Everyone's Guide to Toxics in the Home*; reports such as *Greenpeace Action Community Recycling Start-up Kit* and *Creating a Nuclear Free Zone That Is True to its Name: The Nuclear Free Zone Concept and a Model Treaty* (1989); and several videocassettes.

**green politics,** an umbrella term for a wide range of groups pursuing environmental goals through political action, especially referring to "green parties" that focus primarily on ecological concerns and also often include concerns about nuclear issues, social responsibility, grassroots democracy, and non-violence. Several countries have specific green parties, including New Zealand, Belgium, Italy, France, the United Kingdom, and most notably Germany, from 1983. Many observers have ascribed the German green party's success to its ability to attract and create a coalition among people from the full political spectrum; later many green parties broadened their agendas, as they gained political muscle.

In most other countries, green parties have had less success, especially where politics are under the control of two or three major parties, and green issues are strongly linked with one end of the spectrum, usually the left. In these countries, such as the United States, much green-oriented political action is focused on shaping public opinion and building a popular consensus on environmental issues, which can then become a sufficiently potent force to influence political action by the major parties. Much activity is carried out through a wide range of environmental organizations, which seek new laws and enforcement of old ones on the local, state, and national level (see ENVIRONMENTAL LAWS). However, many people active in the green movement mistrust mainstream organizations, whether environmental or political, and have a more anarchic approach (see DEEP ECOLOGY; SOCIAL ECOLOGY; ECOFEMINISM).

## For more information and action:

- **AMERICANS FOR THE ENVIRONMENT (AFE),** (202-797-6665). Publishes *The Power of the Green Vote* and *The Rising Tide: Public Opinion, Policy and Politics.*
- **NATIONAL AUDUBON SOCIETY,** (212-832-3200; *Audubon Action Line* 202-547-9017).
- **U.S. PUBLIC INTEREST RESEARCH GROUP (PIRG),** (202-546-9707). Publishes *Green Politics: Environmental Initiatives on State and Local Ballots in 1990* (1990).

## Other references:

*Beyond the European Left: Ideology and Political Action in the Belgian Ecology Parties.* Herbert Kitschelt and Staf Hellemans. Duke University Press, 1990.

**green revolution,** the widespread movement to ease chronic food shortages in developing countries through the development and planting of high-yielding varieties (HYVs), primarily grains, using the techniques of BIO-TECHNOLOGY. Developed from several agricultural research centers established in Mexico and elsewhere in the early 1940s under Rockefeller and Ford Foundation auspices, the green revolution was especially associated with Norman BORLAUG, whose work in Mexico from 1944 won the 1970 Nobel Peace Prize. This work had considerable international support, and HYVs were planted widely in developing countries from the mid-1960s. Four early research centers later served as the nucleus for the CONSULTATIVE GROUP ON INTERNATIONAL AGRICULTURAL RESEARCH, formed in 1971.

In those decades of rapidly rising POPULATION and impending FAMINE AND FOOD INSECURITY, the green revolution did indeed help ease chronic hunger in many parts of the world. It was not, however, a complete solution and

in fact raised many other problems. HYVs are highly dependent on irrigation, fertilizers, and PESTICIDES, and so can be used only by those who can afford to provide these, not by the poorest farmers. The accumulating cost of DAMS, irrigation projects, and chemicals contributed to rising Third World debt, much of it for large-scale DEVELOPMENT projects. And because of distribution problems within countries, and export of some grains from some poor countries, the resulting products did not always reach those in need.

In addition, by requiring chemical input, the green revolution led to the ENVIRONMENTAL DEGRADATION of many areas, including SALINIZATION and WATER POLLUTION. Combined with the focus on single crops (see MONOCULTURE), the HYVs also led to a lessening of BIOLOGICAL DIVERSITY, as traditional hardier varieties were replaced and sometimes destroyed. The HYVs were also more vulnerable to molds and other storage problems, so large amounts—sometimes 30 percent or more—were sometimes lost, and further applications of pesticides were needed to save the stored grain.

As these and other problems became apparent, environmentalists pressed for agricultural research to focus more on low-input SUSTAINABLE AGRICULTURE and on fruits and vegetables that form the staple diet of the poor, not primarily grains. (See BIOTECHNOLOGY; also BIOTECHNOLOGY AND GENETIC ENGINEERING INFORMATION AND ACTION GUIDE on page 43.)

**greenways,** undeveloped corridors within developed areas, often along RIVERS and WETLANDS, but also following abandoned railroad lines, utility rights-of-way, canals, and ridgelines. Such corridors provide enormously attractive areas within urban settings, offering oases for frazzled humans, recreation areas, and places to experience natural landscapes, as well as linking historic sites. But the main impetus for greenways comes from the new understanding that large isolated open spaces result in fragmentation of wildlife HABITAT and resulting loss of BIOLOGICAL DIVERSITY. Greenways can provide crucial connecting links between large open spaces, such as parks, WILDLIFE REFUGES, and FORESTS, allowing wildlife to travel for MIGRATION to winter or breeding grounds, to forage, or simply to escape an area that has become too crowded or dangerous. Greenways along water routes are critical for the survival of many aquatic birds and animals. Because of the EDGE EFFECT, diversity of wildlife is encouraged.

Greenways also counteract ENVIRONMENTAL DEGRADATION, holding back and then slowly releasing runoff, thereby reducing flooding; slowing EROSION; controlling sediment buildup (see SEDIMENTATION); and enhancing the environment's natural ability to deal with POLLUTION (see WATER POLLUTION). Natural areas serve to counteract GLOBAL WARMING, but in case of massive CLIMATE CHANGE greenways will offer vital escape routes for wildlife traveling to new habitats, such as those further north.

In some countries, notably parts of Europe, greenways (though not named so) have long been part of the public heritage. But in the United States, because of complicated legal, financial, and jurisdictional questions, creating greenways can be a time-consuming, expensive process, one that requires imagination, good planning, and community-wide cooperation from individual landowners, businesses, organizations, and government agencies. Many greenways have already been established, however, and many others are planned. The environmental organizations who developed BLUEPRINT FOR THE ENVIRONMENT recommended that the FOREST SERVICE coordinate the services involved in creating greenway networks.

## For more information and action:

- **CONSERVATION FUND, THE,** (703-525-6300). Sponsors the *American Greenways* project; publishes *Common Ground,* a bimonthly newsletter.
- **NATIONAL INSTITUTE FOR URBAN WILDLIFE,** (301-596-3311 or 301-995-1119). Publishes *Wildlife Reserves and Corridors in the Urban Environment: A Guide to Ecological Landscape Planning and Resource Conservation* (L.W. Adams and L.E. Dove, 1989).
- **NATIONAL PARK SERVICE,** (202-208-4917). Publishes *The Ecology of Greenways* and *The Economic Benefits of Greenways.*
- **RAILS-TO-TRAILS CONSERVANCY,** (202-797-5400). Publishes *Converting Rails-to-Trails: A Citizen's Manual.*
- **WILDLIFE HABITAT ENHANCEMENT COUNCIL (WHEC),** (301-588-8994). Helps corporations develop wildlife projects, including wildlife corridors.

## Other reference:

*Greenways for America*, Charles E. Little. Johns Hopkins University Press, 1990.

**grey list,** nickname for the HAZARDOUS SUBSTANCES listed in Annex 2 of the CONVENTION ON THE PREVENTION OF MARINE POLLUTION BY DUMPING OF WASTE AND OTHER MATTER (LONDON DUMPING CONVENTION or LDC), for which ocean dumping is allowed only by special permit.

Pinhook Swamp corridor purchased by The Nature Conservancy and the U.S. Forest Service to provide a 15-mile land bridge between Okefenokee National Wildlife Refuge in Georgia and the Osceola National Forest in Florida.

**Source:** Illustration by M.R. Clark, copyright 1990 Defenders of Wildlife, reprinted with permission.

**Group of Ten,** a popular name for 10 environmental organizations that meet informally several times a year to exchange information on environmental and related concerns, though the organizations themselves act together only on occasion, and may disagree with each other on specific issues. The group includes FRIENDS OF THE EARTH, the NATIONAL WILDLIFE FEDERATION, the NATIONAL RESOURCES DEFENSE COUNCIL, the WILDERNESS SOCIETY, the ENVIRONMENTAL DEFENSE FUND, the IZAAK WALTON LEAGUE, the NATIONAL AUDUBON SOCIETY, the NATIONAL PARKS AND CONSERVATION ASSOCIATION, the SIERRA CLUB, and the Sierra Club Legal Defense Fund.

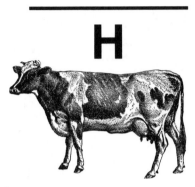

# H

**habitat,** the natural home of an individual or SPECIES of plant or animal; the necessary combination of food, water, cover, and other resources it requires for life. Among these are other living organisms, some of them food sources, as well as conditions such as climate, water, soil, and vegetative cover, available in the right amount and location to be handy for feeding, escape, and breeding. Each species is adapted to certain types and amounts of resources, and if they are not available many members of the species may be weakened and die. Those that survive may do so because their genetic makeup allows them to do so (see BIOLOGICAL DIVERSITY) or because they are able to migrate to another place where the necessary resources are available (see MIGRATION). However, if biological diversity has been lost, if possible migration destinations are no longer available (as when they have been turned into CROPLAND or settlements), if those migration sites no longer have the needed resources, if migration is impossible (as from an island), or if change comes too rapidly for a species to migrate or otherwise adapt (as with rapid CLIMATE CHANGE), the species may be in danger of EXTINCTION (see ENDANGERED SPECIES).

Habitats are classified in various ways, primarily on the basis of the dominant vegetation and its associated environmental conditions; so a habitat in the Pacific Northwest might be described as old-growth temperate coniferous FOREST. Within the world's several general types of biological regions—BIOMES or *major life zones*, such as forest or GRASSLANDS—are found many varied habitats. The immediate surroundings of an individual or community, such as a fallen tree or CAVE entrance, is called a *microhabitat*.

Though many species may occupy the same habitat, each has its own specific needs. Some are highly specialized, such as the PANDAS that require bamboo for food, and some have elaborate needs dependent on a complex set of interrelationships, such as the Douglas fir that is able to get the nutrients it needs when the California red-backed vole eats truffles, in the process spreading truffle spores (see ECOSYSTEM DIVERSITY on page 99). Other species are more flexible, in terms of their needs, and sometimes are able to migrate to other places if their original habitat is disturbed. In general, the more diverse a habitat, the less susceptible it is to insects, disease, and other natural disasters, and the more stable the population of both plants and animals. Diversity in the multitude of individual habitats contributes to the overall biological diversity that is important to the world's health.

Humans have been altering habitats for thousands of years. At its most obvious, conversion of forest or grassland to cropland involves destruction of habitat and loss of biodiversity. In recent decades, however, with the rapid increase in DEVELOPMENT and growth in POPULATION, and consequent DEFORESTATION, DESERTIFICATION, EROSION, and ENVIRONMENTAL DEGRADATION, natural habitats have been lost at an astonishing and alarming rate. Even those habitats not totally destroyed are often so fragmented as to support only a fraction of their previous wildlife. In its 1990 report REDUCING RISKS: SETTING PRIORITIES AND STRATEGIES FOR ENVIRONMENTAL PROTECTION, the ENVIRONMENTAL PROTECTION AGENCY (EPA) classified habitat alteration and destruction as a "relatively high-risk problem," noting that: "Humans are altering and destroying natural habitats in many places worldwide, e.g., by the draining and degradation of wetlands, soil erosion, and the deforestation of tropical and temperate forests.'' Certainly habitat loss is one of the greatest threats to the many endangered species. Although most attention has been focused on the rainforests (see FORESTS), for good reason given the enormous diversity of these areas, significant habitat loss is also found in other general types of habitat, including grasslands, WETLANDS, and other aquatic habitats, such as MANGROVES and CORAL REEFS.

Though the picture is grim, many individuals and organizations have been working throughout the world to preserve existing habitats, through numerous WILDLIFE REFUGES, including BIOSPHERE RESERVES considered to be of particular international importance. Many are also working to revive damaged habitats (see RESTORATION ECOLOGY). Much has been learned, too, about the most effective design for such nature preserves. (See ENDANGERED SPECIES AND BIOLOGICAL DIVERSITY INFORMATION AND ACTION GUIDE on page 104; also ECOSYSTEM; WILDLIFE REFUGES; WILDERNESS; as well as broad types of habitats, such as FORESTS.)

**halogens,** a group of five elements—fluorine, chlorine, bromine, iodine, and astatine—with similarities in chemical structure and all highly reactive, forming new compounds readily, often some of the most TOXIC CHEMICALS known, such as CHLORINATED HYDROCARBONS and many SYNTHETIC ORGANIC CHEMICALS (SOCs). A compound in which one or more hydrogen atoms is replaced by a halogen atom is said to be *halogenated*. Chlorobenzene, for example, is a halogenated compound, formed when chlorine is added to benzene.

**halons,** a group of chemical compounds implicated in destruction of the OZONE LAYER, and therefore scheduled to be banned under the 1990 amended agreement to the MONTREAL PROTOCOL ON SUBSTANCES THAT DEPLETE THE OZONE LAYER, specifically halons 1211, 1301, and 2402, sometimes used as fire-extinguishing chemicals.

**Hanford Nuclear Reservation,** see NUCLEAR WEAPONS ESTABLISHMENT, U.S.

**Hawaiian Patriot oil spill,** leakage of the entire cargo— 30 million gallons (approximately 100,000 tons)—of the OIL tanker *Hawaiian Patriot* into the sea in mid-Pacific 350 miles west of Honolulu, Hawaii, on February 24, 1977. The ship began leaking, then caught fire, and was lost; one crew member died. (See OIL.)

**Hazardous Substance Response Trust Fund,** official name of one of the funds known as SUPERFUND.

**hazardous substances,** see TOXIC CHEMICALS.

**hazardous waste,** any waste from whatever source— home, municipal, agricultural, or industrial—that poses a threat to the environment, including substances that are toxic, readily flammable, corrosive, explosive, or otherwise chemically reactive. Hazardous waste has become a major modern concern, and rightly so considering the large numbers of TOXIC CHEMICALS (and products made from them) that have been introduced into the environment in recent decades, as well as RADIOACTIVE WASTE.

Because of wide concern, hazardous waste has been the subject of numerous ENVIRONMENTAL LAWS, with somewhat varying definitions of hazardous materials. In the United States, under the RESOURCE CONSERVATION AND RECOVERY ACT (RCRA), hazardous waste is defined as ''solid waste, or combinations of solid waste, that because of its quantity, concentration, or physical, chemical or infectious characteristics, may pose a hazard to human health or the environment''; the law also defines these categories more specifically and outlines methods to be used to prevent ''further contamination from improper waste disposal.'' The COMPREHENSIVE ENVIRONMENTAL RESPONSE, COMPENSATION AND LIABILITY ACT (CERCLA) defines *hazardous substance* as ''any substance that, when released into the environment, may present substantial danger to public health, welfare, or the environment''; *extremely hazardous substances* are those that ''could cause serious, irreversible health effects from a single exposure'' and are treated specially in terms of chemical emergency planning. (For a discussion of other laws, see TOXIC CHEMICALS; for a list of such substances, see TOXIC CHEMICALS AND HAZARDOUS SUBSTANCES on page 407.) However, many hazardous substances are not defined as such, and so are not regulated.

Before it was realized how dangerous many of these substances are, much hazardous waste was handled in the same way as other wastes—simply dumped, filled, or poured into the environment, as at LOVE CANAL. Much still is disposed of in that same totally irresponsible way, often illegally, often far from the site of its generation and use. Various international agreements have attempted to deal with the trafficking in and mishandling of hazardous waste, including the CONVENTION ON THE PREVENTION OF MARINE POLLUTION BY DUMPING OF WASTE AND OTHER MATTER. The 1990 Basel Convention on the Transboundary Movement of Waste, sponsored by the UNITED NATIONS ENVIRONMENT PROGRAMME (UNEP), requires signatory countries to give notice of proposed international hazardous waste shipments and obtain prior written consent to receive the shipments, the aim being to ensure that the waste will be "managed in an 'environmentally sound manner' by the receiving country."

In the United States, the Resource Conservation and Recovery Act has attempted to deal with the problem of hazardous waste by establishing a "cradle-to-grave" monitoring system, with documents called *manifests* used for tracing hazardous materials from where it is generated to its final disposal, with requirements for handling at each stage: generation, transport, use, treatment, storage, and disposal. That has established considerably more control over the process and lessened pollution of air, water, and land along the way.

The crucial problem is, however, that there is as yet no satisfactory, environmentally safe way of disposing of most of the hazardous waste generated in the world. The three main types are:

- **organic compounds,** those composed primarily of carbon, hydrogen, and oxygen. Some have been synthesized in the laboratory, while others derive from living or once-living matter, such as OIL (see PETROCHEMICALS). Because the elements in organic compounds are the stuff of life, in theory they can be broken down into harmless, everyday substances such as water and CARBON DIOXIDE by a series of stages: biological decomposition, chemical neutralization, precipitation, and steam stripping, in which the hazardous compounds are vaporized and captured by AIR POLLUTION control equipment (though the residue still remains to be dealt with). However, organics are widespread, insidiously permeate much of the environment, and then are extremely difficult (and therefore expensive) to filter out and treat. (See WATER POLLUTION for approaches to filtering out organics.) The INCINERATION of organic compounds is one increasingly used approach to breaking them down and destroying them; another is BIOREMEDIATION, still in the experimental stage.
- **inorganic compounds,** nonliving, non-carbon-containing substances, notably HEAVY METALS. Because metals are elements, they cannot be destroyed; they may be broken down from complex compounds to their most simple, elemental forms, but these remain and must ultimately be disposed of in the environment in some way. RECYCLING or RESOURCE RECOVERY is the best approach, both to keep inorganic compounds from fouling the environment and to reduce the need for more MINING and yet more destruction. Where that is not possible, inorganic hazardous waste may sometimes be combined with chemical stabilizers to form cementlike blocks; this process, called *solidification*, lessens the amount of LEACHING into the soil.

- **radioactive waste,** matter that gives off RADIATION, for which no proper treatment or disposal method has yet been developed, decades into the nuclear era. Quite apart from the enormously dangerous radioactive waste at NUCLEAR WEAPONS and NUCLEAR ENERGY plants, there is *low-level radioactive waste* (LLRW), which is considered *below regulatory concern* (BRC) and therefore not subject to regulation and special handling.

In the end, however, the hazardous waste ends up in the environment. In the past and still at present, most of it ends up in *surface impoundments*, human-made ponds on industrial sites. Though they have come under some regulatory control, surface impoundments abound and have given us some notable hazardous waste sites. Some abandoned sites have been taken over by the government for clean-up (see SUPERFUND). Unfortunately, clean-up is something of a misnomer, since what goes under that heading is very often simply a partial dilution of toxic material or its removal from one site or medium to another (as from land to air), but with the total amount of toxicity not substantially reduced.

Beyond landfills and surface impoundments, some hazardous waste is pretreated to make it less toxic, and then sent for standard wastewater treatment (see WATER POLLUTION); some is burned (see INCINERATION); some is injected into wells deep underground; and the remainder—including solidified waste and ash from burning—goes into landfills. The trouble with all of these "solutions" is that the material is still often highly toxic and that the various processes release pollutants into air, land, and water. In the United States, for example, the 1976 Resource Conservation and Recovery Act set restrictions and controls on hazardous waste disposal facilities, which were strengthened by the 1984 Hazardous and Solid Waste Amendments (HSWA). Technical requirements for landfills and surface impoundments include the use of liners and a protective cover or cap; monitoring of groundwater quality, for 30 years after facilities are closed; control of EROSION; detection and collection of leachate (see LEACHING); and prevention of rainfall from entering. Many landfills have, in fact, been forced to close because they were unable or unwilling to meet these requirements. The HSWA also extended regulatory control to *small-quantity generators*, such as dry cleaners, laboratories, and vehicle repair shops; where once these could dispose of their hazardous waste in community waste sites, now they can only use those hazardous waste facilities with permits from the ENVIRONMENTAL PROTECTION AGENCY (EPA).

With fewer landfills available, incineration has been widely used as a disposal method, though it leads to significant AIR POLLUTION and results in highly toxic ash. Deep-injection wells are increasingly being used for disposal of hazardous waste, including radioactive waste. Theoretically, these wells are supposed to be drilled below the AQUIFERS and other groundwater sources normally tapped for water, but environmentalists are very concerned that vital WATER RESOURCES will be contaminated, perhaps permanently, by highly toxic materials. In any case, too little is known about the long-term effects of such deep-injection disposal.

Hazardous waste is a classic example of shortsightedness, with enormous amounts of toxic materials being generated with little or no thought as to how, later, to render them harmless to the environment. At present and in the forseeable future, while such methods are being sought, the efforts of many environmentalists and researchers are focused on ways to reduce the amounts of hazardous waste generated, among them:

- lessen use of products that generate hazardous waste, often as part of a wider move to a simpler, more environmentally friendly lifestyle.
- substitute harmless products for harmful ones, as in replacement of biologically based sprays for chemical PESTICIDES.
- make manufacturing processes more efficient, to reduce the amount of toxic substances required or generated.
- recycle toxic materials for use, on the industrial front called RESOURCE RECOVERY, as by capturing heavy metals for reuse in other production processes.
- develop new processes for detoxifying hazardous waste, which is easier said than done.

In the meantime, however, hazardous waste continues to be generated and to pile up in the environment, with no real solution in sight. (See TOXIC CHEMICAL AND HAZARDOUS WASTE INFORMATION AND ACTION GUIDE on page 302, also TOXIC CHEMICALS AND HAZARDOUS SUBSTANCES on page 407, KNOWN HEALTH EFFECTS OF TOXIC CHEMICALS on page 416; SUPERFUND SITES on page 422; STEPS IN CLEANING UP A SUPERFUND SITE on page 294; also TOXIC CHEMICALS; WASTE DISPOSAL; INCINERATION; RECYCLING; LEAKING UNDERGROUND STORAGE TANKS; and various laws mentioned above, including SUPERFUND.)

**heat pump,** a device that not only cools, like an air conditioner, but is reversible to heat as well. In warm weather, it actually operates very much like an air conditioner, gathering excess heat from the indoors and sending it outdoors. In cool weather the machine does the reverse, collecting heat from the outdoors and feeding it into the indoors, a process that is far more energy efficient than using an electric heater indoors.

Used for some thirty years, heat pumps are best suited to midtemperate areas, such as the American South, where their efficiency matches conventional and far more expensive OIL or NATURAL GAS systems. When temperature differences between indoors and outdoors are great (as during a New England winter), heat pumps require more and more electricity to do their work, and in below-freezing temperatures they are nearly useless. Heat pumps can be noisy, drafty, and ineffective in removing humidity, especially when not properly sized and designed for the house, but are generally so efficient that they are presently being installed in about 30 percent of new American homes and are found in nearly all homes in some areas, sometimes installed with subsidies from utility companies. (See ENERGY RESOURCES.)

**heavy metals,** a range of metallic elements of widely differing characteristics and effects on living organisms, including LEAD, MERCURY, ALUMINUM, CADMIUM, COPPER, arsenic, iron, manganese, CHROMIUM, silver, beryllium nickel, selenium, and zinc. Some of these metals are normally found in—and are even necessary in trace amounts to—humans and other living organisms, such as iron, copper, zinc, and manganese. But many are not needed and all are highly toxic to living beings except in the smallest amounts. As chemical elements, rather than compounds, heavy metals cannot be converted or destroyed, and so are extremely difficult to dispose of without harming the environment, as they tend to accumulate in the tissues of living organisms and concentrate in the FOOD CHAIN (see BIOACCUMULATION), especially in marine life, such as shellfish, which can then become highly toxic to humans and others who eat them, as in the Minimata Bay poisoning (see MERCURY).

Relatively small amounts of heavy metals are, like other elements, normally circulated in the great BIOGEOCHEMICAL CYCLES that bind the life of the earth together. But modern industrial activities use far more of these elements than can be readily handled by the environment's normal processes, which easily become overwhelmed. Industrial RECYCLING efforts, such as mandated by the RESOURCE CONSERVATION AND RECOVERY ACT (RCRA), as well as community efforts, are aimed at keeping heavy metals out of the environment, where they would contaminate water, land, and (as when burned) air. Easier said than done, however, because the heavy metals are often part of complex substances that are hard to break down for reuse. Failure to recycle and reuse heavy metals also leads to more MINING and therefore more disruption to the environment, to supply new sources of the metals to meet current needs. Some countries, such as Sweden, are restricting use of some heavy metals, to lessen the problems of HAZARDOUS WASTE, AIR POLLUTION, and WATER POLLUTION.

In their *World Resources 1987*, the WORLD RESOURCE INSTITUTE noted that although scientists have concerns about a wide range of toxic metals, "routine monitoring is usually carried out only for mercury, lead, copper, and cadmium," and even that data is rather fragmentary. Many marine environments are heavily contaminated with heavy metals, including New York harbor, the North Sea, and the MEDITERRANEAN SEA, especially off the French coast. Urban areas are also heavily contaminated, but concentrations of heavy metals are also found in WILDERNESS areas of the United States and Central Europe, often deposited through the mechanism of ACID RAIN, which dissolves heavy metals. Drinking water is routinely monitored for several heavy metals (see SAFE DRINKING WATER ACT; also PRIMARY DRINKING WATER STANDARDS on page 274). Many are also regulated as TOXIC CHEMICALS or HAZARDOUS SUBSTANCES. (See TOXIC CHEMICALS AND HAZARDOUS SUBSTANCES on page 407; KNOWN HEALTH EFFECTS OF TOXIC CHEMICALS on page 416; RANKING OF ENVIRONMENTAL PROBLEM AREAS BY POPULATION CANCER RISK on page 312.)

### For more information and action:

• ENVIRONMENTAL DEFENSE FUND (EDF), (212-505-2100). Publishes *Lurking on the Bottom: Heavy Metals in the Hudson-Raritan Estuary* (Sarah L. Clark, 1990).

**heptachlor,** a highly toxic PESTICIDE (see CYCLODIENES).

**herbicides,** a type of chemical compound used for killing unwanted plants (see PESTICIDES).

**herbivorous,** plant-eating, describing animals that eat plants low on the FOOD CHAIN, rather than eating other animals, as do *carnivores*, or eating both plants and animals, as do *omnivores*. An herbivorous diet makes better use of food energy in natural resources. Though most herbivores are relatively small animals, some quite large beings are herbivores, including ELEPHANTS, RHINOCEROSES, and cows. (See VEGETARIANISM.)

**hexachloride,** a type of PESTICIDE (see CHLORINATED HYDROCARBONS).

**hexachlorobenzene (HCB),** a type of PESTICIDE (see CHLORINATED HYDROCARBONS).

**high-level radioactive waste (HLRW),** fuel that has been irradiated in nuclear reactors, and liquid waste re-

sulting from chemical reprocessing of spent nuclear fuel, often liquid but sometimes solidified (see RADIOACTIVE WASTE).

**high-yielding varieties (HYVs),** plants modified for high production using the techniques of BIOTECHNOLOGY, the basis for the GREEN REVOLUTION.

**Hiroshima and Nagasaki,** two Japanese cities, the targets of the first two atomic bombs used in warfare, beginning the period of fear for the survival of life on earth known as the Nuclear Age. Hiroshima, on Honshu Island, was in the summer of 1945 a city of 350,000 people. Nagasaki, on Kyushu Island, was a city of 230,000. Neither city was a primary military target; both bombings were intended as demonstrations of the killing power of the new atomic weapons, aimed at forcing quick, unconditional Japanese surrender and the end of World War II.

On August 6, 1945, at 8:15 A.M., the *Enola Gay*, a U.S. Air Force B-29 bomber, dropped a single atomic bomb on Hiroshima, which exploded in the air near the center of the city, immediately or very soon afterward killing an estimated 70,000 to 80,000 people, injuring a similar number, and destroying most of the city's structures. Within five years, an estimated 75,000 to 125,000 more had died, of radiation sickness, cancer, and many other bomb-related causes. Tens of thousands more died and many thousands more suffered serious illness and deformity in the decades that followed, including thousands of children unborn at the time of the bombing.

On August 9, a second atomic bombing took place; the American bomber crew had been unable to see Kokura, the intended target, because of cloud cover, and dropped its bomb on Nagasaki, an alternate target. The second bomb immediately or soon thereafter killed 40,000 to 70,000 people, injured a similar number, and destroyed approximately half the city's structures. Within five years an estimated 50,000 to 100,000 more had died, again of radiation sickness, cancer, and other bomb-related causes, with tens of thousands more victims in the decades that followed. In both cities, survivors and their children are still dying because of the bombings that occurred almost half a century ago, at this decisive turning point in world history.

In the decades that have followed, the possibility of an atomic holocaust has always been apparent. The event was memorialized in scores of works, such as John Hersey's book *Hiroshima*, and in such films as Alain Resnais' *Hiroshima, Mon Amour*, while such films as ON THE BEACH, FAIL SAFE, and DR. STRANGELOVE warned of the humanity-destroying dangers of nuclear war. The event also ushered in the Cold War, the decades of armed standoff between the United States and the Soviet Union, with each able to destroy the other and the world, while many other countries also reached for atomic weapons and delivery systems. For many years, the Federation of Atomic Scientists characterized the humanity-destroying nuclear clock as standing at "one minute to midnight," moving the clock back a little as the Cold War ended. But only a little, for NUCLEAR WEAPONS continue to proliferate, and even the world of the great powers is far from stable. (See NUCLEAR WEAPONS; also NUCLEAR ISSUES INFORMATION AND ACTION GUIDE on page 215.)

**Home Energy Rating System (HERS),** an evaluation of the energy efficiency level of a home, including outlining its specific energy-conserving features. (see ENERGY RESOURCES.)

**hot spot,** an area with a high concentration of TOXIC CHEMICALS or other HAZARDOUS SUBSTANCES, including nuclear or other RADIOACTIVE WASTE. These areas, sometimes called *toxic hot spots*, are the focus of major cleanup activities, such as those under SUPERFUND (See SUPERFUND SITES on page 422).

A hot spot is also a region rich in species and in imminent danger of destruction. Such areas are often found on islands, such as MADAGASCAR or parts of the Philippines, including "islands" of relatively untouched habitat within developed lands.

**Houston Ship Channel oil spill,** leakage of an estimated 250,000 gallons (approximately 850 tons) of crude OIL in the Houston Ship Channel after a June 23, 1989 collision between the freighter *Rachel B* and an oil barge. Although over half the spill was recovered and the environmental damage was not great, the accident was perceived by many as part of a much larger oil spill problem, coming as it did on the same day as a major oil spill in NARRAGANSETT BAY, a day before another major spill in the DELAWARE RIVER, and only three months after the March 24, 1989 EXXON VALDEZ disaster. (See OIL.)

**Human Ecology Action League (HEAL)** (P.O. Box 49126, Atlanta, GA 30359; 404-248-1898; Ken Dominy, President), a membership organization founded in 1977 "to serve those whose health has been adversely affected by environmental exposures; to provide information to those concerned about the health effects of chemicals; and to alert the general public about the potential danger of chemicals." HEAL's aims are to "encourage healthy lifestyles that minimize potentially hazardous environmental exposures," often working through local chapters and support groups, sharing information, experiences, and news of new developments. HEAL publishes various materials on chemical sensitivites and ENVIRONMENTAL ILLNESS, including the quarterly magazine *The Human Ecologist,* the brochure *Chemicals Can Affect Your Health,* and numerous resource lists, reading lists, information, sheets and information packs.

**hunting,** the tracking, trapping, and often killing of animals by humans, for food, other products, captive breeding, display, or sport. Hunting was a vital part of the way of life from the earliest human societies; animals provided an important food source, and most other parts of the animals, such as furs, bones, feathers, or horns, were also put to human use. Many INDIGENOUS PEOPLES still build their lives around hunting. Popular impression has it that traditional communities live in a "balanced state of nature," killing only enough for their survival and allowing herds to maintain stable populations; while that is true of some indigenous peoples, it is important to remember that human hunters drove numerous species (such as mammoths) to EXTINCTION long before modern technology.

However, most modern environmentalists focus their concern on hunting by more technologically advanced people, for sport, food, or commercial purposes. Many of the earliest leaders in the conservation movement were hunters (like those in the BOONE AND CROCKETT CLUB), who were disturbed by indiscriminate and unlimited killing of animals, but believed that hunting was a long and deep human tradition, and that a certain amount of hunting was necessary to keep in check animal populations that might otherwise grow so fast as to threaten the natural balance in the region. From such thinking sprang government licensing of hunters and restrictions on hunting, with the limits set by estimates of the health of various game animal populations, and of the optimum size of the population for the CARRYING CAPACITY of the land it occupies. Such considerations are still very much a part of the thinking of most wildlife and range managers, public and private. Conservation-minded hunters are often very active in maintaining or restoring HABITAT for game animals, which may have substantial benefits for other plants and animals as well, (see DUCKS UNLIMITED, for example).

For some environmentalists, however, some different philosophies have developed. One posits that humans have no right to use animals for food or any other purpose (see VEGETARIANISM; DEEP ECOLOGY). Others, perhaps less philosophically rigorous, are primarily concerned about the killing of animals that are biologically close to humans (such as other mammals) or are attractive to humans (such as certain birds). Such views leave open the question of how humans should respond if unchecked animal populations grow out of control, and threaten other animals, plants, or whole habitats. Many environmentalists are also concerned with cruelty to animals in hunting and trapping, focusing for example on banning the use of painful devices such as leghold traps, and seeking through various types of protest to end purely sport hunting, such as organized fox hunting.

But whatever their specific views on other matters, environmentalists certainly agree on the necessity to protect ENDANGERED SPECIES. Threats to species and habitats have increased as humans have developed increasingly effective hunting technology, such as guns or tracking devices; as large-scale commercial markets have developed for animals and animal products; and as human desire for FOREST products and prime land has resulted in destruction of animal habitats, especially with rising POPULATION. Numerous ENVIRONMENTAL LAWS are designed to protect threatened species, limited or prohibiting WILDLIFE TRADE; restricting or barring hunting of specified populations of animals or in certain areas; and ending the market for products of endangered and threatened species. Indigenous peoples are often excepted from restrictions placed on the killing or taking of certain species, even endangered ones. However, such provisions must be carefully monitored for, as they acquire modern technology, many "traditional peoples" can be as dangerous to a species' survival as any other hunter.

Also, because so many animals and animal products are so highly prized, and because the areas where they are found are often very poor, even where animals are protected, illicit hunting, or *poaching*, is a substantial problem. In some WILDLIFE REFUGES, governments have actually hired former poachers as armed guards, to provide for their economic needs and forestall other hunters. Many environmentalists also promote ECOTOURISM as a way of providing economically for local people who would normally make all or part of their living from hunting, so many safaris that once would have featured rifles now are dominated by cameras.

### For more information and action:

- ANIMAL PROTECTION INSTITUTE (API), (916-731-5521). Publishes *Trapping: Can We Allow This Cruel Practice to Continue?*
- BOONE AND CROCKETT CLUB, (703-221-1888). Publishes a quarterly newsletter, *Rules of Fair Chase*, for hunters, and various reference works.
- **Fund for Animals, Inc.** (212-246-2096 or 246-2632). Publishes *The Bloody Business of Fur, An Overview of Killing for Sport,* and *The Destruction of Our Nation's Waterfowl.*
- **Humane Society of the United States (HSUS),** (202-452-

1100). Publishes *Fur Shame: HSUS Campaign Targets Consumers* and *Fur Is Out; Compassion Is In;* fact sheets on wild-caught birds, steel-jaw leghold traps, trapping, and hunter harassment; and brochures such as *Hunted Wildlife* and *Trapped Animals.* (See ANIMAL RIGHTS AND WELFARE INFORMATION AND ACTION GUIDE on page 361.)

- **International Society for Animal Rights (ISAR),** (717-586-2200). Publishes *Surplus Population: A Fallacious Basis for Sport Hunting* and fact sheets on furs. (See ANIMAL RIGHTS AND WELFARE INFORMATION AND ACTION GUIDE on page 361.)
- NATIONAL PARKS AND CONSERVATION ASSOCIATION (NPCA), (202-944-8530).
- NATIONAL INSTITUTE FOR URBAN WILDLIFE, (301-596-3311 or 301-995-1119). Publishes the *Wildlife Habitat Conservation Teachers' Pac* series, covering *Hunting and Wildlife Management.*
- TRAFFIC (TRADE RECORDS ANALYSIUS OF FLORA AND FAUNA IN COMMERCE), (202-293-4800). Monitors global trade in wildlife and wildlife products; publishes *Fur Trade, Elephant Ivory Trade,* and *Primate Trade.*
- WILDLIFE INFORMATION CENTER (WIC), (215-434-1637). Publishes Fact Sheet on *Hunting.*
- WILDLIFE MANAGEMENT INSTITUTE (WMI), (202-371-1808).
- WILDLIFE SOCIETY, THE, (301-897-9770). Publishes *Traps, Trapping, and Furbearer Management.*
- WORLD SOCIETY FOR THE PROTECTION OF ANIMALS (WSPA), (617-522-7000).

(See also ENDANGERED SPECIES; ANIMAL RIGHTS MOVEMENT; VEGETARIANISM.)

**Huntington Beach oil spill,** a spill of an estimated 400,000 gallons (approximately 1,400 tons) of OIL from the tanker *American Trader* on February 7, 1990, which occurred only two miles offshore of Huntington Beach, California, a major recreational area in heavily populated Orange County, south of Los Angeles. By February 15, the 15-mile-long oil slick had struck Huntington Beach and areas south along the shore, causing considerable environmental damage. The spill attracted massive media attention, coming as it did in the wake of the 1989 EXXON VALDEZ disaster and several other highly visible major spills on the Pacific, Gulf, and Atlantic coasts. Once again, television and newspaper photos of oil-drenched, dying seabirds and oil-blackened, unusable beaches called public attention to the growing oil spill problem (See OIL.)

**hydrocarbons (HC),** a massive family of chemicals made up of hydrogen and carbon atoms, in varying proportions and structures. FOSSIL FUELS are largely made up of hydrocarbons, though often with other elements present, such as oxygen, nitrogen, and sulfur. PETROCHEMICALS, hydrocarbons derived from petroleum, are at the center of the modern chemical industry. Hydrocarbons to which chlorine has been added are known as CHLORINATED HYDROCARBONS, and are highly toxic, extremely persistent PESTICIDES. Those to which fluorine has been added are called *hydrofluorocarbons*, such as are used in aerosols, and are implicated in GLOBAL WARMING and depletion of the OZONE LAYER. Hydrocarbons also form the base of many other notable TOXIC CHEMICALS, such as VOLATILE ORGANIC COMPOUNDS (VOCs).

Many hydrocarbons are released into the atmosphere from incomplete combustion, either from fuel-burning power-generating plants or from the exhaust of automobiles and other vehicles running on internal combustion engines; as such they are major contributors to AIR POLLUTION, especially participants in the *photochemical reactions* that produce SMOG. Hydrocarbons are also commonly found in paint spraying, solvent cleaning, printing, and a wide variety of chemical, metal, and other operations. Traditionally hydrocarbons so produced have simply been released into the environment; however, in some countries laws now somewhat restrict such EMISSIONS, as does the high cost of hydrocarbon solvents. In recent years, chemical researchers have developed some hydrocarbons that are less volatile and easier to recover.

**hydrochlorofluorocarbons (HCFCs),** chemical compounds made of hydrogen, chlorine, fluorine, and carbon atoms; a type of SYNTHETIC ORGANIC CHEMICAL often used to substitute for CHLOROFLUOROCARBONS (CFCs), though causing many of the same environmental problems relating to depletion of the OZONE LAYER (only more slowly) and contributing to the GREENHOUSE EFFECT and GLOBAL WARMING. Used as an interim substitute for CFCs, HCFCs are scheduled to be phased out by 2020 if feasible, but banned completely by 2040 at the latest, under the 1990 amended agreement to the MONTREAL PROTOCOL ON SUBSTANCES THAT DEPLETE THE OZONE LAYER. (See also CHLOROFLUOROCARBONS.)

**hydropower,** the energy of flowing water harnessed to human ends. Before the mid-19th century, when FOSSIL FUELS began to dominate, hydropower was one of the main traditional ENERGY RESOURCES used by humans, particularly attractive because it was a RENEWABLE RESOURCE that continued to be available as a natural part of the WATER CYCLE. Clean and relatively nondisruptive to the environment (though the industries it powered often were not), it

was available for use on a small scale, wherever a stream or RIVER of sufficient year-round flow was available.

Waterwheels turned by water flowing through a narrow channel were widely used to produce mechanical energy to grind grain in mills, saw wood, pump water, and perform other such tasks. In the late 19th century, some of these small-scale installations were used instead to produce electricity, turning a rotating shaft connected to an alternator or generator; the resulting electricity could be used directly, stored in batteries, or used to produce electricity of quality equal to that sold by utilities. As COAL and then OIL and NATURAL GAS became the fuels of choice in industrialized countries, these installations were gradually abandoned, most of them falling into ruin, though some have been preserved or later restored, as through historic preservation.

In the 20th century, hydropower has generally meant not such small installations, but huge DAMS with massive turbines, which have become major power-producing systems. Considerable foreign aid for DEVELOPMENT has focused on building such large-scale projects, which also often provide irrigation systems, in Third World countries. Though in earlier decades lauded for bringing cheap power to poor populations, massive hydropower dams have more recently come under heavy fire for major disruptions of the ECOSYSTEMS along the rivers dammed for use, as well as the expulsion of many INDIGENOUS PEOPLES living in the affected areas. Canada's massive JAMES BAY HYDROPOWER PROJECT has, for example, displaced many of the Cree peoples, released into environment MERCURY formerly dormant in rocks, and affected the lives of plants and animals in the region, by changing river patterns. Environmentalists have expressed a whole range of concerns and recommendations about large hydropower projects (see THE SAN FRANCISCO DECLARATION OF THE INTERNATIONAL RIVERS NETWORK on page 79), especially stressing the need for environmental impact assessments before such projects are begun. However, in a world with rapidly increasing POPULATION and strained resources, large-scale hydropower plants offer a source of cheap power that will continue to attract people in many countries.

Since the energy crisis of the 1970s, many people have had renewed interest in small-scale hydropower projects. In the United States, the DEPARTMENT OF ENERGY noted that as of early 1987, over 1,600 small-scale plants were operating, while thousands of other sites are suitable for such projects, in some cases requiring relatively easy retrofitting of existing dams. Some small-scale systems are made more economical by being used also in irrigation, fire control, and drinking water supply.

Both large and small-scale hydropower systems can

cause problems for fish MIGRATION. During the spawning season, schools of fish such as salmon attempt to swim through the site and are killed in the turbines. Provision of a pathway for the migrating fish can prevent this problem but takes extra planning and in some cases also retrofitting.

**For more information and action:**

- **American Rivers** (202-547-6900). Operates *Hydropower Policy Center*. Publishes *Rivers at Risk: The Concerned Citizen's Guide to Hydropower*. (See RIVERS INFORMATION AND ACTION GUIDE on page 270.)
- **CONSERVATION AND RENEWABLE ENERGY INQUIRY AND REFERRAL SERVICE (CAREIRS)**, (800-523-2929, U.S. except AK and HI; for AK and HI, 800-233-3071). Publishes *Small-Scale Hydropower Systems*.

- **CULTURAL SURVIVAL (CS)**, (617-495-2562). Publishes *Hydroelectric Dams on the Xingu River and Indigenous Peoples* (Leinad Ayer O. Santos and Lucia M.M. de Andrade, 1990).
- **FRIENDS OF THE RIVER (FOR)**, (415-771-0400). Runs *Hydromania and Watershed Protection* campaign.
- **NATIONAL CENTER FOR APPROPRIATE TECHNOLOGY (NCAT)**, (406-494-4572).
- **NATURAL RESOURCES AND ENERGY DIVISION (NRED)**, (212-963-6205). Publishes *Joint Hydropower Development* (1988).
- **WORLD BANK** (Public Affairs: 202-473-1782).

(See also GANGES RIVER; GLEN CANYON DAM; JAMES BAY HYDROPOWER PROJECT; NARMADA VALLEY DAM PROJECT; THREE GORGES DAM: TWO FORKS DAM; ALTERNATIVE ENERGY; DAMS; WAVE POWER; ENERGY RESOURCES.)

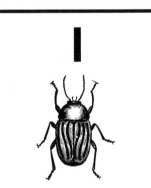

**I*Kare Wildlife Trust,** incorporated name for the INTERNATIONAL WILDLIFE COALITION.

**incineration,** burning of waste in a specially designed combustion chamber. Burning piles of garbage is a traditional method of WASTE DISPOSAL, one that became unacceptable with a rise in the amount of garbage and especially of TOXIC CHEMICALS. Many of these chemicals and products made from them are highly persistent, not breaking down by normal biological processes (see BIODEGRADABLE), and so must be disposed of very carefully if they are not to foul the environment. Many waste management professionals have turned to incineration to do the job.

Much burning of solid waste is done in municipal incin-

erators or standard industrial kilns, boilers, and furnaces. Many of these are *mass burn units*, burning whatever is fed into them; others are *refuse-derived plants*, burning the waste that remains after metals, glass, tires, and other such materials are separated out, with the mixed solid waste often in the form of "pellets" used as fuel. In some places *refuse-derived fuel* (RDF) operations are used to produce heat or electricity, in an approach called COGENERATION.

One major problem with such incineration is AIR POLLUTION. Even when facilities are equipped with SCRUBBERS, many types of substances, some of them toxic, are released into the air. The other major problem is that considerable refuse remains; some of it is so toxic that it meets government definitions of HAZARDOUS WASTE. If it is de-

## On Hazardous Waste Incineration

Hazardous waste incineration is riddled with unknowns, but one thing is certain: the health and the environment of communities in which incinerators are sited are at risk. Incinerators release unknown quantities of unknown chemicals, presenting health threats of unknown magnitude and unknown duration to the people and ecosystems of neighboring communities.

**Source:** Greenpeace Toxics, "Hazardous Waste Incinerators"

rived from household waste, it is generally considered exempt from standards that apply under laws such as the RESOURCE CONSERVATION AND RECOVERY ACT.

For highly toxic substances to be destroyed effectively requires specially designed *high-temperature incinerators.* In assessing the efficiency of such high-temperature incinerators for substances such as SYNTHETIC ORGANIC CHEMICALS, CHLORINATED HYDROCARBONS, and many other types of HAZARDOUS WASTE, the ENVIRONMENTAL PROTECTION AGENCY (EPA) requires a *destruction and removal efficiency* (DRE) of 99.99 percent for some kinds of toxic waste and 99.9999 percent for some other substances, such as PCBs; some incinerators have been given a DRE rating of 99.99999 percent. These are ideal ratings, however, and as many environmentalists have pointed out are assigned after a one-time "trial burn" with selected chemicals, not in everyday operation. And even if the DRE ratings were accurate, GREENPEACE Toxics has pointed out that while in one EPA-contracted study of 10 commercial incinerators, the average incinerator burned 36,865,000 of liquid hazardous waste in one year, that would mean some 3,686 pounds of unburned toxic waste released into the environment.

The problem is that the incineration process must be managed with great care if it is to be properly effective: the products in the incineration chamber must be kept at the right temperature for the right length of time and with sufficient air turbulence to see that all the waste receives adequate amounts of oxygen to ensure destruction. Otherwise the hazardous waste will not be completely destroyed; some will be left in the resulting ash, which goes up the stack as *fly ash* or remains in the chamber as *bottom ash,* later often sent to landfills. Some of the fly ash and vaporized chemicals can be removed by SCRUBBERS, but the remaining toxic chemicals are then transferred to the scrubber water, which is put into ponds (*impoundments*) or released as wastewater. Worse, improper incineration can lead to the formation of new chemicals called *products of incomplete combustion* (PICs), about which little or nothing is known, but some of which one EPA study

stated were "more difficult to destroy and may be more toxic than the parent compound." Among the known PICs identified in just a small portion of stack gases in an EPA study of hazardous waste incinerators were DIOXIN, benzene, phosgene (a poison gas used in World War I), formaldehyde, chloroform, naphthalene, tetrachloroethylene, and furans. In addition, HEAVY METALS such as LEAD and MERCURY, being elements, remain untouched by the incineration, and are simply released into the air, land, or water.

In the United States, EMISSIONS from incinerators are among the targets of the CLEAN AIR ACT, and research continues on ways to improve the efficiency of incinerators. But in the meantime, environmentalists continue to protest the use of incineration and to press for production of less toxic materials, since there exists no truly environmentally safe method for disposing of them. Some countries, notably in Western Europe, incinerate large amounts of waste at sea, and others, including the United States, are considering that as an option. But environmentalists regard that as simply transferring the problem from one medium to another and are attempting to block ocean incineration under international agreements such as the CONVENTION ON THE PREVENTION OF MARINE POLLUTION BY DUMPING OF WASTE AND OTHER MATTER (LONDON DUMPING CONVENTION). A particular fear is that an accidental spill of highly toxic chemicals en route to incineration could kill all life in a massive area.

A wider concern is that materials incinerated are resources lost—resources that must be recreated with considerable effort, expense, and potential damage to the environment. This is true even when heat or energy is derived from the combustion. From this point of view, incineration represents a failure of rational waste disposal, which favors materials recovery and RECYCLING wherever possible, as well as overall reduction. (See INFORMATION AND ACTION GUIDES on WASTE DISPOSAL on page 325; TOXIC CHEMICALS AND HAZARDOUS WASTE on page 407; also WASTE DISPOSAL; TOXIC CHEMICALS; HAZARDOUS WASTE.)

**independent sector,** alternate term for NONGOVERNMEN-
TAL ORGANIZATION.

**indigenous peoples,** the inhabitants of an area before
it came under pressure by modern DEVELOPMENT, often
people following a traditional way of life based on HUNT-
ING, FISHING, gathering, and light agriculture.

Contrary to some popular myths, indigenous peoples are
not uniformly peaceful, benign, and earth-saving; they and
we are all simply human, both intelligent and ignorant,
with good and bad qualities. It is after all the traditional
ancestors of *all* of us who caused the EXTINCTION of the
mammoths many thousands of years ago. Nor have indigenous peoples lived in their homelands from ''time imme-
morial,'' as some writers would have it. Our human
ancestors roamed the continents for thousands of years, as
hunters, invaders, conquerors, and sometimes victims
being pushed from one place to another. The Apache, for
example, arrived in the Southwest from further north only
at around the time Spanish arrived in the Americas; the
name *Apache,* meaning ''enemy,'' was given to them by
other native peoples they had invaded.

Indigenous peoples have, however, been generally good
stewards of the land—certainly far better than most people
in modern civilization. Many have established a sustainable way of life, built on RENEWABLE RESOURCES, not
drawing on them so excessively that they became DECLIN-
ING RESOURCES. They also have a more intimate knowledge of the plants and animals around them, their special
characteristics and their interactions in the ECOSYSTEMS. It
is that way of life that has been virtually destroyed in
many areas of the world. In Europe and North America,
it exists only on the northern fringes and is found in highly
restricted areas elsewhere. In the Third World, which has
had far less development, indigenous ways of life have
survived in many areas, including the fringes of mountain,
forest, and northern tundra. But with rising POPULATION
and increasing hunger for resources, they are being directly threatened—often as part of the wider threat to ecosystems around the world, such as the AMAZON RAIN
FOREST. Some environmentalists focus on saving indigenous peoples, their way of life, and their special knowledge as part of attempts to save whole ecosystems, often
striving to develop markets for products that will not damage the environment and will provide the economic basis
for survival of the indigenous culture.

Indigenous ways of life, which rely on exploitation of
the plant and animal resources of an area, can sometimes
come into conflict with concerns over ENDANGERED SPE-
CIES or animal rights (see ANIMAL RIGHTS MOVEMENT).
Some animal protection laws bar commercial exploitation

by hunters and fishers using modern technology, but allow
exemptions for continuing indigenous use. Arctic hunters
are, for example, allowed to hunt some kinds of WHALES,
even though commercial whaling in those particular whale
species is banned. It is not always easy to strike a balance
between environmental concerns, however. Some ''indigenous'' Arctic hunters have adopted modern technological
weapons and may bring some species close to extinction,
and so the blanket exemption for indigenous peoples may
not be allowed to stand indefinitely.

**For more information and action:**

- **CULTURAL SURVIVAL** (CS), (617-495-2562). Focuses on
  the rights of indigenous peoples and ethnic minorities,
  especially in tropical rain forests; conducts fund-raising
  projects selling rain-forest products; publishes various
  materials including *Indigenous Peoples and Tropical
  Forests: Models of Land Use and Management from
  Latin America* (Jason Clay, 1988) and *Land Rights and
  Indigenous Peoples: The Role of the Inter-American
  Commision on Human Rights* (Shelton Davis, 1988).
- **FRIENDS OF THE EARTH** (**FOE**), (202-544-2600).
- **GREENPEACE** (202-462-1177). Runs the *Tropical For-
  ests Campaign* supporting indigenous peoples
  movements.
- **WORLD BANK** (202-477-1234). Publishes *Tribal Peoples
  and Economic Development: Human Ecologic
  Considerations.*

**Other references:**
*The Gaia Atlas of First Peoples: A Future for the Indige-
nous World.* Julian Burger. Anchor, 1990.

**INFORM, Inc.** (381 Park Avenue South, New York, NY
10016; 212-689-4040; Joanna D. Underwood, President),
an environmental research and education organization
founded in 1973, originally concerned primarily with AIR
POLLUTION but now working also with a wider range of
environmental issues, notably HAZARDOUS WASTE, solid
waste management, WATER POLLUTION, and land, energy,
and water conservation. INFORM ''does not lobby or liti-
gate,'' but examines ''business practices which harm our
air, water, and land resources'' pinpointing ''specific ways
in which practices can be improved;'' the resulting studies
are used by government, environmental organizations, and
concerned business leaders. In additional to participating
in and testifying at conferences, seminars, and legislative
briefings, INFORM publishes various materials, including
a quarterly newsletter *Inform Reports*; reports such as *A
Citizen's Guide to Promoting Toxic Waste Reduction*
(Lauren Kenworthy and Eric Schaeffer, 1990), *Preventing*

*Pollution Through Technical Assistance: One State's Experience* (Mark Dorfman and John Riggio, 1990), and *Drive for Clean Air: Natural Gas and Methanol Vehicles* (James S. Cannon, 1989); and a series of fact sheets such as *Air Pollution and Alternative Fuel Vehicles* and *Source Reduction.*

**INFOTERRA,** a global information network, part of the EARTHWATCH program of the UNITED NATIONS ENVIRONMENT PROGRAMME (UNEP), used by governments, industries, and other researchers in 139 countries. Under INFOTERRA, nations designate institutions to be national focal points (NFPs); in the United States, for example, that is the ENVIRONMENTAL PROTECTION AGENCY (EPA). Each NFP then prepares a "Who's Who" of its national environmental experts and selects the best sources for inclusion in INFOTERRA's *International Directory.* At first, INFOTERRA used such directories only to refer questioners to the nearest appropriate experts; but since 1980 it has answered many queries directly, consulting sources as necessary (including data bases) and analyzing the replies.

**insecticides,** a type of chemical compound used for killing unwanted insects (see PESTICIDES).

**Institute for Food and Development Policy (IFDP),** popularly called *Food First,* (145 Ninth Street, San Francisco, CA 94103; 415-864-8555; Frances Moore Lappé, Executive Director), a private research and education center, a nonprofit membership organization founded in 1975, focusing on "the human-made roots of hunger, poverty, and environmental degradation," stressing that hunger results primarily from "concentrated economic and political power, not scarcity," and hoping to bring about change through active democratic citizen participation, locally, nationally, and globally. Food First operates various programs, such as *Project Public Life* and *The Values Project,* runs a speakers bureau for worldwide audiences, and sometimes conducts special tours, such as *Food and Farm Reality Tours* in California. The Institute also publishes many works, including the quarterly newsletter *Food First News,* educational works, such as *Hunger Myths and Facts, Food First Curriculum* (for grades 4–8), and *Exploding the Hunger Myth: A High School Curriculum*; Development Reports, such as *Help or Hindrance? United States Economic Aid in Central America, The Missing Piece in the Population Puzzle,* and *Brave New Third World? Strategies for Survival in the Global Economy*; Action Alert pamphlets such as *Brazil's Debt and Deforestation—A Global Warning, Myths of African Hunger,* and *Family Farming: Faded Memory or Future Hope*; books

such as *Diet for a Small Planet, Food First: Beyond the Myth of Scarcity, Circle of Poison: Pesticides and People in a Hungry World, Family Farming: A New Economic Vision,* and *A Fate Worse Than Debt: The World Financial Crisis and the Poor*; and audiovisual materials.

**Institute for Local Self-Reliance (ILSR)** (2425 18th Street NW, Washington, DC 20009; 202-232-4108; Neil Seldman, President), an organization founded in 1974 whose slogan is "Mine local resources for self-reliant cities." More generally, it aims to join "technical ingenuity with a sense of community to establish sustainable, environmentally sound forms of consumption and production," promoting "possibilities for self-reliant communities by investigating examples of closed-loop manufacturing, materials policy, materials recovery, energy efficiency, and small-scale production." ILSR seeks to "provide policy makers and community activists with solid alternatives for local self-reliance," stressing local employment, skills training, and additions to the local tax base. It conducts applied research and policy analysis, and provides technical information and assistance to government and private organizations on conservation activities, especially least-cost management for energy utilities and comparative costs of waste management strategies. ILSR publishes various materials including *Proven Profits from Pollution Prevention, Self-Reliant Cities: Energy and the Transformation of Urban America,* and *Substituting Agricultural Materials for Petroleum-Based Industrial Products.*

**integrated pest management (IPM),** an approach that involves analyzing the ECOSYSTEM as a whole and deciding which of all the methods available, in what proportions and combinations, are best to deal with unwanted insects, weeds, and other pests. Methods employed may be:

- **biological,** employing BIOLOGICAL CONTROL, BIOTECHNOLOGY, or GENETIC ENGINEERING;
- **chemical,** using PESTICIDES;
- **cultural,** involving changes in planting patterns or addition of barriers, as to produce an EDGE EFFECT;
- **physical,** quarantining products to prevent entry of new pests; or
- **mechanical,** physically removing weeds or pests from the site.

The final selection of methods is based on ecological principles and research and is tailored to local conditions. Pesticides are regarded as a last resort, to be used only in limited, tightly controlled times and places and to precise ends, not wholesale. Because the aim of IPM is to minimize—and if possible to eliminate—their use, it is sometimes called *least toxic control.*

IPM may be applied in any setting, including CROP-LANDS, FORESTS, rangelands, greenhouses, urban landscapes, buildings, rights-of-way, and medical or veterinary settings. The strategy employed depends on the particular setting and desired result, with the overall objective being to reduce the pest population below the level that causes economic, aesthetic, or health concerns. The criteria involved in selecting optimal methods are:

- **technical-effectiveness,** to control pest damage;
- **cost-effectiveness,** to be affordable and economically advantageous;
- **SUSTAINABILITY,** to be accessible, reliable, and designed for long-term effectiveness; and
- **safety,** to ensure human and environmental health.

Planning IPM programs can be expensive, because they are information-intensive, requiring analysis by scientists who research the biology of target pests, their natural enemies, and how they interact in the environment, and also requiring staff to train farmers. In the United States, various arms of the DEPARTMENT OF AGRICULTURE provide information and assistance on least-toxic alternatives, though their critics charge that they still rely too much on chemicals. International work along the same lines is largely coordinated by the UNITED NATIONS ENVIRONMENT PROGRAMME (UNEP), with much research being conducted under the various centers of the CONSULTATIVE GROUP ON INTERNATIONAL AGRICULTURAL RESEARCH.

However, the application of IPM programs need not be expensive, and they have been used successfully in many parts of the developing world, being in fact more scientifically grounded improvements on approaches used in many poor areas. In developed countries, IPM may even be cheaper to use than pesticide-reliant approaches. In the United States, a Department of Agriculture survey found that some farmers made more profits with IPM than without. The main expense, in all countries, is borne by the government researchers and their agents, who train farmers in the various techniques. Even if minor additional short-term costs are involved with IPM, however, they are far less than the long-term costs (both economic and environmental) of damage to health and the environment and of cleaning up the chemical residue of pesticide use.

IPM approaches may also be applied close to home. In lawn care, for example, an IPM or least-toxic approach would focus on maintaining healthy soil; planting pest-resistant grasses well adapted to the area; aerating the lawn; minimizing thatch (the dense layer of stems and roots on the soil surface); maintaining proper pH and fertil-

ity; watering appropriately for the setting; mowing with sharp, high blades; monitoring the lawn weekly for pests or disease; and if any are found, contacting local groups, such as the County Extension Office, for identification and information on the least toxic methods. IPM may involve accepting less "perfection" of appearance—the occasional dandelion on a lawn, for example, or blemish on an apple—than many have come to expect from pesticide-treated lawns and agricultural products. (See INFORMATION AND ACTION GUIDES on BIOLOGICAL CONTROL AND INTEGRATED PEST MANAGEMENT on page 36; FARMING AND SUSTAINABLE AGRICULTURE on page 226; also ORGANIC FARMING; SUSTAINABLE AGRICULTURE.)

## International Center for Arid and Semiarid Land Studies (ICASALS)

(Box 4620, Texas Tech University, Lubbock, TX 79409; 806-742-2218; Idris R. Traylor, Director), a center created in 1966 for the "interdisciplinary study of arid and semiarid environments and the human relationship to those environments from an international perspective." ICASALS supports research, maintains a library, acts as international information clearinghouse, and provides technical assistance. It also maintains formal affiliations with universities and research centers around the world; sponsors the *Women in Development (WID)* program with the U.S. *Agency for International Development* (AID); administers the world's only master's degree in interdisciplinary arid land studies; serves as headquarters for the *Association for Arid Land Studies (AALS)* (see DESERT AND DESERTIFICATION INFORMATION AND ACTION GUIDE on page 86; arranges for specialized tours and provides discounts on professional publications. It publishes various materials, including the quarterly *ICASALS Newsletter, Arid and Semi-Arid Lands—A Preview, Erosion, Productivity, and Sustainable Agriculture,* and *Urbanization in the Arid Lands.*

## International Council for Bird Preservation (ICBP)

(32 Cambridge Road, Girton, Cambridge CCB3 OPJ, United Kingdom; 0223-277318; Christopher Imboden, Director-General; U.S. Headquarters, c/o WORLD WILDLIFE FUND-U.S.; 202-293-4800), an international organization founded in 1922, devoted "entirely to the conservation of birds and their habitats." A key group in worldwide efforts to protect birds and their MIGRATION routes, the ICBP gathers and disseminates information about endangered birds, maintaining a computerized data bank from which it generates reports; conducts periodic symposia on bird-related issues; seeks to educate the public about endangered birds and their ecological importance; runs the *World Bird Club;* maintains a *Conservation Fund;* runs special campaigns, such as the *Migratory Bird Campaign;*

and develops and carries out priority projects in their *Conservation Programme*, as for the red-tailed PARROT in Brazil, the pink pigeon of Mauritius, or the brush warbler of the Seychelles.

ICBP publishes various materials, including the quarterly newsletter *World Birdwatch*; the annual *ICBP Bulletin*; the periodic *Bustard Studies*: the key series *Bird Red Data Books* (with IUCN—THE WORLD CONSERVATION UNION); monographs such as *Important Bird Areas in Europe* (R.F.A. Grimmett and T.A. Jones, 1989), and *Key Forests for Threatened Birds in Africa* (N.J. Collar and S.N. Stuart, 1988); technical publications such as *Seabird Status and Conservation: A Supplement* (J.P. Croxall, eds., 1991), *Disease and Threatened Birds* (J.E. Cooper, ed., 1989), *Birds to Watch: The ICBP Checklist of Threatened Birds* (N.J. Collar and P. Andrew, 1988), and *Ecology and Conservation of Grassland Birds* (P.D. Goriup, ed., 1988); numerous study reports; and occasional Conservation Red Alert pamphlets on especially threatened birds.

## International Council for the Exploration of the Sea or Conseil International pour l'Exploration de la Mer (ICES or CIEM)

(Palæegade 2–4, DK-1261 Copenhagen K, Denmark; 33 15 42 25; Emory D. Anderson, General Secretary), an intergovernmental organization founded in 1902 as a "scientific forum for the exchange of information and ideas on the seas and its *living* resources and for the promotion and coordination of research undertaken by experts within its seventeen members countries on both sides of the Atlantic." In addition, ICES works closely with regulatory commissions, providing information and advice on conservation and management of fish stocks and shellfish, and on the effects of POLLUTION on the marine environment. This information is funneled to fishery commissions such as the North East Atlantic Fisheries Commission (NEAFC), International Baltic Sea Fisheries Commission (IBSFC), and North Atlantic Salmon Conservation Organization (NASCO), and to marine pollution commissions such as the Oslo Commission for the Prevention of Marine Pollution by Dumping from Ships and Aircraft, the Paris Commission for the Prevention of Marine Pollution from Land-Based Sources, and the Helsinki Commission for the Protection of the Marine Environment of the Baltic Sea Area.

ICES's main activities focus around studies of the water masses of the North Atlantic and the ecological processes within them, and on the types and amounts of marine pollution and its effects on marine life. It also organizes symposia and scientific meetings; maintains international data banks on marine contaminants, fisheries, and oceanographic data; and publishes various materials, including the semiannual newsletter *ICES/CIEM Information*, the periodical *Journal du Conseil*, fishery statistics yearbooks, and numerous scientific reports and papers.

## International Register of Potentially Toxic Chemicals (IRPTC),

an inventory of chemicals of international concern; part of the EARTHWATCH program of the UNITED NATIONS ENVIRONMENT PROGRAMME (UNEP). Not an inventory of all the tens of thousands of chemicals, but a repository of information on those that may have environmental or health effects. National correspondents in some 110 countries gather and transmit to IRPTC information from scientific publications, government reports, research documents, and data banks, making it available to anyone who needs information about the chemical. In addition, IRPTC may also call on a network of international organizations, scientific institutions, and industrial contacts. As of 1990, the IRPTC contained extensive information on the health and environmental effects of over 800 chemicals, including information on manufacture, use, and disposal. It also carries "special files on waste management and disposal, on chemicals currently being tested for toxic effects and on national regulations covering over 8,000 substances," out of the 70,000 now estimated to be in active use, many of which are considered—rightly or wrongly—not harmful.

Working closely with the IRPTC is the *International Programme on Chemical Safety (IPCS)*, operated jointly by UNEP, the World Health Organization (WHO), and the International Labour Organization (ILO). Using information gathered from the IRPTC, the IPCS assesses and evaluates the risks that specific chemicals pose to human health and the environment, producing reports that are then funneled back to the International Register. The International Register can be extraordinarily helpful for developing countries who wish to ensure that they are not having banned or severely restricted chemicals dumped on them (see CIRCLE OF POISON), alerting them to bans and offering guidance and training as necessary. It can also help countries avoid duplicating another's testing efforts or identify new, dimly perceived effects. (See TOXIC CHEMICALS; HAZARDOUS SUBSTANCES.)

## International Transboundary Resources Center (Centro Internacional de Recursos Transfronterizos, or CIRT),

(University of New Mexico, School of Law, Natural Resources Center, 1117 Stanford NE, Albuquerque, NM 87131; 505-277-6424; Albert E. Utton, Director), an international organization founded in 1986 to focus on those natural resources that extend across political boundaries, including "migratory resources such as water, air, energy, and living resources as well as the transboundary environmental impacts of human activities,'' such as the United States/Mexico dispute over the Colorado River (see GRAND CANYON), the ACID RAIN disputes of North America and Europe, or the effects of CHERNOBYL. CIRT publishes various materials, including the quarterly *Transboundary Resources Report* and model international agreements, as concerning AQUIFERS crossed by international political boundaries, or for cooperative U.S.–Mexican development of OIL and NATURAL GAS resources.

**International Wildlife Coalition (IWC)** (634 North Falmouth Highway, P.O. Box 388, North Falmouth, MA 02556; 508-564-9980; Daniel J. Morast, Director), an international association of ''experienced animal welfare advocates, grass-roots lobbyists, scientists, lawyers, and educators . . . committed to countering the abuses of wildlife exploitation worldwide . . . [and] dedicated to promoting a positive educational interaction with wild animals.'' Founded in 1983 from a merger of four animal welfare and wildlife groups, the IWC is incorporated as *I\*Kare Wildlife Trust*; its British affiliate is called *Care for the Wild*. It seeks to halt ''excessive exploitation and needles, cruel slaughter of wild animals,'' focusing on commercial whaling, on unprotected small cetaceans (such as DOLPHINS, PORPOISES, and small WHALES), kangaroos and wallabies, wild cats, fur-bearing animals (seeking to ban the leghold trap and other inhumane killing devices), blood sports, the ivory trade, and protection of critical HABITAT. IWC works through political and international forums, emergency campaigns, and conservation education, such as the *Whale Adoption Project* (see IWC entry in WHALE INFORMATION AND ACTION GUIDE on page 343).

**inversion,** an atmospheric condition in which cool air over an area is trapped by a ''blanket'' of warm air that moves in above it; also called a *temperature inversion* or *thermal atmospheric inversion*. Since warm air normally rises and cool air sinks, the cool air remains in place, gathering ever more pollutants, and often building up the condition called SMOG. The condition normally persists until a new weather system brings winds to sweep the area clear. Inversions are especially common in valleys or bowl-like settings, where the air is easily trapped. Several cities have the dubious distinction of having frequent unhealthy inversions, among them Los Angeles and Mexico City. (See AIR POLLUTION; SMOG.)

**Investor Responsibility Research Center (IRRC)** (1755 Massachusetts Avenue NW, Suite 600, Washington, DC 20036; 202-234-7500; Margaret Carroll, Executive Director), an independent corporation founded in 1972 ''by

and for institutional investors,'' conducting research and publishing ''impartial reports on contemporary business and public policy issues'' that affect corporations and investors. Fields covered include ''corporate governance, global shareholder rights, energy and the environment, military contracting, and multinationals' activities in South Africa and Northern Ireland.'' Its longstanding *Social Issues Service* has covered questions such as animal testing and environmental issues, and in 1990 it launched a separate *Environmental Information Service*, which focuses primarily on environmental profiles of major U.S. corporations, assembling ''key environmental data and indicators that will allow an investor to assess potential environmental risk, a corporation's environmental track record, and its level of environmental awareness.'' IRRC publishes materials on a variety of environmental issues, including *Animal Testing and Consumer Products* (1990), *The Greenhouse Effect: Investment Implications and Opportunities* (1990), *Power Plays: Profiles of America's Leading Renewable Electricity Developers* (1989), and *Stones in a Glass House: CFCs and the Ozone Depletion Controversy* (1988).

**iodine 131,** a radioactive form of the element iodine, commonly found in FALLOUT from nuclear explosions. It has a half-life (see RADIATION) of about eight days and tends to accumulate in the thyroid, so is used in medical diagnosis and therapy. Iodine 131 is often used as a indicator in studying fallout because it is more readily detectable than other radioactive isotopes, despite its short life.

**Iran-Iraq War oil spill,** the worst OIL spill in the history of the Persian Gulf. It began in February 1983, with the blowout of a well in Iran's Nowruz offshore oil field. Iraqi air and sea attacks on March 2 damaged more wells nearby and also the Kharg Island oil facility. Oil from the area continued to foul the Gulf throughout March, by the end of the month totaling an estimated 150,000 barrels, and by the end of April at least 225,000 barrels, and probably a good deal more, though hard facts were impossible to obtain. By the end of May, the prevailing winds that had until then kept the huge oil slick away from the COASTS of Saudi Arabia, Bahrain, and other southern Gulf nations had changed, and very heavy crude oil began to come ashore in large quantities. The flow and environmental disaster continued through the summer of 1983, until the wells were ultimately capped. Although the full extent of the spill was never known, many observers felt that it had been the largest known to date, larger even than the 1979 IXTOC I Gulf of Mexico well blowout, which had been estimated at 600,000 tons (18 times the size of the 1989 *EXXON VALDEZ* disaster off Alaska). It was probably two to three times as large as the 1990 Iraqi oil spill into the

Gulf ordered by Saddam Hussein (see PERSIAN GULF WAR ENVIRONMENTAL DISASTER). (See also OIL.)

**IUCN—THE WORLD Conservation Union (formerly International Union for Conservation of Nature and Natural Resources),** (International Headquarters: Avenue du Mont-Blanc, CH-1196 Gland, Switzerland; 022 64 91 14; Martin W. Holdgate, Director General; U.S. Offices: IUCN-US, c/o WORLD WILDLIFE FUND, 1400 16th Street NW, Washington, DC 20036; 202-797-5454), an international organization founded in 1948 to "provide knowledge and leadership for the sustainable use of the planet's natural resources," unique in that its members include over 60 states, 120 government agencies, and 450 major non-governmental conservation organizations, working together. The IUCN has a global network of more than 3000 scientists and other conservation-oriented professionals, organized into six commissions: *Ecology; Education and Training; Sustainable Development; Environmental Policy, Law and Administration (CEPLA); National Parks and Protected Areas (CNPPA);* and *Species Survival Commission (SSC)* (c/o Chicago Zoological Society, Brookfield Zoo, Brookfield, IL 60513; 708-485-0263, ext. 304; George Rabb, Chairman), from which spun off the now-independent traffic (TRADE RECORDS ANALYSIS OF FLORA AND FAUNA IN COMMERCE) NETWORK.

Through its members and these commissions, the IUCN helps develop international conventions and laws on conservation; it played a key role in formulating measures such as the CONVENTION ON INTERNATIONAL TRADE IN ENDANGERED SPECIES (CITES) and the CONVENTION ON WETLANDS OF INTERNATIONAL IMPORTANCE (Ramsar Convention). With the UNITED NATIONS ENVIRONMENT PROGRAMME (UNEP), the WORLD WIDE FUND FOR NATURE (WWF), and other United Nations organizations, the IUCN helped formulate the general WORLD CONSERVATION STRATEGY (WCS) in 1980, stressing SUSTAINABLE DEVELOPMENT and protection of global resources. The IUCN also operates the *World Conservation Monitoring Centre (WCMC),* (219c Huntingdon Road, Cambridge CB3 ODL, England; 0223 277314), which includes the *Wildlife Trade Monitoring Unit (WTMU);* the *Botanic Gardens Conservation Secretariat (BGCS),* (Descanso House, 199 Kew Road, Richmond, Surrey TW9 3BW, U.K.; 44 81 9400047 or 9488827); and the *Environmental Law Centre (ELC),* (Adenauerallee 214, D-5300 Bonn 1, Federal Republic of Germany; 49 228 26 92 231). In Central America, IUCN operates a service *(SIEP)* to help countries initiate environmental impact assessment procedures. Among IUCN's many publications are the bimonthly *IUCN Bulletin;* a series of *Red Data Books,* standard refer-

ences on threatened species; Action Plans for the conservation of particular threatened species, and the *United Nations List of National Parks and Protected Areas.*

***IXTOC I* oil well blowout,** the largest OIL spill on record. On June 3, 1979, the blowout of the *Ixtoc* I well, in the Gulf of Mexico's Bay of Campeche, began a spill that ultimately dumped an estimated 600,000 tons of crude oil into the bay, off Campeche Province in southern Mexico, causing massive environmental damage. Only the 1983 oil spill into the Persian Gulf from the Nowruz oil field (see IRAN-IRAQ WAR OIL SPILL) rivaled the size of the Ixtoc spill. In 1983, after years of litigation, the Sedco company, owner of the rig at the site of blowout, settled Mexican claims for a little over $2 million. (See also OIL.)

**Izaak Walton League of America (IWLA)** (1401 Wilson Boulevard, Level B., Arlington, VA 22209; 703-528-1818; Jack Lorenz, Executive Director), a membership organization founded in 1922 "to defend the nation's soil, air, woods, waters and wildlife," named after the 17th-century English fisherman and author of *The Compleat Angler.* At the national, state, and local levels, the IWLA seeks to promote citizen involvement in environmental protection, educate the public about emerging threats to natural resources, influence legislators and decisionmakers on conservation concerns, and enforce environmental laws through lawsuits. Its broad range of conservation concerns include clean water, wildlife HABITAT, public land management, farm conservation, protection of natural areas, and enhanced outdoor recreation. Among its programs are *National Conservation Action,* a grassroots action arm; *Save Our Streams,* conducting stream rehabilitation projects and helping to enforce WATER POLLUTION laws locally; *Wetlands Watch,* fostering adoption of WETLANDS by local groups for protection; *Outdoor Ethics,* to "reduce poaching, trespassing, and other illegal and inconsiderate outdoor activities," and to encourage hunter and outdoor education programs; *Izaak Walton League Endowment,* acquiring land to protect it from unsound DEVELOPMENT; as well as regional programs such as *Chesapeake Bay Regional Program, Ohio River Watershed Protection Project, Upper Mississippi River Regional Program,* and *Public Lands Restoration Task Force,* with its *Riparian Enhancement Teams* that voluntarily "help ranchers fence cattle out of riparian (streamside) zones." In addition to the *Uncle Ike Youth Education Program* and the public affairs television program *Make Peace with Nature,* the League publishes various materials, including the quarterly magazine *Outdoor America,* the newsletter *Outdoor Ethics,* the Save Our Streams newsletter *Splash,* and occasional action alerts on critical conservation issues.

**J**

**jaguar,** see LEOPARD.

**James Bay hydropower project,** a massive system of hydroelectric DAMS in northwestern Québec that if completed as planned would include over 200 (some estimate as high as 650) dams and dikes and 23 power stations, involving the diversion of 19 RIVERS. Being built by the Canadian government's Hydro-Québec, it is the world's largest hydropower project, affecting an area as large as New York, Pennsylvania, and New England combined. The project was begun in 1971, without ENVIRONMENTAL IMPACT ASSESSMENT, and over the objections of the local inhabitants, notably the Crees and the Inuit, who lost a fight to stop the project when a court ruled in 1973 that it was too far advanced to stop and that the needs of Québec's millions of residents were more important than the aboriginal rights claimed by the Crees. In fact, as agreements later leaked to the public made clear, Québec had signed cut-rate energy agreement with various metals and chemical companies. The largest potential customers are in the United States, though modest success in energy conservation has made that market less sure; in fact, a major contract with New York State was cancelled in 1992.

More seriously, the environment has been massively disrupted. In areas flooded by the LaGrande River, MERCURY formerly locked in rocks was released to enter the FOOD CHAIN, with disastrous effects. Crees and other natives also charge negative effects on many ECOSYSTEMS, as some rivers are stripped of water and others flooded, in some cases killing herds of animals in the path of torrents of water. Hydro-Québec counters that studies done since the mid-1970s indicate that the project has had positive effects on fish, animals, and birds such as beaver, ducks, pike, and sturgeon.

As environmental concerns have been heightened, in Canada and elsewhere, numerous people have charged that the project is simply too massive, expensive, and environmentally damaging and that it should be stopped now. The Crees have gone back to court, charging that by attempting a large road-building project without environmental review, Hydro-Québec has broken an agreement made in 1975 giving them a say in future projects. Numerous environmental organizations have joined in a *James Bay Coalition* to stop the project, including the EARTH ISLAND INSTITUTE, FRIENDS OF THE EARTH, GREENPEACE, *Humane Society of the United States* (see ANIMAL RIGHTS AND WELFARE INFORMATION AND ACTION GUIDE on page 361), NATIONAL AUDUBON SOCIETY, NATURAL RESOURCES DEFENSE COUNCIL, *Rainforest Action Network* (see FORESTS INFORMATION AND ACTION GUIDE on page 369), and the SIERRA CLUB.

**For more information and action:**

- **James Bay Project** (c/o GREENPEACE, P.O. Box 2032, New York, NY 10013).
- **NATIONAL AUDUBON SOCIETY,** (212-832-3200; Audubon Action Line, 202-547-9017). Has James Bay Hydropower Project.

**Jersey Preservation Trust,** the original organization, founded by Gerald Durrell, from which sprang WILDLIFE PRESERVATION TRUST INTERNATIONAL.

# K

**Kakadu National Park,** massive Australian WILDERNESS park in north central Australia, east of Darwin; it consists of over 4.3 million acres (6,800 square miles), including the 1,300-high and 310-mile-long sandstone escarpment that runs through the park. Over 50 mammal species, 270 bird species, and 1,000 plant species have been reported in the park. The park also holds one of the world's largest groups of cave paintings, some of them dating back 18,000–20,000 years. Most of the park is owned by its Native Australian (Aboriginal) population, and is leased to the national government until 2077. Large scale MINING is being carried on in one section of the park, under a license that expires in the mid-1990s. (See WILDLIFE REFUGE.)

**Katmai National Park and Preserve,** in southern Alaska, the site of the 1912 Mount Katmai volcanic eruption, an explosion so powerful that its blast shot up into the upper atmosphere, and darkened the whole far northern sky around the world for months. In its aftermath, the valley beside the mountain became a volcanic wasteland, to this day known as the Valley of the Ten Thousand Smokes. The whole surrounding area has now become a 4,100,000-acre (6,400-square-mile) national park, notable most of all for its large population of Alaska brown BEARS, who feed on the abundant salmon in the Brooks River and other areas streams. The bears are the world's largest; some stand ten feet tall and weigh up to 1,500 pounds. The park is also a HABITAT for large numbers of beaver and many other kinds of birds and animals, including eagles, ptarmigans, whistling swans, moose, wolverines, and CARIBOU. (See WILDLIFE REFUGE.)

**Kharg 5 oil spill,** leakage of an estimated 19 million gallons (approximately 65,000 tons) of OIL into the Atlantic near the Canary Islands, from the Iranian supertanker *Kharg 5,* after a December 19, 1989 explosion and fire that disabled and nearly sank the ship. The massive spill generated a 100-square-mile oil slick that threatened but did not strike the Moroccan coast, the drifting tanker was towed away from the COAST during salvage operations. (See OIL.)

**Kidepo Valley National Park,** 332,000 acres (519 square miles) of mountains and dry plains in northeastern Uganda, its northwestern boundary the Zaire-Uganda border; the home of many kinds of antelopes, including greater and lesser kudus, elands, oryx, hartebeests, and waterbucks. The ELEPHANT and black RHINOCEROS populations were seriously damaged during the reign of Ugandan dictator Idi Amin (1971–79), but have survived. There are large numbers of giraffes and ZEBRAS, and smaller numbers of a wide range of mammals, such as buffalo, baboons and other primates, hyenas, lynx, LEOPARDS, aardvarks, and CHEETAHS. There are also many varieties of birds and reptiles. (See WILDLIFE REFUGE.)

**Kids for Saving Earth**™**(KSE)** (P.O. Box 47247, Plymouth, MN 55447; 612-525-0002; for information on Target Stores that carry KSE information: 800-800-8800; Tessa Hill, President), an organization founded in 1989 by Clinton Hill, who died of cancer at age 11, and his fellow sixth-graders. That original organization inspired the foundation of over 5,000 similar clubs around the world, with the slogan ''The Pollution Solution.'' Members sign the Kids for Saving Earth™ pledge (see page

**Kids for Saving Earth™ Pledge:**

The Earth is my home. I promise to keep it healthy and beautiful. I will love the land, the air, the water, and all living creatures. I will be a defender of my planet. United with friends, I will save the Earth.

174). KSE encourages students to have an Earth Expo, a fair dedicated to the planet, or an Ecology Carnival; suggests that children mobilize their families, by having them sign a Family Call to Action pledge; and urges them to teach others about saving the earth. KSE also publishes the quarterly *Kids for Saving Earth News*, and the *Kids for Saving Earth Guidebook* on starting a KSE club, which also includes a bibliography of books for young people, ''Eco-Babble'' (a glossary), organizations that can help, and kid-oriented writeups on key issues facing the earth.

**Kluane National Park,** one of Canada's largest national parks and nature preserves, 8,500 square miles in the Yukon, containing part of the St. Elias range, including its highest mountain, 19,500-foot-high Mount Logan. Kluane adjoins Alaska's WRANGEL–ST. ELIAS NATIONAL PARK AND PRESERVE, its 20,600 square miles making it the largest national park area in North America. The wilderness area so preserved forms a very large, complete northern ECOSYSTEM, its CARIBOU herds, thousands of Dall sheep, moose, WOLVES and wolverines, grizzly BEARS and black BEARS, mountain goats, and other land animals able to move freely and safely. It is also a safe haven for a wide range of birds, some of them ENDANGERED SPECIES; the birds here include golden EAGLES, bald EAGLES, peregrine FALCONS, rock ptarmigans, mountain bluebirds, and arctic terns. Although long-term and perhaps ultimately very difficult questions exist about OIL, NATURAL GAS, and mineral extraction throughout western and northern Canada, Kluane and the other Canadian national parks so far continue to be held safely for future generations. (See WILDLIFE REFUGE; WILDERNESS.)

**krill,** a tiny, shrimp-like crustacean that feeds mainly on PLANKTON and occurs in all of the world's oceans. In the Antarctic, krill live in huge numbers, and are the primary food of WHALES, seals (see SEALS AND SEA LIONS), DOLPHINS, and other sea creatures. Beginning in the 1960s, a massive krill take began in southern seas, about 80 percent of it by Soviet and Japanese ships. By 1982, that take had risen to an enormous 582,000 tons, and has varied considerably since. Although the krill are not formally an endangered or threatened species, the size of the take suggests that international limitation is urgently necessary if the krill are to survive in large enough numbers to play their vital role in the FOOD CHAIN of ANTARCTICA. Without enough krill, much of the life of the region is threatened. The krill may also be threatened by the Antarctic hole in the OZONE LAYER, which some environmentalists feel might greatly damage or destroy the krill population, causing immense damage to the food chain (see ANTARCTICA), and therefore to the life of the southern ocean. (See OCEANS.)

**Kruger National Park,** a long, relatively narrow South African nature preserve on the Mozambique-South Africa border, 200 miles long by an average of 22 miles wide, with the Crocodile River as its southern border, the Limpopo River its northern border. On its 5,000,000 acres (7,700 square miles) of rolling country live over 100,000 impalas, 30,000 buffalo, 20,000 ZEBRAS, over 7,000 ELEPHANTS, and large numbers of giraffes, antelopes, LIONS, LEOPARDS, CHEETAHS, and over 110 other mammal species, as well as hundreds of bird species, over 100 reptile species, and over 50 kinds of fish. (See WILDLIFE REFUGE.)

**Krutch, Joseph Wood** (1893–1970), a noted naturalist, for the major part of his career a leading American theatre critic and writer on cultural themes. Krutch retired from his Columbia University teaching position in 1952 and went to live near Tucson, Arizona, in the desert. He then became a leading nature writer and conservationist, his books and television appearances reaching wide audiences and helping to shape the new environmental concerns that were beginning to be felt by millions in many countries, as the modern phase of the long battle to save earth's natural heritage began. Some of his most widely read naturalist works were *The Desert Year* (1952), *The Best of Two Worlds* (1953), *The Voice of the Desert* (1955), *The Great Chain of Life* (1957), *The Gardener's World* (1959), *The World of Animals* (1961), and *Herbal* (1965). He also narrated three television documentaries on nature themes. His autobiography was *More Lives Than One* (1962).

**Kyshtym,** a town in the Urals, about 10 miles away from the Soviet CHELYABINSK nuclear weapons complex. The massive 1957–58 Chelyabinsk-40 nuclear waste explosion is often called the Kyshtym nuclear disaster.

**Lake Nakuru National Park,** the park of the flamingos; in Kenya's Rift Valley, approximately 100 miles from Nairobi. The 24-square-mile park is primarily a bird sanctuary, consisting of the lake and its immediately surrounding areas. Here assemble as many as a million flamingos, providing one of the world's most colorful and massive wildlife displays. Although Lake Nakuru also plays host to hippopotamuses and other large mammals, and to hundreds of bird species, it is the flamingos that draw tourists from around the world. (See WILDLIFE REFUGE; ECOTOURISM.)

**lakes,** inland bodies of standing or slowly moving water, in basins formed by rifts and shifts in the earth (as in Lake BAIKAL); by gouging, as from glaciers or meteorites; by volcanic action, as in craters left following eruptions; by changes in RIVER beds, resulting in isolated ''ox-bow'' lakes; by SEA LEVEL RISES, as in drowned rivers or fjords; or by damming of a RIVER, as through SEDIMENTATION, animal activities (such as beaver DAMS), human activities (such as MINING), wind creation of dunes, or deliberate construction (as of GLEN CANYON DAM). The scientific study of lakes and river is called *limnology*.

A lake is a complex ECOSYSTEM, in which energy is acquired by plants, especially PLANKTON called *algae,* through the process of PHOTOSYNTHESIS, and then is passed up the FOOD CHAIN to larger plants and animals. Dead matter—including *plankton rain*, dead or dying organisms that shower down to the lake bottom—is then broken down by bacteria and other microorganisms for reuse. As part of the earth's massive BIOGEOCHEMICAL CYCLES, the ECOSYSTEM draws on such decomposed elements and other vital elements dissolved in the water, from weathering of rocks, LEACHING from the soil, and to some extent from the air.

Several elements are vital to life processes, but one key indicator of a lake's health is the amount of dissolved oxygen it contains, since oxygen is given off through photosynthesis (see OXYGEN CYCLE) and is then used by animals and also by many microbes breaking down dead matter. If waters are polluted by untreated organic matter or if fertilizer-laden water causes the lake's plants to grow too abundantly, bacteria and other microorganisms may use up large amounts of the lake's oxygen in breaking down the waste matter, as may some animal plankton (*zooplankton*), leaving little or no oxygen for higher animals, such as fish, which may then die off. Unlike rivers, which normally aerate or *oxygenate* water as they flow, lakes cannot so readily recover from this process, called EUTROPHICATION, which can in extreme cases lead to essentially dead lakes, devoid of higher animals. In fact, once excess nutrients are introduced into lakes, they tend to be trapped there and recycled, so eutrophication needs to be recognized and halted early to limit long-term damage. When oxygen is depleted on the lake bottoms, decomposition of dead matter takes place through anaerobic (nonoxygen) processes, which produce gases such as METHANE and hydrogen sulfide that are toxic to animal life.

Lakes are seldom uniform. Rather, those of sufficient depth (about 10 meters, or a little under 40 feet) normally develop layers called *strata*, which have different biochemical characteristics, harbor somewhat different plants and animals, and themselves vary through the seasons. Lakes receive heat from the sun's RADIATION, which is distributed around the upper layer by wind-driven currents and turbulence, keeping the free-floating plankton suspended in the water. In the summer, this heated upper layer is the site of most photosynthetic production; the bottom layer is cold and has little circulation; in the middle is a layer of rapid temperature change. These layers reverse themselves, or *turn over*, as the seasons change and the temperature of the two layers becomes equal. In the temperate zones, lakes generally turn over twice a year. In the autumn as the upper layer gradually cools down, the two layers reverse; through the winter, the bottom layer becomes the warmer one. Then in the spring, the lake turns over again, after the upper layer warms up sufficiently, to return to the summer stratification. In tropical and polar areas, such turning over generally occurs only once a year. The turnover is important because it refreshes the lake. The surface layer, where most photosynthesis takes place, needs nutrients from the bottom. The bottom layer needs dissolved oxygen, more abundant near the surface, which is depleted by microbes decomposing matter.

Often roughly coinciding with turnover, productivity is also seasonal. Various plankton reach a peak of development, or *pulse*, in the spring and to a lesser extent in the fall. If the pulse is so strong that it can be seen with the naked eye, it is called a *bloom*, another result of eutrophication. On the other hand, pollutants that cloud the water may lessen a lake's overall productivity, since it blocks the light necessary for photosynthesis.

Like other ecosystems, a lake is not static, but over time moves through a series of changes called ECOLOGICAL SUCCESSION. A young lake is simply water-covered land with an irregular shoreline. Through wind-driven wave action, the shoreline is gradually smoothed out and beach areas, spits or bars, and an underwater shelf tend to form, through the processes of SEDIMENTATION and EROSION (see COASTS). Shallow areas are increasingly filled in with rooted aquatic plants and sediment. Meanwhile the lake's outlets are eroded, allowing more water to leave and causing the level of the lake to drop. In the end the lake "dies" by becoming a swamp or bog (see WETLANDS). The whole process may take centuries, but for small, shallow lakes—commonly called ponds—it be happen more quickly. Human activities can speed it up markedly, especially where the waters are excessively enriched by nutrient-containing runoff, as from agricultural fertilizer. Then plant growth and the deposition of sediment speed the lake's way to EXTINCTION.

Similarly, a lake can be killed by overuse of its waters, notably for agricultural or drinking purposes, where the inflow does not meet the amount withdrawn. Sometimes then a wasteland is created, with numerous animals and plants killed off and the lake shrunk to a fraction of its size, as is happening to California's MONO LAKE and to the once-huge inland lake, the ARAL SEA. Lakes are often prime recreation areas, for swimming, boating, FISHING, and simply enjoying. But tourism brings its own hazards (see ECOTOURISM), as the damage done by visitors and by the construction of facilities to serve them impinge on the lakes and their habitats.

### For more information and action:

- **AMERICAN WATER RESOURCES ASSOCIATION (AWRA),** (301-493-8600).
- **FRESHWATER FOUNDATION,** (612-449-0092). Supports **Lake and Wetlands Project.** Publishes *A Citizen's Guide to Lake Protection* and *Understanding Your Shoreline: Protecting Rivers, Lakes and Streams.*
- **NATURAL RESOURCES AND ENERGY DIVISION (NRED), UNITED NATIONS,** (212-963-6205). Publishes *River and Lake Basin Development* (1990).
- **NORTH AMERICAN LAKE MANAGEMENT SOCIETY (NALMS),** (202-466-8550). Publishes the bimonthly magazine *Lake Line*; the bimonthly journal *Lake and Reservoir Management*; books and reports, such as *Lake and Reservoir Restoration Guidance Manual* (updated, 1990), *Monitoring Lake and Reservoir Restoration* (1990), *NALMS Management Guide for Lakes and Reservoirs*, *Water Quality Standards for Lakes—A Survey* (1988), and *Lake Conservation Handbook* (1989); and videotapes and slide shows.

### Other references:

*Our Endangered Planet: Rivers and Lakes.* Mary Hoff and Mary M. Rodgers. Lerner, 1991. *Large Lakes: Ecological Structure and Function.* M.M. Tilzer et al., eds. Springer Verlag, 1990. *At the Water's Edge: Nature Study in Lakes Streams and Ponds.* Alan M. Cavancara. Wiley, 1989. *Conservation and Management of Lakes.* J. Salanki and S. Herodek, eds., Stillman, 1989. *Lake.* Lionel Bender. Watts, 1989. (See also WATER RESOURCES; WATER POLLUTION; MONO LAKE; ARAL SEA; GREAT LAKES.)

**Land and Water Conservation Fund Act,** a U.S. federal law passed in 1964 and amended in 1986, establishing the *Land and Water Conservation Fund* (LWCF) to purchase or lease land, under LAND TRUSTS or CONSERVATION EASEMENTS, to protect the environment of the area. About 80 percent of the fund's revenues come from royalties from OFFSHORE DRILLING conducted under federal leases; added to that are money from a motorboat fuel tax and federal surplus property sales. An average of $900 million dollars has been credited to the LWCF's account each year, but Congress has appropriated far less each year than allowed, so that by 1991 approximately $7.8 billion in unappropriated funds had accumulated, according to the WILDERNESS SOCIETY.

Lands acquired under the fund are generally within or bordering existing national parks, FORESTS, or other federal lands, with authority provided by the legislation establishing those lands and the money appropriated by Congress. Prices are usually set by negotiation with the applicable federal agency, sometimes with court intercession, and rarely with condemnation. Where agreement cannot be reached in time to prevent DEVELOPMENT, some private LAND TRUSTS may acquire the land temporarily or permanently (see LAND TRUST AND CONSERVATION EASEMENT INFORMATION AND ACTION GUIDE on page 178). Some of LWCF's funds, up to 60 percent, go to states on a 50–50 matching basis, for local land acquisition and recreational projects.

**land trust (land conservancy),** a private organization that acquires land for the purpose of conserving and protecting natural areas, such as critical wildlife HABITAT, FORESTS, COASTS, or WETLANDS, as well as places of scenic or historic significance. Land may be purchased outright at full market price or in *bargain sales* at less than market value, reducing both the cost to the trust and taxes for the seller; or it may be donated, as through a gift or will, sometimes as a *life estate*, giving the landowner rights to live on the land. Other alternatives include a CONSERVATION EASEMENT, under which land stays privately owned but under legal restrictions as to use and DEVELOPMENT; or *limited development*, in which a part of the property—generally that of the least environmental significance—is developed to finance conservation of the rest. Some land trusts focus on a particular region or kind of land, such as WETLANDS, while others extend their protection to land of all types around the world. Some land trusts do not actually own land, but help to establish and monitor developmental restrictions.

The approach was pioneered primarily in New England in the mid–19th century with a series of "village improvement societies," which sparked early land trusts such as *The Trustees of Reservations (TTOR)*, founded in 1891 to protect "the jewels of the living landscape," still operating locally in Massachusetts, and now owning over 18,000 acres—all open to the public, including Ralph Waldo Emerson's Old Manse—and protecting an additional 7,000 acres through conservation easements. England's National Trust was formed in 1895, and has grown

to be a massive national force and international inspiration, protecting much of its country's natural and historic heritage. From such origins sprang a wide variety of other organizations using the land trust form for conservation ends.

In many cases, land is acquired and a management plan is developed and implemented, to protect, restore, and preserve, as necessary, often with public access being part of the plan. Sometimes the land is acquired only temporarily, as when a group acquires land to block development of land about to be added to a park or WILDLIFE REFUGE. In some cases organizations use conservation easements, leases, or other legal agreements to protect far more land than it has the resources to buy. Some organizations exist solely or primarily as land trusts, while others are wider-ranging conservation organizations with land acquisitions as a "sideline." According to a LAND TRUST ALLIANCE survey, the United States had over 900 land trusts by 1991, up from 53 in 1950, with over 2,700,000 acres protected, including 437,000 acres directly owned, among them wetlands, wildlife habitats, urban gardens and parks, farms, forests, ranches, watersheds, COASTS, RIVER corridors (see GREENWAYS), and trails. Land trusts are funded in a variety of ways, including contributions from individuals, corporations, and foundations; income from endowments; funds raised for special projects; and lines of credit in emergency situations. Governments also purchase land for conservation purposes; in the United States, their funding comes primarily from the LAND AND WATER CONSERVATION FUND, though other arms also use purchases, leases, and conservation easements, including the FISH AND WILDLIFE SERVICE and the MIGRATORY BIRD CONSERVATION COMMISSION. (See LAND TRUST AND CONSERVATION EASEMENT INFORMATION AND ACTION GUIDE on page 178.)

**Land Trust Alliance (LTA)** (900 17th Street, NW, Suite 410, Washington, DC 20006; 202-785-1410; Jean W. Hocker, President and Executive Director), an organization founded in 1982 "by land trusts themselves, as an umbrella for independent, often small and geographically isolated organizations, enabling them to share experiences, increase their effectiveness, gain access to vital information and expertise, raise public awareness of and support for land trust work and accomplish collectively what no individual land trust could do." In particular, the LTA offers workshops for LAND TRUST staff and volunteers and for land conservation professionals, providing "practical information on such topics as land-saving transactions, management of protected land, state and federal policy developments, and legal and organizational matters," as well as low-cost liability insurance through the "Green

## Land Trust and Conservation Easement Information and Action Guide

**For more information and action on land trusts and conservation easements:**

**APPALACHIAN TRAIL CONFERENCE (ACT)**, (304-535-6331). Purchases or protects threatened properties through its *Trust for Appalachian Trail Lands.*

**Archaeological Conservancy, The** (415 Orchard Drive, Santa Fe, NM 87501; 505-982-3278; Mark Michel, President), a national membership conservation organization, founded in 1980, "dedicated to acquiring and permanently preserving the best of the Nation's remaining archaeological sites." More specifically, the Conservancy "identifies the most important remaining ruins in need of preservation; acquires the property by purchase, gift or bargain sale to charity; secures the property and stabilizes the cultural resources *in situ*; prepares a [100-year] management plan and dedicates the property as a permanent archaeological preserve; and educates the general public about the destruction of our cultural heritage and how best to preserve what is left." It sponsors archaeological tours for members and publishes the quarterly *The Archaeological Conservancy Newsletter.*

**DEFENDERS OF WILDLIFE**, (202-659-9510).

**DUCKS UNLIMITED (DU)**, (708-438-4300). Operates the *MARSH (Matching Aid to Restore States Habitat)* program.

**Forest Trust**, (505-983-8992). Conducts a Land Trust program. (See FORESTS INFORMATION AND ACTION GUIDE on page 369.)

**IZAAK WALTON LEAGUE OF AMERICA (IWLA)** (703-528-1818). Operates *Izaak Walton League Endowment*, acquiring land to protect it from unsound development.

**Land Trust Alliance (LTA)**, (202-785-1410). Operates the *Land Conservation Law Institute.* Publishes the quarterly professional journal *Exchange*, the newsletter of land conservation law *The Back Forty*, bimonthly legislative updates, fact sheets on land trusts and land trust projects, the *National Directory of Conservation Land Trusts* (1991), and books such as *Starting a Land Trust* (1990), *Appraising Easements* (rev. ed., 1990), *The Federal Tax Law of Conservation Easements* (Stephen J. Small, 1989), *The Conservation Easement Handbook* (1988), *Preserving Family Lands* (Stephen J. Small, 1988), the brochure *The Land Trust*, and the video *For the Common Good.*

**NATIONAL AUDUBON SOCIETY**, (212-832-3200). Maintains a nationwide sanctuary system.

**NATIONAL PARKS AND CONSERVATION ASSOCIATION (NPCA)**, (202-944-8530). Maintains the *National Park Trust.*

**NATIONAL INSTITUTE FOR URBAN WILDLIFE**, (301-596-3311 or 301-995-1119). Provides technical services on land donations and conservation easements. Certifies *Urban Wildlife Sanctuaries.*

**NATURE CONSERVANCY, THE**, (703-841-5300). Purchases or manages lands needed by earth's rare plants, animals, and natural communities. Publishes the *Nature Conservancy Magazine.*

**RAILS-TO-TRAILS CONSERVANCY (RTC)**, (202-797-5400). Publishes *Purchasing a Rail-Trail: The Most Frequently Asked Questions* (1990) and *Railbanking: What, Where, Why, When and How* (1990).

**Rainforest Alliance**, (212-941-1900). Raises funds to acquire or protect rain forest preserves. (See FORESTS INFORMATION AND ACTION GUIDE on page 369.)

**Save-the-Redwoods League**, (415-362-2352). Purchases available California redwoods lands as preserves. (See FORESTS INFORMATION AND ACTION GUIDE on page 369.)

**SIERRA CLUB**, (415-776-2211 or 202-547-1141). Publishes *How to Gain Funding for Land Acquisition* and *Archaeological Sites Policy.*

**Trust for Public Land (TPL)**, (116 New Montgomery Avenue, 4th Floor, San Francisco, CA 94105; 415-495-4014; Martin J. Rosen, President), a national land conservation organization founded in 1972 to protect "land as a living resource for present and future generations," acquiring "land of environmental, recreational, historic or cultural significance" and holding it until it can be sold to public agencies or nonprofit conservation groups for permanent protection as parks, forests, community gardens, recreation areas, and open space. The TPL helps communities, public agencies, and nonprofit organizations acquire and protect open space, sharing its knowledge of nonprofit land acquisition processes, and "pioneers methods of land conservation and environmentally sound land use." Between 1972 and mid-1990, the TPL participated in 678 projects protecting over 483,000 acres in 37 states. It publishes a periodical report, *Land and People.*

**WILDERNESS SOCIETY, THE**, (202-833-2300). Publishes *Land Acquisition.*

Umbrella Plan" and a telephone consultation and networking service. It also acts as a clearinghouse for land trust information; lobbies at the federal level on issues such as land trust support, federal funding for land acquisition, changes in tax and farm policies, and establishment of a legal enforcement fund for CONSERVATION EASE-MENTS; has a voluntary self-evaluation program, to set and maintain standards and practices among land trusts; and operates the *Land Conservation Law Institute* with the University of California's Hastings College of Law, holding regional seminars and national conferences called National Rallies.

The LTA publishes various materials, including a quarterly professional journal, *Exchange*, the 10-times-a-year newsletter of land conservation law *The Back Forty*, bimonthly legislative updates, the *National Directory of Conservation Land Trusts* (1991), the brochure *The Land Trust*, fact sheets on land trusts and land trust projects, the video *For the Common Good*, and books such as *Starting a Land Trust* (1990), *The Conservation Easement Handbook* (1988), and *Preserving Family Lands* (Stephen J. Small, 1988).

**land use,** the various ways in which land is or may be employed, seen from the human point of view. Traditionally, land use has been classified on the basis of how it is used to serve human needs and desires. In those terms, the main general types of land use are:

- **agriculture,** including pasturing, by far the largest type of land use worldwide, both in terms of total land area and POPULATION employed (see CROPLANDS). Much farmland in urban areas, however, is being taken over for residential, commercial, transportation, and industrial DEVELOPMENT, while new farmlands are often being created out of less fertile land, often at the expense of FORESTS and WETLANDS.
- **forest,** including both privately and publicly owned timberland, as on private farms or public lands. These are being lost at a great rate to other uses, especially when the trees are completely cleared (clear cut) rather than selectively cut, and are a main focus of environmentalists today.
- **mineral resources,** lands used for MINING or extraction of other resources, as of COAL, OIL, NATURAL GAS, or valuable metals. This kind of use is making increasingly heavy inroads on sensitive areas, such as COASTS, forests, and WILDLIFE REFUGES.
- **recreational,** parks and other areas devoted to human leisure enjoyment, including large national parks and other types of playgrounds. To the extent that parks save lands from other kinds of development, recreational uses are favored by environmentalists–but not when the use is so excessive that the land's ECOSYSTEMS are damaged (see ECOTOURISM; WILDLIFE REFUGES).
- **water resources,** lands providing water for irrigation, community use, and HYDROPOWER projects, including the areas (often prime farmlands) beneath large reservoirs created by DAMS. Increasing WATER RESOURCES are necessary for increased population and development, though environmentalists note that much water is wasted, and that water conservation would leave more land for other uses–or for preservation in a natural state.
- **transportation,** lands used for the building of highways, railroads, and airports, the latter requiring increasingly large amounts of flat land, often prime flatland or cleared forest land.
- **urban,** lands used primarily for human structures, including residential areas, factory and other complexes, and commercial districts, and their associated streets and parking lots. It is urban land that is increasing at such an enormous pace. In the affluent countries, increased population, development, and associated transportation needs are gobbling up many farmlands, forest lands, and recreational lands, the phenomenon generally termed *urbanization*. But in poorer countries, too, people increasingly flock to the cities, resulting in the spread of shantytowns around most of the world's major metropolitan areas, often without the associated water, sanitation, and other services required.

Land is often used for several different purposes; in *multiple use*, minerals may be extracted from areas being harvested for timber, for example, or recreational activities may be allowed in certain kinds of forest or farm lands, though environmentalists charge that too often commercial concerns override other considerations.

Land use is a fundamental consideration in ENVIRONMENTAL PLANNING, the first and most basic step of which is to analyze how the land is being used at present, and then to develop an overall plan for how it should be used in the future. It is in these basic areas that environmentalists frequently come into conflict with traditional patterns of development. In real estate, the "highest and best use" of land is the one that makes the property most valuable if resold. From this very limited economic point of view, a piece of land is most valuable when it supports the most income-producing activity; an OIL well or an office tower is considered a better use than "raw" land. It is that view that has caused humans to–as Joni Mitchell put it–"pave paradise, put up a parking lot." Environmentalists argue that this view is not only narrow, but also short-sighted, and does not take into consideration the long-term benefits of the land in its natural, or at least not highly developed state. Using principles of NATURAL RESOURCE ACCOUNTING they hope to give planners the proper ammunition to fight the "development first" approach.

More fundamentally, some environmentalists question the whole idea of land use seen only as service to human needs and desires. They feel that large areas should not be *used* at all, but preserved, though often with some restricted recreational use, and that land should be evaluated from a far wider perspective, in terms of interacting ECOSYSTEMS and the total BIOSPHERE. To preserve BIOLOGICAL DIVERSITY, environmental researchers recommend that regional planning should establish zones for land use, especially focusing on conservation and development of wild SPECIES, and also the most efficient use of land. Much attention has also been focused on the potential disaster involved in converting to a land use inappropriate to the area, and the need to perform long-term planning analysis.

Among the key tools for enforcement of land use policy and environmental planning on the local level are ZONING and building ordinances, supplemented by state and national laws and regulations. Increasingly these are being used on local and national levels to preserve natural areas—undeveloped land of conservation interest, especially forests, WETLANDS, lands overlying AQUIFERS, wildlife areas, scenic sites, trails and trail connectors, and threatened farmland. This trend is buttressed by various international agreements, such as that creating BIOSPHERE RESERVES. In addition, many private groups, too, are using tools such as LAND TRUSTS and CONSERVATION EASEMENTS to restrict land use in ways favorable to the ecosystems involved; these have the advantage of encouraging conservation, since landowners do not lose financially by it, as in zoning or other regulation that provides no compensation for financial loss in leaving land undeveloped.

### For more information and action:

- **AMERCIAN PLANNING ASSOCIATION (APA),** (202-872-0611). Publishes Planning Advisory Service (PAS) reports, such as *Preserving Rural Character* (1990) and *Enforcing Zoning and Land-Use Controls* (1988); bibliographies such as *Federal and State Government Impacts on Local Land Use Policy* (1989) and *Land Information Systems and Land Use Planning* (1988); periodicals such as *Land Use Law & Zoning Digest* and *Zoning News*; and many books.
- **INTERNATIONAL CENTER FOR ARID AND SEMIARID LAND STUDIES (ICASALS),** (806-742-2218). Publishes *Urbanization in the Arid Lands.*
- **RENEW AMERICA,** (202-232-2252). Publishes *Land Use Planning* (1988).
- **RESOURCES FOR THE FUTURE (RFF),** (202-328-5000). Publishes *Multiple-Use Management: The Economics of Public Forestlands.*
- **SIERRA CLUB,** (415-776-2211 or 202-547-1141; legislative hotline, 202-547-5550). Publishes *Transportation Policy* and *Urban Environment Policy.*
- **WESTERN FORESTRY AND CONSERVATION ASSOCIATION (WFCA),** (503-226-4562).
- **WORLD RESOURCES INSTITUTE (WRI),** (202-638-6300). Publishes *Driving Forces: Motor Vehicle Trends and Their Implications for Global Warming, Energy Strategies, and Transportation Planning.*

- **Zero Population Growth (ZPG),** (202-332-2200). Publishes *Bumper to Bumper, Coast to Coast* and *Traffic Congestion.* (See POPULATION RESOURCES INFORMATION AND ACTION GUIDE on page 248.)

### Other references:
*The Greening of Urban Transport: Planning for Walking and Cycling in Western Cities.* R. D. Tolley, ed. Pinter, 1990. *Saving America's Countryside.* Samuel N. Stokes et al. Johns Hopkins University Press, 1989. *America's Suburban Centers: The Land Use-Transportation Link.* Robert Cervero. Unwin and Hyman, 1989. *The Wise Use Agenda.* Alan M. Gottlieb, ed. Free Enterprise, 1989. *Land Use Law,* 2nd ed. Daniel Mandelker. Michie, 1988. *Managing Public Lands in the Public Interest.* Benjamin C. Dysart III and Marion Clawson, eds. Praeger, 1988. (See also ENVIRONMENTAL PLANNING; GREENWAYS; WILDERNESS; WILDLIFE REFUGES.)

**LC$_{50}$ test,** median lethal concentration test (see LD$_{50}$ TEST).

**LD$_{50}$ test (median lethal dose),** a test to determine the DOSAGE LEVEL at which a substance kills half of the test population, usually 50–200 animals; the test substance is normally given by mouth, but may be given by injection or inhalation. The test, developed in 1927 by J.W. Trevan, has been widely used, as in standardizing the doses of various medicinal substances, such as digitalis, insulin, and diphtheria. As such, it has saved many lives and helped researchers identify potentially dangerous substances. However, in recent years, especially with the rise of the ANIMAL RIGHTS MOVEMENT, the LD$_{50}$ test has been reexamined, both in terms of the value of the information supplied, the number of animals needed, and the possibility of alternative approaches, including different types of tests and estimates from computerized statistical analysis.

The *LC$_{50}$ test (median lethal concentration)* is similar, except that it is used to assess the lethally toxic concentration of a substance. Groups of animals are exposed to the test chemical, in food, by inhalation, or (for fish) in water, to determine at what concentration half of them are killed. The test has produced undoubted benefits, to humans and the environment, as it is used to assess the effects and identify possible dangers of TOXIC CHEMICALS such as PESTICIDES, both on humans and on wildlife, and is mandated by law in some cases. But the same criticisms have applied to the LC$_{50}$ as to the LD$_{50}$, spurring searches for alternatives. These include reducing the number of animals and testing human and other animal cells in culture (*in vitro,* literally "in glass"). (See ANIMAL TESTING.)

**leaching,** a process in which water flows or percolates through material, dissolving or otherwise picking up numerous substances on the way, the resulting fluid being called *leachate*. Leaching is a natural process, that happens continually as water from rain or streams flows over or through the land's surface. But if the air and earth through which the water passes is polluted—as in cases of AIR POLLUTION, ACID RAIN, debris from MINING, or waste dumps—then the result will be polluted leachate, which can be toxic to the environment, especially contaminating WATER RESOURCES. and damaging the life that depends on it. To avoid such damage, contaminated leachate is sometimes collected and treated as wastewater before being released into the environment (as in DESALINIZATION), but all too often it is left untreated. Leaching is also sometimes used deliberately in RECYCLING, as part of processes to separate out valuable substances such as COPPER from other matter. (See also ACID RAIN; HEAVY METALS.)

**lead (Pb),** a type of HEAVY METAL in common use for thousands of years, though known for almost as long to have serious health effects. In modern times it has been widely used in gasoline, batteries, alloys, gunshot, paints, and building materials, especially plumbing, and is also a common contaminant from many industrial processes, including MINING and smelting. Recent decades have made clearer lead's devastating effects on health, especially affecting the kidneys, brain, central nervous system (CNS), heart, and circulatory system, by a variety of actions, such as inhibition of the hemoglobin required by oxygen-carrying red blood cells and deactivation of enzymes vital to the brain and nervous system.

Symptoms of lead poisoning include stomach pains, headaches, irritability, shaking, anorexia, anemia, inflammation of the brain, and in extreme cases, coma and death. Diagnosis of poisoning is made by analyzing lead levels in the blood; some medical experts recommend testing for pregnant women and for children annually up to age six. Treatment has traditionally involved a difficult, often painful series of hospital-based injections of medications designed to form chemical bonds with the lead and then flush it from the body; only recently an oral drug was been approved as an alternative. Often, though, lead poisoning goes undiagnosed until significant damage has been done.

Children are especially vulnerable, with lead affecting brain development and overall intellectual functioning, including IQ, memory, and attention span, as well as fetal development in pregnant women. So far unclear is what level of lead is low enough not to be dangerous. In the mid-1960s, government regulations regarded as acceptable a level of 60 micrograms of lead per deciliter (mg/dl) of

blood; that level dropped by stages to 15 mg/dl by 1987, and is expected to fall even further.

Like other heavy metals, lead readily contaminates the environment, often being dissolved by ACID RAIN or by water in the ground, as from industrial or mining sources, or being deposited from particles in the air. It enters the FOOD CHAIN and is stored in the body tissues of wildlife, with increasing concentration at every level in the chain (see BIOACCUMULATION). Animals high on the food chain—such as birds of prey and humans—are especially affected.

Because of its toxicity, levels of lead in the environment are routinely monitored in many countries. In the United States, for example, it is one of the CRITERIA AIR POLLUTANTS for which the ENVIRONMENTAL PROTECTION AGENCY (EPA) sets NATIONAL EMISSIONS STANDARDS FOR HAZARDOUS AIR POLLUTANTS (NESHAPs), under the CLEAN AIR ACT. But even though many industrial countries have restricted uses of lead—phasing out lead in paints and gasoline since the 1970s, for example—lead exists at lower but still significant and often dangerous levels in air, water, and soil, including some areas of eastern North America and Central Europe generally considered as "wilderness." Many industrial workers are exposed to lead-contaminated air. Of particular concern in the home is the lead content of tap drinking water, where old lead plumbing or lead-soldered connections leach significant amounts of lead into home drinking water. The SAFE DRINKING WATER ACT of 1986 banned the use of lead solder and lead materials in public water systems, and a 1988 amendment mandated lead-free solders in drinking water pipes for new homes, and lowered the allowable amount of lead in drinking water. Because lead builds up in water as it sits in pipes, running the water to clear out pipes before drawing water may help, but experts recommend that water should be tested both before use and after flushing, to get a proper reading of lead levels.

Lead is also found in food, from lead-containing PESTICIDES, from contaminated soil, and sometimes from lead solders in cans. Lead soldering is being phased out in some countries, but is still common, though it is generally barred in containers for baby food. Lead solders cannot be seen, but lead-testing kits are available for consumer use. Lead is also a serious contaminant of wine, leaching from lead-foil caps and also from lead-soldering in pipes during processing; a 1991 study found such lead contamination widespread, often exceeding allowable levels in water (see PRIMARY DRINKING WATER STANDARDS on page 274), with imported wines—especially from Italy—having higher levels than U.S.-produced wines. Other common sources of lead in food include imported glazed pottery

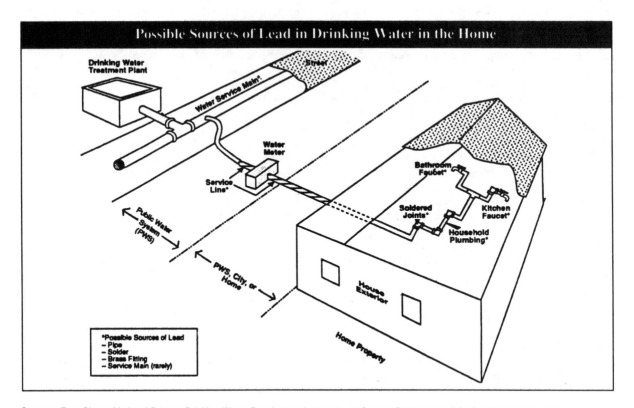

## Possible Sources of Lead in Drinking Water in the Home

Drinking Water Treatment Plant

Street

Water Service Main*

Water Meter

Service Line*

Public Water System (PWS)

PWS, City, or Home

Bathroom Faucet*

Soldered Joints*

Kitchen Faucet*

Household Plumbing*

House Exterior

Home Property

*Possible Sources of Lead
– Pipe
– Solder
– Brass Fitting
– Service Main (rarely)

**Source:** *Fact Sheet: National Primary Drinking Water Regulations for Lead and Copper.* Environmental Protection Agency, 1991.

and crystal glassware, from which lead oxide often leaches into wine.

Lead in old paints is also a great concern, not just (as was long thought) from children eating sweet-tasting paint flakes, but also from lead-laced dust from disintegrating paint flakes, which coat many of the surfaces and toys that children touch and mouth, and not only in poor areas, but also in many old houses in a wide range of areas, in most of which lead paint was routinely used. In the United States the Lead-Based Paint Poisoning Prevention Act of 1971 was intended to attack the toxic threat of lead. But though it required lead paint to be removed from all federally subsidized housing, little has been done, partly because insufficient money was allocated to do the job, which costs several thousand dollars per dwelling.

Experts also disagree about how to handle lead paint. Some say that, as with ASBESTOS, it may be safer to cover lead-based paint, rather than remove it; others say that only postpones the problem. Certainly some methods of dealing with lead paint are themselves dangerous, as when sanding off lead-based paint produces lead-filled dust in-

haled by workers and residents, or when flames used to burn off lead paint product toxic fumes.

Whatever the problems, a 1988 study found that over half the households in the United States still had layers of lead-based paint, and 20 years after the act was passed, an estimated three million children under age six show the effects of excess lead in their blood. Dr. Herbert Needleman, University of Pittsburgh lead poisoning specialist, summed up the tragedy: "Lead poisoning is the most severe environmental disease in this country, and it is totally preventable." In the United States, lead is increasingly monitored as a TOXIC CHEMICAL and HAZARDOUS SUBSTANCE (see TOXIC CHEMICALS AND HAZARDOUS SUBSTANCES on page 407; KNOWN HEALTH EFFECTS OF TOXIC CHEMICALS on page 416).

### For more information and action:

- **ENVIRONMENTAL DEFENSE FUND (EDF),** (212-505-2100). Publishes *Legacy of Lead: America's Continuing Epidemic of Childhood Lead Poisoning* (K.L. Florini et al., 1990).

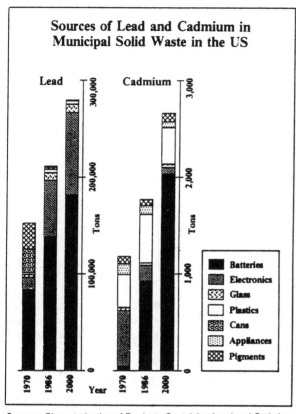

### Sources of Lead and Cadmium in Municipal Solid Waste in the US

**Lead**    **Cadmium**

Legend:
- Batteries
- Electronics
- Glass
- Plastics
- Cans
- Appliances
- Pigments

*Source: Characterization of Products Containing Lead and Cadmium in Municipal Solid Waste in the United States, 1970 to 2000. Environmental Protection Agency, 1989.*

- ENVIRONMENTAL PROTECTION AGENCY (EPA), (202-260-7751 or 202-260-2080).
- NATIONAL WILDLIFE FEDERATION (NWF), (202-797-6800 or 800-245-5484). Publishes *Myths and Facts: Straight Talk on Lead Poisoning and Steel Shot.*

**Other references:**
*Lead Poisoning of America's School Children.* Program Studies, 1991. *The Citizen's Guide to Lead: Uncovering a Hidden Health Hazard.* Barbara Wallace. NC Press (Seven Hills), 1989. *Lead Exposure and Child Development: An International Assessment.* M. Smith, ed. Kluwer Academic, 1989. *Exposure of Infants and Children to Lead* . . . A. Oskarsson. UNIPUB, 1989.
(See also HEAVY METALS; ACID RAIN.)

**leaking underground storage tanks (LUST),** containers holding petroleum products and other TOXIC CHEMICALS, often beneath gas stations and other facilities, from which contents have been oozing and sometimes pouring, to foul water, land, and air. WATER POLLUTION is the most obvious result, but fires and explosions are also real and dangerous possibilities in many places. Leaking underground storage tanks are not new, but the dimensions of the problem have been emerging only in recent years. In the United States alone, the ENVIRONMENTAL PROTECTION AGENCY (EPA) estimates that there are over 2 million underground tanks, about 20 percent of which "are leaking or have the potential to leak," with 63,000 confirmed as of 1990. While the EPA explores, develops, and disseminates new cleanup technologies and funding mechanisms, the primary job of cleaning up of LUST sites is left to the various state and local governments. Actual cleanup is sometimes funded by the Leaking Underground Storage Tank (LUST) trust fund established by the U.S. Congress in 1986.

**For more information and action:**

- AIR AND WASTE MANAGEMENT ASSOCIATION (A&WMA), (412-232-3444). Publishes *Underground Storage Tanks.*
- ENVIRONMENTAL DEFENSE FUND (EDF), (212-505-2100). Publishes *Leaking Underground Storage Tanks—Citizen Action: An Ounce of Prevention* (L. Epstein and K. Stein, Environmental Information Exchange, 1990).
- ENVIRONMENTAL PROTECTION AGENCY (EPA), (202-475-7751 or 202-382-2080).

(See also WATER POLLUTION; also WATER POLLUTION INFORMATION AND ACTION GUIDE on page 330.)

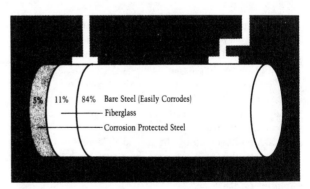

5%    11%    84%    Bare Steel (Easily Corrodes)
— Fiberglass
— Corrosion Protected Steel

### Many Tanks Currently in Use are Unprotected

*Source: Environmental Protection Agency, Office of Underground Storage Tanks.*

**least-toxic control,** an alternative name for INTEGRATED PEST MANAGEMENT.

**Legacy International** (346 Commerce Streeet, Alexandria, VA 22314; 703-549-3630; J.E. Rash, President), an educational organization founded in 1979 that "addresses global issues through programs focusing on environment and development, cross-cultural relations, and conflict resolution," serving as "a catalyst for public and private sector initiatives and for collaboration locally, regionally, and globally." Legacy International is a NONGOVERNMENTAL ORGANIZATION (NGO) affiliated with the United Nations Department of Public Information, and several of its programs (often funded or co-sponsored by government agencies such as the ENVIRONMENTAL PROTECTION AGENCY and the WORLD BANK) have been designed to spur local application of the principles of sustainable DEVELOPMENT embodied in the UN report OUR COMMON FUTURE (the Brundtland Report). Among these are *Youths for Environment and Service (YES)*, offering leadership training on environment and development to young adults, working with community leaders; the *Global Viewpoints Forum*, discussions focusing on critical global issues, notably regional conflicts and environment and development problems; and the *Soviet-American Environmental Initiative*, staffing the 13 offices of the Ecological Center in the Soviet Union, providing "environmental training, information, and technology for grassroots organizations, government, and business in the Soviet Union." With training facilities in Bedford, Virginia, and outposts in Moscow, Stockholm, Izmir (Turkey), and Jerusalem, Legacy International conducts educational programs on Environment and Development, Leadership Development and Conflict Resolution, Outreach and Education, and International Policy Initiatives.

**lemurs,** a primate family that for the past 50–60 million years has evolved in isolation on the island of MADAGASCAR, off the southeastern coast of Africa. Earlier, there were primitive lemurs in Europe, Asia, and Africa; but the lemurs of Madagascar, while descended from the same ancestors as the African primates, evolved quite separately, and provide fascinating insights into the evolution of all the primates, including humanity. Over 40 lemur SPECIES had evolved by the time people settled on Madagascar about 2,000 years ago; there may have been earlier human visitors, but they do not seem to have left a lasting imprint on the island.

By the mid-20th century, HUNTING, loss of HABITAT, and the new animals and diseases introduced into the island by its human occupants had destroyed half the lemur species, and all of the 20 to 22 that remain are greatly endangered. It is possible that a few more species have survived; for example, the hairy-eared dwarf lemur, the smallest of all the primates, was thought to be extinct—until one was discovered alive on Madagascar in April 1989.

Yet the situation is desperate, and worsening. In only the past 25 years, the POPULATION of Madagascar has doubled, from 6 million to 12 million people, with no change in wasteful slash-and-burn agricultural practices. The result is an accelerating ecological disaster, with the island's once-massive central highland FOREST nearly destroyed, total destruction soon to come and the hillsides eroding away, their vital topsoil ultimately flowing into the sea. Their HABITAT is disappearing, while unrestrained HUNTING of lemurs continues; if this persists, the lemurs will soon be gone. Some small conservation areas have been set aside by the government, and conservationists (barred from the country from 1975–85) have resumed their effort to save the lemurs and the island's many other ENDANGERED SPECIES. International support has also come, in the form of a pioneering DEBT-FOR-NATURE SWAP with the U.S. government. But as of early 1991 little of immediate practical value had been achieved; habitat, lemurs, and other species were continuing to disappear very quickly, and it was very clear that one of the world's most immediate ecological crises existed on Madagascar, which might very well destroy the utterly unique lemur population of the island.

**For more information and action:**

- IUCN—THE WORLD CONSERVATION UNION, (202-797-5454). Publishes *Lemurs of Madagascar and the Comoros: The IUCN Red Data Book* (1990).
- WILDLIFE PRESERVATION TRUST INTERNATIONAL (WPTI), (215-222-3636).
- WORLD WILDLIFE FUND (WWF), (202-293-4800).

(See also ENDANGERED SPECIES; also ENDANGERED AND THREATENED WILDLIFE AND PLANTS on page 372.)

**leopards,** the only big cat species still widespread, with an estimated 90,000–100,000, most of them of the *North African leopard* subspecies, ranging throughout sub-Sahara Africa and south Asia, with small numbers also found in northern Africa and central Asia. The leopard, often alternatively called a *panther*, is listed as threatened in sub-Sahara Africa, and endangered elsewhere. Loss of HABITAT to explosively expanding African POPULATIONS may come close to destroying the SPECIES early in the 21st century. More immediate, but less catastrophic dangers stem from trophy hunters, for whom leopards are preferred targets.

Three other species are not strictly classified as leopards, but are generally perceived as leopards. All three, unfortunately, are highly prized for their skins, and are attacked by poachers, who find ready markets in several countries, even though the trade is illegal.

- The **jaguar,** a New World equivalent of the Old World leopard, once ranged from what is now the southwestern United States through all of Central and South America. Its *Arizona Jaguar* subspecies is now almost extinct, and its several other subspecies, which include the *Yucatán, Panama, Amazon, Peruvian,* and *Paraná* jaguars, now range in much smaller numbers from the Yucatan south, increasingly threatened by habitat loss and hunters.
- The **snow leopard,** found in the high mountains of central Asia, is greatly threatened by hunters, and may not long survive if large sums continue to be paid for their skins.
- The South Asian **clouded leopard,** a forest dweller, is threatened by the accelerating DEFORESTATION of the region, as well as by hunters.

**For more information and action:**

- **International Snow Leopard Trust (ISLT)** (4949 Sunnyside Avenue North, Seattle, WA 98103; Helen Freeman, President; 206-632-2421), a membership foundation for individuals concerned with "the conservation of the snow leopard and its mountain habitat," which works on cooperative projects in Central Asian countries and offers special travel opportunities and discounts on publications and products. It publishes various materials, including the newsletter *Snowline*, pamphlets *A Review of the Status and Ecology of the Snow Leopard*, *An Annotated Bibliography of Literature on the Snow Leopard*, and proceedings from International Snow Leopard Symposia.
- **World Wildlife Fund (WWF),** (202-293-4800).

**Other references:**
*Vanishing Tracks: Four Years among the Snow Leopards of Nepal.* Darla Hillard. Morrow, 1989.
(See also ENDANGERED SPECIES; also ENDANGERED AND THREATENED WILDLIFE AND PLANTS on page 372.)

**lindane (Y-hexachlorocyclohexane),** a type of PESTICIDE (see CHLORINATED HYDROCARBONS).

**lions,** majestic CARNIVOROUS mammals once widespread throughout Europe, Africa, and Asia, and possessed of a powerful mythological and religious presence for much of human history, but now found in quantity only in the WILDLIFE REFUGES of sub-Sahara Africa. Fewer than 200 Asiatic lions survive in India's Gir wildlife sanctuary.

The lions continue to exert an enormous pull, for tourists on "safari" rather than for the gun-toting hunters who nearly destroyed them in the course of unrestrained trophy HUNTING. Now they are "shot" by cameras at Tanzania's SERENGETI NATIONAL PARK; Africa's greatest wildlife sanctuary; at South Africa's KRUGER NATIONAL PARK; and at a dozen other African sanctuaries, such as Kenya's AMBOSELI, TSAVO, MERU, and MASAI MARA preserves. African lions are not listed as endangered or threatened; but political instability in those countries now providing safe havens for the lions could very easily threaten all remaining lion populations, since all depend entirely on human protection. (See also ENDANGERED SPECIES; also ENDANGERED AND THREATENED WILDLIFE AND PLANTS on page 372.)

**Living Sea, The**, see Jacques-Yves COUSTEAU.

**London Dumping Convention (LDC),** see CONVENTION ON THE PREVENTION OF MARINE POLLUTION BY DUMPING OF WASTE AND OTHER MATTER.

**Love Canal,** notorious chemical dump site at Niagara Falls, New York. From 1942 to 1953, the Hooker Chemical Company dumped an estimated 21,000 to 22,000 tons of chemical waste there, much of it highly toxic, and including DIOXIN. In 1953, the company donated the property to the local school district, in the terms of the transfer trying to block any further liability stemming from the dump. A school and houses were built on the dump site, although chemicals continued to ooze up through the surface for decades. In 1978, attributing high rates of illness and birth defects to the chemicals at the site, New York State forced evacuation of 240 families from the area. Later, over 500 homes near but not directly at the dump site were also evacuated. Those evacuated were compensated for their losses, after long negotiation with the chemical company. In 1980 the site became the first federal environmental disaster area, and a decade-long cleanup effort began. In 1988, New York State called 236 evacuated homes safe for reoccupancy, and in 1990 the ENVIRONMENTAL PROTECTION AGENCY cleared the homes for sale to new owners. Many environmentalists sharply disagreed with the decision to open the area around the dump site, now renamed Black Creek Village, to new occupancy, but many people bid for the homes, sold as bargains. (See TOXIC CHEMICALS; also TOXIC CHEMICAL AND HAZARDOUS SUBSTANCE INFORMATION AND ACTION GUIDE on page 302.)

**low-input sustainable agriculture (LISA),** a general term for farming practices that emphasize use of resources available on the farm itself over those purchased off the farm, the implication being "low *external* input." The term is, however, sometimes used simply to refer to a lowered or reduced level of dependence on—and more efficient use of—externally purchased materials, such as PESTICIDES and chemical fertilizers, with the focus on eco-nomic savings over environmental advantages. (See SUSTAINABLE AGRICULTURE.)

**low-level radioactive waste (LLRW),** radioactive waste materials other than high-level radioactive waste, transuranic waste, spent fuel, or mill tailings from radio-active substances such as uranium (see RADIOACTIVE WASTE).

# M

**Madagascar,** an island nation off the southeastern coast of Africa, a classic example of the havoc that can be wrought by a combination of runaway POPULATION growth and wasteful and destructive land cultivation practices, with damage to the land, its people, and its other species.

As the population of the country ballooned, from 6 million to 12 million in only 25 years, traditional slash-and-burn agricultural techniques continued to be used. By now almost all of Madagascar's once-abundant central highlands FOREST has been burned and cut away, leaving an ecological disaster behind, the EROSION cutting away at the hillsides, the RIVERS that run down to the sea filled with disappearing topsoil, and the harbors silting up. An extraordinarily damaging cycle is in process, with more and more people getting less and less out of the land, as farmers are no longer able to leave land degraded by slash-and-burn techniques to lie fallow for a decade or more to recover naturally, but instead must plant poor-yielding crops far too soon.

As the damage has accelerated, Madagascar's extraordinary animal and plant population has suffered greatly, with many plants and SPECIES endangered, and some EXTINCTION already taking place. Madagascar lies 250 miles off the African coast, and, at approximately 225,000 square miles, is the fourth largest of the world's islands. Because of its isolation, size, and subtropical location, it has had an extraordinary and in many instances unique profusion of animals and plants, including over 40 species of LEMURS (only 20 or so still surviving), hundreds of other animal and bird species, over 900 identified orchid species, and an estimated 10,000 plant species in all. The entire ECOSYSTEM is now endangered.

From the mid-1980s, Madagascar's government has engaged in a conservation effort, though one seriously hampered by lack of funds. At the same time, conservationists from the rest of the world, barred from the country from 1975 to 1985, have focused world attention on the island's much-compromised ecosystem. The "save the lemurs" campaign, important in itself, has also helped to focus world attention on wider problems. In 1989, the U.S. government announced that it would provide a $1 million grant for a DEBT-FOR-NATURE SWAP, with Madagascar receiving $2.1 million in relief from its national debt in exchange for its development of such conservation efforts as park ranger training, wildlife preservation, and new tree plantings. In 1990, CONSERVATION INTERNATIONAL concluded a similar, but wider agreement with Madagascar, which included the purchase at a discount of a total of $5 million in outstanding trade credit as well as bank credit. Early results have been somewhat promising, although out-of-control population growth, slash-and burn agriculture, and massive erosion continue as before.

**For more information and action:**

- INTERNATIONAL COUNCIL FOR BIRD PRESERVATION (ICBP) (United Kingdom: 0223-277318; U.S. Headquarters, c/o WORLD WILDLIFE FUND-US; 202-293-4800). Publishes *A Wildlife Survey of Marojejy Nature Reserve, Madagascar* (1988).
- IUCN—THE WORLD CONSERVATION UNION, (202-797-5454). Publishes *Primates of Madagascar and the Comoros: The IUCN Red Data Book* (1990) and *Madagascar: An Environmental Profile* (M.D. Jenkins, ed., 1987.)
- WILDLIFE PRESERVATION TRUST INTERNATIONAL (WPTI) (215-222-3636).
- WORLD WILDLIFE FUND (WWF), (202-293-4800).
(See also WILDLIFE REFUGE; ECOTOURISM.)

**malathion,** a common type of PESTICIDE (see ORGANOPHOSPHATE).

## Man and the Biosphere Program (MAB), (U.S. arm:
U.S. MAB Secretariat, OES/EGC/MAB, Department of State, Washington, DC 20520-7818; 703-235-2946; Roger E. Soles, Executive Director), an international program established by the United Nations in 1970 (replacing the earlier International Biological Program, or IBP) to formally bring together the previously diffuse national and international research, conservation, and training activities. MAB's main objective is "to develop a scientific basis linking the natural and social sciences for the rational use of the biosphere—that portion of the Earth which contains living organisms—and for the improvement of the relationship between humans and their environment." Taking an "integrated, interdisciplinary, problem-focused research approach," MAB seeks to make a "bridge between fundamental science and technological applications." These activities are focused on BIOSPHERE RESERVES, over 280 areas set aside in over 70 countries, of the more than 110 countries participating in the MAB program. Each country defines and organizes the specific activities to be carried on under the MAB program. The United States program, for example, has chosen to focus on five general areas—High Latitude Ecosystems, Human Dominated Systems, Marine and Coastal Ecosystems, Temperate Ecosystems, and Tropical Systems—and the cross-disciplinary research by social and biological/physi-

cal scientists working in its 46 biosphere reserves is organized under those five programs, each with its own goals. (See BIOSPHERE RESERVE.)

**manatees and dugongs,** greatly endangered large (500– to–2,000-pound) sea mammals, both also known as "sea cows." As recently as the mid-1930s, *West Indian manatees*, *West African manatees*, and *Amazonian manatees* were plentiful, as were the Indian Ocean and eastern Pacific *dugongs*, but these COAST- and river-dwelling, gentle, quite helpless herbivores have by now been hunted almost to EXTINCTION. Of a set of populations that orginally numbered at least in the hundreds of thousands, only a few thousand are left. A related species, *Stellar's Sea Cow*, was hunted to extinction in the Bering Sea by the mid-1700s.

All three manatee species and the dugongs are listed as ENDANGERED SPECIES by many nations. But poaching is still common outside the United States, pushing the species even further toward extinction. There are also new hazards all over the world, as from powerboats and toxic wastes, and as part of the "incidental kill" resulting from commercial FISHING, as when gill nets set out to capture other sea creatures entangle and kill manatees and dugongs.

The West Indian manatee population of the southeastern United States, now down to as few as 1,200, may have the best chance of survival, because of accelerated government and private efforts to save the manatees. But even that chance is slim, as deaths caused by collisions with the almost 2 million vessels operating off the southeastern coast and on its waterways continue to climb, as DEVELOPMENT continues to destroy necessary manatee HABITATS, and as manatee calf death rates continue to climb, possibly because of toxic wastes.

**For more information and action:**

- AMERICAN CETACEAN SOCIETY (ACS), (213-548-6279).
- ELSA WILD ANIMAL APPEAL (EWAA), (818-761-8387).
(See also ENDANGERED SPECIES; ENDANGERED AND THREATENED WILDLIFE AND PLANTS on page 372.)

**manganese (Mn),** a type of HEAVY METAL necessary to many living things, including humans, with its absence sometimes limiting growth, but which in larger amounts can be unhealthy, especially affecting the nervous system. As a pollutant, manganese is treated as a TOXIC CHEMICAL and HAZARDOUS SUBSTANCE (see TOXIC CHEMICALS AND HAZARDOUS SUBSTANCES on page 407; KNOWN HEALTH EFFECTS OF TOXIC CHEMICALS on page 416). It is, however, an important industrial metal, used in alloys such as stainless steel, and rather a rare one. One of the main reasons that the United States has not (as of this 1992 writing) signed the CONVENTION ON THE LAW OF THE SEA is because of potential limitation of seabed MINING rights for manganese.

**mangroves,** distinctive flooded FORESTS of trees on "stilts" in the low-lying coastal mudflats and tidal swamps bordering tropical rain forests, where the salt-water-tolerant, evergreen trees are able to take hold in a watery environment, notably on the COASTS of Africa, South America, and southern and southeastern Asia. Mangrove forests have great BIOLOGICAL DIVERSITY and are also enormously productive, playing key roles in the FOOD CHAIN and life cycles of various aquatic animals, such as shrimp and numerous fish, including many on which the local human population depend, for their food or livelihood. Because of their extensive root systems, mangroves also are important in stabilizing the shoreline and water quality of the coasts, sometimes being cultivated deliberately for that purpose, as in parts of Thailand and the United States.

Mangroves are under significant threat however, from several quarters:

- **logging,** especially clear-cutting, rather than selective culling, for forest products.
- **stripping,** as when mangroves are used by the local population for FUELWOOD.
- **loss of freshwater sources,** as when DAMS or heavy irrigation projects are built inland.
- **conversion to** AQUACULTURE, as when swamps are converted into brackish-water fish ponds, common in Southeast Asia.
- **conversion to** CROPLAND, as when land is drained and "reclaimed," as done extensively in Ecuador in recent years.
- **tourism and recreation,** when coastal areas are attractive to seasonal visitors.
- **development,** as for urban settlements, industrial complexes, mining operations, or ports.
- **silting,** build-up of sediment from runoff, the normal process of SEDIMENTATION, but much accelerated by inland EROSION.
- **dredging and dumping,** deposition of soil and waste products, often pollutants, in nearby land and waters.

Because loss of the mangroves has such major effects, especially on aquatic life and the people dependent on it, numerous countries have moved to protect at least some mangrove ECOSYSTEMS, though many environmentalists question the commitment to action and the quality of the management of even the relatively few protected mangrove areas. (See also WETLANDS; COASTS; FORESTS.)

**Manu National Park,** an extraordinarily diverse 3,800,000-acre (5,900-square-mile) Peruvian nature preserve, which extends from the 14,800-foot level in the Andes to the basin of the Manu River, on the western edge of the huge Amazon basin. The park is also a United Nations World Heritage Site. With an additional 350,000 acres of reserve, the area is a United Nations BIOSPHERE RESERVE.

The wide range of altitudes and landforms found at Manu, from high mountains to tropical FOREST, mean that a very wide range of animals and plants are found here. An estimated 1,500 bird species are found in Manu, along with such animals as jaguars (see LEOPARDS), armadillos, Andean deer, giant otters, BEARS, tapirs, MONKEYS, and peccaries, some of them threatened SPECIES in more thickly settled areas of Peru. Little DEVELOPMENT has yet come to the area, and it is not yet seriously threatened by the kind of massive slash-and-burn farming and land clearing for ranching purposes that endangers some of the Brazilian portion of the AMAZON RAIN FOREST. However, much of the countryside of southern Peru, in which Manu is located, is all or partially controlled by the Shining Path (*Sendero Luminoso*) insurgency, which greatly limits environmentally harmful development, but also limits both administration of the area as a national park and visitor access to the area. (See WILDLIFE REFUGE; WILDERNESS.)

**Maralinga,** British nuclear test site in South Australia, used from 1953 to 1963 for a series of then-secret nuclear bomb tests. The Native Australian (Aboriginal) community occupying the test site area was relocated during the testing years, and the British attempted a cleanup of the contaminated test site area in 1967, before the Australian government took control of the area. But later Australian government studies, undertaken when some Aborigines began to return to tribal lands in the mid-1980s, showed the test site still very seriously contaminated with plutonium pellets, and also revealed contamination of an estimated 300 square kilometers surrounding the test site, which had continued to be occupied by thousands of Aborigines throughout the testing period, with consequent RADIATION-related illnesses, including cancer and leukemia. In 1991, tribal leaders began a campaign aimed at forcing effective cleanup of the area and compensation of those made ill, as did ex-service personnel claiming radiation-related illnesses.

During the 1950s, British nuclear tests occurred in several other Australian locations, including the Emu test range and the Monte Bello Islands. Hydrogen and atomic bomb tests occurred at Christmas Island in the South Pacific, later generating many hundreds of compensation claims from radiation-damaged British veterans. (See NUCLEAR TESTING.)

**margin of safety (MOS),** see TOLERANCE LEVELS.

**Marine Mammal Commission** (1825 Connecticut Avenue NW, Suite 512, Washington, DC 20009; 202-653-6237; John R. Twiss, Jr., Executive Director), a U.S. federal commission set up, under the MARINE MAMMAL PROTECTION ACT originally passed in 1972, as an independent agency of the Executive Branch, charged with "developing, reviewing, and making recommendations on actions and policies for all Federal agencies with respect to marine mammal protection and conservation and for carrying out a research program" on marine mammals such as DOLPHINS, MANATEES, sea OTTERS, polar BEARS, PORPOISES, SEALS AND SEA LIONS, and WHALES. The Commission often works closely with other national and international agencies, notably the *National Marine Fisheries Service* (see NATIONAL OCEANOGRAPHIC AND ATMOSPHERIC ADMINISTRATION), FISH AND WILDLIFE SERVICE, *International Whaling Commission* (see WHALE INFORMATION AND ACTION GUIDE on page 343), the Department of Commerce (as regarding FISHING), the Department of the Interior (as regarding permits to take or import marine mammals for research or public display), and the DEPARTMENT OF AGRICULTURE's Animal and Plant Health Inspection Service (as regarding setting "standards and regulations for the humane handling, care, treatment and transportation of marine mammals").

The commission publishes an annual report, for both government and the public, reviewing domestic and international activities affecting marine mammals, each year focusing on those species in most critical danger. Under 1988 amendments to the act, the Commission became more directly involved in the national and international questions of so-called "incidental kill" of marine mammals during commercial fishing, such as dolphin killed by tuna fishers; with increasing numbers of whales being killed supposedly for "research purposes," to circumvent the whaling ban under the IWC; and with the extensive damage to marine mammals by the use of DRIFTNETS in fishing. The Commission has developed guidelines to control such incidental kills, which are to govern commercial fishing operations from late 1993 on. It is also involved in assessing the effects of materials such as PLASTICS, pollution from OIL spills (such as *EXXON VALDEZ*), and such commercial activities as OFFSHORE DRILLING and seabed MINING, issuing ENVIRONMENTAL IMPACT STATEMENTS for proposed lease sales. In addition to its annual report, numerous reports of research projects are generated from Commission-sponsored activities.

**Marine Mammal Protection Act,** a U.S. federal law passed in 1972, and amended in 1988, to protect, conserve, and encourage international research on marine mammals. It imposed a moratorium on the taking and import of marine mammals and products made from them. Permits may be granted for exemptions, as for scientific research, public display, and taking "incidental" to commercial FISHING, a question of considerable controversy given the widespread use of DRIFTNETS. Guidelines are set for the incidental take, and the permit is subject to withdrawal if it exceeds U.S. standards (from 1990 set at 1.25 times the number of U.S. fishing vessels). These and other interim exemptions are subject to monitoring and annual review. INDIGENOUS PEOPLES of Alaska are granted an exception for subsistence taking and handicrafts.

The Act also outlaws the taking, possession, or import of marine mammals or their products, except where permitted by international treaty; however, importing pregnant or lactating females, young that are nursing or under eight months old, or species designated as depleted, is unlawful, except by research permit. Permits are limited in time, specifying the number and kind of animals that can be taken, where and how, and sometimes (as for display or research) also for care after capture. For violations, civil penalties range up to $10,000 per violation, with forfeiture of the animal or product generally considered sufficient if importation is for "personal use." Knowing violation can lead to a fine up to $20,000 and up to a year in prison, per violation. In addition, the cargo of the violating vessel or vehicle can be confiscated and held for a fine up to $25,000, with rewards of up to $2,500 paid to informers (other than public officials).

Various federal or state agencies may be involved in enforcement of the Act. However, in general, responsibility for *Cetaceans* (such as WHALES, DOLPHINS, and PORPOISES) and pinnipeds (aquatic animals such as SEALS AND SEA LIONS, which use flippers for locomotion, except WALRUSES) is under the Department of Commerce, specifically the *National Marine Fisheries Service* (see NATIONAL OCEANOGRAPHIC AND ATMOSPHERIC ADMINISTRATION), while other marine mammals are under the Department of the Interior, specifically the FISH AND WILDLIFE SERVICE.

Also under the Act, the MARINE MAMMAL COMMISSION was established as an independent executive agency, supplemented by a committee of scientific advisors on marine mammals, to develop and monitor actions, policy, and research regarding marine mammals, including existing laws and treaties, conditions, methods of protection, conservation, humane taking, and permit applications. Where both apply, the Marine Mammal Protection Act—regarded as the more restrictive—takes precedence over the ENDAN-

GERED SPECIES ACT. (See also ENDANGERED SPECIES; BIOLOGICAL DIVERSITY; ENVIRONMENTAL LAW; ANIMAL RIGHTS MOVEMENT; WILDLIFE TRADE; also specific marine mammals.)

**Masai Mara National Reserve,** 450,000-acre (700-square-mile) game reserve in southern Kenya; its southern boundary is the Kenya-Tanzania border, where it meets Tanzania's SERENGETI NATIONAL PARK. Masai Mara's inner area, of about 200 square miles, is a national park; the balance of the reserve is used for cattle grazing by the Masai.

This is one of Africa's major wildlife sanctuaries, plains country with a profusion of animals, and in that respect remains much as it was before the European conquest of East Africa. Masai Mara and the Serengeti park are the homes of large numbers of LIONS, ELEPHANTS, hartebeests, gnus (wildebeests), hippopotamuses, LEOPARDS, CHEETAHS, steinboks, impalas, gazelles, black RHINOCEROSES (though poachers have made inroads here, too), and a score of smaller mammals; many of these are fast disappearing elsewhere in Africa. Hundreds of bird SPECIES are also found in the reserve. (See ECOTOURISM; WILDLIFE REFUGE.)

**maximum acceptable tolerance concentration (MATC),** see TOLERANCE LEVELS.

**maximum contaminant level (MCL),** the largest amount of a potentially harmful substance that the ENVIRONMENTAL PROTECTION AGENCY (EPA) allows to be present in drinking water before action is scheduled to be taken; sometimes called the *maximum permissible contaminant level* (MPCL) or *goal*. MCLs are scheduled to be phased out between 1990 and 1993 and superseded by NATIONAL PRIMARY DRINKING WATER REQUIREMENTS (NPDWRs). (See SAFE DRINKING WATER ACT [SDWA]; TOLERANCE LEVELS.)

**media,** in environmental usage, an umbrella term for the areas in which pollutants or other substances may appear—that is, air, land, or water. (See MULTIMEDIA ENFORCEMENT.)

**Mediterranean Sea,** one of the great cradles of humanity, but also one of the most seriously threatened marine environments on earth. Stretching 2,300 miles from Gibraltar to Turkey, with an average width of 400 miles, its low rate of evaporation, lack of major currents, and relative shallowness make it far more like a huge LAKE than an OCEAN, and make it greatly vulnerable to human attack. Over 100 million people live on or near its shores, and in summer that number swells to well over 200 million, as tourists flock in from all over the world. Seventeen countries discharge sewage and industrial wastes into the sea, from the Nile to the Ebro, some of it from such large urban areas as Cairo, Rome, Naples, Marseilles, and Athens. An estimated 70 to 85 percent of that waste is untreated, some of it highly toxic and all of it destructive of the life of the sea.

Some progress has been made in the battle to save and restore the Mediterranean, most notably in such areas as international cooperation to clean up after OIL spills and to attempt to reduce TOXIC CHEMICAL discharges into the sea, as developed through the United Nations–sponsored Mediterranean Action Plan and the 1976 Convention for the Protection of the Mediterranean Sea Against Pollution (Barcelona Convention). But POPULATION and tourism continue to increase, and with them the huge unchecked, untreated discharges into the sea that are destroying it as a center of life. POLLUTION grows; EUTROPHICATION continues to deplete the oxygen in the sea, and algal blooms such as those which struck much of the western ADRIATIC coast in the late 1980s accelerate the loss of life-giving oxygen. For the Mediterranean, environmentalists quite correctly hammer out danger.

**For more information and action:**

- **Commission Internationale pour l'Exploration Scientifique de la Mer Méditerranée (CIESM) or International Commission for Scientific Exploration of the Mediterranean Sea (ICSEM),** (16 Boulevard de Suisse, MC-98030 Monte Carlo, Monaco; 93.30.38.79; François Doumenge, Secretary-General), an international organization founded in 1910, which conducts oceanographic exploration of the Mediterranean; Jacques Cousteau was Secretary-General for 22 years, until 1988. CIESM holds meetings and publishes scientific papers. Members work on specialized Scientific Committees: Benthos, Salt Water Lakes and Lagoons, Marine Geology and Geophysics, the Fight Against Marine Pollution, Marine Microbiology and Biochemistry, Island Environment, Chemical Oceanography, Physical Oceanography, Plankton, Marine Radioactivity, Marine Vertebrates, and Cephalopods. Since 1972 a special focus has been *Studies on Marine Pollution in the Mediterranean* including disposal of RADIOACTIVE WASTE in the sea. CIESM also works closely with other international organizations, as with the UNITED NATIONS PROGRAMME FOR THE ENVIRONMENT (UNEP) on its Action Plan for the Mediterranean.
- **COUSTEAU SOCIETY,** (804-627-1144). Projects include a "health report" on the Mediterranean Sea with the

International Commission for the Scientific Exploration of the Mediterranean.

- **WORLD BANK,** (202-477-1234). Publishes *Environmental Program for the Mediterranean: Preserving a Shared Heritage and Managing a Common Resource.*

**Other references:**

*Saving the Mediterranean: The Politics of International Environmental Cooperation.* Peter M. Haas. Columbia University Press, 1990. (See also OCEANS.)

**Mee, Margaret** (1909–1988), English botanist, artist, explorer, and conservationist, who spent 36 years (1956–1988) in the AMAZON RAIN FOREST, observing, collecting, and painting rarely seen flowers, including the rare moonflower cactus, which blooms only one night a year. Her work brought her a deep understanding of the Amazonian ECOSYSTEM and a horror of the effects of destruction of the rain FOREST, and she became a leading figure in the fight to save the rain forest and the flora and fauna living there. Her paintings were published in *Flowers of the Brazilian Forests* (1968) and *Flowers of the Amazon* (1970), and her diaries and other artwork appeared just before her death in *In Search of Flowers of the Amazon Forests.*

***Mega Borg* oil spill,** leakage of an estimated 4.3 million gallons (approximately 15,000 tons) of light crude OIL from the burning Norwegian supertanker *Mega Borg* into the Gulf of Mexico, 57 miles off the Texas coast southeast of Galveston, on June 8 to 15, 1990. While the tanker was off-loading its cargo into a smaller tanker, a small explosion of unknown origin generated a powerful explosion in the ship's pump room and a massive oil fire that burned out of control for several days and was not finally extinguished for a week. Four crew members were killed, and there was a strong possibility that the entire 38 million gallons of oil in the ship at the time of the fire would spill into the Gulf of Mexico. But the fire was brought under control, and much of the oil that spilled was consumed in the fire or evaporated, rather than spilling and then remaining in the sea. The accident marked one of the earliest uses of oil-eating bacteria in the open sea as part of the environmental cleanup effort following the spill (see BIOREMEDIATION). Such bacteria had been used on the beaches of Prince William Sound after the 1989 EXXON VALDEZ spill, and were later used in July 1990, after a barge-ship collision and subseqent oil spill (see GALVESTON BAY OIL SPILL). (See also OIL.)

**Mendes, Chico (Francisco Mendes Filho),** environmental activist, president of the Brazilian rubber tappers union, murdered in December 1988 over his attempts to stop destruction of the AMAZON Rain Forest.

**mercury (Hg),** a type of HEAVY METAL, a silvery liquid that can have extremely toxic effects on humans and other living beings. In nature, mercury occurs in stable compounds that cause no particular problems; for over 3,500 years, however, humans have been ''liberating'' mercury from these compounds for industrial and agricultural uses—though its dangers have been known for much of that time. The Roman naturalist Pliny noted the rate of deaths among miners of the red sulfide ore of mercury used for color; and the phrase ''mad as a hatter'' refers to the neurological effects of the mercury used by 19th-century makers of felt hats. In the 20th century, mercury has had a wide range of uses. It is a powerful fungicide (see PESTICIDES), so mercury compounds, especially methyl mercury, have been used in agriculture and in the paper industry; it is also widely used in PLASTICS, batteries, electronic products, and paints, and is released during processes such as MINING, burning of FOSSIL FUELS such as COAL and OIL, metal smelting, and the making of steel and cement. Once in the environment, mercury enters the FOOD CHAIN and through the process of BIOACCUMULATION is increasingly concentrated in large animals at the top of the food chain, such as fish, birds, and humans. ORGANIC COMPOUNDS such as methyl mercury are fat-soluble and accumulate in the kidneys, interfering with basic metabolic processes, and in the brain, affecting coordination, and often causing tremors and slurred speech. In severe cases, mercury contamination leads to delirium, convulsions, coma, and death, as in Minamata, Japan, in the 1950s and early 1960s, where many people became ill and some died as the result of eating fish contaminated with mercury from a nearby plant.

Because of its dangers, mercury is a highly regulated substance. In the United States, it is one of the air pollutants for which the ENVIRONMENTAL PROTECTION AGENCY (EPA) sets NATIONAL EMISSION STANDARDS FOR HAZARDOUS AIR POLLUTANTS (NESHAPs), under the CLEAN AIR ACT (CAA), and mercury compounds are listed as hazardous air pollutants under the 1990 amendments to CAA (see HEALTH EFFECTS OF THE REGULATED AIR POLLUTANTS on page 8). Mercury in water is covered by the SAFE DRINKING WATER ACT (see PRIMARY DRINKING WATER STANDARDS on page 274) and the CLEAN WATER ACT (CWA). More generally, it is treated as a TOXIC CHEMICAL and HAZARDOUS SUBSTANCE (see TOXIC CHEMICALS AND HAZARDOUS SUBSTANCES on page 407; KNOWN HEALTH EFFECTS OF TOXIC CHEMICALS on page 416). Many uses of mercury have been barred; in 1990, for example, the

EPA negotiated an agreement with the paints and coatings industry to eliminate mercury from interior paints and to place warning labels on mercury-containing exterior paints.

Even so, the mercury problem remains and is worsening—and would continue to do so in many areas even if all current mercury-producing activities were halted. Like other heavy metals, once released into the environment, from whatever source, mercury remains there as a contaminant. Batteries and paints containing mercury become HAZARDOUS WASTE if discarded in the environment; however, INCINERATION of such products, including old painted wood, simply releases mercury into the air, as does continued burning of fossil fuels. In addition, ACID RAIN and OZONE pollution—both increasing problems in recent decades—trigger environmental conversion of mercury into methyl mercury.

Mercury is also a home health hazard, present in some paints, thermometers, barometers, batteries, and electronic devices. As such it is a variable but potentially dangerous factor in indoor AIR POLLUTION. Controversy also exists about its adverse effects from its use in the silver amalgam of dental fillings, though the National Institutes of Health in 1991 reported that the amounts used were too small to cause concern. (See HEAVY METAL; TOXIC CHEMICALS; HAZARDOUS WASTE.)

**Meru National Park,** in central Kenya, north of Mt. Kenya; the 450,000-acre (700-square-mile) preserve made world-famous by Joy ADAMSON in *Born Free.* Her camp, the home of Elsa the lioness, was in the southeastern corner of the park, on the Tana River. Meru is also notable for its white RHINOCEROS, so endangered by poachers, and for its WILDERNESS area, in which the only approach to wildlife is made on foot, rather than safely and swiftly by motor vehicle. Large animals are abundant in the park, including ELEPHANTS, rhinoceroses (black and white), hippopotamuses, giraffes, LIONS, LEOPARDS, CHEETAHS, buffalo, ZEBRAS, and gazelles, along with many smaller animals and hundreds of bird species, including many varieties of egret, heron, stork, ibis, vulture, kite, eagle, buzzard, bustard, plover, sandpiper, dove, cuckoo, kingfisher, bee-eater, hornbill, hoopoe, owl, honeyguide, swift, woodpecker, lark, flycatcher, wheatear, warbler, swallow, sunbird, weaver, and whydah. (See ECOTOURISM; WILDLIFE REFUGE.)

**methane ($CH_4$),** a flammable gas; a type of HYDROCARBON, with each molecule being formed of one carbon and four hydrogen atoms. Methane is produced by the partial decay of organic matter, as of plants in WETLANDS, landfills, or rice paddies, and also in the digestive tract of domesticated animals such as cattle. This form of production is sometimes deliberately exploited (see BIOFUELS). In geological time, some of this methane becomes trapped underground and forms the main constituent of NATURAL GAS. During the MINING of COAL and the tapping of OIL and natural gas sources, methane often leaks into the air, and in underground mining released concentrations of the gas can kill miners or set off explosions. Some methane is also produced by the burning of FORESTS and SAVANNAS, as when tropical forests are cleared. Though produced by natural processes, the accelerated release of methane into the air, including leakage of natural gas during transmission and distribution, is an environmental concern because it is one of the gases held responsible for the GREENHOUSE EFFECT, possibly resulting in GLOBAL WARMING.

**methyl chloroform (MC),** a type of SYNTHETIC ORGANIC CHEMICAL implicated in destruction of the OZONE LAYER and so scheduled to be phased out by 2005, under the MONTREAL PROTOCOL ON SUBSTANCES THAT DEPLETE THE OZONE LAYER. MC itself had been a substitute for some earlier solvents, notably trichloroethylene (TCE), which contributed to AIR POLLUTION, especially SMOG.

**Mexico City natural gas explosion,** the explosion of a Mexico City NATURAL GAS plant on November 19, 1984, triggered by the explosion of a nearby gasoline truck, the combination killing an estimated 450 people and destroying much of the surrounding area. (See NATURAL GAS.)

**migration,** movement from one place to another with more favorable conditions, especially more food, warmer temperatures, and more abundant water. Migration may be one-way, as when humans migrate permanently for economic reasons or animals find a new area more favorable than their original home, especially when environmental changes make an area no longer suitable for habitation.

But the best-known migrations are those that are regular patterns of movement, returning periodically to their place of origin, and may be undertaken by animals as diverse as insects, fish, butterflies, marine mammals, birds, and land mammals. Such migrations are made in various time frames, including daily, as in response to light changes; monthly, following the phases of the moon; yearly, with seasonal changes; or once-in-a-lifetime, as with saltwater salmon returning to freshwater streams for spawning. Individuals may migrate separately, joining up at breeding grounds, but many animals migrate in groups along well-defined routes, often running north-south, but also up-down (as on a mountain, with seasonal changes) or even east-west (as with birds from Continental Europe wintering in the more temperate British Isles).

Migration routes have been studied intensively, from the 1920s through banding or tagging of birds and then other animals, and more recently also through use of sonor, radar, radio transmitters, and other such devices. Among the best-known routes are those north-south corridors, or *flyways*, followed seasonally by birds; in North America, the four main flyways are the Pacific, Central, Mississippi, and Atlantic Flyways. The longest known migration is made by Arctic terns, which nest in Greenland and northern North America, and a few months later fly to Antarctica, some by way of Europe, for an annual round trip of at least 25,000 miles.

Unfortunately, migrating animals are extremely vulnerable to changes in environmental conditions along their routes and in their intended destinations. If conditions are no longer favorable in the places where they usually feed or nest, many animals will die and the population, and perhaps the whole SPECIES, may be put at risk. Numerous national and international efforts have been mounted to try to assure the continued health of migrating populations. Agreements such as the CONVENTION ON THE CONSERVATION OF MIGRATORY SPECIES OF WILD ANIMALS (the Bonn Convention) and the CONVENTION ON WETLANDS OF INTERNATIONAL IMPORTANCE, ESPECIALLY AS WATERFOWL HABITAT (the Ramsar Convention or Wetlands Convention) are attempts in this direction (see ENVIRONMENTAL LAWS). In addition, many environmental organizations (such as DUCKS UNLIMITED) have attempted to maintain or restore vital feeding and nesting grounds on migration routes. With rising POPULATION cutting into natural areas, many environmentalists have turned to the idea of GREENWAYS, to allow passage from one area to another. A particular long-term concern is the possible effect of CLIMATE CHANGE, whether GLOBAL WARMING or GLOBAL COOLING, on migrating species, since changing conditions may make their normal stopping places no longer favorable.

**For more information and action:**

- **American Littoral Society,** (201-291-0055). Publishes brochure on tagging fish. (See COASTS INFORMATION AND ACTION GUIDE on page 62.)
- **AMERICAN ORNITHOLOGISTS' UNION (AOU),** (202-357-1970).
- **DUCKS UNLIMITED (DU),** (708-438-4300). Has projects to maintain or restore vital habitats along migration flyways.
- **ENVIRONMENTAL DEFENSE FUND (EDF),** (212-505-2100).
- **FISH AND WILDLIFE SERVICE (FWS),** (202-208-4717;

Artic Tern Migration Routes

**Source:** "Bird Banding: The Hows and Whys." U.S. Fish and Wildlife Service, Department of the Interior, 1986.

*Federal Wildlife Reference Service,* 301-492-6403 or 800-582-3421). Publishes *Migration of Birds.*
- **INTERNATIONAL COUNCIL FOR BIRD PRESERVATION (ICBP),** (United Kingdom: 0223-277318; U.S. Headquarters, c/o WORLD WILDLIFE FUND—US; 202-293-4800). Runs the *Migratory Bird Campaign*; publishes the quarterly newsletter *World Birdwatch,* the annual *ICBP Bulletin,* and the key *Bird Red Data Books.*
- **NATIONAL AUDUBON SOCIETY,** (212-832-3200; *Audubon Action Line,* 202-547-9017). Conducts the *Christmas Bird Count.* Publishes the periodicals *Audubon, American Birds, Audubon Activist,* and *Audubon Wildlife Report.*
- **NATIONAL INSTITUTE FOR URBAN WILDLIFE,** (301-596-3311 or 301-995-1119).
- **WILDLIFE MANAGEMENT INSTITUTE (WMI),** (202-371-1808).
- **WILDLIFE SOCIETY, THE,** (301-897-9770).

**Migratory Bird Conservation Commission** (Interior Building, Washington, DC 20240; 703-358-1716; William F. Hartwig, Secretary), a U.S. federal commission established under the Migratory Bird Conservation Act of 1929, with its staff drawn from the FISH AND WILDLIFE SERVICE, and its members from the Congress and specified Cabinet agencies, including the Secretaries of Interior and Agriculture, and the Administrator of the ENVIRONMENTAL PROTECTION AGENCY (EPA). The Commission passes on the purchase or rental of land and/or water sites recommended for acquisition by the Secretary of the Interior.

Funds for such acquisitions come from the *Migratory Bird Conservation Fund*, which receives revenues from the sale of Duck Stamps (officially Migratory Bird Hunting and Conservation Stamps, under a 1934 authorizing act) which waterfowl hunters are required to buy each year, and also from appropriations under the 1961 Wetlands Loan Act and the 1986 Emergency Wetlands Resources Act, as well as from "receipts from the sale of products from and rights-of-way across national wildlife refuges, disposals of refuge land, and reverted Federal Aid funds." The Fund also finances (without requiring approval from the Commission) acquisition of "small natural wetlands with associated uplands located mainly in the Prairie Pothole Region of the upper Midwest," lands called "Water fowl Production Areas." (See PLIGHT OF THE PRAIRIE POTHOLES on page 341.) The Commission publishes an annual report on its activities; in 1991, the Department of Interior purchased or rented 62,177 acres of "major migratory bird conservation areas" at a cost of $16,299,727, and an additional 28,229 acres of Waterfowl Production Areas at a cost of $5,447,742. In addition, during 1990, the Commission approved the establishment of the East Grasslands Wildlife Management Area in 36,550 acres of what was once 4 million acres of wetlands in northern California, "to preserve critical breeding, migration, and wintering habitat in the Pacific Flyway," especially important to numerous species of ducks, and also geese and sandhill CRANES.

**Migratory Species Convention,** see CONVENTION ON THE CONSERVATION OF MIGRATORY SPECIES OF WILD ANIMALS.

**mining,** the extraction of resources from under or out of the ground, including "soft rock" minerals such as COAL and "hard rock" minerals such as COPPER, iron, gold, silver, and uranium. Minerals are DECLINING RESOURCES, being used up faster than they are being replaced by the earth's natural processes (see BIOGEOCHEMICAL CYCLES), so in this industrialized age, with its expanding POPULATION and appetite for metals and energy, humans have been expanding older mines and opening up many new ones, with increasing damage to the environment.

Some key minerals are quite rare, and the search for

and extraction of them can come into direct conflict with environmental desires to preserve threatened ECOSYSTEMS. In recent years, for example, a gold rush has threatened parts of the AMAZON RAIN FOREST; desire to tap minerals such as MANGANESE in the seabed threatens aquatic life (see COASTS; EXCLUSIVE ECONOMIC ZONES); and in the United States coal mining has defaced many stretches of public lands leased by the BUREAU OF LAND MANAGEMENT (BLM), sometimes critically dubbed the Bureau of Livestock and Mining. Only after a bitter fight was ANTARCTICA declared off limits to mining, and even then only for 50 years.

Traditionally, coal and many other minerals were mined by individual workers digging by hand in underground rooms or tunnels, with pillars and other supports to keep the ceiling from collapsing. In the 20th century, miners have been aided by power tools, including continuous cutting machines. But *underground mining* or *deep mining* still poses many dangers for miners, including collapse of overlying rock; explosion or suffocation from encountering pockets of METHANE; exposure to RADIATION from radioactive minerals (such as uranium) and releases of the gas RADON; and dangerous AIR POLLUTION. In some areas, refuse from mining is piled in huge slag heaps; these and underground beds, if once set afire, may burn for years, fouling the nearby land, air, and water. HEAVY METALS, acidic matter, and other toxic substances are released that pollute the land, air, and water. When old or weak mine structures collapse, the ground above them may subside, also damaging the environment. Mining also requires the building of roads and rail lines for transport of coal and heavy machinery, further damaging the environment.

Unlike traditional mining, where most polluting material is kept underground, *surface mining* or *strip mining* is a major modern destroyer of the environment; it is an approach to mining that has been used increasingly in recent years. Instead of digging underground, miners remove the *overburden*—the overlying rock and soil—to expose the coal, which can then be removed by heavy machinery, often much more cheaply and with less hazard to miners but at great cost to the environment. In *contour mining* or *collar mining*, used in hilly areas such as the Appalachians, the strips are removed in narrow bands, following the slope and curve of the land. In *area mining* or *furrow mining*, used in flat or rolling country such as the Western Great Plains, strips are relatively straight and parallel, with the debris from one strip being thrown into the pit formed by removal of coal from the previous strip. In *open pit mining*, the overburden is heaped up on the side of an ever-deepening pit. One new approach being explored is *in situ mining*, in which chemicals are used to extract

## On the Need for Minerals

Hundreds of the things we do each day, from driving a car to opening a can of soup, depend on products made from minerals. It is now necessary to provide 40,000 pounds of new minerals every year to each American. The average newborn citizen will consume over 1,050 pounds of lead, 1,050 pounds of zinc, 1,750 pounds of copper, 4,550 pounds of aluminum, 91,000 pounds of iron and steel, 360,500 pounds of coal, and over a million pounds of stone, sand, gravel, cement, and clay over the course of his or her lifetime.

**Source:** U.S. Bureau of Mines.

minerals from underground deposits without the necessity of digging up the earth. Modern technology has also allowed underwater mining, primarily on parts of the continental shelf leased for the purpose. This greatly concerns environmentalists because of the fragility of coastal ecosystems, already under enormous stress from land-based POLLUTION.

Strip mining is a disaster to the environment. In a process of total ENVIRONMENTAL DEGRADATION, plant and animal life lose their homes; complex ecosystems are destroyed; topsoil is lost to EROSION or buried under piles of nonfertile soil and rock; and acidic and toxic matter is brought to the surface, releasing heavy metals and other toxic substances into the environment. All these affect not just the immediate environment but the areas downstream and downwind. Mining is assessed and ranked among the 31 environmental problem areas in the ENVIRONMENTAL PROTECTION AGENCY's report UNFINISHED BUSINESS: A COMPARATIVE ASSESSMENT OF ENVIRONMENTAL PROBLEMS.

In recent years, in some countries, laws have been passed requiring that mining companies carry on their operations more carefully. The 1977 Surface Mining Control Reclamation Act (SMCRA) in the United States requires that companies restore the land to an equal or better environmental state than before mining. Mining companies may, for example, be required to separate out the top soil and replace it after the coal has been removed; to rebury acidic and toxic materials; to placed polluted groundwater in artificial ponds called *impoundments*, to lessen WATER POLLUTION; to restructure the land to its original contours; and to revegetate the land. Environmentalists complain, however, that mine operators are often required only to plant reclaimed land in grasses, not with the variety of trees and plants found before disruption; that some of the fill used in hilly areas is not durable, but is quickly lost to EROSION; and that some firms have been granted exemptions from even minimal compliance.

In the United States, apart from SMCRA, mining for metals on public lands is covered by the grossly outdated 1872 Mining Law, under which any person who locates an unclaimed valuable mineral deposit on federal land can simply file a claim for it and thereby be granted free access to the claim site and use of the site for mining or development. Before 1976, claimants could begin mining immediately, without informing anyone. Rights to the claim are maintained indefinitely as long as the claimant can show that at least $100 worth of work is done on the claim annually; with evidence of a valuable deposit and a total of $500 in work, the miner can purchase the land for the 1872 price: $5 an acre for a lode claim and $2.50 for a placer claim. In the late 1980s, about 3,000 mining claims for mineral rights on six million acres were on file for lands in the National Park System alone.

The 1872 Mining Law contains no bar to claiming and destroying even unique and sensitive ecosystems, including CAVES, WILDLIFE REFUGES, and WILDERNESS areas, and no requirements for protection or restoration of the environment (though more general regulations from other laws, such as the CLEAN AIR ACT and CLEAN WATER ACT, may apply). The federal government can formally withdraw certain lands from mineral development, but in the 1980s the Department of the Interior's policy was to have no such withdrawals.

Not surprisingly, in the United States and elsewhere, environmentalists are seeking stronger enforcement and further legislation to require mining permits; set performance standards; ensure usage of the more environmentally safe technologies; bar mining in sensitive or protected areas; encourage recovery of minerals now lost in the processing of other minerals (as cobalt is lost during the processing of lead); require posting of a financial guarantee to ensure that the mine operator will restore the land but not at public expense; and study long-term effects of mining activities, including impoundments. Beyond that, environmentalists call for a reevaluation of LAND USE policy regarding public lands with regard to mining and other potentially harmful activities, especially by requiring ENVIRONMENTAL IMPACT STATEMENTS. They also recommend

## Mining Information and Action Guide

**For more information and action on mining:**
BUREAU OF LAND MANAGEMENT (BLM), (202-208-5717).

**Bureau of Mines** (Office of Public Information, Bureau of Mines, U.S. Department of Interior, 2401 E Street NW, Washington, DC 20241; 202-501-9770; T.R. Ary, Director), a U.S. federal agency, primarily focusing on nonfuel minerals, founded in 1910 to study "the safety of miners," which now also "conducts research and collects information concerning almost every activity involved in removing minerals from the earth and making them into useful products." It works with other federal agencies to assess whether minerals occur on public lands, as with the U.S. Geological Survey on lands being considered for designation as parks, WILDLIFE REFUGES, or WILDERNESS areas; and the BUREAU OF LAND MANAGEMENT and FOREST SERVICE, on the lands they manage. More widely it gathers and evaluates information about global mineral resources; answers questions and publishes the brochure *Bureau of Mines: The Minerals Source* and numerous research, statistical, and analytical studies on minerals and mining.

**Environmental Law Institute (ELI),** (202-328-5150; publications office: 202-939-3844). Publishes *Environmental Regulation of Coal Mining: SMCRA's Second Decade* (James M. McElfish, Jr., and Ann Beier, 1990). (See ENVIRONMENTAL LAW INFORMATION AND ACTION GUIDE on page 116.)

ENVIRONMENTAL PROTECTION AGENCY (EPA), (202-260-7751 or 202-260-2080).

FRIENDS OF THE EARTH, (202-544-2600). Publishes *The Strip Mining Handbook* (Mark Squillace, 1990).

INFORM, INC., (212-689-4040).

NATIONAL INSTITUTE FOR URBAN WILDLIFE, (301-596-3311 or 301-995-1119). Publishes *Environmental Reclamation and the Coal Surface Mining Industry* (D.L. Leedy et al.).

NATURAL RESOURCES AND ENERGY DIVISION (NRED), (212-963-6205). Publishes *Small-Scale Coal Mining in Developing Countries* (1989).

NATURAL RESOURCES DEFENSE COUNCIL (NRDC), (212-727-2700).

**Office for Ocean Affairs and the Law of the Sea (OALOS),** (212-963-6424). Maintains a computerized minerals database (MINDAT). (See CONVENTION ON THE LAW OF THE SEA.)

RESOURCES FOR THE FUTURE (RFF), (202-328-5000). Publishes *World Mineral Exploration: Trends and Economic Issues* (John E. Tilton et al., eds., 1988).

SIERRA CLUB, (415-776-2211 or 202-547-1141; legislative hotline, 202-547-5550). Publishes *Coal Mining Policy.*

SOIL AND WATER CONSERVATION SOCIETY OF AMERICA (SWCS), (515-289-2331 or 800-THE-SOIL [843-7645]).

---

that the government reclaim many more abandoned earlier mining sites and buy back mineral rights not presently being used, to prevent future DEVELOPMENT.

In some areas previously ruined by mining activities, methods such as RESTORATION ECOLOGY are being used to try to restore life, in the United States often coming under the Abandoned Mine Land Fund. But the original ecosystems, once destroyed, can never be fully recreated. Because of this, environmentalists have been stressing RECYCLING, RESOURCE RECOVERY, and general reduction of demand for minerals, to back down from the ever-increasing need to open up new mines and destroy yet more environments. (See MINING INFORMATION AND ACTION GUIDE above; also COAL; MERCURY.)

**mirex,** a type of PESTICIDE (see CHLORINATED HYDROCARBONS).

**molluscicides,** a type of chemical compound used for killing unwanted molluscs such as snails, clams, whelks, mussels, and oysters (see PESTICIDES).

**monkeys,** relatively small members of the primate fam-

ily, found in over 130 SPECIES, mainly in the tropical areas of Africa, Asia, and South and Central America. All species are at risk, although fewer than 25 monkey species and subspecies are listed as endangered or threatened by the United States FISH AND WILDLIFE SERVICE. For all the monkey species, the great threat is loss of HABITAT. Most monkeys are FOREST dwellers; for them, it is the loss of rain forest and other forest habitats that can destroy entire species. For some species, additional dangers include killing for food by humans, and capture for export to ZOOS and as pets. All three dangers happened to the greatly endangered *Brazilian golden (golden lion) tamarin* and *pied tamarin*, both now near EXTINCTION in the wild. Similarly threatened are such species as the *Brazilian muriqui (woolly spider monkey)*, the *Andean yellow-tailed woolly spider monkey*, and several Old World monkeys.

**For more information and action:**

• WILDLIFE PRESERVATION TRUST INTERNATIONAL (WPTI), (215-222-3636).
• WORLD WILDLIFE FUND (WWF), (202-293-4800).

(See also ENDANGERED SPECIES; ENDANGERED AND THREATENED WILDLIFE AND PLANTS on page 372.)

**monkeywrenching,** a term for a wide range of actions taken by radical environmental activists to disrupt and halt damage to the environment; sometimes also called *ecotage*, *ecological sabotage*, or (by critics) *ecoterrorism*. Actions performed by monkeywrenchers include sit-ins, as in front of bulldozers or in offices; "decommissioning" machinery, as by pouring sand in a bulldozer's gas tank or damaging OIL exploration equipment; ramming whaling ships to damage or sink them; pulling up surveyor's stakes; chaining themselves to or camping in trees; cutting down fences, power lines, and billboards; spiking trees, by driving long metal spikes into them, to bar logging; and spiking roads, to damage and deter off-road vehicles and close FOREST roads. The name comes from Edward ABBEY's 1976 novel *The Monkey Wrench Gang*, in which a group of environmentalists plot to blow up the GLEN CANYON DAM to "free" the RIVER, burn billboards, and carry out other antidevelopment actions.

Monkeywrenching is most commonly associated with EARTH FIRST!—whose co-founder, David FOREMAN, wrote *Ecodefense: A Field Guide to Monkeywrenching* (1985)— but is also employed by other radical environmentalist groups, such as the SEA SHEPHERD CONSERVATION SOCIETY. Many monkeywrenchers compare themselves to Resistance fighters in World War II, seeing environmental damage as equivalent to the Holocaust and other war crimes. In general, monkeywrenching actions are meant to be violent towards machinery being used for despoliation and industrialization, but nonviolent towards human beings. As Foreman put it: "Ecodefense is primarily defensive. It says, 'Stay out of this place, leave it alone.' It is nonviolent." To avoid injury by loggers and sawyers, some monkeywrenchers mark spiked trees, or send letters warning that trees have been spiked; some do not, however, and at least one mill worker was seriously injured when his chain saw shattered as it hit a buried spike.

Opinions about monkeywrenching vary widely. Some in the environmentalist movement, while saying such actions are "not for them," note that monkeywrenchers have received enormous publicity and halted damage to some areas—some go so far as to call them the "conscience of the environmental movement." But others feel that they are irresponsible at best and have tarnished the reputation of environmentalism. Their severest critics regard monkeywrenchers as simply environmental terrorists.

**For more information and action:**

- **EARTH FIRST! (E.F.!),** (Direct Action Fund, 415-376-7329).

- **SEA SHEPHERD CONSERVATION SOCIETY,** (213-373-6979).

**Other references:**

*Green Rage: Radical Environmentalism and the Unmaking of Civilization.* Christopher Manes. Little, Brown, 1991. *Ecodefense: A Field Guide to Monkeywrenching.* Dave Foreman. Ned Ludd Books, 1985. Address: P.O. Box 5141, Tucson, AZ 85703.

**monoculture,** planting large areas of land with a single crop, sometimes with a single strain. The advantage to farmers is that the crop will be relatively uniform—a known quantity. Such single strains are, however, more vulnerable to pests and disease, lacking the genetic variability that might make them adaptable to new dangers (see BIOLOGICAL DIVERSITY). With monoculture, farmers are also more dependent on PESTICIDES, since they lose the natural protection they get from a variety of plants and animals (see EDGE EFFECT), and therefore lose the chance to exercise BIOLOGICAL CONTROL.

**Mono Lake,** an 80-square-mile California LAKE, approximately 100 miles south of Lake Tahoe and east of YOSEMITE NATIONAL PARK. The lake, with its large brine shrimp population, is an important stop on the Pacific Flyway (see MIGRATION), especially for tens of thousands of phalaropes and hundreds of thousands of grebes, among the hundreds of SPECIES of migrating birds found there in the spring, summer, and autumn. It is also a breeding place for many water birds, including tens of thousands of California gulls.

The lake is a seriously threatened body of water, as the city of Los Angeles continues to draw water from its tributary streams. Formerly, its normal evaporation was replaced by water from nearby streams, and its size and content were, as in all such bodies of water, a balance struck between evaporation and inflowing water. With that balance gone, its surface area has gone down to 65 square miles, and its salt and alkali contents are reaching levels that will soon make it dangerous to its wildlife. This is basically the same process as that at work in the much larger ARAL SEA, although their situation is far worse, given the range of factors at work there. (See LAKE; SALINIZATION.)

**Montreal Protocol on Substances that Deplete the Ozone Layer,** a 1987 international agreement to phase out substances destructive to the earth's OZONE LAYER. In 1990, an amended protocol was accepted in London by 93 nations, including some (such as China and India) not party to the original, agreeing to phase out five key CHLO-

ROFLUOROCARBONS (CFCs 11, 12, 113, 114, and 115), carbon tetrachloride, and nonessential uses of the fire-extinguishing halon gases (Halons 1211, 1301, and 2402) by 2000 and METHYL CHLOROFORM (MC) by 2005. HYDRO-CHLOROFLUOROCARBONS (HCFCs) proposed as interim substitutes (even though they also attack the ozone layer, albeit more slowly) are to be used only where no other feasible alternatives exist, to be phased out by 2020 if feasible, and completely banned by 2040 at the latest. The 1990 agreement also established the Montreal Protocol Multilateral Fund to help developing countries "finance the transition from ozone-depleting chemicals." (See OZONE LAYER.)

**Morrison Institute for Population and Resource Studies, The Dean and Virginia** (Stanford University, Herrin Labs, Room 467, Stanford, CA 94305; 415-723-7518; Marcus W. Feldman, Principal Investigator and Director), a center for interdisciplinary study of POPULATION growth and such related "global issues as conservation of the environment and natural resources, and sustainable socio-economic development," including problems such as "environmental degradation, resource depletion, urbanization, poverty, health, migration, illiteracy, governance, and, ultimately, national and international economic viability, security and peace." The Institute conducts research projects and workshops; develops new courses and educational materials; maintains library and speaker resources; and sponsors international exchange of faculty and students between the United States and Third World countries.

The Institute also publishes policy papers on population-related issues, such as *Population Biology, Conservation Biology, and the Future of Humanity* (Paul R. Ehrlich), *Population as a Contributor to International Security* (Marcus W. Feldman), *An Exploratory Model of the Impact of Rapid Climate Change on the World Food Situation* (Gretchen C. Daily and Paul R. Ehrlich), *Environmental Ethics: Converging Views on a Small Planet* (Timothy C. Weiskel), and *Global Change and Carrying Capacity: Implications for Life on Earth* (Paul R. Ehrlich et al).

**Moruroa,** South Pacific nuclear test site, in French Polynesia, activated after French nuclear testing in Algeria was terminated by the successful Algerian war of independence. Approximately 40 open-air nuclear tests were conducted on Moruroa from 1966 to 1974 and a reported five more on neighboring Fangataufa. Underground testing continued thereafter. The tests were regarded as potentially contaminating by neighboring Pacific and Pacific Rim governments, including those of New Zealand and Australia, a concern that seemed well-founded from the start, as the extremely "dirty," very large test explosion of September

1966 deposited radioactive debris as far as Western Samoa, 2,000 miles downwind. Opposition also developed from world environmental organizations, including GREENPEACE; their yacht, the *Vega,* was seized by the French navy in international waters, while attempting to disrupt French nuclear tests. In July 1985, the Greenpeace ship RAINBOW WARRIOR was sunk by French agents, while in the harbor of Auckland, New Zealand, before setting out on a planned voyage of nuclear-test disruption; a Greenpeace cameraman was killed. The event triggered a major international incident. Two French agents were arrested by the New Zealand government, and convicted of manslaughter; they were later freed after mediation by United Nations Secretary General Javier Pérez De Cuéllar, and French agreement to $7 million in damages. (See NUCLEAR TESTING.)

**Mountain Zebra National Park,** South African mountain ZEBRA preserve in the Cape Province; its 16,000 acres (25 square miles) are the home of over 200 mountain zebras, an ENDANGERED SPECIES that was nearly extinct by the late 1940s. In the fenced-in preserve are also many smaller animals, as well as over 200 bird species. (See WILDLIFE REFUGE.)

**Mt. Kenya National Park,** in central Kenya, a park that comprises the upper slopes and twin peaks of Mount Kenya (Batian and Nelion), starting at the 11,000-foot level. The 145,000-acre (227-square mile) park includes an extraordinary succession of environments, with high bamboo FOREST giving way to alpine moorlands above the forest level, and then to the glacial areas that are the snow-capped top of the mountain. Protected here are the rare black RHINOCEROS, along with such mammals as ELEPHANTS, ZEBRAS, giant forest hogs, bush pigs, duikers, bongos, bushbucks, hare, porcupines, genets, civets, jackals, hyenas, mongoose, LEOPARDS, hyrax, and more, as well as a considerably number of bird species, including the rare green ibis and kestrels, kites, falcons, and several varieties of eagle, sunbird, dove, kingfisher, cuckoo, owl, swift, wagtail, flycatcher, and thrush. (See ECOTOURISM; WILDLIFE REFUGE.)

**Muir, John** (1838–1914), the pioneering naturalist and nature writer for whom California's Muir Woods national monument and Glacier Bay's Muir Glacier are named, and a key figure in the American conservation movement. Muir's first trip to California's YOSEMITE Valley was in 1868; he lived mainly in Yosemite from 1868 to 1874. In 1879, he first visited Alaska's GLACIER BAY. From 1880 he campaigned for the establishment of Yosemite as a national park, in a series of widely read magazine articles, and in 1890 Congress voted the park into existence. A year later, Congress made the decision to establish protected national FOREST areas. From 1896, as an advisor to the National Forestry Commission, Muir played a major role in saving large tracts of western forest for future generations, strongly resisting encroachment and generating public support in a long series of conservationist articles. In the early 1900s, in a crucial period for the future of the United States WILDERNESS heritage, he strongly influenced Theodore Roosevelt's forest reserve policy.

Muir is best remembered for Yosemite—and for a long series of lyrical nature books, including *The Mountains of California* (1894), *Our National Parks* (1901), *Stickeen* (1909), *My First Summer in the Sierra* (1911), *The Yosemite* (1912), and *Travels in Alaska* (1915).

**mulimedia enforcement,** an approach to enforcing ENVIRONMENTAL LAWS that involves consolidating violations from all media—air, water, or land—into a single complaint, to maximize environmental benefits, rather than enforcing violations separately; a strategy adopted only recently in the U.S. by the ENVIRONMENTAL PROTECTION AGENCY (EPA).

**multiple chemical sensitivites (MCS),** a type of ENVIRONMENTAL illness.

**Murchison Falls (Kabalega) National Park,** a Ugandan park bisected by a 75-mile-long section of the Nile River, above Murchison Falls, much of its northwestern boundary being on Lake Albert and Zaire. The wildlife of the 950,000-acre (1,450-square-mile) Ugandan nature preserve was seriously attacked by unrestrained poaching during the reign of Ugandan dictator Idi Amin (1971–79), with great damage suffered by the ELEPHANTS, black RHINOCEROSES, and the almost extinct white rhinoceros, as well as by other large animals living in the park. The park is also home to baboons, CHIMPANZEES, several other kinds of primates, aardvarks, Cape buffalo, giraffes, several kinds of antelopes, LIONS, and LEOPARDS, as well as to many kinds of birds, reptiles, and fish. (See WILDLIFE REFUGE.)

**mutagen,** a substance that causes a mutation, or alteration, in the basic genetic structure (see RISK ASSESSMENT). (See also HEALTH EFFECTS OF REGULATED AIR POLLUTANTS on page 8; and KNOWN HEALTH EFFECTS OF TOXIC CHEMICALS on page 416.)

**N**

**Nagasaki,** see HIROSHIMA AND NAGASAKI.

**Narmada Valley Dam Project,** the massive, highly controversial Indian government multi-dam plan for northeastern India's Narmada Valley. With WORLD BANK financing, the 50-year plan is to build 32 major DAMS and over 3,000 smaller dams in the Narmada River basin, to irrigate approximately 20,000 square miles currently populated by over 12 million farmers, supply over 2,500 mega-

watts of electricity to northern India, and definitively eliminate recurrent drought in the basin. Critics of the plan assert that the project will flood 1,500 square miles, make 1 million people homeless, destroy tribal cultures in the basin (see INDIGENOUS PEOPLES), and run the risk of disastrous earthquakes in the area. (See DAMS.)

**Narragansett Bay oil spill,** leakage of an estimated 400,000 gallons (approximately 1,400 tons) of light fuel

OIL from the Greek tanker *World Prodigy* into Narragansett Bay near Newport, Rhode Island, when the tanker grounded on a reef on June 23, 1989. Although some environmental damage was done to the bay area, much of the light oil evaporated or dissipated quickly, while some was contained by booms. The accident further focused public attention on oil spills, coming soon after the March 24, 1989, EXXON VALDEZ disaster, and also on the same day as another major oil spill (see HOUSTON SHIP CHANNEL OIL SPILL), and a day before a third major oil spill (see DELAWARE RIVER OIL SPILL.) The three June 23–24 spills were treated in the media and perceived by many as almost a single disaster, and certainly as evidence of the urgency of the oil spill problem. (See OIL.)

**National Ambient Air Quality Standards (NAAQSs),** standards set under the CLEAN AIR ACT by the ENVIRONMENTAL PROTECTION AGENCY (EPA) for *criteria air pollutants,* those that pose a general threat to the quality of outdoor (ambient) air, including OZONE, PARTICULATE MATTER, CARBON MONOXIDE, SULFUR DIOXIDE, LEAD, and NITROGEN DIOXIDE. (See CLEAN AIR ACT; also HEALTH EFFECTS OF THE REGULATED AIR POLLUTANTS on page 8.)

**National Audubon Society** (950 Third Avenue, New York, NY 10022; 212-832-3200; Peter A.A. Berle, President; *Audubon Action Line* 202-547-9017, a legislative hotline for taped information on current environmental bills before Congress), a key membership organization founded in 1886 by George Bird Grinnell, originally focusing primarily on birds, especially opposing the killing of birds for their decorative feathers, but now having much wider concerns, dedicated to "long-term protection and the wise use of wildlife, land, water, and other natural resources; the promotion of rational strategies for energy development and use; the protection of life from pollution, radiation, and toxic substances; and the solution of global problems caused by overpopulation and the depletion of natural resources," recognizing that "all forms of life are interdependent and that the diversity of nature is essential to the economic and environmental well-being of all peoples."

The Society maintains a nationwide sanctuary system protecting 250,000 acres of natural HABITAT for birds, wildlife, and plants; seeks to educate the public, as through education centers, television specials, workshops, conferences, seminars, and the *Audubon Adventures* program for young children; operates summer ecology camps for adults and children; and runs travel-study programs and field seminars in the United States for students exploring natural and social issues. Through its own professional staff the Society conducts extensive scientific studies and field research on environmental concerns; pursues litigation on environmental matters before the courts; and seeks to develop public policy on the environment, through its *Environmental Policy Analysis Department,* and to influence passage and enforcement of laws through dialogue with and testimony before federal, state, and local agencies and legislative committees, often in cooperation with other conservation organizations, at home and abroad, as with the INTERNATIONAL COUNCIL FOR BIRD PRESERVATION.

Among the Society's major activities are the *Christmas Bird Count,* in which over 40,000 birders gather key information on the distribution and number of American birds; the *Citizens Acid Rain Monitoring Network,* coordinating measurements from 350 monitors around the country; and the *Audubon Activist Network,* available to members who wish to "take political and personal action . . . on behalf of the environment." In addition to developing an Audubon Energy Plan, current policy projects include exploring risks at THREE MILE ISLAND; the Platte River and its habitat; the implications of BIOTECHNOLOGY and CLIMATE CHANGE; the impacts of OIL and NATURAL GAS development on wildlife in Alaska and elsewhere; the health effects of AIR POLLUTION and health effects of magnetic fields; and threats from the JAMES BAY HYDROPOWER PROJECT. Many of the Society's activities are coordinated through its nine regional and five state offices, staffed by professional conservationists, or through local chapters.

The Society publishes various materials, including the magazine *Audubon;* the ornithological journal *American Birds;* a monthly news-journal *Audubon Activist;* the annual professional reference work *Audubon Wildlife Report,* an overview of wildlife management in the United States, and the activities of the federal and state agencies responsible for it, a series of action alerts or information sheets, such as *Planet Earth: Coming to the Rescue* and *From Outrage to Action: The Story of the National Audubon Society,* and flyers on National Audubon Society High-Priority Campaigns, such as *Arctic National Wildlife Refuge, Ancient Forests of the Northwest, Saving the Wetlands,* and *The Platte: A River Under Seige.*

**For more information:**

*The Audubon Ark: A History of the National Audubon Society.* Frank Graham, Jr., with Carl W. Buchheister. Knopf, 1990.

**National Campers and Hikers Association (NCHA)** (4804 Transit Road, Building 2, Depew, NY 14043, 716-668-6242; Joseph Vasut, President; in Canada: 52 West 22nd Street, Hamilton, Ontario L9C 4N5), a membership organization for campers of all ages who are concerned with the natural environment. The NCHA promotes safety techniques and campsite etiquette, provides Disaster Awareness and Emergency Preparedness Training, offers scholarships, encourages participation in community projects such as tree-plantings and litter-pickups, offers conservation workshops, maintains a Wildlife Refuge Program, and provides general information, advice, and assistance on camping and hiking interests, and other subjects such as the gypsy moth, the golden eagle, and new hiking trails. It also publishes various materials, including the monthly *Camping Today,* and offers members discounts and discount catalogs.

**National Center for Appropriate Technology (NCAT),** (3040 Continental Drive, P.O. Box 3838, Butte, MT 59702; 406-494-4572), an organization incorporated in 1976 to "help communities find better ways to do things to improve the quality of life, using skills and resources at hand," originally focusing on energy but from 1986 also addressing the need for a more "sustainable and environmentally benign agricultural industry." NCAT manages APPROPRIATE TECHNOLOGY TRANSFER FOR RURAL AREAS (ATTRA) and also publishes various materials.

**National Center for Atmospheric Research (NCAR)** (3215 Marine Street, P.O. Box 3000, Boulder, CO 80307; 303-497-1000; Information Services, 303-497-8600; Robert Serafin, Director), a mostly-government-funded research center, established in 1960 and operated by the University Corporation for Atmospheric Research (UCAR), a university consortium providing support and laboratory facilities to university and NCAR scientists, mostly at Boulder, in the Mesa Laboratory at Mesa Verde National Park (with exhibits and hiking trails open to visitors), but also at other facilities around the world. Research is primarily carried on in four scientific divisions (each with its own sub-sections and projects): *Atmospheric Chemistry Division (ACD),* focusing on the transport cycle of chemicals between the earth and the lower atmosphere, and its effects on life; *Climate and Global Dynamics Division (CGD),* focusing on long-term, large-scale interactions between the atmosphere and the earth; *High Altitude Observatory (HAO),* focusing on studies of the sun and its influence on earth's weather; and *Mesoscale and Microscale Meteorology (MMM) Division,* focusing on the short-term, short-range dynamics of chemical and physical processes governing the weather. Supporting these are the *Atmospheric Technology Division (ATD)* providing specialized facilities and tools for weather detection and the *Scientific Computing Division (SCD)* supplying supercomputer services.

**National Coalition for Marine Conservation (NCMC)** (P.O. Box 23298, Savannah, GA 31403; 912-234-8062; Ken Hinman, Executive Director), a membership organization founded in 1973 by people believing that "the living resources of the sea are one of nature's most precious gifts, to be used wisely and shared equitably, for the enjoyment and benefit of this and future generations," with members including "fishermen, boaters, divers, wildlife enthusiasts, scientists, and others, working together to conserve ocean fish and protect their environment." The NCMC supports development of fishery management plans and national OCEAN and fisheries policy; gathers and disseminates information about fish and fish conservation, as through national conferences and forums; seeks to influence public policy and legislation, as regarding overfishing, reduction of "by-catch" in DRIFTNETS, and protection of WETLANDS, CORAL REEFS, and other key HABITATS; sponsors game fish tagging programs and promotes release FISHING; and pursues international cooperation through ocean-wide agreements, as regarding tuna and salmon, often through international conferences. It also publishes various materials, including the newsletter *Marine Bulletin,* the bimonthly newsletter *Currents,* the periodic summary of current issues *Ocean View,* and a series of Marine Recreational Fisheries books, such as *Planning the Future of Billfishes.*

**National Emissions Standards for Hazardous Air Pollutants (NESHAPs),** standards set under the CLEAN AIR ACT by the ENVIRONMENTAL PROTECTION AGENCY (EPA) for hazardous air pollutants, such as arsenic, ASBESTOS, benzene, beryllium, MERCURY, radionuclides, VINYL CHLORIDE, and coke oven emissions. (See CLEAN AIR ACT; also HEALTH EFFECTS OF THE REGULATED AIR POLLUTANTS on page 8.)

**National Environmental Education Act,** a U.S. federal law passed in 1990 establishing "a non-profit national environmental education and training foundation to be funded through government grants and private gifts" and authorizing and funding education activities nationwide, especially for elementary and secondary school children.

**National Environmental Health Organization (NEHA)** (720 South Colorado Boulevard, South Tower, Suite 970, Denver, CO 80222; 303-756-9090), a professional organization of environmental health practitioners, founded in 1937, and linked with international counterparts in the *International Federation of Environmental Health.* NEHA maintains specialized sections: Air/Land/Water, Environmental Health Mangement, Food Protection, General Environmental Health, Injury Prevention/Occupational Health, Institutional/Environmental Health, Solid and Hazardous Waste, and International Environmental Health. It offers professional credentials for registered environmental health specialists and conducts educational conferences. It also publishes the peer-reviewed quarterly *Journal of Environmental Health,* and various professional and educational books and manuals.

## National Environmental Policy Act (NEPA), a U.S.

federal law passed in 1969, under which the government is directed to "use all practicable means . . . to create and maintain conditions in which man and nature can exist in productive harmony." Sometimes called "our basic national charter for protection of the environment," NEPA was the first general U.S. environmental law to call for government to consider environmental protection in making any decisions concerning "major Federal actions significantly affecting the quality of the human environment," with regulations designed to "help public officials make decisions that are based on understanding of environmental consequences, and take actions that protect, restore, and enhance the environment."

NEPA requires that an ENVIRONMENTAL IMPACT STATEMENT be filed for any major construction project that involves federal funds; it does not, however, require that an agency block an action that might harm the environment, nor does it require that the agency ensure that steps are taken to minimize harm (though other laws may do so). Under NEPA, the COUNCIL ON ENVIRONMENTAL QUALITY (CEQ) was set up as an independent agency in the White House, to advise and assist the president on environmental policy and on the preparation of an annual report on environmental quality, and to set regulations regarding the Act.

**For more information and action:**

• **Environmental Law Insitute (ELI),** (202-328-5150; publications office: 202-939-3844). Publishes *NEPA Deskbook* (1989). (See ENVIRONMENTAL LAW INFORMATION AND ACTION GUIDE on page 116.) (See also ENVIRONMENTAL LAW.)

## National Institute for Urban Wildlife, (10921 Trotting

Ridge Way, Columbia, MD 21044; 301-596-3311 or 301-995-1119; Gomer E. Jones, President), a membership organization founded in 1973 "dedicated to the conservation of wildlife in urban, suburban and developing areas." Through its professional staff and research associates, the Institute conducts research on relationships between people and wildlife seeking to "discover and disseminate practical procedures for maintaining, enhancing or controlling wildlife species" in urban or urbaninzing settings, while also building "an appreciation for and understanding of wild-

life and wildlife needs" and a "positive conservation ethic through local community and neighborhood educational programs."

The Institute provides technical services to urban planners, developers, land managers, government agencies, and homeowners on topics such as environmental assessments and impact statements for land DEVELOPMENT, open space planning and management, aquatic space planning and management, recreational planning, experimental design, urban WETLANDS enhancement, terrestrial and aquatic field research, data analysis, literature research, environmental education and training, attracting backyard wildlife, natural resources management, donations of land dedicated to wildlife purposes, and CONSERVATION EASEMENTS.

Among the Institute's other programs are certifications of a network of *Urban Wildlife Sanctuaries* on private and public lands (from half an acre to over 100 acres) and maintenance of a *National Roster of Urban Wildlife Sanctuaries.* As part of its *Nature Center Services Program,* the *Association of Nature Center Adminstrators (ANCA)* offers a series of urban wildlife symposia and an awards program for contributions to wildlife conservation in a metropolitan environment.

The Institute also publishes various materials, including the quarterlies *Urban Wildlife News* and *Urban Wildlife Manager's Notebook;* the *Wildlife Habitat Conservation Teacher's Pac* series; and books, booklets, and reports such as *A Guide to Urban Wildlife Management* (D.L. Leedy and L.W. Adams) and *Wildlife Reserves and Corridors in the Urban Environment: A Guide to Ecological Landscape Planning and Resource Conservation* (L.W. Adams and L.E. Dove, 1989).

## National Institute of Environmental Health Sciences (NIEHS) (P.O. Box 12233, Mail Drop A2–01,

Research Triangle Park, NC 27709; 919-541-3345; Kenneth Olden, Director), a key U.S. government biomedical research center to investigate the health effects of environmental agents, founded in 1966 as the Division of Environmental Health Sciences, renamed in 1969. Much research is done on site, including some of the crucial early studies of the effects of pollutants such as PCBs, DIOXIN, and HEAVY METALS. NIEHS's work is concerned with the effects of toxic chemical, biological, and physical factors on human health, especially the neurological system, behavior, pulmonary disease, and genetics, as well as molecular biophysics and pharmacology, with particular focus on the actual mechanism by which environmental agents work at the molecular and cellular levels.

NIEHS also administers numerous Public Health Service

(PHS) grants and awards funding work by other environmental health science researchers at colleges, universitites, research centers, marine and freshwater biomedical centers, and the like. Since 1978, it has coordinated all toxicology studies of the U.S. Department of Health and Human Services (HHS), under the *National Toxicology Program (NTP)*, including the National Center for Toxicological Research of the Food and Drug Administration (FDA), the National Institute for Occupational Safety and Health (NIOSH) of the Centers for Disease Controls (CDC), and parts of the National Cancer Institute (NCI), eventually transferred to NIEHS. In support of this program, NIEHS developed two additional programs, the *Division of Toxicology Research and Testing (DTRT)* and the *Biometry and Risk Assessment Program (BRAP)*, specializing in mathematical, statistical, and epidemiological research, experimental design, computer science, and data analysis.

Under SUPERFUND, the NIEHS has helped shape a training curriculum for people working with HAZARDOUS WASTE, and developed a basic interdisciplinary research program on hazardous waste problems, including the movement and fate of chemicals at waste sites, disposal or destruction methods, and assessments of health and ecological toxic effects. It also carries out testing, under an interagency agreement, with the *Agency for Toxic Substances and Disease Registry* of the Public Health Service.

Seeking expanded knowledge of the environmental health sciences, which may make for better regulations, legislation, and public health policy, NIEHS feels it has a central role in communication of scientific research results, as by hosting numerous major conferences, maintaining a massive toxicology source library, and publishing the scientific journal *Environmental Health Perspectives,* booklets such as *National Institute of Environmental Health Sciences Research Programs* and *Issues and Challenges in Environmental Health,* and brochures.

## National Oceanic and Atmospheric Administration (NOAA)

(11400 Rockville Pike, Rockville, MD 20852; 301-443-8910; Public Affairs Office: 202-377-8090; John A. Knauss, Deputy Under Secretary for Oceans and Atmosphere, and Administrator of NOAA), an arm of the U.S. Department of Commerce, established in 1970 to provide information on and oversee management of the physical environment and oceanic life. The NOAA includes several main components, among them:

- **National Marine Fisheries Service (NMFS)** (Silver Spring Metro Center 1, 1335 East-West Highway, Silver Spring, MD 20910; 301-27-2239; William Fox, Assistant Administrator), established in 1970 to manage the living marine resources of the U.S. within the nation's

EXCLUSIVE ECONOMIC ZONE (EEZ). The NMFS collects and analyzes information about human and natural effects on the marine environment, makes and carries out conservation and management plans, and provides financial assistance to states and industries for fisheries development. It publishes materials such as *Fisheries of the United States, 1990* (1991).

- **Office of Ocean and Coastal Resource Management (OCRM)** (1825 Connecticut Avenue NW, Suite 700, Washington, DC 20235; 202-606-4111; Trudy Coxe, Director), the agency that provides grant aid to states in planning and management for coastal areas; it includes the *Coastal Zone Information Center* (202-606-5115), established under the Coastal Zone Management Act (CZMA) of 1972, to "reduce conflicts among competing land and water use in the coastal zone, while protecting fragile coastal resources," including the *Coastal Zone Management (CZM)* program and the *National Estuarine Reserve Research System (NERRS)*.

- **National Environmental Satellite, Data and Information Service (NESDIS),** which itself includes the:

- **National Oceanographic Data Center (NODC),** (202-634-5539), which gathers, analyzes, interprets, stores, and disseminates worldwide oceangraphic data, on topics such as temperature, salinity, and pH readings; marine POLLUTION; PLANKTON production; OCEAN currents; and wind and wave data.

- **Ocean Pollution Data and Information Network (OPDIN),** (202-673-1500), which is designed to facilitate access to ocean pollution and data information generated by 11 participating federal departments and agencies. Information can be accessed through its *National Marine Pollution Information System (NMPIS)* or *Automated Electronic System for Ocean Pollution (AESOP),* (both 202-606-4539).

- **National Environmental Data Referral Service (NEDRES),** (202-673-5548), which provides access to computerized databases of worldwide environmental information and also publishes various "data catalogs" on the information available.

- **National Status and Trends Program for Marine Environmental Quality (NS&T)** (11400 Rockville Pike, Rockville, MD 20852; 301-443-8655), part of the NOAA's *Office of Oceanography and Marine Assessment,* which conducts systematic observations of coastal and estuarine areas to assess the effects of human activities on environmental quality, and provide the basis for management plans to improve these areas.

- **National Sea Grant College Program** (6010 Executive Boulevard, Rockville, MD 20852; 301-443-8923), which supports programs to develop marine resources.

The NOAA and its various arms publish numerous technical publications; periodic reports to Congress; guides to environmental information, such as the *Handbook of Federal Systems and Services for Marine Pollution Data and Information* (1988); a series of Water Quality Fact Sheets (with the U.S. Geological Survey); summary works such as *State-Issued Fish Consumption Advisories: A National Perspective, Coastal Degradation and Fish Population Losses, Assessing Human Health Risks from Chemically Contaminated Fish and Shellfish: A Guidance Manual, National Estuarine Inventory, West Coast of North America Data Atlas,* and *Lake Ontario: A Great Lake in Transition;* practical guides such as the quarterly *Mariners Weather Log,* and citizen-oriented works such as *National Directory of Citizen Volunteer Environmental Monitoring Programs* (1990), and a series of environmental guides to U.S. coastal recreation areas.

**National Park Service (NPS)** (U.S. Department of the Interior, Washington, DC 20240; James M. Ridenour, Director; Office of Public Inquiry, P.O. Box 37127, Washington, DC 20013; 202-208-4917), an agency of the U.S. Department of the Interior, established by the U.S. Congress in 1916 to administer "the several national parks and national monuments which are now under the jurisdiction of the Department of the Interior . . . and of such other national parks and reservations of like character as may be hereafter created by Congress," its purposes being to "conserve the scenery and the natural and historic objects and the wild life therein and to provide for the enjoyment of the same" so as to "leave them unimpaired for the enjoyment of future generations"; to manage the National Park System; and to "cooperate with other federal agencies, Indians, states, and local governments, private citizens and organizations in the preservation and interpretation of our Nation's natural and cultural heritage." By 1990 the National Park System had grown to include over 350 natural, historical, recreational, and cultural parks, covering over 79 million acres, not only in the 50 states, but also in Washington, DC; Puerto Rico; Guam; the Virgin Islands; and the Trust Territories.

Among its many functions are performing a wide range of surveys, including the National Survey of Historic Sites and Buildings, Historic American Buildings Survey, and the Historic American Engineering Record Survey; maintaining a national archeological salvage program; and carrying out studies of prospective environmental education landmarks, natural and historical themes, natural and historical resources of the National Park System, and historic federal property declared surplus or proposed for demolition. The NPS maintains registers of National Historic Landmarks, National Natural Landmarks, and National Environmental Education Landmarks and prepares periodic Nationwide Outdoor Recreation Plans to guide future policy. In addition to regional offices and planning and training centers, the NPS includes divisions such as the *Job Corps, Civilian Conservation Centers,* and *Youth Conservation Corps.*

The Service publishes numerous materials, including *National Park System: Map and Guide;* the annual *The National Parks: Camping Guide;* handbooks on the major natural and historic places; and brochures and flyers on most individual national park sites.

**National Parks and Conservation Association (NPCA)** (1015 31st Street, NW, Washington, DC 20007; 202-944-8530; Paul C. Pritchard, President), a membership organization founded in 1919 "to protect and improve America's national parks and to educate the public about the need to preserve this country's great natural and historical heritage." Among the NPCA's recent activities have been its 1990 nationwide March for Parks; publication of its blueprint for the future, the three-volume *National Park System Plan* (1988); actions to expand national parks, such as the EVERGLADES; independent studies of research and resource management in national parks; support for the 1988 creation of the National Park of American Samoa, to save a remnant of tropical rain FOREST; support for reintroduction of the WOLF to YELLOWSTONE NATIONAL PARK; and efforts to protect the Florida PANTHER. It has a long history of opposition to potentially damaging proposed DAM projects, as at GRAND CANYON; to real estate development "whittling away at historic Revolutionary and Civil War battlefield areas"; to overuse of park trails to the detriment of wildlife HABITATS; to opening of parks to HUNTING and trapping; and to archaeological looting and vandalism at prehistoric and more modern sites.

Through its national and regional offices, the NPCA works in concert with the NATIONAL PARK SERVICE and with other environmental groups, as in the Everglades Coalition, the Yellowstone Coalition, and the Clean Air Coalition, on a wide range of issues, including AIR POLLUTION, ACID RAIN, WATER POLLUTION, ENDANGERED SPECIES, damage to coastal areas by off-road vehicles, and expansion and strengthening the park and WILDLIFE REFUGE system, as by government acquistion of private "inholdings" within parks, to prevent damaging development. It supports passage of an American Heritage Trust Act to legislate such acquisitions "to protect our historic and natural heritage," with funds to be provided from royalties from offshore OIL drilling, though it opposes MIN-

ING and oil drilling proposals that threaten parks, such as YELLOWSTONE, DENALI, and GLEN CANYON.

The NCPA also maintains the *National Park Trust,* a revolving fund for acquiring national park land; maintains a *Park Watchers Program,* a "nationwide network of local activists who monitor park threats"; coordinates a *Contact Program,* through which members convey to public officials information from NPCA action alerts; offers a public information service, the *Park Education Center;* conducts "Behind the Scenes" members tours to selected national parks; and publishes various materials, including the bimonthly magazine *National Parks* and periodic legislative updates and action alerts, and publishes or distributes numerous other guidebooks, videotapes, audiotapes, and gift items.

## National Primary Drinking Water Requirements (NPDWRs), limits set by the ENVIRONMENTAL PROTECTION AGENCY for the largest amount of a potentially harmful substance allowed to be present in drinking water, before action is scheduled to be taken. NPDWRs replace MAXIMUM CONTAMINANT LEVELS (MCLs), scheduled to be phased out between 1990 and 1993. (See SAFE DRINKING WATER ACT [SDWA]; TOLERANCE LEVELS.)

## National Priorities List (NPL), a list of U.S. abandoned HAZARDOUS WASTE sites to be dealt with under SUPERFUND. (For a full listing, see SUPERFUND SITES on page 422.)

## National Recycling Coalition (NRC) (1101 30th Street NW, Suite 305, Washington, DC 20007; 202-625-6406; David Loveland, Executive Director), a coalition of individuals, small and large businesses, environmental groups, nonprofit organizations, state recycling associations, and state and local governments, founded in 1978, "dedicated to developing lasting solutions to the nation's solid waste problems," believing that "all parties must work together to develop and implement sound public policies." The NRC seeks to increase "public understanding of and support for effective recycling and conservation programs," and promotes implementation of appropriate laws and regulations, especially to proper procurement guidelines for recycled products as required by the RESOURCE CONSERVATION AND RECOVERY ACT (RCRA). It provides hands-on assistance and technical education, as through its *Peer Match* program, including technical councils, in which "members with similar concerns . . . [can] address issues unique to their programs" and are also put in touch with professional recyclers whose assistance matches their needs. The NRC hosts the annual National Recycling Congress, and maintains the Recycling Advisory Council

(RAC) to "establish sound recycling and resource management policies." It also publishes various materials, including the bimonthly newsletter *The NRC Connection,* and *National Policy on Recycling and Policy Resolutions.*

## National Wildlife Federation (NWF) (1400 16th Street NW, Washington, DC 20036; 202-797-6800 or 800-245-5484; Jay D. Hair, President), a conservation education organization founded in 1936, "committed to wildlife, conservation and a healthier environment," promoting "the wise use of natural resources," and believing that "our natural heritage can be protected only through continued awareness, understanding and action." Working on such issues as "clean air, pure water, endangered species, and the protection of vital wildlife habitat," the NWF seeks to influence state and national conservation policies "through administrative, legislative, and, as a last resort, legal channels," working through their "nationwide network of state affiliates and members," and maintains natural resource law and science centers. It also sponsors *Conservation Summits®,* weeklong outdoor discovery programs led by naturalists and other specialists for NWF members—adults, families, singles, and educators, for whom there are special programs on teaching techniques; *Wildlife Camps®,* two-week-long sessions for children 9–13; *Teen Adventures,* wilderness sessions for those 14- to 17-including backpacking, camping, and nature experiences; *Leadership Training Programs,* teaching teens 14–17 the skills needed to assist counselors in Wildlife Camps; *Nature Quest® Leadership Training,* certified 3-day programs for camp directors, nature and science counselors, naturalists, and outdoor educators; and *Washington Action Workshop,* teaching the skills needed to "lobby lawmakers and work effective on environmental issues in your area."

The NWF publishes the annuals *Conservation Directory* and *Environmental Quality Index;* the quarterly *Legislative Update;* the bimonthlies *National Wildlife* and *International Wildlife,* including the *Wildlife Digest Newsletter;* the triweekly *Enviroaction;* the monthlies *Ranger Rick* (for ages 6–12) and *Your Big Backyard* (for ages 3–5); numerous Fact Sheets on environmental topics; and working bibliographies and scientific works on various animals. It also publishes numerous practical and useful educational materials for parents and educators, including the *Citizens Action Guide, The NWF Activist Kit, The Backyard Naturalist, The Gardening with Wildlife® Kit, Backyard Wildlife Habitat Information Packet, Environment: A Place at the Table, Our Threatened Heritage* (a video and booklet), classroom materials for *Wildlife Week,* and the *Nature Scope® Series,* an education activity series for use with children in grades K–8, covering 18 environmental issues, such as *Rain Forests: Tropical Treasures; Endangered Species: Wild and Rare;* and *Pollution: Problems and Solutions.*

**natural gas,** a naturally occurring, burnable gas that includes primarily METHANE (approximately 50 to 99 percent), along with other HYDROCARBONS, as well as hydrogen sulfide, CARBON DIXOIDE, nitrogen, and helium. It is generally considered to be the cleanest of the FOSSIL FUELS, contributing less to AIR POLLUTION than COAL or OIL. However, recent studies have suggested that leakage of natural gas during transmission and distribution may contribute disproportionately to the GREENHOUSE EFFECT and so perhaps to GLOBAL WARMING. If the estimates of 1-to-3-percent leakage are confirmed, natural gas will be far less environmentally attractive, since methane traps 30 to 70 times more heat than CARBON DIOXIDE.

Like other fossil fuels, natural gas is generally believed to have been formed from partly decomposed plant matter converted by heat, pressure, and chemical reactions into hydrocarbons over millions of years—the geological equivalent of *swamp gas* or *marsh gas.* Certainly natural gas deposits often occur with oil and coal. Some scientists, however, believe that natural gas comes from deep within the earth. Whatever its origin, pressure forces it upward through sand and porous rock until it pours into reservoirs created by shifts in the earth's crust, where it is trapped by a cap or done of impermeable rock. The largest known deposits of natural gas are in the United States, Canada, the former Soviet Union, and the Middle East.

In decades past, energy-rich countries often used to simply "flare off," or burn at the well head, natural gas released from oil wells. Only as people have come to realize that fossil fuels are DECLINING RESOURCES have some of these countries tapped their natural gas. Sometimes it is simply "reinjected" into underground tanks for storage until needed, as in abandoned mines or in naturally occurring spaces such as AQUIFERS or porous rock. Since natural gas fields produce best when drawn on at a steady rate, such storage areas are often filled during the summer, when demand is low, and drawn down with heavier use in the winter.

Traditionally natural gas has been carried cross-country and sometimes underwater by pipeline. Natural gas may also be chilled down to liquid form, which takes considerably less space. This may be transported by pipeline or by special seagoing liquefied natural gas (LNG) carriers, in heavily insulated cryogenic tanks chilled to −162 degrees Celsius Cryogenic processing may also be used to separate out hydrocarbons from nonburning elements, such as helium, nitrogen, and carbon dioxide, to produce a high-efficiency fuel.

Some forms of natural gas are synthesized from coal or oil (see SYNTHETIC FUELS) or from solid waste and waste water, which under appropriate conditions naturally produce methane (see BIOFUELS). In some parts of the world, natural gas—synthesized or from underground—is being used as an alternative fuel, as in automobiles.

Apart from the ecological damage of setting up and maintaining production sites, and its contribution to the greenhouse effect, the main environmental danger from natural gas is that of leaks from pipelines and storage tanks and resulting explosions. In fact, the development of liquefied natural gas was shelved for years after the 1944 CLEVELAND NATURAL GAS EXPLOSION of an LNG storage tank, which killed perhaps 125 people and destroyed 50 city blocks; LNG development was dusted off only during the 1970s energy crisis, being especially attractive to energy-poor regions such as Japan and Europe. Pockets of natural gas have also been a danger to coal miners for centuries, and explosions sometimes rock structures built over abandoned fossil fuel fields, as in some parts of downtown Los Angeles.

### For more information and action:

- **INTERNATIONAL TRANSBOUNDARY RESOURCES CENTER (CENTRO INTERNACIONAL DE RECURSOS TRANSFRONTERIZOS, or CIRT),** (505-277-6424). Publishes a model international agreement for development of gas resources.
- **NATIONAL WILDLIFE FEDERATION (NWF),** (202-797-6800 or 800-245-5484). Publishes *The Arctic Refuge and Oil and Gas Development.*
- **NATURAL RESOURCES DEFENSE COUNCIL (NRDC),** (212-727-2700). Publishes materials on oil and natural gas.
- **SIERRA CLUB,** (415-776-2211 or 202-547-1141; legislative hotline, 202-547-5550). Publishes brochures on oil and gas policies.

(See also FOSSIL FUELS; BIOFUELS; SYNTHETIC FUELS; ENERGY RESOURCES; ENERGY RESOURCES INFORMATION AND ACTION GUIDE on page 110.)

**natural resource accounting,** a relatively new approach that treats natural resources as assets that can be depreciated, the aim being to have such resources (including nonhuman species) considered as part of cost accounting in analyzing the effects of any action affecting the environment. The approach was developed to counter the long-dominant traditional approach of treating natural resources and nonhuman species as expendable commodities, which did not need to be considered as "costs" in short-term economic plans. (See ENVIRONMENTAL PLANNING; LAND USE.)

## Natural Resources and Energy Division (NRED), United Nations

(United Nations, New York, NY 10017; 212-963-6205; Dunja Pastizzi-Feren'cic, Director), one of the two arms of the United Nations Department of Technical Co-operation for Development (UNDTCD), established to aid developing countries in solving their environmental problems, and to coordinate UN programs in the areas of energy, water, and mineral resources. Main concerns include the combustion of FOSSIL FUELS and the resulting GREENHOUSE EFFECT, CLIMATE CHANGE, and ACID RAIN; scarcity of FUELWOOD and resulting DESERTIFICATION; wasted water, as from leaking pipes or excess irrigation; the need to reduce water demand while continuing to meet human needs; WATER POLLUTION; and the need to minimize and properly dispose of solid and liquid wastes from MINING.

The NRED seeks to ensure that UN projects, many funded by the UNITED NATIONS DEVELOPMENT PROGRAMME (UNDP), properly consider ecological and environmental impacts, often aiding developing countries in making environmental impact assessments. It publishes or distributes various materials, including the *Energy Newsletter,* and reports such as *Energy Issues and Options for Developing Countries* (1989), *National Energy Information Systems* (1988), and *Joint Hydropower Development* (1988).

## Natural Resources Defense Council (NRDC)

(40 West 20th Street, New York, NY 10111, 212-727-2700; John H. Adams, Executive Director; 90 New Montgomery Street, #620, San Francisco, CA 94105; 415-777-0220), a nonprofit membership organization, founded in 1970, staffed primarily by lawyers and scientific specialists, which employs litigation and public advocacy on a wide range of environmental issues, acting as a watchdog over government agencies and supplying vital scientific information to the public, including AIR POLLUTION, WATER POLLUTION, CLIMATE CHANGE, TOXIC CHEMICALS, PESTICIDES, LAND USE, nuclear safety, ENDANGERED SPECIES, BIOLOGICAL DIVERSITY, ENERGY CONSERVATION, rain forests and other FORESTS, COASTS, Alaska, WILDLIFE REFUGES and WILDERNESS, focusing primarily on the United States, and on international environmental issues, especially those affected by U.S. foreign policy, as through foreign aid or multilateral DEVELOPMENT banks.

The NRDC publishes a wide range of materials, including *The Amicus Journal;* the *NRDC Newsline;* books such as *The Right to Know More: Toxic Releases into the*

*Environment* (Deborah Sheiman, 1991), *The Rainforest Book: How You Can Save the World's Ranforest* (Scott Lewis with NRDC, 1990), *Areas of Critical Environmental Concern: Promise vs. Reality* (Faith Campbell and Johanna Wald, 1989), and *A Who's Who of American Toxic Air Polluters: A Guide to More Than 1,500 Factories in 46 States Emitting Cancer-Causing Chemicals* (Deborah A. Sheiman et al, 1989); and NRDC Earth Action Guides such as *Reducing, Recycling, and Rethinking Garbage* and *Saving the Ozone Layer.*

## Nature Conservancy, The

(1815 North Lynn Street, Arlington, VA 22209; 703-841-5300; Frank D. Boren, President), an international membership organization founded in 1951 dedicated to "preserving Earth's rare plants, animals, and natural communities by protecting the lands they need to survive," with the lands so protected now totaling over 5 million acres of land, mostly in the United States but also in Canada and the CARIBBEAN. The Conservancy may purchase lands directly (sometimes adding them only until other agencies or organizations are ready to assume responsibility for them) or provides funds to manage such lands.

Through its headquarters and its numerous regional, field, and chapter offices, it also works with other environmental organizations and government agencies to develop biological inventories, seeking to "collect, verify, and disseminate information on the occurrences and status of rare species and exemplary ecosystems," particular aims being to identifying the "rarest of the rare," those SPECIES most in need of protection, and to help federal agencies designate lands as "research natural areas," "areas of critical environmental concern," or "special interest areas."

Among the Conservancy's recent projects are *Parks in Peril,* an international campaign targeting 200 key tropical ECOSYSTEMS in Latin America and the Caribbean parks and reserves, covering 91 million acres, for which they seek funds to ensure adequate management; DEBT-FOR-NATURE SWAPS in Costa Rica, Dominican Republic, and Ecuador; an agreement with the Department of Defense to allow the Conservancy to do a biological inventory and provide management assistance for over 25 million acres of public lands; and development of a series of state-by-state computerized biological inventories, which has served as a model for similar programs elsewhere, as in Latin America and the Caribbean. Its activities may range from buying a prime stretch of tallgrass prairie in Oklahoma to creating new preserves on Hawaii in an Islands of Life Campaign, from expanding the acreage of the National Key Deer Wildlife Refuge to assisting Latin American and Caribbean countries to do their own biological inventories and protection programs. The Conservancy publishes the *Nature Conservancy Magazine*.

**nematicides,** a type of chemical compound used for killing roundworms and threadworms, many of them parasites (see PESTICIDES).

**Nevada Test Site,** U.S. atomic weapons desert test site approximately 120 kilometers (75 miles) northwest of Las Vegas; from 1951 to 1958, over 100 atmospheric nuclear test explosions at the site generated heavy radioactive FALLOUT "downwind," for distances of up to 200 miles, contaminating large areas, and causing greatly increased RADIATION-connected illnesses in the area for decades. Somewhat less contaminating underground tests continued after 1958. (See NUCLEAR WEAPONS ESTABLISHMENT F, U.S.; NUCLEAR TESTING; *The Conqueror*.)

**New York harbor oil spills,** five OIL spills during the first half of 1990, three of them major, all occurring in the Arthur Kill and Kill Van Kull, narrow waterways feeding the immense complex of New Jersey and Staten Island, New York, OIL and chemical plants on the western side of New York harbor. On January 1, 1990 a leaking Exxon pipeline spilled 567,000 gallons of fuel oil into the Arthur Kill, at Linden, New Jersey. On February 28, a leaking barge spilled 24,000 gallons of heating oil into the Kill Van Kull, off Bayonne, New Jersey. On March 1, a leaking barge spilled 3,500 gallons of heavy crude oil into the Arthur Kill, again off Linden. On March 6, a barge explosion and fire spilled an estimated 200,000 gallons of heating oil into the Arthur Kill, again at Linden. And on June 7 the British supertanker *Nautilus* ran aground while docking at Bayonne, spilling 260,000 gallons of heating oil into the Kill Van Kull.

The spills totaled an estimated 1,045,000 gallons (approximately 3,600 tons). The cumulative effect of these disasters reversed much of the ecological comeback that had been occurring in the area in the previous decade, as seabirds and fish began to return to this greatly damaged portion of the Atlantic shore. The spills also attracted national media attention, coming soon after the 1989 *Exxon Valdez* disaster and several other recent major and very damaging oil spills on the Pacific and Gulf coasts. (See OIL.)

**niche,** in ECOLOGY, the general "slot" or place of an organism within its HABITAT. The actual physical space an organism occupies is called its *habitat niche,* while the role it plays in relation to other organisms, as in a FOOD CHAIN, is called its *ecological niche.* Organisms that occupy the same niches in similar but geographically separated areas—such as bacteria acting as decomposers in two different old-growth temperate hardwood forests—are called *ecological equivalents.*

**nitrates,** nitrogen-containing compounds (often with a combination of one nitrogen and three oxygen atoms, abbreviated as $NO_3$). Formed naturally from NITRITES as part of the NITROGEN CYCLE, nitrates are vital for plant growth, and they are a prime constituent of both natural manures and artificial fertilizers. However, excess nitrates can cause POLLUTION. Nitrates are highly soluble, and when they percolate through the soil they can contaminate groundwater. Excess nitrates in RIVERS, LAKES and other bodies of water can cause so much plant growth as to totally disrupt the ECOSYSTEM and sometimes kill off all marine life, a process called EUTROPHICATION. Nitrates can also cause problems to humans if they are chemically converted back to nitrites.

**nitrites,** nitrogen-containing compounds that naturally occur in the soil; as part of the NITROGEN CYCLE, nitrites are converted to NITRATES, which are vital to plant growth. However, in the human body, nitrites can cause health problems, interfering with the vital blood-carrying function of blood and possibly causing cancer. Nitrites, and also related compounds called *nitrosamines,* are readily formed in the digestive system from water polluted by dissolved nitrates. Nitrites are also used as food preservatives, especially in curing meats.

**nitrogen cycle,** the process by which living organisms extract from the environment the nitrogen that is essential to life (see BIOGEOCHEMICAL CYCLES). Although the earth's atmosphere is almost 80 percent nitrogen, most plants and animals cannot use nitrogen directly, but only after it has been converted into one or more nitrogen compounds, a process called *nitrogen fixation* or *nitrification*. This can only be done by some kinds of bacteria and algae, which convert gaseous nitrogen ($N_2$) into ammonia ($NH_3$). Some plants use the ammonia directly, while others must wait until soil bacteria convert it further, into NITRITES or NITRATES. Either way, the nitrogen then becomes available for use in forming life-sustaining amino acids and proteins.

The reverse part of the cycle occurs when microorganisms break down dead plant and animal matter, some into nitrogen and other compounds (a process called *denitrification,*) others into ammonia and other products, (a process called *ammonification,*) with nitrogen being released back into the atmosphere. Nitrification and denitrification generally form a relatively balanced cycle, but wide-scale use of fertilizers in recent decades has upset that balance, sometimes leading to EUTROPHICATION, in which excess nitrogen in LAKES, RIVERS, and along COASTS encourages so much plant production that oxygen is depleted and fish die. The long-term effect of that imbalance, including the buildup of nitrates, nitrites, and ammonia in the biosphere, are still being explored.

**For more information and action:**

• NITROGEN FIXING TREE ASSOCIATION (NFTA), (800-956-7985).

**nitrogen dioxide (NO₂)**, a poisonous, pungent gas readily formed when nitric oxide (NO) is brought together with HYDROCARBONS (chemical compounds of hydrogen and carbon) and sunlight, producing a *photochemical reaction*. These conditions are readily found anywhere in the modern world where automobiles are to be found, because nitric oxide is formed in internal combustion engines and exhausted into the air, where various hydrocarbons are to be found. The nitrogen dioxide then formed disperses in the air, where its yellowish-brown cast contributes to the formation of SMOG; it also reacts with water droplets to form nitric acid (HNO₃), a major constituent of ACID RAIN.

Nitrogen dioxide also results from various industrial activities, notably the manufacture of fertilizers and explosives, and from some natural events, such as lightning. At sufficient concentrations, nitrogen dioxide can be deadly, but its most usual action is more insidious, damaging the respiratory systems of those who breathe it, contributing to lung diseases such as emphysema, and attacking the vegetation, soil, buildings, and other materials that exist in it. In the United States, it is one of the CRITERIA AIR POLLUTANTS for which the ENVIRONMENTAL PROTECTION AGENCY (EPA) sets NATIONAL AMBIENT AIR QUALITY STANDARDS (NAAQSs), under the CLEAN AIR ACT, and nitrogen oxides are among the main targets of the 1990 amendments to that act. CATALYTIC CONVERTERS are used to help diminish nitrogen oxides in automobile exhaust. (See also AIR POLLUTION; ACID RAIN; CLEAN AIR ACT.)

**Nitrogen Fixing Tree Association (NFTA)** (P.O. Box 680, Waimanalo Research Station, University of Hawaii, 41–6948 Ahiki Street, Waimanalo, HI 96795; 808-956-7985; Gregory Sullivan, President), a membership organization founded in 1980, that "encourages the international research, development and communication of N-fixing trees to help meet the needs of people in the developing countries for fuelwood, fertilizer, fodder, food, timber, medicinal and other products." The NFTA acts as an information center "on all aspects of NFT biology, planting and use"; operates an Outreach Program providing technical assistance, information and initial project funds; has area representatives (ARs) working in "critical areas of the world" to coordinate NFT activities with local associ-

ates; provides training, consultation, and grants for small-scale forestry projects; encourages research and improvement, as through the *Cooperative Planting Program (CPP)* and their own tree improvement program; maintains a germ plasm preservation program to help maintain BIOLOGICAL DIVERSITY; sponsors workshops; and publishes various materials, including the *NFT Highlights* and the *NFTA News;* the annuals *Nitrogen Fixing Tree Research Reports* and *Leucaena Research Reports;* books and field manuals; and various brochures such as *Why Nitrogen Fixing Trees* and others on specific NFT species.

**Noatak National Preserve,** in northern Alaska, a 6,500,000-acre (10,100-square-mile) portion of the Brooks Range, cut for 210 miles by the course of the Noatak River. Abutting the preserve to the south is the 1,750,000-acre (2,700-square-mile) Kobuk Valley National Park; to the east is the 8,500,000-acre (13,300-square-mile) GATES OF THE ARCTIC NATIONAL PARK AND PRESERVE. The three preserves, taken together, comprise an enormous northern WILDERNESS that is a major world natural heritage asset. The United Nations has named Noatak an international BIOSPHERE RESERVE.

Noatak sustains a wide range of Arctic animals in its basin, including Dall sheep, grizzly BEARS, moose, CARIBOU, wolverines, WOLVES, and loons, and has such fish as northern pike and Arctic char. Its basin also supports the life of several hundred plant species, a very unusual number for the far north. (See TUNDRA; WILDLIFE REFUGES; WILDERNESS.)

**noise pollution,** sounds that in kind, loudness, or intensity jeopardize health and welfare, closely associated with POPULATION growth, urbanization and the associated traffic, industry, machinery, appliances, and the clamor of human activity. Noise pollution can damage hearing, disrupt sleep, impair learning, increase stress and anxiety, and foster antisocial behavior. But because these effects are not generally seen as serious or as linked to noise pollution, the problem is often disregarded.

In the United States, Congress enacted a Noise Control Act (NCA) in 1972 (amended in 1978), to promote an environment free from harmful noise. Under the administration of the ENVIRONMENTAL PROTECTION AGENCY (EPA), the *Office of Noise Abatement Control* (ONAC) was to coordinate research, identify types of noise requiring control, set standards, control activities, and disseminate information about the health effects of noise pollution, safe noise levels, noisy products and techniques, and noise control. At that time, the EPA estimated that 34 million people were exposed to nonoccupational noise capable of causing hearing loss, that 44 million lived in areas with annoyingly high levels of transportation noise (including aircraft), and that 21 million were faced with disruptive amounts of construction noise.

ONAC made a start, setting guidelines in some areas, conducting some educational programs, and coordinating with local and state noise-abatement programs. However, it was disbanded in 1981, as part of President Reagan's deregulation moves, to surprisingly little protest from Congress or the public. Since then (as of this writing) the EPA has not received (nor in recent years asked for) funding to enforce federal noise regulations, though the law remains on the books.

Not surprisingly, a 1991 commission report noted that the problem had only increased, especially with the proliferation of loud toys and portable stereo headset systems. Noise abatement programs in the United States today are largely in state and local hands, though many of these programs have also quietly died. Ironically, ONAC guidelines (where they exist) are by law given precedence over state and local standards, so though the federal guidelines are now out of date and inadquate, the Act prevents state governments from setting stricter standards. Even when active, the federal program had done little or nothing about labeling of noisy products, or about ensuring government purchase of low-noise products.

**For more information and action:**

•NATIONAL ENVIRONMENTAL HEALTH ORGANIZATION **(NEHA),** (303-756-9090). Publishes *Measuring Environmental Noise.*

**non-attainment areas,** localities that do not meet federal or other pollution control standards for a specific pollutant; as opposed to *attainment areas,* which do (see AIR POLLUTION).

**noncompliance,** the condition of not having met set standards, such as having more than specified acceptable levels of pollutant in EMISSIONS; localities or industries that *do* meet the standards are said to be *in compliance* (see AIR POLLUTION).

**nongovernmental organization (NGO),** any organization that is not directly affiliated with government, including environmental and development groups, business and industry, trade unions, scientific and academic organizations, youth and adult citizen's groups, and INDIGENOUS PEOPLES groups. Though "NGO" is widespread in environment-speak, especially among international environmental organizations, more recently some have come to prefer the term *independent sector.* Some such groups join together, especially on the international front, as in the Conference of Non Governmental Organizations in Consultative Status with the United Nations Economic and Social Council (CONGO), the African NGOs Environment Network, or the Independent Sector Coordinating Committee on Environment and Development (ISCCED), which includes the NATIONAL AUDUBON SOCIETY, NATIONAL WILDLIFE FEDERATION, WORLD RESOURCES INSTITUTE, the SIERRA CLUB, and other such key groups.

**nonrenewable resources,** an alternative term for DECLINING RESOURCES.

**North American Lake Management Society (NALMS)** (1000 Connecticut Avenue NW, Suite 202, Washington, DC 20036; 202-466-8550; Judith F. Taggert, Executive Secretary; mailing address, P.O. Box 217, Merrifield, VA 22116), a membership organization founded in 1980 by people who study and manage LAKES and reservoirs, and are concerned about how lakes and reservoirs are affected by captured pollutants and sediments, how to restore those affected by these stresses, and how to protect those not yet affected. NALMS holds an annual international symposium, specialty conferences, and regional workshops; provides expert referral services; encourages networking among chapters and with other organizations; and offers travel grants and internships. It also publishes various materials, including the magazine *Lake Line,* the journal *Lake and Reservoir Management;* books and reports such as *Lake and Reservoir Restoration Guidance Manual* (1990), *Monitoring Lake and Reservoir Restoration* (1990), *Lake Conservation Handbook* (1989), and *NALMS Management Guide for Lakes and Reservoirs;* and audiovisual materials.

**North Sea,** the shallow 220,000-square-mile sea, an arm of the Atlantic, long a major set of shipping lanes and commercial fisheries. Its strong currents and exchange of water with the Atlantic make it a healthy sea, rather than a closed system deeply threatened by 20th-century environmental hazards.

However, these hazards do pose considerable threats to the life of the sea. Among them are OIL spills from the hundreds of wells now in the sea and from the tankers in its sea-lanes, including such spectacular disasters as that of the *TORREY CANYON* in 1967 and *AMOCO CADIZ* in 1978, as well as the thousands of smaller spills that supply the main body of oil in the sea. Added to these are the huge flow of municipal and industrial waste, some of it toxic, from the RHINE, Thames, and other European rivers, airborne pollutants, incinerator wastes, and the chemical pollutants still legally dumped into the sea by British companies—all posing a clear threat to sea life. Fish contamination and red tides have been observed off the Norwegian, Danish, German, Dutch, and Belgian coasts.

Since the mid-1980s, the countries of the North Sea have been taking substantial antipollution measures in the North Sea. Sewage sludge dumping has been prohibited by most North Sea countries, as has chemical dumping, with the notable exception of Britain, which promises to prohibit chemical dumping in the early 1990s. Fewer pollutants are arriving in the sea from the Thames, although the flow of pollutants from the Rhine and other mainland rivers is only slightly lessened, if at all. In the early 1990s, there seems room for hope that the North Sea countries can greatly lessen the pollution of the sea. (See OCEANS.)

**Nowruz,** Iranian OIL field, site of a massive blowout in 1983 (see IRAN-IRAQ WAR OIL SPILL).

**nuclear energy,** power released from the atom, either by splitting the atom (*nuclear fission*) or fusing atoms (*nuclear fusion*), the latter still very much in the development stage. At the beginning of the "atomic era," nuclear fission was for many the hope of limitless power, low energy cost, and a clean future; instead it has turned out to be in both human and economic terms incalculably expensive and extraordinarily dirty. Commercially produced nuclear energy has generated not only substantial amounts of electricity but also a massive worldwide campaign to resist new nuclear energy plants and close existing ones, and to find ways to dispose safely of the mountains of RADIOACTIVE WASTE that have piled up during three decades of operation and continue to pile up every day.

Worldwide views of atomic energy have been made even more negative by the shockingly inhuman four-decades-long performance of the several military establishments testing and producing atomic weapons, much of which is still coming to light, including the Soviet Union's cover-up of the massive nuclear waste explosion at the CHELYABINSK nuclear weapons complex and a dozen lesser disasters; the American denials of the callous NEVADA TEST SITE exposures and of what was happening to lethal wastes at such plants as Hanford, Rocky Flats, Savannah River, and Fernald (see NUCLEAR WEAPONS ESTABLISHMENTS, U.S.); the British performances at SELLAFIELD and MARALINGA; and the French at MORUROA.

But it was the commercial production of atomic energy that generated the accidents that were to fully destroy worldwide public confidence in nuclear energy. In 1979, the partial core meltdown and near-disaster at THREE MILE ISLAND focused world attention on nuclear energy hazards. In 1986, the CHERNOBYL MELTDOWN brought the world directly to the kind of nuclear disaster long predicted by nuclear energy opponents, with hundreds of immediate deaths and tens of thousands of further deaths to follow. More than 200,000 people were evacuated from poisoned areas by mid-1991 and 120,000 were still to follow. Radioactive FALLOUT effects are still damagingly evident as far away as Scotland and the land and animal life of thousands of square miles occupied by 4 million people has been poisoned for decades and centuries to come.

The magnitude of the Chernobyl disaster made a mockery of 25 years of careful cost comparisons between nuclear power and other kinds of power. In a very real way, the huge human and economic costs already incurred, and the prospect of clearing up or sealing away the radioactive waste already created and accumulated had already made it clear the nuclear energy was by far the most expensive kind of energy. But after Chernobyl, with its massive human and economic costs to be carried forward to future generations, commercial nuclear energy could no longer be viewed as a major long-term energy source, no matter how persuasively its proponents argued that new and untried techniques would "almost certainly" greatly reduce risks. In essence, most of the world responded after Chernobyl that no level of nuclear energy risk was acceptable—and further, that governments, atomic scientists, and atomic industry people were not to be trusted to make such statements, given the record and the problems still unaddressed.

The net result was that the building of new commercial atomic plants dried up in most of the world, and that now-aging first generation nuclear plants began closing faster than anticipated. By the end of 1989, International Atomic Agency figures showed 426 commercial nuclear reactors in operation, with 96 more under construction. But 46 of these were in the Soviet Union and Eastern Europe and seven more in India, and by early 1991 it was quite clear that most of these would never be completed. The United States, with 110 commercial reactors then in operation, had only four under construction, with more than 50 aging reactors reaching their licensed age of 40 years in the next quarter century; some of these were already encountering major problems, as had the 16 less-than-40-year-old reactors previously closed. Only France and Japan continued to strongly develop commercial atomic energy programs. France, with 75 percent of its electricity requirements met by nuclear reactors, and Japan, 28 percent nuclear, continued to build new reactors. But in early 1991 Japanese nuclear accidents cast a pall on future nuclear energy plans, leaving France alone in its decision to press ahead. Whether that decision continues to hold may depend on whether or not future nuclear accidents cripple French resolve in this area.

For the rest of the world, withdrawal from commercial nuclear energy seems in prospect. But not immediately; much has been invested in nuclear energy, there are strong vested political and economic interests, and massive new energy needs lie ahead. Almost 20 percent of U.S. electricity is nuclear-generated, as is 22 percent of British, over 30 percent of German, and 12 percent of the former Soviet Union, with the figures for some smaller countries going even higher. Nuclear energy proponents and political leaders, point out that the practical alternatives so far are mainly FOSSIL FUELS, with COAL especially releasing huge amounts of CARBON DIOXIDE into the air of a planet threatened by GLOBAL WARMING. How quickly the world is able to back away from commercial nuclear energy will depend to some extent on how quickly major ALTERNATIVE ENERGY sources and energy conservation measures can be brought into play. (See also NUCLEAR ISSUES INFORMATION AND ACTION GUIDE on page 215; MAJOR NUCLEAR DISASTERS AND INCIDENTS below also NUCLEAR WEAPONS; NUCLEAR WEAPONS ESTABLISHMENT, U.S.; RADIATION.)

## Major Nuclear Disasters and Incidents

**1945** **The first atomic bomb test,** code-named Trinity, occurred on July 16, 1945, at the Alamogordo Bombing Range, in the New Mexico desert; the first radioactive fallout was recorded as far east as New England.

**1945** **Hiroshima and Nagasaki,** two Japanese cities, were the targets of the first two atomic bombs used in warfare; Hiroshima was bombed on August 6, 1945, Nagasaki on August 9, 1945. In all, 110,000–150,000 people died immediately or soon after the bombing, while 125,000–175,000 more have died since, and many are still dying. (See also HIROSHIMA AND NAGASAKI.)

**1946** **Bikini Atoll tests,** the explosions of two atomic bombs in the air over Bikini lagoon, took place on July 1 and July 25, 1946, in the tests code-named Operation Crossroads. They were the first of over 70 atomic weapons tests at Bikini and Eniwetok atolls, two island groups in the Marshall Islands, which in aggregate heavily contaminated islands as much as 200 miles downwind. (See also BIKINI AND ENIWETOK.)

**1951** **Nuclear tests began at the Nevada Test Site,** in the desert northwest of Las Vegas. Over 100 atmospheric nuclear device tests were conducted from 1951 to 1958, generating radioactive fallout that contaminated wide surrounding areas with a population of 100,000. (See also NEVADA TEST SITE.)

**1952** **British nuclear tests began,** with an atom bomb explosion at the Monte Bello Islands, off the western coast of Australia, on October 3, 1952. (See also MARALINGA.)

**1952** **Chalk River, Ontario,** was the site of a partial meltdown within the core of a Canadian experimental reactor on December 2, 1952, the first such on record, and a precursor of much that would follow.

**1953** **Maralinga** was the site of the beginning of British nuclear weapons tests on the mainland of southern Australia, used from 1953 to 1963 for a series of thensecret and highly contaminating nuclear bomb tests— and the beginning of radiation-related illnesses and dislocation for thousands of Aborigines in a wide area. (See also MARALINGA.)

**1954** *The Conqueror* was filmed at St. George, Utah, in a heavily contaminated area downwind of the Nevada Test Site; in later years many of the movie's cast and crew were cancer victims, among them John Wayne, Susan Hayward, Pedro Armendariz, and Agnes Moorehead. (See also *The* CONQUEROR.)

**1954** **The first hydrogen bomb** was exploded on the island of Bikini, on March 1, 1954, in the test codenamed Castle-Bravo; its fallout severely contaminated Rongelop, 100 miles away, and several other islands in the Marshalls. (See also BIKINI AND ENIWETOK.)

**1957** **The Sellafield (then named Windscale) nuclear accident** occurred on October 7–12, 1957. A fire at this major British plutonium plant, in the reactor core of Pile No. 1, released large amounts of radioactive iodine and polonium, contaminating large areas and causing many later deaths. The accident was kept secret by the British government for decades. (See also SELLAFIELD.)

**1957** **The Chelyabinsk disaster** resulted from a huge nuclear waste explosion at this Soviet nuclear complex in the Urals, near Kyshtym, which contaminated hundreds of square miles, and caused thousands of casualties. It was kept secret by the Soviet government, revealed by Zhores Medvedev in 1976, and admitted only in 1988. (See also CHELYABINSK.)

**1960** **French nuclear testing began** at Reggane, in thenFrench Algeria, on February 13, 1960.

**1961** **In an Idaho Falls, Idaho, reactor explosion,** a steam explosion in the overheated core of a nuclear reactor killed three atomic plant workers on January 3, 1961.

**1964** **Chinese nuclear testing began** at a test site in the Lop Nor desert, in western Xinjiang province, on October 16, 1964. The first Chinese hydrogen bomb was exploded in the Lop Nor, in 1967.

**1966** **French nuclear tests began at Moruroa,** the French South Pacific nuclear test site, in French Polynesia; from 1966 to 1974, 40 to 45 atmospheric tests, many of them highly contaminating and all of them highly controversial, were carried out at Moruroa and nearby Fangataufa. (See also MORUROA.)

**1966** **The Fermi reactor partial meltdown occurred** in a nuclear breeder reactor at the Enrico Fermi nuclear plant, located only 30 miles southwest of Detroit, on Lake Michigan, on October 5, 1966; it was a near-disaster that might have contaminated much of the Detroit area.

**1979  At the Three Mile Island nuclear plant,** 10 miles from the Pennsylvania state capitol at Harrisburg, the March 28, 1979, nuclear fuel and partial core meltdown came very close to becoming the kind of nuclear disaster that struck at Chernobyl in 1986. (See also THREE MILE ISLAND.)

**1985  *Rainbow Warrior,*** the Greenpeace ship, was sunk by French agents in the harbor of Auckland, New Zealand, in July 1985, while preparing to disrupt scheduled French South Pacific nuclear tests; the sinking triggered a major international incident between New Zealand and France. (See also RAINBOW WARRIOR.)

**1986  The Chernobyl meltdown took place** at the Chernobyl nuclear power station, on the Priapat River north of Kiev in the Ukraine, on April 26, 1986. A powerful steam explosion, core fire, and huge hydrogen explosion contaminated much of the eastern Soviet Union and Europe. Hundreds died immediately or soon after the blast, thousands of longer-term casualties resulted, and hundreds of square miles were greatly contaminated. (See also CHERNOBYL MELTDOWN.)

(See also NUCLEAR WEAPONS ESTABLISHMENTS, U.S.)

---

**Nuclear Regulatory Commission (NRC or USNRC)** (Washington, DC 20555; 301-492-7000; Kenneth M. Carr, Chairman), a U.S. federal agency created under the 1947 Energy Reorganization Act; it took over the regulatory functions of the former Atomic Energy Commission (AEC), while the AEC's other functions were transferred to the Energy Research and Development Administration (ERDA) of the DEPARTMENT OF ENERGY. The NRC is responsible for establishing regulations, standards, and guidelines governing the various licensed uses of nuclear facilities and materials; reviewing and licensing construction and operation of nuclear facilities, as well as possession and use of nuclear materials, as for medical, industrial, educational, research, and other purposes; inspection, investigation, and enforcement of agency regulations and other requirements; carrying out "confirmatory research programs in the areas of safety, safeguards and environmental assessment," and licensing export and import of nuclear facilities, equipment, and materials. These functions are carried out under three main operations offices—Nuclear Reaction Regulation; Nuclear Material Safety and Safeguards (NMSS); and Nuclear Regulatory Research—along with other advisory offices and committees. It shares responsibility with the Department of

Transportation (DOT) for shipping of radioactive materials, with the DOT focusing on packages containing small amounts of radioactivity, called Type A packages, as well as carriers and conditions of transport, while the NRC regulates shipping containers for large amounts of radioactivity, so-called Type B packages. The NRC publishes various materials, including fact sheets such as "The Nuclear Regulatory Commission," "Nuclear Material Safety and Safeguards," and "Research Programs at the Nuclear Regulatory Commission;" brochures such as "Below Regulatory Concern;" and numerous technical reports.

**nuclear testing,** the experimental explosion of NUCLEAR WEAPONS, the source of a great many extraordinarily lethal effects, with deaths and illnesses resulting, sometimes for no better reason than wilful ignorance or concern over adverse "public relations," a mounting to casual mass murder. A worldwide reaction against the radioactive FALLOUT caused by air and water NUCLEAR WEAPONS tests brought about the 1963 Soviet-American-British Nuclear Test Ban Treaty, which banned atmospheric, underwater, or outer space testing by those countries. But before that happened a great deal of damage had been done, as at the NEVADA TEST SITE, where warnings and evacuations, rather than the reassurances that were given, could have saved hundreds and perhaps thousands of lives. Similarly, the hydrogen bomb tests at Bikini (see BIKINI AND ENIWETOK) caused damaging fallout on islands hundreds of miles away. Thousands of equally unnecessary deaths and illnesses were caused by the nuclear tests of several other nations, as by Soviet tests in Siberia, Chinese tests in western China's Lop Nor desert; British tests at Australia's MARALINGA test range; and the extremely dirty—that is, fallout-producing—French tests at MORUROA in French Polynesia, which like the Chinese tests continued long after other nations agreed to stop such tests. Underground nuclear weapons testing by many nations continues, with significant damage to surrounding environments. (See also NUCLEAR ENERGY; NUCLEAR WEAPONS; NUCLEAR WEAPONS ESTABLISHMENTS, U.S.; RADIATION; also NUCLEAR ISSUES INFORMATION AND ACTION GUIDE on page 215; MAJOR NUCLEAR DISASTERS AND INCIDENTS on page 212.)

**nuclear weapons,** the considerable range of weapons developed for the delivery of nuclear explosive devices, beginning with the nuclear fission atomic bombs dropped on HIROSHIMA AND NAGASAKI, on August 6 and 9, 1945, which together immediately killed 110,000 to 150,000 people, and within a few years killed 125,000 to 225,000 more due to RADIATION, cancer, and other bombing-related injuries. Victims and their children are still dying today from the effects of the bombs.

In 1952, during the early years of the U.S.–U.S.S.R. Cold War, the United States developed the hydrogen bomb, which used an atomic bomb to trigger a much more powerful nuclear fusion device. Both nations, and several other nations that joined the international nuclear arms race, including Britain, France, China, India, South Africa, and Israel, then proceeded to develop a considerable variety of missiles and battlefield weapons capable of delivering nuclear warheads. For almost four decades, the governments and military forces of the United States and Soviet Union stood ready to destroy their own peoples, all of humanity, and many other life-forms, at a few minutes notice. With the end of the Cold War in the late 1980s, the immediate danger of worldwide destructions receded; and the United States and the Soviet Union negotiated several key agreements, including the critically important 1987 Intermediate Nuclear Forces (INF) Treaty, in which for the first time the two superpowers agreed to destroy a whole class of nuclear weapons. But even after this and several other agreements aimed at cutting conventional and nuclear weapons, both the United States and the former Soviet Union still possess far more than enough weapons and delivery systems to destroy human society and much of life on earth.

Nuclear weapons production has also been enormously and often unnecessarily destructive, creating massive quantities of deadly RADIOACTIVE WASTE, as at CHELYABINSK and other Soviet and Eastern European locations; at Hanford, Sellafield, Rocky Flats, Fernald, and a dozen other Western nuclear arms plant locations; and at French, Chinese, and other nuclear arms production sites. (See NUCLEAR ISSUES INFORMATION AND ACTION GUIDE on page 215; MAJOR NUCLEAR DISASTERS AND INCIDENTS on page 212 also NUCLEAR ENERGY; NUCLEAR TESTING; NUCLEAR WEAPONS ESTABLISHMENT, U.S.; RADIATION.)

**nuclear weapons establishment, U.S.,** a nationwide group of United States NUCLEAR WEAPONS plants, test sites, RADIOACTIVE WASTE storage facilities, dump sites, and laboratories, many of them enormous sources of environmental contamination. By the early 1990s, at least 122 contaminated sites had been identified by the federal government, including 17 major sites in 12 states; more will follow, as the full story of the nuclear weapons complex unfolds. Federal cleanup cost estimates have run as high as $200 billion, although many observers feel that total costs will prove much higher. Beyond the cost of cleanup, a good deal of the damage done may very well prove irreversible, in that some areas will remain contaminated for thousands of years.

In the late 1980s, as court cases and the Freedom of Information Act forced open previously closed federal records, and as new federal policies were initiated, it became quite clear that many federal officials and companies operating weapons plants on government contracts had condoned and participated in widespread cover-ups of accidents and systematic, secret pollution of areas near nuclear weapons plants and test sites. In a landmark 1985 legal action, 14,000 residents of the area around the Fernald, Ohio nuclear weapons plant sued the National Lead Company, former operator of the plant, for damages resulting from the secret dumping into their water and release into their air of radioactive uranium dust. The case was settled by the federal DEPARTMENT OF ENERGY in 1989 for up to $78 million after new government policies went into effect.

State and federal agencies also began to press enforcement actions in the late 1980s and early 1990s, as in the ENVIRONMENTAL PROTECTION AGENCY (EPA) fining of the Energy Department for failure to live up to Fernald cleanup agreements and FBI and EPA raids on the Rocky Flats, Colorado, nuclear plant in search of criminal violations. State and private legal actions were also pressed in many other areas, including Washington State, Nevada, Ohio, and Colorado. Yet the cleanup job proceeded slowly and very expensively, with the true nature of the federal government commitment always in question, as when the Energy Department in February 1991 unilaterally announced that construction of a plant to process hazardous, possibly explosive RADIOACTIVE WASTES stored in leaking tanks at the Hanford nuclear plant would be postponed for one to two years.

Some of the U.S. nuclear weapons sites that have attracted greatest attention are:

• **Hanford Nuclear Reservation,** a 575-square-mile weapons complex on the Columbia River, near Richland, Washington, which from 1944 supplied plutonium for atomic bombs. From late 1944 through 1955, plant operators secretly released an estimated 530,000 curies of radioactive iodine, the equivalent of a major nuclear accident, into the air above the plant, while from 1944 through at least the late 1960s releasing millions of curies of radioactive materials directly into the Columbia River. In the 1950s, millions of gallons of radioactive materials were also dumped directly into the ground. The net effect was secretly to poison the air, water, and FOOD CHAIN of the area. At the same time, millions of gallons of highly concentrated radioactive waste were stored in tanks, in increasingly unstable condition and by the early 1990s posing an imminent threat of a chemical explosion that might cause a major nuclear catastrophe, similar to the 1957–58 Soviet CHELYABINSK (Kyshtym) nuclear waste explosion, which contaminated at least 400 square miles in the Ural mountains, with hundreds and perhaps thousands of casualties.

## Nuclear Issues Information and Action Guide

**For more information and action on nuclear issues:**

AMERICAN PLANNING ASSOCIATION **(APA),** (202-872-0611). Publishes *Community Emergency Response to Nuclear Power Plant Accidents* (1988).

ECOLOGICAL SOCIETY OF AMERICA **(ESA),** (301-530-7005).

ENVIRONMENTAL AND ENERGY STUDY INSTITUTE **(EESI),** (202-628-1400). Publishes policy reports such as *Review of "Advanced" Nuclear Reactor Designs* (1990).

FRIENDS OF THE EARTH **(FOE),** (202-544-2600).

GREENPEACE, (202-462-1177). Has a *Nuclear Campaign* and a *Below Regulatory Concern (BRC) Project.* Publishes reports such as *Creating a Nuclear Free Zone That Is True to Its Name: The Nuclear Free Zone Concept and a Model Treaty* (1989), *French Nuclear Testing 1960–88* (1989), the *Greenpeace Book of the Nuclear Age* (John May, 1989) action factsheets such as *Disarmament, Campaign for a Comprehensive Test Ban Treaty, Campaign to End Nuclear Weapons Production, Nuclear Power, French Nuclear Testing in Polynesia,* and *Nuclear Power and Foreign Oil;* and videocassettes.

**Investor Responsibility Research Center (IRRC),** (202-234-7500).

**Natural Resources Defense Council (NRDC),** (212-727-2700). Publishes *Phasing Out Nuclear Weapons: A Report to the President and Congress From the Belmont Conference on Nuclear Test Ban Policy* (1989) and *The Nuclear Weapons Databook* in several volumes (1987–89).

PACIFIC INSTITUTE FOR STUDIES IN DEVELOPMENT, ENVIRONMENT, AND SECURITY, (415-843-9550).

RESOURCES FOR THE FUTURE **(RFF),** (202-328-5000).

SIERRA CLUB, (415-776-2211 or 202-547-1141; legislative hotline, 202-547-5550). Publishes *High-Level Nuclear Waste Policy, Low-Level Nuclear Waste Policy, Nuclear Power Policy, Decommissioning Nuclear Reactors Policy, Nuclear Exports Policy,* and *Nuclear Weapons Policy.*

UNION OF CONCERNED SCIENTISTS **(UCS),** (617-547-5552 or 202-332-0900). Has the *Professionals' Coalition for Nuclear Arms Control.* Publishes the quarterly *Nucleus;* books and reports such as *The Verification Revolution* (Allan Krass, 1989); briefing papers such as *Antisatellite Weapons, Chemical Weapons and Arms Control, Dismantling Nuclear Weapons Under the INF Treaty, Nuclear Proliferation, Nuclear Reaction Containment: Sieve or Shield?* and *The Tritium Problem;* and the brochure *Nuclear Power: Past and Future.*

**U.S. PUBLIC INTEREST RESEARCH GROUP (PIRG),** (202-546-9707). Publishes *Below Regulatory Concern, But Radioactive and Carcinogenic* (1990).

WORLDWATCH INSTITUTE, (202-452-1999).

**Other references:**

*The Nuclear Lion: What Every Citizen Should Know About Nuclear Power and Nuclear War.* J. Jagger. Plenum, 1991. *Nuclear Power Reactors in the World.* International Atomic Energy Agency (IAEA; Vienna), 1989. After Three Mile Island and Chernobyl. G.M. Ballard. Elsevier, 1988.

---

- **Fernald nuclear plant,** on the Great Miami River, 18 miles northwest of Cincinnati, Ohio, at which plant operators had for decades been secretly releasing radioactive uranium waste into the water, air, and ground, while at the same time storing highly concentrated liquid radioactive waste in leaking concrete tanks.
- **Rocky Flats nuclear plant,** near Denver, Colorado, a plutonium-producing plant closed in 1988 because of multiple safety concerns and operating problems, as well as severe radioactive waste disposal problems. The plant's history included loss of deadly plutonium into the air through fires, leakage of plutonium into the plant's air ducts, and leakage into the environment of stored radioactive wastes, all shrouded by "national security" secrecy for decades.
- **Savannah River nuclear plant,** near Aiken, South Carolina, a large tritium and plutonium-producing plant with a three-decades-long history of concealed nuclear accidents, including potentially catastrophic core and fuel-rod melt-

downs, and contamination of the plant and surrounding area, as well as secret radioactive waste discharges into the environment.
- **Nevada Test Site,** a desert area approximately 120 kilometers (75 miles) northwest of Las Vegas, at which over 100 atmospheric nuclear device tests were conducted from 1951 to 58, generating radioactive FALLOUT that contaminated areas up to 200 miles east and 100 miles north of the test range, the "downwind" areas, with a population of approximately 100,000. Underground tests continued at the site after 1958, some of which were "vented" into the air, creating radioactive clouds that contaminated smaller areas. At no time was that population or any portion of the area evacuated or warned of the very serious hazards associated with the tests. One especially well known group of Nevada Test Site victims were some of the cast and crew of the 1956 film *The Conqueror,* filmed in 1954 near St. George, Utah, in the contaminated downwind area. As unusually high incidences of cancer and leukemia

developed among those living in the areas contaminated by the tests, a series of legal actions for compensation developed, but ultimately, in 1988, the U.S. Supreme Court ruled that the federal government was immune to suits resulting from the tests.

In the decades since the early atomic weapons tests of the 1940s, many groups of radiation-damaged people have formed organizations to pursue their interests, among them ''Downwinders'' from near the Nevada Atomic Test Site, the 14,000 at Fernald, tens of thousands more at Hanford and other nuclear sites, and several veterans' organizations. (See also NUCLEAR ISSUES INFORMATION AND ACTION GUIDE on page 215; also MAJOR NUCLEAR DISASTERS AND INCIDENTS page 212; also NUCLEAR WEAPONS; RADIATION; RADIOACTIVE WASTE.)

**nuclear winter,** the theory that a massive worldwide CLIMATE CHANGE, involving worldwide cooling, widespread crop failures, and mass life-form EXTINCTIONS could result from full-scale nuclear warfare between any powers able to deliver large numbers of intercontinental nuclear missiles. The theory suggests that the massive set of explosions generated by full-scale nuclear war would lift large quantities of matter pulverized into very small particles into the atmosphere, which would rise high into the stratosphere, spread worldwide, and stay up for a month or more, perhaps as long as several years. The particles, blocking the sun and subjecting the planet to a worldwide radioactive FALLOUT, might generate a situation in which plants at the base of the FOOD CHAIN might not be able to get life-giving sunlight, thereby threatening the entire chain of life, while fallout might destroy much of life in the northern hemisphere.

The highly influential theory was in a general sense born out of Luis and Walter Alverez's 1980 theory of mass extinctions following a meteorite crash into earth 65 million years ago. Such scientists as Paul J. Crutzen, Carl Sagan, and Richard Turco developed the nuclear winter theory and models in the early 1980s. Turco, Sagan, James Pollard, and Owen Toon fully introduced the theory in a 1983 article in *Science* magazine, and an interdisciplinary group which included Sagan published the centrally important paper *Long-Term Biological Consequences of Nuclear War* in 1984. Subsequently, Sagan became the best known exponent of the theory.

In January 1991, before the massive oil well fires were set by the Iraqi army during the Persian Gulf War, Crutzen warned that such fires might be set, and might result in a smaller version of the nuclear winter. Sagan, Turco, and others later joined him, suggesting that the burning oil smoke could superheat surrounding air and lift itself high into the atmosphere. By the summer of 1991, that had not happened; the fires were causing massive regional human and environmental damage, but had not developed the kind of high plume needed to spread the pall worldwide. (See PERSIAN GULF WAR ENVIRONMENTAL DISASTER; also NUCLEAR ISSUES INFORMATION AND ACTION GUIDE on page 215.)

**nutrient cycles,** an alternative name for BIOGEOCHEMICAL CYCLES.

**O**

**Ocean Alliance** (Fort Mason, Building E, San Francisco, CA 94123; 415-441-5970), a California-based organization formed by the merger of the *Whale Center* with the San Francisco chapter of the *Oceanic Society* (see FRIENDS OF THE EARTH), their mission being "the protection of all marine mammals and their ocean habitat." The Ocean Alliance seeks stronger protection from laws such as the ENDANGERED SPECIES ACT, the MARINE MAMMAL PROTECTION ACT, and the Marine Sanctuary Program; a ban on all commercial whaling, use of DRIFTNETS, and OFFSHORE DRILLING; lessening of OCEAN pollution; and creation of new national marine sanctuaries. It operates an *Adopt-A-Whale* program for the California gray WHALES, under which a person adopts a gray whale and names it, receiving an adoption certificate, a photograph, biographical information, and quarterly updates on the MIGRATION, feeding, and breeding of gray whales. The Ocean Alliance also operates the WhaleBus, a "classroom on wheels" that visits school, libraries, and community groups in northern California.

**oceans,** the bodies of water that contain most of the earth's water and serve as home to the unique ECOSYSTEMS that live in the salty water, as well as playing major roles in the regulation of the earth's climate and in the great BIOGEOCHEMICAL CYCLES by which basic elements are recycled for use and reuse. Oceans are not uniform or static, but have layers that vary widely in temperatures, salt content, and productivity; great swirling currents, such as the Gulf Stream, that have their own distinguishing characteristics; and huge connected salt-water areas such as the MEDITERRANEAN SEA and Gulf of Mexico. Included in marine ecosystems are the COASTS, with their estuaries, bays, tidepools, seaweed communities, and MANGROVES. The energy in the ocean's movements can sometimes be harnessed for human use (see WAVE POWER).

The seawater characteristic of ocean ecosystems has a relatively high concentration of dissolved salts; nearly 78 percent (by weight) is sodium chloride, with much smaller amounts of compounds such as magnesium chloride, magnesium sulfate, calcium sulfate, potassium sulfate, magnesium bromide, calcium carbonate, and many other substances. (For comparison with freshwater, see WATER RESOURCES or DESALINIZATION.) Unlike freshwater contaminated by ACID RAIN, ocean water is slightly alkaline (see PH), primarily because of the large amounts of dissolved carbon-containing compounds called *carbonates*. Most of the elements required for life are found in abundance in ocean waters, though some elements—notably phosphorus, nitrogen, and silicon, but occasionally also iron and MANGANESE—are often in short supply and can limit growth. The concentrations of the various elements vary widely, however, as the ocean is continuously being churned by entry of water from RIVERS, by melting of ice, by upwelling of deeper water, and by heating and evaporation of the surface sea waters. The Pacific, for example, has nearly twice the amount of nitrogen and phosphorus as the North Atlantic, at comparable depths, with the South Atlantic and Antarctic oceans falling in between, and the Mediterranean having the lowest levels of any major body of seawater.

Like land ecosystems, marine ecosystems are supported

## Oceans Information and Action Guide

**For more information and action on oceans:**
AMERICAN OCEANS CAMPAIGN (AOC), (213-576-6162). Runs *American Oceans Conservation Committee (AOCC)*. Publishes the newsletter *Making Waves*.
CENTER FOR MARINE CONSERVATION (CMC), (202-429-5609). Has *Marine Habitat Program*. Publishes the quarterly newsletters *Marine Conservation News* and *Sanctuary Currents*; *A Nation of Oceans* (stressing marine sanctuaries), and *The Ocean: Consider the Connections* for children grade K-8.
CLEAN OCEAN ACTION (COA), (201-872-0111). Publishes *Clean Ocean Advocate*.
FRIENDS OF THE EARTH (FOE), (202-544-2600). Publishes *Ocean Watch*.
GREENPEACE, (202-462-1177). Greenpeace Action runs the *Ocean Ecology Campaign* and the *Nuclear Campaign*, to rid the sea of nuclear weapons and nuclear reactors. Publishes videocassettes such as *Troubled Waters* (1989) on nuclear weapons at sea.
INTERNATIONAL COUNCIL FOR THE EXPLORATION OF THE SEA OR CONSEIL INTERNATIONAL POUR L 'EXPLORATION DE LA MER (ICES or CIEM) (Copenhagen K, Denmark: 33 15 42 25). Maintains oceangraphic data bank; publishes numerous scientific reports and papers.
OCEAN ALLIANCE, (415-441-5970).
**Office for Ocean Affairs and the Law of the Sea (OALOS)** (212-963-6424). Maintains computerized Law of the Sea Information System (LOSIS) and the country marine profile data base (MARPRO). Publishes the *Law of the Sea Bulletin*, an annual review of ocean affairs (law and policy), and various analytical studies and technical reports such as *The Law of the Sea: A Select Bibliography* (1989) and *The Law of the Sea: Current Developments in State Practice* (1989). (See CONVENTION ON THE LAW OF THE SEA.)
SCRIPPS INSTITUTION OF OCEANOGRAPHY, (619-534-3624). Operates *Center for Coastal Studies (CCS)*.
SEA WORLD RESEARCH INSTITUTE (SWRI), (619-226-3870).
UNITED NATIONS ENVIRONMENT PROGRAMME (UNEP), (212-963-8138 or -8098). Publishes *The State of the Marine Environment* (1990).
WOODS HOLE OCEANOGRAPHIC INSTITUTION (WHOI), (508-548-1400; Associates Office 508-457-2000, ext. 2392). Operates the *Marine Policy Center (MPC)*, the *Center of Marine Exploration (CME)*, and the *Coastal Research Center (CRC)*.

---

by energy from the sun: the heat that warms the ocean and the light that fuels the life-sustaining process of PHOTOSYNTHESIS. Apart from the relatively small amount reflected, most of the sun's RADIATION is absorbed by the upper layer of the ocean, the site of the ocean's main biological productivity. The primary producers are microscopic plant forms of PLANKTON called *phytoplankton,* including some algae and fungi, which during photosynthesis combine various elements found in seawater (including dissolved CARBON DIOXIDE) to "fix" energy, and are then eaten by equally tiny animal plankton called *zooplankton*. These form the basis of the complex oceanic FOOD CHAIN that ultimately feeds large fish and marine mammals—and often humans. At every step, bits of dead or excreted matter shower down to the depths of the ocean, supplying nutrients to living beings in the cooler, less productive lower depths. After its last use, the waste matter begins to decompose, being attacked by bacteria; this process takes oxygen from the water and releases carbon dioxide, later used in further production. Where oxygen is depleted, anaerobic bacteria undertake decomposition, releasing hydrogen sulfide (and METHANE) into the water. Either way, decomposition returns to the water many of the elements previously taken up by the phytoplankton. Some of these are returned to the surface of the ocean by upwelling, notably near the equator, or transported far distances by major currents, but often they remain concentrated near the ocean floor.

In the temperate and high latitudes's productivity generally varies seasonally, with the major burst of growth in the spring; a leveling out in the summer, often due to lack of key nutrients; a lesser peak in the autumn; then decline during the winter, with lack of light, partly because of increased turbulence in the water. In tropical and subtropical latitudes, productivity is at a more level and often somewhat lower rate, except where nutrients from upwelling of waters bring vital elements to the surface and allow more productivity, as around the equator and on the western coasts of continents. The most productive areas are the shallower coastal waters, where sunlight reaches the ocean floor, and rooted plants and other kinds of algae join phytoplankton as primary producers. This *neritic zone,* extending from the COAST to the edge of the continental shelf, is enriched by nutrients such as PHOSPHATES and NITRATES flowing in from nearby rivers, and welling up from the sea floor. This also applies to estuaries, coastal waters subject to both river and tidal currents, and to coastal marshes, including mangroves.

The largest consumers in ocean food chains are the actively swimming animals, such as fish, crabs, and squid, and marine mammals such as WHALES, DOLPHINS, and POR-POISES; these are called *nekton organisms*. The other main group of consumers are the *benthos organisms,* primarily mud-dwelling animals on the sea floor, such as sponges, shrimp, and sea urchins in the deep sea. In coastal areas, called *littoral zones,* these benthos beings include clams, oysters, snails, mussels, and barnacles, with CORAL REEFS in warmer waters. Because of wide variations in light, temperature, salinity, nutrients, and the sea floor itself, littoral creatures often form many small, relatively independent, and often rather vulnerable ecosystems. By contrast, conditions at the deep-sea floor have relatively constant salinity and temperature, and little light, mostly in the blue-violet range; the number and variety of organisms decreases with the depth of the water.

The oceans are vast, and the popular view has long held that nothing humans did would be more than a "drop in the ocean," so many people have regarded the oceans as a giant WASTE DISPOSAL site. But human activities now have such far-reaching effects that the oceans and their enormous productivity may also be affected. PESTICIDES, TOXIC CHEMICALS, HEAVY METALS, OIL, and other HAZARD-OUS WASTE, including RADIOACTIVE WASTE, increasingly invade the oceans—which are, after all, the ultimate repository of all the solid material produced by EROSION or otherwise entering the freshwater system (see SEDIMENTA-TION). Many of these are deliberately dumped, along with large amounts of dredged sediment and normal waste. AIR POLLUTION also contributes to the ocean's load of wastes, both from air currents moving off land and also from IN-CINERATION of waste at sea. Coastal areas, sites of most of the world's fisheries, are the most affected, receiving large amounts of hazardous pollutants from land as well as excess nutrients. This can lead to overgrowth and depletion of oxygen in the water, a process called EUTROPHICA-TION; in coastal waters this sometimes results in a seasonal "red tide" or "brown tide," a heavy growth of algae, certainly unsightly but also often toxic, to marine life as well as humans. The ocean depths still remain relatively unaffected, though traces of toxic chemicals are found even in the deepest waters. But as scientists have come to understand the violent turbulence that often affects ocean floors, fears have increased about the long-term dangers posed by the drums of toxic and radioactive waste now lying at the bottom of the sea. Such concerns as these have prompted international agreements to limit POLLUTION of the ocean, notably the CONVENTION ON THE PREVENTION OF MARINE POLLUTION BY DUMPING OF WASTE AND OTHER MATTER (LONDON DUMPING CONVENTION or LDC).

Also of enormous concern is the effect on the oceans, and therefore on the earth's climate, of possible GLOBAL WARMING. Even without that, periodic shifts in the ocean winds, connected in complicated and as-yet not fully understood ways with ocean temperature and currents, produce massive changes such as the El Niños of the southern Pacific, changes in winds and currents; these cause extremely disruptive shifts in the climate over land, producing rain in normal deserts and drought where rain usually predominates. What further effects might result from significant climate changes are unknown, but potentially disastrous. Changes in the temperature of the ocean might cause large-scale die-offs of plants, fish, and marine mammals that live only in narrow temperature ranges. Ocean currents might also be shifted, and with them the fisheries that supply approximately 14 percent of the world's animal protein, in some areas (such as Japan) nearly 60 percent. Warming of the sea water would cause oceans to expand and the sea level to rise; levels are rising in any case, due to long-term melting of polar and glacier ice (see SEA LEVEL RISE). Breeding grounds in estuaries could also be affected or destroyed by sea level rise or an associated change in the salinity of the water.

As international bodies of water, the world's oceans are the subjects of many agreements; a key multinational agreement is the CONVENTION ON THE LAW OF THE SEA, OR LAW OF THE SEA CONVENTION (LOSC). Most maritime nations have declared EXCLUSIVE ECONOMIC ZONES (EEZs), extending about 200 miles from their borders; except as limited by other agreements, these are reserved for their exclusive control and exploitation of resources, such as OFFSHORE DRILLING, also an issue of great concern to environmentalists. Many international agreements are directed at conserving the resources of the ocean, especially regarding FISHING and whaling (see WHALES), and at limiting or ending practices that result in the accidental killing of marine beings, as with DRIFTNETS or the dumping of PLASTIC debris. (See OCEANS INFORMATION AND ACTION GUIDE on page 218; also COASTS; WATER POLLUTION; WAVE POWER; and specific conventions noted above.)

**offshore drilling,** the extraction of resources from the seabed, generally OIL and NATURAL GAS. From its first use in the 1930s in the Gulf of Mexico, offshore drilling has been focused primarily in relatively shallow waters near the COAST on the outer continental shelf but in increasingly deeper waters as technology has advanced. From stable (though movable and often floating) drilling platforms, exploratory holes are drilled into the seabed. Unlike on land, where a test hole may be converted immediately into a producing hole, exploratory wells offshore are plugged, and they are tapped for full-scale use only after a permanent production platform is in place. Oil and natural gas are generally shipped by pipeline to refineries.

Some of the world's most notable oil spills have occurred from offshore drilling (see MAJOR OIL SPILLS AND INCIDENTS, right), including the 1969 SANTA BARBARA OIL WELL BLOWOUT, which fouled 20 miles of California coastline, and the 1979 IXTOC I OIL WELL BLOWOUT, the world's largest oil spill so far, which spewed 600,000 tons of oil into the Gulf of Mexico. It was the Santa Barbara blowout in particular that spurred widespread concern about offshore drilling—and criticism of the federal government's policy of leasing offshore lands for oil and natural gas exploration. Except for the risk of explosion, natural gas does not pose the same environmental risks, since it evaporates into the atmosphere.

Beyond such massive disasters, however, are day-to-day polluting activities. On most drilling platforms, all the mud and pulverized rock from the drilling; waste generated from platform life, including untreated human waste; and oils and other chemicals used at any stage of the process, including motor oils and lubricants, are simply dumped unceremoniously into the water. U.S. federal law requires sewage to be treated before being released into the water. In a few rare situations, notably in Mobile Bay in response to Alabama's ''zero-discharge'' rules, drilling platforms collect all waste and ship it on barges to land-based treatment plants. But in general the day-to-day POLLUTION continues, with the threat of massive spills, along coasts with their extremely sensitive life.

Environmentalists who seek to ban further exploration and exploitation of oil and gas resources through offshore drilling are often joined in their call by the people who live along the coasts, and especially by those communities whose livelihood depends on the health of the coastal waters, as for recreation and FISHING. Many also seek the establishment of marine sanctuaries, where offshore drilling and other DEVELOPMENT would be permanently banned. In the United States, leasing of federally controlled waters—beginning three miles from shore in most states—is handled by the Department of the Interior, but environmental regulation is primarily under the ENVIRONMENTAL PROTECTION AGENCY. The EPA considered pollution from offshore drilling as one of the main environmental problems in the 1987 EPA report UNFINISHED BUSINESS: A COMPARATIVE ASSESSMENT OF ENVIRONMENTAL PROBLEMS. Partly in response to public pressure, the Bush administration in 1990 backed away from the previous Reagan policy of wholesale leasing. (See also OIL; NATURAL GAS; OCEANS; COASTS; also OIL AND OIL POLLUTION INFORMATION AND ACTION GUIDE on page 222.)

## Major Oil Spills and Incidents

**1967** ***Torrey Canyon*** ran aground off Cornwall, England, on March 18, 1967, ultimately spilling most of its 118,000-ton crude-oil cargo and causing a massive environmental disaster that fouled 175 miles of British and French coastline. (See also TORREY CANYON OIL SPILL.)

**1969** Offshore oil well blowout off Santa Barbara, California, on February 8, 1968, leaked an estimated 800,000 gallons (approximately 2,700 tons) of crude oil that fouled 20 miles of California coastline; the resulting environmental disaster became a major incident in the long, continuing controversy over offshore drilling. (See also SANTA BARBARA OIL WELL BLOWOUT.)

**1976** ***Argo Merchant*** ran aground off Nantucket on December 15, 1976, spilling 7.5 million gallons (approximately 25,000 tons) of fuel oil that greatly damaged nearby New England fishing grounds. (See also ARGO MERCHANT OIL SPILL.)

**1976** ***Hawaiian Patriot*** leaked oil and caught fire in the mid-Pacific on February 24, 1977, spilling 30 million gallons (approximately 100,000 tons). (See also HAWAIIAN PATRIOT OIL SPILL.)

**1976** ***Urquiola*** ran aground off La Coruña, Spain, on May 12, 1976, spilling 60–70,000 tons of crude oil and fouling 50–60 miles of the Spanish coastline. (See also URQUIOLA OIL SPILL.)

**1977** **Bravo 14 well in the Ekofisk field** blew out on April 22, 1977, spilling 8 million gallons (approximately 27,000 tons) of crude oil into the North Sea. (See also EKOFISK OIL WELL BLOWOUT.)

**1978** ***Amoco Cadiz*** ran aground at Portsall, Brittany, on March 17, 1978, spilling its whole cargo of 226,000 tons of crude oil, and causing a massive ecological disaster that fouled 200 miles of the French coast. (See also AMOCO CADIZ OIL SPILL.)

**1979** ***Atlantic Empress*** and ***Aegean Captain*** collided off Tobago on July 19, 1979, killing 27 and spilling 370,000 tons of oil into the Caribbean; it was the largest shipping spill on record. (See also ATLANTIC EMPRESS-AEGEAN CAPTAIN OIL SPILL.)

**1979** ***Ixtoc 1*** blew out on June 3, 1979, beginning a 600,000 ton oil spill into the Mexican Bay of Campeche in the Gulf of Mexico; it is the largest oil spill on record. (See also IXTOC I WELL BLOWOUT.)

**1983** ***Castillo de Bellver*** caught fire off Cape Town on August 6, 1983, and then broke up, killing three people and spilling 250,000 tons of crude oil. (See also CASTILLO DE BELLVER FIRE.)

**1983** **Well blowout during the Iran-Iraq War** in February 1983 and subsequent Iraqi attacks generated a massive oil spill from the Nowruz field in the Persian Gulf, estimated at 600,000 tons, with an accompanying ecological disaster. (See also IRAN-IRAQ WAR OIL SPILL.)

**1984** *Alvenus* ran aground at Lake Charles, Louisiana, on July 30, 1984, spilling an estimated 1.8 million gallons (approximately 6,000 tons) of heavy crude oil into the Gulf of Mexico. (See also *ALVENUS* OIL SPILL.)

**1985** *Grand Eagle* ran aground in the Delaware River on September 28, 1985, spilling an estimated 450,000 gallons (approximately 1,500 tons) of crude oil into the river. (See also *GRAND EAGLE* OIL SPILL.)

**1986** *Amazon Venture* ran aground on the Savannah River near Savannah, Georgia, on December 4, 1986, spilling an estimated 500,000 gallons (approximately 1,700 tons) of fuel oil. (See also SAVANNAH RIVER OIL SPILL.)

**1988** *Ashland Oil* storage tank collapse on January 2, 1988, spilled 700,000–750,000 gallons (approximately 2,400–2,500 tons) of diesel fuel into the Monongahela River near Pittsburgh, causing a water supply in many cities and towns downriver. (See also ASHLAND OIL SPILL.)

**1988** *Piper Alpha* oil rig exploded and caught fire in the North Sea on July 6, 1988, killing 167 people. (See also *PIPER ALPHA* EXPLOSION.)

**1989** *Presidente Rivera* grounded in the Delaware River on June 24, 1989, spilling an estimated 300,000 gallons (approximately 1,000 tons) of heating oil into the river. (See also DELAWARE RIVER OIL SPILL.)

**1989** *Exxon Valdez* grounded in Prince William Sound, off Valdez, Alaska, on March 24, 1989, spilling over 11 million gallons (approximately 37,000 tons) of oil into the sound; it was the worst such disaster in American history. (See also *EXXON VALDEZ* disaster.)

**1989** *Houston Ship Channel* collision between the *Rachel B* and a barge on June 23, 1989, spilled an estimated 250,000 gallons (approximately 850 tons) of crude oil into the channel. (See also HOUSTON SHIP CHANNEL OIL SPILL.)

**1989** *Kharg 5* caught fire off the Canary Islands on December 19, 1989, spilling an estimated 19 million gallons of oil (approximately 65,000 tons). (See also *KHARG 5* OIL SPILL.)

**1989** *World Prodigy* grounded in Narragansett Bay off Newport, Rhode Island, on June 23, 1989, spilling an estimated 400,000 gallons (approximately 1,400 tons) of fuel oil. (See also NARRAGANSETT BAY OIL SPILL.)

**1990** *Shinoussa* collided with two barges in Galveston Bay on July 28, 1990, spilling an estimated 500,000 gallons (approximately 1,700 tons) of heavy crude oil. (See also GALVESTON BAY OIL SPILL.)

**1990** *American Trader* suffered a hull tear two miles off Huntington Beach, California, on February 7, 1990, spilling an estimated 400,000 gallons (approximately 1,400 tons) of oil. (See also HUNTINGTON BEACH OIL SPILL.)

**1990** *Mega Borg* exploded and caught fire in the Gulf of Mexico off Galveston on June 8, 1990, killing four people and spilling an estimated 4.3 million gallons (approximately 15,000 tons) of crude oil. (See also *MEGA BORG* OIL SPILL.)

**1990** *New York Harbor* suffered five oil spills, totaling over one million gallons (approximately 3,400 tons) during the first half of 1990, three of them major, and all occurring in the Arthur Kill and Kill Van Kull. (See also NEW YORK HARBOR OIL SPILLS.)

**1991** *Persian Gulf War environmental disaster* began on January 23, 1991, with the deliberate Iraqi oil spill at Sea Island Terminal, and ultimately included a massive oil spill, the setting of many hundreds of oil well fires, and a resulting set of massive ecological disasters. (See also PERSIAN GULF WAR ENVIRONMENTAL DISASTER.)

---

**oil (petroleum),** a naturally occurring type of FOSSIL FUEL; an oil composed mostly of HYDROCARBONS, but with varying amounts of oxygen, nitrogen, and sulfur compounds. The industrialized world's dependence on oil, and its contribution to AIR POLLUTION, the GREENHOUSE EFFECT, GLOBAL WARMING, WATER POLLUTION, TOXIC CHEMICALS, and other problem areas have made oil use a major concern for environmentalists.

Petroleum is believed to have been formed from organic matter, buried under sediment that gradually became rock, over millions of years reacting and changing under pressure. As the liquid oil formed, pressure forced it upward into porous rocks and naturally formed reservoirs, often in gaps formed when the earth's crust moved and was trapped in place by a cap or dome of impermeable rock. Generally NATURAL GAS, often found associated with petroleum, forms the top layer in the reservoir; below that is the oil, sometimes containing dissolved gases; and below that saltwater remnants of ancient seas, perhaps 10 to 50 percent of the reservoir. Some other oils—nonflowing, and not considered true petroleum—are found in oil-permeated shale and sandstone deposits called *tar sands*.

Crude oils, as they come from the ground, range in color from black, brown, or green to amber. They vary widely in other respects as well, in their specific gravity (weight per given volume), pour point (the lowest temperature at which they will pour), viscosity (rate of flow through a given size pipe), and content of salts, HEAVY METALS, and sulfur. Oils that are highly corrosive when heated, have a high sulfur content, and produce large amounts of hydrogen sulfide during processing are called *sour crude* and are said to need "sweetening"; these are

## Oil and Oil Pollution Information and Action Guide

For more information and action on oil and oil pollution:

AMERICAN OCEANS CAMPAIGN (AOC), (213-576-6162).

ARCTIC INSTITUTE OF NORTH AMERICA (AINA) of the University of Calgary, (403-220-7515).

ECOLOGICAL SOCIETY OF AMERICA (ESA), (301-503-7005).

ENVIRONMENTAL LAW INSTITUTE (ELI), (202-328-5150; publications office, 202-939-3844). Publishes *Oil Pollution Deskbook* (1991). (See ENVIRONMENTAL LAW.)

GREENPEACE, (202-462-1177). Greenpeace Action runs the *Ocean Ecology Campaign.*

International Transboundary Resources Center (Centro Internacional de Recursos Transfronterizos, or CIRT), (505-277-6424). Publishes model international agreement for co-operative U.S.–Mexican development of oil and gas resources.

IUCN—THE WORLD CONSERVATION UNION, (202-797-5454).

NATIONAL AUDUBON SOCIETY, (212-832-3200; *Audubon Action Line* 202-547-9017). Current policy projects include exploring impacts of oil and gas development on wildlife in Alaska and elsewhere.

NATIONAL PARKS AND CONSERVATION ASSOCIATION (NPCA), (202-944-8530). Supports use of royalites from offshore oil drilling to fund land aquisition but opposes mining and oil drilling proposals that threaten parks.

Natural Resources and Energy Division (NRED), United Nations, (212-963-6205).

NATIONAL WILDLIFE FEDERATION (NWF), (202-797-6800 or 800-245-5484). Publishes *The Arctic Refuge and Oil and Gas Development.*

Natural Resources Defense Council (NRDC), (212-727-2700). Publishes *Looking for Oil in All the Wrong Places: Facts About Oil, Natural Gas, and Efficiency Resources* (Robert Watson, 1991), *Tracking Arctic Oil: The Environmental Price of Drilling in the Arctic National Wildlife Refuge* (1991), *Amazon Crude* (Judy Kimerling, 1991), *Coastal Alert: Ecosystems, Energy, and Offshore Oil Drilling* (Dwight Holing, 1990), *Fact Sheet on Oil and Conservation Resources* (R. Watson, 1988), and *Oil in the Arctic: The Environmental Record of Oil Development on Alaska's North Slope* (L. Speer et al., 1988).

Ocean Alliance, (415-441-5970). Seeks to ban offshore oil drilling.

Renew America, (202-232-2252).

SIERRA CLUB (415-776-2211 or 202-547-1141; legislative hotline, 202-547-5550). Publishes *Onshore Oil and Gas Policy, What You Can Do to Help Protect Our Coasts from Offshore Oil Development,* and *Offshore Oil and Gas Policy.*

(See also MAJOR OIL SPILLS AND INCIDENTS on page 220; also entries on specific oil spills, such as the *EXXON VALDEZ.*)

---

typical of oils from West Texas and the Middle East. Low-sulfur, relatively noncorrosive oils, which produce little hydrogen sulfide, are called *sweet crude,* as from Louisiana, Libya, and Nigeria.

The most economical way to move oil from field to refinery is by pipeline. Oil is transported by relatively small pipelines to central holding locations, from which it is moved by larger "trunk" lines, studded en route with pumping stations, meters, and samplers. But much of the world's oil is transported by water, on barges or tankers. In the United States, for example, about half goes by pipeline, half by water.

At the refinery, after sodium chloride and other salts are removed to lessen corrosivity, the oil is treated in various ways. In general, heat, pressure, and catalysts are used to separate out various groups of hydrocarbons (called *fractions*). Other treatments are used to increase the octane and anti-knock qualities of the refined oil, to make it more efficient as a fuel; and sulfur and nitrogen may be replaced with hydrogen, producing a cleaner fuel.

It is the resulting products that have come to be so essential to the modern industrialized world. Most forms of transportation rely on oil-derived fuels, as do industry,

agriculture, and many homes. Petroleum is also the source of PETROCHEMICALS, including SYNTHETIC ORGANIC CHEMICALS and PESTICIDES. Even after the warning of the energy crisis of the 1970s, industrialized countries continued their dependence on oil. This has been so even though oil is now widely understood to be a rapidly DECLINING RESOURCE. Existing oil reserves are classed as proven, possible, or potential; the amount actually made available from any one area depends on its production efficiency and on governmental policy.

How much oil actually remains is a matter of great debate. Some say that oil reserves may last only about 60 years at late 1980s rates of use, though yet-to-be-developed technology could extend production from areas now regarded as depleted, using present techniques. But even if the end of the reserves is years or decades further away, as the amounts of oil decline, it will become more expensive, because of both increasing production costs and supply-and-demand. For many people, the decline in oil reserves calls for intensification of the search for and exploitation of new oil fields, wherever they may be. For environmentalists, however, it points up the necessity to develop alternatives for processes now entirely oil-reliant, instead of destroying the environment for what will be, in any case, only a stopgap measure.

Though enormously efficient, convenient, and flexible—qualities that gave it its present predominance—oil poses environmental problems at every stage. In fields tapped for production, whether on land or at sea, ECOSYSTEMS in the area are disturbed and often destroyed by the arrival of drilling rigs, by roads and pipelines built for transport, and by other human activities. In areas where large amounts of oil have been removed, the land may subside, and there is some evidence that removal can trigger local earthquakes. Leaks of oil foul the environment, polluting land, air, and water, at every stage—at the drilling site, along pipelines, at transfer points to and from tankers, at refineries and storage areas, and in the storage of refined fuels, only in recent years recognized as a major problem (see LEAKING UNDERGROUND STORAGE TANKS).

Most notable are the massive leaks that have begun to catch the world's attention (some of the largest actually occurred before the world was watching so closely; see MAJOR OIL SPILLS AND INCIDENTS on page 220), but in fact the bulk of the POLLUTION from oil comes from the everyday releases of oil all along its production, transportation, and processing route, often in the shipping lanes along extremely vulnerable coastal areas. Under public pressure, some oil installations have been planned with environmental concerns in mind, such as the Alaska pipeline, designed to minimize the effects on herds of CARIBOU and other animals in the region; yet the end of the pipeline saw one of the worst modern accidents, the *EXXON VALDEZ OIL SPILL*. Environmentalists quite rightly question the will—and, even where the will exists, the capacity—of humans to control environmental damage from oil production, transport, and refining. In the United States, the 1990 Oil Pollution Act is intended to "facilitate oil-spill prevention activities, improve federal and state preparedness, set strict liabilities for cleanup costs, and expand oil-pollution research and development," under the direction of the ENVIRONMENTAL PROTECTION AGENCY (EPA) and the U.S. Coast Guard.

Of particular concern is the pressure to extend oil exploration and exploitation on sensitive public lands, such as WILDLIFE REFUGES and WILDERNESS, and in coastal areas, where government controls and regulates leasing. Many environmentalists urge that federal agencies apply ENVIRONMENTAL IMPACT STATEMENTS to areas being considered for oil leasing, using these to assess which areas should be opened for leasing and which withheld, especially banning exploration in wild and scenic RIVER areas, other MIGRATION corridors and GREENWAYS, and other environmentally sensitive areas. Where leases have already been granted,

they urge the government to trade, suspend, or buy back leases and to add protective regulations to those that remain, requiring that the leaseholders offer minimal disruption to wildlife HABITAT, employ EROSION control measures, protect WATER RESOURCES, and revegetate the area after use. Many environmentalists are especially concerned about OFFSHORE DRILLING and its threats to the fragile coastal ecosystems. (See OIL AND OIL POLLUTION INFORMATION AND ACTION GUIDE on page 222; also MAJOR OIL SPILLS AND INCIDENTS on page 220; also ENERGY RESOURCES; OFFSHORE DRILLING; FOSSIL FUELS; ALTERNATIVE FUELS.)

**Okefenokee Swamp,** U.S. National Wildlife Refuge in southeastern Georgia and northern Florida; its 620 square miles of swampland, marsh, LAKE, and woods, much of it set aside as a national refuge in 1937, supply safe haven to a wide variety of wildlife and plant life, including over 200 kinds of birds, scores of mammal, amphibian, and reptile SPECIES, and hundreds of plant species. Okefenokee is the home of an estimated 10,000 to 15,000 ALLIGATORS, deer, black BEARS, bobcats, white ibises, sandhill CRANES, many varieties of orchids, and much more—it is one of the world's most notable WILDLIFE REFUGES. (See WETLANDS).

**old-growth forest,** mature FORESTS of long standing, some hundreds, even over a thousand years old. (See FORESTS.)

**Olympic Rain Forest,** the temperate rain FOREST of Washington State's Olympic Peninsula. A 50-mile stretch of the seacoast is national park land, as is the whole center of the peninsula, the national park covering over 1,000 square miles of seashore, rain forest, and mountains, rising to 7,965-foot Mount Olympus. The forests surrounding the parkland at the center of the peninsula are heavily logged, though some are national forests, where logging has been impeded in recent years by the long controversy over the preservation of the northern spotted OWL. The protected seashore supports a wide range of life, including sea OTTERS, SEALS AND SEA LIONS, several clam, mussel, snail, and crab SPECIES, and a considerable number of fishing shorebirds, including gulls, bald EAGLES, grebes, murres, cormorants, and great blue herons. Inland, the national park offers safe haven to a large herd of Roosevelt elk, black BEAR, several deer species, mountain lions, beaver, bobcats, raccoons, and such birds as rosy finches, mountain bluebirds, hummingbirds, and thrushes. In the park are also found the kinds of old-growth forests that are fast being cut down in the logging areas around the park, including hemlock, spruce, cottonwood, bigleaf maples, and western red cedar. At Olympic, the national seashore and inland national parklands have so far been held for future generations, while the long, profoundly important argument between loggers and conservationists continues nearby. (See FORESTS.)

**omnivorous,** plant- and flesh-eating, describing animals that eat both plants low on the FOOD CHAIN, as do *herbivores*, and animals high on the food chain, as do *carnivores*. Humans are omnivorous, though many become largely herbivorous for philosophical reasons or for economic ones, since a plant-based diet makes far more efficient use of the food energy in natural resources (See VEGETARIANISM.)

***On the Beach,*** a 1959 fiction film, based on the 1957 Nevil Shute novel, set in Australia as people wait for the atomic cloud that will end all life on earth, after the nuclear war that had finally come. Stanley Kramer's very powerful and influential anti-war film starred Gregory Peck, Ava Gardner, Fred Astaire, and Anthony Perkins.

**orangutan,** with GORILLAS and CHIMPANZEES one of the three types of great apes, which of all the animal SPECIES are the most closely related to humanity. Orangutans are great red apes, forest-dwellers who are found only on Sumatra and Borneo. Highly respected by the peoples of the area, they are an ENDANGERED SPECIES largely because of loss of HABITAT, as exploding human POPULATIONS and accelerating rain FOREST clearance proceed side by side. Once orangutan babies were widely taken as pets and for ZOOS, but now they are protected species in Indonesia and Malaya, with considerable populations protected in several national parks and wildlife on Sumatra and Borneo. However, rain forests on both islands are disappearing fast, and there are considerable pressures to log the protected areas, as well as to develop them, with HYDROPOWER and other public and private projects. The future of the orangutans will probably depend on the will of the Indonesian and Malayan governments to keep their wildlife preserves wild. (See also ENDANGERED SPECIES; also ENDANGERED AND THREATENED WILDLIFE AND PLANTS on page 372.)

**organic compound,** any substance containing carbon. Carbon-containing compounds form the chemical basis of all living things, including carbohydrates, lipids (fats), proteins, and nucleic acids (DNA and RNA). An organic compound is also any substance that has been derived from living organisms, such as FOSSIL FUELS. Organic gases are highly reactive—that is, they readily participate in chemical reactions, including the photochemical reactions involving sunlight that result in SMOG. Organic compounds are more numerous on earth than *inorganic*

*compounds,* which lack carbon and are not of the essence of life. Some of the most promising, versatile, useful, and also some of the most dangerous chemicals of recent decades have been organic compounds. The UNITED NATIONS ENVIRONMENT PROGRAMME (UNEP) estimates that since 1950 production of organic chemicals has jumped from 7 million tons a year to about 250 million tons. (See CHLORINATED HYDROCARBONS; HYDROCARBONS; SYNTHETIC ORGANIC CHEMICALS; VOLATILE ORGANIC COMPOUNDS.)

**organic farming,** a system of agriculture production that avoids the use of PESTICIDES and sythetic fertilizers, and (where livestock are involved) also feed additives and growth regulators such as hormones. As the United States DEPARTMENT OF AGRICULTURE has described it: "To the maximum extent feasible, organic farming systems rely on crop rotations, crop residues, animal manures, legumes, green manures, off-the-farm organic wastes, mechanical cultivation, mineral-bearing rocks, and aspects of biological pest control to maintain soil productivity and tilth, to supply plants nutrients, and to control insects, weeds, and other pests.''

Organic farming is virtually synonymous with traditional farming. Though pre-20th-century farmers did sometimes use certain toxic substances, often containing HEAVY METALS such as MERCURY, it was not until the mid-20th century that the world saw the main explosion in the production of pesticides and other SYNTHETIC ORGANIC CHEMICALS, which have since so fouled the global environment. As the dangers of these substances have come to be better understood—and as many consumers have sought to find chemical-free foods—increasing numbers of farmers have been turning away from pesticide use, employing instead a wide variety of methods, many involving BIOLOGICAL CONTROL or INTEGRATED PEST MANAGEMENT.

Organic farmers may use sprays, but they are biologically derived, such as *fertilizing sprays* made from plant teas, minerals, sea kelp, or compost (see COMPOSTING); *soap sprays* formulated to control pests; *oil and mineral sprays* to suffocate spores and pest eggs, especially on fruit trees; and *botanical sprays,* plant-derived liquids used against insect pests. These are not harmful to food, because (unlike synthetic chemicals) they are broken down quickly and naturally by sunlight, oxygen, and microorganisms, and any remaining residue is quickly washed off the agricultural products.

There is no single, standardized set of terms to reflect the different types of ''organic'' growing practices by farmers. Among the most common labels in use are:

• **organic,** in general applied to crops grown without synthetic chemical pesticides and fertilizers, though some naturally derived pesticides and fertilizers are allowed. In some areas the term may be defined by law; in California, for example, the term *organic* can be applied only to food grown on land to which no synthetic chemicals have been applied for at least a year before planting. In such places, farmers, distributors, and grocers are often required to keep records documenting their organic farming practices.

- **certified organic,** applied only to those foods for which a certification organization has verified the records documenting organic farming practices. In California, for example, the *California Certified Organic Farmers (CCOF)* association (see ORGANIC FARMING AND SUSTAINABLE AGRICULTURE INFORMATION AND ACTION GUIDE on page 226) inspects farmers' records, including a 10-year LAND USE history, and the results of periodic soil tests for pesticide residues. Sometimes, through a phenomenon called *pesticide drift* (pesticide being blown in from other farms), pesticide residues occur even on organically grown crops; if produce is tested and found to contain more than 10 percent of the legal residue limit for conventional crops, they are not allowed to be labeled *organic*.

- **transitional organic,** meaning that the crops are grown without synthetic chemicals being applied to them, but with residues still remaining on the ground during the specified waiting period before the term *organic* can be applied.

- **unsprayed** or **no spray,** meaning that no synthetic pesticides were sprayed directly on the crop, though some may have been applied before planting or through irrigation. Farmers using this label on their crops are not required to keep any records of their growing practices.

- **integrated pest management**, meaning that farmers used various methods of pest control, with minimal or at least lessened pesticide use. Again, no records are required to document these practices.

- **no detected residues,** meaning that samples of the food have been tested in a laboratory and been found to contain less than one-tenth of the allowable maximum tolerance of the specified pesticides reported to be used on the farm. Such testing is often done under contract, as by some supermarket chains in California. The laboratory sometimes inspects the farms to ensure that no other pesticides are being used; however, critics note that laboratories are able to screen for less than 50 percent of the pesticides legally available to farmers, and many secondary compounds formed as pesticides "decay" also go undetected.

- **pesticide-free,** an undefined, unrestricted label; an undocumented personal statement by the farmer that no synthetic pesticides were used in growing the food. It is a misleading label, since—even if pesticides were not used—they may still be present from pesticide drift or residues in the ground.

An Organic Food Production Act, which defines *organically produced,* sets uniform standards, and provides for enforcement, has been proposed in the U.S. Congress. Consumers should note, however, that no label can guarantee that a food contains absolutely no pesticide residues; that would be virtually impossible, for traces of pesticides are found virtually everywhere in the world, including ANTARCTICA, even when they were never used directly. In addition, except for *organic, certified organic,* and *transitional,* none of the above labels conveys any information about use of chemical fertilizers.

Beyond the question of labels, however, is the stance of organic farmers. As the California Certified Organic Farmers association put it: " 'Organic' means far more than a set of legal statutes and far more than simply not applying certain chemicals to crops and animals . . . [It] means a completely different approach to agriculture and agricultural resources [by farmers who have] made a commitment to restore the ecological balance to their soil and to employ only those farming practices that promote stable, sustainable methods of growing food."

A related movement is *biodynamic agriculture,* which goes beyond organic farming to use specific and precisely prepared herbs and minerals. The biodynamic approach also involves a spiritual philosophy relating humans, plant and animal life, and the cosmos as intertwining parts of agriculture. In Europe, where the movement was founded, the Demeter Association certifies food grown by biodynamic agriculture.

In the short term, organic farming involves more management, planning, and labor, which means that organically grown produce generally costs more for the farmer to produce and for the consumer to buy. In addition, organic produce accounts for a relatively small percentage of the total food market—in the United States, only about 2 to 3 percent—and so organic farmers and distributors are less able to take advantage of volume economies in marketing and transportation. Some communities have attempted to aid organic farmers and themselves through COMMUNITY SUPPORTED AGRICULTURE, helping to defray the uncertainties and extra expenses incurred by small organic farmers.

In the longer term, however, organic farming is far less expensive than chemical-dependent farming, once the wider social costs are included, such as the health costs of contaminated food, soil, and drinking water; the costs of testing and monitoring chemical residues in the food

## Organic Farming and Sustainable Agriculture
## Information and Action Guide

For more information and action on sustainable agriculture and organic farming:

**Agroecology Program** (University of California, Santa Cruz, CA 95064; 408-459-4140; Stephen Gliessman, Director), a university program offering undergraduate and graduate degrees in sustainable agriculture, as well as public education and research. The school maintains a list of universities, colleges, and institutes that teach agroecology or related subjects, in North America and Europe; manages a model farm and garden open to the public, and also publishes various materials, including the semiannual newsletter *The Cultivar* and the brochure *Pesticide Perspectives.*

**Alternative Farming Systems Information Center** (National Agricultural Library [NAL], Room 304, 10301 Baltimore Boulevard, Beltsville, MD 20705; 301-344-3724 or 344-3559), a service of the U.S. DEPARTMENT OF AGRICULTURE, providing numerous Quick Bibliographies, such as *Alternative Farming Systems—Economic Aspects* (K. Schneider), *Societal Impacts of Adoption of Alternative Agricultural Practices* (J. MacLean, 1990), and *Sustainable or Alternative Agriculture* (J. MacLean, 1990); Special Reference Briefs such as *Organic Certification* (J. Gates, 1989); Agri-Topics such as *Organic Gardening* (J. Gates, 1989); Search Tips Series such as *Searching AGRICOLA for . . . Low Input or Sustainable Agriculture* (K. Schneider, 1988), on searching agricultural computer data bases; Bibliographies and Literature of Agriculture, such as *Tracing the Evolution of Organic/Sustainable Agriculture: A Selected and Annotated Bibliography (J. Gates, 1988);* and *List of Organizations Concerned with Organic Farming, Gardening and Horticulture* (J. Rafats, 1989); and videotapes of interviews on alternative farming, which may be borrowed.

**APPROPRIATE TECHNOLOGY TRANSFER FOR RURAL AREAS (ATTRA),** (501-442-9824 or 800-346-9140).

**California Certified Organic Farmers (CCOF),** (P.O. Box 8136, Santa Cruz, CA 95061; 408-423-2263; Bob Scowcroft, Executive Director), a membership organization founded in 1973 "to promote and verify organic farming practices, supporting all efforts for a healthier, sustainable agricultural system." Working through local chapters with a statewide coordinating office, CCOF establishes standards and conducts grower certification programs. Growers must meet the standards of both CCOF and the California Organic Food Act of 1982; however, CCOF "welcomes the participation of 'transitional' growers who intend to make a gradual conversion of their operation to organic practices." It also publishes the quarterly *CCOF Statewide Newsletter,* including legislative updates, market conditions, and technical information.

**CENTER FOR SCIENCE IN THE PUBLIC INTEREST (CSPI),** (202-332-9110). Publishes a directory of mail-order sources of organically grown foods and *Organic Agriculture: What the States Are Doing* (Dan Howell, 1989).

**Committee for Sustainable Agriculture (CSA)** (27 South Main Street, P.O. Box 1300, Colfax, CA 95713; 916-346-2777; Otis Wollan, Executive Director), a membership organization that developed out of the first Ecological Farming Conference in 1981, its aims being: "To achieve a safe food supply and a cleaner environment through dissemination of information about farming, food processing, and marketing techniques that conserve and replenish soil resources, and decrease the use of toxic and synthetic chemicals." CSA sponsors an annual Ecological Farming Conference and other conferences on organic farming, conducts tours to organic farms, and publishes various materials, including the quarterly journal *Organic Food Matters* and *Organic Marketing News and Information Service (OMNIS),* a weekly for farmers, listing wholesale and retail prices for organically grown food.

**CONSULTATIVE GROUP ON INTERNATIONAL AGRICULTURAL RESEARCH (CGIAR OR CG),** (202-473-8951). Sponsors various

---

supply; and the expense of cleaning up contaminated environments. In addition, critics point out that chemical-dependent agriculture receives millions of dollars in federal subsidies, generally not available to organic farmers, partly because the subsidies apply to one-crop fields (see MONOCULTURE), while organic farmers generally use various forms of *intercropping*—interspersing rows of two or more types of crops—as part of natural pest control and soil-building techniques. U.S. environmentalists have strongly recommended that the Department of Agriculture change its policies to provide equal subsidies for organic farmers. (See ORGANIC FARMING AND SUSTAINABLE AGRICULTURE INFORMATION AND ACTION GUIDE above; also SUSTAINABLE AGRICULTURE; BIOLOGICAL CONTROL; INTEGRATED PEST MANAGEMENT; COMMUNITY SUPPORTED AGRICULTURE.)

**organochlorines,** an alternate name for CHLORINATED HYDROCARBONS.

**organophosphates (OPs),** a group of PESTICIDES, compounds that include carbon, hydrogen, and phosphorus; among them are parathion, malathion, HETP, and TEPP (tetraethyl pyrphosphate). They are generally used as insecticides and acaricides (to kill members of the *Arachnida*

key international agricultural research centers working for sustainable agriculture, especially in developing countries.

COORDINATION IN DEVELOPMENT (CODEL), (212-870-3000). Publishes *Environmentally Sound Small Scale Agriculture Projects* (1988).

ENVIRONMENTAL AND ENERGY STUDY INSTITUTE (EESI), (202-628-1400). Publishes *The Economics of Sustainable Agriculture* (1990).

ENVIRONMENTAL DEFENSE FUND (EDF), (212-505-2100). Publishes *Biotechnology's Bitter Harvest: Herbicide-Tolerant Crops and the Threat to Sustainable Agriculture.*

FRIENDS OF THE EARTH (FOE), (202-544-2600).

HUMAN ECOLOGY ACTION LEAGUE (HEAL), (404-248-1898). Publishes resource list on *Organic Food, Natural Gardening, Lawn Care, Pest Control.*

**Institute for Alternative Agriculture (IAA)** (9200 Edmonston Road, Suite 117, Greenbelt, MD 20770; 301-441-8777; I. Garth Youngberg, Executive Director), a membership organization established in 1983 "to facilitate the adoption of low-cost, resource-conserving, and environmentally sound farming methods." The IAA sponsors research and education outreach programs, including an annual symposium; acts as a "contact for farmers and others who seek information on diversified, sustainable farming systems," especially government agencies and committees; seeks to act as a resource about and speaks for alternative agriculture to legislators and educational and farm organizations; and publishes various scientific materials, including the monthly newsletters *Alternative Agriculture News* and *Alternative Agriculture Resources Report* (for the agriculture education and research community), and the quarterly *American Journal of Alternative Agriculture.*

KIDS FOR SAVING EARTH™ (KSE), (612-525-0002 or 800-800-8800).

NATIONAL CENTER FOR POLICY ALTERNATIVES, (202-387-6030). Publishes *What Sustainable Agriculture Has to Offer the Management of Global Warming* (Erik Jansson, 1989).

**National Coalition Against Misuse of Pesticides (NCAMP),** (202-543-5450). Publishes brochures and flyers such as *Pest Control Without Toxic Chemicals,* and a series of fact sheets on least-toxic control of pests and pesticide chemicals. (See PESTICIDES INFORMATION AND ACTION GUIDE on page 238.)

NATURAL RESOURCES DEFENSE COUNCIL (NRDC), (212-727-2700). Publishes *Harvest of Hope: The Potential of Alternative Agriculture to Reduce Pesticide Use* (Jennifer Curtis, 1991) and *Reaping the Revenue Code: Why We Need Sensible Tax Reform Policy for Sustainable Agriculture* (Justin R. Ward et al., 1989).

PACIFIC INSTITUTE FOR STUDIES IN DEVELOPMENT, ENVIRONMENT, AND SECURITY, (415-843-9550). Sponsors Program on Sustainable Development.

RODALE INSTITUTE, (215-967-5171). Conducts research and publishes *New Farm* magazine; *International Ag-Sieve* books such as *How to Grow Vegetables Organically;* booklets such as *Controlling Weeds Without Chemicals;* and numerous reports.

WINROCK INTERNATIONAL INSTITUTE FOR AGRICULTURAL DEVELOPMENT, (501-727-5435 or 703-525-9430).

**Zero Population Growth (ZPG),** (202-332-2200). Publishes *Sustainability: The Global Challenge.* (See POPULATION INFORMATION AND ACTION GUIDE on page 248.)

**Other references:**

*Organically Grown Food: A Consumer's Guide.* Theodore Wood Carlat. Available from: Wood Marketing, 1916 Brooks, Suite 315, Missoula, MT 59801; 213-659-3877. *Small-Scale Agriculture in America: Race, Economics, and the Future.* Ejigou Demisse. Westview, 1990. *Planting the Future—A Resource Guide to Sustainable Agriculture in the Third World.* Minneapolis, 1989. *Alternative Agriculture.* National Research Council. National Academy Press, 1989. *Healthy Harvest III: A Directory of Sustainable Agriculture and Horticulture Organisations, 1988–1989.* Available from Potomac Valley Press, 1424 16th Street, NW, #105, Washington, DC 20036.

---

and *Acarina* families, notably mites and ticks) in farm fields, often applied by crop dusting or spraying. Discovered during nerve-gas research, organophosphates disrupt the nervous system, specifically by blocking the action of the enzyme acetylcholinesterase, which controls the transmission of nerve impulses, bringing death to their intended (and sometimes unintended) victims; because of that, they are called *cholinesterase-inhibitors.*

In humans, OPs enter the body by various routes, including the digestive tract, skin, lungs, and mucous membranes. Symptoms of exposure to organophosphates start with excess salivation and sweating, headache, cramps, nausea, diarrhea, and tightness in the chest; in sufficient doses symptoms progress quickly to spasms, convulsions, paralysis, and death. The hypothetical "average" adult might be killed by as little as a few drops to a tablespoon of parathion, but some people are far more susceptible, with children being especially sensitive; the "lowest toxic dose" for parathion is less than 0.1 ounce. Unlike CHLORINATED HYDROCARBONS, organophosphates are BIODEGRADABLE, being stored only briefly in the tissues of living organisms and breaking down relatively quickly in bodies and in the environment. But being so highly toxic, organophosphates are marked for "restricted use" by the

ENVIRONMENTAL PROTECTION AGENCY. Some organophosphates may also be MUTAGENS and CARCINOGENS. Many environmentalists and other citizens object to any use at all for such toxic substances. Malathion (along with methyl bromide) has been the center of a considerable controversy over their use against the Mediterranean fruit fly (medfly), as in California and Guatemala.

**For more information and action:**

- **Northwest Coalition for Alternatives to Pesticides (NCAP)** (503-344-5044). Publishes fact sheet *Malathion.* (See PESTICIDES INFORMATON AND ACTION GUIDE on page 238.)

(See also PESTICIDES; also TIPS FOR DEALING WITH PESTICIDES on page 242.)

**osprey (fish hawk),** large fish-eating bird of prey, found worldwide mainly in coastal waters, but also sometimes on inland waterways. From the 1950s through the early 1970s, DDT and other PESTICIDES built up in the FOOD CHAIN, causing calcium deficiencies that thinned the eggshells of ospreys and many other SPECIES, all but destroying their ability to reproduce in some parts of the world, and especially in eastern North America. After the 1972 ban on DDT by the ENVIRONMENTAL PROTECTION AGENCY, the amount of DDT in the food chain began to diminish, and the ability to reproduce slowly began to return, as did the ospreys to such coastal areas as eastern Long Island, where osprey-lovers built hundreds of nesting platforms to attract the returning birds.

**For more information and action:**

- **International Osprey Foundation, The (TIOF)** (P.O. Box 250, Sanibel, FL 33957; 813-472-5218; David Loveland, President), an international organization founded in 1981 for professionals and amateurs "dedicated to studying the problem of restoring osprey numbers to a stable population, making recommendations to enhance the continued survival of the osprey, and initiating educational programs." TIOF offers research grants and publishes a newsletter, working bibliography, and *Osprey Platforms and Their Construction.*

**Other reference:**

*Ospreys: A Natural and Unnatural History.* Alan F. Poole. Cambridge University Press, 1989.

(See also ENDANGERED SPECIES; also ENDANGERED AND THREATENED WILDLIFE AND PLANTS on page 372.)

**otter, California sea,** a remnant of the once-large northern Pacific sea otter population, which before commercial hunting began in the mid-1700s inhabited coastal waters in a great arc that stretched from northern Japan to Alaska to Baja California. Highly prized for their skins, the sea otters were hunted very close to EXTINCTION by the early 20th century, and were saved only by the 1911 North Pacific Fur Seal Convention, signed by the United States, Japan, Great Britain, and Russia. Some sea otters survived, in isolated pockets along the northern COASTS of the arc, and approximately 50 off the coast of central California.

The California sea otter population has grown to approximately 1,800 since then, with the help of state regulations against the use of gill nets that "incidentally" catch and kill otters while other sea creatures are being hunted. But there are major new threats to the coast-dwelling life of the sea otter off California and the rest of the North American Pacific coast, including toxic wastes, the sewage of expanding human populations, the OIL spills resulting from OFFSHORE DRILLING, and such disasters as the 1989 *EXXON VALDEZ* OIL SPILL in Alaska's Prince William Sound. An attempt to relocate some sea otters to new grounds off St. Nicholas Island in California's Channel Islands has had only limited success, and the future of the California sea otter remains in question.

Five of the eleven other otter SPECIES are listed as endangered by the United States FISH AND WILDLIFE SERVICE, including the South American *giant, southern river, marine,* and *long-tailed* otters, and the *Cameroon clawless* otter. The giant otter, once found by the hundreds of thousands in the waterways of the Amazon basin, has by now been hunted to very near extinction.

**For more information and action:**

- **AMERICAN CETACEAN SOCIETY (ACS),** (213-548-6279). Publishes *A Raft of Sea Otters.*
- **Animal Protection Institute** (916-731-5521). (See ANIMAL RIGHTS AND WELFARE INFORMATION AND ACTION GUIDE on page 361.)
- **CENTER FOR MARINE CONSERVATION (CMC),** (202-429-5609).
- **ELSA WILD ANIMAL APPEAL (EWAA),** (818-761-8387).
- IUCN—**THE WORLD CONSERVATION UNION,** (202-797-5454). Publishes *Otters: An Action Plan for Their Conservation.*
- **PACIFIC WHALE FOUNDATION (PWF),** (808-879-8860; for orders 800-WHALE-1-1 [942-5311]. Publishes *A Raft of Sea Otters* and books for young children.
- **SIERRA CLUB,** (415-776-2211 or 202-547-1141; legislative hotline, 202-547-5550). Publishes *Song of the Sea Otter.*

(See also ENDANGERED SPECIES; also ENDANGERED AND THREATENED WILDLIFE AND PLANTS on page 372.)

## Our Common Future: Seven Goals

- Reviving economic growth.
- Changing the quality of growth.
- Meeting essential needs for jobs, food, energy, water, and sanitation.
- Ensuring a sustainable level of population.

- Conserving and enhancing the resource base.
- Reorienting technology and managing risk.
- Merging environment and economics in decision-making.

**Source:** *Our Common Future*, the final report of the World Commission on Environment and Development, 1987.

---

**Our Common Future (Brundtland Report),** the title of the final report of the World Commission on Environment and Development, published in 1987, endorsed by the United Nations General Assembly, and intended to serve governments and other institutions as a basis for future policy regarding the environment and DEVELOPMENT, especially with its ''call for a new era of growth and sustainable development based on an equitable distribution of benefits,'' including provision of technical and support assistance where needed. The Commission was an independent body created by the United Nations in 1983 and chaired by Norwegian leader Mrs. Gro Harlem Brundtland, with a mandate to ''re-examine the critical issues of environment and development and formulate new and concrete action proposals to deal with them, to assess and propose new forms of international cooperation that could break out of existing patterns and foster needed change; and to raise the level of understanding and commitment everywhere.'' On publication of its report, the Commission itself ceased to exist, though its initiatives have inspired many other organizations, in particular the Centre for Our Common Future (see below).

### For more information and action:

- **Centre for Our Common Future** (Palais Wilson, 52, rue des Pâquis, Ch-1201, Geneva, Switzerland, [022] 732 71 17; Warren H. Lindner, Executive Director), an international organization founded in 1988 to foster the goals articulated in the World Commission on Environment and Development's report, *Our Common Future*. The Centre acts as an information clearinghouse on the report's recommendations; offers advice and encouragement to individuals and organizations; holds public forums; and publishes the quarterly *Brundtland Bulletin*, the monthly *Network '92*, the book *Signs of Hope*, and other print and audiovisual materials.
- **GLOBAL TOMORROW COALITION (GTC),** (202-628-4016). Seeks to ''broaden outreach and understanding of reports like *Our Common Future*.''

- **LEGACY INTERNATIONAL,** (703-549-3630). Conducts programs designed to spur local application of the principles of sustainable development embodied in *Our Common Future*.

**Outer Continental Shelf Lands Act,** a U.S. federal law passed in 1953 and amended in 1990, asserting federal control of DEVELOPMENT of mineral resources in the outer continental shelf (OCS)—the level, relatively shallow underwater plain that extends out from the COAST—including the seabed and subsoil, and attempting to ensure that operations there do not harm the environment, with states involved in policy and planning decisions. The Act is primarily administered by the Department of the Interior (DOI) and Department of Commerce (DOC), with annual reports submitted to Congress on short- and long-term environmental effects, and on the adequacy of health and safety regulations. DOI administers the regulation of leases up to 10 years and under 5,760 acres, offered through competitive sealed bidding, and may suspend or cancel them if activities are harmful to the environment, aquatic life, mineral resources, or national security. It also approves pipeline rights-of-way to transport mineral resources, with capacity expansion under the Federal Energy Regulatory Commission (FERC). DOC develops and administers regulations regarding hazardous working conditions. DOI and DOC, with the army, enforces regulations under the Act.

The Act calls for leasing operations to use the best available and safest economically feasible technologies, and also requires that state governors be provided with information about leases within three miles of shore, with 27 percent of the income from that area going to the state and the rest to the U.S. Treasury. The law contains restrictions designed to limit potentially dangerous releases of HYDROCARBONS, and requires leaseholders to provide all data and information from lease operations to the government, which DOI will use in making a biannual report to Congress on estimated total discovered crude OIL and NATURAL GAS reserves.

Geophysical exploration plans must be approved in advance and modified if necessary so as not to disrupt lease operations or aquatic life, cause POLLUTION, or disturb historical objects. Before beginning operations for any lease outside the Gulf of Mexico, lease holders must submit development and production plans for approval, describing shore facilities and operations, including environmental and safety protection measures. States must also approve plans that affect coastal zone management (see COASTS), and specifically leases or permits may not be granted within 15 miles of the Point Reyes Wilderness, without approval from California.

The Act carries civil and criminal penalties for violations. Citizens may bring suit against violators (including government agencies) with 60 days advance notice, waived in cases of emergency risk to public health and safety. The Act established a Fishermen's Contingency Fund, to compensate for losses. Original provisions on OIL pollution were repealed and replaced by the Oil Pollution Act of 1990 (see OIL).

**overgrazing,** the process by which domesticated animals and wildlife eat more plants than are able to regenerate in an area, notably in natural GRASSLANDS or areas where deforested land is used for pasturing animals. The result is significant ENVIRONMENTAL DEGRADATION. More specifically, as plant cover is lost, the area becomes open to EROSION and is less able to capture and hold vital moisture. The area becomes progressively drier and loses increasing amounts of topsoil to wind and water; meanwhile, more desirable species are replaced by less edible ones, so the land is less able to support human and other animal life. Overgrazing is a major concern in areas of significant POPULATION pressure, where farmers and herders are pushed into marginal lands, or where herders are unable to follow their traditional pattern of moving freely to successive pastures, allowing each to regenerate in turn. Overgrazing is also a concern where the short-term economic benefits are unbalanced by longer-term views of the ecological balance vital to the region, as in the conflict between ranchers pasturing their domesticated livestock on public lands and environmentalists seeking protection for wildlife in these supposedly protected areas. (See also GRASSLANDS; DESERTIFICATION; WILDLIFE REFUGES.)

**owl, northern spotted,** a medium-sized predator found in the old-growth FORESTS of the Pacific Northwest, from southwestern British Columbia through northern California. The environmental variety found in such forests provides nesting and roosting places, as well as protection from other predators; these owls do not fare well in other kinds of forests. In decline in recent decades, largely because of loss of essential old-growth forest HABITAT because of logging, the Pacific Northwest spotted owl population in the early 1990s was estimated at 2,000 to 3,000 pairs.

Much of the remaining old-growth forest in the United States portion of the Pacific Northwest is on federal forest land, such forests on private land long having been cut down by loggers. A dispute between environmentalists and loggers raged throughout the 1980s, generating lawsuits that in 1989 stopped most old-growth cutting on federal land. In June 1990 the FISH AND WILDLIFE SERVICE put the northern spotted owl on the endangered species list, and very sharply limited further old-growth logging on federal land, in an effort to preserve the habitat of the northern spotted owl. In the process, the remaining, irreplaceable old-growth forest was reprieved, as well.

As required by law, the federal government then attempted to develop a plan to preserve the owl, which was to include restrictions on logging throughout federal forest lands. But the federal FOREST SERVICE continued to lease federal land to loggers for cutting, before such a plan had been completed and approved by the federal courts. In May 1991, environmentalist lawsuits once again blocked old-growth forest logging on federal lands, this time through an injunction, until owl preservation plans were developed. (See also ENDANGERED SPECIES; also ENDANGERED AND THREATENED WILDLIFE AND PLANTS on page 372.)

**oxidant,** a substance that contains oxygen and readily makes it available for chemical reactions, which form new substances, as in the *photochemical reaction* that takes place in sunlight, and triggers the formation of SMOG.

**oxygen cycle,** the process by which living organisms obtain the oxygen necessary for life (see BIOGEOCHEMICAL CYCLES). Oxygen is a key part of the energy processes that fuel life. During PHOTOSYNTHESIS, green plants use CARBON DIOXIDE, water, and the sun's energy to store carbon in energy-rich compounds, releasing oxygen into the atmosphere. Many other "higher" forms of life—including humans—breathe in the oxygen and use it in their own energy-storing and energy-producing processes (giving off carbon dioxide). Oxygen as OZONE ($O_3$) also forms a layer high in the atmosphere, which protects living organisms from ultraviolet RADIATION (see OZONE LAYER). But too much oxygen is toxic to some organisms, and ozone near the ground contributes significantly to AIR POLLUTION. Oxygen can also be depleted, killing oxygen-dependent animals, as during EUTROPHICATION. In fact, one of the standard measures of WATER POLLUTION is *biochemical oxygen demand (BOD);* if water containing a high proportion of untreated organic matter (as in sewage) is pumped into a waterway, bacteria and microorganisms may use up all the water's oxygen in breaking down the waste matter, leaving no oxygen for fish and other aquatic animals.

## On Ozone

Ozone is an extraordinarily dangerous pollutant. Few realize that two one-hundredths of a gram of ozone is a lethal dose. Put at its very simplest, this means that a single 14-ounce can of hair spray filled with pure ozone could kill 14,000 people . . . . Ozone is nearly as effective at destroying lungs as mustard gas.

**Source:** Centers for Disease Control.

---

**ozone (O$_3$),** a poisonous, colorless gas (dark-blue in liquid form) in which the molecules each consist of three oxygen atoms. In the two-atom form generally found in the air and dissolved in water, oxygen is not only beneficial but essential to human and most other animal life. High in the atmosphere, the three-oxygen-atom ozone forms the OZONE LAYER, which helps shield life on earth from damaging ultraviolet RADIATION from the sun. But on the ground, ozone is a severe pollutant, irritating eyes, nose, and throat, and damaging the respiratory system, and is especially harmful to people with cardiorespiratory problems. (See HEALTH EFFECTS OF THE REGULATED AIR POLLUTANTS on page 8.) It is one of numerous air pollutants formed from automobile exhausts and industrial emissions in the presence of sunlight, in a series of what chemists call *photochemical reactions,* and is a key component of SMOG, generally along with NITROGEN DIOXIDE.

Ozone is one of the CRITERIA AIR POLLUTANTS for which the ENVIRONMENTAL PROTECTION AGENCY (EPA) sets NATIONAL AMBIENT AIR QUALITY STANDARDS (NAAQSs), under the CLEAN AIR ACT. Standards are far from being met in many areas; in 1988 the United States had 90 urban areas that fell short of the standard for ozone or smog. Ozone can also be a significant *indoor* air pollutant, as ozone-laden outdoor air is sucked indoors, and can be especially harmful to children exercising strenuously in homes or schools with no air conditioning. Various technologies, including activated charcoal, can be used to filter ozone from indoor air. On occasion however, ozone has its uses, being one alternative to CHLORINATION for disinfecting water.

### For more information and action:

• **Air and Waste Management Association (A&WMA),** (412-232-3444). Publishes *The Scientific and Technical Issues Facing Post-1967 Ozone Control Strategies* (George T. Wolff et al., eds. 1989), *Meteorological Aspects of the Ozone Problem* (1989), *Ozone Control by Emission Blending* (1989), and *Long-Term Ozone Exposure and Health Effects* (1989).

### Other references:

*Global Alert: The Ozone Pollution Crisis.* Jack Fishman and Robert Kalish. Plenum, 1990.

(See also OZONE LAYER; AIR POLLUTION; ACID RAIN.)

## How Ozone Is Destroyed

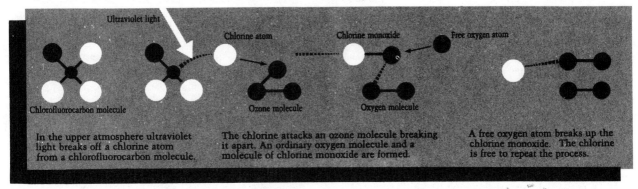

In the upper atmosphere ultraviolet light breaks off a chlorine atom from a chlorofluorocarbon molecule.

The chlorine attacks an ozone molecule breaking it apart. An ordinary oxygen molecule and a molecule of chlorine monoxide are formed.

A free oxygen atom breaks up the chlorine monoxide. The chlorine is free to repeat the process.

**Source:** *Environmental Progress and Challenges.* Environmental Protection Agency, *1988.*

## Ozone Layer Information and Action Guide

**For more information and action on the ozone layer:**
AIR AND WASTE MANAGEMENT ASSOCIATION (A&WMA), (412-232-3444). Publishes *Meteorological Aspects of the Ozone Problem* (1989) and *Stratospheric Ozone Depletion—Control Strategies and Technologies* (1989).
AMERICAN PLANNING ASSOCIATION (APA), (202-872-0611). Publishes *Ozone in the Troposphere and the Stratosphere* (1988).
ENVIRONMENTAL DEFENSE FUND (EDF), (212-505-2100). Publishes *Ominous Future Under the Ozone Hole: Assessing Biological Impacts in Antarctica* (M. Voytek, 1989), *Global Lessons from the Ozone Hole* (M. Oppenheimer, 1988), and *Protecting the Ozone Layer: What You Can Do* (S.L. Clark, Environmental Information Exchange, 1988).
ENVIRONMENTAL PROTECTION AGENCY (EPA), (202-260-7751 or 202-260-2080).
FRIENDS OF THE EARTH (202-544-2600). Publishes *Saving Our Skins—Technical Potential and Policies for the Elimination of Ozone-Depleting Chlorine Compounds* (Arjun Makhijani et al., 1988) and an atmospheric ozone newsletter.
KIDS FOR SAVING EARTH™ (KSE), (612-525-0002 or 800-800-8800).
NATIONAL CENTER FOR ATMOSPHERIC RESEARCH (NCAR), (303-497-1000; Information Services, 303-497-8600).

NATIONAL WILDLIFE FEDERATION (NWF), (202-797-6800 or 800-245-5484). Publishes Fact Sheet *Ozone Depletion*.
NATURAL RESOURCES DEFENSE COUNCIL (NRDC), (212-727-2700). Publishes *A Who's Who of American Ozone Depletors: A Guide to 3,014 Factories Emitting Three Ozone-Depleting Chemicals* (Deborah A. Sheiman et al., 1990), *Public Enemy No. 1,1,1: A Who's Who of Consumer Products That Contain the Ozone-Depleting Chemical 1,1,1-Trichloroethane* (Deborah A. Sheiman and David D. Doniger, 1990), and the *NRDC Earth Action Guide: Saving the Ozone Layer.*
RESOURCES FOR THE FUTURE (RFF), (202-328-5000).
U.S. PUBLIC INTEREST RESEARCH GROUP (PIRG), (202-546-9707). Publishes *As the World Burns: Documenting America's Failure to Address the Ozone Crisis* (1989).
WORLD RESOURCES INSTITUTE, (202-638-6300). Publishes *Protecting the Ozone Shield: Strategies for Phasing Out CFCs During the 1990s* (Irving Mintzer et al., 1990).
WORLD WILDLIFE FUND (WWF), (202-293-4800). Publishes *Ozone Diplomacy: New Directions in Safeguarding the Planet* (Richard E. Benedick, 1991).

**Other references:**

*The Hole in the Sky.* John Gribbin. Bantam/Corgi, 1988.

---

**ozone layer (ozonosphere or stratospheric ozone),** a band of concentrated OZONE (molecules containing three atoms of oxygen, abbreviated $O_3$) in the stratosphere, an upper layer in the earth's atmosphere, about 50,000 to 120,000 feet high. Though on earth ozone is a poisonous gas, and a main contributor to AIR POLLUTION, especially SMOG, stratospheric ozone serves an enormously beneficial function. It is formed in the stratosphere by RADIATION from the sun, and helps to shield life on earth from some of the sun's potentially destructive ultraviolet (UV) RADIATION. Some scientists, indeed, believe that life as we know it could have evolved only with the protective ozone shield in place.

Unfortunately, at least from the early 1970s, scientists had suspicions that the ozone layer was being depleted. By the 1980s it became clear that the ozone shield was indeed thinning in some places—a 1991 report noted that wintertime ozone in the northern latitudes has dropped by 3 percent in the last two decades—and at times even has a seasonal hole in it, notably over ANTARCTICA. While the causes and extent of the depletion are not fully known, most scientists believe that various chemicals in the air are responsible for depleting the ozone layer.

The most widely agreed-upon culprit is the family of chlorine-based compounds, most notably CHLOROFLUORO-CARBONS (CFCs) and chlorinated solvents (see CLORINATED HYDROCARBONS) such as carbon tetrachloride and METHYL CHLOROFORM, as well as the fire-extinguishing chemicals HALONS. Chlorine molecules are highly active and readily break apart the three-atom ozone into the two-atom form of oxygen generally found close to earth, in the lower atmosphere. Natural events also help deplete the ozone layer, notably chlorine from volcanic eruptions and changes in the solar cycle, as the sun creates less ozone when it emits less radiation.

Thinning of the ozone shield and increasing ultraviolet radiation raise the risk of skin cancer and cataracts, are implicated in suppression of the human immune system, and damage other animals and plants, especially aquatic life and crops such as soybeans. The urgency of the problem spurred the 1987 signing of the MONTREAL PROTOCOL ON SUBSTANCES THAT DEPLETE THE OZONE LAYER, amended and considerably extended in 1990. Worldwide data on the ozone layer is gathered by the GLOBAL ENVIRONMENT MONITORING SYSTEM (GEMS) from various sources. (See OZONE LAYER INFORMATION AND ACTION GUIDE above.)

# P

**Pacific Institute for Studies in Development, Environment, and Security** (1681 Shattuck Avenue, Suite H, Berkeley, CA 94709; 415-843-9550), a nonprofit, public benefit corporation, founded in 1987, to study the connections among "international security, global environmental change, and economic development" and to facilitate communications between concerned individuals and groups. The Institute also serves to educate policymakers and the public, seeking to bridge the gap between "specialized academic disciplines, policymakers, and practitioners." It sponsors various programs, including Program on Sustainable Development, focusing on Third World experiences; Program on Global Environment, on climatic change and associated effects; and Program on International Security, on the geopolitics of the arms race, Third World debt and development, and environmental consequences. In addition, the Institute publishes various materials, including testimony before Congressional committees, papers, articles, chapters, and books, such as *When Nations Clash—Raw Materials, Ideology, and Foreign Policy.*

**Pacific Whale Foundation (PWF)** (Kealia Beach Plaza, 101 North Kihei Road, Suite 25, Kihei, Maui, HI 96753; 808-879-8860; for orders 800-WHALE-1-1 [942-5311]; Gregory D. Kaufman, President), a membership organization founded in 1980 to "educate the public, from a scientific perspective, about conservation issues relating to marine mammals and their ocean environment." As a research, education and conservation organization, PWF conducts systematic field studies, focusing especially on WHALES and DOLPHINS, and aims to "bring learning to life" through its educational programs, including experiential learning programs aboard its two ocean-going vessels *Whale One* and *Whale II*. In addition to whalewatching, natural history cruises, and snorkeling trips, PWF also offers research internships; conducts Ocean Outreach educational programs; works with other organizations and agencies in "developing conservation policies and plans for endangered marine life" and maintains an *Adopt-A-Whale* Program. It also publishes various materials, including *Hawaii's Humpback Whales: A Complete Whalewatchers Guide* (Gregory D. Kaufman and Paul H. Forestell), *Dolphins and Porpoises* (Richard Ellis), *A Pod of Killer Whales, A Pod of Gray Whales, A Raft of Sea Otters, Seals and Sea Lions, Tidepools,* and books for young children, such as *Discovering Marine Mammals.*

**panda, giant,** a greatly endangered, extraordinarily popular species, seen throughout the world as "cuddly" models for many teddy bears of all sizes, and greatly sought for exhibitions. Once found by the tens of thousands in the upland bamboo FORESTS of East Asia, loss of HABITAT and HUNTING have reduced the number of surviving giant pandas to between 700 and 1,000 in the wild, all in China. Approximately 100 more survive in captivity. Sometimes called "bamboo bears" (after their main diet component) or "panda bears," giant pandas are now generally thought not to be bears, but part of the racoon family.

Pandas are a protected species in China, which has provided 14 sanctuary areas, and in recent years has even instituted and carried through the death penalty for panda poachers. But panda pelts have come to be worth as much as $20,000 in the internationally illegal WILDLIFE TRADE, with more available purchasers than there are pelts, especially in Japan, and also in several other countries. As long as a ready panda pelt market exists, the giant panda will continue to be in danger of imminent EXTINCTION.

In the long term, giant pandas are also threatened by the needs of the growing Chinese POPULATION, at 1.1 billion by far the largest on earth. Continuing encroachment on already-small bamboo forest panda preserves will continue to destroy the remaining pandas even if hunting is successfully stopped. Any Chinese political instability can also threaten the pandas; were they to be left unprotected for even a little while, poachers would very quickly kill as many as possible, and in the process drive the pandas very close or all the way to extinction in the wild.

On the hopeful side, panda breeding programs in captivity do exist, and have been moderately successful, although the Chinese government has seemed less than eager to assist breeding programs abroad. In recent years, some environmentalist groups, including animal rights organizations, have attempted to block continuing international exchanges of pandas for moneymaking exhibitions for ZOOS, on the grounds that the exchanges are illegal trade in ENDANGERED SPECIES. (See also ENDANGERED SPECIES; also ENDANGERED AND THREATENED WILDLIFE AND PLANTS on page 372.)

**panther, Florida,** the southern subspecies of the American panther, which once ranged throughout much of North America. The Florida panther, which once lived in the wet FORESTS of the southeast, from the Mississippi valley to the Atlantic coast, is now found only in southern Florida, largely in the EVERGLADES and Big Cypress wildlife refuges, and in the new Florida Panther National Wildlife Refuge. An estimated 25 to 50 of the panthers survive in the wild; these are threatened by loss of HABITAT, which is drying up as DEVELOPMENT proceeds, by automobiles passing through their too-small refuges, and by disease. Survival of the species in the wild seems possible, but will be greatly helped if current attempts to develop a captive breeding population succeed. The Florida panther is the state's official animal, intended to be a symbol of its people's determination to conserve their natural heritage. (See also ENDANGERED SPECIES; also ENDANGERED AND THREATENED WILDLIFE AND PLANTS on page 372.)

**parathion,** a common type of PESTICIDE (see ORGANOPHOSPHATE).

**parrots,** a group of over 300 bird SPECIES, variously known as parrots, budgerigars, parakeets, macaws, cocka-

toos, and more; at least 25 are ENDANGERED SPECIES, and the number of seriously threatened species has climbed to at least 75, with more species becoming extinct, endangered, and threatened every year.

There are two massive, sustained worldwide attacks on the parrot species taking place simultaneously. The first is the worldwide trade in "exotic" birds for pets, which deeply affects parrots and many other bird species, as well. The trade is substantial: for example, a total of at least one million wild birds were imported into the United States and the European Community in 1990, with some of them selling for hundreds and even thousands of dollars. At least 250,000 parrots were imported into the United States alone. Such birds as the hyacinth macaw, the world's largest parrot, sell for tens of thousands of dollars; its population is down to a few thousand in the AMAZON RAIN FOREST. In the early 1990s, a powerful worldwide movement has developed to stop the importation of wild birds, led by such organizations as the DEFENDERS OF WILDLIFE, the WORLD WILDLIFE FUND, and the Royal Society for the Protection of Birds.

The second massive attack on the parrot species affects many other tropical bird species, as well. It is the continuing destruction of their rain forest HABITAT, and however well the sale of parrots and other species can be limited, in the long run, unchecked rain FOREST destruction can destroy most of the enormous variety of parrot species now on earth. Saving significant portions of the tropical rain forest may be the hardest task of all, for it will be made possible only with a sustained, successful attack on the massive overpopulation and poverty questions that plague almost all of the countries of the tropical rain forest belt.

**For more information and action:**

- **DEFENDERS OF WILDLIFE,** (202-659-9510).
- **INTERNATIONAL COUNCIL FOR BIRD PRESERVATION (ICBP),** (United Kingdom: 0223-277318; U.S. Headquarters, c/o WORLD WILDLIFE FUND—US; 202-293-4800).
- **RARE CENTER FOR TROPICAL BIRD CONSERVATION,** (215-568-0420).
- **WILDLIFE PRESERVATION TRUST INTERNATIONAL (WPTI),** (215-222-3636).
- **WORLD WILDLIFE FUND (WWF),** (202-293-4800).

(See also ENDANGERED SPECIES; also ENDANGERED AND THREATENED WILDLIFE AND PLANTS on page 372.)

**particulate matter,** tiny bits of solid or liquid material suspended in the air, many of which are small enough to irritate the eyes and enter the lungs, causing irritation and damage to the respiratory system. The particles are often chemically complex and can be toxic, including various kinds of HYDROCARBONS, other compounds, and HEAVY METALS. In sufficient concentration these particles can also harm visibility. Particulate matter is one of the CRITERIA AIR POLLUTANTS for which the ENVIRONMENTAL PROTECTION AGENCY (EPA) sets NATIONAL AMBIENT AIR QUALITY STANDARDS (NAAQSs), under the CLEAN AIR ACT. (See HEALTH EFFECTS OF THE REGULATED AIR POLLUTANTS on page 8.) Focus is especially on matter less than 10 micrometers in diameter ($PM_{10}$), since these are small enough to be inhaled into the lungs.

**For more information and action:**

• **Air and Waste Management Association (A&WMA),** (412-232-3444). Publishes *Visibility and Fine Particles* (1990); *PM-10: Implementation of Standards* (C.V. Mathai and David H. Stonefield, eds., 1988).

(See AIR POLLUTION.)

**passenger pigeon,** an extinct bird that provides a classic cautionary tale, for as recently as the mid-1800s a seemingly inexhaustible population of hundreds of millions and perhaps as many as 2 billion of these North American wild pigeons lived in eastern North America, from the Great Plains to the Atlantic and from Québec to Texas. Mass killings by hunters, loss of HABITAT to settlers, and perhaps disease combined to destroy them; by the early 20th century, they were extinct in the wild. The last known passenger pigeon, a female who had been named Martha, died at the Cincinnati Zoo on September 1, 1914. (See EXTINCTION.)

**PCBs (polychlorinated biphenyls),** a group of SYNTHETIC ORGANIC CHEMICALS, carbon-containing human-made compounds with chlorine added. Long before their danger was recognized, PCBs were used in many areas, as insulating materials, flame retardants, dye carriers (as in carbonless copy paper), paints, inks, dyes, lubricants, hydraulic fluids, plasticizers, and most importantly, heat transfer fluids in electrical transformers and capacitors.

Unfortunately, PCBs were later found to be highly toxic; they damage skin and the liver; are potentially CARCINOGENIC; can cause reproductive problems; and can be more immediately life-threatening in sufficient concentrations. If heated or burned (except at extremely high temperatures with complete combustion), they give off even more toxic compounds, such as DIOXIN and polychlorinated dibenzofuran (PCDF). PCBs also proved to be highly persistent in the environment, building up in the FOOD CHAIN, so much so that by the mid-1980s the ENVIRONMENTAL PROTECTION AGENCY estimated that nearly

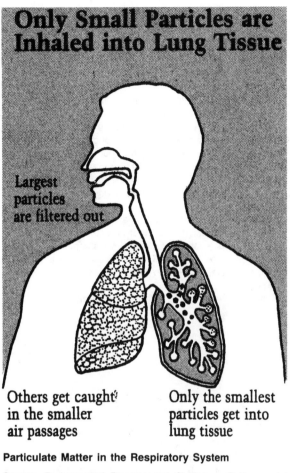

**Particulate Matter in the Respiratory System**

**Source:** *Environmental Progress and Challenges.* Environmental Protection Agency, 1988.

100 percent of the United States population had a trace of PCBs in their bodies. This was so, even though the use of PCBs, except in totally enclosed electrical equipment, was banned for most uses from 1976 in the United States and European Community (EC).

Despite the ban, PCBs are still widespread; though often found concentrated in industrial pollutants, PCBs are also found in old, dilapidated, often leaking electrical equipment throughout the world. Even where PCB-containing installations have been identified, problems remain as to how to destroy PCBs safely. The difficulty is such that the EPA, which regulates cleanup and disposal of PCBs after spills, has developed new technology for the attempt, including mobile incinerators and various chemical and biological approaches.

## Tale of the Hudson River PCBs

The Hudson River provides a classic example of environmental damage due to chemical dumping, and of the clash of powerful commercial interests with public interests. From 1946–77, two General Electric plants, upriver just south of Glen Falls at Fort Edward and Hudson Falls, dumped thousands of pounds of extremely toxic PCBs into the Hudson River. The PCBs sank to the bottom, beginning a long, slow journey downriver, ultimately polluting the whole course of the river, as far south as New York Harbor. In 1973, a dam at Fort Edwards was removed, speeding the PCB flow downriver.

In the early 1970s, it became clear that PCBs were a carcinogen in animals, and enough of a threat for New York State to ban commercial striped bass fishing in the Hudson, to warn against eating nine other kinds of fish found in the river, and to urge only very limited consumption of several other kinds of fish. In 1976, General Electric paid a $3 million fine to the state, and in 1977 stopped dumping PCBs into the river.

For the next 15 years, state legislators and officials de-

bated the issue of removing the PCBs—and took no concrete steps to do so, beyond abortive attempts to set up landfill for the PCBs that needed to be dredged up from 40 miles of riverbed, from Hudson Falls to Troy. At issue was the estimated $280 million (more by the time the work will finally be done) needed to do the dredging, as well as the landfill arrangements. The state made plans to dredge the river and then present General Electric with the bill for the job, as provided by the federal Superfund law. But in the spring of 1990 these plans were stopped by the state legislature, which decided—after 15 years—to wait for a further federal review of the situation. General Electric, which favored waiting and not paying, suggested bioremediation, in this instance an attempt to attack the toxic sludge with bacteria; state environmental officials suggested that after 15 years the time for further study and stalling had passed.

As of this writing, most of the PCBs still rested at the bottom of the river, contaminating the chain of life, though some cleanup was begun in mid-1991.

---

Two incidents illuminate the problem of dealing with PCBs:

- In June 1979, PCB-laced fluid from a transformer in a feed-processing firm leaked into animal feed, 1.9 million pounds of which was in the next few months sent to Minnesota, Montana, Idaho, Washington, North Dakota, and Utah farms. By mid-September 1979, over a million eggs and 400,000 chickens were destroyed, some with over 50 times the allowed amount of PCBs (see TOLERANCE LEVELS), in addition to the products of numerous bakeries and other food plants using eggs or chickens.
- In 1981, an explosion in the basement of an office building in Binghamton, New York, cracked an electrical transformer. The resulting fire partly burned PCB-containing material, converting some of it into dioxins and PCDFs, and the air-conditioning system quickly distributed the ash throughout the building. The office block was immediately sealed off, and even years later was considered unsafe to enter without protective clothing. The cost of complete decontamination of the building was estimated at $19 million.

Conflicts of interest—business and political—also complicate cleanup of PCB contamination; for example, see TALE OF THE HUDSON RIVER PCBs above. In 1989, the ENVIRONMENTAL PROTECTION AGENCY (EPA) put into ef-

fect new regulations establishing ''a 'cradle-to-grave' tracking and reporting system to ensure safe storage and disposal'' of PCBs. However, PCBs continue to be widely used in the developing world, with use increasing into the 1990s, especially in Latin America. (See also TOXIC CHEMICALS; HAZARDOUS WASTE.)

**pelican, brown,** American water bird, found off the California, Gulf, and Atlantic COASTS. Once numerous, the species was decimated by chemical POLLUTION, mainly by DDT and endrin (see CHLORINATED HYDROCARBONS), from the late 1950s through the early 1970s. Along the Louisiana and Texas coasts, endrin directly poisoned tens of thousands of brown pelicans, almost extinguishing them. Off the Gulf Coast, DDT concentrations caused calcium deficiencies in the eggs of pelicans and many other SPECIES, further attacking the species. Off the California coast, illegal DDT dumping into sewage systems all but destroyed the ability of the pelicans to reproduce. After the 1972 ban on DDT by the ENVIRONMENTAL PROTECTION AGENCY, the amount of DDT in the chain of life began to diminish, and the pelicans' ability to reproduce slowly began to return. The Florida brown pelican population had been least damaged by DDT; now it flourished once again, though always threatened by other forms of POLLUTION and HABITAT loss to developers on the coastal islands on which brown pelicans nest. The California brown pelicans began to return, as did pelican populations off the Carolinas, Texas, and Alabama, while a transfer of pelicans to their old breeding grounds off Louisiana proved successful. However, all but the Florida brown pelicans are still listed as ENDANGERED SPECIES, for their numbers are still small—and for all brown pelicans, habitat loss and toxic waste are growing dangers. (See also ENDANGERED SPECIES; also ENDANGERED AND THREATENED WILDLIFE AND PLANTS on page 372.)

**Persian Gulf War environmental disaster,** the combined impact of two acts committed by the Iraqi armed forces, as ordered by Saddam Hussein. The first was a major OIL spill, generated by the Iraqis beginning on January 23, 1991, by discharging oil at the Sea Island Terminal, 10 miles off the coast of Kuwait; at the Mina al-Bakr terminal, offshore nearer Kuwait; and from several tankers at Al-Ahmadi. American bombers struck at pipelines connecting Al-Ahmadi and Sea Island on January 27, in an attempt to stop the flow of oil, but were at best only partially successful. Estimates of the size of the total spill varied widely, from the wartime Allied claim that it was the greatest spill in history, larger even than the 1979 600,000-ton Gulf of Mexico IXTOC I WELL BLOWOUT, to far more conservative postwar estimates ranging as low as 70,000 tons. Whatever the final figure, it was still a massive spill, and especially destructive in the shallow waters of the upper Persian Gulf. Several months after the spill, some estimated that more than 20,000 seabirds had been killed by the spreading oil slick, and that the waters and shore of the Gulf would be poisoned for many years.

The second environmental disaster created by the Iraqis was the setting afire of an estimated 650 Kuwaiti oil wells, creating an enormous disaster in Kuwait and a regional environmental disaster of the first magnitude, as a pall of black, oily smoke spread south and west toward the countries of the Gulf and southwest Asia. In the spring of 1991 at least 500 wells were still burning, the last one was not extinguished until November 1991. The worldwide disaster predicted by some, much like a NUCLEAR WINTER, did not come, and seemed quite unlikely, as the smoke cloud did not rise into the upper atmosphere, being partly attenuated by some regional conditions, and has so far tested as less toxic that some had expected. But the longer-term effects of both the oil spill and the well fires could not yet be predicted, and the short-term effects were disastrous for the life and environment of the region. (See also IRAN-IRAQ WAR OIL SPILL; OIL.)

**pesticides (biocides),** substances used to reduce or eliminate unwanted plants or animals, especially insects; the subject of enormous public concern in recent de-

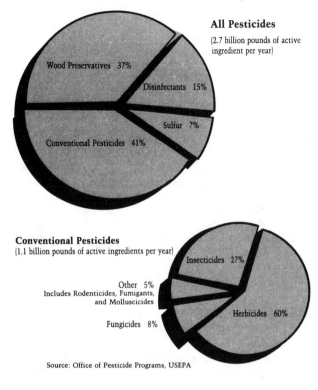

**Pesticide Use in the U.S.** (1986 Estimates)

**All Pesticides**
(2.7 billion pounds of active ingredient per year)

Wood Preservatives 37%
Disinfectants 15%
Sulfur 7%
Conventional Pesticides 41%

**Conventional Pesticides**
(1.1 billion pounds of active ingredients per year)

Insecticides 27%
Other 5% Includes Rodenticides, Fumigants, and Molluscicides
Herbicides 60%
Fungicides 8%

Source: Office of Pesticide Programs, USEPA

**Source:** Environmental Protection Agency, *Office of Pesticide Programs.*

cades. "Pesticide" is actually a popular umbrella term for a wide variety of specific "control chemicals," often used together, including *herbicides* (against plants), *insecticides* (against insects in general), *fungicides* (against fungi), *acaricides* (against members of *Acarina* and *Arachnida* families, notably mites, ticks, and spiders), *nematicides* (against roundworms and threadworms, many of them parasites), *molluscicides* (against molluscs such as snails, clams, whelks, mussels, and oysters), *termiticides* (against termites), *rodenticides* (against rodents such as rats or mice), *avicides* (against birds), and *bactericides* (against bacteria). According to the *VNR Scientific Encyclopedia*, over 100,000 chemical formulations are known as possible pesticides, about half of them insecticides.

Pesticides have been used for a wide variety of purposes. Herbicides help eliminate unwanted plants, generically known as weeds, some of which may harbor crop pests, provide a base for the buildup of viral disease and fungi (especially by retaining moisture), and

## Pesticides Information and Action Guide

**For more information and action on pesticides:**
**Alternative Farming Systems Information Center,** (301-344-3724 or 301-344-3559). Provides numerous Quick Bibliographies, such as *Herbicide Resistance* (K. Schneider, 1989) and *Herbicides: Ecological Effects* (J. MacLean, 1989). (See ORGANIC FARMING AND SUSTAINABLE AGRICULTURE INFORMATION AND ACTION GUIDE on page 226.)

CENTER FOR SCIENCE IN THE PUBLIC INTEREST **(CSPI),** (202-332-9110). Publishes *Nutrition Action Healthletter, Chemical Cuisine Poster*; brochures such as *Guess What's Coming to Dinner: Contaminants in Our Food;* and a directory of mail-order sources of organically grown foods.

**Concern, Inc.** (202-328-8160). Publishes *Pesticides: A Community Action Guide.*

ECOLOGICAL SOCIETY OF AMERICA **(ESA),** (301-530-7005).

ENVIRONMENTAL LAW INSTITUTE **(ELI),** (202-328-5150; publications office, 202-939-3844). (See ENVIRONMENTAL LAW.)

ENVIRONMENTAL PROTECTION AGENCY **(EPA),** (Public Information Center, 202-260-7751 or 202-260-2080). Publishes *Termiticides* (1988). Operates *National Pesticide Telecommunications Network (NPTN) Hotline* (800-858-PEST [7378]; in Texas: 806-743-3091; 24 hours a day, 365 days a year), and the *National Poison Control Center Hotline,* (202-625-3333).

FOOD AND DRUG ADMINISTRATION **(FDA),** (301-443-1544 or 302-443-3170). Operates the *National Center for Toxicological Research.* Reviews and approves or rejects chemicals used in foods, drugs, and cosmetics.

GREENPEACE, (202-462-1177). Runs *Toxic Campaign*; publishes *Exporting Banned Pesticides: Fueling the Circle of Poison* (1989) and the Action Factsheet *Pesticides.*

HUMAN ECOLOGY ACTION LEAGUE **(HEAL),** (404-248-1898). Publishes information packet *Experts Speak on Pesticides* and information sheets on chemical sensitivities.

INSTITUTE FOR FOOD AND DEVELOPMENT POLICY **(IFDP),** popularly called *Food First*, (415-864-8555). Publishes *Circle of Poison: Pesticides and People in a Hungry World.*

INTERNATIONAL COUNCIL FOR BIRD PRESERVATION **(ICBP)** (United Kingdom: 0223-277318; U.S. Headquarters, c/o WORLD WILDLIFE FUND—U.S.; 202-293-4800). Publishes *The Impact of Pesticides on Palearctic Migratory Birds in Western Sahel* (1989).

KIDS FOR SAVING EARTH™ **(KSE),** (612-525-0002 800-800-8800).

**National Coalition Against Misuse of Pesticides (NCAMP),** (701 E Street, SE, Suite 200, Washington, DC 20003; 202-543-5450; Jay Feldman, National Coordinator), a membership organization founded in 1981 by a "broad coalition of health, environmental, labor, farm, consumer and church groups, and individuals who share common concerns about the potential hazards associated with pesticides." NCAMP seeks to "focus public attention on the very serious pesticides poisoning problem," promotes "reduced pesticide exposure through alternative pest management strategies that use few or no toxic chemicals," "advocates public policies that better protect the public from pesticide exposure," and supplies information on alternative methods of pest control. It publishes various materials, including the newsletter *Pesticides and You (PAY);* a monthly *NCAMP's Technical Report;* books and booklets such as *Pesticide in Contract Lawn Maintenance* (Rachel Carson Council) and *NCAMP's Library Aid for Students of Pesticide Issues*, a series of *pesticides reviews—Health and Environmental Effects and Alternatives*, as on chlordane, lawn care, and wood preservatives, brochures and flyers, such as *Pesticide Safety: Myths and Facts, Pesticides and Your Fruits and Vegetables,* and *Agriculture: Soil Erosion, Pesticides, Sustainability;* and a "how-to" series on *Taking Action to Control Pesticides and Promote Alternatives.*

NATURAL RESOURCES DEFENSE COUNCIL **(NRDC),** (212-727-2700). Publishes *For Our Kid's Sake: How to Protect Your Child Against Pesticides in Food* (1989), *Intolerable Risk: Pesticides in Our Children's Food* (Bradford H. Sewell and Robin M. Whyatt, 1989), and *Pesticide Alert: A Guide to Pesticides in Fruits and Vegetables* (L. Mott and K. Snyder, 1988).

---

can weigh down and damage fences and other structures (as kudzu does). By using herbicides, farmers and gardeners are also freed from the need to remove weeds mechanically or manually to promote growth of desired crops. Directed toward insects and other fauna, pesticides can have public health benefits, as in preventing the spread of diseases such as malaria or Lyme disease; economic benefits, as in preventing damage to crops or to organic materials such as wood or cloth in other settings; and "welfare" benefits (see WELFARE EFFECTS),

as in preventing discomfort, annoyance, or injury to humans, pets, or livestock. Pesticides indeed have so many useful purposes that they were in the early days of their discovery and use regarded as "miracle chemicals," capable of transforming daily life; Paul Müller, who in 1939 discovered the pesticide potential for DDT, for example, was awarded the 1948 Nobel Prize for Chemistry for his benefits to humanity.

Before DDT, many pesticides were inorganic substances, often containing HEAVY METALS such as COPPER,

**Northwest Coalition for Alternatives to Pesticides (NCAP)** (P.O. Box 1393, Eugene, OR 97440; 503-344-5044; Norma Grier, Executive Director), a grassroots membership organization founded in 1977 by the union of 17 citizen pesticide reform groups in five states: California, Idaho, Montana, Oregon, and Washington. NCAP aims "to offer alternatives to pesticides" and "to strengthen grassroots organizations and grassroots support." Its concerns encompass "pesticide dependence in forest, agriculture, roadside, aquatic, and urban settings." NCAP gathers and exchanges information on pesticide issues with other organizations and agencies; responds to queries; attempts to influence public policy; and publishes various materials, including the quarterly *Journal of Pesticide Reform;* information packets such as *Getting to the Roots of Pesticide Reform* (Tom Lamar, 1990), *2,4-D Information Packet* (Sally Claggett, 1990), *Glyphosate Information Packet* (Susan Allen, 1990), *Pesticide Exposure and the Role of the Physician* (Jennifer Curtis, 1988), *Blowin' in the Wind: Pesticide Drift* (Sandra Ely and Francis Eatherington, 1989), *Pesticides in Our Food: From Alar and Apples to Alternative Agriculture* (Becky Riley, 1989), and *Teaching Ideas: Pesticide Awareness and the Concept of Integrated Pest Management* (Becky Riley, 1989); and fact sheets on specific pesticides.

**Pesticide Action Network, North America Regional Center (PANNA)** (P.O. Box 610, San Francisco, CA 94101; 415-541-9140); Monica Moore, Executive Director, international coalition of over 300 nongovernmental organizations "working to stop pesticide misuse and global pesticide proliferation," formerly called the Pesticide Education Action Project, founded in 1982 runs PANNA the Dirty Dozen Campaign to replace the most notorious "pesticides with sustainable, ecologically sound alternatives." It also publishes various materials, including the quarterly newsletter *Global Pesticide Campaigner (GPC),* the bi-monthly *PANNA Outlook,* posters on the Dirty Dozen Campaign and circle of poisons, and books such as *Problem Pesticides, Pesticide Problems: A Citizen's Action Guide to the UN Food and Agriculture Organization's (FAO) International Code of Conduct on the Distribution and Use of Pesticides, The FAO Code: Missing Ingre-*dients, *The Pesticide Code Monitor, Monitoring the International Code of Conduct on the Distribution and Use of Pesticides in North America, Escaping From the Pesticide Treadmill: Alternatives to Pesticides in Developing Countries, Breaking the Pesticide Habit: Alternatives to 12 Hazardous Pesticides,* and *Pills, Pesticides and Profits: The International Trade in Toxic Substances.*

RENEW AMERICA, (202-232-2252). Publishes *Pesticide Contamination* (1988).

RESOURCES FOR THE FUTURE (RFF), (202-328-5000). Includes research arms *Quality of the Environment Division,* and *National Center for Food and Agricultural Policy.* Publishes *Pesticide Policy, Production Risk, and Producer Welfare: An Econometric Approach to Applied Welfare Economics* (John M. Antle, 1988).

SIERRA CLUB, (415-776-2211 or 202-547-1141; legislative hotline, 202-547-5550). Publishes *Pest Management Policy.*

THRESHOLD, INTERNATIONAL CENTER FOR ENVIRONMENTAL RENEWAL (602-432-7353). Operates the *Malathion Project* in Baja California, Mexico.

U.S. PUBLIC INTEREST RESEARCH GROUP (PIRG), (202-546-9707). Publishes *Presumed Innocent: A Report on 69 Cancer-Causing Pesticides Allowed in Our Food* (1990), *Guess What's Coming to Dinner?: A Study of Carcinogenic Pesticides Allowed in 16 Foods and Found in Groundwater* (1989), *Pesticides in Groundwater: EPA Files Reveal Tip of Deadly Iceberg (1988),* and PAC Studies such as *Pesticide PAC Study* (1988).

WILDLIFE INFORMATION CENTER, (215-434-1637). Publishes *Lawn Care Chemicals.*

WORLD RESOURCES INSTITUTE, (202-638-6300).

**Other references:**

*The Effect of Pesticides on Human Health.* Scott Baker and Chris Wilkinson, eds., Princeton Scientific Publishing, 1990. *Environmental Law: Pesticides and Toxic Substances,* 3 vols., William H. Rodgers, Jr. West (St. Paul, MN), 1988.

(See also BIOLOGICAL CONTROL AND INTEGRATED PEST MANAGEMENT INFORMATION AND ACTION GUIDE on page 36.)

---

LEAD, MERCURY, and zinc, as well as tin and arsenic. Many such substances are still used, but DDT ushered in the age of SYNTHETIC ORGANIC CHEMICALS (SOCs), often used with considerable effectiveness as pesticides. Pesticides helped countries all over the world grow enough food to feed the exploding POPULATIONS of the 20th century; in fact, the GREEN REVOLUTION, widely credited with averting disastrous international FAMINE AND FOOD INSECURITY, did so by developing high-yielding grains extremely vulnerable to pests and therefore highly dependent on pesticides.

Unfortunately, it was not clear until recent decades how powerful, dangerous, or persistent many of these pesticides really were. Only gradually through the second half of the 20th century has it become clear that many pesticides remain in the environment for years and in some cases decades, being taken up in nature's great BIOGEOCHEMICAL CYCLES, entering the FOOD CHAIN, and through BIOACCUMULATION building up in the bodies of larger animals, often with devastating effects. Among humans, cancer is one of the best known and most feared effects from pesticide, but damage to the other major organ systems—heart, lungs, kidneys, liver, and central nervous system—is also common. Children are thought to be especially at risk because their diet is made up of more pesticide-containing foods than that of adults, and they are more susceptible to cancer and brain damage. The number of people injured or killed each year by pesticides is unknown, since no proper records are kept, but estimates range up to 10,000 deaths and 1 million injuries.

Some warnings came early, notably Rachel CARSON's *Silent Spring*, but full-scale pesticide use continued and increased. Pesticides have now been carried throughout the world by wind and water, and traces are found even in ANTARCTIC, far from actual use. In the 1987 ENVIRONMENTAL PROTECTION AGENCY (EPA) report UNFINISHED BUSINESS: A COMPARATIVE ASSESSMENT OF ENVIRONMENTAL PROBLEMS, pesticides was third-ranked among 31 environmental problem areas for population cancer risks and ecological risks, and also ranked high as a non-cancer risk (see tables near UNFINISHED BUSINESS entry on page 316.)

Living beings are also affected by pesticide use in a wide variety of other ways. DDT, for example, was found to inhibit absorption of calcium, making the eggshells of many birds too thin to survive incubation, so its use brought to the brink of EXTINCTION numerous birds, such as the California CONDOR, whooping CRANE, bald EAGLE, peregrine FALCON, OSPREY, and brown PELICAN, some of which are only reviving now in places where DDT has been banned.

Nor are pesticides—even without these dangers—all they were hoped to be. Some insects have developed a resistance to pesticides, while some plants have lost their natural resistance to insects, both factors leading to the use of ever more pesticides to achieve the same effect. Even where pesticides are successful in attacking a "target" species, many non-target species are killed as well, and the whole balance of the crop ECOSYSTEM goes awry.

Not all pesticides are equally dangerous. Some are targeted for specific plants or insects, being termed *narrow spectrum*, while *wide spectrum* pesticides act more indiscriminately. Some are BIODEGRADABLE, effective for only a few days and then breaking down in the environment. These are less dangerous but also less effective, unless used during a precise time in the life cycle of target plants or animals, such as only before the plant emerges, or during a key developmental stage of an insect. Some pesticides work by contact, while others enter and disrupt the plant or animal's system.

Pesticides come in many different forms, including granules, powders, dusts, slurries, sprays, and other forms, sometimes mixed by the chemical manufacturers,

sometimes by the local supplier or user. The people actually making, mixing, and using the pesticides are especially at risk. Although pesticides are most commonly thought of in relation to use on crops, they are also widely used in and around homes, posing great danger to people whose lawns and gardens are "treated" and constituting a dangerous part of AIR POLLUTION, outdoors and in. For information on protecting yourself in and around the home, see TIPS FOR DEALING WITH PESTICIDES on page 242.

Governments increasingly monitor the amounts and effects of pesticides in the environment. In the United States, this process is an EPA responsibility, under such laws as the FEDERAL INSECTICIDE, FUNGICIDE AND RODENTICIDE ACT (FIFRA), TOXIC SUBSTANCES CONTROL ACT (TSCA or TOSCA), SAFE DRINKING WATER ACT (SDWA), CLEAN WATER ACT (CWA), and CLEAN AIR ACT (CAA). MAXIMUM CONTAMINANT LEVELS are set (see PRIMARY DRINKING WATER STANDARDS on page 274) and sites found to be dangerously contaminated may be cleaned up under a variety of laws, such as the COMPREHENSIVE ENVIRONMENTAL RESPONSE, COMPENSATION AND LIABILITY ACT (CERCLA) and the EMERGENCY PLANNING AND COMMUNITY RIGHT-TO-KNOW ACT (EPCRA), and its SUPERFUND amendments.

However, as numerous environmentalists have pointed out, the EPA monitors only a small fraction of pesticides; the large majority are not monitored, and in many cases their probable effects on the environment are unknown or incompletely known. In the wake of the SHASTA LAKE PESTICIDE DISASTER, for example, it was found that the EPA had received warnings of health dangers from at least 10 pesticides but had failed to take action—in some cases, as in Shasta Lake's metam sodium, they had failed even to read the reports.

In industrialized countries, some pesticides known to be extremely toxic in the environment have been taken off the market. (See PESTICIDES BANNED IN THE UNITED STATES on page 241.) However, in many other countries, such pesticides continue to be used; DDT, for example, is widely used in the Third World, notably in Latin America, Africa, and on the Indian subcontinent. Many pesticide-contaminated foods are then imported into industrialized countries, completing what some have called the CIRCLE OF POISON.

Even where pesticides have been banned, many persist in the environment. According to the EPA, the groundwater of at least 30 states contains 50 or more pesticides, many of them CARCINOGENS, and the U.S. General Accounting Office reported that over 140 pesticides and other

## Pesticides Banned in the United States

Note: *Oncogenicity* means causes tumors; *mutagenicity* means causes mutations; *carcinogenicity* means causes cancer; *teratogenicity* means causes major birth defects; *fetotixicity* means causes toxicity to the unborn fetus. Also note that, since this table was published, the EPA has banned several other pesticides, including R-11, EBDC, and Diazinon.

| Pesticides | Use | Concerns | Pesticides | Use | Concerns |
|---|---|---|---|---|---|
| **Aldrin** | Insecticide | Oncogenicity | **Heptachlor** (Agricultural uses; termiticide uses suspended or cancelled) | Insecticide | Oncogenicity; mutagenicity; reproductive effects |
| **Chlordane** (Agricultural uses, termiticide uses suspended or cancelled) | Insecticide/ termites, ants | Oncogenicity; reduction in non-target and endangered species | | | |
| | | | **Kepone** | Insecticide | Oncogenicity |
| **Compound 1080** (Livestock collar retained, rodenticide use under review) | Coyote control; rodenticide | Reductions in non-target and endangered species; no known antidote | **Lindane** (Indoor smoke bomb cancelled; some uses restricted) | Insecticide/ vaporizer | Oncogenicity; teratogenicity; reproductive effects; acute toxicity; other chronic effects |
| **DDT and related compounds** | Insecticide | Ecological (eggshell thinning); carcinogenicity | **Mercury** | Microbial uses | Cumulative toxicant causing brain damage |
| **Dibromochloro-propane (DBCP)** | Soil fumigant—fruits and vegetables | Oncogenicity; mutagenicity; reproductive effects | **Mirex** | Insecticide/fire ant control | Nontarget species; potential oncogenicity |
| **Dieldrin** | Insecticide | Oncogenicity | **Silvex** | Herbicide/forestry rights-of-way, weed control | Oncogenicity; teratogenicity; fetotoxicity |
| **Dinoseb** (in hearings) [later cancelled] | Herbicide/crop desiccant | Fetotoxicity; reproductive effects; acute toxicity | | | |
| **Endrin** (Avicide use retained) | Insecticide/avicide | Oncogenicity; teratogenicity; reductions in nontarget and endangered species | **Strychnine** (Rodenticide use and livestock collar retained) | Mammalian predator control; rodenticide | Reductions in nontarget and endangered species |
| | | | **2,4,5-T** | Herbicide/forestry rights-of-way, weed control | Oncogenicity; teratogenicity; fetotoxicity |
| **Ethylene dibromide (EDB)** (Very minor uses on citrus for export retained) | Insecticide/ fumigant | Oncogenicity; mutagenicity; reproductive effects | **Toxaphene** (Livestock dip retained) | Insecticide—cotton | Oncogenicity; reduction in nontarget species; acute toxicity to aquatic organisms; chronic effects on wildlife |

**Source:** *A Number of Pesticides Have Been Taken Off the Market,* from *Environmental Progress and Challenges: EPA's Update.* Environmental Protection Agency, 1988.

drugs, many of which also cause cancer or birth defects, are found in meat products after slaughter. In 1990, the EPA tested drinking-water wells for 127 pesticides and NITRATES; in the same year, it also issued rules to regulate 26 pesticides, an improvement that still dealt with only a fraction of the problem. However, the EPA noted that

in 1989 and 1990 it had cancelled approximately 20,000 pesticide products "for failure to pay new annual registration maintenance fees or to supply required scientific data." The EPA has encouraged (under the 1990 Farm Bill) funding for a program to support registration of pesticides used on "minor" or specialty crops, and another

## Tips for Dealing with Pesticides

Pesticides are *not* "safe." They are produced specifically because they are toxic to something. By heeding *all* the following tips, you can reduce your risks when you use pesticides.

### Handling Pesticides

- All pesticides legally marketed in the United States must bear an EPA-approved label; check the label to make sure it bears an EPA registration number.
- Before using a pesticide, read the entire label. Even if you have used the pesticide before, read the label again—don't trust your memory. Use of any pesticide in any way that is not consistent with label directions and precautions is subject to civil and/or criminal penalties.
- Do not use a "restricted use" pesticide unless you are a formally trained, certified pesticide applicator. These products are too dangerous to be used without special training.
- Follow use directions carefully. Use only the amount directed, at the time and under the conditions specified, and for the purpose listed. Don't think that twice the dosage will do twice the job. It won't. What's worse, you may harm yourself, others, or whatever you are trying to protect.
- Look for one of the following signal words on the front of the label. It will tell you how hazardous a pesticide is if swallowed, inhaled, or absorbed through the skin.
  - "Danger" means highly poisonous.
  - "Warning" means moderately hazardous.
  - "Caution" means least hazardous.
- Wear the items of clothing the label requires: for example, long sleeves and long pants, impervious gloves, rubber (not canvas or leather) footwear, hat, and goggles. Personal protective clothing usually is available at home building supply stores.
- If you must mix or dilute the pesticide, do so outdoors or in a well-ventilated area. Mix only the amount you need and use portions listed on the label.
- Keep children and pets away from areas where you mix or apply pesticides.
- If a spill occurs, clean it up promptly. Don't wash it away.

Instead, sprinkle with sawdust, vermiculite, or kitty litter; sweep into a plastic garbage bag; and dispense with the rest of your trash.
- Remove pets (including birds and fish) and toys from the area to be treated. Remove food, dishes, pots, and pans before treating kitchen cabinets, and don't let pesticides get on these surfaces. Wait until shelves dry before refilling them.
- Allow adequate ventilation when applying pesticides indoors. Go away from treated areas for *at least* the length of time prescribed by the label. When spraying outdoors, close the windows of your home.
- Most surface sprays should be applied only to limited areas; don't treat entire floors, walls, or ceilings.
- Never place rodent or insect baits where small children or pets can reach them.
- When applying spray or dust outdoors, cover fish ponds, and avoid applying pesticides near wells. Always avoid over-applications when treating lawn, shrubs, or gardens. Runoff or seepage from excess pesticide usage may contaminate water supplies. Excess spray may leave harmful residues on home-grown produce.
- Keep herbicides away from nontarget plants. Avoid applying any pesticide to blooming plants, especially if you see honeybees or other pollinating insects around them. Avoid birds' nests when spraying trees.
- Never spray or dust outdoors on a windy day.
- Never smoke while applying pesticides. You could easily carry traces of the pesticide from hand to mouth. Also, some products are flammable.
- Never transfer pesticides to containers that are not intended for them, such as empty soft drink bottles or other containers that children might associate with something to eat or drink. Keep pesticides in containers that clearly and prominently identify the contents. Properly refasten all childproof caps.
- Shower and shampoo thoroughly after using a pesticide product. Wash the clothing that you wore when applying the product separately from the family laundry. To prevent

---

program to help farmers improve their pesticide and nutrient management practices, to reduce problems with LEACHING and POLLUTION of runoff. In 1989 it also initiated a new program with the FISH AND WILDLIFE SERVICE and the DEPARTMENT OF AGRICULTURE to protect ENDANGERED SPECIES from the effects of pesticide use, ranking species on "status, vulnerability, and recovery potential."

As pesticide dangers have become ever clearer, more people are turning to alternative ways of dealing with pests

and unwanted plants. Among the main kinds of alternatives are BIOLOGICAL CONTROL, INTEGRATED PEST MANAGEMENT (IPM), and ORGANIC FARMING. These have in common a "systems" approach to pest management, seeing a farm or section of a farm as a "crop ecosystem," and using wherever possible natural controls for unwanted pests, such as planting borders of plants toxic to certain insects. These are sometimes more expensive approaches in the short-term, but become less so when considering the

tracking chemicals inside, also rinse boots and shoes before entering your home.

- Before using a pesticide product, know what to do in case of accidental poisoning.
- To remove residues, use a bucket to triple-rinse tools or equipment, including any containers or utensils used to mix the chemicals. Then pour the rinse water into the pesticide container and reuse the solution by applying it according to the pesticide product label directions.
- Evaluate the results of your pesticide use.

## Storing Pesticides

- Buy only enough product to carry you through the use season, to reduce storage problems.
- Store pesticides away from children and pets. A locked cabinet in a well-ventilated utility area or garden shed is best.
- Store flammable liquids outside living quarters and away from an ignition source.
- Never put pesticides in cabinets with, or near, food, medical supplies, or cleaning materials. Always store pesticides in their original containers, complete with labels that list ingredients, directions for use, and antidotes in case of accidental poisoning.
- Avoid storing pesticides in places where flooding is possible, or in open places where they might spill or leak into the environment. If you have any doubt about the content of a container, dispose of it with your trash.

## Disposing of Pesticides

- The best way to dispose of a small, excess amount of pesticide is to use it—apply it—according to directions on the product label. If you cannot use it, ask your neighbor whether he/she can use it. If all the pesticides cannot be used, first check with your local health department or solid waste management agency to determine whether your community has a household hazardous waste collection program or any other program for handling disposal of pesticides.
- If no community programs exist, follow label directions regarding container disposal. To dispose of less than a full container of a liquid pesticide, leave it in the original container, with the cap securely in place to prevent spills or leaks. Wrap the container in several layers of newspapers and tie securely. Then place the package in a covered trash can for routine collection with municipal refuse. If you do not have a regular trash collection service, take the package to a permitted landfill (unless your municipality has other requirements). **Note:** No more than one gallon of liquid pesticide should be disposed of in this manner.

- Wrap individual packages of dry pesticide formulations in several layers of newspaper, or place the package in a tight carton or bag, and tape or tie it closed. As with liquid formulations, place the package in a covered trash can for routine collections. **Note:** No more than five pounds of pesticide at a time should be disposed of in this manner.
- Do *not* pour leftover pesticide down the sink or into the toilet. Chemicals in pesticides could interfere with the operation of wastewater treatment systems or could pollute waterways, because many municipal systems cannot remove all pesticide residues.
- An empty pesticide container can be as hazardous as a full one because of residues remaining inside. Never reuse such a container. When empty, a pesticide container should be carefully rinsed and thoroughly drained. Liquids used to rinse the container should be added to the sprayer or to the container previously used to mix the pesticide and used according to label directions.
- Empty product containers made of plastic or metal should be punctured to prevent reuse. (Do not puncture or burn a pressurized product container—it could explode.) Glass containers should be rinsed and drained, as described above, and the cap or closure replaced securely. After rinsing, an empty mixing container or sprayer may also be wrapped and placed in the trash.
- If you have any doubts about proper pesticide disposal, contact your state or local health department, your solid waste management agency, or the regional EPA office.

**Source:** *Citizen's Guide to Pesticides.* Environmental Protection Agency, 1990.

---

cost of repairing—where that is even possible—damage to the environment. One approach to handling the up-front costs is COMMUNITY SUPPORTED AGRICULTURE (CSA). The EPA also noted that in 1989–90 it registered 10 new biologically based pesticides, almost one-third of all new registrations during that period.

In BLUEPRINT FOR THE ENVIRONMENT, U.S. environmentalists urged that the EPA "sponsor, develop and promote Integrated Pest Management techniques to help reduce chemical inputs"; "require registrants [manufacturers] to develop Best Management Practices [BMPs] designed to prevent ground water contaminations"; monitor ground and surface water in high-pesticide-use locations; set up a single system for gathering and disseminating information on pesticide poisonings; fulfill its obligation to "protect endangered species from the adverse impacts of pesticide exposure"; "ensure that all tolerance levels are supported by full health and safety data and that these tolerances ensure that all consumers, especially children and the elderly, are protected from risk of cancer and other serious adverse health effects''; develop non-lethal techniques for their Animal Damage Control (ADC) program; ensure that all pesticides are fully reregistered within the next few years; and consider crop surpluses when determining the benefit of high-risk products, restructuring risk-benefit analyses to ''replace yield goals with profit-per-acre goals,'' and eliminating the bias against alternative pest controls, the goal being less pesticide use. (See PESTICIDES INFORMATION AND ACTION GUIDE on page 238; also TOXIC CHEMICALS AND HAZARDOUS SUBSTANCES INFORMATION AND ACTION GUIDE on page 407; KNOWN HEALTH EFFECTS OF TOXIC CHEMICALS on page 416; also specific pesticides, such as AGENT ORANGE; ALAR; CARBAMATES; CHLORINATED HYDROCARBONS; CYCLODIENES; DDT; DIOXIN; HEAVY METALS; ORGANOPHOSPHATES; TRIBUTYL TIN; 2,4-D; 2,4,5-T.)

**Peterson, Roger Tory** (1908– ), U.S. ornithologist, illustrator, and nature writer. Peterson's first book, *Field Guide to the Birds; Giving Field Marks of All Species Found in Western North America* (1934), which he wrote and illustrated, became the ''bible'' of three generations of American birdwatchers, whose ever-expanding numbers provided much of the basis for the new American ecological movements that developed in mid-century. He followed it with such works as *A Field Guide to Western Birds* (1941); the long and popular Field Guide series, which he began editing in 1946; the equally popular American Naturalist series; and a wide range of other works, some of them describing his field trips in search of birds, as in *Birds of America* (1948), *Wild America* (1955), and *Penguins* (1979), reflecting his long interest in Antarctic wildlife. He has also served as president of the INTERNATIONAL COUNCIL FOR BIRD PRESERVATION (ICBP).

**petrochemical,** a susbstance or material derived from petroleum, and so a type of HYDROCARBON, a chemical made of hydrogen and carbon atoms. Petrochemicals are at the heart of the modern chemical industry, being the basis for many ''miracle'' substances, but also the source of considerable chemical POLLUTION. Among the best known petrochemicals are acetic acid, acetone, benzene, formaldehyde, ethylene, ethylene dichloride, methanol, phenol, polyethylene, polyvinyl chloride, styrene, toluene, VINYL CHLORIDE, and xylene. Many petrochemicals have been linked to cancer; the Louisiana industrial corridor, where 20 percent of the United States' petrochemicals are produced, has even been dubbed ''Cancer Alley,'' because of unusually high rate of cancer. Various individuals and organizations there have brought suit against chemical

manufacturers for vinyl chloride exposure. Two cases settled out of court called for payment of a $1 million penalty to the federal government and an additional $250,000 for university research into the health effects of hazardous air pollutants. (See TOXIC CHEMICALS; also TOXIC CHEMICALS AND HAZARDOUS SUBSTANCES on page 407; KNOWN HEALTH EFFECTS OF TOXIC CHEMICALS on page 416.)

**pH,** a chemist's measure of how acid or alkaline a solution is. On a scale of 0 to 14, 7 indicates neutrality. As the numbers decrease from 7 they denote increasingly acid substances; ACID RAIN is generally considered to be rain with a pH of 5.6 or below. Vinegar has a pH of 3 to 4 and lemon juice 1 to 2. (See illustrations at ACID RAIN.) As the numbers increase from 7, they denote increasingly alkaline substances, such as carbonates and bicarbonates—well known from television commercials for doing what alkaline substances do best: neutralize acids. Baking soda has a pH of 8 to 9. OCEANS are largely alkaline because they contain large amounts of dissolved carbonates. The ''pH'' actually stands for ''pHydrion,'' which refers to the concentration of hydrogen ions in the solution, expressed mathematically in logarithms.

**phenoxy herbicides,** a family of PESTICIDES that includes 2,4-D and 2,4,5-T, which in a 50–50 mixture are the constituents of AGENT ORANGE.

**phosphates,** phosphorus-containing compounds that occur naturally and are vital for plant growth, but which in excess can cause POLLUTION. In LAKES, RIVERS and some other bodies of water, they can cause so much plant growth as to kill off marine life, a process called EUTROPHICATION. Phosphates (along with NITRATES) are commonly found in fertilizers, as well as in sewage; but one of the main sources of phosphates has been in detergents, long a target of environmentalists.

### For more information and action:

• **Chesapeake Bay Foundation (CBF),** (301-268-8816) Publishes *Detergents, Phosphorus, and the Bay*. (See CHESAPEAKE BAY.)

**photosynthesis,** the process by which green (chlorophyll-containing) plants use the sun's energy to convert water and CARBON DIOXIDE into oxygen and energy-rich carbohydrates (see BIOGEOCHEMICAL CYCLES).

*Piper Alpha* **explosion,** a series of explosions, followed by a massive fire, that destroyed the Occidental Petroleum Company North Sea OIL rig *Piper Alpha,* off Aberdeen, Scotland, on July 6, 1988, killing 167 people. It was the worst disaster since the beginning of NORTH SEA drilling operations in 1968, though there had been other such disasters in the previous decade, such as the destruction of the *Ocean Ranger* oil drilling rig in a storm off St. John's, Newfoundland, in 1982, killing 84, and the sinking of a "floating hotel" for North Sea oil rig workers in a storm off Stavanger, Norway, in 1980, killing 123.

**plankton,** a general name for the large and diverse body of tiny plants and animals that form much of the basis of life in the sea, and which gather vital energy for life through the process of PHOTOSYNTHESIS. Most basic is the plant life, called *phytoplankton,* which feeds the body of small animal forms called *zooplankton.* Plankton begins the FOOD CHAIN, and therefore the whole chain of life in the sea, as when the masses of KRILL in Antarctic seas feed on plankton and are themselves the primary food of many larger sea creatures (see illustration at ANTARCTICA). Some environmental scientists have suggested that the loss of protective OZONE, and in particular the hole in the Antarctic OZONE LAYER, may cause genetic damage and perhaps adverse mutations to the plankton in Antarctic seas, with possibly harmful results for all the life in those seas. There are also warnings that because phytoplankton use large amounts of CARBON DIOXIDE, their lesser numbers might mean more carbon dioxide in the atmosphere, which might contribute to GLOBAL WARMING. Concern has also grown about similar effects in other parts of the world, as recent evidence continues to suggest widespread ozone depletion. (See OCEANS.)

**plastics,** a whole family of chemical compounds that are easily molded and worked during manufacture—hence the name—but hold their shape afterward; some derive from natural substances, while others are synthesized in the laboratory, many from petroleum (see PETROCHEMICALS). Because of their versatility and durability, plastics have been used for a wide range of consumer products since their commercial introduction in the late 1920s. But by the 1970s, it had become clear that plastics were *too* durable, since they persisted in the environment long after their useful life was ended, choking landfills, littering the landscape, especially roadsides and COASTS, and killing many land and sea animals who tried to eat the plastic or became entangled in plastic devices. Many of the DRIFTNETS used so indiscriminately in commercial FISHING are made of plastic.

In response to environmental concerns, scientists have developed some types of plastics that are BIODEGRADABLE, breaking down by natural processes in the environment. Critics charge, however, that these are biodegradable only over decades and when exposed to light and air, so the POLLUTION is not effectively reduced. Even then, the prod-

uct is not fully biodegradable, but leaves chemical fragments behind. While research continues, many shoppers seek to avoid plastic products or packaging, where possible (see GREEN CONSUMERISM).

Some communities are trying a RECYCLING approach to the plastics problem. These focus on two types of plastic, which make up over 80 percent of all plastics used in consumer products in the United States: polyethylene terephthalate (PET), used in large soda bottles, and high-density polyethylene, used in milk bottles. However, most plastics are not as appropriate for recycling, since (unlike glass or aluminum) they cannot be used to make products of the same type. In addition, the hundreds of different kinds of plastics all have their own chemical specifications for recycling and cannot readily be distinguished and separated. (For more details, see RECYCLING.) Recycled plastics may, however, be mixed together and used to produce lower-quality plastics or burned for energy (see COGENERATION; INCINERATION).

The industrial production and use of plastics is also of environmental concern, since many plastics manufacturers release large amounts of TOXIC CHEMICALS into the environment. Some plastics, such as polyvinyl chloride (PVC), can give off toxic fumes and by-products, such as DIOXINS, when burned. In addition, some plastics, such as polystyrene foam products, are made with chemicals that damage the OZONE LAYER, including CHLOROFLUOROCARBONS.

### For more information and action:

- **CENTER FOR MARINE CONSERVATION (CMC),** (202-429-5609). Has *Marine Debris and Entanglement Program.* Publishes *Citizen's Guide to Plastic in the Ocean: More Than a Litter Problem, Marine Wildlife Entanglement in North America,* and slide show *Marine Debris and Entanglement.*
- **ENVIRONMENTAL DEFENSE FUND (EDF),** (212-505-2100). Publishes *Degradable Plastics: The Wrong Answer to the Right Question* (R.A. Denison and J. Wirka, 1989).
- **GREENPEACE,** (202-462-1177). Publishes "Plastics: An Environmental Menace" and *Breaking Down the Degradable Plastics Scam* (1990).
- **KIDS FOR SAVING EARTH™ (KSE),** (612-525-0002 or 800-800-8800).

(See also RECYCLING; WASTE DISPOSAL.)

**plover, piping,** once a common North American shorebird, this species of plover ranged along the Atlantic seaboard from northern Canada to the CARIBBEAN, and in mid-continent from the northern Great Plains to the Gulf coast. Unrestrained HUNTING and loss of HABITAT to growing human POPULATIONS took an enormous toll: by the mid-1980s, less than 1,000 breeding pairs were estimated as surviving on the Atlantic COAST, less than 100 pairs in the northern plains and GREAT LAKES, and substantial but much reduced numbers in western Canada. Joint Canadian and U.S. efforts now aim to protect plover habitats, especially those on public lands, and especially during breeding season, and some success has been reported, although loss of habitat to hydroelectric plants and developers, and disturbance of habitat by off-the-road recreation vehicles and holiday activities continues. On the whole, though, the possibility that the piping plover will be saved seems good. (See also ENDANGERED SPECIES; also ENDANGERED AND THREATENED WILDLIFE AND PLANTS on page 372.)

**pollution,** broadly, a concentration of substances that—in kind or amount—are beyond an environment's capacity to handle through its normal processes. Looked at from a different perspective, pollution is a concentration sufficient to make the environment less healthy or less suitable for use, by human or other life. In a natural environment, substances are processed through an elaborate, intertwining network of BIOGEOCHEMICAL CYCLES, being picked up by plants, traveling through the FOOD CHAIN to larger and more complex organisms, then as the circle is completed being decomposed into simpler forms for later reuse. Such substances are said to be BIODEGRADABLE, since they can be broken down by the environment's normal biological systems. Pollution occurs when the environment becomes overloaded beyond the capacity of these normal processing systems. This can occur with

- excess amounts of normally innocuous or even helpful substances, such as nutrients (see EUTROPHICATION);
- excess amounts of substances that are harmless and perhaps even necessary in tiny amounts but toxic in concentration, such as iron, COPPER, zinc, or MANGANESE;
- synthetic (human-made) compounds that are poisonous in the environment, often even in trace amounts, such as DDT, DIOXIN, PCBs, PBBs, SYNTHETIC ORGANIC CHEMICALS (SOCs), VOLATILE ORGANIC COMPOUNDS (VOCs), CHLORINATED HYDROCARBONS, and other TOXIC CHEMICALS; and
- materials in any amounts that resist biodegradation, or decomposition in the natural cycles, such as PLASTICS and highly persistent chemicals like DDT and other chlorinated hydrocarbons.

So it is that a substance, such as copper or nitrogen fertilizer, that is helpful and encourages natural processes in modest amounts, can sometimes become a pollutant, and substances used for one effect in one place can often

persist to clog and disrupt natural systems elsewhere. Some pollutants kill living organisms outright; other *sublethal pollutants* do not kill, but cause long-term biological damage and make organisms more vulnerable to disease.

In these last few decades, as throughout history, most approaches to pollution have focused on sufficiently diluting or dispersing it so that the pollutants will be at harmless levels and the environment will handle them naturally, an approach summed up by the phrase, "Dilution is the solution to pollution." However, the pollutants have increased so much in amount and toxicity that this approach is now sharply in question, and many environmentalists are focusing their effort on *source reduction*—that is, on cutting the actual amount of pollution produced.

Traditionally, most attention has focused on *point source pollution*, where pollutants are produced from a stationary location, such as industrial plants, mines, or municipal works. Many of the laws passed in recent decades have focused on such point sources, in attempts to reduce the amounts of pollutants spewed into the air, water, and land. While these laws have had only modest success, at best, in some areas, the other main kind of pollution has proved even harder to deal with: *nonpoint source pollution*, which cannot be traced to a specific spot. Among common nonpoint sources are automobile EMISSIONS, fertilizer runoff, sediment from construction or EROSION, PLASTIC packaging, gases from aerosol cans, even cooking fumes from restaurants and backyard barbeques.

Some nonpoint sources can be attacked by laws directed at industry, such as banning CHLOROFLUOROCARBONS in aerosol cans or requiring automobile manufacturers to install emissions controls. But many kinds of nonpoint source pollution can only be dealt with by changing the ideas, attitudes, approaches, and habits of the society's individuals. That has been the aim of much education, by governments, schools, and especially environmental organizations in recent years. Numerous organizations (including many in this book) are involved in the effort to combat pollution, and in monitoring the amount of pollution—and so the relative health—of the earth.

Pollution does not stay in one place, but is carried around the world by air and water, as well as by living organisms, which even in ANTARCTICA show traces of pollutants such as PCBs. But some pollution is deliberately moved abroad. Companies restricted by pollution-control regulations at home sometimes move their plants to other less restrictive countries, as was the case with the plant involved in the BHOPAL chemical disaster. Or, while remaining at home, they may sell abroad products that are classed in their own countries as too dangerous for sale, such as banned PESTICIDES. In some cases, HAZARDOUS

WASTE may also be shipped abroad, generally from industrialized countries to developing countries willing to accept such waste for a fee, despite the hazards. All such practices are called *export of pollution.* When such pollutants turn up again in the originating country, as when food is imported that contains banned pesticides, the process is said to be completing a CIRCLE OF POISON.

### For more information and action:

- **Alternative Farming Systems Information Center,** (301-344-3724 or 344-3559). Provides Quick Bibliographies *Nonpoint Source Pollution, an Agricultural Concern* (J. MaClean, 1989). (See ORGANIC FARMING AND SUSTAINABLE AGRICULTURE INFORMATION AND ACTION GUIDE on page 226.)
- **ENVIRONMENTAL PROTECTION AGENCY (EPA)** (Public Information Center, 202-260-7751 or 202-260-2080). Publishes *A Family Guide to Pollution Prevention* (1990).
- **NATIONAL WILDLIFE FEDERATION (NWF),** (202-797-6800 or 800-245-5484). Publishes *Pollution: Problems and Solutions,* for children in grades K-8.
- **INSTITUTE FOR LOCAL SELF-RELIANCE (ILSR),** (202-232-4108). Publishes *Proven Profits from Pollution Prevention.*
- **UNITED NATIONS ENVIRONMENT PROGRAMME (UNEP),** (212-963-8138).
- **WORLD RESOURCES INSTITUTE (WRI),** (202-638-6300). Publishes *Environmental Pollution: A Long-Term Perspective* (James Gustave Speth, 1988) and a biannual *World Resources.*

(See also ACID RAIN, AIR POLLUTION, HAZARDOUS WASTE, NOISE POLLUTION, PESTICIDES, RADIOACTIVE WASTE, TOXIC CHEMICALS, WATER POLLUTION.)

**polychlorinated biphenyls (PCBs),** see PCBs.

**population,** the rapidly expanding number of humans on earth, so many that humanity has become a threat to many of earth's other life-forms, and threatens its own future, as well. Throughout the world, and especially in the developing countries that are the home of most of humanity, overpopulation, the destruction of the natural world, and the worsening of the conditions of life for hundreds of millions of people happen side by side, and not at all by chance; humanity has made some advances in food production, but has hardly begun to solve the set of problems that have come with overpopulation, and grow worse every day.

At the turn of the 20th century, in 1900, there were 1.61 billion people on earth. In 1960, there were over 3.02 billion, an increase of almost 88 percent. By 1990,

the population had grown to 5.3 billion, 3.3 times (330 percent) the 1900 figure. The United Nations estimates a world population of 7.6 to 9.4 billion by 2025, with a medium and generally used estimate of 8.5 billion. The 8.5 billion estimate is 5.28 times (528 percent) the 1900 figure. The continuing population explosion indicated by these figures is even worse than it seems, for population is growing fastest in some of the poorest developing countries, where there is little ability to handle the needs of these huge new populations, where damage to the natural world is great and growing, and where most people are young, meaning that birth rates may go down somewhat in coming decades but that large numbers of women of child-bearing age will guarantee that total births will go up well into the 21st century. UN population projections indicate that the populations of the world's more developed countries will increase by less than 200 million through 2025, but that 3 billion more people from less developed countries will by then have entered the world's population.

The size, speed, and location of this explosive population growth has already brought many kinds of disasters; unchecked, it will bring far more. A few illustrations:

- Saving the AMAZON RAIN FOREST has been a high priority for most of two decades, generating a worldwide campaign and some limited successes. But the population of Brazil grew approximately 333 percent from 1940 to 1990, from 45 million to over 150 million, and that is the main reason the Brazilian government encouraged settlement and clearance of some parts of the Amazon from the 1960s on, endangering the hundreds of thousands of SPECIES in the rain FOREST. United Nations estimates project a Brazilian population increase to 245 million by 2025, with the population of São Paulo topping 20 million before the year 2000, large numbers of its people living in shantytowns around the city, without sanitation, adequate food, or health care, as is already true for millions. In those circumstances, there can be little possibility that the great natural areas of the Amazon basin will long survive, for all eight nations sharing the basin face precisely the same population and poverty problems, and will certainly reach for every bit of mineral and forest wealth they can get in the basin—and soon. Unless these problems are quickly addressed by a worldwide effort, at best only a few Amazon park and preserve areas will survive long into the next century.
- The same kinds of urban problems occur throughout the world, as tens of millions flock to the major cities, not as a step up to better lives as in the Europe and North America of the 19th and 20th centuries, but into destitu-

## Population Information and Action Guide

**For more information and action on population:**

INSTITUTE FOR FOOD AND DEVELOPMENT POLICY (IFDP), popularly called *Food First*, (415-864-8555). Publishes *The Missing Piece in the Population Puzzle*.

MORRISON INSTITUTE FOR POPULATION AND RESOURCE STUDIES, (415-723-7518). Publishes policy papers on population-related issues, such as *Population Biology, Conservation Biology, and the Future of Humanity* (Paul R. Ehrlich).

**Population Council, The** (1 Dag Hammarskjold Plaza, New York, NY 10017; 212-644-1300; George Zeidenstein, President), an international organization established in 1952 that "applies science and technology to the solution of population problems in developing countries," working with governments, nongovernmental organizations, and private foundations on "population policy, family planning and fertility, reproductive health and child survival, women's roles and status, contraceptive introduction, and development of human and institutional resources." The council sponsors research in the social and health sciences, as in contraceptive technology, and disseminates information through conferences, seminars, workshops, and its numerous publications, including the quarterly *Population and Development Review* and the bi-monthly *Studies in Family Planning*; newsletters such as *Norplant® Worldwide, Alternatives* (in Spanish and English), and *African Alternatives* (in French and English); and review supplements on special themes, such as *Resources, Environment, Population: Present Knowledge, Future Options* (Kingsley Davis and Mikhail S. Bernstam, eds., 1990) and *Rural Development and Population: Institutions and Policy* (Geoffrey McNicoll and Mead Cain, eds., 1990); as well as research working papers, pamphlets, brochures, reports, and computer software, generally available in several languages.

**Population Crisis Committee (PCC)** (1120 19th Street NW, Suite 550, Washington, DC 20036; 202-659-1833; J. Joseph Speidel, President), a private organization founded in 1966 that "seeks to stimulate public awareness, understanding and action towards the reduction of population growth rates in developing countries through voluntary family planning and other actions needed to solve world population problems," offering "authoritative analysis of the impact and im-

portance of U.S. policies and financial support for international population assistance programs." The PCC seeks to educate legislators and policy-makers, and to identify and support "innovative, cost-effective and replicable" grassroots family planning projects in developing countries. It also publishes and distributes various materials, including population policy information sheets such as *RU-486* (1989) and *Demand for Family Planning: Fact and Fiction* (1988), and studies and reports (often in English, Spanish, and French editions) such as *1990 Report on Progress Towards Population Stabilization* and *Population Pressures Abroad and Immigration Pressures at Home* (1990).

**Population-Environment Balance** (1325 G Street NW, Suite 1003, Washington, DC 20005; 202-879-3000; Rose M. Hanes, Executive Director), a membership organization founded in 1973 as *The Environmental Fund to Balance*, renamed in 1986, aiming to stabilize the population of the United States, to safeguard the land's CARRYING CAPACITY, and also supporting "a responsible immigration policy," "increased funding for contraceptive research and availability," and "a woman's right to reproductive choice." It seeks to educate and influence the general public and policymakers about the adverse impact of population growth and to "achieve a national commitment to population stabilization," especially encouraging "replacement-level" birth rates and immigration quotas; institution of a "population impact report" for all major federal actions (similar to an ENVIRONMENTAL IMPACT STATEMENT); and inclusion of "population stabilization provisions in environmental protection legislation." It publishes the quarterly newsletter *Balance Report*, various action alerts and updates on population stabilization activities, and *Balance Data* sheets such as *Water Availability and Population Growth, Population Growth and Farmland Loss, Global Warming and Population Growth,* and *Why Excess Immigration Damages the Environment*.

**Population Institute** (110 Maryland Avenue NE, Washington, DC 20002; 202-544-3300; Werner Fornos, President), an international organization, established in 1969, "primarily concerned with bringing the world's population into balance with its resources and environment, creating population stability and enhancing the quality of life," especially focusing

---

tion, hunger, and disease. Cholera, once thought nearly eradicated, in 1990 blossomed in the swollen slums of Lima, and turned into an epidemic that caused 200,000 cases and 8,000 deaths in Peru. Mexico City already has 17 million people, and will probably have 20 to 25 million in the first quarter of the 21st century, the vast majority of them slum-dwellers. Even now, the city's

air is very nearly unbreathable, and it is ripe for a cholera epidemic of its own. Cairo, Delhi, Calcutta, Bombay, and a score of other newly-massive cities face the same kinds of catastrophic futures.

- The recurring cyclone and flood disasters that have taken well over half a million lives in Bangladesh during the past three decades are tied directly to Indian and Bangla-

on "those developing countries where the problems of over-population are most critical." The institute seeks to educate the public about the relationship between the population crisis and environmental problems, to develop the leadership to solve these problems, and to mobilize "the needed response to the Third World's urgent pleas for birth-control assistance," including promotion of smaller families and increasing the availability of family planning information and services globally. The Institute maintains a computerized Population Research Service and publishes various materials, including the bimonthly POPLINE; a global directory of women's organizations implementing population strategies; a videotape; and a series of monographs, such as *The Apocalyptic Cycle: Overpopulation, Illiteracy, Poverty* (1990), *The Long, Dry Season: Population and Water* (1990), *Population and Global Survival: A Vision for the Nineties* (1988; also in audiocassette), and *Population and Environment: The Growing Imbalance, the Growing Imperative* (1988).

**Population Reference Bureau (PRB)** (777 14th Street NW, Suite 800, Washington, DC 20005; 202-639-8040; Thomas W. Merrick, President), a scientific and education organization, founded in 1929, that "gathers, interprets and disseminates information about population," seeking to "increase awareness and understanding of population trends and their implications" among legislators, public officials, teachers, students, and the business community, and others concerned about national and work affairs. Stressing "hard facts and sober analysis," the PRB sponsors research on population policy and related policy development activities; provides technical support to organizations in developing countries; and provides information and public education services, as through workshops, meetings, seminars, and direct responses to queries. It also publishes various materials, including the newsletter *Population Today*; the annual *United States* and *World Population Data Sheets*; occasional series such as *Population Trends and Public Policy* and *Working Papers; Population Handbooks* (in U.S., International, French, and Arabic editions); teaching kits such as *World Population: Fundamentals of Growth* (2nd edition, 1990), *World Population: Toward the Next Century* (3rd edition, 1989), and *World Population: Facts in Focus* (1988); the quarterly *Population Bulletin* of in-depth studies on various topics; and other policy, trends, and analysis reports.

**RESOURCES FOR THE FUTURE (RFF),** (202-328-5000).
**SIERRA CLUB,** (415-776-2211 or 202-547-1141; legislative hotline, 202-547-5550). Publishes *What You Can Do to Help Stabilize World Population, Population Policy*, and *Population Report*.
**WINROCK INTERNATIONAL INSTITUTE AGRICULTURAL DEVELOPMENT,** (501-727-5435 or 703-525-9430). Publishes *Population Growth and Sustainable Agricultural Production: An Emerging Agenda* (Robert D. Havener, 1989).
**WORLD BANK,** (202-47-1234). Publishes *Population Pressure, the Environment, and Agricultural Intensification, Population Change and Economic Development, Population Growth Rate,* and *Population Terminology*.
**WORLD RESOURCES INSTITUTE (WRI),** (202-638-6300).
**Zero Population Growth (ZPG),** (1400 16th Street, NW, Washington, DC 20036 Suite 320, 202-332-2200; Susan Weber, Executive Director), a membership organization founded in 1968 by Paul EHRLICH, who remains honorary president, advocating stabilization of the world's population, to "develop a sustainable balance of people, resources and the environment." Working independently and with other organizations, ZPG sponsors education programs; works for family planning and other population issues domestically and internationally; combats misinformation about population and related issues; and sponsors an Activist Program for members. ZPG publishes various materials, including the bimonthly newsletter *The ZPG Reporter* and the quarterly newsletter *Activist*; teaching kits such as *For Earth's Sake* and *U.S.A. by Numbers*, brochures and background reports such as *The Population Challenge*; fact sheets such as *Setting a Limit, Demographic Facts of Life in the U.S.A.*, and *Population and the Greenhouse Effect*; and books such as *U.S.A. By Numbers: A Statistical Portrait of the United States*; the video *World Population*; and legislative alerts.

**Other references:**

*The Population Explosion*. Paul R. Ehrlich and Anne H. Erhlich. Simon and Schuster, 1990. *Population Matters: People, Resources, Environment, and Immigration*. Julian L. Simon. Transaction (New Brunswick, NJ), 1989. *World Population Prospects 1988*. United Nations Population Division. United Nations, 1989.

---

desh overpopulation (see BANGLADESH DISASTERS). DEFORESTATION of the Himalayas and along the whole course of the GANGES and Brahmaputra rivers, and the creation of new delta land formed by washed-away topsoil, coupled with poverty-induced settlement of excess population on the new islands so created—with Bangladesh government incentives—has created a huge, very

poor, quite helpless farming population in the cyclone-prone delta. There is no place to go; Bangladesh had 51 million people in 1960, 115 million by early 1990, and the UN projects it will have 235 million people by 2025. India went from 442 million in 1960 to 853 million in early 1990, and is projected to rise to 1.445 billion by 2025. Should those population predictions for both countries prove true—and in all probability they will—massive human and ecological disasters can be expected on the subcontinent.

• On a much smaller scale, but equally telling, the population of MADAGASCAR more than doubled from 5.3 to 12 million between 1960 and 1990, and is predicted to rise to an astonishing 33 million by 2025, though it is very hard to see how the island can even begin to support that many people. At 12 million, and employing traditional slash-and-burn agricultural practices, Madagascar's ongoing ecological disaster has almost destroyed the once-massive central highland forest and will soon deforest the entire island—resulting in the balance of the hillsides then following the great amount of topsoil that has already flowed into the sea. In those circumstances, Madagascar's remaining LEMURS and many other unique remaining SPECIES are quite likely to follow the wide range of island SPECIES already extinct. The destruction of HABITAT is particularly dramatic on Madagascar, but is a well-established pattern worldwide. Kenya shows an equally large population increase, as do Ethiopia, Zaire, and a dozen other African countries. Perhaps some of their world heritage wildlife preserves will survive population pressures, for they generate hard currency; but they too are threatened, as pressures will increase with population growth, and sustained political instability can destroy them.

Increasing populations bring a wide range of other problems, as well, from the larger amounts of sewage, toxic waste, and other discharges into the world's RIVERS, LAKES, and OCEANS to the increased use of FOSSIL FUELS in more developed as well as less developed countries.

Some environmentalists also maintain that population pressures greatly contribute to the growth of such problems as ACID RAIN, the GREENHOUSE EFFECT, GLOBAL WARMING, and perhaps will eventually lead to a series of civilization-destroying breakdowns and regional wars, as nations compete for ever-scarcer resources. Those conclusions are disputed by others, in and outside the environmental movement, who want more data before themselves reaching those conclusions. Some also point out that the pace of change in science and technology makes it impossible to predict the wider course of future events; for example, cheap and clean solar power, if and when discovered, could greatly affect all of the POLLUTION, pollution cleanup, food production, and population distribution questions facing humanity, and advances already foreseeable in GENETIC ENGINEERING and medicine may greatly affect all food, sustenance, and health matters.

The intertwined questions of contraception and abortion are often expressed as sharply and abrasively political,

moral, and religious questions in many countries. In the United States, abortion is a major political issue, and in those countries where women's rights movements have developed fertility rates have declined, reflecting greater status and independence. But other factors are at work, as well. In most of the more developed countries, fertility rates continue to decrease, regardless of apparent moral and political questions. Catholic Italy, for example, has the lowest fertility rate in the world, with an estimated two thirds of its women using contraception and a substantial abortion rate, regardless of Catholic Church strictures. That is true of Catholic France, as well, and especially since adoption of RU 486, the very effective abortion pill developed by the French.

In a worldwide and long-term sense, the question of population control seems to most national leaders facing very hard questions to be scarcely a moral one. In many of the less developed countries with very high fertility rates, population control is seen as a simple matter of survival. China, the most populous country in the world at 1.1 billion people, continues to institute birth control campaigns periodically, some of them quite coercive and not acceptable to the democracies. But the desire to control population is no less strong in many other countries; Indonesia and Brazil, for example, have made strong and successful public education campaigns in the late 1980s and early 1990s, with some Indonesian Muslims reversing a traditional antisterilization position. India has made several less successful attempts to control its population growth, but can be expected to try again and again, for without population control all the hydroelectric and other projects and what has been the notably effective building of a grain reserve will come to nothing. For all of the world's less developed nations, and therefore for the more developed nations as well, the related questions of overpopulation and population control remain central. (See POPULATION INFORMATION AND ACTION GUIDE on page 248; also DEVELOPMENT.)

**porpoises,** marine mammals far less gregarious, numerous, and well known than their DOLPHIN cousins, but which face many of the same kinds of hazards. Although COAST dwellers, most members of the six porpoise SPECIES feed far enough out to sea to become entangled in the purse-seine DRIFTNETS that have "incidentally" killed millions of dolphins in the last three decades. Closer to shore, they also become entangled in floating abandoned driftnets (ghostnets), and are also entrapped and incidentally killed in gill nets and other fishing devices, as well as becoming poisoned by the toxic wastes and OIL spills that threaten all other seacoast dwellers.

The *Dall's porpoise*, a Pacific coast dweller in a wide arc stretching from northern Japan to Baja California, is particularly threatened off the coast of Japan, where harpoon FISHING has greatly increased in recent years, probably to replace sharply restricted whaling. Although the species is not yet listed as threatened, it soon will be if current overfishing continues. In the United States, porpoises are protected under the MARINE MAMMAL PROTECTION ACT, administered by the MARINE MAMMAL COMMISSION. (See DOLPHIN AND PORPOISE INFORMATION AND ACTION GUIDE on page 91; also ENDANGERED SPECIES; also ENDANGERED AND THREATENED WILDLIFE AND PLANTS on page 372.)

**precycling,** refusal to buy products that cannot be reused; an approach to RECYCLING that starts before purchase, with choice of reusable items over unrecyclable products, especially those designed for wasteful disposal, such as disposable diapers or polystyrene foam containers (see GREEN CONSUMERISM).

**President's Commission on Environmental Quality (PCEQ),** a U.S. commission established by President George Bush in 1991 (see COUNCIL ON ENVIRONMENTAL QUALITY).

**primary standards,** in relation to POLLUTION, those levels set in relation to human health (as under the SAFE DRINKING WATER ACT or CLEAN AIR ACT), as opposed to *secondary standards*, which refer to WELFARE EFFECTS, affecting plants, animals, buildings, and materials.

**pronghorn (American antelope),** a conservation success story, and a SPECIES saved. Found only in North America, and once ranging from central Mexico north to central Canada and from the midwest to the Pacific northwest, there were an estimated 30 to 40 million pronghorns in the 1850s. With the settlement of the West came mass killings of pronghorns, and with farming and sheepherding came fatal loss of HABITAT, as well. Although by the early 1920s pronghorn HUNTING had been banned in many Western states, the damage was done; there were only 15,000 to 20,000 pronghorns left in North America by the mid-1920s, and the species was headed for EXTINCTION.

But the 1930s saw a revival of interest in conservation, even with the financial constraints forced by the Great Depression. The federal government set aside over 800,000 acres in Nevada and Oregon, creating a national game range and two national refuges for the last of the American antelope herds, and began the long restocking process that by the early 1990s had established herds totaling over 300,000 pronghorns, from northern Mexico through the western states to western Canada.

**For more information and action:**

• WILDLIFE SOCIETY, THE (301-897-9770). Publishes *American Pronghorn Antelope*.

(See also ENDANGERED SPECIES; also ENDANGERED AND THREATENED WILDLIFE AND PLANTS on page 372.)

**propoxur,** a type of CARBAMATE, a family of chemical compounds containing carbon and nitrogen, many of them used as PESTICIDES.

**Przewalski's horse,** the wild horse of inner Asia, the root stock from which the domestic horse is thought to have descended; also called the *Wild horse* or *Asian horse*. Although the domestic horse is found worldwide, Przewalski's horse is now believed to be extinct in the wild, with only 200 to 300 surviving in captivity. The two wild ass species, the *African wild ass* and the *Asian wild ass*, closely related to the horses as part of the *Equus* genus, are also ENDANGERED SPECIES. ZEBRAS are part of the same family.

# Q

**Queen Elizabeth (Rwenzori) National Park,** Ugandan FOREST, LAKE, and wildlife preserve; its 600,000 acres (950 square miles) of valley floor are in the southern portion of the country's western rift valley, and include Lakes Edward and George, connected by the Kazinga Channel. The park's western boundary is the Zaire-Uganda border. During the reign of Ugandan dictator Idi Amin (1971–79), the park's ELEPHANT, hippopotamus, and endangered black RHINOCEROS populations were seriously attacked by unrestrained poaching, though all three species survived. The park is the home of large herds of buffalo, several kinds of antelopes, and topis, as well as several kinds of mongooses, LEOPARDS, LIONS, CHIMPANZEES, baboons, several MONKEY species, jackals, hyenas, aardvarks, anteaters, porcupines, and many bird, reptile, and fish species. (See WILDLIFE REFUGE.)

# R

**radiation,** energy emitted as waves or particles; also the process of emitting such energy. Radiation is ever-present in the universe and has been so all the while life evolved on earth. Some types and amounts of radiation are, in fact, essential to life. During the process of PHOTOSYNTHE-SIS, plants obtain life-sustaining energy from light (other-wise known as *visible radiation*); the rhythm and cycles of living beings are regulated by changes in the light; vision is dependent on light; *infrared radiation* warms the earth; and even potentially destructive *ultraviolet radiation* is important in creating vitamin D. As with so much else in the environment, the problem comes with changes in the amount, types, and intensity of the radiation.

Much of what we call radiation exists in a range called the *electromagnetic spectrum*, with the different types of radiation distinguished by their frequency and wavelength. Radiation with the longest wavelengths and lowest frequencies are *radiowaves* and *microwaves*, followed by *infrared radiation* (heat). Near the middle of the spectrum is *visible radiation* (light). Beyond that is *ultraviolet (UV) radiation*; then come the types of radiation with the shortest wavelengths and highest frequencies: *X-rays, gamma rays,* and *cosmic rays*.

The latter four types together are called *ionizing radiation*, because as they penetrate substances they tend to cause electrons to become ''excited'' and ''escape'' from the chemical bonds that normally hold them within an atom, a process called *ionization*. Both the remaining atoms and the loose electrons are then charged particles and are highly active chemically. In the bodies of living organisms this kind of chemical activity can cause much damage and often wreak havoc, depending on the organism and the type of radiation. The ionization danger is greatest from X-rays and gamma rays, which penetrate deeply enough to cause genetic effects. Ultraviolet radiation does not penetrate body tissues as deeply, though it can cause considerable superficial damage, as can other kinds of radiation, including infrared, which can burn, and microwaves, the effects of which are not fully known.

Among humans the main general effects of radiation are an accelerated rate of mutation; lessened fertility; increased risk of some diseases, notably cancer and cataracts; and a lowered life expectancy. Effects are especially pronounced in areas of cell proliferation, including that of the reproductive cells, blood-forming tissue, the basal layer of the skin, and the intestinal lining. In sufficiently large doses radiation can kill immediately, though the amount necessary varies. In some settings radiation is used for sterilization, instead of heat: food is also sometimes sterilized by irradiation, a use about which much controversy exists and much remains to be known. Ultraviolet radiation has long been used as a disinfectant, as in hospitals, and in water treatment plants, as an alternative to CHLORINATION.

Radiation also exists in streams of particles from atoms that have been broken apart, naturally or artificially (as in a nuclear device). Such particles include the parts of an atom—protons, electrons, positrons, neutrons, and nuclei—as well as other energy-packed particles such as *alpha particles* and *beta particles*. Such particles are emitted as part of a natural process of disintegration, during which radioactive substances gradually break down. The length of time it takes for half of a given amount of a substance to break down is called its *half-life*, an important figure in calculating the amount of time a substance's radiation will still be dangerous.

Radiation is measured in various ways. A *Roentgen* is a unit used in measuring the amount of ionization—that is, the number of charged ions—created by radiation in a given substance. A more common measure is the *rad*, a unit of the amount of radiation absorbed in tissues. In judging the *relative biological effectiveness* (RBE) of a particular type of radiation, the unit most often used is the *rem*, which stands for *Roentgen equivalent man*. One rem is the dose that would produce in a human the biological effects of one rad of X rays. These are the types of units governments and others use in calculating what are acceptable limits of radiation exposure for workers, for the general public, and for other living organisms. Another measure, the *curie*, is a unit of radioactivity, assessing the speed of a radioactive substance's disintegration.

All living beings absorb radiation all the time. Much of this *background radiation* (see BACKGROUND LEVELS) comes from the sun and other stars in the form of cosmic rays. These vary to some extent by geography and by events in the universe, such as sunspots or flares. Some off-earth radiation is screened out by the atmosphere; in particular, the OZONE LAYER screens out some ultraviolet radiation. However, modern chemical use is thinning that protective shield, which may lead to increased cancer, especially of the skin, and cataracts. CHLOROFLUOROCARBONS (CFCs) have been implicated as a clear and present danger to the ozone layer, and therefore to humans and many other life-forms, so a concerted worldwide effort is now under way to stop further additions of destructive CFCs to the atmosphere. A telling indication to many is the increase in the incidence of skin cancer that has occurred in recent years, which is widely attributed to the loss of ozone layer protection. That conclusion has yet to be fully proven by rigorous clinical studies, but taken all together, the evidence is compelling enough and the hazards posed by ozone-layer loss are enormous enough to justify massive, quick action to protect the ozone layer from further attack. Naturally occurring radiation may be dangerous in other ways, as well, as when high-flying air crews are subjected to less than safe concentrations, especially over the poles, where natural radiation from off-earth is highest.

Background radiation also results from natural *radioisotopes*—radioactive forms of common substances. Among those normally occurring in the environment are radium and the particles into which it disintegrates (called *radium daughters*), along with thorium, potassium-40, carbon-14, and hydrogen-3 (tritium). These are found in the soil and rocks, in the air as dust, and in water, from all of which sources they are taken up by plants, and so enter the FOOD CHAIN. By the process of BIOACCUMULATION, the long-lasting radioisotopes increasingly concentrate in bodies as they go up the food chain. MINING, building construction, and other disruption of the soil and rocks tends to increase the amount of radioactive matter released into the environment from these sources, though the extent of the problem has been clear only in recent years. RADON—a colorless, odorless radioactive gas that seeps into homes from underlying soil and rocks—is now known to be more prevalent in new homes than in older ones in the same area, because of the more recent disturbance in the earth. Burning COAL has been found to release into the air particles of the radioactive minerals, especially radium. And several studies in 1990 made it clear that OIL drilling has for many decades drawn radium-contaminated water up with oil and caused radium contamination in thousands of U.S. oil well locations.

The other main source of radiation—and the one totally within human control—is from artificial, human-created uses. Many of these are beneficial, such as X-rays and radioisotopes that have revolutionized medical treatment and diagnosis in the 20th century. Such devices can, however, be overused and pose dangers to the technicians as well as patients. This began to be a matter of intense concern in the 1920s, when radium was found to be a deadly poison. Until then it had been hailed as an extraordinarily beneficial substance and used for treating cancer and a wide range of other illnesses, in popular remedies and in such industrial applications as watch dial painting.

With the coming of nuclear fission, NUCLEAR WEAPONS, NUCLEAR TESTING, and NUCLEAR ENERGY have come massive new sources of very dangerous radiation. The atomic bombings of HIROSHIMA AND NAGASAKI, which ushered in the nuclear age, have so far killed 235,000 to 375,000 people, most of them beyond the close-up blast area, due to radiation and radiation-related illnesses. Survivors and their children are still dying, and many of them suffer from radiation-related cancers, respiratory disorders, genetic impairments, and a wide range of other diseases. The nuclear-created radiation sources that have since been developed include all of the world's nuclear weapons and nuclear energy plants, the FALLOUT and residual radiation from hundreds of atomic weapons tests, and the CHERNOBYL and CHELYABINSK disasters, among others. They also include the tremendously dangerous high-level wastes, dangerous transuranic wastes, and masses of low-level, yet still dangerous, wastes that are by-products of nuclear manufacturing processes and that have found their way into the land and water of many countries; the huge mounds of radioactive tailings that dot the western United States and other uranium-mining areas; and the highly radioactive spent atomic fuel that still sits beside the world's nuclear reactors (see RADIOACTIVE WASTE).

All of these nuclear dangers have been major sources of death and disease for several decades; all for decades were defended by the governments that produced them as far less dangerous than they really were. The will to clean up the worst of them began to grow only in the late 1980s and early 1990s, as increasingly mistrustful citizen's organizations, and in some countries new governments, began to force effective action. A few examples follow:

• In February 1990, a trailblazing British study established statistical links between the very high incidence of childhood leukemia in west Cumbria and the exposure to radiation of men working at the SELLAFIELD nuclear plant, raising very serious questions for nuclear plant workers throughout the world and suggesting that currently ''acceptable'' levels of radiation exposure at Sellafield were in fact far from acceptable.
• In July 1990, after extremely damaging disclosures about secret radiation releases from the Hanford nuclear weapons plant in the state of Washington (see NUCLEAR WEAPONS ESTABLISHMENT, U.S.), the DEPARTMENT OF ENERGY finally agreed to release the health records of 44,000 former Hanford workers.
• In January 1991, the U.S. government finally moved responsibility for radiation studies regarding the 600,000 who have worked in the nuclear weapons industry from the Department of Energy to the Department of Health and Human Services, ending for at least a time the ability of those who made nuclear weapons to control health studies in that area.

The extent and impact of radiation from such sources as medical treatments, X-rays, computer terminals and television screens, power lines, and other industrial uses is a matter of intense worldwide debate. X-rays and some other medical uses have long been recognized as possible sources of radiation damage, while the debate still rages as to screens and power lines. Concern over power-line radiation, called *electromagnetic radiation* or *emissions*, grew a great deal from the late 1970s, as studies reported a sharply increased risk of cancer for children who lived near power lines, and for electrical plant workers. In December 1990, the ENVIRONMENTAL PROTECTION AGENCY identified a possible causal link between extremely low-level electromagnetic fields and leukemia, lymphoma, and brain cancer. Research continues; meanwhile, elementary prudence indicates that exposure to electricity should be minimized, as in homes near power lines, television sets

very close to viewers, electric blankets, and beds and chairs near power distribution inlets to homes.

**For more information and action on electromagnetic emissions:**

• **FOOD AND DRUG ADMINISTRATION (FDA),** (301-443-1544 or 301-443-3170) Operates the *Bureau of Radiological Health*.
• **HUMAN ECOLOGY ACTION LEAGUE (HEAL),** (404-248-1898). Publishes reading list on *Electromagnetics*.
• **NATIONAL AUDUBON SOCIETY,** (212-832-3200; *Audubon Action Line* 202-547-9017). Current policy projects include exploring health effects of magnetic fields.
• **NATIONAL ENVIRONMENTAL HEALTH ORGANIZATION (NEHA),** (303-756-9090).

**Other references:**
*Deadly Deceit: Low-Level Radiation, High-Level Cover-Up.* Jay M. Gould and Benjamin A Goldman. Four Walls Eight Windows, 1990. *Living with Radiation: The Risk, the Promise.* Henry N. Wagner, Jr., and Linda E. Ketchum. Johns Hopkins University Press, 1989. *Currents of Death: Power Lines, Computer Terminals, and the Attempt to Cover Up Their Threat to Your Health.* Paul Brodeur. Simon & Schuster, 1989.
(For other types of radiation, see NUCLEAR ISSUES INFORMATION AND ACTION GUIDE on page 215; also RADON.)

**radioactive waste,** waste that emits RADIATION, at a high or low level. From the beginning of the atomic era, radioactive waste has presented an unresolved and growing set of problems. In the early 1990s, those problems seemed not much closer to solution and their magnitude had become clearer. Where NUCLEAR WEAPONS have been produced, the reprocessing of spent fuel to recover plutonium and uranium has produced extremely radioactive waste, called *high-level radioactive wastes* (HLRW), usually stored in liquid form, though sometimes solidified, which will remain dangerous for thousands of years. Weapons plants and nuclear power plants also produce radioactive wastes that are far less radioactive and that lose much of their radioactivity in no more than tens of years; some industrial and medical activities also produce such radioactive wastes, all collectively called *low-level radioactive wastes* (LLRW). But some otherwise low-level wastes also carry small quantities of longer-lived and more radioactive materials; these are called *transuranic wastes* (so-called because their atomic numbers are higher than that of uranium), and they need to be treated nearly as carefully as the high-level wastes. The leftover portions of uranium ore from which nuclear fuel is taken, called *tailings*, are also highly radioactive; piles of mill tailings measured in hundreds of millions of tons dot nuclear-ore waste sites all over the world.

Beyond that, there are throughout the world, wherever there are nuclear weapons or power plants, highly radioactive stores of spent nuclear fuel. Most of this fuel is still stored where it was used, one of several reasons that the hundreds of closed nuclear plants around the earth are and will remain some of the most contaminated places on the planet.

The liquid high-level nuclear waste storage sites at Hanford and Savannah River (see NUCLEAR WEAPONS ESTABLISHMENT, U.S.) are especially dangerous, having already experienced leaks; they pose the risk of the kind of massive nuclear waste explosion that occurred at the Soviet CHELYABINSK plant in 1957–58. From the late 1980s, Hanford and Savannah River have had enormous publicity, and they are announced federal cleanup targets, although progress has been slow. But they are only the tip of the iceberg; by the early 1990s at least 122 contaminated sites had been identified by the federal government, including 17 major sites in 12 states. Estimated cleanup costs were at least $200 billion, probably a low figure that does not take into account the human and economic costs already incurred.

Nor was a solution in sight: the federal Waste Isolation Pilot Plant (WIPP), the first American permanent high-level nuclear waste storage facility, scheduled to open in 1988, was by the spring of 1992 still not open, as critics—some of them inside the government—raised major safety questions. Growing stores of transuranic wastes posed less urgent, but equally difficult and unsolved, problems. Storage facilities for low-level nuclear wastes were inadequate, and it was proving almost impossible to find sites for other such facilities, as public mistrust of HAZARDOUS WASTE, nuclear power, and government reassurance grew very rapidly. The 1980 Low-Level Radioactive Waste Policy Act, which required that by 1986 each state should have made provision for disposing of its LLRW, was amended in 1985 and its deadline postponed to 1993, when it was clear the target would not be met. Nor did the highly questionable suggested disposal of these and other hazardous wastes under the seabed find much favor, in the United States or abroad, as too many safety questions remained inadequately answered. Much low-level radioactive waste has, in fact, simply been dumped into the ocean over the years and now lies at the bottom in disintegrating containers.

In much of the rest of the world, nuclear waste disposal is even less advanced. It was clear that enormous quantities of nuclear waste have been generated in the countries that made up the former Soviet Union and Eastern Europe,

but the long, arduous, expensive cleanup job had in most countries hardly even reached the data-gathering stage; all or almost all remained to be done.

**For more information and action:**

- AMERICAN PLANNING ASSOCIATION (APA), (202-872-0611).
- GREENPEACE (202-462-1177). Runs the Below Regulatory Concern (BRC) Project.
- NATIONAL ENVIRONMENTAL HEALTH ORGANIZATION (NEHA), (303-756-9090). Publishes *Low-Level Radioactive Waste Regulation—Science, Politics & Fear.*

(See NUCLEAR ISSUES INFORMATION AND ACTION GUIDE on page 215; MAJOR NUCLEAR DISASTERS AND INCIDENTS on page 212; also NUCLEAR ENERGY; NUCLEAR WEAPONS; NUCLEAR WEAPONS ESTABLISHMENT, U.S., RADIATION; HAZARDOUS WASTE.)

**radon,** an odorless, colorless toxic gas that occurs naturally in rocks, soil, and groundwater. The gas from the decay of uranium is the culmination of a series of steps, through to the decay of radium-226 and the release of radon, which quickly breaks down in air but leaves a residue of toxic particles, called *radon daughters*; these, when inhaled, release RADIATION that can damage lungs and help lead to lung cancer. Radon and its particles dissipate quickly in the open air but can constitute a major cancer hazard indoors. Radon has been known to be toxic since at least the 1960s, when studies began to indicate that OIL drilling had drawn radium-contaminated water up with oil, but the full scope of the contamination, extending to many thousands of locations worldwide, became clear only in the 1990s.

That radon can also seep into homes became known in the 1960s, when Colorado homes built with materials containing uranium mill tailings were found to be contaminated. It was also found in new housing in Sweden, in Florida, and then in several other locations during the 1970s. In Florida it came into homes built on uranium-rich phosphate-laden reclaimed land. But it was in 1984, after Pennsylvania nuclear engineer Stanley Watrous set off radiation-measuring devices at his nuclear plant, because of radon contamination picked up at his home, that the huge size of the problem became apparent. The ENVIRONMENTAL PROTECTION AGENCY (EPA) estimates that 5,000 to 20,000 additional cancer deaths caused by radon occur yearly in the United States alone—and that estimate may not yet fully reflect the impact of radon generated by oil drilling.

As to homes and other radon-contaminated structures, the severity of radon contamination varies widely, largely

## Radon Risk Evaluation Chart

| pCi/1 | WL | Estimated lung cancer deaths due to radon exposure (out of 1000) | Comparable exposure levels | | Comparable risk |
|---|---|---|---|---|---|
| 200 | 1 | 440—770 | 1000 times average outdoor level | | More than 60 times non-smoker risk |
| | | | | | 4 pack-a-day smoker |
| 100 | 0.5 | 270—630 | 100 times average indoor level | | 2,000 chest x-rays per year |
| 40 | 0.2 | 120—380 | | | 2 pack-a-day smoker |
| 20 | 0.1 | 60—210 | 100 times average outdoor level | | 1 pack-a-day smoker |
| 10 | 0.05 | 30—120 | 10 times average indoor level | | 5 times non-smoker risk |
| 4 | 0.02 | 13—50 | | | |
| | | | | | 200 chest x-rays per year |
| 2 | 0.01 | 7—30 | 10 times average outdoor level | | |
| | | | | | Non-smoker risk of dying from lung cancer |
| 1 | 0.005 | 3—13 | Average indoor level | | |
| | | | | | 20 chest x-rays per year |
| 0.2 | 0.001 | 1—3 | Average outdoor level | | |

Note: Measurement results are reported in one of two ways.
1) pCi/l(Picocuries per liter) - measurement of *radon gas*
2) WL(Working levels) - measurement of *radon decay products*

**Source:** Environmental Protection Agency, Office of Air and Radiation Programs.

according to terrain. Early indications were that the Reading Prong, an underlying geological structure in Pennsylvania and several other eastern states, was a major source of radon. Since then, many other highly contaminated areas have been found worldwide.

In a period in which much emphasis has been placed on energy saving and making structures "tight," especially in colder areas, radon has posed a particularly difficult problem. But the risks are great—so great that in some cases highly contaminated homes have been vacated—that the EPA recommends a series of possible steps to prevent and reduce radon contamination, even though these will add greatly to energy use and cost. Public interest in this environmental hazard is so great that a substantial portion of the EPA booklet has been excerpted in this book (see RADON REDUCTION METHODS on page 451). For a comparative assessment of the risk associated with radon, see the tables associated with UNFINISHED BUSINESS: A COMPARATIVE ASSESSMENT OF ENVIRONMENTAL PROBLEMS (page 309), which ranks 31 environmental problem areas, including radon.

### For more information and action:

- AIR AND WASTE MANAGEMENT ASSOCIATION (A&WMA), (412-232-3444).
- AMERICAN COUNCIL FOR AN ENERGY-EFFICIENT ECONOMY (ACEEE) (202-429-8873). Publishes *Residential Indoor Air Quality and Energy Efficiency* (Peter du Pont and John Morrill, 1989), including *The Radon Story*.
- AMERICAN PLANNING ASSOCIATION (APA), (202-872-0611).
- **Conservation and Renewable Energy Inquiry and Referral Service (CAREIRS), (800-523-2929, U.S. except AK and HI; for AK and HI, 800-233-3071). Publishes *Residential Indoor Air Pollution*.**
- ENVIRONMENTAL DEFENSE FUND (EDF), (212-505-2100).
- ENVIRONMENTAL PROTECTION AGENCY (EPA), (202-260-7751 or 202-260-2080). Maintains *Radon Hotline* (800-505-RADON [767-72366]) and *Radon Information Line*, (703-356-5346).

### Other references:

*Indoor Air Pollution: Radon, Bioaerosols, and VOCs.* Jack G. Kay et al. Lewis, 1991. *The Indoor Radon Problem.* Douglas G. Brookins. Columbia University Press, 1990. *The Complete Book of Home Environmental Hazards.* Roberta Altman. Facts on File, 1990. *Facts on Radon and Asbestos.* Ron Taylor. Watts, 1990. *Radon: Risk and Remedy.* David J. Brenner. Freeman, 1989.

**Rails-to-Trails Conservancy (RTC)** (1400 16th Street N W, Washington, DC 20036, 202-797-5400; David Burwell, President), a membership organization founded in 1985 by trails enthusiasts, seeking to keep abandoned railroad rights-of-way for public use as trails, which often become key parts of GREENWAY systems. While not seeking curtailment of railroad service or abandonment of trackage, RTC monitors railroad corridors for already or about-to-be abandoned section, acting in coordination with recreation and conservation groups, public and private agencies, and community groups to help save them for public use, assisting such groups in following complicated legal procedures. RTC also works to publicize rails-to-trails issues; seeks funding programs and simplified regulations to promote rail-trail conversions; sponsors conferences and meetings; and publishes various materials, including the quarterly newsletter *Trailblazer*; books and booklets such as *Converting Rails-to-Trails: A Citizen's Manual, RTC Legal Manual,* and *A Guide to America's Rail-Trails;* fact sheets and studies such as *How to Get Involved with the Rails-to-Trails Movement* (1990), *Purchasing a Rail-Trail: The Most Frequently Asked Questions* (1990), ''Rails with Trails'' *A New Alternative for Recreation Planning?* (1989), and *The Economic Benefits of Rails-to-Trails Conversions to Local Economies* (1989); and spotlights on various specific trails.

**Rainbow Warrior,** the GREENPEACE ship sunk by French agents in the harbor of Auckland, New Zealand, in July 1985. The ship was preparing for a voyage aimed at disrupting scheduled French South Pacific nuclear tests. The sinking, and the death of the Greenpeace cameraman aboard, triggered a major international incident. Two French agents were arrested by the New Zealand government and convicted of manslaughter; they were later freed after mediation by United Nations secretary general Javier Pérez de Cuéllar and a French agreement to pay $7 million in damages. (See also NUCLEAR TESTING.)

**Rain forest,** see FOREST and AMAZON RAIN FOREST.

**Ramsar Convention,** an alternate name for the CONVENTION ON WETLANDS OF INTERNATIONAL IMPORTANCE, ESPECIALLY AS WATERFOWL HABITAT.

**RARE Center for Tropical Bird Conservation** (1529 Walnut Street, Philadelphia, PA 19102; 215–568–0420; John Guarnaccia, Executive Director), a membership organization founded in 1973 that seeks to ''ensure that endangered tropical birds and their habitats are secured for future generations.'' It works primarily in Latin America and the Caribbean, focusing on endangered birds because of their value as environmental indicators and because ''by emphasizing the needs of notable species'' they can ''galvanize local government and public support for preservation of the entire habitat.'' Working with local governments and conservation organizations in host countries, the RARE Center undertakes various special programs including HABITAT protection, research, education, and training; it also publishes the *Rare Center News.*

**realm,** any of the major biogeographical regions of the earth, each characterized by a distinct pattern of plants and animals. The concept was originally proposed in 1876 by Alfred Russel Wallace, who suggested that climate and terrain presented virtually impassable barriers dividing each area from the others. His basic realms were:

- **Nearctic**—North America, from the Arctic regions (including Greenland) south to roughly the Mexican border.
- **Palearctic**—Europe and most of Asia (excluding India and Southeast Asia), plus Iceland, northwest Africa, and most of Arabia; by far the largest realm.
- **Neotropical**—Mexico, Central America, and South America.
- **Ethiopian**—Africa (except the northwest portion) and southwest Arabia.
- **Oriental**—the Indian subcontinent, Southeast Asia, and the western half of the East Indies.
- **Australian**—Australia, the eastern half of the East Indies, and the South Pacific, including Hawaii. The last two realms show strikingly different animal types on either side of what is now called ''Wallace's Line,'' along the strait between the islands of Bali and Lombok.

In the 20th century, biogeographers have generally accepted the idea of realms but modify their number and borders, depending on their purposes. One widely accepted grouping of the world's biogeographical regions is that summarized by the WORLD RESOURCES INSTITUTE and the International Institute for Environment and Development in their *World Resources 1986,* including the following realms:

- **Nearctic**—roughly like Wallace's Nearctic, but including a ''tongue'' of land stretching down through Mexico and into Central America, excluding coastal regions and the southern tips of Florida and Baja California.
- **Palearctic**—roughly like Wallace's, but including all of Arabia and northern Africa; still the largest realm, stretching all the way east to Japan, and also including islands off northwest Africa, such as the Canaries and Madeira.
- **Neotropical**—like Wallace's, but excluding the central uplands of Mexico and northern Central America and including the southern tips of Florida and Baja California; this realm also includes the CARIBBEAN and Pacific coastal islands such as the GALAPAGOS.
- **Afrotropical**—like Wallace's Ethiopian, except excluding all of northern Africa and Arabia; this realm includes Indian Ocean islands such as MADAGASCAR, the Mascarenes, the Comores, and Aldabra, and southern Atlantic islands such as Ascension and St. Helena.
- **Indomalayan**—like Wallace's Oriental. This realm includes islands in the Indian Ocean, such as the Seychelles, Amirantes, the Laccadives, and the Maldives; those in the Bay of Bengal, such as the Andaman and Nicobar islands; and much of the East Indies, excluding those in the Oceanian Realm (below).
- **Oceanian**—the southernmost of the East Indies, includ-

ing Papua New Guinea, Micronesia, Polynesia, and the islands of the southern Pacific, among them Hawaii, New Caledonia, and East Melanesia.

- **Australian**—Australia and Tasmania.
- **Antarctic**—Antarctica, New Zealand, and nearby southern Atlantic islands such as the Falklands (Malvinas) and South Georgia. Biologists looking at plants or animals alone, rather than whole biogeographical communities, have other groupings, sometimes called *kingdoms* or *life zones,* with somewhat different borders.

**recycling,** the gathering of waste material after the end of its useful life and reprocessing it for reuse in the same or different products. This generally refers to sortable and separable consumer products such as cans, glass or plastic bottles and jars, and newspapers and other paper products. Recycling of waste in industrial settings is more often called RESOURCE RECOVERY (especially when related to TOXIC CHEMICALS) or *materials recovery.* Many organic materials—those living or once-living—can be recycled by taking advantage of natural BIOGEOCHEMICAL CYCLES, in a method called COMPOSTING.

Recycling has considerable advantages:

- It reduces the total amount of waste, so less needs to be handled as solid waste and less ends up in already overflowing landfills (see WASTE DISPOSAL).
- It makes the remaining solid waste more suitable for INCINERATION, since removing metals and glass reduces the amount of HEAVY METALS released during combustion or left in ash; it also burns more efficiently, which is especially valuable in COGENERATION plants, where the heat from incineration is used, not wasted.
- It reduces the need for new raw materials, and so helps preserve the natural environment from destructive processes such as MINING and use of WATER RESOURCES.
- It lessens the amount of energy needed to manufacture certain products—those for which significantly less energy is needed for recovering recycled matter than for processing the original raw material.
- It lessens AIR POLLUTION and WATER POLLUTION, especially from the industrial processes needed to produce the raw materials and from incineration of waste that contains recyclables.

For materials to be candidates for recycling, they must be separated out from other trash and must be usable in the same or other products—enough so that a market exists or can be developed for the recyclables. Recycling programs often are community projects and sometimes are fundraising projects for community groups; for some materials, however, an insufficient market exists, so communi-

ties must pay to have some recyclable materials taken away until they or others are able to develop or find a market for the used materials. (See HOW TO GET INVOLVED IN RECYCLING on page 260.) Recycling programs depend on the will of the community to follow through on the separating and collecting; in some areas, response is weak and enforcement lacking, so the community must fall back on other approaches, such as INCINERATION, as New York City felt obliged to do in 1991, despite protests from environmental groups.

The most commonly recycled materials are:

- **aluminum,** recycling's greatest success story, partly because the metal is so expensive to produce from bauxite ore and so easy to recover from used cans. Recycled for over 20 years, a ton of aluminum cans in 1990 was valued at over $1,000 in the United States. In 1990, 9.65 million tons of cans—54.9 billion cans—were recycled, a recycling rate of 63.6 percent and rising.
- **steel,** the only product in which recycling was routine before the rise of the recent environmental movement, with a wide-scale scrap metal industry focusing on abandoned cars and appliances. Because steel food cans have a coating of tin inside, to prevent rust, they have not traditionally been reused, since tin mars the steel; but the amounts of tin used have lessened, so food cans are increasingly being recycled. In 1990, 9 billion steel cans were recycled in the United States, up from 5 billion in 1988, with prices ranging from $40 to $70 a ton.
- **glass,** suitable for reuse, since making new glass from crushed glass (called *cullet*) uses less energy and produces less air pollution than making glass "from scratch." Glass must be sorted by color, with clear glass being the most valuable and green glass (as in beer bottles) the most variable in price, from $10 to $60 a ton in 1991. In the United States, over 11 million tons of glass are recycled annually, or over 7.5 percent of all glass produced annually. Several states have funded specific glass recycling programs.
- **paper,** the largest element of solid waste in the United States—about 40 percent—including newspapers, cardboard boxes, computer printouts, and other paper and paperboard products. Roughly 30 percent of this is presently being recycled. Newspaper recycling programs are widespread; for a time in the late 1980s, the market demand for used paper was smaller than the supply, so many communities had to pay for removal of used paper, in some areas $25 a ton. In areas with high landfill fees—for example, $70 a ton—this was still a saving. However, some communities found that by "upgrading" their old paper, by removing paper bags and slick maga-

## How to Get Involved in Recycling

**Practical Suggestions:**

- Start a compost pile.
- Don't bag your grass clippings or leaves (during the summer, grass clippings account for 17 percent of residential solid waste).
- Use a regular cup for coffee at work and home rather than a disposable one.
- Purchase long-lasting, durable items rather than disposable ones.
- Buy recycled products.
- Buy the economy size. You will probably save money, and it will reduce the number of containers being thrown away.
- Be an informed shopper by buying products that last or can be easily repaired.
- Buy products using the smallest amount of packaging materials.
- Tell local manufacturers and businesses that you look for the recycling symbol on their products, packages, and paper.
- Use rechargeable batteries, cloth dish towels and napkins instead of paper ones, and refillable ink pens.
- Recycle unwanted appliances and clothing by giving them to charitable groups or thrift stores for resale.

**Starting a Recycling Program:**

Locate recycling centers in your area. Start by checking the Yellow Pages under recycling, resource recovery, or the specific item, such as glass, paper, aluminum, or plastic. Check with your local and state governments; try the Department of Environmental Resources. Some important questions to ask the recycling center include:

- Rates.
- Hours of operation.
- Procedures for cashing in the products.
- Do they offer assistance to groups that use recycling as a fund-raising project?
- Are there any promotional resources available, such as posters, bumpers, stickers, fliers, or films?

**Organizing a Recycling Program:**

Get enthusiastic and delegate responsibility by having different people plot strategies, produce materials, collect and deliver materials to recycling centers, and maintain records.

- Have a contest among members.
- Set an overall goal.
- Recruit the aid of local businesses.
- Pass out promotional/descriptive material at highly visible locations, such as shopping, civic, or community centers.
- Use the media—newspapers, radio, or television—to promote your program.

**Source:** "Recycling Waste to Save Energy." U.S. Department of Energy, 1989. Compiled from materials produced by the Aluminum Association and Fairfax County, VA, Department of Public Works.

---

zines, their market revived. Used newsprint can be used for other newsprint. Higher-grade used paper is often used to make grocery bags, stationery, household tissues and towels, diapers, and other sanitary products, as well as book and magazine paper.

- **plastics,** relatively new as a recycling item, largely because there are hundreds of different kinds of plastics and it is hard and expensive to distinguish between and separate them; also, each has different chemical specifications for recycling. In addition, plastics cannot be recycled into the original product (as can glass, aluminum, steel, and paper) but must be used in lesser-quality mixed plastic products such as fences, benches, picnic tables, traffic-sign posts, floating docks, and flooring. However, because plastics are such a persistent environmental pollutant, a number of states have a refund-for-deposit system to encourage recycling of the soda bottles made of polyethylene teraphthalate (PET), the main candidate for plastics recycling. In the United States, roughly 20 percent of all PET bottles are recycled each year; PET and high-density polythylene (such as that used in milk bottles) make up about 80 percent of all consumer plastics, and so are the focus for recycling. Some other types of plastic are burned to provide high-energy combustion in cogeneration plants, though critics are concerned about the toxic emissions from this incineration.

In general, the recycling process works like this: The people in the community separate out their recyclables from their other household trash, either placing them out for curbside pickup or delivering them to collection centers. When already separated out, they are sold in bulk in the recycling market. When recyclables such as bottles and cans are mixed together, they are often sent to a materials recovery center, where they are separated, decontaminated, and compressed into bales ready for sale and shipment to the appropriate mills.

Environmentally aware shoppers generally prefer to buy products that are recycled (see GREEN CONSUMERISM).

Consumers should be aware, however, that use of the term *recycled* is not regulated in most areas, so it can be used on products that are made not from consumer waste, but scrap from the normal production process, which many environmentalists would like to see more properly labeled as *reprocessed industrial material.* Various governments have or are planning guidelines for the use of labels such as *recycled* or *recycled content* so consumers are properly informed.

Of course, if recycling is just catching on in the affluent "throwaway" world, it has been the way of life from the beginning of human society in most parts of the world. From Moscow to Calcutta to Mexico City, humans routinely save, modify, trim, use, trade, and sell everything from empty milk cartons to torn stockings to ancient automobiles. (See RECYCLING AND COMPOSTING INFORMATION AND ACTION GUIDE on page 262; also WASTE DISPOSAL; COMPOSTING.)

### Reducing Risks: Setting Priorities and Strategies for Environmental Protection, a 1990 report of the

Science Advisory Board's Relative Risk Reduction Strategies Committee to William K. Reilly, head of the ENVI-

RONMENTAL PROTECTION AGENCY (EPA); a summary document supported by nearly 400 pages of appendices. A followup to the EPA's landmark 1987 report UNFINISHED BUSINESS: A COMPARATIVE ASSESSMENT OF ENVIRONMENTAL PROBLEMS, *Reducing Risks* was prepared in response to the EPA's request to "assess and compare different environmental risks in light of the most recent scientific data . . . to examine strategies for reducing major risks and to recommend improved methodologies for assessing and comparing risks and risk reduction options in the future." Unlike most Science Advisory Board reports, which focus on evaluating scientific and engineering data, the committee stressed that at the EPA's request "our review of *Unfinished Business* and our analysis of risk reduction options have led us to make findings and recommendations that are more policy-oriented than is usually the case." It proposed steps that the EPA (involving the Congress and the rest of the country) can take to reduce environmental risks, stressing the need to use "all the tools at its disposal in an integrated, targeted approach to protecting human health, welfare, and the ecosystem." *Reducing Risks* attempted to correct an imbalance in *Unfinished Business,* which largely ignored urgent ecological problems such as

## Municipal solid waste disposal and recovery, per capita, 1960–1988.

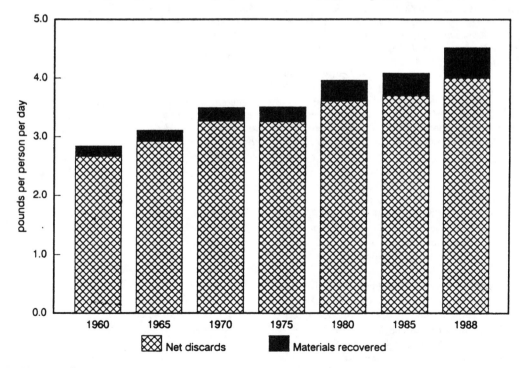

Source: *Environmental Quality.* The 21st Annual Report of the Council on Environmental Quality, 1991.

## Recycling and Composting Information and Action Guide

For more information and action on recycling and composting:

**Alternative Farming Systems Information Center**, (301-344-3724 or 344-3559). Provides Quick Bibliography *Composts and Composting of Organic Wastes* (J. MacLean, 1989). (See ORGANIC FARMING AND SUSTAINABLE AGRICULTURE INFORMATION AND ACTION GUIDE on page 226.)

**CONSERVATION AND RENEWABLE ENERGY INQUIRY AND REFERRAL SERVICE (CAREIRS)**, (800-523-2929, U.S. except AK and HI; for AK and HI, 800-233-3071). Publishes *Recycling to Save Energy*.

**Earthworm, Inc.: The Greater Boston Recyclers** (186 South Street, Boston, MA 02111; *Recycling Hotline*: 617-426-7344), an organization founded in 1970 to be a "viable recycling enterprise, minimize waste, and create environmentally useful jobs" and "to promote conservation by providing individuals, communities, and businesses with accurate and practical information on recycling and waste reduction." While its actual recycling activities are centered on the Greater Boston area, Earthworm provides consulting services, technical assistance, and public education to a much wider area, though still primarily in the Northeast, including projects with the ENVIRONMENTAL PROTECTION AGENCY. Earthworm maintains a specialty library and a recycling database; organizes annual educators' conferences; does public presentations to schools and community organizations; and publishes the newsletter *Earthworm Recycling Guide*.

**ENVIRONMENTAL DEFENSE FUND (EDF)**, (212-505-2100). Publishes *Recycling Community Action Guide* (rev. ed., 1990), *Recycling and Incineration: Evaluating the Choices* (R. Denison and J. Ruston, eds., 1990), and *Coming Full Circle: Successful Recycling Today* (N. Cohen et al., 1988).

**GREENPEACE**, (202-462-1177). Has a *Garbage Prevention Plan*. Publishes *Greenpeace Action Community Recycling Start-up Kit*, *Market Development: The Key to Successful Recycling* (1989), and *Sham Recyclers, Part I: Hazardous Waste Incineration in Cement and Aggregate Kilns* (1989).

**INSTITUTE FOR LOCAL SELF-RELIANCE (ILSR)**, (202-232-4108). Publishes *Beyond 40 Percent: Record-Setting Recycling and Composting Programs* and *Beyond 25 Percent: Materials Recovery Comes of Age*.

**KIDS FOR SAVING EARTH™ (KSE)**, (612-525-0002; 800-800-8800).

**NATIONAL RECYCLING COALITION (NRC)**, (202-625-6406). Provides *Peer Match* program; publishes the bimonthly newsletter *The NRC Connection, National Policy on Recycling and Policy Resolutions,* and offers discounts on four key recycling magazines.

**NATURAL RESOURCES DEFENSE COUNCIL (NRDC)**, (212-727-2700). Publishes *NRDC Earth Action Guide: Reducing, Recycling, and Rethinking Garbage*.

**RODALE INSTITUTE**, (215-967-5171). Publishes *Compost*.

**U.S. Public Interest Research Group (PIRG)**, (202-546-9707).

**WORLD BANK**, (202-477-1234). Publishes *Recycling from Municipal Refuse: A State-of-the-Art Review and Annotated Bibliography* and *Co-Composting of Domestic Solid and Human Wastes*.

**WILDLIFE INFORMATION CENTER**, (215-434-1637). Publishes *Selected Recycling References*.

**Zero Population Growth (ZPG)**, (202-332-2200). Publishes *Recycling*. (See POPULATION INFORMATION AND ACTION GUIDE on page 248.)

**Other References:**

*How to Start a Recycling Center.* Available from California Waste Management Board (CWMB), 1020 Ninth Street, Sacramento, CA 95814. *Recycling and Incineration: Evaluating the Choices.* Richard A. Denison and John Ruston, eds. Island Press, 1990. *Organic Waste Recycling.* Congral Polprasert. Wiley, 1989.

---

critical wildlife HABITATS and BIOLOGICAL DIVERSITY, and also corrected some of the 1987 report's inappropriate or faulty economic assumptions.

In summary, its main recommendations are:

- EPA should target its environmental protection efforts on the basis of opportunities for the greatest risk reduction.
- EPA should attach as much importance to reducing ecological risk as it does to reducing human health risk.
- EPA should improve the data and analytical methodologies that support the assessment, comparison, and reduction of different environmental risks.

- EPA should reflect risk-based priorities in its strategic planning process.
- EPA should reflect risk-based priorities in its budget priorities.
- EPA—and the nation as a whole—should make greater use of all the tools available to reduce risk.
- EPA should emphasize pollution prevention as the preferred option for reducing risk.
- EPA should increase its efforts to integrate environmental considerations into broader aspects of public policy in as fundamental a manner as are economic concerns.
- EPA should work to improve public understanding of

environmental risks and train a professional work force to help reduce them.

- EPA should develop improved methods to value natural resources and to account for long-term environmental effects in its economic analysis.

**For more information:**

- ENVIRONMENTAL PROTECTION AGENCY (EPA), (202-260-7751 or 202-260-2080).

**regenerative agriculture,** a general term referring to farming practices that build up the biological productivity of the soil, while maintaining stable, high levels of production and with little or no impact on the environment beyond the field or farm concerned. (See SUSTAINABLE AGRICULTURE.)

**Renewable Natural Resources Foundation (RNRF)** (5430 Grosvenor Lane, Bethesda, MD 2814; 301-493-9101; Robert Dwain Day, Executive Director), an organization established in 1972 to "advance science and public education in renewable natural resources; promote the application of sound, scientific practices in managing and conserving renewable natural resources; foster coordination and cooperation among professional, scientific, and educational organizations having leadership responsibilities for renewable natural resources;" and develop the *Renewable Natural Resources Center*, an office park and complex for RNRF member organizations and other nonprofit organizations. Members are "professional, scientific and educational organizations that have, among their primary purposes, the advancement of sciences and public education in renewable natural resources and/or the application of scientific knowledge to the management of renewable natural resources," the aim being to enhance opportunities for communication and cooperation, as in sharing information and experiences about renewable natural resource issues and association management. Individuals, as well as other organizations, institutions, companies, and foundations may become Associates. RNRF publishes the quarterly *Renewable Resources Journal* on public policy issues related to natural resources management and conservation.

**renewable resources,** a supply of resources that occurs naturally and cannot be used up, such as SOLAR ENERGY, WATER RESOURCES, or WAVE POWER, as opposed to nonrenewable or DECLINING RESOURCES that are finite supplies that diminish with use, such as OIL and COAL. Renewable resources include the whole range of living organisms—fish and wildlife and the plant sources of food and energy—as well as the organic and inorganic materials that are circulated through BIOGEOCHEMICAL CYCLES, such as the WATER CYCLE, CARBON CYCLE, NITROGEN CYCLE, OXYGEN CYCLE, and SULFUR CYCLE. Though such resources are continually replenished, modern use of resources has outstripped the environment's ability to recycle materials for further use; the result has been POLLUTION and shortage of natural resources, often requiring further activities—such as MINING or building DAMS—that also damage the environment. Underlying the whole concept of conservation, and more particularly SUSTAINABILITY, is the aim of bringing human use of resources back into line with the environment's ability to replenish them.

**For more information and action:**

- RENEWABLE NATURAL RESOURCES FOUNDATION (RNRF), (303-493-9101).
- RESOURCES FOR THE FUTURE (RFF), (202-328-5000). Publishes *America's Renewable Resources: A Historical Perspective on Their Use and Management* (Kenneth D. Frederick and Roger A. Sedjo, eds., 1991).

**Renew America** (1400 16th Street NW, Suite 710, Washington, DC 20036; 202-232-2252; Richard Wiles, Executive Director), a membership organization that "collects, verifies, and disseminates information on solutions to America's environmental problems," encouraging "cooperation among environmental interests, individuals, activists, communities, industry and government to solve our country's most pressing environmental problems." Renew America maintains the *Environmental Success Index*, a "clearinghouse of success stories that provides individuals, public interest groups, the media, industry, and policymakers with information on programs that are solving America's environmental problems," the aim being to coordinate and disseminate information on model programs for replication in other communities. Renew America also offers Searching for Success awards to successful environmental programs in areas such as AIR POLLUTION reduction; community environmental education; conservation of agricultural resources; drinking water protection; energy efficiency; environmental beautification; fish conservation; food safety; FOREST protection and urban forestry; hazardous materials reduction and recycling; institutional environmental education; groundwater protection; growth management; public lands and open space protection; range conservation; renewable energy; solid waste reduction and recycling; surface water and WETLANDS protection; transportation efficiency; and wildlife conservation.

It also publishes various materials, including the *Environmental Success Index* (1991), *The Emerging Environmental Consensus* (1991), and *Searching for Success: Meeting Community Needs Through Environmental Lead-*

*ership* (1990); "report cards" on the environmental programs and policies in each of the 50 states; and focus papers on specific issues.

**reproductive effects,** changes in the processes of conception and birth caused by environmental hazards, such as TOXIC CHEMICALS and RADIATION (see RISK ASSESSMENT).

**Resource Conservation and Recovery Act (RCRA),** a U.S. federal law passed in 1976 to provide for safe treatment and disposal of HAZARDOUS WASTE, and also the key federal law regulating municipal solid WASTE DISPOSAL. Its predecessor, the Resource Recovery Act of 1970, provided funds for RECYCLING materials and mandated a full investigation of the country's hazardous waste management practices. RCRA, passed six years later, continued those provisions and was expanded to cover the disposal of used OIL and waste, defining solid waste to include hazardous waste and also closing most open dumps.

RCRA requires the ENVIRONMENTAL PROTECTION AGENCY (EPA) to identify hazardous wastes and to regulate their generation, transportation, treatment, storage, and disposal, by establishing a "cradle-to-grave" tracking system. The EPA was slow in setting up rules to implement the law, until the LOVE CANAL case galvanized public pressure in 1978. Even so, the agency did not issue the first rules—defining which waste is hazardous and setting handling standards—until 1980. Amendments passed in 1984 banned land disposal of untreated hazardous waste after May 1990; closed loopholes that had allowed INCINERATION of toxic materials in industrial and apartment furnaces; and expanded EPA's regulatory responsibility to cover an estimated 600,000 generators of small quantities of hazardous substances, including petroleum products. Left largely unregulated was medical waste, responsible for much of the summer beach washups, though a regional pilot tracking program was established in 1988, with the EPA charged with setting up a limited regulatory program, including labeling, segregation from other wastes, and proper packaging for disposal.

RCRA focuses on the day-to-day management practices of the hazardous waste industry; by contrast, the COMPREHENSIVE ENVIRONMENTAL RESPONSE, COMPENSATION, AND LIABILITY ACT (CERCLA) and its SUPERFUND amendments deal with cleanup of hazardous substances from spills and inactive and abandoned disposal sites. RCRA covers hazardous waste, or "waste streams," in general; by contrast, disposal of particular hazardous chemicals, such as PCBs, would come under the TOXIC SUBSTANCES CONTROL ACT (TSCA). Transportation of hazardous mate-

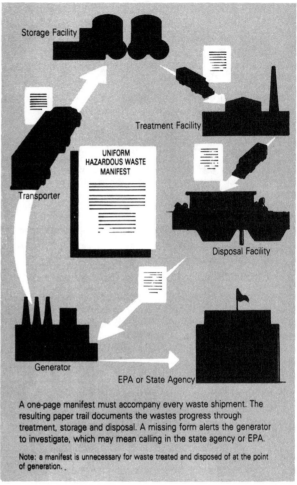

**"Cradle to Grave": The Hazardous Waste Manifest Trail**

Storage Facility

Treatment Facility

UNIFORM HAZARDOUS WASTE MANIFEST

Transporter

Disposal Facility

Generator

EPA or State Agency

A one-page manifest must accompany every waste shipment. The resulting paper trail documents the wastes progress through treatment, storage and disposal. A missing form alerts the generator to investigate, which may mean calling in the state agency or EPA.

Note: a manifest is unnecessary for waste treated and disposed of at the point of generation.

**Source:** *Meeting the Environmental Challenge.* Environmental Protection Agency, 1990.

rials comes under the Hazardous Materials Transportation Act, administered by the U.S. Department of Transportation, which sets regulations for labeling, packaging, and spill reporting.

RCRA has been shown to have some bite. In 1990, the Texas-based Formosa Plastics corporation agreed to pay a $3.4 million penalty—the largest ever collected by the EPA for violations of the federal hazardous and solid waste law—and establish a $1 million trust fund for environmental education. The RCRA is up for review and reauthorization in the early 1990s.

**For information and action:**

• **Environmental Law Institute (ELI),** (202-328-5150;

publications office, 202-939-3844). Publishes *RCRA Deskbook* (1991) (See ENVIRONMENTAL LAW INFORMATION AND ACTION GUIDE on page 116.)

**resource recovery,** the process of extracting or separating and diverting material from solid waste and either converting it to energy or preparing it for reuse. The aim is to reduce the amount of solid waste generated and overall consumption of resources, by reusing recovered material. In recent decades, resource recovery has become a main focus within WASTE DISPOSAL in general and on the community level is the inspiration for RECYCLING. In the United States, it is at the federal level covered under the RESOURCE CONSERVATION AND RECOVERY ACT. (See WASTE DISPOSAL; HAZARDOUS WASTE.)

**Resources for the Future (RFF)** (1616 P Street NW, Washington, DC 20036; 202–328–5000; Robert W. Fri, President), a research organization, established in 1952, specializing in natural resources and the environment, stressing economics and the other social sciences but using also "the insights of the natural sciences." The RFF seeks to take a "nonpartisan, objective stance on all specific policy issues," while advocating "more efficient, equitable, and effective policies in general" and seeking to "inform and improve policy debates about resource and environmental issues by disseminating the results of its research" to policymakers, scholars, and those members of the public concerned with the policy debates (materials are not canted toward students or the general public).

RFF's often-interdisciplinary work is organized into four divisions:

• **Energy and Natural Resources Division,** focusing on energy policy and the management of renewable resources, including CLIMATE CHANGE, OIL markets and energy security, regulatory issues in NATURAL GAS and electricity, relationships between energy and environment, outer space as an economic resource, the changing material requirements of industry, and improvement of management practices in agriculture, water, and forestry;

• **Quality of the Environment Division,** focusing on the management of natural and environmental resources, including cost-benefit analysis of environmental and other health and safety regulations, valuations of natural resources, strategies for the management of toxic wastes, studies of groundwater contamination, PESTICIDES, regional resource management models, and analyses of industry's response to regulation;

• **National Center for Food and Agricultural Policy,** focusing on emerging policy issues, especially relating to U.S. agriculture's links to environmental quality and nat-

ural resources, food safety and quality, and health, but also including the international dimension;

• **Center for Risk Management,** focusing on the management of risks to health and the environment in modern society, including uncertainty in RISK ASSESSMENT, trends in industrial accidents, the safety of waste INCINERATION, and the valuation of life-saving programs.

The RFF provides small grants for research; operates a summer internship program; and sponsors seminars, conferences, colloquia, and policy briefings. It publishes numerous materials on a wide range of topics, including the quarterly *Resources*, a continuing series of discussion papers from the research divisions, and many books, reports, and studies such as *America's Renewable Resources: A Historical Perspective on Their Use and Management* (Kenneth D. Frederick and Roger A. Sedjo, eds., 1991) and *Public Policies for Environmental Protection* (Paul R. Portney, ed., 1990).

**restoration ecology,** a relatively new specialty involving attempts to recreate or revive lost or severely damaged ECOSYSTEMS. Often involving both scientific professionals and amateurs, it is a hands-on approach to righting some previous environmental wrongs, especially reversing damaging trends and rebuilding HABITATS so that ENDANGERED SPECIES can revive and BIOLOGICAL DIVERSITY can be maintained. Two classic examples of restoration ecology are reconstructions of an oak-and-grassland SAVANNA in Northbrook, Illinois, and a prairie in the 100-acre ring formed by the underground Fermi National Accelerator Laboratory at Batavia, Illinois, both projects of the Illinois chapter of the NATURE CONSERVANCY, whose leaders are also active in the SOCIETY FOR ECOLOGICAL RESTORATION (see below).

Ecological restoration is still in relative infancy, but its practitioners have learned that it is easier to reassemble the flora than the fauna into a working ecosystem, so they have tended to focus on the plant portions of ecosystems. This often starts with a few key plants, called *matrix species*, which sometimes remain only in odd corners such as in cemeteries or near railroad rights-of-way. When the plant mix is right for the ecosystem, insects, birds, small animals, and sometimes larger animals as well often return and revive on their own, though some management may be needed to ensure that invading plants and animals do not destroy the reconstructed system.

Restoration projects are also under way in WETLANDS, LAKES, RIVERS, FORESTS, and even CORAL REEFS. In the United States, under the federal government's "no net loss" policy, developers are sometimes allowed to destroy wetlands, if they at the same time restore or create another; since this is done using techniques developed by restoration ecology, the discipline has been subject to some criticism. But restoration ecologists themselves stress that nothing can substitute for preservation, and that the newly reconstructed ecosystems are only shadows of the originals, which they firmly believe should be maintained. A closely related discipline is CONSERVATION BIOLOGY.

## For more information and action:

- NATURE CONSERVANCY, (703-841-5300).
- NATIONAL INSTITUTE FOR URBAN WILDLIFE, (301-596-3311 or 301-995-1119). Publishes *Environmental Reclamation and the Coal Surface Mining Industry* (D. L. Leedy et al.)
- SOCIETY FOR ECOLOGICAL RESTORATION, (608-262-9547). Publishes the semiannual *Restoration & Management Notes*.
- SOIL AND WATER CONSERVATION SOCIETY OF AMERICA (SWCS), (515-289-2331 or 800-THE-SOIL [843-7645]).

## Other references:

*Restoration Ecology: A Synthetic Approach to Ecological Research.* William R. Jordan III et al., eds. Cambridge University Press, 1990. *Environmental Restoration: Science and Strategies for Restoring the Earth.* John J. Berger, ed. Island Press, 1989.

**Rhine River,** the historic, beautiful, extraordinarily polluted river that flows from the Alps through Switzerland, Germany, France, and the Netherlands, ultimately discharging large quantities of pollutants into the NORTH SEA. Approximately 40 million people live in the heavily industrialized Rhine basin; the sewage of such cities as Basel, Strasbourg, Mannheim, Bonn, Frankfurt, and Düsseldorf joins the heavy chemical, chloride, and metal discharges from the potash mines of the Alsace and the industrial plants that line the banks of the river.

Beginning in 1963, some international antipollutant action began on the Rhine, mainly in the form of research, study, and nonbinding recommendations generated by an international commission set up by the four countries. In 1976, further international conventions began to focus on TOXIC CHEMICAL and chloride POLLUTION of the river. Some small progress resulted, in the area of toxic chemical discharges, but little effective enforcement action resulted.

That become painfully clear with the November 1, 1986, SANDOZ CHEMICAL SPILL, when a fire at the Sandoz warehouse upriver from Basel caused a massive flow of highly contaminated water full of toxic wastes into the Rhine. An estimated 500,000 fish and much of the other life of the river were killed, and a water use emergency was generated downriver from the spill. In the aftermath of the fire, as a huge international protest focused attention on the Rhine and its polluters, it became apparent that many companies were routinely dumping pollutants into the river, some of them highly toxic, and also not reporting accidents. For example, Ciba-Geigy admitted spilling 100 gallons of highly toxic atrizine into the river on October 30, before the Sandoz fire, after the presence of atrizine—a substance not stored at Sandoz—was picked up by newly effective monitoring downriver.

After the Sandoz disaster, a great deal of international study and recommendation was generated by several international bodies, including the United Nations and the European Community, spurred by a strengthening green movement (see GREEN POLITICS) in all four countries and throughout Europe. How effectively the Rhine can be restored will become apparent in the years directly ahead. (See RIVER.)

**rhinoceros,** a large single- or double-horned HERBIVOROUS mammal that only a century ago numbered in the millions in the wild, throughout Africa, India, and Southeast Asia; now perhaps 10,000 to 11,000 are left in all, in five greatly ENDANGERED SPECIES. The rhinos have suffered a long, sustained attack by hunters, who continue to kill them for their horns, which are then used for a variety of supposedly medicinal purposes throughout Africa and Asia, as aphrodisiacs in some areas, and as ceremonial daggers in Yemen. Although the rhino horn trade has been outlawed by international agreement since the 1970s, illegal trade in rhino horns continues, with horns worth more and more as they become rarer, and with poachers armed with automatic weapons often able to defeat small numbers of lightly armed game wardens in protected areas. Rhinos have also suffered loss of HABITAT to explosively growing African and Asian human POPULATIONS.

Only 2,000 to 3,000 of the sub-Saharan *black rhinoceros* remain, where once there were 2 to 3 million, and poachers continue to kill more black rhinos than are bred, further reducing an already critically small species. Attempts to save the black rhinos center on the creation of closely guarded game preserves and the breeding of young rhinos in captivity, for later return to the wild.

Such efforts have had some success in South Africa, where a *white rhinoceros* population very close to EXTINCTION has been rebuilt to a population of 4,000 to 5,000. But that success rests very heavily on South African political stability, for without close guarding and enforcement, poachers would quickly wipe out the white rhinos.

Similarly, the *Indian rhinoceros* has been brought back from near-extinction to a population of over 2,000, but continuing civil unrest crossing over into guerrilla warfare in northern India has endangered preservation areas, and with them the Indian rhino. The southeast Asian *Javan rhinoceros* remains very close to extinction, with less than 100 left in the wild, and little being done to save the species. The southeast Asian *Sumatran rhinoceros* is also very close to extinction, although perhaps 500 to 600 remain in the wild.

**For more information and action:**

- TRAFFIC (TRADE RECORDS ANALYSIS OF FLORA AND FAUNA IN COMMERCE), (202-293-4800), Publishes *Rhinoceros Trade*.
- WORLD SOCIETY FOR THE PROTECTION OF ANIMALS (WSPA), (617-522-7000).

(See also ENDANGERED SPECIES; also ENDANGERED AND THREATENED WILDLIFE AND PLANTS on page 372; ANIMAL RIGHTS AND WELFARE INFORMATION AND ACTION GUIDE on page 361.)

**Right-to-Know Act,** an alternate name for the EMERGENCY PLANNING AND COMMUNITY RIGHT-TO-KNOW ACT.

**risk assessment,** evaluation of the hazards to the environment, including human health, from exposure to a substance, such as a PESTICIDE. Quantitative and qualitative data on the toxicity of the substance is combined with data about exposure, to give an overall assessment of hazard. Beyond life-and-death questions, various types of effects are considered in risk assessment, most importantly changes in the processes of conception and birth, called *reproductive effects*. If the change affects the basic genetic structure—causing a mutation—it is called *mutagenic*; if it causes birth defects, specifically, structural defects of prenatal origin, it is called *teratogenic*; if it causes abnormal, uncontrolled growth—a cancer—it is called *carcinogenic*. In the United States, much of the key work on assessment of risks from environmental agents is carried out or sponsored by the NATIONAL INSTITUTE OF ENVIRONMENTAL HEALTH SCIENCES. In practice, such assessments are extraordinarily difficult, especially for individual cases, because humans and other living organisms are exposed to so many different substances, individuals respond differently depending on age and other factors, and the effects of some substances may not be seen for decades. One extraordinary national exercise in general risk assessment was the 1987 ENVIRONMENTAL PROTECTION AGENCY (EPA) report UNFINISHED BUSINESS: A COMPARATIVE ASSESSMENT OF ENVIRONMENTAL PROBLEMS. (See also DOSAGE LEVELS.)

**river,** a system of water channels with branches feeding into a main stream, which eventually empties into a LAKE or OCEAN, in the process draining the higher ground on either side, known as its *watershed*. As they run downhill, rivers and streams continually scour their channels (see EROSION), lowering the level of the bottom and also creating loose gravel and other sediment that is carried along by the rushing water and deposited downstream (see SEDIMENTATION), along the low, flat floor of the lower river valley, in *alluvial* or *flood plains*, or in a wide, flat, triangle-shaped *delta* at the mouth of the river. This eroding action can be enormously damaging all along the river system during floods, but the sediment deposited downstream is often extremely fertile. This leads to a classic environmental balancing act, one often involving questions of whether or not to dam the river (see DAMS).

The water in a river system comes from surface water—that is, drainage of precipitation and melting ice and snow—and from groundwater (see WATER RESOURCES). The surface water varies seasonally, peaking in the spring, and is the main source of the system's sediment load. The groundwater, having percolated through the soil and rock, carries much of a stream's dissolved matter (see LEACHING), such as HEAVY METALS; it also flows more steadily and is the main source of a river system's water during the dry seasons. The typical river system in a mountainous temperate zone such as Europe or North America starts with steep, rapidly flowing, cold streams in sharply V-shaped valleys, with pools and riffles, of the type where trout are often found. The streams gradually become less steep and warmer, and run in slightly wider valleys with a narrow flood plain; these gradually grow into meandering rivers with wide, flat valleys and flood plains, and often deltas at the river mouth.

The study of LAKES and rivers is called *limnology*, and in their deep pools and other relatively still waters, river ECOSYSTEMS have much in common with lakes. Their main energy is derived from PLANKTON, especially algae, through the process of PHOTOSYNTHESIS, and then passes through the FOOD CHAIN to higher animals; dead and other waste matter later showers to the bottom in a *plankton rain*, ultimately being broken down by microbes for reuse in nature's great BIOGEOCHEMICAL CYCLES. The swiftly flowing sections of river systems, however, are characterized by different types of plants and animals, those more adapted to low temperatures and high amounts of dissolved oxygen (see OXYGEN CYCLE).

Like lakes, rivers can also be subject to EUTROPHICATION, which is a kind of POLLUTION that results from over-enrichment of the waters. Organic matter such as household sewage, paper pulp, or detritus from a canning factory produces an oversupply of nutrients to the river ecosystem. Bacteria are needed to break down this waste matter, a process that uses up oxygen, often leaving too little for oxygen-dependent animals, such as fish, which may then die off. The flow of water, especially in rapids, tends to aerate or *oxygenate* the water, so (except in dry periods) rivers have more natural capacity than lakes to recover from organic pollution, if it is not in excessive amounts.

Other kinds of pollution can be more serious. PESTICIDES, dissolved heavy metals, TOXIC CHEMICALS, and other HAZARDOUS WASTE can damage rivers and their many types of HABITATS, sometimes killing directly (as in the SHASTA LAKE PESTICIDE DISASTER), sometimes indirectly, as when MERCURY or DDT is passed up the food chain (see BIOACCUMULATION) to fish and birds, who then are unable to reproduce or themselves survive. In particular, untreated and unobstructed flows of industrial and municipal wastewater place enormous strain on rivers, which in some cases have become no longer living ecosystems but flow-ing streams of pollution, like Ohio's Cuyahoga River, which in 1969 was so polluted that it actually caught fire.

Because in their long, winding routes they pass many human communities, rivers are also subject to heavy use, as for drinking water, industrial use, and agricultural irrigation. The impact on the rivers and its habitats is enormous. In some places, rivers that once flowed proudly now peter out into the sand, and with them go the wildlife they once supported, including many ENDANGERED SPECIES. And the need will not diminish, for POPULATION pressure keeps increasing. Many of the international dam projects under discussion are to provide water for homes, industries, and farms, as well as cheap sources of power (see HYDROPOWER). Around the world, the environmentalists' desire to save the environment is pitted directly against the needs of rising populations, many of them impoverished. In heavily populated areas, the condition of the rivers is also worsened by general ENVIRONMENTAL

## Contamination of Surface Water

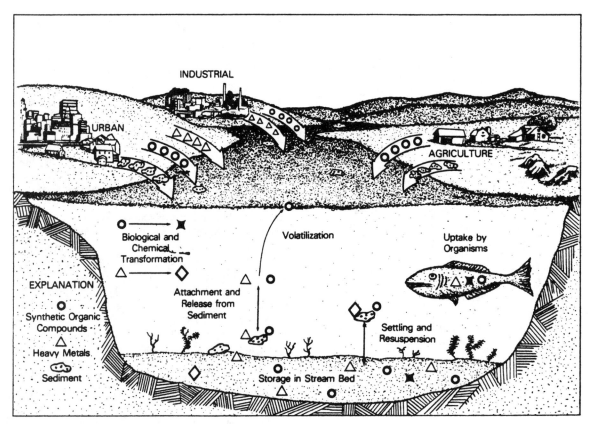

**Source:** "Water Fact Sheet: Toxic Substances Hydrology Program: Surface-Water Contamination." U.S. Geological Survey, Department of the Interior, 1989.

DEGRADATION, including DEFORESTATION and OVERGRAZING, both of which increase erosion.

Rivers are also prime sources of recreation and livelihood for many people, frequently with recreational FISHING in the upper reaches and commercial fishing in the lower river, and in the WETLANDS, bays, and estuaries nearby, where pollution from other sources has not killed the aquatic population altogether. The TWO FORKS DAM on the South Platte River was finally vetoed by the ENVIRONMENTAL PROTECTION AGENCY (EPA) partly because it would have destroyed prime recreational fishing areas and also wetlands on the flyways of endangered migratory birds (see MIGRATION).

Rivers are main avenues of navigation, as well, and many have been altered to suit the needs of commercial shipping, including the building of canals (many themselves now "endangered" by the passage of time). But heavy use of rivers by tourists (see ECOTOURISM), fishermen, and shippers also places stress on the river, with again the need to balance the desire to maintain the river habitats pitted against the human desire to enjoy them and to live off their bounty. Often the conflict is between upstream users and downstream users, whether the subject is water use, water quality, hydropower, environmental quality, sedimentation, or flood control.

The problems are further complicated when river systems are shared by two or more countries, such as the GANGES, Indus, Amazon, St. Lawrence, and Nile rivers. Reduced flow, from heavy use or dams upstream, can increase salinity of both the river water and adjoining coastal lands, as the ocean's salt water penetrates further inland. Users downstream from dams also miss the benefit of fertile sediment once deposited downstream, as in the Nile.

Numerous organizations and governments have sought to protect river systems in different ways. A series of international agreements have been developed to help countries prevent jointly used rivers from being destroyed, degraded, or depleted of their ecosystems and SPECIES. For some systems, such as the RHINE RIVER, the damage is so deep and of such long standing that recovery is a massive undertaking; there have been successes, however, notably the Thames River, once virtually dead, which is now in the process of being restored.

## Riparian Areas

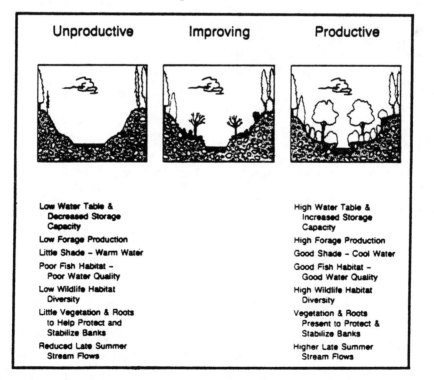

| Unproductive | Improving | Productive |
|---|---|---|

Low Water Table & Decreased Storage Capacity

Low Forage Production

Little Shade – Warm Water

Poor Fish Habitat – Poor Water Quality

Low Wildlife Habitat Diversity

Little Vegetation & Roots to Help Protect and Stabilize Banks

Reduced Late Summer Stream Flows

High Water Table & Increased Storage Capacity

High Forage Production

Good Shade – Cool Water

Good Fish Habitat – Good Water Quality

High Wildlife Habitat Diversity

Vegetation & Roots Present to Protect & Stabilize Banks

Higher Late Summer Stream Flows

**Source:** *State of the Public Rangelands 1990.* Bureau of Land Management, Department of the Interior.

## Rivers Information and Action Guide

**For information and involvement about rivers:**

AMERICAN CANAL SOCIETY, (771-843-4035). Publishes the quarterly *American Canals.*

**American Rivers** (801 Pennsylvania Avenue NW, Suite 303, Washington, DC 20003; 202-547-6900; Kevin J. Coyle, President), a membership organization founded in 1973 "devoted exclusively to preserving the nation's outstanding rivers and its landscapes," seeking to preserve rivers, protect streamside acres, and block dams. *Its Hydropower Policy Center* seeks a national policy that balances DEVELOPMENT of needed dams on some rivers with preservation for others. In addition to its annual list of the Ten Most Endangered Rivers, American Rivers publishes various materials, including the quarterly newsletter *American Rivers*; action alerts on river conservation issues; lists of river outfitters, fishing guides, canoe and kayak manufacturers and retailers that support river conservation; and books such as *Rivers at Risk: The Concerned Citizen's Guide to Hydropower* (John D. Echeverria et al.), *The American Rivers Guide to Wild and Scenic River Designation: A Primer on National River Conservation* (Kevin J. Coyle), and *The American Rivers Outstanding Rivers List* (John D. Echeverria and Jamie Fosburgh).

**AMERICAN WILDLANDS ALLIANCE (AWL),** (303-771-0380). Maintains *Wildlands Conservation Program (WCP); River Defense Fund; Wildland Economic Research Program,* and *Watershed and Riparian Rehabilitation.*

**BUREAU OF LAND MANAGEMENT (BLM),** (202-208-5717). Manages many rivers under the Wild and Scenic Rivers Act.

**CULTURAL SURVIVAL (CS),** (617-495-2562).

**EARTH FIRST! (E.F.!),** (Direct Action Fund, 415-376-7329). Opposes construction of new DAMS and advocates destruction of many others, such as GLEN CANYON.

**EARTH ISLAND INSTITUTE,** (415-788-3666). Sponsors the *International Rivers Network.*

**FRESHWATER FOUNDATION,** (612-449-0092). Publishes *Understanding Your Shoreline: Protecting Rivers, Lakes and Streams.*

**FRIENDS OF THE RIVER (FOR),** (415-771-0400). Conducts the *100 Rivers Campaign; Water Policy Reform* campaign; and *Hydromania and Watershed Protection* campaign.

**International Rivers Network (IRN)** (301 Broadway, Suite B, San Francisco, CA 94133; 415-986-4694; Phil Williams, President), an international organization founded in 1988 to "stop construction of dams that destroy the environment" and to build "a united front for environmentally sound, socially just water resource development." Among its main aims are "reclamation and restoration of rivers . . . ravaged by pollution and bad development; preservation of the world's last wild rivers; freedom of information, and an end to the secrecy of development banks and aid agencies; public participation in development decisions which affect the lives and future of entire communities; [and] promotion of environmentally sound development policies." The IRN is a project of *The Tides Foundation,* and is affiliated with FRIENDS OF THE EARTH (International); it publishes or distributes various materials, including the bimonthly newsletter *World Rivers Review* and books such as *Damming the Narmada: India's Greatest Planned Environmental Disaster* (Claude Alvares and Ramesh Billorey, 1988).

**IZAAK WALTON LEAGUE OF AMERICA (IWLA),** (703-528-1818). Operates *Save Our Streams* project.

**NATIONAL INSTITUTE FOR URBAN WILDLIFE,** (301-596-3311 or 301-995-1119). Publishes the *Wildlife Habitat Conservation Teacher's Pac* series, covering *Rivers and Streams.*

**NATURAL RESOURCES AND ENERGY DIVISION (NRED), UNITED NATIONS,** (212-963-6205). Publishes *River and Lake Basin Development* (1990).

**SIERRA CLUB,** (415-776-2211 or 202-547-1141; legislative hotline, 202-547-5550). Publishes the *National Wild and Scenic Rivers System.*

**TROUT UNLIMITED,** (703-281-1100).

**WORLD BANK,** (202-477-1234). Publishes *Dam Safety and the Environment, Dams and the Environment: Considerations in World Bank Projects,* and *Reservoir Sedimentation: Impact, Extent, and Mitigation.*

**Other references:**

*Better Trout Habitat: A Guide to Stream Restoration and Management.* Christopher J. Hunter. Island Press, 1990. *Rivers at Risk: The Concerned Citizen's Guide to Hydropower.* John D. Echeverria et al. Island Press, 1989.

(Note: Many rivers and river basins have their own regional organizations, such as the Potomac or the Connecticut. These may be found in the general directories listed in the GREEN BOOKSHELF on page 480.)

---

In the United States, various organizations exist to deal jointly with major river systems, especially cleaning up and restoring the lower rivers. In recent decades, however, much attention has been focused on those rivers that are still relatively untouched and unspoiled, covered under the WILD AND SCENIC RIVERS ACT of 1968. Environmentalists have also been seeking additional protection for rivers by the FOREST SERVICE, BUREAU OF LAND MANAGEMENT, or other federal agencies, as part of the National Forest System or other public lands. Because many rivers cross jurisdictional as well as political boundaries, environmentalists in the BLUEPRINT FOR THE ENVIRONMENT recommended establishment of a Joint Interagency Office of River Protection to coordinate planning, technical assistance, and

## Most Endangered American Rivers

Every year, the conservationist organization *American Rivers* (see RIVERS INFORMATION AND ACTION GUIDE on page 270) compiles a list of America's Most Endangered Rivers. The 1991 list was headed by the Colorado River in Arizona, threatened by the operation of the GLEN CANYON DAM, and included the upper Mississippi; the Snake and the Columbia in the Pacific Northwest; the Alsek and Tatshenshini in Alaska; the American in California; the Susquehanna in Pennsylvania; the New in North Carolina; the Gunnison in Colorado; and the Passaic in New Jersey. All were threatened by such dangers as hydroelectric DAMS, WATER POLLUTION, land DEVELOPMENT, and MINING. The 1990 list was topped by the Klamath River in Oregon, threatened by the Salt Caves hydropower diversion, and included the South Platte in Colorado (reprieved in 1991 by the vetoing of the TWO FORKS DAM), the Bruneau and Jarbridge in Idaho, the Cahaba in Alaska, the Jemez in New Mexico, the James in Missouri, and again the Passaic, the Penobscot, the Alsek, and the Tatshenshini.

---

management programs regarding river protection. Many river habitats are now being restored or preserved through local GREENWAYS programs. (See RIVERS INFORMATION AND ACTION GUIDE on page 270; also WATER RESOURCES; WATER POLLUTION; WETLANDS; WILD AND SCENIC RIVERS ACT; DAMS; FISHING; GREENWAYS; also MOST ENDANGERED AMERICAN RIVERS above; and SAN FRANCISCO DECLARATION OF THE INTERNATIONAL RIVERS NETWORK on page 79.)

**Rocky Flats nuclear plant,** see NUCLEAR WEAPONS ESTABLISHMENT, U.S.

**Rocky Mountain Institute (RMI),** (1739 Snowmass Creek Road, Snowmass, CO 81654; 303-927-3851), a nonprofit resource policy center, founded in 1982 by energy analysts Hunter Lovins (President and Executive Director) and Amory Lovins (Director of Research). RMI seeks to "foster the efficient and sustainable use of resources as a path to global security," seeking to prevent POLLUTION or threatened resources "by displacing harmful activities with environmentally benign, at least equally desirable, and *more cost-effective* substitutes." RMI works in "five interrelated programs: Energy, Water, Agriculture, Economic Renewal (an innovative approach to local development), and Redefining National Security," seeking a "secure world, based not on military force, privation, and fear, but on the efficient and equitable distribution of energy food, water, strategic materials, and information." It offers the Competitek Subscription Service for consultation on use and misuse of electricity, and publishes the triannual *Rocky Mountain Institute Newsletter*; books such as *Practical Home Energy Savings, Water Efficiency for Your Home: Products and Advice Which Save Water, Energy, and Money* (John C. Woodwell), *Resource-Efficient Housing: An Annotated Bibliography* (Robert Sardinsky and the RMI), and *Energy Unbound: A Fable for America's Future* (L. Hunter Lovins, Amory B.

Lovins, and Seth Zuckerman; available from SIERRA CLUB); and numerous reprints of articles, papers, and interviews.

**Rodale Institute** (222 Main Street, Emmaus, PA 18098; 215-967-5171), an organization associated with Rodale Press, funded partly by contributions, that focuses on "people helping people improve their lives, land and communities by increasing their inherent capacities for regeneration and enhancement," doing so "by working with them in successful programs for farms working in harmony with nature, thriving communities, a cleaner environment, and the prevention of famine." Rodale Institute oversees the *Rodale Research Center (RRC)* and works with over 25 cooperating research farms; operates the *Farmers Own Network for Education (FONE),* enhancing communication among farmers doing regenerative farming, so innovative farmers can be models for others; has a *Community Regeneration Network,* to give practical aid to old cities, industries, and rural communities; and has several projects in Africa, Asia, and Latin America, notably the *Famine Prevention Project,* seeking ways of saving and regenerating soil, using water more efficiently, encouraging AGROFORESTRY, developing drought-resistant food plants, and new uses for existing crops. The Institute also publishes the quarterly *Partner Report; New Farm* magazine; *International Ag-Sieve* (part of its *International Information Exchange Network*); books in the New Farm Library such as *How to Grow Vegetables Organically*; booklets such as *Controlling Weeds Without Chemicals* and *Using Manure Resources Wisely*; and numerous reports.

**rodenticides,** a type of chemical compound used for killing unwanted rodents, such as rats and mice (see PESTICIDES).

**Rwenzori National Park,** alternate name for QUEEN ELIZABETH NATIONAL PARK.

# S

**Safe Drinking Water ACT (SDWA),** a U.S. federal law passed in 1974, and amended in 1986, authorizing the ENVIRONMENTAL PROTECTION AGENCY (EPA) to set minimum national standards for drinking water, designed to protect public health and welfare from contaminants. Covered are "every public water supply in the country serving at least 15 service connections or 25 or more people."

Primary Drinking Water Standards set under the original 1974 act were called *maximum contaminant levels* (MCLs), or the largest amount or concentration allowable in drinking water for various hazardous substances and other contaminants. (See PRIMARY DRINKING WATER STANDARDS on page 274.) Each MCL is to be set as close as possible to another (but nonenforceable) SDWA standard, the *maximum contaminant level goal* (MCLG), orginally called *recommended maximum contaminant level* (RMCL), described as a "health goal equal to the maximum level of a contaminant which is not expected to cause any adverse health effects over a lifetime of exposure and includes a margin of safety."

When measurement is not technically or economically feasible, the EPA has the option of adopting a *National Primary Drinking Water Regulation* (NPDWR), requiring a specific treatment method to control the contaminant. During the 1990s, all MCLs are scheduled to be replaced by NPDWRs, while (under the 1986 amendments) the EPA is required to set standards for dozens more contaminants. In 1990, the EPA issued rules to regulate 26 PESTICIDES and 36 other contaminants in drinking water that "when effective . . . will more than double the number of pollutants subject to federal standards." Many more pollutants are still unregulated, however; in the EPA's own 1990 survey of drinking water wells alone, 127 pesticides and NITRATES were measured.

Local public water systems (PWSs) are required to monitor their drinking water periodically "for contaminants with MCLs and for a broad range of other contaminants as specified by the EPA." Enforcement of the standards, monitoring, and reporting are the responsibility of the individual states, but the 1986 amendments require the EPA to act when the state fails or is too slow to do so, and authorizes substantial civil penalties against the worst violators, termed *significant noncompliers*.

The Safe Drinking Water Act and its amendments also authorize the EPA to set *secondary drinking water standards*, regarding public "welfare," by "providing guidelines regarding the taste, odor, color, and aesthetic aspects of drinking water which do not present a health risk." These nonenforceable guidelines are called *suggested levels*. (See SECONDARY DRINKING WATER STANDARDS on page 276.) The "EPA recommends them to the States as reasonable goals, but federal law does not require water systems to comply with them," though some individual states have enforceable regulations regarding these concerns.

The 1986 amendments also ban all future use of LEAD pipe and lead solder in public drinking water systems and require public water systems to "tell their users of the potential sources of lead contamination, its health effects, and the steps they can reasonably take to mitigate lead contamination." In addition, they extend federal protection for groundwater, "by establishing programs to protect critical ground-water sources of drinking water, to protect areas around wells that supply public drinking water systems, and by regulating the underground injection of wastes above and below drinking water sources.''

Requirement does not necessarily mean enforcement, however. Many citizens have sharply criticized the EPA for failing to properly enforce the Safe Drinking Water Act. Environmentalists in BLUEPRINT FOR THE ENVIRONMENT put it bluntly, averring that ''EPA and state enforcement of the SDWA has been virtually nonexistent,'' with action taken against only a ''tiny fraction of the violating water suppliers,'' and even against *significant noncompliers* (the worst offenders) only a third of the time. And although the law requires that the public served by a noncomplier be notified of the violation, they noted that this requirement was ''often ignored,'' and urged that EPA's enforcement program be ''reorganized, reinvigorated, and funded at a higher level.'' Programs intended to protect groundwater supplies have generally been underfunded or entirely unfunded (see AQUIFERS).

In addition, many environmentalists have criticized the EPA for exempting from the SDWA requirements over 100,000 PWSs as not serving ''year-round residents,'' although these include schools, hospitals, factories, seasonal resorts, summer camps, and roadside restaurants. They urge a change in interpretation, and also a new program to protect rural water users and others on small or ''noncommunity'' water systems. They also suggest that contaminant standards should be based on higher consumption rates and revised to reflect not just exposure through drinking water, but also through showering, cooking, and washing. Stressing that many SYNTHETIC ORGANIC CHEMICALS are dangerous but have no standards under the SDWA, they also suggest that the EPA establish *total synthetic organic chemicals* (TSOC) standards, to protect against exposure to multiple contaminants in drinking water.

### For more information and action:

- **Environmental Law Institute (ELI),** (202–328–5150; publications office, 202-939-3844). Publishes *Clean Water Deskbook* (rev. ed., 1991). (See ENVIRONMENTAL LAW INFORMATION AND ACTION GUIDE on page 116.)
- **ENVIRONMENTAL PROTECTION AGENCY (EPA),** (Public Information Center, 202-260-7751 or 202-260-2080). Operates *Safe Drinking Water Hotline* (202-382-5533; toll-free (outside DC, except AK), 800-426-4791). Publishes *Is Your Drinking Water Safe?* (1989).

(See also WATER RESOURCES; WATER POLLUTION; ENVIRONMENTAL LAW.)

**Safe Energy Communication Council (SECC)** (1717 Massachusetts Avenue NW, Suite LL215, Washington, DC 20036; 202-483-8491; Scott Denman, Director), a national environmental coalition founded in 1980 ''to lead the fight for energy sources we can live with.'' SECC's aim is to provide grassroots and national energy and environmental groups with ''essential leadership through established and effective energy information programs, publications, media workshops, strategy consultation, and technical assistance,'' as through the *Media Strategy Consultation Program* to provide a coordinated response for workable media strategies and effective educational campaigns, and its *Information Dissemination Program*, providing factual material about economically and environmentally sound energy options for the press, public officials, and grassroots activists, as well as providing interviews, background information, and referrals to reporters, writers, and editors on a wide range of energy and environment issues. SECC conducts media training workshops for environmental, energy, consumer, and other public activists and volunteers, covering how to ''develop an effective overall media strategy, write press releases that work, get reporters to respond favorably to your story, sharpen TV and radio interview skills, choose and use the right media technique to meet your special needs, and create PSAs [Public Service Announcements], op-eds, and other methods of reaching new audiences.''

It also publishes various materials, including the bimonthly graphics service *ENfacts*, providing topical energy and environmental information in graphical form; *MYTHBusters*, a series of brief ''point-counterpoint'' reports on specific issues, such as GLOBAL WARMING, foreign OIL dependence, RADIOACTIVE WASTE, energy efficiency, renewable energy, and nuclear reactor safety; and *VIEWPOINT*, a bimonthly commentary providing in-depth discussion of current energy and environmental issues, such as *Energy Efficiency: Giving the U.S. a Competitive Edge* (Claudine Schneider) and *Higher Gas Mileage—And a Better Environment* (Bill Magavern).

**Sahel,** the part-GRASSLANDS, part-DESERT area immediately south of the Sahara, extending from Senegal east through portions of Mauritania, Mali, Upper Volta, Niger, Nigeria, Chad, Sudan, and in recent decades also Ethiopia. Since the 1960s, massive POPULATION growth and an ill-considered widescale international effort to dig wells that would provide water for the area combined to convert a formerly nomadic cattle-raising people into a much larger cattle-raising and subsistence-farming people. Crop-rotation practices soon broke down and the number of cattle increased. While this was happening, a long period

## Primary Drinking Water Standards

Note: MCL is the Maximum Contaminant Level, expressed in milligrams per liter, unless otherwise noted. For more information, see SAFE DRINKING WATER ACT.

| Contaminants | Health Effects | MCL* | Sources |
|---|---|---|---|
| **Microbiological** | | | |
| Total Coliforms (Coliform bacteria, fecal coliform, streptococcal, and other bacteria) | Not necessarily disease-producing themselves, but can be indicators of organisms that cause assorted gastroenteric infections, dysentery, hepatitis, typhoid fever, cholera, and others; also interfere with disinfection process. | 1 per 100 milliliters** | Human and animal fecal matter |
| Turbidity | Interferes with disinfection. | 1 to 5 NTU** | Erosion, runoff, and discharges |
| **Inorganic Chemicals** | | | |
| Arsenic | Dermal and nervous system toxicity effects | .05 | Geological, pesticide residues, industrial waste and smelter operations |
| Barium | Circulatory system effects | 1 | |
| Cadmium | Kidney effects | .01 | Geological, mining and smelting |
| Chromium | Liver/kidney effects | .05 | |
| Lead | Central and peripheral nervous system damage; kidney effects; highly toxic to infants and pregnant women | .05** | Leaches from lead pipes and lead-based solder pipe joints |
| Mercury | Central nervous system disorders; kidney effects | .002 | Used in manufacture of paint, paper, vinyl chloride, used in fungicides, and geological |
| Nitrate | Methemoglobinemia ("blue-baby syndrome") | 10 | Fertilizer, sewage, feedlots, geological |
| Selenium | Gastrointestinal effects | .01 | Geological, mining |
| Silver | Skin discoloration (Argyria) | .05 | Geological, mining |
| Fluoride | Skeletal damage | 4 | Geological, additive to drinking water, toothpaste, foods processed with fluorinated water |
| **Organic Chemicals** | | | |
| Endrin | Nervous system/kidney effects | .0002 | Insecticide used on cotton, small grains, orchards (cancelled) |
| Lindane | Nervous system/kidney effects | .004 | Insecticide used on seed and soil treatments, foliage application, wood protection |
| Methoxychlor | Nervous system/kidney | .1 | Insecticide used on fruit trees, vegetables |
| 2,4-D | Liver/kidney effects | .1 | Herbicide used to control broad-leaf weeds in agriculture, used on forests, range, pastures, and aquatic environments |
| 2,4,5-TP Silvex | Liver/kidney effects/ | .01 | Herbicide (cancelled in 1984) |

| Contaminants | Health Effects | MCL* | Sources |
|---|---|---|---|
| Toxaphene | Cancer risk | .005 | Insecticide used on cotton, corn, gin |
| Benzene | Cancer | .005 | Fuel (leaking tanks), solvent commonly used in manufacture of industrial chemicals, pharmaceuticals, pesticides, paints and plastics |
| Carbon tetrachloride | Possible cancer | .005 | Common in cleaning agents, industrial wastes from manufacture of coolants |
| ρ-Dichlorobenzene | Possible cancer | .075 | Used in insecticides, moth balls, air deodorizers |
| 1,2-Dichloroethane | Possible cancer | .005 | Use in manufacture of insecticides, gasoline |
| 1,1-Dichloroethane | Possible cancer | .007 | Use in manufacture of plastics, dyes, perfumes, paints, SOCs [synthetic organic compounds] |
| 1,1,1-Trichloroethane | Nervous system problems | .2 | Used in manufacture of food wrappings, synthetic fibers |
| Trichloroethylene (TCE) | Possible cancer | .005 | Waste from disposal of dry-cleaning materials and manufacture of pesticides, paints, waxes, and varnishes, paint strippers, metal degreasers |
| Vinyl chloride | Cancer risk | .002 | Polyvinylchloride pipes and solvents used to join them, waste from manufacturing plastics and synthetic rubber |
| Total trihalomethanes (TTHM) (chloroform, bromoform, bromodichloromethane, dibrochloromethane) | Cancer risk | .1 | Primarily formed when surface water containing organic matter is treated with chlorine |

**Radionuclides**

| | | | |
|---|---|---|---|
| Gross alpha particle activity | Cancer | 15 pCi/L | Radioactive waste, uranium deposits |
| Gross beta particle activity | Cancer | 4 mrem/yr | Radioactive waste, uranium deposits |
| Radium 226 & 228 (total) | Bone cancer | 5 pCi/L | Radioactive waste, geological |

**Other substances**

| | | | |
|---|---|---|---|
| Sodium | Possible increase in blood pressure in susceptible individuals | None*** (20 mg/ 1 reporting level) | Geological, road salting |

*Effective December 1990, the present total coliforms MCL will be superseded by these National Primary Drinking Water Requirements (NPDWRs): 95% of samples taken shall be free of any coliforms; small systems can have one contaminated sample in 39. The present turbidity MCLs will be superseded by NPDWRs, which will be phased in between December 1990 and June 1993. These NPDWRs regulate *Giardia lamblia* (99.9% reduction), viruses (99.99% reduction), *Legionellae*, hetertrophic bacteria, and turbidity. The revised turbidity limits are 5 NTU [turbidity units] in the source water to avoid filtration; 0.5 NTU 95% of the time and 5 NTU at all times for conventional or direct filtration; 1 NTU 95% of the time and 5 NTU at all times for slow sand or diatomaceous earth filters.

**Agency considering substantially lower number.

***Monitoring is required and data is reported to health officials to protect individuals on highly restricted sodium diets.

**Source:** *Is Your Drinking Water Safe?* Environmental Protection Agency, 1989.

## Secondary Drinking Water Standards

Note: These are nonenforceable federal guidelines; see SAFE DRINKING WATER ACT.

| Contaminants | Suggested Levels | Contaminant Effects | Contaminants | Suggested Levels | Contaminant Effects |
|---|---|---|---|---|---|
| pH | 6.5–8.5 | Water is too corrosive | Zinc | 5 mg/1 | Taste |
| Chloride | 250 mg/1 | Taste and corrosion of pipes | Fluoride | 2.0 mg/1 | Dental fluorosis (a brownish discoloration of the teeth) |
| Copper | 1 mg/1 | Taste and staining of porcelain | Color | 15 color units | Aesthetic |
| Foaming agents | 0.5 mg/1 | Aesthetic | Corrosivity | Noncorrosive | Aesthetic and health related (Corrosive water can leach pipe materials, such as lead, into drinking water.) |
| Sulfate | 250 mg/1 | Taste and laxative effects | | | |
| Total dissolved solids (hardness [vs. softness of water]) | 500 mg/1 | Taste and possible relation between low hardness and cardiovascular disease; also an indicator of corrosivity (related to lead levels in water); can damage plumbing and limit effectiveness of soaps and detergents. | Iron | 0.3 mg/1 | Taste and staining of laundry |
| | | | Manganese | 0.05 mg/1 | Taste and staining of laundry |
| | | | Odor | 3 threshold odor number | Aesthetic |

**Source:** *Is Your Drinking Water Safe?*, Environmental Protection Agency, 1989.

of drought hit the entire area. The net result was long-term OVERGRAZING of diminishing pasturelands, and the DESERTIFICATION of large areas; in some areas the Sahara moved south as much as 150 to 200 miles. A long famine began, its effects much worsened by the political instability of many of the countries involved (see FAMINE AND FOOD INSECURITY).

On the political side, the decades-long Ethiopian–Eritrean civil war, which began in 1962, used up resources greatly needed for famine relief, as famine, disease, and war generated a flood of refugees. As a result, an estimated 1 to 2 million refugees died, many of them because one side or the other in the civil war sometimes refused to admit foreign famine relief. During the long period of drought and famine, there were also long civil wars in Nigeria, Chad, and Somalia. The combatants in Nigeria in some periods refused to let foreign aid reach the Sahel refugees. In 1992, foreign aid was reaching some of the millions of Sahel refugees, but war continued in several Sahel countries. No solution that promised to return the

refugees to their now seriously degraded lands was in sight.

### For more information and action:

• **Comité Permanent Interetats de Lutte contre la Sécheresse dans le Sahel (CILSS, or Permanent Interstate Committee for Drought Control in the Sahel)** (B.P. 7049, Ouagadougou, Burkina Faso; 33-42-52, 33-43-55, 33-48-70; Ali Djalbord Diard, Executive Director), an international organization focusing on the environmental health of the Sahel. CILSS maintains the *Centre for Agrometeorology*; operates a research and training arm *Institute du Sahel* (Institute of the Sahel, B.P. 1530, Bamako, Mali; 22-21-48); coordinates *Operation Hydrology*; runs the computerized *Sahelian Scientific and Technical Documentation and Information Network (RESADOC)*; and publishes a journal *Reflets Sahéliens*, newsletters, and bibliographies, all in French.

• IUCN–THE WORLD CONSERVATION UNION, (202-797-5454). Publishes *The IUCN Sahel Studies* (M. Norton

Griffiths and P. Rydén, eds., 1989; in English or French).

- UNITED NATIONS DEVELOPMENT PROGRAMME (UNDP), (212-906-5000). Has U.N. Sudano-Sahelian Office (UNSO).
- WORLD BANK, (202-477-1234). Publishes *Desertification Control and Renewable Resource Management in the Sahelian and Sudanian Zones of West Africa.*
- WORLD RESOURCES INSTITUTE (WRI), (202-638-6300). (See also GRASSLANDS; also DESERT AND DESERTIFICATION INFORMATION AND ACTION GUIDE on page 86.)

**salinization,** accumulation of salts in soil or water, making it unable to support plant life; a kind of ENVIRONMENTAL DEGRADATION. Like the WATER RESOURCES that supply its moisture, soil contains varying amounts of salts. In many areas, especially where rainfall is average or abundant, and the drainage good, these are dissolved, flushed out of the soil, and carried away into surface water or groundwater. But in some areas, salts tend to accumulate in soil, especially in dry areas or along COASTS, and human activities can accelerate these processes.

In arid or semiarid areas, waters are often more salty than other freshwater because evaporation of surface waters leaves behind salt; the waters in Egypt's Aswan Dam, for example, are estimated to be 10 percent more salty than the water entering it. Use of this more concentrated solution for irrigation adds salt to the land. In addition, continual irrigation tends to "waterlog" the land and raise the water table, which on the way up dissolves salts and adds them to the upper level of soil; the result is what some call "wet deserts." Such problems can be somewhat controlled if the land is allowed to lie fallow periodically, to allow the salts to be flushed out naturally and to recover. But often land is kept irrigated and cultivated continually, with increasing salt content and decreasing agricultural returns. Indeed, one of the main concerns about large-scale DAMS and associated intensive irrigation projects is precisely that salinization often results, degrading the environment and undercutting the efforts to make the land more productive—with the net result of massive expenditure for DEVELOPMENT sometimes near zero.

Local approaches to salinization include lining irrigation channels, installing drainage ditches to prevent waterlogging of the soil, and digging wells to lower the water table. These generally have only local effects, however, since salts remain in the system and are deposited downstream. In such ways, river systems in some major agricultural valleys have become increasingly saline, including the Indus, the Tigris and Euphrates, the Rio Grande, the Colorado, China's North Plain, California's San Joaquin

Valley, and Australia's Murray River. More general DESALINIZATION techniques exist, but they are often too expensive for wide-scale use, though that may change in the future if less costly methods are developed; if cheap, renewable energy becomes available; or if the need for freshwater becomes great enough.

In a linked problem, salinization can also result from overuse of surface waters, drawing down the level of LAKES and ponds, and leaving behind heavy salt deposits that from the air look like snow, two classic cases being the ARAL SEA in Central Asia and California's MONO LAKE. If these deposits include many carbonates, they will tip the soil balance toward alkalinity (see PH). At sufficient concentrations, the soil becomes so salty or alkaline that no plants can grow there, and sometimes so hard and crusty that it could not be cultivated in any case. In some areas, winds may also pick up the salt deposits, later dropping them on other lands.

On sea COASTS, salinization occurs when sea water intrudes into freshwater zones. Coastal areas often include WETLANDS that have brackish or somewhat salty water, such as MANGROVES. But EROSION upstream and changing patterns of SEDIMENTATION downstream can lead to increased floods, bringing salt water into coastal lands, making them for a time unusable for the area's normal agriculture. If floods recur too frequently, as in the repeated BANGLADESH DISASTERS, the lands may be lost to cultivation for long periods or permanently. Salt water can also invade coastal areas as the sea level rises relative to the land. That can occur as a global phenomenon (see SEA LEVEL RISE) or as a local event, as when groundwater is so heavily drawn on that the ground subsides (see AQUIFERS). Either way, ECOSYSTEMS and agriculture dependent on freshwater will be damaged and eventually killed by the excess salts.

**For more information and action:**

- CONSULTATIVE GROUP ON INTERNATIONAL AGRICULTURAL RESEARCH (CGIAR or CG), (202-473-8951). Works closely with the International Irrigation Management Institute (IIMI).
- UNITED NATIONS ENVIRONMENT PROGRAMME (UNEP), (212-963-8138 or -8098).
- WORLD RESOURCES INSTITUTE, (202-638-6300).

**Sandoz chemical spill,** a November 1, 1986 fire at Sandoz AG's warehouse 956, on the RHINE RIVER, upriver from Basel, Switzerland, that caused a massive leak of contaminated water into the Rhine. The warehouse had contained 840 tons of insecticides and other TOXIC CHEMICALS; some of these mixed with the large quantities of water poured onto the fire to dump an estimated 30 tons of highly toxic waste into the river, some of it containing MERCURY, an extraordinarily toxic substance. On November 7, further leakage from the damaged warehouse into the Rhine was also reported.

The spill caused a water-use crisis on the Rhine, in one of Europe's most heavily populated areas and most used waterways. By November 3, thousands of dead fish were appearing in the Rhine, and on November 4, Wiesbaden, Germany, stopped taking water from the river, as did many other towns and cities downstream, in Switzerland, France, Germany, and Luxembourg. In total, an estimated 500,000 fish in the river were killed, as well as much else in the life of the river. As an international protest grew, it also became clear that several companies on the Rhine had also been dumping toxic wastes into the river, some routinely and some as the result of unreported accidents, as in the spill of 100 gallons of highly toxic atrizine into the river by Ciba-Geigy on October 30, just before the Sandoz fire. (See TOXIC CHEMICALS.)

**Santa Barbara oil well blowout,** the leakage of an estimated 800,000 gallons (approximately 2,700 tons) of crude OIL from an offshore rig off Santa Barbara, California, from January 31 to February 8, 1969. The oil slick quickly came ashore, fouling 20 miles of heavily populated California coastline and causing the deaths of hundreds of seabirds and much life in the sea. OFFSHORE DRILLING in the area had been highly controversial, with just this sort of accident predicted by conservationists. The blowout triggered a major battle, one of many on the issue, which resulted in somewhat greater oil industry responsibility for cleanups after such disasters, and placed some practical political obstacles in the way of unrestricted offshore drilling. In 1971, four oil companies paid $4.5 million to settle the claims of owners of California property damaged as a result of the Santa Barbara well blowout. Criminal charges against the companies were dealt with by single-count guilty pleas and token fines. (See OIL.)

**SARA,** an abbreviation for the SUPERFUND Amendments and Reauthorization Act of 1986, Title III.

**Savannah River nuclear plant,** see NUCLEAR WEAPONS ESTABLISHMENT, U.S.

**Savannah River oil spill,** leakage of an estimated 500,000 gallons (approximately 1,700 tons) of fuel OIL from the Liberian tanker *Amazon Venture* into the Savannah River near Savannah, Georgia, on December 4–7, 1986. The oil slick created by the spill did considerable environmental damage to wildlife and their environment at the Savannah National Wildlife Refuge. (See OIL.)

**savannas (savannahs),** transitional regions between FORESTS and relatively dry regions; a kind of GRASSLAND that takes varied forms, but generally has widely separated trees interspersed with grasses and shrubs. Savannas often develop in regions that are subject to recurrent fires, either from natural causes or human intervention. In tropical zones, as in Africa or South America, the trees are often deciduous, dropping their leaves in the long dry season following summer rains, but may also be evergreen; the shrubby or grassy low growth is often dense, deeply rooted to tap underground water, and tends to form a mat, with a flammability that tends to maintain the savanna. Savanna trees commonly have a distinctive umbrella crown and gnarled Y-shaped trunk. Along stream edges trees tend to grow more closely together, forming what are called *gallery forests*; savannas may also contain pockets of forest, called *relics*, from earlier periods.

Savannas are found widely in Africa, notably in East Africa; in South America, in Venezuela and Brazil (where the term is *campo cerrado*); and in Australia. African savannas, lying between tropical rain forests and semiarid regions, and dominated by acacia, have been the focus of enormous environmental attention, since they are home to numerous large wild animals, such as ZEBRAS, ELEPHANTS, antelopes, and giraffes. Many of the best known WILDLIFE REFUGES in the world, such as those on the SERENGETI Plain, are largely savanna. In areas with heavy POPULATION pressure, however, savannas are under attack because the land is well suited to many crops, such as coffee, fruit trees, millet, and sorghum.

Savannas are also found in temperate zones and colder regions. While *temperate savannas* can be quite productive, such as those that once existed as transitions between forests and prairies in Illinois (see RESTORATION ECOLOGY), *cold savannas* are much poorer agriculturally. These are regions of high altitude (as in the South American *páramo*) or transition areas between forests and TUNDRA, whose scattered evergreens, mosses, lichens, and low woody plants are most hospitable to herds of wild animals such as CARIBOU and reindeer. (See GRASSLANDS; FORESTS; TUNDRA.)

**Scripps Institution of Oceanography** (University of California, La Jolla, CA 92093; 619-534-3624; Edward A. Frieman, Director), a research and teaching institution founded as an independent biological research laboratory in 1903, becoming part of the University of California in 1912; it is a key resource for those seeking knowledge about the marine environment. In addition to offering graduate training in oceanographic studies and numerous programs for children and adults the Institution sponsors research programs in a wide range of scientific areas including ''studies of global warming and long-term climate change, the marine food chain, earthquake prediction, pharmaceuticals from sea life and coastal ocean processes.'' It maintains a fleet of research craft; operates an aquarium-museum for the public and an experimental aquarium for research; maintains a diving facility, a pier acting as an observation platform, and underwater research areas; and also has other specialized facilities.

Scripps also operates a research division, *Center for Coastal Studies (CCS)* (Mail Code A-033, c/o Scripps; D.L. Inman, Director), which conducts scholarly studies of the coastal environment, and advises on coastal protection and sediment management, with areas studied including waves, currents and tides in nearshore and estuarine waters; sediment transport by waves, winds, and rivers; fluid-sediment interactions, and marine archaeology. It also offers occasional expeditions, such as a snorkeling and natural history expedition to Hawaii; whale-watching off Baja California; or diving in Fiji. It publishes a quarterly newsletter *Calendar*, irregular collections of scientific papers in the *Bulletin of the Scripps Institution of Oceanography*, and other specialized reports.

**scrubbers,** popular name for a wide variety of devices used to remove pollutants from EMISSIONS before they are released into the air. In general, the pollutant-laden air is passed through a device containing certain chemicals, designed to react with the unwanted pollutants—that is, to form new compounds that separate, or *precipitate out*, from the rest—and so remove them from the exhaust. In one common scrubber to remove SULFUR DIOXIDE, the industrial exhaust is passed through a device containing a SLURRY of water and lime or another calcium-based material. As the pollutant-laden exhaust passes through the slurry, sulfur dioxide dissolves in it and is removed from the air. Unfortunately, there remains the problem of disposing of the sulfur-contaminated slurry; also such devices are easily fouled by calcium deposits.

For such reasons, the approaches much preferred are *regenerative*—that is, they focus on RESOURCE RECOVERY. An approach using a magnesium slurry separates out the sulfur dioxide in such a fashion as to turn it into a marketable product, while the magnesium compound can be reused. Considerable attention has been focused on developing such self-perpetuating, to some extent self-supporting, scrubbers, using a wide variety of chemicals, among them some containing sodium and ammonia. (See AIR POLLUTION; ACID RAIN.)

**sea cows,** see MANATEES.

**sea-level rise,** an increase in the proportion of the earth's water that is in the OCEANS, as opposed to being in RIVERS, LAKES, AQUIFERS, or stored in ice; and so, the covering of more land by water. Though the total amount of water on earth is believed to have been generally constant for millions of years, the sea level has changed dramatically with changes in the earth's climate. During the great ice ages, large amounts of water were tied up in ice sheets and glaciers, resulting in much lower ocean levels; in between, as the earth warmed, ocean levels rose again. Since the last ice age, over 10,000 years ago, the earth has been in an interglacial period. During that period, the ocean level has been slowly rising, at variable rates estimated as between 1 and 10 centimeters (approximately .4 to 4 inches) a century. Many coastal sites inhabited by early humans are now underwater; the mouths of old rivers are ''drowned'' by rising OCEAN waters; low-lying islands have sunk beneath the waves; and what were once peninsulas are now islands, such as Britain, which was joined to the mainland until about 5500 B.C. This natural, long-term process has been occurring for thousands of years.

Recently, however, many observers have become concerned that human activities may be speeding up the process. The sea level has risen an estimated 10 to 15 centimeters (4 to 6 inches) in the past century, at the somewhat faster pace of about 1 to 1.5 millimeters (almost .04 to .06 inches) a year; a 1990 National Research Council report gave the current rate at 1 to 2 millimeters a year. Even those who agree on the increased rate of sea-level rise cannot be sure of its cause, but many point out that it has coincided with the heavy use of FOSSIL FUELS. They suggest a chain of events, beginning with accumulations of various pollutants in the air, which cause a GREENHOUSE EFFECT, which results in GLOBAL WARMING, which in turn causes more rapid melting of the earth's ice storehouse of water. The chain of events is not entirely clear, but some scientists are predicting substantial increases in sea level rise in the next century, with estimates ranging from 20 to 200 centimeters (8 to 80 inches).

If this scenario is correct and the sea level continues to rise faster, the result could be a relatively rapid swamping of all current coastal areas, the sites of some of the heaviest concentrations of humans and their works, as well as enormously rich and varied WETLANDS habitats, with incalculable consequences for civilization and the environment. This would mean not only the loss of habitations and habitats—the ENVIRONMENTAL PROTECTION AGENCY (EPA) estimates that in the United States alone a three-foot rise in sea level could swamp an area the size of Massachusetts—but also increased EROSION and the saltwater contamination of river mouths, adjoining lands, and aquifers supplying water for remaining coastal areas. Low-lying islands, river deltas, and coastal sand bars would be the most vulnerable, especially to major storms and floods, and would be among the first to be inundated. Elaborate systems of dikes, like those now used in the Netherlands, would afford only temporary relief, and in any case would be far-too-expensive options for poor countries like Bangladesh.

In a 1989 survey, the UNITED NATIONS ENVIRONMENT PROGRAMME (UNEP) identified the 10 countries most vulnerable to sea-level rise: Bangladesh, Egypt, The Gambia, Indonesia, the Maldives, Mozambique, Pakistan, Senegal, Surinam, and Thailand—all generally poor, heavily populated areas that could ill afford to lose massive amounts of living space and CROPLANDS. Even rich cities, such as Miami or Charleston, South Carolina, however, would have massive problems, not the least of which would be trying to maintain uncontaminated freshwater supplies. Substantial worldwide changes in sea level can also contribute to further CLIMATE CHANGE, causing other massive disruptions to earth and its life.

The facts about sea-level rise are not entirely clear. At least one 1989 study found that the Greenland ice sheet was growing, rather than melting. And a 1991 book, *Sea Levels, Land Levels and Tide Gauges* (see below) by two researchers from the WOODS HOLE OCEANOGRAPHIC INSTITUTION, questioned the accuracy of measurements of sea-level rise, pointing out that tide gauges may be thrown off and their data obscured by local conditions, including human activities that affect COASTS (such as EROSION, loss of WETLANDS, and construction of jetties) and movements of the earth's crust. This is because some areas are sinking and others rising, responding to the pushes and pulls of continental plates, and in some cases, land is still "rebounding" from the long-ago withdrawal of glaciers. Most agree, however, that the potential problems are extremely serious, and that it is important to act now to minimize POLLUTION that may contribute to sea-level rise, since its effects are not reversible.

A localized form of sea-level rise can occur when a region draws too heavily on its WATER RESOURCES, depleting groundwater, and allowing soil and rock to collapse. Such subsidence can cause significant environmental and property damage, also making the area far more vulnerable to floods and drainage problems. Some areas locally experience the reverse, *sea-level drop*, where local shifts in the earth's crust tilt the region upward, or where SEDIMENTATION raises the level of a delta.

## For more information and action:
- **American Littoral Society,** (201-291-0055). (See COASTS INFORMATION AND ACTION GUIDE on page 62.)

- **ENVIRONMENTAL PROTECTION AGENCY (EPA),** (202-260-7751 or 202-260-2080).
- **NATURAL RESOURCES DEFENSE COUNCIL (NRDC),** (212-727-2700).

**Other references:**
*Sea Levels, Land Levels, and Tide Gauges.* K.O. Emery and David G. Aubrey. Springer-Verlag, 1991. *Sea Level Rise: Animator and Terminator of Coastal Marshes.* W. Roland Gehrels and Stephen P. Leatherman. Vanci Bibliography (Monticello, IN), 1991. *The Rising Tide: Global Warming and World Sea Levels.* Lynne T. Edgerton. Island Press, 1990.
(See also CLIMATE CHANGE; COASTS; GLOBAL WARMING; AQUIFERS.)

**seals and sea lions,** various CARNIVOROUS marine mammals, all part of the same family, which includes *walruses*, sometimes termed *pinnipeds* because they use flippers for locomotion. Many of these 33 SPECIES have long been hunted, and some are still important to several Eskimo peoples. Commercial HUNTING began in the early 1700s, with the great Atlantic harp seal and walrus herds of the Arctic and sub-Arctic the first to be attacked. By the late 1700s, northern and southern fur seals were being attacked, as well; during the late 1700s and early 1800s, for example, at least two million fur seals were killed at the Pribilof Islands, off Alaska, while in the same period at least one million fur seals were killed in the Antarctic and sub-Antarctic by hunters operating mainly in the Falklands and off New Georgia Island. By the early 20th century, northern and southern fur and elephant seals were close to extinction, as were several less numerous species. Several other species were seriously threatened.

With the 1911 North Pacific Fur Seal Convention and subsequent international agreements, several greatly threatened species were saved and then recovered, including the *northern* and *southern fur seals*, the *harp seal*, the *northern* and *southern elephant seal*, and the *Pacific walrus*. But the *Atlantic walrus* never came back fully; nor did several other *fur seal* species, which are still threatened.

Though they are not an ENDANGERED SPECIES, the mass clubbing to death of baby harp seals has caused enormous worldwide revulsion and forced restriction of the practice by the Canadian government. It has played a significant role in the spreading of the ANIMAL RIGHTS MOVEMENT in recent years.

All three kinds of *monk seals*—the *Caribbean*, the *Hawaiian*, and *Mediterranean*—are greatly endangered species. The Caribbean monk seal is very nearly extinct; currently, there is little hope that the species will survive. The Mediterranean monk seal population seems down to only a few hundred, and these few survivors are greatly at risk from POLLUTION, "incidental" kill through entanglement with nets, and loss of HABITAT. Probably between 1,000 and 2,000 Hawaiian monk seals still survive, most of them in the northwest islands of the chain, and some also off the main islands in the group. In the United States, the MARINE MAMMAL COMMISSION (operating under the MARINE MAMMAL PROTECTION ACT) and the FISH AND WILDLIFE SERVICE are attempting to foster recovery of the seals, even while they are further endangered by increased FISHING and incidental kill, so the future of the species remains in doubt.

Threatened species also include the *Guadalupe fur seal* off California and western Mexico, and the *Steller sea lion* (northern sea lion), which lives in the northern Pacific, from California to Siberia. The *northern sea lion* has only very recently become threatened, as its population dropped sharply, for reasons that are so far unclear.

### For more information and action:

- AMERICAN CETACEAN SOCIETY (ACS), (213-548-6279). Publishes *Seals and Sea Lions*.
- CENTER FOR MARINE CONSERVATION (CMC), (202-429-5609). Has *Species Recovery Program*.
- ELSA WILD ANIMAL APPEAL (EWAA), (818-761-8387).
- GREENPEACE, (202-462-1177).
- PACIFIC WHALE FOUNDATION (PWF), (808-879-8860; for orders, 800-WHALE-1-1 [942-5311]). Publishes *Seals and Sea Lions*.
- SEA SHEPHERD CONSERVATION SOCIETY, (213-373-6979).
- SEA WORLD RESEARCH INSTITUTE (SWRI), (619-226-3870).

### Other references:

*Sea Lion.* Franklin A. Leib. NAL-Dutton, 1991. *Fur Seal Island: An Environment in Peril.* Paul Thomas. Paul & Co., 1991. *The Pinnipeds: Seals, Sea Lions, and Walruses.* Marianne Riedman. University of California Press, 1990.
(See also ENDANGERED SPECIES; MARINE MAMMAL PROTECTION ACT; ENDANGERED AND THREATENED WILDLIFE AND PLANTS on page 372; also ANIMAL RIGHTS AND WELFARE INFORMATION AND ACTION GUIDE on page 361.)

### Sea Shepherd Conservation Society

(P.O. Box 7000-S, Redondo Beach, CA 90277; 213-373-6979 or P.O. Box 48446, Vancouver, BC V7XX 1A2, Canada; 604-688 SEAL [7325]; Paul Watson, Founder), an international direct-action organization founded in 1977, devoted to conserving and protecting marine wildlife and HABITAT. Originally focused on WHALES, the Society soon extended its activities to include smaller marine mammals and birds. It came to prominence in 1979 and 1980, when the *Sea Shepherd I* rammed and sank several European whalers FISHING in violation of international regulations, and again in 1984 when it sank two of Iceland's four whaling ships and destroyed a whale processing factory. Other recent actions include blockading sealing fleets off Canada and Scotland's Orkney Islands; boycotting tuna caught by methods that also kill DOLPHIN; and ramming and severely damaging a fleet of six Japanese DRIFTNET ships.

The crews of Sea Shepherd vessels are largely volunteers, sometimes paying $1,500 in order to participate in an action campaign. The Society also offers occasional paid "nonconfrontational voyages" for members who want to gain seagoing experience and see DOLPHINS and whales on the way. The Society publishes a quarterly newsletter *Sea Shepherd Log* and occasional other alerts and releases.

**sea turtle,** see TURTLES, SEA.

### Sea World Research Institute (SWRI)

(Hubbs Marine Research Institute, 1700 South Shores Road, San Diego, CA 92109; 619-226-3870; Frank A. Powell, Jr., Executive Director), a nonprofit marine research organization, founded in 1963 by the Sea World Park as the Mission Bay Research Foundation, focusing on wise use of OCEAN environments. Its work "encompasses conservation, resource management education, ecology of marine animals, animal behavior, and mariculture," and its recent projects include studies of marine mammals around the California Channel Islands, studies of MONO LAKE's ecology, especially as a bird staging area, a program to raise and release white sea bass, and bioacoustics studies of WHALES and DOLPHINS. SWRI publishes the quarterly newsletters *Currents* and *The Helmsmen Quarterly,* and offers donors special events and tours.

**secondary standards,** in relation to POLLUTION, those levels set in relation to plants, animals, buildings, and

---

### Who Are the Sea Shepherds?

We are the investigators, documentors and enforcers of laws protecting the oceans. We are the shock troops of the movement which seeks to expose and remove those elements which are dangerously disrupting the ecological and biological status quo of the natural oceanic ecosystems.

—Paul Watson, Founder, Sea Shepherd Society, 1990

materials (see WELFARE EFFECTS), as opposed to *primary standards,* which affect human health, as under the SAFE DRINKING WATER ACT or CLEAN AIR ACT.

**sedimentation,** deposit of particles on the floor of bodies of water, such as RIVERS, LAKES, and OCEANS. These include organic matter—tiny living organisms or their once-living remains—and inorganic matter, such as bits of rock and soil washed away through EROSION, particles spewed forth by volcanoes, or naturally occurring chemical compounds precipitated out of the water. All of these types of matter in various degrees are present in water, generally kept suspended by currents and other turbulence, and by upwelling of bottom waters. But gradually, in the long term, they sink through the water to settle to the bottom. There they form a layer rich in life-sustaining nutrients. On the deep sea floor, they are little used. But in shallower areas, or where upwelling of currents brings sediment to the surface, they are important in sustaining biological productivity, since they are the source of the vital substances needed for PHOTOSYNTHESIS.

Unfortunately, the natural process of sedimentation has been much accelerated by human activities, especially those leading to increased erosion of land, causing some severe problems. Much larger loads of sediment are being carried into the world's bodies of waters. These limit the productivity of the waters, by screening out some of the light needed for photosynthesis. They also speed up the natural process of building up the bottoms of lakes and rivers, shortening their natural life spans. Shallower river beds lead to increased flooding, as the river's water can no longer be contained in its banks and spreads onto the surrounding countryside. Embankments can help to control floods, but if the process continues, the rivers may come to be some feet above the surrounding countryside. Then, if flooding does occur, as of China's Yellow River in 1991, it is far more disastrous. Rivers used for navigation, such as the Mississippi, also require routine but expensive dredging to clear sediment from the shipping channels.

Much of a river's sediment is deposited at the mouth of the river, as the water slows down at sea level, forming highly productive deltas of land. However, when rivers are dammed upstream, the sediment drops where the water stops—at the DAM. In areas where erosion is heavy, as in China or the Indian Subcontinent, this can mean that the dam fills up with silt, and is no longer able to function. One of the concerns about the NARMADA VALLEY DAM PROJECT is that heavy silting may shorten the active life of the dam, providing too small a return for the massive expense and dislocation in-

volved in the project. And, as an illustration of the complicated international nature of many sedimentation questions, Bangladesh opposes the Narmada Valley project because the dam will block the fertile sediment that its downstream farmers rely on.

According to a UNITED NATIONS ENVIRONMENT PROGRAMME (UNEP) report, sedimentation is also a major contributor to coastal pollution, perhaps even more than OIL spills or toxic-waste dumping. (See EROSION.)

**selenium (Se),** a type of HEAVY METAL.

**Sellafield,** the major British nuclear production plant, formerly called *Windscale,* on the Cumbrian coast of northwest England, facing the Irish Sea. It began operations in 1950, producing plutonium from 1952. A major nuclear accident occurred at the plant on October 7, 1957, when a fire in the reactor core of Pile No. 1 released large amounts of radioactive iodine and polonium into the air, contaminating the plant and surrounding areas. Following the accident, livestock in surrounding areas were destroyed, as was over 500,000 gallons of milk.

The disaster, which caused at least 30 later deaths from cancer (some estimates have run as high as 1,000 additional deaths), was kept secret by the British government, which for decades denied that anything more than a minor radioactive discharge had taken place. Earlier that year and throughout the 1950s, strontium-90 discharges had contaminated large surrounding areas. These discharges were also kept secret, as were the majority of the significant nuclear accidents occurring at the plant in the decades that followed. The plant was also a major OCEAN polluter, dumping large quantities of RADIOACTIVE WASTE into the Irish Sea, often far more then was officially announced.

In February 1990, a trailblazing study by Dr. Thomas Gardner of Southampton University established clear statistical links between the very high incidence of childhood leukemia in west Cumbria and the exposure to RADIATION of men working at the Sellafield nuclear plant, raising very serious questions for nuclear plant workers throughout the world, and suggesting that currently "acceptable" levels of radiation exposure at Sellafield were in fact far from acceptable, and in need of sharp downward revision. (See also NUCLEAR WEAPONS; also MAJOR NUCLEAR DISASTERS AND INCIDENTS on page 212.)

**Serengeti National Park,** Africa's greatest wildlife sanctuary, world-famous for the number and variety of its large animals, so many of them fast disappearing elsewhere on a continent facing enormous overpopulation, disease, famine, and poverty problems, all made worse by recurrent wars and civil wars. The 3,600,000-acre (5,600-square-mile) park is in north central Tanzania, its western edge only five miles from Lake Victoria and its northern boundary the Kenya–Tanzania border, with Kenya's MASAI MARA NATIONAL RESERVE beginning on the Kenya side.

On the Serengeti plains live hundreds of thousands and perhaps millions of wildebeests, ZEBRAS, and gazelles; the winter MIGRATIONS of an estimated million wildebeests and hundreds of thousands of zebras have provided some of the world's most memorable wildlife photography. Here too are substantial numbers of LIONS, LEOPARDS, CHEE-TAHS, black RHINOCEROS, hippopotamus, giraffes, impalas, and scores of other animals, as well as hundreds of bird species, including many varieties of ibis, grebe, pelican, heron, egret, stork, flamingo, duck, teal, goose, vulture, kestrel, eagle, goshawk, frankolin, bustard, plover, sandpiper, courser, dove, kingfisher, hornbill, owl, lark, pipit, flycatcher, warbler, swallow, shrike, sunbird, and weaver. (See ECOTOURISM; WILDLIFE REFUGE.)

**Seveso,** an Italian town, the site of a July 10, 1976 chemical explosion at the Givaudan plant, owned by Hoffman-La Roche. The explosion released a cloud of DIOXIN-carrying gas, which contaminated 7 square miles, forced evacuation of the town, killed hundreds of animals, and allegedly caused hundreds of dioxin-related birth defects and illnesses in later years. In April 1983, 41 barrels of dioxin-contaminated waste from the Seveso site were covertly dumped by a WASTE-DISPOSAL contractor in a small French town, while Italian, French, and German environmental authorities mounted a continent-wide search for the extremely dangerous materials. Ultimately found, they were incinerated by Hoffman-La Roche. (See TOXIC CHEMICALS.)

**Shasta Lake pesticide disaster,** the spill of approximately 19,500 gallons of the PESTICIDE metam sodium, marketed as Vapam, when a tanker car derailed, plunged into the Sacramento River, and ruptured, on July 14, 1991. The resulting chemical blob, which grew to half a mile long and 200 yards wide, swirled downstream, destroying "every living thing in the river," according to a California wildlife expert, and by July 17th had entered Shasta Lake, California's largest reservoir, even more vulnerable at 55 percent of its capacity during a long-term drought.

Though clearly highly toxic, the pesticide was not listed with the federal Department of Transportation as a regulated substance, so train crews were neither required to carry the chemical in a double-hulled tanker nor given information on handling it in case of an accident. William

K. Reilly, head of the ENVIRONMENTAL PROTECTION AGENCY (EPA), noted that the spill should trigger a review of what he called "totally anachronistic" pesticide regulations.

The local town of Dunsmuir was evacuated and about 200 people treated for symptoms such as nausea, headaches, rashes, respiratory problems, and eye irritation. But little else was done immediately, apart from testing and removing dead fish and birds, because little was known about how the land-based chemical would react in water in such large amounts. Clean-up attempts were begun in Lake Shasta and were expected to then move upriver. But their success and the long-term impact of the disaster on northern California's drinking water and on the life of the prime recreation area, with its premier trout fishing, are yet to be known. It was later disclosed that metam sodium (which when mixed with water forms the highly toxic methyl-isothiocyanate) was one of at least 10 dangerous pesticides about which the EPA had previously received warnings of health dangers (in this case, birth defects) and took no action. In August 1991, the California EPA urged pregnant women in the area to be tested to see if their fetuses had brain or spinal abnormalities. (See also PESTICIDES.)

**sick building syndrome,** a type of ENVIRONMENTAL ILLNESS.

**Sierra Club** (730 Polk Street, San Francisco, CA 94109; 415-776-2211; Michael L. Fischer, Executive Director; or 408C Street, NE, Washington, DC 20002; 202-547-1141; legislative hotline, 202-547-5550, for taped information on current environmental bills before Congress), a key environmental organization, founded in 1892 by John MUIR, which "promotes conservation of the natural environment by influencing public policy decisions—legislative, administrative, legal, and electoral." The Club's statement of purpose is: "To explore, enjoy, and protect the wild places of the earth; to practice and promote the responsible use of the earth's ecosystems and resources; to educate and enlist humanity to protect and restore the quality of the natural and human environment; and to use all lawful means to carry out these objectives."

The Sierra Club has 57 chapters, divided into 378 groups, and several affiliated programs, including:

- **Sierra Club Legal Defense Fund** (415-576-6100; Frederic Sutherland, Executive Director), which "brings environmental litigation on behalf of the Sierra Club and other environmental organizations";
- **Sierra Club Books** (100 Bush Street, 13th Floor, San

Francisco, CA 94104; 415-291-1600), publishing numerous environmentally oriented books and calendars;

- **Sierra Club Political Committee** (415-776-2211), established in 1976 to ''promote environmental candidates for public office, and educate the public about the Club's environmental priorities'';
- **Sierra Club Foundation** (415-291-1800; Stephen M. Stevick, Director), established in 1960 ''to fund non-legislative activities, including research, public education, and publishing'';
- **International Program,** run from its Washington office.

The Club uses lobbying, expert testimony, grassroots activism, and public education in its various campaigns. Recent campaigns include the Clean Air Act Authorization; Arctic National Wildlife Refuge Protection; BLM Wilderness/Desert National Parks; National Forests/National Parks Protection; Toxics: Resource Conservation and Recovery Act Reauthorization; Global Warming/Greenhouse Effect; and International Development Lending Reform. It also sponsors numerous outings, on the national, chapter, and group levels, including inner-city outings for ''urban youth, disabled, and seniors.''

The Sierra Club also publishes numerous materials, including periodicals such as the bimonthly magazine *Sierra*, the biweekly *National News Report* focusing on environmental legislation, the *Hazardous Materials/Water Resources Newsletter*, the *Public Lands Newsletter*, and various chapter and group newsletters, and brochures such as *How to Become an Environmental Activist, Environmental Protection Begins at Home, Platform for the Environment, Sierra Club Policies, Common Future Action Plan, Urban Environment Policy, How to Be a Wildlife Activist, Sierra Club History, Sierra Club History of Accomplishments, Sierra Club Organizational Summary,* and *Sierra Club: A Guide.* It also publishes numerous books, such as *Shopping for a Better World, Women and Wilderness, Starting Small in the Wilderness, Animals in Their Places, Voices for the Earth,* and the *Naturalist's Guide Series*; and other publications, such as *Sierra Magazine: Public Lands issue,* and *Library Periodicals Listing.*

**Silent Spring,** see Rachel CARSON.

**Silent World, The,** see Jacques-Yves COUSTEAU.

**Silkwood, Karen** (1946–74), U.S. atomic plant worker, employed at the Kerr-McGee Cimarron works, a plutonium-producing plant near Oklahoma City, Oklahoma. She was a health-and-safety committee member in the plant's Oil, Chemical, and Atomic Workers Union local, deeply involved in attempting to prove that Kerr-McGee was producing defective materials and contaminating the plant and

its surrounding environment. Silkwood died in an automobile accident while on her way to meet a union official and a *New York Times* reporter, carrying a body of documents aimed at proving her charges. Her documents were never found. Although local officials ruled her death accidental, there were widespread, though unproven allegations, that she had been murdered and her documents stolen.

Shortly before her death, Silkwood had been discovered to be RADIATION-contaminated; after her death, her family brought a civil suit against Kerr-McGee, and a related case against the federal government, charging company responsibility for the radiation contamination and violation of her civil rights by the company and the government. The latter charges were dismissed, but her estate won a $10.5 million damage award against Kerr-McGee on the contamination charges. The award was reversed by an appeal court, upheld in principle by the Supreme Court, and later settled out of court, for a reported $1.4 million.

Meryl Streep played Karen Silkwood in the 1983 film *Silkwood,* directed by Mike Nichols, and with a cast that included Cher, Kurt Russell, Craig T. Nelson, and Ron Silver. Silkwood's death, her family's pursuit of the case against Kerr-McGee, and the powerful film, seen by millions throughout the world, combined to turn some American public opinion even more against nuclear power and the nuclear power industry.

Kerr-McGee was back in the public eye on January 6, 1986, when a container of nuclear material burst at its Gore, Oklahoma, Sequoyah Fuels plant, killing one person and injuring over 100, as the resulting uranium-bearing gas emissions contaminated the air and ground in and near the plant. (See NUCLEAR ENERGY; also MAJOR NUCLEAR DISASTERS AND INCIDENTS on page 212.)

**silver (Ag),** a type of HEAVY METAL.

**sludge,** the solid-and-liquid residue that is left after as much liquid as possible is removed, as from waste water in a treatment plant, with a consistency ranging from a SLURRY to wet mud to fairly dry soil. Sludge sometimes also refers to the organic (living or once-living) matter on the bottom of RIVERS or LAKES. The composition of sludge varies widely with the source of the waste water, which may be domestic, commercial, industrial, or storm water. Whatever the source, solids suspended in the water are allowed to settle out and are then treated to stabilize them, destroy harmful bacteria, and reduce odor.

The resulting sludge is a nutrient-rich organic product that can be used in a variety of ways. It can undergo COMPOSTING; it can be burned, for simple disposal or to produce heat or energy (see INCINERATION); it can be chemically stabilized to become a low-grade fertilizer, cover material for landfills, or back-fill in land-reclamation projects; it can be turned into uniform-sized pellets, to fertilize and condition soil; it can be combined with other substances to produce *biobricks*; or it can be spread directly on the land.

Such uses are large-scale, modernized applications of what have been traditional ways of RECYCLING human waste, and as such they fit the profile of activities generally recommended by environmentalists. The catch is that much waste water is contaminated by TOXIC CHEMICALS, so using sludge in this way may simply be spreading poisons further and deeper into the environment. Environmentalists urge that sludge from waste water at least not be used on fields where crops are being grown for human consumption, though some are concerned about any environmental use, because final disposition cannot be controlled. (See WASTE DISPOSAL).

**slurry,** a mixture of liquid and insoluble matter, such as are used in some POLLUTION control devices called SCRUBBERS.

**smog,** originally conditions of smoke and fog combined, but now more widely referring to murky, heavily polluted air, especially laden with SULFUR DIOXIDE, NITROGEN DIOXIDE, and other pollutants commonly produced by automobiles and industrial manufacturers. Sunlight exacerbates the situation, triggering a *photochemical reaction*, in which nitric oxide produced by automobile exhaust is transformed into the toxic, pungently sweetish-smelling nitrogen dioxide. Smog irritates and damages the eyes, throat, and respiratory system, but in extreme cases—especially when people already have cardiorespiratory problems—it can trigger a fatality. It is most dangerous in conditions of temperature INVERSION, in which the heavily polluted smog is trapped over an area. If CRITERIA AIR POLLUTANTS are high enough, a *smog alert* may be issued, warning people of potential danger in the area. (See AIR POLLUTION.)

**snail darter,** a small freshwater fish, which became the center of a major environmental confrontation during the 1970s. Apparently unknown to science until first found in the Little Tennessee River in 1973, in an area to be flooded by the Tennessee Valley Authority's Tellico Dam, the snail darter was in 1975 declared an ENDANGERED SPECIES. A series of federal court decisions, culminating in a 1978 Supreme Court decision, then ruled that completion of the DAM would be in violation of the 1973 ENDANGERED SPECIES ACT. In 1978 Congress amended that Act, but the Congressional Committee created by the amended Act

would not exempt the dam from compliance with the law. Congress in 1979 specifically made an exception for the Tellico Dam, which was completed.

The snail darter survived, as it turned out; a mid-1970s transplant of the species into a nearby river worked well, and additional snail darter populations were found during the 1980s in several other Tennessee, Georgia, and Alabama streams. (See also ENDANGERED SPECIES; also ENDANGERED AND THREATENED WILDLIFE AND PLANTS on page 372.)

**social ecology,** in the environmental movement, that "wing" focusing on social issues, including militarism and racism, and political organization, including traditional conservationists and preservationists. Social ecology has been part of the main stream of environmentalism in the last few decades, but has sometimes been criticized as *anthropocentric*, or human-centered. Criticism often comes from the other main wing, DEEP ECOLOGY, which has a more philosophical bent and stresses the value of all SPECIES (not just because they may be useful or attractive to humans), a stance sometimes called *biocentric*.

In practice, though, social ecology and deep ecology are simply part of a spectrum of opinion, and people tending in differing directions work together in the whole range of environmental activities. Sometimes more troublesome within social ecology is the question of whether to reach wide—to take on the whole globe and all the questions affecting it—or to focus sharply and locally in places and on issues that can be directly affected.

Within the scientific community, social ecology more often refers to the study of the social behavior of organisms in groups, such as GORILLAS in the wild or humans in organizations.

### For more information:

*The Philosophy of Social Ecology: Essays on Dialectical Naturalism.* Murray Bookchin. Black Rose, 1990. *Social Ecology: Exploring Post-Industrial Society.* Martin Large. Anthroposophic, 1990.
(See also ECOLOGY.)

**Social Investment Forum (SIF)** (430 First Avenue North, Suite 290, Minneapolis, MN 55401; 612-333-8338; Brad Lehrman, Executive Director), a national professional association for investment advisors, financial planners, fund managers, and other individuals and organizations involved in investing, founded in 1981, which developed and encourages the practice of SOCIALLY RESPONSIBLE INVESTING (SRI). A project of the Forum, the COALITION FOR ENVIRONMENTALLY RESPONSIBLE ECONOMIES (CERES) formulated (with other groups) the VALDEZ

PRINCIPLES, ''intended to guide corporations in the establishment of environmentally sound policies.'' The Forum sponsors quarterly meetings around the country on social investment issues and opportunities, in addition to local chapter meetings; serves as an information clearinghouse on SRI, tracing the performance of socially invested assets; seeks to expand understanding about the concepts and practices of SRI; and publishes the quarterly *The Forum Newsletter*, *The Social Investment Services Guide*, and an annotated semiannual membership guide.

**socially responsible investing (SRI),** a concept developed by the SOCIAL INVESTMENT FORUM, proposing that social as well as financial criteria be considered before making an investment decision; when environmental concerns are paramount, sometimes called *environmental investing*. Favorable criteria under SRI might include a corporation's ''strong corporate citizenship,'' quality employee relations, and safe and useful products, for example; conversely corporations that pollute the environment or, manufacture weapons would be viewed more negatively in SRI terms. Because of public interest, some financial counselors specialize in investing in companies that have a favorable social or environmental approach; when the companies themselves stress that in their public relations, it is sometimes called *environmental advertising*. Increasingly, all investment counselors are having to consider the possible negative or positive effects of a company's actions as they affect the environment.

**For more information and action:**

- ENVIRONMENTAL HAZARDS MANAGEMENT INSTITUTE **(EHMI),** (603-868-1496). Publishes magazine *HazMat World*, which has an environmental stock index.
- INVESTOR RESPONSIBILITY RESEARCH CENTER (IRRC), (202-234-7500). Operates an *Environmental Information Service*.
- SIERRA CLUB, (415-776-2211 or 202-547-1141; legislative hotline, 202-547-5550). Publishes *Socially Responsible Investing*.
- SOCIAL INVESTMENT FORUM (SIF), (612-333-8338). Publishes the quarterly *The Forum Newsletter* and *The Social Investment Services Guide*.

## Society for Ecological Restoration (SER) (University of Wisconsin, Arboretum, 1207 Seminole Highway, Madison, WI 53711; 608-262-9547; William R. Jordan III, Supervisor of Administration and Editor), an interdisciplinary organization of professionals and amateurs founded in 1987, focusing on the restoration and subsequent management of damaged areas—urban, rural, and wilderness—''as a science and art [and] a conservation

strategy.'' The SER seeks to gather and disseminate information to public and professionals, and publishes the semiannual *Restoration & Management Notes*, the quarterly *SER News*, proceedings from annual conference (print and audio), and *Landscape Architecture Programs Directory*.

**sodbuster provision,** a part of the 1985 Food Security Act (Farm Bill) aimed at protecting soil from EROSION, under which farmers would risk losing commodity price supports and other federal farm aid if they produce destructive crops on highly erodable fields.

## Soil and Water Conservation Society of America (SWCS) (7515 NE Ankeny Road, R. R. #1, Ankeny, IA 50021; 515-289-2331; 800-THE-SOIL [843-7645]; Verlon K. (Tony) Vrana, Executive Vice President), a scientific and educational membership organization, founded in 1945 as the *Soil Conservation Society of America*, devoted to the ''conservation of land, water, and related resources to meet the needs of present and future generations by creating a variety of forums to identify, analyze, and formulate workable recommendations on land and water management policy and issues,'' with chapters throughout North America. In 1982 it sparked the founding of the WORLD ASSOCIATION OF SOIL AND WATER CONSERVATION. The SWCS sponsors annual meetings; has multidisciplinary working groups on special interests; holds conferences on land and water management concerns; offers awards for contributions in land and water conservation; and provides scholarships and research grants.

It also publishes various materials, including the bimonthly multidisciplinary *Journal of Soil and Water Conservation (JSWC)*; the bimonthly *Conservogram*; a middle-school-age computer program, *Farm and Food Bytes: Soil and Water Conservation*; cartoon-style booklets (with teacher's guides) oriented toward school-age children; and books.

**soil conservation,** management of the land so as to retain and enhance the productive capability of the soil, especially soil that is vulnerable to accelerated EROSION—the breaking down, carrying away, and later deposition of soil—due to human activities.

Soil is the layer of bonded particles of sand, silt, and clay that covers the land surface of the earth. Most soils develop multiple layers. The *topsoil* or *surface soil* is the most productive; it contains organic matter—decomposed plant and animal remains—that provides vital nutrients for plant PHOTOSYNTHESIS, the basis of the FOOD CHAIN. Below the topsoil is the *subsoil*, much less productive, partly because it contains much less organic matter. Below that is the *parent* or *underlying material*, the bedrock or other geologic material from which the soil is ultimately formed. The general rule of thumb is that it takes about 30 years to form one inch of topsoil from subsoil; it takes much longer than that for subsoil to be created from parent material, the length of time depending on the nature of the underlying matter. As human activities accelerate erosion, the topsoil is, of course, the first layer to go. But if erosion is heavy, more topsoil may be lost than is created through normal processes (see EROSION), making land ever less productive.

As a result, conservationists in developed and developing countries alike focus considerable attention on soil conservation. Their management plans look at four major properties of soil:

- **texture,** the proportion of sand, silt, and clay particles in soil. Clay particles have stronger bonds than silt or sand, but once broken apart they erode more readily. The size of the particles also affects the soil's erodability. In any area, the texture of the soil is a given, which it is impractical to change significantly.
- **slope,** the steepness of the land—another given—with the erosive power of runoff increasing with the steepness of the slope and with runoff exerting increasing force on soil particles, breaking them apart more readily, and carrying them farther away.
- **soil structure,** the size, shape, and arrangement of clusters of soil particles called *aggregates*, which themselves form larger clumps called *peds*. In an undisturbed landscape, soil develops a unique, fairly stable structure, but that can be changed—positively or negatively—by various agricultural practices. In general, the more the air space between the aggregates, the more water can infiltrate the soil, and the less erosion there is. Excessive tilling of the land breaks down peds and aggregates, lessening air space and erosion resistance. This can be minimized by reducing the frequency and depth of tillage, avoiding tilling when the soil is wet, and increasing the soil's content of organic matter.
- **organic matter,** the decomposed or decomposing remains of plants and animals, the presence of which helps not only fertility, but also soil structure, especially ability to store water. In previously undisturbed land, such as greeted farmers in North America, organic matter was plentiful. But there and throughout the world, if crops are grown year after year, without intervening years of crops (such as alfalfa) that restore nutrients and rebuild the soil, the nutrients and organic matter become depleted, crop failures become frequent, and land is eventually abandoned. Soil low in nutrients can be tilled, but this is more difficult, more expensive, less productive, and generally requires substantial amounts of fertilizer.

It is the object of soil conservation—and of SUSTAINABLE AGRICULTURE—to use management practices that allow land to remain in productive use.

A wide variety of techniques are used in soil conservation plans, among them:

- **crop residue management,** leaving standing stubble and other crop residues in the field, after harvesting without tillage, through the nongrowing season, when the erosion hazard is greatest.
- **conservation tillage,** tilling so as to leave crop residue on the soil surface to reduce erosion. In a *no-till* system, the soil is not disturbed before planting, and even then only a narrow slot is made, where the crop seed is to be inserted. In a *mulch till* system, the land is plowed before planting, but with machinery designed to keep large amounts of crop residues on the surface.
- **permanent grass or tree plantings,** covering the ground with healthy grasses or trees. Reforestation is the best possible erosion control, best suited for areas not suitable for crops. In the United States, such plantings are encouraged in highly erodible areas under the CONSERVATION RESERVE PROGRAM (CRP).
- **crop rotations,** planting grass or legume crops in an alternating pattern with other crops, to help build soil nutrients and control erosion.
- **cover crops,** planting of a protective crop after the harvesting of the main crop, to help prevent wind erosion until the next planting.
- **wind barriers,** planting occasional rows of plants—from perennial grasses to rows of trees—between fields or interspersed with row crops to retain moisture and lessen wind damage. The plants need to be chosen for the particular area; how much area they protect effectively depends partly on the height and density of the barrier. Such barriers and windbreaks also serve to provide some natural pest protection, as through the EDGE EFFECT. In general, rows of crops and windbreaks or barriers should be at right angles to the prevailing winds, to trap and hold particles moved by wind erosion.
- **stripcropping,** alternating equal-width strips of row crops or fallow with strips of wind-resistant crops, with all planted at right angles to the prevailing winds, providing not only soil protection but also crop rotation. When the wind-resistant strips are not as wide as the other strips, they are generally called *buffer strips*. A similar approach involves planting raised ridges of crops in fields, with the rows running at right angles to prevailing winds to absorb wind energy and trap moving soil particles.
- **contouring and terracing,** tilling and planting on the contour of the land, especially on short, gentle slopes,

to lessen soil movement. Where the slope is long or steep, terracing can be used to divide the field into shorter slopes, to minimize soil movement. Terraces may be formed by earth embankments, channels, or a combination of the two, with channels used to trap water and hold it so it can soak into the ground.

The techniques of soil conservation are also applied to the restoration of degraded areas, such as those damaged by OVERGRAZING or MINING. In the United States, for exampole, the SOIL CONSERVATION SERVICE focuses on not just soil and water conservation, but also natural resource surveys and community resource protection and management, offering nationwide assistance through the nearly 3,000 locally organized and run Soil and Water Conservation districts. (See EROSION AND SOIL CONSERVATION INFORMATION AND ACTION GUIDE on page 122); ORGANIC FARMING AND SUSTAINABLE AGRICULTURE INFORMATION AND ACTION GUIDE on page 226; also EROSION; SUSTAINABLE AGRICULTURE.)

**Soil Conservation Service (SCS)** (P.O. Box 2890, Washington, DC 20013; Director, Public Information Division, 202-447-5240), a key conservation agency under the United States DEPARTMENT OF AGRICULTURE, working in three main areas: "soil and water conservation, natural resource surveys, and community resource protection and management." The SCS is charged with carrying out national soil and water conservation programs, working with more than 2.3 million landowners and operators in the nearly 3,000 locally organized and operated soil and water conservation districts around the country and with other agencies.

The SCS also leads flood prevention programs, to reduce costly upstream floods; in cooperation with other state and federal agencies, conducts the *National Cooperative Soil Survey*, including preparation of maps of agricultural, forested, and built-up areas, describing the physical and chemical characteristics of the soils in each area (generally a county), on which land treatments and conservation planning in general are based; makes snow surveys in the West to forecast water supplies; and implements the *Land Evaluation and Site Assessment (LESA)* system of evaluating land and providing information for land use assessments. In addition, it carries out special programs such as the *Great Plains Conservation Program (GPCP)*, to protect the drought-prone Great Plains against wind EROSION; the *Rural Abandoned Mine Program (RAMP)*, to aid landowners in reclaiming abandoned coal-mined land; the *Resource Conservation and Development (RC&D) Program*, to help local multicounty areas develop resources and protect their environment; and numerous wa-

tershed projects, including the *Emergency Watershed Protection (EWP)* program, providing technical and financial assistance when natural disasters, such as fire and flood, damage watershed areas.

The SCS also assists with RIVER basin studies and carries out periodic national inventories of soil, water, and related resources, as required by the Soil and Water Resources Conservation Act of 1977. In addition, it carries on international exchange programs to train visitors from abroad, with technical specialists sent to work on projects in foreign countries; provides assistance in environmental education and recreation development; and seeks conservation plants to solve soil and WATER RESOURCE problems.

**solar energy,** power from the sun that can be harnessed for human use. In the widest sense, the sun's energy supports all life on earth, through its heating rays and the energy that is "fixed" by plants through the process of PHOTOSYNTHESIS. Most of the energy available on earth derives from the sun, including the chemical energy in plants, which nourishes all life and is the basis for both BIOFUELS and FOSSIL FUELS; WIND POWER, fueled by air masses heated to differing temperatures by the sun's RADIATION; and HYDROPOWER, part of the WATER CYCLE powered by the sun's radiation. But more precisely, solar energy is a range of technologies that attempt to tap the sun's energy more directly.

Solar energy is the hope of the world. The reason for this is simple: The photosynthesis behind all the growth of all the plants in the world—which supplies all our food, wood, and other plant products, and also all fossil fuels—taps only six-hundredths of 1 percent of the solar radiation to reach the earth. Clearly, if current researchers we are able to develop ways to tap more of the sun's radiation directly, the world's energy problems would be solved.

Researchers are exploring various approaches to do just that, among them:

- **solar collectors,** sometimes called **passive solar,** in which stationary panels are used to absorb and extract heat from sunshine, generally to heat water or interior spaces. Such solar panels have been added to many houses since the energy crisis of the 1970s. They are generally used with backup home heating systems for especially cold days or cloudy stretches.
- **solar thermal electric generation,** more sophisticated systems in which trough-shaped solar collectors track the sun and concentrate both its heat and light, sometimes with mirrors, using it to heat OIL, which in turn heats water to create steam that drives a turbine generator. Since the mid-1980s, several plants have been in operation in California; they are built in modules, and so can

be constructed far more quickly and inexpensively than conventional power plants. An alternative form, used since the 1970s, also in California and in Spain, uses a central receiver and can reach much higher temperatures. Another approach, for which a plant was being converted in 1991, is to use huge mirrors to reflect and concentrate the sun's rays to heat molten salt, instead of oil.

- **photovoltaic (PV),** in which individual particles of light, called *photons*, are absorbed by a semiconductor, creating an electric current directly. PV systems have enormous potential. They produce no POLLUTION or noise; have no moving parts and minimal maintenance; require no water, being suitable for arid and isolated areas; and can operate on any scale, from portable modules to massive power plants. Because of this, PV systems can be located near users, meaning less electricity is lost in transport, so they can come to be cost-effective even in relatively cloudy or high-latitude areas. At its present stage of development, PV-produced electricity is far more expensive than that from conventional sources, except in places far removed from existing power lines, though researchers have been reporting rapid progress in making more efficient *solar cells*. PVs may also have considerable potential in developing countries, where rural electrification is minimal, so the cost of electricity from conventional sources would have to include the building of power lines. In the United States, large-scale PV use is being explored in a joint government–industry project called Photovoltaics for Utility Scale Applications (PVUSA); similar projects are under way in Japan and various European countries.

The main problem with solar energy is its variability, and therefore the need for storage and backup. Some researchers have focused on adapting solar thermal electrical systems to high-temperature storage, to provide backup and also to maximize output; others use a fossil-fuel-based system, often using NATURAL GAS, generally considered the cleanest. For photovoltaic systems, batteries are generally used for storage and diesel generators for backup.

Another promising approach is to use solar electricity to break apart water ($H_2O$) into its hydrogen and oxygen components. The resulting hydrogen is a clean fuel and provides a convenient way of storing solar energy, which can be used when needed for transportation, for heating, and even for producing electricity and heat in batterylike *fuel cells*. Hydrogen also can be transported by pipeline, with less cost and loss of energy than electricity transmitted by wire; so it can be economically produced at the cheapest production points (such as DESERTS) and then

readily shipped to distant usage sites. More than that, when solar-derived hydrogen is burned, it simply combines with oxygen to turn back into water, producing no pollutants of any kind. Solar hydrogen is expected to be especially attractive where land and water—and therefore BIOMASS for fuel use—are restricted.

Beyond the conversion of sunlight, many people also use the aptly named GREENHOUSE EFFECT in their homes and indoor gardens, using glass to trap the light in greenhouses and *sunspaces*, to heat indoor areas directly and to enhance the growing of plants indoors.

### For more information and action:

- CONSERVATION AND RENEWABLE ENERGY INQUIRY AND REFERRAL SERVICE (CAREIRS), (800-523-2929, U.S. except AK and HI; for AK and HI, 800-233-3071). Publishes *Sunspaces* and provides information on various forms of solar energy.
- DEPARTMENT OF ENERGY (DOE), (202-586-5000).
- ENVIRONMENTAL PROTECTION AGENCY (EPA), (202-475-7751 or 202-382-2080). Publishes *Investing in Success* (Photovoltaic Energy Technology Division, 1989).
- NATIONAL CENTER FOR APPROPRIATE TECHNOLOGY (NCAT), (406-494-4572).
- SIERRA CLUB, (415-776-2211 or 202-547-1141; legislative hotline, 202-547-5550). Publishes *Suncell*.
- UNION OF CONCERNED SCIENTISTS (UCS), (617-547-5552 or 202-332-0900). Publishes the brochure *Solar Power: Energy for Today and Tomorrow*.
- WORLD RESOURCES INSTITUTE (WRI), (202-638-6300). Publishes books on solar energy.

(See also ENERGY RESOURCES.)

***Soylent Green,*** a 1973 science fiction film, set in New York City in 2022, when the world has become immensely overcrowded, resources have been terribly depleted, the natural world is only a memory, and humanity has been reduced to seeing films of an earlier, greener earth as a great privilege and eating an artificial food (soylent green) that in the end turns out to be made at least in part of recycled humans. Edward G. Robinson and Charlton Heston starred, in a cast that included Brock Peters, Leigh Taylor-Young, Chuck Connors, and Joseph Cotton. The film was based on Harry Harrison's novel *Make Room! Make Room!*

**species,** a group of closely related, physically similar beings that can interbreed freely. In taxonomy—the hierarchy of biological classification—*species* is the category just below *genus*, but in practice the dividing lines between species, and sometimes between subspecies or varieties, are sometimes unclear and at issue.

Organisms that are part of a region's natural flora and fauna are called *native* or *indigenous species*. Those that are associated with the fully mature, or *climax* form of the community (see ECOLOGICAL SUCCESSION) are called *climax species*; fragments of these remaining after a major disturbance (as from fire or human intervention) are called *relicts*.

Organisms not native to a particular area are called *exotic* or *introduced species*. They can wreak havoc when brought deliberately or by accident into a new area where they have no natural enemies or where they compete more aggressively than other organisms in the habitat; classic examples abound, including Dutch ELM disease, the zebra mussel in the GREAT LAKES, and goats to many islands. Where, on the other hand, new species adapt well, so they can perpetuate themselves without special help, such as Kentucky bluegrass or starlings, they are said to be *acclimatized* or *naturalized*.

Plants and animals not original to a region, that arrive after the area is disturbed, as by heavy grazing or fire, are called *invader species*, while those native species that are the first to recolonize a disturbed area are called *pioneer species*. Those that are especially adapted to highly variable, unpredictable, or transient environments are called *opportunistic species*, especially ephemeral plants. All of the plants and animals found in a particular area, whether native or introduced, are called *resident species*.

Within a particular area, *dominant species* are those plants and animals that—because of their number, coverage, or size—strongly influence or control the conditions of other species in an area. Plant species especially sought after by grazing animals, as on rangelands, are called *preferred* or *ice cream species*. In an area being managed, those species (especially plants) that contribute positively toward the management objectives are termed *desired* or *desirable species*. Those that do not, such as those plant species not readily eaten by animals, are called *undesirable* or *noxious species*. Those that can produce sickness, death, or impaired health in animals that eat them are termed *toxic* or *poisonous*.

Where changes in a species are believed to reflect the relative health of other species or of the whole ECOSYSTEM being observed, it is called an *indicator species*. A prime example was the striped bass (rockfish), whose decline in the late 1970s signaled problems in CHESAPEAKE BAY, and the spotted OWL, whose decline indicated significant loss of BIOLOGICAL DIVERSITY in the Pacific Northwest old-growth FORESTS. An *indicator* or *key species* may also be one used to show the stage of development or regeneration of an ecosystem, of to indicate a degree of use by other species, such as plant species used to help managers assess the level of grazing use in rangeland.

If the survival of several other species depends on that of a single species, it may be called a *keystone species*. Where a species plays an important role in more than one ecosystem, it is called a *mobile link species*. When the continued existence of a species is in question, it is regarded as an ENDANGERED SPECIES, a matter of strong concern to conservationists, especially where the species is biologically unique—that is, the only representative of its genus or family, such as the giant PANDA. A species found only in a very restricted geographic range is termed *endemic* or *narrowly endemic*, and is especially at risk.

Loss of HABITAT is a major concern with endangered species because large natural ecosystems tend to have more species than small ones. That relationship has even been expressed in a mathematical equation called the *species-area relationship*. Another general rule is that *species richness* varies with the type of region, being greatest in warm or wet places, such as tropical forests, and least in cold or dry places, such as the poles. (See ENDANGERED SPECIES; BIOLOGICAL DIVERSITY.)

**speciesism,** the view that members of one species—that is, humans—are prejudiced against members of other species, a concept popularized by animal-rights philosopher Peter Singer (see ANIMAL RIGHTS MOVEMENT).

**Stockholm Declaration,** an alternate name for the DECLARATION OF THE CONFERENCE ON THE HUMAN ENVIRONMENT.

**stork, wood,** only half a century ago a common sight on the United States south Atlantic and Gulf coasts, the wood stork is now listed as an ENDANGERED SPECIES in the United States, Mexico, and Central and South America. In the United States, the wood stork population is down from an estimated 60,000 to 70,000 in the 1930s to approximately 10,000 to 12,000 in the early 1990s. The main and continuing problem is loss of essential WETLANDS and shallow water fishing HABITAT to expanding human POPULATIONS, as DEVELOPMENT and waterways projects take over former wood stork breeding and FISHING grounds. Some attempts are going forward to create shallow, artificial lakes stocked with fish for stork-feeding purposes. (See also ENDANGERED SPECIES; also ENDANGERED AND THREATENED WILDLIFE AND PLANTS on page 372.)

**strontium 90,** a radioactive form of the metal strontium, commonly found in FALLOUT from nuclear explosions. It has a half-life (RADIATION) of about 26 years and tends to accumulate in bones, sometimes replacing calcium there.

**Student Conservation Association (SCA)** (Box 550, Charlestown, NH 03603; 603-826-4301; Scott D. Izzo, President), an educational organization founded 1957 that "provides opportunities for student and adult volunteers to assist in the stewardship and conservation of natural resources," serving in a variety of programs in "national parks, forests, wildlife refuges, and other public lands," both fostering volunteerism and commitment to a conservation ethic and also providing leadership and technical training for conservation careers.

Working with conservation agencies, SCA identifies tasks appropriate for and then recruits annually about 1,500 volunteers, with deliberate inclusion of people from the full spectrum of socioeconomic backgrounds and "special youth populations, including those who are disadvantaged, developmentally or learning disabled, or at-risk"; it also provides technical training in WILDERNESS management and trail construction for resource managers. Living in coeducational tent camps in backcountry areas, students, who must be at least 16, work in groups of 6 to 10 students with one to two adult supervisors on outdoor projects, such as trail construction and maintenance, improvement of timber stands or wildlife HABITATS, building and repairing fences, archaeological field surveying, and construction of structures such as shelters, privies, and bridges. During the four- to five-week project, students also receive informal education on native plants and animals, geology, environmental issues, ecological principles, and low-impact camping techniques. There are no tuition costs, and food, lodging, and group equipment are provided by SCA; but participants must arrange for their own transportation to and from the program area and provide their own personal gear, though financial aid is available for those in need, and SCA loans bed packs. Working under contract to SCA and trained in special workshops, adult supervisors act as group leaders, project foremen, expedition leaders, and environmental educators, being responsible for virtually every aspect of the program at their location, including all program logistics, such as food and equipment.

The SCA also annually recruits about 900 resource assistants (RAs), 18 years or older, who work for about 12 weeks with the resource staff of cooperating agencies, such as the NATIONAL PARK SERVICE, FOREST SERVICE, FISH AND WILDLIFE SERVICE, BUREAU OF LAND MANAGEMENT, state park and wildlife agencies, and private natural resource agencies. Openings (about 75 percent of them for the summer months) are listed and any special qualifications described in semiannual position listings; selections are made on a competitive basis, being first screened by SCA and the final selection made by the agency's personnel staff. The RA program neither requires tuition nor offers salaries, but it does provide a travel grant to and from the program, by least expensive mode of transportation; free housing, generally at an apartment or trailer with other RAs or seasonal staff; a stipend for food and basic living expenses, not covering entertainment and personal costs; and an allowance for a uniform, if required. In addition to career-training experience, some colleges accept the RA program for internship requirements or elective credits. SCA also publishes the monthly *Earth Work* for and about current and future conservation professionals, which includes *Job Scan*, a listing of natural resource and environmental job opportunites coast to coast.

**Student Environmental Action Coalition (SEAC)**, (P.O. Box 1168, Chapel Hill, NC 27514; 919-967-4600; Miya Yoshitani, National Coordinator), a student-led, student-staffed grassroots organization founded in 1988 "dedicated to building power among students involved in environmental and social justice action . . . through education resources, building coalitions and encouraging cooperative actions, challenging the traditional definition of 'environment,' and using effective strategies and tactics." Concerned about a wide range of issues, including the OZONE LAYER, depletion of rain FORESTS, GLOBAL WARMING and CLIMATE CHANGE, TOXIC CHEMICALS and disasters such as Bhopal, ENVIRONMENTAL RACISM, ENERGY RESOURCES, AIR POLLUTION, WATER POLLUTION, HAZARDOUS WASTE, and WASTE DISPOSAL, the SEAC organizes national conferences and marches, lobbies for strong legislation, and conducts various other campaigns, such as a National Energy Strategy and opposition to the JAMES BAY HYDROPOWER PROJECT.

SEAC also urges corporate accountability, and seeks to change campuses, by "reducing resource use, improving the curriculum, and changing their investment practices." Associated with the SEAC is the *People of Color Caucus*,

---

### On Student Environmental Action

Those running the show right now are mortgaging our future for a short-term spree of consumption. They will be dead and buried when the environmental and economic bills come due. It is our right and our responsibility as young people to speak out against these wrongs. We must take back our future which is being stolen from us.

**Source:** "The Student Environmental Action Coalition" brochure.

---

which seeks to "address issues of racial inequity inside and outside of SEAC." SEAC publishes a newsletter *Threshold* and practical guides such as *SEAC Organizing Guide, SEAC High School Organizing Guide, SEAC Student Environmental Action Guide* (published by Earthworks), and *SEAC Campus Environmental Audit.*

**sulfur cycle,** the process by which living organisms obtain the sulfur necessary for life (see BIOGEOCHEMICAL CYCLES). Sulfur is a vital element in all proteins, but is released from the environment for use in living things only by the action of microorganisms, usually working in oxygen-poor soils, bogs, and swamps. These produce sulfides such as the foul-smelling hydrogen sulfide, which are then incorporated in living organisms, and make their way through the FOOD CHAIN. Eventually, sulfur is returned to the earth as dead plant or animal matter, which is once again broken down by bacteria and fungi. This delicate, not thoroughly understood process has been somewhat disturbed by human activities, especially the burning of FOSSIL FUELS and large-scale slash-and-burn clearing of the land, which release SULFUR DIOXIDE as part of AIR POLLUTION and ACID RAIN.

**sulfur dioxide (SO$_2$),** a poisonous gas formed primarily from the burning of fuel that contains sulfur, notably FOSSIL FUELS such as untreated COAL, OIL and NATURAL GAS (in order of decreasing sulfur content), and also from volcanoes. Several other sulfur oxides are formed under these circumstances, but sulfur dioxide is of special concern because such large amounts are emitted—an estimated three tons of sulfur dioxide for every hundred tons of coal or coke burned, for example. Being corrosive, sulfur dioxide is damaging to the respiratory systems of those who breathe it, as well as to the vegetation, soil, buildings, and other materials that exist in air laden with it, being a key culprit in ACID RAIN. As such, sulfur dioxide is one of the CRITERIA AIR POLLUTANTS for which the ENVIRONMENTAL PROTECTION AGENCY (EPA) sets NATIONAL AMBIENT AIR QUALITY STANDARDS (NAAQSs), under the CLEAN AIR ACT. Most approaches to the sulfur dioxide problem focus on the use of SCRUBBERS. In 1990, the EPA set new rules requiring an 80 percent reduction of sulfur in diesel fuel by 1993; under the Clean Air Act, firms can trade unused allowances for sulfur dioxide EMISSIONS.

**For more information and action:**

- ENVIRONMENTAL DEFENSE FUND (EDF), (212-505-2100). Publishes *CO$_2$ and SO$_2$: Consistent Policy Making in a Greenhouse* (D. Dudek et al., 1990). (See also ACID RAIN; AIR POLLUTION.)

## Utilities Are the Primary Source of Sulfur Dioxide Emissions

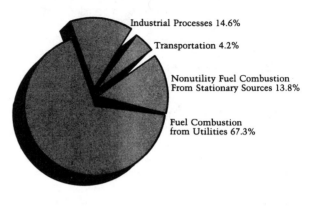

Industrial Processes 14.6%

Transportation 4.2%

Nonutility Fuel Combustion From Stationary Sources 13.8%

Fuel Combustion from Utilities 67.3%

**Superfund,** popular name for U.S. federal funds to finance cleanup of abandoned and inactive HAZARDOUS WASTE dump sites. The COMPREHENSIVE ENVIRONMENTAL RESPONSE, COMPENSATION, AND LIABILITY ACT of 1980 originally established two funds, the Post-Closure Liability Trust Fund, financed by a tax on receipt of hazardous waste at a qualified hazardous waste disposal facility, and the Hazardous Substance Response Trust Fund, financed by a tax on U.S.-refined or imported crude OIL and chemical feedstocks. (The name "superfund" reportedly came from an earlier oil industry proposal that would have had oil companies contributing to a "superfund for supertankers" but would have released them from all liability.)

Little was done with the Superfund in the early 1980s, with public charges of Environmental Protection Agency mismanagement causing considerable controversy during Anne Gorsuch Burford's tenure, just as the TIMES BEACH situation was emerging. After various resignations and firings, the EPA changed its policies to speed cleanup of contaminated sites under Superfund. Progress was still too slow, however, and in 1986 Congress passed the Superfund Amendments and Reauthorization Act (SARA, or Title III), as part of the EMERGENCY PLANNING AND COMMUNITY RIGHT-TO-KNOW ACT (EPCRA).

SARA increased the fund from its original $1.6 billion to $8.5 billion over five years, and authorized use of fund monies along with contributions from *potentially responsible parties* (PRPs), in what was called *mixed fundings.* SARA also stressed permanent remedies at Superfund sites, setting schedules for beginning cleanup work and studies, with cleanup work for a minimum of 375 sites scheduled to begin by 1991. Targets for long-term remedial action are listed on a *National Priorities List (NPL),* updated at least annually. (For a full list of sites, see SUPEREFUND SITES on page 422.)

Under SARA, the *Agency for Toxic Substances and Disease Registry* performs health assessments at Superfund sites, lists hazardous substances found there, prepares toxicological profiles on them, identifies gaps in research on health effects, and publishes its findings (see NATIONAL INSTITUTE OF ENVIRONMENTAL HEALTH SCIENCES).

Responding to continuing criticism from Congress and oversight offices, the Bush administration in the early 1990s began to push for enforcement, and to compel PRPs to pay for cleanups. The EPA has been attempting to follow the precept "the polluter pays," both in initial handling and later for government-handled cleanup, with cases being referred to the Department of Justice for recovery of cleanup costs from responsible parties where possible. In 1990, the EPA completed its National Contingency Plan, "emphasizing quick action to control immediate dangers, expanded use of in-place treatment technologies, increased public participation, and improved processes for selecting cleanup remedies." It also revised its Hazard Ranking System—the criteria used to evaluate potential Superfund sites—to include factors reflecting the impact of biological and soil contamination. For an overview of how a Superfund site is handled, see STEPS IN CLEANING UP A SUPERFUND SITE on page 294.

Many environmentalists charge, however, that still too little is being done—that thousands more sites need to be added to the National Priorities List, and that the cleanup of such sites often fails to solve the problem, since the contaminated material may only be stored elsewhere, sometimes polluting a new site (see HAZARDOUS WASTE). The Environmental Law Institute, which produced *An Analysis of State Superfund Programs* for the

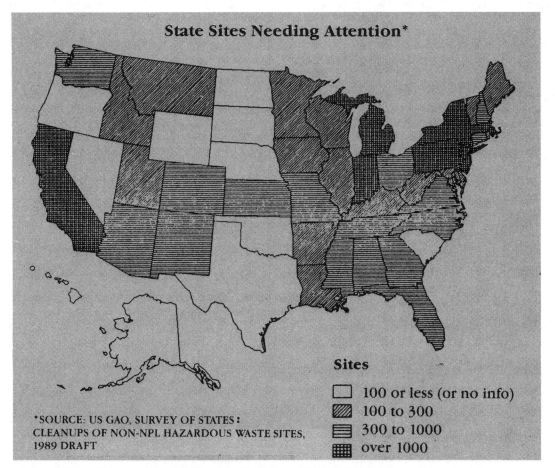

**State Sites Needing Attention***

**Sites**

☐ 100 or less (or no info)
▨ 100 to 300
▤ 300 to 1000
▦ over 1000

*SOURCE: US GAO, SURVEY OF STATES: CLEANUPS OF NON-NPL HAZARDOUS WASTE SITES, 1989 DRAFT

**Source:** *Survey of States: Cleanups of Non-NPL Hazardous Waste Sites, 1989 Draft.* U.S. Government Accounting Office.

## Steps in Cleaning Up a Superfund Site

**The Initial Warning.** Individuals report abandoned hazardous waste sites or incidents of illegal dumping to the EPA's *National Response Center* (800-424-8802). Whether it is a citizen reporting half-buried barrels, a police officer reporting a midnight dumper, or a facility manager making a required report, these are entered into the computerized data base CERCLIS, which by 1987 had 25,000 suspected sites, at least 2,500 of which were expected to require cleanup under Superfund.

**Identification and Preliminary Assessment.** The EPA gathers information about the sites from local, state, and federal records, including geological survey maps, assessing the size of the site, identity of potentially responsible parties, the types and quantities of substances involved, local water and weather conditions, and the likely impact on the environment.

**Site Inspection.** If preliminary assessment suggests a possible threat to human health or the environment, inspectors visit the site to rank its hazard potential. They look for obvious signs, such as leaking storage drums, or dead or discolored vegetation; take samples of soil and water, if appropriate; and check how the site might pollute the environment (as through runoff), or whether children have access to the site.

**Ranking Sites for the National Priorities List.** Sites that may require long-term remedial action under Superfund are placed on the NPL, which contains the worst known abandoned or uncontrolled hazardous waste sites in the United States. Among the factors considered in the ranking are type of substance, quantity, and toxicity; the number of people potentially exposed; the likely pathways of exposure; and the importance and vulnerability of the underlying supply of groundwater.

**Remedial Investigation.** NPL sites are investigated through field study, involving extensive sampling and laboratory analysis, generating more precise data on the types and quantities of the waste, the soil types and water drainage patterns, and threats to the environment or human health. The aim of the investigation is to select the cleanup strategy best suited to the particular site.

**Feasibility Study and Cleanup.** To tailor cleanup action precisely to the needs of the individual site, the feasibility study analyzes its needs and evaluates alternative cleanup approaches on the basis of their relative effectiveness and cost. The selected remedy is outlined in a Record of Decision.

**Removal Actions.** If a site poses imminent hazards, as of fire or explosion or contamination of a drinking water supply, the EPA may initiate short-term removal actions, such as actually digging up and removing wastes for safe disposal, or installing security fencing (as may also be done for other sites, not on the NPL), even before the actual planned cleanup is begun.

**Source:** Adapted from *Superfund: Looking Back, Looking Ahead.* Environmental Protection Agency, 1987.

---

EPA, reports that there are more than 28,000 hazardous waste sites nationwide needing attention, but fewer than 1,300 are listed for federal funding. Many states have developed their own superfund programs to supplement the federal one.

### For more information and action:

- **Environmental Law Institute (ELI),** (202-328-5150; publications office, 202-939-3844). Publishes *Superfund Deskbook* (rev. ed., 1990), *Enhancing State Superfund Capabilities: Nine-State Study* (1990), *Toward a More Effective Superfund Enforcement Program* (1989, 2 vols.), and *An Analysis of State Superfund Programs: 50-State Study* (1989; available through the ENVIRONMENTAL PROTECTION AGENCY). (See ENVIRONMENTAL LAW INFORMATION AND ACTION GUIDE on page 116.)
- **ENVIRONMENTAL PROTECTION AGENCY (EPA),** (Public Information Center, 202-260-7751 or 202-260-2080).
- **NATIONAL INSTITUTE OF ENVIRONMENTAL HEALTH SCIENCES (NIEHS),** (919-541-3345).
- **U.S. PUBLIC INTEREST RESEARCH GROUP (PIRG),** (202-546-9707). Publishes *Right Train—Wrong Track: Failed Leadership in the Superfund Program* (1988).

(See also COMPREHENSIVE ENVIRONMENTAL RESPONSE, COMPENSATION, AND LIABILITY ACT.)

**sustainability,** in general, the wise, appropriate, and efficient use of resources, so that population and demand do not outrun or damage the environment's long-term life-supporting ability. That implies focusing wherever possible on RENEWABLE RESOURCES rather than on DECLINING RESOURCES, such as OIL. (See SUSTAINABLE AGRICULTURE; ENERGY RESOURCES; DEVELOPMENT.)

**sustainable agriculture,** a view of farming that sees agriculture as a total system, not separate from but part of the wider environment, stressing the long-term conservation of resources and balance of the human need for food with concerns for the environment. It is a very general term, and definitions vary.

For many people, sustainable agriculture emphasizes use of RENEWABLE RESOURCES drawn from the farm itself, rather than DECLINING RESOURCES purchased externally, such as PESTICIDES and chemical fertilizers, which are often environmentally damaging as well. In general, the less purchased or brought in from the farm, the more sustainable the agricultural system. Substantial (or even modest) reduction in the use of resources from off the farm is sometimes called LOW INPUT SUSTAINABLE AGRICULTURE (LISA).

Some views of sustainable agriculture stress stewardship of the land for future generations and preservation of the family farm (see CROPLANDS). Others stress equity and social justice, going far beyond simply sustaining the soil to focus on the rural poor's access to land and farm credit, especially in developing countries, as well as the right of farm workers to respect and a decent standard of living.

Still other views of sustainable agriculture stress the wider set of interactions between the agricultural ECOSYSTEM and social, economic, geographic, and political systems, as well as general respect for the BIOSPHERE. As the University of California at Santa Cruz's Agroecology Program put it: "A sustainable agriculture is one which recognizes the whole-systems nature of food, feed and fiber production in equitably balancing the concerns of environmental soundness, social justice, and economic viability among all sectors of the public, including international and intergenerational peoples," stressing that "sustainability must extend not only globally but indefinitely in time." Put more briefly, the Agroecology Program defines sustainable agriculture as being:

- **environmentally sound,** employing practices that neither degrade the environment nor exhaust nonrenewable resources;
- **socially equitable,** with the costs and benefits of agriculture shared fairly and reflecting the needs of society at large; and
- **economically viable,** taking into account *all* costs incurred by agricultural practices, not just for a few years but for the long term.

For many environmentalists, however, the only truly sustainable agricultural approach is ORGANIC FARMING, which eliminates the use of pesticides, chemical fertilizers, and (where livestock is involved) feed additives and growth regulators such as hormones. Many point out that organic farming means more than "input substitution," or simply not applying certain chemicals to crops and animals; it implies a completely different approach to agriculture and agricultural resources, including a commitment to restoring the ecological balance to the soil.

Critics of dominant agricultural approaches charge that researchers and policy-makers have emphasized the highest yields at the lowest cost, without reference to the future health and maintenance of the agricultural system. They urge that research programs and practices be reevaluated in light of the principles of AGROECOLOGY and shifted to include environmental quality, food safety, the health and welfare of people in the farm community, the quality of rural life, humane treatment of livestock, and conservation of soil, water, air, and genetic resources, also taking into account the long-term effects of different agricultural strategies on the agroecosystem in its social, economic, and political context. Many stress the need to go beyond purely technological solutions, even those labeled *sustainable*, to examine how application of these solutions will affect the community—how they will actually be used, who will benefit from them, and who will be hurt by them—and what their impact will be on wider processes such as GLOBAL WARMING, SALINIZATION, or DESERTIFICATION.

Sustainable agriculture was a major concern of the 1980 WORLD CONSERVATION STRATEGY and is a key focus of the CONSULTATIVE GROUP ON INTERNATIONAL AGRICULTURAL RESEARCH (CGIAR), especially since rising POPULATIONS continue to pose questions of FAMINE AND FOOD INSECURITY, despite the technological (and generally nonsustainable) innovations of the GREEN REVOLUTION and BIOTECHNOLOGY. The overall aim of such international movements is to maintain food production while protecting the environment, especially to relieve pressure on the most fragile ecosystems. For CGIAR's sustainable agriculture subcommittee, sustainable agriculture is "the successful management of resources for agriculture to satisfy changing human needs, while simultaneously maintaining or enhancing the natural resource base and conserving natural resources." (See ORGANIC FARMING AND SUSTAINABLE AGRICULTURE INFORMATION AND ACTION GUIDE on page 226; see also ORGANIC FARMING; BIOLOGICAL CONTROL.)

**swampbuster provision,** a part of the 1985 Food Security Act (Farm Bill) aimed at protecting WETLANDS, under which farmers would risk losing federal benefits if they produce crops on converted wetlands.

**swan, trumpeter,** the world's largest swan and something of a conservation success story. Once numerous throughout North America, the trumpeter was an ENDANGERED SPECIES in the United States by 1900, although there continued to be Canadian and Alaskan populations totaling several thousand birds. In the early 1930s, less than 100 trumpeter swans were known to live in the U.S., in the high plateau country of Montana and Wyoming, some of them in YELLOWSTONE NATIONAL PARK. In 1935, with establishment of the federal Red Rock Lakes Migratory Waterfowl Refuge in southern Montana's Centennial Valley, a concerted, very successful effort to save and restore the trumpeter swan began. With strongly enforced anti-hunting laws in Canada and the United States, the SPECIES continues to flourish in Alaska and Canada, and the U.S. population of well over 1,000 trumpeters has made it possible to take it off the endangered species list. (See also ENDANGERED SPECIES; also ENDANGERED AND THREATENED WILDLIFE AND PLANTS on page 372.)

**synergy,** in general, the process of working together, so that the result is greater than or different from the sum of the individual parts. Relating to TOXIC CHEMICALS or other pollutants, synergy refers to the effect of two or more substances acting together being greater and sometimes altogether different than the two acting separately. People exposed long-term to either *environmental tobacco smoke* (ETS) or ASBESTOS, for example, have much higher cancer rates than people not exposed; but those exposed to *both* ETS and asbestos may have their risk of cancer increased tenfold. Traditionally, in the setting of safety standards, chemicals have been tested in isolation, but in the real world they mix together with other environmental contaminants, sometimes spawning new and unexpected compounds, about which little or nothing is known. Organizations and agencies such as the ENVIRONMENTAL PROTECTION AGENCY (EPA) are only beginning to take synergy into account when setting safety standards. (See TOXIC CHEMICALS.)

**synthetic fuels (synfuels),** fuels formed of HYDROCARBONS created through conversion of solid fuels (notably COAL) into gaseous and liquid forms. These are easier and cheaper to transport, and more flexible and efficient to use than the original solid fuels; they are also far cleaner to use, since contaminants such as sulfur and HEAVY METALS are largely removed in the process. When created from recently living organic matter, called BIOMASS, synthetic fuels are often called BIOFUELS.

Synfuels received enormous attention in the 1970s, at the time of the energy crisis, but as the crisis eased most countries withdrew support for synfuel research, with the notable exception of South Africa. In the United States, the quasi-federal U.S. Synthetic Fuels Corporation was formed to explore such conversions but was phased out in 1986, having authorized only $1.3 billion of its original $14.9 billion spending authority.

A wide variety of methods may be used to convert coal to gas or fuel, a process sometimes called *coal gasification* or *coal conversion*, but these may be grouped in four basic ways:

- **pyrolysis,** removal of carbon from coal, to alter the hydrogen-to-carbon ratio; a kind of distillation.
- **hydroliquefaction,** adding hydrogen to alter the hydrogen-to-carbon ratio.
- **direct synthesis** of hydrocarbons from CARBON MONOXIDE and hydrogen.
- **underground coal gasification,** in which heating and pyrolysis are actually done on site, eliminating the need for transport and plant treatment; especially good for sites unsuitable for MINING.

With increasing concern about AIR POLLUTION and ACID RAIN, attention may turn once again toward synfuels, especially as increasing regulation makes use of traditional fuels more expensive and synthetic fuels therefore more economically viable.

Several new approaches have been developed, among them:

- the **integrated coal-gasification combined cycle (IGCC) system,** in which coal is converted to a gas, which is then burned and used to drive both steam and gas turbines.
- the **steam-injected gas turbine (STIG),** in which synthetic gases (or NATURAL GAS) are burned to drive a gas turbine, with the exhaust gases from the turbine used to produce steam, which is injected into the combustion chamber, rather than driving a steam turbine.
- the **intercooled STIG (ISTIG)** in which the combustion air is cooled before being pressurized between stages of the process, to work at higher efficiency.

Burning of synthetic fuels derived from fossil fuels will still contribute to the GREENHOUSE EFFECT and GLOBAL WARMING, since CARBON DIOXIDE is released into the air, so energy conservation remains an environmental priority. However, if biomass is used as an energy resource and produced in a sustainable way—that is, so that as much is grown as is used—then the carbon dioxide released will be used up by plants during the process of PHOTOSYNTHESIS and will not damage the environment.

### For more information and action:

- **DEPARTMENT OF ENERGY (DOE),** (202-357-8300).
- **INFORM, INC.** (212-689-4040).
- **NATURAL RESOURCES AND ENERGY DIVISION (NRED), UNITED NATIONS** (212-963-6205).

(See BIOFUELS; FOSSIL FUELS; COAL; ENERGY RESOURCES.)

**synthetic organic chemicals (SOCs),** an umbrella phrase for human-made compounds that contain carbon; also called *synthetic organic compounds.* Among these are the best-known PESTICIDES, including CHLORINATED HYDROCARBONS (organochlorines), such as DDT; ORGANOPHOSPHATES (organic phosphates), such as parathion and malathion; industrial chemicals such as chlorinated biphenyls (see PCBs); ozone-destroying CHLOROFLUOROCARBONS; and organometals such as TRIBUTYL TIN (TBT). Despite their danger, so many SOCs exist that standards have not been set for exposure for many of them, as under the SAFE DRINKING WATER ACT (SDWA), which has set requirements for only about 50 out of the hundreds of SOCs. In 1990, under the CLEAN AIR ACT, the ENVIRONMENTAL PROTECTION AGENCY (EPA) issued new rules covering 149 SOCs (included in TOXIC CHEMICALS AND HAZARDOUS SUBSTANCES on page 407), designed to reduce by 70 percent EMISSIONS from synthetic organic chemical plants. (See ORGANIC COMPOUNDS; TOXIC CHEMICALS.)

**Tarragona propylene gas explosion,** the explosion of a truck carrying propylene gas on July 11, 1978, at Tarragona, Spain. As it crashed, the truck went off the road into a heavily populated campsite by the sea, and then exploded, killing 145 people and injuring hundreds more as fire swept the site.

**Teale, Edwin Way** (1899–1980), U.S. nature writer, naturalist, and photographer, whose work and thinking shaped the sensibilities of two generations of American nature lovers. By example, as much as through his writing, he was one of those who provided the moral basis for the modern American ecological movement.

Much of his early work was on insects, beginning with his first book, *Grassroot Jungles* (1937), a set of his own insect photographs, with his comments. In the mid-1940s, he moved to wider naturalist concerns, beginning with *The Lost Woods* (1945). In 1951, he began the four-book series that was by far his best-known work, in which he traveled with the American seasons, his journeys taking him 70,000 to 80,0000 miles, and resulting in *North With the*

*Spring* (1951), *Autumn Across America* (1956), *Journey Into Summer* (1960), and his Pulitzer Prize-winning *Wandering Through Winter* (1963). *Springtime in Britain* (1970) recorded an 11,000-mile journey through a British season. His later work also included *A Walk Through the Year* (1978).

**teratogen,** a substance that causes birth defects, specifically structural defects of prenatal origin (see RISK ASSESSMENT). (See also HEALTH EFFECTS OF REGULATED AIR POLLUTANTS on page 8; and KNOWN HEALTH EFFECTS OF TOXIC CHEMICALS on page 416.)

**Texas City explosions,** three explosions on April 15 to 16, 1957, resulting when the French freighter *Grandcamp* caught fire while in the harbor of Texas City, Texas. Shortly after dawn, the ammonium nitrate fertilizer in its cargo exploded, raining fiery fragments on a highly combustible Monsanto chemical plant a short distance away, which then also exploded, destroying most of the center of the city. That night, the ammonium nitrate fertilizer cargo of the freighter *High Flyer* also blew up in the harbor, causing massive additional damage. In all, an estimated 800 to 1,000 people died in the three chemically generated explosions. (See TOXIC CHEMICALS.)

**theoretical maximum residue contribution (TMRC),** see TOLERANCE LEVELS.

**30 Per Cent Club,** a group of countries, including Norway, Sweden, and Canada, who are major victims of—and are trying to help combat—ACID RAIN, by reducing SULFUR DIOXIDE emissions by 30 percent (see CONVENTION ON LONG-RANGE TRANSBOUNDARY AIR POLLUTION).

**33/50 Project,** a U.S. program to voluntarily reduce pollution from 17 high-priority TOXIC CHEMICALS, including benzene, CADMIUM, carbon tetrachloride, chloroform, chromium, cyanide, dichloromethane, LEAD, MERCURY, methyl ethyl ketone, methyl isobutyl ketone, nickel, tetrachloroethylene, toluene, 1,1,1-trichloroethane, trychloroethylene, and xylenes. Sponsored by the ENVIRONMENTAL PROTECTION AGENCY (EPA), the program seeks to have chemical, petroleum, paper, and transportation industries reduce the "total releases and transfers" of the chemicals to air, water, and land by one-third (33 percent) by 1992, and by one-half (50 percent) by 1995.

**Three Gorges Dam** (Chang Jiang Dam), the huge, highly controversial DAM across the Yangtze (Chang Jiang) planned by the Chinese government. The plan is to build the world's largest concrete dam, 475 feet high and 1.6 miles long, which would generate 18 million kilowatts of power, providing much needed power for central China; end the flooding of the Yangtze, which has claimed hundreds of thousands of lives in the 20th century; open the Yangtze to navigation and trade all the way to Chongqing; and create a 350-mile-long lake above the dam. The dam would also flood the lands of an estimated 700,000 to 800,000 people (some estimates run as high as 3 million), and all but destroy the scenic beauty of China's historic Yangtze River gorges. Many are also concerned about the environmental impacts of the project, especially as regards the fish in the river and the loss of yearly silt flow into the Yangtze delta, which may cause seawater intrusion into the farmlands of the delta. (see DAMS; RIVERS; also RIVERS INFORMATION and ACTION GUIDE on page 270.)

**Three Mile Island nuclear accident,** the March 28, 1979 nuclear fuel and partial core meltdown at then-new Unit 2, one of two reactors at the nuclear power plant on the island, 10 miles from the Pennsylvania state capitol at Harrisburg. Starting at 4:00 A.M., a series of equipment failures and human errors caused the reactor to overheat and meltdown to begin, the accident coming close to causing the kind of massive hydrogen explosion and widescale nuclear disaster that occurred at CHERNOBYL in 1986. But at Three Mile Island, no major steam or hydrogen gas explosion occurred, and the plant's containment structure was not breached, though some outside observers claim that there was a hydrogen explosion on March 28.

How much RADIATION escaped from the plant is still a highly controversial matter. Plant operators and federal and state regulatory authorities have stated that EMISSIONS were negligible, while some outside observers have claimed substantial contamination of surrounding areas, with greatly increased incidence of cancer in the next decade. Richard Thornburgh, then governor of Pennsylvania, was concerned enough about possible FALLOUT to order evacuation of pregnant women and children in the area immediately surrounding the plant, though waiting two days to do so. By then, stimulated by national and international media coverage of the accident, hundreds of thousands of people had fled from wide areas of central Pennsylvania.

Whatever the human and environmental damage caused by the accident, a major casualty of the event was the United States nuclear industry. The industry was already under sharp attack for alleged widespread environmental contamination, especially from its NUCLEAR WEAPONS plants. After Three Mile Island, the nuclear industry saw new plant starts shrink to nearly zero, while new, much more expensive safety requirements caused plant costs to skyrocket.

The film *The China Syndrome,* made in the summer of 1978, was released shortly after the Three Mile Island accident, and had an enormous impact on audiences throughout the world. It dealt with a nearly disastrous nuclear accident at a United States nuclear plant, the whole sequence of events described being extraordinarily close to what happened at Three Mile Island. In the film, the protagonists triumphed over incompetent plant management to avert the accident; at Three Mile Island, the accident happened; and at Chernobyl in 1986, the accident was a major nuclear catastrophe, with land and people poisoned for generations to come. (See also NUCLEAR ENERGY; also MAJOR NUCLEAR DISASTERS AND INCIDENTS on page 212.)

**threshold,** the lowest dose to produce measurable effects (see DOSAGE LEVEL), or the lowest level at which harmful effects can be discerned, as of a pollutant.

**Threshold, International Center for Environmental Renewal** (Naturequest Center, Drawer CU, Bisbee, AZ 85603; 602-432-7353; John P. Milton, Chairman), a foundation established in 1972 that carries out various projects in "environmental research, education, technical assistance, planning, and public information," at the local, regional, national, and international levels, its aim being to serve as "a catalyst for innovative work to harmonize people, nature, and spirit." Threshold's main current project is the *Environmental Crisis Fund* designed to "dispatch funds directly to projects dealing with and in environmentally critical areas," among them the *Malathion Project* in Baja California, Mexico, and the *Coral Reef Project* focusing on the Gulf of Mexico and the eastern tropical Pacific. Other recent projects include a 1987 coalition-building conference on tropical rain forests in New Delhi, India; a survey to protect the Dog River in central Georgia; development of an environmentally sound resource plan for the Coolfont Conference Center in Berkeley Springs, West Virginia; and contribution to "the human ecology of national park planning" regarding Nepal's Chitawan National Park.

**tigers,** the big Asian cats that until the late 19th century roamed freely throughout much of southern Asia, from the Near East to the Pacific, and as far north as Manchuria and southeastern Siberia, numbering in the tens of thousands. The *Siberian tiger* is the largest of the cats, some weighing over 800 pounds, and the *Indian tiger* the most numerous; the other six subspecies are the *Balinese, Sumatran, Javan, Indochinese, South Chinese*, and *Caspian* tigers. All are powerful hunters, some of whom have acquired a taste for hunting humans, as well as their more usual quarry; all have generated myths and legends that permeate the history of the peoples who have lived with them.

All eight tiger species are now endangered by HUNTING and loss of habitat, and some are believed to be extinct in the wild, including the Javan, Balinese, and Caspian tigers. Fewer than 200 Siberian tigers are thought to survive in their natural range and the Sumatran tiger is similarly close to EXTINCTION in the wild.

In 1972, the Indian government, with the help of the WORLD WILDLIFE FUND, set up 11 tiger reserves, and Nepal and other countries in the area also took conservationist steps. The Fund reported in 1989 that the Indian tiger population had grown from 1,800 to 4,000 from 1977 through 1989, providing a major victory in the struggle to save the tigers. However, the explosive growth of Indian and other south and southeast Asian human POPULATIONS continues to apply great pressure to the tiger preserves and other tiger HABITATS. Political instability also threatens all conservationist action in the area; were the tigers and other protected species left unprotected for even a little while, poachers might very easily destroy all that has so far been accomplished.

**For more information and action:**

• **ELSA WILD ANIMAL APPEAL (EWAA),** (818-761-8387).

(See also ENDANGERED SPECIES; also ENDANGERED AND THREATENED WILDLIFE AND PLANTS on page 372.)

**Times Beach,** a small town in Missouri, about 30 miles southwest of St. Louis, with a population of 2,400 in the early 1980s. In 1971, its unpaved roads (like many other such roads throughout the state) had been covered with dust-controlling oil that contained highly toxic DIOXIN, originating as a waste product from the production of AGENT ORANGE and other chemicals at a plant elsewhere in Missouri. The danger was not understood at the time, but soil tests taken in November 1982 showed dangerously high levels of dioxin contamination in the town, causing the U.S. Centers for Disease Control to urge at least temporary evacuation of the town while further tests were made. In February 1983, the federal government offered to buy the entire town and relocate its residents, using $33 million of SUPERFUND money. In April 1985, the now almost vacant town was closed.

In the early 1990s, the problem of how to dispose of the dioxin-contaminated layer of earth at Times Beach and many other dioxin-contaminated sites in eastern Missouri provoked a major controversy in the area, as federal officials moved to incinerate the soil, over local opposition concerned about possible airborne toxic waste. Under a 1990 consent decree signed by Missouri, the federal government, and Syntex Agribusiness, Inc., the ENVIRONMENTAL PROTECTION AGENCY affirmed its plan to return Times Beach "to beneficial use," along with 27 other dioxin-contaminated sites in Missouri. (See TOXIC CHEMICALS; SUPERFUND.)

**Title III,** a nickname for the Superfund Amendments and Reauthorization Act (SARA) of 1986 (see SUPERFUND), an extension of the EMERGENCY PLANNING AND COMMUNITY RIGHT-TO-KNOW ACT (EPCRA).

**tolerance level,** legal limits for the residual amount of a chemical (such as a PESTICIDE) to be found in food. Tolerance levels are set by government agencies such as the FOOD AND DRUG ADMINISTRATION (FDA) and the ENVIRONMENTAL PROTECTION AGENCY (EPA), based on the results of testing (mostly ANIMAL TESTING). DOSAGE LEVELS are determined at which little or no effects were observed; these are adjusted to human equivalency doses, with a *margin of safety* (MOS) then built in.

Establishment of tolerance levels is part of overall RISK ASSESSMENT, or evaluation of the hazards to the environment, including human health, from exposure to a substance, such as a pesticide. Quantitative and qualitative data on the toxicity of the substance is combined with data about exposure, to give an overall assessment of hazard. These calculations involve assessing the *theoretical maximum residue contribution* (TMRC), or the amount of a chemical that would be present in the average daily diet if all foods involving that chemical had amounts at the tolerance level.

In assessing safety for humans, and for organisms inadvertently affected by exposure to a substance, the highest concentration allowable is called the *maximum acceptable tolerance concentration* (MATC), while the highest amount allowable in drinking water is called the MAXIMUM CONTAMINANT LEVEL (MCL), a measure being phased out between 1990 and 1992 and replaced by NATIONAL PRIMARY DRINKING WATER REQUIREMENTS (NPDWRs). For natural or synthetic substances, the maximum amount of a substance that—based on the current evidence—humans can receive daily without lifetime risk is the ACCEPTABLE DAILY INTAKE (ADI). A maximum for a limited number of brief periods, as to RADIATION, is called the *short-term exposure limit* (STEL).

In relation to AIR POLLUTION, standards focus on the *permissible exposure level* (PEL). The highest allowable air concentration in which workers are presumed to work for 40 hours a week for many years without ill effects is called the *threshold limit value* (TLV) or (with a factor for varying amounts of exposure during the workday) the *threshold limit value—time weighted average* (TLV-TWA).

Critics charge that the government's tolerances are set too high for safety, for the general population and also workers; and that the tolerances do not fully take into account the cumulative effect of toxic residues from a wide variety of sources in the environment (see BIOACCUMULATION), especially persistent substances such as CHLORINATED HYDROCARBONS, and the unanticipated effects of two or more chemicals combined (see SYNERGY). Problems associated with these have spurred wide efforts to reduce chemical use, as through ORGANIC FARMING and BIOLOGICAL CONTROL of pests. Tolerance levels are also criticized for not recognizing elevated risks of adverse health effects among children, pregnant women, and the elderly. Serious questions have also been raised about the necessity and manner of using animals in toxicity testing. (See also PESTICIDES; ANIMAL TESTING.)

**Torrey Canyon oil spill,** leakage of much of the 118,000-ton crude OIL cargo of the tanker *Torrey Canyon* into the sea off Cornwall, England, after the tanker went aground on Pollard's Rock on March 18, 1967. After the grounding, an attempt was made to salvage the ship, while its cargo continued to leak and form large oil slicks that moved toward the English coast. The ship broke up on March 26 to 27, during a salvage attempt, and was belatedly set afire by aircraft on March 28, in an attempt to burn off some of the remaining oil. By then, an environmental disaster was well under way, which would in the following three months foul 175 miles of seashore, 120 in Britain and 55 more in France, resulting in the deaths of many thousands of seabirds and much other damage to the ecology of the affected area. (See OIL.)

**Tortuguero National Park,** Costa Rican nature preserve on the CARIBBEAN shore, 56 miles north of Puerto Limón; inland, its 45,000 acres (70 square miles) include palm swamps and rain FOREST. Tortuguero was established primarily as a WILDLIFE REFUGE for the Atlantic green TURTLE, and also is a refuge for hundreds of varieties of birds and for such animals as jaguars (see LEOPARDS), kinkajous, mountain lions, PARROTS, macaws, ocelots, and tapirs.

In 1954, the CARIBBEAN CONSERVATION CORPORATION (CCC) began its long-term study of the green turtle breeding grounds on the Tortuguero beach, and since then has contributed to the worldwide effort to conserve these and other turtles. In the 1960s, thousands of turtle hatchlings were flown from Tortuguero to other Caribbean beaches, to help restore seriously threatened turtle populations. Two of its most visible continuing programs have involved the tagging, with the help of volunteers, of thousands of green turtles and leatherback turtles, in a long-term study of their migration patterns.

In the late 1980s, Tortuguero became a heavily visited ecotourist destination—and with that came some problems, for scores of tourists crowded around a nesting sea turtle can very well cause the turtle to abandon its nest and flee. That is especially so° at night, as even a single flashlight can frighten and rout a nesting turtle. (See TURTLES; ECOTOURISM; WILDLIFE REFUGES.)

**total allergy syndrome,** a type of ENVIRONMENTAL ILLNESS.

**toxaphene,** a type of PESTICIDE (see CHLORINATED HYDROCARBONS).

**toxic chemicals,** substances that can have adverse effects on human health and the environment. For much of human history, chemicals have been used with little or no regulation, except for known deadly poisons. But the 20th century has seen a proliferation of chemicals, many of still-unknown impact, especially involving SYNTHETIC ORGANIC CHEMICALS (SOCs). The UNITED NATIONS ENVI-

RONMENT PROGRAMME (UNEP) estimates that about 70,000 chemicals are in common use today, with about 1,000 new ones being introduced each year. How many of these are toxic, and to what organisms in what circumstances and to what degree, is a wide-open question. Only in recent years has information begun to be required about such chemicals; even then, information is spotty, focuses primarily on human health (though often resulting from ANIMAL TESTING), often stresses acute over chronic, long-term effects, and tells little about the impact on the environment.

In addition, many other toxic chemicals are formed as by-products of manufacturing, such as DIOXIN, or of use, especially products of incomplete combustion (PICs), such as PCBS. Many more are formed by the mix of chemicals in the environment, sometimes acting together to form substances of greater or quite different effects (see SYNERGY), seldom recognized until damage has been done in the environment and "ecodetectives" try to track down what caused the damage and how. Many toxic substances are not manufactured at all, though they may be released into the environment by human activities, such as MINING; these include RADON and HEAVY METALS, such as LEAD and MERCURY.

Governments have in recent years attempted to gain more information as to the health and environmental effects of the known manufactured chemicals, to identify those that are toxic, and to monitor and regulate where and how they are manufactured, stored, used, and disposed of. In the United States, toxic chemicals are covered by many laws, most notably:

- the 1938 Food, Drug, and Cosmetic Act, prohibiting the sale of "adulterated" or "misbranded" foods, drugs, devices, or cosmetics;
- the 1947 FEDERAL INSECTICIDE, FUNGICIDE, AND RODENTICIDE ACT (FIFRA), amended in 1970 and 1972, which requires PESTICIDES to be registered for specific uses only;
- the 1960 Federal Hazardous Substances Act, which established labeling requirements for consumer products containing hazardous substances;
- the 1972 Consumer Products Safety Act (see CONSUMER PRODUCT SAFETY COMMISSION), authorizing a ban on substances that pose an "unreasonable" risk;
- the 1976 TOXIC SUBSTANCES CONTROL ACT (TSCA OR TOSCA), which regulates specific toxic substances not otherwise regulated, such as pesticides;

**Environmental distribution of TRI releases and transfers, 1988.**

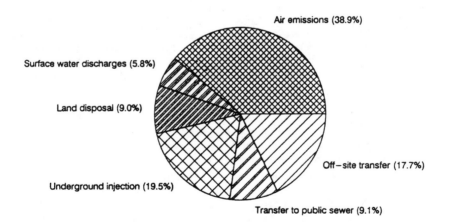

Note: TRI = Toxics Release Inventory. Total releases and transfers = 6,241 million pounds.

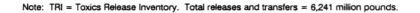

**Source:** *Environmental Quality.* The 21st Annual Report of the Council on Environmental Quality, 1991.

## Toxic Chemical and Hazardous Waste Information and Action Guide

**For more information and action on toxic chemicals and hazardous waste:**

AIR AND WASTE MANAGEMENT ASSOCIATION (A&WMA), (412-232-3444). Publishes books such as *Hazardous Waste Management in the '90s: Moving from Remediation to Practical Prevention Strategies* (1990), *Hazardous Waste Minimization* (Harry M. Freeman, ed., 1989), and numerous training manuals, videotapes, and technical works.

AMERICAN PLANNING ASSOCIATION (APA), (202-872-0611). Publishes bibliographies *Industrial Pollution* (1988) and *Resource Recovery* (1988).

CENTER FOR SAFETY IN THE ARTS (CSA) (Five Beekman Street, New York, NY 10038; 212-227-6220; Chris Proctor, Director), an organization founded to gather and disseminate information about hazardous chemicals in arts and crafts; formerly the *Center for Occupational Hazards*. Through its *Art Hazards Information Center*, it offers precautions, suggests alternatives, and makes referrals. It also maintains a library and publishes various materials, including the *Art Hazard News,* reprints of articles, lists of acceptable arts and craft materials, and data sheets on specific types of art hazards and precautions.

CENTER FOR SCIENCE AND TECHNOLOGY FOR DEVELOPMENT (CSTD), UNITED NATIONS, (212-963-8435).

Chesapeake Bay Foundation (CBF), (301-268-8816). Publishes *A Guide to Household Hazardous Waste*. (See CHESAPEAKE BAY.)

CONSUMER PRODUCT SAFETY COMMISSION (CPSC), (301-492-6580; Hotline 800-638-CPSC [2772]).

ENVIRONMENTAL DEFENSE FUND (EDF), (212-505-2100).

ENVIRONMENTAL HAZARDS MANAGEMENT INSTITUTE (EHMI), (603-868-1496). Trains public, industry and agency officials in the safe handling and management of hazardous materials and hazardous wastes; publishes the monthly magazine *HAZMAT World*, and the biweekly newsletters, *Environmental*

*Manager's Compliance Advisor* (EMCA) and *OSHA Compliance Advisor* (OCA), as well as a useful household hazardous waste "wheel."

**Environmental Law Institute (ELI),** (202-328-5150; publications office, 202-939-3844). (See ENVIRONMENTAL LAW INFORMATION AND ACTION GUIDE on page 116.)

ENVIRONMENTAL PROTECTION AGENCY (EPA), (Public Information Center, 202-260-7751 or 202-260-2080). Operates *Chemical Emergency Preparedness Program (CEEP) Hotline* (202-479-2449 or toll-free number (except AK and DC) 800-535-0202); *Inspector General's Whistle Blower Hotline* (202-382-4977 or 800-424-4000); *Resource Conservation and Recovery ACT (RCRA)/Superfund Hotline*, 202-382-3000; toll-free (outside DC, 800-424-9348); *Toxic Substances Control Act Assistance Information Service*, 202-554-1404; and *National Pesticides Telecommunications Network (NPTN)* (806-743-3091, toll-free (outside TX), 800-858-PEST [7378]).

FOOD AND DRUG ADMINISTRATION (FDA), (301-443-1544 or 301-443-3170). Operates the *National Center for Toxicological Research*. Reviews and approves or rejects chemicals used in or on foods, drugs, or cosmetics.

FRIENDS OF THE EARTH (FOE), (202-544-2600). Publishes *Community Plume Chemical Safety Newsletter*.

GREENPEACE, (202-462-1177). Runs the *Toxics Campaign*, the *Waste Project*, and the *Below Regulatory Concern (BRC) Project*. Publishes *A Citizen's Toxic Waste Audit Manual* (1990), *The International Trade in Waste: A Greenpeace Inventory* (1990), *A Shot in the Dark: Underground Injection of Hazardous Waste* (1990), *We All Live Downstream: The Mississippi River and the National Toxics Crisis* (1989), *The Politics of Penta* (1989), and *Burnt Offerings II* (1988), and numerous Action Fact Sheets and videocassettes.

HUMAN ECOLOGY ACTION LEAGUE (HEAL), (404-248-1898). Publishes information sheets on chemical sensitivities.

INFORM, Inc., (212-689-4040). Publishes books such as *A Cit-*

---

- the 1976 RESOURCE CONSERVATION AND RECOVERY ACT (RCRA), which regulates HAZARDOUS WASTE in general, as part of solid waste, and focuses on recovery and reuse;
- the 1977 CLEAN WATER ACT, which focuses on toxics in water;
- the 1980 COMPREHENSIVE ENVIRONMENTAL RESPONSE, COMPENSATION, AND LIABILITY ACT (CERCLA), which focuses on spills and abandoned and inactive hazardous waste sites (the most serious sites being handled under SUPERFUND, under 1986 amendents);
- the 1986 EMERGENCY PLANNING AND COMMUNITY RIGHT-TO-KNOW ACT (EPCRA), which focuses on chemical inventories and planning for emergencies;

- the 1990 CLEAN AIR ACT, which seeks to reduce toxic pollutant EMISSIONS from industry.

Not surprisingly, with such a patchwork of laws, a variety of definitions exists relating to toxic substances. But in general, as under CERCLA, a *hazardous substance* is defined as "any substance that, when released into the environment, may present substantial danger to public health, welfare, or the environment," while an *extremely hazardous substance* (under CERCLA as amended) is a substance that "could cause serious, irreversible health effects from a single exposure." Other laws and agencies have slightly different definitions—the Occupational

izen's Guide to Promoting Toxic Waste Reduction (Lauren Kenworthy and Eric Schaeffer, 1990), *Toxics in Our Air* (Nancy Lilenthal, 1990), *Trading Toxics Across State Lines* (Nancy Lilenthal, 1990), a series of directories of organic chemical manufacturing plants; numerous Action Fact Sheets, such as *Source Reduction.*

KIDS FOR SAVING EARTH™ (KSE), (612-525-0002 or 800-800-8800).

NATIONAL ENVIRONMENTAL HEALTH ORGANIZATION (NEHA), (303-756-9090). Publishes books and manuals such as *Hazardous Materials Management, Toxicology Primer, Low-Level Radioactive Waste Regulation—Science, Politics and Fear, Hazardous Materials Dictionary, Health Effects from Hazardous Waste Sites,* and *Environmental Impacts of Hazardous Waste Treatment, Storage and Disposal Facilities.*

NATIONAL INSTITUTE OF ENVIRONMENTAL HEALTH SCIENCES (NIEHS), (919-541-3345). Key biomedical research center to investigate the health effects of environmental agents. Coordinates toxicology studies under the *National Toxicology Program (NTP).*

NATIONAL WILDLIFE FEDERATION (NWF), (202-797-6800 or 800-245-5484). Publishes *Phantom Reduction: Tracking Toxic Trends* and *Reducing the Risk of Chemical Disaster.*

NATURAL RESOURCES DEFENSES COUNCIL (NRDC), (212-727-2700). Publishes *The Right to Know More: Toxic Releases into the Environment* (Deborah Sheiman, 1991) and *Toxic Chemicals Activists Kit* (D. Sheiman, 1988).

RENEW AMERICA, (202-232-2252). Publishes *Food Safety (1989).*

RESOURCES FOR THE FUTURE (RFF), (202-328-5000). Includes research arms *Quality of the Environment Division* and *Center for Risk Management.*

SIERRA CLUB, (415-776-2211 or 202-547-1141; legislative hotline, 202-547-5550). Recent campaigns include Toxics: Resource Conservation and Recovery Act Reauthorization. Publishes the *Hazardous Materials/Water Resources Newsletter,* "Toxic Air Pollutants Policy," "Toxics," and *For Our Kids' Sake.*

STUDENT ENVIRONMENTAL ACTION COALITION (SEAC), (919-967-4600).

U.S. PUBLIC INTEREST RESEARCH GROUP (PIRG), (202-546-9707). Publishes *Toxic Truth and Consequences: The Magnitude of and the Problems Resulting from America's Use of Toxic Chemicals* (1991) and *An Ounce of Toxic Pollution Prevention: Rating States' Toxics Use Reduction Laws* (1991).

WATER ENVIRONMENT FEDERATION (WEF), (703-684-2400 or 800-666-0206). Publishes *Hazardous Waste Site Remediation Management* (1990), *Hazardous Waste Treatment Processes Including Environmental Audits and Waste Reduction* (1990), *Hazardous Waste Site Remediation: Assessment and Characterization* (1988), and brochures such as *Household Hazardous Waste: What You Should and Shouldn't Do* and *Hazardous Waste Reduction.*

WOODS HOLE OCEANOGRAPHIC INSTITUTION (WHOI), (508-548-1400; Associates Office: 508-457-2000, ext. 2392). Operates the *Coastal Research Center (CRC).*

WORLD BANK (202-477-1234). Publishes *Safe Disposal of Hazardous Wastes: The Special Needs and Problems of Developing Countries.*

WORLD ENVIRONMENT CENTER (WEC), (212-683-4700). Publishes *Household Hazardous Waste Wheel.*

**Other references:**

*Chemical Exposures: Low Levels and High Stakes.* Nicolas Ashford and Claudia Miller, M.D. Van Nostrand Reinhold, 1991. *A Citizen's Guide to Understanding Measurements of Toxic and Radioactive Concentrations.* James Chapman. Citizens Environmental Coalition, 1990. Address: 33 Central Avenue, Albany, NY 12210; 518-462-5527. *Fighting Toxics: A Manual for Protecting Your Family, Community, and Workplace.* Gary Cohen and John O'Connor, eds., Island Press, 1990. *Managing Toxic Wastes.* Michael Kronenwetter. Messner, 1989. (See also PESTICIDES; NUCLEAR ENERGY; NUCLEAR WEAPONS ESTABLISHMENT, U.S.; WASTE DISPOSAL.

Safety and Health Administration (OSHA) inventories *hazardous chemicals*, for example, and other laws focus on *toxic chemicals* and chemical categories—and slightly different lists of substances are covered. (For a comparative list of toxic chemicals covered under TSCA, CERCLA, and the Clean Air Act, see TOXIC CHEMICALS AND HAZARDOUS SUBSTANCES on page 407; see also KNOWN HEALTH EFFECTS OF TOXIC CHEMICALS on page 416.) Environmentalists are very much aware, however, that far too little is known about the short- and long-term effects of toxic chemicals, singly and in the "chemical stews" that exist in many parts of our environment. In the United States, government testing is primarily carried out under

a variety of laws and interagency agreements by the NATIONAL INSTITUTE OF ENVIRONMENTAL HEALTH SCIENCES.

Much governmental effort has focused on limiting the amounts of toxic chemicals released into the environment, and on diluting their presence in the environment. However, some toxic chemicals—for example, CHLORINATED HYDROCARBONS such as DDT—are not BIODEGRADABLE but are highly persistent, building up in the FOOD CHAIN by the process of BIOACCUMULATION. Such substances must be banned completely if the environment is to be able to heal itself. Easier said than done, however, for synthetic chemicals—many of them later discovered to be toxic—are found all around us. Citizen's groups are working actively to use the laws on the books—and to push for new ones—that would increase the amount of information about and regulation of potentially toxic synthetic chemicals *before* they are introduced into the environment.

On the personal level, individuals can screen their own households and workplaces for toxics, being particularly watchful of plastics, solvents (as in glues, cleaners, polishers, thinners, paints, and correction fluids), aerosols (not just those with CHLOROFLUOROCARBONS), wood preservatives (as in furniture and building materials), some insulations and plywoods (such as those containing formaldehyde), and pesticides in general, including bug-killers and garden sprays. It is generally possible to replace these with natural substances (see BIOLOGICAL CONTROL; also ALTERNATIVES TO TOXIC PRODUCTS USED IN THE HOME, right), some of which are commercially available, since the environmentally oriented market has grown. Toxic substances often lurk in surprising places, notably in arts and crafts materials, including those used by children. Children, along with the elderly, pregnant women, and the chronically ill, are among those most vulnerable to damage from toxic chemicals.

Many homes and workplaces—including many new "tight" office buildings containing many synthetic materials—can sometimes be so polluted with toxic chemicals that they cause the people who live and work there to become ill (see ENVIRONMENTAL ILLNESS). Workers who actually manufacture, work with, or use toxic chemicals are often at the most risk, since their levels of exposure are often both high and long-term. In the United States, they receive some protection under regulations administered by the Occupational Safety and Health Administration, but in many places around the world, they have little or no protection from toxic chemicals.

Toxic chemicals are a concern not only in the industrialized world but also in developing countries. In fact, many toxic chemicals long banned in most industrialized countries, including pesticides such as DDT, are being sold in increasing amounts in Latin America, Africa, and Asia. Many governmental agencies and environmental organizations are seeking to end such export of POLLUTION, by providing information to toxic chemical users in developing countries. Most notably, the UNITED NATIONS ENVIRONMENT PROGRAMME (UNEP), as part of its EARTHWATCH program, maintains the INTERNATIONAL REGISTER OF POTENTIALLY TOXIC CHEMICALS (IRPTC), an inventory of chemicals of international concern. Working with the World Health Organization (WHO) and the International Labour Organization (ILO), it also operates the *International Programme on Chemical Safety (IPCS)*.

Obeying no boundaries, toxic chemicals are often the subject of dispute between countries, as where they share the same WATER RESOURCES or receive toxic EMISSIONS through the air. They have been the subject of numerous international agreements. Many of these focus on questions of disposal (see HAZARDOUS WASTE), such as the CONVENTION ON THE PREVENTION OF MARINE POLLUTION BY DUMPING OF WASTE AND OTHER MATTER (LONDON DUMPING CONVENTION or LDC). (See TOXIC CHEMICALS AND HAZARDOUS WASTE INFORMATION AND ACTION GUIDES on page 302; also PESTICIDES; AIR POLLUTION; WATER POLLUTION; and specific types of chemicals, such as CHLORINATED HYDROCARBONS or HEAVY METALS.)

## Alternatives to Toxic Products Used in the Home:

| Instead of: | Try: |
|---|---|
| Abrasive cleaners | 1/2 lemon dipped in borax. |
| Ammonia-based cleaners | Vinegar, salt and water mixture; or baking soda and water. |
| Disinfectants | 1/2 cup borax in 1 gallon water |
| Drain cleaners | 1/4 cup baking soda and 1/4 cup vinegar in boiling water |
| Enamel or oil-based paints | Latex or water-based paints |
| Floor or furniture polish | Mixture of 1 part lemon juice and 2 parts olive or vegetable oil |
| Furniture strippers | Sandpaper |
| House plant insecticide | Dishwater or bar soap and water |
| Mothballs | Cedar chips; lavender flowers |
| Rug and upholstery cleaners | Dry cornstarch |
| Silver cleaners | Boiling water with baking soda, salt, a piece of aluminum |
| Toilet cleaners | Baking soda and a toilet brush |

**Source:** Adapted from *Household Hazardous Waste Wheel.* Environmental Hazards Management Institute.

**Toxic Releases Inventory,** a report of routine releases of TOXIC CHEMICALS into the environment, based on information submitted to the ENVIRONMENTAL PROTECTION AGENCY (EPA), as required by the EMERGENCY PLANNING AND COMMUNITY RIGHT-TO-KNOW ACT of 1986. (For a list of chemicals covered, see TOXIC CHEMICALS AND HAZARDOUS SUBSTANCES on page 407; for an overview of their health effects, see KNOWN HEALTH EFFECTS OF TOXIC CHEMICALS on page 416.)

### Toxic Substances Control Act (TSCA or TOSCA),

a U.S. federal law passed in 1976 that authorizes the ENVIRONMENTAL PROTECTION AGENCY (EPA) to monitor and control the risks posed by commercial chemical substances that are not otherwise regulated as either drugs, food additives, cosmetics, tobacco, nuclear material, firearms and ammunition, or PESTICIDES (covered under other federal laws). TSCA requires that the EPA be notified before any new chemical is manufactured, by the filing of a *premanufacture notice* (PMN) outlining the chemical's name, structure, production process, intended uses, and other available information about the health and environmental effects of the chemical. The law authorizes the EPA to regulate the production, use, or disposal of such chemicals, including requiring the manufacturer to test for cancer and other possible effects from the chemical. Manufacturers are required to maintain records of adverse effects among their workers, and in general report any new information suggesting substantial risk from the substance, by filing a *substantial risk notice*. EPA's authority also extends to new uses developed for existing chemicals and also chemicals newly imported into the United States.

In addition, the EPA is charged with controlling the risks from over 65,000 existing chemicals—those on the market before the law passed. If these are found to pose unreasonable public health and environmental risks, the EPA may regulate their manufacture, processing, distribution, use, and disposal, including labeling, restrictions on use, and outright bans. Other government agencies (generally an Interagency Testing Committee, or ITC) may recommend and citizens can petition that certain chemicals should be tested. The disposal of a specific hazardous chemical, such as PCBs, comes under TSCA; by contrast, the disposal of a range of hazardous chemicals, or a "waste stream," is covered by the RESOURCE CONSERVATION AND RECOVERY ACT (RCRA). (For a list of the toxic chemicals covered under TSCA, see TOXIC CHEMICALS AND HAZARDOUS SUBSTANCES on page 407.)

Under TSCA, the EPA also carries on numerous other programs, such as the *National Human Monitoring Program*, tracking levels of PCBs and DDT in human body tissue, and chemical exposure studies, such as evaluation of risks from formaldehyde and chlorinated solvents (see CHLORINATED HYDROCARBONS). As part of its TSCA responsibilities, the EPA also maintains a chemical inventory of all commercial chemical substances that are, or have been, manufactured or imported into the United States since January 1, 1975, a list to which all new

chemicals are added. Along with the FEDERAL INSECTICIDE, FUNGICIDE, AND RODENTICIDE ACT, TSCA also gives the EPA responsibility for regulating products of BIOTECHNOLOGY.

Critics point out that, under TSCA, the EPA should—but does not yet—have the authority to require testing of a chemical without first having to declare the chemical an "unreasonable risk." They also note that, where regulatory authority is unclear, the EPA generally defers to other agencies, such as the Occupational Safety and Health Administration (OSHA), which sometimes fail to act regarding a chemical hazard. The BLUEPRINT FOR THE ENVIRONMENT recommends that the EPA reassert its authority over any substance found to pose an unreasonable risk. (See TOXIC CHEMICALS; PESTICIDES; HAZARDOUS WASTE; ENVIRONMENTAL LAW.)

### TRAFFIC (Trade Records Analysis of Flora and Fauna in Commerce),

(USA offices: c/o World Wildlife Fund—U.S. 1250 24th Street, NW, Washington, DC 20037; 202-293-4800; Ginette Hemley, Director; TRAFFIC International: c/o World Conservation Monitoring Centre, 291c Huntingdon Road, Cambridge CB3 ODL, United Kingdom; 44-223-277427; Jorgen B. Thomsen, Director), an international network that monitors global trade in wildlife and wildlife products, from 10 worldwide offices, the USA office being operated by the WORLD WILDLIFE FUND and the international offices being associated with IUCN-THE WORLD CONSERVATION UNION. More specifically, TRAFFIC focuses on the trade regulations of the CONVENTION ON INTERNATIONAL TRADE IN ENDANGERED SPECIES (CITES), tracking and reporting on traded wildlife species; helping governments comply with CITES provisions; developing training materials and enforcement tools for wildlife-trade enforcement officers; pressing for stronger enforcement under national wildlife trade laws, in the United States often working with the FISH AND WILDLIFE SERVICE and other government agencies; and seeking protection for newly threatened species. TRAFFIC is also active in educating the public about conservation and wildlife trade, using media campaigns, traveling exhibits such as *Cargo to Extinction*, education kits for students, and publications such as the *Buyer Beware!* brochure warning tourists about prohibited wildlife products, as well as fact sheets such as *Elephant Ivory Trade*, *U.S. Imports of Wildlife*, and *World Trade in Wildlife*.

### Trans-Siberian Railroad gas pipeline explosion, a

June 3, 1989, Soviet railroad disaster, in which a leaking gas pipeline running close to the Trans-Siberian railroad line exploded, near Ufa, in the Urals. The force of the explosion derailed a passing passenger train, pushing it into a second passenger train coming in the opposite direction; both heavily laden trains were wrecked. At least 500 people died, including many young children who were not required to have tickets, making the casualty count approximate. (See NATURAL GAS.)

**transuranic waste,** radioactive waste from substances whose atomic number is higher than that of uranium (see RADIOACTIVE WASTE).

**tributyl tin (TBT),** a type of SYNTHETIC ORGANIC CHEMICAL, a human-made carbon-containing compound with tin added; part of a group of *organometals*. From the mid-1960s, TBT was used against fungi, molluscs, and marine plants, especially in boat paint and wood preservatives, but also in anti-odor socks. But by the 1980s, researchers had found that TBT had severely contaminated many estuaries and bays, damaging shellfish, such as oysters, and other marine life. TBT may also affect the immune and reproductive systems of many invertebrates, including humans. As a result, governments in various countries have moved to ban TBT. (See TOXIC CHEMICALS; also TOXIC CHEMICALS AND HAZARDOUS SUBSTANCES on page 407.)

**Tropical Resources Institute (TRI)** (Yale University, School of Forestry and Environmental Studies, 205 Prospect Street, New Haven, CT 06511; 203-432-5109), an institute founded in 1983, largely funded by foundations, grants, and contracts, to encourage "current and future environmental leaders to study tropical resource issues from applied management and policy perspectives," emphasizing interdisciplinary and international approaches to tropical resource management and conservation. TRI offers courses and internships, and oversees research and service projects, with four specializations: tropical biology and ECOLOGY; AGROFORESTRY and social forestry; wildlife and wildland management; and policy, planning, and economics of rural development. It maintains a library and other information resources on environmental issues, and publishes the quarterly *TRI News* and numerous working papers.

**Trout Unlimited** (800 Follin Lane, Suite 250, Vienna, Virginia 22180; 703-281-1100; Charles Gauvin, Executive Director), a membership organization founded by Michigan anglers in 1959, but now national in scope, with international affiliations and cooperative agreements with other organizations around the world, its main early concerns being loss of HABITAT, water quality, and displacement of wild trout by hatchery-raised trout. Trout Unlimited's mission is "to conserve, restore and enhance North America's trout, salmon and steelhead—the ultimate indicators of good water and habitat quality—and their watersheds."

Working through local chapters, members assist state and federal agencies with research and field projects such as stream habitat improvement projects, "cleaning up streams and restoring degraded trout and salmon habitat; participating in water-quality surveillance programs; calling for identification, protection, and careful management of quality trout and salmon waters; seeking recognition and maintenance of the genetic integrity of native trout, salmon, and steelhead stocks; encouraging integrated watershed management through wise land-use practices; supporting clean air and clean water legislation; sponsoring scientific meetings and seminars; and promoting international cooperation in devising solutions to common problems facing trout and salmon throughout the world." Trout Unlimited also offers educational programs for the public, including young people; sponsors fishing clinics and courses; offers public testimony; and publishes various materials, including the quarterly magazine *Trout* and the quarterly newsletter *Action Line*.

**Tsavo National Park,** Kenya's largest WILDLIFE REFUGE, most notable for its large ELEPHANT herds. The park occupies 5,100,000 acres (8,000 square miles) in southeastern Kenya, with its southern boundary on the Kenya-Tanzania border. This is a major African refuge; protected here are LIONS, LEOPARDS, CHEETAHS, antelopes, gazelles, ZEBRAS, black RHINOCEROS, giraffes, hartebeests, impalas, and a score of other mammals, many of which are disappearing fast elsewhere in Africa. Hundreds of bird species are also found in the park. The park is cut in two by the main Nairobi-Mombasa road and railroad; the northeastern section is named Tsavo Park East and the southwest Tsavo Park West. (See ECOTOURISM; WILDLIFE REFUGE.)

**tundra,** cold, treeless plains, such as are characteristic of the Arctic regions north of the taiga FOREST; one of the world's main land BIOMES, or major life zones. Tundra regions generally have low temperatures year round, even during the summer averaging under 50 degrees F; strong winds; low precipitation; and thin, shallow, often waterlogged soil, oddly featured from continual freezing and thawing, and overlying a permanently frozen layer called *permafrost*. Tundra vegetation consists mainly of lichens, mosses, grasses, close-to-the-ground "cushion" plants, and shrubs or dwarf trees. Plant SPECIES are opportunistic and highly adaptable—many are able to live in any of several HABITATS—but not many are found in any one place. Tundra also has relatively few species of animals, but these sometimes exist in very large numbers, as in vast migratory herds of CARIBOU or cyclically burgeoning populations of lemmings (see MIGRATION). Among the other wildlife common in the tundra are the polar BEAR,

## Arctic Information and Action Guide

For more information and action about the Arctic:

ARCTIC INSTITUTE OF NORTH AMERICA (AINA) of the University of Calgary, (403-220-7515). Operates the *Arctic Science and Technology Information System (ASTIS)*; publishes a quarterly journal *Arctic*; quarterly newsletter *Information North* and books, reports, and numerous technical papers.

CLIMATE INSTITUTE (CI) (316 Pennsylvania Avenue SE, Suite 403, Washington, DC 20003; 202-547-0104). Publishes *The Arctic and Global Change* (1990). (See GLOBAL WARMING AND CLIMATE CHANGE INFORMATION AND ACTION GUIDE on page 144.)

NATIONAL AUDUBON SOCIETY, (212-832-3200; *Audubon Action Line*, 202-547-9017). Publishes *Arctic National Wildlife Refuge*.

NATURAL RESOURCES DEFENSE COUNCIL (NRDC), (212-727-

2700). Publishes *Tracking Arctic Oil: The Environmental Price of Drilling in the Arctic National Wildlife Refuge* (1991).

SIERRA CLUB, (415-776-2211 or 202-547-1141; legislative hotline, 202-547-5550). Publishes *Arctic Refuge* and *Alaska Report*.

WILDERNESS SOCIETY, THE (202-833-2300). Publishes *Arctic National Wildlife Refuge: America's Serengeti*.

WOODS HOLE OCEANOGRAPHIC INSTITUTION (WHOI), (508-548-1400; Associates Office, 508-457-2000, ext. 2392). Operates the *Marine Policy Center (MPC)*, including Arctic studies.

Other references:

*The Arctic and Antarctica: Roof and Floor of the World*. Alice Gilbreath. Macmillian, 1988.

---

musk ox, reindeer, foxes, and WOLVES, along with numerous birds. Except for the ptarmigan, most birds migrate seasonally to their summer Arctic breeding grounds, such as the snowy owl, ducks, geese, terns, and plovers. Tundra is also found in small sections of ANTARCTICA (elsewhere, perpetually ice-and-snow-covered), and in high mountain ranges such as the Alps, though there the tundra has no permafrost, is generally wetter from summer rains, and has more permanent residents, such as mountain goats and mountain sheep.

Tundra flora and fauna have adapted themselves to a difficult and fluctuating environment. Compared to other land biomes, the tundra ECOSYSTEM has a relatively simple FOOD CHAIN—but that also means it is readily susceptible to disruption by outside influences, including human activities such as OIL drilling, MINING, HUNTING, or tourism. Some such activities are carried on in Arctic tundra regions, as in Siberia and in Alaska (notably the oil pipeline), though less so in the Canadian far north. However, large parts of the tundra have been protected in WILDLIFE REFUGES; among those described in this book are the ARCTIC NATIONAL WILDLIFE REFUGE, AUYUITTUQ, GATES OF THE ARCTIC NATIONAL PARK AND PRESERVE, and NOATAK NATIONAL PRESERVE. (See ARCTIC INFORMATION AND ACTION GUIDE above.)

**turtles, sea,** a group of marine reptile SPECIES; several sea turtle species are the object of much environmentalist concern in this period. One of the best known of these is the *green sea turtle*, a deep-sea, long-lived warm water sea dweller that before the European conquest of the Americas was numerous from Bermuda to the CARIBBEAN

and from west Africa to the northern coast of South America. Weighing up to 450 pounds, and highly prized for their meat and shells, they were hunted to near-extinction in many areas by the mid-20th century. Although now protected from hunters by many nations, widespread poaching continues where enforcement is ineffective. In the modern period, many green sea turtles have also been ''incidentally'' killed by entangling fishnets set up to catch other sea creatures. Loss of nesting HABITAT has also become a major problem: Green sea turtles need quiet, clean, sandy beaches with some vegetation for nesting, and loss of such coastal nesting places on both sides of the Atlantic has meant a long-term additional threat to the species.

Despite efforts to save the green sea turtles of the Florida coast, only small numbers remain, and there they are listed as an ENDANGERED SPECIES. Recovery has been much more successful in the Caribbean, and especially at Tortuguero Beach (see TORTUGUERO NATIONAL PARK), in Costa Rica, site of the world's largest surviving green sea turtle refuge. There, since 1954, the CARIBBEAN CONSERVATION CORPORATION (CCC) has been studying the turtles and participating in a multinational effort to reestablish them on other beaches throughout the Caribbean, with considerable success.

The National Marine Fisheries Service (see NATIONAL OCEANIC AND ATMOSPHERIC ADMINISTRATION) has also been involved in efforts to save these and other sea turtles, by requiring that shrimpboats place turtle excluder devices in the mouths of their nets; the move, sharply resisted by Gulf of Mexico commercial FISHING interests, has considerably reduced the number of sea turtles killed by the nets.

The *hawksbill turtle* was in the early 1990s the center of

an international storm. This species has been increasingly threatened by the Japanese tortoise shell industry, employing approximately 2,000 people, which uses shells secured by partially cooking the live turtles to soften the shells and then tearing the shells off the living turtles, which are then often put back into the sea—where they are thought by some to survive and grow new shells, but in actuality soon die. Prodded by environmentalists, the United States government in 1991 threatened to place trade sanctions on Japan if the tortoise shell industry was not stopped. Japan had signed the CONVENTION OF INTERNATIONAL TRADE IN ENDANGERED SPECIES, but had refused to recognize the hawksbill turtle as an endangered species. Japan had promised to stop the trade in five years, but the U.S. had demanded a halt within one year. In May 1991, Japan did agree to list the hawksbill as endangered, and announced that the trade would be stopped, but did not supply a hard timetable for the stoppage. The United States postponed imposition of trade sanctions, but the issue remained wide open, as the Japanese tortoise shell trade continued.

The *leatherback*, largest of the sea turtles, is also an endangered species in southeastern U.S. coastal waters, for much the same reasons as the green sea turtle, and also because a main diet item is the jellyfish, which closely resembles some of the lethal PLASTIC debris now found in coastal waters. One other very notable related near-extinction was that of the huge *Galapagos tortoise*, killed by the millions by whalers.

**For more information and action:**

- CARIBBEAN CONSERVATION CORPORATION (CCC), (904-373-6441). Operates the Green Turtle Research Station; has an *Adopt-A-Turtle Program* (800-678-7853); and publishes quarterly newsletter *Velador*.
- CENTER FOR MARINE CONSERVATION (CMC), (202-429-5609). Has *Marine Debris and Entanglement Program*; promotes Turtle Excluder Devices (TEDs); campaigns to control artificial light on Florida beaches that interferes with sea turtles nesting. Publishes *Sea Turtle Coloring Book* for children K-4 (in English and Spanish), *Status of the Kemp's Ridley*, slide shows on *Sea Turtles* and *The Turtle Excluder Device*, and fact sheets on sea turtles.
- EARTH ISLAND INSTITUTE, (415-788-3666). Sponsors the *Sea Turtle Restoration Project*.
- ELSA WILD ANIMAL APPEAL (EWAA), (818-761-8387).
- GREENPEACE, (202-462-1177). Greenpeace Action runs the *Ocean Ecology Campaign*. Operates the *Sea Turtle Beach Patrol*.
- IUCN—THE WORLD CONSERVATION UNION, (202-797-

5454). Publishes *Tortoises and Freshwater Turtles: An Action Plan for Their Conservation* (David Stubb, comp., 1989) and *Conservation Biology of Tortoises* (Ian R. Swingland and Michael W. Klemens, eds., 1989).

(See also ENDANGERED SPECIES; also ENDANGERED AND THREATENED WILDLIFE AND PLANTS on page 372.)

**twentieth century illness,** a type of ENVIRONMENTAL ILLNESS.

**Two Forks Dam,** a long-planned dam across the South Platte River, 30 miles north of Denver, Colorado, at Cheesman Canyon, between two forks of the river. The city of Denver had planned to dam the river to provide water for its growing northern suburbs; environmentalists had opposed the dam, which would have destroyed WETLANDS that were also a prime recreational area, noted particularly for its trout FISHING.

Plans for the dam went forward throughout the 1980s, with U.S. Army Corps of Engineers approval of a permit to build the dam coming in 1989. The regional ENVIRONMENTAL PROTECTION AGENCY (EPA) office had also indicated that it would approve the project. But in November 1990, newly appointed EPA head William K. Reilly refused to authorize the dam, because of adverse environmental impact. Proponents of the plan continued to press a political fight for the project, however, and also threatened court action. (See DAM.)

**2,4-D (2, 4-dichlorophenoxyacetic acid),** a chemical compound used as a herbicide, often for weed control in FORESTS and rights-of-way, and long thought to be harmless to humans; a type of PESTICIDE. While a related herbicide, 2,4,5-T, was banned (the two had formed the notorious 50–50 mixture called AGENT ORANGE), 2,4-D continued to be widely used. After the banning of several other herbicides (see PESTICIDES BANNED IN THE UNITED STATES on page 000), 2,4-D became the third most widely used pesticide in the United States by the early 1990s, with the ENVIRONMENTAL PROTECTION AGENCY (EPA) estimating 52 to 67 million pounds used in 1987. However, more recent studies at the National Cancer Institute strongly suggest that 2,4-D may cause cancer in humans. Some critics argued that data from ANIMAL TESTING does not support that contention, though a 1991 study found that dogs whose owners used 2,4-D as a lawn herbicide were 1.3 to 2 times as likely to develop lymphatic cancer. As of spring 1992, the EPA was considering a special review of 2,4-D, as provided under the FEDERAL INSECTICIDE, FUNGICIDE, AND RODENTICIDE ACT (FIFRA). Both 2,4-D and 2,4,5-T are known as *phenoxy herbicides*.

## For more information and action:
- **Northwest Coalition for Alternatives to Pesticides (NCAP),** (503-344-5044). Publishes *2,4-D Information Packet* (Sally Claggett, 1990).

(See PESTICIDES INFORMATION AND ACTION GUIDE on page 238.)

**2,4,5-T (2,4,5-trichlorophenoxyacetic acid),** a type of PESTICIDE; a chemical compound used as a herbicide, often for weed control in FORESTS and rights-of-way. At first believed harmless to humans, 2,4,5-T was found to cause cancer and birth defects, and to be toxic to unborn babies; it is also often contaminated with DIOXIN. As a result, it has been banned by several countries, in the United States by the ENVIRONMENTAL PROTECTION AGENCY (EPA) in 1985. However, it is still used in the Third World, as part of the CIRCLE OF POISON. Perhaps the best-known use of 2,4,5-T was in a 50–50 mix with 2,4-D, the result being the defoliant AGENT ORANGE, used during the Vietnam War. Both 2,4-D and 2,4,5-T are known as *phenoxy herbicides*. (See PESTICIDES.)

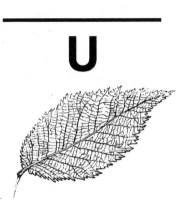

# U

**underground storage tanks,** see LEAKING UNDERGROUND STORAGE TANKS (LUST).

**Unfinished Business: A Comparative Assessment of Environmental Problems,** a landmark 1987 report by and for the ENVIRONMENTAL PROTECTION AGENCY (EPA) that attempts to assess "the relative risks to human health and the environment posed by various environmental problems," acknowledged as "subjective and based on imperfect data," but intended as "a credible first step toward a promising method of analyzing, developing, and implementing environmental policy." Accepting the importance of applying the EPA's "finite resources where they will have the greatest effect," the project staff attempted to assess the relative kinds of risk associated with major environmental problems.

The "universe" of major environmental problems was divided into 31 problem areas (these are not listed in ranked order; numbers are for reference to associated tables only):

1—CRITERIA AIR POLLUTANTS from mobile and stationary sources (including acid precipitation);
2—hazardous/toxic air pollutants;
3—other air pollutants (including fluorides, total reduced sulfur, and substances not included above that emit odors);
4—RADON (indoor air only);
5—indoor AIR POLLUTION other than radon;
6—RADIATION from sources other than indoor radon;
7—substances suspected of depleting the stratospheric OZONE LAYER, such as CFCS;
8—CARBON DIOXIDE and GLOBAL WARMING;
9—direct, point-source discharges (such as industrial) to surface waters;
10—indirect, point-source discharges (from publicly owned treatment works, or POTWs, to surface waters;
11—nonpoint-source discharges to surface waters;
12—contaminated SLUDGE (including municipal and SCRUBBER sludge);
13—discharges to estuaries, coastal waters, and OCEANS from all sources;
14—discharges to WETLANDS from all sources;
15—drinking water as it arrives at the tap (including TOXIC CHEMICALS, LEAD from pipes, biological contaminants, radiation, etc.);

16—active HAZARDOUS WASTE sites (including hazardous waste storage tanks; groundwater and other MEDIA);

17—inactive hazardous waste sites (SUPERFEUND; groundwater and other media);

18—nonhazardous municipal waste sites (groundwater and other media);

19—nonhazardous industrial waste sites (including utilities; groundwater and other media);

20—MINING waste (including OIL and NATURAL GAS extraction wastes);

21—accidental release of toxic chemicals (all media);

22—accidental OIL spill;

23—releases from storage tanks (includes product and petroleum tanks, above, on, or underground);

24—other groundwater contamination (including septic systems, road salt, injection wells, etc.);

25—PESTICIDE residues on foods eaten by humans and wildlife;

26—application of pesticides (risks to applicators, which includes workers who mix and load, as well as apply, and also consumers who apply pesticides);

27—other pesticide risks (including LEACHING and runoff of pesticides and agricultural chemicals, air deposition from spraying, etc.);

28—new toxic chemicals;

29—BIOTECHNOLOGY (environmental releases of genetically altered materials);

30—exposure to consumer products;

31—worker exposure to chemicals.

Each of these 31 problems was analyzed and ranked in relation to four different kinds of risk: cancer risks, noncancer health risks, ecological effects, and WELFARE EFFECTS (by definition effects other than ecological, such as damage to materials, recreation, natural resources, public and community property, groundwater supplies, and aesthetics). *Not* considered were "the economic or technical controllability of the risks; the qualitative aspects of the risks that people find important, such as the degree to which the risks are voluntary, familiar, or equitable; the benefits to society of the activities that cause the environmental problems; and the statutory and public mandate (or lack thereof) for EPA to deal with the risks," noting that some problems fall under other agencies.

The result was an annotated ranking of the problems for each type of risk, and a summary discussion of the 31 problems, discussing each of the types of risk associated with them. Not all problems were ranked for every type of risk, since for some sufficient data was not available, and in some cases the risk did not apply (indoor air pollution presented little or no ecological risk, for example, and so was not con-

sidered in the ranking). For the RANKING OF ENVIRONMENTAL PROBLEM AREAS BY ECOLOGICAL RISKS, see page 311; BY POPULATION CANCER RISK, see page 312; BY WELFARE EFFECTS, see page 317; and BY NONCANCER RISKS, see page 316.

Among the report's general conclusions were that:

- no problems ranked consistently "high" or "low" across all risk types, and that whether or not an environmental problem is classed as major depends on which type of risk or adverse effect is being considered.
- the "risks and EPA's current program priorities do not always match," noting that the EPA's "priorities appear more closely aligned with public opinion than with estimated risks," and that the EPA seems to have been "more concerned about pollution that affects public health, as opposed to protection of natural habitats and ecosystems, in all programs except surface water protection."
- "statutory authorities do not match neatly with risks," notably that in relation to consumer and worker exposure to chemicals, the EPA shares jurisdiction with other agencies, and that in some high-risk areas—such as indoor air pollution, carbon dioxide, global warming, and nonpoint sources of WATER POLLUTION—no federal agency has extensive statutory authority.
- "national rankings do not necessarily reflect local situations—local analyses are needed."
- "some chemicals show up as major concerns in multiple problem areas, notably lead, chromium, formaldehyde, solvents, and some pesticides," suggesting "the need for integrated strategies to deal with them."
- more research is needed in several areas.
- the EPA should study other areas important to setting priorities, noting that some serious environmental problems—such as radon and indoor air pollution—had only recently been "discovered."

In addition, the project staff reviewed data on public concerns, to see how they compared with the project ranking. They found that some problems ranked high in *Unfinished Business*—such as carbon dioxide and global warming, tied for first in the ecological effects rankings—were perceived as relatively low-risk by the public (that may well have changed since 1987). Conversely, topics that top the public's list of concerns—such as hazardous waste, water pollution, toxic chemical releases, and air pollution—were seen by project staff as posing relatively less risk than other problems, such as radon, which shared the top spot on the cancer-risk rankings.

The 1990 EPA report REDUCING RISKS: SETTING PRIORITIES AND STRATEGIES FOR ENVIRONMENTAL PROTECTION was a followup report, expanding, correcting, and building on *Unfinished Business*.

## Ranking of Environmental Problem Areas by Ecological Risks

Notes: Numbers in parentheses refer to the environmental problem areas listed in the entry on *UNFINISHED BUSINESS: A COMPARATIVE ASSESMENT OF ENVIRONMENTAL PROBLEMS.* Within each rank, problems are presented in numerical order by problem number; they are not ranked within categories.

| Rank | Environmental Problem | Rationale for Ranking Position |
|------|----------------------|--------------------------------|
| 1 | Stratospheric ozone depletion (7) CO$_2$ and global warming (8) | *Intensity of Impact*: High (can severely damage all natural systems, particularly primary productivity). *Scale of impact*: Biospheric. *Ecosystem recovery*: Recovery period extremely long; impacts may be irreversible. *Control*: Effective controls require coordinated, international effort that will be very difficult to obtain. *Uncertainty*: Effects of ozone depletion uncertain; ecological response to global warming is well characterized. Rate and timing of the problem is uncertain. |
| 2 | Physical alteration of aquatic habits (13/14) Mining, gas, oil extraction, and processing wastes (20) (Risks from problems 13/14 and 20 are similar, but 20 includes terrestrial impacts.) | *Intensity of impact*: High (can both degrade and completely destroy ecosystem structure and functions). Mining poses severe impacts on water ecosystems. *Scale of impact*: Local to regional. *Ecosystem recovery*: Physical impacts are generally irreversible. *Control*: Low degree of controllability. *Uncertainty*: High degree of certainty associated with effects. |
| 3 | Criteria air pollutants (1) Point-source discharges (9/10) Nonpoint-source discharges and in-place toxics in sediment (11) Pesticides (25–27) | *Intensity of impact*: High (tend to affect ecsytem functions directly and indirectly affect ecosystem structure). *Scale of Impact*: Local and regional. |

| Rank | Environmental Problem | Rationale for Ranking Position |
|------|----------------------|--------------------------------|
| | (While problems 1, 9/10, 11, and 25 to 27 do not share common characteristics, they are rank-grouped together.) | *Ecosystem Recovery*: Impacts are generally reversible. *Control*: Degree of control varies among the problems in this rank group; more controllable than rank group #1 *Uncertainty*: Some uncertainty, but much is known about these effects. |
| 4 | Toxic air pollutants (2) | *Intensity of impact*: Medium. Growing evidence to indicate that toxic air pollutants are responsible for ecological damage. *Scale of impact*: Local to regional. *Ecosystem recovery*: Unknown. *Control*: Unknown, but likely to be difficult. *Uncertainty*: Substantial. |
| 5 | Contaminated sludge (12) Inactive hazardous waste sites (17) Municipal waste sites (18) Industrial nonhazardous waste sites (19) Accidental releases of toxics (21) Oil spills (22) Other groundwater contamination (24) | *Intensity of Impacts*: Medium (many sources; impacts generally low, but can be high locally. *Ecosystem recovery*: Uncertain. *Control*: Variable. *Uncertainty*: Moderate. (Overall these problems have localized releases and effects.) |
| 6 | Radiation other than radon (6) Active hazardous waste sites (16) Underground storage tanks (23) (These problems are characterized by a few large releases, a high degree of control for 6 and 16.) | *Intensity of impacts*: Usually low, though could be moderate to severe locally in unusual circumstances. *Scale of impact*: Local. *Ecosystem recovery*: Uncertain. *Uncertainty*: Moderate. |

**Source:** *Unfinished Business: A Comparative Assessment of Environmental Problems: Overview Report.* Environmental Protection Agency, 1987.

## Ranking of Environmental Problem Areas by Population Cancer Risk

Note: The five categories represent decreasing magnitude of cancer risk, with Category 1 representing problem areas with the highest relative risk, and Category 5 representing problems for which no cancer risk has been identified. Problems are also ranked numerically within each category. (see Unfinished Business.)

### Category 1

| Rank | Problem Area | Substances/ Exposures Investigated | Comments |
|---|---|---|---|
| 1 (tied) | Worker exposure to chemicals | Formaldehyde Tetrachloroethylene Asbestos Methylene chloride | Ranked highest of any single environmental problem, along with indoor radon-based on work group consensus. About 250 cancer cases were estimated annually from four substances, but workers face potential exposures to over 20,000 substances. Individual risk can be very high. |
| 1 (tied) | Indoor radon | Radon and is decay products | Also ranked the highest. Current estimates are 5,000 to 20,000 lung cancers annually from exposures within homes. Some of these are a consequence of the joint action of radon and tobacco smoke. Individual risks can be very high. |
| 3 | Pesticide residue on foods | 1 Herbicide 3 Fungicides 1 Insecticide 1 Growth regulator | Cancer incidence estimate of about 6,000 annually, based on exposure to 200 potential oncogens [tumor-causing agents] (one-third of total pesticides in use). Assessment does not account for so-called inert materials in pesticides. |
| 4 (tied) | Indoor air pollutants other than radon | Tobacco smoke Benzene ρ-Dichlorobenzene Chloroform Carbon tetrachloride Tetrachloroethylene Trichloroethylene | Quantitative assessment estimates 3,500 to 6,500 cancers annually. Environmental tobacco smoke is responsible for the majority. Risks from organics estimated on the basis of monitoring 600 U.S. homes. Individual risks can be very high. Potential for some double counting with Consumer Exposure to Chemicals and with Drinking Water. |
| 4 (tied) | Consumer exposure to chemicals | Formaldehyde Methylene chloride ρ-Dichlorobenzene Asbestos | The risk from these four chemicals is about 100 to 135 cancers annually. There are an estimated 10,000 chemicals in consumer products. Even though exposures are generally intermittent, risks are believed to be high, given the concentrations to which individuals are exposed. Consumers are exposed through such products as cleaning fluids, pesticides, particleboard and other building materials, and numerous asbestos-containing products. Considerable double counting with Indoor Air Pollution and Other Pesticide Risks. |
| 6 | Hazardous/toxic air pollutants | 20 substances, classes of substances, or waste streams | A quantitative assessment of 20 substances estimates approximately 2,000 cancer cases annually. This is a subset of the large total number of pollutants to which people are exposed in ambient air. Individual risks can be very high. Potential for some double counting with Active Hazardous Waste Sites, Municipal Hazardous Waste Sites, and Contaminated Sludge. |

### Category 2

| Rank | Problem Area | Substances/ Exposures Investigated | Comments |
|---|---|---|---|
| 7 | Depletion of stratospheric ozone | Increased UV [ultraviolet] radiation (chlorofluorocarbons, halon 1301, chlorocarbons) | Current nonmelanoma and melanoma skin cancer deaths at 10,000 annually. Ozone depletion projected to result in steadily increasing risks, with an additional 10,000 annual deaths projected for the year 2100. This is ranked Category 2 because of the uncertainties concerning estimates of future risk. If estimates are correct, would rank higher. Needs further research. |

| Rank | Problem Area | Substances/ Exposures Investigated | Comments |
|------|--------------|-----------------------------------|----------|
| 8 | Hazardous Waste Sites—Inactive | Trichloroethylene Vinyl chloride Arsenic Tetrachloroethylene Benzene 1,2-Dichloroethane | Nationwide cancer incidence from six chemicals at just over 1,000 annually. Considerable uncertainty, since nationwide risk estimates are based on extrapolating from 35 sites to about 25,000 sites nationwide. Individual risks can be very high. Potential for some double counting with drinking water. |
| 9 | Drinking water | Ingestion and/or inhalation of 23 substances | Quantitative assessment estimates 400–1,000 cancer cases annually, based on home surveys of public water systems. Most cases are from radon and trihalomethanes. Potential for some double counting with Indoor Radon, Indoor Air Pollution, and several categories related to contaminated groundwater. |
| 10 | Application of pesticides | 1 Herbicide 3 Fungicides 1 Insecticide 1 Growth regulator | Approximately 100 cancers annually estimated by a method analogous to that used for Pesticide Residues on Food. Small population exposed, but uniformly high risks. |
| 11 | Radiation other than indoor radon | Occupational exposures Consumer products Industrial emissions | Risks associated with medical exposures and natural background levels excluded; would rank higher if these were included. Two-thirds of assessed risk of 360 annual cancers results from building materials. Individual risks can be very high. Nonionizing radiation not considered due to lack of data. |
| 12 | Other pesticide risks | Consumer use Professional exterminator use | Few quantitative estimates available. Consensus estimate of 150 cancers annually, based loosely on discussion of termiticide risks. Less data here than for other pesticide areas. |
| 13 | Hazardous Waste Sites—Active | Several carcinogens from each of the following: Hazardous waste storage tanks Hazardous waste in boilers/furnaces Hazardous waste incineration Waste oil | No nationwide risk estimates are available, but probably fewer than 100 cases annually. Risk estimates are sensitive to assumptions regarding the proximity of future wells to waste sites. Solid waste management units were excluded from analysis. Individual risks can be very high. Possible double counting with Drinking Water and Hazardous/Toxic Air Pollutants. |
| 14 | Nonhazardous waste sites—industrial | Arsenic 1,1,2,2-Tetrachloroethane Chloroform Benzene | No analysis of cancer incidence. Instead, based on the consensus of the work group. Judged less severe than hazardous waste, worse than municipal. Potential for some double counting with Drinking Water. |
| 15 | New toxic chemicals | None | Very difficult to assess future uses of new chemicals and the risks of using chemicals never manufactured. Consensus was that this problem poses moderate risks. |

**Category 3**

| Rank | Problem Area | Substances/ Exposures Investigated | Comments |
|------|--------------|-----------------------------------|----------|
| 16 | Nonhazardous waste sites—municipal | Several pollutants/ waste streams from the following: Municipal landfills Municipal sludge incineration Municipal waste incineration | Quantitative estimate of about 40 cancers annually. This estimate does not include risks from municipal surface impoundments. Potential for some double counting with Hazardous/Toxic Air Pollutants, Contaminated Sludge, and Drinking Water. |

| Rank | Problem Area | Substances/ Exposures Investigated | Comments |
|------|--------------|-----------------------------------|----------|
| 17 | Contaminated sludge | Up to 22 carcinogens from the following: Land application Distribution and marketing Landfilling Incineration Ocean disposal | Analyses and regulatory development are ongoing. Preliminary results estimate approximately 40 cancers annually. Most of this risk comes from incineration and landfilling. Potential for some double counting with Hazardous/Toxic Air Pollutants, Nonpoint Source Discharges to Surface Water, and Nonhazardous Waste Sites—Municipal. |
| 18 | Mining waste | Arsenic Cadmium | Estimate of 10–20 cancer cases annually largely due to arsenic. Severity of problem is relatively low because remote locations expose a relatively small population. This assessment excludes oil and gas operations. Individual risks can be very high. Potential for double counting with Drinking Water. |
| 19 | Releases from storage tanks | Benzene | Preliminary analysis suggests relatively low cancer incidence (1 annually), but exposure modeling not as conservative as several other solid waste problems (behavior that limits exposure is assumed). Potential for double counting with Drinking Water. |
| 20 | Nonpoint-source discharges to surface water | None | Judged to be more serious than other surface water categories, but no quantitative analysis is available. |
| 21 | Other groundwater contamination | Methylene chloride from septic systems | Generally, risks from other groundwater contamination are not estimated due to a lack of information with respect to sources, their locations, and concentration levels. Individual risks generally less than $10^{-6}$, with rough estimate of population risk well under 1 case per year. However, this is an estimate of a small portion of total risk, as we examined one chemical at just one of many sources (septic systems). Potential for some double counting with Drinking Water. |
| 22 | Criteria air pollutants | Lead Ozone Particulate matter Nitrogen oxides Sulfur oxides Carbon monoxide | This assessment excludes carcinogenic particles and VOCs [volatile organic compounds] (controlled to reduce ambient ozone), which are considered under Hazardous/Toxic Air Pollutants. Ranked relatively low because none of the criteria pollutants has been adequately shown to cause cancer. If any are shown to be carcinogenic (e.g., lead), or if VOCs and carcinogenic particles are included in the definition of Criteria Air Pollutants, this problem would move to a higher category. |

**Category 4**

| | | | |
|------|--------------|-----------------------------------|----------|
| 23 | Direct point-source discharges to surface water. | None | No quantitative assessment is available. Only ingestion of contaminated seafood was considered, since the impact of drinking water was covered elsewhere. |
| 24 | Indirect point-source discharges to surface water. | None | Same as above. |
| 25 | Accidental releases—None toxic | None | Because of the short duration of personal exposure to accidental releases, cancer risk judged to be very small. Long-term effects on groundwater exposures were not considered here. Noncancer health effects are of much greater concern. Nature of substances and exposures ranks this problem above oil spills. |
| 26 | Accidental releases—oil spills | None | See above. Oil spills will be of greater concern for welfare and ecological effects. |

| Rank | Problem Area | Substances/ Exposures Investigated | Comments |
|---|---|---|---|
| **Category 5 (listed alphabetically)** | | | |
| | Biotechnology | None | Dilemma of ranking this problem is similar to that for new chemicals, but even less information is available. No known instances of carcinogenic bioengineered substances. |
| | $CO_2$ and global warming | None | Cancer is not considered a significant aspect of this environmental problem. No assessment was undertaken. |
| | Other air pollutants | None | By definition, carcinogenic pollutants in the outdoor air are considered under Hazardous/Toxic Air Pollutants. Therefore, no cancer risk was assessed here. |
| **Not ranked** | | | |
| | Discharges to estuaries, coastal waters, and oceans | None | This category represents a conglomeration of other categories. The work group chose not to rank it to minimize double counting. |
| | Discharges to wetlands | None | See Discharges to Estuaries, Coastal Waters, and Oceans, above. |

**Source:** *Unfinished Business: A Comparative Assessment of Environmental Problems: Overview Report.* Environmental Protection Agency, 1987

---

## For more information:

• ENVIRONMENTAL PROTECTION AGENCY (EPA), (202-260-7751 or 202-260-2080).

**Union of Concerned Scientists (UCS)** (26 Church Street, Cambridge, MA 02238; 617-547-5552; or 1616 P Street NW, Suite 310, Washington, DC 20036; 202-332-0900; Howard Ris, Executive Director), an independent membership organization, founded by MIT faculty and students in 1969, of "scientists and other citizens concerned about the impact of advanced technology on society." Programs of UCS focus on "national energy policy, national security policy, arms control, and nuclear power safety," advocating "energy strategies that minimize risks to public health and safety, provide for efficient and cost-effective use of energy resources, and minimize damage to the global environment," and "defense policies and negotiated arms agreements that reduce the risk of nuclear war, benefit U.S. security interests, and enhance the nation's economic strength." It has three UCS Action Networks: the *Scientists Action Network*, for scientists active in grassroots educational and lobbying programs; the *Legislative Alert Network*, alerting members of coming votes, so they can contact their legislators; and the *Professionals' Coalition for Nuclear Arms Control*, for scientists, physicians, lawyers, and design professionals seeking to advance arms-control education and legislation. The UCS

sponsors research on energy and defense programs; recommends new directions in government policy; is active in lobbying and litigation, notably in Washington, DC; maintains a speaker's bureau; and seeks to educate the public, as through conferences, curricula, and appearances at hearings and on news programs.

The UCS also publishes various materials, including the quarterly *Nucleus*; books and reports such as *Cool Energy: The Renewable Solution to Global Warming* (Michael Brower, 1990); videocassettes such as *Greenhouse Crisis: The American Response* (1989); briefing papers such as *The Greenhouse Effect*; and brochures such as *How You Can Fight Global Warming: An Action Guide, How You Can Influence Government Energy Policy,* and *Nuclear Power: Past and Future.*

**United Nations Department of Technical Cooperation for Development (UNDTCD)** (United Nations Secretariat, New York, NY 10017), a major division of the United Nations Secretariat, which includes two subsidiaries: the NATURAL RESOURCES AND ENERGY DIVISION (NRED) and the CENTRE FOR SCIENCE AND TECHNOLOGY FOR DEVELOPMENT (CSTD).

**United Nations Conference on Environment and Development (UNCED),** the "Earth Summit" held in Rio de Janeiro in June 1992, attended by delegates from over 175 countries, widely regarded as the largest summit

## Ranking of Environmental Problem Areas by Non-cancer Risks

Note: Numbers in parentheses refer to the environmental problem areas listed in the entry on *UNFINISHED BUSINESS: A COMPARATIVE ASSESSMENT OF ENVIRONMENTAL PROBLEMS*. A dash in a column indicates that the work group did not believe it had sufficient information to fill out these columns.

| Problem Area | Level of Confidence | % of Problem Covered | Problem Area | Level of Confidence | % of Problem Covered |
|---|---|---|---|---|---|
| **High Noncancer Risks** | | | **Low Noncancer Risks** | | |
| Criteria air pollutants (1) | High | 30–100 | Direct discharges—industrial (9) | Medium | 3–10 |
| Hazardous air pollutants (2) | Medium | <3 | Contaminated sludge (12) | Medium | 30–100 |
| Indoor air pollutants—not radon (5) | Medium | 30–100 | To wetlands (14) | – | – |
| Drinking water (15) | High | 30–100 | Active hazardous waste sites (16) | Medium | 10–30 |
| Accidental releases—toxics (21) | High | 30–100 | Inactive hazardous waste sites (17) | Medium | 10–30 |
| Pesticide residues on food (25) | Medium | <3 | Mining waste (20) | Low | 30–100 |
| Application of pesticides (26) | High | 3–10 | Releases from storage tanks (23) | – | – |
| Consumer product exposure (30) | Medium | 3–10 | | | |
| Worker exposure to chemicals (31) | High | <3 | **Unranked** | | |
| | | | Other air pollutants (3) | – | – |
| **Medium Noncancer Risks** | | | CO$_2$ and global warming (8) | – | – |
| | | | Accidental releases—oil spills (22) | – | – |
| Radon—indoor air (4) | Low | 30–100 | Other groundwater contamination (24) | – | – |
| Radiation—not radon (6) | Medium | 30–100 | New toxic chemicals (28) | – | – |
| UV [ultraviolet] radiation/ ozone depletion (7) | Low | 30–100 | Biotechnology (29) | – | – |
| Indirect discharge (POTWs) (10) | Medium | 3–10 | | | |
| Nonpoint sources (11) | – | | | | |
| To estuaries, coastal water, oceans (13) | Medium | 30–100 | | | |
| Municipal nonhazardous waste sites (18) | Medium | 10–30 | | | |
| Industrial nonhazardous waste sites (19) | Low | 30–100 | | | |
| Other pesticide risks (27) | Medium | 10–30 | | | |

**Source:** *Unfinished Business: A Comparative Assessment of Environmental Problems: Overview Report.* Environmental Protection Agency, 1987.

gathering in history, with more than 100 heads of state attending. Long in planning, the conference took on even more importance with the ending of the Cold War, with widespread pressure to redirect money from military expenditures toward protecting the environment and aiding DEVELOPMENT among the poorer nations of the world, two goals that go hand in hand. The conference took up the whole range of environmental concerns, most notably BIOLOGICAL DIVERSITY, the OZONE LAYER, loss of FORESTS,

and GLOBAL WARMING and CLIMATE CHANGE; several key treaties were (at this writing) scheduled to be signed, with questions remaining as to which ones the large industrialized countries, such as the United States, would sign.

**United Nations Development Programme (UNDP)** (One United Nations Plaza, New York, NY 10017; 212-906-5000; William H. Draper, III, Administrator), the key agency within the United Nations system for coordinating

## Ranking of Environmental Problem Areas by Welfare Effects

Note: In UNFINISHED BUSINESS, the EPA report from which this table was taken, "welfare effects" by definition referred to effects other than ecological, generally those to which some monetary value could be ascribed, such as damage to materials, recreation, natural resources, public and community property, groundwater supplies, and aesthetics.

**Rank Environmental Problem Area**

**High Effects**

1 Criteria air pollutants from mobile and stationary sources (including acid precipitation
2 Nonpoint-source discharges to surface waters (includes effect from pesticides)
3 Indirect point-source discharges (POTWs) to surface waters
4 To estuaries, coastal waters, and oceans from all sources (includes effects from pesticides)
5 $CO_2$ and global warming
6 Stratospheric ozone depletion
7 Other air pollutants (odors and noise)
8 Direct point-source discharges (industrial, etc.) to surface waters

**Medium Effects**

9 Hazardous waste sites—inactive (Superfund)
10 Nonhazardous waste sites—municipal
11 Hazardous waste sites—active (RCRA)
12 To wetlands from all sources
13 Other pesticide risks—leaching and runoff of pesticides and agricultural chemicals, air deposition from spraying, etc.
14 Biotechnology

**Low Effects**

15 Nonhazardous waste sites—industrial
16 Releases from storage tanks (including product and petroleum tanks that are above, on, and underground)
17 Accidental releases of toxics
18 Accidental oil spills
19 Drinking water as it arrives at the tap
20 Radon—indoor only
21 Mining wastes (including oil and gas extraction wastes)
22 Contaminated sludge
23 Hazardous/toxic air pollutants

**Minor Effects**

Other groundwater contamination
Radiation other than radon
Indoor air pollutants other than radon
Pesticide residuals on foods eaten by humans
Applicators of pesticides (risks to applicators and consumers)
New toxic chemicals
Consumer product exposure
Worker exposure to chemicals

**Source:** *Unfinished Business: A Comparative Assessment of Environmental Problems: Overview Report.* Environmental Protection Agency, 1987.

---

funding, planning, and organization of technical assistance for development, the aims of its projects being to "help build self-reliance and develop the human and natural resources required to meet basic needs and for economic growth." Successor to the earlier *Expanded Programme of Technical Assistance for Economic Development of Under-Developed Countries (EPTA)*, established in 1950, UNDP has a network of over 110 offices worldwide, and works in collaboration with governments, which provide funding and set policy guidelines and priorities. Through specialized agencies, which serve as "knowledge and experience banks," UNDP aids in planning, evaluating, and implementing projects, as in obtaining expert services or equipment, or arranging for specialized training abroad; as coordinator, UNDP mobilizes resources for multilateral DEVELOPMENT assistance, provides administrative and other support, administers special-purpose funds and programs, and helps developing countries prepare for "fol-

low-up capital investment." The UNDP administers six separately funded programs:

- **United Nations Capital Development Fund (UNCDF),** which provides small-scale capital assistance to the world's least-developed countries.
- **United Nations Sudano-Sahelian Office (UNSO),** which promotes sustainable development in 22 countries in sub-Saharan Africa, especially focusing on protecting the soil and controlling desertification.
- **United Nations Revolving Fund for Natural Resources Exploration (UNRFNRE),** which funds explorations for mineral deposits, notably in Africa, Asia, and Latin America.
- **United Nations Development Fund for Women (UNIFEM),** which provides direct project support for activities promoting women's concerns, women being seen as key to long-term development.

- **United Nations Fund for Science and Technology for Development (UNFSTD),** which aids countries in making use of the most current scientific and technological advances, also promoting international cooperation among research institutions.
- **United Nations Volunteers (UNVs),** which funds field workers in specific participatory development projects.

A key part of the UNDP is the Special Unit for *Technical Co-operation among Developing Countries (TCDC),* which fosters national and collective self-reliance of developing countries. The UNDP publishes the annual *Human Development Report,* the quarterly *Source,* and reports such as *World Development* and *Safe Water 2000.*

## United Nations Environment Programme (UNEP)

(International Headquarters: P.O. Box 30552, Nairobi, Kenya; (254 2) 333930/520600; UNEP Regional Office for North America, 2 United Nations Plaza, New York, NY 10017; 212-963-8138 or -8098; Mostafa Kamal Tolba, Executive Director), an international agency of the United Nations, formed in 1973 as a result of the 1972 Stockholm Conference of Human Environment, to help nations, non-GOVERNMENTAL ORGANIZATIONS, and other UN agencies "protect the environment by distributing education materials and by serving as a coordinator and catalyst of environmental initiatives," sometimes dubbed the "environmental conscience of the UN system." UNEP has a wide range of concerns, among them depletion of the world's OZONE LAYER; CLIMATE CHANGE; WASTE DISPOSAL; HAZARDOUS WASTES, including OCEAN dumping; TOXIC CHEMICALS; BIOLOGICAL DIVERSITY; AIR POLLUTION; WATER POLLUTION; FORESTS and DEFORESTATION; DESERTS and DESERTIFICATION; ENVIRONMENTAL DEGRADATION in general; DEVELOPMENT; ENERGY RESOURCES including FUELWOOD; and the earth's BIOGEOCHEMICAL CYCLES.

At the heart of UNEP is *Earthwatch,* a three-pronged program, designed to monitor and measure environmental problems in a uniform way, the aim being to produce global information that can be used for assessment and decision-making. The three parts of the Earthwatch program are the GLOBAL ENVIRONMENT MONITORING SYSTEM (GEMS); the global information system INFOTERRA; and the INTERNATIONAL REGISTER OF POTENTIALLY TOXIC CHEMICALS (IRPTC).

UNEP operates a number of other international programs, including the *Regional Seas Programs,* which seeks to preserve and protect shared areas such as the CARIBBEAN, MEDITERRANEAN, South Pacific, and Persian Gulf; and the *International Geosphere-Biosphere Programme (IGBP),* which conducts special projects and workshops on biogeochemical cycles and publishes reports.

UNEP's *Industry and Environment Office (IEO)* seeks to advise industry on environment-related issues, maintaining a data base on national POLLUTION standards and publications on industry and the environment; answering queries; and publishing numerous materials, including the quarterly review, *Industry and the Environment,* and detailed guidelines, reports and technical reviews "on the environmental impacts of different industrial sectors and on such cross-sectoral issues as environmental impact assessment, the siting of industry, and environmental auditing. "The IEO also operates the *International Cleaner Production Information Clearinghouse (ICPIC),* which gathers and disseminates to industry (through newsletter and computerized data base) information on clean technology, and *Awareness and Preparedness for Emergencies at Local Level (APELL),* aiming to help avoid situations like BHOPAL by alerting communities to industrial hazards and helping them develop emergency response plans.

With the World Health Organization (WHO) and the International Labour Organization (ILO), UNEP also operates the *International Programme on Chemical Safety (IPCS),* which works closely with the IRPTC. With UNESCO, UNEP also operates a network of six regional *Microbiological Resource Centres (MIRCENs),* to conserve, develop, and use microbes essential in maintaining biological diversity and also biogeochemical cycles. Within the United Nations, UNEP also coordinates activities under the *System-Wide Medium-Term Environment Programme (SWMTEP),* which is a six-year plan under which UN systems can streamline or expand existing programs and identify what still needs to be done, the work being coordinated within each agency by the Designated Official for Environmental Matters.

UNEP is a key organization on the international environmental front, as in planning for the 1992 UN Conference on Environment and Development (UNCED) in Brazil; organizing with the World Meteorological Organization (WMO) the 1990 Intergovernmental Panel on Climate Change (IPCC); helping to resolve international environmental crises such as that resulting from the Persian Gulf War; and helping to shape and gain adoption of the major international treaties (see ENVIRONMENTAL LAW) of the last two decades, including the CONVENTION ON INTERNATIONAL TRADE IN ENDANGERED SPECIES OF WILD FAUNA AND FLORA (CITES; 1973), the CONVENTION ON THE CONSERVATION OF MIGRATORY SPECIES OF WILD ANIMALS (Bonn Convention; 1979), the Vienna Convention for the Protection of the Ozone Layer (1985; see OZONE

LAYER), and the Basel Convention on the Control of Transboundary Movements of Hazardous Wastes and their Disposal (1989; see HAZARDOUS WASTE).

UNEP also publishes various materials, including the bimonthly *Our Planet*, occasional issues of the *Environmental Events Record*, and the annual *Register of International Treaties*.

### For more information and action:

• **US/UNEP (U.S. Committee for the United Nations Environment Program,** 2013 Q Street, NW, Washington, DC 20009; 202-483-4805; Richard Hellman, President), a private membership organization established in 1984 as *Friends of UNEP (FUNEP)* to "help make sure that UNEP is well known and well supported in its critical work." US/UNEP provides a link between UNEP and United States environmental organizations and seeks to educate the public and public officials on key environmental issues such as depletion of the ozone layer, the greenhouse effect, and toxic chemicals, especially conveying UNEP's positions on such questions. It organizes annual World Environment Day celebrations; offers awards to environmental achievers; and publishes the quarterly newsletter *FUNEP Focus*, covering UNEP and international environmental issues.

## U.S. Public Interest Research Group (PIRG) (215 Pennsylvania Avenue SE, Washington, DC 20003; 202-546-9707; Gene Karpinski, Director), a donation-funded independent research and lobbying organization for national environmental and consumer protection, established in 1983 as a national lobbying office by a union of state PIRGs, some of which date back to 1971. Its recent research and lobbying activities have focused on TOXIC CHEMICALS, sustainable energy, RECYCLING, waste reduction, RADIOACTIVE WASTE, consumer protection, and open government, as well as working toward passage of the CLEAN AIR ACT amendments of 1990, the CLEAN WATER ACT, and a 1990 law strengthening the CONSUMER PRODUCT SAFETY COMMISSION.

The U.S. PIRG publishes various materials, including the quarterly newsletter *Citizen Agenda*; books and reports such as *Toxic Truth and Consequences: The Magnitude of and the Problems Resulting from America's Use of Toxic Chemicals* (1991), *Below Regulatory Concern, But Radioactive and Carcinogenic* (1990), *Presumed Innocent: A Report on 69 Cancer-Causing Pesticides Allowed in Our Food* (1990), and *As the World Burns: Documenting America's Failure to Address the Ozone Crisis* (1989); various PAC Studies documenting industry-financed lobbies and contributions to block or blunt environmental legislation; and fact sheets on issues of concern.

*Urquiola* **oil spill,** leakage of 60,000 to 70,000 tons of crude OIL into the sea on May 12, 1976, after the Spanish tanker *Urquiola* ran aground, exploded, and sank while entering the port of La Coruna, on the northwestern Spanish coast. Oil slicks from the wreck fouled 50 to 60 miles of the Spanish coast, greatly damaging shellfish beds that were an important part of the local fishing industry and causing considerable other environmental damage. (See OIL.)

# V

**Valdez Principles,** a set of 10 guidelines (see page 321) for corporate responsibility, written ''to encourage the development of positive programs designed to prevent environmental disasters and degradation,'' by setting forth ''broad standards for evaluating activities by corporations that directly or indirectly impact the Earth's biosphere,'' and ''to help investors make informed decisions around environmental issues.'' The principles were developed in 1989 by the COALITION FOR ENVIRONMENTALLY RESPONSIBLE ECONOMIES (CERES), a project of the SOCIAL INVESTMENT FORUM, in collaboration with environmental groups, churches, labor unions, and other concerned private and public organizations. Recognizing that the issues covered by the principles are complex, CERES regards the principles as a ''long-term process rather than a static statement,'' and expresses the hope that signatory companies will work with them to more specifically elaborate and implement them, the intent being to ''create a voluntary mechanism of corporate self-governance that will maintain business practices consistent with the goals of sustaining our fragile environment for future generations, within a culture that respects all life and honors its interdependence.''

## For more information and action:

- **COALITION FOR ENVIRONMENTALLY RESPONSIBLE ECONOMIES (CERES),** (617-451-0927).
- **SOCIAL INVESTMENT FORUM,** (612-333-8338).

(See also SOCIALLY RESPONSIBLE INVESTING.)

**vegetarianism,** the philosophy or practice of having a diet that excludes red meat, often also excluding poultry and fish, and sometimes eggs and dairy products as well. A fully vegetarian diet—in ecological terms termed HERBIVOROUS—consists only of plants and plant products; being lower on the FOOD CHAIN, it makes far more efficient use of the energy ''fixed'' by plants during the process of PHOTOSYNTHESIS. For people in many parts of the world, a vegetarian diet is a practical necessity, because food resources are limited. Many others choose a vegetarian diet for religious or philosophical reasons, such as some people in the ANIMAL RIGHTS MOVEMENT, who may also avoid other uses of animal products, including the wearing of leather or furs. With widespread use of hormones in meat-producing animals, and with the BIOACCUMULATION OF PESTICIDES, HEAVY METALS, and other TOXIC CHEMICALS in animals high on the food chain, many people have in recent decades also adopted a form of vegetarianism to limit their intake of harmful substances.

There are several types of vegetarian diets:

- **semivegetarian,** excluding red meat, but allowing some poultry and fish;
- **lacto-ovovegetarian,** excluding meat, poultry, and fish, but allowing eggs, milk, cheese, and other dairy products;
- **lactovegetarian,** excluding all animal products except milk, cheese, and other dairy products;
- **vegan,** also called *strict* or *pure vegetarian,* excluding animal products in any form; butter or milk are *not* allowed for cooking.
- **fruitarian,** excluding not only all animal products but also any products that require destruction of the plant for harvesting, and restricting the diet to only those plant

# Valdez Principles

By adopting these Principles, we publicly affirm our belief that corporations and their shareholders have a direct responsibility for the environment.

We believe that corporations must conduct their business in a manner that leaves the earth healthy and safe. We believe that corporations must not compromise the ability of future generations to sustain their needs.

We recognize this to be a long-term commitment to update our practices continually in light of advances in technology and new understandings in health and environmental science. We intend to make consistent, measurable progress in implementing these Principles and to apply them wherever we operate throughout the world.

**The Valdez Principles**

1. **Protection of the Biosphere.** We will minimize and strive to eliminate the release of any pollutant that may cause environmental damage to the air, water, or earth or its inhabitants. We will safeguard habitats in rivers, lakes, wetlands, coastal zones, and oceans and will minimize contributing to the greenhouse effect, depletion of the ozone layer, acid rain, or smog.
2. **Sustainable Use of Natural Resources.** We will make sustainable use of renewable natural resources, such as water, soils, and forests. We will conserve nonrenewable natural resources through efficient use and careful planning. We will protect wildlife habitat, open spaces, and wilderness, while preserving biodiversity.
3. **Reduction and Disposal of Waste.** We will minimize the creation of waste, especially hazardous waste, and wherever possible recycle materials. We will dispose of all wastes through safe and responsible methods.
4. **Wise Use of Energy.** We will make every effort to use environmentally safe and sustainable energy sources to meet our needs. We will invest in improved energy efficiency and conservation in our operations. We will maximize the energy efficiency of products we produce and sell.
5. **Risk Reduction.** We will minimize the environmental, health and safety risks to our employees and the communities in which we operate by employing safe technologies and operating procedures and by being constantly prepared for emergencies.
6. **Marketing of Safe Products and Services.** We will sell products or services that minimize adverse environmental impacts and that are safe as consumers commonly use them. We will inform consumers of the environmental impacts of our products or services.
7. **Damage Compensation.** We will take responsibility for any harm we cause to the environment by making every effort to fully restore the environment and to compensate those persons who are adversely affected.
8. **Disclosure.** We will disclose to our employees and to the public incidents relating to our operations that cause environmental harm or pose health or safety hazards. We will disclose potential environmental, health or safety hazards posed by our operations, and we will not take any action against employees who report any condition that creates a danger to the environment or poses health and safety hazards.
9. **Environmental Directors and Managers.** We will commit management resources to implement the Valdez Principles, to monitor and report upon our implementation efforts, and to sustain a process to ensure that the Board of Directors and Chief Executive Officer are kept informed of and are fully responsible for all environmental matters. We will establish a Committee of the Board of Directors with responsibility for environmental affairs. At least one member of the Board of Directors will be a person qualified to represent environmental interests to come before the company.
10. **Assessment and Annual Audit.** We will conduct and make public an annual self-evaluation of our progress in implementing these Principles and in complying with applicable laws and regulations throughout our worldwide operations. We will work toward the timely creation of independent environmental audit procedures, which we will complete annually and make available to the public.

**Source:** SOCIAL INVESTMENT FORUM.

---

products that fall off naturally, such as nuts, beans, peas, corn, cucumbers, tomatoes, berries, and fruits such as apples, pears, and peaches.

People following a vegetarian diet must take care to get the proper amount and mix of proteins, minerals, and vitamins, especially because most plant sources contain only some of the amino acids for proteins (most animal sources contain all). So vegetarians, especially those following a vegan or fruitarian diet, must learn which foods to combine (rice and beans, for example) to obtain the full range of proteins needed.

### For more information and action:

• **American Vegan Society (AVS)** (P.O. Box H, Malaga, NJ 08328; 609-694-2887; H. Jay Dinshah, President), an organization of people following the vegan diet and using no animal clothing. It publishes the quarterly *Ahimsa* and books such as *Compassion, the Ultimate Ethic: An Exploration of Veganism* 3rd ed., (Victoria Moran, 1991).

- INSTITUTE FOR FOOD AND DEVELOPMENT POLICY (IFDP), popularly called *Food First*, (415-864-8555). Publishes *Diet for a Small Planet*.
- INTERNATIONAL SOCIETY FOR ANIMAL RIGHTS (ISAR) (717-586-2200). Publishes fact sheet on vegetarianism. (See ANIMAL RIGHTS AND WELFARE INFORMATION AND ACTION GUIDE on page 361.)
- Jewish Vegetarian Society—America (JVS) (P.O. Box 5722, Baltimore, MD 21208; 301-486-4948; Izak Luchinsky, Board Chairman), an organization of vegetarian Jews, which gathers and disseminates information on the religious basis for vegetarianism, its advantages, and the arguments against meat-eating. It provides information on vegetarian culture, facilities, and services; maintains a hotline; and publishes various materials, including a monthly newsletter, the quarterly *Jewish Vegetarian*, *Directory of Vegetarian Restaurants and Hotels*, and bibliographies and reviews of books on vegetarianism.
- North American Vegetarian Society (NAVS) (P.O. Box 72, Dolgeville, NY 13329; 518-568-7970; Brian Graff, Secretary), an organization of individuals and groups concerned with vegetarianism. It seeks to educate the public and publishes the quarterly *Vegetarian Voice* and *Facts of Vegetarianism*.
- Student Action Corps for Animals (SACA) (202-543-8983). (See ANIMAL RIGHTS AND WELFARE INFORMATION AND ACTION GUIDE on page 361.)
- Vegetarian Information Service (VIS) (P.O. Box 5888, Bethesda, MD 20814; 301-530-1737; Alex Hershaft, President), an organization devoted to gathering and disseminating information on vegetarianism and its environmental, ethical, economic, health, and social advantages. It seeks to educate the public and influence public policy, publishing various materials.

## Other references:

*Food for Thought: The Vegetarian Philosophy*. Amanda Mitra. Nucleus, 1991. *The Vegetarian Teen*. Charles A. Salter. Millbrook Press, 1991. *Simply Vegan*. Debra Wasserman and Reed Mangels. Vegetarian Resc, 1991. *The Sexual Politics of Meat: A Feminist-Vegetarian Critical Theory*, 2nd ed. Carol J. Adams. Continuum, 1991. *With the Grain: The Essentially Vegetarian Way*. Ellen H. Brown. Carroll and Graf, 1990. *Any Which Way But Meat*. Lilly and Belote, 1990. *A Vegetarian Sourcebook: The*

*Nutrition, Ecology, and Ethics of a Natural Foods Diet*, 3rd ed. Keith Akers. Vegetarian Press, 1989. *The New Vegetarians*. Rynn Berry. Pythago Books, 1989. *The New Vegetarians: Promoting Health and Protecting Life*. P.R. Amato and S.A. Partridge. Plenum, 1989.

**vicuña,** a South American member of the camel family, which numbered in the millions before the European invasion of the Americas in the 1500s. The vicuña lives in the high Andes, grazing above the 12,000-foot level. Unfortunately, vicuñas were highly prized for their skins, and hunted almost to EXTINCTION before becoming a protected SPECIES in the late 1960s, their population at that point down to less than 15,000. Once protected, they recovered, to an early 1990s population of 80,000 to 90,000. Given the growing worldwide revulsion to fur coats and other fur clothing—or at least of choosing such clothing—their chances of survival seem excellent, though possible political instability might make large-scale poaching possible, and there are still some ready markets for fur garments. Vicuña have received protection under several international treaties, notably in 1969, 1979, and 1981, especially between Bolivia and Argentina. (See also ENDANGERED SPECIES; ANIMAL RIGHTS MOVEMENT; also ENDANGERED AND THREATENED WILDLIFE AND PLANTS on page 372.)

**vinyl chloride (VC),** a colorless gas, a kind of PETROCHEMICAL, used in the manufacture of polyvinyl chloride, an ingredient in PLASTICS. Known to cause liver cancer and linked with lung cancer, nervous disorders, and other illnesses, vinyl chloride is one of the hazardous air pollutants for which the ENVIRONMENTAL PROTECTION AGENCY (EPA) sets NATIONAL EMISSION STANDARDS FOR HAZARDOUS POLLUTANTS (NESHAPs), under the CLEAN AIR ACT. It is also monitored under the SAFE DRINKING WATER ACT (see PRIMARY DRINKING WATER STANDARDS on page 274), and several other acts (see TOXIC CHEMICALS AND HAZARDOUS SUBSTANCES on page 407; also KNOWN HEALTH EFFECTS OF TOXIC CHEMICALS on page 416.)

**volatile organic compounds (VOCs),** carbon-containing compounds that readily evaporate at low temperatures. Some of the best known VOCs are benzene, carbon tetrachloride, and chlorform, but over 250 are in common use in modern society, among them many PETROCHEMICALS. VOCs are often found in industrial EMISSIONS and also in many home, automotive, and hobby products, such as paint strippers and solvents used in cleaning and painting, other cleaners and disinfectants, aerosol sprays, air "fresheners," new furnishings, including carpeting and drapes, newly dry-cleaned clothes, environmental tobacco smoke, mothballs, and stored fuels such as kerosene or gasoline. VOCs contribute strongly to AIR POLLUTION, helping to trigger formation of SMOG; they are also prime causes of indoor air pollution. In or out of the home, VOCs cause headaches, loss of coordination, nausea, and eye, nose, and throat irritation. Susceptibility to or high concentration of VOCs can lead to more severe problems, including liver and kidney damage, central nervous system problems, and in extreme cases even death. In 1990, the ENVIRONMENTAL PROTECTION AGENCY (EPA) issued new rules designed to reduce by over 75 percent, or 29,000

tons annually, emissions of volatile organic chemicals from HAZARDOUS WASTE treatment, storage, and disposal facilities; and by 5 percent annually from emissions from automobiles and light trucks.

**For more information:**

*Indoor Air Pollution: Radon, Bioaerosols, and VOCs.* Jack G. Kay et al. Lewis, 1991.

(See also CHLORINATED HYDROCARBONS; ORGANIC COMPOUNDS; SMOG; AIR POLLUTION.)

# W

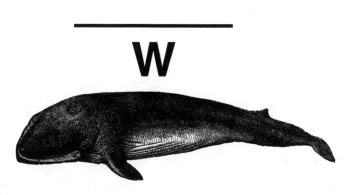

**walruses,** see SEALS AND SEA LIONS.

**waste disposal,** the management and final handling of matter that is past its useful life. Humans have always been known by their garbage. Much of what we know about early human societies comes from archaeological examination of ancient garbage dumps, called *middens*, and anyone who reads about daily life in history knows that at every stage humans have always had enormous amounts of garbage, underfoot and all around them. That is still true in the poorest parts of developing countries, and it poses a significant hazard to human health and to the environment.

But in the 20th century in most industrialized countries, all that changed; with modern approaches to sanitation, garbage and other human waste were removed away from many living and working areas. This was healthier for humans but turned out to be a little different for the environment, as most waste was simply diverted into waterways, heaped and often burned on garbage dumps (now often called *surface impoundments*), or dumped into areas

called *landfills*, often former WETLANDS being filled in for anticipated future use. The result has, in many cases, been so massive as to overwhelm and sometimes directly kill life in the local environment. In the United States alone, 6 billion tons of waste are produced each year, half of it from agriculture and nearly 40 percent from MINING and milling.

But what is new about the modern garbage crisis is not the amount, great as it is, but its toxicity and its persistence. Aside from HEAVY METALS and other waste from relatively small-scale MINING and industrial processes, most waste in earlier times was BIODEGRADABLE—that is, it could and did break down in the environment as part of natural processes (see BIOGEOCHEMICAL CYCLES.) However, in the 20th century, humans began to routinely use products that were made from or produced TOXIC CHEMICALS—SYNTHETIC ORGANIC CHEMICALS, PESTICIDES, PLASTICS, and many other hazardous substances. Many of these are poisonous to start with; some become poisonous under certain situations, such as when they are burned (as PCBs form from DIOXIN) or when they come into contact with

**Material discards in the municipal waste stream, by volume, 1988.**

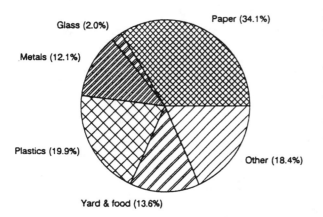

Glass (2.0%)
Paper (34.1%)
Metals (12.1%)
Plastics (19.9%)
Other (18.4%)
Yard & food (13.6%)

**Source:** *Meeting The Environmental Challenge.* Environmental Protection Agency, 1990.

waste water (see WATER POLLUTION) produce decontaminated water and SLUDGE—solid residue after water is largely removed from waste water—which is then treated as a kind of solid waste. Solid waste is generally divided into *municipal solid waste*, produced by homes, institutions, and businesses, and *industrial solid waste*, produced by industrial processes.

Solid waste may also be defined as *hazardous* or *nonhazardous*. HAZARDOUS WASTE is defined in various ways and requires special handling for disposal; under the RESOURCE CONSERVATION AND RECOVERY ACT (RCRA), it is any solid that "may pose a hazard to human health or the environment" because of its "quantity, concentration, or physical, chemical or infectious characteristics." Nonhazardous waste (also under RCRA) is defined by default as "solid wastes, including municipal wastes, household hazardous waste, municipal sludge, and industrial and

certain other chemicals (or with water), forming a sort of chemical stew of unknown toxicity. Many of them, such as plastics and pesticides, persist in the environment for years, decades, and beyond; some also enter the FOOD CHAIN, being passed along in concentration in the bodies of larger animals (see BIOACCUMULATION). When such toxic materials predominate, affected garbage is called HAZARDOUS WASTE and is subjected to special treatment. But in truth, all waste today—like virtually all human life—is contaminated to some extent by such chemicals. This, apart from the sheer bulk of the garbage produced by the aptly named "throwaway society," is what gives the modern garbage crisis its special urgency and what must be considered in assessing the value of various approaches to the problem of waste disposal.

Waste is classified in various ways. *Solid waste* includes such kinds of garbage as paper and paperboard, yard wastes, food wastes, glass, metals, PLASTICS, and the like, but it also includes semisolid, liquid, and even gaseous wastes in containers. The other main kind of waste is *waste water*, the used water or *effluent* flowing from homes (including septic systems), industries, businesses, municipalities, agricultural activities, and mining, OIL, and NATURAL GAS operations. The various methods of treating

**6 Billion Tons of Waste Are Generated in the U.S. Each Year (excludes high-level radioactive waste)**

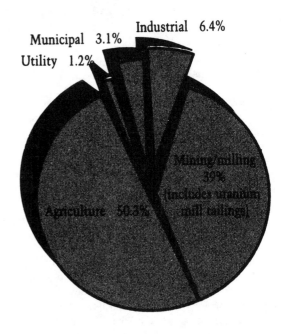

Municipal 3.1%
Industrial 6.4%
Utility 1.2%
Mining/milling 39% (includes uranium mill tailings)
Agriculture 50.3%

**Source:** Environmental Protection Agency, Office of Solid Waste.

# Waste Disposal Information and Action Guide

**For more information and action on waste disposal:**

AIR AND WASTE MANAGEMENT ASSOCIATION (A&WMA), (412-232-3444). Publishes the scientific monthly *Journal of the Air & Waste Management Association*; books such as *Waste Minimization* (1990); and numerous training manuals, videotapes, technical papers, reprints, and books such as, *Emission Control and Waste Management, Factors in Decision-making for Solid Waste or Refuse Disposal, Thermal Treatment of Contaminated Soils and Sludges* and *Measuring Toxic Emissions from Municipal and Hazardous Waste Combustion*.

AMERICAN PLANNING ASSOCIATION (APA), (202-872-0611). Publishes *Solid Waste Management: Planning Issues and Opportunities* (1990); and bibliographies.

CENTRE FOR SCIENCE AND TECHNOLOGY FOR DEVELOPMENT (CSTD), UNITED NATIONS, (212-963-8435).

CONCERN, INC., (202-328-8160). Publishes *Household Waste: Issues and Opportunities* and *Waste: Choices for Communities*.

CONSERVATION AND RENEWABLE ENERGY INQUIRY AND REFERRAL SERVICE (CAREIRS), (800-523-2929, U.S. except AK and HI; for AK and HI, 800-233-3071). Provides fact sheets, brochures, bibliographies, and information on municipal waste.

ENVIRONMENTAL AND ENERGY STUDY INSTITUTE (EESI), (202-628-1400). Publishes *Municipal Solid Waste Legislation: Issues for the 101st Congress* (1990).

ENVIRONMENTAL DEFENSE FUND (EDF), (212-505-2100). Publishes *Recycling and Incineration: Evaluating the Choices* (R. Denison and J. Ruston, eds., 1990), *Incinerator Monitoring: The Critical Link Between Source and Receptor* (R. Denison, 1990), *Supermarkets and the Environment in the 1990's.* (J. Prince, 1990), and *A Hole in the Ground with Grass on Top: The Inadequacy of EPA's Proposed Design Standards for New Municipal Solid Waste Landfills* (K.F. Florini et al., 1989).

FRIENDS OF THE EARTH (FOE), (202-544-2600).

GREENPEACE, (202-462-1177). Has *Garbage Prevention Plan.* Publishes *Greenpeace Action Community Recycling Start-up Kit, Citizens Waste Audit Manual* (1990) and *The International Trade in Wastes: A Greenpeace Inventory*, 4th ed. (Jim Vallette, 1989); Action Factsheets such as *Municipal Solid Waste Incinerators*; and the videocassette *The Rush to Burn* (1989).

INFORM, INC., (212-689-4040). Publishes *Technologies for Minimizing the Emission of $NO_x$ from MSW Incinerators* (Marjorie J. Clarke, 1989), *Improving Environmental Performance of MSW Incinerators* (Marjorie J. Clarke, 1988), *Garbage: Practices, Problems, and Remedies* (Joanna Underwood et al., 1988); and the Fact Sheets *Source Reduction*.

INSTITUTE FOR LOCAL SELF-RELIANCE (ILSR), (202-232-4108). Publishes *Beyond 25 Percent: Materials Recovery Comes of Age, Salvaging the Future: Waste-Based Production, Directory of Waste Utilization Technologies in Europe and the United States*, and *An Environmental Review of Incineration Technologies*.

KIDS FOR SAVING EARTH® (KSE), (612-525-0002 or 800-800-8800).

NATIONAL ENVIRONMENTAL HEALTH ORGANIZATION (NEHA), 303-756-9090).

NATURAL RESOURCES DEFENSE COUNCIL (NRDC), (212-727-2700). Publishes *NRDC Earth Action Guide: Reducing, Recycling, and Rethinking Garbage*.

NATIONAL WILDLIFE FEDERATION (NWF), (202-797-6800 or 800-245-5484). Publishes Fact Sheet *Stop Making Garbage*.

RESOURCES FOR THE FUTURE (RFF), (202-328-5000). Includes research arms *Quality of the Environment Division*, and *Center for Risk Management*. Publishes *Managing Ash From Municipal Waste Incinerators* (Alyce M. Ujihara and Michael Gough, 1990).

SIERRA CLUB (415-776-2211 or 202-547-1141; legislative hotline, 202-547-5550). Publishes *What You Can Do to Help Solve the Garbage Crisis, Solid Waste Policy, More About Homes and Garbage*, and *How Much Do You Know About Garbage?*

STUDENT ENVIRONMENTAL ACTION COALITION (SEAC), (919-967-4600).

WATER ENVIRONMENT FEDERATION (WEF), (703-684-2400 or 800-666-0206). Publishes Manuals of Practice (MOPs) such as *Sludge Incineration: Thermal Destruction of Residues* (1991), *Hazardous Waste Treatment Processes Including Environmental Audits and Waste Reduction* (1990), *Beneficial Use of Waste Solids* (1989), *Incineration* (1988), and *Sludge Conditioning* (1988); technical publications; and courses for waste water professionals.

WORLD RESOURCES INSTITUTE (WRI), (202-638-6300). Publishes *Cleaning Up: U.S. Waste Management Technology and Third World Development* (John Elkington and Jonathan Shopley, 1989).

WORLDWATCH INSTITUTE, (202-452-1999).

WORLD WILDLIFE FUND (WWF), (202-293-4800). Publishes *Getting at the Source: Strategies for Reducing Municipal Solid Waste* (1991).

**Zero Population Growth (ZPG),** (202-332-2200). Publishes *The Garbage Crisis*. (See POPULATION INFORMATION AND ACTION GUIDE on page 248.)

**Other references:**

*Waste Management: Towards a Sustainable Society*. O.P. Kharbanda and E.A. Stallworthy. Auburn House/Greenwood (Westport, CT), 1990. *War On Waste: Can America Win its Battle with Garbage?* Louis Blumberg and Robert Gottlieb. Island Press, 1989. *Rush to Burn: Solving America's Garbage Crisis*. Newsday. Island Press, 1989.

(See also RADIOACTIVE WASTE; RECYCLING; COMPOSTING; TOXIC CHEMICALS; HAZARDOUS WASTE.

commercial wastes that are not hazardous.'' The catch is that all of these sources today contain toxic substances to a greater or lesser extent, though all are classed as ''nonhazardous.'' Hazardous substances, of course, require special handling (see HAZARDOUS WASTE), though so many hazardous substances are mixed in with regular waste—items such as batteries, solvents, cleansers, pesticides, and other substances containing toxic chemicals—that much goes into the environment untouched; among these are low-level RADIOACTIVE WASTE, considered *below regulatory concern* (BRC).

Traditionally, most municipal solid waste has been placed in landfills—in the United States, about 80 percent. However, landfills are rapidly filling up, and few people want to have a new landfill opened near them; this attitude is sometimes called the Solid Waste Syndrome, or TISE (''take it somewhere else''). At the remaining landfills, the *tipping fees*—the amount that must be paid to dump a certain amount of waste—are rising sharply. As a result, many communities are turning toward RECYCLING and INCINERATION. Many export their waste to other states, with states sometimes exporting one kind of waste and importing another, depending on the availability of specially designed facilities for different kinds of waste.

Industrial waste, too, was traditionally dumped or poured on the land and into the water. A series of antipollution laws, such as the CLEAN WATER ACT, have checked that to some extent, but much industrial waste—especially that classed as nonhazardous—is still largely unregulated. Much industrial solid waste is disposed of on-site in landfills or ponds *surface impoundments)*, sometimes being spread or piled on the land; some is sent to off-site landfills or to waste water treatment plants; a good deal, some of it quite illegally, continues to be discharged directly into nearby surface waters.

Some individuals and organizations, of course, solve their waste-disposal problems by dumping their waste on land or at sea regardless of any law. It is these unauthorized dumpings that have given us some of the worst environmental hazards, especially when hazardous waste is involved. They have also been responsible for the widespread fouling of our COASTS, as municipal, medical, and industrial waste washes up on our shores.

Underlying all approaches to waste disposal, however, is the need for *source reduction*—simply lessening the amount of material that finds its way into the *waste stream*. This is very much a problem of affluent societies, since poorer countries tend to regard as reusable and even precious some items routinely thrown away in rich nations. A classic example is the yard waste (leaves, grass clip-

pings, and the like) that forms over 20 percent of the waste in the United States; this can be, and many places is used in COMPOSTING or less formally retained to return nutrients to the land, rather than wasting resources of all kinds in its disposal. Similarly, many products are overpackaged and the packages then wastefully disposed of, rather than being recycled in a formal way or reused in an innovative, informal way. Considerable environmental pressure is being exerted to cut down on packaging and to make it more recyclable. (See WASTE DISPOSAL INFORMATION AND ACTION GUIDES on page 325; also TOXIC CHEMICALS; HAZARDOUS WASTE; RECYCLING; INCINERATION; PLASTICS; SLUDGE.)

**water cycle (hydrological cycle),** the circulation of water from OCEANS to air to ground and underground and then back to the oceans again. From the surface of the earth's waters—about 85 percent from the oceans, the rest from RIVERS, LAKES, and WETLANDS—water evaporates into the air, is carried by the wind for tens or even hundreds of miles, and then returns to the earth's surface as precipitation. Of this, some is used by plants, in the life-sustaining process of PHOTOSYNTHESIS, of which part is quickly returned to the air; some falls on the surface and runs off into river systems; some percolates through the soil into groundwater, only later joining surface water in running back into the oceans, completing the cycle; and the majority simply returns directly to the oceans, which cover over 70 percent of the earth. At any one time, over 97 percent of the earth's water is found in the oceans, with the rest as either ice, water vapor, or freshwater.

Like the other main BIOGEOCHEMICAL CYCLES, the water cycle is vital for life, being required by plants in the process of PHOTOTSYNTHESIS and also directly by animals. Water's unparalleled ability to dissolve substances also makes it vital as a supplier of essential minerals, though making it also highly vulnerable to POLLUTION. Looking at the earth as a whole, the water cycle evens out, with the amount of precipitation—estimated to average about 34 inches a year—balanced by the amount of evaporation. However, parts of the earth are involved in the cycle in very different ways and proportions, with an arid area having extremely little evaporation or precipitation, and a tropical rain FOREST having a great deal of both.

Though the overall global balance will not be affected, human activities can alter the precise pattern of the water cycle in any particular area; for example, DEFORESTATION can lead to increased runoff of water, with less being available for human use. Similarly, CLIMATE CHANGE can affect the pattern of precipitation in an area, and more widely can affect the amount of water in the oceans as compared to the land, as when SEA LEVEL RISE follows GLOBAL WARMING. (See BIOGEOCHEMICAL CYCLES; WATER RESOURCES.)

**water pollution,** the presence of unwanted substances in water beyond levels acceptable for health or aesthetics. These may include organic (living or once-living) matter, HEAVY METALS, minerals (some desirable), sediment, bacteria, and viruses, as well as newer kinds of pollutants, especially TOXIC CHEMICALS such as PESTICIDES, SYNTHETIC ORGANIC CHEMICALS, and VOLATILE ORGANIC COMPOUNDS. Water is never "pure," but always contains some other substances. (For a description of pure water, as well as soft, hard, brackish, and brine, see WATER RESOURCES.) What needs to be determined is at what level the various substances pose a threat to human or environmental health or offend human standards of acceptability. That is not a question individuals are well-equipped to answer, and governments generally have the responsibility for defining *maximum contaminant levels* (MCLs) for pollutants.

In the United States, MCLs for drinking water are set under the SAFE DRINKING WATER ACT (SDWA). Those MCLs most important to health are called PRIMARY DRINKING WATER STANDARDS (see page 274). Other standards relate more to aesthetics, including characteristics such as color, taste, odor, hardness, salinity, PH, and turbidity (murkiness); these are covered by SECONDARY DRINKING WATER STANDARDS (see page 276). However, the number of different and new contaminants released into our water systems has grown far faster than the ability of government or citizens' groups to keep up with them. There are, in fact, hundreds of pollutants now found in drinking water, but as of 1991 only 60 of them were regulated by the SDWA; For many of them, tests are never done and may not even exist. Even the nature of some pollutants (especially secondary compounds, formed by the reaction of multiple chemicals in water) is unknown.

Some contaminants come from natural sources, including salts and minerals from the ground and RADON gas, but human activities are responsible for the increasing presence of these and many other contaminants in water. Among the major sources of water pollution are:

• MINING **and drilling** for OIL or NATURAL GAS, which re-

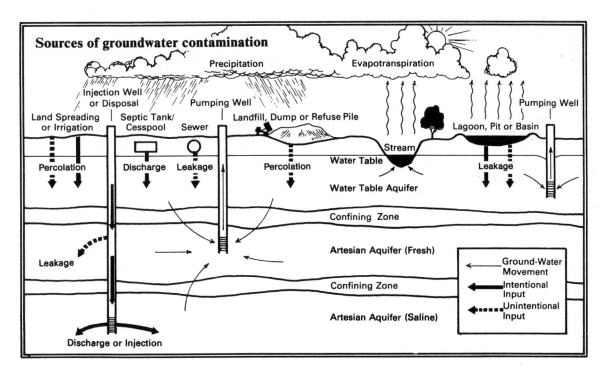

**Source:** Environmental Protection Agency.

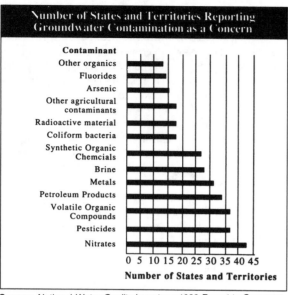

**Number of States and Territories Reporting Groundwater Contamination as a Concern**

Contaminant

- Other organics
- Fluorides
- Arsenic
- Other agricultural contaminants
- Radioactive material
- Coliform bacteria
- Synthetic Organic Chemcials
- Brine
- Metals
- Petroleum Products
- Volatile Organic Compounds
- Pesticides
- Nitrates

0 5 10 15 20 25 30 35 40 45
**Number of States and Territories**

**Source:** *National Water Quality Inventory: 1988 Report to Congress.* Environmental Protection Agency, 1990.

leases heavy metals and sometimes radioactive matter into the environment and causes acidity, EROSION, and resulting SEDIMENTATION; oil drilling in some places also produces a salty brine, which pollutes surface and groundwaters. Construction causes some of the same problems. Much waste is totally unregulated.

- **agriculture and forestry,** especially where pesticides are used, which then leach into the groundwater, and where practices encourage erosion and sedimentation. These *non-point sources* are so far little regulated, though in the United States they are expected to be targeted by the scheduled revisions of the CLEAN WATER ACT. Factory farms (see FACTORY FARMING) are also major sources of pollution, from the large and concentrated amounts of animal waste they produce.
- **municipal, governmental, and industrial waste,** in landfills, dumps, deep injection wells, ponds called *surface impoundments*, and LEAKING UNDERGROUND STORAGE TANKS (see WASTE DISPOSAL; HAZARDOUS WASTE). From such sources, pollutants—many from hazardous waste or RADIOACTIVE WASTE sites—leach into the ground, often contaminating surface and groundwater, including the vital underground reservoirs called AQUIFERS. These are *point sources*, which have been the main focus of the Clean Water Act; this has had notable effects on biological pollutants, though the amount and toxicity of the chemical pollutants has outstripped many efforts to control them.
- **water and sewage treatment plants,** which help reduce

water pollution but can add contaminants of their own (see below).

- **household products** improperly disposed of, such as cleaners, automotive oil and antifreeze, batteries, paint removers and solvents, and lawn and garden products, especially pesticides. Some of these reach the water supply through septic tanks or cesspools.

Those pollutants classified as hazardous waste or pesticides have come under increasing regulation, under laws such as the RESOURCE CONSERVATION AND RECOVERY ACT (RCRA), the COMPREHENSIVE ENVIRONMENTAL RESPONSE, COMPENSATION, AND LIABILITY ACT (CERCLA) and its related SUPERFUND amendments, and the FEDERAL INSECTICIDE, FUNGICIDE, AND RODENTICIDE ACT (FIFRA). Also, some state and local governments have put into place more stringent measures to protect their water supplies from pollution.

In many parts of the world, people drink water as it comes to them, from wells, RIVERS, LAKES, and the like even when those same sources are used for bathing, washing, and FISHING, and by animals, as well. Untested and untreated water is, in fact, a major human and environmental health problem in many parts of the world, and regions with substantial water pollution also generally have high infant and adult mortality rates. Even in affluent countries, many small, private systems receive little or no treatment or testing; these include *noncommunity* systems, defined under the SDWA as those providing services for less than a year, such as campgrounds, but also including some schools. Many environmentalists have protested such exclusions and urge widening of testing and treatment.

People using uncovered systems—in the United States including the approximately 40 million people served by private wells—may need to arrange for private testing. This can often be done for a nominal fee through the state, county, or local department of public health, state department of environmental resources, or state university laboratories, or by private laboratories for more variable fees. CONCERN, Inc., in their Community Action Guide *Drinking Water*, suggests obtaining a copy of the state drinking water standards as a guide and testing at least once a year for bacteria and NITRATES, and less frequently (except when problems are suspected) for other kinds of contaminants, depending on the area; iron, MANGANESE, and ALUMINUM would be tested for in mining areas, for example, as would commonly used pesticides in agricultural areas.

Even for larger water systems, serving communities year-round, frequency of testing varies widely. Under the

SDWA, for example, community water systems serving more than 4.7 million people are tested for bacteria with 500 samples per month; however, systems serving 25 to 1,000 people are required to be tested for bacteria only once a month. Community systems using groundwater are required to test for inorganic chemicals once every three years but are not required to test for organic chemicals under federal law (though some states require such testing), except for trihalomethanes (THMs), formed when organic matter in the water reacts with chlorine used as a disinfectant. Whatever the size, systems also generally test for turbidity, the cloudiness caused by large amounts of silt, clay, or other particles; the hazard is that, in large numbers, these particles can hamper disinfection and allow disease-causing bacteria to survive.

Treatment systems vary widely, but an overview of standard water treatment in large supply systems would include these steps:

- **coagulation,** using chemicals to create small jellylike particles called *floc*, which collect dirt and other solids suspended in the water.
- **flocculation,** gentle mixing of the water so floc particles clump together.
- **settling,** slowing the larger floc particles and sediment so they fall to the bottom, creating SLUDGE.
- **filtration,** passing water through a granular medium, such as sand or crushed hard COAL.
- **disinfection,** various processes to kill potentially disease-causing bacteria and other microorganisms. Generally this is done by adding chlorine (see CHLORINATION), though trihalomethanes are sometimes formed. Alternatives that do not form THMs, but are somewhat less convenient and more expensive, are using OZONE, ultraviolet light (see RADIATION), chlorine dioxide, or chloramines.
- **corrosion control,** the addition of chemicals (such as quicklime) to reduce the water's acidity, to prevent corrosion in water pipes and consequent additions of metals to the water.
- **fluoridation,** the addition of fluoride, to help prevent tooth decay. Though commonly used in water-treatment facilities and credited with the great increase in dental health, some questions continue to be raised about adverse effects, including an arthritislike disorder from excess fluorine and questions about possible links to cancer.

Where appropriate, other procedures may be used to rid water supplies of synthetic organic compounds (SOCs), volatile organic compounds (VOCs), and inorganic chemicals, often at the stage after sand filtration, such as:

- **granular activated carbon (GAC),** beds of carbon substances such as coal or coke, through which water is passed. This removes many SOCs and most VOCs, except vinyl chloride, and also improves taste and odor.
- **aeration,** in which air is passed through water, or droplets of water are forced through air, so VOCs will evaporate and be removed. The most effective type of aeration is *packed tower aeration*, in which water is pumped into the top of a tower, to flow through packing material, while air comes up through the material. This process also removes some inorganic chemicals. The process must be carefully managed so that it does not then release toxic EMISSIONS into the air.

These and other approaches may also help to reduce trihalomethanes in the water.

People whose water supply is not being treated, or is being inadequately tested and treated, must treat the water themselves, either at the *point of entry*, where it enters the house, or the *point of use*, at the faucet used for drinking and cooking water. No single home water-treatment device treats all sorts of pollution problems; it must be selected to deal with specific problems. Consumers should note that home treatment devices are not at present tested or regulated by the federal government, nor do such branches as the ENVIRONMENTAL PROTECTION AGENCY (EPA) recommend any. In addition, those chosen must be installed, monitored, changed, and maintained very carefully, if they are to work effectively. That said, the main types of devices used for home water treatment are:

- **activated carbon filters,** which are designed to remove organic contaminants, not bacteria or inorganic chemicals, and in fact may provide a bacteria breeding ground and so are recommended only where water has already been disinfected. Under-the-counter models with solid carbon blocks are more effective than those used at the faucet, but both are better than those using granular carbon and powdered carbon. All must be changed frequently, as their contaminant-holding capacity is limited.
- **reverse osmosis systems,** in which water is forced by tap pressure through a cellophanelike membrane; it is most effective at removing inorganic chemicals, such as LEAD or NITRATE'S, and needs the filter changed regularly. It may be combined with a presediment filter and a carbon filter to also remove organic chemicals and generally improve taste and odor. Systems range from counter-top models to house-wide systems, costing several hundred dollars to over a thousand dollars. Reverse osmosis units are also enormous water-wasters, with 75 to 90 percent of the water they process going down the drain and only 10 to 25 percent filtered for use.

## Water Pollution Information and Action Guide

**For more information and action on water pollution:**

**Alternative Farming Systems Information Center,** (301-344-3724 or 344-3559). Provides Quick Bibliography *Ground Water Contamination* (H. Gilbert, 1990). (See ORGANIC FARMING AND SUSTAINABLE AGRICULTURE INFORMATION AND ACTION GUIDE on page 226.)

**AMERICAN WATER RESOURCES ASSOCIATION (AWRA),** (301-493-8600). Publishes *Aquatic Organisms as Indicators of Environmental Pollution* (Joan A. Browder, ed., 1988).

**Chesapeake Bay Foundation (CBF),** (301-268-8816). Publishes *Your Boat and the Bay* and *Septic Systems and the Bay.* (See CHESAPEAKE BAY.)

**CLEAN WATER ACTION,** (202-457-1286).

**CONSERVATION FOUNDATION,** (202-293-4800).

**CONSERVATION FUND, The** (703-525-6300). Sponsors the *Spring and Groundwater Resources Institute.*

**ENVIRONMENTAL AND ENERGY STUDY INSTITUTE (EESI),** (202-628-1400). Publishes *Farm Policies to Protect Groundwater: A Midwestern Perspective* (1990) and *Groundwater Protection and the 1990 Farm Bill* (1990).

**ENVIRONMENTAL DEFENSE FUND (EDF),** (212-505-2100). Publishes *Polluted Coastal Waters: The Role of Acid Rain* (D. Fisher et al., 1988).

**ENVIRONMENTAL HAZARDS MANAGEMENT INSTITUTE (EHMI),** (603-868-1496). Publishes a useful "water sense wheel."

**ENVIRONMENTAL LAW INSTITUTE (ELI),** (202-328-5150). (See ENVIRONMENTAL LAW.)

**ENVIRONMENTAL PROTECTION AGENCY (EPA)** Public Information Center, 202-260-7751 or 202-260-2080). Operates *Safe Drinking Water Hotline,* (202-382-5533 or toll-free (outside DC), 800-428-4791).

**FRESHWATER FOUNDATION,** (612-449-0092). Publishes *Nitrates and Groundwater: A Public Health Concern, Waste Is a Water Problem: What You Can Do About Solid Waste, Water Filters: Their Effect on Water Quality, Hazardous Waste in Our Home—and in Our Water,* and *Understanding Your Septic System.*

**FRIENDS OF THE EARTH (FOE),** (202-544-2600). Publishes *Bottled Water; Sparkling Hype at a Premium Price* (Sandra Marquardt, 1989).

**GREENPEACE, (202-462-1177).** Greenpeace Action runs the *Ocean Ecology Campaign,* and the *Toxics Campaign,* which publishes *We All Live Downstream: The Mississippi River and the National Toxics Crisis* (1989), *Water for Life: The Tour of the Great Lakes* (1989), and *Mortality and Toxics Along the Mississippi River* (1988). Greenpeace also publishes Action Factsheets and videocassettes.

**HUMAN ECOLOGY ACTION LEAGUE (HEAL),** (404-248-1898). Publishes *Water Testing* and *Water Treatment.*

**INTERNATIONAL COUNCIL FOR THE EXPLORATION OF THE SEA or Counseil International pour l'Exploration de la Mer (ICES OR CIEM)** (Copenhagen K, Denmark: 33 15 42 25).

**IZAAK WALTON LEAGUE OF AMERICA (IWLA),** (703-528-1818).

**KIDS FOR SAVING EARTH™ (KSE),** (612-525-0002 or 800-800-8800).

**National Coalition Against Misuse of Pesticides (NCAMP),** (202-543-5450). Publishes *The Great American Water Debate* (See PESTIDES INFORMATION AND ACTION GUIDE on page 238.)

**NATIONAL ENVIRONMENTAL HEALTH ORGANIZATION (NEHA)** (303-756-9090). Publishes *Groundwater Quality Protection, Groundwater Contamination: Sources, Control and Preventive Measures, On Site Wastewater Disposal, Septic Tank System Effects on Groundwater Quality, Groundwater Pollution Control* and *Drinking Water Health Advisories—Pesticides.*

---

- **distillers,** which remove bacteria and inorganic compounds, including heavy metals, minerals, and salts; they are much less effective at removing organic chemicals, including pesticides, and so are often used with carbon filters. Distillers vary widely, but all need regular cleaning.

Consumers are advised to test their water independently, if they have suspicions or questions about its quality, and to select one or a combination of these or other systems to meet their particular needs. Service contracts are recommended, since all such systems require regular service.

Where consumers consider their water supply dangerous or questionable, many buy bottled water for drinking and sometimes cooking as well. They may not be getting what they bargained for, however. Bottled water is regulated not by the EPA, but by the Food and Drug Administration (FDA). For all the talk about "mountain springs" and the like, some 25 percent of bottled waters from the United States use community water systems as their water source. The rest draw from groundwater sources, but FDA regulations specify only that the source be "protected," not that it be identified. In the United States, water not already chlorinated is disinfected with ozone, often has minerals removed, and is sometimes distilled. Domestic bottling facilities are regulated like food plants, while imported bottled water is tested only at random on entry. In general, FDA testing on bottled water covers fewer contaminants, tests less often, and has less stringent certification and reporting requirements for laboratories and bottlers than

NATIONAL PARKS AND CONSERVATION ASSOCIATION (NPCA), (202-944-8530).

NATIONAL WILDLIFE FEDERATION (NWF), (202-797-6800 or 800-245-5484) Publishes *An Environmental Agenda for Clean Water: Prevent, Protect and Enforce.*

NATURAL RESOURCES AND ENERGY DIVISION (NRED), UNITED NATIONS, (212-963-6205).

NATURAL RESOURCES DEFENSE COUNCIL (NRDC), (212-727-2700). Publishers *Ebb Tide for Pollution: Actions for Cleaning Up Coastal Waters* (1989) and *Poison Runoff: A Guide to State and Local Control of Nonpoint Source Water Pollution* (Paul Thompson et al., 1989).

NORTH AMERICAN LAKE MANAGEMENT SOCIETY (NALMS), (202-466-8550). Publishes the bimonthly magazine *Lake Line*, the bimonthly journal *Lake and Reservoir Management*, books, reports, and videos.

RESOURCES FOR THE FUTURE (RFF), (202-328-5000).

SIERRA CLUB, (415-776-2211 or 202-547-1141; legislative hotline, 202-547-5550). Publishes the *Hazardous Materials/ Water Resources Newsletter* and *Water Policy.*

UNITED NATIONS DEVELOPMENT PROGRAMME (UNDP), (212-906-5000). Publishes *Safe Water 2000.*

UNITED NATIONS ENVIRONMENT PROGRAMME (UNEP), (212-963-8139). Publishes *International Conventions on the Prevention of Marine Pollution: Coastal Strategies* (M. Nauke, 1991) and *Assessment of Freshwater Quality* (Global Environmental Monitoring System [GEMS] and World Health Organization [WHO], 1988).

U.S. PUBLIC INTEREST RESEARCH GROUP (PIRG), (202-546-9707). Publishes *Permit to Pollute: Violations of the Clean Water Act by the Nation's Largest Facilities* (1991).

WATER ENVIRONMENT FEDERATION (WEF), (703-684-2400 or 800-666-0206). Sponsors an annual conference on water quality and pollution control technology and issues; provides administrative support for *Water Quality 2000.* For the general public it publishes a Water Environment Curriculum with videos and student and teacher guides for grades 5–9, including *Surface Water Unit, The Groundwater Video Adventure, The Wastewater Treatment Video,* and *Saving Water— The Conservation Unit*; the video *Careers in Water Quality* for high school students; and brochures such as *Let's Save the Environment, Clean Water: A Bargain At Any Cost, Nature's Way: How Wastewater Treatment Works For You, Groundwater: Why You Should Care, Nature Recycles Water . . . We Can Too, Clean Water For Today: What Is Wastewater Treatment?* and *Stop Water Pollution!* It also publishes numerous technical works and materials for wastewater professionals.

WORLD BANK, (202-477-1234). Publishes *Environmental Health Components for Water Supply, Sanitation, and Urban Projects, Wastewater Management for Coastal Cities: The Ocean Disposal Option, Water Pollution Control: Guidelines for Project Planning and Financing,* and *Wastewater Irrigation in Developing Countries: Health Effects and Technical Solutions.*

**Other references:**

*Practical Handbook of Ground-Water Monitoring.* David M. Nielsen, ed. Lewis, 1991. *Surveillance of Drinking Water Quality in Rural Areas.* Barry Lloyd and Richard Helmer. Wiley, 1991. *Drinking Water Quality: Standards and Controls.* John De Zuane. Van Nostrand Reinhold, 1990. *Global Freshwater Quality: A First Assessment.* Michel Meybeck et al., eds. Blackwell Reference (Oxford, U.K.), 1990.

(See also CHLORINATION; WATER RESOURCES; HEAVY METALS; ACID RAIN; TOXIC CHEMICALS; HAZARDOUS WASTE; WASTE DISPOSAL).

---

the EPA does for community water under SDWA, so bottled water does not necessarily meet federal drinking water standards. Also, mineral water, soda, seltzer, and flavored water are ill-defined, if at all, and exempted from meeting maximum containment level (MCL) standards. In addition, some volatile organic compounds, such as benzene and toluene, can get into the water during the bottling process. Consumers who use bottled water may wish to seek those brands that provide guarantees that they meet federal EPA water quality standards.

While the greatest attention is focused on drinking water, environmentalists are also concerned that wastewater—all the water from a community's domestic, commercial, and industrial use—be treated in such a way that it also does not pollute the environment. In water or on land,

waste is decomposed and broken down in natural BIOGEOCHEMICAL CYCLES, by decomposers such as bacteria that return nutrients to the ground. This process uses bacteria, so one widespread measure of water pollution is *biological* (or *biochemical*) *oxygen demand* (BOD)—the amount of oxygen that bacteria will use in consuming the waste in wastewater. If the BOD is too high, the bacteria will use up most or all of the oxygen in the water, leaving none for plants and animals; this process is called EUTROPHICATION. A major aim of wastewater treatment is to lessen the BOD and to remove from the water any substances that cannot be consumed by bacteria and that might be harmful to the environment, such as pesticides and heavy metals. In addition, wastewater must be disinfected, to kill disease-causing microorganisms (*pathogens*).

Wastewater is carried to treatment plants by a network of pipes. Those that carry only domestic, industrial, and commercial wastewater are called *sanitary sewers*, while those that also carry stormwater runoff are called *combined sewers*. Where possible, stormwater is kept separate, since during heavy rains the large amounts of water can disrupt the wastewater plant's operations and make treatment less effective. Wastewater, whether from municipal or industrial sources, is sent to treatment plants, where solids are separated from the liquid; both are treated to destroy harmful bacteria and reduce odor, the end result ideally being water that is cleansed and purified for reintroduction into the environment and sludge, a nutrient-rich organic product with wide uses. More precisely, wastewater is first screened and then allowed to settle, so that suspended solids either drop to the bottom or float to the top, where they can be removed. The remaining wastewater goes to an aeration tank, where air encourages growth of bacteria and other microorganisms that consume the waste; more solids are removed, and the remaining water is then disinfected, generally by CHLORINATION, and then released into the environment.

Some industrial installations—those that produce pollutants designated as *incompatible* with standard treatments—are not allowed to feed their waste into such *publicly owned treatment works* (POTWs), but must make their own arrangements for treating their wastewater. In the United States, under the Clean Water Act, such plants must operate either a private treatment plant to treat water for release in the environment or a *pretreatment plant* designed to remove unacceptable substances from the wastewater before it is fed into the public treatment plant, often paying a fee for use of public facilities.

But beyond testing and treatment, citizens are concerned about preventing water pollution from occurring and worsening. Many of the laws noted above and the agencies charged with administering them are aimed at doing just that. In the United States, over 3,000 soil and water conservation districts operate under local management, with advice and counsel from the SOIL CONSERVATION SERVICE, often mapping water sources, especially AQUIFERS vulnerable to pollution. Localities use this information as the basis for LAND USE decisions to protect the water. These may include decisions on siting WASTE DISPOSAL facilities and wastewater treatment plants; controlling the rate of DEVELOPMENT, including the number of septic tanks built in growing areas; protecting sensitive areas by CONSERVATION EASEMENTS and LAND TRUSTS, as from heavy use of pesticides and chemical fertilizers on farms; planning for retention or channeling of urban runoff; and developing regional approaches to protecting watershed areas. In addi-

tion, they focus considerable attention on hazardous chemicals manufacturing and disposal sites, restricting and closely monitoring underground storage tanks, and arranging for collection and RECYCLING or treatment of household hazardous waste.

The problem is that everything, sooner or later, ends up in the water system. The OCEANS have so far shown considerable capacity for absorbing pollution, but rivers, lakes, and coastal waters have been under enormous environmental stress. The only sure way to ease that stress is at the source: by reducing and eliminating sources of pollution affecting our vital water supplies. (See WATER POLLUTION INFORMATION AND ACTION GUIDE on page 330; also WATER RESOURCES; OCEANS; LAKES; COASTS; RIVERS.)

**Water Environment Federation (WEF)** (601 Wythe Street, Alexandria, VA 22314; 703-684-2400; for membership information and orders: 800-666-0206; Quincalee Brown, Executive Director), an international professional membership organization of water-quality experts, more precisely a federation of over 70 member associations around the world, its aim being ''the preservation and enhancement of water quality worldwide; until recently called the *Water Pollution Control Federation (WPCF)*. WEF was founded in 1928 as the Federation of Sewage Works Association, publishing the *Sewage Works Journal*, and is still a key organization in wastewater services, but now ''provides technical services and educational resources to members, the government, and the general public'' on a much broader range of water-quality issues. It has various technical committees, including Nonpoint Source Pollution, Groundwater, Collections Systems, and Technical Practice, as well as the WEF Research Foundation, and also provides administrative support for *Water Quality 2000*, a cooperative effort with dozens of other environmental, scientific, professional, and government organizations.

WEF sponsors an annual conference on water quality and POLLUTION-control technology and issues; specialty conferences on topics such as toxicity, landfills, and surface water quality; periodic Washington briefings, bringing together government officials and water-quality experts to discuss current trends and issues; and a Pacific Rim Conference focusing on environmental problems in countries around the Pacific. It also maintains an on-line computer service and publishes many other materials, including periodicals such as the monthly *Water Environment and Technology*, the bimonthly *Research Journal of the Water Pollution Control Federation*, and the monthly *Operations Forum* for wastewater operations professionals, and specialized newsletters for professionals, including the *Safety and Health Bulletin*, and the *Washington Bulletin* on water-quality regulation and legislation.

WEF provides continuing education training programs workshops, and seminars, publishing audiovisual courses and study guides (often developed with other organizations), and also distributes "Safety and health videos provided by municipalities involved in water pollution control." Among its numerous professional publications are Manuals of Practice (MOPs), technical publications, and reference works. Among its publications for the general public are a Water Environment Curriculum with videos and student and teacher guides for grades 5 to 9, children's coloring book *Let's Save Water*, slide shows, videos, films, and brochures, such as *Let's Save the Environment* and *Clean Water: A Bargain At Any Cost*.

**water resources,** all of the waters in, on, or around earth, in whatever form—in liquids as in LAKES, RIVERS, OCEANS, or underground in AQUIFERS; in gases, as in the atmosphere; or in solids, in the form of ice and snow. In the widest sense, the earth's water resources are inexhaustible, for water is in, above, below, and all around us (see WATER CYCLE), with water covering 70 percent of the earth's surface. However, most of that—over 97 percent of all the water on earth—is salt water in the oceans, unavailable for most land uses without DESALINIZATION, which is impractically expensive on a large scale in most areas of the world. As it is, most humans and other land-based life must make do with freshwater that makes up under 3 percent of the earth's water—in fact, far less than that, since nearly three-quarters of that is tied up in polar or glacial ice. Even this small percentage would be sufficient to serve the needs of life on earth—except not that it is often not available when and where it is needed.

"Pure" freshwater ($H_2O$) is made up of molecules having two hydrogen and one oxygen atom each. But because water is a nearly universal solvent, pure water does not exist in the real world. In fact, its ability to dissolve substances is actually essential to all plant and animal life, especially in providing the elements needed for the energy-fixing, life-sustaining process of PHOTOSYNTHESIS. Water is more properly seen as a solution, with a composition that varies with the qualities of the air, soil, and rock it has traveled through—and also with the nature and types of pollutants introduced into it. It is an essential part of earth's great BIOGEOCHEMICAL CYCLES, and participates in its own crucial water cycle. Some of the most common substances naturally found in water are calcium, magnesium, sodium, potassium, bicarbonate, chloride, sulfate, and dissolved CARBON DIOXIDE and oxygen. Freshwater is distinguished by its relatively low content of dissolved

minerals, in general under 1,000 parts per million (ppm) of total dissolved solids (TDS), though 500 ppm is generally the target for drinking water. "Soft" freshwater has markedly less dissolved calcium and magnesium than "hard" freshwater. By contrast, seawater has 10,000 to 36,000 ppm TDS, with over 75 percent of that (by weight) being sodium chloride (NaCl); water between 1,000 to 10,000 ppm TDS is termed *brackish*, such as water in MANGROVES or tidal areas; while water above 36,000 ppm TDS is labeled *brine*, such as the concentrated solution left after the process of desalinization or from MINING waste.

In addition to the water in the atmosphere, freshwater available for use by humans and other life exists either as surface water or groundwater. Surface water is the runoff draining from the highest points through springs, lakes, streams, and rivers to the lowest points, at sea level, where it feeds into the oceans, the whole area drained being called the *watershed*. Groundwater is freshwater that percolates into the ground, and is trapped and held for a time in soil-and-rock systems called AQUIFERS; when the aquifers are confined between two layers and therefore under pressure, they are called ARTESIAN SYSTEMS. Making up most of the freshwater available for use, groundwater is the source of wells and springs, and its underground flow and continual dissolving action helps create CAVES, which remain important storage places for subsurface water. During dry periods, such as the summer or drought years, groundwater gradually drains out of the soil and rocks and into streams, and the water table—the "ceiling" of the water-saturated zone—drops.

Through the mechanism of the water cycle, groundwater resources are continually being replenished or "recharged," with the "renewal period" for rivers being about 12 to 20 days, while that for groundwater is more in the range of 280 days. However, if the groundwater is used faster than it is recharged, the aquifer gradually begins to decline, a process variously called *water mining*, *drawing down*, or *overdraft*. If this situation persists, groundwater changes from a RENEWABLE RESOURCE into a DECLINING RESOURCE, with potentially grave long-term consequences for the region. Over-extraction of water can lead to subsidence of lands, including shifts that can damage roads, bridges, and buildings; dramatic sinkhole collapses; and in coastal areas localized SEA LEVEL RISE, at the same time often introducing ground-based contamination into normally protected aquifers. Subsidence generally causes so much contraction in the volume of the aquifer that it can never regain its former water-holding capacity, even if it is recharged. Renewal periods are also important when considering contamination, since pollutants in groundwater tend to persist and have far wider effects than

## Water Resources Information and Action Guide

**For more information and action about water resources:**
**Alternative Farming Systems Information Center,** (301-344-3724 or 344-3559). Provides the quick bibliography *Ground Water Contamination* (H. Gilbert, 1990). (See ORGANIC FARMING AND SUSTAINABLE AGRICULTURE INFORMATION AND ACTION GUIDE on page 226.)
**AMERICAN PLANNING ASSOCIATION (APA),** (202-872-0611). Publishes *Protecting Nontidal Wetlands* (David G. Burke et al., 1989), and bibliography *Groundwater Quality: Trends Toward Regional Management* (1988).
**AMERICAN WATER RESOURCES ASSOCIATION (AWRA),** (301-493-8600). Publishes *Redefining National Water Policy: New Roles and Directions* (Stephen M. Born, ed., 1989), *Water Management in the 21st Century* (A. Ivan Johnson and Warren Viessman, Jr., eds., 1989) and *Water: Laws and Management* (Frederick E. David, ed., 1989), and a series of Regional Aquifer System Analysis (RASA) Program Studies with the U.S. Geological Survey (see AQUIFERS).
**CENTRE FOR SCIENCE AND TECHNOLOGY FOR DEVELOPMENT (CSTD), UNITED NATIONS,** (212-963-8435).
**Chesapeake Bay Foundation (CBF),** (301-268-8816). Publishes *Water Conservation: Wasted Water Means Wastewater.* (See CHESAPEAKE BAY.)
**CLEAN WATER ACTION** (202-459-1286).
**CONCERN, INC.,** (202-328-8160). Publishes *Groundwater: A Community Action Guide* and *Drinking Water: A Community Action Guide.*
**CONSERVATION FOUNDATION,** (202-293-4800).
**CONSERVATION FUND, THE,** (703-525-6300). Sponsors the *Spring and Groundwater Resources Institute.*
**ENVIRONMENTAL AND ENERGY STUDY INSTITUTE (EESI),** (202-628-1400). Publishes *Groundwater Protection and the 1990 Farm Bill* (1990).
**ENVIRONMENTAL HAZARDS MANAGEMENT INSTITUTE (EHMI),** (603-868-1496). Publishes useful "wheel" on water.
**ENVIRONMENTAL LAW INSTITUTE (ELI),** (202-328-5150); publications office: 202-939-3844). Publishes *Clean Water Desk-book* (rev. ed., 1991). (See ENVIRONMENTAL LAW INFORMATION AND ACTION GUIDE on page 116.)
**ENVIRONMENTAL PROTECTION AGENCY (EPA),** (Public Information Center, 202-260-7751 or 202-260-2080). Operates *Safe Drinking Water Hotline* (202-382-5533 or toll-free (outside DC), 800-428-4791.
**FRESHWATER FOUNDATION,** (612-449-0092). Publishes *Freshwater Journal, Facets of Freshwater Newsletter, U.S. Water News, Watershed Management: A Community Commitment,* and *Groundwater: Understanding Our Hidden Resource.*
**FRIENDS OF THE EARTH (FOE),** (202-544-2600). Publishes *Groundwater Newsletter* and *Bottled Water: Sparkling Hype at a Premium Price* (Sandra Marquardt, 1989).
**FRIENDS OF THE RIVER (FOR),** (415-771-0400). Conducts *Water Policy Reform* campaign, and *Hydromania and Watershed Protection* campaign.
**INFORM, INC.,** (212-689-4040). Publishes model international agreements concerning aquifers and reports such as *Winning with Water: Soil-Moisture Monitoring for Efficient Irrigation* (Gail Richardson and Peter Mueller-Beilschmidt, 1988).
**INTERNATIONAL CENTER FOR ARID AND SEMIARID LAND STUDIES (ICASALS),** (806-742-2218). Publishes *Making Rain in America: A History.*
**INTERNATIONAL TRANSBOUNDARY RESOURCES CENTER (Centro Internacional de Recursos Transfronterizos,** or *CIRT),* (505-277-6424).
**IZAAK WALTON LEAGUE OF AMERICA (IWLA),** (703-528-1818).
**KIDS FOR SAVING EARTH™ (KSE),** (612-525-0002 or 800-800-8800).
**NATIONAL WATER RESOURCES ASSOCIATION (NWRA)** (3800 North Fairfax Drive, Suite #4, Arlington, VA 22203; 703-524-1544; James W. Trull, President), an organization of associations and individuals concerned with the "optimum development and use of our water and land resources," seeking "to help achieve a critical balance in water use and the protection and preservation of the environment," its main concerns

---

when pollutants are confined to more quickly renewing rivers (see WATER POLLUTION).

On reaching the sea, freshwater mixes with the more salty seawater, at the mouths of rivers, in coastal WETLANDS, to some extent in inland subsurface waters, and during floods and powerful storms on nearby lowlands. One of the main concerns about sea-level rise is the extent to which salt water will penetrate into and contaminate coastal lands, underground water resources, and ECOSYSTEMS dependent on freshwater. Freshwater normally lies on top of salt water in aquifers; but if too much freshwater

is drawn out too quickly, the salt water will come to the top, contaminating the system, sometimes permanently. The same can happen with polluted water from other nearby sources. (Other kinds of contamination are discussed under WATER POLLUTION.)

Once it drains into the sea, water is—until the cycle comes around again—lost to land ecosystems. A number of human activities tend to speed runoff, rather than encourage retention of water in the ground. Where the land is stripped of plant cover, soil is eroded and less water is absorbed into the environment. Instead, more water runs

being "water development, conservation, flood control, power, recreation, and wastewater issues while retaining a firm commitment to cost effectiveness and wise use of available resources." NWRA's mission is "the promotion of wise water and land policies; recognition of attendant economic and ecological effects; preservation of responsibilities and rights of individuals and organizations in the encouragement of beneficial use of water; and the achievement of an equitable allocation of costs to develop, conserve and protect water and land resources for the national good." It also publishes a directory.

**NATIONAL WILDLIFE FEDERATION,** (202-797-6887). Publishes *Danger on Tap* (1988).

**NATURAL RESOURCES AND ENERGY DIVISION (NRED), UNITED NATIONS,** (212-963-6205). Publishes or distributes *Ground Water Economics* (1988) and *Water Resources Planning to Meet Long-Term Demand: Guidelines for Developing Countries* (1988).

**NATURAL RESOURCES DEFENSE COUNCIL (NRDC),** (212-727-2700).

**NORTHWEST COALITION FOR ALTERNATIVES TO PESTICIDES (NCAP),** (503-344-5044). Publishes *Every Drop Matters: A Guide to Preventing Groundwater Contamination* (Neva Hassanein and Ivy Cotler, 1989). (See PESTICIDES INFORMATION AND ACTION GUIDE on page 238.)

**Population-Environment Balance,** (202-879-3000). Publishes *Water Availability and Population Growth.* (See POPULATION INFORMATION AND ACTION GUIDE on page 248.)

**RENEW AMERICA,** (202-232-2252). Publishes focus papers *Drinking Water (1989)* and *Surface Water Protection* (1988).

**RESOURCES FOR THE FUTURE (RFF),** (202-328-5000). Includes research arms, *Energy and Natural Resources Division* and *Quality of the Environment Division.* Publishes *Markets for Federal Water: Subsidies, Property Rights, and the Bureau of Reclamation* (Richard W. Wahl, 1989).

**ROCKY MOUNTAIN INSTITUTE (RMI),** (303-927-3851) Publishes *Water Efficiency for Your Home: Products and Advice Which Save Water, Energy, and Money* (John C. Woodwell).

**SIERRA CLUB,** (415-776-2211 or 202-547-1141; legislative hotline, 202-547-5550.) Publishes the *Hazardous Materials/Water Resources Newsletter* and *Water Policy.*

**SOIL AND WATER CONSERVATION SOCIETY OF AMERICA (SWCS),** (515-289-2331 or 800-THE-SOIL [843-7645]). Publishes a bimonthly multidisciplinary *Journal of Soil and Water Conservation (JSWC)*; the bimonthly *Conservogram*; a middle-school-age computer program *Farm and Food Bytes: Soil and Water Conservation*; cartoon-style booklets and guides oriented toward school-age children, and books.

**TROUT UNLIMITED,** (703-281-1100).

**U.S. PUBLIC INTEREST RESEARCH GROUP (PIRG),** (202-546-9707).

**WATER ENVIRONMENT FEDERATION (WEF),** (703-684-2400 or 800-666-0206). Publishes a Water Environment Curriculum with videos and student and teacher guides.

**WORLD ASSOCIATION OF SOIL AND WATER CONSERVATION (WASWC),** (605-627-9309; May–October 218-864-8506).

**WORLD BANK,** (202-477-1234). Publishes *Water for Rural Communities: Helping People Help Themselves, Community Piped Water Supply Systems in Developing Countries,* and *Appropriate Technology for Water Supply and Sanitation.*

**WORLD RESOURCES INSTITUTE (WRI),** (202-638-6300).

**ZERO POPULATION GROWTH (ZPG),** (202-332-2200). Publishes *Water Wars* and *In Troubled Waters.* (See POPULATION INFORMATION AND ACTION GUIDE on page 248.)

**Other references:**

*Water Resources Planning.* Andrew A. Dzuirk. Rowman & Littlefield, 1990. *The Water Encyclopedia,* 2nd ed. Frits van der Leeden et al. Lewis, 1990. *Overtapped Oasis: Reform or Revolution for Western Water.* Marc Reisner and Sarah Bates. Island Press, 1990. *Water and the Future of the Southwest.* Zachary A. Smith, ed. University of Arizona Press, 1989. *Urban Surface Water Management.* Stuart G. Walesh. Wiley, 1989. *Troubled Waters: New Policies for Managing Water in the American West.* Mohamed T. El-Ashry and Diana C. Gibbons. Cambridge University Press, 1988. *Water Law,* 2nd ed. William Goldfarb. Lewis, 1988.

(See also RIVERS; CAVES).

---

off into river systems, increasing the likelihood of floods in areas where water is generally plentiful; the SEDIMENTATION patterns also change with more silt in the river. The highest areas of a watershed—which often have the steepest slopes and the greatest rainfall—are the most susceptible to EROSION, so it is important that forests and pastures in such areas be kept intact. Where such areas have been cleared, as by logging or OVERGRAZING, and flooding and heavy silting have resulted, environmentalists generally regard reforestation and other land recovery measures as far preferable to attempting to make

changes to the river itself, such as digging deeper channels, which may further disrupt the area. Paving, as of highways, shopping centers, and driveways, also leads to increased runoff, as water cannot penetrate the soil and be absorbed.

In areas where water is relatively scarce, different problems occur. Water sources are increasingly tapped to supply drinking water for human habitation, industry, and agriculture, often beyond the region's natural ecosystems. Where the demand is heavy enough, the surface and underground water systems become depleted, so the natural life is increasingly damaged or killed. As plants die off, the ground becomes less able to absorb water, further accelerating the drying up of the region, a process called DESERTIFICATION. When heavy erosion and desertification are combined, the result can be an extremely disruptive *drought-flood cycle*. With overuse of surface water, evaporating water may leave behind deposits of once-dissolved salts, making the land unusable for agriculture, in a process called SALINIZATION, a classic example being the ARAL SEA.

The amount of precipitation and therefore runoff varies widely, not only from region to region, but over time, with periodic droughts seeming to go in cycles, such as 2–3, 5–7, 11–13, and 22–28 years. Though there is no general agreement about the length and causes of these cycles, some suggest that drought cycles of 11–13 years are linked to changes in solar activity. Periodic shifts in climate patterns, such as the changed wind and current patterns called *El Ñino* in the Pacific, also change precipitation patterns around the world in so-far-unpredictable ways, with droughts then being found in normally rainy areas, and rain found in what are usually deserts.

Because of the variations in distribution and seasonal availability of water resources, humans have long built DAMS to store water for use as needed and to divert water from areas of plenty to those of need, as well as to control potential flood waters, to drain WETLANDS for cultivation or settlement, to supply energy (see HYDROPOWER), and increasingly to dilute polluted water. Once largely local, these have in the 20th century become massive regional dams and water transfer projects, to meet the demands of heavy DEVELOPMENT and rising POPULATION around the world. These have brought enormous benefits, but have also created enormous problems, such as destroying downstream HABITATS, changing sedimentation patterns, and disrupting the lives of INDIGENOUS PEOPLES in the area. As a result many environmentalists have been urging great care in building dams (see SAN FRANCISCO DECLARATION OF THE INTERNATIONAL RIVERS NETWORK on page 79, for example), and stressing the need for water conservation— and by reducing waste of water to lessen the need for more dams. This is especially important because the need for water is growing even faster than the mushrooming world population, given the patterns of modern life—especially because large amounts of water are being used in dealing with POLLUTION.

That being said, however, communities around the world with existing and growing populations, and agricultural, industrial, and municipal needs, are faced with supplying water to their people and environments. Many communities draw from existing surface water sources, such as lakes or rivers, often with dams or reservoirs constructed as storage areas, but many others must tap into groundwater sources, especially in relatively dry areas such as the American Southwest. In affluent areas, water is generally conveyed by open or closed conduits to water treatment plants, where it is treated to be safe and palatable (see WATER POLLUTION), and then conveyed to users by a system of pipes, using pumps to transmit water under pressure or to lift it to gravity-feed distribution reservoirs. However, in rural areas and in less-developed countries, water is often drawn as needed from community wells, often with little or no governmental monitoring of quality.

Though not free, water is still relatively inexpensive in many areas, except where high demand and low availability have combined to produce costly water storage and supply systems, as in Los Angeles. As such costs rise with even heavier demand—or if cheaper, renewable ALTERNATIVE ENERGY sources are developed—the techniques of DESALINIZATION will become more economical, and those countries on or near the oceans will have available a far larger, inexhaustible supply of water. (See WATER RESOURCES INFORMATION AND ACTION GUIDE on page 334; see also AQUIFERS; LAKES; RIVERS; OCEANS; WATER POLLUTION).

**wave power,** energy from the motion of sea waves, which can be used to generate electricity and so harnessed for human use. Wave power has long attracted researchers, but experimental projects have had little governmental support, except during a brief period following the 1970's energy crisis. This is partly because of fears that wave energy installations will be expensive, large, obstructive to ships, and vulnerable to storm damage.

Some approaches are designed for use on the shore, acting as an energy-generating breakwater, such as Britain's first wave-power station, which opened on the island of Islay in 1991. This station uses an air chamber, closed except to the sea, operating something like a piston. As waves surge into the chamber, air is pushed through turbines, generating electricity; as they recede, air is sucked back into the chamber, also used to turn turbines.

Other wave power approaches are designed to be established offshore. Among these is a ''circular clam,'' formed of a series of air bags linked in a circle; as waves strike, they squeeze air from the air bags through turbines. The ''solo duck'' is an offshore device that generates electricity by bobbing up and down, as does the Salter Duck system, which uses a battery of smaller bobbing devices to the same end.

Another form of ocean energy is *tidal power*, which

uses the rise and fall of the tide in bays and estuaries. A DAM is built across the bay and filled by the rising tide, then closed when the tide ebbs; then the water is released, turning turbines to generate electricity. In some installations, water is used to turn turbines with both rise and fall of the tide. However, such installations share the defects of other dams in disruption of delicate coastal life and increases in SEDIMENTATION.

The durability and cost-competitieness of these and other ocean energy approaches are yet to be determined. Certainly, the initial capital outlay is considerable. But as costs for traditional FOSSIL FUELS rise, along with concern about resulting POLLUTION, wave and tidal energy approaches may become increasingly attractive.

**For more information or action:**
CONSERVATION AND RENEWABLE ENERGY INQUIRY AND REFERRAL SERVICE (CAREIRS), (800-523-2929, U.S. except AK and HI; for AK and HI, 800-233-3071).

(See also ALTERNATIVE ENERGY; DAMS; HYDROPOWER; ENERGY RESOURCES.)

**welfare effects,** in relation to POLLUTION, those effects that are thought not to affect health but primarily crops, livestock, vegetation, and buildings. It often refers to effects to which some monetary value could be ascribed—such as damage to materials, recreation, natural resources, public and community property, groundwater supplies, and aesthetics, including appearance, taste, and visibility—but for which no one pays or receives compensation directly. (See RANKINGS OF ENVIRONMENTAL PROBLEM AREAS BY WELFARE EFFECTS, on page 317.) In relation to PARTICULATE MATTER, for example, to the extent that it irritates or damages the lungs or eyes, it is considered to affect health; but its clouding of visibility, as part of AIR POLLUTION, would be considered a welfare effect.

**Western Forestry and Conservation Association (WFCA)** (4033 Southwest Canyon Road, Portland, OR 97221; 503-226-4562; Richard Zabel, Executive Director), a membership organization founded in 1909 to provide a common meeting ground for individuals, businesses, and government agencies on social, technological, and natural resource concerns about forestry in western North America, its aims being to "promote the practice of forestry and the development of conservation on Western forest lands, provide an open forum for exchanging and disseminating forestry and conservation information, and bring about cooperation among federal, state and provincial governments, private forest industry, small woodland owners, and natural resource conservation groups." WFCA sponsors an annual Western Forestry Conference,

promoting "a cross pollination of the science and technology of forestry across many disciplines," through its six standing technical committees: Economics, Stand Management, Forest Health, Fire, Reforestation, and Land Use. WFCA sponsors "an annual issues study tour where infield analysis emphasizes a current forestry issue," and publishes a quarterly newsletter *Western Banner*, and has annual conference proceedings.

**wetlands,** environments characterized by shallow or fluctuating water levels and abundant aquatic and marsh plants, including a wide variety of areas under many names, such as marshes, salt marshes, swamps, bayous, bogs, potholes, sloughs, fens, bottomland forests, wet meadows, and ponds, often the late stages in the life cycle of LAKES. The main kinds of wetlands are:

- **freshwater marshes,** including shoreline wetlands, small woodland marshes, prairie potholes, springfed pools, river oxbows, bogs, and even artificially constructed marshes, varying in size from a few square yards to thousands of acres. Freshwater marshes are generally found in depressions in the landscape, often near lakes or RIVERS, receiving water from rainfall, runoff from the surrounding area, groundwater (see AQUIFERS), surface springs, or streams. Freshwater wetlands are dominated by plants like cattails, bulrushes, grasses, sedges, smartweeds, waterlilies, and underwater pondweeds.
- **lake and shoreline marshes,** the most common type of freshwater marsh, consisting of narrow bands of vegetation around lake borders or behind lake beaches. These are commonly breeding grounds for lake fish, but are frequently filled in during DEVELOPMENT.
- **bogs,** a type of freshwater wetland characterized by accumulations of dead and decaying vegetation, often intertwined with roots of living plants to form a mat, which develops into *peat*, used as garden fertilizer or an alternative fuel source (see BIOFUELS). Bogs are generally dominated by sphagnum mosses, insect-eating plants, and specialized shrubs, such as leatherleaf and bog birch, while trees such as black spruce, larch, and northern white cedar grow on the edges. Relatively nutrient-poor and unproductive, bogs do produce crops of cranberries and blueberries.
- **prairie potholes,** special types of freshwater marshes consisting of shallow depressions scooped out by retreating glaciers in the last ice age, varying in size from less than an acre to several square miles. In the North American prairies, these are seasonally dry or flooded, but are important both as breeding places for waterfowl—sometimes even being dubbed the "duck fac-

tory''—and also for replenishing moisture in the soil and groundwater, and for floodwater control. Many have been drained and filled in, though efforts are being made by many environmentalists to halt that (see below; also MIGRATION, also PLIGHT OF THE PRAIRIE POTHOLES on page 341).

- **swamps,** areas wet part of the year and dry the rest, and dominated by woody vegetation, such as cedars, maples, ashes, willows, and alders in the northern United States, and bald cypress, tupelo gum, and oaks in the south, many alongside the Mississippi. Swamp trees are often dormant during the wet season.
- **salt marshes,** marshes of salty or brackish (somewhat less salty) water along COASTS, often dominated by salt-tolerant plants such as cord-grasses. These are prime spawning and nursery grounds for fish and shellfish, as well as waterfowl and other wildlife.
- **artificial marshes,** marshes re-created in drained areas or created where not previously existing, as by building dikes on uplands or across parts of lakes and controlling water levels by pumping or other manipulation. Such marshes are common where most natural marshes have been lost, and are often built and maintained by government wildlife agencies or private groups, such as HUNTING clubs.

In addition to these are MANGROVES, types of warm-climate, brackish wetlands discussed separately.

Wetlands were little regarded for much of human history, often feared as dangerous, seen as little more than dumpsites, or useful only if drained and developed. Because of such thinking, the FISH AND WILDLIFE SERVICE estimates that over 100,000,000 acres of wetlands have been destroyed in the United States alone, with over 54 percent of the wetlands that existed in colonial times now gone forever. Only in recent decades have conservationists and environmentalists come to realize the many values of wetlands.

Some have called them the ''cradle of life,'' and with good reason. Wetlands are prime sites for breeding of waterfowl, freshwater fish, marine fish, shellfish, fur-bearing animals and other wildlife, and also form nurseries and permanent HABITATS for many of these same beings. In the United States, for example, wetlands are home to perhaps one-third of those listed as threatened or ENDANGERED SPECIES, and coastal marshes are key spawning and nursery grounds for about two-thirds of the shellfish and commercial and sport species of marine fish. Millions of waterfowl breed in North American wetlands, and rely on them for food on their seasonal MIGRATIONS, as do many songbirds.

Wetlands also provide protection and stability for human and other inland environments:

- by storing water, they help control floods and lessen downstream destruction;
- by keeping the water table high, they block intrusion of salt water, while protecting water supplies (see WATER RESOURCES);
- by holding water, they replenish soil moisture and groundwater supplies, preventing the subsidence that can occur when groundwater is depleted;
- by removing silt and filtering out or absorbing many pollutants, they act as natural water purifiers;
- by slowing water currents and absorbing wave and storm energy, they hinder EROSION of the shoreline;
- by reducing the height of waves and so blunting the force of storms, they help prevent property damage and EROSION.

In addition, wetlands offer unspoiled environments for enjoying and learning about nature, and for activities such as hiking, fishing, hunting, and photography. Bottomland forests and some other wetlands are also rich sources of timber.

Though the value of wetlands is today more widely understood, the threats are still many and varied, including:

- **conversion to CROPLAND,** involving filling in (and sometimes first logging) wetlands to create land for agricultural production. The Fish and Wildlife Service, in its *National Wetlands Trends Analysis* of the United States from the mid-1950s to mid-1970s, found that 11 million acres of inland marshes, forested wetlands, and shrub swamps were lost, mostly due to agriculture, and others have been ''so degraded by pollution and hydrological changes that they no longer perform many of their natural functions.'' They noted that 2.3 million acres of such wetlands were *added*, mostly by the building of farm ponds—though environmentalists point out that such artificially created wetlands are often of different types, and also do not have the same BIOLOGICAL DIVERSITY as established wetlands, and therefore lack the same value to the environment.
- **conversion to AQUACULTURE,** which involves changing the free-flowing wetlands into controlled fish nurseries. In many warm, heavily populated countries, large areas of mangroves are being lost to aquaculture, in a long-term conflict of environmental interest.
- **conversion to construction sites,** with filling of wetlands to provide sites for housing developments, industry, and tourist facilities, including marinas. With rising POPULA-

# Wetlands Information and Action Guide

**For more information and action on wetlands:**

AMERICAN FISHERIES SOCIETY (AFS), (301-897-8616).

AMERICAN PLANNING ASSOCIATION (APA), (202-872-0611). Publishes *Protecting Nontidal Wetlands* (1988).

AMERICAN WATER RESOURCES ASSOCIATION (AWRA), (301-493-8600). Has technical working group on wetlands. Publishes *Wetlands: Concerns and Successes* (David W. Fisk, ed., 1989).

**Convention on Wetlands of International Importance Especially as Waterfowl Habitat (Ramsar Convention or Convention Relative aux Zones Humides d'Importance Internationale Particulierement Comme Habitats des Oiseaux d'Eau), Ramsar Convention Bureau** (Avenue du Mont-Blanc, CH-1196 Gland, Switzerland; (022/ 64 91 14; Daniel Navid, Secretary General; or Slimbridge, Gloucester GL2 7BX, United Kingdom), the organization that administers the Ramsar Convention, the international agreement signed at Ramsar, Iran, in 1971, under UNESCO auspices. The Ramsar Convention Bureau is administered by the IUCN (International Union for Conservation of Nature and Natural Resources, also called the World Conservation Union), including IUCN's subsidiary bureau, the World Conservation Monitoring Centre (WCMC). The Bureau publishes the quarterly newsletter *Ramsar, the Directory of Wetlands of International Importance*, and other materials.

DEPARTMENT OF AGRICULTURE (USDA), (202-447-2791).

DUCKS UNLIMITED (DU), (708-438-4300). Runs the *Marsh (Matching Aid to Restore States Habitat)* program.

ENVIRONMENTAL DEFENSE FUND (EDF), (212-505-2100). Publishes *Carolina Wetlands: Our Vanishing Resource*.

**Environmental Law Institute (ELI),** (202-328-5150; publications office, 202-939-3844). Publishes the bimonthly *National Wetlands Newsletter, Wetlands Protection: The Role of Economics* (Paul F. Scodari, 1990), and *Implementation of the "Swampbuster" Provisions of the Food Security Act of 1985* (1990). (See ENVIRONMENTAL LAW INFORMATION AND ACTION GUIDE on page 116.)

ENVIRONMENTAL PROTECTION AGENCY (EPA), (Public Information Center, 202-260-7751 or 202-260-2080).

FISH AND WILDLIFE SERVICE (FWS), (202-208-4717; publications unit: 703-358-2156; for publications, 703-358-1711; Federal Wildlife Reference Service, 301-492-6403 or 800-582-3421). Provides information through the *Federal Wildlife Reference Service (FWRS)*. Conducts the *National Wetlands Inventory*, and publishes from it the *National Wetlands Trends Analysis, Wetlands of the United States: Current Status and Recent Trends*, and numerous wetland maps (which can be purchased by calling 800-USA-MAPS[872-6277]).

FRESHWATER FOUNDATION, (612-449-0092). Supports *Lake and Wetlands Project*.

INTERNATIONAL COUNCIL FOR BIRD PRESERVATION (ICBP), (202-293-4800).

IUCN—THE WORLD CONSERVATION UNION, (202-797-5454). Publishes *Directory of African Wetlands* (Robert Mepham and Susan Mepham, 1990), *The Legal Aspects of the Protection of Wetlands: Proceedings of an International Conference* (IUCN Environmental Law Centre staff, eds., 1989; in English and French), and *A Directory of Asian Wetlands* (Derek A. Scott, comp., 1989).

IZAAK WALTON LEAGUE OF AMERICA (IWLA), (703-528-1818). Operates *Wetlands Watch*.

MIGRATORY BIRD CONSERVATION COMMISSION, (703-358-1716). Operates funds to restore and enhance wetlands.

NATIONAL AUDUBON SOCIETY, (212-832-3200; *Audubon Action Line*, 202-547-9017). Publishes the *Wetlands Tool Kit* for the Audubon Activist *Wetlands Campaign* and *Saving the Wetlands*.

NATIONAL COALITION FOR MARINE CONSERVATION (NCMC), (912-234-8062.)

NATIONAL INSTITUTE FOR URBAN WILDLIFE, (301-596-3311 or 301-995-1119). Publishes the *Wildlife Habitat Conservation Teacher's Pac* series, covering *Wetlands Conservation and Use*.

NATIONAL WILDLIFE FEDERATION, (202-797-8000 or 800-245-5484). Publishes *Wetlands: Increasing Our Wetland Resources* (1988).

SIERRA CLUB (415-776-2211 or 202-547-1141; legislative hotline, 202-547-5550). Publishes *Wetlands Policy* and *Water Policy*.

WATER ENVIRONMENT FEDERATION (WEF), (703-684-2400 or 800-666-0206). Publishes *Wetlands*.

WILDLIFE INFORMATION CENTER, (215-434-1637). Publishes *Wetlands: Important to Wildlife and People*.

WILDLIFE MANAGEMENT INSTITUTE (WMI), (202-371-1808).

WORLD WILDLIFE FUND (WWF) (202-293-4800). Publishes *Statewide Wetlands Strategies: A Guide to Protecting and Managing the Resource* (1991), *Protecting America's Wetlands* (1988), and *Issues in Wetlands Protection*.

**Other references:**

*Wetlands: A Threatened Landscape.* Michael Williams, ed. Basil Blackwell, 1991. *Wetland Creation and Restoration: The Status of the Science.* Jon A. Kusler and Mary E. Kentula, eds. Island Press, 1990. *Wetlands: Mitigating and Regulating Development Impacts.* David Salvesen. Urban Land Institute, 1990.

(See also LAKES; RIVERS; COASTS; MANGROVES; WATER RESOURCES.)

TION and the attraction of waterside vacation sites around the world, this kind of DEVELOPMENT will continue to be a major pressure on wetlands in many areas, such as Florida and around the CARIBBEAN SEA.

- **conversion to open water,** using dredging and channelization to create deepwater habitats from wetlands. Such loss in the United States between the mid-1950s and mid-1970s accounted for over 372,000 acres of coastal wetlands.
- **building of DAMS,** involving channelization and development of deepwater habitats where shallow ones once existed. The addition of 1.4 million acres of deepwater habitats created by construction of inland lakes and reservoirs in the United States from the mid-1950s to mid-1970s entailed destruction of large amounts of wetlands, though it also created others.

Other hazards do not threaten wetlands' immediate existence, but its health and long-term existence. The building of levees, navigation channels (as to coastal OIL and NATURAL GAS drilling sites), and dams trap upstream the sediment that is normally deposited downstream in wetlands—and which is, in fact, needed to maintain the level of the wetlands against the long-term trends of erosion and compaction of soil. With loss of the sediment, coastal wetlands experience a local SEA LEVEL RISE, an effect exaggerated in areas that have overuse of water or large-scale extraction of underground reserves (as of oil, natural gas, sulfur, salt, and phosphate), which also can lead to subsidence of the land. This can mean loss of wetlands, loss of other valuable lands, and contamination of water supplies by salt water. Channel dredging can allow saltwater intrusion into formerly freshwater or brackish marshes, and piling up the *spoils* (dredged material) on the banks creates dry land out of wetlands, and also islands or bars that block the natural flow of water. When these contain pollution, the unhealthy and toxic material is trapped in the wetlands and poisons the environment. The building of highways, railroad lines, drainage ditches for mosquito control, and the like also affect the health of existing wetlands. On the other hand, some of the same techniques—such as ditching, diking, pumping, and control of water flow—can be used to restore and maintain existing wetlands, as part of properly conceived wetlands management.

As the public has come to understand the importance of wetlands and the severity of the threats against them, numerous governments and environmental organizations have taken steps to halt the loss. On the international level, the main agreement is the 1971 CONVENTION ON WETLANDS OF INTERNATIONAL IMPORTANCE ESPECIALLY AS WATERFOWL HABITAT (Ramsar Convention), which provided for coverage of key wetlands sites around the world. As of 1990, approximately 30,500,000 hectares (76,250,000 acres) were covered in over 500 sites (for a full list, see WETLANDS OF INTERNATIONAL IMPORTANCE on page 395).

Numerous other programs also exist on the national, state, and local level. In the United States, many programs involve purchasing or leasing key wetlands to protect them, under LAND TRUST or CONSERVATION EASEMENT programs. The 1934 *Migratory Bird Hunting and Conservation Stamp Act*, which established the *Migratory Bird Conservation Fund*, with revenue from the sale of "Duck Stamps" required of waterfowl hunters each year; the 1961 *Wetlands Loan Act*; and the 1986 *Emergency Wetlands Resources Act* all provide funds under which the MIGRATORY BIRD CONSERVATION COMMISSION acquires, enhances, or restores wetlands. Similarly, the 1964 LAND AND WATER CONSERVATION FUND ACT and the 1989 *Wetlands Conservation Fund Act* also established funds used for wetlands, to which are added revenues from the sale of products from and rights-of-way across national wildlife refuges, disposals of refuge land, and reverted Federal Aid funds.

Various other federal branches have perceived the severity of the problem and begun to address it. The ENVIRONMENTAL PROTECTION AGENCY (EPA) has been focusing on early identification of valuable wetlands areas, on support for grassroots programs, and development of technical expertise to prevent further deterioration. In 1990 they signed agreements with the Army Corps of Engineers "aimed at mitigating wetlands loss," regarding administration of the CLEAN WATER ACT, and at removing 'prior converted' croplands from permitting requirements." Under the *swampbuster provision* of the 1985 Food Security Act (Farm Bill), farmers would risk losing federal benefits if they produce crops on converted wetlands, though this has not so far been widely enforced. The 1990 Farm Bill, shaped by the Congress, the EPA, and the DEPARTMENT OF AGRICULTURE, established a wetlands reserve program of one million acres, "providing long-term and permanent easements on farmland restored to wetlands." The 1991 EPA veto of the TWO FORKS DAM was partly to save the wetlands of the area, as were several other recent vetoes. In addition, many private organizations also buy or lease land or easements to protect wetlands. (See WETLANDS INFORMATION AND ACTION GUIDE on page 339.)

**Wetlands Convention,** an alternate name for the CONVENTION ON WETLANDS OF INTERNATIONAL IMPORTANCE, ESPECIALLY AS WATERFOWL HABITAT.

## Plight of the Prairie Potholes

Approximately half of the wetlands originally in the contiguous United States have been lost since the time of the European settlement. In the two decades between 1955 and 1975 alone, more than 11 million acres were lost and other wetlands have been so degraded by pollution and hydrological changes that they no longer perform many of their natural functions.

Nebraska's Rainwater Basin, a vital link in America's migratory flyway, has lost over 90 percent of its wetlands. And in North Dakota, the prairie potholes that remain are crowded with ducks and geese battling for nesting sites, struggling to survive against the onslaught of disease and predators that find easy sport in the cramped breeding grounds. Today the terrible toll of generations of uninformed, unthinking, and incremental destruction of wetlands is all too clear.

**Source:** *Environmental Stewardship: EPA's First Two Years in the Bush Administration* (1991).

---

**whales,** marine mammals in the *Cetacean* order, many of them very large—including the largest animal on earth—though some smaller ones called whales are actually DOLPHINS or PORPOISES. Late in the 20th century, as some kinds of whales neared EXTINCTION after a centuries-long attack upon them by whalers, a worldwide campaign began to save what remained of the great whales. This group of sea-dwelling mammal species had long been highly prized for commercial reasons; now they began to be even more highly prized for their intelligence and beauty—and as one of earth's vital life forms.

Whales have been hunted by people for at least 4,000 years off the Arctic shores of Alaska and Siberia. Norwegian whalers sailed the Atlantic off Scandinavia at least as early as 900 A.D., and Basques hunted right whales in the Bay of Biscay from about 1,000 A.D., ultimately following the diminishing population of whales across the North Atlantic, and hunted off Labrador and Greenland before Columbus discovered America. By the late 1500s, English and Dutch whalers were also operating in the North Atlantic, and by the 1650s were joined by American whalers out of New England, all of them HUNTING and killing right and humpback whales. The Japanese also began commercial whaling in the early 1600s.

During the 1700s and 1800s, larger and faster ships, able to process whale blubber into whale oil on board, followed and continued to destroy Atlantic Arctic whale populations, taking an enormous toll of right, humpback, and bow whales. They hunted sperm whales throughout the Atlantic. Whalers moved into the Pacific late in the 1700s; by the late 1860s, they had almost destroyed the gray and bowhead whales in the Pacific, and had greatly damaged the sperm whale population.

In 1868, Sven Foyn invented the explosive harpoon, fired by a small cannon, making it even easier to kill whales. At the same time, steamships began to replace sailing ships, and the much faster steamships, armed with explosive harpoons, became able to hunt and almost destroy the 150-ton blue whale, the largest animal ever to inhabit earth, and then successively turned to the 80-ton fin whale and the 30-ton sei whale. From the base established in South Georgia Island, in the South Atlantic, whalers hunted and killed these species in the South Atlantic and Antarctic during the first quarter of the 20th century. Then, with the invention of the factory ship in 1925, the killing intensified, and by the mid-1960s the blue whale, fin whale, and sei whale were all ENDANGERED SPECIES.

Establishment of the International Whaling Commission (see WHALE INFORMATION AND ACTION GUIDE on page 343) in 1946 reflected growing worldwide concern over the impending extinction of the great whales. But the commission had little power, and the killing continued, with large Japanese and Soviet factory fleets leading the way.

By the 1960s, a massive worldwide effort to save the whales had begun, led by environmentalist organizations. That movement bore fruit in 1972, with the United Nations Conference on the Human Environment call for a 10-year moratorium on whaling; although not adopted then, it greatly encouraged the worldwide campaign to save the whales. In the same year came the United States MARINE MAMMAL PROTECTION ACT, which outlawed the importing and killing of marine mammals or products derived from them, with some small exceptions. The act is administered by the MARINE MAMMAL COMMISSION.

In 1982, the campaign to save the whales scored a major victory, with the decision of the International Whaling Commission to impose a worldwide ban on whaling, fully effective in 1986. That prohibition has been largely effective, although the whalers of several countries, including Japan and the Soviet Union, have continued to kill hundreds of small Mincke whales allegedly for "scientific study." But by the early 1990s, several countries, including Japan, Iceland, and Norway, were demanding a resumption of whaling. In 1990, for example, Japan called for an end to the moratorium on whale killing. In 1991, Iceland took steps to withdraw from the International Whaling Commission, after the commission refused to reinstitute whaling, and Norway threatened to follow suit.

Although their survival is not at this time immediately threatened by whaling, all of the great whales are still very much endangered species. They will become greatly at risk if large-scale whaling is resumed. The great whales in the southern seas are also at risk because of the huge KRILL take, largely by Japanese and Soviet factory fleets. The chain of life in the seas around ANTARCTICA includes masses of PLANKTON, on which feed enormous numbers of tiny, shrimplike krill, which in turn are the primary food of whales, SEALS AND SEA LIONS, dolphins, and other sea creatures. The greatest modern danger to the entire life of the sea around Antarctica lies in such krill take, which if unchecked can threaten the entire FOOD CHAIN. If the krill population is destroyed, or even seriously diminished, many other species, and certainly the whales, are seriously threatened.

In the early 1980s, another major threat emerged. This was the worldwide threat created by the hole in the OZONE LAYER, in all probability created by the presence of chlorine released from CHLOROFLUOROCARBONS (CFCs), widely used as a coolant and in several other commercial applications. Some environmentalists believed that loss of protective ozone might destroy the plankton that feeds the krill population, causing immense damage to the food chain, and therefore to the life of the southern ocean.

These are the endangered and threatened whale species, all of them great whales, as listed by the United States FISH AND WILDLIFE SERVICE:

- **The blue whale**, by far the largest land or sea creature ever known, is found in all the world's oceans, though mostly in Antarctic seas. Its worldwide population before heavy commercial hunting began in the early 1900s was an estimated 180,000 to 245,000, and may have been much higher. From 1920 to 1959 the total reported world blue whale catch was over 320,000 of these great whales. Late 1980s estimates showed only 7,000 to 20,000 surviving blue whales worldwide, with some estimates even lower—and that was with something of a comeback that began in the early 1960s, when whaling began to be slowed by the Save the Whales campaign and international action. There is general agreement that the blue whale came close to extinction, and its future is by no means assured.
- **The humpback whale** sings its extraordinary songs in all the world's oceans. Once a population of at least 100,000,

this species also came very close to extinction, probably down to less than 5,000 worldwide. But the humpback whale has made a notable comeback in the North Atlantic, off the coast of North America, and as many as 10,000 now sing in the world's seas, although they are still endangered, not least by toxic wastes from MINING and other industrial sources; oil spills, such as the 1976 ARGO MERCHANT oil spill off Nantucket; and the ever-increasing amounts of sewage that find their way into the Atlantic from the heavily settled North Atlantic coast of North America.

- **The bowhead whale** barely survived the centuries-long attack of the whalers, and its survival is still very much in doubt. Bowheads were once found in all the northern seas; estimates of their population before commercial hunting began run from 50,000 to 100,000. Now they are found in some quantity only in the western Arctic, off North America, where 3,000 to 5,000 survive. The Alaska Eskimo bowhead whale hunt along the Alaska coast each spring, which occurs as the whales head east, was made an exception to the worldwide whale hunt ban (see INDIGENOUS PEOPLES). The number taken each year, along with the number mortally wounded but not taken, seems enough to prevent a bowhead population comeback, leaving the species greatly endangered, with conservationists urging an end or at least a sharp limitation of the whale hunt before it is too late. These whales, like all seacoast dwellers, also face the kinds of major environmental hazards caused by such oil spills as the 1989 EXXON VALDEZ disaster in Alaska's Prince William Sound and the ever-increasing flow of waste, some of it toxic, into the world seas and waterways. Off Alaska, there are also the enhanced dangers that come with mining and further oil exploration, both matters of great and increasing concern to environmentalists. The bowhead whale continues to be a greatly endangered species.
- **The right whale** once swam in all the earth's seas; Basque sailors in the Bay of Biscay began a thousand-year-long attack on the right whale about 1,000 A.D., and today only 3,000 to 4,000 survive worldwide, out of a population estimated to have been between 100,000 and 300,000. Right whales came very close to extinction before the worldwide ban on whaling began; their future is still uncertain, and made even more so because their mating and birthing occurs largely off coastlines, in waters threatened by such environmental hazards as sewage, toxic industrial wastes, and oil spills.
- **The fin (or finback) whale**, at 80 tons second only in size to the great blue whale, was the second choice of whalers operating in Antarctic seas. Like the blue and the sei, the fin became easy prey for whalers after the invention of the explosive harpoon and fast steamship; its worldwide population, estimated at 450,000 to 475,000 before the 20th cen-

# Whale Information and Action Guide

**For more information and action on whales:**

**AMERICAN CETACEAN SOCIETY (ACS),** (213-548-6279). Publishes the newsletter *Whale News*: quarterly journal *Whale-watcher*; educational tools *Gray Whale Teaching Kit* and *Whale Fact Pack*; various videocassettes; and books such as *Whale Zoo Book, Wild Whales, The Book of Whales, Whale Nation, Coloring Book of Sea Mammals, A Pod of Gray Whales, A Pod of Killer Whales,* and *A Guide to the Photographic Identification of Individual Whales: Based on Their Natural and Acquired Markings.*

**Animal Protection Institute,** (916-731-5521). Publishes *Whales.* *(See* ANIMAL RIGHTS AND WELFARE INFORMATION AND ACTION GUIDE *on page 361.)*

**CENTER FOR MARINE CONSERVATION (CMC),** (202-429-5609). Has *Marine Habitat Program.* Produces slide shows and fact sheets on whales.

**CETACEAN SOCIETY INTERNATIONAL (CSI),** (203-563-6444). Publishes the newsletter *The Connecticut Whale* and the book *Introduction to Whales and Other Cetaceans* (in English and Spanish); arranges whalewatching trips.

**COUSTEAU SOCIETY,** (806-627-1144). Maintains the *Marine Mammal Stranding Program* and *Marine Mammal Events Program.*

**EARTH ISLAND INSTITUTE,** (415-788-3666). Sponsors the *International Marine Mammal Project.*

**ELSA WILD ANIMAL APPEAL (EWAA),** (818-761-8387).

**ENVIRONMENTAL INVESTIGATION AGENCY (EIA),** (202-483-6621). Investigates environmental abuse; publishes various materials, including *The Global War Against Small Cetaceans, A Second Report* (1991).

**GREENPEACE** (202-462-1177). Runs the *Ocean Ecology Campaign.* Publishes the Action Factsheet *Japanese Whaling* and a videocassette.

**International Whaling Commission (IWC)** (The Red House, Station Road, Histon, Cambridge CB4 4NP, England; 0223 233971), an organization established under the *International Convention for the Regulation of Whaling,* "to provide for the proper conservation of whale stocks and thus make possible the orderly development of the whaling industry." The IWC reviews and revises as needed the Convention measures that govern international whaling, protecting certain species, designating specified areas as whale sanctuaries, setting seasonal catch limits, prescribing open and closed seasons and areas, setting limits on the size of whales that may be killed, and prohibiting capture of suckling calves and female whales accompanied by calves. The IWC fosters and funds whale research, publishing numerous scientific reports; it also maintains subcommittees on infractions and on aboriginal subsistence whaling. At present only large whales hunted commercially are covered by the Convention; though many members feel that smaller whale species, dolphins, and porpoises should also be covered, member countries have not reached agreement to do so.

**INTERNATIONAL WILDLIFE COALITION (IWC)** (505-564-9980). Operates the *Whale Adoption Project.* Publishes the quarterly newsletter *Whalewatch*; books such as *New England Whales, Whales and Man: Adventures with the Giants of the Deep, Wings in the Sea, The Humpback Whale, Crystal: The Story of a Real Baby Whale,* and *Humphrey the Wrong Way Whale*; and audio and visual materials.

**IUCN—THE WORLD CONSERVATION UNION,** (202-797-5454). Publishes *Dolphins, Porpoises and Whales of the World: The IUCN Red Data Book* (1990) and *Dolphins, Porpoises, and Whales: An Action Plan for the Conservation of Biological Diversity: 1988–1992* (W.F. Perrin, comp., 1988).

**Ocean Alliance,** (415-441-5970). Has an *Adopt-A-Whale* program for the California gray whales. Operates the *WhaleBus.*

**PACIFIC WHALE FOUNDATION (PWF),** (808-879-8860; for orders, 800-WHALE-1-1 [942-5311]). Offers whalewatches and experiential learning programs aboard its two ocean-going vessels *Whale One* and *Whale II*; maintains an *Adopt-A-Whale* Program; and publishes *Hawaii's Humpback Whales: A Complete Whalewatchers Guide* (Gregory D. Kaufman and Paul H. Forestell), *Marine Mammals of Australasia, A Pod of Killer Whales, A Pod of Gray Whales,* and for young children *Discovering Marine Mammals, Gentle Giants of the Sea, A Whale's Tale, The Whale Who Wanted to Be Small,* and *The Wonderful Journey* (the last two by Gill McBarnet).

**SEA SHEPHERD CONSERVATION SOCIETY,** (213-373-6979). Uses direct action against illegal whalers; offers whale-watching voyages.

**Sea World Research Institute (SWRI),** (619-226-3870).

**SIERRA CLUB,** (415-776-2211 or 202-547-1141; legislative hotline, 202-547-5550). Publishes *The Delicate Art of Whale Watching* (Joana M. Varawa, 1991).

**WILDLIFE INFORMATION CENTER,** (215-434-1637). Publishes *Selected Whale References.*

**WORLD SOCIETY FOR THE PROTECTION OF ANIMALS (WSPA),** (617-522-7000).

**Other references:**

*Men and Whales.* Richard Ellis. Knopf, 1991. *Where the Whales Are: Your Guide to Whale-Watching Trips in North America.* Patricia Corrigan. Globe Pequot, 1991. *The Last Whales.* Lloyd Abbey. Grove Weidenfeld, 1990. *Can the Whales Be Saved?* Philip Whitfield. Viking, 1989. *Whales of the World.* Nigel Bonner. Facts on File, 1989. *Celebrating Whales.* Nick Beilenson. Peter Pauper, 1989. *Jacques Cousteau: Whales.* Jacques-Yves Cousteau and Yves Paccalet. Abrams, 1988. *Voyage to the Whales.* Hal Whitehead. Dutton, 1988. *The Whale: Going . . . Going . . . Gone?* Marion Phillips. Exposition-Phoenix, 1988.

(See also ANIMAL RIGHTS AND WELFARE INFORMATION AND ACTION GUIDE, on page 361.)

tury, is down to 100,000 to 115,000, and it was in the process of being hunted to extinction, saved only by the worldwide campaign to save the whales and resulting ban on whaling. The worldwide fin whale kill from 1920 to 1979 was an estimated 790,000.

• **The sei whale**, less than half the size of the fin, was the third choice of Antarctic whalers, and like them became easy prey after the invention of the explosive harpoon and fast steamship. Its estimated worldwide population was between 100,000 and 200,000 early in the 20th century; in the mid-1980s, saved by the worldwide ban on whaling and after something of a comeback, there were an estimated 35,000 to 55,000, most of them in the northern hemisphere, with only 10,000 in southern seas, where there had earlier been 60,000 to 65,000. With the blue whale nearly extinct, and the fin whale in the process of being hunted to extinction, whalers in the 1960s stepped up their attacks on the smaller sei whales. Of the reported 280,000 seis killed between 1920 and 1979, 210,000 of them, or 75 percent, were killed between 1960 and 1979. There can be no doubt that the seis were on the verge of being hunted to extinction when they were saved by the ban on whaling.

• **The gray whale** was hunted to extinction in the north Atlantic very early, perhaps by the early 1700s. It is a coast dweller off North America and East Asia; as the California gray whale it has become familiar to west coast Canadians and Americans, as large schools of whales travel in spring and fall between Alaska and Baja California. Not a very numerous whale species, the California gray whales were nearly extinct by the late 1850s, as whalers killed them for their blubber, the source of whale oil. Only the turn to petroleum instead of whale oil saved the few gray whales that survived. But since then, the California gray whales have made a full comeback, their estimated 15,000 now what it was before heavy commercial whaling began. In this period, the gray whale is no longer threatened by whalers. But because the gray whales migrates so close to land, often as little as a mile offshore, they are particularly vulnerable to toxic wastes, from mining and other industrial sources; oil spills, such as the 1989 *Exxon Valdez* oil spill off Alaska; well blowouts, such as those that have often occurred off the California shore; and the ever-increasing amounts of sewage that find their way into the Pacific from the heavily settled California coast.

• **The sperm whale** is by far the most numerous of all the great whale species, with an estimated one million sperm whales living in all the oceans, down from the estimated 1,400,000 to 1,500,000 before commercial whaling began. But it has not always been so. By the 1860s, American whalers sailing out of New England had greatly damaged the world's sperm whale population, and all but destroyed the great white variety that were the model for Herman Melville's *Moby Dick*. The sperm whale made a comeback only after petroleum replaced whale oil as a light source. But in the 20th century several sperm whale-derived products became money-makers in commerce—and the mass killing of sperm whales began again. From 1950 to 1979, a period of only 30 years, at least 590,000 sperm whales were killed by whalers, the trend making this an endangered species, and one saved only by the worldwide ban on whaling.

(See WHALE INFORMATION AND ACTION GUIDE on page 343; also ENDANGERED SPECIES; DOLPHINS; PORPOISES; also ENDANGERED AND THREATENED WILDLIFE AND PLANTS on page 372.)

**Wild and Scenic Rivers Act,** a U.S. federal law passed in 1968 that called upon all federal agencies, in the course of their land and WATER RESOURCE planning, to consider which "outstandingly remarkable" free-flowing rivers might be appropriate for special protection under the Act, for present and future generations. For RIVERS designated federal Wild and Scenic Rivers, DAMS and other restrictive water projects are prohibited, and immediately surrounding lands are also protected from some activities (such as OVERGRAZING or logging on the river bank) that might lead to degradation of the river environment.

On federal lands, covered rivers are classified as

• **wild,** with little or no shoreline DEVELOPMENT and no roads, essentially WILDERNESS, with no logging or new MINING claims allowed;
• **scenic,** with overall natural character, but limited access and DEVELOPMENT, with some controlled logging and mining allowed; or
• **recreational,** with existing residential and commercial development and roads, with regulated logging and mining.

Private lands are not covered in the same way, and can only be protected by federal agencies acquiring the land or using CONSERVATION EASEMENTS, or by working with state and local authorities and private organizations. The work of evaluating rivers has proceeded slowly, however. The NATIONAL PARK SERVICE (NPS) developed by 1982 a *Nationwide Rivers Inventory (NRI)* listing over 1,500 river segments (about 2 percent of miles of river in the country) that had potential for inclusion in the system. But by early 1991 only 123 rivers (about .2 percent), mostly in the West, had actually been covered.

Environmentalists in BLUEPRINT FOR THE ENVIRONMENT note that evaluation of rivers is fragmented among federal agencies and recommend that a Joint Interagency Office of River Protection be formed to coordinate such evalua-tions, as well as offer technical assistance to state and local groups, and overall protection, urging that development be allowed on NRI rivers "only if there is no prudent and feasible alternative." As late as 1989, environmentalists were calling for assurances that, before a HYDROPOWER project was federally approved on a river in the Inventory, time would be allowed for study of the river for possible inclusion into the system. Under the law, the NPS offers technical assistance for river assessment and protection, including GREENWAYS programs, to those state and local organizations that have their own river protection programs; the United States FOREST SERVICE is empowered to do the same, but its work has not been funded.

**wilderness,** a natural area, relatively untouched by human activities. The U.S. Wilderness Act of 1964 defines a wilderness as "an area where the earth and its community of life are untrammeled by man, where man himself is a visitor who does not remain." Many areas of the world can still be regarded as wilderness, though they are becoming more restricted and isolated; except for special areas such as offshore islands, such areas generally need to be quite large—the Wilderness Act suggests at least 5,000 contiguous acres with no roads. These may be any type of area, including FORESTS, COASTS, WETLANDS, RIVERS, LAKES, DESERTS, mountains, and canyons.

No area in the world, even the most remote and seemingly wild, is free of human influence, if only because of the TOXIC CHEMICALS that are carried throughout the world by AIR POLLUTION and ACID RAIN. But in areas designated as wilderness, the main attempt by environmentalists is to allow only temporary intrusions by humans. Under the Wilderness Act, some kinds of activities are banned, notably logging, use of off-road vehicles, and permanent DEVELOPMENT, including roads, DAMS, and buildings. Activities allowed include hiking, camping, rafting or canoeing, swimming, horseback riding, cross-country skiing, FISHING, and scientific studies; also allowed, but considered more controversial, are HUNTING, MINING, and grazing of livestock. Environmentalists worldwide work to limit potentially damaging activities, and to seek protection for wilderness areas under various laws and agreements. The aim is to protect not just specific ENDANGERED SPECIES, but whole natural ECOSYSTEMS and HABITATS, for the future. (See WILDLIFE REFUGE AND WILDERNESS INFORMATION AND ACTION GUIDE on page 349; also WILDLIFE REFUGE; BIOSPHERE RESERVE; ENDANGERED SPECIES.)

**Wilderness Society, The,** (900 17th Street NW, Washington, DC 20006; George T. Frampton Jr., President), a membership organization founded in 1935, devoted "to the cause of saving and restoring America's public lands—a priceless heritage of wild country, beauty, and biological diversity." Through its Washington headquarters and 16 regional offices, the Society has been active in "passing legislation to protect wild and scenic rivers and national seashores; enlarging the national park system; creating landmark bills to regulate the management of national forests, wildlife refuges, and the millions of acres administered by the Bureau of Land Management, establishing the Alaska Lands Act of 1980, and . . . adding to the National Wilderness Preservation System."

The Society carries on research in its Resource Planning and Economics Department; seeks to educate the public, the media, and legislators through its Public Affairs Department; and acts as an advocate through its Conservation Department, evaluating and seeking to influence national policy on conservation. Among the "strategic issues in wilderness protection" on which the Society is currently focusing are "saving the ancient forests of the Pacific Northwest; shaping a national energy policy to conserve America's resources; ending the subsidized destruction of our public lands; rescuing our national parks and their surrounding ecosystems; safeguarding our great northern forest lands; preserving western wilderness; and defending endangered species and strengthening our national wildlife refuges."

The Society publishes the quarterly magazine *Wilderness*, and various other materials, including fact sheets such as *National Wilderness Preservation System*, *Wilderness Management*, *The Grand Canyon*, *Ancient Forests of the Pacific Northwest*, *Arctic National Wildlife Refuge: America's Serengeti*, *Antarctica*, *The Everglades*, *The Adirondacks*, *Global Warming*, *Grazing on Public Lands*, *Land Acquisition*, *Tongass National Forest: America's Vanishing Rain Forest*, and *Yosemite National Park*.

**Wildfowl Trust of North America (WTNA)** (P.O. Box 519, Grasonville, MD 21638; 301-827-6694; Benedict J. Hren, Executive Director), a membership organization founded in 1979 and "dedicated to fostering a public stewardship toward our dwindling wetland resources and their highly visible wildfowl," ducks, geese, and swans. At its 300-acre site on the CHESAPEAKE BAY, a WETLAND ecosystem designated a "critical area" by the Smithsonian, the Trust operates the Horsehead Wetlands Center as a base for conservation, educational programs for adults and children, research, and recreation, with natural areas including concealed blinds, towers, and a boardwalk for wildlife viewing. WTNA publishes a semiannual newsletter.

**Wildlife Conservation International (WCI)** (c/o New York Zoological Society, The Zoological Park, Bronx, NY

10460; 212-220-5100; George Schaller, Director of Science), an international conservation program, founded in 1895 as a division of the *New York Zoological Society*. WCI seeks to "preserve biological diversity and to protect significant fragments of nature," focusing its efforts on "key species whose conservation will assure the survival of entire ecological communities and ecosystems." WCI conservation biologists work in projects around the world, gathering data, developing plans for protecting endangered wildlife and HABITATS, training local conservationists, and working with local governments and communities on long-term conservation plans. WCI publishes the bimonthly magazine *Wildlife Conservation*, including numerous special features such as the Conservation Hotline, Zoo World, Elephant Watch, Survival Status, and Grassroots Action, and the brochure *Protecting the World's Tropical Forests*.

## Wildlife Habitat Enhancement Council (WHEC)

(1010 Wayne Avenue, Suite 1240, Silver Spring, MD 20910; 301-588-8994; Joyce M. Kelly, Executive Director), an organization founded in 1987 to help corporations improve their lands for wildlife, with members including corporations, conservation organizations, and wildlife consultants. Among the largely volunteer, low-cost, employee-run wildlife projects developed by corporations are provision of food, water, and cover for wildlife; planting native grasses and shrubs; halting streamside EROSION; restoring prairies and WETLANDS (see RESTORATION ECOLOGY); creating wildlife viewing and photo opportunities; helping threatened and ENDANGERED SPECIES by enhancing BIOLOGICAL DIVERSITY; and creating wildlife corridors (see GREENWAYS). According to WHEC, corporations own one-third of all the private land in the United States; by 1991, it had helped develop over 106 wildlife conservation projects on 130,000 acres.

WHEC has developed the Corporate Wildlife Habitat Certification program to give public credit for corporate efforts on behalf of wildlife, where they meet WHEC standards, including a formal wildlife management plan, a suitable provision to meet the plan, and the implementation of conservation efforts. WHEC publishes various materials, including the quarterly newsletter *WIN—Wildlife in the News*; the annual *International Registry of Certified Corporate Wildlife Habitat and Management Plans*, and the brochure *A New Partnership for America*.

## Wildlife Information Center

(629 Green Street, Allentown, PA 18102; 215-434-1637; Donald S. Heintzelman, President), an organization founded in 1986 and dedicated to "the protection and conservation of wildlife around the world through advocacy . . . dissemination of wildlife information, and nonintrusive, descriptive research on wild-

life demographics and behavior." It strongly advocates "wildlife protection and encourages nonharmful interaction with wildlife such as observation, photography, sound recording, drawing and painting, and wildlife tourism," and opposes "harmful treatment of wildlife such as hunting, trapping, and environmental pollution." In particular, the center opposes WILDLIFE TRADE, use of the leghold trap, killing of WHALES and WOLVES, HUNTING mourning doves and TUNDRA swans, and expansion of HUNTING and trapping in urban parks, national WILDLIFE REFUGES, and other recreational areas. The Center opposes lists of game species and hunting seasons and is concerned also with ACID RAIN, destruction of tropical FOREST habitats, PESTICIDE use, DEVELOPMENT of wildlife HABITATS, and ENDANGERED SPECIES.

The Center offers a program of wildlife education at various levels, including public school teachers, and also including lectures and wildlife walks; it also actively petitions federal agencies for rule changes regarding wildlife protection, often working with other wildlife organizations. It publishes various materials, including the newsletters *Educational Hawkwatcher, Wildlife Activist, Wildlife Conservation Reports,* and *Wildlife Book Review*; and wildlife conservation reports, including *"Hands-Off" Wildlife Research Techniques: A Synoptic Review* (Donald S. Heintzelman, 1990) and *Wildlife in Traveling Animal Shows: An Examination and Critique* (Donald S. Heintzelman and Carola Seiler, 1989). It also publishes bibliographies, fact sheets, and action alerts on individual SPECIES and emergency wildlife issues.

## Wildlife Management Institute (WMI)

(Suite 725, 1101 14th Street NW, Washington, DC 20005; 202-371-1808; Rollin D. Sparrowe, President), a private scientific and educational organization founded by businessmen and sportsmen in 1911 and "dedicated to the restoration, sound management, and wise use of natural resources in North America." Working with government agencies, colleges and universities, and other environmental organizations, WMI "strives to gain greater accommodation of wildlife in our growing society; to maintain sufficient, suitable habitats for all wildlife species in North America," as by encouraging public and private landowners to develop wildlife HABITAT and public recreation access programs; to help wildlife directly, as by saving and restoring WETLANDS and developing sound land and water plans; to improve wildlife administration, as by evaluating the effectiveness of state and federal programs and agencies, including regulations relating to *flyways* (see MIGRATION), and promoting educational programs for hunters; and to establish facts for management, as by underwriting research and field studies. WMI believes that "regulated hunting of designated wildlife populations has significant economic and recreational benefits," being often "the most practical, expeditious, and/or cost-effective method of keeping wildlife populations numbers in balance with habitat and public demands," while urging that hunters "police their own ranks [and] avoid abusing public sensitivities."

WMI sponsors an annual North American Wildlife and Natural Resources Conference; testifies before Congress, though not a lobbying organization; and publishes various materials, including the biweekly newsletter, *Outdoor News Bulletin*; booklets and brochures; periodic special releases; transactions of conferences; and various books made available through commercial or university publishers.

## Wildlife Preservation Trust International (WPTI)

(34th Street and Girard Avenue, Philadelphia, PA 19104; 215-222-3636; Bill Konstant, Executive Director), an international organization founded in 1973 by naturalist Gerald Durrell, stemming from his activities in the *Jersey Wildlife Preservation Trust*, on the English Channel isle of Jersey, where from 1959 he established a specialized ZOO for breeding in captivity animals facing EXTINCTION in the wild. WPTI's symbol is the now-extinct DODO. Its objectives are: "to support the propagation of rare and endangered species in captivity as an aid to their survival," their reintroduction into restored HABITATS, research on them in captivity and in the wild, especially in developing countries, professional training of zoologists and conservation biologists, and formulation of "strategies and policy activities for the conservation of endangered species and their habitats."

WPTI provides professional training at the *International Training Center for the Conservation and Captive Breeding of Endangered Species*, founded on Jersey in 1979, as part of its "New Noahs Program"; offers grants, scholarships, and internships, especially to biologists from developing countries; runs conferences and workshops; sponsors research projects; maintains the *Dodo Club*, offering students junior membership in WPTI and a three-times-a-year newsletter *Dodo Dispatch*; and outlines annual action plans focusing on "The Rarest of the Rare," such as (in 1990–91) the black lion tamarin (see MONKEYS), the muriqui or woolly spider monkey, the Berenty LEMUR, Livingstone's fruit BAT, the MADAGASCAR ploughshare or angonoka, the Mauritius kestrel, the Mauritius pink pigeon, several reptiles from Round Island, and several PARROTS.

WPTI also publishes various materials, including *State of the Ark* (Lee Durrell), *Travels in Search of Endangered Species* (Jeremy J.C. Mallinson), and books for children.

**wildlife refuges,** areas set aside for the conservation, protection, and better management of fish and wildlife; sometimes also called *wildlife ranges, game ranges, wildlife management areas,* or *waterfowl production areas.* Life forms in a wildlife refuge include not only ENDANGERED SPECIES but also a wide range of other animals, with focus on in recent years whole ECOSYSTEMS. Internationally, such refuges go under many names, many being classed as BIOSPHERE RESERVES; the laws under which they operate vary widely. Where endangered species are involved, various international ENVIRONMENTAL LAWS are in effect, such as the CONVENTION ON INTERNATIONAL TRADE IN ENDANGERED SPECIES (CITES), CONVENTION ON THE CONSERVATION OF MIGRATORY SPECIES OF WILD ANIMALS (the Bonn Convention), and the CONVENTION ON WETLANDS OF INTERNATIONAL IMPORTANCE, ESPECIALLY AS WATERFOWL HABITAT (the Ramsar Convention or Wetlands Convention).

The shape and size of wildlife refuges can be very important. As environmental researchers have learned, in general, a larger refuge is better than a smaller one (see EDGE EFFECT); a single refuge is better than the same acreage in several smaller preserves; clusters of small, separate preserves are better grouped close together than dispersed or in a line; small, separate preserves are better if connected by strips of land (*habitat corridors*, such as GREENWAYS), to provide passage from one to the other; and a circular refuge, with every external point roughly equidistant from the center, is better than a linear or triangular shape. These approaches to shaping a wildlife refuge will allow the largest breeding populations to survive.

For an endangered species, such an approach can have its hazards, however. If a species is found only in a single HABITAT, the "all-your-eggs-in-one-basket" approach can leave the population vulnerable to disease, natural disasters, and other hazards, such as an OIL spill. And the use of habitat corridors can expose species to disease from the outside world (as from livestock) and to the increased likelihood of poaching.

In the United States, the *National Wildlife Refuge System* was begun in 1903 by President Theodore Roosevelt, who by executive order declared Florida's Pelican Island off-limits, to protect its egrets, herons, and other birds from the hat industry's excessive use of their feathers. Within nine decades, the U.S. system of wildlife refuges grew to cover nearly 90 million acres of refuge land of every description, including COASTS, DESERTS, mountains, FORESTS, and LAKES, all administered by the FISH AND WILDLIFE SERVICE, in addition to numerous other hatcheries and research areas, and private lands included in many of the refuges.

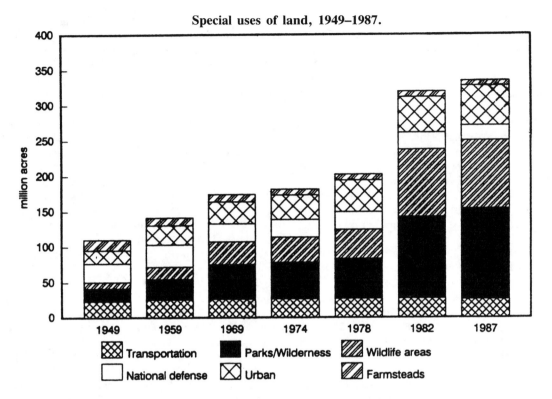

**Special uses of land, 1949–1987.**

Legend:
- ⊠ Transportation
- ▨ Parks/Wilderness
- ▨ Wildlife areas
- ☐ National defense
- ⊠ Urban
- ▨ Farmsteads

Source: *Environmental Quality*. The 21st Annual Report of the Council on Environmental Quality, 1991.

Contrary to much popular opinion, most wildlife refuges are *not* designed to protect all members of a particular species from harm; rather, they are intended to provide an area where the wildlife populations can be managed to maintain a stable population, but with HUNTING and FISH-ING allowed. In fact, conservation-oriented hunting and fishing groups have often played a key role in the establishment and maintenance of wildlife refuges. Refuges are open to many other activities as well, including camping, water sports, hiking, off-road vehicles, and wildlife observation. Unfortunately, some of these activities can be harmful to the refuge's plant and animal life; where refuges attract many visitors, these can cause significant ENVI-RONMENTAL DEGRADATION, sometimes termed *visitor abuse* (see ECOTOURISM).

More troublesome is the fact that the 1996 National Wildlife Refuge Act gives the Secretary of the Interior the power to "permit any use of any area within the system for any purpose . . . whenever he determines that such use is compatible with the major purposes for which such areas were established." Even though many refuges are closed to public access during the breeding season, or are used only for research, this power has been interpreted so broadly that many wildlife refuges are leased for commercial or government activities such as oil and NATURAL GAS drilling, logging, stock grazing, and military exercises. Environmentalists urge that such activities are incompatible with the purposes of the refuges and should be banned; also that new refuges should be formed, and old ones cleared of private lands, many of which are developed or can threaten adjoining park areas with POLLUTION. To protect these lands from the most damaging kinds of invasions, especially vehicular traffic and permanent DEVELOPMENT, environmentalists urge that refuge lands be designated as WILDERNESS, as is allowed under the 1964 National Wilderness Act.

In the United States, various other kinds of areas have been set aside for limited use, among them:

• **National Forest System,** administered by the FOREST SERVICE, which includes some 191 million acres in 156 national forests, including areas prime for plants and wildlife, as well as scenic areas popular for human recreation. About 32 million acres of these have been desig-

## Wildlife Refuge and Wilderness Information and Action Guide

**For more information and action on wildlife refuges and wilderness:**

**AFRICAN WILDLIFE FOUNDATION,** (202-265-8393 or 800-344-TUSK [8875]).

**AMERICAN WILDLANDS ALLIANCE (AWL),** (303-771-0380). Operates *Wildlands Conservation Program (WCP), Wildland Economic Research Program,* and *Ancient Forests of the Interior West.* Publishes the quarterly journal *On the Wild Side* and alerts on key issues.

**EARTH FIRST! (E.F.!)** (Direct Action Fund, 415-376-7329). Supports preservation of all remaining wilderness and restoration of previous areas of wilderness.

**Humane Society of the United States (HSUS),** (202-452-1100). Publishes *Refuge Wildlife Under Siege!* and *National Wildlife Refuges: A Cruel Hoax.* (See ANIMAL RIGHTS AND WELFARE IINFORMATION AND ACTION GUIDE on p. 361)

**IUCN—THE WORLD CONSERVATION UNION,** (202-797-5454). Publishes *1990 United Nations List of National Parks and Protected Areas* (1990), *New Challenges for the World's Protected Area System* (Jim Thorsell, comp., 1988) and *Protected Landscapes* (John Foster, 1988).

**NATIONAL AUDUBON SOCIETY,** (212-832-3200; *Audubon Action Line,* 202-547-9017). Maintains a nationwide sanctuary system. Publishes the annual professional reference work *Audubon Wildlife Report,* and flyers on National Audubon Society High-Priority Campaigns, such as *Arctic National Wildlife Refuge.*

**NATIONAL CAMPERS AND HIKERS ASSOCIATION (NCHA),** (716-668-6242). Maintains *Wildlife Refuge Program.*

**NATIONAL INSTITUTE FOR URBAN WILDLIFE,** (301-596-3311 or 301-995-1119). Certifies properties as part of the *Urban Wildlife Sanctuary* network, maintains a *National Roster of Urban Wildlife Sanctuaries,* and publishes *Wildlife Reserves and Corridors in the Urban Environment: A Guide to Ecological Landscape Planning and Resource Conservation* (L.W. Adams and L.E. Dove, 1989).

**NATIONAL PARKS AND CONSERVATION ASSOCIATION (NPCA),** (202-944-8530).

**NATIONAL WILDLIFE REFUGE ASSOCIATION (NWRA),** (10824 Fox Hunt Lane, Potomac, MD 20854; 301-983-1238; Ginger Merchant Meese, Executive Vice President), a membership organization founded in 1975, the "only conservation organization focused solely on the National Wildlife Refuge System," and dedicated to its protection, perpetuation, and expansion. Working with other organizations and networks, NWRA "monitors and works to improve federal agency administration of the nation's wildlife refuges," advocating increased funding and stronger legislative guidance, helping develop a system management plan, assisting individual refuges with particular needs, and seeking to eliminate "secondary uses of refuges that are incompatible with their primary purposes." NWRA publishes the quarterly newsletter *Blue Goose Flyer.*

**RESOURCES FOR THE FUTURE (REF),** (202-328-5000).

**SIERRA CLUB** (415-776-2211 or 202-547-1141; legislative hotline, 202-547-5550). Recent campaigns include BLM Wilderness/Desert National Parks and National Forests/National Parks Protection. Publishes *Protecting National Parks and Forests, How to Be a Wildlife Refuge Advocate, Wildlife Policy, Wildlife Needs You, How to Be a Wildlife Activist, Vicious Cycles, Off-Roads Vehicles Policy, Public Range Policy, Public Lands User Fees Policy, Archaeological Sites Policy, Wildfire Management Policy, Wilderness Management Policy; National Forest System, National Park System, National Trails System, National Wild and Scenic Rivers System, National Wilderness Preservation System,* and *National Wildlife Refuge System.*

**TROPICAL RESOURCES INSTITUTE,** (203-432-5116). Publishes *Planning and Management of a Biosphere Reserve* (Alan Ragins, 1988).

**WILDERNESS SOCIETY, THE,** (202-833-2300). Publishes fact sheets *National Wilderness Preservation System* and *Wilderness Management.*

**WILDLIFE SOCIETY, THE,** (301-897-9770).

**WORLD BANK,** (202-477-1234). Publishes *Wildlands: Their Protection and Management in Economic Development* and *Living with Wildlife: Wildlife Resource Management with Local Participation in Africa.*

**WORLD WILDLIFE FUND (WWF),** (202-293-4800). Has *Wildlands and Human Needs Program.* Conducts debt-for-nature swaps.

**Other references:**

*Nature Reserves: Island Theory and Conservation Practice.* Craig L. Shafer. Smithsonian Institution Press, 1990. *Economics of Protected Areas: A New Look at Benefits and Costs.* John A. Dixon and Paul B. Sherman. Island Press, 1990.

---

nated as wilderness areas, but many others are available for logging, grazing, MINING of COAL and other minerals, and oil and natural gas exploitation.

• **National Park System,** administered by the NATIONAL PARK SERVICE (NPS), which was begun with the 1872 establishment of YELLOWSTONE NATIONAL PARK, is funded by the LAND AND WATER CONSERVATION FUND, and now covers over 80 million acres in over 350 separate units, including parks, monuments, preserves, seashores, lakeshores, and riverways. Large sections have been designated as wilderness, though most of that lies in Alaska (see ARCTIC NATIONAL WILDLIFE REFUGE). These, too, are threatened by visitor abuse and commercial exploitation.

• **National Trails System,** a network of scenic, historic, recreational, and connecting or side trails, administered jointly by the National Park Service, BUREAU OF LAND MANAGEMENT (BLM), and Forest Service, established by the 1968 National Trails System Act, the first two being the Appalachian and Pacific Crest trails. Trails are not as protected as parks, refuges, and wilderness. They often do not have a permanent right-of-way, and may be diverted or even severed, as by DEVELOPMENT, road construction, or private owners closing their land to hikers. Volunteer user groups, called *trail conferences* or *trail councils,* often aid in planning, development, maintenance, and protection of the trails, working with the many government jurisdictions involved; a classic model is the APPALACHIAN TRAIL CONFERENCE. A vexing question on many trails is whether to allow mountain bikes; some trail conferences encourage nonmotorized biking.

• **National Wild and Scenic Rivers System,** established by the 1968 Wild and Scenic Rivers Act and administered by various local, state, or federal agencies, notably the National Park Service, Bureau of Land Management, and Forest Service. It now covers over 70 rivers, but most of the river mileage is in Alaska. (see RIVERS).

Many environmental organizations focus all or part of their activities on increasing the size and level of protections of these various parks, refuges, and recreation areas, so as to forestall additional loss of wildlife and natural areas, and to help restore areas that have been damaged.

Worldwide, attention is especially focused on wildlife refuges, often called biosphere reserves, in areas populated by endangered or threatened species. As rising human POPULATION causes increasing pressure to convert natural areas into CROPLANDS or residential areas, animal populations become more restricted and isolated. To ease the economic pressure on people in poor countries, many environmental groups are organizing DEBT-FOR-NATURE SWAPS, providing aid or debt relief for countries that maintain natural habitats, and promoting ecotourism, making wildlife refuges "pay" by bringing in tourist dollars.

Even where HUNTING is illegal and WILDLIFE TRADE banned or strictly monitored, many wildlife refuges still lose animals to illegal hunting, or *poaching.* Some countries (often with the aid of outside funds) are hiring armed ex-poachers to act as guards in wildlife refuges, to discourage others. But long-term protection for wildlife refuges depends heavily on economic and political stability around the world, and on continuing strength of will. (See WILDLIFE REFUGE AND WILDERNESS INFORMATION AND ACTION GUIDE on page 349, also WILDERNESS.)

**Wildlife Society, The** (5410 Grosvenor Lane, Bethesda, MD 20814; 301-897-9770; Harry E. Hodgdon, Executive Director), an organization of "professionals serving the resource management fields, especially wildlife ecology and management," founded in 1936 as the Society of Wildlife Specialists, renamed a year later, and now organized into seven regional sections with dozens of regular and student chapters. Its main objectives are "to develop and promote sound stewardship of wildlife resources and the environments upon which wildlife and humans depend; to undertake an active role in preventing human-induced environmental degradation; to increase awareness and appreciation of wildlife values; and to seek the highest standards in all activities of the wildlife profession." The Society offers certification for wildlife biologists; acts as a clearinghouse for information on wildlife research and programs; sponsors conferences and continuing education; works with other organizations and agencies on conservation matters; and consults with colleges on wildlife curricula.

It also publishes various materials, including the quarterlies *The Journal of Wildlife Management* and *Wildlife Society Bulletin;* the bimonthly newsletter *The Wildlifer;* a series of wildlife monographs; leaflets such as *A Wildlife Conservation Career for You* and *Conservation Policies of The Wildlife Society,* outlining the Society's positions on topics such as urban wildlife, forest management, trapping, human populations, and management of living natural resources; and books such as *Readings in Wildlife Conservation* and *Waterfowl Ecology and Management: Selected Readings.*

**wildlife trade,** a worldwide, largely illegal trade, often in endangered and threatened species, pursued by poachers and other traffickers, selling increasingly valuable animal skins, ivory, shells, coral, and other goods to what are in many countries still large, ready-to-buy markets, even after two decades of a worldwide campaign against the traffic. That campaign began to take hold in the late 1960s, and in 1973 scored two major victories. The multinational CONVENTION ON INTERNATIONAL TRADE IN ENDANGERED SPECIES OF FLORA AND FAUNA (CITES), which has become a powerful weapon in the fight to save endangered and threatened species, was signed in Washington in March 1973, and went into effect in January 1975. IUCN–WORLD CONSERVATION UNION reports on the legal and illegal animal trade through its World Conservation Monitoring Center, as does the WORLD WILDLIFE FUND through its TRAFFIC offices. In the United States, the ENDANGERED SPECIES ACT became law in 1973. Although lax enforcement of the law has often drawn criticism from environmentalists, the Act has provided a solid basis for an increasingly effective U.S. movement to save endangered and threatened animals and plants.

The trade goes on, however; estimates of the annual size of the illegal wildlife trade run from $2 billion to $5 billion, while the legal trade in what are in reality greatly threatened but not yet listed species is much larger. Three examples of the scope and tremendously damaging nature of the trade:

- The century-long attack on Africa's ELEPHANTS continues. There remain only 100 endangered Cape elephants, 40,000 to 50,000 Asian elephants, and 400,000 to 600,000 left of a 1.3 million African bush elephant population—and the number is dropping sharply every year, as poachers kill thousands of elephants and illegally sell their increasingly valuable ivory tusks, in spite of new laws that in some areas even include the death penalty. In 1989, CITES dropped an ill-considered attempt to legalize a controlled ivory trade, and voted a worldwide ban on the trade, while the United States and the European Community banned imports of raw or worked ivory. Yet several African countries continued to export ivory, and areas such as Hong Kong, China, Japan, and Singapore continued to import it, feeding the worldwide illegal ivory trade—and making both the African bush elephant and Asian elephant greatly threatened species.
- The worldwide PARROT population is under sustained attack because of loss of essential tropical HABITATS. But a more immediate attack is the international trade in wild birds; CITES reported a worldwide trade of almost 700,000 parrots in 1986, and in 1990 at least 250,000 parrots were imported into the United States alone. The early 1990s worldwide campaign to save the parrots and other wild birds, coupled with the campaign to secure more humane transport practices, has had some limited success, but the number of parrot ENDANGERED SPECIES continues to climb, in 1990 reaching at least 75 of 300 species.
- The hawksbill turtle has been increasingly threatened by Japanese tortoise shell products manufacturers; the live turtles are partially cooked to soften their shells, which are then torn off the living turtles, which are often put back into the sea—where they are thought by some to survive and grow new shells, but in actuality soon die. Japan, a CITES signatory, refused to recognize the hawks-

bill turtle as an endangered species. The U.S. government in 1991 threatened to place trade sanctions on Japan, which ultimately agreed to list the hawksbill as endangered and announced in May 1991 that the trade would be stopped, but did not supply a hard timetable for doing so. Sanctions were postponed, but only that, while the United States awaited Japanese action to end the trade.

In early 1991, the World Wildlife Fund reported that in spite of executions for poaching, the Chinese illegal trade in endangered animals was flourishing, with exceedingly rare giant PANDAS, LEOPARDS, egrets, hummingbirds, and more all freely offered at high prices in the South Chinese illegal rare animal market.

Given the large amounts of money to be made in illegal wildlife trade markets, it is clear that any attempt to save endangered and threatened species from poachers and trades will depend on strong, consistent enforcement and on worldwide pressure applied to those nations that continue to encourage or condone that trade.

### For more information and action:

- **African Wildlife Foundation,** (202-265-8393 or 800-344-TUSK [8875]).
- **Environmental Investigation Agency (EIA),** (202-483-6621). Investigates environmental abuse. Publishes various materials, including *To Save an Elephant* (Allan Thornton and Dave Currey, 1991) and *Wild Bird Imports for Pet Trade, An EEC Overview* (1990).
- **Humane Society of the United States (HSUS),** (202-452-1100). Publishes *Close-Up* reports such as *The Animal Slave Trade—Brutality on the Road to Research*, *Remember the Elephants . . . Forget Ivory* and *Save the Chimpanzee—Humankind's Sibling Species*; model legislation for captive wild animal protection; reports such as *The Trade in Live Wildlife: Mortality and Transport Conditions* and *The Bird Business*; and brochures *Wild Birds Should Fly Free, Captive Wildlife,* and *Hunted Wildlife.* (See ANIMAL RIGHTS AND WELFARE INFORMATION AND ACTION GUIDE on page 361.)
- **INTERNATIONAL WILDLIFE COALITION (IWC),** (508-564-9980).
- **IUCN—THE WORLD CONSERVATION UNION,** (202-797-5454). Publishes the quarterly *TRAFFIC Bulletin*.
- **TRAFFIC (TRADE RECORDS ANALYSIS OF FLORA AND FAUNA IN COMMERCE),** (202-293-4800). Monitors global trade in wildlife and wildlife products. Publishes numerous materials including *Buyer Beware!, U.S. Imports of Wildlife, World Trade in Wildlife, Fur Trade, Primate Trade, Watch Out for Wildlife Products—The Caribbean,* and *Watch Out for Wildlife Products—Mexico.*

- **WILDLIFE INFORMATION CENTER,** (215-434-1637). Publishes *Importation and Sale of Live Wild Birds.*
- **WORLD WILDLIFE FUND (WWF),** (202-293-4800). Seeks to block illegal wildlife trade and helps monitor it through the offices of TRAFFIC. Publishes the periodical *TRAFFIC (U.S.A.),* and books such as *Whose Business Is It? A Guide to International Trade in Wildlife* (Sarah Gates Fitzgerald, 1988).

**Other references:**

*Significant Trade in Wildlife: A Review of Selected Species listed in CITES Appendix II. Vol. 1: Mammals.* Steven Broad et al., eds. *Vol 2: Reptiles and Invertebrates.* Richard Luxmoore et al., eds. *Vol. 3: Birds* Tim Inskipp et al., eds. CITES, 1988.

**wind power,** energy ultimately derived from the sun's warming of the atmosphere, with the differing temperatures of air masses giving rise to wind currents; therefore a kind of RENEWABLE RESOURCE, unlike FOSSIL FUELS. Humans have been using wind power for at least 15 centuries, generally with small windmills, in which the wind moved "sails" and produced mechanical energy, such as could be used to turn millstones to grind grains. Scientific historians have estimated that at one point there were as many as six million windmills operating around the world, mostly on small farms. In the early and mid-20th century, these were mostly abandoned with the arrival of convenient and relatively low-cost electricity, expanded widely through rural electrification programs.

From as far back as the 1920s, experimenters built large *aerogenerators*, windmills that converted wind energy into electricity, which could then be fed into existing electrical networks. But it was not until the energy crisis of the 1970s that attention was once again focused on this ALTERNATIVE ENERGY source. Since then the focus has been shifted from large aerogenerators to *wind farms*, arrays of smaller wind turbines used as generators to produce electricity. Designs for these take advantage of new lightweight materials and design advances. Small-scale wind turbines or wind farms are found in many areas of the world, the best sites being those on an unobstructed hill or mountainous coast with a high annual wind speed, but they still have not gone into wide commercial use, partly because funding for development dried up as the immediate energy crisis seemed to ease.

One problem with wind power is that, even in appropriate areas, wind turbines generally operate only about 30 percent of the time. Often these are used to directly produce electricity, which is used or sold to a network, with the supplier then being able to draw electricity from the network during the wind turbines' "down times." Where not connected to a network, users face questions of storage, generally with cumbersome, costly batteries, and backup, such as diesel engines. Some researchers have explored other ways of using wind power, as to pump water into storage, to run small-scale irrigation systems, to compress air and store it in CAVES or AQUIFERS, to run modern wind-powered ships, or to produce hydrogen and other alternative fuels.

**For more information and action:**

- **CONSERVATION AND RENEWABLE ENERGY INQUIRY AND REFERRAL SERVICE (CAREIRS),** (800-523-2929, U.S. except AK and HI; for AK and HI, 800-233-3071). Publishes *Wind Energy Systems.*.
- **NATIONAL CENTER FOR APPROPRIATE TECHNOLOGY (NCAT),** (406-494-4572).
- **WORLDWATCH INSTITUTE,** (202-452-1999).

**Windscale,** the earlier name of the British nuclear production plant at SELLAFIELD. (See SELLAFIELD; also MAJOR NUCLEAR DISASTERS AND INCIDENTS on page 212.)

**Winrock International Institute for Agricultural Development** (Headquarters: Route 3, Morrillton, AK 72110; 501-727-5435; or 1611 North Kent Street, Arlington, VA 22209; 703-525-9430; Robert D. Havener, President), an international organization funded primarily by grants and contracts from private and public agencies, founded "to alleviate human hunger and poverty through agricultural development" and SUSTAINABLE AGRICULTURE, seeking to assist "people and nations to produce food and fiber more efficiently while conserving the natural resource base to support future generations." It was formed in 1985 from the merger of three international development institutions that "shared a common heritage stemming from the philanthropic traditions of the Rockefeller family": the *Agricultural Development Council (A/D/C),* founded in 1953; the *International Agricultural Development Service (IADS),* founded in 1975; and the *Winrock International Livestock Research and Training Center (WILRTC),* established in 1975. Winrock International's three main areas of operation are:

- **human resource development,** providing training and research programs in developing countries;
- **technical cooperation,** aiding in generation and transfer of appropriate agricultural technologies;
- **planning and analysis,** aiding in use and management of renewable resources.

Winrock's activities extend around the globe, with several dozen professionals posted on projects in various countries, especially in Asia and Africa, but also in Latin America and the rural United States, with special focus on agricultural systems improvement, including livestock, crops, and AGROFORESTRY; natural resources management, including SOIL CONSERVATION, water management, and small-scale irrigation; and operational programs, including education, marketing systems, and area-development projects. Winrock also publishes various materials, including profiles on its many projects, and books such as *Aid, Trade, and Farm Policies: A Sourcebook on Issues and Interrelationships* (Wayne E. Swegle and Polly C. Ligon, eds., 1989), *Food, Hunger, and Agricultural Issues* (Deborah Clubb and Polly C. Ligon, eds., 1989), *Population Growth and Sustainable Agricultural Production: An Emerging Agenda* (Robert D. Havener, 1989), and *The Role of State Governments in Agriculture* (Enrique Ospina and Cami S. Sims, eds., 1988).

**wolves,** CARNIVOROUS mammals once common in North America, Europe, and Asia; regarded as one of the historic enemies of humankind because of their attacks on livestock and occasional attacks on humans, and so for centuries the object of sustained and successful attack.

There are two wolf species:

- The endangered **red wolf** was last found in the southeastern United States. It has become extinct in the wild, and is now being reintroduced by the United States FISH AND WILDLIFE SERVICE in the southeast, in a very limited way and with great sensitivity to the concerns of local farmers.
- The **gray wolf (timber wolf)** is still numerous in the WILDERNESS areas of Alaska, western Canada, and northern Asia, and is found in many subspecies, including the Asian *tundra wolf* and *steppe wolf*. In the "lower 48" United States, there are gray wolf populations in northern Minnesota, Michigan, and Wisconsin, and the gray wolf is listed as an ENDANGERED SPECIES everywhere but Minnesota, where it is listed as threatened. The U.S. Fish and Wildlife Service also plans to reintroduce the gray wolf into YELLOWSTONE NATIONAL PARK; the plan has been strongly resisted by local farmers and ranchers, who still regard the wolf as a natural enemy.

**For more information and action:**

- **EARTH FIRST!** (E.F.!), (Direct Action Fund, 415-376-7329). Has *Wolf Action Network*.
- **ELSA WILD ANIMAL APPEAL (EWAA),** (818-761-8387).
- **WILDLIFE INFORMATION CENTER,** (215-434-1637). Publishes *Selected Wolf References.(See also* ENDANGERED SPECIES; also ENDANGERED AND THREATENED WILDLIFE AND PLANTS on page 372)

**Wood Buffalo National Park,** at 17,300 square miles Canada's largest national park, straddling the Alberta-Northwest Territories border, created in 1922 as a refuge for North America's last remaining herd of *wood bison*. The herd was later interbred with plain bison, and the interbred BUFFALO herd now numbers over 12,000. A few hundred wood bison also survive as a separate SPECIES in the park. The huge park is also a safe haven for a wide range of other northern wildlife, and is famous as the place at which the whooping CRANES were saved. At Wood Buffalo, in 1954, was found the only known surviving breeding population of whooping cranes, previously thought extinct. The rare and endangered cranes, with a strong Canadian–U.S. cooperative effort that included breeding in captivity and return to the wild, now number over 200, and have also been established in other locations. (See WILDLIFE REFUGES.)

**Woods Hole Oceanographic Institution (WHOI)** (Woods Hole, MA 02543; 508-548-1400; Associates Office, 508-457-2000, ext. 2392; Craig E. Dorman, Director), a key marine research and educational institution, chartered in 1931 as a private organization, though much of its funding comes from government contracts, especially from the National Science Foundation and the Office of Naval Research. WHOI explores all aspects of OCEAN science, carrying on both basic and applied research, often in multidisciplinary ways, joining the specialties of ocean engineering, biology, chemistry, geology, geophysics, and physical geography, to study such questions as the types, distributions, and life cycles of marine organisms; food supply in the oceans; the composition of seawater and its role in the earth's BIOGEOCHEMICAL CYCLES; the impact of contaminants on these processes; and the ways that variations in temperature, salinity, and pressure, as well as winds, the earth's rotation, and the pull of the sun and moon, affect the ocean and in turn interact with the world's climate.

Legal and policy issues about human use of the sea are investigated by WHOI's *Marine Policy Center (MPC),* directed by James M. Broadus III, which has recently concentrated on four areas: global CLIMATE CHANGE; ocean use and protection; marine technology; and Arctic Studies. The *Center of Marine Exploration (CME),* directed by Robert D. Ballard, focuses on technology for deep-sea exploration, especially unmanned systems; it has also been much involved in marine archaeology, sponsoring international discussions on "ethics and policy pertaining to the discovery, exploration, and exploitation of undersea cultural resources, namely shipwrecks." Much of WHOI's deep-sea exploration is carried on in its own research vessels, including the well-known *Alvin*. The *Coastal Research Center (CRC)*, directed by David G. Aubrey, focuses on five main areas: the impact of global climate change on the coastal zone; circulation, transport, and uptake of TOXIC CHEMICALS; improved measuring instruments; rapid response, as to hurricane; and education. WHOI runs graduate degree programs, often in conjunction with a nearby university, and also provides undergraduate summer programs and post-doctoral fellowship grants.

An *Associates Program* for "all persons, corporations, and institutions interested in the science of the sea and the work" of WHOI was begun in 1952. Associate members are invited to WHOI's seminars, symposia, and special events, to learn about research directly from the scientists, and receive WHOI's quarterly publications *Ocean Views* and *Oceanus*.

### World Association of Soil and Water Conservation (WASWC)

(317 Marvin Avenue, Volga, SD 57071; 605-627-9309; May–October, 218-864-8506; William Moldenhauer, Executive Secretary), an international organization founded in 1982 by the SOIL AND WATER CONSERVATION SOCIETY OF AMERICA, "dedicated to encouraging the wise use and conservation of soil and WATER RESOURCES so that these resources can be used to sustain mankind forever." It seeks to develop an information exchange on the conservation and use of soil and water resources around the world, through publications, conferences, workshops, and meetings; studies policies and recommend actions; and encourages research and demonstration projects. The Society publishes a newsletter and books in concert with the Soil and Water Conservation Society.

### World Bank

(1818 H Street NW, Washington, DC 20433; 202-477-1234), a key international DEVELOPMENT organization, self-described as a "multilateral lending agency," established in 1944 at the Bretton Woods meeting, originally to rebuild war-torn Western Europe, but quickly refocused on the economic needs of developing countries, especially after the post-war decolonialization. With over 150 member countries, the World Bank actually consists of four closely intertwined institutions:

- **International Bank for Reconstruction and Development (IBRD),** which lends money to developing countries with relatively high per capita incomes; it is funded primarily by the sale of bonds on world financial markets. This is the original arm, founded in 1944.
- **International Development Association (IDA),** which provides assistance "on concessional terms" to poorer developing countries, unable to borrow from the IBRD;

it is funded primarily by contributions from more affluent member countries. This was founded in 1960.
- **International Finance Corporation (IFC),** which promotes growth in developing countries by investing (with others) in private commercial enterprises, through loans or equity financing.
- **Multilateral Investment Guarantee Agency (MIGA),** which encourages foreign investment in developing countries by offering foreign investors guarantees against "loss caused by noncommercial risks."

From its founding through at least the 1960s, the World Bank's emphasis was on funding massive projects, such as DAMS, irrigation networks, or highways. Recognizing that "the benefits of such large projects did not adequately reach all members of society," the Bank since then has focused somewhat more on projects that "raise productivity and living standards of the rural and urban poor," among them those providing "seeds, agricultural advice, financial credit, and access roads to individual farmers." Since the 1970s, with mounting indebtedness among developing countries, the Bank has supported "broad national economic reform programs and initiative to improve the economic efficiency of specific sectors such as agriculture, education, and banking."

Unfortunately, the rising debt has created an additional set of pressures, which threaten not only the stability of some governments, but also the environment in general. Many environmentalists have criticized the World Bank for "throwing money at problems," and supporting massive solutions to problems, without carefully assessing beforehand the long-term effects of choices on the society and the environment. But the Bank's supporters point out that its work has helped raise the average life expectancy and standard of living in developing countries, even at a time of rapidly increasing POPULATION. The Bank sees its 1990s development agenda as "committed to equitable and sustainable growth," and emphasizing five themes:

- Reducing world poverty
- Protecting the environment
- Helping people achieve their full potential through better education, improved nutrition, and family planning
- Assisting countries reduce their debts and make their economies more efficient
- Strengthening the private sector.

In the 1990s, the largest amount of World Bank lending goes to agriculture and rural development, energy, policy reform and technical assistance, and transportation (in that order); lesser amounts go to education, development finance companies, industries and small enterprises, urban

## World Conservation Strategy—Its Objectives

The aim of the World Conservation Strategy is to achieve the three main objectives of living resource conservation:

- **to maintain essential ecological processes and life-support systems** (such as soil regeneration and protection, the recycling of nutrients, and the cleansing of waters) on which human survival and development depend.
- **to preserve genetic diversity** (the range of genetic material found in the world's organisms), on which depend the functioning of many of the above processes and life-support systems, the breeding programmes necessary for

the protection and improvement of cultivated plants, domesticated animals and microorganisms, as well as much scientific and medical advance, technical innovation, and the security of the many industries that use living resources.

- **to ensure the sustainable utilization of species and ecosystems** (notably fish and other wildlife, forests, and grazing land), which support millions of rural communities as well as major industries.

**Source:** *World Conservation Strategy* (1980).

---

development, population, health and nutrition, water supply and sewerage, telecommunications, and public sector management. Many loans, however, provide aid to several sectors at once, and the Bank asserts that "almost half of the loans approved in 1990 contained environmental components." The modern World Bank stresses that it "does more than lend money," helping also to "build expertise and knowledge in developing countries, so they can better manage their development."

The World Bank sees itself as "the preeminent publisher of books on development." In addition to its annual *World Development Report*, it publishes hundreds of public information booklets on a very wide range of development-related issues, as well as computer software programs, videocassettes, several periodicals, many country studies, and public information booklets, all of them listed in its *Index of Publications*, a book in itself.

**World Charter for Nature,** an international declaration of two dozen principles of conservation by which human actions affecting nature are to be guided and judged. The document—an example of "soft" ENVIRONMENTAL LAW—was adopted by the United Nations General Assembly in 1982, the only dissenting vote being the United States, which objected to some mandatory language in the supposedly nonbinding document.

**World Commission on Environment and Development (WCED),** an independent body created by the United Nations in 1983, chaired by Norwegian leader Mrs. Gro Harlem Brundtland, which was disbanded after publishing its final report, OUR COMMON FUTURE, also called the Brundtland Report (1987).

**World Conservation Monitoring Centre (WCMC),** an organization that maintains data bases on ENDANGERED

SPECIES and their HABITATS, operated jointly by the GLOBAL ENVIRONMENT MONITORING SYSTEMS (GEMS), WORLD WILDLIFE FUND (WWF, or the World Wide Fund for Nature), and IUCN—THE WORLD CONSERVATION UNION.

**World Conservation Strategy: Living Resource Conservation for Sustainable Development (WCS),** a key report published in 1980, prepared by the International Union for Conservation of Nature and Natural Resources (now called IUCN—THE WORLD CONSERVATION UNION) with the advice, cooperation, and financial assistance of the UNITED NATIONS ENVIRONMENT PROGRAMME (UNEP) and the WORLD WILDLIFE FUND (WWF), and in collaboration with the Food and Agriculture Organization of the United Nations (FAO) and the United Nations Educational, Scientific, and Cultural Organization (UNESCO). The WCS assumes that "human beings . . . must come to terms with the reality of resource limitation and the carrying capacities of ecosystems, and must take account of the needs of future generations," and that "the object of conservation is to ensure earth's capacity to sustain development and to support all life." Noting the "almost limitless capacity of human beings for building creation, matched by equally great powers of destruction and annihilation," and "the global interrelatedness of actions, with its corollary of global responsibility," the WCS aims to provide "both an intellectual framework and practical guidance for the conservation actions necessary," calling for global coordination and solidarity to implement its programs. The strategy was quickly adopted in some 30 countries and was influential in many more. (See WORLD CONSERVATION STRATEGY—ITS OBJECTIVES above.) As of this writing, the original organizations were preparing an updated Strategy for the 1990s, in a report tentatively titled *Caring for the World: A Strategy for Sustainability*, which focuses especially on stabilizing POPULATION and reducing the resource demand for high-income societies, so as not to exceed the CARRYING CAPACITY of the BIOSPHERE.

**For more information and action:**

• IUCN—THE WORLD CONSERVATION UNION, (202-797-5454).

**World Environment Center (WEC)** (419 Park Avenue, Suite 1800, New York, NY 10016; 212-683-4700; Antony G. Marcil, President), an international non-advocacy organization founded in 1974 that "contributes to sustainable development by strengthening environmental management and industrial health and safety practices worldwide." Funded by "governments, national and international agencies, industry, foundations, and private citizens," and often working with other environmental organizations and government agencies, WEC specializes in providing volunteer expert technical services and information exchange programs "for the benefit of both the private and public sectors worldwide," as through its *International Environment and Development Service (IEDS)*. It publishes various materials, including the *WEC Network News*, a newsletter on IEDS, the booklet *Chlorine Safety Pays* and a *Household Hazardous Waste Wheel*.

**World Future Society (WFS)** (4916 St. Elmo Avenue, Bethesda, MD 20814; 301-656-8274; Edward Cornish, President), a membership organization founded in 1966 for "the study of alternative futures," its aim being to act as "an impartial clearinghouse for a variety of different views and . . . not [to] take positions on what will or should happen in the future." The Society holds meetings around the United States, often on special themes, and offers distinguished service awards. It publishes various materials, including the bimonthly magazine *The Futurist*; the newsletter *Newsline; Future Survey: A Monthly Abstract of Books, Articles, and Reports Concerning Forecasts, Trends, and Ideas about the Future;* and books such as *The 1990s and Beyond* (1990).

**World Glacier Monitoring Service,** an international organization gathering data on glaciers worldwide, operated jointly by GLOBAL ENVIRONMENT MONITORING SYSTEMS (GEMS), UNESCO and the Swiss Federal Institute of Technology.

**World Natural Heritage Sites,** natural areas considered to be of "outstanding universal value," listed under the 1972 CONVENTION CONCERNING THE PROTEC-

TION OF THE WORLD CULTURAL AND NATURAL HERITAGE, the aim being to promote international cooperation in safeguarding them. Nations propose natural and cultural sites that are already protected within their borders; these are then evaluated by the World Heritage Committee for listing. Natural heritage sites selected are those that have scientifically or aesthetically outstanding physical and biological formations; geological or physiographical formations and areas composing the HABITAT of threatened plant or animal SPECIES of outstanding value to science or conservation; and natural sites outstanding for science, conservation, or natural beauty. (See LIST OF WORLD NATURAL HERITAGE SITES on page 406); also ENVIRONMENTAL LAW.)

**World Nature Association (WNA)** (P.O. Box 673, Woodmoor Station, Silver Spring, MD 20901; Donald H. Messersmith, President), a membership organization of professional and amateur naturalists of widely varying backgrounds, founded in 1969. From dues and contributions, WNA funds various conservation projects around the world, largely carried on by volunteer naturalists and most too small to be funded by governments or larger groups. Annual meetings are held alternately in the United States and elsewhere in the world, generally to coincide with birding or other nature study tours. WNA publishes a semiannual newsletter *World Nature News*.

**World Resources Institute (WRI)** (1709 New York Avenue NW, Suite 700, Washington, DC 20006; 202-638-6300; John H. Adams, Executive Director), a key independent, international policy research center, founded in 1982, to provide sound information, analysis, and policy recommendations to governments, organizations and individuals on issues concerning the environment, development, and resource management. WRI conducts numerous policy research programs, recently on FORESTS and biodiversity; economics and institutions; climate, energy and POLLUTION; resource and environmental information; technology; and special initiatives in institutions and governance. It also operates the *Center for International Development and Environment*, formerly the North American arm of the INTERNATIONAL INSTITUTE FOR ENVIRONMENT AND DEVELOPMENT (IIED).

WRI publishes numerous materials on topics such as agriculture and PESTICIDE safety, ACID RAIN, BIOLOGICAL DIVERSITY, energy, environmental pollution, forests, CLIMATE CHANGE, AIR POLLUTION, OZONE, sustainable DEVELOPMENT, and water, land, and other natural resources, as well as publishing a biannual *World Resources* report, most recently in collaboration with the UNITED NATIONS ENVIRONMENT PROGRAMME (UNEP) and the UNITED NA-

TIONS DEVELOPMENT PROGRAMME (UNDP). Among its recent publications are *Lessons Learned in Global Environmental Governance* (Peter H. Sand, 1990) and *Taking Stock: The Tropical Forest Action Plan After Five Years* (Robert Winterbottom, 1990).

## World Society for the Protection of Animals (WSPA)

(29 Perkins Street, P.O. Box 190, Boston, MA 02130; 617-522-7000; Richard Steiner, President; International Headquarters: Park Place, 10 Lawn Lane, London SW8 1UD, United Kingdom; 071-793-0540; Gordon Walwyn, Director General), an international membership organization that seeks to "relieve the suffering of all animal life throughout the world," often working with other environmental groups around the world and for its activities given unique consultative status by the United Nations. Much of WSPA's work is in disaster relief, working much as the Red Cross does after hurricanes, earthquakes, floods, fires, and other major international disasters, such as BHOPAL and the PERSIAN GULF WAR ENVIRONMENTAL DISASTER, including treating the few survivors from the Kuwait Zoo.

WSPA sponsors humane education projects, for adults and children, as through school-age Kindness Clubs in Africa; and conducts public information campaigns on issues such as leghold traps, bull fighting, dog fighting, animal stoning (as in Spain), wearing furs, WILDLIFE TRADE, saving ENDANGERED SPECIES such as the WHALE and the RHINOCEROS, and humane treatment of animals intended for human consumption (as in Korea and the Philippines). It also helps develop and lobbies for effective animal welfare legislation, and publishes various public information leaflets on animal welfare issues.

WSPA was incorporated in 1981 by the merger of the *International Society for the Protection of Animals (ISPA)*, founded in 1959, and the *World Federation for the Protection of Animals (WFPA)*, founded in 1950.

## Worldwatch Institute

(1776 Massachusetts Avenue NW, Washington, DC 20036; 202-452-1999; Lester R. Brown, President), an independent, nonprofit organization founded in 1974 to "help raise understanding of global environmental issues to the point where the public will support the policies needed to create an environmentally sustainable global economy." It publishes various materials, including the bimonthly magazine *World Watch*, the annual book *State of the World*, and a notable series of Worldwatch Papers analyzing vital issues.

## World Wide Fund for Nature (WWF),

international organization originally known as the WORLD WILDLIFE FUND, still its name in the United States.

## World Wildlife Fund (WWF)

(WWF-US, 1250 24th Street, NW, Washington, DC 20037; 202-293-4800; Kathryn S. Fuller, President), a key international conservation organization founded in 1961, now known internationally (except in Canada, Australia, and the United States) as the *World Wide Fund for Nature*. WWF acts with numerous other United States organizations in a WWF network "to conserve the natural environment and ecological processes essential to life," paying "particular attention to endangered wildlife and to natural habitats important for human welfare." Using an approach to conservation based "on practical and scientifically based principles," with hundreds of projects conducted or supported around the world, WWF "protects endangered wildlife and habitats and helps preserve the earth's biological diversity through fieldwork, scientific research, institutional development, wildlife trade monitoring, public policy initiatives, technical assistance and training, environmental education, communications, and more."

WWF's United States arm has since 1985 been affiliated with the *Conservation Foundation*, stressing social science and policy analysis, which operates the *Osborn Center for Conservation and Development*, stressing "the wise management and efficient use of renewable resources" as a "central element in the economic development plans of developing nations." WWF also monitors international trade in wild plants and animals through the offices of TRAFFIC, part of an international network in cooperation with the IUCN—THE WORLD CONSERVATION UNION.

Recent WWF concerns have included programs to save the African ELEPHANT, especially banning ivory imports under the CONVENTION ON INTERNATIONAL TRADE IN ENDANGERED SPECIES (CITES); to preserve tropical rain forest (see FORESTS); scientific research to "identify conservation priorities in each of the earth's biogeographical regions" (see REALMS); to "halt overexploitation of otherwise renewable resources," in the Wildlands and Human Needs Program; to "create new parks and reserves before . . . critical ecosystems are destroyed" (see WILDLIFE REFUGES); blocking illegal WILDLIFE TRADE, through TRAFFIC offices; to conserve HABITATS before they have been degraded and some species faced with EXTINCTION, as in the Himalayan kingdom of Bhutan; and DEBT-FOR-NATURE SWAPS.

WWF publishes numerous materials, including periodicals such as the *WWF Letter, TRAFFIC (U.S.A.)*, and *Tropical Forest Conservation*; booklets such as *Speaker and News Media Sourcebook: A Guide to Experts in Domestic and International Environmental Issues*, for news media, policymakers, and organizations; educational materials, research papers, and books jointly published with organizations such as IUCN, including *The Gaia Atlas of*

*Future Worlds: Challenge and Opportunity in an Age of Change* (Norman Myers, 1991), *Options for Conservation: The Different Roles of Nongovernmental Conservation Organizations* (Sarah Fitzgerald, 1991), *The Official World Wildlife Fund Guide to Endangered Species of North America* (2 vols., 1990; published by Beacham Publishing), and *WWF Atlas of the Environment* (Geoffrey Lean et al., 1990); and audiovisual materials.

**Wrangel-St. Elias National Park and Preserve,** the largest national park area in the United States, its 13,200,000 acres (20,600 square miles) containing substantial portions of two mountain ranges, the Wrangel Mountains and the very high St. Elias Mountains, with Mount St. Elias at 18,000 feet and many others over 15,000 feet high. In its southern portion, it abuts Canada's KLUANE NATIONAL PARK, which contains 19,500-foot-high Mount Logan, the highest mountain in the St. Elias range. Both parks are the home of many bird and animal SPECIES, able to live freely in a large complete ECOSYSTEM, including many thousands of Dall sheep, CARIBOU herds, moose, grizzly BEARS and black bears, mountain goats, and such birds as golden eagles, bald EAGLES, peregrine FALCONS, rock ptarmigans, mountain bluebirds, and arctic terns. But all is not entirely idyllic here; there is continuing tension between conservationists and hunters, who want more of the land opened up for HUNTING; and between conservationists and miners, many of whom have rights pre-dating the setting aside of the area for park purposes. (See WILD-LIFE REFUGES; WILDERNESS.)

# X–Y–Z

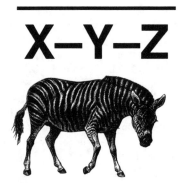

**Yellowstone National Park,** an extraordinarily important place in the history of the long campaign to save the natural world for future generations, in 1872 being made the world's first national park. The over 3,400-square-mile park in northwestern Montana, now also a WORLD NATURAL HERITAGE SITE, is in mountain country, most of it a 7,000–8,000-foot-high plateau, with several peaks over 10,000 feet high. It draws between 2.5 and 3 million visitors every year, most of them coming to see Old Faithful and some of the other 300 geysers for which the park is world-famous, along with its hot springs, hot lakes, hot mudholes, and steam holes. They also come to see the Grand Canyon of the Yellowstone—and the grizzly BEARS and black bears, such an important part of what has come to be mythic status for Yellowstone.

The park shelters a great many other animals, as well, including an estimated 20,000 elk and 2,000 bison (see BUFFALO), as well as moose, bighorn sheep, wolverines, cougars, coyotes, PRONGHORNS, and many smaller mammals, as well as white pelicans, trumpeter SWANS, sandhill CRANES, golden eagles, bald EAGLES, and OSPREYS. The United States FISH AND WILDLIFE SERVICE also plans to reintroduce the once-abundant gray wolf (see WOLVES) into Yellowstone, over the angry objections of local ranchers, who feel that their livestock will be attacked by the predators.

Yellowstone is the largest of the national parks in the "lower 48" states; but it is also extremely crowded from mid-May through mid-September, and during the 1980s, like many other U.S. national parks, was the victim of a federal policy that encouraged commercial exploitation and further crowding. Its traffic problems are not as severe as those of the Yosemite Valley, a narrow funnel that on Memorial Day in 1985 experienced gridlock and forced restriction of automobile traffic in the park, but the kinds of traffic jams experienced during peak periods make it probable that measures to protect the park's environment from damage will soon be necessary.

**For more information and action:**

• **Greater Yellowstone Coalition (GYC)** (P.O. Box 1874, 13 South Willson, Bozeman, MT 59771; 406-586-1593; Edward M. Lewis, Executive Director), an organization founded in 1983 by various environmental organizations and individuals seeking "to ensure the long-term well-being of the natural and human resources of Greater Yellowstone." GYC hold workshops, annual conferences, and field trips; runs the *Greater Yellowstone Tomorrow (GYT)* project and *Snake River Watershed Project*; has joined in a multi-organization grizzly bear project; and publishes the quarterly *Greater Yellowstone Report* and special *EcoAction* alerts. (See also WILDLIFE REFUGES; WILDERNESS.)

**Yosemite National Park,** one of the world's most popular nature preserves, and a WORLD NATURAL HERITAGE SITE. Yosemite is a tribute to the devotion of pioneer naturalist and conservationist, John MUIR, who first visited the Yosemite Valley in 1868, and had the satisfaction of seeing the establishment of Yosemite National Park in 1890.

The 1,170-square-mile park saves several world-famous places for future generations, including the seven-mile-long, mile-wide Yosemite Valley, almost 4,000 feet above sea level, with the solid granite, 7,500-foot-high El Capitan at one end and 8,500-foot-high Half Dome at the other. Yosemite Falls, 13 times as high as Niagara at over 2,400 feet, is the highest waterfall in North America. The park also includes such landmark places as the Mariposa Grove, with its 2,700-year-old, 100-feet-around, 200-foot-tall Grizzly Giant sequoia, the Merced and Tolumne sequoia groves, and Tolumne Meadows. One of North America's greatest parks, it is also one of the historic places of the world conservation movement.

Yosemite is not primarily a WILDLIFE REFUGE; but it does shelter a considerable number of animals, including black BEARS, mule deer, wolverines, porcupines, beaver, raccoons, skunks, and such birds as kingfishers, quail, grouse, purple finches, and woodpeckers. It also shelters such trees as incense cedars, ponderosa pines, black oaks, Douglas firs, and the mountain flowers that bloom in profusion every spring.

During the 1980s, some parts of Yosemite became se-

verely threatened by the park's popularity, and by commercial exploitation. With 3.5 million visitors a year pouring into and through the narrow Yosemite Valley, and with federal encouragement of luxury hotels and other facilities in the park, the valley and several other park areas became overcrowded—so extraordinarily overcrowded that after a Memorial Day 1985 traffic gridlock in Yosemite Valley, restrictions were set on the movement of motor vehicles in the park, and by the early 1990s, restrictions on the number of people entering the park were seriously being considered. When a major set of forest fires struck the park in August 1990, an estimated 10,000 tourists were trapped in the valley, and were evacuated the next day, the park then being closed for 10 days while the fire, which gutted 25,000 acres, was brought under control.

In a development related to the commercial exploitation of the park, the National Park Foundation takes over control of the park concessions from 1993, by agreement between the Department of the Interior and the new Japanese owners of the current concessionaire. The foundation has announced its intention to reduce the number of structures in the Yosemite Valley, as part of a move to limit further damage.

**For more information and action:**

• **WILDERNESS SOCIETY, THE,** (202-833-2300). Publishes *Yosemite National Park.*

(See also WILDLIFE REFUGES.)

**zebras,** horselike mammals once numerous in eastern and southern Africa, which are threatened by loss of HABITAT to explosively expanding human POPULATIONS, as well as by poachers. Large numbers of *plains zebras* do survive in protected areas, as on the SERENGETI plains, with its hundreds of thousands of zebras; at South Africa's KRUGER NATIONAL PARK; and several other parks and WILDLIFE REFUGES. But both of the other zebra species are at great risk. *Grevy's zebra*, ranging through east and central Africa, is greatly endangered by poachers for its highly prized skin and will survive only if strong enforcement saves it and other similarly endangered animals. The *mountain zebra*, ranging through southern Africa, was thought to have become extinct as early as the 1940s, but a few survived to become a protected species in such wildlife refuges as South Africa's MOUNTAIN ZEBRA NATIONAL PARK, now the home of over 200 mountain zebras. (See ENDANGERED SPECIES, also ENDANGERED AND THREATENED WILDLIFE AND PLANTS on pg. 372).

**zero population growth,** the stabilization of a POPULATION at its current level, with birth and death rates for several generations canceling each other out. The birth rate is at a "replacement reproduction" level a little higher than the death rate, allowing for infant mortality and other early death factors. Zero population growth is a theoretical construct and a population control goal; as a practical matter, diminishing birth rates are likely to vary on the way down to levels that will reduce populations, while diminishing death rates can accelerate on the way down due to scientific and medical developments or be adversely affected by war, epidemic disease, and other major factors. (See POPULATION; also POPULATION INFORMATION AND ACTION GUIDE on page 248, including an organization called Zero Population Growth.)

**zoning,** a key instrument for implementing ENVIRONMENTAL PLANNING, involving the division of a community into districts with different regulations regarding LAND USE, including the type of construction allowed, and specific limits on characteristics such as height and area of buildings; the types of uses to which they may be put, such as residential, industrial, or commercial (including mixed use, as when a complex contains offices, shops, and apartments); and the density of buildings in an area. Zoning is used to maintain or develop a certain character in an area, and also is increasingly used (though often belatedly so) to separate districts for reasons of environmental health, as by keeping residential areas separate from possibly dangerous industrial facilities. Zoning cannot, however, restore a town and undo damage once done once DEVELOPMENT has proceeded unchecked, so environmentalists urge that even small towns and rural areas develop zoning regulations in advance of major development. (See ENVIRONMENTAL PLANNING; LAND USE; DEVELOPMENT.)

**zoo,** a collection of captive animals; sometimes more formally called a *zoological park* or, where marine animals are involved, an *aquarium*. Traditionally zoos have been established for the display of animals, scientific research, education, and the breeding of particular SPECIES. For centuries most captive animals were simply kept in cages, often small and unkempt, and were exposed to abuse, from visitors or keepers. But in the 20th century, the trend has been toward more open areas, with room for roaming, with increased concern for treatment of the animals, in zoos, aquariums, and also circuses.

With the rise of the ANIMAL RIGHTS MOVEMENT, some people have come to feel that zoos—however spacious—are simply prisons, and should be abolished, with all animals being freed into the wild. However, the 20th century has seen such a massive toss of HABITAT, and as a result so many ENDANGERED SPECIES, that "the wild" no longer exists as an option for some zoo animals. Indeed, some animals have come so close to actual EXTINCTION that none of their species any longer exists in the wild.

In these circumstances, zoos have become important sites for the preservation and—it is hoped—restoration of many species, through *captive breeding* (see BIOLOGICAL DIVERSITY). The knowledge and experience developed in modern zoos and aquariums may hold the key to the continued survival for such species, in terms of reproduction and also ways of helping them in the future survive in much changed, often polluted environments.

Many zoos and aquariums remain on a collision course with some animal rights activists, however. In late 1991, several aquariums even felt obliged to go to court, charging that three animal rights groups had falsely portrayed their motives in attempting to rescue stranded WHALES and DOLPHINS. They stress the importance of such rescue missions, and of their role in educating new generations about wildlife and natural environments.

**For more information and action:**

- **AMERICAN ASSOCIATION OF ZOO KEEPERS (AAZK),** (913-272-5821, ext. 31). Publishes the monthly *Animal Keepers' Forum*, the *Conservation, Preservation and Restoration Committee Bulletin*, and *Zookeeping as a Career*.
- **AMERICAN SOCIETY OF ZOOLOGISTS (ASZ),** (805-492-3585). Publishes the journal *American Zoologists* and *Careers in Animal Biology*.
- **International Society for Animal Rights (ISAR)** (717-586-2200). Conducts Zoowatch campaign. Publishes fact sheets on zoos. (See ANIMAL RIGHTS AND WELFARE INFORMATION AND ACTION GUIDE on page 361.)
- **WILDLIFE CONSERVATION INTERNATIONAL (WCI),** (212-220-5100). Publishes the magazine *Wildlife Conservation*.

# Special Information Section

## Animal Rights and Welfare Information and Action Guide

**For more information and action on animal rights and welfare:**

**American Anti-Vivisection Society (AA-VS)** (Suite 204 Noble Plaza, 801 Old York Road, Jenkintown, PA 19046; 215-887-0816), a membership organization, founded in 1883, of people seeking "the end of animal use in research, testing and education," by working to educate the public and influence policymakers, encouraging protests and boycotts of firms that exploit animals, suggesting alternative courses of action, and supporting and reporting on research in non-animal testing. It publishes various materials, including the monthly *AV Magazine*; brochures such as *Animals in Education: An Outline for Student Activists, The Call to Compassion, The Casebook of Experiments with Living Animals, Don't Tread*

*On Our Genes, Halt Animal Patents, Pet Owners Beware, Pilate Washes His Hands, Point/Counterpoint: Responses to Pro-Vivisection Arguments, Stop—Why We Oppose Vivisection, and What Can I Do to Help?*; audiovisual materials, such as the film *Suffer the Animals;* and books on animal research and related issues.

**AMERICAN ASSOCIATION OF ZOO KEEPERS (AAZK)** (913-272-5821, ext. 31).

**American Humane Association (AHA), Animal Protection Division** (63 Inverness Drive East, Englewood, CO 80112; 303-792-9900; or P.O. Box 1266, Denver, CO 80201; Dennis J. White, Director, Animal Protection Division), a membership organization of individuals and animal-related agencies concerned about preventing "cruelty, neglect, abuse, and exploitation of animals," founded in 1877. The organization promotes legislation to "prevent abuse of pet animals, wildlife, animals used in biomedical research and testing, farm animals," and animals used in entertainment, sports, fighting, and related situations; and provides training programs for local animal care and control agencies. The AHA provides emergency relief for animal victims of natural disasters, and offers information and referral services. It has established guidelines for treatment of animals on motion picture sets, supervising when allowed, and rates movies based on their treatment of animals. The AHA publishes numerous materials, including the quarterly magazine *Advocate*, the bimonthly *American Humane Shoptalk* for animal care and control professionals, *Directory of Animal Care and Control Agencies, Helping Animals Through Legislative Activism*, and pamphlets such as the "Care Of . . ." series for pet owners, *Who Would Hurt them?*, and *Genetic Engineering.*

**American Fund for Alternatives to Animal Research (AFAAR)** (175 West 12th Street, Suite 16G, New York, NY 10011; 212-989-8073; Ethel Thurston, Trustee), an organization founded in 1977 dedicated to finding non-animal alternatives for tests and other projects (as in schools) currently involving animals. Provides grants for developing non-animal tests and encourages use of computer simulations, for dissections, providing several electronic animal dummies free for use in veterinary colleges for practicing cardiac pulmonary resuscitation. It publishes *AFAAR News Abstracts* and leaflets.

**American Society for the Prevention of Cruelty to Animals (ASPCA)** (441 East 92nd Street, New York, NY 10128; 212-876-7700; Roger Caras, President), the oldest animal-protection society in the United States, founded by Henry Bergh and incorporated in 1866, "to provide effective means for the prevention of cruelty to animals throughout the United States." Its areas of concern include companion animals, animals in research and testing, those raised for food, wild animals, entertainment and work animals, and those in education. The ASPCA seeks to increase public awareness of alternatives to cruelty, through education, media exposure, and print and video publications, such as the magazine *ASPCA Reports*, pamphlets, informational flyers, and brochures on animal protection and care of companion animals, and "ASPCA Updates" on various topics, including *Puppy Mills, Rodeo Cruelty, Veal Calf Facts, Animals in Research, Fur Facts and Fallacies,* and *ASPCA Guidelines for Student Experiments Involving Animals.*

**Animal Legal Defense Fund (ALDF)** (1363 Lincoln Avenue, San Rafael, CA 94901; 415-459-0885; Joyce S.A. Tischler, Executive Director; *Dissection Hotline*, 800-922-FROG [3764]), a member-supported "nationwide network of over 250 attorneys dedicated to protecting and promoting animal rights" providing the legal services in defense against animal abuse and exploitation in research laboratories, on farms, or in the wild. For students (and others) opposing animal dissection, the ALDF publishes the brochure *Objecting to Dissection: A College Students' Handbook.* The ALDF also publishes the quarterly newsletter *The Animals' Advocate* and *ALDF Updates.*

**Animal Protection Institute (API)** (2831 Fruitridge Road, P.O. Box 22505, Sacramento, CA 95822; 916-731-5521; Duf Fischer, Executive Director), a membership organization seeking humane treatment for animals, focusing especially on stopping slaughter of animals such as WHALES and harp seals, protecting ENDANGERED SPECIES, avoiding overpopulation of cats and dogs, and barring leg-hold traps. The API gathers and disseminates information through educational programs and publications, such as the quarterly magazine *Mainstream*; books such as *Animal Activist's Handbook, Product Testing: A Way Without Animals,* and *Animals in Research* and brochures and flyers such as *Factory Farming, Everyperson's Guide to Animal Rights, Taking Animals Out of the Labs, Trapping: Can We Allow This Cruel Practice to Continue?, Poultry: Life and Death on the Factory Line, Endangered Species, Whales, The Harp Seal,* and *Children's Reading List.* The group also sponsors wildlife-viewing safaris in East Africa.

**Animal Welfare Information Center (AWIC)** (National Agricultural Library [NAL], Beltsville, MD 20705; 301-344-3212; Public Services Desk, 301-344-3755; Jean Larson, Coordinator), a center established under the 1986 ANIMAL WELFARE ACT as part of the National Agricultural Library (NAL) as a clearinghouse for information and publications on animal welfare. AWIC helps enquirers answer specific questions; eases access to NAL animal-care collections; provides referrals to individuals and organizations; performs free or minimal-cost data base searches (as of NAL's AGRICOLA), provides conference facilities and hosts training sessions for groups or individuals; and offers speakers and/or exhibits for training sessions, conferences, and workshops. AWIC's *Document Delivery Service* arranges for interlibrary loan of books and audiovisuals through libraries; provides photocopies of otherwise inaccessible journal articles and microforms; and helps locate books or journals not in the NAL holdings. AWIC also publishes many materials, including Quick Bibliographies, such as *Animal Welfare Legislation and Regulation, Ethical and Moral Issues Relating to Animals, Laboratory Animal Facilities and Management, Transport and Handling of Livestock,* and *Welfare of Experimental Animals*; Special Reference Briefs, such as *Animal Care and Use Committees, Animal Euthanasia, The Draize Eye-Irritancy Test,* and *The $LD_{50}$ (Median Lethal Dose) and $LC_{50}$ (Median Lethal Concentration) Toxicity Tests* (fact sheets such as *Resources for Information on Alternatives and Animal Welfare;* and other publications such as *Animal-Related Computer Simulation Programs for Use in Education and Research, Audio Visuals Relating to Animal Care, Use and Welfare,* and reviews of bills and public laws related to animal welfare.

**Animal Welfare Institute (AWI)** (P.O. Box 3650, Washington, DC 20007; 202-337-2332; Christine Stevens, President), an organization founded in 1951 that aims "to reduce the sum total of pain and fear inflicted on animals by man," specifically seeking humane treatment of laboratory animals and development of non-animal tests, humane science teaching and use of non-animal experiments, trapping reform, ban on trade in exotic pets, regulation of shipping conditions for all animals, preservation of species and habitats, and reform of conditions for food animals, such as factory farms, advocating "humane slaughter." It has run the Save the Whales Campaign since 1971 and awards the annual Albert Schweitzer medal for achievement in animal welfare. AWI's companion organization for lobbying, primarily on the federal and international level, is the **Society for Animal Protective Legislation (SAPL)** (P.O. Box 3719, Washington, DC 20007; 202-337-2334; Madeleine Bemelmans, President), which focuses entirely on passage of animal protection legislation. AWI publishes or distributes various materials, including books such as *Animal Welfare Institute Quarterly, Animals and Their Legal Rights, The Endangered Species Handbook, The Bird Business Beyond the Laboratory Door, Comfortable Quarters for Laboratory Animals, Facts About Furs*; an annotated bibliography for members of Institutional Animal Care and Use Committees, and various brochures and reprints.

**Beauty Without Cruelty International (BWC)** (11 Limehill Road, Tunbridge Wells, Kent YN1 1LJ, England); **BWC USA** (175 West 12th Street, 16G, New York, NY 10011; 212-989-8073; Ethel Thurston, Chairwoman), an organization opposed to the use of clothing or cosmetics involving animal slaughter or testing. BWC publishes the newsletter *The Compassionate Shopper, Action Alert*, and *Please Excuse Me for Approaching You—I See You Are Wearing Fur*, and lists of "animal-friendly" (cruelty-free) products and companies.

**Center for Animals and Public Policy (CAPP)** (Tufts University School of Veterinary Medicine, 200 Westboro Road, North Grafton, MA 01536; 508-839-5302, ext. 4750; Andrew N. Rowan, Director), an organization founded in 1983 "to coordinate and focus programs dealing with ethical, legal, scientific, and social issues relating to the status of animals in society." The Center conducts programs on the whole range of "interactions between animals and society that are amenable to scholarly and scientific study," including "veterinary ethics, veterinary jurisprudence, companion animal demographics and control, human/animal relations, wildlife policy issues, animal research ethics," BIOTECHNOLOGY, animal behavior programs, and grief counseling. The Center sponsors seminars and conferences, supports research, and publishes various materials, including the *Tufts Center for Animals & Public Policy Newsletter*, the journal *Anthrozoos, The Alternatives Report*, and proceedings of conferences and workshops.

**Doris Day Animal League (DDAL)** (900 Second Street NE, Suite 303, Washington, DC 20002; 202-842-3325; Holly Hazard, Executive Director), a membership organization founded in 1987 by actress Doris Day that acts as a "citizens' lobbying organization, formed to focus public attention on the needless suffering of many animals in commercial

testing facilities and laboratories." DDAL's main legislative goals are to ban the LD-$_{50}$ TEST, to outlaw the DRAIZE EYE-IRRITANCY TEST (see also ANIMAL TESTING for both), and to stop pound seizure of animals for experimentation. It publishes the *DDAL Newsletter*, the periodical *Animal Guardian*, and legislative alerts.

**ELSA WILD ANIMAL APPEAL (EWAA)** (818-761-8387). Publishes *Wildlife Education Kits*.

**ENVIRONMENTAL INVESTIGATION AGENCY (EIA),** (202-483-6621). Publishes *To Save an Elephant* (1991); and reports such as *The Global War Against Small Cetaceans, A Second Report* (1991), and *Wild Bird Imports for Pet Trade, An EEC Overview* (1990).

**Fund for Animals, Inc.** (200 West 57th Street, New York, NY 10019; 212-246-2096 or 246-2632; Cleveland Amory, President), an organization founded in 1967 as "a national anti-cruelty society . . . to fight the imposition of fear and suffering on all animals, wild and domestic." Active on a whole range of animal rights issues, the Fund publishes various materials, including the periodical *The Fund for Animals*; the brochure *The Armchair Activist*; and a series of Fact Sheets, such as *The Bloody Business of Fur, An Overview of Killing for Sport*, and *The Destruction of Our Nation's Waterfowl*.

**Hastings Center** (255 Elm Road, Briarcliff Manor, NY 10510; 914-762-8500; Daniel Callahan, Director), an organization founded in 1969 to carry on research, education, and consultation on "difficult moral issues in our society," often ethical issues relating to life and death. Its *Animal, Human and Environmental Ethics* project explores "deepening concerns about the interplay of the wider environment with human health and well-being and new images of the significance of the nonhuman world." It offers many publications including *Animals, Science and Ethics* (1990)

**Humane Society of the United States (HSUS)** (2100 L Street NW, Washington, DC 20037; 202-452-1100; John A. Hoyt, President), a charitable, contribution-supported organization, founded in 1954, devoted to protecting animals. HSUS seeks to educate the public, as through its Professional Education Training Seminars (PETS) and its *National Association for the Advancement of Humane Education (NAAHE)* division. Through its bioethics division, the *Center for Respect of Life and Environment (CRLE)*, it fosters discussion of ethical concerns and animal rights; and through its *Institute for the Study of Animal Problems* it carries on scientific investigations allowing HSUS to "challenge more effectively the exploitation of animals by science and industry." It also carries out legal and investigative work and seeks to influence legislation, nationally and through its regional offices.

The HSUS publishes a wide range of materials, including the periodicals *HSUS News, Animal Activist Alert, Shelter Sense* (for animal work professionals), *Children & Animals* (for educators), *Kind News* (for children at elementary and secondary levels), *International Journal for the Study of Animal Problems*, and periodic *Close-Up Reports* such as *Dolphin Death: Thousands Drown in Tuna Nets, Crisis in the Oceans, Refuge Wildlife Under Siege!, National Wildlife Ref-*

uges: A Cruel Hoax, Fur Shame: HSUS Campaign Targets Consumers, Fur Is Out; Compassion Is In, Save the Chimpanzee—Humankind's Sibling Species, The Animal Slave Trade—Brutality on the Road to Research, Remember the Elephants . . . Forget Ivory, HSUS Exposes Livestock Transportation Cruelty, Investigations in Action, Animal Companions—The Promise Kept; The Promise Broken, and Dogfighters on the Run.

HSUS also publishes fact sheets on key animal rights and welfare issues, such as animal exploitation, laboratory animals, LD-$_{50}$ acute toxicity and DRAIZE EYE-IRRITANCY TESTS, alternatives to animals in testing and research, wild-caught birds, steel-jaw leghold traps, FACTORY FARMING, and horse and dog racing; model legislation, as for wildlife management, trapping, protection against livestock cruelties, responsible animal regulation, and captive wild animal protection; guidelines on various topics, such as animal shelter policies, cruelty investigation, and euthanasia; educational materials for children, such as Captive Wild Animals and Does the Idea of Dissecting or Experimenting on Animals in Biology Class Disturb you?; reports such as Alternatives to Current Uses of Animals in Research, Safety Testing, and Education: A Layman's Guide, The Trade in Live Wildlife: Mortality and Transport Conditions, Factory Farming, Introduction to Animal-Cruelty Investigation, and The Bird Business; brochures and pamphlets such as Laboratory Animals, Understanding the Animal Welfare Act, The Production of White Veal as an Animal-Welfare Issue, Wild Birds Should Fly Free, The Shame of Fur, Captive Wildlife, Hunted Wildlife, Trapped Animals, and Humane Shopper's Guide; reprints of articles on key issues; and audiovisual materials.

**In Defense of Animals (IDA)** (816 West Francisco Boulevard, San Rafael, CA 94901; 415-453-9984; Report Animal Abuse Hotline, 415-453-9994, 24 hours a day, seven days a week; Elliot M. Katz, D.V.M., President), a membership organization founded in 1984 to act as advocate to end animal suffering. Animal activist campaigns involve nonviolent demonstrations and rallies, letter writing and lobbying, legal actions, publicity-seeking actions such as occupying a construction crane at an animal laboratory, and support of World Laboratory Animal Liberation Week. IDA publishes various materials, including the newsletter In Defense of Animals and brochures and flyers on topics of concern, such as Report Animal Abuse, Fashion Shouldn't Cost an Arm and a Leg, A Shocking Story of Animal Abuse: A Military Disgrace, From Your Back Yard to an Animal Torture Chamber, Behind Closed Doors, What Do NIMH Funds Really Pay For? and Just Say No! to the Alcohol, Drug Abuse, and Mental Health Administration.

**Institute of Laboratory Animal Resources (ILAR)** (Commission on Life Sciences, 2100 Constitution Avenue, Washington, DC 20418; 202-334-2590; Tom Wolfle, Director), a coordinating agency and international resource for gathering and disseminating information on laboratory animals, especially advising the scientific community on humane and appropriate care and use of animals and on the strengths and weaknesses of alternatives to ANIMAL TESTING. Part of the National Research Council, ILAR promotes use of animal or nonanimal alternatives, as appropriate to the research situation; advises on refinement of research methodologies; and maintains a computerized database, Animal Models and Genetic Stocks Information Program. It seeks to educate the scientific and educational community on production, care, and breeding of animals and on recognizing and alleviating pain, through conferences and symposia as well as through its publications, such as the quarterly ILAR News, Guide for the Care and Use of Laboratory Animals, Animals for Research—A Directory of Sources, and Principles and Guidelines for the Use of Animals in Precollege Education.

**International Foundation for Ethical Research (IFER)** (79 West Monroe, Suite 514, Chicago, IL 60603; 312-419-6990; Michael J. Bello, Executive Director), an organization established in 1985 by people "seeking viable, scientifically valid alternatives to the use of live animals in research, testing and teaching," advocating not "immediate, indiscriminate abandonment of animal models," but "a process that will allow for planned, steady progress in this area. Its guidelines are dubbed the 4 R's: "Refinement—any improvement in the optimal well-being of animals used in research; Reduction—a decrease in the number of animals used while enhancing the yield of information; Replacement—a scientifically valid substitute for current live animal methodologies; Responsibility—the reevaluation of the course science is taking with animal models, the recognition of society's heightened awareness of the use of animals in research, the development of new technologies, the implementation of new methodologies, and the furthering of personal accountability." IFER sponsors research; gathers and disseminates information, through lectures, workshops, seminars, and symposia; and publishes a quarterly newsletter.

**International Fund for Animal Welfare (IFAW)** (P.O. Box 193, 411 Main Street, Yarmouth Port, MA 02675; 508-362-4944; Brian Davies, Founder), an international member-supported organization founded in 1969, originally to stop the "brutal harp and hood seal commercial slaughter by Canadian and Norwegian hunters" in Canada's Gulf of St. Lawrence, but since widened to become a general animal welfare organization, whose mission is "to promote and ensure the just and kind treatment of animals as sentient beings," which "includes improving the quality of the lives of animals and their environment, preserving animals from extinction, [and] preventing and abolishing animal cruelty." IFAW operates the ketch Song of the Whale to carry out nonintrusive research on marine life; conducts various campaigns around the world, such as actions against steel leg-hold traps, brutal dog- and cat-butchering in Asia, and inhumane treatment of iguanas in Nicaragua; and publishes action alerts and fact sheets on topics of concern, such as killing of ELEPHANTS for their ivory, commercial whaling, and ANIMAL TESTING for cosmetics.

**International Society for Animal Rights (ISAR)** (421 South State Street, Clarks Summit, PA 18411; 717-586-2200; Helen Jones, President), a membership organization founded in

1959 and funded by contributions and grants, its aims being "exposing and alleviating animal abuse and exploitation." Its recent Zoowatch campaign seeks to expose local zoos as "animal prisons" and to document its charges that they sell zoo animals to research laboratories, private HUNTING preserves, and circuses, as well as to other zoos. ISAR publishes a bimonthly newsletter, *ISAR Report*; guides for activists, such as *The Argument for Abolition* (Steven Tiger) on animal experimentation, *How to Take Your Tax Money Away from Vivisectors*, *How to Use the Freedom of Information Act*, for information on animal experimentation, and *What You should Know About Grassroots Lobbying*; fact sheets, brochures, and flyers on animals rights issues, including furs, dog labs, DOLPHINS, nonviolence, rodeos, seals, student activists, circuses, zoos, the Pet Theft Act, the Federal Animal Welfare Act, cosmetic testing, cruelty-free products, and animal addiction experiments; and various books and booklets.

**INTERNATIONAL WILDLIFE COALITION (IWC)**, (508-564-9980).

**INVESTOR RESPONSIBILITY RESEARCH CENTER (IRRC)**, (202-234-7500). Publishes *Animal Testing and Consumer Products* (1990).

**Johns Hopkins Center for Alternatives to Animal Testing (CAAT)** (615 North Wolfe Street, Baltimore, MD 21205; 301-955-3343; Alan Goldberg, Director), an organization established in 1981 to develop and disseminate "basic scientific knowledge concerning innovative non-whole animal methods to evaluate fully the safety of commercial and therapeutic products" focusing primarily on developing *in vitro* toxicity testing methods; communicating new developments to scientific, governmental, business, and other concerned organizations; validating and promoting the use of alternative testing methods, understanding that "in vitro methods act in concert with whole animal and clinical studies to advance our knowledge base, develop new products and drugs and treat, cure, and prevent disease." CAAT conducts symposia and publishes various technical reports and a newsletter.

**National Alliance for Animal Legislation (NAAL)** (P.O. Box 75116, Washington, DC 20013; 703-684-0654; Peter G. Linck, Executive Director), a "grassroots organization devoted to promoting legislation which will improve the quality of life for all living beings," founded in 1985. Not relying on professional lobbyists working in Washington, DC, the Alliance has developed a national grassroots network of animal advocates, many of whom are trained for their work in the Alliance's workshops or seminars, often funded by the related *National Alliance for Animals' Education Fund*. The Alliance publishes the periodical newsletter *Capitol Hill Report* and various *Alliance Alerts*.

**National Anti-Vivisection Society (NAVS)** (53 West Jackson Boulevard, Suite 1550, Chicago, IL 60604; 312-427-6065; George J. Trapp, Managing Director), an organization founded in 1929 by people interested in animal welfare. The NAVS *Campaign for Life* seeks "systematic reduction and replacement of animal experimentation aimed at total elimination," fostering alternatives to animal research, seeking to eliminate pound seizure of animals for laboratories, bringing lawsuits on behalf of animals, and seeking to educate the public through schools, public service programs, and publications. These include the *NAVS Bulletin*; books and booklets, such as *Personal Care With Principle: A Guide to Choosing Cruelty Free Cosmetics and Products from Major Manufacturers* and *A Critique of Animal Experiments on Cocaine Abuse*; fact sheets on topics such as pound seizure, cosmetic testing, alternatives to animal-based research, lethal dose 50 percent test, Draize Eye and Skin Irritancy tests, dissection, and psychological research; and brochures and pamphlets such as *The Campaign for Life, Alternatives to Animal Research and Testing, Animal Shelter? Or Halfway House to Horror?, Reverence for Life: An Ethic for High School Biology Curricula* (George K. Russell), *School Project Packet*, and *Some of Us Don't See Eye to Eye*.

**People for the Ethical Treatment of Animals (PETA)**, (P.O. Box 42516, Washington, D.C. 20015; 301-770-7444; Kim Stallwood, Executive Director), an organization founded in 1980 to establish and defend the rights of all animals, following "the simple principle that animals are not ours to eat, wear or experiment on," and focusing on areas such as FACTORY FARMING, ANIMAL TESTING, HUNTING and the fur trade, FISHING, ZOOS, and circuses. PETA works through "public education, research and investigations, legislation, special events, direct action, grassroots organizing," and "exposing cruelty wherever it occurs." It publishes the bimonthly *PETA News*, periodic action alerts and updates, and other informative materials on animal rights concerns, such as *Animals Rights—Why Should It Concern Me?* and *Take a Step Toward Compassionate Living*.

**Progressive Animal Welfare Society (PAWS)** (P.O. Box 1037, Lynnwood, WA 98946; 206-742-4142; Tim Greyhavens, Executive Director), a Washington State–based membership organization founded in 1967, "dedicated to promoting and protecting the rights, interests and well-being of all animals. "To that end PAWS will "provide shelter, adoption, and lost and found services for companion animals; work to end companion animal overpopulation; care for and return injured, orphaned and displaced wildlife to their natural homes; combat animal abuse and exploitation through public campaigns, legislation, litigation and direct action; promote respect for all life through the education of adults and children." In addition to its shelter, PAWS operates HOWL, a wildlife rehabilitation center for injured animals in Washington State, which publishes *Howlings*, and has a volunteer animal rights activist arm, *PAWS Action*, which publishes the *PAWS Action Letter*. PAWS publishes its own newsletter, *Paws News*.

**Scientists Center for Animal Welfare (SCAW)** (4805 St. Elmo Avenue, Bethesda, MD 20814; 301-654-6390; Lee Krulisch, Executive Director), an organization founded to educate the public and scientific and educational institutions about humane and responsible use of animals in research, testing, and education. SCAW sponsors conferences, maintains a speakers' bureau, and publishes various materials, including a quarterly newsletter *Laboratory Animal Welfare: A Bibliog-*

raphy, *Field Research Guidelines, Effective Animal Care and Use Committees, Science and Animals, Addressing Contemporary Issues*, and conference proceedings.

**Student Action Corps for Animals (SACA)** (P.O. Box 15588, Washington, DC 20003; 202-543-8983; Rosa Feldman, Director), national "advocacy, education, and information organization—in the animal rights movement—dedicated exclusively to empowering young people in high school to work effectively for animal rights and liberation." Founded in 1981 with mostly student membership, it offers counseling by telephone helpline (above) or mail, refers students to legal assistance when necessary, and acts as a student communication network. It began the national "Say No to Dissection" campaign in 1984. SACA publishes various materials, including the quarterly *SACA News* and brochures and flyers. *Say No to Dissection, Suggestions for High School Student Animal Rights Groups*, and *1•0•1 Non-Animal Biology Lab Methods (Animals Are Not Tools for a Lab)*.

**United Action for Animals (UAA)** (205 East 42nd Street, New York, NY 10017; 212-983-5315; [Miss] MacDonald White, President), a membership organization founded in 1967 "to end the shocking and tragic waste of billions of animal lives and taxpayer dollars on duplicative, inconclusive, and wasteful animal experiments." The UAA seeks to expose the "research myth" that all animal research is life-saving; to

"replace live animals in research using currently available, modern methods"; and to foster the cause of "research accountability and responsibility towards animal life in both the private and public sectors." It publishes various materials, including the newsletter *UAA Reports* and brochures such as *Animal Welfare Act: Unreported Crimes?, Facts About Research Accountability, Animal Agony in Addiction Research*, and *Science Gone Insane*.

**Wildlife Information Center** (215-434-1637). Publishes *Wildlife in Traveling Animal Shows: An Examination and Critique*.

**World Society for the Protection of Animals (WSPA)** (617-522-7000).

**Other references:**

*The Animal Rights Handbook: Everyday Ways to Save Animal Lives*. ASPCA and Living Planet Press, 1990. *Victims of Vanity*. Lynda Dickinson. Sterling, 1990. *Animal Liberation*. Peter Singer. Random House, 1990. *The Unheeded Cry: Animal Consciousness, Animal Pain and Science*. Bernard E. Rollin. Oxford University Press, 1989. *The Rights of Nature: A History of Environmental Ethics*. Roderick Nash. University of Wisconsin Press, 1989. *Animal Liberators*. Susan Sperling. University of California Press, 1988.

## Ecotourism Information and Action Guide

**For more information and action on ecotourism:**

**African Wildlife Foundation (AWF),** (202-265-8393 or 800-344-TUSK [8875]). Offers African safaris.

**American Hiking Society (AHS)** (703-385-3252). Sponsors volunteer trailbuilding vacations. Publishes *Helping Out in the Outdoors* (a directory of volunteer projects on public lands).

**American Littoral Society (ALS),** (201-291-0055). Sponsors field trips, including weekend camping, birding, canoeing or boating, and diving trips, as along the Atlantic or in the Caribbean. (See Coasts Information and Action Guide.)

**Animal Protection Institute (API),** (916-731-5521). Sponsors wildlife-viewing safaris into East Africa. (See Animal Rights and Welfare Information and Action Guide, page 361.)

**American Wildlands alliance (AWL),** (303-771-0380). Operates the *Eco-Adventure Connection*, offering "'wild country experiences" in natural areas of the world, focusing on the "people, flora, fauna, geology, history, and conservation issues" of each area.

**Appalachian Mountain Club (AMC),** (617-523-0636). Offers day-trips, excursions, and volunteer projects.

**Appalachian Trail Conference (ATC),** (304-535-6331). Trains volunteers in maintaining the Appalachian Trail. Publishes *Appalachian Trailway News*.

**Archaeological Conservancy, The,** (505-982-3278). Sponsors archaeological tours for members. (See Land Trust and Conservation Easement Information and Action Guide on page 178.)

**Biological Journeys** (1696 Ocean Drive, McKinleyville, CA 95521; 707-839-0178 or 415-527-9622 or U.S. except CA 800-548-7555; Ronn Storro-Patterson and Ron LeValley, Founders), an organization that provides whale watching and natural history tours, notably on the Pacific coast and in South America. The firm also helps plan independent natural history travel to these and other regions.

**Cab International (CABI),** (602-621-7897 or 800-528-4841). Key source of bibliographic information on tourism.

**Caribbean Conservation Corporation (CCC),** (904-373-6441). Sponsors volunteer research programs in Costa Rica.

**Center for Responsible Tourism** (2 Kensington Road, San Anselmo, CA 94960; 415-258-6594; Virginia Hadsell, Director), an organization that seeks to promote socially responsible tourism, formerly called *North American Coordinating Center for Responsible Tourism*. It publishes various materials, including the newsletter *Responsible Traveling*; directories and reports such as *Alternative Tourism: Third World Travel Directory* (Betty Stott, ed.), *Guidelines for Planning Travel/Study Experiences* (Robert Reber), and *Tourism and*

*Ecology: The Impact of Travel on a Fragile Earth*; and reports on prostitution and tourism in parts of East Asia.

**CETACEAN SOCIETY INTERNATIONAL** (CSI), (203-563-6444). Arranges whale-watching trips.

**Cheeseman's Ecology Safaris** (20800 Kittredge Road, Saratoga, CA 95070; 408-867-1371 or 741-5330; Doug Cheeseman [Zoologist/Ecologist] and Gail Cheeseman [Naturalist/Birder], Directors), an organization offering wildlife tours to key natural sites in places such as Central and South America, Alaska, East Africa, the Seychelles, MADAGASCAR, New Guinea, India, and Australia, as well as WHALE trips in Monterey Bay. They aim to promote conservation through ecotourism, helping small groups of travelers appreciate the world's biodiversity (through pre-trip get-togethers, as well as the tour itself) and providing infusion of tourism money to encourage the host country to maintain natural areas. Funds from one tour a year are returned to the host country.

**CONSERVATION INTERNATIONAL (CI)**, (202-429-5660). Has ECO-TOURISM program, sponsoring small-scale travel to special environments, to benefit both conservation and local communities.

**Earthwatch (Center for Field Research)** (680 Mt. Auburn Street, P.O. Box 403, Watertown, MA 02272; 617-926-8200; Brian A. Rosborough, President), a membership organization founded in 1971 that matches paying volunteers (which make up its *EarthCorps*) and scientific researchers. By mid-1990, Earthwatch reported that it had provided over 23,000 volunteers and $15 million in funds and equipment to scientists working on over 1,000 projects in over 85 countries, "to solve problems on the frontier of knowledge" and "to document a changing world." Earthwatch's stated mission is "to improve human understanding of the planet, the diversity of its inhabitants, and the processes which affect the quality of life on earth," working "'to sustain the world's environment, monitor global change, conserve endangered habitats and species, explore the vast heritage of our peoples, and foster world health, and international cooperation." It publishes a bimonthly magazine, *Earthwatch*.

**Ecotourism Society, The** (801 Devon Place, Alexandria, VA 22314; 703-549-8979; Megan Epler Wood, Executive Director), an organization founded by people concerned with ECO-TOURISM. It carries out special projects, such as the *Galapagos Campaign* to redesign plans for resource management and visitor education and safety; offers seminars, such as the Ecotourism Management Seminar, including ecotourism and its role in sustainable development, and publishes various materials, including a newsletter, "The New Ethic in Adventure Travel," "Ecotourism: The Uneasy Alliance," and *Ecotourism: The Potentials and Pitfalls*.

**ENVIRONMENTAL DEFENSE FUND (EDF)**, (212-505-2100). Publishes *Paradise Lost: The Need for Environmental Regulation of Tourism in Antarctica* (B. Manheim, 1990).

**FRIENDS OF THE EARTH (FOE)**, (202-544-2600). Offers ecotours through Oceanic Society Expeditions, the environmental travel arm of the Oceanic Society.

**FRIENDS OF THE RIVER (FOR)**, (415-771-0400). Offers rafting trips on Western RIVERS, and abroad, with discounts to members and a portion of the trip price going to fund FOR's campaigns.

**Journeys** (3516 NE 155th Street, Seattle, WA 98155; 206-365-0686; 800-345-HIKE [4453]; Kurt Kutay, Director), a travel organization founded in 1976, arranging both group and individual tours to visit "natural environments, wildlife, archaeological sites and indigenous cultures," especially in Asia, Africa, and the Americas. Journeys maintains a nonprofit *Earth Preservation Fund (EPF)*, with a portion of the cost of each trip being donated to conservation or community development projects in host countries; staff members and sometimes travelers also volunteer time for local EPF projects.

**NATIONAL AUDUBON SOCIETY**, (212-832-3200). Operates summer ecology camps for adults and children, and runs travel-study programs and field seminars in the United States exploring natural and social issues.

**NATIONAL CAMPERS AND HIKERS ASSOCIATION (NCHA)**, (716-668-6242). Arranges for European camping passports, and sponsors "'travelongs," or caravans around the world.

**NATIONAL PARK SERVICE**, (202-208-4917).

**NATIONAL PARKS AND CONSERVATION ASSOCIATION (NPCA)**, (202-944-8530). Conducts "Behind the Scenes" member tours in U.S. national parks.

**Oceanic Society Expeditions (OSE)** (Fort Mason Center, Building E, Room 240, San Francisco, CA 94123; 415-441-1106 or 800-326-7491; Birgit Winning, President), an organization founded in 1972 as the environmental arm of the Oceanic Society, which in 1990 merged with FRIENDS OF THE EARTH; it seeks to help protect "wilderness areas by contributing to an economy that is in harmony with conservation." Reflecting concerns such as tropical deforestation, protection of the OCEANS, and preservation of BIOLOGICAL DIVERSITY and EN-DANGERED SPECIES, the organization offers tours to places of outstanding environmental interest, such as such as the AMA-ZON RAIN FOREST, the ARCTIC NATIONAL WILDLIFE REFUGE, GA-LAPAGOS ISLANDS, and MADAGASCAR. Some tours offered with the California Academy of Sciences combine cultural education and natural sciences or research expeditions, as to the Bahamas (on DOLPHINS) or southeast Alaska (on WHALES).

**PACIFIC WHALE FOUNDATION (PWF)**, (808-879-8860; for orders 800-WHALE-1-1 [942-5311]). Offers experiential learning programs, WHALE watchers, natural history cruises, and snorkeling trips aboard its two ocean-going vessels *Whale One* and *Whale II*.

**RAILS-TO-TRAILS CONSERVANCY**, (202-797-5400).

**Sacred Passage** (Drawer CZ, Bisbee, AZ 85603; 602-432-7353; John Milton, Contact), an organization that arranges for guided solo WILDERNESS tours, primarily on the southern coasts of Mexico's Baja, California, on the Pacific or the Sea of Cortez, but also elsewhere. Participants travel with a guide and group, and spend a three-day training period learning "specific forms of meditation and awareness training" as well as camping and safety skills, before going off solo on a spot of their own choosing on private retreat land, where adequate water and shelter is available. Participants' "safety and solitude are ensured through a buddy system," under which a guide or companion can check on them daily "without having to make visual or auditory contact," but is available to respond in case of emergency. After seven days they return to the group and guide for two days of "bridging back" into human culture. Sacred Passage also arranges for couples' passages, and other special gatherings, as for a solar eclipse viewing and celebration.

**Safaricentre International** (3201 North Sepulveda Boulevard, Manhattan Beach, CA 90266; 213-546-4411; U.S. except CA, 800-223-6046; CA, 800-624-5342; Canada 800-233-6046), an organization that offers "adventure/specialty travel arrangements around the world," its motto being "for any safari under the sun," with customized safari plans available. They claim to have "the widest range of safaris in Kenya, Egypt, Uganda, Tanzania, Rwanda, Zaire, Zambia, Zimbabwe, Botswana, and Namibia, as well as trans-Saharan and overland expeditions in Africa;" other destinations for ecological safaris and wildlife watching include Brazil, Peru, Venezuela, Argentina, Bolivia, Ecuador, and the Galapagos Islands in South America, and India, Nepal, Malaysia, and Papua New Guinea in Asia.

**Sanctuary Travel Services** (3701 East Tudor Road, Anchorage, AK 99507; 907-561-1212 or 800-247-3149, outside Anchorage; John Victors, President), a full-service travel agency founded in 1986 "to provide the very best in travel related services to the general public, and to raise funds to benefit our natural environment," through a program under which "non-profit environmental organizations receive 20% of the agency's commissions in exchange for promotion of Sanctuary Travel Services to members and supporters," with over $100,000 raised in the first three years.

Scripps Institution of Oceanography, (619-534-3624). Offers occasional expeditions, such as a snorkeling and natural history expeditions to Hawaii, whale-watching off Baja California, or diving in Fiji.

Sierra Club, (415-776-2211 or 202-547-1141; legislative hotline, 202-547-5550). Sponsors numerous outings, on the national, chapter, and group levels, including Inner City Outings for "urban youth, disabled, and seniors." Publishes *Outings Catalog, Sierra Club Inner City Outings, Outdoor Recreation Organizations, Sierra Club Wayfinding Book*, and *Sierra Club Summer Book.*

**Smithsonian Research Expeditions** (Smithsonian National Associate Program, 490 L'Enfant Plaza SW, Suite 4210, Washington, DC 20560; 202-287-3210; Ann Kirking Post, Acting Program Manager), a program of research expeditions in which people "contribute their labor and financial support to projects led by Smithsonian scientists, curators and research associates," gaining experience in "hands-on research" as they work in "field settings, laboratories, and archives to collect, organize and interpret data."

Student Conservation Association (SCA), (603-826-4301). Arranges for student and adult volunteers to work in a variety of programs in national parks, forests, wildlife refuges, and other public lands," deliberately including many disadvantaged young people.

Tropical Resources Institute (203-432-5116). Publishes *Biological and Social Aspects of Eco-Tourism: The Monteverde Case . . .* (David Tobias, 1989).

**Voyagers International** (P.O. Box 915, Ithaca, NY 14851; 607-257-3091; David Blanton, Managing Director), a company founded in 1982 that "organizes worldwide tours for leading nonprofit nature and conservation organizations throughout the United States and Canada," going "beyond standard package tours [to] provide in-depth experiences that focus on the natural history and traditional culture of an area," seeking to "provide low-impact travel that is environmentally sound and culturally sensitive." Voyagers International focuses on natural history, nature photography, and independent travel, avoiding "'crowded tourist lodges," and has its own schedule of small-sized nature and photo tours in addition to specially designed tours of environmental organizations, such as the Wildlife Preservation Trust International, and various state and local Audubon societies. Voyagers International is active in fundraising for the East African Wild Life Society (of which their director is the North American representative), the Darwin Research Station on the Galapagos, and other nonprofit conservation organizations, and contributes to various others, supporting the host countries' economies by using local guides. The firm publishes a semiannual newsletter and brochures, and supplies background readings on the natural history, conservation efforts, and traditional culture of the places being visited.

**Wilderness Travel** (801 Allston Way, Berkeley, CA 94710; 415-548-0420; 800-247-6700; Bill Abbott, Managing Director and cofounder), an organization that offers small-group nature-oriented adventure tours, from "back-country basic" to luxury, around the world, including Asia, Africa, Europe, South America (including the Galapagos Islands), and the Pacific. Wilderness Travel "actively promotes cultural preservation, conservation, and environmental protection . . . by supporting a number of environmental and cultural projects and organizations, promoting minimum-impact camping and travel in the field, and actively encouraging cross-cultural ties." Wilderness Travel also specializes in "designing and coordinating private trips for families, groups of friends, universities, museums, zoos, professional groups, and other non-profit organizations."

World Bank (202-477-1234). Publishes *Tourism: Passport to Development? Perspectives on the Social and Cultural Effects of Tourism in Developing Countries.*

World Wildlife Fund (WWF), (202-293-4800). Publishes *Ecotourism: The Potentials and Pitfalls*, 2 vols. (Elizabeth Boo, 1990).

## Other references:

*Environmental Vacations: Volunteer Projects to Save the Planet*, 2nd ed. Stephanie Ocko. John Muir, 1992.

## Forests Information and Action Guide

**For more information and action on forests:**

AIR AND WASTE MANAGEMENT ASSOCIATION (A&WMA), (412-232-3444). Publishes *Effects of Air Pollution on Western Forests* (1989).

**Alternative Farming Systems Information Center,** (301-344-3724) or 344-3559). Provides Quick Bibliographies *Air Pollution Effects on Crops and Forests* (J. Gates, 1990), *Ecology of Tropical Rainforests* (J. Gates, 1990) and *Agroforestry Systems* (J. Maclean, 1989). (See ORGANIC FARMING AND SUSTAINABLE AGRICULTURE INFORMATION AND ACTION GUIDE on page 226.)

**American Forestry Association (AFA)** (1516 P Street NW, Washington, DC 20005; 202-667-3300; mailing address: P.O. Box 2000, Washington, DC 20013; R. Neil Sampson, Executive Vice-President), an organization of "citizen conservationists" and natural resource professionals, founded in 1875, which promotes the "protection, wise management, and enjoyment of forest resources in America and throughout the world" and has worked for decades to create and widen the U.S. network of public lands and parks; to stop "indiscriminate logging and uncontrolled wildfires"; and to support professional forestry schools, agencies, and forest fire prevention programs, as well as aid to private nonindustrial forest landowners. The AFA provides technical assistance on trees, sponsors action projects, seeks to influence public policy and legislative reform, provides environmental and forestry educational programs, and sponsors WILDERNESS experiences and other educational tours.

Among the major AFA campaigns are *Global ReLeaf*, a public education program focusing on tree planting and reduction of deforestation, to combat CLIMATE CHANGE; *Friends of the National Forests*, encouraging local groups to protect individual FORESTS; *Urban and Community Forestry*, in support of community trees; *America's Historic Forests*, a program for planting community groves of trees descended from historic and famous trees; and *The National Register of Big Trees*, a listing of the largest tree of every species in the United States.

The AFA publishes various materials, including the bimonthly magazine *American Forests*, the action-oriented bimonthly newsletter *Urban Forests*, a biweekly *Resource Hotline*, and many other materials, including *Tree and Shrub Transplanting Manual* (E.B. Himelick, 1991), *Shading Our Cities* (Sarah Ebenreck *and* Gary Moll, eds., 1989), *National Register of Big Trees, Famous and Historic Trees, Save Our Trees Citizen Action Guide, Tree Care Handbook*, and *Woodland Steward*, and brochures such as *Global ReLeaf Action Guide* and *Forests and Forestry in the USA*.

**AMERICAN WILDLANDS ALLIANCE (AWL),**(303-771-0380). Maintains *Timber Management Policy Reform Program (TMPRP)* and *Ancient Forests of the Interior West*.

**CAB INTERNATIONAL (CABI),** (602-621-7897 or 800-528-4841).

**Children of the Green Earth** (Box 31087, Seattle, WA 98103, 206-781-0852; Michael Soulé, Director), an organization founded in 1982 by the late forester Richard St. Barbe Baker to encourage the reforestation of the earth, in particular sponsoring "tree-planting partnerships between groups and individuals in North America and people in other lands where assistance is needed," through which "children can link up with other children in far off lands and share their love of trees and nature." It publishes various materials, including the quarterly *Children of the Green Earth Newsletter*, each featuring "'one region of the world, with tree lore, current tree-planting work, and a two-page children's section of stories, interesting facts and games which can be reproduced for classroom use." It also publishes *The Green Book* (Soulé, ed.), a resource guide for those working with children, a series of guides for teachers, booklets for children, and audiovisual materials.

**Commonwealth Forestry Association (CFA)** (Oxford Forestry Institute, South Parks Road, Oxford OX1 3RB, England; [44 865] 275072), an organization of professionals, public, and organizations concerned with conservation, development, and management of forests; once focused on the British Commonwealth, but now global in orientation. It publishes the quarterly *Commonwealth Forestry Review* and *Commonwealth Forestry Handbook*.

CONSERVATION INTERNATIONAL (CI), (202-429-5660). Prepared the *Rain Forest Imperative*.

CONSULTATIVE GROUP ON INTERNATIONAL AGRICULTURAL RESEARCH (CGIAR or CG), (202-473-8951).

COORDINATION IN DEVELOPMENT (CODEL), (212-870-3000).

CULTURAL SURVIVAL (CS), (617-495-2562). Publishes *Logging Against the Natives of Sarawak* (1989) and *Indigenous Peoples and Tropical Forests: Models of Land Use and Management from Latin America* (Jason Clay, 1988).

EARTH FIRST! (E.F.!) (Direct Action Fund, 415-376-7329). Has *Rainforest Action Group*.

EARTH ISLAND INSTITUTE, (415-788-3666). Sponsors the *Friends of the Ancient Forest* project and the *Rainforest Health Alliance*.

**Forest Farmers Association, Inc.** (Suite 120, 4 Executive Park East, P.O. Box 95385, Atlanta, GA 30347; 404-325-2954; B. Jack Warren, Executive Vice-President), a membership organization founded in 1941 to serve the interests of people owning or managing timberland in the 15 southern states, its goals being "protection or and promotion of the wise use of the South's timber resources." The Association oversees the *Forest Farmers Association Education and Research Foundation*, "to develop and publish technical and practical information of interest to private timberland owners, to initiate, encourage and sponsor educational programs in forest resource management and other related subjects for timberland owners and the public in general, and to sponsor research projects in forestry and publish or aid in publication of the results of research." It also lobbies through its legislative program; stages an annual Southern Forestry Conference; and publishes various materials, including the *Forest Farmer Manual* and the magazine *Forest Farmer*.

**Forest History Society (FHS)** (701 Vickers Avenue, Durham, NC 27701; 919-682-9319; Harold K. Steen, Executive Director), a membership organization, established in 1946 and affiliated with Duke University, that "explores the history of resources such as timber, water, soil, forage, fish and wildlife, recreation, and scenic values" for "today's diverse forest communities." Members include scholars, foresters, land-use planners, conservationists, industrialists, and scientists from many disciplines. The FHS maintains a library, archives, and compute data bases; encourages research; organizes meetings, symposia, conferences, and field trips; offers discounts on FHS and other forest-level publications; and publishes various materials, including the quarterly journal *Forest and Conservation History*, the quarterly newsletter *The Cruiser*, and books.

**Forest Trust** (P.O. Box 9238, Santa Fe, NM 87504; 505-983-8992; Henry H. Carey, Director), a project of the *Tides Foundation* (873 Sutter Street, San Francisco, CA 94109), "dedicated to the practical task of protecting America's forests," regarding them as assets of national importance and seeking to "'build value' in natural resources by amplifying the integrity, resilience, and productivity of forest and range ecosystems," by "providing land management services and resources protection strategies to private landowners, conservation organizations, public agencies, and rural communities." It conducts research, provides technical assistance, and offers training, through its *National Forest Program* and its other programs focusing on four areas: Forestry Development for Rural Communities, including their Mora Training Center and an Economic Development Unit, helping to create "sustainable economic opportunities based on forestry and forest products"; National Forest Planning and Policy, working with the FOREST SERVICE (sometimes under contract) and environmental organizations; Land Trust, directly protecting productive forest and range lands, as through CONSERVATION EASEMENTS and land acquisition; and Land Management, helping private landowners and ranchers "to increase the value of their property, to apply high standards of environmental management, to reduce carrying costs, and to realize increased enjoyment from the land." The Trust publishes the quarterly *Forest Trust* and occasional *National Updates*.

**FRIENDS OF THE EARTH (FOE)**, (202-544-2600).

**GREENPEACE**, (202-462-1177). Runs the *Tropical Forests Campaign*. Publishes Action Factsheets *Tropical Rainforests, Hawaiian Rainforests, Global Rates of Tropical Deforestation*, and *Tropical Forest Sarawak Action Alert*.

**INSTITUTE FOR FOOD AND DEVELOPMENT POLICY (IFDP)**, popularly called *Food First* (415-864-8555). Publishes *Brazil's Debt and Deforestation—A Global Warning*.

**INTERNATIONAL COUNCIL FOR BIRD PRESERVATION (ICBP)** (United Kingdom: 0223-277318; U.S. Headquarters, c/o WORLD WILDLIFE FUND—US; 202-293-4800). Publishes *An Introduction to Tropical Rain Forests* (T.C. Whitmore, Oxford University Press, 1990) and *Key Forests for Threatened Birds in Africa* (N.J. Collar and S.N. Stuart, 1988).

**IUCN—THE WORLD CONSERVATION UNION**, (202-797-5454). Publishes numerous materials on forest resources.

**International Society of Tropical Foresters (ISTF)** (5400 Grosvenor Lane, Bethesda, MA 20814; 301-897-8720; Warren T. Doolittle, President), a professional organization, founded in 1950 and reactivated in 1979, "committed to the protection, wise management, and rational use of the world's tropical forests." ISTF acts as an information exchange on tropical forests for its international membership, often working through local and regional chapters; conducts workshops and symposia; and publishes various materials, including the quarterly newsletter *ISTF News* (in English and Spanish) and a membership directory.

**KIDS FOR SAVING EARTH™ (KSE)**, (612-525-0002; 800-800-8800).

**NATIONAL AUDUBON SOCIETY**, (212-832-3200; *Audubon Action Line* 202-547-9017 Publishes flyers on its *Ancient Forests of the Northwest* Campaign).

**NATIONAL PARKS AND CONSERVATION ASSOCIATION (NPCA)**, (202-944-8530).

**NATIONAL WILDLIFE FEDERATION (NWF)**, (202-797-6800 or 800-245-5484). Publishes *Rain Forests: Tropical Treasures* as part of its *NatureScope® Series*, an education activity series for use with children in grades K-8.

**National Woodland Owners Association** (NWOA) (374 Maple Avenue, East, Suite 204, Vienna, VA 22180; 703-255-2700; Keith A. Argow, President), a membership organization of small nonindustrial woodland owners founded in 1983, seeking to help promote "good non-industrial private forestry for pleasure and profit," with activities "independent of the forest products industry and forestry agencies." The NWOA keeps members up-to-date on new programs and forestry laws; represents members' interests in Washington, DC; and provides information about the 22 affiliated state forestry/woodland owner associations. Members with 20 acres or more (in 26 states) receive an introductory, one-time consultation from a certified professional forester, in cooperation with the *National Forestry Network*. The NWOA publishes the quarterly magazine *National Woodlands*, including the *Conservation News Digest*, and the *Woodland Report*.

**NATURAL RESOURCES DEFENSE COUNCIL (NRDC)**, (212-727-2700). Maintains a *Tropical Forests Working Group*. Publishes *The Rainforest Book: How You Can Save the World's Rainforest* (Scott Lewis with NRDC, 1990), *Taxing the Tree Farm: Sensible Policies for Sensible Private Forestry* (F. Benfield et al., 1988), and children's books *The Rainforest Book: How You Can Save the World's Rainforests* and *Color the Rainforest*.

**NITROGEN FIXING TREE ASSOCIATION (NFTA)**, (808-956-7985). Runs *Cooperative Planting Program (CPP)*. Publishes *Why Nitrogen Fixing Trees*.

**Rainforest Action Network (RAN)** (301 Broadway, Suite A, San Francisco, CA 94133; 415-398-4404; Randall Hayes, Director), a nonprofit activist organization of people working to save the world's rain forests, formerly part of EARTH ISLAND INSTITUTE. RAN works with other environmental and human rights organizations on major campaigns and encourages formation of local *Rainforest Action Groups (RAGs)* to exert pressure at the grassroots level, using "negotiation to resolve problems, public pressure, direction action, such as letter writing campaigns, boycotts, consumer action campaigns, demonstrations, and selective bans." RAN publishes monthly *Action Alerts* on topics of urgent concern, fact sheets and other educational materials on specific issues, and a quarterly *World Rainforest Report*, issued jointly with like-minded international groups.

**Rainforest Alliance** (270 Lafayette Street, Room 512, New York, NY 10012; 212-941-1900; Chris Wille and Diane Jukofsky, Co-Directors), an organization founded in 1986, with projects mostly managed by volunteers, aiming to "conserve the diversity of life by raising funds to acquire or protect rainforest preserves." The Alliance seeks to education the public, acts as an information clearinghouse, coordinates activities with local groups and international agencies, and publishes the quarterly newsletter, *The Canopy*.

**RENEW AMERICA**, (202-232-2252). Publishes *Forest Management* (1989).

**RESOURCES FOR THE FUTURE (RFF)**, (202-328-5000). Includes research arm *Energy and Natural Resources Division*. Publishes *The Long-Term Adequacy of World Timber Supply* (Roger A. Sedjo and Kenneth S. Lyon, 1990) and *Multiple-Use Management: The Economics of Public Forestlands* (Michael D. Bower and John V. Krutilla, 1989).

**Save-The-Redwoods League** (114 Sansome Street, Room 605, San Francisco, CA 94104; 415-362-2352; John B. Dewitt, Executive Director), a membership organization founded in 1918, dedicated to conserving California's redwood forests for public enjoyment, purchasing available redwood lands at their fair market value and setting them aside as redwood parks or natural perserves, often incorporating them into existing parks. The League publishes various materials, including semiannual bulletins and pamphlets on redwoods.

**SIERRA CLUB**, (415-776-2211 or 202-547-1141; legislative hotline, 202-547-5550). Recent campaigns include National Forests/National Parks Protection. Publishes *Forest Primeval, Lessons of Rainforest, View from the Oak, Protecting National Parks and Forests, What You Can Do to Save Tropical Rainforests, Rainforests Policy,* and *National Forest System*.

**Society of American Foresters (SAF)** (5400 Grosvenor Lane, Bethesda, MD 20814; 301-897-8720; William H. Banzhas, Executive Vice-President), a professional membership organization founded in 1900 that aims "to advance the science, technology, education, and practice of professional forestry and to use the knowledge and skills of the profession to benefit society." The Society has numerous state and regional societies and local chapters, and over two dozen specialized working groups, serving as a forum for presentation and exchange of technical information, in the general areas of forest ecology and biology, forest resources protection, forest resources measurements, forest production and utilization, silviculture, managerial and decision sciences, and social and related arts and sciences. It also sponsors conferences, workshops, and symposia on forestry and related natural-resource topics; provides accreditation of professional degree programs in forestry; and formulates policy statements on forest policies. It publishes various materials, including the periodicals *Journal of Forestry, Forest Science*, and the *Northern, Southern* and *Wester Journals of Applied Forestry*, and numerous technical publications.

**TreePeople** (12601 Mulholland Drive, Beverly Hills, CA 90210; 818-753-4600; Andy Lipkis, President), a California-based membership organization founded by Lipkis in 1973 that "fosters environmental stewardship through personal involvement, community action, and global awareness," most specifically encouraging planting of trees and acting as a clearinghouse of information on urban forestry issues. Among TreePeople's recent projects are the Citizen Forestry program, training Citizen Foresters in planting and maintaining urban trees; the Environmental Leadership Program, educating California schoolchildren; and supplying fruit trees to several African countries. Its citizen foresters' training manual was expanded into *The Simple Act of Planting a Tree: A Citizen Forester's Guide to Healing Your Neighborhood, Your City, and Your World* (TreePeople with Andy Lipkis and Katie Lipkis; Tarcher, 1990).

**TROPICAL RESOURCES INSTITUTE (TRI)**, (203-432-5109). Offers courses and internships, and oversees research and service projects related to tropical forest resources; publishes the quarterly *TRI News* and numerous working papers.

**WESTERN FORESTRY AND CONSERVATION ASSOCIATION (WFCA)**, (503-226-4562).

**WILDERNESS SOCIETY, THE** (202-833-2300). Publishes *Ancient Forests of the Pacific Northwest* and *Tongass National Forest: America's Vanishing Rain Forest*.

**WILDLIFE CONSERVATION INTERNATIONAL (WCI)**, (212-220-5100). Publishes the bimonthly magazine *Wildlife Conservation* and the brochure *Protecting the World's Tropical Forests*.

**WILDLIFE INFORMATION CENTER**, (215-434-1637). Publishes *Forest Fragmentation and Wildlife Loss* and *Tropical Forests*.

**WINROCK INTERNATIONAL INSTITUTE FOR AGRICULTURAL DEVELOPMENT** (501-727-5435 or 703-525-9430). Publishes *Multipurpose Tree Species for Small Farm Use* (Dale Withington, 1988).

**WORLD BANK** (202-477-1234). Publishes *People and Trees: The Role of Social Forestry in Sustainable Development*.

**World Forestry Center** (4033 SW Canyon Road, Portland, OR 97221; 503-228-1367; Eric B. Landis, Director), a nonprofit education organization aiming to increase understanding of the importance of FORESTS and forest resources; mounts exhibits and has a model tree farm; operates the

*World Forest Institute (WFI)*, an international information clearinghouse for professionals, offering a computerized data base, Forest Information International (FI$^2$), and the Wood Products Information Center, which publishes a quarterly newsletter *Wood Design Focus*.

**WORLD RESOURCES INSTITUTE (WRI)**, (202-638-6300). Conducts *Program in Forests and Biodiversity*; publishes *Reforesting America: Combatting Global Warming?* (Mark C. Trexler and William R, Moomaw, 1990), *Taking Stock: The Tropical Forest Action Plan After Five Years* (Robert Winterbottom, 1990), and *The Forest for the Trees? Government Policies and the Misuse of Forest Resources* (Robert Repetto, 1988).

**WORLD WILDLIFE FUND (WWF)**, (202-293-4800). Publishes *Tropical Forest Conservation, Responding to Tropical Deforestation: An Eruption of Crises/An Array of Solutions* (Brian Johnson, 1991), *Tropical Rainforests of West Africa: Their Ecology–Endangerment–Conservation* (Claude Martin, 1991), and *Vanishing Rain Forests Education Kit* (1989).

**Zero Population Growth (ZPG)**, (202-332-2200). Publishes *Deforestation*. (See POPULATION INFORMATION AND ACTION GUIDE on page 248.)

**Other references:**

*On forests in general:*
*Forests: A Naturalists Guide to Trees and Forest Ecology.* Laurence C. Walker. Wiley, 1990. *World Deforestation in the Twentieth Century.* John F. Richards and Richard P. Tucker, eds. Duke University Press, 1990. *Entering the Grove*. Kim Stafford. Gibbs-Smith, 1990. *Forest Primeval: The Natural History of an Ancient Forest.* Chris Maser. Sierra Club Books, 1989. *Shading Our Cities: A Resource Guide for Urban and Community Forests.* Gary Moll and Sara Ebenreck, eds. Island Press, 1989. *Fragile Majesty: The Battle for North America's Last Great Forest.* Keith Erwin. The Mountaineers, 1989. *Ancient Forests of the Pacific Northwest.* Elliot A. Norse. Island Press, 1989. *Secrets of the Old Growth Forest.* David Kelly. Gibbs-Smith, 1988. *The Forest.* David Bellamy. C.N. Potter, 1988. *The Forest and the Trees: A Guide to Excellent Forestry.* Gordon Robinson. Island Press, 1988. *The Hidden Life of the Forest.* David M. Schwartz. Crown, 1988. *Public Policies and the Misuse of Forest Resources.* Robert Repetto and Malcolm Gillis, eds. Cambridge University Press, 1988.

**On tropical and rain forests:**

*Trees of Life: Saving Tropical Forests and Their Biological Wealth.* Kenton Miller and Laura Tangley. Beacon, 1991. *The Last Rain Forests: A World Conservation Atlas.* Mark Collins, ed. Oxford University Press, 1990. *Conserving Rain Forests.* Martin Banks. Steck-Vaughn, 1990. *The Rainforest Book: How You Can Save The World's Rainforests.* Scott Lewis with the Natural Resources Defense Council. Living Planet, 1990. *The World Is Burning.* Alex Shoumatoff. Little, Brown, 1990. *Lessons of the Rainforest.* Suzanne Head and Robert Heinzman, eds. Sierra Club Books, 1990. *The Tropical Rainforest: A World Survey of Our Most Valuable Endangered Habitats—With a Blueprint for Its Survival.* Arnold Newman. Facts On File, 1990. *Saving the Tropical Forests.* Judith Gradwohl and Russell Greenberg. Island Press, 1988. *The Future of the Tropical Rain Forest.* Malenie J. McDermott, ed. Oxford Forestry Institute (Oxford, U.K.), 1988.

---

## Endangered and Threatened Wildlife and Plants

Note: These lists are adapted from the FISH AND WILDLIFE SERVICE'S publication *Endangered and Threatened Wildlife and Plants*, dated April 15, 1990. Animals are listed by their common names, with alternate and italicized scientific names in parentheses; for plants, the scientific name is given first, then the common name. Where the scientific name alone is given, there is no common name.

The geographic description indicates the species' historic range. *E* means endangered; *T* means threatened. Unless otherwise noted, these designations apply throughout a species' historic range. The number in parentheses is the year the species was first listed as endangered or threatened.

Lists of endangered species kept by IUCN—THE WORLD CONSERVATION UNION differ somewhat from the U.S. list, partly because of differing definitions (see ENDANGERED SPECIES). There are, of course, many other known endangered and threatened species, in the United States and around the world, that have not been officially "listed" by any agency; and many unknown flora and fauna that are on the verge of disappearing without ever having been "discovered" by the scientific world.

### Endangered and Threatened Wildlife

**Mammals**

**anoa**
- lowland (*Bubalus depressicornis* or *B. anoa depressicornis*), Indonesia, E (1970).
- mountain (*Bubalus quarlesi* or *B, anoa quarlesi*), Indonesia, E (1976).

**antelope,** giant sable (*Hippotragus niger variani*), Angola, E (1976). (See also BONTEBOK and SAIGA, below.)

**argali** (*Ovis ammon hodgsoni*), Tibet and Himalayas in China, E (1976).

**armadillo**
- giant (*Priodontes maximus* or *Priodontes giganteus*), Venezuela and Guyana to Argentina, E (1976).

- pink fairy (*Chlamyphorus truncatus*), Argentina, E (1970).

**ass**
- African wild (*Equus asinus* or *Equus africanus*), Somalia, Sudan, and Ethiopia, E (1970).
- Asian wild (onager kulan or *Equus hemionus*), southwestern and central Asia, E (1970).

**avahi** (*Avahi laniger* or *Lichanotus laniger*), Madagascar (Malagasy Republic), E (1970).

**aye-aye** (*Daubentonia madagascariensis*), Madagascar (Malagasy Republic), E (1970).

**babirusa** (*Babyrousa babyrussa*), Indonesia, E (1976).

**baboon,** gelada (*Theropithecus gelada*), Ethiopia, T (1976).

**bandicoot**
- barred (*Perameles bougainville*), Australia, E (1970).
- desert (*Perameles eremiana*), Australian, E (1973).
- lesser rabbit (*Macrotis leucura*), Australia, E (1970).
- pig-footed (*Chaeopus ecaudatus*), Australia, E (1970).
- rabbit (*Macrotis lagotis*), Australia, E (1970).

**banteng** (*Bos javanicus*), southeast Asia, E (1970).

**bat**
- Bulmer's fruit (flying fox or *Aproteles bulmerae*), Papua New Guinea, E (1984).
- bumblebee (*Craseonycteris thonglongyai*), Thailand, E (1984).
- gray (*Myotis grisescens*), central and southeast United States, E (1976).
- Hawaiian hoary (*Laisurus cinereus semotus*), Hawaii, E (1970).
- Indiana (*Myotis sodalis*), eastern and midwestern United States, E (1967).
- little Mariana fruit (*Pteropus tokudae*), Guam, E (1984).
- Mariana fruit (*Pteropus mariannus mariannus*), western Pacific Ocean islands, including Guam, Rota, Tinian, Saipan, and Agiguan, E in Guam (1984).
- Mexican long-nosed (*Leptonycteris nivalis*), New Mexico, Texas, Mexico, and Central America, E (1988).
- Ozark big-eared (*Plecotus townsendii ingens*), Arkansas, Missouri, and Oklahoma, E (1979).
- Rodrigues fruit (flying fox or *Pteropus rodricensis*), Rodrigues Island in Indian Ocean, E (1984).
- Sanborn's long-nosed (*Leptonycteris sanborni* or *Leptonycteris yerbabuenae*), Arizona, New Mexico, Mexico, and Central America, E (1988).
- Singapore roundleaf horseshoe (*Hipposideros ridleyi*), Malaysia, E (1984).
- Virginia big-eared (*Plecotus townsendii virginianus*), Kentucky, North Carolina, Virginia, and West Virginia, E (1979).

**bear**
- Baluchistan (*Ursus thibetanus gedrosianus*), Iran and Pakistan, E (1986).
- brown (*Ursus arctos arctos*), Palearctic realm (see REALM on page 258 ), E in Italy (1976).
- brown (*Ursus arctos pruinosus*), Tibet (China), E (1976).
- brown or grizzly (*Ursus arctoc* or *Ursus arctos horribilis*), Holarctic (see REALM on page 258), T in United States, in 48 adjacent states (1967).
- brown or grizzly (*Ursus arctos* or *Ursus arctos nelsoni*), Holarctic (see REALM on page 258), E in Mexico (1970).

**beaver** (*Castor fiber birulai*), Mongolia, E (1976).

**bison,** wood (*Bison bison athabascae*), Canada and northwestern United States, E in Canada (1970).

**bobcat** (*Felis rufus escuinapae*), Central Mexico, E (1976). (See also CAT, below.)

**bontebok** (antelope or *Damaliscus dorcas dorcas*), South Africa, E (1976).

**camel,** Bactrian (*Camelus bactrianus* or *Camelus ferus*), Mongolia and China, E (1976).

**caribou,** woodland (*Rangifer tarandus caribou*), Canada and the United States (Arkansas, Idaho, Maine, Michigan, Minnesota, Montana, New Hampshire, Vermont, Washington, and Wisconsin), E in British Columbia, Idaho, and Washington (1983).

**cat**
- Andean (*Felis Jacobita*), Argentina, Bolivia, Chile, and Peru, E (1976).
- black-footed (*Felis nigripes*), southern Africa, E (1976).
- flat-headed (*Felis planiceps*), Malaysia and Indonesia, E (1976).
- Iriomote (*Felis [Mayailurus] iriomotensis*), Iriomote Island and Ryukyu Islands of Japan, E (1979).
- leopard, (*Felis bengalensis bengalensis*), India and southeast Asia, E (1976).
- marbled (*Felis marmorata*), Nepal, southeast Asia, and Indonesia, E (1976).
- Pakistan sand (*Felis margarita scheffeli*), Pakistan, E (1984).
- Temminck's (golden cat or *Felis temmincki*), Nepal China, southeast Asia, and Sumatra in Indonesia, E (1976).
- tiger (*Felis tigrinus*), Costa Rica to northern Argentina, E (1972).

(See also BOBCAT, above; COUGAR, JAGUAR, JAGUARUNDI, LEOPARD, LYNX, MARGAY, NATIVE-CAT, OCELOT, PANTHER, PUMA, SERVAL, and TIGER, below.)

**chamois,** Apennine (*Rupecapra rupicapra ornata*), Italy, E (1976).

**cheetah** (*Acinonyx jubatus*), Africa to India, E (1970).

**chimpanzee**
- (*Pan troglodytes*), Africa, E (1976).
- pygmy chimpanzee (*Pan paniscus*), Zaire, E (1976).

**chinchilla** (*Chinchilla brevicaudata boliviana*), Bolivia, E (1976).

**civet** Malabar large-spotted (*Viverra megaspila civettina*), India, E (1979).

**cochito** (Gulf of California harbor porpoise or *Phocoena sinus*), Gulf of California off Mexico, E (1985).

**cougar,** eastern (*Felis concolor couguar*), eastern North America, E (1973).

**deer**
- Bactrian (*Cervus elaphus bactrianus*), U.S.S.R. and Afghanistan, E (1979).
- Barbary (*Cervus elaphus barbarus*), Algeria, Morocco, and Tunisia, E (1979).
- Bawean (*Axis porcinus kuhli* or *Cervis porcinus kuhli*), Indonesia, E (1970).
- Cedros Island mule (*Odocoileus hemionus cedrosensis*), Cedros Island of Mexico, E (1975).
- Columbian white-tailed (*Odocoileus virginianus leucurus*), Washington and Oregon, E (1967).
- Corsican red (*Cervus elaphus corsicanus*), Corsica and Sardinia, E (1979).
- Eld's brow-antlered (*Cervus eldi*), India to southeast Asia, E (1970).
- Formosan sika (*Cervus nippon taiouanus*), Taiwan, E (1979).
- hog (*Axis porcinus annamiticus* or *Cervus porcinus annamiticus*), Cambodia (Kampuchea), Laos, Thailand, and Vietnam, E (1976).
- key (*Odocoileus virginianus clavium*), Florida, E. marsh (*Blastocerus dichotomus*), Argentina, Bolivia, Brazil, Paraguay, and Uruguay, E (1967).
- McNeill's (*Cervus elaphus macneilii*), Tibet and Sinkiang (central Asian China), E (1970).
- musk—(*Moschus*—all species), central and eastern Asia, E in Afghanistan, Bhutan, Burma, India, Nepal, Pakistan, Sikkim, Tibet (China) and the Yunnan region of China (1976).
- North China sika (*Cervus nippon mandarinus*), the Shantung and Chihli provinces of China, E (1979).
- pampas (*Ozotoceros bezoarticus*), Argentina, Brazil, Bolivia, Paraguay, and Uruguay, E (1976).
- Persian fallow (*Dama dama meropotamica*), Iran and Iraq, E (1970).
- Philippine (*Axis porcinus calamianesis* or *Cervus porcinus calamianensis*), Calamian Islands of the Philippines, E (1976).
- Ryukyu sika (*Cervus nppon kermae*) Ryukyu Islands of Japan, E (1979).
- Shansi sika (*Cervux nippon grassianus*), Shansi Province of China, E (1979).
- South China sika (*Cervus nippon kopschi*), southern China, E (1979).
- swamp (barasingha or *Cervus duvauceli*), India and Nepal, E (1970).

- Visayan (*Cervus alfredi*), Philippines, E (1988).
- Yarkand (*Cervus elaphus yarkandensis*), Sinkiang (central Asian China), E (1979).
(See also STAG, page 378.)

**dhole** (Asiatic wild dog or *Cuon alpinus*), China, India, Korea, U.S.S.R., and southeast Asia, E (1970). (See also DOG, below.)

**dibbler** (*Antechinus apicalis*), Australia, E (1970).

**dog,** African wild (*Lycaon pictus*), sub-Saharan Africa, E (1984). (See also DHOLE, above.)

**dolphin,** Chinese river (whitefin or *Lipotes vexillifer*), China E (1989).

**drill** (*Papio leucophaeus*), equatorial west Africa, E (1976).

**dugong** (*Dugong dugon*), East Africa to southern Japan; E everywhere except in U.S. trust territories (1970).

**duiker, Jentink's** (*Cephalophus jentinki*), Ivory Coast, Liberia, and Sierra Leone, E (1979).

**eland,** Western giant (*Taurotragus derbianus derbianus*), Senegal to Ivory Coast, E (1979).

**elephant**
- African (*Loxodonta africana*), Africa, T (1978).
- Asian (*Elaphas maximus*), south-central and southeast Asia, E (1976).

**ferret,** black-footed (*Mustela nigripes*), western North America, E (1967).

**fox**
- Northern swift (*Vulpes velox hebes*), northern plains of United States and Canada, E in Canada (1970).
- San Joaquin kit (*Vulpes macrotis mutica*), California E (1967).
- Simien (*Cans [Simenia] simensis*), Ethiopia, E (1979).

**gazelle**
- Arabian (*Gazella gazella*), Arabian and Sinai peninsulas and Palestine (Israel), E (1979).
- Clark's (Dibatag or *Ammodorcas clarkei*), Ethiopia and Somalia, E (1970).
- Cuvier's (*Gazella cuvieri*), Algeria, Morocco, and Tunisia, E (1970).
- Mhorr (*Gazella dama mhorr*), Morocco, E (1970).
- Moroccan (Dorcas or *Gazella dorcas massaesyla*), Algeria, Morocco, and Tunisia, E (1970).
- Pelzein's (*Gazella dorcas pelzelni*), Somalia, E (1979).
- Rio de Oro Dama (*Gazella dama lozanoi*), western Sahara, E (1970).
- sand (*Gazella subgutturosa marica*), Arabian Peninsula and Jordan, E (1979).
- Saudi Arabian (*Gazella dorcas saudiya*), Arabian Peninsula, Iraq, Israel, Jordan, and Syria, E (1979).
- slender-horned (Rhim or *Gazella leptoceros*), E (1970).

**gibbons** (*Hylobates*—all species, including *Nomascus*), China, India, and southeast Asia, E (1970).

**goat,** wild (Chiltan markhor, *Capra aegagrus*, or *falconeri chiltanensis*), southwestern Asia, E in the Chiltan Range of Pakistan (1976).

**goral** (*Nemorhaedus goral*), east Asia, E (1976).

**gorilla** (*Gorilla gorilla*), central and western Africa, E (1970).

**hare,** hispid (*Caprolagus hispidus*), Bhutan, India, and Nepal, E (1976).

**hartebeest**
• Swayne's (*Alcelaphus buselaphus swaynei*), Ethiopia and Somalia, E (1970).
• Tora (*Alcelaphis buselaphus tora*), Egypt, Ethiopia, and the Sudan, E (1979).

**hog,** pygmy (*Sus salvanius*), Bhutan, India, Nepal, and Sikkim, E (1970).

**horse,** Przewalski's (*Equus przewalskii*), Mongolia and China, E (1976).

**huemul**
• North Andean (*Hippocamelus antisensis*), Argentina, Bolivia, Chile, Ecuador, and Peru, E (1976).
• South Andean (*Hippocamelus bisulcus*) Argentina and Chile, E (1976).

**hutia**
• Cabrera's (*Capromys angelcabrerai*), Cuba, E (1976).
• dwarf (*Capromys nana*), Cuba, E (1986).
• large-eared (*Capromys auritus*), Cuba, E (1986).
• little earth (*Capromys sanfelipensis*), Cuba, E (1986).

**hyena**
• Barbary (*Hyaena hyaena barbara*), Algeria, Morocco, and Tunisia, E (1970).
• brown (*Hyaena brunnea*), southern Africa, E (1970).

**ibex**
• Pyrenean (*Capra purenaica pyrenaica*), Spain, E (1970).
• Walia (*Capra walie*), Ethiopia, E (1970).

**impala,** black-faced (*Aepyceros melampus petersi*), Angola and Namibia, E (1970).

**indri** (*Indri indri*—whole genus), Madagascar (Malagasy Republic), E (1970).

**jaguar** (*Panthera onca*), Arizona, New Mexico, Texas, and Central and South America; E from Mexico south (1972).

**jaguarundi**
• (*Felis yaguaroundi cacomitli*), Texas and Mexico, E (1976).
• (*Felis yagouaroundi fossata*), Mexico and Nicaragua, E (1976).
• (*Felis yagouaroundi panamensis*), Costa Rica, Nicaragua, and Panama, E (1976).
• *Felis yagouaroundi tolteca*), Arizona and Mexico, E (1976).

**kangaroo**
• eastern gray (*Macropus giganteus*—all subspecies except *tasmaniensis*), Australia, T (1974).
• red (*Macropus [Megaleia] rufus*), Australia, E (1974).
• Tasmanian forester (*Macropuis giganteus tasmaniensis*), Tasmania (Australia), E (1973).
• western gray (*Macropus fuliginosus*), Australia, T (1974).

**kouprey** (*Bos sauveli*), Cambodia (Kampuchea), Laos, Thailand, and Vietnam, E (1970).

**lachwe,** red (*Kobus leche*), southern Africa, T (1970).

**langur**
• capped (*Presbytis pileata*), Bangladesh, Burma (Myanmar), and India, E (1976).
• Douc (*Pygathrix nemaeus*), Cambodia (Kampuchea), Laos, and Thailand, E (1970).
• entellus (*Presbytis nemaeus*), Bangladesh, India, Kashmir, Pakistan, Sikkim, Sri Lanka (Ceylon), and Tibet (China), E (1976).
• Francois' (*Presbytis francoisi*), Cambodia, Laos, Thailand, and the Kwangsi region of China, E (1976).
• golden (*Presbytis geei*), Assam (India), and Bhutan, E (1976).
• long-tailed (*Presbytis potenziani*), Indonesia, T (1976).
• Pagi Island (*Nasalis [Simias] concolor*), Indonesia, E (1970).
• purple-faced (*Presbytis senex*), Sri Lanka (Ceylon), T (1976).
• Tonkin snub-nosed (*Pygathrix [Rhinopithecue] avunculus*), Vietnam, T (1976).

**lemurs** (Lemuridae, including Cheirogaleidae and Lepilemuridae; all members of genera *Lemur, Phaner, Hapalemus, Lepilemur, Microcebus, Allocebus, Cheriogaleus,* and *Varecia*), Madagascar (Malagasy Republic), E (1970).

**leopard**
• clouded (*Neofelis nebulosa*), southeast and south-central Asia and Taiwan, E (1970).
• (*Panthera pardus*), Africa and Asia; T in Africa in the wild from Gabon, the Congo, Zaire, Uganda, and Kenya and south; E elsewhere (1970).
• snow (*Panthera uncia*), Central Asia, E (1972).

**linsang,** spotted (*Prinodon pardicolor*), Assam (India), Burma (Myanmar), Cambodia (Kampuchea), Laos, Nepal, and Vietnam, E (1976).

**lion,** Asiatic (*Panthera leo persica*), Turkey to India, E (1970).

**loris,** lesser slow (*Nycticebus pygmaeus*), Cambodia (Kampuchea), Laos, and Vietnam, T (1976).

**lynx** Spanish (*Felis pardina* or *Lynx pardina*), Portugal and Spain, E (1970).

**macaque**
• Formosan rock (*Macaca cyclopis*), Taiwan, T (1976).

- Japanese (*Macaca fuscata*), Shikoku, Kyushu, and Honshu islands of Japan, T (1976).
- lion-tailed (*Macaca silenus*), India, E (1970).
- stump-tailed (*Macaca arctoides*), Assam (India) to southern China, T (1976).
- Toque (*Macaca sinica*), Sri Lanka (Ceylon), T (1976).

**manatee**
- Amazonian (*Trichechus inunguis*), Amazon River basin of South America, E (1970).
- West African (*Trichechus senegalensis*), coastal West Africa, from Senegal River to Cuanza River, T (1979).
- West Indian (Florida manatee or *Trichechus manatus*), southeast United States, Caribbean Sea, and South America, E (1967).

**mandrill** (*Papio sphinx*), equatorial West Africa, E (1976).

**mangabey**
- Tana River (*Cercocebus galeritus*), Kenya, E (1970).
- white-collared (*Cercocebus torquatus*), Senegal to Ghana and Nigeria to Gabon, E (1976).

**margay** (*Felis wiedii*), Texas and Central and South America, E from Mexico south (1972).

**markhor**
- Kabal (*Capra falconeri megaceros*), Afghanistan and Pakistan, E (1976).
- straight-horned (*Capra falconeri jerdoni*), Afghanistan and Pakistan, E (1976).

**marmoset**
- buff-headed (*Callithrix flaviceps*), Brazil, E (1984).
- buffy tufted-ear (*Callithrix jacchus aurita*), Brazil, E (1986).
- cotton-top (*Saguinus oedipus*), Costa Rica to Colombia, E (1976).
- Goeldi's (*Callimico goeldii*), Brazil, Bolivia, Colombia, Ecuador, and Peru, E (1970).

**marmot,** Vancouver Island (*Marmota vancouverensis*), Vancouver Island (Canada), E (1984).

**marsupial,** eastern jerboa (*Antechinomys laniger*), Australia, E (1970).

**marsupial-mouse**
- large desert (*Sminthopsis psammophtlia*), Australia, E (1970).
- long-tailed (*Sminthopsis longicaudata*), Australia, E (1970).

**marten,** Formosan yellow-throated (*Martes flavigula chrysospila*), Taiwan, E. (1970).

**monkey**
- black colobus (*Colobus satanas*), Cameroon, the Congo, Equatorial Buinea, and Gabon, E (1976).
- black howler (*Alouatta pigra*), Belize, Guatemala, and Mexico, T (1976).

- Diana (*Cercopithecus diana*), coastal West Africa, E (1976).
- howler (*Alouatta palliata* or *Alouatta villosa*), Mexico to South America, E (1976).
- L'hoest's (*Cercopithecus lhoesti*), Cameroon and upper eastern Congo River basin, E (1976).
- Preuss's red colobus (*Colobus badius preussi*), Cameroon, E (1984).
- proboscis (*Nasalis larvatus*), Borneo, E (1976).
- red-backed squirrel (*Saimiri oerstedii*), Costa Rica and Panama, E (1970).
- red-bellied (*Cercopithecus erythrogaster*), western Nigeria, E (1976).
- red-eared nose-spotted (*Cercopithecus erythrotis*), Cameroon, Nigeria, and Fernando Po, E (1976).
- spider (*Ateles geoffroyi frontatus*), Costa Rica and Nicaragua, E (1970).
- spider (*Ateles geoffroyi panamensis*), Costa Rica and Panama, E (1970).
- Tana River red colobus (*Colobus rufomitratus* [or *badius*] *rufomitratus*), Kenya, E (1970).
- woolly spider (*Brachyteles arachnoides*), Brazil, E (1970).
- yellow-tailed woolly (*Lagothrix flavicauda*), Andes Range in northern Peru, E (1976).
- Zanzibar red colobus (*Colobus kirki*), Tanzania, E (1970).

**mouse**
- Alabama beach (*Peromyscus polionotus ammobates*), Alabama, E (1985).
- Anastasia Island beach (*Peromyscus polionotus phasma*), Florida, E (1989).
- Australian native (*Zyzomys pedunculatus* or *Notomys pedunculatus*), Australia, E (1976).
- Australian native (*Notomyx aquilo*), Australia, E (1976).
- Choctawhatchee beach (*Peromyuscus polionotus allophrys*), Florida, E (1985).
- Field's (*Pseudomys fieldi*), Australia, E (1970).
- Gould's (*Pseudomys gouldii*), Australia, E (1973).
- Key Largo cotton (*Peromyscus gossypinus allapaticola*), Florida, E (1983).
- New Holland (*Pseudomyx novaehollandiae*), Australia, E (1970).
- Perdido Key beach (*Peromyscus polionotus trissyllepsis*), Alabama and Florida, E (1985).
- salt marsh harvest (*Reithrodontomys raviventris*), California, E (1970).
- Shark Bay (*Pseudomys praeconis*), Australia, E (1970).
- Shortridge's (*Pseudomys shortridgei*), Australia, E (1970).
- Smoky (*Pseudomys fumeus*), Australia, E (1970).
- southeastern beach (*Peromyscis polionotus niveiventris*), Florida, T (1989).
- western (*Pseudomys occidentalis*), Australia, E (1970).

**muntjac,** Fea's (*Muntiacus feae*), Australia, E (1979).

**native-cat,** eastern (*Dasyurus viverrinus*), Australia, E (1973).

**numbat** (*Myrmecobius fasciatus*), Australia, E (1970).

ocelot (*Felis pardalis*), Arizona, Texas, and Central and South America, E (1972).

orangutan, (*Pongo pygmaeus*), Borneo and Sumatra, E (1970).

oryx, Arabian (*Oryx leucoryx*), Arabian Peninsula, E (1970).

otter
- Cameroon clawless (*Aonyx* [or *Paraonyx*] *congica microdon*), Cameroon and Nigeria, E (1970).
- giant (*Pteronura brasiliensis*), South America, E (1970).
- long-tailed (*Lutra longicaudis*, including *platensis*), South America, E (1970).
- marine (*Lutra felina*), Peru south to the Straits of Magellan, E (1976).
- southern river (*Lutra provocax*), Argentina and Chile, E (1976).
- southern sea (*Enhydra lutris nereis*), Pacific coast from Washington to Baja California, T (1977), except California coast from Point Conception to Mexican border.

panda, giant (*Ailuropoda melanoleuca*), China, E (1984).

pangolin (scaly anteater or *Manis temmincki*), Africa, E (1976).

panther, Florida (*Felis concolor coryi*), United States, from Lousiana and Arkansas east to South Carolina and Florida, E (1967).

planigale
- little (*Planigale ingrami subtillissima*), Australia, E (1970).
- southern (*Planigale tenuirostris*), Australia, E (1970).

porcupine, thin-spined (*Chaetomys subspinosus*), Brazil, E (1970).

possum
- Leadbeater's (*Gymnobelideus leadbeateri*), Brazil, E (1986).
- mountain pygmy (*Buramys parvus*), Australia, E (1970).
- scaly-tailed (*Wyulda squamicaudata*), Australia, E (1970).

prairie dog
- Mexican (*Cynomys mexicanus*), Mexico, E (1970).
- Utah (*Cynomys parvidens*), Utah, T (1973).

pronghorn
- peninsular (*Antilocapra americana peninsularis*), Baja, California, E (1975).
- Sonoran (*Antilocapra americana sonoriensis*), Arizona and Mexico, E (1967).

pudu (*Pudu pudu*), southern South America, E (1976).

puma, Costa Rican (*Felis concolor costaricensis*), Costa Rica, Nicaragua, Panama, E (1976).

quokka (*Setonix brachyurus*), Australia, E (1973).

rabbit
- Ryukyu (*Pentalagus furnessi*), Ryukyu Islands of Japan, E (1979).
- volcano (*Romerolague diazi*), Mexico, E (1970).

rat
- false water (*Xeromys myoides*), Australia, E (1970).
- Fresno kangaroo (*Dipodomys nitratoides exilis*), California, E (1985).
- giant kangaroo (*Dipodymis ingens*), California, E (1987).
- Morro Bay kangaroo (*Dipodymys heermanni morroensis*), California, E (1970).
- Stephens' kangaroo (*Dipodomys stephensi*, including *D. cascus*), California, E (1988).
- stick-nest (*Leporillus conditor*), Australia, E (1973).
- Tipton kangaroo (*Dipodomys nitratoides nitratoides*), California, E (1988).

rat-kangaroo
- brush-tailed (*Bettongia penicillata*), Australia, E (1970).
- Gaimard's (*Betongia gaimardi*), Australia, E (1973).
- Lesuer's (*Bettongia leseuer*), Australia, E (1970).
- plain (*Caloprymnus campestris*), Australia, E (1970).
- Queensland (*Bettongia tropica*), Australia, E (1970).

rhinoceros
- black (*Diceros bicornis*), sub-Saharan Africa, E (1980).
- great Indian (*Rhinoceros unicornis*), India and Nepal, E (1970).
- javan (*Rhinoceros sondaicus*), Bangladesh, Burms (Myanmar), Cambodia (Kampuchea), Indonesia, Laos, Malaysia, Sikkim, Thailand, and Vietnam, E (1970).
- northern white (*Ceratotherium simum cottoni*), Central African Republic, Sudan, Uganda, and Zaire, E (1970).
- Sumatran (*Dicerorhinus* [or *Didermoceros*] *sumatrensis*), Bangladesh to Vietnam to Indonesia (Borneo), E (1970).

saiga, Mongolian (antelope or *Saiga tatarica mongolica*), Mongolia, E (1976).

saki
- southern bearded (*Chiropotes satanas satanas*), Brazil, E (1986).
- white-nosed (*chiropotes albinasus*), Brazil, E (1970).

sea lion, Steller (northern sea lion or *Eumetopias jubatus*), Pacific coast of North America, from California to Alaska, also Canada, U.S.S.R., and north Pacific Ocean, T (1990).

seal
- Caribbean monk (*Monachus tropicalis*), Caribbean Sea and Gulf of Mexico, E (1967).
- Guadalupe fur (*Arctocephalus townsendi*), Farallon Islands of California south to Islas Revillagigedo of Mexico, T (1985).
- Hawaiian monk (*Monachus schauinslandi*), Hawaii, E (1976).
- Mediterranean monk (*Monachus monachus*), Mediterranean and Black seas and northwest coast of Africa, E (1970).

**seledang** (gaur or *Bos gaurus*), Bangladesh, India, and southeast Asia, E (1970).

**serow** (*Capricornis sumatraensis*), Sumatra and east Asia, E (1976).

**serval,** Barbary (*Felis serval constantina*), Algeria, E (1970).

**shapo** (*Ovis vignei vignei*), Kashmir, E (1976).

**shou** (*Cervus elaphus wallichi*), Bhutan and Tibet, E (1970).

**shrew,** Dismal Swamp southeastern (*Sorex longirostris fisheri*), Virginia and North Carolina, T (1986).

**siamang** (*Symphalangus syndactylus*), Indonesia and Malaysia, E (1976).

**sifakas** (*Propithecus*—all species), Madagascar (Malagasy Republic), E (1970).

**sloth,** Brazilian three-toed (*Bradypus torquatus*), Brazil, E (1970).

**solenodon**
• Cuban (*Solenodon [Atopogale] cubanus*), Cuba, E (1970).
• Haitian (*Solenodon paradoxus*), Dominican Republic and Haiti, E (1970).

**squirrel**
• Carolina northern flying (*Glaucoms sabrinus coloratus*), North Carolina and Tennessee, E (1985).
• Delmarva Peninsula fox (*Sciurus niger cinereus*), Delmarva Peninsula (U.S. to southeast Pennsylvania), E in all, except Sussex County, Delaware (1967).
• Mount Graham red (*Tamiasciurus hudsonicus grahamensis*), Arizona, E (1987).
• Virginia northern flying (*Glaucomys sabrinus fuscus*), Virginia and West Virginia, E (1985).

**stag**
• Barbary (*Cervus elaphus barbarus*), Algeria and Tunisia, E (1970).
• Kashmir (*Cervus elaphus hanglu*), Kashmir, E (1970).

**suni,** Zanzibar (*Neotragus* [or *Nesotragus*] *moschatus moschatus*), Zanzibar and nearby islands, E (1979).

**tahr,** Arabian (*Hemitragus jayakari*), Oman, E (1970).

**tamaraw** (*Bubalus mindorensis*), Philippines, E (1970).

**tamarin**
• golden-rumped (golden-headed tamarin, golden-lion marmoset, or *Leontopithecus* [or *Leontideus*]—all species), Brazil, E (1970).
• pied (*Saguinus bicolor*), Brazil, E (1976).
• white-footed (*Saguinus leucopus*), Colombia, T (1976).

**tapir**
• Asian (*Tapirus indicus*), Burma (Myanmar), Cambodia (Kamphuchea), Indonesia, Laos, Malaysia, Thailand, and Vietnam, E (1976).

• Brazilian (*Tapirus terrestris*), Colombia and Venezuela south to Paraguay and Argentina, E (1970).
• Central American (*Tapirus bairdii*), southern Mexico to Colombia and Ecuador, E (1970).
• mountain (*Tapirus pinchaque*), Colombia, Ecuador, and possibly Peru and Venezuela, E (1970).

**tarsier,** Philippine (*Tarsius syrichta*), Philippines, T (1976).

**tiger**
• (*Panthera tigris*), temperate and tropical Asia, E (1970).
• Tasmanian (Thylacine tiger of *Thylacinus cynocephalus*), Australia, E (1970).
(See also CAT, page 373.)

**uakari**—all species (*Cacajao*—all species), Brazil, Colombia, Ecuador, Peru, and Venezuela, E (1970).

**urial** (*Ovis musimon* [or *orientalis*] *ophion*), Cyprus, E (1976).

**vicuña** (*Vicugna vicugna*), Andes Range of South America, E (1970).

**vole**
• Amargosa (*Microtus californicus scirpensis*), California, E (1984).
• Hualapai Mexican (*Microtus mexicanus hualpaiensis*), Arizona, E (1987).

**wallaby**
• branded hare (*Lagostrophus fasciatus*), Australia, E (1970).
• brindled nail-tailed (*Onychogalea fraenata*), Australia, E (1970).
• crescent nail-tailed (*Onychogalea lunata*), Australia, E (1970).
• Parma (*Macropus parma*), Australia, E (1970).
• Western hare (*Lagorchestes hirsutus*), Australia, E (1970).
• yellow-footed rock (*Petrogale xanthropus*), Australia, E (1973).

**whale**
• blue (*Balaenoptera musculus*), Oceanic, E (1970).
• bowhead (*Balaena mysticetus*), Oceanic (northern latitudes only), E (1970).
• finback (*Balaenoptera physalus*), Oceanic, E (1970).
• gray (*Eschrichtius robustus*), northern Pacific Ocean, coastal waters and Bering Sea, formerly northern Atlantic Ocean, E (1970).
• humpback (*Megaptera novaengliae*), Oceanic, E (1970).
• right (*Balaena glacialis*), Oceanic E (1970).
• *Sei* (*Balaenoptera borealis*), Oceanic, E (1970).
• sperm (*Physeter catodon*), Oceanic, E (1970).

**wolf**
• gray (*Canis lupus*), Holarctic (see REALM on page 258), 48 adjacent states in U.S. and Mexico, T in Minnesota, E elsewhere (1967).

- maned (*Chrysocyon brachyurus*), Argentina, Bolivia, Brazil, Paraguay, and Uruguay, E (1970).
- red (*Canis rufus*), southeastern United States, west to central Texas, E everywhere except Dare, Tyrrell, Hyde, and Washington counties in North Carolina (1967).

**wombat,** hairy-nosed (Barnard's wombat, Queensland hairnosed wombat, or *Lasiorhinus krefftii*, formerly *L. barnardi* and *L. gillespiei*), Australia, E. (1970).

**woodrat,** Key Largo (*Neotoma floridana smalli*), Florida, E (1983).

**yak,** wild (*Bos grunniens*), India and Tibet, E (1970).

**zebra**
- Grevy's (*Equus grevyi*), Ethiopia, Kenya, and Somalia, T (1979).
- Hartmann's mountain (*Equus zebra hartmannae*), Angola and Namibia, T (1979).
- mountain (*Equus zebra zebra*), South Africa, E (1976).

**Birds**

**akepa**
- Hawaii (honeycreeper or *Loxopx coccineus coccineus*), Hawaii, E (1970).
- Maui (honeycreeper or *Loxops coccineus ochraceus*), Hawaii, E (1970).

**akialoa,** Kauai (honeycreeper or *Hemignathus procerus*), Hawaii, E (1967).

**akiapolaau** (honeycreeper or *Hemignathus munroi* [or *wilsoni*]), Hawaii, E (1967).

**albatross,** short-tailed (*Diomedia albatrus*), northern Pacific Ocean, including Japan, U.S.S.R., Hawaii, and mainland U.S. Pacific Coast, E everywhere except U.S. (1970).

**blackbird,** yellow-shouldered (*Aelaius xanthomus*), Puerto Rico, E (1976).

**bobwhite,** masked (quail or *Colinus virginianus ridgwayi*), Arizona and Sonora (Mexico), E (1967).

**booby,** Abbott's (*Sula abbotti*), Christmas Island (Indian Ocean), E (1976).

**bristlebird**
- Western (*Dasyornis brachypterus longirostris*), Australia, E (1970).
- western rufous (*Dasyornis broadbenti littoralis*), Australia, E (1976).

**broadbill,** Guam (*Myiagra freycineti*), Guam (western Pacific Ocean), E (1984).

**bulbul,** Mauritius olivaceous (*Hypsipetes borbonicus olivaceus*), Mauritius (Indian Ocean), E (1970).

**bullfinch,** Sao Miguel (finch or *Phyrrhula phyrrhula murina*), Azores Islands (eastern Atlantic Ocean), E (1970).

**bushwren,** New Zealand (*Xenicus longipes*), New Zealand, E (1970).

**cahow** (Bermuda petrel or *Pterodroma cahow*), Bermuda (northern Atlantic Ocean), E (1970).

**caracara,** Audubon's crested (*Polyborus plancus audubonii*), United States—Arizona, Florida, Louisiana, New Mexico, and Texas—south to Panama, and Cuba, T in Florida (1987).

**condor**
- Andean (*Vultur gryphus*), Columbia to Chile and Argentina, E (1970).
- California (*Gymnogyps californianus*), Oregon, California, and Baja California, E. in U.S. only (1967).

**coot,** Hawaiian (alae keo keo or *Fulica americana alai*), Hawaii, E (1970).

**cotinga**
- banded (*Cotinga maculata*), Brazil, E (1976).
- white-winged (*Xipholena atropurpurea*), Brazil, E (1976).

**crane**
- black-necked (*Grus nigricollis*), Tibet, E (1967).
- Cuba sandhill (*Grus canadensis nesiotes*), Cuba (West Indies), E (1967).
- hooded (*Grus monacha*), Japan and former Soviet Union, E (1970).
- Japanese (*Grus japonensis*), China, Japan, Korea, and former Soviet Union, E (1970).
- Mississippi sandhill (*Grus canadensis pulla*), Mississippi, E (1973).
- Siberian white (*Grus leucogeranus*), Siberia (former Soviet Union) to India, China, and Iran, E (1970).
- white-naped (*Grus vipio*), Mongolia, E (1967).
- whooping (*Grus americana*), Canada, United States (Rocky Mountains east to Carolinas), and Mexico, E (1967).

**creeper**
- Hawaii (*Oreomystis* [or *Loxops*] *mana*), Hawaii, E (1975).
- Molokai (kakawahie, *Paroreomyza* [or *Oreomystis,* or *Loxops*] *flammea*), Hawaii, E (1970).
- Oahu (alauwahio or *Paroreomyza* [or *Oreomystis,* or *Loxops*] *maculata*), Hawaii, E (1970).

**crow**
- Hawaiian ('alala or *Corvus hawaiiensis* [or *tropicus*]), Hawaii, E (1967).
- Mariana (*Corvus kubaryi*), Guam and Rota (western Pacific Ocean), E (1984).

**cuckoo-shrike**
- Mauritius (*Coquus* [or *Coracina*] *typicus*), Mauritius (Indian Ocean), E (1970).
- Reunion (*Coquus* [or *Coracina*] *newtoni*), Reunion (Indian Ocean), E (1970).

**curassow**
- razor-billed (*Mitu* [or *Crax*] *mitu mitu*), eastern Brazil, E (1976).
- red-billed (*Crax blumenbachii*), Brazil, E (1970).

**curlew**, Eskimo (*Numenius borealis*), Alaska and northern Canada to Argentina, E (1967).

**dove**
- cloven-feathered (*Drepanoptila holosericea*), New Caledonia (southwest Pacific Ocean), E (1970).
- Grenada gray-fronted (*Leptotila rufaxilla wellsi*), Grenada (West Indies), E (1970).

**duck**
- Hawaiian (koloa or *Anas wyvilliana*), Hawaii, E (1967).
- Laysan (*Anas laysanensis*), Hawaii, E (1967).
- pink-headed (*Rhodonessa caryophyllacea*), India, E (1976).
- white-winged wood (*Cairina scutulata*), India, Indonesia, Malaysia, and Thailand, E (1970).

**eagle**
- **bald** (*Haliaeetus leucocephalus*), North America south to northern Mexico, T in Michigan, Minnesota Oregon, Washington, and Wisconsin; E in rest of 48 adjacent states in U.S. (1967).
- Greenland white-tailed (*Haliaeetus albicilla groenlandicus*), Greenland and adjacent Atlantic islands, E (1976).
- harpy (*Harpis harpyja*), Mexico south to Argentina, E (1976).
- Philippine (monkey-eating eagle or *Pithecophaga jefferyi*), Philippines, E (1970).
- Spanish imperial (*Aquila heliaca adalberti*), Algeria, Morocco, and Spain, E (1970).

**egret,** Chinese (*Egretta eulophotes*), China and Korea, E (1970).

**falcon**
- American peregrine (*Falco peregrinus anatum*), nests from central Alaska across northwest-central Canada to central Mexico, and winters south to South America, E (1970).
- Arctic peregrine (*Falco peregrinus tundrius*), nests from northern Alaska to Greenland, and winters south to Central and South America, T (1970).
- Eurasian peregrine (*Falco peregrinus peregrinus*), Europe, Eurasia south to Africa and Middle East, E (1976).
- northern aplomado (*Falco femoralis septentrionalis*), Arizona, New Mexico, Texas, Mexico, and Guatemala, E (1986).
- peregrine (*Falco peregrino*), worldwide, except Antarctica and most Pacific islands, E in the world in 48 adjacent states of U.S. (1984).

**finch**
- Laysan (honeycreeper or *Telespyza* [or *Psittirostra*] *cantans*), Hawaii, E (1967).
- Nihoa (honeycreeper or *Telespyza* [or *Psittirostra*] *ultima*), Hawaii, E (1967).

**flycatcher**
- Euler's (*Empidonax euleri johnstonei*), Grenada (West Indies), E (1970).
- Seychelles paradise (*Terpsiphone corvina*), Seychelles Islands (Indian Ocean), E (1970).
- Tahiti (*Pomarea nigra*), Tahiti (southern Pacific Ocean), E (1970).
(See also GRASSWREN, MONARCH, and SCARLET-BREASTED ROBIN, below.)

**fody,** Seychelles (weaver-finch or *Foudia sechellarum*), Seychelles Islands (Indian Ocean), E (1970).

**frigatebird,** Andrew's (*Fregata andrewsi*), eastern Indian Ocean, E (1976).

**goose**
- Aleutian Canada (*Branta canadensis leucopareia*), Pacific Northwest coast, including California, Oregon, Washington, and Alaska, and Japan, E (1967).
- Hawaiian (nene or *Nesochen* [or *Branta*] *sandvicensis*), Hawaii, E (1967).

**goshawk,** Christmas Island (*Accipter fasciatus natalis*), Christmas Island (Indian Ocean), E (1970).

**grackle,** slender-billed (*Quisicalus* [or *Cassidix*] *palustris*), Mexico, E (1970).

**grasswren,** Eyrean (flycatcher or *Amytornis goyderi*), Australia, E (1970).

**grebe,** Atitlan (*Podilymbus gigas*), Guatemala, E (1970).

**greenshank,** Nordmann's (*Tringa guttifer*), former Soviet Union and Japan south to Malaya and Borneo, E (1976).

**guan,** horned (*Oreophasis derbianus*), Guatemala and Mexico, E (1970).

**gull**
- Audouin's (*Larus audouinii*), Mediterranean Sea, E (1970).
- relict (*Larus relictus*), China and India, E (1976).

**hawk**
- Anjouan Island sparrow (*Accipiter francesii pusillus*), Comoro Islands (Indian Ocean), E (1970).
- Galapagos (*Buteo galapagoensis*), Galapagos Islands, E (1970).
- Hawaiian (lo or *Buteo soltarius*), Hawaii, E (1967).

**hermit,** hook-billed (hummingbird or *Glaucis* [or *Ramphodon*] *dohrnii*), Brazil, E (1976).

**honeycreeper,** crested ('akohekohe or *Palmeria dolei*), Hawaii, E (1967). (See also AKEPA, AKIALOA, AKIAPOLAAU, and FINCH, above; NUKUPU'U, 'O'U, PALILA, PARROTBILL, and PO'OULI below.)

**honeyeater,** helmeted (*Meliphaga cassidix*), Australia, E (1970). (See also 'O'O, below.)

**hornbill,** helmeted (*Rhinoplax vigil*), New Caledonia (South Pacific Ocean), E (1976).

**ibis,** Japanese crested (*Niponia nippon*), China, Japan, Korea, and former Soviet Union, E (1970).

**jay,** Florida scrub (*Aphelocoma coerulescens coerulescens*), Florida, T (1987).

**kagu** (*Rhynochetos jubatus*), New Caledonia (South Pacific Ocean), E (1970).

**kakapo** (owl-parrot or *Strigops habroptilus*), New Zealand, E (1970).

**kestrel**
• Mauritius (*Falco punctatus*), Mauritius (Indian Ocean), E (1970).
• Seychelles (*Falco araea*), Seychelles Islands (Indian Ocean), E (1970).

**kingfisher,** Guam Micronesian (*Halcyon cinnamomina cinnamomina*), Guam, (western Pacific Ocean), E (1984).

**kite**
• Cuba hook-billed (*Chondroheirax uncinatus wilsonii*), Cuba (West Indies), E (1970).
• Everglade snail (*Rostrhamus sociabilis plumbeus*), Florida and Cuba, E (1967).
• Grenada hook-billed (*Chondrohierax uncinatus mirus*), Grenada (West Indies), E (1970).

**kokako** (wattlebird or *Callaeas cinerea*), New Zealand, E (1970).

**macaw**
• glaucous (*Andorhynchus glaucus*), Brazil, Paraguay, and Uruguay, E (1976).
• indigo (*Anodorhynchus leari*), Brazil, E (1976).
• little blue (*Cyanopsitta spixii*), Brazil, E (1976).

**magpie-robin,** Seychelles (thrush or *Copsychus sechellarum*), Seychelles Islands (Indian Ocean), E (1970).

**malkoha,** red-faced (cuckoo or *Phoenicophaeus phyrrhocephalus*), Sri Lanka (Ceylon), E (1970).

**mallard,** Mariana (*Anas oustaleti*), Guam and Mariana Islands (western Pacific Ocean), E (1977).

**megapode**
• Maleo (*Macrocephalon maleo*), Celebes (Indonesia), E (1970).
• Micronesian (*Megapodius laperouse*), Palau Island and Mariana Islands (western Pacific Ocean), E (1970).

**millerbird,** Nihoa (old world warbler or *Acrocephalus familiaris kingi*), Hawaii, E (1967).

**monarch,** Tinian (old world flycatcher or *Monarcha takatsukasae*), Mariana Islands (western Pacific Ocean), T (1970).

**moorhen**
• Hawaiian common (gallinule or *Gallinula chloropus sandvicensis*), Hawaii E (1967).
• Mariana common (gallinule or *Gallinula chloropus guami*), Guam, Pagan, Saipan, and Tinian (western Pacific Ocean), E (1984).

**nightjar,** Puerto Rican (Puerto Rican whip-poor-will or *Caprimulgus noctitherus*), Puerto Rico, E (1973).

**nukupu'u** (honeycreeper or *Hemignathus lucidus*), Hawaii, E (1967).

**'o'o,** Kauai ('o'o 'a'a, honeyeater, or *Moho braccatus*), Hawaii, E (1967).

**ostrich**
• Arabian (*Struthio camelus syriacus*), Jordan and Saudi Arabia, E (1970).
• West African (*Struthio camelus spatzi*), Spanish Sahara, E (1970).

**'o'u** (honeycreeper or *Psittirostra psittacea*), Hawaii, E (1967).

**owl**
• Anjouan scops (*Otus rutilus capnodes*), Comoro Island (Indian Ocean), E (1970).
• giant scops (*Otus gurneyi*), Marinduque and Mindanao islands (Philippines), E (1976).
• Seychelles (*Otus insularis*), Seychelles Islands (Indian Ocean), E (1970).

**owlet,** Morden's (Sokoke or *Otus ireneae*), Kenya E (1970).

**palila** (honeycreeper or *Loxioides* [or *Psittirostra*] *bailleui*), Hawaii, E (1967).

**parakeet**
• Forbes' (*Cyanoramphus auriceps forbesi*), New Zealand, E (1970).
• golden (*Aratinga guarouba*), Brazil, E (1970).
• golden-shouldered (golden-hooded parakeet or *Psephotus chrysopterygius*), Australia, E (1970).
• Mauritius (*Psittacula echo*), Mauritius (Indian Ocean), E (1970).
• ochre-marked (*Pyrrhura cruentata*), Brazil, E (1970).
• orange-bellied (*Neophema chrysogaster*), Australia, E (1970).
• paradise (beautiful parakeet or *Psephotus pulcherrimus*), Australia, E (1970).
• scarlet-chested (splendid parakeet or *Neophema splendida*), Australia, E (1970).
• turquoise (*Neophema pulchella*), Australia, E (1970).

**parrot**
• Australian (*Geopsittacus occidentalis*), Australia, E (1970).
• Bahaman or Cuban (*Amazona leucocephala*), Bahamas, Cayman Islands, and Cuba (West Indies), E (1970).
• ground (*Pezoporus wallicus*), Australia, E (1973).

- imperial (*Amazona imperialis*), Dominica (West Indies), E (1970).
- Puerto Rican (*Amazona vittata*), Puerto Rico, E (1967).
- red-browed (*Amazona rhodocorytha*), Brazil, E (1970).
- red-capped (*Pionopsitta pileata*), Brazil, E (1976).
- red-necked (*Amazona arausiaca*), Dominica (West Indies), E (1979).
- red-spectacled (*Amazona pretrei pretrei*), Argentina and Brazil, E (1976).
- St. Lucia (*Amazona versicolor*), St. Lucia (West Indies), E (1970).
- St. Vincent (*Amazona guildingii*), St. Vincent (West Indies), E (1970).
- thick-billed (*Rhychopsitta pachrhyncha*), Arizona, New Mexico, and Mexico, E in Mexico (1970).
- vinaceous-breasted (*Amazona vinacea*), Brazil, E (1976).

**parrotbill,** Maui (honeycreeper or *Pseudonestor xanthophrys*), Hawaii, E (1967).

**pelican,** brown (*Pelecanus occidentalis*), Carolinas to Texas, California, coastal Central and South American, and the West Indies, E except Florida and Alabama Atlantic Coast (1970).

**penguin,** Galapagos (*Spheniscus mendiculus*), Galapagos Islands, E (1970).

**petrel,** Hawaiian dark-rumped (*Pterodroma phaeopygia sandwichensis*), Hawaii, E (1970).

**pheasant**
- bar-tailed (*Syrmaticus humaie*), Burma (Myanmar) and China, E (1970).
- Blyth's tragopan (*Tragopan blythii*), Burme (Myanmar), China, and India E (1970).
- brown eared (*Crossoptilon mantchuricum*), China, E (1970).
- Cabot's tragopan (*Traopan caboti*), China, E (1970).
- Chinese moral (*Lophophorus ihuysii*), China, E (1970).
- Edward's (*Lophura edwardsi*), Vietnam, E (1970).
- Elliot's (*Syrmaticus ellioti*), China, E (1976).
- imperial (*Lophura imperialis*), Vietnam, E (1970).
- Mikado (*Syrmaticus mikado*), Taiwan, E (1970).
- Palawan peacock (*Polyplectron emphanum*), Philippines, E (1970).
- Sclater's monal (*Lophophorus sclateri*), Burma, China, and India, E (1970).
- Swinhoe's (*Lophura swinhoii*), Taiwan, E (1970).
- western tragopan (*Tragopan melanocephalus*), India and Pakistan, E (1970).
- white eared (*Crossoptilon crossoptilon*), Tibet and India, E (1970).

**pigeon**
- Azores wood (*Columba palumbus azorica*), Azores Islands (eastern Atlantic Ocean), E (1970).
- Chatham Island (*Hemiphaga novaeseelandiae chathamensis*), New Zealand, E (1970).

- Minoro zone-tailed (*Ducula mindorensis*), Philippines, E (1976).
- Puerto Rican plain (*Columba inornata wetmorei*), Puerto Rico, E (1970).

**piping-guan,** black-fronted (*Pipile jacutinga*), Argentina, E (1976).

**pitta, Koch's** (*Pitta kochi*), Philippines, E (1976).

**plover**
- New Zealand shore (*Thinornis novaeseelandiae*), New Zealand, E (1970).
- piping (*Charadrius melodus*), Great Lakes, northern Great Plains, and Atlantic and Gulf coasts of United States, Canada, Mexico, and West Indies (including Bahamas, Puerto Rico, and Virgin Islands), E in Great Lakes watershed areas and province of Ontario, T elsewhere (1985).

**po'ouli** (honeycreeper or *Melamprosops phaeosoma*), Hawaii, E (1975).

**prairie-chicken,** Attwater's greater (*Tympanuchus cupido attwateri*), Texas, E (1967).

**quail,** Merriam's Montezuma (*Cyrtonuz montezimae merriami*), Vera Cruz region of Mexico, E (1976).

**quetzel,** resplendent (*Pharomachrus mocinno*), E (1976).

**rail**
- Aukland Island (*Rallus pectoralis muelleri*), New Zealand, E (1970).
- California clapper (*Rallus longirostric obsoletus*), California, E (1970).
- Guam (*Rallus Owstoni*), Guam and experimental populations on Rota (both western Pacific Ocean), E (1970).
- light-footed clapper (*Rallus longirostris levipes*), California and Baja California, E in United States only (1970).
- Lord Howe wood (*Tricholimnas sylvstris*), Lord Howe Island (Australia), E (1976).
- Yuma clapper (*Rallus longirostris yumanensis*), Arizona, California, and Mexico, E in United States only (1967).

**rhea,** Darwin's (*Pterocnemia pennata*), Argentina, Bolivia, Peru, and Uruguay, E (1970).

**robin**
- Chatham Island (*Petroica traversi*), New Zealand, E (1970).
- scarlet-breasted (flycatcher or *Petroica multicolor multicolor*), Norfolk Island (Australia), E (1970).

**rockfowl**
- grey-necked (*Picathartes oreas*), Cameroon and Gabon, E (1970).
- white-necked (*Picathartes gymnocephalus*), Togo to Sierra Leone (Africa), E (1970).

**roller,** long-tailed ground (*Uratelornis chimaera*), Madagascar (Malagasy Republic), E (1970).

**scrub-bird,** noisy (*Atrichornis clamosus*), Australia, E (1970).

**shama,** Cebu black (thrush or *Copsychus niger cebuensis*), Philipines, E (1970).

**shearwater,** Newell's Townsend's ('a'o, formerly Manx shearwater; *Puffinus auricularis*, formerly *P. newelli*), Hawaii, T (1975).

**shrike,** San Clemente loggerhead (*Lanius ludovicianus mearnsi*), California, E (1977).

**siskin,** red (*Carduelis* [or *Spinus*] *cucullata*), South America, E (1976).

**sparrow**
• Cape Sable seaside (*Ammodramus* [or *Ammospiza*] *maritimus mirabilis*), California, E (1967).
• dusky seaside (*Ammodramus* [or *Ammospiza*] *maritimus nigrescens*), Florida, E (1967).
• Florida grasshopper (*Ammodramus savannarum floridanus*), Florida, E (1986).
• San Clemente sage (*Amphispiza belli clementeae*), California, T (1977).

**starling**
• Ponape mountain (*Aplonis pelzelni*), Carolina Islands (western Pacific Ocean), E (1970).
• Rothschild's (myna or *Leucopsar rothschildi*), Bali (Indonesia), E (1970).

**stilt,** Hawaiian (ae'o or *Himantopus mexicanus* [or *himantopus*] *knudseni*), Hawaii, E (1970).

**stork**
• oriental white (*Ciconia ciconia boyciana*), China, Japan, Korea, and U.S.S.R., E (1970).
• wood (*Mycteria americana*), United States from California, Arizona, and Texas to the Carolinas, Mexico, and Central and South America, E (1984).

**swiftlet,** Mariana gry (Vanikoro or *Aerodramus* [or *Collocalia*] *vanikorensis bartschi*), Agiguan, Guam, Rota, Saipan, and Tinian (western Pacific Ocean), E (1984).

**teal**
• Campbell Island flightless (*Anas aucklandica nesiotis*), Campbell Island (New Zealand), E (1976).
• California least (*Sterna antillarum* [or *albifrons*] *browni*), California and Mexico, E (1970).
• least (*Sterna antillarum*), California, Mississippi River basin, and Atlantic and Gulf Coasts of the United States, Mexico and Bahamas and the Greater and Lesser Antilles in the West Indies; winters in Central and northern South America, E in Mississippi River basin and many parts of the U.S. except within 50 miles of coast, E (1985).
• roseate (*Sterna dougallii dougallii*), tropical and temperate coasts of Atlantic Basin and East Africa, E in Bermuda, Atlantic Coast of United States south to North Carolina, and Canadian provinces of Newfoundland, Nova Scotia, and Quebec, T elsewhere in Western Hemisphere and adjacent oceans, including Puerto Rico and Virgin Islands (1987).

**thrasher,** white-breasted (*Ramphocinclus brachyurus*), St. Lucia and Martinique (West Indies), E (1970). (See also TREMBLER, below.)

**thrush**
• large Kauai (*Myadestes* [or *Phaeornis*] *myadestinus*), Hawaii, E (1970).
• Mokolai (olomao'o or *Myadestes* [or *Phaeornis*] *lanaiensis* [or *obscurus*] *rutha*), Hawaii, E (1970).
• New Zealand (wattlebird or *Turnagra capensis*), New Zealand, E (1970).
• small Kauai (puaiohi or *Myadestes* [or *Phaeornis*] *palmeri*), Hawaii E (1967).

**tinamou,** solitary (*Tinamus solitarus*), Argentina, Brazil, and Paraguay, E (1976).

**towhee,** Inyo California (brown towhee or *Pipilo crissali* [or *fuscus*] *eremophilus*), California, T (1987).

**trembler,** Martinique (thrasher or *Cinclocerthia ruficauda gutturalis*), Martinique (West Indies), E (1970).

**vireo**
• black-capped (*Vireo atricapillus*), Kansas, Louisiana, Nebraska, Oklahoma, Texas, and Mexico, E (1987).
• least Bell's (*Vireo bellii pusillus*), California and Mexico, E (1986).

**wanderer,** plain (collared-hemipode or *Pedionomous torquatus*), Australia, E (1973).

**warbler (old world)**
• nightingale reed (*Acrocephalus luscinia*), western Pacific Ocean, E in Mariana Islands, E (1970).
• Rodrigues (*Bebrornis rodericanus*), Rodrigues Islands (Mauritius), E (1970).
• Seychelles (*Bebrornis sechellensis*), Seychelles Islands (Indian Ocean), E (1970).

**warbler (wood)**
• Bachman's (*Vermivora bachmanii*), southeastern United States and Cuba, E (1967).
• Barbados yellow (*Dendroica petechia petechia*), Barbados (West Indies), E (1970).
• Kirtland's (*Dendroica kirtlandii*), Bahamas (West Indies), Canada, and the United States, especially Michigan, E (1967).
• Semper's (*Leucopeza semperi*), St. Lucia (West Indies), E (1970).

**whipbird,** Western (*Psophodes nigrogularis*), Australia, E (1970).

**white-eye**
• bridled (*Zosterops conspicillatus conspicillatus*), Guam (western Pacific Ocean), E (1984).
• Norfolk Island (*Zosterops albogularis*), Norfolk Islands (Indian Ocean), E (1976).
• Ponape greater (*Rukia longirostra* [or *sanfordi*]), Caroline Islands (western Pacific Ocean), E (1970).

- Seychelles (*Zosterops modesta*), Seychelles Islands (Indian Ocean), E (1970).

**woodpecker**
- imperial (*Campephilus imperialis*), Mexico, E (1970).
- ivory-billed (*Campephilus principalis*), Cuba and south-central and southeastern United States, E (1970).
- red-cockaded (*Picoides* [or *Dendrocopos*] *borealis*), south-central and southeastern United States, E (1970).
- Tristam's (*Dryocopus javensis richardsi*), Korea, E (1970).

**wren**
- Guadeloupe house (*Troglodytes aedon guadeloupensis*), Guadeloupe (West Indies), E (1970).
- St. Lucia house (*Troglodytes aedon mesoleucus*), St. Lucia (West Indies), E (1970).

## Reptiles

**alligator**
- American (*Alligator mississippiensis*), southeastern United States, T (1967).
- Chinese (*Alligator sinensis*), China, E (1976).

**anole,** Culebra Island giant (*Anolis roosevelti*), Culebra Island (Puerto Rico), E (1977).

**boa**
- Jamaican (*Epicrates subflavus*), Jamaica, E (1970).
- Mona (*Epicrates monensis monensis*), Puerto Rico, T (1978).
- Puerto Rican (*Epicrates inornatus*), Puerto Rico, E (1970).
- Round Island (*Bolyeria multocarinata*), Mauritius (Indian Ocean), E (1980).
- Round Island (*Casarea dussumieri*), Mauritius (Indian Ocean), E (1980).
- Virgin Islands tree (*Epicrates monensis granti*), Virgin Islands (United States and British, West Indies), E (1970).

**caiman**
- Apaporis River (*Caiman crocodilus apaporiensis*), Colombia, E (1976).
- black (*Melanosuchus niger*), Amazon River basin, E (1976).
- broad-snouted (*Caiman latirostris*), Argentina, Brazil, Paraguay, and Uruguay, E (1976).
- Yacare (*Caiman crocodilus yacare*), Argentina, Bolivia, Brazil, and Peru, E (1970).

**chuckwalla,** San Esteban Island (*Sauromalus various*), Mexico, E (1980).

**crocodile**
- African dwarf (*Osteolaemus tetraspis tetraspis*), West Africa, E (1976).
- African slender-snouted (*Crocodylus cataphractus*), western and central Africa, E (1971).
- American (*Crocodylus acutus*), Florida, Mexico, Central and South America, and Caribbean, E (1975).

- Ceylon mugger (*Crocodylus palustris kimbula*), Sri Lanka (Ceylon), E 1976.
  Congo dwarf (*Osteolaemus tetraspis osborni*), Congo River drainage basin, E (1976).
- Cuban (*Crocodylus rhombifer*), Cuba, E (1970).
- Morelet's (*Crocodylus moreleti*), Belize, Guatemala, and Mexico, E (1970).
- mugger (*Crocodylus palustris palustris*), Bangladesh, India, Iran, and Pakistan, E (1976).
- Nile (*Crocodylus niloticus*), Africa and the Middle East, T in Zimbabwe, elsewhere, E (1970).
- Orinoco (*Crocodylus intermedius*), Orinoco River basin (South America), E (1970).
- Philippine (*Crocodylus novaeguineae mindorensis*), Philippine Islands, E (1976).
- saltwater (estuarine crocodile or *Crocodylus porosus*), Australia, Papua New Guinea, southeast Asia, and Pacific Islands, E everywhere except Papua New Guinea, E (1979).
- Siamese (*Crocodylus siamensis*), southeast Asia and Malay Peninsula, E (1976).

**gavial** (gharial or *gavialis gangeticus*), Bangladesh, Burma (Myanmar), India, Nepal, and Pakistan, E (1970).

**gecko**
- day (*Phelsuma edwardnewtoni*), Mauritius (Indian Ocean), E (1970).
- Monito (*Sphaerodactylus micropithecus*), Puerto Rico, E (1982).
- Round Island day (*Phelsuma guentheri*), Mauritius (Indian Ocean), E (1970).
- Serpent Island (*Cyrtodactylus serpensinsula*), Mauritius (Indian Ocean), T (1983).

**iguana**
- Acklins ground (*Cyclura rileyi nuchalis*), Bahamas (West Indies), T (1983).
- Allen's Cay (*Cyclura cychlura inornata*), Bahamas (West Indies), T (1983).
- Andros Island ground (*Cyclura cychlura cychlura*), Bahamas (West Indies), T (1983).
- Anegada ground (*cyclura pinguis*), Anegada Island (British Virgin Islands, West Indies), E (1970).
- Barrington land (*Conolophus pallidus*), Galapagos Islands, E (1970).
- Cayman Brac ground (*Cyclura nubila caymanensis*), Cayman Islands (West Indies), E (1983).
- Cuban ground (*Cyclura nubila nubila*), Cuba and introduced population in Puerto Rico, T in Cuba (1983).
- Exuma Island (*Cyclura cychlura figginsi*), Bahamas (West Indies), T (1983).
- Fiji banded (*Brachylophus fisciatus*), Fiji and Tongs (Pacific Ocean), E (1980).
- Fiji crested (*Brachylophus vitiensis*), Fiji (Pacific Ocean), E (1980).
- Grand Cayman ground (*Cyclura nubila lewisi*), Cayman Islands (West Indies), E (1983).

- Jamaican (*Cyclura collei*), Jamaica (West Indies), E (1983).
- Mayaguana (*Cyclura carinata bartschi*), Bahamas (West Indies), T (1983).
- Mona ground (*Cyclura stejnegeri*), Mona Island (Puerto Rico, West Indies), T (1978).
- Turks and Caicos (*Cyclura carinata carinata*) Turks and Caicos Islands (West Indies), T (1983).
- Watling Island ground (*Cyclura rileyi rileyi*), Bahamas (West Indies), E (1983).
- White Car ground (*Cyclura rileyi cristata*), Bahamas (West Indies), T (1983).

### lizard

- blunt-nosed leopard (*Gambelia* [or *Crotaphytus*] *silus*), California, E (1967).
- Coachella Valley fringe-toed (*Uma inornata*), California, T (1980).
- Hierro giant (*Gallotia simonyi simonyi*), Canary Islands, E (1984).
- Ibiza wall (*Podarcis pityusensis*), Balearic Islands, T (1984).
- Island night (*Xantusia* [or *Klauberina*] *riversiana*), California, T (1977).
- St. Croix ground (*Ameiva polops*), Virgin Islands, E (1977).

### monitor

- Bengal (*Varanus bangalensis*), Afghanistan, Burma (Myanmar), India, Iran, Iraq, Malaysia, Sri Lanka (Ceylon), Thailand, and Vietnam, E (1976).
- desert (*Varanus griseus*), North Africa to Near East, northwest India, and Caspian Sea through former Soviet Union to Pakistan, E (1976).
- Komodo island (*Varanus komodoensis*). Komodo, Padar, Rintja, and western Flores Island (Indonesia), E (1976).
- yellow (*Varanus flavescents*), West Pakistan through India to Bangladesh, E (1976).

**python,** Indian (*Python molurus molurus*), Sri Lanka (Ceylon) and India, E (1976).

### rattlesnake

- Aruba Island (*Crotalus unicolor*), Aruba Island (Netherland Antilles), T (1983).
- New Mexican ridge-nosed (*Crotalus willardi obscurus*), New Mexico and Mexico, T (1978).

### skink

- blue-tailed mole (*Eumeces egregius lividus*), Florida, T (1987).
- Round Island (*Leiolopisma telfairi*), Mauritius (Indian Ocean), T (1983).
- sand (*Neoseps reynoldsi*), Florida, T (1987).

### snake

- Atlantic salt marsh (*Merodia fasciata taeniata*), Florida, T (1977).
- Concho water (*Nerodia harteri paucimaculata*), Texas, T (1986).
- eastern indigo (*Drymarchon corais couperi*), Alabama,

Florida, Georgia, Mississippi, and South Carolina, T (1978).
- San Francisco garter (*Thamnophis sirtalis tetrataenia*), California, E (1967).

**tartaruga** (*Podocnemis expansa*), Orinoco and Amazon river basins (South America), E (1970).

**terrapin,** river (Tuntong or *Batagur baska*), Bangladesh, Burma (Myanmar), India, Indonesia, and Malaysia, E (1970).

**tomistoma** (*Tomistoma schlegelii*), Indonesia and Malaysia, E (1976).

### tortoise

- angulated (*Geochelone yniphora*), Madagascar (Malagasy Republic), E (1976).
- Bolson (*Gopherus flavomarginatus*), Mexico, E (1979).
- desert (*Gopherus* [or *Xerobates* or *Scaptochelys*] *agassizii*), Arizona, California, Nevada, Utah, and Mexico, T (1980).
- Galapagos (*Geochelone elephantopus*), Galapagos Islands, E (1970).
- gopher (*Gopherus polyphemus*), Alabama, Florida, Georgia, Louisiana, Mississippi, and South Carolina, T west of Mobile and Tombigbee rivers in Alabama, Mississippi, and Lousiana (1987).
- radiated (*Geochelone* [or *Testudo*] *radiata*), Madagascar (Malagasy Republic), E (1970).

**tracaja** (*Podocnemis unifilis*), Orinoco and Amazon river basins (South America), E (1970).

### turtle

- Alabama red-bellied (*Pseudemys alabamensis*), Alabama, E (1987).
- aquatic box (*Terrapene coahuila*), Mexico, E (1973).
- black softshell (*Trionyx nigricans*), Bangladesh, E (1976).
- Burmese peacock (*Morenia ocellata*), Burma (Myanmar), E (1976).
- Central American river (*Dermatemys mawii*), Belize, Gautemala, and Mexico, E (1983).
- Cuatro Cienegas softshell (*Trionyx ater*), Mexico, E (1976).
- flattened musk (*sternotherus depressus*), Alabama, T in Black Warrior River system, upstream from Bankhead Dam (1987).
- geometric (*Psammobates geometricus* or Geochelone geometrica), South Africa, E (1976).
- green sea (*Chelonia mydas*, including *agassizi*), circumglobal in tropical and temperate seas and oceans, E breeding colony populations in Florida and Pacific coast of Mexico, T elsewhere (1970).
- hawksbill sea (carey turtle or *Eretmochelys imbricata*), tropical seas, E (1970).
- Indian sawback (*Kachiga tecta tecta*), India, E (1976).
- Indian softshell (*Trionyx gangeticus*), India and Pakistan, E (1976).
- Kemp's (or Atlantic) ridley sea (*Lepidochelys kempii*), tropical and temperate seas in the Atlantic Basin, including the Gulf of Mexico, E (1970).

- leatherback sea (*Dermochelys coriacea*), tropical, temperate, and subpolar seas, E (1970).
- loggerhead sea (*Caretta caretta*), circumglobal in tropical and temperate seas and oceans, T (1978).
- olive (or Pacific) ridley sea (*Lepidochelys olivacea*), tropical and temperate seas in the Pacific Basin, E breeding colony populations on Pacific coast of Mexico, T elsewhere (1978).
- peacock softshell (*Trionyx hurum*), Bangladesh and India, E (1976).
- Plymouth red-bellied (*Pseudemys [or Chrysemys] rubriventris bangsi*), Massachusetts, E (1980).
- ringed sawback (*Graptemys oculifera*), Louisiana and Mississippi, T (1986).
- shortnecked (western swamp turtle or *Pseudomydura umbrina*), Australia, E (1970).
- spotted pond (*Geoclemys [or Damonia] hamiltonii*), Pakistan and northern India, E (1976).
- three-keeled Asian (*Malenochelys [or Geoemyda or Nicoria] tricarinata*), central India to Bangladesh and Burma (Myanmar), E (1976).

**viper,** Lar Valley (*Vipera latfii*), Iran, E (1983).

**Amphibians**

**coqui,** golden *(Eleutherodactylus jasperi)*, Puerto Rico, T (1977).

**frog**
- Israel painted (*Discoglossus nigriventer*), Israel, E (1970).
- Panamanian golden (*Atelopus various zeteki*), Panama, E (1976).
- Stephen Island (*Leiopelma hamiltoni*), New Zealand, E (1970).

**salamander**
- Cheat Mountain *(Plethodon nettingi)*, West Virginia, T (1989).
- Chinese giant (*Andrias davidianus davidianus*), western China, E (1976).
- desert slender (*Batrachoseps aridus*), California, E (1973).
- Japanese giant (*Andrias davidianus japonicus*), Japan, E (1976).
- Red Hills (*Phaeognathuis hubrichti*), Alabama, T (1976).
- San Marcos (*Eurycea nana*), Texas, T (1980).
- Santa Cruz long-toed (*Ambystoma macrodactylum croceum*), California, E (1967).
- Shenandoah (*Plethodon shenandoah*), Virginia, E (1989).
- Texas blind (*Typhlomolge rathbuni*), Texas, E (1967).

**toad**
- African viviparous (*Nectophrynoides*—all species), Cameroon, Ethiopia, Guinea, Ivory Coast, Liberia, and Tanzania, E (1976).
- Cameroon (*Bufo superciliaris*), equatorial Africa, E (1976).
- Houston (*Bufo houstonensis*), Texas, E (1970).
- Monte Verde (*Bufo periglenes*), Costa Rica, E (1976).
- Puerto Rican crested (*Peltophryne lemur*), Puerto Rico and the British Virgin Islands, T (1987).
- Wyoming (*Bufo hemiophrys baxteri*), Wyoming, E (1984).

**Fishes**

**ala balik** (trout or *Salmo platycephalus*), Turkey, E (1970).

**ayumodoki** (loach or *Hymenophysa* for *Botia]* *curta*), Japan, E (1970).

- **blindcat,** Mexican (catfish or *Prietella phreatophila*), Mexico, E (1970).

- **bonytoungue,** Asian (*Sclerophages formosus*). Indonesia, Malaysia, and Thailand, E (1977).

**catfish**
- giant (*Pangasianodon gigas*), Thailand, E (1970).
- (*Pangasius sanitwongsei*), Thailand, E (1970).
- Yaqui (*Ictalurus pricei*), Arizona and Mexico, T (1987).
(See also BLINDCAT, MEXICAN, above, and NEKOGIGI, below.)

**cavefish**
- Alabama (*Speoplatyrhinus poulsoni*), Alabama, E (1977).
- Ozark (*Amblyopsis rosae*), Arizona, Missouri, and Oklahoma, T (1984).

**chub**
- bonytail (*Gila elegans*), Arizona, California, Colordao, Nevada, Utah, and Wyoming.
- Borax Lake (*Gila boraxobius*), Oregon, E (1982).
- Chihuahua (*Gila nigrescens*), New Mexico and Chihuahua, in Mexico, T (1983).
- humpback (*Gila cypha*), Arizona, Colorado, Utah, and Wyoming, E (1967).
- Hutton tui (*Gila bicolor*, all species), Oregon T (1985).
- Mohave tui (*Gila bicolor mohavensis*), California, E (1970).
- Owens tui (*Gila bicolor synderi*), California, E (1985).
- Pahranagat roundtail [or bonytail] (*Gila robusta jordani*), Nevada, E (1970).
- slender (*Hybopsis cahni*), Tennessee and Virginia, T (1977).
- Sonora (*Gila ditaenia*), Arizona and Mexico, T (1986).
- spotfin (*Cyprinella [or Hybopsis] monacha*), Alabama, Georgia, North Carolina, Tennessee, and Virgina, T (1977).
- Virgin River (*Gila robusta semidnuda*), Arizona, Nevada, and Utah, E (1989).
- Yaqui (*Gila purpurea*), Arizona and Mexico, E (1984).

**cicek** (minnow or *Acanthorutilus handlirschi*), Turkey, E (1970).

**cui-ui** (*Chasmistes cujus*), Nevada, E (1967).

**dace**
- Ash Meadows speckled (*Rhinichthys osculus nevadensis*), Nevada, E (1982).
- blackside (*Phoxinus cumberlandensis*), Kentucky and Tennessee, T. (1987).
- Clover Valley speckled (*Rhinichthys osculus oligoporus*), Nevada, E (1989).
- desert (*Eremichthys acros*), Nevada, T (1985).

- Foskett speckled (*Rhinichthys osculus*, all species), Oregon, T (1974).
- Independence Valley speckled (*Rhinichthys osculus lethoporus*), Nevada, T (1989).
- Kendall Warm Springs (*Rhinichthys osculus thermalis*), Wyoming, E (1970).
- Moapa (*Moapa coriacea*), Nevada E, (1967).

**darter**
- amber (*Percina antesella*), Georgia and Tennessee, E (1985).
- bayou (*Etheostoma rubrum*), Mississippi, T (1975).
- boulder (Elk River darter or *Theostoma capiti*), Alabama and Tennessee, E (1988).
- fountain (*Etheostoma fonticola*), Texas, E (1970).
- leopard (*Percina pantherina*), Arkansas and Oklahoma, T (1978).
- Maryland (*Etheostoma sellare*), Maryland, E (1967).
- Niangua (*Etheostoma nianguae*), Missouri, T (1985).
- Okaloosa (*Etheostoma okaloosae*), Florida, E (1973).
- slackwater (*Etheostoma boschungi*), Alabama and Tennessee, T (1977).
- snail (*Percina tanasi*), Alabama, Georgia, and Tennessee, T (1975).
- watercress (*Etheostoma nuchale*), Alabama, E (1970).

**gambusia**
- Big Bend (*Gambusia gaigei*), Texas, E (1967).
- Clear Creek (*Gambusia heterochir*), Texas, E (1967).
- Pecos (*Gambusia nobilis*), New Mexico and Texas, E (1970).
- San Marcos (*Gambusia georgei*), Texas, E (1980).

**killifish,** Pahrump (*Empetrichthys latos*), Nevada, E (1967).

**logperch**
- Conasauga (*Percina jenkinsi*), Georgia and Tennessee, E (1985).
- Roanoke (*Percina rex*), Virginia, E (1989).

**madtom**
- Scioto (*Noturus trautmani*), Ohio, E (1975).
- Smoky (*Noturus baileyi*), Tennessee, E (1984).
- yellowfin (*Noturus flavipinnis*), Tennessee and Virginia, T except for limited experimental populations (1977).

**minnow,** loach (*Tiaroga cobitis*), Arizona, New Mexico, and Mexico, T (1986).

**nekogigi** (catfish or *Coreobagrus ichikawai*), Japan, E (1970).

**pupfish**
- Ash Meadows Amargosa (*Cyprinodon nevadensis mionectes*), Nevada, E (1982).
- Comanche Springs (*Cyprinodon elegans*), Texas, E (1967).
- desert (*Cyprinodon macularius*), Arizona, California, and Mexico, E (1986).
- Devils Hole (*Cyprinodon diabolis*), Nevada, E (1967).
- Leon Springs (*Cyprinodon bovinus*), Texas, E (1980).

- Owens (*Cyprinodon radiosus*), California, E (1967).
- Warm Springs (*Cyprinodon navadensis pectoralis*), Nevada, E (1970).

**salmon,** chinook (*Oncorhynchus tshawytscha*), Pacific Ocean, T in Sacramento River, California, for winter run (1990).

**sculpin,** pygmy (*Cottus pygmaeus*), Alabama, T (1989).

**shiner**
- beautiful (*Cyprinella* [or *notropis*] *formosa* [or *formosus*]), Arizona, New Mexico, and Mexico, T (1984).
- Cape Fear (*Notropis mekistocholas*), North Carolina, E (1987).
- Pecos bluntnose (*Notropis simus peconsensis*), New Mexico, T (1987).

**silverside,** Waccamaw (*Menidia extensa*), North Carolina, T (1987).

**spinedace**
- Big Spring (*Lepidomeda mollispinis pratensis*), Nevada, T (1985).
- Little Colorado (*Lepidomeda vittat*), Arizona, T (1987).
- White River (*Lepidomeda albivallis*), Nevada, T (1985).

**springfish**
- Hiko White River (*Crenichthys baileyi grandis*), Nevada, E (1985).
- Railroad Valley (*Crenichthys nevadae*), Nevada, T (1986).
- White River (*Crenichthys baileyi baileyi*), Nevada, E (1985).

**squawfish,** Colorado (*Ptychocheilus lucius*), Arizona, California, Colorado, New Mexico, Nevada, Utah, Wyoming, and Mexico, E except experimental populations in Arizona (1967).

**stickleback,** unarmored threespine (*Gasterosteus aculetaus williamsoni*), California, E (1970).

**sturgeon,** shortnose (*Acipenser brevirostrum*), Atlantic Coast of U.S. and Canada, E (1967).

**sucker**
- June (*Chasmistes liorus*), Utah, E (1986).
- Lost River (*Deltistes luxatus*), California and Oregon, E (1988).
- Modoc (*Catostomus microps*), California, E (1985).
- short-nose (*Chasmistes brevirostris*), California and Oregon, E (1988).
- short-nose (*Chasmistes brevirostris*), California and Oregon, E (1988).
- Warner (*Catostomus warnerensis*), Oregon, T (1985).

**tango,** Miyako (Tokyo bitterling or *Tanakia tango*), Japan, E (1970).

**temolek,** ikan (minnow or *Probarbus jullieni*), Cambodia, Laos, Malaysia, Thailand, and Vietnam, E (1976).

**topminnow,** Gila [incl. Yaqui] (*Poeciliopsis occidentalis*), Arizona, New Mexico, and Mexico, E in U.S. (1967).

**totoaba** (seatrout, weakfish, or *Cynoscion macdonaldi*), Gulf of California off Mexico, E (1979).

**trout**
- Apache (Arizona trout or *Oncorhynchus* [or *Salmo*] *apache*), Arizona, T (1967).
- Gila (*Oncorhynchus* [or *Salmo*] *gilae*), Arizona and New Mexico, E (1967).
- greenback cutthroat (*Oncorhynchus* [or *Salmo*] *clarki stomias*), Colorado, T (1967).
- Lahonton cutthroat (*Onchorhynchus* [or *Salmo*] *clarki henshawi*), California, Nevada, and Oregon, T (1970).
- Little Kern golden (*Onchorhynchus* [or *Salmo*] *aguabonita whitei*), California, T (1978).
- Paiute cutthroat (*Oncorhynchus* [or *Salmo*] *clarki seleniris*), California, T (1967).

**woundfin** (*Plagopterus argentissimus*), Arizona, Nevada, and Utah, E except experimental populations in Gila River system (1970).

**Snails**

**shagreen,** Magazine Mountain (*Mesodon magazinensis*), Arizona, T (1989).

**snail**
- Chittenango ovate amber (*Succinea chittenangoensis*), New York, T (1978).
- flat-spired three-toothed (*Triodopsis platysayoides*), West Virginia, T (1978).
- Iowa Pleistocene (*Discus macclintocki*), Iowa, E (1978).
- Manus Island tree (*Papustyla pulcherrima*), Admiralty (Manus) Island, Pacific Ocean, E (1970).
- noonday (*Mesodon clarki nantahala*), North Carolina, T (1978).
- Oahu tree (*Achatinella*, all species), Hawaii, E (1981).
- painted snake coiled forest (*Anguispira picta*), Tennessee, T (1978).
- Stock Island (*Orthalicus reses*, not including *nesodryas*), Florida, E (1978).
- Virginia fringed mountain (*Polyygyriscus virginianus*), Virginia, E (1978).

**Clams**

**fatmucket,** Arkansas (*Lampsilis powelli*), Arkansas, T (1990).

**mussel**
- Curtus' (*Pleurobema curtum*), Alabama and Mississippi, E (1987).
- dwarf wedge (*Alasmidonta heterodon*), Connecticut, District of Columbia, Delaware, Maryland, Massachusetts, North Carolina, New Hampshire, New Jersey, Pennsylvania, Virginia, Vermont, and New Brunswick, Canada, E (1990).

- Judge Tait's (*Pleurobema taitianum*), [same as above], E (1987).
- Marshall's (*Pleurobema marshalli*), [same as above], E (1987).
- penitent (*Epiostoma* [or *Dysomia*] *penita*), [same as above], E (1987).
- ring pink (golf stick pearly mussel or *Obovaria retusa*), Alabama, Illinois, Indiana, Kentucky, Ohio, Pennsylvania, Tennessee, and West Virginia, E (1989).

**pearlshell,** Louisiana (*Margaritifera hembeli*), Lousiana, E (1988).

**pearly mussel**
- Alabama lamp (*Lampsilis virescens*), E (1976).
- Appalachian monkeyface (*Quadrula sparsa*), Tennessee Virginia, E (1976).
- birdwing (*Conradilla caelata*), Tennessee and Virginia, E (1976).
- cracking (*Hemistena* [or *Lastena*] *lata*), Alabama, Illinois, Indiana, Kentucky, Ohio, Tennessee, and Virginia, E (1989).
- Cumberland bean (*Villosa* [or *Micromya*] *trabalis*), Kentucky and Tennessee, E (1976).
- Cumberland monkeyface (*Quardula intermedia*), Alabama, Tennessee, and Virginia), E (1976).
- Curtis' (*Epioblamsa* [or *Dysnomia*] *florentina curtisi*), Missouri, E (1976).
- dromedary (*Dromus dromus*), Tennessee and Virginia, E (1976).
- green-blossom (*Epioblasma* [or *Dysnomia*] *torulosa gubernaculum*), Tennessee and Virginia, E (1976).
- Higgin's eye (*Lampsilis higginsi*), Illinois, Indiana, Iowa, Kentucky, Ohio, Pennsylvania, and Tennessee, E (1976).
- little-wing (*Pegias fabula*), Alabama, Kentucky, North Carolina, Tennessee, and Virginia, E (1988).
- Nicklin's (*Megalonaias nicklineana*), Mexico, E (1976).
- orange-footed (pimple back or *Plethobasus cooperianus*), Alabama, Indiana, Iowa, Kentucky, Ohio, Pennsylvania, and Tennessee, E (1976).
- pale lilliput (*Toxolasma [or Carunculina] cylindrellus*), Alabama and Tennessee, E (1976).
- pink mucket (*Lampsilis orbiculata*), Alabama, Illinois, Indiana, Kentucky, Missouri, Ohio, Pennsylvania, Tennessee, and West Virginia, E (1976).
- Tampico (*Cyrtonaias tampicoensis tecomatensis*), Mexico, E (1976).
- tubercled-blossom (*Epioblasma* [or *Dysnomia*] *torulosa torulosa*), Illinois, Indiana, Kentucky, Tennessee, and West Virginia, E (1976).
- turgid-blossom (*Epioblasma* [or *Dysnomia*] *turgidula*), Alabama and Tennessee, E (1976).
- white cat's paw (*Epioblasma* [or *Dysnomia*] *sulcata delicata*), Indiana, Michigan, and Ohio, E (1976).
- white wartyback (*Plethobasus cicatricosus*), Alabama, Indiana, and Tennessee, E (1976).

- yellow-blossom (*Epioblasma* [or *Dysnomia*] *florentina florentina*), Alabama and Tennessee, E (1976).

**pigtoe**
- fine-rayed (*Fusconaia cuneolus*), Alabama, Tennessee, and Virginia, E (1976).
- rough (*Pleurobema plenum*), Indiana, Kentucky, Tennessee, and Virginia, E (1976).
- smooth (*Fusconaia edgariana*), Alabama, Tennessee, and Virginia, E (1989).

**pocketbook**
- fat (*Potamilus* [or *Proptera*] *capax*), Arkansas, Indiana, Missouri, and Ohio, E (1976).
- speckled (*Lampsilils streckeri*), Arkansas, E (1989).

**riffle shell,** tan (*Epioblasma walkeri*), Kentucky, Tennessee, and Virginia, E (1977).

**spinymussel**
- James River [or Virginia] (*Pleurobema* [or *Fusconia*, or *Elliptio*, or *Canthyria*] *collina*), Virginia and West Virginia, E (1988).
- Tar River (*Elliptio* [or *Canthyria*] *steinstansana*), North Carolina, E (1985).

**stirrup shell** (*Quadrula stapes*), Alabama and Mississippi, E (1987).

### Crustaceans

**amphipod,** Hay's Spring (*Stygobromus hayi*), District of Columbia, E (1982).

**crayfish**
- (*Cambarus zophonastes*), Arizona, E (1987).
- Nashville (*Orconectes shoupi*), Tennessee, E (1986).
- Shasta [or placid] (*Pacifastacus fortis*), California, E (1988).

**isopod**
- Madison Cave (*Antrolana lira*), Virginia, T (1982).
- Socorro (*Thermosphaeroma* [or *Exosphaeroma*] *thermophilus*), New Mexico, E (1978).

**shrimp**
- Alabama cave (*Palaemonias alabamae*), Alabama, E (1988).
- California freshwater (*Syncaris pacifica*), California, E (1988).
- Kentucky cave (*Palaemonias ganteri*), Kentucky, E (1983).

### Insects

**beetle**
- American burying (Giant carrion beetle or *Nicrophorus americanus*), eastern Canada and eastern United States south to Florida and west to South Dakota and Texas, E (1989).
- delta green ground (*Elaphrus viridis*), California, T (1980).

- Kretschmarr Cave mold (*Texasmaurops reddelli*), Texas, E (1988).
- Tooth Cave ground (*Rhadine persephone*), Texas, E (1988).
- valley elderberry longhorn (*Desmocerus californicus dimorphus*), California, T (1980).

**butterfly**
- bay checkerspot (*Euphydryas editha bayensis*), California, T (1987).
- El Segundo blue (*Euphilotes* [or *Shijimiaeoides*] *battoides allyni*), California, E (1976).
- Lange's metalmark (*Apodemia mormo langei*), California, E (1976).
- lotis blue (*Lycaeides argyrognomon lotis*), California, E (1976).
- mission blue (*Icaricia icarioides missionensis*), California, E (1976).
- Oregon silverspot (*Speyeria zerene hippolyta*), Oregon and Washington, T (1980).
- Palos Verdes blue (*Glaucopsyche lygdamus palosverdesensis*), California, E (1980).
- Queen Alexandra's birdwing (*Triodes* [or *Orhithoptera*] *alexandrae*), Papua New Guinea, E (1989).
- San Bruno elfin (*Callophrys mossii bayensis*), California, E (1976)
- Schaus swallowtail (*Heraclides* [or *Papilio*] *aristodemus ponceanus*), Florida, E (1976).
- Smith's blue (*Euphilotes* [or *Shijimiaeoides*] *enoptes smithi*], California, E, (1976).

**moth,** Kern primrose sphinx (*Euroserpinus euterpe*), California, T (1980).

**naucorid,** Ash Meadows (*Ambrysus amargosus*), Nevada, T (1985).

**skipper,** Pawnee montane (*Hesperia leonardus* [or *pawnee*] *montana*), Colorado, T (1987).

### Arachnids

**harvestman,** Bee Creek cave (*Texella reddelli*), Texas, E (1988).

**pseudoscorpion,** Tooth Cave (*Microcreagris texana*), Texas, E (1988).

**spider,** Tooth cave (*Leptoneta myopica*), Texas, E (1988).

## Endangered and Threatened Plants
Note: For more information on 16 of the most endangered plants in the United States, see GONE TOMORROW? on page 107.

### Acanthaceae (Acanthus family)
*Justicia cooleyi* (Cooley's water-willow), Florida, E (1989).

### Agavaeae (Agave family)
*Agave arizonica* (Arizona agave), Arizona, E (1984).

### Alismataceae (Water-plantain family)
- *Sagittaria fasciculata* (bunched arrowhead), North and South Carolina, E (1979).

- *Sagittaria secundifolia* (Kral's water-plantain), Alabama and Georgia, T (1990).

## Amaranthaceae (Amaranth family)
*Achyranthes splendens* var. *rotundata*, Hawaii, E (1986).

## Anacardiaceae (Cashew family)
*Rhus michauxii* (Michaux's sumac), North and South Carolina and Georgia, E (1989).

## Annonaceae (Custard-apple family)
- *Asimina tetramera* (four-petal pawpaw), Florida, E (1986).
- *Deeringothamnus pulchellus* (beautiful pawpaw), Florida, E (1986).
- *Deerintoghamnus rugelii* (Rugel's pawpaw), Florida, E (1986).

## Apiaceae (Parsley family)
- *Eryngium constancei* (Loch Lomond coyote-thistle), California, E (1985).
- *Eryngium cuneifolium* (snakeroot), Florida, E (1987).
- *Lomatium bradshawii* (Bradshaw's desert-parsley), Oregon, E (1988).
- *Oxypolis canbyi* (Canby's dropwort), Delaware, Georgia, Maryland, and North and South Carolina, E (1986).
- *Ptilimnium nodosum* or *P. fluviatile* (harperella), Alabama, Georgia, Maryland, North and South Carolina, and West Virginia, E (1988).

## Apocynaceae (Dogbane family)
- *Amsonia kearneyana* (Kearney's blue-star), Arizona, E (1989).
- Cycladenia humilis var. *jonesii* (Jones cycladenia), Arizona and Utah, T (1986).

## Aquifoliaceae (Holly family)
*Ilex cookii* (Cook's holly), Puerto Rico, E (1987).

## Arecaceae (Palm family)
*Calyptronoma rivalis* (Palma de manaca) Puerto Rico, T (1990).

## Aristolochiaceae (Heartleaf family)
*Hexastylis naniflora* (dwarf-flowered heartland), North and South Carolina, T (1989).

## Asclepieadaceae (Milkwood family)
- *Asclepias meadii* (Mead's milkweed), Illinois, Indiana, Iowa, Kansas, Missouri, and Wisconsin, T (1988).
- *Asclepias welshii* (Welsh's milkweed), Arizona and Utah, T (1987).

## Aspleniaceae (Spleenwort family)
- *Phyllitis scolopendrium* var. *americana* or *P. japonica* all species *a.* (American hart's-tongue fern), Alabama, Michigan, New York, Tennessee, and Ontario, Canada, T (1989).
- *Polystichum aleuticum* (Aleutian shield-fern or Aleutian holly-fern), Alaska, E (1988).

## Asteraceae (Aster family)
- *Argyroxiphium sandwichense* all species *sandwicense* (ahinahina or Mauna Kea silversword), Hawaii, E (1986).
- *Bidens cuneata* (cuneate bidens), Hawaii, E (1984).
- *Boltonia decurrens* (decurrent false aster), Illinois and Missouri, T (1988).
- *Chrysopsis floridana* or *Heterotheca f.* (Florida golden aster), Florida, E (1986).
- *Cirsium pitcheri* (Pitcher's thistle), Illinois, Indiana, Michigan, Wisconsin, and Ontario, Canada, T (1988).
- *Cirsium vinaceum* (Sacramento Mountains thistle), New Mexico, T (1987).
- *Echinacea tennesseensis* (Tennessee purple cornflower), Tennessee, E (1979).
- *Enceliopsis nudicaulis* var. *currugata* (Ash Meadows sunray), Nevada, T (1985).
- *Erigeron maguirei* var. *maguirei* (Maguire daisy), Utah, E (1985).
- *Erigeron rhizomatus* (Zuni [or Rhizome] (fleabane), New Mexico, T (1985).
- *Grindelia fraxinopratensis* (Ash Meadows gumplant), California and Nevada, T (1985).
- Hymenoxys acaulis var. *glabra* (Lakeside daisy), Ohio, Illinois, and Ontario, Canada, T (1988).
- Hymenoxys texana (Texas prairie dawn-flower or Texas bitterweed), Texas, E (1986).
- *Liatris helleri* (Heller's blazingstar), North Carolina, T (1987).
- *Liatris ohlingerae* (scrub blazingstar), Florida, E (1989).
- *Lipochaeta venosa*, Hawaii, E (1979).
- *Marshallia mohrii*, (Mohr's Barbara's buttons), Alabama and Georgia, T (1988).
- *Pityopsis ruthii*, *Heterotheca r.* or *Chrysopsis r.* (Ruth's golden aster), Tennessee, E (1985).
- *Senecio franciscanus* (San Francisco Peaks groundsel), Arizona, T (1983).
- *Solidago albopilosa* (white-haired goldenrod), Kentucky, T (1988).
- Solidago houghtonii (Houghton's goldenrod), Michigan and Ontario, Canada, T (1988).
- *Solidago shortii* (Short's goldenrod), Kentucky, T (1988).
- *Solidago spithamaea* (Blue Ridge goldenrod), North Carolina and Tennessee, T (1985).
- *Stephanomeria malheurensis* (Malheur wire-lettuce), Oregon, E (1982).
- *Thymophylla tephroleuca* or *Dyssodia t.* (ashy dogweed), Texas, E (1984).
- *Townsendia aprica* (Last Chance townsendia), Utah, T (1985).

## Berberidaceae (Barberry family)
*Berberis sonnei* or *Mohania s.* (Truckee barberry), California, E (1979).

## Betulaceae (Birch family)
*Betula uber* (Virginia round-leaf birch), Virginia, E (1978).

## Bignoniaceae (Bignonia family)

*Crescentia portoricensis* (Higuero de Sierra), Puerto Rico, E (1987).

## Boraginaceae (Borage family)

*Amsinckia grandiflora* (large-flowered fiddleneck), California, E (1985).

## Brassicaceae (Mustard family)

- *Arabis mcdonaldiana* (McDonald's rock-cress), California, E (1978).
- *Arabis serotina* (shale barren rock-cress), Virginia and West Virginia, E (1989).
- *Cardamine micranthera* (small-anthered bittercress), North Carolina, E (1989).
- *Erysium capitatum* var. *angustatum* (Contra Costa wallflower), California, E (1978).
- *Glaucocarpum suffrutescens* (toad-flax cress), Utah, E (1987).
- *Lesquerella congesta* (Dudley Bluffs bladderpod), Colorado, T (1990).
- *Lesquerella filiformis* (Missouri bladderpod), Missouri, E (1987).
- Lesquerella pallida (white bladderpod), Texas, E (1987).
- *Physaria obcordata* (Dudley Bluffs twinpod), Colorado, T (1990).
- *Theylpodium stenopetalum* (slender-petaled mustard), California, E (1984).
- *Warea amplexifolia* (wide-leaf warea), Florida, E (1987).
- *Warea carteri* (Carter's mustard), Florida, E (1987).

## Buxaceae (Boxwood family)

*Buxus vahlii* (Valh's boxwood), Puerto Rico, E (1985).

## Cactaceae (Cactus family)

- *Ancistrocactus tobuschii, Echinocactus t,* or *Mammillaria t.* (Tobusch fishhook cactus), Texas, E (1979).
- *Cereus eriophorus* var. *fragrans* (fragrant prickly-apple), Florida, E (1985).
- *Cereus robinii* (Key tree-cactus), Florida and Cuba, E (1984).
- *Coryphantha minima, C. nellieae, Escobaria, n.,* or *Mammillaria n.* (Nellie cory cactus), Texas, E (1979).
- *Coryphantha ramillosa* (bunched cory cactus) Texas and Coahuila, Mexico, T (1979).
- *Coryphantha robbinsoru, Cochiseia r.,* or *Escobaria r.* (Cochise pincushion cactus), Arizona and Sonora, Mexico, T (1986).
- *Coryphantha sneedii* var. *leei, Escobaria l,* or *Mammillaria l.* (Lee pincushion cactus), New Mexico, T (1979).
- *Coryphantha sneedii* var. *sneedii, Escobaria s,* or *Mammillaria s.* (Sneed pincushoin cactus), Texas and New Mexico, E (1979).
- *Echinocactus horizonthalonius* var. *nicholii* (Nichol's Turk's head cactus), Arizona, E (1979).
- *Echinocereus chisosensis* var. *chisosensis* or *E. reichenbachii* var *c.* (Chisos Mountain hedgehog cactus), Texas, T (1988).

- *Ethinocereus fendleri* var. *kuenzleri, E Kuenzleri,* or *E. hempelii* (Kuenzler hedgehod cactus), New Mexico, E (1979).
- *Echinocereus lloydii* or *E. roetteri* var. *l.* (Lloyd's hedgehog cactus), Texas, E (1979).
- *Echinocereus reichenbachii* var. *albertii* or *E. melancocentrus* (black lace cactus), Texas, E (1979).
- *Echinocereus triglochidiatus* var. *arizonicus* or *E. arizonicus* (Arizona hedgehog cactus), Arizona, E (1979).
- *Echinocereus triglochidiatus* var. *inermis, E. coccineus* var. *i.,* or *E. phoeniceus* var. *i.* (spineless hedgehog cactus), Colorado and Utah, E (1979).
- *Echinocereus viridiflorus* var. *davissi* or *E. davisii* (Davis' green pitaya), Texas, E (1979).
- *Neolloydia mariposensis, Echinocactus m.,* or *Echinomastus m.* (Lloyd's Maripose cactus), Texas and Coahvila, Mexico, T (1979).
- *Pediocactus bradyi* or *Toumeya b.* (Brady pincushion cactus), Arizona, E (1979).
- *Pediocactus despainii* (San Rafael cactus), Utah, E (1987).
- *Pediocactus knowtonii, P. bradyi* var. *k.,* or *Toumeya k.* (Knowlton cactus), New Mexico and Colorado, E (1970).
- *Pediocactus peeblesianus* var. *peeblesianus, Echinocactus p., Navajoa p., Toumeya p.,* or *Utahia p.* (Peebles Navajo cactus), Arizona, E (1979).
- *Pediocactus sileri, Echinocactus s.,* or *Utahia s.* (Siler pincushion cactus), Arizona and Utah, E (1979).
- *Sclerocactus glaucus, Echinocactus g., E. sublaucus, E. whipplei* var. *g., Pediocactus g., S franklinii,* or *S. whipplei* var. *g.* (Iunta Basin hookless cactus) Colorado and Utah, T (1979).
- *Sclerocactus mesawe-verdae, Coloradoa m., Echinocactus m.,* or *Pediocactus m.* (Mesa Verde cactus), Colorado and New Mexico, T (1979).
- *Sclerocactus wrightiae* or *Pediocactus w.* (Wright fishhook cactus), Utah, E (1979).

## Campanulaceae (Bellflower family) *Campanula robinsiae* (Brooksville [or Robins'] bellflower), Florida, E (1989).

## Caryophyllaceae (Pink family)

- *Arenaria cumberlandensis* (Cumberland sandwort), Kentucky and Tennesssee, E (1988).
- *Geocarpon minimum,* Arizona and Missouri, T (1987).
- *Paronychia chartacea* or *Nyachia pulvinata* (papery whitlow-wort), Florida T. (1987).
- Schiedea adamantis (Diamond Head schiedea), Hawaii, E (1984).

## Chenopodiaceae (Goosefoot family) *Nitrophila mohavensis* (Amargosa niterwort), California, E (1985).

## Cistaceae (Rockrose family) *Hudsonia montana* (mountain golden heather), North Carolina, T (1980).

## Convolvulaceae (Morning-glory family) *Bonamia grandifloria* (Florida bonamia), Florida, T (1987).

**Crassulaceae (Stonecrop family)** *Dudleya traskiae* (Santa Barbara Island liveforever), California, E (1978).

**Cucurbitaceae (Gourd family)** *Tumamoca macdougalii* (Tumamoc globe-berry), Arizona and Sonora, Mexico E (1986).

**Cupressaceae (Cypress family)**
- *Cupressus abramsiana* (Sata Cruz cypress), California, E (1987).
- *Fitzroya cupressoides* (Chilean false larch [or alerce]), Argentina and Chile, T (1979).

**Cyatheaceae (Tree-fern family)** *Cyathea dryoperoides* (elfin tree fern), Puerto Rico, E (1987).

**Cyperaceae (Sedge family)** *Carex specuicola* (Navajo sedge), Arizona, T (1985).

**Ericaceae (Heath family)**
- *Arctostaphylos pungens* var. *ravenii* or *A. hookeri* all speciesr. (Presidio [or Raven's] manzanita), California, E (1979).
- *Rhododendron chapmanii* (Chapman rhododendron), Florida, E (1979).

**Euphorbiaceae (Spurge family)**
- *Chamaesyce deltoidea* all species *deltoidea* or *Euphorbia d.* all species *d.* (spurge), Florida, E (1985).
- *Chamaesyce garberi* or *Euphorbia g..*, Florida, T (1985).
- *Chamaesyce skottsbergii* var. *kalaeloana* or *Euphorbia s.* var. *k.* (Ewa Plains akoko), Hawaii, E (1982).
- *Jatropha costaricensis* (Costa Rican jotropha), Costa Rica, E (1984).

**Fabaceae (Pea family)**
- *Amorpha crenulata* (crenulate lead-plant), Florida, E (1985).
- *Apioa priceana* (Price's potato-bean), Alabama, Illinois, Kentucky, Mississippi, and Tennessee, T (1990).
- *Astragalus humillimus* (Mancos milk-vetch), Colorado and New Mexico, E (1985).
- *Astragalus montii* or *A. limnocharis* var. *m.* (heliotrope milk-vetch), Utah, T (1987).
- *Astragalus osterhouti* (Osterhout milk-vetch), Colorado, E (1989).
- *Astragalus phoenix* (Ash Meadows milk-vetch), Nevada, T (1985).
- *Astragalus robbinsii* var. *jesupi* (Jesup's milk-vetch), New Hampshire and Vermont, E (1987).
- *Baptisia arachnifera* (hairy rattleweed), Georgia, E (1978).
- *Caesalpinia kavaeiense* or *Mezoneuron k.* (Uhiuhi), Hawaii, E (1986).
- *Cassia mirabilis*, Puerto Rico, E (1990).
- *Galactia smallii* (Small's milkpea), Florida, E (1985).
- *Hoffmannseggia tenella* (slender rush-pea), Texas, E (1985).
- *Lespedeza leptostachya* (prairie bush-clover), Iowa, Illinois, Minnesota, and Wisconsin, T (1987).
- *Lotus dendroideus* all species *traskiad* or *L. scoparius* all

species *t.* (San Clemente Island broom), California, E (1977).
- *Lupinus aridorum* (scrub lupine), Florida, E (1987).
- *Oxytropis campestris* var. *chartacea* (Fassett's locoweed), Wisconsin, T (1988).
- *Serianthes nelsonii* (Hayun lagu [on Guam] or Tronkon guafi [on Rota]), Guam and Rota (western Pacific Ocean).
- *Stahlia monosperma* (Cobana negra), Puerto Rico and Dominican Republic, T (1990).
- *Trifolium stoloniferum* (running buffalo clover), Arizona, Illinois, Indiana, Kansas, Kentucky, Missouri, Ohio, and West Virginia, E (1987).
- *Vicia menziesii* (Hawaiian vetch), Hawaii, E (1978).

**Fagaceae (Oak family)** *Quercus hinckleyi* (Hinckley's oak), Texas, T (1988).

**Flacourtiaceae (Flaucourtia family)** *Banara vanderbiltii* (Palo de Ramon), Puerto Rico, E (1987).

**Frankeniaceae (Frankenia family)** *Frankenia johnstonii* (Johnston's frankenia), Texas and Neuvo Leon, Mexico, E (1984).

**Gentianaceae (Gentian family)** *Centaurium namophilum* (spring-loving centaury), California and Nevada, T (1985).

**Goodeniaceae (Goodenia family)** *Scaevola coriacea* (dwarf naupaka), Hawaii, E (1986).

**Hydrophyllaceae (Waterleaf family)**
- *Phacelia argillacea* (clay phacelia), Utah, E (1978).
- *Phacelia formosula* (North Park phacelia), Colorado, E (1982).

**Hypericaceae (St. Johns-Wort family)** *Hypericum cumulicola* (Highlands scrub hypericum), Florida, E (1987).

**Icacinacea (Icacina family)** *Ottoschulzia rhodoxylon* (Palo de rosa), Puerto Rico and Dominican Republic, E (1990).

**Iridiaceae (Iris family)** *Iris lacustris* (dwarf lake iris), Michigan, Wisconsin, and Ontario, Canada, T (1988).

**Isoetaceae (Quillwort family)**
- *Isoetes melanospora* (black-spored quilllwort), Georgia and South Carolina, E (1988).
- *Isoetes tegetiformans* (mat-forming quillwort), Georgia, E (1988).

**Lamiaceae (Mint family)**
- *Acenthomintha obovata* all species *duttonii* (San Mateo thornmint), California, E (1985).
- *Dicerandra christmanii* (Garrett's mint), Florida, E (1985).
- *Dicerandra comutissima* (longspurred mint), Florida, E (1985).
- *Dicerandra frutescens* (scrub mint), Florida, E (1985).
- *Dicerandra immaculata* (Lakela's mint), Florida, E (1985).
- *Haplostachys haplostachya* var. *angustifolia*, Hawaii, E (1979).

- *Hedeoma apiculatum* (McKittrick pennyroyal), Texas and New Mexico, T (1982).
- *Hedeoma todsenii* (Todsen's pennyroyal), New Mexico, E (1981).
- *Pogogyne abramsii* (San Diego mesa mint), California, E (1978).
- *Scuttellaria montana* (large-flowered skullcap), Georgia and Tennessee, E (1986).
- *Stenogyne angustifolia*, var. *angustifolia*, Hawaii, E (1979).

**Lauraceae (Laurel family)** *Lindera melissifolia* (pondberry), Alabama, Arkansas, Florida, Georgia, Louisiana, Missouri, Mississippi, and North and South Carolina, E (1986).

**Liliaceae (Lily family)**
- *Erythronium propullans* (Minnesota trout lily), Minnesota, E (1986).
- *Harperocallis flava* (Harper's beauty), Florida, E (1979).
- *Helonias bullata* (swamp pink), Delaware, Georgia, Maryland, New Jersey, New York, North and South Carolina, and Virginia, T (1988).
- *Trillium persistens* (persistent trillium), Georgia and South Carolina, E (1978).
- *Trillium reliquum* (relict trillium), Alabama, Georgia, and South Carolina, E (1988).

**Loasaceae (Loasa family)** *Mentzelia leucophylls* (Ash Meadows blazing-star), Nevada, T (1985).

**Malvaceae (Mallow family)**
- *Abutilon menziesii* (ko'oloa'ula), Hawaii, E (1986).
- *Callirhoe scabriuscula* (Texas poppy-mallow), Texas, E (1981).
- *Hibiscadelphus distans* (Kauai hau kuahiwi), Hawaii, E (1986).
- *Iliamna corei* (Peter's Mountain mallow), Virginia, E (1986).
- *Kokia cookei* (Cooke's kokio), Hawaii, E (1979).
- *Kokia drynarioides* (koki'o, hau-hele'ula, or Hawaii tree cotton), Hawaii, E (1984).
- *Malacothamnus clementinus* (San Clemente Island bush-mallow), California, E (1977).
- *Sidalcea pedata* (Pedate checker-mallow), California, E (1984).

**Meliaceae (Mahogany family)** *Trichliia triacantha* (bariaco), Puerto Rico, E (1988).

**Nyctaginaceae (Four-o'clock family)**
- *Abronia macrocarpa* (large-fruited sand-verbena), Texas, E (1988).
- *Mirabilis macfarlanei* (MacFarlane's four-o'clock), Idaho and Oregon, E (1979).

**Oleaceae (Olive family)** *Chionanthus pygmaeus* (pygmy fringe-tree), Florida, E (1987).

**Onagraceae (Evening-primrose family)**
- *Camissonia benitensis* (San Benito evening-primrose), California, T (1985).

- *Oenothera avita* all species *eurekensis* (Eureka Valley evening-primrose), California, E (1978).
- *Oenothera deltoides* all species *howellii* (Antioch Dunes evening-primrose), California, E (1978).

**Orchiaceae (Orchid family)**
- *Isotria medeoloides* (small whorled pogonia), Connecticut, District of Columbia, Delaware, Georgia, Illinois, Massachusetts, Maryland, Maine, Michigan, Montana, New Hampshire, New Jersey, New York, North Carolina, Pennsylvania, South Carolina, Tennessee, Virginia, Vermont, and Ontario, Canada, E (1982).
- *Platanthera leucophaea* (Eastern prairie fringed orchid), Arkansas, Iowa, Illinois, Indiana, Maine, Michigan, Montana, Nebraska, New Jersey, New York, Ohio, Oklahoma, Pennsylvania, Virginia, Wisconsin, and Ontario and New Brunswick, Canada, T (1989).
- *Platanthera praeclara* (Western praiarie fringed orchid), Iowa, Minnesota, Missouri, Nebraska, North Dakota, Oklahoma, Kansas, South Dakota, and Manitoba, Canada, T (1989).
- *Spiranthes parksii* (Navasota ladies'-tresses), Texas, E (1982).

**Papaveraceae (Poppy family)**
- *Arctomecom humilis* (dwarf bear-poppy), Utah, E (1979).
- *Argemone pleicantha* all species *pinnatisecta* (Sacramento prickly-poppy), New Mexico, E (1989).

**Pinaeae (Pine family)** *Abeis guatemalensis* (Guatemalan fir or pinabete), Guatemala, Hondura, Mexico, and El Salvador, T (1979).

**Piperaceae (Pepper family)** *Peperomia wheeleri* (Wheeler's peperomia), Puerto Rico, E (1987).

**Poaceae (Grass family)**
- *Panicum fauriei* var. *carteri* (Carter's panicgrass), Hawaii, E (1983).
- *Swallenia alexandrae* (Eureka Dune grass), California, E (1978).
- *Tuctoria mucronata* or *Orcuttia m.* (Solano grass), California, E (1978).
- *Zizania texana* (Texas wild-rice), Texas, E (1978).

**Polemoniaceae (Phlox family)** *Eriastrum densifolium* all species *sanctorum* (Santa Ana River wooly-star), California, E (1987).

**Polygalaceae (Milkwort family)** *Polygala smallii* (tiny polygala), Florida, E (1985).

**Polygonaceae (Buckwheat family)**
- *Dodecahema leptoceras* or *Centrostegia l.* (slender-horned spineflower), California, E (1987).
- *Eriogonum gypsophilum* (gypsum wild-buckwheat), New Mexico, T (1981).
- *Eriogonum ovalifolium* var. *williamsiae* (steamboat buckwheat), Nevada, E (1986).

- *Eriogonum pelinophilum* (clay-loving wild-buckwheat), Colorado, E (1984).
- *Polygonella basiramia* or *P. ciliata* var. *b.* (wireweed), Florida, E (1987).

### Primulaceae (Primrose family)
- *Lysimachia asperulaefolia* (rough-leaved loosestrife), North and South Carolina, E (1987).
- *Primula maguirei* (Maguie primrose), Utah, T (1985).

### Ranunculaceae (Buttercup family)
- *Aconitum noveboracense* (northern wild monkshood), Iowa, New York, Ohio, and Wisconsin, T (1978).
- *Clematis socialis* (Alabama leather flower), Alabama, E (1986).
- *Delphinium kinkiense* (San Clemente Island larkspur), California, E (1977).
- *Ranunculus acriformis* var. *aestivalis* or *R. acris* var. *aestivalis* (autumn buttercup), Utah, E (1989).
- *Thalictrum cooleyi* (Cooley's meadowrue), Florida and North Carolina, E (1989).

### Rhamnaceae (Buckthorn family)
- *Gouania hillebrandii*, Hawaii, E (1984).
- *Ziziphus celata* (Florida ziziphus), Florida, E (1989).

### Rosaceae (Rose family)
- *Geum radiatum* (spreading avens), North Carolina and Tennessee, E (1990).
- *Ivesia kingii* var. *eremica* (Ash Meadows ivesia), Nevada, T (1985).
- *Poentilla robbinsiana* (Robbins' cinquefoil), New Hampshire and Vermont, E (1980).
- *Prunus geniculata* (scrub plum), Florida, E (1987).
- *Purchis subintegra* or *Cowania s.* (Arizona cliffrose), Arizona, E (1984).

### Rubiaceae (Coffee family)
- *Gardenia brighamii* (na'u or Hawaiian gardenia), Hawaii, E (1985).
- *Hedyotis purpurea* var. *montana* (Roan Mountain bluet), North Carolina and Tennessee, E (1990).

### Rutaceae (Citrus family) *Zanthosylum thomasianum* (St. Thomas prickly-ash), Puerto Rico and Virgin Islands, E (1985).

### Santalaceae (Sandalwood family) *Santalum freycinetianum* var. *lanaiense* (Lanai sandalwood or iliahi), Hawaii E (1986).

### Sarraceniaceae (Pitcher-plant family)
- *Sarracenia oreophila* (green pitcher-plant), Alabama, Georgia, and Tennessee, E (1979).
- *Sarracenia rubra* all species *alabamansis* or *S. alabemensis* all species *a.* (Alabama canebrake pitcher-plant), Alabama, E (1989).
- *Sarracenia rubra* all species *jonesii* or *S. jonesii* (mountain sweet pitcher-plant), North and South Carolina, E (1988).

### Saxifragaceae (Saxifrage family) *Ribes echinellum* (Micosukee gooseberry), Florida and South Carolina, T (1985).

### Scrophulariaceae (Snapdragon family)
- *Agalinis acuta* (sandplain gerardia), Connecticut, Massachusetts, Maryland, New York, and Rhode Island, E (1988).
- *Amphianthus pusillus* (little amphianthus), Alabama, Georgia, and South Carolina, T (1988).
- *Castilleja grisea* (San Clemente Island Indian paintbrush), California, E (1977).
- *Cordylanthus maritimus* all species *maritimus* (salt marsh bird's beak), California and Baja California, Mexico, E (1978).
- *Cordylanthus palmatus* (palmate-bracted bird's beak), California, E (1986).
- *Pedicularis furbishiae* (Furbish lousewort), Maine, and New Brunswick, Canada, E (1978).
- *Penstemon haydenii* (blowout penstemon), Nebraska, E (1987).
- *Penstemon penlandii* (Penland beardtongue), Colorado, E (1989).

### Solanaceae (Nightshade family)
- *Goetzea elegans* (beautiful goetzea or matabuey), Puerto Rico, E (1985).
- *Solanum drymophilium* (erubia), Puerto Rico, E (1988).

### Styrcaceae (Styrax family) *Styrax texana* (Texas snowbells), Texas, E (1984).

### Taxaceae (Yew family) *Torreya taxifolia* (Florida torreya), Florida and Georgia, E (1984).

### Thymelaeaceae (Mezereum family) *Daphnopsis hellerana*, Puerto Rico, E (1988).

### Verbenaceae (Verbena family) *Cornutia obovata* (Palo de Nigue), Puerto Rico, E (1988).

---

## Plants and Animals No Longer Listed
These are plants and animals that once were listed by the U.S. Fish and Wildlife Service as endangered and threatened, but have since been taken off the list, because of extinction, recovery, or discovery that the original listing was in error. The reasons are given in each entry below, with the date of the "delisting" given in parentheses.

**butterfly, Bahama swallowtail** (*Heracilides* [or *Papilio*] *andraemon bonhotei*), Florida and Bahamas, original data in error (1984).

**cactus, purple-spined hedgehog** (*Echinocereus engelmannii* var. *purpureus*), Utah, recovered (1989).

**cisco, longjaw** (*Coregonus alpenae*), Lakes Michigan, Huron, and Erie, extinct (1982).

**dove, Palau** (*Gallicolumba canifrons*), Palau Islands (western Pacific Ocean), recovered (1985).

**duck, Mexican** (*Anas "diazi"*), Arizona, New Mexico, and Texas to central Mexico, original data in error (1978).

**fantail, Palau** (Old World flycatcher or *Rhipidura lepida*), Palau Islands (western Pacific Ocean), recovered (1985).

**gambusia, Amistad** (*Gambusia amistadensis*), Texas, extinct (1987).

**milk-vetch, Rydberg** (*Astragalus perianus*), Utah, recovered (1989).

**owl, Palau** (*Pyroglaux* or [Otus] *podargina*), Palau Islands (western Pacific Ocean), recovered (1985).

**pearly mussel, Sampson's** (*Epioblasma* [or *Dysnomia*] *sampsoni*), Illinois and Indiana, extinct (1984).

**pike, blue** (*Stizostedion vietreum glacum*), Lakes Erie and Ontario, extinct (1983).

**pupfish, Tecopa** (*Cyprinodon nevadensis calidae*), California, extinct (1983).

**sparrow, Santa Barbara song** (*Melospiza melodia graminea*), California, extinct (1983).

**treefrog, Pine Barrens** (*Hyla andersonii*), Alabama, Florida, New Jersey, and North and South Carolina, original data in error (1983).

**turtle, Indian flap-shelled** (*Lissemys punctata punctata*), Bangladesh, India, and Pakistan, original data in error (1984).

---

## Wetlands of International Importance

Below is a list of all the WETLANDS covered under the CONVENTION ON WETLANDS OF INTERNATIONAL IMPORTANCE ESPECIALLY AS WATERFOWL HABITAT (the 1971 Ramsar Convention), as of September 1990. The 506 wetlands are alphabetized by name under each country; the date in parentheses is the year listed. A more detailed listing (giving longitude, latitude, and hectares covered) or a full-scale directory may be obtained from the Ramsar Convention Bureau (see WETLANDS). Such a listing is also included in *The 1990 United Nations List of National Parks and Protected Areas*. (See IUCN—THE WORLD CONSERVATION UNION.)

### Algeria
Lac Oubeïra (1983)
Lac Tonga (1983)

### Australia
Albacutya Lake (1982)
Apsley Marshes (1983)
Argyle and Kununurra lakes (1990)
Barmah Forest (1982)
Bool and Hacks lagoons (1985)
Coongie Lakes (1987)
The Coorong and lakes Alexandrina and Albert (1985)
Corner Inlet (1982)
Coubourg Peninsula (1974)
East Coast Cape Barren Island lagoons (1982)
Eighty-mile Beach (1990)
Forrestdale and Thomsons lakes (1990)
Gippsland Lakes (1982)
Gunbower Forest (1982)
Hattah-Kulkyne lakes (1982)
Jocks Lagoon (1982)
Kakadu National Park, Stage I (1980)
Kakadu National Park, Stage II (1989)
Kerang Wetlands (1982)
Kooragang Nature Reserve (1984)
Lake Crescent, NW corner (1982)
Logan Lagoon (1982)
Lower Ringarooma River (1982)
Macquarie Marshes Nature Reserve (1986)
Moulting Lagoon (1982)
Ord River Floodplain (1990)
Peel-Yalgorup System (1990)
Pittwater-Orielton Lagoon (1982)
Port Phillip Bay, W shoreline, and Bellarine Peninsula (1982)
Riverland (1987)
Roebuck Bay (1990)
Sea Elephant Conservation Area (1982)
Toolibin Lake (1990)
Towra Point Nature Reserve (1984)
Vasse-Wonnerup System (1990)
Warden Lake System (1990)
Western District Lakes (1982)
Western Port (1982)

### Austria
Donau-March-Auen (1982)
Lower Inn reservoirs (1982)
Neusiedlersee (1982)
Rheindelta, Bodensee (1982)
Untere Lobau (1982)

### Belgium
Le Blankaart (1986)
Kalmthouse Heide (1986)
La Marais d'Harchies (1986)
Les Schorren de l'Escaut à Doel et à Zandvliet (1986)
Les Vlaamse Banken dans les eaux côtières (1986)
Le Zwin (1986)

### Bolivia
Laguna Colorado (1990)

**Bulgaria**
Arkoutino (1975)
Atanassovo Lake (1984)
Durankulak Lake (1984)
Srebarna (1975)

**Burkina Faso**
Mare aux Hippopotames (1990)
Mare d'Oursi (1990)
Parc national du "W" (1990)

**Canada**
Alaksen (1982)
Beaverhill Lake (1987)
Chignecto (1985)
Delta Marsh (1982)
Dewey Soper (1982)
Grand Codroy Estuary (1987)
Hay-Zama Lakes (1982)
I'lle Verte, Baie de (1987)
Last Mountain Lake, N part (1982)
Long Point (1982)
Malpeque Bay (1988)
Mary's Point (1982)
McConnell River (1982)
Musquodoboit Harbour Outer Estuary (1987)
Oak-Hammock Marsh (1987)
Old Crow Flats (1982)
Peace-Athabasca Delta (1982)
Pelee, Point (1987)
Polar Bear Pass (1982)
Polar Bear Provincial Park (1987)
Queen Maud Gulf (1982)
Quill Lakes (1987)
Rasmussen Lowlands (1982)
Saint-François, Lac (1987)
Shepody Bay (1987)
Southern Bight—Minas Basin (1987)
Southern James Bay Sanctuaries (1987)
St. Clair (1985)
Tourmente, Cap (1981)
Whooping Crane Summer Range (1982)

**Chad**
Réserve de la Biosphère de Lac Fitri (1990)

**Chile**
Carlos Andwandter Sanctuary (1981)

**Czechoslovakia**
Čičov dead arm (1990)

Lednice fish ponds (1990)
Modrava peabogs (1990)
Novozámeck'y and Břehyně ponds (1990)
Pariz marshes (1990)
Sennéfish ponds (1990)
Sür (1990)
Třeboň fish ponds (1990)

**Denmark**
Anholt Island sea area (1977)
Ertholmene Islands E of Bornholm (1977)
Fejo and Femo Isles, water SE of (1977)
Fiilsø (1977)
Hirsholmene (1977)
Horsens Fiord and Endelave (1977)
Karrebæk, Dybsø, and Avnø fiords (1977)
Lillebælt (1977)
Lolland and Falster, waters between, including Rødsand, Guldborgsund, and Bøtø Nor (1977)
Laesø (1977)
Maribo lakes (1977)
Nakskov Fiord and Inner Fiord (1977)
Nissum Bredning with Narbøre and Agger peninsulas (1977)
Nissum Fiord (1977)
Nordre Rønner (1977)
Naerea Coast and Æbelø area (1977)
Praestø Fiord, Jungshoved Nor, Ulfshale and Nyord (1977)
Randers and Mariager fiords, part (1977)
Rinkøbing Fiord (1977)
Sejerø Bugt (1977)
Skaelskdør Nor and Glaemø, waters off (1977)
South Funen Archipelago (1977)
Stadil and Vestastadil fiords (1977)
Stavns Fiord adjacent waters (1977)
Ulvedybet and Nibe Bredning (1977)
Vadehavet (The Waddensea) (1987)
Vejlerne and Løgstør Bredning (1977)
(See also GREENLAND, below)

**Egypt**
Lake Bardawil (1988)
Lake Burullus (1988)

**Finland**
Aspkär (1974)
Björkör and Lagskär (1974)
Koitilaiskaira (1974)
Krunnit (1974)

Maartimoaapa—Lumiaapa (1974)

Patvinsuo (1974)

Ruskis (1974)

Signilskär (1974)

Söderskär and Langoren (1974)

Valassaaret and Björkögrunden (1974)

Viikki (1974)

### France

La Camargue (1986)

### Gabon

Petit Loango (1986)

Setté Cama (1986)

Wongha-Wonghé (1986)

### Germany

Ammersee (1976)

Berga-Kelbra Storage Lake (1978)

Bodensee: Wollmatingen reed-bed with NE part of Ermatingen Basin; Giehren Marsh with Bay of Hegne on the Gnadensee; and Mindelsee near Radolfzell (1976)

Chiemsee (1976)

Diepholzer Lowland Marsh and peat bogs (1976)

Donau water-meadows and peat bogs (1976)

Dümmersee (1976)

Elbe (Lower) and Barnkrug-Otterndorf (1976)

Elbe water-meadows between Schnackenburg and Lauenburg (1976)

Galenbecker See (1978)

Hamburgisches Wattenmeer, Nationalpark (1983)

Havel River (Lower) And Gülper See (1978)

Inn (Lower) between Haiming and Neuhaus (1976)

Ismaning Reservoir and fish ponds (1976)

Krakower Obersee (1978)

Lech-Donau Winkel: Feldheim Reservoir on the Lech and Bertoldsheim Reservoir on the Donau (1976)

Müritz See, E shore (1978)

Oder Valley near Schwedt (1978)

Ostfriesisches Wattenmeer and Dollart (1976)

Peitz Ponds (1978)

Rhine between Eltville and Bingen (1976)

Rieselfelder Münster (1983)

Rügen/Hiddensee and E part of Zingst Peninsula (1978)

Starnberger See (1976)

Steinhuder Meer (1976)

Unterer Niederrhein (1983)

Wattenmeer, Elbe-Weser-Dreieck (1976)

Wattenmeer, Jadebusen Western Weser Mouth (1976)

Weserstaustufe Schlüsselburg (1983)

### Ghana

Owabi (1988)

### Greece

Amvrakikos Gulf (1975)

Axios-Aliakmon-Loudias Delta (1975)

Evros Delta (1975)

Kerkini Lake (1975)

Kotichi Lagoon (1975)

Mesolonghi lagoons (1975)

Mikra Prespa and Megali Prespa lakes (1975)

Mitrikou Lake and adjoining lagoons (1975)

Nestos Delta and Gumburnou Lagoon (1975)

Visthonis Lake and Porto Lagos Lagoon (1975)

Volvis and Langada lakes (1975)

### Greenland

Aqajarua-Sullorsuag (1988)

Eqalummiut Nunaat-Nassuttuup Nunaa (1988)

Heden (1988)

Hochstetter Forland (1988)

Ikkatoq (1988)

Kilen (1988)

Kitsissunnguit (1988)

Kuannersuit Kuussuat (1988)

Naternaq (1988)

Qinguata Marraa-Kuussuaq (1988)

Ydre Kitsissut (1988)

### Guatemala

Lagune del Tigre (1990)

### Guinea Bissau

Lagoa de Cufada (1990)

### Hungary

Balaton Lake (1989)

Bodrogzug (1978)

Fertö Lake (1989)

Hortobágy (1979)

Kardoskut (1979)

Kis-balaton (1979)

Kiskunság (1979)

Mártély (1979)

Ócsa (1989)

Pusztaszer (1979)

Szaporca (1979)

Tata Old Lake (1989)
Velence-Dinnyés (1979)

**Iceland**
M'yvatn-Laxá Region, part of (1977)
Thjorsarver (1990)

**India**
Chilka Lake (1981)
Harike Lake (1980)
Keoladeo National Park (1981)
Loktak Lake (1980)
Sambhar Lake (1980)
Wular Lake (1980)

**Iran**
Alagol, Ulmagol, and Ajigol lakes (1975)
Amirkelayeh Lake (1975)
Anzali Mordab Complex (1975)
Bandar Kiashahr Lagoon and mouth of Sefid Rud (1975)
Gavkhouni Lake and marshes of the lwoer Zaindeh Rud (1975)
Gori Lake (1975)
Hamoun-e-Puzak, south end (1975)
Hamoun-e-Saberi (1975)
Khuran Straits (1975)
Kobi Lake (1975)
Miankaleh Peninsula, Gorgan Bay, and Lapoo-Zaghmarz Ab-bandans (1975)
Neiriz Lakes and Kanjan marshes (1975)
Oroomiyeh Lake (1975)
Parishan Lake and Dasht-e-Arjan (1974)
Rud-e-Gaz and Rud-e-Hara Deltas (1975)
Rud-e-Shur, Rud-e-Shirin, and Rud-e-Minab deltas (1975)
Shadegan Marshes and tidal mud-flats of Khor-al Amaya and Khor Musa (1975)
Shur Gol, Yadegarlu, and Dorgeh Sangi lakes (1975)

**Ireland**
Baldoyle Estuary (1988)
Castlemaine Harbour (1990)
Clara Bog (1988)
Coole/Garryland (1990)
Easkey Bog (1990)
Gearagh, The (1990)
Knockmoyle/Sheskin (1987)
Lough Barra Bog (1987)
Meenachullion Bog (1990)
Mongan Bog (1988)

North Bull Island (1988)
Owenboy (1987)
Owenduff Catchment (1986)
Pettigo Plateau (1986)
Pollardstown Fen (1990)
Raheenmor Bog (1988)
Raven Nature Reserve (1986)
Rogerstown Estuary (1989)
Slieve Bloom Mountains (1986)
Tralee Bay (1989)
Wexford (1984)

**Italy**
Alberete, Punte (1976)
Angitola, Bacino dell'-(1989)
Averto, Valle (1989)
Bellochio, Sacca de (1976)
Bertuzzi, Valle (1981)
Bolghieri, Palude di (1976)
Boscone, Isola (1989)
Brabbia, Palude (1984)
Burano, Lago di (1976)
Cabras, Stagno di (1979)
Cagliari, Stagno di (1976)
Campootto e Bassarone, Valle (1979)
Caprolace, Lago di (1976)
Cavanata, Valle (1978)
Cellarda, Vincheto di (1976)
Cervia, Saline de (1981)
Cesine, Le (1977)
Colfiorito, Palude di (1976)
Comprensorio de Comacchio, Valli residue del (1981)
Corru S'Ittiri Fishery—Stagno de San Giovanni e Marceddi (1979)
Fogliano, Lago di (1976)
Gela, Il Biviere di (1988)
Gorino, Valle di (1981)
Marano Lagunare—Foci dello Stella (1979)
Margherita di Savoia, Salina de (1979)
Mezzola, Lago di-Pian di Spagna (1976)
Mincio, Valli del (1984)
Mistras, Stagno di (1982)
Molentargius, Stagno di (1976)
Monaci, Lago di (1976)
Nazzano, Lago di (1976)
Orbetello, Lagune di, N part (1976)
Ortazzo and adjacent territories (1981)

Ostiglia, Paludi di (1984)
Pauli Maiori, Stagno di (1979)
Pialassa della Baiona (1981)
Sabaudia, Lago di (1976)
Sale Porcus, Stagno di (1982)
Santa, Valle (1976)
S'Ena Arrubia, Stagno (1976)
Torbiere d'Iseo (1984)
Torre Guaceto (1981)
Tovel, Lago di (1980)
Vendicar, Riserva naturale (1989)
Villetta Barrea, Lago di (1976)

**Japan**
Izu-numa and Uchi-numa (1985)
Kushiro-shitsugen (1980)
Kutcharo-ko (1989)

**Jordan**
Azraq Oasis (1977)

**Kenya**
Lake Nakuru National Park (1990)

**Mali**
Lac Horo (1987)
Séri (1987)
Walado Debo/Lac Debo (1987)

**Malta**
Ghadira (1988)

**Mauritania**
Banc de'Arquin (1982)

**Mexico**
Ría Lagartos, Yucatán (1986)

**Morroco**
d'Affennourir, Lac (1980)
Khnifiss Bay or Puerto Cansado (1980)
Sidi-Bourhaba, Merja (1980)
Zerga, Merja (1980)

**Nepal**
Koshi Toppu (1987)

**Netherlands**
Biesbosch, De, part (1980)
Boschplaat, De (1980)
Engbertskijksvenen (1989)
Griend, De (1980)
Groote Peele, de (1980)
Naardermeer, Het (1980)

Oosterschelde (1987)
Oostvaardersplassen (1989)
Wadden Sea (1984)
Weerribben, De (1980)
Zwanenwater (1988)

**Netherlands Antilles**
Gotomeer, Het (1980)
Klein Bonaire Island and adjacent sea (1980)
Lac, Het (1980)
Pekelmeer, Het (1980)
Slagbaai, De (1980)
Spaans Lagoen, Het (1980)

**New Zealand**
Farewell Spit (1976)
Kopuatai Peat Dome (1989)
Thames, Firth of (1990)
Waituna Lagoon (1976)
Whangamarino (1989)

**Niger**
Parc national de "W" (1987)

**Norway**
Åkersvika (1974)
Forlandsøyane (1985)
Ilene and Presterødkilen (1985)
Jaeren (1985)
Kurefjorden (1985)
Nordre Øyeren (1985)
Øra (1985)
Ørlandet (1985)
Stabbursneset (1985)
Tautra and Svaet (1985)
(See also SPITZBERGEN, below.)

**Pakistan**
Drigh Lake (1976)
Haleji Lake (1976)
Kandar Dam (1976)
Khabbaki Lake (1976)
Kheshki Reservoir (1976)
Kinjhar (Kalri) Lake (1976)
Malugul Dhand (1976)
Tanda Dam (1976)
Thanadarwala (1976)

**Poland**
Kara's Lake (1984)
Luknajno Lake (1977)

Siedem Wysp (1984)
S'lo'nsk (1984)
Swidwie Lake (1984)

**Portugal**
Formosa Sound (1980)
Tagus Estuary (1980)

**Senegal**
Djoudj (1977)
Gueumbeul (1986)
Ndiaël, Bassin du (1977)
Saloum, Delta du (1984)

**South Africa**
Barberspan (1975)
Blesbokspruit (1986)
Hoop Vlei, De (1975)
Langebaan (1988)
Mond, De (Heuningnes Estuary) (1986)
St. Lucia System (1986)
Turtle Beaches/Coral Reefs of Tongaland (1986)

**Spain**
Cadiz, Laguna de—Lagune de Medina and Lagune Salada del
  Puerto (1989)
Daimiel, Las Tablas de (1982)
Doñana (1982)
Fuentapiedra, Laguna de (1983)
Gata, Salinas del Cabo de (1989)
Hondo, Pantano de el (1989)
Mallorca, S'Albufera de (1989)
Mata y Torrevieja, Salinas de la (1989)
Odiel, Marismas del (1989)
Ortigueira y Ladrido, Rias de (1989)
Prat de Cabanes—Torreblanca (1989)
Santa Pola, Salinas de (1989)
Sur de Cordoba, Lagune de—Lagune de Zoñar, Laguna
  Amarga, and Laguna del Rincón (1989)
Umia-Grove (Complejo Intermareal O), La Lanzada, Punta
  Correirón, y Lagoa Bodeira (1989)
Valencia, L'Albufera de (1989)
Vega o del Pueblo, Laguna de (1989)
Villafáfila, Lagunas de (1989)

**Spitzbergen**
Dunøyane (1985)
Gasøyane (1985)
Isøyane (1985)
Kongsfjorden (1985)

**Sri Lanka**
Bundala Sanctuary (1990)

**Suriname**
Coppename Rivermouth (1985)

**Sweden**
Ånnsjön (1974)
Åsnen (1989)
Dättern Bay (1989)
Falsterbo—Bay of Foteviken (1974)
Gammelstadsviken (1974)
Getterön (1974)
Gotland, isles off Faludden, Grötlingboholme and Rone Ytter-
  holmen, Laus Holmar, and Skenholmen (1974)
Helga River: Hammarsjön and Egeside, and Araslövssjön
  (1974)
Hjälstaviken (1974)
Hornborgasjön (1974)
Hovran Area (1989)
Kilsviken Bay (1989)
Klingavälsån-Krankesjön (1974)
Kvismaren (1974)
Laidaure (1974)
Mosse and Kävsjön, Store (1974)
Öland, coastal areas of: Stora Ören—Gammalsbyören, Egby-
  Kapelludden, and Södviken (1974)
Östen Lake (1989)
Ottenby (1974)
Persöfjärden (1974)
Sjaunja Kaitum (1974)
Stifgjorden Bay (1989)
Stockholm Outer Archipelago (1989)
Svartån River: Lake Gorgen—Nötmyran and Fläcksjön—Gus-
  sjön (1989)
Tåkern (1974)
Tärnasjön (1974)
Tavvavouma (1974)
Tjålmejaure-Laisdalen (1974)
Träslövsläge—Morups Tånge (1989)
Umeälv River Delta (1989)

**Switzerland**
Fanel Bay and le Chablais (1976)
Magadino, Bolle di (1982)

**Tunisia**
Ichkeul (1980)

**Turks and Caicos**
Turks and Caicos (1990)

**Uganda**
Lake George (1988)

**Former Soviet Union**
Issyk-kul Lake (1976)
Kandalaksha Bay (1976)
Karkinitski Bay: intertidal areas of the Dounai, and Yagorlits and Tendrov Bays (1976)
Khanka Lake (1976)
Kirov Bay (1976)
Kourgaldzhin and Tengiz lakes (1976)
Krasnovodsk and North-Cheleken bays (1976)
Matsalu Bay (1976)
Sivash Bay (1976)
Turgay and Irgiz, lakes of the lower (1976)
Volga Delta (1976)

**United Kingdom**
Abberton Reservoir (1981)
Alt Estuary (1985)
Bridgend Flats (1988)
Bridgwater Bay (1976)
Bure Marshes (1976)
Cairngorm Lochs (1981)
Chesil Beach and the Fleet (1985)
Chichester and Langstone harbors (1987)
Claish Moss (1981)
Cors Fochno and Dyfi (1976)
Dee Estuary, The (1985)
Derwent Ings (1985)
Din Moss—Hoselaw Loch (1988)
Druidibeg, a'Machair, and Stilligary lochs (1976)
Duin, Loch-an (1990)
Eilean Ne Muice Duighe (Duich Moss) (1988)
Eye, Loch (1986)
Fala Flow (1990)
Feur Lochain (1990)
Glac-na-Criche (1990)
Gladhouse Reservoir (1988)
Gruinart Flats (1988)
Hickling Broad and Horsey Mere (1976)
Holburn Moss (1985)
Irthinghead Mires (1985)
Leighton Moss (1985)
Leven, Loch (1976)
Lindisfarne (1976)
Lintrathen, Loch of (1981)
Lomond, Loch (1976)

Martin Mere (1985)
Minsmere—Walberswick (1976)
Neagh and Beg loughs (1976)
Norfolk Coast, N part (1976)
Ouse Washes (1976)
Pagham Harbour (1988)
Rannoch Moore (1976)
Rockcliffe Marshes (1986)
Rostherne Mer (1981)
Severn (Upper) Estuary (1988)
Silver Flowe (1981)
Skene, Loch of (1986)
Swale, The (1985)
Wash, The (1988)
(See also TURKS AND CAICOS, above.)

**United States of America**
Ash Meadows (1986)
Cache—Lower White rivers (1989)
Chesapeake Bay (1987)
Cheyenne Bottoms (1988)
Everglades, The (1987)
Forsythe (Edwin B.) National Wildlife Refuge (1986)
Izembek (1986)
Okefenokee (1986)

**Uruguay**
Ba'nado del Este y Franja Costera (1984)

**Venezuela**
Cuare (1988)

**Vietnam**
Red River Estuary (1988)

**Yugoslavia**
Obedska Bara (1977)
Ludasko Lake (1977)

## Biosphere Reserves

Below is a list of the BIOSPHERE RESERVES listed under the MAN AND THE BIOSPHERE program as of 1990, categorized by country in order of date listed (given in parentheses). A more detailed listing (giving longitude, latitude, and hectares covered) can be found in the *1990 United Nations List of National Parks and Protected Areas* (see IUCN—THE WORLD CONSERVATION UNION).

**Algeria**
Parc National du Tassili (1986)

**Argentina**

Reserva de la Biofera San Guillermo (1980)
Reserva Natural de Vida Silvestre Laguna Blanca (1982)
Parque Costero del Sur (1984)
Reserva Ecológica de Ñacuñán (1986)
Reserva de la Bioshera de Pozuelos (1990)

**Australia**
Croajingolong (1977)
Danggali Conservation Park (1977)
Kosciusko National Park (1977)
Macquarie Island Nature Reserve (1977)
Prince Regent River Nature Reserve (1977)
Southwest National Park (1977)
Uluru (Ayers Rock—Mount Olga) National Park (1977)
Unnamed conservation park of South Australia (1977)
Yathong Nature Reserve (1977)
Fitzgerald River National Park (1978)
Hattah-Kulkyne National Park and Murray-Kulkyne Park (1981)
Wilson's Promontory National Park (1981)

**Austria**
Gossenkollesee (1977)
Gurgler Kamm (1977)
Lobau Reserve (1977)
Neusiedler See-Österreichischer Teil (1977)

**Benin**
Réserve de la biosphère la Pendjari (1986)

**Bolivia**
Parque Nacional Pilón-Lajas (1977)
Reserva Nacional de Fauna Ulla Ulla (1977)
Beni (1986)

**Bulgaria**
Parc National Steneto (1977)
Réserve Alibotouch (1977)
Réserve Bistrichko Branichté (1977)
Réserve Boatine (1977)
Réserve Djendema (1977)
Réserve Doupkata (1977)
Réserve Doupki-Djindjuritza (1977)
Réserve Kamtchia (1977)
Réserve Koupena (1977)
Réserve Mantaritza (1977)
Réserve Maritchini ezera (1977)
Réserve Ouzounboudjak (1977)
Réserve Parangalitza (1977)
Réserve Srébarna (1977)
Réserve Tchervenata aténa (1977)

Réserve Tchoupréné (1977)
Réserve Tssaritchina (1977)

**Burkina Faso**
Forêt classée de la mare aux hippopotames (1986)

**Byelorussia**
Berezinskiu Zapovednik (1978)

**Cameroon, United Republic of**
Parc national de Waza (1979)
Parc national de la Benoué (1981)
Réserve forestière et de faune du Dja (1981)

**Canada**
Mont St Hilaire (1978)
Waterton Lakes National Park (1979)
Long Point Biosphere Reserve (1986)
Riding Mountain Biosphere Reserve (1986)
Réserve de la biosphère de Charlevoix (1988)
Niagara Escarpment Biosphere Reserve (1990)

**Central African Republic**
Basse-Lobaye Forest (1977)
Bamingui-Bangoran Conservation Area (1979)

**Chile**
Parque Nacional Fray Jorge (1977)
Parque Nacional Juan Fernández (1977)
Parque Nacional Torres del Paine (1978)
Parque Nacional Laguna San Rafael (1979)
Parque Nacional Lauca (1981)
Reserva de la Biosfera Araucarias (1983)
Reserva de la Biosfera La Campana-Peñuelas (1984)

**China**
Changbai Mountain Nature Reserve (1979)
Dinghu Nature Reserve (1979)
Wolong Nature Reserve (1979)
Fanjingshan Mountain Biosphere Reserve (1986)
XXilin Gol Natural Steppe Protected Area (1987)
Fujian Wuyishan Nature Reserve (1987)
Bogdhad Mountain Biosphere Reserve (1980)

**Colombia**
Cinturón Andino Cluster Biosphere Reserve (1979)
Sierra Nevada de Santa Marta (incl. Tayrona National Park) (1979)
El Tuparro Nature Reserve (1979)

**Congo**
Parc national d'Odzala (1977)
Réserve de la biosphère de Dimonika (1988)

**Côte d'Ivoire (Ivory Coast)**
Parc national de Taï (1977)
Parc national de la Comoé (1983)

**Cuba**
Sierra del Rosario (1984)
Baconão (1987)
Cuchillas del Toa (1987)
Peninsula de Guanahacabibes (1987)

**Czechoslovakia**
Krivoklátsky Protected Landscape Area (1977)
Slovensky Kras Protected Landscape Area (1977)
Třeboň Basin Protected Landscape Area (1977)
Palava Protected Landscape Area (1986)
Sumava Biosphere Reserve (1990)
Polana Bosphere Reserve (1990)

**Denmark**
North-east Greenland National Park (1977)

**Ecuador**
Archipiélago de Colón (Galápagos) (1984)
Reserva de la Biosfera de Yasuni (1989)

**Egypt**
Omayed Experimental Research Area (1981)

**France**
Atoll de Taiaro (1977)
Réserve de la biosphère de la Vallée du Fango (1977)
Réserve nationale de Camargue BR (1977)
Réserve de la biosphère d'Iroise (1988)
Réserve de la biosphère de PN des Cévennes (1984)
Réserve de la biosphère des Vosges du Nord (1988)

**Gabon**
Réserve naturelle intégrale d'Ipassa-Makokou (1983)

**Germany**
Middle Elbe Biosphere Reserve (1979)
Vessertal Nature Reserve (1979)
Bayerischer Wald National Park (1981)

**Ghana**
Bia National Park (1983)

**Greece**
Gorge of Samaria National Park (1981)
Mount Olympus National Park (1981)

**Guinea**
Réserve de la biosphère des Monts Nimba (1980)
Réserve de la biosphère du massif du Ziama (1980)

**Hungary**
Aggtelek Biosphere Reserve (1979)
Hortobágy National Park (1979)
Kiskunság Biosphere Reserve (1979)
Lake Fertö Biosphere Reserve (1979)
Pilis Biosphere Reserve (1980)

**Indonesia**
Cibodas Biosphere Reserve (Gunung Gede-Pangrango) (1977)
Komodo (1977)
Lore Lindu (1977)
Tanjung Puting (1977)
Gunung Leuser (1981)
Siberut Nature Reserve (1981)

**Iran**
Arasbaran Protected Area (1976)
Arjan Protected Area (1976)
Geno Protected Area (1976)
Golestan National Park (1976)
Hara Protected Area (1976)
Kavir National Park (1976)
Lake Oromeeh National Park (1976)
Miankaleh Protected Area (1976)
Touran Protected Area (1976)

**Ireland**
North Bull Island (1981)
Killarney National Park (1982)

**Italy**
Collemeluccio-Montedimezzo (1977)
Forêt Domaniale du Circeo (1977)
Miramare Marine Park (1979)

**Japan**
Mount Kakusan (1980)
Mount Odaigahara and Mount Omine (1980)
Shiga Highland (1980)
Yakushima Island (1980)

**Kenya**
Mount Kenya Biosphere Reserve (1978)
Mount Kulal Biosphere Reserve (1978)
Malindi-Watamu Biosphere Reserve (1979)
Kiunga Marine National Reserve (1980)

**Korea, People's Democratic Republic of**
Mount Paikdu Biosphere Reserve (1989)

**Korea, Republic of**
Mount Sorak Biosphere Reserve (1982)

**Madagascar**

Réserve de la biosphère du Mananara Nord (1990)

**Mali**

Parc national de la Boucle du Baoulé (etc.) (1982)

**Mauritius**

Macchabee/Bel Ombre Natural Reserve (1977)

**Mexico**

Reserva de la Michilia (1977)

Reserva de Mapimi (1977)

Montes Azules (1979)

Reserva de la Biósfera de Sian Ka'an (1986)

Reserva de la Biósfera ''El Cielo'' (1986)

Reserva de la Biósfera Sierra Manantlán (1988)

**Netherlands**

Waddensea Area (1986)

**Nigeria**

Omo Strict Natural Reserve (1977)

**Norway**

North-east Svalbard Nature Reserve (1976)

**Pakistan**

Lal Suhanra National Park (1977)

**Panama**

Parque Nacional Froterizo Darién (1983)

**Peru**

Reserve del Manu (1977)

Reserva del Noroeste (1977)

Reserva du Huascaráran (1977)

**Philippines**

Puerto Galera Biosphere Reserve (1977)

Palawan Biosphere Reserve (1990)

**Poland**

Babia Gora Biosphere Reserve (1976)

Bialowieza National Park (1976)

Lukajno Lake Reserve (1976)

Slowinski National Park (1976)

**Portugal**

Paul do Boquilobo Biosphere Reserve (1981)

**Romania**

Pietrosul Mare Nature Reserve (1979)

Retezat National Park (1979)

Rosca-Letea Reserve (1979)

**Rwanda**

Parc national des Volcans (1983)

**Senegal**

Forêt classée de Samba Dia (1979)

Delta du Saloum (1980)

Parc national du Niokolo-Koba (1981)

**Spain**

Reserve de Grazalema (1977)

Reserva de Ordesa-Vinamala (1977)

Parque Natural del Montseny (1978)

Reserva de la Biosfera de Doñana (1980)

Reserva de la Biosfera de la Mancha Humeda (1980)

Las Sierras de Cazorla y Segura BR (1983)

Reserva de la Biosfera de las Mariasmas del Odiel (1983)

Reserva de la Biosfera del Canal y los Tiles (1983)

Reserva de la Biosfera del Urdaibai (1984)

Reserva de la Biosfera Sierra Nevada (1986)

**Sri Lanka**

Hurulu Forest Reserve (1977)

Sinharaja Forest Reserve (1978)

**Sudan**

Dinder National Park (1979)

Radom National Park (1979)

**Sweden**

Lake Torne Area (1986)

**Switzerland**

Parc national Suisse (1979)

**Tanzania, United Republic of**

Lake Manyara National Park (1981)

Serengeti-Ngorongoro Biosphere Reserve (1981)

**Thailand**

Sakaerat Environmental Research Station (1976)

Hauy Tak Teak Reserve (1977)

Mae Sa-Kog Ma Reserve (1977)

**Tunisia**

Parc national de Djebel Bou-Hedma (1977)

Parc national de Djebel Chambi (1977)

Parc national de l'Ichkeul (1977)

Parc national des Iles Zembra et Zembretta (1977)

**Uganda**

Queen Elizabeth (Rwenzori) National Park (1979)

**Ukrain**

Chernomorskiy Zapovednik (1984)

Askaniya-Nova Zapovednik (1985)

**Former Soviet Union**

Chatkal Mountains Biosphere Reserve (1978)

Kavkazskiy Zapovednik (1978)
Oka River Biosphere Reserve (1978)
Repetek Zapovednik (1978)
Sikhote-Alin Zapovednik (1978)
Tsentral'nochernozem Zapovednik (1978)
Astrakhanskiy Zapovednik (1984)
Kronotskiy Zapovednik (1984)
Laplandskiy Zapovednik (1984)
Sayano-Shushenskiy Zapovednik (1984)
Sokhondinskiy Zapovednik (1984)
Voronezhskiy Zapovednik (1984)
Tsentral'nolesnoy Zapovednik (1985)
Lake Baikal Region Biosphere Reserve (1986)
Tzentralnosibirskii Biosphere Reserve (1986)
West Estonian Archipelago Biosphere Reserve (1990)

## United Kingdom

Beinn Eighe National Nature Reserve (1976)
Braunton Burrows National Nature Reserve (1976)
Caerlaverock National Nature Reserve (1976)
Cairnsmore of Fleet National Nature Reserve (1976)
Dyfi National Nature Reserve (1976)
Isle of Rhum National Nature Reserve (1976)
Loch Druidibeg National Nature Reserve (1976)
Moor House-Upper Teesdale Biosphere Reserve (1976)
North Norfolk Coast Biosphere Reserve (1976)
Silver Flowe-Merrick Kells Biosphere Reserve (1976)
St. Kilda National Nature Reserve (1976)
Claish Moss National Nature Reserve (1977)
Taynish National Nature Reserve (1977)

## United States of America

Aleutian Islands National Wildlife Refuge (1976)
Big Bend National Park (1976)
Cascade Head Experimental Forest Scenic Research Area (1976)
Central Plains Experimental Range (CPER) (1976)
Channel Islands Biosphere Reserve (1976)
Coram Experimental Forest (incl. Coram NA) (1976)
Denali National Park and Biosphere Reserve (1976)
Desert Experimental Range (1976)
Everglades National Park (incl. Ft. Jefferson NM) (1976)
Fraser Experimental Forest (1976)
Glacier National Park (1976)
H.J. Andrews Experimental Forest (1976)
Hubbard Brook Experimental Forest (1976)

Jornada Experimental Range (1976)
Luquillo Experimental Forest (Caribbean NF) (1976)
Noatak National Arctic Range (1976)
Olympic National Park (1976)
Organ Pipe Cactus National Monument (1976)
Rocky Mountain National Park (1976)
San Dimas Experimental Forest (1976)
San Joaquin Experimental Range (1976)
Sequoia-Kings Canyon National Parks (1976)
Stanislaus-Tuolunme Experimental Forest (1976)
Three Sisters Wilderness (1976)
Virgin Islands National Park and Biosphere Reserve (1976)
Yellowstone National Park (1976)
Beaver Creek Experimental Watershed (1978)
Konza Prairie Research Natural Area (1979)
Niwot Ridge Biosphere Reserve (1979)
The University of Michigan Biological Station (1979)
Hawaii Islands Biosphere Reserve (1980)
Isle Royale National Park (1980)
Big Thicket National Preserve (1981)
Guanica Commonwealth Forest Reserve (1981)
California Coast Ranges Biosphere Reserve (1983)
Central Gulf Coastal Plain Biosphere Reserve (1983)
South Atlantic Coastal Plain Biosphere Reserves (1983)
Mojave and Colorado Deserts Biosphere Reserves (1984)
Carolinian-South Atlantic Biosphere Reserve (1986)
Glacier Bay-Admiralty Island Biosphere Reserve (1986)
Central California Coast Biosphere Reserve (1988)
New Jersey Pinelands Biosphere Reserve (1988)
Southern Appalachian Biosphere Reserve (1988)
Champlain-Adirondack Biosphere Reserve (1989)
Mammoth Cave Area (1990)

## Uruguay

Bañados del Este (1976)

## Yugoslavia

Réserve écologique du Bassin de la Rivière Tara (1976)
Velebit Mountain (1977)

## Zaire

Réserve Floristique de Yangambi (1976)
Réserve forestière de Luki (1979)
Vallée de la Lufira (1982)

**Source:** *1990 United Nations List of National Parks and Protected Areas.* IUCN, 1990.

## World Natural Heritage Sites

Below is a list of the WORLD NATURAL HERITAGE SITES listed under the 1972 CONVENTION CONCERNING THE PROTECTION OF THE WORLD CULTURAL AND NATURAL HERITAGE as of 1990, categorized by country in order of date listed (given in parentheses). Those with an asterisk(*) are mixed natural/cultural sites, included on the basis of "beauty resulting from the man/nature interaction, rather than natural features alone."

**Algeria**
Tassili N-Ajjer (1982)

**Argentina**
Los Glaciares National Park (1981)
Iguazú National Park (1984)

**Australia**
Great Barrier Reef (1981)
Kakadu National Park (Stage I—1981, Stage II—1987)
Willandra Lakes Region (1981)
Lord Howe Island Group (1982)
Tasmania Wilderness (1982; extended 1989)
Australian East Coast Temperate and Subtropical Rainforest Parks (1986)
Uluru (Ayers Rock) National Park (1987)
Wet Tropics of Queensland (1988)

**Brazil**
Iguaçu National Park (1986)

**Bulgaria**
Srébarna National Park (1983)
Pirin National Park (1983)

**Cameroon**
Dja Faunal Reserve (1987)

**Canada**
Nahanni National Park (1978)
Dinosaur Provincial Park (1979)
Kluane-Wrangell/St. Elias National Park (1979; with USA)
Wood Buffalo National Park (1983)
Canadian Rocky Mountain Parks (1984)
Gros Morne National Park (1987)

**Central African Republic**
Pacnational national de Manovo-Grounda-St. Floris (1988)

**China**
Mount Taishan (1987)*

**Costa Rica**
Talamanci Range–La Amistad Reserves (1983)

**Côte d'Ivoire (Ivory Coast)**
Mount Nimba Strict Nature Reserve (1982; with Guinea)
Comoé National Park (1983)
Taï National Park (1982)

**Ecuador**
Galápagos Islands (1978)
Sangay National Park (1983)

**Ethiopa**
Simien National Park (1978)

**France**
Cape Girolata, Cape Porto, and Scandola Nature Reserve in Corsica (1983)
Mont-Saint-Michel and its bay (1979)*

**Greece**
Meteora (1988)*
Mount Athos (1988)*

**Guinea**
Mount Nimba Strict Nature Reserve (1982; with Côte d'Ivoire)

**Honduras**
Rio Plátano Biosphere Reserve (1982)

**India**
Kaziranga National Park (1985)
Keoladeo National Park (1985)
Manas National Park (1985)
Sundarbans National Park (1987)
Nanda Devi National Park (1988)

**Malawi**
Lake Malawi National Park (1984)

**Mali**
Bandiagara (1989)*

**Mauritania**
Banc d'Arguin National Park (1989)

**Mexico**
Sian Ka'an Biosphere Reserve (1987)

**Nepal**
Sagarmatha National Park (1979)
Royal Chitwan National Park (1984)

**New Zealand**
Fiordland National Park (1986)
Westland/Mount Cook National Parks (1986)

**Panama**

Darién National Park (1981)

**Peru**

Sanctuário histórico de Machu Picchu (1983)

Huascarán National Park (1985)

Manu National Park (1987)

**Poland**

Bialowieza National Park (1979)

**Senegal**

Djoudj National Bird Sanctuary (1981)

Niokolo-Koba National Park (1981)

**Seychelles**

Aldabra Atoll (1982)

Vallée de Mai Nature Reserve (1983)

**Spain**

Garajonay National Park (1986)

**Sri Lanka**

Sinharaja Forest Reserve (1988)

**Tanzania**

Ngorongoro Conservation Area (1979)

Serengeti National Park (1981)

Selous Game Reserve (1982)

Mt. Kilimanjaro National Park (1987)

**Tunisia**

Ichkeul National Park (1980)

**Turkey**

Göreme National Park (1985)

Hierapolis-Pamukkale (1988)[*]

**United Kingdom**

Giant's Causeway (1986)

St. Kilda (1986)

Henderson Island (1988)

**United States of America**

Yellowstone National Park (1978)

Everglades National Park (1979)

Grand Canyon National Park (1979)

Kluane-Wrangell/St. Elias National Park (1979; with Canada)

Redwood National Park (1980)

Mammoth Cave National Park (1981)

Olympic National Park (1981)

Great Smoky Mountains National Park (1983)

Yosemite National Park (1984)

Hawaii Volcanoes National Park (1987)

**Yugoslavia**

Kotor (1979)[*]

Ohrid (1979)[*]

Plitvice Lakes National Park (1979)

Durmitor National Park (1980)

Skocjan Caves (1986)

**Zaire**

Virunga National Park (1979)

Garamga National Park (1980)

Kahuzi-Biega National Park (1980)

Salonga National Park (1984)

**Zambia**

Victoria Falls (Mosi-oa-Tunya) (1989; with Zimbabwe)

**Zimbabwe**

Mana Pools National Park, Sapi and Chewore Safari areas (1984)

Victoria Falls (mosi-oa-Tunya) (1989; with Zambia)

## Toxic Chemicals and Hazardous Substances

The table below shows the toxic chemicals and hazardous substances covered under three key United States laws. More specifically, it includes:

- the hazardous substances listed under §104(i) of the COMPREHENSIVE ENVIRONMENTAL RESPONSE, COMPENSATION, AND LIABILITY ACT (CERCLA, or SUPERFUND), as amended by SARA §110;
- the toxic chemicals listed under §313 of the SUPERFUND Amendments and Reauthorization Act (SARA or Title III), included in the EMERGENCY PLANNING AND COMMUNITY RIGHT-TO-KNOW ACT (EPCRA);
- the hazardous air pollutants listed under §7412(b) of the CLEAN AIR ACT of 1990.

The three lists have been combined, with hazardous substances in the column headed "HS," toxic chemicals in the column headed "TC," and hazardous air pollutants under "HAP."

Where a popular name is widely used—as in 2,4-D—the chemical is listed under that name, rather than the full chemical name. (This has been done partly to make it easier to use this table in connection with KNOWN HEALTH EFFECTS OF TOXIC CHEMICALS on page 416.) Alternate names are listed following "aka" (also known as). The CAS (Chemical Abstract Services) Number is given in the righthand column, where one has been assigned.

Entries are alphabetized under the name of the chemical; where the name begins with a number, or with formula prefixes such as "alpha," "cis," "trans," or "N," it is alphabetized under the first main word in the formula name. The original sources (see end of table) also provide information on other rules relating to these and other chemicals.

| Chemical Name | HS | TC | HAP | CAS# |
|---|---|---|---|---|
| Acenaphthene | x | | | 83329 |
| Acenaphthylene | x | | | 208968 |
| Acetaldehyde | | x | x | 75070 |
| Acetamide; aka: Ethanamide | | x | x | 60355 |
| Acetone | x | x | | 67641 |
| Acetonitrile | | x | x | 75058 |
| Acetophenone | | | x | 98862 |
| 2-Acetylaminofluorene | | x | x | 53963 |
| Acrolein | x | x | x | 107028 |
| Acrylamide; aka: 2-Propenamide | | x | x | 79061 |
| Acrylic acid | | x | x | 79107 |
| Acrylonitrile | x | x | x | 107131 |
| Aldrin | x | x | | 309002 |
| Allyl chloride | | x | x | 107051 |
| Aluminum (fume or dust) | | x | | 7429905 |
| Aluminum oxide | | x | | 1344281 |
| 1-Amino-2-methylanthraquinone | | x | | 82280 |
| 2-Aminoanthraquinone | | x | | 117793 |
| 4-Aminoazobenzene | | x | | 60093 |
| 4-Aminobiphenyl | | x | x | 92671 |
| Ammonia | x | x | | 7664417 |
| Ammonium nitrate (solution) | | x | | 6484522 |
| Ammonium sulfate (solution) | | x | | 7783202 |
| Aniline; aka: Benzenamine | x | x | x | 62533 |
| 0-Anisidine | | x | x | 90040 |
| p-Anisidine | | x | | 104949 |
| o-Anisidine hydrochloride | | x | | 134292 |
| Anthracene | x | x | | 120127 |
| Antimony | x | x | | 7440360 |
| Antimony compounds | | x | x | – |
| Antimony tris (iso-octyl mercaptoacetate); aka: ATOM | | x | | 27288444 |
| Aramite | x | | | 140578 |
| Arsenic | x | x | | 7440382 |
| Arsenic compounds | | x | x | – |
| Asbestos | x | | x | 1332214 |
| Asbestos (asbestiform varieties of chrysotile (serpentine); crocidolite (rieeckite); amosite (cummingtonitegrunerite); anthophyllite; tremolite; and actinolite) | | x | | – |
| Atrazine | x | | | 1912249 |
| Auramine | | x | | 492808 |
| Barium | x | x | | 7440393 |
| Barium compounds | x | x | | – |
| Benzal chloride; aka: Benzene, dichloromethyl- | | x | | 98873 |
| Benzamide | | x | | 55210 |
| Benzenamine, 2-nitro-; aka: 2-Nitroaniline, or o-Nitroaniline | x | | | 88744 |
| Benzenamine, 3-nitro-; aka: m-Nitroaniline | x | | | 99092 |
| Benzenamine, 4-chloro-; aka: 4-Chloroaniline | x | | | 106478 |
| Benzene (HAP includes benzene from gasoline) | x | x | x | 71432 |
| Benzene, bromo- | | x | | 108861 |
| Benzene, chloromethyl- | | x | | 100447 |
| Benzene, 1,2-dinitro-; aka: o-Dinitrobenzene | | x | | 528290 |
| Benzene, 1,3-dinitro-; aka: m-Dinitrobenzene | | x | | 99650 |
| Benzene, 1,4-dinitro; aka: p-Dinitrobenzene | | x | | 100254 |
| Benzene, methyldinitro-; aka: Dinitrotoluene (mixed isomers) | | x | | 25321146 |
| Benzene, pentachloro- | x | | | 608935 |
| Benzene, 1,2,3-trichloro-; aka: 1,2,3-Trichlorobenzene | x | x | | 108907 |
| 1,2-Benzenedicarboxylic acid, dicyclohexyl ester | x | | | 84617 |
| 1,4-Benzenediol; aka: Hydroquinone | | x | | 122319 |
| Benzidine; aka: [1,1'Biphenyl]-4-4'-diamine | x | x | x | 92875 |
| 1,3-Benzodioxole, 5-(1-propenyl)-; aka: Isosafrole | | x | | 120581 |
| Benzo[a]anthracene | x | | | 56553 |
| Benzo[b]fluoranthene | x | | | 205992 |
| Benzo[k]fluoranthene | x | | | 207089 |
| Benzo[g,h,i]perylene | x | | | 193395 |
| Benzo[a]pyrene | x | | | 50328 |
| Benzoic acid | x | | | 65850 |

| Chemical Name | HS | TC | HAP | CAS# |
|---|---|---|---|---|
| p-Benzoquinone; aka: or | | | | |
| 2,5-Cyclohexadiene-1,4- | | | | |
| dione, or Quinone | | x | x | 106514 |
| Benzotrichloride; aka: Ben- | | | | |
| zene, trichloromethyl- | | x | x | 98077 |
| Benzoyl chloride | | x | | 98884 |
| Benzoyl peroxide | | x | | 94360 |
| Benzyl alcohol | x | | | 100516 |
| Benzyl chloride | | | x | 100447 |
| Beryllium | x | x | | 7440417 |
| Beryllium compounds | | x | x | – |
| Biphenyl; aka: 1,1-Biphenyl | | x | x | 92524 |
| Bis(2-ethylhexyl) adipate | | x | | 103231 |
| Boron | x | | | 7440428 |
| Boron compounds | x | | | – |
| Bromochlorodifluoromethane; | | | | |
| aka: Halon 1211 | | x | | 421012 |
| Bromoform; aka: Methane, | | | | |
| tribromo- | x | x | x | 75252 |
| 1-Bromo-4-phenoxybenzene | x | | | 101553 |
| Bromotrifluoromethane; aka: | | | | |
| Halon 1301 | | x | | 75638 |
| 1,3-Butadiene | | x | x | 106990 |
| 1,3-Butadiene, 2-chloro-; aka: | | | | |
| Chloroprene | | x | | 126998 |
| Butyl acrylate; aka: 2-Propen- | | | | |
| oic acid, butyl ester | | x | | 141322 |
| n-Butyl alcohol; aka: | | | | |
| Butanol | | x | | 71363 |
| sec-Butyl alcohol | | x | | 78922 |
| tert-Butyl alcohol | | x | | 75650 |
| Butyl benzyl phthalate; aka: | | | | |
| 1,2-Benzenedicarboxylic | | | | |
| acid, butyl phenylmethyl | | | | |
| ester; Benzyl butyl phthal- | | | | |
| ate; or BBP | x | x | | 85687 |
| 1,2 Butylene oxide; aka: 1,2- | | | | |
| Epoxybutane | | | x | 106887 |
| Butyraldehyde; aka: | | | | |
| Butanal | | x | | 123728 |
| Cadmium | x | x | | 7440439 |
| Cadium compounds | | x | x | – |
| Calcium cyanamide | | x | x | 156627 |
| Caprolactam | | | x | 105602 |
| Captan | | x | x | 133062 |

| Chemical Name | HS | TC | HAP | CAS# |
|---|---|---|---|---|
| Carbaryl; aka: Sevin | x | x | x | 63252 |
| Carbon disulfide | x | x | x | 75150 |
| Carbon tetrachloride | x | x | x | 56235 |
| Carbonyl sulfide | | x | x | 463581 |
| Catechol | | x | x | 120809 |
| Chloramben | | x | x | 133904 |
| Chlordane | | x | x | 57749 |
| Chlorine | | x | x | 7782505 |
| Chlorine dioxide | | x | | 10049044 |
| Chloroacetic acid | | x | x | 79118 |
| 2-Chloroacetophenone | | x | x | 532274 |
| Chlorobenzene | | x | | 108907 |
| Chlorobenzilate | | x | x | 510156 |
| Chlorodibenzodioxins | x | | | – |
| Chlorodibenzofurans | x | | | – |
| Chlorodifluoromethane | x | | | 75456 |
| Chloroform; aka: Methane, | | | | |
| trichloro | x | x | | 67663 |
| p-Chloro-m-cresol | x | | | 59507 |
| Chloromethyl methyl ether; | | | | |
| aka: Methane, | | | | |
| chloromethoxy- | | x | x | 107302 |
| Chlorophenols | | x | | – |
| 2-Chlorophenol | x | | | 95578 |
| 4-Chlorophenyl phenyl | x | | | 7005723 |
| Chloroprene | | | x | 126998 |
| Chlorothalonil | | x | | 1897456 |
| Chromium | x | x | | 7440473 |
| Chromium compounds | | x | x | – |
| Chrysene | x | | | 218019 |
| C.I. Acid Blue 9, diammon- | | | | |
| ium salt | | x | | 2650182 |
| C.I. Acid Blue 9, disodium | | | | |
| salt | | x | | 3844459 |
| C.I. Acid Green 3 | | x | | 4680788 |
| C.I. Basic Green 4 | | x | | 569642 |
| C.I. Basic Red 1 | | x | | 989388 |
| C.I. Direct Black 38; aka: | | | | |
| 2,7-Naphthalenedisulfonic | | | | |
| acid, 4-amino-3-[ [4'-[ (2,4- | | | | |
| diaminophenyl)azo] | | | | |
| [1,1'-biphenyl]-4-yl] | | | | |
| azo]-5-hydroxy-6- | | | | |
| (phenylazo)-, | | | | |
| disodium salt | | x | | 1937377 |

| Chemical Name | HS | TC | HAP | CAS# |
|---|---|---|---|---|
| C.I. Direct Blue 6; aka: 2,7-Naphthalenedisulfonic acid, 3,3'- [[1,1'-biphenyl]-4,4'-diylbis(azo) ]bis[5-amino-4-hydroxy-, tetrasodium salt | | x | | 2602462 |
| C.I. Disperse Yellow 3 | | x | | 2832408 |
| C.I. Food Red 5 | | x | | 3761533 |
| C.I. Food Red 15 | | x | | 81889 |
| C.I. Pigment Green 7 | | x | | 1328536 |
| C.I. Solvent Orange 7 | | x | | 3118976 |
| C.I. Solvent Yellow 3 | | x | | 97563 |
| C.I. Solvent Yellow 14 | | x | | 842079 |
| C.O. Vat Yellow 4 | | x | | 128665 |
| Cobalt | x | x | | 7440484 |
| Cobalt compounds | x | x | x | – |
| Coke oven emissions | | x | | – |
| Copper | x | x | | 7440508 |
| Copper compounds | | x | | – |
| Copper, [1,3,8,16,18,24-hexabromo-2,4,9,10,11,15,17,22,23,25-decachloro-29H, 31HH-phthalocyaninato(2-)-N (29), N (30), N (31), N (32)]-, (SP-4-2)-; aka: C.I. Pigment Green 36 | x | | | 14302137 |
| Copper, [29H, 31H-phthalocyaninato(2-)-N (29), N (30), N (31), N (32) ]-, (SP-4-1)-; aka: C.I. Pigment Blue 15 | | x | | 147148 |
| Creosote | x | x | | 8001589 |
| p-Cresidine | | x | | 120718 |
| Cresoles Creslylic acid (isomers and mixture); aka: Phenol, methyl- | x | x | x | 1319773 |
| m-Cresol; aka: Phenol, 3-methyl- | | x | x | 108394 |
| o-Cresol; aka: Phenol, 2-methyl- | x | x | x | 95487 |
| p-Cresol; aka: Phenol, 4-menthyl- | x | x | x | 106445 |
| Cumene | | | x | 98828 |
| Cumene hydroperoxide; aka: Hydroperoxide, 1-methyl-1-phenylethyl- | | x | | 80159 |
| Cupferron | | x | | 135206 |
| Cuprate(2-), [5-[ [4'-[ [2,6-di-hydroxy-3- [ (2-hydroxy-5 sulfophenyl)azo] phenyl] azo] [1,1'-biphenyl]-4-yl ]lazo]-2-hydroxybenzoato (4-) ]-, disodium | | x | | 16071866 |
| Cyanide | x | x | | 57125 |
| Cyanide compounds | | x | x | – |
| Cyclohexane | | x | | 110827 |
| Cyclohexane, 1,2,3,4,5,6-hexachloro-, (1alpha, 2alpha, 3beta, 4alpha, 5beta, 6beta)- | x | | | 319846 |
| Cyclohexanone | x | | | 108941 |
| Cyclonite; aka: RDX | x | | | 121824 |
| DDE | | | x | 3547044 |
| 4,4'-DDE, DDT, DDD | x | | | 72559 |
| Decabromodiphenyl oxide; aka: Decabromodiphenyl ether | | x | | 1163195 |
| Diallate | x | | | 2303164 |
| 2,4-Diaminoanisole; aka: 1,3-Benzenediamine, 4-methoxy-; or m-Phenylenediamine, 4-methoxy- | | x | | 615054 |
| 2,4-Diaminoanisole sulfate; aka: 1,3-Benzenediamine, 4-methoxy-, sulfate (1:1) | | x | | 39156417 |
| 4,4'-Diaminodiphenyl ether | | x | | 101804 |
| 2,4-Diaminotoluene; aka: 2,4-Toluene diamine, or 1,3-Benzenediamine, 4-methyl-, of 1,3-Diamino-4-methylbenzene | | x | x | 95807 |
| Diazomethane | | x | x | 334883 |
| Dibenzo[a,h]anthracene | x | | | 53703 |
| Dibenzofurans | x | x | x | 132649 |
| Dibromotetrafluoroethane; aka: Halon 2402 | | x | | 124732 |
| 1,2-Dibromo-3-chloropropane | | | x | 961281 |
| Dibutyl phthalate; aka: 1,2-Benzenedicarboxylic acid, dibutyl ester; or Di-n-butyl phthalate | x | x | x | 84742 |

| Chemical Name | HS | TC | HAP | CAS# |
|---|---|---|---|---|
| Dichlorobenzene; aka: Benzene, dichloro (mixed isomers) | | x | | 25321226 |
| m-Dichlorobenzene; aka: Benzene, 1,3-dichloro- | x | x | | 541731 |
| o-Dichlorobenzene; aka: Benzene, 1,2-dichloro | x | x | | 95501 |
| p-Dichlorobenzene; aka: Benzene, 1,4-dichloro- | x | x | | 106467 |
| 1,4-Dichlorobenzene(p) | | | x | 106467 |
| 3,3'-Dichlorobenzidine | x | x | x | 91941 |
| Dichlorobromomethane; aka: Methane, bromodichloro- | x | x | | 75274 |
| Dichlorodifluoromethane; aka: CFC-12 | x | x | | 75718 |
| 1,2-Dichloroethylene | x | x | | 540590 |
| cis-1,2-Dichloroethylene | x | | | 156592 |
| Dichloroethyl ether; aka: Bis(2-chloroethyl) | x | x | x | 111444 |
| Dichloroisopropyl ether; aka: Propane, 2,2'-oxybis[1-chloro-; aka: Bis(2-chloro-1-methylethyl) ether, or Bis(2-chloroisopropyl) ether | | x | | 108601 |
| Dichloromethylether; aka: Bis(chloromethyl) ether | x | x | x | 542881 |
| 2,4-Dichlorophenol | x | x | | 120832 |
| 2,4-D; aka: 2,4-Dichlorophenoxyacetic acid (HS includes salts and esters) | x | x | x | 94757 |
| 1,3-Dichloropropene | | | x | 542756 |
| cis-1,3-Dichloropropene | x | | | 10061015 |
| trans-1,3-Dichloropropene | x | | | 10061026 |
| Dichlorotetrafluoroethane; aka: CFC114 | | x | | 76142 |
| Dichlorvos | | x | x | 62737 |
| Dicofol | | x | | 115322 |
| Dieldrin/aldrin | x | | | 60571 |
| 1:2:3:4-Diepoxybutane; aka: 2,2'-Bioxirane | | x | | 1464535 |
| Diethanolamine | | | | 111422 |
| Diethyl sulfate | | | x | 64675 |
| Di(ethylhexyl) phthlate; aka: 1,2-Bis(2-ethylhexyl) phthalate; or Benzenedicarboxylic acid, bis(2-ethylhexyl) ester, or DEHP | x | x | x | 117817 |
| Diethyl phthalate; aka: 1,2-Benzenedicarboxylic acid, diethyl ester | x | x | | 846627 |
| 3,3'-Dimethoxybenzidine | | x | x | 119904 |
| Dimethyl aminoazobenzene; aka: 4- Dimethylaminoazobenzene | | x | x | 60117 |
| N,N-Dimethylaniline; aka: N,N-Dimethyl aniline | | x | x | 121697 |
| 3,3'-Dimethylbenzidine; aka: o-Tolidine | | x | x | 119937 |
| Dimethylcarbamyl chloride | | x | x | 79447 |
| Dimethyl formamide; aka: DMF, or Formamide, N,N-dimethyl- | x | | x | 68122 |
| 1,1-Dimethylhydrazine | | x | x | 57147 |
| 2,4-Dimethylphenol | x | x | | 105679 |
| 1,2-Dimethyl phthalate; aka: Benzenedicarboxylic acid, dimethyl ester; or Dimethylphthalate | x | x | x | 131113 |
| Dimethyl sulfate | | x | | 77781 |
| 4,6-Dinitro-o-cresol; aka: 4,6-Dinitro-2-methylphenol (HAP includes salts) | x | x | x | 534521 |
| 2,4-Dinitrophenol | x | x | x | 51285 |
| 2,4-Dinitrotoluene | x | x | x | 121142 |
| 2,6-Dinitrotoluene | x | x | | 606202 |
| Di-n-octyl phthalate; aka: 1,2-Benzenedicarboxylic acid, dioctyl ester | x | x | | 117840 |
| Di-n-propylnitrosamine; aka: 1-Propanamine, N-nitroso-N-propyl; or Nitrosodipropylamine | x | x | | 621647 |
| 1,4-Dioxane; aka: 1,4-Diethyleneoxide; or Dioxane | x | x | x | 123911 |
| 1,2-Diphenylhydrazine; aka: Hydrazine, 1,2-diphenyl-; or Hydrazobenzene | x | x | x | 122667 |
| Disulfoton | x | | | 298044 |
| Endosulfan; aka: Alpha, beta, sulfate | x | | | 115297 |
| Endrin aldehyde/endrin | x | | | 7221934 |
| Epichlorohydrin; aka: Oxirane, chloromethyl-, or 1-Chloro-2,3-epoxypropane) | | x | x | 106898 |

| Chemical Name | HS | TC | HAP | CAS# |
|---|---|---|---|---|
| Ethanamine, N-ethyl-; aka: diethylamine | | x | | 109897 |
| Ethane, 1,1-dichloro-; aka: Ethylidene dichloride | x | | x | 75343 |
| Ethane, 1,1'-[methylenebis (oxy) ]bis[2-chloro-; aka: Bis(2- chloroethoxy)methane | x | | | 111911 |
| Ethanol, 2,2'-iminobis-; aka: Diethanolamine | | x | | 111422 |
| Ethene, (2-chloroethoxy); aka: 2-Chloroethyl vinyl ether | x | | | 110758 |
| Ethene, 1,2-dichloro-, (E)-; aka: 1,2-trans- Dichloroethene | x | | | 156606 |
| Ethyl acrylate; aka: 2-Propen-oic acid, ethyl ester | | x | x | 140885 |
| Ethyl benzene; aka: Benzene, ethyl- | x | x | x | 100414 |
| Ethyl carbamate; aka: Urethane | | x | | 51796 |
| Ethyl chloride; aka: Ethane, chloro | x | x | x | 75003 |
| Ethyl chloroformate | | x | | 541413 |
| Ethylene | | x | | 74851 |
| Ethylene dibromide; aka: 1,2-Dibromoethane, or EDB | x | x | x | 106934 |
| Ethylene dichloride; aka: Ethane, 1,2-dichloro- | x | x | x | 107062 |
| Ethylene glycol | x | x | x | 107211 |
| Ethylene glycol monoethyl ether; aka: 2-Ethoxyethanol | | x | | 110805 |
| Ethyleneimine; aka: Aziridine, or Ethylene imine | | x | x | 151564 |
| Ethylene oxide; aka: Oxirane | x | x | x | 75218 |
| Ethylene thiourea | | x | x | 96457 |
| Fluometuron | | x | | 2164172 |
| Fluoranthene | | x | | 206440 |
| Fluorene | x | | | 86737 |
| Fluorides/fluorine/hydrogen fluoride | x | | | 16984488 |
| Fluorotrichloromethane; aka: Trichlorofluoromethane, or CFC-11 | x | x | | 75694 |
| Formaldehyde | x | x | x | 50000 |

| Chemical Name | HS | TC | HAP | CAS# |
|---|---|---|---|---|
| Freon 113; aka: Ethane, 1,1,2-trichloro-1,2,2,- trifluoro-, or Chlorinated fluorocarbon | x | x | | 76131 |
| Glycol ethers | | x | x | − |
| Heptachlor (Heptachlor/Hep-tachlor epoxide under HS) | x | x | x | 76448 |
| Heptachlor epoxide | x | | | 1024573 |
| Heptane | x | | | 142825 |
| Hexachlorobenzene | x | x | x | 118741 |
| Hexachlorobutadiene; aka: 1,3-Butadiene, 1,1,2,3,4,4- hexachloro- | x | x | x | 87683 |
| Hexachlorocyclopentadiene; aka: 1,3-Cyclopentadiene, 1,2,3,4,5,5-hexa-chloro- | x | x | x | 77474 |
| Hexachloroethane; aka: Eth-ane, hexachloro- | x | x | x | 67721 |
| Hexachloronaphthalene; aka: Naphthalene, hexachloro- | | x | | 1335871 |
| Hexamethylene-1,6- diisocyanate | | | x | 822060 |
| Hexamethylphosphoramide | | x | x | 680319 |
| Hexane | x | | x | 110758 |
| Hydrazine | x | x | x | 302012 |
| Hydrazine sulfate | | x | | 10034932 |
| Hydrochloric acid | | x | x | 7647010 |
| Hydrogen cyanide; aka: Hydrocyanic acid | | x | | 749008 |
| Hydrogen fluoride; aka: Hydrofluoric acid | | x | x | 7664393 |
| Hydrogen sulfide | x | | x | 7783064 |
| Hydroquinone | | | x | 123319 |
| Indeno[1,2,3-cd]pyrene | x | | | 193395 |
| Isobutyraldehyde | | x | | 78842 |
| Isophorone; aka: 2-Cyclo-hexen-1-one, 3,5,5-trimethyl- | x | | x | 78591 |
| Isopropyl alcohol; aka: Iso-propanol or 2-Propanol | | x | | 67630 |
| 4,4'-Isopropylidenediphenol; aka: Phenol, 4,4'-(1-methylethylidene)bis-; aka: Bisphenol A | | x | | 80057 |

| Chemical Name | HS | TC | HAP | CAS# |
|---|---|---|---|---|
| Lead | x | x | | 7439921 |
| Lead compounds | | x | x | – |
| Lindane (HAP includes all isomers) | | x | x | 58899 |
| Malathion | x | | | 121755 |
| Maleic anhydride; aka: 2,5-Furandione | | x | x | 108316 |
| Maneb | | x | | 12427382 |
| Manganese | x | x | | 7439965 |
| Manganese compounds | | x | x | – |
| MBI; aka: 4,4'-Methyl-enebis(N,N-dimethylbenzenamine) | | x | | 101688 |
| Melamine | | x | | 108781 |
| Mercury | x | x | | 7439976 |
| Mercury compounds | | x | x | – |
| Methane, bromochloro- | x | | | 74975 |
| Methane, dibromochloro-; aka: Chlorodibromomethane | x | | | 124481 |
| 4,4'-Methylenebis(N,N-dimethylbenzenamine) | | x | | 101611 |
| Methylene bromide; aka: Methane, dibromo- | | x | | 74953 |
| Methylene chloride; aka: Methane, dichloro-, or Dichloromethane | x | x | x | 75092 |
| 4,4-Methylenedianiline; aka: Benzenamine, 4,4'-methylenebis-, or MDA | | x | x | 101779 |
| Methanol | x | x | x | 67561 |
| Methoxychlor | x | x | x | 72435 |
| 2-Methoxyethanol | | x | | 109864 |
| Methyl acrylate; aka: 2-Propenoic acid, methyl ester | | x | | 96333 |
| Methyl bromide; aka: Bromomethane, or Methane, bromo- | x | x | x | 74839 |
| Methyl n-butyl ketone; aka: 2-Hexanone | x | | | 591786 |
| Methyl chloride; aka: Methane, chloro- | x | x | x | 74873 |
| 1-Methylethylbenzene; aka: Cumene, or Benzene, (1-methylethyl)- | | x | | 98828 |
| Methyl ethyl ketone; aka: 2-Butanone or MEK | x | x | x | 78933 |
| Methyl hydrazine; aka: Methylhydrazine | | x | x | 60344 |
| Methyl iodide; aka: Iodomethane | | x | x | 74884 |
| Methyl isobutyl ketone; aka: 2-Pentanone, 4-methyl-, or Hexone | x | x | x | 108101 |
| Methyl isocyanate | | x | x | 624839 |
| 4-4'-Methylenebis(2-chlorobenzenamine); aka: 4,4'- Methylenebis (2-chloroaniline), or MBOCA | x | x | x | 101144 |
| Methylene diphenyl diisocyanate; aka: Benzene, 1,1'-methylenebis[4-isocyanato-, Methylenebis (phenylisocynate), or MDI | | x | x | 101688 |
| Methyl methacrylate; aka: 2-Propenoic acid, 2-methyl-, methyl ester | x | x | x | 80626 |
| 2-Methylnaphthalene | x | | | 91576 |
| Methyl tert-butyl ether; aka: Propane, 2-methoxy-2-methyl- | | x | x | 1634044 |
| Michler's ketone | | x | | 90948 |
| Mineral fibers (includes mineral fiber emissions from places manufacturing or processing glass, rock, slag, or other mineral-derived fibers, avg. under 1 micrometer) | | | x | – |
| Mirex | x | | | 2385855 |
| Molybdenum | x | | | 7439987 |
| Molybdenum trioxide; aka: Molybdenum oxide | | x | | 1313275 |
| (Mono)chloropentafluoroethane; aka: CFC115 | | x | | 76153 |
| Mustard gas; aka: Ethane, 1,1'-thiobis[2-chloro- | x | x | | 505602 |
| Naphthalene | x | x | x | 91203 |
| alpha-Naphthylamine; aka: 1-Naphthylamine | | x | | 134327 |

| Chemical Name | HS | TC | HAP | CAS# |
|---|---|---|---|---|
| beta-Naphthylamine | | x | | 91598 |
| Nickel | x | x | | 7440020 |
| Nickel compounds | | x | x | – |
| Nitrates/nitrites | x | | | 14797558 |
| Nitric acid | | x | | 7697372 |
| Nitrilotriacetic acid | | x | | 139139 |
| Nitrobenzene; aka: Benzene, | | | | |
|   nitro- | x | x | x | 98953 |
| 4-Nitrobiphenyl | | x | x | 92933 |
| Nitrofen | | x | | 1836755 |
| Nitrogen mustard; aka: | | | | |
|   Mechlorethamine | x | x | | 51752 |
| Nitroglycerin | | x | | 55630 |
| 5-Nitro-o-anisidine | | x | | 99592 |
| Nitrophenol | x | | | 25154556 |
| 2-Nitrophenol | x | x | | 88755 |
| 4-Nitrophenol; aka: | | | | |
|   p-Nitrophenol | x | x | x | 100027 |
| 2-Nitropropane | | x | x | 79469 |
| N-Nitrosodiethylamine | | x | | 55185 |
| N-Nitrosodimethylamine | x | x | x | 62759 |
| N-Nitrosodiphenylamine | x | x | | 86306 |
| p-Nitrosodiphenylamine | | x | | 156105 |
| N-Nitrosodi-n-butylamine; | | | | |
|   aka: 1-Butanamine, | | | | |
|   N-butyl-N-nitroso-; or | | | | |
|   Nitrosodibutylamine | | x | | 924163 |
| N-Nitroso-N-ethylurea | | x | | 759739 |
| N-Nitroso-N-methylurea | | x | | 684935 |
| N-Nitrosomethylvinylamine | | x | | 4549400 |
| N-Nitrosomorpholine | | x | x | 59892 |
| N-Nitrosonornicotine | | x | | 16543558 |
| N-Nitrosopiperidine | | x | | 100754 |
| Octane | x | | | 111659 |
| Octachloronaphthalene; aka: | | | | |
|   Naphthalene, octachloro- | | x | | 2234131 |
| Osmium tetroxide | | x | | 20816120 |
| Oxirane, ethyl- | | x | | 106887 |
| Parathion; aka: DNTP | x | x | x | 56382 |
| PCBs-Aroclor 1016 | x | | | 12674112 |
| PCBs-Aroclor 1221 | x | | | 11104282 |
| PCBs-Aroclor 1232 | x | | | 11141165 |
| PCBs-Aroclor 1242 | x | | | 53469219 |
| PCBs-Aroclor 1248 | x | | | 12672296 |
| PCBs-Aroclor 1254 | x | | | 11097691 |

| Chemical Name | HS | TC | HAP | CAS# |
|---|---|---|---|---|
| PCBs-Aroclor 1260 | x | | | 11096825 |
| Pentachloronitrobenzene; aka: | | | | |
|   Quintozene or PCNB | | x | x | 82688 |
| Pentachlorophenol; aka: PCP | x | x | x | 87865 |
| n-Pentane | x | | | 109660 |
| Peracetic acid | | x | | 79210 |
| Phenanthrene | x | | | 85018 |
| Phenol | x | x | x | 108952 |
| p-Phenylenediamine; aka: 1,4- | | | | |
|   Benzenediamine, p-Dia- | | | | |
|   minobenzene, or p-PDA | | x | x | 106503 |
| 2-Phenylphenol | | x | | 90437 |
| Phosgene | x | x | x | 75445 |
| Phosphine | | | x | 7803512 |
| Phosphoric acid | | x | x | 7664382 |
| Phosporous (yellow or white) | | x | | 7723140 |
| Phthalic anhydride | | x | x | 85449 |
| Picric acid | | x | | 88891 |
| Plutonium-239 | x | | | 15117483 |
| Polybrominated biphenyls; | | | | |
|   aka: PBBs (brominated | | | | |
|   biphenyl molecules having | | | | |
|   the molecular formula CC | | | | |
|   (12)H (x)Br (y), where × | | | | |
|   + y = 10 and y ranges | | | | |
|   from 1 to 10) | x | x | | – |
| Polychlorinated biphenyls; | | | | |
|   aka; PCBs (any chemical | | | | |
|   substance that is limited to | | | | |
|   the biphenyl molecule that | | | | |
|   has been chlorinated to var- | | | | |
|   ing degrees, or any com- | | | | |
|   bination of substances | | | | |
|   which contains such sub- | | | | |
|   stances), or Arochlors | | x | x | 1336363 |
| Polycyclic organic matter (or- | | | | |
|   ganic matter with more | | | | |
|   than one benzene ring, with | | | | |
|   a boiling point at or above | | | | |
|   100°C) | | x | | – |
| Propane, 1,2,-dibromo-3- | | | | |
|   chloro- | x | x | | 96128 |
| 1,3-Propane sultone; aka: Pro- | | | | |
|   pane sultone, or 1,2-Oxa- | | | | |
|   thiolane, 2,2-dioxide | | x | x | 1120714 |

| Chemical Name | HS | TC | HAP | CAS# |
|---|---|---|---|---|
| Propane, 1,2,3-trichloro | x | | | 96184 |
| 2-Propen-l-ol; aka: Allyl alcohol | | x | | 107186 |
| 1-Propene, 1,3-dichloro-; aka: 1,3-Dichloropropylene | | x | | 542756 |
| 1-Propene, 2,3-dichloro- | | x | | 78886 |
| beta-Propiolactone | | x | x | 57578 |
| Propionaldehyde | | x | x | 123386 |
| Propoxur; aka: Baygon | | x | x | 114261 |
| Propylene; aka: Propene | | x | | 115071 |
| Propylene dichloride; aka: Propane, 1,2-dichloro- | x | x | x | 78875 |
| Propyleneimine; aka: 1,2-Propylenimine, or 2-Methyl aziridine | | x | x | 75558 |
| Propylene oxide; aka: Oxirane, methyl- | | x | x | 75569 |
| Pyrene; aka: Benzo [def]phenanthrene | x | | | 129000 |
| Pyridine | | x | | 110861 |
| Quinoline | | x | x | 91225 |
| Radionuclides (including radon) | | | x | – |
| Radium | x | | | 7440144 |
| Radium compounds | x | | | – |
| Radon and its compounds (HAP under Radionuclides, above) | x | | x | 10043922 |
| Saccharin (manufacturing) | | x | | 81072 |
| Safrole | | x | | 94597 |
| Selenium | x | x | | 7782492 |
| Selenium compounds | | x | x | – |
| Silver | x | x | | 7440224 |
| Silver compounds | | x | | – |
| Sodium sulfate (solution) | | x | | 7757826 |
| Strontium | x | | | 7440246 |
| Styrene; aka: Benzene, ethenyl- (Styrene monomer) | x | x | x | 100425 |
| Styrene oxide; aka: Oxirane, phenyl- | | x | x | 96093 |
| Sulfur dioxide | x | | | 7446095 |
| Sulfuric acid | x | x | | 7664939 |
| Sulfuric acid, diethyl ester; aka: Diethyl sulfate | | x | | 64675 |

| Chemical Name | HS | TC | HAP | CAS# |
|---|---|---|---|---|
| Sulfuric acid, dimenthyl ester | | x | | 77781 |
| Terephthalic acid | | x | | 100210 |
| 2,3,7,8-Tetrachlorodibenzo-p-dioxin; aka: Tetrachloro-dibenzo-p-dioxin | x | | x | 1746016 |
| 1,1,2,2-Tetrachloroethane; aka: Ethane, 1,1,2,2,-tetrachloro- | x | x | x | 79345 |
| Tetrachloroethylene; aka: Per-chloroethylene, or Eth-ene, terachloro- | | x | x | 127184 |
| Tetrachlorvinphos | | x | | 961115 |
| Tetrahydrofuran | x | | | 109999 |
| Thallium | x | | | 7440280 |
| Thallium compounds | | x | | – |
| Thioacetamide | | x | | 62555 |
| 4,4'-Thiodianiline | | x | | 139651 |
| Thiourea | | x | | 62566 |
| Thorium | x | | | 7440291 |
| Thorium compounds | x | | | – |
| Thorium dioxide | | x | | 1314201 |
| Tin | x | | | 7440315 |
| Titanium dioxide | | x | | 13463677 |
| Titanium tetrachloride | | x | x | 7550450 |
| Toluene; aka: Benzene, methyl- | x | x | x | 108883 |
| Toluenediamine; aka: Benzen-ediamine, ar-methyl-; or Diaminotoluene | | x | | 25376458 |
| Toluene diisocynate (mixed isomers); aka: Benzene, 1,3-diisocyanatomethyl- | x | x | | 26471625 |
| Toluene-2,4-diisocyanate; aka: Benzene, 2,4-diisoc-yanato-1-methyl-, or 2,4-Toluene diisocyanate | | x | x | 584849 |
| Toluene-2,6-diisocyanate; aka: Benzene, 1,3-diisoc-yanato-2-methyl- | | x | | 91087 |
| o-Toluidine; aka: Benzena-mine, 2-methyl- | x | | x | 95534 |
| o-Toluidine hydrochloride | | x | | 636215 |
| Toxaphene; aka: Chlorinated camphene | x | x | x | 8001352 |
| 2,4,5-T | x | | | 93765 |

| Chemical Name | HS | TC | HAP | CAS# |
|---|---|---|---|---|
| 2,4,5-TP acid; aka: Silvex | x | | | 93721 |
| Triaziquone | | x | | 68768 |
| Trichlorfon | | x | | 52686 |
| 1,2,4-Trichlorobenzene; aka: Benzene, 1,2,4-trichloro- | x | x | x | 120821 |
| 1,1,1-Trichloroethane; aka: Methyl chloroform; or Ethane, 1,1,1-trichloro- | x | x | x | 71556 |
| 1,1,2-Trichloroethane; aka: Ethane, 1,1,2-trichloro- | x | x | x | 79005 |
| Trichloroethylene; aka: Trichloroethene | x | x | x | 79016 |
| 2,4,5,-Trichlorophenol | x | x | x | 95954 |
| 2,4,6-Trichlorophenol | x | x | x | 88062 |
| Triethylamine | | x | | 121448 |
| Trifluralin | | x | x | 1582098 |
| 1,2,4-Trimethylbenzene; aka: Benzene, 1,2,4-trimethyl- | | x | | 95636 |
| 2,2,4-Trimethylpentane; aka: Pentane, 2,2,4-trimethyl- | | x | x | 540841 |
| 1,3,5-Trinitrobenzene | x | | | 99354 |
| Trinitrophenylmethylnitramine | x | | | 479458 |
| 2,4,6-Trinitrotoluene | x | | | 118967 |
| Tris (2,3-dibromopropyl) phosphate | | x | | 136727 |
| Tritium | x | | | 10028178 |
| Uranium | x | | | 7440611 |
| Uranium compounds | x | | | – |
| Vanadium (fume or dust) | x | x | | 7440622 |
| Vinyl acetate; aka: Acetic acid, ethenyl ester | x | x | x | 108054 |
| Vinyl bromide; aka: Ethene, bromo- | | x | ⌣ | 593602 |
| Vinyl chloride (monomer) | x | x | x | 75014 |
| Vinylidene chloride; aka: 1,1-Dichloroethylene, or 1,1-Dichloroethene | x | x | x | 75354 |
| Xylenes; aka: Benzene, di-methyl- (Total xylenes—HS; isomers and mixtures-HAP) | x | x | x | 1330207 |
| m-Xylene; aka: Benzene, 1,3-dimethyl- | | x | x | 108383 |
| o-Xylene; aka: Benzene, 1,2-dimethyl- | | x | x | 95476 |

| Chemical Name | HS | TC | HAP | CAS# |
|---|---|---|---|---|
| p-Xylene; aka: Benzene, 1,4-dimethyl- | | x | x | 106423 |
| 2,6-Xylidine | | x | | 87627 |
| Zinc (fume or dust) | x | x | | 7440666 |
| Zinc borate hydrate; aka: ZB-2335 | | x | | 12513278 |
| Zinc compounds | | x | | – |
| Zineb | | x | | 12122677 |

**Sources:** *Chemicals on Reporting Rules (CORR) Database*, dated 6/30/90, compiled by the Office of Toxic Substances (OTS), Existing Chemical Assessment Division, Chemical Screening Branch. Also *Clean Air Act of 1990*; available in *U.S. Environmental Laws* (Bureau of National Affairs, 1991).

## Known Health Effects of Toxic Chemicals

Below is a table summarizing the known health effects of some key TOXIC CHEMICALS, specifically those covered listed under §313 of the SUPERFUND Amendments and Reauthorization Act (SARA or Title III). Releases of any of these chemicals must be reported to the ENVIRONMENTAL PROTECTION AGENCY for its annual TOXICS RELEASE INVENTORY, made available to the public. This overview was first appeared in INFORM, Inc.'s *A Citizen's Guide to Promoting Toxic Waste Reduction* (Lauren Kenworthy and Eric Schaeffer, 1990), and is reprinted with their permission.

| Chemical Name | CAS Number | Carcinogenicity | Heritable genetic and chromosomal mutations | Developmental toxicity (including teratogenicity) | Reproductive toxicity | Acute toxicity | Chronic (system) toxicity | Neurotoxicity | Environmental toxicity | Bioaccumulation | Persistence in the Environment |
|---|---|---|---|---|---|---|---|---|---|---|---|
| Acetaldehyde | 75-07-0 | x | | | | | x | | x | | |
| Acetamide | 60-35-5 | x | | | | | | | | | x |
| Acetone | 67-64-1 | | | | | x | | x | | | |
| Acetonitrile | 75-05-8 | | | x | x | x | x | | | | x |
| 2-Acetylamino-fluorene | 53-96-3 | x | | | | | | | | | |
| Acrolein | 107-02-8 | | | x | x | | x | | | | |
| Acrylamide | 79-06-1 | x | | x | x | x | x | x | | | |
| Acrylic acid | 79-10-7 | | | | | | x | | | | |
| Acrylonitrile | 107-13-1 | x | | x | x | x | | x | | | |
| Aldrin | 309-00-2 | x | | x | x | x | x | | x | x | |
| Allyl chloride | 107-05-1 | x | | x | | x | x | x | x | | |
| alpha-Naphthylamine | 134-32-7 | x | | | | | | | | | |

| Chemical Name | CAS Number | Carcinogenicity | Heritable genetic and chromosomal mutations | Developmental toxicity (including teratogenicity) | Reproductive toxicity | Acute toxicity | Chronic (system) toxicity | Neurotoxicity | Environmental toxicity | Bioaccumulation | Persistence in the Environment |
|---|---|---|---|---|---|---|---|---|---|---|---|
| Aluminum oxide | 1344-28-1 | | | | | | x | | | | |
| Aluminum (fume or dust) | 7429-90-5 | | | | | | | | | | |
| 1-Amino-2-methyl-anthraquinone | 82-28-0 | x | | | | | | | | | |
| 4-Aminoazobenzene | 60-09-3 | x | | | | | | | | | |
| 4-Aminobiphenyl | 92-67-1 | x | | | | | | | | | |
| Ammonia | 7664-41-7 | | | | | x | x | | x | | |
| Ammonium nitrate (solution) | 6484-52-2 | | | | | | x | | | | |
| Ammonium sulfate (solution) | 7783-20-2 | | | | | | | | x | | |
| Aniline | 62-53-3 | x | | | | x | x | | x | | |
| o-Anisidine hydrochloride | 134-29-2 | x | | | | | | | | | |
| o-Anisidine | 90-04-0 | x | | | | | x | x | | | |
| p-Anisidine | 104-94-9 | | | | | | | | | | |
| Anthracine | 120-12-7 | | | | | | x | | x | x | |
| Antimony | 7440-36-0 | | | | x | | | | | | |
| Arsenic | 7440-38-2 | x | | | | | | | | | |
| Asbestos (friable) | 1332-21-4 | x | | | | | x | | | | |
| Auramine | 492-80-8 | x | | | | | | | | | |
| Barium | 7440-39-3 | | | | | | | | | | |
| Benzal chloride | 98-87-3 | x | | | x | | | | | | |
| Benzamide | 55-21-0 | | | | | | | | | | |
| Benzene | 71-43-2 | x | | x | x | | x | | x | | |
| Benzidine | 92-87-5 | x | | | | x | x | | | | |
| p-Benzoquinone | 106-51-4 | | | | | x | | | x | | |
| Benzotrichloride | 98-07-7 | x | | | | | x | | | | |
| Benzoyl chloride | 98-88-4 | | | | | | | | x | | |
| Benzoyl peroxide | 94-36-0 | | | | | | | | | | |
| Benzyl chloride | 100-44-7 | x | | x | | x | x | x | x | | |
| Beryllium | 7440-41-7 | x | | | | | x | | | | |
| Biphenyl | 92-52-4 | | | x | | | x | | x | | |
| Bis(2-ethylhexyl) adipate | 103-23-1 | x | x | | | | | | | | |
| Bromoform | 75-25-2 | | | | | x | x | x | | | |
| 1,3-Butadiene | 106-99-0 | x | | x | x | | x | | | | |
| 1-Butanol | 71-36-3 | | | | | | x | | | | |
| Butyl acrylate | 141-32-2 | | | | | | | | x | | |
| sec-Butyl alcohol | 78-92-2 | | | | | | | | | | |
| tert-Butyl alcohol | 75-60-5 | | | | | | | | | | |
| Butyl benzyl phthalate | 85-68-7 | | | | | | x | | x | | |
| 1,2-Butylene oxide | 106-88-7 | | | | | | | | | | |
| Butyraldehyde | 123-72-8 | | | | | | | | x | | |
| Cadmium | 7440-43-9 | x | | x | x | x | x | | x | | |
| Calcium cyanamide | 156-62-7 | | | | | | x | x | | | |
| Captan | 133-06-2 | x | x | x | x | x | | x | | x | |
| Carbaryl | 63-25-2 | | | x | x | x | x | x | x | x | x |
| Carbon disulfide | 75-15-0 | | | x | x | | x | x | x | | x |
| Carbon tetrachloride | 56-23-5 | x | | x | | | x | | x | | x |
| Carbonyl sulfide | 463-58-1 | | | | | | x | | | | |
| Catechol | 120-80-9 | | | | | | x | | x | | |
| Chloramben | 133-90-4 | x | | | | | | | | | |
| Chlordane | 57-74-9 | x | | x | x | x | x | x | | x | |
| Chlorine | 7782-50-5 | | | | | | x | x | x | | |
| Chlorine dioxide | 10049-04-4 | | | | | | x | x | | | |
| Chloroacetic acid | 79-11-8 | | | | | | x | | | | |
| 2-Chloroacetophenone | 532-27-4 | | | | | | x | | | | |
| Chlorobenzene | 108-90-7 | | | | | | x | | x | | |
| Chlorobenzilate | 510-15-6 | x | | | | | | | x | | |
| Chloroform | 67-66-3 | x | | x | x | | x | | x | | x |
| Chloromethyl methyl ether | 107-30-2 | x | | | | | x | | | | |
| Chloropene | 126-99-8 | x | x | x | | | x | x | | | |
| Chlorothalonil | 1897-45-6 | x | | | | | | | x | | |
| Chromium | 7440-47-3 | x | | | | | x | | x | | |
| Cobalt | 7440-48-4 | | | | | | x | | | | |
| Copper | 7440-50-8 | | | | | x | x | | x | | |
| p-Cresidine | 120-71-8 | x | | | | | | | | | |
| m-Cresol | 108-39-4 | | | | | | x | | x | | |
| o-Cresol | 95-48-7 | | | | | | x | | x | | |
| p-Creol | 106-44-5 | | | | | | x | | x | | |
| Cresol (mixed isomers) | 1319-77-3 | | | | | | x | x | x | | |

| Chemical Name | CAS Number | Carcinogenicity | Heritable genetic and chromosomal mutations | Developmental toxicity (including teratogenicity) | Reproductive toxicity | Acute toxicity | Chronic (system) toxicity | Neurotoxicity | Environmental toxicity | Bioaccumulation | Persistence in the Environment |
|---|---|---|---|---|---|---|---|---|---|---|---|
| Cumene hydroperoxide | 80-15-9 | | | | | x | | | x | | |
| Cupferron | 135-20-6 | x | | | | | | | | | |
| Cyanide compounds | 57-12-5 | | | | | | | | x | | |
| Cyclohexane | 110-82-7 | | | | | | | | x | | |
| C.I. Acid Blue 9, di-ammonium salt | 2650-18-2 | | | | | | | | | | |
| C.I. Acid Blue 9, di-sodium salt | 3844-45-9 | x | | | | | | | | | |
| C.I. Acid Green 3 | 4680-78-8 | x | | | | | | | | | |
| C.I. Basic Green 4 | 569-64-2 | | | | | | x | | x | | |
| C.I. Basic Red 1 | 989-38-8 | x | | | | | | | | | |
| C.I. Direct Black 38 | 1937-37-7 | x | | | | | | | | | |
| C.I. Direct Blue 6 | 2602-46-2 | x | | x | | | | | | | |
| C.I. Direct Brown 95 | 16071-86-6 | x | | | | | | | | | |
| C.I. Disperse Yellow 3 | 2832-40-8 | x | | | | | | | | | |
| C.I. Food Red 15 | 81-88-9 | x | | | | | | x | | | |
| C.I. Food Red 5 | 3761-53-3 | x | | | | | | | | | |
| C.I. Solvent Orange 7 | 3118-97-6 | | | | | | | | | | |
| C.I. Solvent Yellow 14 | 842-07-9 | x | | | | | | | | | |
| C.I. Solvent Yellow 3 | 97-56-3 | x | | | | | | | | x | |
| C.I. Vat Yellow 4 | 128-66-5 | x | | | | | | | | | |
| 2,4-D | 94-75-7 | | | x | x | x | x | | x | | |
| Decabromodiphenyl-oxide | 1163-19-5 | x | | | | | | | | | |
| Diallate | 2303-16-4 | x | | x | | | | | x | | |
| 2,4-Diaminoanisole | 615-05-4 | x | | | | | | | | | |
| 2,4-Diaminoanisole sulfate | 39156-41-7 | x | | | | | | | | | |
| 4,4'-Diaminodiphenyl ether | 101-80-4 | x | | | | | | x | | | |
| 2,4-Diaminotoluene | 95-80-7 | x | x | | | | | | | | |
| Diazomethane | 334-88-3 | | | | | | | | | | |
| Dibenzofuran | 132-64-9 | | | | | | | | | | |
| 1,2-Dibromo-3-chloropropane | 96-12-8 | x | | x | x | x | x | x | | | |
| Dibutyl phthalate | 84-74-2 | x | | x | x | | x | | | x | x |
| Dichlorobenzene | 25321-22-6 | x | | | | | | x | | x | x |
| m-Dichlorobenzene | 541-73-1 | | | | | | | x | | | |
| o-Dichlorobenzene | 95-50-1 | | | | | | | | | x | x |
| p-Dichlorobenzene | 106-46-7 | x | | | | | | x | | x | x |
| 3,3'-Dichlorobenzidine | 91-94-1 | x | | | | | | | | | |
| Dichlorobromomethane | 75-27-4 | | | | | | | | | | x |
| Dichloroethyl ether | 111-44-4 | | | | | x | x | | | | |
| 1,1-Dichloroethylene | 75-35-4 | x | | x | x | | x | | x | | |
| Dichloroisoprophyl ether | 108-60-1 | x | | | | x | x | | | | |
| Dichloromethyl ether | 542-88-1 | x | | | | | x | | | | |
| 2,4-Dichlorophenol | 120-83-2 | | | | | | | x | | | |
| 1,3-Dichloropropene | 542-75-6 | x | | | | x | x | | x | | |
| Dichlorvos | 62-73-7 | | | | x | x | x | | x | | x |
| Dicofol | 115-32-2 | x | | | | | x | | x | | |
| 1:2,3:4-Diepoxybutane | 1464-53-5 | x | x | | | | x | | | | |
| Diethanolamine | 111-42-2 | x | | | | | | | x | | |
| Diethyl sulfate | 64-67-5 | x | x | | | | | | | | |
| Diethylhexyl phthalate | 117-81-7 | x | | x | x | x | | | x | x | x |
| Diethylphthalate | 84-66-2 | | | | | | | x | | | |
| 3,3'-Dimethoxybenzidine | 119-90-4 | x | | | | | | | | | |
| Dimethyl sulfate | 77-78-1 | x | x | | | | x | | x | | |
| 4-Dimethylaminoazobenzene | 60-11-7 | x | | | | | x | x | | | x |
| N,N-Dimethylaniline | 121-69-7 | | | | | | | x | x | | |
| 3,3'-Dimethylbenzidine | 119-93-7 | x | | | | | | | | | |
| Dimethylcarbomyl chloride | 79-44-7 | x | | | | | x | | | | |

| Chemical Name | CAS Number | Carcinogenicity | Heritable genetic and chromosomal mutations | Developmental toxicity (including teratogenicity) | Reproductive toxicity | Acute toxicity | Chronic (system) toxicity | Neurotoxicity | Environmental toxicity | Bioaccumulation | Persistence in the Environment |
|---|---|---|---|---|---|---|---|---|---|---|---|
| 1,1-Dimethylhydrazine | 57-14-7 | x |  | x |  |  | x |  |  |  |  |
| 2,4-Dimethylphenol | 105-67-9 |  |  |  |  |  | x |  |  |  |  |
| Dimethylphthalate | 131-11-3 |  |  | x |  |  | x |  |  |  |  |
| 2,4-Dinitrophenol | 51-28-5 |  |  | x | x | x | x |  | x |  |  |
| 2,4-Dinitrotoluene | 121-14-2 | x |  |  |  | x | x |  |  |  |  |
| 2,6-Dinitrotoluene | 606-20-2 |  |  |  |  | x | x |  |  |  |  |
| 4,6-Dinitro-o-cresol | 534-52-1 |  |  |  |  | x | x |  |  |  |  |
| Dioxane | 123-91-1 | x |  |  |  |  |  |  |  |  |  |
| 1,2-Diphenylhydrazine | 122-66-7 | x |  |  |  |  | x |  |  |  |  |
| Di-n-octylphthalate | 117-84-0 |  |  |  |  | x | x |  |  | x |  |
| Di-n-propylnitrosamine | 621-64-7 | x |  |  |  |  |  |  |  |  |  |
| Epichlorohydrin | 106-89-8 | x | x |  | x | x | x |  | x | x |  |
| Ethyl acrylate | 140-88-5 | x |  | x |  |  | x | x |  |  | x |
| Ethyl carbamate (urethane) | 51-79-6 | x | x |  |  |  |  |  |  |  |  |
| Ethyl chloride | 75-00-3 |  |  |  |  |  |  |  |  |  |  |
| Ethyl chloroformate | 541-41-3 |  |  |  |  | x |  |  |  |  |  |
| Ethylbenzene | 100-41-4 |  |  |  | x | x | x |  | x |  |  |
| Ethylene | 74-85-1 |  |  |  |  |  | x |  |  |  |  |
| Ethylene dibromide | 106-93-4 | x | x | x | x | x | x |  | x |  |  |
| Ethylene dichloride | 107-06-2 | x | x |  |  |  |  |  |  |  | x |
| Ethylene glycol | 107-21-1 |  |  |  |  |  | x |  |  |  |  |
| Ethylene glycol monoethyl ether | 110-80-5 |  |  | x |  | x | x |  |  |  |  |
| Ethylene oxide | 75-21-8 | x | x | x | x | x | x |  | x |  | x |
| Ethyleneimine | 151-56-4 | x | x |  | x | x | x |  | x |  | x |
| Ethylenethiourea | 96-45-7 | x | x | x | x |  | x |  |  |  |  |
| Fluometuron | 2164-17-2 | x |  |  |  |  | x | x |  |  |  |
| Formaldehyde | 50-00-0 | x | x |  |  | x | x | x |  |  |  |
| Freon 113 | 76-13-1 |  |  |  |  |  | x |  |  |  |  |
| Heptachlor | 76-44-8 | x |  |  | x | x |  |  | x | x |  |
| Hexachlorobenzene | 118-74-1 | x |  | x | x | x | x |  | x | x |  |
| Hexachlorocyclopentadiene | 77-47-4 |  |  | x |  |  |  |  |  |  |  |
| Hexachloroethane | 67-72-1 | x |  | x | x |  | x |  |  |  |  |
| Hexachloronaphthalene | 1335-87-1 |  |  |  |  |  |  |  |  |  |  |
| Hexamethylphosphoramide | 680-31-9 | x | x |  |  | x |  |  |  |  |  |
| Hydrazine | 302-01-2 | x |  |  |  | x |  |  | x |  |  |
| Hydrazine sulfate | 10034-93-2 | x |  |  |  |  |  |  |  |  |  |
| Hydrochloric acid | 7647-01-0 |  |  |  |  | x | x |  |  |  |  |
| Hydrogen cyanide | 74-90-8 |  |  |  |  | x | x |  | x |  |  |
| Hydrogen fluoride | 7664-39-3 | x | x | x | x | x | x |  |  |  |  |
| Hydroquinone | 123-31-9 |  |  |  |  | x | x |  | x |  |  |
| Isobutyraldehyde | 78-84-2 |  |  |  |  |  | x |  |  |  |  |
| Isopropyl alcohol | 67-63-0 | x |  |  |  |  | x | x |  |  |  |
| 4,4'-Isopropylidenediphenol | 80-05-7 |  |  |  |  |  |  |  |  |  |  |
| Lead | 7439-92-1 |  |  |  |  | x | x |  | x |  |  |
| Lindane | 58-89-9 | x |  |  | x | x | x | x |  | x | x |
| Maleic anhydride | 108-31-6 |  |  |  |  |  |  |  |  |  |  |
| Maneb | 1247-38-2 |  |  | x | x |  | x | x | x |  |  |
| Manganese | 7439-96-5 |  |  |  |  |  |  | x |  |  |  |
| MBI | 101-68-8 |  |  |  |  |  |  |  |  |  |  |
| Melamine | 108-78-1 | x |  |  |  |  | x |  |  |  |  |
| Mercury | 7439-97-6 |  |  |  |  | x |  | x | x | x |  |
| Methanol | 67-56-1 |  |  |  |  |  |  | x |  |  |  |
| Methoxychlor | 72-43-5 |  |  |  |  | x | x |  | x | x | x |
| 2-Methoxyethanol | 109-86-4 |  |  | x | x |  |  | x |  |  |  |
| Methyl acrylate | 96-33-3 |  |  |  |  |  |  | x |  |  |  |
| Methyl bromide | 74-83-9 |  |  |  |  | x | x | x | x |  | x |
| Methyl chloride | 74-87-3 |  |  |  |  | x | x |  | x |  | x |
| 1-Methyl ethyl benzene (Cumene) | 98-82-8 |  |  |  |  |  | x | x | x |  |  |
| Methyl ethyl ketone (MEK) | 78-93-3 |  | x |  | x |  | x | x |  |  |  |
| Methyl hydrazine | 60-34-4 | x |  |  |  | x | x |  | x |  |  |
| Methyl iodide | 74-88-4 | x |  |  |  |  |  | x |  |  | x |
| Methyl isobutyl ketone | 108-10-1 |  |  |  |  |  | x | x |  |  |  |
| Methyl isocyanate | 624-83-9 |  |  |  |  | x |  |  |  |  |  |
| Methyl methacrylate | 80-62-6 |  |  |  | x |  | x |  |  |  |  |

| Chemical Name | CAS Number | Carcinogenicity | Heritable genetic and chromosomal mutations | Developmental toxicity (including teratogenicity) | Reproductive toxicity | Acute toxicity | Chronic (system) toxicity | Neurotoxicity | Environmental toxicity | Bioaccumulation | Persistence in the Environment |
|---|---|---|---|---|---|---|---|---|---|---|---|
| Methyl tert-butyl ether | 1634-04-4 | | | | | | | | | | |
| Methylene bromide | 74-95-3 | | | | | | | x | | | |
| Methylene chloride | 75-09-2 | x | | | | | | | | | x |
| 4,4'-Methylenebis (2-chloroaniline) | 101-14-4 | x | | | | | | | | | |
| 4,4'-Methylenebis (N,N-dimethyl) | 101-61-1 | x | | | | | | | | | |
| 4,4'-Methylenedianiline | 101-77-9 | | | | | | x | | | | |
| Michler's ketone | 90-94-8 | x | | | | | | | | | |
| Molybdenum trioxide | 1313-27-5 | | | | | x | x | x | | | |
| Mustard gas | 505-60-2 | x | x | | | x | | | | | |
| Naphthalene | 91-20-3 | | | | | | | | | x | x |
| beta-Naphthylamine | 91-59-8 | x | | | | | | | | | |
| Nickel | 7440-02-0 | x | | x | x | | x | x | | | |
| Nitric acid | 7697-37-2 | | | | | | x | | | | |
| Nitrilotriacetic acid | 139-13-9 | x | | | | | x | | | | |
| Nitrobenzene | 98-95-3 | | | | x | x | x | | x | | |
| 4-Nitrobiphenyl | 92-93-3 | x | | | | | | | | | |
| Nitrofen | 1836-75-5 | x | | x | x | | x | x | x | | |
| Nitrogen mustard | 51-75-2 | x | x | x | x | x | | | | | |
| Nitroglycerin | 55-63-0 | | | | | | | | x | | |
| 2-Nitrophenol | 88-75-5 | | | | | | x | x | x | | |
| p-Nitrophenol | 100-02-7 | | | | | | x | x | x | x | |
| 2-Nitropropane | 79-46-9 | x | | x | x | x | x | | | | |
| N-Nitrosodiethylamine | 55-18-5 | x | | x | x | x | x | | | | |
| N-Nitrosodimethylamine | 62-75-9 | x | | x | | | x | | | | |
| N-Nitrosodiphenylamine | 86-30-6 | x | | | | | | | x | | |
| p-Nitrosodiphenylamine | 156-10-5 | x | | | | | | | | | |
| N-Nitrosodi-n-butylamine | 924-16-3 | x | | | | | | | | | |
| N-Nitrosomethylvinylamine | 4549-40-0 | x | x | | | x | | | | | |
| N-Nitrosomorpholine | 59-89-2 | x | x | x | | x | | | | | |
| N-Nitrosonornicotine | 16543-55-8 | x | | | | | | | | | |
| N-Nitrosopiperidine | 100-75-4 | x | x | | | x | x | | | | |
| N-Nitro-N-ethylurea | 759-73-9 | x | x | x | | | | | | | |
| N-Nitroso-N-methylurea | 684-93-5 | x | x | x | | | x | | | | |
| 5-Nitro-o-anisidine | 99-59-2 | x | | | | | | | | | |
| Octachloronaphthalene | 2234-13-1 | | | | | | x | | | x | |
| Osmium tetroxide | 20816-12-0 | | | | | | x | | | | |
| Parathion | 56-38-2 | | | | x | x | x | x | | x | |
| PCBs | 1336-36-3 | x | | | | | | | | | |
| Pentachloronitrobenzene (PCNB) | 82-68-8 | x | x | | | | x | | | x | x |
| Pentachlorophenol | 87-86-5 | | x | x | | | x | | | x | x |
| Peracetic acid | 79-21-0 | | | | | x | x | | | | |
| Phenol | 108-95-2 | | x | | | | x | | x | x | |
| p-Phenylenediamine | 106-50-3 | | | x | | | x | | | | |
| 2-Phenylphenol | 90-43-7 | x | | | | | | | | | |
| Phosgene | 75-44-5 | | | | | | x | | | | x |
| Phosphoric acid | 7664-38-2 | | | | | | | | | | |
| Phosphorous (yellow or white) | 7723-14-0 | | | | | x | x | x | | x | |
| Phthalic anhydride | 85-44-9 | | | | | | | | x | | |
| Picric acid | 88-89-1 | | | | | | | | x | | |
| 1, 3-Propane sultone | 1120-71-4 | x | | | | | | | | | |
| beta-Propiolactone | 57-57-8 | x | x | | x | | | | | | |
| Propionaldehyde | 123-38-6 | | | | | | | x | | x | |
| Proxpur | 114-26-1 | | | | | | | x | | | |
| Propylene | 115-07-1 | | | | | | | | | | |
| Propylene dichloride | 78-87-5 | x | | | x | | x | | | | |
| Propylene oxide | 75-56-9 | x | x | | | x | x | x | x | | x |
| Propyleneimine | 75-55-8 | x | | | | | x | | | | |
| Pyridine | 110-86-1 | | | | | | | | | x | |
| Quinoline | 91-22-5 | | | | | | | | | x | |

| Chemical Name | CAS Number | Carcinogenicity | Heritable genetic and chromosomal mutations | Developmental toxicity (including teratogenicity) | Reproductive toxicity | Acute toxicity | Chronic (system) toxicity | Neurotoxicity | Environmental toxicity | Bioaccumulation | Persistence in the Environment |
|---|---|---|---|---|---|---|---|---|---|---|---|
| Saccharine | 81-07-2 | x | x | x | x | | | | | | |
| Safrole | 94-59-7 | x | | x | | x | | | | | |
| Selenium | 7782-49-2 | | | | | x | x | | x | | |
| Sodium hydroxide (solution) | 1310-73-2 | | | | | | | | x | | |
| Sodium sulfate (solution) | 7757-82-6 | | | | | | | | x | | |
| Styrene | 100-42-5 | x | x | | | | x | | x | | |
| Styrene oxide | 96-09-3 | x | | x | x | | | | | | |
| Sulfuric acid | 7664-93-9 | | | | | x | x | | x | | |
| Terephthalic acid | 100-21-0 | | | | | | x | x | | | |
| 1,1,2,2-Tetrachloroethane | 79-34-5 | x | | x | | | x | | x | | |
| Tetrachloroethyllene | 127-18-4 | x | | x | x | | x | | x | | x |
| Tetrachlorvinphos | 961-11-5 | x | | | | | | | | | |
| Thallium | 7440-28-0 | | | | | | | | | | |
| Thioacetamide | 62-55-5 | x | x | | | | x | | | | |
| 4,4'-Thiodianiline | 139-65-1 | x | | x | | | | | | | |
| Thiourea | 62-56-6 | x | | x | x | x | | | | | |
| Thorium dioxide | 1314-20-1 | | | | | | | | | | |
| Titanium dioxide | 13464-67-7 | | | | | | | | | | |
| Titanium tetrachloride | 7550-45-0 | | | | | | x | | | | |
| Toluene | 108-88-3 | | | | | x | x | | x | | |
| Toulenediamine | 25376-45-8 | x | x | | | | x | | | | |
| Toulene-2,4-diisocyanate | 584-84-9 | | | | | x | | | | | |
| Toulene-2,6-diisocyanate | 91-08-7 | | | | | x | x | | | | |
| o-Toluidine hydrochloride | 636-21-5 | x | | | | | | | | | |
| o-Toluidine | 95-53-4 | x | | | | | x | | x | | |
| Toxaphene | 8001-35-2 | x | | x | x | x | x | x | x | | |
| Triaziquone | 68-76-8 | x | x | | x | | | | | | |
| Trichlorfon | 52-68-6 | | | x | x | x | x | | x | | x |
| 1,2,4-Trichlorobenzene | 120-82-1 | | x | | | x | | | x | x | |
| 1,1,1-Trichloroethane | 71-55-6 | | x | | | | x | | x | | x |
| 1,1,2-Trichloroethane | 79-00-5 | x | | | | | x | | x | | |
| Trichloroethylene | 79-01-6 | x | | x | x | | x | | | | |
| 2,4,5-Trichlorophenol | 95-95-4 | | | | | | x | | x | | |
| 2,4,6-Trichlorophenol | 88-06-2 | x | | | | | | x | | | |
| Trifluralin | 1582-09-8 | x | | x | x | | x | | x | x | |
| 1,2,4-Trimethylbenzene | 95-63-6 | | | | | | | | x | | |
| Tris (2,3-dibromopropyl) phosphate | 126-72-7 | x | x | x | | x | | | | | |
| Vanadium (fume or dust) | 7440-62-2 | | | | | | | | | | |
| Vinyl acetate | 108-05-4 | | | | | | x | | x | | |
| Vinyl bromide | 593-60-2 | | | | | | | | | | |
| Vinyl chloride | 75-01-4 | x | x | x | x | | x | | | | |
| m-Xylene | 108-38-3 | | | | | x | | x | x | | |
| o-Xylene | 95-47-6 | | | | | x | x | x | x | | |
| p-Xylene | 106-42-3 | | | | | x | | | x | | |
| Xylene (mixed isomers) | 1330-20-7 | | | | | | x | | | | |
| 2,6-Xylidine | 87-62-7 | | | | | | | x | | | |
| Zinc (fume or dust) | 7440-66-6 | | | | | | | | x | | |
| Zineb | 12122-67-7 | | | | | | | | | x | |

## Superfund Sites

Below is a list of the final or proposed sites on the NATIONAL PRIORITIES LIST (NPL), those 1,211 sites eligible for remedial action funded under the COMPREHENSIVE ENVIRONMENTAL RESPONSE, COMPENSATION, AND LIABILITY ACT (CERCLA) of 1980, as amended by the SUPERFUND Amendments and Reauthoriation Act (SARA) of 1986. For each site, the table shows when it was proposed or announced for the list, and when it was finally placed on the list. (Sites previously on the list but now deleted, are not included.)

NOTES (indicated by letters in the right margin of table):
A = Based on issurance of health advisory by Agency for Toxic Substances and Disease Registry (if scored, HRS [Hazard Ranking System] need not be >28.50).
C = Construction completion category [sites where "remedial activities have been completed but deletion is not yet appropriate"].
F = Federal facility, not eligible for SUPERFUND-financed response. ["EPA's policy is to place Federal facility sites on the NPL if they have an HRS score of 28.50 or greater, even if the Federal facility also is subject to the correction action authorities of RCRA Subtitle C. In that way, those sites could be cleaned up under CERCLA, if appropriate."]
R = Listed here because owners have demonstrated an inability to finance corrective action; normally subject to Subtitle C of the Resource Conservation and Recovery Act (RCRA), under which owners can be forced legally to take corrective action.
S = State top priority (if scored, HRS score need not be >28.50).

| Site name | City/County | Date Prop'd | Date Final |
|---|---|---|---|
| **Alabama** (12 Final + 0 Proposed = 12) | | | |
| Alabama Army Ammunition Plant | Childersburg | 10/84 | 7/87 F |
| Anniston Army Depot (Southeast Industrial Area) | Anniston | 10/84 | 3/89 F |
| Ciba-Geigy Corp. (McIntosh Plant) | McIntosh | 9/83 | 9/84 |
| Interstate Lead Co (ILCO) | Leeds | 9/85 | 6/86 |
| Mowbray Engineering Co. | Greenville | 12/81 | 9/83 |

| Site name | City/County | Date Prop'd | Date Final |
|---|---|---|---|
| Olin Corp. (McIntosh Plant) | McIntosh | 9/83 | 9/84 |
| Perdido Ground Water Contamination | Perdido | 12/81 | 9/83 |
| Redwing Carriers, Inc. (Saraland) | Saraland | 6/88 | 2/90 |
| Stauffer Chemical Co. (Cold Creek Plant) | Bucks | 9/83 | 9/84 |
| Stauffer Chemical Co. (LeMoyne Plant) | Axis | 9/83 | 9/84 |
| T.H. Agriculture & Nutrition Co. (Montgomery Plant) | Montgomery | 6/88 | 8/90 |
| Triana/Tennessee River (once listed as Triana (Redstone) Arsenal) | Limestone/ Morgan | 10/81 | 9/83 |
| **Alaska** (6 Final + 0 Proposed = 6) | | | |
| Alaska Battery Enterprises | Fairbanks N. Star Bor. | 6/88 | 3/89 |
| Arctic Surplus | Fairbanks | 10/89 | 8/90 |
| Eielson Air Force Base | Fairbanks N. Star Bor. | 7/89 | 11/89 F |
| Elmendorf Air Force Base | Greater Anchorage Bo. | 7/89 | 8/90 F |
| Fort Wainwright | Fairbanks N. Star Bor. | 7/89 | 8/90 F |
| Standard Steel & Metals Salvage Yard (USDOT) | Anchorage | 7/89 | 8/90 F |
| **Arizona** (10 Final and 0 Proposed = 10) | | | |
| Apache Powder Co. | St. David | 6/86 | 8/90 |
| Hassayampa Landfill | Hassayampa | 6/86 | 7/87 |
| Indian Bend Wash Area | Scottsdale/ Tmpe/Phnx | 12/82 | 9/83 |
| Litchfield Airport Area | Goodyear/ Avondale | 12/82 | 9/83 |
| Luke Air Force Base | Glendale | 7/89 | 8/90 F |

| Site name | City/County | Date Prop'd | Date Final |
|---|---|---|---|
| Motorola, Inc. (53nd St. Plant) | Phoenix | 10/84 | 10/89 |
| Nineteenth Avenue Landfill | Phoenix | 10/81 | 9/83 |
| Tucson International Airport Area | Tucson | 7/82 | 9/83 |
| Williams Air Force Base | Chandler | 7/89 | 11/89 F |
| Yuma Marine Corps Air Station | Yuma | 6/88 | 2/90 F |
| **Arkansas** (10 Final + 0 Proposed = 10) | | | |
| Arkwood, Inc. | Omaha | 9/85 | 3/89 |
| Fruit Industries | Walnut Ridge | 10/81 | 9/83 |
| Gurley Pit | Edmondson | 12/82 | 9/83 |
| Industrial Waste Control | Fort Smith | 12/82 | 9/83 |
| Jacksonville Municipal Landfill | Jacksonville | 1/87 | 7/87 |
| Midland Products | Ola/Birta | 10/84 | 6/86 |
| Mid-South Wood Products | Mena | 10/81 | 9/83 C |
| Monroe Auto Equipment Co. (Paragould Pit) | Paragould | 10/89 | 8/91 |
| Rogers Road Municipal Landfill | Jacksonville | 1/87 | 7/87 |
| Vertac, Inc. | Jacksonville | 10/81 | 9/83 |
| **California** (88 Final + 3 Proposed = 91) | | | |
| Advanced Micro Devices, Inc. (Bldg 915) | Sunnyvale | 6/88 | 8/90 |
| Advanced Micro Devices, Inc. | Sunnyvale | 10/84 | 6/86 |
| Aerojet General Corp. | Rancho Cordova | 10/81 | 9/83 |
| Applied Materials | Santa Clara | 10/84 | 7/87 |
| Atlas Asbestos Mine | Fresno County | 9/83 | 9/84 |
| Barstow Marine Corps Logistics Base | Barstow | 7/89 | 11/89 F |
| Beckman Instruments (Porterville Plant) | Porterville | 10/84 | 6/86 |
| Brown & Bryant, Inc. (Arvin Plant) | Arvin | 6/88 | 10/89 |
| Camp Pendleton Marine Corps Base | San Diego County | 7/89 | 11/89 F |
| Castle Air Force Base | Merced | 10/84 | 7/87 F |
| Celtor Chemical Works | Hoopa | 12/82 | 9/83 C |
| Coalinga Asbestos Mine | Coalinga | 9/83 | 9/84 |
| Coast Wood Preserving | Ukiah | 12/82 | 9/83 |
| Crazy Horse Sanitary Landfill | Salinas | 6/88 | 8/90 |
| CTS Printex, Inc. | Mountain View | 6/88 | 2/90 |
| Del Amo Facility | Los Angeles | 7/91 | |
| Del Norte Pesticide Storage | Crescent City | 9/83 | 9/84 |
| Edwards Air Force Base | Kern County | 7/89 | 8/90 F |
| El Toro Marine Corps Air Station | El Toro | 6/88 | 2/90 F |
| Fairchild Semiconductor Corp. (Mt. View Plant) (once listed as Fairchild Camera & Instrument Corp.) | Mountain View | 10/84 | 2/91 |
| Fairchild Semiconductor Corp. (So. San Jose Plant) (once listed as Fairchild Camera & Instrument Corp.) | South San Jose | 10/84 | 10/89 |
| Firestone Tire & Rubber Co. (Salinas Plant) | Salinas | 10/84 | 7/87 |
| Fort Ord | Marine | 7/89 | 2/90 F |
| Fresno Municipal Sanitary Landfill | Fresno | 6/88 | 10/89 |

| Site name | City/County | Date Prop'd | Date Final | Site name | City/County | Date Prop'd | Date Final |
|---|---|---|---|---|---|---|---|
| George Air Force Base | Victorville | 7/89 | 2/90 F | McClellan Air Force Base (Ground Water Contamination) | Sacramento | 10/84 | 7/87 F |
| Hewlett-Packard (620–640 Page Mill Rd.) | Palo Alto | 6/88 | 2/90 | McColl | Fullerton | 12/82 | 9/83 |
| Hexcel Corp. | Livermore | 6/88 | 8/90 | MGM Brakes | Cloverdale | 12/82 | 9/83 |
| Industrial Waste Processing | Fresno | 10/89 | 8/90 | Modesto Ground Water Contamination | Modesto | 6/88 | 3/89 |
| Intel Corp. (Mt. View Plant) | Mountain View | 10/84 | 6/86 | Moffett Naval Air Station | Sunnyvale | 4/85 | 7/87 F |
| Intel Corp. (Santa Clara III) | Santa Clara | 10/84 | 6/86 | Monolithic Memories | Sunnyvale | 10/84 | 7/87 |
| Intel Magnetics | Santa Clara | 10/84 | 6/86 | Montrose Chemical Corp. | Torrance | 10/84 | 10/89 |
| Intersil Inc./Siemens Components | Cupertino | 6/88 | 8/90 | National Semiconductor Corp. | Santa Clara | 10/84 | 7/87 |
| Iron Mountain Mine | Redding | 10/81 | 9/83 | Newmark Ground Water Contamination | San Bernardino | 6/88 | 3/89 |
| Jasco Chemical Corp. | Mountain View | 6/88 | 10/89 | | | | |
| J.H. Baxter & Co. | Weed | 10/84 | 10/89 | Norton Air Force Base | San Bernadino | 10/84 | 7/87 F |
| Jibboom Junkyard | Sacramento | 12/82 | 9/83 C | Operating Indus-tries, Inc., Landfill | Monterey Park | 10/84 | 6/86 |
| Koppers Co., Inc. (Oroville Plant) | Oroville | 9/83 | 9/84 | | | | |
| Lawrence Liv-ermore Na-tional Laboratory (USDOE) | Livermore | 10/84 | 7/87 F | Pacific Coast Pipe Lines | Fillmore | 6/88 | 10/89 |
| | | | | Raytheon Corp. | Malaga | 12/82 | 9/83 |
| Lawrence Liv-ermore Na-tional Laboratory (Site 300) (USDOE) | Livermore | 7/89 | 8/90 F | Riverbank Army Ammunition Plant | Riverbank | 6/88 | 2/90 F |
| Liquid Gold Oil Corp. | Richmond | 12/82 | 9/83 | Sacramento Army Depot | Sacramento | 10/84 | 7/87 F |
| Lorentz Barrel & Drum Co. | San Jose | 10/84 | 10/89 | San Fernando Val-ley (Area 1) | Los Angeles | 10/84 | 6/86 |
| Louisiana-Pacific Corp. | Oroville | 10/84 | 6/86 | San Fernando Val-ley (Area 2) | Los Angeles/ Glendale | 10/84 | 6/86 |
| March Air Force Base | Riverside | 7/89 | 11/89 F | San Fernando Val-ley (Area 3) | Glendale | 10/84 | 6/86 |
| Mather Air Force Base (once listed as Mather Air Force Base (AC&W Disposal Site) | Sacramento | 10/84 | 11/89 F | San Fernando Val-ley (Area 4) | Los Angeles | 10/84 | 6/86 |
| | | | | San Gabriel Valley (Area 1) | El Monte | 9/83 | 5/84 |
| | | | | San Gabriel Valley (Area 2) | Baldwin Park Area | 9/83 | 5/84 |

| Site name | City/County | Date Prop'd | Date Final |
|---|---|---|---|
| San Gabriel Valley (Area 3) | Alhambra | 9/83 | 5/84 |
| San Gabriel Valley (Area 4) | Le Puente | 9/83 | 5/84 |
| Selma Treating Co. | Selma | 12/82 | 9/83 |
| Sharpe Army Depot | Lathrop | 10/84 | 7/87 |
| Sola Optical USA, Inc. | Petaluma | 6/88 | 2/90 |
| South Bay Asbestos Area (once listed as Alviso Dumping Area) | Alviso | 10/84 | 6/86 |
| Southern California Edison Co. (Visalia Poleyard) | Visalia | 11/87 | 3/89 |
| Spectra-Physics, Inc. | Mountain View | 6/88 | 2/91 |
| Stoker Company | Imperial | 7/91 | |
| Stringfellow | Glen Avon Heights | 10/81 | 9/83 |
| Sulphur Bank Mercury Mine | Clear Lake | 6/88 | 9/83 |
| Synertek, Inc. (Bldg 1) | Santa Clara | 6/88 | 10/89 |
| Teledyne Semiconductor | Mountain View | 10/84 | 7/87 |
| T.H. Agriculture & Nutrition Co. (once listed as Thompson-Haywood Chemical Co.) | Fresno | 10/84 | 6/86 |
| Tracy Defense Depot | Tracy | 7/89 | 8/90 F |
| Travis Air Force Base | Solano County | 7/89 | 11/89 F |
| Treasure Island Naval Station— Hunters Point Annex | San Francisco | 7/89 | 11/89 F |
| TRW Microwave, Inc. (Bldg 825) | Sunnyvale | 6/88 | 2/90 |
| United Heckathorn Co. | Richmond | 10/89 | 3/90 |
| Valley Wood Preserving, Inc. | Turlock | 6/88 | 2/90 |

| Site name | City/County | Date Prop'd | Date Final |
|---|---|---|---|
| Waste Disposal, Inc. | Santa Fe Springs | 6/86 | 7/87 |
| Watkins-Johnson Co. (Stewart Div.) | Scotts Valley | 1/87 | 8/90 |
| Western Pacific Railroad Co. | Oroville | 10/89 | 8/90 |
| Westinghouse Electric Corp (Sunnyvale Plant) | Sunnyvale | 10/84 | 8/90 |
| Westminster Tract #2633 | Westminster | 7/91 | |
| **Colorado** (16 Final + 0 Proposed = 16) | | | |
| Air Force Plant PJKS | Waterton | 7/89 | 11/89 F |
| Broderick Wood Products | Denver | 9/83 | 9/84 |
| California Gulch | Leadville | 12/82 | 9/83 |
| Central City-Clear Creek | Idaho Springs | 7/82 | 9/83 |
| Chemical Sales Co. | Denver | 6/88 | 8/90 |
| Denver Radium Site | Denver | 10/81 | 9/83 |
| Eagle Mine | Minturn/Redcliff | 10/84 | 6/86 |
| Lincoln Park | Canon City | 9/83 | 9/84 |
| Lowry Landfill | Arapahoe County | 7/82 | 9/83 |
| Marshall Landfill | Boulder County | 7/82 | 9/83 S |
| Rocky Flats Plant (USDOE) | Golden | 10/84 | 10/89 F |
| Rocky Mountain Arsenal | Adams | 10/84 | 7/87 F |
| Sand Creek Industrial | Commerce City | 12/82 | 9/83 |
| Smuggler Mountain | Pitkin County | 10/84 | 6/86 |
| Uravan Uranium Project (Union Carbide Corp.) | Uravan | 10/84 | 6/86 |
| Woodbury Chemical Co. | Commerce City | 7/82 | 9/83 |
| **Connecticut** (15 Final + 0 Proposed = 15) | | | |
| Barkhamsted-New Hartford Landfill | Barkhamsted | 6/88 | 10/89 |
| Beacon Heights Landfill | Beacon Falls | 12/82 | 9/83 |

| Site name | City/County | Date Prop'd | Date Final |
|---|---|---|---|
| Cheshire Ground Water Contamination (once listed as Cheshire Associates Property) | Cheshire | 6/88 | 8/90 |
| Durham Meadows | Durham | 6/88 | 10/89 |
| Gallup's Quarry | Plainfield | 6/88 | 10/89 |
| Kellogg-Deering Well Field | Norwalk | 9/83 | 9/84 |
| Laurel Park, Inc. (once listed as Laurel Park Landfill) | Naugatuck Borough | 10/81 | 9/83 S |
| Linemaster Switch Corp. | Woodstock | 6/88 | 2/90 |
| New London Submarine Base | New London | 10/89 | 8/90 F |
| Nutmeg Valley Road | Wolcott | 1/87 | 3/89 |
| Old Southington Landfill | Southington | 9/83 | 9/84 |
| Precision Plating Corp. | Vernon | 6/88 | 10/89 |
| Revere Textile Prints Corp. | Sterling | 6/86 | 10/89 |
| Solvents Recovery Service of New England | Southington | 12/82 | 9/83 |
| Yaworski Waste Lagoon | Canterbury | 12/82 | 9/83 |

**Delaware** (20 Final + 0 Proposed = 20)

| Site name | City/County | Date Prop'd | Date Final |
|---|---|---|---|
| Army Creek Landfill (once listed as Delaware Sand & Gravel-Llangolen Army Creek Landfills) | New Castle County | 10/81 | 9/83 |
| Chem-Solv, Inc. | Cheswold | 1/87 | 8/90 |
| Coker's Sanitation Service Landfills | Kent County | 4/85 | 7/87 |
| Delaware City PVC Plant (once listed as Stauffer Chemical Co.) | Delaware City | 10/81 | 9/83 |

| Site name | City/County | Date Prop'd | Date Final |
|---|---|---|---|
| Delaware Sand & Gravel Landfill (once listed as Delaware Sand & Gravel—Llangollen Army Creek Landfills) | New Castle County | 10/81 | 9/83 |
| Dover Air Force Base | Dover | 10/84 | 3/89 F |
| Dover Gas Light Co. | Dover | 1/87 | 10/89 |
| E.I. Du Pont de Nemours & Co., Inc. (Newport Pigment Plant Landfill) | Newport | 1/87 | 2/90 |
| Halby Chemical Co. | New Castle | 9/85 | 6/86 |
| Harvey & Knott Drum, Inc. | Kirkwood | 7/82 | 9/83 |
| Kent County Landfill (Houston) | Houston | 6/88 | 8/90 |
| Koppers Co., Inc; (Newport Plant) | Newport | 10/89 | 8/90 |
| NCR Corp. (Mills-boro Plant) | Millsboro | 4/85 | 7/87 |
| New Castle Spill (once listed as TRIS Spill) | New Castle County | 12/82 | 9/83 |
| Sealand Limited | Mount Pleasant | 6/88 | 9/90 |
| Standard Chlorine of Delaware, Inc. | Delaware City | 9/85 | 7/87 |
| Sussex County Landfill No. 5 | Laurel | 6/88 | 10/89 |
| Tybouts Corner Landfill | New Castle County | 10/81 | 9/83 S |
| Tyler Refrigeration Pit | Smyrna | 6/86 | 2/90 |
| Wildcat Landfill | Dover | 12/82 | 9/83 |

**Florida** (51 Final + 1 Proposed = 52)

| Site name | City/County | Date Prop'd | Date Final |
|---|---|---|---|
| Agrico Chemical Co. | Pensacola | 6/88 | 10/89 |
| Airco Plating Co. | Miami | 6/88 | 2/90 |
| Alpha Chemical Corp. | Galloway | 10/81 | 9/83 C |

| Site name | City/County | Date Prop'd | Date Final | Site name | City/County | Date Prop'd | Date Final |
|---|---|---|---|---|---|---|---|
| American Creosote Works, Inc. (Pensacola Plant) (once listed as American Creosote Works) | Pensacola | 10/81 | 9/83 | Hipps Road Landfill | Duval County | 9/83 | 9/84 |
| | | | | Hollingsworth Solderless Terminal | Fort Lauderdale | 10/81 | 9/83 |
| | | | | Homestead Air Force Base | Homestead | 7/89 | 8/90 F |
| | | | | Jacksonville Naval Air Station | Jacksonville | 7/89 | 11/89 F |
| Anaconda Aluminum Co./Milgo Electronics Corp. | Miami | 10/89 | 8/90 | Kassauf-Kimerling Battery Disposal (once listed as Timber Lake Battery Disposal) | Tampa | 10/81 | 9/83 |
| Anodyne, Inc. | North Miami Beach | 6/88 | 2/90 | | | | |
| B&B Chemical Co., Inc. | Hialeah | 6/88 | 8/90 | Madison County Sanitary Landfill | Madison | 6/88 | 8/90 |
| Beulah Landfill | Pensacola | 6/88 | 2/90 | Miami Drum Services (once listed as part of Biscayne Aquifer) | Miami | 10/81 | 9/83 |
| BMI-Textron | Lake Park | 6/88 | 2/90 | | | | |
| Broward County—21st Manor Dump | Fort Lauderdale | 7/91 | | | | | |
| Brown Wood Preserving | Live Oak | 12/82 | 9/83 | Munisport Landfill | North Miami | 12/82 | 9/83 |
| Cabot/Koppers | Gainesville | 9/83 | 9/84 | Northwest 58th Street Landfill (once listed as part of Biscayne Aquifer) | Hialeah | 10/81 | 9/83 |
| Cecil Field Naval Air Station | Jacksonville | 7/89 | 11/89 F | | | | |
| Chemform, Inc. | Pompano Beach | 6/88 | 10/89 | | | | |
| City Industries, Inc. | Orlando | 10/84 | 10/89 | Peak Oil Co./Bay Drum Co. | Tampa | 10/84 | 6/86 |
| Coleman-Evans Wood Preserving Co. | Whitehouse | 10/81 | 9/83 | Pensacola Naval Air Station | Pensacola | 7/89 | 11/89 F |
| Davie Landfill (once listed as Broward County Solid Waste Disposal Facility) | Davie | 10/81 | 9/83 | Pepper Steel & Alloys, Inc. | Medley | 9/83 | 9/84 |
| | | | | Petroleum Products Corp. | Pembroke Park | 4/85 | 7/87 |
| Dubose Oil Products Co. | Cantonment | 10/84 | 6/86 | Picketville Road Landfill | Jacksonville | 10/81 | 9/83 |
| Florida Steel Corp. | Indiantown | 12/82 | 9/83 | Pioneer Sand Co. | Warrington | 10/81 | 9/83 |
| Gold Coast Oil Corp. | Miami | 10/81 | 9/83 | Piper Aircraft/Vero Beach Water & Sewer Department | Vero Beach | 6/86 | 2/90 |
| Harris Corp. (Palm Bay Plant) (once listed as Harris Corp./ Development Utilities) | Palm Bay | 4/85 | 7/87 | Reeves Southeast Galvanizing Corp. | Tampa | 10/81 | 9/83 |
| | | | | Sapp Battery Salvage | Cottondale | 10/81 | 9/83 |

| Site name | City/County | Date Prop'd | Date Final |
|---|---|---|---|
| Schuykill Metals Corp. | Plant City | 12/82 | 9/83 |
| Sherwood Medical Industries | Deland | 12/82 | 9/83 |
| Sixty-Second Street Dump | Tampa | 12/82 | 9/83 |
| Standard Auto Bumper Corp. | Hialeah | 6/88 | 10/89 |
| Sydney Mine Sludge Ponds | Brandon | 6/86 | 10/89 |
| Taylor Road Landfill | Seffner | 10/81 | 9/83 |
| Tower Chemical Co. | Clermont | 10/81 | 9/83 |
| Whitehouse Oil Pits | Whitehouse | 10/81 | 9/83 |
| Wilson Concepts of Florida, Inc. | Pompano Beach | 6/88 | 3/89 |
| Wingate Road Municipal Incinerator Dump | Fort Lauderdale | 6/88 | 8/90 |
| Woodbury Chemical Co. (Princeton Plant) | Princeton | 6/88 | 8/90 |
| Yellow Water Road Dump | Baldwin | 9/85 | 6/86 |
| Zellwood Ground Water Contamination | Zellwood | 10/81 | 9/83 |

**Georgia** (13 Final + 0 Proposed = 13)

| Site name | City/County | Date Prop'd | Date Final |
|---|---|---|---|
| Cedartown Industries, Inc. | Cedartown | 6/88 | 2/90 |
| Cedartown Municipal Landfill | Cedartown | 6/88 | 3/89 |
| Diamond Shamrock Corp. Landfill | Cedartown | 1/87 | 8/90 |
| Firestone Tire & Rubber Co. (Albany Plant) | Albany | 6/88 | 10/89 |
| Hercules 009 Landfill | Brunswick | 9/83 | 9/84 |
| Marine Corps Logistics Base | Albany | 7/89 | 11/89 F |
| Marzone Inc./Chevron Chemical Co. | Tifton | 6/88 | 10/89 |

| Site name | City/County | Date Prop'd | Date Final |
|---|---|---|---|
| Mathis Brothers Landfill (South Marble Top Road) | Kensington | 1/87 | 3/89 |
| Monsanto Corp. (Augusta Plant) | Peach County | 9/83 | 9/84 |
| Powersville Site | Peach County | 9/83 | 9/84 |
| Robins Air Force Base (Landfill #4/Sludge Lagoon) | Houston County | 10/84 | 7/87 F |
| T.H. Agriculture & Nutrition Co. (Albany Plant) | Albany | 6/88 | 3/89 |
| Woolfolk Chemical Works, Inc. | Fort Valley | 6/88 | 8/90 |

**Guam** (1 Final + 0 Proposed = 1)

| Site name | City/County | Date Prop'd | Date Final |
|---|---|---|---|
| Ordot Landfill | Guam | 10/81 | 9/83 S |

**Hawaii** (2 Final + 1 Proposed = 2)

| Site name | City/County | Date Prop'd | Date Final |
|---|---|---|---|
| Pearl Harbor Naval Complex | Pearl Harbor | 7/91 | F |
| Schofield Barracks | Oahu | 7/89 | 8/90 F |

**Idaho** (9 Final + 0 Proposed = 9)

| Site name | City/County | Date Prop'd | Date Final |
|---|---|---|---|
| Arrcom (Drexler Enterprises) | Rathdrum | 12/82 | 9/83 |
| Bunker Hill Mining & Metallurgical | Smelterville | 12/82 | 9/83 |
| Eastern Michaud Flats Contamination | Pocatello | 5/89 | 8/90 |
| Idaho National Engineering tory (USDOE) | Idaho Falls | 7/89 | 11/89 F |
| Kerr-McGee Chemical Corp. (Soda Springs Plant) | Soda Springs | 5/89 | 10/89 |
| Monsanto Chemical Co. (Soda Springs Plant) | Soda Springs | 5/89 | 8/90 |
| Mountain Home Air Force Base | Mountain Home | 7/89 | 8/90 F |
| Pacific Hide & Fur Recycling Co. | Pocatello | 9/83 | 9/84 |
| Union Pacific Railroad Co. | Pocatello | 9/83 | 9/84 |

| Site name | City/County | Date Prop'd | Date Final |
|---|---|---|---|
| **Illinois** (36 Final + 1 Proposed = 37) | | | |
| A & F Material Reclaiming, Inc. | Greenup | 7/82 | 9/83 |
| Acme Solvent Reclaiming, Inc. (Morristown Plant) | Morristown | 7/82 | 9/83 |
| Adams County Quincy Landfills 2 & 3 | Quincy | 6/88 | 8/90 |
| Amoco Chemicals (Joliet Landfill) | Joliet | 6/88 | 2/90 |
| Beloit Corp. | Rockton | 6/88 | 8/90 |
| Belvidere Municipal Landfill | Belvidere | 12/82 | 9/83 |
| Byron Salvage Yard | Byron | 12/82 | 9/83 |
| Central Illinois Public Service Co. | Taylorville | 6/88 | 8/90 |
| Cross Brothers Pail Recycling | Pembroke Township | 12/82 | 9/83 |
| DuPage County Landfill/ Blackwell Forest Preserve | Warrenville | 6/88 | 2/90 |
| Galesburgkoppers Co. | Galesburg | 12/82 | 9/83 |
| H.O.D. Landfill | Antioch | 9/85 | 2/90 |
| Ilada Energy Co. | East Cape Girardeau | 6/88 | 10/89 |
| Interstate Pollution Control, Inc. | Rockford | 6/88 | 3/89 |
| Johns-Manville Corp. | Waukegan | 12/82 | 9/83 |
| Joliet Army Ammunition Plant (Load-Assembly-Packing Area) | Joliet | 4/85 | 3/89 F |
| Joliet Army Ammunition Plant (Manufacturing Area) | Joliet | 10/84 | 7/87 F |
| Kerr-McGee (Kress Creek/West Branch of DuPage River) | DuPage County | 10/84 | 2/91 |
| Kerr-McGee (Reed-Keppler Park) | West Chicago | 10/84 | 8/90 |
| Kerr-McGee (Residential Areas) | West Chicago/ DuPage County | 10/84 | 8/90 |
| Kerr-McGee (Sewage Treatment Plant) | West Chicago | 10/84 | 8/90 |
| LaSalle Electric Utilities | LaSalle | 12/82 | 9/83 |
| Lenz Oil Service, Inc | Lemont | 6/88 | 10/89 |
| MIG/Dewane Landfill | Belvidere | 10/89 | 8/90 |
| NL Industries/Taracorp Lead Smelter | Granite City | 10/84 | 6/86 |
| Ottawa Radiation Areas | Ottawa | 7/81 | |
| Outboard Marine Corp. | Waukegan | 10/81 | 9/83 S |
| Pagel's Pit | Rockford | 10/84 | 6/86 |
| Parsons Casket Hardware Co. | Belvidere | 1/87 | 7/87 |
| Sangamo Electric Damp/Crab Orchard National Wildlife Refuge (USDOI) | Carterville | 10/84 | 7/87 F |
| Savanna Army Depot Activity | Savanna | 10/84 | 3/89 F |
| Southeast Rockford Ground Water Contamination | Rockford | 6/88 | 3/89 |
| Tri County Landfill Co./Waste Management of Illinois, Inc. | South Elgin | 6/86 | 3/89 |
| Velsicol Chemical Corp. (Illinois) | Marshall | 12/82 | 9/83 |
| Wauconda Sand & Gravel | Wauconda | 7/82 | 9/83 |
| Woodstock Municipal Landfill | Woodstock | 6/88 | 10/89 |
| Yeoman Creek Landfill | Waukegan | 6/88 | 3/89 |

| Site name | City/County | Date Prop'd | Date Final |
|---|---|---|---|
| **Indiana** (33 Final + 0 Proposed = 33) | | | |
| American Chemical Service, Inc. | Griffith | 9/83 | 9/84 |
| Bennett Stone Quarry | Bloomington | 9/83 | 9/84 |
| Carter Lee Lumber Co. | Indianapolis | 6/88 | 3/89 |
| Columbus Old Municipal Landfill#1 | Columbus | 9/85 | 6/86 |
| Conrail Rail Yard (Elkhart) | Elkhart | 6/88 | 8/90 |
| Continental Steel Corp. | Kokomo | 6/88 | 3/89 |
| Douglas Road/ Uniroyal, Inc., Landfill | Mishawaka | 6/86 | 3/89 |
| Envirochem Corp. | Zionsville | 12/82 | 9/83 |
| Fisher-Calo | LaPorte | 12/82 | 9/83 |
| Fort Wayne Reduction Dump | Fort Wayne | 10/84 | 6/86 |
| Galen Myers Dump/Drum Salvage | Osceola | 6/88 | 3/89 |
| Himco Dump | Elkhart | 6/88 | 2/90 |
| Lakeland Disposal Service, Inc. | Claypool | 6/88 | 3/89 |
| Lake Sandy Jo (M & M Landfill) (once listed as Lake Sandy Jo) | Gary | 12/82 | 9/83 |
| Lemon Lane Landfill | Bloomington | 12/82 | 9/83 |
| Main Street Well Field | Elkhart | 12/82 | 9/83 |
| Marion (Bragg) Dump | Marion | 12/82 | 9/83 |
| MIDCO I | Gary | 12/82 | 9/83 |
| MIDCO II | Gary | 10/84 | 6/86 |
| Neal's Dump (Spencer) | Spencer | 10/84 | 6/86 |
| Neal's Landfill (Bloomington) | Bloomington | 10/81 | 9/83 |
| Ninth Avenue Dump | Gary | 12/82 | 9/83 |
| Northside Sanitary Landfill, Inc. | Zionsville | 9/83 | 9/84 |
| Prestolite Battery Division | Vincennes | 9/85 | 10/89 |
| Reilly Tar & Chemical Corp. (Indianapolis Plant) | Indianapolis | 9/83 | 9/84 |
| Seymour Recycling Corp. | Seymour | 10/81 | 9/83 S |
| Southside Sanitary Landfill | Indianapolis | 6/86 | 3/89 |
| Tippecanoe Sanitary Landfill, Inc. | Lafayette | 6/88 | 8/90 |
| Tri-State Plating | Columbus | 9/85 | 6/86 |
| Waste, Inc., Landfill | Michigan City | 4/85 | 7/87 |
| Wayne Waste Oil | Columbia City | 12/82 | 9/83 |
| Wedzeb Enterprises, Inc. | Lebanon | 12/82 | 9/83 |
| Whiteford Sales & Service Inc./ NationaLease | South Bend | 6/88 | 8/90 |
| **Iowa** (20 Final + Proposed = 20) | | | |
| Aidex Corp. | Council Bluffs | 10/81 | 9/83 S |
| Des Mounes TCE (once listed as DICO) | Des Moines | 12/82 | 9/83 |
| E.I. Du Pont de Nemours & Co., Inc. (County Road#23) | West Point | 6/88 | 8/90 |
| Electro-Coatings, Inc. | Cedar Rapids | 6/88 | 10/89 |
| Fairfield Coal Gasification Plant | Fairfield | 6/88 | 8/90 |
| Farmers' Mutual Cooperative | Hospers | 6/88 | 8/90 |
| Iowa Army Ammunition Plant | Middletown | 7/89 | 8/90 F |
| John Deere (Ottumwa Works Landfill) | Ottumwa | 6/88 | 2/90 |
| LaBounty Site | Charles City | 12/82 | 9/83 C |
| Lawrence Todtz Farm | Camanche | 9/85 | 6/86 |

| Site name | City/County | Date Prop'd | Date Final |
|---|---|---|---|
| Lehigh Portland Cement Co. | Mason City | 6/88 | 8/90 |
| Mid-American Tanning Co. | Sergeant Bluff | 6/88 | 3/89 |
| Midwest Manufacturing/North Farm | Kellogg | 9/85 | 6/86 |
| Northwestern States Portland Cement Co. | Mason City | 6/88 | 8/90 |
| Peoples Natural Gas Co. | Dubuque | 6/88 | 8/90 |
| Red Oak City Landfill | Red Oak | 6/86 | 3/89 |
| Shaw Avenue Dump | Charles City | 9/85 | 7/87 |
| Sheller-Globe Corp. Disposal | Keokuk | 5/89 | 8/90 |
| Vogel Paint & Wax Co. | Orange City | 10/84 | 6/86 |
| White Farm Equipment Co. Dump | Charles City | 6/88 | 8/90 |
| **Kansas** (11 Final + 0 Proposed = 11) | | | |
| 29th & Mead Ground Water Contamination | Wichita | 6/88 | 2/90 |
| Arkansas City Dump | Arkansas City | 10/81 | 9/83 S |
| Big River Sand Co. | Wichita | 10/84 | 6/86 |
| Cherokee County (once listed as Tar Creek, Cherokee County) | Cherokee County | 12/82 | 9/83 |
| Doepke Disposal (Holliday) | Johnson County | 12/82 | 9/83 |
| Fort Riley | Junction City | 7/89 | 8/90 F |
| Hydro-Flex Inc. | Topeka | 6/88 | 3/89 |
| Johns' Sludge Pond | Wichita | 12/82 | 9/83 |
| Obee Road | Hutchinson | 1/87 | 9/83 |
| Pester Refinery Co. | El Dorado | 6/88 | 3/89 |
| Strother Field Industrial Park | Cowley County | 10/84 | 6/86 |
| **Kentucky** (17 Final + 2 Proposed = 19) | | | |
| A.L. Taylor (Valley of Drums) | Brooks | 10/81 | 9/83 C,S |

| Site name | City/County | Date Prop'd | Date Final |
|---|---|---|---|
| Airco | Calver City | 9/83 | 9/84 |
| B.F. Goodrich | Calvert City | 12/82 | 9/83 |
| Brantley Landfill | Island | 6/88 | 2/90 |
| Caldwell Lace Leather Co., Inc. | Auburn | 6/88 | 9/90 |
| Distler Brickyard | West Point | 12/82 | 9/83 |
| Distler Farm | Jefferson County | 7/82 | 9/83 |
| Fort Hartford Coal Co. Stone Quarry | Olaton | 6/88 | 8/90 |
| General Tire & Rubber Co. (Mayfield Landfill) | Mayfield | 6/88 | 2/90 |
| Green River Disposal, Inc. | Maceo | 6/88 | 8/90 |
| Howe Valley Landfill | Howe Valley | 6/86 | 7/87 |
| Lee's Lane Landfill | Lousville | 7/82 | 9/83 |
| Maxey Flats Nuclear Disposal | Hillsboro | 10/84 | 6/86 |
| National Electric Coil Co./Cooper Industries | Dayholt | 7/91 | |
| National Southwire Aluminum Co. | Hawesville | 7/91 | |
| Newport Dump | Newport | 12/82 | 9/83 C |
| Red Penn Sanitation Co. Landfill | Peewee Valley | 6/88 | 3/89 |
| Smith's Farm | Brooks | 10/84 | 6/86 |
| Tri-City Disposal Co. | Shepherdsville | 6/88 | 3/89 |
| **Louisiana** (11 Final + 0 Proposed = 11) | | | |
| Bayou Bonfouca | Slidell | 12/82 | 9/83 |
| Bayou Sorrel Site | Bayou Sorel | 7/82 | 9/84 |
| Cleve Reber | Sorrento | 12/82 | 9/83 |
| Combustion, Inc. | Denham Springs | 6/86 | 8/90 |
| D.L. Mud, Inc. | Abbeville | 6/88 | 10/89 |
| Dutchtown Treatment Plant | Ascension Parish | 1/87 | 7/87 |
| Gulf Coast Vacuum Services | Abbeville | 6/88 | 3/89 |

| Site name | City/County | Date Prop'd | Date Final |
|---|---|---|---|
| Louisiana Army Ammunition Plant | Doyline | 10/84 | 3/89 F |
| Old Inger Oil Refinery | Darrow | 7/82 | 9/83 S |
| PAB Oil & Chemical Service, Inc. | Abbeville | 6/88 | 3/89 |
| Petro-Processors of Louisiana Inc. | Scotlandville | 9/83 | 9/84 |
| **Maine** (9 Final + 0 Proposed = 9) | | | |
| Brunswick Naval Air Station | Brunswick | 10/84 | 7/87 F |
| Loring Air Force Base | Limestone | 7/89 | 2/90 F |
| McKin Co. | Gray | 12/82 | 9/83 |
| O'Connor Co. | Augusta | 12/82 | 9/83 |
| Pinette's Salvage Yard | Washburn | 12/82 | 9/83 |
| Saco Municipal Landfill | Saco | 6/88 | 2/90 |
| Saco Tannery Waste Pits | Saco | 12/82 | 9/83 |
| Union Chemical Co., Inc. | South Hope | 4/85 | 10/89 |
| Winthrop Landfill | Winthrop | 10/81 | 9/83 |
| **Maryland** (10 Final + 0 Proposed = 10) | | | |
| Aberdeen Proving Ground (Edgewood Area) | Edgewood | 4/85 | 2/90 F |
| Aberdeen Proving Ground (Michaelsville Landfill) | Aberdeen | 4/85 | 10/89 F |
| Anne Arundel County Landfill | Glen Burnie | 6/88 | 2/91 |
| Bush Valley Landfill | Abingdon | 6/88 | 3/89 |
| Kane & Lombard Street Drums | Baltimore | 10/84 | 6/86 |
| Limestone Road | Cumberland | 12/82 | 9/83 |
| Mid-Atlantic Wood Preservers, Inc. | Harmans | 10/84 | 6/86 |
| Sand, gravel & Stone | Elkton | 12/82 | 9/83 |

| Site name | City/County | Date Prop'd | Date Final |
|---|---|---|---|
| Southern Maryland Wood Treating | Hollywood | 10/84 | 6/86 |
| Woodlawn County Landfill | Woodlawn | 1/87 | 7/87 |
| **Massachusetts** (25 Final + 0 Proposed = 25) | | | |
| Atlas Tack Corp. | Fairhaven | 6/88 | 2/90 |
| Baird & McGuire | Holbrook | 12/82 | 9/83 |
| Cannon Engineering Corp. (CEC) | Bridgewater | 12/82 | 9/83 |
| Charles-George Reclamation Trust Landfill | Tyngsborough | 10/81 | 9/83 |
| Fort Devens | Fort Devens | 7/89 | 11/89 F |
| Fort Devins—Sudbury Training Annex | Middlesex County | 7/89 | 2/90 F |
| Groveland Wells | Groveland | 12/82 | 9/83 |
| Haverhill Municipal Landfill | Haverhill | 10/84 | 6/86 |
| Hocomonco Pond | Westborough | 12/82 | 9/83 |
| Industri-Plex (once listed as Mark Phillip Trust | Woburn | 10/81 | 9/83 |
| Iron Horse Park | Billerica | 9/83 | 9/84 |
| New Bedford Site | New Bedford | 7/82 | 9/83 S |
| Norwood PCBs | Norwood | 10/84 | 6/86 |
| Nyanza Chemical Waste Dump | Ashland | 10/81 | 9/83 |
| Otis Air National Guard Base/ Camp Edwards | Falmouth | 7/89 | 11/89 F |
| Plymouth Harbor/ Cannon Engineering Corp. (once listed as Plymouth Harbor/ Cordage) | Plymouth | 12/82 | 9/83 |
| PSC Resources | Palmer | 12/81 | 9/83 |
| Re-Solve, Inc | Dartmouth | 10/81 | 9/83 |
| Rose Disposal Pit | Lanesboro | 10/84 | 6/86 |
| Salem Acres | Salem | 10/84 | 6/86 |
| Spack Landfill | Norton/Attleboro | 10/84 | 6/86 |
| Silresim Chemical Corp. | Lowell | 7/82 | 9/83 |
| Sullivan's Ledge | New Bedford | 9/83 | 9/84 |

| Site name | City/County | Date Prop'd | Date Final |
|---|---|---|---|
| Wells G & H | Woburn | 12/82 | 9/83 |
| W.R. Grace & Co. Inc. (Acton Plant) | Acton | 12/82 | 9/83 |
| **Michigan** (77 Final + 0 Proposed = 77) | | | |
| Adams Plating | Lansing | 6/88 | 3/89 |
| Albion-Sheridan Township Landfill | Albion | 6/88 | 10/89 |
| Alied Paper, Inc./ Portage Creek/ Kalamazoo River | Kalamazoo | 5/89 | 8/90 |
| American Anodco, Inc. | Ionia | 6/86 | 3/89 |
| Anderson Development Co. | Adrian | 12/82 | 9/83 |
| Auto Ion Chemicals, Inc. | Kalamazoo | 12/82 | 9/83 |
| Avenue "E" Ground Water Contamination | Traverse City | 10/84 | 6/86 |
| Barrels, Inc. | Lansing | 1/87 | 10/89 |
| Bendix Corp./Allied Automotive | St. Joseph | 6/88 | 2/90 |
| Berlin & Farro | Swartz Creek | 7/82 | 9/83 |
| Bofors Nobel, Inc. | Muskegon | 6/88 | 3/89 |
| Burrows Sanitation | Hartford | 9/83 | 9/84 |
| Butterworth #2 Landfill | Grand Rapids | 12/82 | 9/83 |
| Cannelton Industries, Inc. | Sault Sainte Marie | 6/88 | 3/89 |
| Carter Industrials, Inc. | Detroit | 6/88 | 3/89 |
| Cemetery Dump | Rose Center | 12/82 | 9/83 |
| Charlevoix Municipal Well | Charlevoix | 12/82 | 9/83 |
| Chem Central | Wyoming Township | 12/82 | 9/83 |
| Clare Water Supply | Clare | 9/83 | 9/84 |
| Cliff/Dow/Dump | Marquette | 12/82 | 9/83 |
| Duell & Gardner Landfill | Dalton Township | 12/82 | 9/83 |
| Electrovoice | Buchanan | 9/83 | 9/84 |
| Folkertsma Refuse | Grand Rapids | 6/86 | 3/89 |

| Site name | City/County | Date Prop'd | Date Final |
|---|---|---|---|
| Forest Waste Products | Otisville | 12/82 | 9/83 |
| G & H Landfill | Utica | 7/82 | 9/83 |
| Grand Traverse Overall Supply Co. | Greilickville | 12/82 | 9/83 |
| Gratio County Landfill | St. Louis | 10/81 | 9/93 S |
| H. Brown Co., Inc. | Grand Rapids | 4/85 | 6/86 |
| Hedblum Industries | Oscoda | 12/82 | 9/83 |
| Hi-Mill Manufacturing Co. | Highland | 6/88 | 2/90 |
| Ionia City Landfill | Ionia | 12/82 | 9/83 |
| J & L Landfill | Rochester Hills | 6/86 | 3/89 |
| K & L Avenue Landfill | Oshtemo Township | 12/82 | 9/83 |
| Kaydon Corp. | Muskegon | 6/88 | 2/90 |
| Kent City Mobile Home Park | Kent City | 9/85 | 7/87 |
| Kentwood Landfill | Kentwood | 12/82 | 9/83 |
| Kysor Industrial Corp | Cadillac | 9/85 | 10/89 |
| Liquid Disposal, Inc. | Utica | 7/82 | 9/83 |
| Mason County Landfill | Pere Marquette Township | 12/82 | 9/83 |
| McGraw Edison Corp. | Albion | 12/82 | 9/83 |
| Metal Working Shop | Lake Ann | 1/87 | 2/90 |
| Metamora Landfill | Metamora | 9/83 | 2/90 |
| Michigan Disposal Service (Cork Street Landfill) | Kalamazoo | 10/84 | 2/90 |
| Motor Wheel, Inc. | Lansing | 10/84 | 6/86 |
| Muskegon Chemical Co. | Whitehall | 6/88 | 2/90 |
| North Bronson Industrial Area | Bronson | 10/84 | 6/86 |
| Northernaire Plating | Cadillac | 7/82 | 9/83 |
| Novaco Industries | Temperance | 12/82 | 9/83 |
| Organic Chemicals, Inc. | Grandville | 12/82 | 9/83 |

| Site name | City/County | Date Prop'd | Date Final |
|---|---|---|---|
| Ossineke Ground Water Contamination | Ossineke | 12/82 | 9/83 |
| Ott/Story/Cordova Chemical Co. | Dalton Township | 7/82 | 9/83 |
| Packaging Corp. of America | Filer City | 12/82 | 9/83 |
| Parsons Chemical Works, Inc. | Grand Ledge | 6/88 | 3/89 |
| Peerless Plating Co. | Muskegon | 6/88 | 8/90 |
| Petoskey Municipal Well Field | Petoskey | 12/82 | 9/83 |
| Rasmussen's Dump | Green Oak Township | 12/82 | 9/83 |
| Rockwell International Corp. (Allegan Plant) | Allegan | 4/85 | 7/87 |
| Rose Township Dump | Rose Township | 7/82 | 9/83 |
| Roto-Finish Co., Inc. | Kalamazoo | 10/84 | 6/86 |
| SCA Independent Landfill | Muskegon Heights | 12/82 | 9/83 |
| Shiawassee River | Howell | 12/82 | 9/83 |
| South Macomb Disposal Authority (Landfills #9 and #9a) | Macomb Township | 10/84 | 6/86 |
| Southwest Ottawa County Landfill | Park Township | 12/82 | 9/83 |
| Sparta Landfill | Sparta Township | 12/82 | 9/83 |
| Spartan Chemical Co. | Wyoming | 12/82 | 9/83 |
| Spirgelberg Landfill | Green Oak Township | 12/82 | 9/83 |
| Springfield Township Dump | Davisburg | 12/82 | 9/83 |
| State Disposal Landfill, Inc. | Grand Rapids | 6/88 | 2/90 |
| Sturgis Municipal Wells | Sturgis | 9/83 | 9/84 |
| Tar Lake | Mancelona Township | 12/82 | 9/83 |
| Thermo-Chem, Inc. | Muskegon | 10/84 | 6/86 |

| Site name | City/County | Date Prop'd | Date Final |
|---|---|---|---|
| Torch Lake | Houghton County | 10/84 | 6/86 |
| U.S. Aviex | Howard Township | 12/82 | 9/83 |
| Velsicol Chemical Corp. (Michigan) | St. Louis | 12/82 | 9/83 |
| Verona Well Field | Battle Creek | 7/82 | 9/83 |
| Wash King Laundry | Pleasant Plains Township | 12/82 | 9/83 |
| Waste Management of Michigan (Holland Lagoons) | Holland | 10/84 | 6/86 |

**Minnesota** (42 Final + 0 Proposed = 42)

| Site name | City/County | Date Prop'd | Date Final |
|---|---|---|---|
| Adrian Municipal Well Field | Adrian | 10/84 | 6/86 |
| Agate Lake Scrapyard | Fairview Township | 10/84 | 6/86 |
| Arrowhead Refinery Co. | Hermantown | 9/83 | 9/84 |
| Boise Cascade/ Onan Corp./ Medtronics, Inc. | Fridley | 9/83 | 9/84 |
| Burlington Northern (Brainerd/ Baxter Plant) | Brainerd/Baxter | 7/82 | 9/83 |
| Dakhue Sanitary Landfill | Cannon Falls | 10/89 | 8/90 |
| East Bethel Demolition Landfill | East Bethel Township | 9/85 | 6/86 |
| FMC Corp. (Fridley Plant) | Fridley | 7/82 | 9/83 |
| Freeway Sanitary Landfill | Burnsville | 9/85 | 6/86 |
| General Mills/ Henkel Corp. | Minneapolis | 9/83 | 9/84 |
| Joslyn Manufacturing & Supply Co. | Brooklyn Center | 9/83 | 9/84 |
| Koch Refining Co./ N-Ren Corp. | Pine Bend | 10/84 | 6/86 |
| Koppers Coke | St. Paul | 10/81 | 9/83 |

| Site name | City/County | Date Prop'd | Date Final |
|---|---|---|---|
| Kummer Sanitary Landfill | Bemidji | 10/84 | 6/86 |
| Kurt Manufacturing Co. | Fridley | 10/84 | 6/86 |
| LaGrand Sanitary Landfill | LaGrand Township | 6/86 | 7/87 |
| Lehillier/Mankato Site | Lehillier/ Mankato | 7/82 | 9/83 |
| Long Prairie Ground Water Contamination | Long Prairie | 10/84 | 6/86 |
| MacGillis & Gibbs Co./Bell Lumber & Pole Co. | New Brighton | 9/83 | 9/84 |
| Naval Industrial Reserve Ordnance Plant | Fridley | 10/84 | 11/89 F |
| New Brighton/ Arden Hills | New Brighton | 7/82 | 9/83 |
| NL Industries/Taracorp/Golden Auto (once listed as National Lead Taracorp) | St. Louis Park | 10/81 | 9/83 |
| Nutting Truck & Caster Co. | Faribault | 9/83 | 9/84 |
| Oak Grove Sanitary Landfill | Oak Grove Township | 10/84 | 6/86 |
| Oakdale Dump | Oakdale | 10/81 | 9/83 |
| Olmsted County Sanitary Landfill | Oronoco | 10/84 | 6/86 |
| Perham Arsenic Site | Perham | 9/83 | 9/84 |
| Pine Bend Sanitary Landfill (once listed as Pine Bend Sanitary Landfill/Crosby American Demolition Landfill) | Dakota County | 10/84 | 6/86 |
| Reilly Tar & Chemical corp. (St. Louis Park Plant) | St. Louis Park | 10/81 | 9/83 S |
| Ritari Post & Pole | Sebeka | 1/87 | 7/87 |
| South Andover Site (once listed as Andover Sites) | Andover | 10/81 | 9/83 |
| Dump (once listed as St. Augusta Sanitary Landfill/St. Cloud Dump) | St. Augusta Township | 9/85 | 7/87 |
| St. Louis River Site | St. Louis County | 9/83 | 9/84 |
| St. Regis Paper Co. | Cass Lake | 9/83 | 9/84 |
| Twin Cities Air Force Reserve Base (Small Arms Range Landfill) | Minneapolis | 1/87 | 9/84 F |
| Union Scrap Iron & Metal Co. | Minneapolis | 9/83 | 9/84 C |
| University of Minnesota (Rosemount Research Center) | Rosemount | 10/84 | 6/86 |
| Waite Park Wells | Waite Park | 9/85 | 6/86 |
| Washington County Landfill | Lake Elmo | 9/83 | 9/84 |
| Waste Disposal Engineering | Andover | 7/82 | 9/83 |
| Whittaker Corp. | Minneapolis | 9/83 | 9/84 |
| Windom Dump | Windom | 10/84 | 6/86 |
| **Mississippi** (2 Final + 0 Proposed = 2) | | | |
| Flowood Site | Flowood | 9/83 | 9/84 S |
| Newsom Brothers/ Old Reichhold Chemicals, Inc. | Columbia | 10/84 | 6/86 |
| **Missouri** (22 Final + 0 Proposed = 22) | | | |
| Bee Cee manufacturing Co. | Malden | 10/84 | 6/86 |
| Conservation ical Co. | Kansas City | 4/85 | 10/89 |
| Ellisville Site | Ellisville | 10/81 | 9/83 S |
| Fulbright Landfill | Springfield | 10/81 | 9/83 |
| Kem-Pest Laboratories | Cape Girardeau | 1/87 | 10/89 |

| Site name | City/County | Date Prop'd | Date Final |
|-----------|-------------|-------------|------------|
| Lake City Army Ammunition Plant (Northwest Lagoon) | Independence | 10/84 | 7/87 F |
| Lee Chemical | Liberty | 10/84 | 6/86 |
| Minker/Stout/ Romaine Creek (once listed as Arena 2: Fills 1 and 2) | Imperial | 12/82 | 9/83 |
| Missouri Electric Works | Cape Girardeau | 6/88 | 2/90 |
| North-U Drive Well Contamination | Springfield | 10/84 | 6/86 |
| Oronogo-Duenweg Mining Belt | Jasper County | 6/88 | 8/90 |
| Quality Plating | Sikeston | 10/84 | 6/86 |
| Shenandoah Stables (once listed as Arena 1: Shenandoah Stables) | Moscow Mills | 12/82 | 9/83 |
| Solid State Circuits, Inc. | Republic | 10/84 | 6/86 |
| St. Louis Airport/ Hazelwood Interim Storage/ Futura Coatings Co. | St. Louis County | 5/89 | 10/89 |
| Syntex Facility | Verona | 12/82 | 9/83 |
| Times Beach Site | Times Beach | 3/83 | 9/83 |
| Valley Park TCE | Valley Park | 4/85 | 6/86 |
| Weldon Spring Former Army Ordnance Works | St. Charles County | 7/89 | 2/90 |
| Weldon Spring Quarry/Plant/ Pits (USDOE/ Army) (once listed as Weldon Spring Quarry (USDOE/Army) | St. Charles County | 10/84 | 7/87 F |
| Westlake Landfill | Bridgeton | 10/89 | 8/90 |
| Wheeling Disposal Service Co. Landfill | Amazonia | 1/87 | 10/89 |

| Site name | City/County | Date Prop'd | Date Final |
|-----------|-------------|-------------|------------|
| **Montana** (8 Final = 0 Proposed = 8) | | | |
| Anaconda Co. Smelter | Anaconda | 12/82 | 9/83 |
| East Helena Site (once listed as East Helena Smelter) | East Helena | 9/83 | 9/84 |
| Idaho Pole Co. | Bozeman | 10/84 | 6/86 |
| Libby Ground Water Contamination | Libby | 12/82 | 9/83 |
| Milltown Reservoir Sediments | Milltown | 12/82 | 9/83 |
| Montana Pole and Treating | Butte | 6/86 | 7/87 |
| Mouat Industries | Columbus | 10/84 | 6/86 |
| Silver Bow Creek/ Butte Area (once listed as Silver Bow Creek) | Silver Bow/Deer Lodge | 12/82 | 9/83 |
| **Nebraska** (6 Final + 2 Proposed = 8) | | | |
| 10th Street Site | Columbus | 10/89 | 8/90 |
| Cleburn Street Well | Grand Island | 7/91 | |
| Cornhusker Army Ammunition Plant | Hall County | 10/84 | 7/87 F |
| Hastings Ground Water Contamination | Hastings | 10/84 | 6/86 |
| Lindsay Manufacturing Co. | Lindsay | 10/84 | 10/89 |
| Nebraska Ordnance Plant (Former) | Mead | 10/89 | 8/90 |
| Sherwood Medical Co. | Norfolk | 7/91 | |
| Waverly Ground Water Contamination | Waverly | 10/84 | 6/86 |
| **Nevada** (1 Final + 0 Proposed = 1) | | | |
| Carson River Mercury Site | Lyon/Churchill County | 10/89 | 8/90 |
| **New Hampshire** (16 Final + 1 Proposed = 17) | | | |
| Auburn Road Landfill | Londonderry | 12/82 | 9/83 |

| Site name | City/County | Date Prop'd | Date Final |
|---|---|---|---|
| Coakley Landfill | North Hampton | 10/84 | 6/86 |
| Dover Municipal Landfill | Dover | 12/82 | 9/83 |
| Fletcher's Paint Works & Storage | Milford | 6/88 | 3/89 |
| Holton Circle Ground Water Contamination | Londonderry | 6/88 | 3/89 |
| Kearsage Metallurgical Corp.(once listed as Kearsage Metallurgical Corp.) | Conway | 9/83 | 9/84 |
| Keefe Environmental Services (once listed as KES) | Epping | 10/81 | 9/83 |
| Mottolo Pig Farm | Raymond | 4/85 | 7/87 |
| New Hampshire Plating Co. | Merrimack | 7/91 | R |
| Ottati & Goss/ Kingston Steel Drum (once listed as Ottati & Goss) | Kingston | 10/81 | 9/83 |
| Pease Air Force Base | Portsmouth/ Newington | 7/89 | 2/90 F |
| Savage Municipal Water Supply | Milford | 9/83 | 9/84 |
| Somersworth Sanitary Landfill | Somersworth | 12/82 | 9/83 |
| South Muncipal Water Supply Well | Peterborough | 9/83 | 9/84 |
| Sylvester | Nashua | 10/81 | 9/83 S |
| Tibbets Road | Barrington | 4/85 | 6/86 |
| Tinkham Garage | Londonderry | 12/82 | 9/83 |

**New Jersey** (108 Final + 1 Proposed = 109)

| Site name | City/County | Date Prop'd | Date Final |
|---|---|---|---|
| A.O. Polymer | Sparta Township | 12/82 | 9/83 |
| American Cyanamid Co. | Bound Brook | 12/82 | 9/83 |
| Asbestos Dump | Millington | 12/82 | 9/83 |
| Beachwood/ Berkley Wells | Berkley Township | 12/82 | 9/83 |
| Bog Creek Farm | Howell Township | 12/82 | 9/83 |
| Brick Township Landfill | Brick Township | 12/82 | 9/83 |
| Bridgeport Rental & Oil Services | Bridgeport | 10/81 | 9/83 |
| Brook Industrial Park | Bound Brook | 6/88 | 10/89 |
| Burnt Fly Bog | Marlboro Township | 10/81 | 9/83 |
| Caldwell Trucking Co. | Fairfield | 12/82 | 9/83 |
| Chemical Control | Elizabeth | 10/81 | 9/83 |
| Chemical Insecticide Corp. | Edison Township | 10/89 | 8/90 |
| Chemical Leaman Tank Lines, Inc. (once listed as Chemical Leaman Tank Liners, Inc.) | Bridgeport | 9/83 | 9/84 |
| Chemsol, Inc. | Piscataway | 12/82 | 9/83 |
| Ciba-Geigy Corp. (once listed as Toms River Chemical) | Toms River | 12/82 | 9/83 |
| Cinnaminson Township (Block 702) Ground Water Contamination | Cinnaminson Township | 10/84 | 6/86 |
| Combe Fill North Landfill | Mount Olive Township | 12/82 | 9/83 |
| Combe Fill South Landfill | Chester Township | 12/82 | 9/83 |
| Cosden Chemical Coatings Corp. | Beverly | 1/87 | 7/87 |
| CPS/Madison Industries | Old Bridge Township | 12/82 | 9/83 |
| Curcio Scrap Metal, Inc. | Saddle Brook Township | 1/87 | 7/87 |
| Dayco Corp./L.E. Carpenter Co. | Wharton Borough | 4/85 | 7/87 |
| Delilah road | Egg Harbor Township | 9/83 | 9/84 |
| Denzer & Schafer X-Ray Co. | Bayville | 12/82 | 9/83 |

| Site name | City/County | Date Prop'd | Date Final |
|---|---|---|---|
| De Rewal Chemical Co. | Kingwood Township | 9/83 | 9/84 |
| Diamond Alkali Co. | Newark | 9/83 | 9/84 |
| D'Imperio Property | Hamilton Township | 10/81 | 9/83 |
| Dover Municipal Well 4 | Dover Township | 12/82 | 9/83 |
| Ellis Property | Evesham Township | 12/82 | 9/83 |
| Evor Phillips Leasing | Old Bridge Township | 12/82 | 9/83 |
| Ewan Property | Shamong Township | 9/83 | 9/84 |
| Fair Lawn Well Field | Fair Lawn | 12/82 | 9/83 |
| Federal Aviation Administration Technical Center (USDOT) | Atlantic County | 7/89 | 8/90 F |
| Florence Land Re-contouring Landfill | Florence Township | 9/83 | 9/84 |
| Fort Dix (Landfill Site) | Pemberton Township | 10/84 | 7/87 F |
| Fried Industries | East Brunswick Township | 10/84 | 6/86 |
| Garden State Cleaners Co. | Minotola | 6/88 | 3/89 |
| GEMS Landfill | Gloucester Township | 7/82 | 9/83 |
| Glen Ridge Radium Site | Glen Ridge | 10/84 | 2/85 |
| Global Sanitary Landfill | Old Bridge Township | 6/88 | 3/89 |
| Goose Farm | Plumstead Township | 10/81 | 9/83 |
| Helen Kramer Landfill | Mantua Township | 7/82 | 9/83 |
| Hercules, Inc (Gibbstown Plant) | Gibbstown | 12/82 | 9/83 |
| Higgins Disposal | Kingstown | 6/88 | 8/90 |
| Higgins Farm | Franklin Township | 6/88 | 3/89 |

| Site name | City/County | Date Prop'd | Date Final |
|---|---|---|---|
| Hopkins Farm | Plumstead Township | 9/83 | 9/84 |
| Imperial Oil Co., Inc/Champion Chemicals | Morganville | 12/82 | 9/83 |
| Industrial Latex Corp. | Wallington Borough | 6/88 | 3/89 |
| Jackson Township Landfill | Jackson Township | 12/82 | 9/83 |
| JIS Landfill | Jamesburg/So. Brunswick | 12/82 | 9/83 |
| Kauffman & Min-teer, Inc. | Jobstown | 6/88 | 3/89 |
| Kin-Buc Landfill | Edison Township | 10/81 | 9/83 |
| King of Prussia | Winslow Township | 12/89 | 9/83 |
| Landfill & Develop-ment CO. | Mount Holly | 9/83 | 9/84 |
| Lang Property | Pemberton Township | 12/82 | 9/83 |
| Lipari Landfill | Pitman | 10/81 | 9/83 |
| Lodi Municipal Well | Lodi | 10/84 | 8/90 |
| Lone Pine Landfill | Freehold Township | 10/81 | 9/83 |
| Mannheim Avenue Dump | Galloway Township | 12/82 | 9/83 |
| Maywood Chemical Corp. | Maywood/ Rochelle Park | 12/82 | 9/83 |
| Metaltec/ Aerosystems | Franklin Borough | 12/82 | 9/83 |
| Monitor Devices/In-tercircuits, Inc. | Wall Township | 4/85 | 6/86 |
| Monroe Township Landfill | Monroe Township | 12/82 | 9/83 |
| Montclair/West Or-ange Radium Site | Montclair/West Orange | 10/84 | 2/85 |
| Montgomery Town-ship Housing Development | Montgomery Township | 12/82 | 9/83 |
| Myers Property | Franklin Township | 12/82 | 9/83 |
| Nascolite Corp. | Millville | 9/83 | 9/84 |

| Site name | City/County | Date Prop'd | Date Final | Site name | City/County | Date Prop'd | Date Final |
|---|---|---|---|---|---|---|---|
| Naval Air Engineering Center | Lakehurst | 9/83 | 7/87 F | Swope Oil & Chemical Co. | Pennsauken | 7/82 | 9/83 |
| Naval Weapons Station Earle (Site A) | Colts Neck | 10/84 | 8/90 F | Syncon Resins | South Kearny | 7/82 | 9/83 |
| NL Industries | Pedricktown | 12/82 | 9/84 | Tabernacle Drum Dump | Tabernacle Township | 9/83 | 9/84 |
| Pepe Field | Boonton | 12/82 | 9/83 | Universal Oil Products (Chemical Division) | East Rutherford | 12/82 | 9/83 |
| Picatinny Arsenal | Rockaway Township | 7/89 | 2/90 F | | | | |
| Pijak Farm | Plumstead Township | 10/81 | 9/83 | Upper Deerfield Township Sanitary Landfill | Upper Deerfield Township | 9/83 | 9/84 |
| PJP Landfill | Jersey City | 12/82 | 9/83 | U.S. Radium Corp. | Orange | 12/82 | 9/83 |
| Pohatcong Valley Ground Water Contamination | Warren County | 6/88 | 3/89 | Ventron/Velsicol | Wood Ridge Borough | 9/83 | 9/84 |
| Pomona Oaks Residential Wells | Galloway Township | 10/84 | 6/86 | Vineland Chemical Co., Inc. | Vineland | 9/83 | 9/84 |
| Price Landfill | Pleasantville | 10/81 | 9/83 S | Vineland State School | Vineland | 12/82 | 9/83 |
| Radiation Technology, Inc. | Rockaway Township | 9/83 | 9/84 | Waldick Aerospace Devices, Inc. | Wall Township | 9/83 | 9/84 F |
| Reich Farms | Pleasant Plains | 12/82 | 9/83 | White Chemical Corp. | Newark | 5/91 | A |
| Renora, Inc. | Edison Township | 12/82 | 9/83 | Williams Property | Swainton | 12/82 | 9/83 |
| Ringwood Mines/ Landfill | Ringwood Borough | 12/82 | 9/83 | Wilson Farm | Plumstead Township | 9/83 | 9/84 |
| Rockaway Borough Well Field | Rockaway Township | 12/82 | 9/83 | Witco Chemical Corp. (Oakland Plant) | Oakland | 6/88 | 10/89 |
| Rockaway Township Wells | Rockaway | 12/82 | 9/83 | | | | |
| Rocky Hill Municipal Well | Rocky Hill Borough | 12/82 | 9/83 | Woodland Route 532 Dump | Woodland Township | 9/83 | 9/84 |
| Roebling Steel Co. | Florence | 12/82 | 9/83 | Woodland Route 72 Dump | Woodland Township | 9/83 | 9/84 |
| Sayreville Landfill | Sayreville | 12/82 | 9/83 | W.R. Grace & Co., Inc./Wayne Interim Storage Site (USDOE) (once listed as W.R. Grace & Co., Inc. (Wayne Plant) | Wayne Township | 9/83 | 9/84 F |
| Scientific Chemical Processing | Carlstadt | 12/82 | 9/83 | | | | |
| Sharkey Landfill | Parsippany/ Troy Hills | 12/82 | 9/83 | | | | |
| Shieldalloy Corp. | Newfield Borough | 9/83 | 9/84 | | | | |
| South Brunswick Landfill | South Brunswick | 12/82 | 9/83 | **New Mexico** (10 Final + 0 Proposed = 10) | | | |
| South Jersey Clothing Co. | Minotola | 6/88 | 10/89 | AT & SF (Clovis) | Clovis | 10/81 | 9/83 |
| Spence Farm | Plumstead Township | 10/81 | 9/83 | Cal West Metals (USSBA) | Lemitar | 6/88 | 3/89 F |

| Site name | City/County | Date Prop'd | Date Final |
|---|---|---|---|
| Cimarron Mining Corp. | Carrizozo | 6/88 | 10/89 |
| Cleveland Mill | Silver City | 6/88 | 3/89 |
| Homestake Mining Co. | Milan | 10/81 | 9/83 |
| Lee Acres Landfill (USDOI) | Farmington | 6/88 | 8/90 F |
| Pagano Salvage | Los Lunas | 6/88 | 10/89 |
| Prewitt Abandoned Refinery | Prewitt | 6/88 | 8/90 |
| South Valley | Albuquerque | 7/82 | 9/83 S |
| United Nuclear Corp. | Church Rock | 10/81 | 9/83 |
| **New York** (83 Final + 1 Proposed = 84) | | | |
| Action Anodizing, Plating, & Pol- ishing Corp. | Copiague | 6/88 | 3/89 |
| American Thermo- stat Co. | South Cairo | 12/82 | 9/83 |
| Anchor Chemicals | Hicksville | 10/84 | 6/86 |
| Applied Environ- mental Services | Glenwood Landing | 10/84 | 6/86 |
| Batavia Landfill | Batavia | 10/81 | 9/83 |
| BEC Trucking | Town of Vestal | 10/84 | 6/86 |
| BioClinical Labora- tories, Inc. | Bohemia | 6/86 | 3/89 |
| Brewster Well Field | Putnam County | 12/82 | 9/83 |
| Brookhaven Na- tional Labora- tory (USDOE) | Upton | 7/89 | 11/89 F |
| Byron Barrel & Drum | Byron | 10/84 | 6/86 |
| C & J Disposal Leasing Co. Dump | Hamilton | 6/88 | 3/89 |
| Carroll & Dubies Sewage Disposal | Port Jervis | 6/88 | 2/90 |
| Circuitron Corp. | East Farming dale | 6/88 | 3/89 |
| Claremont Polychemical | Old Bethpage | 10/84 | 6/86 |
| Clothier Disposal | Town of Granby | 10/84 | 6/86 |
| Colesville Munici- pal Landfill | Town of Colesville | 10/84 | 6/86 |

| Site name | City/County | Date Prop'd | Date Final |
|---|---|---|---|
| Conklin Dumps | Conklin | 6/86 | 3/89 |
| Cortese Landfill | Village of Narrows burg | 10/84 | 6/86 |
| Endicott Village Well Field | Village of Endicott | 10/84 | 6/86 |
| Facet Enterprises, Inc. | Elmira | 10/81 | 9/83 |
| FMC Corp. (Dublin Road Landfill) | Town of Shelby | 10/84 | 6/86 |
| Forest Glen Mobile Home Subdivision | Niagara Falls | 8/89 | 11/89 A |
| Fulton Terminals | Fulton | 12/82 | 9/83 |
| GE Moreau | South Glen Falls | 12/82 | 9/83 |
| General Motors (Central Foundry Div.) | Massena | 9/83 | 9/84 |
| Genzale Plating Co. | Franklin Square | 6/86 | 7/87 |
| Goldisc Recordings, Inc. | Holbrook | 10/84 | 6/86 |
| Griffiss Air Force Base | Rome | 10/84 | 7/87 F |
| Haviland Complex | Town of Hyge Park | 10/84 | 6/86 |
| Hertel Landfill | Plattekill | 10/84 | 6/86 |
| Hooker (102nd Street) | Niagara Falls | 12/82 | 9/83 |
| Hooker (Hyde Park) | Niagara Falls | 12/82 | 9/83 |
| Hooker (S Area) | Niagara Falls | 12/82 | 9/83 |
| Hooker Chemical/ Ruco Polymer Corp | Hicksville | 10/84 | 6/86 |
| Hudson River PCBs | Hudson River | 9/83 | 9/84 |
| Islip Municipal San- itary Landfill | Islip | 1/87 | 3/89 |
| Johnstown City Landfill | Town of Johnstown | 10/84 | 6/86 |
| Jones Chemicals, Inc. | Caledonia | 6/88 | 2/90 |
| Jones Sanitation | Hyde Park | 1/87 | 7/87 |
| Katonah Municipal Well | Town of Bedford | 10/84 | 6/86 |
| Kenmark Textile Corp. | Farmingdale | 10/84 | 6/86 |

| Site name | City/County | Date Prop'd | Date Final | Site name | City/County | Date Prop'd | Date Final |
|---|---|---|---|---|---|---|---|
| Kentucky Avenue Well Field | Horseheads | 7/82 | 9/83 | Robintech, Inc./ National Pipe Co. | Town of Vestal | 10/84 | 6/86 |
| Liberty Industrial Finishing | Farmingdale | 10/84 | 6/86 | Rosen Brothers Scrap Yard/ Dump | Cortland | 6/88 | 3/89 |
| Li Tungsten Corp. | Glen Cove | 7/91 | | Rowe Industries Ground Water Contamination | Noyack/Sag Harbor | 6/86 | 7/87 |
| Love Canal | Niagara Falls | 10/81 | 9/83 | | | | |
| Ludlow Sand & Gravel | Clayville | 12/82 | 9/83 | Sarney Farm | Amenia | 10/84 | 6/86 |
| Malta Rocket Fuel Area | Malta | 6/86 | 7/87 | Sealand Restoration, Inc. | Lisbon | 10/89 | 8/90 |
| Marathon Battery Corp. | Cold Springs | 10/81 | 9/83 | Seneca Army Depot | Romulus | 7/89 | 8/90 F |
| Mattiace Petro- chemical Co., Inc. | Glen Cove | 6/88 | 3/89 | Sidney Landfill | Sidney | 6/88 | 3/89 |
| | | | | Sinclair Refinery | Wellsville | 7/82 | 9/83 |
| Mercury Refining Co. | Colonie | 12/82 | 9/83 | SMS Instruments, Inc. | Deer Park | 10/84 | 6/86 |
| Nepera Chemical Co., Inc. | Maybrook | 10/84 | 6/86 | Solvent Savers | Lincklaen | 12/82 | 9/83 |
| Niagara County Refuse | Wheatfield | 10/81 | 6/86 | Suffern Village Well Field | Village of Suffern | 10/84 | 6/86 |
| Niagara Mohawk Power Corp. (Saratoga Springs Plant) | Saratoga Springs | 6/88 | 2/90 | Syosset Landfill | Oyster Bay | 12/82 | 9/83 |
| | | | | Tri-Cities Barrel CO., Inc. | Port Crane | 5/89 | 10/89 |
| North Sea Munici- pal Landfill | North Sea | 10/84 | 6/86 | Vestal Water Sup- ply Well 1-1 (once listed with Well 4-2 as one site) | Vestal | 12/82 | 9/83 |
| Old Bethpage Landfill | Oyster Bay | 10/81 | 9/83 | | | | |
| Olean Well Field | Olean | 10/81 | 9/83 | Volney Municipal Landfill | Town of Volney | 10/84 | 6/86 |
| Pasley Solvents & Chemicals, Inc. | Hempstead | 10/84 | 6/86 | Warwick Landfill | Warwick | 9/85 | 3/89 |
| Plattsburgh Air Force Base | Plattsburgh | 7/89 | 11/89 F | Wide Beach Development | Brant | 12/82 | 9/83 |
| Pollution Abatement Services | Oswego | 10/81 | 9/83 S | York Oil Co. | Moira | 7/82 | 9/83 |
| Port Washington Landfill | Port Washington | 12/82 | 9/83 | **North Carolina** (22 Final + 0 Proposed = 22) | | | |
| Preferred Plating Co. | Farmingdale | 10/84 | 6/86 | ABC One Hour Cleaners | Jacksonville | 6/88 | 3/89 |
| Radium Chemical Co., Inc. | New York City | 8/89 | 11/89 A | Aberdeen Pesticide Dumps | Aberdeen | 1/87 | 3/89 |
| Ramapo Landfill | Ramapo | 12/82 | 9/83 | Benfield Industries, Inc. | Hazelwood | 6/88 | 10/89 |
| Richardson Hill Road Landfill/ Pond | Sidney Center | 6/86 | 7/87 | Bypass 601 Ground Water Contamination | Concord | 10/84 | 6/86 |

| Site name | City/County | Date Prop'd | Date Final |
|---|---|---|---|
| Camp Lejeune Military Reservation (once listed as Camp Lejeune Marine Corps Base) | Onslow County | 6/88 | 10/89 F |
| Cape Fear Wood Preserving | Fayetteville | 6/86 | 7/87 |
| Carolina Transformer Co. | Fayetteville | 1/87 | 7/87 |
| Celanese Corp. (Shelby Fiber Operations) | Shelby | 10/84 | 6/86 |
| Charles Macon Lagoon & Drum Storage | Cordova | 1/87 | 7/87 |
| Chemtronics, Inc. | Swannanoa | 12/82 | 9/83 |
| FCX, Inc. (Statesville Plant) | Statesville | 6/88 | 2/90 |
| FCX, Inc. (Washington Plant) | Washington | 6/88 | 3/89 |
| Geigy Chemical Corp. (Aberdeen Plant) | Aberdeen | 6/88 | 10/89 |
| Hevi-Duty Electric Co. | Goldsboro | 5/89 | 8/90 |
| Jadco-Hughes Facility | Belmont | 10/84 | 6/86 |
| Jadco-Hughes Facility | Belmont | 10/84 | 6/86 |
| JFD Electronics/ Channel Master | Oxford | 6/88 | 10/89 |
| Koppers Co., Inc. (Morrisville Plant) | Morrisville | 6/88 | 3/89 |
| Martin-Marietta Sodyeco, Inc. | Charlotte | 12/82 | 9/83 |
| National Starch & Chemical Corp. | Salisbury | 4/85 | 10/89 |
| New Hanover County Airport Burn Pit | Wilmington | 6/88 | 3/89 |
| North Carolina State University (Lot 86, Farm Unit#1) | Raleigh | 10/84 | 6/86 |

| Site name | City/County | Date Prop'd | Date Final |
|---|---|---|---|
| Potter's Septic Tank Service Pits | Maco | 6/88 | 3/89 |
| **North Dakota** (2 Final 0 Proposed = 2) | | | |
| Arsenic Trioxide Site | Southeastern ND | 10/81 | 9/83 S |
| Minot Landfill | Minot | 6/88 | 3/89 |
| **Ohio** (33 Final + 0 Proposed = 33) | | | |
| Allied Chemical & Ironton Coke | Ironton | 12/82 | 9/83 |
| Alsco Anaconda | Gnadenhutten | 10/84 | 6/86 |
| Arcanum Iron & Metal | Darke County | 12/82 | 9/83 |
| Big D Campground | Kingsville | 12/82 | 9/83 |
| Bowers Landfill | Circleville | 12/82 | 9/83 |
| Buckeye Reclamation | St. Clairsville | 12/82 | 9/83 |
| Chem-Dyne | Hamilton | 10/81 | 9/83 S |
| Coshocton Landfill | Franklin Township | 12/82 | 9/83 |
| E.H. Schilling Landfill | Hamilton Township | 12/82 | 9/83 |
| Feed Materials Production Center (USDOE) | Fernald | 7/89 | 11/89 |
| Fields Brook | Ashtabula | 10/81 | 9/83 |
| Fultz Landfill | Jackson Township | 12/82 | 9/83 |
| Industrial Excess Landfill | Uniontown | 10/84 | 6/86 |
| Laskin/Poplar Oil Co. (once listed as Poplar Oil Co.) | Jefferson Township | 7/82 | 9/83 |
| Miami County Incinerator | Troy | 9/83 | 9/84 |
| Mound Plant (USDOE) | Miamisburg | 7/89 | 11/89 F |
| Nease Chemical | Salem | 12/82 | 9/83 |
| New Lyme Landfill | New Lyme | 12/82 | 9/83 |
| Old Mill (once listed as Rock Creek/Jack Webb) | Rock Creek | 12/82 | 9/83 |
| Ormet Corp. | Hannibal | 9/85 | 7/87 |
| Powell Road Landfill | Dayton | 9/83 | 9/84 |

| Site name | City/County | Date Prop'd | Date Final |
|---|---|---|---|
| Pristine, Inc. | Reading | 12/82 | 9/83 |
| Reilly Tar & Chemical Corp. (Dover Plant) | Dover | 6/88 | 8/90 |
| Republic Steel Corp. Quarry | Elyria | 10/84 | 6/86 |
| Sanitary Landfill Co. (Industrial Waste Disposal Co., Inc.) | Dayton | 10/84 | 6/86 |
| Skinner Landfill | West Chester | 12/82 | 9/83 |
| South Point Plant | South Point | 9/83 | 9/84 |
| Summit National | Deerfield Township | 10/81 | 9/83 |
| TRW, Inc. (Minerva Plant) | Minerva | 6/86 | 3/89 |
| United Scrap Lead Co., Inc. | Troy | 9/83 | 9/84 |
| Van Dale Junkyard | Marietta | 10/84 | 6/86 |
| Wright-Patterson Air Force Base | Dayton | 6/88 | 10/89 F |
| Zanesville Well Field | Zanesville | 12/82 | 9/83 |
| **Oklahoma** (10 Final + 0 Proposed = 10) | | | |
| Compass Industries (Avery Drive) (once listed as Compass Industries) | Tulsa | 9/83 | 9/84 |
| Double Eagle Refinery Co. | Oklahoma | 6/88 | 3/89 |
| Fourth Street Abandoned Refinery | Oklahoma City | 6/88 | 3/89 |
| Hardage/Criner (once listed as Criner/ Hardage Waste Disposal) | Criner | 10/81 | 9/83 |
| Mosley Road Sanitary Landfill | Oklahoma City | 6/88 | 2/90 |
| Oklahoma Refining Co. | Cyril | 6/88 | 2/90 |
| Sand Springs Petrochemical Complex | Sand Springs | 10/84 | 6/86 |

| Site name | City/County | Date Prop'd | Date Final |
|---|---|---|---|
| Tar Creek (Ottawa County) | Ottawa County | 10/81 | 9/83 |
| Tenth Street Dump/ Junkyard | Oklahoma City | 1/87 | 7/87 |
| Tinker Air Force Base (Soldier Creek/Building 3001) | Oklahoma City | 4/85 | 7/87 F |
| **Oregon** (8 Final + 0 Proposed = 8) | | | |
| Allied Plating, Inc. | Portland | 1/87 | 2/90 |
| Gould, Inc. | Portland | 12/82 | 9/83 |
| Joseph Forest Products | Joseph | 6/88 | 3/89 |
| Martin-Marietta Aluminum Co. | The Dalles | 10/84 | 6/86 |
| Teledyne Wah Chang | Albany | 12/82 | 9/83 |
| Umatilla Army Depot (Lagoons) | Hermiston | 10/84 | 7/87 F |
| Union Pacific Railroad Co. Tie Treating Plant | The Dalles | 10/89 | 8/90 |
| United Chrome Products, Inc. | Corvallis | 9/83 | 9/84 |
| **Pennsylvania** (95 Final + 2 Proposed = 97) | | | |
| A.I.W. Frank/Mid-County Mustang | Exton | 6/88 | 10/89 |
| Aladdin Plating | Scott Township | 1/87 | 7/87 |
| Ambler Asbestos Piles | Ambler | 10/84 | 6/86 |
| AMP, Inc. (Glen Rock Facility) | Glen Rock | 6/88 | 10/89 |
| Avco Lycoming (Williamsport Division) | Williamsport | 1/87 | 2/90 |
| Bally Ground Water Contamination | Bally Borough | 6/86 | 7/87 |
| Bell Landfill | Terry Township | 6/88 | 10/89 |
| Bendix Flight Systems Division | Bridgewater Township | 9/85 | 7/87 |
| Berkley Products Co. Dump | Denver | 6/88 | 3/89 |
| Berks Landfill | Spring Township | 6/88 | 10/89 |
| Berks Sand Pit | Longswamp Township | 9/83 | 9/84 |

| Site name | City/County | Date Prop'd | Date Final | Site name | City/County | Date Prop'd | Date Final |
|---|---|---|---|---|---|---|---|
| Blosenski Landfill | West Cain Township | 12/82 | 9/83 | Hellertown turing Co. | Hellertown | 1/87 | 3/89 |
| Boarhead Farms | Bridgeton Township | 6/88 | 3/89 | Henderson Road | Upper Merion Township | 9/83 | 9/84 |
| Brodhead Creek | Strouds burg | 12/82 | 9/83 | Hranica Landfill | Buffalo Township | 10/81 | 9/83 |
| Brown's Battery Breaking | Shoemakersville | 10/84 | 6/86 | Hunterstown Road | Straban Township | 10/84 | 6/86 |
| Bruin Lagoon | Bruin Borough | 10/81 | 9/83 | Industrial Land | Williams Township | 9/83 | 9/84 |
| Butler Mine Tunnel | Pittston | 6/86 | 7/87 | Jacks Creek/Sitkin Smelting & Re- fining, Inc. | Maitland | 6/88 | 10/89 |
| Butz Landfill | Stroudsburg | 6/88 | 3/89 | | | | |
| C & D Recycling | Foster Township | 9/85 | 7/87 | Keystone Sanitation Landfill | Union Town ship | 4/85 | 7/87 |
| Centre County Kepone | State College Boro | 12/82 | 9/83 | Kimberton Site | Kimberton Borough | 12/82 | 9/83 |
| Commodore Semi- conductor Group | Lower Provi- dence Township | 1/87 | 10/89 | Lackawanna Refuse | Old Forge Borough | 12/82 | 9/83 |
| Craig Farm Drum | Parker | 12/82 | 9/83 | Lansdowne Radia- tion Site | Lansddowne | 4/85 | 9/85A |
| Crossley Farm | Hereford Township | 7/91 | | Letterkenny Army Depot (Prop- erty Disposal Of- fice Area) | Franklin County | 4/85 | 3/89 F |
| Croydon TCE | Croydon | 9/85 | 6/86 | | | | |
| CryoChem, Inc. | Worman | 6/86 | 10/89 | | | | |
| Delta Quarries & Disposal, Inc./ Stotler Landfill | Antis/Logan Townships | 6/86 | 10/89 | Letterkenny Army Depot | Chambersburg (Southeast Area) | 10/84 | 7/87 F |
| Dorney Road Landfill | Upper Macungie Township | 9/83 | 9/84 | Lindane Dump | HarrisonTownsh ip | 10/81 | 9/83 |
| Douglassville Disposal | Douglassville | 12/82 | 9/83 | Lord-Shope Landfill | Girard Township | 10/81 | 9/83 |
| Drake Chemical | Lock Haven | 7/82 | 9/3 | Malvern TCE | Malvern | 12/82 | 9/83 |
| Dublin TCE Site | Dublin Borough | 10/89 | 8/90 | McAdoo Associates | McAdoo Borough | 10/81 | 9/83 |
| Eastern Diversified Metals | Hometown | 6/86 | 10/89 | Metal Banks | Philadelphia | 12/82 | 9/83 |
| East Mount Zion | Springettsbury Township | 9/83 | 9/84 | Middletown Air Field | Middletown | 10/84 | 6/86 |
| Elizabethtown Landfill | Elizabethtown | 6/88 | 3/89 | Mill Creek Dump | Erie | 9/83 | 9/84 |
| Fischer & Porter Co. | Warminster | 12/82 | 9/83 | Modern Sanitation Landfill | Lower Windsor Township | 10/84 | 6/86 |
| Havertown PCP | Haverford | 12/82 | 9/83 | Moyers Landfill | Eagleville | 12/82 | 9/83 |
| Hebelka Auto Sal- vage Yard | Weisenberg Township | 6/86 | 7/87 | MW Manufacturing (once listed as Domino Salvage Yard) | Valley Township | 10/84 | 6/86 |
| Heleva Landfill | NorthWhitehallT ownship | 12/82 | 9/83 | | | | |

| Site name | City/County | Date Prop'd | Date Final |
|---|---|---|---|
| Naval Air Development Center (8 Waste Areas) | Warminster Township | 10/84 | 6/86 |
| North Penn—Area 1 (once listed as Gentle Cleaners, Inc./Granite Knitting Mills, Inc.) | Souderton | 1/87 | 3/89 |
| North Penn—Area 2 (once listd as Ametek, Inc. (Hunter Spring Division) | Hatfield | 1/87 | 10/89 |
| North Penn—Area 5 (once listed as American Electronics Laboratories) Montgomery Township | | 1/87 | 3/89 |
| North Penn—Area 6 (once listed as J.W. Rex Co./Allied Paint Manufacturing Co., Inc./Keystone Hydraulics) | Lansdale | 1/87 | 3/89 |
| North Penn—Area 7 (once listed as Spra-Fin, Inc.) | North Wales | 1/87 | 3/89 |
| North Penn—Area 12 (once listed as Transicoil, Inc.) | Worcester | 1/87 | 2/90 |
| Novak Sanitary Landfill | South Whitehall Township | 1/87 | 10/89 |
| Occidental Chemical Corp./Firestone Tire & Ruber Co. | Lower Pottsgrove Township | 6/88 | 10/89 |
| Ohio River Park | Neville Island | 10/89 | 8/90 |
| Old City of York Landfill | Seven Valleys | 12/82 | 9/83 |
| Osborne Landfill | Grove City | 7/82 | 9/83 |
| Palmerton Zinc Pile | Palmerton | 12/82 | 9/83 |

| Site name | City/County | Date Prop'd | Date Final |
|---|---|---|---|
| Paoli Rail Yard | Paoli | 1/87 | 8/90 |
| Publicker Industries Inc. | Philadelphia | 5/89 | 10/89 |
| Raymark | Hatboro | 6/88 | 10/89 |
| Recticon/Allied Steel Corp. | East Coventry Township | 6/88 | 10/89 |
| Resin Disposal | Jefferson Borough | 12/82 | 9/83 |
| Revere Chemical Co. | Nockamixon Township | 9/85 | 7/87 |
| River Road Landfill (Waste Management, Inc.) | Hermitage | 1/87 | 10/89 |
| Rodale Manufacturing Co., Inc. | Emmaus Borough | 7/91 | |
| Route 940 Drum Dump (once listed as Pocono Summit) | Pocono Summit | 9/85 | 7/87 |
| Saegertown Industrial Area | Saegertown | 6/88 | 2/90 |
| Salford Quarry | Salford Township | 1/87 | 8/90 |
| Shriver's Corner | Straban Township | 10/84 | 6/86 |
| Stanley Kessler | King of Prussia | 12/82 | 9/83 |
| Strasburg Landfill | Newlin Township | 6/88 | 3/89 |
| Taylor Borough Dump | Taylor Borough | 9/83 | 9/84 C |
| Tobyhanna Army Depot | Tobyhanna | 7/89 | 8/90 F |
| Tonolli Corp | Nesquehoning | 6/88 | 10/89 |
| Tysons Dump | Upper Merion Township | 9/83 | 9/84 |
| Walsh Landfill | Honeybrook Township | 9/83 | 9/84 |
| Westinghouse Electric Corp. (Sharon Plant) | Sharon | 6/88 | 8/90 |
| Westinghouse Elevator Co. Plant | Gettysburg | 10/84 | 6/86 |
| Westline Site | Westline | 12/82 | 9/83 |
| Whitmoyer Laboratories | Jackson Township | 10/84 | 6/86 |

| Site name | City/County | Date Prop'd | Date Final |
|---|---|---|---|
| William Dick Lagoons | West Caln Township | 1/87 | 7/87 |
| York County Solid Waste and Refuse Authority Landfill | Hopewell Township | 4/85 | 7/87 |

**Puerto Rico** (9 Final + 0 Proposed = 9)

| Site name | City/County | Date Prop'd | Date Final |
|---|---|---|---|
| Barceloneta Landfill | Florida Afuera | 12/82 | 9/83 |
| Fibers Public Supply Wells | Jobos | 9/83 | 9/84 |
| Frontera Creek | Rio Abajo | 12/82 | 9/83 |
| GE Wiring Devices | Juana Diaz | 12/82 | 9/83 |
| Juncos Landfill | Juncos | 12/82 | 9/83 |
| Naval Security Group Activity | Sabana Seca | 6/88 | 10/89 F |
| RCA Del Caribe | Barceloneta | 12/82 | 9/83 |
| Upjohn Facility | Barceloneta | 9/83 | 9/84 |
| Vega Alta Public Supply Wells | Vega Alta | 9/83 | 9/84 |

**Rhode Island** (11 Final + 1 Proposed = 12)

| Site name | City/County | Date Prop'd | Date Final |
|---|---|---|---|
| Central Landfill | Johnston | 10/84 | 6/86 |
| Davis (GSR) Landfill | Glocester | 4/85 | 6/86 |
| Davis Liquid Waste | Smithfield | 10/81 | 9/83 |
| Davisville Naval Construction Battalion Center | North Kingstown | 7/89 | 11/89 F |
| Landfill & Resource Recovery, Inc. (L&RR) | North Smithfield | 12/82 | 9/83 |
| Newport Naval Education & Training Ctr. | Newport | 7/89 | 11/89 F |
| Peterson/Puritan, Inc. | Lincoln/ Cumberland | 12/82 | 9/83 |
| Picillo Farm | Coventry | 10/81 | 9/83 S |
| Rose Hill Regional Landfill | South Kingstown | 6/88 | 10/89 |
| Stamina Mills, Inc. (once listed as Forestdale-Stamina Mills, Inc.) | North Smithfield | 12/82 | 9/83 |
| Western Sand & Gravel | Burrillville | 10/81 | 9/83 |

| Site name | City/County | Date Prop'd | Date Final |
|---|---|---|---|
| West Kingston Town Dump/ URI Disposal Area | South Kingstown | 7/91 | |

**South Carolina** (23 Final + 0 Proposed = 23)

| Site name | City/County | Date Prop'd | Date Final |
|---|---|---|---|
| Beaunit Corp. (Circular Knit & Dyeing Plant) | Fountain Inn | 6/88 | 2/90 |
| Carolawn, Inc. | Fort Lawn | 12/82 | 9/83 |
| Elmore Waste Disposal | Greer | 6/88 | 3/89 |
| Geiger (C & M Oil) | Rantoules | 9/83 | 7/84 |
| Golden Strip Septic Tank Service | Simpsonville | 1/87 | 7/87 |
| Helena Chemical Co. Landfill | Fairfax | 6/88 | 2/90 |
| Independent Nail Co. | Beaufort | 9/83 | 9/84 C |
| Kalama Specialty Chemicals | Beaufort | 9/83 | 9/84 |
| Koppers Co., Inc. (Florence Plant) | Florence | 9/83 | 9/84 |
| Leonard Chemical Co., Inc. | Rock Hill | 9/83 | 9/84 |
| Lexington County Landfill Area | Cayce | 6/88 | 10/89 |
| Medley Farm Drum Dump | Gaffney | 6/86 | 3/89 |
| Palmetto Recycling, Inc. | Columbia | 1/87 | 7/87 |
| Palmetto Wood Preserving | Dixiana | 9/83 | 9/84 |
| Para-Chem Southern, Inc. | Simpsonville | 10/89 | 8/90 |
| Rochester Property | Travelers Rest | 6/86 | 10/89 |
| Rock Hill Chemical Co. | Rock Hill | 6/88 | 2/90 |
| Sangamo Weston, Inc./Twelve-Mile Creek/Lake Hartwell PCB Contamination) | Pickens | 1/87 | 2/90 |
| Savannah River Site (USDOE) | Aiken | 7/89 | 11/89 F |

| Site name | City/County | Date Prop'd | Date Final | | Site name | City/County | Date Prop'd | Date Final |
|---|---|---|---|---|---|---|---|---|
| SCRDI Bluff Road | Columbia | 10/81 | 9/83 | | **Texas** (28 Final + 1 Proposed = 29) | | | |
| SCRDI Dixiana | Cayce | 7/82 | 9/83 | | Air Force Plant#4 (General Dynamics) | Fort Worth | 10/84 | 8/90 F |
| Townsend Saw Chain Co. | Pontiac | 6/88 | 2/90 | | Bailey Waste Disposal | Bridge City | 10/84 | 6/86 |
| Wamchem, Inc. | Burton | 9/83 | 9/84 | | Bio-Ecology Systems, Inc. | Grand Prairie | 10/81 | 9/83 |
| **South Dakota** (3 Final + 1 Proposed = 4) | | | | | Brio Refining Co. | Friendswood | 10/84 | 3/89 |
| Annie Creek Mine Tailings | Lead | 7/91 | | | Crystal Chemical Co. | Houston | 7/82 | 9/83 |
| Ellsworth Air Force Base | Rapid City | 10/89 | 8/90 F | | Crystal City Airport | Crystal City | 10/84 | 6/86 |
| Whitewood Creek | Whitewood | 10/81 | 9/83 S | | Dixie Oil Processors, Inc. | Friendswood | 6/88 | 10/89 |
| Williams Pipe Line Co. Disposal Pit | Sioux Falls | 10/89 | 8/90 | | French, Ltd. | Crosby | 10/81 | 9/83 |
| **Tennessee** (14 Final + 0 Proposed = 14) | | | | | Geneva Industries/ Fuhrmann Energy | Houston | 9/83 | 9/84 |
| American Creosote Works, Inc. (Jackson Plant) (once listed as American Creosote Works) | Jackson | 10/84 | 6/86 | | Highlands Acid Pit | Highlands | 7/82 | 9/83 |
| | | | | | Koppers Co., Inc. (Texarkana Plant) | Texarkana | 10/84 | 6/86 |
| Amnicola Dump | Chattanooga | 12/82 | 9/83 | | Lone Star Army Ammunition Plant | Texarkana | 10/84 | 7/87 F |
| Arlington Blending & Packaging | Arlington | 1/87 | 7/87 | | | | | |
| Carrier Air Conditioning Co. | Collierville | 6/88 | 2/90 | | Longhorn Army Ammunition Plant | Karnack | 7/89 | 8/90 F |
| Gallaway Pits | Gallaway | 12/82 | 9/83 | | Motco, Inc | La Marque | 10/81 | 9/83 S |
| Lewisburg Dump | Lewisburg | 12/82 | 9/83 | | North Cavalcade Street | Houston | 10/84 | 6/86 |
| Mallory Capacitor Co. | Waynesboro | 1/87 | 10/89 | | Odessa Chromium#1 | Odessa | 10/84 | 6/86 |
| Milan Army Amunition Plant | Milan | 10/84 | 7/87 F | | Odessa Chromium#2 (Andrews Highway) | Odessa | 10/84 | 6/86 |
| Murray-Ohio Dump | Lawrenceburg | 12/82 | 9/83 | | | | | |
| Murray-Ohio Manufacturing Co. (Horseshoe Bend Dump) | Lawrenceburg | 6/88 | 8/90 | | Pantex Plant (USDOE) | Pantex Village | 7/91 | F |
| North Hollywood Dump | Memphis | 10/81 | 9/83 S | | Pesses Chemical Co. | Fort Worth | 10/84 | 6/86 |
| Oak Ridge Reservation (USDOE) | Oak Ridge | 7/89 | 11/89 F | | Petro-Chemical Systems, Inc. (Turtle Bayou) | Liberty County | 10/84 | 6/86 |
| Velsicol Chemical Corp. (Hardeman County) | Toone | 12/82 | 9/83 | | Sheridan Disposal Services | Hempstead | 6/86 | 3/89 |
| Wrigley Charcoal Plant | Wrigley | 6/88 | 3/89 | | | | | |

| Site name | City/County | Date Prop'd | Date Final |
|---|---|---|---|
| Sikes Disposal Pits | Crosby | 10/81 | 9/83 |
| Sol Lynn/Industrial Transformers | Houston | 10/84 | 3/89 |
| South Cavalcade Street | Houston | 10/84 | 6/86 |
| Stewco, Inc. | Waskom | 10/84 | 6/86 |
| Texarkana Wood Preserving Co. | Texarkana | 4/85 | 6/86 |
| Tex-Tin Corp. | Texas City | 6/88 | 8/90 |
| Triangle Chemical Co. | Bridge City | 12/82 | 9/83 C |
| United Creosoting Co. | Conroe | 9/83 | 9/84 |
| **Utah** (11 Final + 1 Proposed = 12) | | | |
| Hill Air Force Base | Ogden | 10/84 | 7/87 F |
| Midvale Slag | Midvale | 6/86 | 2/91 |
| Monticello Mill Tailings (USDOE) | Monticello | 7/89 | 11/89 F |
| Monticello Radioactively Contaminated Properties | Monticello | 10/84 | 6/86 |
| Ogden Defense Depot | Ogden | 7/91 | F |
| Petrochem Recycling Corp./Ekotek, Inc. | Salt Lake City | 10/84 | 6/86 |
| Portland Cement (Kiln Dust 2 & 3) | Salt Lake City | 10/84 | 6/86 |
| Rose Park Sludge Pit | Salt Lake City | 10/81 | 9/83 S |
| Sharon Steel Corp. (Midvale Tailings) (once listed as Sharon Steel Corp. (Midvale Smelter)) | Midvale | 10/84 | 8/90 |
| Tooele Army Depot (North Area) | Tooele | 10/84 | 8/90 F |
| Utah Power & Light/American Barrel Co. | Salt Lake City | 5/89 | 10/89 |
| Wasatch Chemical Co. (Lot 6) | Salt Lake City | 1/87 | 2/91 |

| Site name | City/County | Date Prop'd | Date Final |
|---|---|---|---|
| **Vermont** (8 Final + 0 Proposed = 8) | | | |
| Bennington Municipal Sanitary Landfill | Bennington | 6/88 | 3/89 |
| BFI Sanitary Landfill (Rockingham) | Rockingham | 6/88 | 10/89 |
| Burgess Brothers Landfill | Woodford | 6/88 | 3/849 |
| Darling Hill Dump | Lyndon | 6/88 | 10/89 |
| Old Springfield Landfill | Springfield | 12/82 | 9/83 |
| Parker Sanitary Landfill | Lyndon | 6/88 | 2/90 |
| Pine Street Canal | Burlington | 10/81 | 9/83 S |
| Transitor Electronics, Inc. | Bennington | 6/88 | 10/89 |
| **Virginia** (20 Final + 0 Proposed = 20) | | | |
| Abex Corp. | Portsmouth | 6/88 | 8/90 |
| Arrowhead Associates/Scovill Corp. | Montross | 6/88 | 2/90 |
| Atlantic Wood Industries, Inc. | Portsmouth | 6/86 | 2/90 |
| Avtex Fibers, Inc. | Front Royal | 10/84 | 6/86 |
| Buckingham County Landfill (once listed as Love's Container Service Landfill) | Buckingham | 4/85 | 10/89 |
| C & R Battery Co., Inc. | Chesterfield County | 1/87 | 7/87 |
| Chisman Creek | York County | 10/81 | 9/83 C |
| Culpeper Wood Preservers, Inc. | Culpeper | 10/84 | 10/89 |
| Defense General Supply Center | Chesterfield County | 10/84 | 7/87 F |
| Dixie Caverns County Landfill | Salem | 1/87 | 10/89 |
| First Piedmont Corp. Rock Quarry (Route 710) (once listed as First Piedmont Corp. Rock Quarry) | Pittsylvania County | 4/85 | 7/87 |

| Site name | City/County | Date Prop'd | Date Final |
|---|---|---|---|
| Greenwood Chemical Co. | Newton | 1/87 | 7/87 |
| H & H Inc., Burn Pit | Farrington | 1/87 | 7/87 |
| L.A. Clarke & Son | Spotsylvania County | 10/84 | 6/86 |
| Rentokil, Inc. (Virginia Wood Preserving Division) | Richmond | 1/87 | 3/89 |
| Rhinehart Tire Fire Dump | Frederick County | 10/84 | 6/86 |
| Saltville Waste Disposal Ponds | Saltville | 12/82 | 9/83 |
| Saunders Supply Co. | Chuckatuck | 1/87 | 10/89 |
| Suffolk City Landfill | Suffolk | 6/88 | 2/90 |
| U.S. Titanium | Piney River | 12/82 | 9/83 |
| **Washington** (45 Final + 4 Proposed = 49) | | | |
| ALCOA (Vancouver Smelter) | Vancouver | 6/88 | 2/90 |
| American Crossarm & Conduit Co. | Chehalis | 6/88 | 10/89 |
| American Lake Gardens | Tacoma | 9/83 | 9/84 |
| Bangor Naval Submarine Base | Silverdale | 7/89 | 8/90 F |
| Bangor Ordiance Disposal | Bremerton | 10/84 | 7/87 F |
| Bonneville Power Administration Ross Complex (USDOE) | Vancouver | 7/89 | 11/89 F |
| Centralia Municipal Landfill | Centralia | 6/88 | 8/90 |
| Colbert Landfill | Colbert | 12/82 | 9/83 |
| Commencement Bay, Near Shore/Tide Flats | Pierce County | 10/81 | 9/83 |
| Commencement bay, South Tacoma Channel | Tacoma | 10/81 | 9/83 |
| Fairchild Air Force Base (4 Waste Areas) | Spokane County | 6/88 | 3/89 F |

| Site name | City/County | Date Prop'd | Date Final |
|---|---|---|---|
| FMC Corp. (Yakima Pit) | Yakima | 12/82 | 9/83 |
| Fort Lewis (Landfill No. 5) | Tacoma | 10/84 | 7/87 F |
| Fort Lewis Logistics Center | Tillicum | 7/89 | 11/89 F |
| Frontier Hard Chrome, Inc. | Vancouver | 12/82 | 9/83 |
| General Electric Co. (Spokane Shop) | Spokane | 6/88 | 10/89 |
| Greenacres Landfill | Spokane County | 9/83 | 9/84 |
| Hamilton Island Landfill (USA/COE) | North Bonneville | 7/91 | |
| Hanford 100-Area (USDOE) | Benton County | 6/88 | 10/89 F |
| Hanford 100-Area (USDOE) | Benton County | 6/88 | 10/89 F |
| Hanford 200-Area (USDOE) | Benton County | 6/88 | 10/89 F |
| Hanford 200-Area (USDOE) | Benton County | 6/88 | 10/89 F |
| Harbor Island (Lead) | Seattle | 12/82 | 9/83 |
| Hidden Valley Landfill (Thun Field) | Pierce County | 6/86 | 3/89 |
| Kaiser Aluminum Mead Works | Mead | 12/82 | 9/83 |
| Lakewood Site | Lakewood | 12/82 | 9/83 |
| McChord Air Force Base (Wash Rack/Treatment Area) | Tacoma | 10/84 | 7/87 F |
| Mica Landfill | Mica | 10/84 | 6/86 |
| Midway Landfill | Kent | 10/84 | 6/86 |
| Moses Lake Wellfield Contamination | Moses Lake | 7/91 | |
| Naval Air Station, Whidbey Island (Ault Field) | Whidbey Island | 9/85 | 2/90 F |
| Naval Air Station, Whidbey Island (Seaplane Base) | Whidbey Island | 9/85 | 2/90 F |

| Site name | City/County | Date Prop'd | Date Final |
|---|---|---|---|
| Naval Undersea Warfare Engineering Station (4 Waste Areas) | Keyport | 6/86 | 10/89 F |
| North Market Street (once listed as Tosco Corp. (Spokane Terminal) | Spokane | 6/88 | 8/90 |
| Northside Landfill | Spokane | 10/84 | 6/86 |
| Northwest Transformer | Everson | 10/84 | 6/86 |
| Northwest Transformer (South Harkness Street) | Everson | 6/88 | 2/90 |
| Old Inland Pit | Spokane | 6/86 | 2/90 |
| Pacific Car & Foundry Co. | Renton | 6/88 | 2/90 |
| Pasco Sanitary Landfill | Pasco | 6/88 | 2/90 |
| Pesticide Lab (Yakima) | Yakima | 12/82 | 9/83 |
| Queen City Farms | Maple Valley | 9/83 | 9/84 |
| Seattle Municipal Landfill (Kent Highlands) | Kent | 6/88 | 8/90 |
| Silver Mountain Mine | Loomis | 10/84 | 6/86 |
| Tulalip Landfill | Marysville | 7/91 | |
| Vancouver Water Station #4 Contamination | Vancouover | 7/91 | |
| Western Processing Co., Inc. | Kent | 7/82 | 9/83 |
| Wyckoff Co./Eagle Harbor | Bainbridge Island | 9/85 | 7/87 |
| Yakima Plating Co. | Yakima | 6/88 | 3/89 |
| **West Virginia** (5 Final + 0 Proposed = 5) | | | |
| Fike Chemical, Inc. | Nitro | 12/82 | 9/83 |
| Follansbee Site | Follansbee | 12/82 | 9/83 |
| Leetown Pesticide | Leetown | 12/82 | 9/83 |
| Ordnance Works Disposal Areas | Morgantown | 10/84 | 6/86 |
| West Virginia Ordnance | Point Pleasant | 10/81 | 9/83 S |

| Site name | City/County | Date Prop'd | Date Final |
|---|---|---|---|
| **Wisconsin** (39 Final + 0 Proposed = 39) | | | |
| Algoma Municipal Landfill | Algoma | 6/86 | 7/87 |
| Better Brite Plating Co. Chrome & Zinc Shop | DePere | 10/89 | 8/90 |
| City Disposal Corp. Landfill | Dunn | 9/83 | 9/84 |
| Delevan Municipal Well #4 | Delavan | 9/83 | 9/84 |
| Eau Claire Municipal Well Field | Eau Claire | 9/83 | 9/84 |
| Fadrowski Drum Disposal | Franklin | 10/84 | 6/86 |
| Hagen Farm | Stoughton | 9/85 | 7/87 |
| Hechimovich Sanitary Landfill | Williamstown | 6/88 | 3/89 |
| Hunts Disposal Landfill | Caledonia | 6/86 | 7/87 |
| Janesville Ash Beds | Janesville | 9/83 | 9/84 |
| Janesville Old Landfill | Janesville | 9/83 | 9/84 |
| Kohler Co. Landfill | Kohler | 9/83 | 9/84 |
| Lauer I Sanitary Landfill | Menomonee Falls | 9/83 | 9/84 |
| Lemberger Landfill, Inc. (once listed as Lemberger Fly Ash Landfill) | Whitelaw | 9/85 | 6/86 |
| Lemberger Transport & Recycling Madison Metropolitan Sewerage District Lagoons | Blooming Grove | 6/88 | 2/90 |
| Master Disposal Service Landfill | Brookfield | 9/83 | 9/84 |
| Mid-State Disposal, Inc. Landfill | Cleveland Township | 9/83 | 9/84 |
| Moss-American (Kerr-McGee Oil Co.) | Milwaukee | 9/83 | 9/84 |
| Muskego Sanitary Landfill | Muskego | 9/83 | 9/84 |

| Site name | City/County | Date Prop'd | Date Final |
|---|---|---|---|
| National Presto In- dustries, Inc. | Eau Claire | 10/84 | 6/86 |
| Northern Engraving Co. | Sparta | 9/83 | 9/84 C |
| N.W. Mauthe Co., Inc. | Appleton | 6/88 | 3/89 S |
| Oconomowoc Elec- troplating Co. Inc. | Ashippin | 9/83 | 9/84 |
| Omega Hills North Landfill | Germantown | 9/83 | 9/84 |
| Onalaska Municipal Landfill | Onalaska | 9/83 | 9/84 |
| Sauk County Landfill | Excelsior | 6/88 | 10/89 |
| Schmalz Dump | Harrison | 9/83 | 9/84 |
| Scrap Processing Co., Inc. | Medford | 9/83 | 9/84 |
| Sheboygan Harbor & River | Sheboygan | 9/85 | 6/86 |
| Spickler Landfill | Spencer | 10/84 | 6/86 |
| Stoughton City Landfill | Stoughton | 10/84 | 6/86 |
| Tomah Armory | Tomah | 1/87 | 7/87 |
| Tomah Fairgrounds | Tomah | 1/87 | 7/87 |
| Tomah Municipal Sanitary Landfill | Tomah | 6/86 | 3/89 |

| Site name | City/County | Date Prop'd | Date Final |
|---|---|---|---|
| Waste Management of Wisconsin, Inc. (Brookfield Sanitary Landfill) | Brookfield | 6/88 | 8/90 |
| Waste Research & Reclamation Co. | Eau Claire | 9/83 | 9/84 |
| Wausau Ground Water Contamination | Wausau | 4/85 | 6/86 |
| Wheeler Pit | LaPrairie Township | 9/83 | 9/84 |
| **Wyoming** (3 Final + 0 Proposed = 3) | | | |
| Baxter/Union Pa- cific Tie Treating | Laramie | 12/82 | 9/83 |
| F.E. Warren Air Force Base | Cheyenne | 7/89 | 2/90 F |
| Mystery Bridge Rd/ U.S. Highway 20 | Evansville | 6/88 | 8/90 |

Total: 1188 Final + 23 Propsoed = 1211 Total Sites

**Source:** *Background Information: National Priorities List, Proposed Rule.* U.S. Environmental Protection Agency, Office of Solid Waste and Emergency Response, Office of Emergency and Remedial Response Hazardous Site Evaluation Division (OS-230), July 1991. Publication 9320.7-041.

## Radon Reduction Methods

### General Information

#### EPA Research

The U.S. Environmental Protection Agency is now studying ways of reducing elevated levels of radon in houses. While much research is still in progress, EPA has already learned much that can be of immediate use to homeowners. Additional information will be published as it becomes available.

This is intended for homeowners who have already tested their houses for radon and decided that they need to take some action, as well as for those who are still uncertain. The information provided should be helpful for homeowners who have the skills and equipment needed for "do-it-yourself" radon reduction work, as well as for homeowners who decide to hire contractors to perform the needed work.

It should be noted that the radon reduction methods described in this booklet are concerned primarily with radon that enters a house from the underlying soil (as a component of "soil gas"). The methods have undergone short-term field testing by EPA and/or other research groups and are currently being evaluated for long-term performance and durability.

#### Background Information

If you need general information on radon in houses or if you are uncertain about the meaning of your test results, read the introductory EPA booklet, *A Citizen's Guide to Radon: What It Is And What To Do About It* (OPA-86-004).

For more detailed information on the installation of radon reduction systems, you should consult one of the following manuals. They will be especially useful if you plan to do the work yourself.

• *Application of Radon Reduction Methods* (EPA/625/5-88/024) is the most up-to-date publication for homeowners seeking guidance on how to diagnose a radon problem and select and design a reduction method. Step-by-step guidance on system design, installation, and operation is included.

• *Radon Reduction Techniques for Detached Houses: Technical Guidance* (Second Edition) (EPA/625/5-87/019) is a more technical reference manual that provides detailed information on the sources of radon and its health effects, and guidance for the selection, design, and installation of radon reduction systems. This manual is primarily for the professional radon reduction contractor or do-it-yourself homeowner.

If you are building a new house and are interested in radon prevention methods, refer to the EPA guide, *Radon Reduction in New Construction, An Interim Guide* (OPA-87-009) or the more detailed EPA publication *Radon-Resistant Residential New Construction* (EPA-600/8-88-087).

To obtain copies of any of the above documents, contact your State Radiation Program Office or EPA regional office.

## What You Should Do and When

### Confirmation of Radon Levels

At present, EPA is advising homeowners to test their houses for radon using a short-term (two- to seven-day) screening measurement device. If the initial test results show 4 picocuries per liter (pCi/L) of the gas, or more, follow up measurements should be taken to confirm. If the follow-up measurements also indicate levels over 4 pCi/L, homeowners should take radon reduction actions.

Most homeowners whose initial measurement falls below 4 pCi/L will probably let the matter rest at that point. However, EPA reminds you that the greater the reduction in radon, the greater the reduction in health risk. That is why the Agency encourages even homeowners with radon levels below 4 pCi/L to reduce them still further, although techniques currently available may not be able to achieve such reductions.

If you have further questions about how to interpret your initial and follow-up radon measurements, consult *A Citizen's Guide to Radon.*

### How Soon to Take Action

If follow-up measurements confirm elevated radon levels in the living area of your house, action to reduce the levels is recommended in the following time frame:

• **Less than about 4 pCi/L:** Although radon levels in this range may represent a significant health risk, only limited information on cost-effective reduction methods for this range is currently available. Increasing ventilation and limiting the time spent in areas of the house with higher radon concentrations may help reduce risks.

• **4 to 20 pCi/L:** Action should be undertaken to reduce radon levels as low as possible within a year or two.

• **20 to 200 pCi/L:** Action should be undertaken to reduce radon levels as low as possible within several months.

• **Greater than 200 pCi/L:** Action should be undertaken to reduce radon levels within several weeks. If this is not feasible, a temporary increase in ventilation or a temporary relocation should be considered.

### The Four Major ways to Reduce Radon

Radon reduction methods described in this section fall into four different categories based upon their operating principles: soil gas suction, sealing, house pressure control, and house ventilation. It is useful to think of the first three as preventive, and the last as an after-the-fact response to radon. These methods are often used in combination.

All four methods are described in detail in Part Two, as are air cleaners and the problem of radon in water. It should be noted here that the cost, complexity, and potential for reducing radon vary considerably among the four methods, depending on a number of factors. When evaluating the various alternatives, you should consider the level of reduction needed, the house type, installation and operation costs, pros and cons of system maintenance, and local climate and geology.

In general, with moderate to high radon levels (more than 20 pCi/L), current experience suggests that soil gas suction—especially subslab suction—is the most appropriate radon reduction technique. In fact, subslab suction systems are often installed in houses with low to moderate radon levels (less than 20 pCi/L) because of their reliable performance and potential for maximum radon reduction. Nevertheless, if the radon is low to moderate, you might consider natural house ventilation and sealing of suspected radon entry routes because of the lower installation costs involved.

### Before Choosing A Radon Reduction Method

Selecting the right radon reduction method for a specific house can be a complicated decision. You have to take into account such factors as the source of the radon and how the specific characteristics of the house affect radon entry, questions that can often be answered through a series of diagnostic observations and measurements.

Remember this key point: Each house is unique. A radon reduction technique that is successful in one house may not work as well even in a seemingly similar house because of variations in the underlying soils, specific house design features, and occupant activities. Such differences affect the results obtained by using the radon reduction methods described in this guide. That is why a detailed house inspection is so important in diagnosing a radon problem.

You should carefully inspect your house before choosing a radon reduction method. A typical inspection includes the identification of potential radon entry routes (e.g., cracks in slabs or walls, open sumps, etc.) and those house design features or appliances that may enhance radon entry (e.g., air-consuming appliances, chimneys, etc).

When more detailed diagnostic inspections are required, these are often done by radon reduction contractors. For example, if house ventilation is under consideration, the rate of natural air infiltration into the house might be measured. A radon reduction contractor would have the knowledge, expertise, and equipment to do so.

The more extensive the diagnostic information collected, the better one is able to assess a home's needs and select an effective radon reduction method, although increased diagnostics can also increase your costs.

### What to Look For in a Radon Reduction Method

There is a very wide range of radon reduction options. Choosing among them can be overwhelming for many homeowners.

In choosing the system right for your situation and your budget, you should keep in mind the following guidelines:

- The system should be a permanent part of the structure with a long life expectancy.
- Natural house ventilation (e.g., opening of windows) should be considered only a temporary solution.

- A warning device should be installed on all active (fan-assisted) systems to warn of system failure.

- System components should be fully and accurately labeled (what each component is, who to contact for service, etc.).

- The system should not reduce the comfort of the living space; nor should it be intrusive or noisy.

- Energy costs should be minimized.

- Radon levels should be reduced to the lowest possible levels.

- Radon levels should be monitored annually under all systems.

### Different Approaches to Radon Reduction
### Easy Preliminary Steps

If you are unable to install a permanent radon reduction system as soon as the EPA suggests, you can still take some steps that might reduce radon levels at little cost. These steps, which are discussed more fully in the "Radon-Reduction Methods" section, include increasing your house's ventilation and sealing suspected routes of radon entry.

### Do-It-Yourself Techniques

Homeowners with skill and experience in house repairs might consider installing a do-it-yourself radon reduction system. The steps involved are often similar to common construction and house repair practices. If a homeowner feels comfortable with the principles behind the system, then he or she might consider installing it to save money. The first step in planning a do-it-yourself installation is to obtain a copy of the manual: *Application of Radon Reduction Methods*. (EPA/625/5-88/024)

### Phased and Combined Installations

Depending on the initial radon level measured in the home and the amount of radon reduction desired, you might consider installing your system in phases. An easily installed system with a relatively low installation cost can be attempted and then added

to if necessary. One approach might include an increase in house ventilation and sealing of suspected radon entry routes. These relatively simple techniques are especially attractive for a homeowner-installed system, or when radon levels are relatively low and an expensive system is not desired for the initial attempt at radon reduction.

Phased installation also provides you protection against contractors who may try to install a more expensive system than is really needed. Of course, if simple methods ultimately prove ineffective, you should go ahead and invest in a more complex system, such as subslab suction.

When attempting to lower highly elevated radon levels, it may be necessary to install a combination of methods. For example, multiple methods may be necessary when both your underlying soil and your well water are radon sources (see "Radon in Water" on page 463).

### Selecting a Radon Reduction Contractor

If you are unable to reduce radon levels enough through do-it-yourself steps, you should consider hiring a contractor experienced in radon reduction. Since radon reduction is a new field, it is unlikely that contractors in every part of the country will have extensive experience in this kind of work. You should request references and ask your Better Business Bureau about the experience and credentials of any contractor you consider.

To obtain local lists of radon reduction contractors, contact your state radiological health officials or local public health officials. Some states require that contractors work be licensed or certified. Local building trade associations, realtors' associations, local building supply houses, chambers of commerce, home improvement firms, and neighbors also may be able to supply information on contractors in your area.

When evaluating and comparing contractors, you should consider:

- In how many houses has the contractor installed radon reduction systems?

- What results were achieved?

- Will the contractor provide references?

- What types of diagnostic testing does the contractor do before designing and installing the radon reduction system?

- Will the contractor take the time to explain exactly what the work will entail?

- How will the contractor determine system performance?

- What type of guarantee, if any, does the contractor provide?

- How does the contractor's cost estimate compare with those of other contractors?

**Post-Installation Testing**

Both short-term and long-term testing of radon levels are important following installation of the radon reduction system.

Short-term testing is needed shortly after the installation of a reduction system to determine if radon levels have been adequately reduced. A two- to seven-day measurement taken at least one day after system installation is usually the best way to initially test the system's effectiveness. This is because a longer-term measurement may not provide information quickly enough if radon levels have not been satisfactorily lowered. However, once a short-term test indicates a system is working, a long-term device may be desired to check your system's long-term effectiveness. Some contractors may take short-term post-installation measurements using a continuous radon monitor. If so, readings should be gathered for a period of no less than two days.

In addition to monitoring radon levels, post-installation diagnostic measurements should be made to ensure that active (fan-assisted) systems are operating properly. Potential modifications for better system operation and increased radon reduction may also be identified by the diagnostic tests. If the need for additional radon reduction is indicated, it may be possible to modify the existing system. If not, it may be necessary to install an entirely new system.

Once the system has been fine-tuned and is working properly, annual use of alpha track or electric (long-term) detectors or seasonal use of charcoal canisters or electric (short-term) detectors is recommended to monitor the system's continuing performance. Long-term monitoring of radon is important because radon levels can vary significantly between seasons and over a period of years.

If you feel that you might forget to place or remove the detectors used for long-term monitoring, you may also want to consider installing an automatic warning device or indicator. Such devices, which are now commercially available, alert the homeowner if radon levels exceed a certain limit. Further information can be obtained from your state's radon program office.

## Radon Reduction Methods

### Preventing Radon Entry
### Soil Gas Suction

Soil gas suction—especially subslab suction—is the most widely used of all radon reduction methods because of its effectiveness in *preventing* the entry of radon gas into homes. It works by drawing away radon from under and around the house before it can enter the structure.

The objective of soil gas suction is to reduce the air pressure under the house's concrete slab, or in its block walls, to a pressure lower than that in the house. This reverses the flow of radon; instead of seeping into the house, it is sucked out.

Where radon reductions of at least 80 percent are required, some form of active (fan-assisted) soil gas suction is usually necessary and always highly desirable. To enhance the system's effectiveness and to reduce the energy costs resulting from increased exhaust of air from the house into the soil, major openings in the slab and walls should always be sealed. In such cases, soil gas suction is used in conjunction with the sealing techniques described in the next section.

Subslab permeability (also known as "subslab communication"), often mentioned in discussions of soil gas suction, refers to the ability of air to move through the material underlying the house. Material with a large particle size such as clean coarse gravel is more permeable than a material of small particle size such as a clay soil. Soil gas suction techniques are most successful in houses with good subslab permeability.

Types of soil gas suction include subslab suction (the most popular), drain tile suction, and block wall suction.

- **Subslab:** For subslab suction, pipes are inserted through the slab directly into the crushed rock or soil. A fan sucks radon-containing soil gas from under the slab through the pipes, releasing it into the outdoor air. In a crawl space with an earthen floor, this can be done by applying suction under a membrane such as a polyethylene sheet laid over the soil.

- **Drain Tile:** In some houses, water is directed away from the foundation by perforated pipes called drain tiles installed beside the foundation of the house. The tiles usually drain either to an above-grade discharge spot located away from the house, or to an internal sump. If these drain tiles form a complete loop around the exterior or interior of the footings, they may be used to draw radon away from the surrounding soil. Since drain tiles are usually located near major radon entry routes, drawing soil gas away via the drain tiles can reduce or prevent radon entry into the house. If the permeability of the underlying soil or aggregate is sufficient, it is possible that suction on the tiles can extend underneath the entire slab.

- **Block Wall:** The concrete blocks used to construct many basement walls contain hollow spaces that are normally connected both vertically and horizontally. Radon from the soil, entering the wall through joints, pores, and cracks, can move through these hollow spaces and enter the basement through similar openings on the interior side, or through uncapped openings in the top row of blocks. Block wall suction removes the radon from these void spaces before it can enter the house by creating a zone of lower pressure that reverses the direction of soil gas flow.

Maintenance requirements, fan noise, and operating costs associated with active soil gas suction systems can be avoided if the soil gas suction system is designed to run passively, without a fan. Such systems rely on temperature differences and wind to create a natural suction in the vent stack. There are insufficient data at present for a sound assessment of the effectiveness of passive soil gas suction techniques, and optimal designs cannot be recommended until more information becomes available. However, initial data have not been encouraging.

The soil gas suction systems covered in this section are active systems (operated under suction).

It may be possible to operate some of these systems by applying pressure rather than suction to the soil gas in the space under slabs or within block walls, but the effectiveness of pressurization has not been widely confirmed in the field. In fact, there is some evidence to indicate that pressure might cause radon, soil moisture, termite control pesticides, and odors to enter the living space.

The principles of operation for each type of soil gas suction system are described below in more complete detail.

### Subslab Suction

**When To Use:** Subslab suction tends to be most effective with slabs with underlying clean, coarse gravel or permeable soil. Even if the permeability underneath the slab is not good, subslab suction may still be applicable, depending on the number and location of suction pipes and the use of a suitable fan. Before undertaking subslab suction, it is a good idea to measure air movement under the slab to make sure that the area has adequate permeability.

**Reductions:** Subslab suction systems can reduce radon levels by 80 to 99 percent when permeability underneath the slab is good, in most cases by over 90 percent.

**How to Install:** Installation of such system is not a simple do-it-yourself job, although homeowners with the necessary skills and equipment may be able to do it successfully, especially when it is known that a good layer (e.g., four inches) of crushed rock or permeable soil lies beneath the slab.

Individual polyvinylchloride (PVC) pipes are inserted verti-

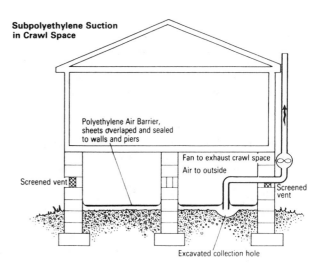

**Subpolyethylene Suction in Crawl Space**

Polyethylene Air Barrier, sheets overlaped and sealed to walls and piers

Fan to exhaust crawl space Air to outside

Screened vent

Screened vent

Excavated collection hole

cally through the slab from inside the house in order to reach the soil beneath it. The number of pipes needed depends on the permeability of the material underneath the slab and on the strength and location of the radon source (if subslab permeability is very good, one suction pipe may be sufficient).

A fan connected to the pipes draws the soil gas out from under the house. Fans are commonly located in an attic area or on the exterior of the house. The exhaust ends of these pipes are extended to roof level and placed away from any windows or vents that could allow the radon to re-enter the house. To increase the effectiveness of a subslab suction system, an effort should always be made to seal all major openings in the slab and walls. To ensure that the system is drawing enough air, it should include an easily checked pressure gauge in the piping.

In basements with a sump, the sump pit can be used as a ready-made hole through the slab. The sump should be capped with an air-tight cover, fitted with a water trap if needed, and then vented. The effectiveness of suction on the sump will depend on the permeability of the material underneath the slab, the presence of drain tiles emptying into the sump, and the strength and location of the radon source.

In crawl spaces, the earthen floor can be covered with membrane (such as polyethylene sheets) and sealed around the perimeter. Then the radon in the soil gas beneath the sheets can be actively sucked out to the outdoors. In small crawl spaces with few support pillars, some sub-membrane suction systems have worked effectively without sealing.

**Cost and Maintenance:** Contractor installation should cost about $800 to $2,000, depending on the number of suction pipes. If subslab permeability is poor or if the slab area is finished living space, costs could be higher. For a do-it-yourself installation, materials (i.e., fans, pipes, etc.) might cost

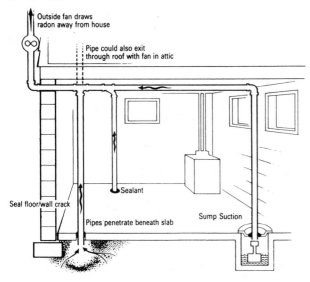

**Subslab Suction**

Outside fan draws radon away from house

Pipe could also exit through roof with fan in attic

Sealant

Seal floor/wall crack

Pipes penetrate beneath slab

Sump Suction

as little as $300. Typical annual operating costs would be about $30 for the fan and about $100 for the heating and cooling penalty resulting from the increase in ventilation. Maintenance includes fan inspections and repairs, sealing inspections, and, if a pressure gauge has been installed in the piping, a check to see that the suction in the pipes is within the desired range.

## Drain Tile Suction

**When To Use:** Where tiles are present, drain tile suction is often a cost-effective approach to reducing elevated radon levels. Usually, the system can be installed in an unobtrusive location, and thus is an especially attractive option in houses where the lower level is finished living space.

These systems work best when the drain tiles form a complete loop around the house. Unless the homeowner observed construction of the house or has a set of house plans detailing drain tile locations, it is often difficult to determine the exact extent of the drain tile loop. Often, drain tile loops either are not complete or some of them have been blocked or damaged. As a result, part of the substructure may not be effectively treated by a drain tile suction system.

**Reductions:** If the drain tile loop is relatively complete, radon reductions of 90 to 99 percent may be obtained. If there is only a partial drain tile loop, reductions may be much lower, depending on subslab permeability.

**How to Install:** If the tiles drain to an above-grade discharge area, an exhaust fan can be attached to a PVC collection pipe to draw radon out of the soil. To maintain an effective airtight system, a water-filled trap or reverse flow valve must be installed in the collection pipe beyond where the fan is attached. The water trap must be placed below the frost line and must be kept filled with water.

If the tiles drain to a sump inside the house, the sump should be capped with an airtight cover and suction drawn from the sump cavity. Ideally, the exhaust fan should be located outside the house to avoid leakage of radon into the house. Non-submersible pumps (if present) should be replaced by submersible units to facilitate sealing and to avoid rusting of the pump motor. (Note: the presence of a sump does not necessarily mean that the house has drain tiles discharging into the sump.)

**Cost and Maintenance:** Costs vary widely, depending on the characteristics of your house and the finish desired for the area around the installation. For a contractor-installed system draining to an above-average discharge, costs would range from about $700 to $1,500; for a contractor-installed system draining to an internal sump, the range is $800 to $2000. For a homeowner-installed system, material costs (i.e., fan, pipes, etc.) are about $300. Annual operating costs include about $30 for the fan and roughly $100 for the heating or cooling costs resulting from increased house ventilation. Maintenance for a drain tile suction system includes periodic fan inspec-

## Drain Tile Suction where Tile Drains to an Above-Grade Discharge

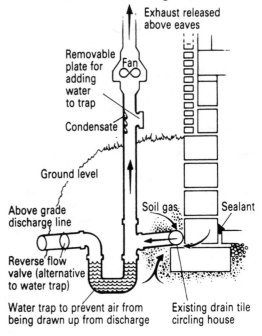

Exhaust released above eaves

Removable plate for adding water to trap

Fan

Condensate

Ground level

Above grade discharge line

Reverse flow valve (alternative to water trap)

Water trap to prevent air from being drawn up from discharge

Soil gas

Sealant

Existing drain tile circling house

tions and repairs, sealing inspections, and periodic filling of water traps (if applicable).

## Block Wall Suction

**When to Use:** Block wall suction can only be used in houses built with hollow-block foundation walls. Because its effectiveness can be difficult to predict, consideration should first be given to a subslab suction system, unless the house has poor subslab permeability. In houses where subslab suction does not adequately treat the block walls, subslab and wall suction might applied in combination.

Block wall ventilation can be costly. It is most applicable when initial radon readings are moderate to high. Another disadvantage associated with block wall suction is that *all* major wall openings must be adequately sealed in order for the technique to be effective. In addition, the leakiness of the walls may cause a greater increase in heating and cooling costs than either subslab or drain tile suction, although such added costs may be reduced by painting or coating the interior block walls.

**Reductions:** Radon reductions can be as high as 90 to 99 percent, provided that the walls are adequately sealed, and there are no major radon entry routes remote from the under-

### Block Wall Suction (Pipe-in-Wall Approach)

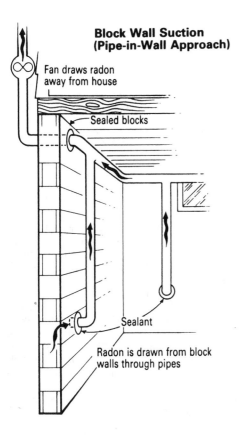

Fan draws radon away from house

Sealed blocks

Sealant

Radon is drawn from block walls through pipes

finished basement costs from about $1,500 to $2,500; a baseboard system in a similar basement could cost as much as $2,000 to $3,000. If the basement is finished living space, the costs could increase. Materials for a do-it-yourself installation cost about $300 to $1000 for a wall suction system and considerably more for a baseboard system. Annual operating costs for a block wall suction system would be about $30 to $60 for the fan and about $200 to $500 for additional heating and cooling costs resulting from the additional ventilation.

Maintenance requirements include fan inspections and repairs, sealing inspections, and checks to ensure that combustion appliances are not backdrafting. Backdrafting can occur when the suction of the radon venting system causes air to be drawn back down flue pipes or chimneys. If backdrafting is observed, one might consider operating the system under pressure. However, pressurization could cause soil moisture, termite control pesticides, and odors to enter the living space.

### Sealing Radon Entry Routes

Sealing, closure, or isolation of radon entry routes limits the flow of radon gas into the house. Radon can move through cracks infloor slabs and walls, areas of exposed soil (such as

lying slab. If the walls are not sufficiently sealed or the slab is badly cracked, 50 to 70 percent reductions are more typical.

**How to Install:** There are two alternative approaches to block wall suction. The simplest approach is to insert one or two PVC pipes into each wall and to draw radon out with fans vented to the outdoors. Another way involves installing a plastic or sheet-metal baseboard duct around the perimeter of the basement floor/wall crack. Holes are drilled into the hollow spaces in the block wall behind the duct. The baseboard approach generally results in better suction and tends to be less obtrusive but is more expensive; it is most appropriate where the hollow portions of the block wall are not continuous, when drainage problems exist, or when a perimeter (French) drain is present. With either system, the exhaust ends of all pipes should extend to roof level and be placed away from windows, doors, or vents that could allow the radon to re-enter the house.

To improve performance and reduce operating costs, all major openings must be sufficiently sealed. In some houses, adequate sealing is difficult, if not impossible. (See "Sealing Radon Entry Routes," above right.)

**Cost and Maintentance:** Installing exhaust pipes in an un-

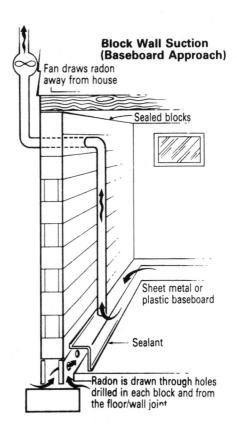

### Block Wall Suction (Baseboard Approach)

Fan draws radon away from house

Sealed blocks

Sheet metal or plastic baseboard

Sealant

Radon is drawn through holes drilled in each block and from the floor/wall joint

an earthen crawl space floor), untrapped floor drains, sumps, perimeter (French) drains, and open block tops in hollow-block foundation walls. Also, floor and wall cracks, below-grade utility penetrations, and pores in block walls can sometimes let in significant amounts of radon since they are often distributed over wide areas.

**When to Use:** Sealing, closure, or isolation of radon entry routes can be applied to any substructure type. In fact, sealing of major accessible entry routes *should* be considered an essential part of most approaches to radon reduction.

The effectiveness of sealing is limited by our ability to identify, access, and seal major radon entry routes. Complete sealing is often impractical. In some houses, certain areas will be difficult, if not impossible to reach and/or seal without significant expense. Hard-to-reach areas include: tops of block walls, spaces between block walls and exterior brick veneer, openings concealed by masonry fireplaces and chimneys, the floor above a crawl space, and below-ground areas that have been converted into living space. In addition, settling foundations, seismic activity, and expanding floor cracks continually open new entry routes and reopen old ones. Another limitation of sealing is that bonding between the sealant and the surface is often difficult to make and maintain.

In a house with low to moderate radon levels (less than 20 pCi/L), sealing can be a relatively economical first attempt at radon reduction, if the work can be done by the homeowner. It may reduce radon to acceptable levels. However, in houses with high radon levels, sealing alone usually will not reduce radon levels to below 4 pCi/L.

**Reductions:** Radon reductions observed when only sealing is used vary widely between houses, depending on the importance of the entry routes sealed, the nature of the remaining unsealed entry routes, and the effectiveness of the sealants chosen and the way they were applied. Radon reductions resulting from extensive sealing efforts are typically 50 to 70 percent, although reductions of as high as 90 percent have been observed.

**How to Install:** Once radon entry routes are identified, the methods and materials depend on the specific entry routes. Selection of an appropriate sealant and proper surface preparation are critical.

Large areas of exposed soil, such as those found in crawl spaces, can sometimes be effectively covered and sealed with a polyethylene sheet. It is also possible, if needed, to vent the air under the sheet to the outdoors, using a fan (see the "Soil Gas Suction" section, page 454). In extreme cases, a concrete slab can be poured over areas of exposed soil and then treated as a basement suitable for subslab suction.

Drainage areas such as sumps, floor drains, and perimeter drains are also significant radon entry routes. Sumps can be capped and sealed to reduce radon entry. If needed for drainage, a drain trap can be installed in the sump. Floor drains can also be rebuilt to include a trap. Traps allow water that collects on basement floors to drain away but eliminate the entry of radon. If you use a water trap, keep it full of water to maintain its effectiveness.

When capping and sealing a sump, it might be advisable to install a vent so that the air trapped in the sump is ex-

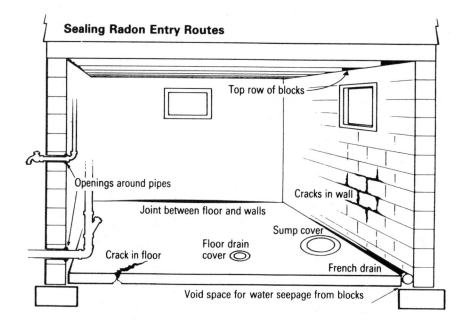

**Sealing Radon Entry Routes**

Top row of blocks

Openings around pipes

Cracks in wall

Joint between floor and walls

Sump cover

Crack in floor

Floor drain cover

French drain

Void space for water seepage from blocks

hausted to the outdoors (see "Soil Gas Suction" page 454). Using a sump hole as the location for subslab suction is often very effective in reducing radon levels.

Perimeter (French) drains can be sealed with flowable urethane sealant. Cracks, joints, and utility penetrations are most effectively sealed with polyurethane caulking materials. Field testing has shown that latex-based caulks—even silicone—do not adhere well to these surfaces. Proper surface preparation is critical. Manufacturer's instructions should always be carefully followed to ensure a good bond.

Paints or other pore-filling coatings are useful for large, porous surfaces such as hollow-block basement walls; however, surface cracks should first be treated with caulking material to prevent leakage. Three or more coats of Latex paint will probably be required to fully seal block pores; one of two coats of waterproof paint or epoxy paint might be equally effective. Another option for cracked or porous walls and other large surface areas is applying a radon-impermeable film sealed with caulking or tape at the joints.

Uncapped tops of hollow-block walls are also significant means for radon entry; if accessible, they should be sealed with mortar or urethane foam, or covered by strips of wood cemented over the openings.

**Cost and Maintenance:** Some do-it-yourself sealing can be accomplished with materials costing $100 or less. More extensive efforts, such as the application of coatings and membranes by a contractor, can cost as much as $500. The cost for a contractor to install a sump cover would be about $100. If a trap is needed, costs may increase by several hundred dollars. It might cost as much as $500 for a contractor to add a water trap to a floor drain. In many cases, however, the work can be done much less expensively by the homeowner.

Maintenance includes periodic inspections and resealing if a crack reopens or if settling causes new entry routes to occur. If a water drain trap is installed, it should be refilled as necessary.

### House Pressure Control

A primary factor contributing to the flow of radon into a house is the lower air pressure of the house's substructure relative to its underlying soil. This phenomenon—known as "house depressurization"—can be caused by homeowner activities and appliance usage, house design and construction features, as well as weather conditions. If house depressurization is minimized or eliminated, then radon entry will be reduced. In fact, if the lower levels of the house can be maintained at an air pressure higher than that of the underlying soil gas, then the flow of radon can be stopped. The process of maintaining a higher pressure in the house relative to the underlying soil is called "house pressurization."

While house pressurization should work in theory, actual experience with this technique is still limited. Testing is now underway to provide additional information, but until more conclusive data are available, house pressure control techniques should only be applied if they are low-cost. Otherwise, soil gas suction techniques should be considered.

**When to Use:** Simple, low-cost corrective steps can sometimes be implemented by the homeowner in a house that is suitable. House pressure control techniques are most effective in houses with tight basements and and/or heated crawl spaces. These systems are most effective in houses that have no combustion appliances upstairs. In addition, the homeowner must understand the system and keep lower-level doors and windows closed.

**Reductions:** Radon reductions based on house pressure control techniques vary, depending on the characteristics of the house, but can be significant when the pressure is neutralized (i.e., when indoor air pressure matches outdoor or subslab pressure) or maintained at a positive level (i.e., the indoor pressure is kept higher than the outdoor or subslab pressure). In some situations, EPA has seen radon reductions of up to 90 percent effective from systems maintaining a positive pressure level. However, these techniques are still being refined, and more definitive data will not be available until further research is completed.

**Avoidance of House Depressurization—How to Install:** Exhaust fans, such as window fans, kitchen fans, bathroom fans, attic fans, clothes dryers, and whole-house fans, can be significant sources of house depressurization. If these exhaust fans must be used, consider opening windows near the fan, or in some cases, reorienting the fan to blow back into the house.

Fireplaces, coal or wood stoves, central furnaces, water heaters, and other vented combustion devices can also cause significant house depressurization. The installation of a permanent system for supplying outdoor air will assist in reducing house depressurization caused by these air-consuming appliances.

If you install air-supply ductwork for appliances, you should make sure that it includes a barometric damper to prevent cold air from entering when the appliance is not being operated. The outside opening for the ductwork should also be screened to bar pests and debris. Many combustion units are designed to accept outside air, but for others modification may violate codes and be unsafe. You can try directing outdoor air to a point near a gas furnace or enclosing the furnace in a room that is vented to the outdoors, or—as a temporary solution—you can keep windows open near the appliance to facilitate the influx of outdoor air.

To reduce depressurization caused by central, forced-air heating and cooling systems, seal off any cold-air return registers that are in your basement or crawl space. Where accessible, cold-air return ducting in your basement or crawl space should be carefully taped or caulked to reduce any leakage of radon-containing air into the ducts. (Note: All return air ducts are under negative pressure when the air-handling fan is operating.)

Depressurization caused by wind can be reduced by opening windows on more than one side of the house (see "House Ventilation," page 460). Closing air-flow by-passes between floors, such as stair wells, utility penetrations, and laundry chutes, may also reduce radon entry by limiting house depressurization.

**House Pressurization—How to Install:** Although house pressurization techniques are experimental, experience has shown that the lower level of a house, such as a basement or crawl space, may be pressurized by blowing air in from either the upstairs living space or the outside.

To enhance the effectiveness of house pressurization, you should make an effort to seal as many major openings as possible between the basement and upper floors, and limit the opening of doors and windows in the pressurized area.

In order to reduce fan noise and vibrations in the living area, the pressurizing fan can be located on the floor of the basement or crawl space with ducting connecting the fan to the outdoor air supply.

**Cost and Maintenance:** The cost of avoiding house depressurization will be fairly low if the system can be installed by the homeowner. In some cases, there may be an increase in appliance operating cost due to the temperature difference of the outside air being drawn in.

Contractor installation of a house or basement pressurization system could cost as much as $1,000 to $2,500, and possibly more if additional sealing is needed. Additional electricity costs for fan operation would be roughly $40 a year. Heating and cooling penalties caused by increased ventilation would be as much as $500 a year.

## Getting Rid of Radon Once It's Already In

### House Ventilation

Some natural ventilation occurs in all houses as outside air is drawn in through cracks and openings. Indoor is replaced by outdoor air about once every half hour in a leaky house and about once every 10 hours in a tight house. In technical terms, these are referred to as 2.0 and 0.1 air changes per hour, respectively. Typical U.S. houses exchange air about once every 1 to 2 hours (1 to 0.5 air changes per hour). By increasing house ventilation, you can reduce radon levels and also combat other indoor air pollutants (such as termite or other pest-control treatments).

An increase in house ventilation—by opening lower-level windows, doors, and vents or by blowing outdoor air into the house—reduces radon levels both by replacing indoor air with outdoor air and by reducing the forces that draw radon into the house. Since the mechanism responsible for radon entry is a lower air pressure in the house relative to the surrounding soil, neutralization of that pressure through house ventilation can help to reduce indoor radon levels.

Ventilation can be increased either naturally (by opening doors, windows, or vents) or by using a fan, but in most climates, those two methods can lead to loss of indoor heat or air conditioning. To save on your utility bills, you may want to install a heat recovery ventilator (HRV)—also called an air-to-air heat exchanger—which will increase house ventilation while recovering some of your heat during winter or your air conditioning during summer.

### Natural and Forced-Air Ventilation

**When To Use:** Natural and forced-air (fan-assisted) ventilation can generally be used in almost any house and usually can be implemented directly by the homeowner. Forced-air ventilation may be preferable if you want to maintain a certain air exchange rate independent of weather conditions. Basements and crawl spaces can be easily ventilated and can often be closed off from the rest of the house. In fact, natural ventilation of the crawl space is one of the first radon reduction options to be considered in crawl space houses.

The major disadvantages of natural and forced-air ventilation are increased energy costs and/or discomforts during extreme weather conditions, security concerns (e.g., from open windows), and the increased entry of unfiltered outdoor air into the house. Natural and forced air ventilation are only practical, permanent, year-round solutions to elevated radon levels if the area to be ventilated is completely closed off from the living space, such as a crawl space or an unused basement. However, for houses with very high indoor radon levels, ventilation can be an effective short-term radon reduction approach until permanent radon reduction measures can be taken.

Other problems more specific to forced-air ventilation are excessive fan noise (depending on system design) and the potential for moisture to condense and freeze inside the exterior walls during cold weather.

**Reductions:** Although natural or forced-air ventilation is capable of significant radon reductions, the reduction is highly variable and depends on the specific house. Ventilation would, for instance, tend to have more of an effect in reducing radon levels in a tight house than a leaky house.

**How to Install:** When using natural or forced-air ventilation, always ventilate the lowest level of the house that is in contact with the soil—if possible, a basement or crawl space. Ventilating only the upper levels of a house should be avoided since it might actually increase radon levels by causing radon-containing soil gas to be pulled in through the lower levels. Windows and vents should be opened on all sides of a house or, at a minimum, on opposite sides.

Possible designs for forced-air ventilation include the installation of inward-blowing fans in windows and vents, or the use of duts from outside vents connected to existing furnace ducting so as to supply additional fresh air to the house. The operation of exhaust fans—such as a whole house fan—is not recommended since they tend to reduce the pressure in the house and thus increase radon entry.

When installing a forced-air ventilation system, always place the fan so that air is blown into the house. The fan(s) should be large enough to provide at least 500 to 1,000 cubic feet per minute (cfm) of air depending on the initial radon level, the reduction desired, as well as house size and leakiness.

If the ventilated area, such as a crawl space or basement, is to be closed off from the living space, utility pipes should

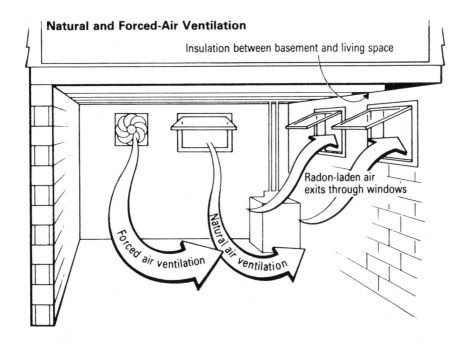

**Natural and Forced-Air Ventilation**

Insulation between basement and living space

Radon-laden air exits through windows

Forced air ventilation

Natural air ventilation

be properly insulated to prevent freezing. A homeowner might also consider insulating the floor area between the substructure and living space to reduce heating or cooling costs and increase comfort levels.

**Cost and Maintenance:** Unless materials are needed to keep windows or vents open, or to prevent unauthorized entry through these openings, there are no installation costs for natural ventilation. However, the homeowner can expect an increase in heating or cooling costs of 10 percent to over 300 percent during weather extremes. The only maintenance requirements are the occasional adjustments to open windows, doors, or vents for comfort or other reasons. Ventilation could vary from the costs of a fan (about $30 to $200) to the modification of a central furnace to supply fresh air (as much as $1000). Operation costs related to increased heating or cooling are comparable to those for natural ventilation. The cost of electricity or fan operation could range from about $50 to almost $300 a year. Depending on the system, maintenance would include periodic inspection and perhaps lubrication of the fan(s), along with fan repairs, if necessary. If the system includes a filter, it will need periodic cleaning.

**Heat Recovery Ventilation**

**When to Use:** Heat recovery ventilators (HRV) are most useful in climates with cold winters and/or hot, humid summers. They may be installed in any substructure type and can be designed to ventilate all or part of a house.

The primary advantages of the HRV are reduced heating or cooling costs (depending on season) associated with natural and forced-air ventilation, and greater levels of personal comfort during weather extremes. HRVs ensure a constant degree of ventilation throughout the year and avoid potential house security problems associated with open windows. HRVs can also improve air quality in houses afflicted with other pollutant sources or with inadequate air exchange rates.

For an HRV to be a reasonable mitigation option, the savings resulting from the reduced energy penalty should more than offset the initial cost of the HRV. Therefore, in areas of relatively mild climate, it may be less expensive to reduce radon levels through natural or forced-air ventilation. Before a decision is made to install an HRV, the unit should be evaluated for potential energy savings and radon reduction. The costs should then be compared with those of other available options.

**Reductions:** Radon reductions generally range from 50 to 75 percent with 200 to 400 cfm of HRV capacity. If an HRV is intended as the only technique to reduce radon levels to below 4 pCi/L, then the initial radon level in the house should be no greater than about 10 pCi/L. As with natural and forced-air ventilation, reductions would tend to be greater in a tight house.

**How to Install:** In general, HRVs are either ducted systems with supply and return ducts servicing different parts of the house, or wall-mounted units similar to wall-mounted air-conditioning units. Fully ducted systems should be designed and installed by an experienced heating, ventilating, and air-condi-

## Heat Recovery Ventilation (HRV)

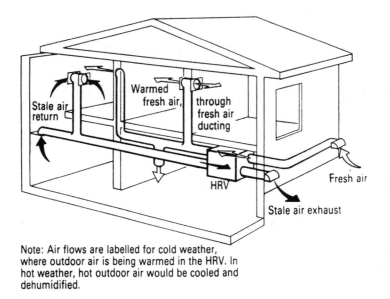

Note: Air flows are labelled for cold weather, where outdoor air is being warmed in the HRV. In hot weather, hot outdoor air would be cooled and dehumidified.

tioning (HVAC) contrator since the system's effectiveness in reducing indoor radon levels is sensitive to proper installation, ducting, and adjustment. Wall mounted units are usually less complex and can sometimes be homeowner-installed. The expected radon reduction will be moderate with a fully ducted HRV and lower with a wall-mounted unit since the distribution of fresh air is not as effective with a wall unit.

HRVs typically include two fans, one blowing air into the house and the other pulling an equal amount of indoor air outdoors. About 50 to 80 percent of the heat (or cold) from the outgoing air is transferred to the indoor air. Since the HRV blows air out, its primary mechanism for radon reducton is through dilution of the indoor air. As a result, its ability to reduce radon levels through pressure neutralization is limited. To assist in sustaining a positive indoor air pressure, an HRV can intentionally be operated on an unbalanced basis so that the inflow is greater than the exhaust; however, this reduces the overall energy efficiency of the system.

The core and the fan of an HRV unit can be installed in an inconspicuous part of the house, such as a basement or utility room. In selecting a location, however, make sure that the installation of the ductwork is kept as simple as possible. To achieve sufficient air circulation, care should be taken to position the ducting so that the fresh-air supply is well removed from the stale-air return.

In comparing different HRVs, you should consider several factors. The fans should be properly sized for maximum flow with minimum power consumption, and there should be ade-

quate controls to prevent freezing of the coils in cold climates. The HRV should be capable of removing humidity when used in hot, humid climates. Also, a good HRV should recover 70 to 80 percent of the energy from the exhausted air.

**Cost and Maintenance:** The total installed cost for a ducted HRV unit delivering up to 150 to 200 cfm of air would typically range from about $800 to $2,500. Increasing the capacity from 300 to 400 cfm could increase the cost by roughly 25 to 50 percent, or by as much as 100 percent if a second 150 to 200 cfm unit is installed.

Annual operating costs for an HRV are seasonal—greatest during extremes of hot or cold weather—with the fan alone costing about $50 a year to operate. Assuming that the HRV is 50 to 80 percent energy efficient, the heating or cooling penalty will be only 20 to 50 percent of the penalty that would have occurred without the HRV.

Annual servicing of the HRV by a trained technician would cost about $50 to $100, and the cost of filter and fan replacement will vary between units.

### Air Cleaners

The radon reduction methods described in this section concentrate on methods of preventing radon gas from entering the house and removing it once it has already entered.

The health risks from radon are associated with the products of radon decay, and not the radon itself. Air cleaners are devices that either mechanically filter or electrostatically remove particles from the air. They are commonly used to condition indoor air for a variety of health and comfort reasons. Since radon decay products will rapidly attach to other particles in household air, there have been attempts to market air cleaners to reduce radon decay products in indoor air. While air cleaners can reduce the total concentration of radon decay products, they can actually *increase* the concentration of unattached decay products, possibly increasing the health risk.

EPA does not endorse the use of air cleaners as a method of reducing radon decay products in indoor air because this technology has not been demonstrated to be effective in reducing the health risks associated with radon. However, EPA believes that the available data do not warrant discontinuing the use of air cleaners already installed. Further research should lead to more definitive Agency guidance.

Some people also ask if the radon gas itself can be removed from the indoor air. While some research has been done on using charcoal to filter indoor air, more research is needed before the EPA can recommend such a technology.

## Radon in Water

In some parts of the country, radon in well water can be a significant contributor to elevated levels of indoor radon. The only known health concern involving radon in well water is the airborne radon that is released when the water is drawn up through pipes and agitated as it pours into sinks, tubs, and appliances. Household activities that use hot water, such as showering and washing dishes or clothes, can cause significant releases of waterborne radon into the air, particularly in the household areas where the water is used.

In general, 10,000 pCi/L of radon in water will contribute roughly 1 pCi/l of airborne radon throughout the house. In some areas, water from private wells or small community water systems can contain sufficient radon to contribute significantly to elevated levels within a house.

Elevated levels of radon in well water can be addressed by ventilating the house near the points of water usage; however, removing radon from the well water prior to use is preferable. Radon levels in water can be reduced either by a granulated activated carbon (GAC) unit or by aeration of the water. Typical systems cost about $1,000-$2,000 for a GAC unit and about $2,500 to $4,500 for an aeration unit. For more detailed information on radon in well water, refer to the EPA booklet, *Removal of Radon from Household Water* (OPA-87-011).

**Source:** *Radon Reduction Methods; A Homeowner's Guide*, 3rd ed. Environmental Protection Agency, 1989.

## Environmental Alphabet

Some have called it "ecobabble." Environmental organizations, government agencies, and scientists all have this in common: they tend to use—and sometimes overuse—a great many abbreviations, acronyms, and initialisms. For everyone who has ever been confused, stymied, or put off by references to NGOs, $LD_{50}$, EDB, $SO_2$, or NAAQS, here is a handy guide to the shorthand used in the world of environmental concerns.

Where a name has varying forms, alternative or additional words are placed in parentheses, for example:

**BOD,** biochemical (or biological) oxygen demand.
**MCL(G),** maximum containment level (goal).

**AAAS,** American Association for the Advancement of Science.
**AABGA,** American Association of Botanical Gardens and Arboreta.
**AALS,** Association of Arid Lands Studies.
**AARC,** Alliance for Acid Rain Control.
**AARD,** Agency for Agricultural Research and Development.
**AA-VS,** American Anti-Vivisection Society.
**AAZK,** American Association of Zoo Keepers.
**AAZPA,** American Association of Zoological Parks and Aquariums.
**ABA,** American Bar Association, or American Birding Association.
**ABF,** America the Beautiful Fund.
**ABS,** acrylonitrile butadiene styrene, or alkylbenzene sulfonate.
**ACA,** American Conservation Association, or ammoniacal copper arsenate.
**ACC,** Administrative Committee on Coordination.
**ACCA,** American Cave Conservation Association.
**ACD,** Atmospheric Chemistry Division.
**ACE,** Alliance for Clean Energy.
**ACEC,** areas of critical environmental concern.

**ACEEE,** American Council for an Energy Efficient Economy.
**ACH,** air changes per hour.
**AChE,** acetylcholinesterase.
**ACIC,** American Committee for International Conservation.
**ACM (ACBM),** asbestos-containing material (or building material).
**ACMP,** Advisory Committee on Marine Pollution.
**ACOPS,** Advisory Committee on Pollution of the Sea.
**ACP,** Air Carcinogen Policy.
**ACQUIRE,** Aquatic Information Retrieval.
**ACR,** acreage conservation reserve.
**ACS,** American Cetacean Society, American Chemical Society, Agricultural Cooperative Service, or American Canal Society.
**ACTS,** Asbestos Contractor Tracking System.
**ACWA,** American Clean Water Association.
**ADB,** African Development Bank, or Asian Development Bank.
**ADC,** Animal Damage Control.
**ADI,** acceptable daily intake.
**AE,** acid equivalent.
**AEA,** Atomic Energy Act.

**AEC,** Atomic Energy Commission.

**AEE,** Alliance for Environmental Education.

**AEM,** acoustic emission monitoring.

**AESOP,** Automated Electronic System for Ocean Pollution.

**AFA,** American Forestry Association.

**AFAAR,** American Fund for Alternatives to Animal Research.

**AFS,** American Fisheries Society.

**AFT,** American Farmland Trust.

**AGID,** Association of Geoscientists for International Development.

**AGRICOLA,** Agricultural Online Access.

**AHA,** American Humane Association.

**AHERA,** Asbestos Hazard Emergency Response Act.

**AHH,** arythydrocarbon hydroxylase.

**AHS,** American Hiking Society.

**AI,** active ingredient.

**AICE,** American Institute of Chemical Engineers.

**AICP,** American Institute of Certified Planners.

**AID,** Agency for International Development.

**AIDS,** acquired immune deficiency syndrome.

**AINA,** Arctic Institute of North America.

**AKA,** also known as.

**Al,** aluminum.

**AL,** acceptable level.

**ALA,** American Lung Association.

**ALARA,** as low as reasonably achievable.

**ALDF,** Animal Legal Defense Fund.

**ALIC,** Arid Land Information Center.

**ALS,** American Littoral Society.

**AMA,** American Medical Association.

**AMC,** Appalachian Mountain Club.

**AMS,** American Meteorological Society, Agricultural Marketing Service, or ammonium sulfamate.

**ANF,** a-naphthoflavone.

**ANSI,** American National Standards Institute.

**ANSS,** American Nature Study Society.

**ANWR,** Arctic National Wildlife Refuge.

**AOC,** area of concern, or American Oceans Campaign.

**AOML,** Atlantic Oceanographic and Meteorological Laboratory.

**AOU,** American Ornithologists' Union.

**APA,** American Planning Association.

**APCD(A)/AQMD,** Air Pollution Control District (or Association)/Air Quality Management District.

**APELL,** Awareness and Preparedness for Emergencies at Local Level.

**APHA,** American Public Health Association.

**APHIS,** Animal and Plant Health Inspection Service.

**API,** Animal Protection Institute, or American Petroleum Institute.

**APPEN,** Asian-Pacific People's Environment Network.

**AQCR,** Air Quality Control Region.

**AR,** area representative.

**ARAR,** applicable or relevent and appropriate standards, limitations, criteria, and requirements.

**ARB,** Air Resources Board.

**ARC,** Appalachian Regional Commission.

**ARCC,** American Rivers Conservation Council.

**ARENA,** Applied Research Ethics National Association.

**ARIC,** Air Resources Information Clearinghouse, or Acid Rain Information Clearinghouse.

**ARIP,** Accidental Release Information Program.

**ARL,** Air Resources Laboratory.

**ARM,** Air Resources Management, or Animal Rights Mobilization.

**ARO,** alternate regulatory option.

**ARS,** Agricultural Research Service.

**ARZ,** auto-restricted zone.

**ASA,** American Standards Association.

**ASCS,** Agricultural Stabilization and Conservation Service.

**ASDWA,** Association of State Drinking Water Administrators.

**ASEH,** American Society for Environmental History.

**ASF,** Americans for Safe Food, or Atlantic Salmon Federation.

**ASHAA,** Asbestos in Schools Hazard Abatement Act.

**ASHRAE,** American Society of Heating, Refrigerating, and Air-Conditioning Engineers.

**ASMFC,** Atlantic States Marine Fisheries Commission.

**ASPCA,** American Society for the Prevention of Cruelty to Animals.

**ASRL,** Atmospheric Sciences Research Laboratory.

**ASTIS,** Arctic Science and Technology Information System.

**ASTM,** American Society for Testing and Materials.

**ASTSWMO,** Association of State and Territorial Solid Waste Management Officials.

**ASZ,** American Society of Zoologists.

**AT,** advanced treatment, or alpha track.

**ATA,** American Trucking Association.

**ATAS,** Advance Technology Alert System.

**ATC,** Appalachian Trail Conference.

**ATD,** Atmospheric Technology Division.

**ATERIS,** Air Toxics Exposure and Risk Information System.

**ATF,** Alcohol, Tobacco, and Firearms Division of the U.S. Treasury.

**ATOM,** antimony tris(isooctyl mercaptoacetate).

**ATP,** adenosinetriphosphate.

**ATSDR,** Agency for Toxic Substances and Disease Registry.

**ATTF,** Air Toxics Task Force.

**ATTRA,** Appropriate Technology Transfer for Rural Areas.

**AVRDC,** Asian Vegetable Research and Development Center.

**AWA,** American Wilderness Alliance (now American Wildlands).

**AWF,** African Wildlife Foundation.

**AWI,** Animal Welfare Institute.

**AWIC,** Animal Welfare Information Center.

**AWL,** American Wildlands Alliance.

**A&WMA,** Air and Waste Management Association.

**A/WPR,** Air/Water Pollution Report.

**AWRA,** American Water Resources Association.

**AWWA,** American Water Works Association.

**BACT,** best available control technology.

**BADEA,** Arab Bank for Economic Development in Africa.

**BADT,** best available demonstrated technology.

**BaP** or **BAP,** benzo-a-pyrene.

**BAPMoN,** Background Air Pollution Monitoring Network.

**BARI,** Bangladesh Agricultural Research Institute.

**BART,** best available retrofit technology.

**BAT,** best available technology.

**BATEA,** best available technology economically achievable (or available).

**BBF,** broadbed and furrow system.

**BBP,** benzyl butyl phthalate.

**BCI,** Bat Conservation International.

**BCT,** best control technology, or best conventional pollutant control technology.

**BDAT,** best demonstrated achievable technology.

**BDT,** best demonstrated technology.

**Be,** beryllium.

**BEAR,** Biological Effects of Atomic Radiation.

**BEIR,** Biological Effects of Ionizing Radiation.

**BEJ,** best expert judgment.

**BGCS,** Botanical Gardens Conservation Secretariat.

**BGMV,** bean golden mosaic virus.

**BIC,** Bank Information Center.

**BIRC,** Bio-Integral Resource Center.

**BLM,** Bureau of Land Management.

**BMP,** best management practices.

**BNA,** ß-naphthylamine.

**BNF,** biological nitrogen fixation.

**BOD,** biochemical (or biological) oxygen demand.

**BOD5,** BOD over five days.

**BOF,** basic oxygen furnace.

**BOM,** Bureau of Mines.

**BOP,** basic oxygen process.

**BOR,** Bureau of Reclamation.

**BOSEX,** Baltic Open Sea Experiment.

**BOSTID,** Board on Science and Technology for International Development.

**BOYSNC,** beginning of year significant non-compliers.

**BPA,** Bonneville Power Administration.

**BPJ,** best professional judgment.

**BPT,** best practicable technology, best practicable control technology, or best practicable treatment.

**BQ,** Becquerel.

**BR,** biosphere reserve.

**BRAP,** Biometry and Risk Assessment Program.

**BRC,** below regulatory concern.

**BRF,** Bioresources Research Facility.

**BRI,** building-related illness.

**BSI,** British Standards Institution.

**BSO,** benzene-soluble organics.

**B.t.,** Bacillus thuringiensis.

**BTU OR Btu,** British thermal unit.

**BTZ,** below the treatment zone.

**BUN,** blood urea nitrogen.

**BWC,** Beauty Without Cruelty.

**C,** Celsius (formerly centigrade) temperature scale.

**Ca,** calcium.

**CA,** cooperation agreements, or corrective action.

**CAA,** Clean Air Act, or compliance assurance agreement.

**CAAT,** Center for Alternatives to Animal Testing (Johns Hopkins).

**CABEI,** Central American Bank for Economic Integration.

**CABI,** CAB (Commonwealth Agricultural Bureaux) International.

**CAC,** Crop Advisory Committees.

**CAER,** Community Awareness and Emergency Response.

**CAFE,** corporate average fuel economy standard.

**CAFO,** consent agreement/final order.

**CAG,** Carcinogen Assessment Group.

**CAI,** Comité Arctique International.

**CAIR,** Comprehensive Assessment Information Rules.

**CAMCORE,** Central American and Mexico Coniferous Resources Cooperative.

**CAMP,** continuous air monitoring program.

**CAP,** criteria air pollutant, corrective action plan, or cost allocation procedure.

**CAPA,** critical aquifer protection area.

**CAPP,** Center for Animals and Public Policy.

**CAR,** corrective action report.

**CAREIRS,** Conversation and Renewable Energy Inquiry and Referral Service.

**CAS,** Chemical Abstract Service, or Center for Automotive Safety.

**CASAC,** Clean Air Scientific Advisory Committee.

**CAST,** Council for Agricultural Science and Technology.

**CATIE,** Centro Agronómico Tropical de Investigación y Ensañanza.

**CATS,** corrective action track system.

**CAU,** carbon absorption unit.

**CBA,** Chesapeake Bay Agreement, or cost benefit analysis.

**CBDS,** Carcinogenesis Bioassay Data System.

**CBI,** compliance biomonitoring inspection, or confidential business information.

**CBRA(S),** Coastal Barriers Resources Act (or System).

**CC,** charcoal canister.

**CCA,** chromated copper arsenate.

**CCAA,** Canadian Clean Air Act.

**CCAMLR,** Commission for the Conservation of Antarctic Marine Living Resources.

**CCAP,** Center for Clean Air Policy.

**CCC,** Caribbean Conservation Corporation.

**CCEA,** Conventional Combustion Environmental Assessment.

**CCHW,** Citizens Clearinghouse for Hazardous Wastes.

**CCIC,** Canadian Council for International Cooperation.

**CCID,** Confidential Chemicals Identification System.

**CCL₄,** carbon tetrachloride.

**CCMS/NATO,** Committee on Challenges of a Modern Society/North Atlantic Treaty Organization.

**CCOF,** California Certified Organic Farmers.

**CCRO,** Central Coordination and Referral Office.

**CC/RTS,** Chemical Collection/Request Tracking System.

**CCS,** Center for Coastal Studies.

**CCTP,** Clean Coal Technology Program.

**Cd,** cadmium.

**CD,** climatological data.

**CDB,** Caribbean Development Bank.

**CDC,** Centers for Disease

Control, or Conservation Data Centers.

**CDD,** chlorinated dibenzo-p-dioxin.

**CDF,** chlorinated dibenzofuran.

**CDSS,** Country Development Strategy Statements.

**CEARC,** Canadian Environmental Assessment Research Council.

**CEB,** chemical element balance.

**CEC,** Commission of European Communities.

**CEE,** Center for Environmental Education.

**CEEM,** Center for Energy and Environmental Management.

**CEI,** Center for Environmental Information, or compliance evaluation inspection.

**CEIP,** Coastal Energy Impact Program.

**CELRF,** Canadian Environmental Law Research Foundation.

**CEM(S),** continuous emission monitoring (system).

**CEN,** Canadian Environmental Network.

**CEPLA,** Commission on Environmental Policy, Law and Administration.

**CEPP,** Chemical Emergency Preparedness Plan.

**CEQ,** Council on Environmental Quality.

**CERCLA,** Comprehensive Environmental Response, Compensation, and Liability Act.

**CERCLIS,** CERCLA Information System.

**CERES,** Coalition for Environmentally Responsible Economies.

**CERI,** Center for Environmental Research Information.

**CERP,** Conservation Education and Research Program.

**CF,** Conservation Foundation.

**CFA,** Commonwealth Forestry Association, or Consumer Federation of America.

**CFC,** chlorofluorocarbon.

**CFM,** chlorofluoromethane, or cubic feet per minute.

**CRF,** Code of Federal Regulations.

**CFS,** cubic feet per second.

**CGIAR** (or **CG**), Consultative Group on International Agricultural Research.

**CGTB,** Cellular and Genetic Toxicology Branch.

**CH$_2$O** (or **HCHO**), formaldehyde.

**CH$_4$,** methane.

**CHABA,** Committee on Hearing and Bio-Acoustics.

**CHAMP,** Community Health Air Monitoring Program.

**CHEC,** Commonwealth Human Ecology Council.

**CHEMTRACK,** Chemical Information and Tracking System.

**CHEMTREC,** Chemical Transportation Emergency Center.

**CHESS,** Community Health and Environmental Surveillance System.

**CHIP,** Chemical Hazard Information Profile.

**Ci,** Curie.

**CI,** Conservation International, Climate Institute, compression ignition, or confidence interval.

**CIAQ,** Council on Indoor Air Quality.

**CIAT,** Centro Internacional de Agricultura Tropical (International Center for Tropical Agriculture).

**CIBC,** CAB (Commonwealth Agricultural Bureaux) International Institute of Biological Control.

**CICIS,** Chemicals-in-

Commerce Information System.

**CID,** Consortium for International Development.

**CIDA,** Canadian International Development Agency.

**CIDIE,** Committee of International Development Institutions on the Environment.

**CIE,** CAB (Commonwealth Agricultural Bureaux) International Institute of Entomology.

**CIEM,** Conseil International pour l'Exploration de la Mer (International Council for the Exploration of the Sea).

**CIESM,** Commission Internationale pour l'Exploration Scientifique de la Mer Méditerranée.

**CILLS,** Comité Permanent Inter-Etats de Lutte contre la Sécheresse dans le Sahel.

**CIMMYT,** Centro Internacional de Mejoramiento de Maiz y Trigo (International Maize and Wheat Improvement Center).

**CINTRAFOR,** Center for International Trade in Forest Resources.

**CIP,** Centro Internacional de la Papa (International Potato Center).

**CIRT,** Centro Internacional de Recursos Transfronterizos (International Transboundary Resources Center).

**CIS,** Chemical Information System, or Contracts Information System.

**CISTOD,** Confederation of International Scientific and Technological Organizations for Development.

**CITES,** Convention on International Trade in Endangered Species of Wild Flora and Fauna.

**CLC,** capacity limiting constituents.

**CLEATS,** Clinical Laboratory for Evaluation and Assessment of Toxic Substances.

**CLEVER,** Clinical Laboratory for Evaluation and Validation of Epidemiological Research.

**CLF,** Conservation Law Foundation.

**CLIPS,** Chemical List Index and Processing System.

**CMA,** Chemical Manufacturers Association.

**CMAS,** Confédération Mondiale des Acticités Subaquatiques (World Underwater Federation).

**CMB,** chemical mass balance, or Comparative Medicine Branch.

**CMC,** Conservation Monitoring Center, or Center for Marine Conservation.

**CME,** Center for Marine Exploration.

**CMEA,** Council for Mutual Economic Assistance.

**CME(L),** Comprehensive Monitoring Evalution (Log) of groundwater.

**CMP,** Cellular and Molecular Pharmacology.

**CNPPA,** Commission on National Parks and Protected Areas.

**CNS,** central nervous system.

**CO,** carbon monoxide.

**CO$_2$,** carbon dioxide.

**CO$_3$,** carbonate.

**COA,** Clean Ocean Action.

**COCO,** Contractor-Owned/Contractor-Operated.

**COD,** chemical oxygen demand.

**CODEL,** Coordination in Development.

**COE,** Corps of Engineers.

**COH,** coefficient of haze.

**CONGO,** Conference of Non-Governmental Organizations in Consultative

Status (to the United Nations).

**COP,** coefficient of performance.

**CORR,** Chemicals on Reporting Rules.

**CP,** controlled point, or constructive placement.

**CPB,** Chemical Pathology Branch.

**CPC,** Center for Plant Conservation.

**CPER,** Central Plains Experimental Range.

**CPF,** carcinogenic potency factor.

**CPL,** Council of Planning Librarians.

**CPM,** counts per minute (in measuring particle ionization.)

**CPP,** Cooperative Planting Program.

**CPPS,** Comisión Permanente del Pacífico Sur.

**CPR,** Center for Public Resources, or Conserve, Preserve, and Restore.

**CPSC,** Consumer Product Safety Commission.

**Cr,** chromium.

**CRAMRA,** Convention on the Regulation of Antarctic Mineral Resource Activities.

**CRC,** Coastal Research Center.

**CRF,** Cave Research Foundation.

**CRGO,** Competitive Research Grants Office.

**CRIS,** Current Research Information Program.

**CRLE,** Center for Respect of Life and Environment.

**CRP,** Conservation Reserve Program.

**CRR,** Center for Renewable Resources.

**CRRI,** Central Rice Research Institute.

**CRWC,** Connecticut River Watershed Council.

**CS,** Cultural Survival, or Cousteau Society.

**CSA,** Committee for Sustainable Agriculture, or community supported agriculture.

**CSCAR,** Citizens for the Sensible Control of Acid Rain.

**CSDHA,** Centre for Social Development and Humanitarian Affairs.

**CSI,** Cetacean Society International; or compliance sampling inspection.

**CSIN,** Chemical Substances Information Network.

**CSMA,** Chemical Specialties Manufacturers Association.

**CSO,** combined sewer overflow.

**CSPA,** Council of State Planning Agencies.

**CSPI,** Center for Science in the Public Interest.

**CSRL,** Center for the Study of Responsive Law.

**CSRS,** Cooperative State Research Service.

**CSTD,** Centre for Science and Technology for Development.

**CTARC,** Chemical Testing and Assessment Research Commission.

**CTB,** Computer Technology Branch.

**CTBT,** Comprehensive Test Ban Treaty.

**CTD,** conductivity-temperature-depth.

**CTEB,** Carcinogenesis and Toxicologic Evaluation Branch.

**CTG,** control technique guidelines (or guidance).

**Cu,** copper.

**CUP,** conditional use permit.

**CW,** Congress Watch.

**CWA,** Clean Water Act, or Clean Water Action.

**CWLM,** continuous working level monitor, or cumulative working level months.

**CWTC,** Chemical Waste Transportation Council.

**CZIC,** Coastal Zone Information Center.

**CZM(A),** Coastal Zone Management (Act).

**CZMP,** Coastal Zone Management Program.

**dB,** decibel.

**DBCP,** dibromochloropropane.

**DBRA,** Division of Biometry and Risk Assessment.

**DCBTF,** 3,4-dichloro-benzotrifluoride.

**DCO,** delayed compliance order.

**DC/PAC,** Desertification Control Programme Activity Centre.

**DCPU,** Development Planning and Co-operation Unit.

**DDAL,** Doris Day Animal League.

**DDM,** diaminodiphenyl methane.

**DDT,** dichloro-diphenyl-trichloromethane.

**DDVP,** dichlorvos.

**DECC,** diethylcarbamoyl chloride.

**DED,** Dutch elm disease.

**DEHP,** di(ethylhexyl)phthlate.

**DERT,** Division of Extramural Research and Training.

**DES,** diethylstilbestrol.

**DI,** diagnostic inspection.

**DIESA,** Department of International Economic and Social Affairs.

**DIR,** Division of Intramural Research.

**DMCC,** dimethylcarbamoyl chloride.

**DMF,** dimethyl formamide.

**DMR,** downy mildew resistant.

**DNA,** deoxyribonucleic acid.

**DNTP,** Parathion.

**DO,** dissolved oxygen.

**DOC,** disaster operations center, or Department of Commerce.

**DOD,** Department of Defense.

**DOE,** Department of Energy.

**DOEM,** Designated Official for Environmental Matters.

**DOI,** Department of the Interior.

**DOJ,** Department of Justice.

**DOL,** Department of Labor.

**DOS,** Department of State.

**DOT,** Department of Transportation.

**DOW,** Department of Wildlife.

**DPA,** Deepwater Ports Act.

**DQO,** data quality objective.

**DRE,** destruction and removal efficiency.

**DRU,** Desert Research Unit.

**DSA,** disaster support area.

**DTBP,** 2,6-di-tert-butyl phenol.

**DTCD,** Department of Technical Co-operation for Development.

**DTRT,** Division of Toxicology Research and Testing.

**DU,** Ducks Unlimited.

**DWS,** drinking water standard.

**EA,** endangerment assessment, enforcement agreement, environmental action, environmental assessment, or environmental audit.

**EAG,** Exposure Assessment Group.

**EAP,** Environmental Action Plan.

**EAWLS,** East African Wild Life Society.

**EB,** emissions balancing, or Epidemiology Branch.

**EC,** effective concentration, Environment Canada, or European Community.

**ECA,** Economic Community for Africa.

**ECE,** Economic Commission for Europe.

**ECG,** Ecosystem Conservation Group.

**ECHH,** electro-catalytic hyper-heaters.

**ECL,** environmental chemical laboratory.

**ECLA,** Economic Commission for Latin America.

**ECPA,** Electric Consumers Protection Act.

**ECRA,** Economic Cleanup Responsibility Act.

**ED,** fective dose, erythema dose, or Department of Education.

**ED$_{50}$,** effective dose for 50 percent of the tested subjects.

**EDA,** Economic Development Administration, or Emergency Declaration Area.

**EDB,** ethylene dibromide.

**EDC,** ethylene dichloride.

**EDD,** Enforcement Decision Document.

**EDF,** Environmental Defense Fund.

**EDRS,** Enforcement Document Retrieval System.

**EDS,** Energy Data System.

**EDTA,** ethylene diamine triacetic acid.

**EDZ,** emission density zoning.

**EE,** ecosystem evaluation.

**EEA,** energy and environment analysis.

**EEC,** European Economic Commission.

**EEI,** Edison Electric Institute.

**EENET,** Emergency Education Network.

**EER,** excess emission report.

**EERL,** Eastern Environmental Radiation Laboratory.

**EERU,** Environmental Emergency Response Unit.

**EES,** Energy Extension Service.

**EESI,** Environment and Energy Study Institute.

**EESL,** Environmental Ecological and Support Laboratory.

**EETFC,** Environmental Effects, Transport and Fate Committee.

**EETU,** Environmental Education and Training Unit.

**EF,** emission factor.

**EF!,** Earth First!

**EFTC,** European Fluorocarbon Technical Committee.

**EGR,** exhaust gas recirculation.

**EHC,** Environmental Health Committee.

**EHMI,** Environmental Hazards Management Institute.

**EHS,** environmental health sciences, or extremely hazardous substance.

**EI,** emissions inventory, or environmental (or ecological) illness.

**EIA,** environmental impact assessment, or economic impact assessment.

**EID,** European Investment Bank.

**EIL,** environmental impairment liability.

**EIR,** environmental impact report, or endangerment information report.

**EIS,** environmental inventory system, or environmental impact statement.

**EIS/AS,** Emissions Inventory System/Area Source.

**EIS/PA,** Emissions Inventory System/Point Source.

**EL,** exposure level.

**ELC,** Environmental Law Centre.

**ELCI,** Environment Liaison Centre International.

**ELI,** Environmental Law Institute.

**ELISA,** enzyme-linked immunosorbent assay.

**ELIU,** Environmental Law and Institutions Unit.

**ELR,** Environmental Law Reporter.

**EMAP,** Environmental Monitoring and Assessment Program.

**EMBRAPA,** Empresa Brasiliera de Pesquisa Agropecuaria (Brazilian Agricultural Research Bureau).

**EMF,** electromagnetic fields.

**EMI,** Emergency Management Institute.

**EMR,** Environmental Management Report.

**EMS,** Enforcement Management System, or emergency medical services.

**EMSL,** Environmental Monitoring Support (or Systems) Laboratory.

**EMTS,** Environmental (or Exposure) Monitoring Test Site.

**EO,** ethylene oxide.

**EOC,** Emergency Operating Center.

**EP,** environmental profile, extraction procedure, or earth protectors.

**EPA,** Environmental Protection Agency.

**EPAA,** Environmental Programs Assistance Act.

**EPACASR,** EPA Chemical Activities Status Report.

**EPCRA,** Emergency Planning and Community Right-to-Know Act.

**EPD,** Emergency Planning District.

**EPF,** Earth Preservation Fund.

**EPH,** epibromohydrin.

**EPI,** Environmental Policy Institute.

**EPIC,** erosion productivity impact calculator.

**EPO,** Estuarine Programs Office.

**EPOCA,** Environmental Project on Central America.

**EPR,** error-prone repair.

**EPRI,** Electric Power Research Institute.

**EPTC,** Extraction Procedure Toxicity Characteristic.

**ERAMS,** Environmental Radiation Ambient Monitoring System.

**ERC,** Emergency Response Commission, or emissions reduction credit.

**ERCS,** Emergency Response Cleanup Services.

**ERDA,** Energy Research and Development Administration.

**ERD&DAA,** Environmental Research, Development and Demonstration Authorization Act.

**ERL,** Environmental Research Laboratory.

**ERMS,** Emergency Radiation Monitoring System.

**ERNS,** Emergency Response Notification System.

**ERP,** Enforcement Response Policy.

**ERS,** Economic Research Service.

**ERT,** Emergency Response Team.

**ES,** enforcement strategy, or Extension Service.

**ESA,** Endangered Species Act, or Ecological Society of America.

**ESC,** Endangered Species Committee.

**ESCA,** electron spectroscopy for chemical analysis.

**ESCAP,** Economic and Social Commission for Asia and the Pacific.

**ESCWA,** Economic and Social Commission for Western Asia.

**ESECA,** Energy Supply and Environmental Coordination Act.

**ESH,** environmental safety and health.

**ESP,** electrostatic precipitator, or Economic Support Funds.

**ESR,** electron spin resonance.

**ESTA,** environmentally sound technology assessment.

**ET(P),** emissions trading (policy).

**ETS,** environmental tobacco smoke.

**ETU,** ethylene thiourea.

**EUP,** Environmental Use Permit.

**EWAA,** Elsa Wild Animal Appeal.

**EWCC,** Environmental Workforce Coordinating Committee.

**ExEx,** expected exceedance.

**EXTOXNET,** Extension Toxicology Network.

**F,** Fahrenheit temperature scale.

**FAA,** Foreign Assistance Act, or Federal Aviation Administration.

**FAM** or **FACM,** friable asbestos-containing material.

**FAO,** Food and Agriculture Organization.

**FAPS,** Federal Aid Primary System.

**FAS,** Foreign Agricultural Service.

**FATES,** FIFRA and TSCA Enforcement System.

**FAUS,** Federal Air Urban System.

**FBC,** fluidized bed combustion.

**FC,** fluorocarbon.

**FCAP,** fluor chrome arsenic phenol.

**FCC,** fluid catalytic converter, or Federal Communications Commission.

**f/cc,** fibers per cubic centimeters of air.

**FCCU,** fluid catalytic cracking unit.

**FCIP,** Federal Crop Insurance Program.

**FCO,** Federal Coordinating Officer.

**FCS,** Farm Credit System.

**FDA,** Food and Drug Administration.

**FDF,** fundamentally different factors.

**FDL,** Final Determination Letter.

**Fe,** iron.

**FE,** fugitive emissions.

**FEA,** Federal Energy Administration.

**FEDS,** Federal Energy Data System.

**FExF,** forced expiratory flow.

**FEIS,** Fugitive Emissions Information System.

**FEMA,** Federal Emergency Management Agency.

**FEMAC,** Federación Mesoamericana de Asociaciones Conservacionistas No-Gubernamentales.

**FEMA-REP-1,** FEMA Response Plans and Preparedness in Support of Nuclear Power Plants.

**FEMA-REP-2,** FEMA Guidance for Developing State and Local Radiological Emergency Response Plans and Preparedness for Transportation Action.

**FEPCA,** Federal Energy Policy and Conservation Act, or Federal Environmental Pesticide Control Act.

**FERC,** Federal Energy Regulatory Commission.

**FEV (FEV 1),** forced expiratory volume (in one second).

**FEVI,** front end volatility index.

**FFAR,** Fuel and Fuel Additive Registration.

**FFDCA,** Federal Food, Drug, and Cosmetic Act.

**FFFSG,** fossil fuel fired steam generator.

**F/FRED,** Forestry/Fuelwood Research and Development Project.

**FGD,** flue gas desulfurization.

**FGIS,** Federal Grain Inspection Service.

**FHA,** Farmers Home Administration.

**FHS,** Forest History Society.

**FHWA,** Federal Highway Administration.

**FI$^2$,** Forest Information International.

**FIC,** Federal Information Center.

**FID,** flame ionization detector.

**FIFRA,** Federal Insecticide, Fungicide, and Rodenticide Act.

**FIM,** friable insulation material.

**FIP,** final (or federal) implementation (or information) plan.

**FIPS,** Federal Information Procedures System.

**FIT,** field investigation team.

**FILM,** federal land manager.

**FLP,** flashpoint.

**FLPMA,** Federal Land Policy and Management Act.

**FM,** friable material.

**F/M,** food to microorganism ratio.

**FMC,** Federal Maritime Commission.

**FmHA,** Farmers Home Administration.

**FML,** flexible membrane liner.

**FMVCP,** Federal Motor Vehicle Control Program.

**FNR,** Forestry, Natural Resources, and the Environment Office.

**FNS,** Food and Nutrition Service.

**FNSI** or **FONSI,** finding of no significant impact.

**FoA,** Friends of Animals.

**FOE,** Friends of the Earth.

**FONE,** Farmers Own Network for Education.

**FOR,** Friends of the River.

**FORAST,** forest response to anthropogenic stress.

**FP,** fine particulate.

**FPA,** Federal Pesticide Act, or Federal Powers Act.

**FPC,** Federal Power Commission.

**FPD,** flame photometric detector.

**FPEIS,** Fine Particulate Emissions Information System.

**FPPA,** Farmland Protection Policy Act.

**FR,** Federal Register.

**FRAME,** Fund for the Replacement of Animals in Medical Research.

**FRC,** Federal Radiation Council.

**FRDS,** Federal Reporting Data System.

**FREDS,** Flexible Regional Emissions Data System.

**FRES,** Forest Range Environmental Study.

**FS,** feasbility study, or Forest Service.

**FSA,** Food Security Act.

**FSIS,** Food Safety and Inspection Service.

**FSR,** farming systems research.

**FST,** Farming Systems Trial.

**FTC,** Federal Trade Commission.

**FTP,** federal test procedure.

**FUA,** Fuel Use Act.

**FURS,** Federal Underground Injection Control Reporting System.

**FVC,** forced vital capacity.

**FVMP,** Federal Visibility Monitoring Program.

**FWPCA,** Federal Water Pollution Control Act (or Administration).

**FWS,** Fish and Wildlife Service.

**FWS/ESO,** Fish and Wildlife Service, Endangered Species Office.

**GAC** or **GAC(T),** granulated (or groundwater) activated carbon (treatment).

**GAIA,** Green Alternative Information for Action.

**GAO,** General Accounting Office.

**GC/MS,** gas chromatograph/mass spectrograph.

**GDP,** gross domestic product.

**GEMS/PAC,** Global Environment Monitoring System Programmed Activity Centre.

**GESAMP,** Group of Experts on the Scientific Aspects of Marine Pollution.

**GEU,** genetic evaluation and utilization.

**GFF,** glass fiber filter.

**GI,** gastrointestinal.

**GIS,** Geographic Information Systems, or Global Indexing System.

**GIT,** gastrointestinal tract.

**GLC,** glass liquid chromatography.

**GLERL,** Great Lakes Environment Research Laboratory.

**GLNPO,** Great Lakes National Program Office.

**GLOBE,** Global Legislators Organization for a Balanced Environment.

**GLU,** Great Lakes United.

**GLWQA,** Great Lakes Water Quality Agreement.

**GMCC,** global monitoring for climatic change.

**g/mi,** grams per mile.

**GOCO,** government-owned/contractor operated.

**GOGO,** government-owned/government-operated.

**GOTV,** get out the vote.

**GPAD,** gallons per acre per day.

**GPG,** grams per gallon.

**GPO,** Government Printing Office.

**GPR,** ground-penetrating radar.

**GPS,** Groundwater Protection Strategy.

**GRGL,** groundwater residue guidance level.

**GRID,** Global Resources Information Database.

**GRIN,** Germplasm Resources Information Network.

**GRU,** genetic resources unit.

**GSA,** General Services Administration.

**GTC,** Global Tomorrow Coalition.

**GTN,** Global Trend Network.

**GVP,** gasoline vapor pressure.

**GW(M),** groundwater (monitoring).

**GWPS,** groundwater protection standard (or strategy).

**GWSS,** Groundwater Supply Survey.

**Gy,** Gray, a measure of ionizing radiation.

**H,** Henry's Law Constant.

**H₂O,** water.

**H₂S,** hydrogen sulfide.

**H₂SO₄,** sulfuric acid.

**HA,** health advisory.

**HAD,** Health Assessment Document.

**HAO,** High Altitude Observatory.

**HAP(EMS),** hazardous air pollutant (enforcement management system).

**HAPPS,** HAP Prioritization System.

**HATREMS,** hazardous and trace emissions system.

**HAZMAT,** hazardous materials.

**HAZOP,** Hazard and Operability Study.

**HC,** hydrocarbon, or hazardous constitutients.

**HCB,** hexachlorobenzene.

**HCCPD,** hexachlorocyclopentadiene.

**HCFC,** hydrochlorofluorocarbons.

**HCHO** (or **CH₂O**), formaldehyde.

**HCO₃,** bicarbonate.

**HCP,** hypothermal coal process.

**HCS,** Hazard Communication Standard.

**HDD,** heavy-duty diesel.

**HDE,** heavy-duty engine.

**HDG,** heavy-duty gasoline-powered vehicle.

**HDPE,** high-density polyethelene.

**HDT** or **HDV,** heavy-duty truck (or vehicle).

**HEAL,** Human Exposure Assessment Location, or Human Ecology Action League.

**HEI,** Health Effects Institute.

**HEM,** human exposure modeling.

**HEPA,** high-efficiency particulate air.

**HERL,** Health Effects Research Laboratory.

**HERS,** hyperion energy recovery system.

**HEX-BCH,** hexachloronorbornadiene.

**Hg,** mercury.

**HHE,** human health and the environment.

**HHS,** U.S. Department of Health and Human Services.

**HHV,** higher heating value.

**HI,** hazard index.

**HLW** or **HLRW,** high-level radioactive waste.

**HMIS,** Hazardous Materials Information System.

**HMP,** habitat management plan.

**HMPA,** hexamethylphosphoric triamide.

**HMS,** highway mobile source.

**HMTA** (or **R**), Hazardous Materials Transportation Act (or Regulation).

**HNIS,** Human Nutrition Information Service.

**HNS,** hazardous and noxious substances.

**HO,** halogenated organic carbons.

**HON,** hazardous organic NESHAP.

**HOV,** high-occupancy vehicle.

**HP,** horsepower.

**HPF,** Historic Preservation Fund.

**HPLC,** high-performance liquid chromatography.

**HPV,** high-priority violator.

**HRC,** Human Resources Council.

**HRS,** Hazard Ranking System.

**HRUP,** high risk urban problem.

**HRV,** heat-recovery ventilation.

**HS,** hydrogen sulfide.

**HSDB,** Hazardous Substance Data Base.

**HSL,** Hazardous Substance List.

**HSUS,** Humane Society of the United States.

**HSWA,** Hazardous and Solid Waste Amendments.

**HT,** hypothermally treated.

**HTP,** high temperature and pressure.

**HUD,** Department of Housing and Urban Development.

**HVAC,** heating, ventilation, and air conditioning.

**HVIO,** high-volume industrial organics.

**HW,** hazardous waste.

**HWDMS,** Hazardous Waste Data Management System.

**HWERL,** Hazardous Waste Engineering Research Laboratory.

**HWGTF,** Hazardous Waste Groundwater Task Force (or Treatment Facility).

**HWLT,** hazardous waste land treatment.

**HWM,** hazardous waste management.

**HWRTF,** Hazardous Waste Restrictions Task Force.

**HWTC,** Hazardous Waste Treatment Council.

**HYRV,** high-yielding rice variety.

**HYV,** high-yielding varieties.

**HYWV,** high-yielding wheat variety.

**Hz,** hertz (one cycle per second).

**IA** or **IAG,** interagency agreement.

**IAA,** Institute for Alternative Agriculture.

**IAAC,** Interagency Assessment Advisory Committee.

**IACUC,** Institutional Animal Care and Use Committee.

**IAEA,** International Atomic Energy Agency, United Nations.

**IAP,** indoor air polution, or incentive awards program.

**IARC,** International Agricultural Research Centers, or International Agency for Research on Cancer.

**IASA,** International Alliance for Sustainable Agriculture.

**IATDB,** Interim Air Toxics Data Base.

**IBA,** Industrial Biotechnology Association.

**IBPGR,** International Board for Plant Genetic Resources.

**IBRD,** International Bank for Reconstruction and Development.

**IBSFC,** International Baltic Sea Fisheries Commission.

**IBSRAM,** International Board for Soil Research and Management.

**IC(A)P,** inductively coupled (argon) plasma.

**ICARDA,** International Center for Agricultural Research in the Dry Areas.

**ICASALS,** International Center for Arid and Semi-arid Land Studies.

**ICBN,** International Commission on the Biological Effects of Noise.

**ICBP,** International Council for Bird Preservation.

**ICC,** International Chamber of Commerce, or Interstate Commerce Commission.

**ICCAT,** International Commission for the Conservation of Atlantic Tuna.

**ICE,** internal combustion engine, or industrial combustion emissions.

**ICEA,** Working Group on an International Commission for Environmental Assessment.

**ICES,** International Council for the Exploration of the Sea.

**ICIMOD,** International Centre for Integrated Mountain Development.

**ICIPE,** International Centre of Insect Physiology and Ecology.

**ICLARM,** International Center for Living Aquatic Resources Management.

**ICP,** Institutional Conservation Program.

**ICPIC,** International Cleaner Production Information Clearinghouse.

**ICPRB,** Interstate Commission on the Potomac River Basin.

**ICR,** information collection request, or International Congress of Radiology.

**ICRAF,** International Council for Research in Agroforestry.

**ICRE,** ignitability, corrosivity, reactivity, extraction.

**ICRISAT,** International Crops Research Institute for the Semi-Arid Tropics.

**ICRP,** International Commission on Radiological Protection.

**ICS,** Institute for Chemical Studies, or intermittent

control strategies (or system).

**ICSEAF,** International Commission for the Southeast Atlantic Fisheries.

**ICSEM,** International Commission for Scientific Exploration of the Mediterranean Sea.

**ICSU,** International Council of Scientific Unions.

**ICTA,** Instituto de Ciencias y Tecnologías Agropecuarias (Institute of Agricultural Science and Technology).

**ICVA,** International Council of Voluntary Agencies.

**ICWM,** Institute for Chemical Waste Management.

**IDA,** In Defense of Animals.

**IDB,** Inter-American Development Bank.

**IDC,** International Development Conference.

**IDLH,** immediately dangerous to life and health.

**IEA,** International Energy Agency.

**IEB,** International Environment Bureau.

**IECA,** International Erosion Control Association.

**IEDS,** International Environment and Development Service.

**IEMP,** Integrated Environmental Management Project.

**IEO,** Industry and Environment Office.

**IES,** Institute for Environmental Studies.

**IFAD,** International Fund for Agricultural Development, United Nations.

**IFAW,** International Fund for Animal Welfare.

**IFB,** invitation for bid.

**IFC,** International Facilitating Committee.

**IFCAM,** industrial fuel choice analysis model.

**IFDC,** International Fertilizer Development Center.

**IFDP,** Institute for Food and Development Policy.

**IFER,** International Foundation for Ethical Research.

**IFIS,** Industry File Information System.

**IFPP,** industrial fugitive process particulate.

**IFPRI,** International Food Policy Research Institute.

**IGBP,** International Geosphere-Biosphere Programme.

**IGCI,** Industrial Gas Cleaning Institute.

**IIEC,** International Institute for Energy Conservation.

**IIED,** International Institute for Environment and Development.

**IMMI,** International Irrigation Management Institute.

**IITA,** International Institute of Tropical Agriculture.

**IJC,** International Joint Commission (on the Great Lakes).

**ILAR,** Institute of Laboratory Animal Resources.

**ILCA,** International Livestock Center for Africa.

**ILRAD,** International Laboratory for Research on Animal Diseases.

**ILSR,** Institute for Local Self-Reliance.

**I/M,** inspection and maintenance.

**IMF,** International Monetary Fund.

**IMO,** International Maritime Organization.

**IMPACT,** integrated model of plumes and atmosphere in complex terrain.

**IMPROVE,** Interagency Monitoring of Protected Visual Environment.

**IMS,** Institute of Museum Services.

**INF,** Intermediate Nuclear Forces.

**INIA,** Instituto Nacional de Investigaciones Agropecuarias (National Institute for Agricultural Research).

**INIBAP,** International Network for the Improvement of Banana and Plantain.

**INIPA,** Instituto Nacional de Investigación y Promoción Agropecuaria (National Agricultural Research and Development Institute).

**INT,** intermittent.

**INTECOL,** International Association for Ecology.

**IOC,** Intergovernmental Oceanographic Commission.

**IP,** inhalable particles, or information packets (packages).

**IPCC,** Intergovernmental Panel on Climate Change.

**IPCS,** International Program on Chemical Safety.

**IPM,** integrated pest management, or inhalable particulate matter.

**IPP,** Intermedia Priority Pollutant, Implementation Planning Program, or Interated Plotting Package.

**IPPC,** International Plant Protection Convention.

**IR,** infrared.

**IRDC,** International Development Research Centre.

**IRDP,** Integrated Regional Development Planning.

**IRG,** interagency review group.

**IRIS,** Integrated Risk Information System, or Instructional Resources Information System.

**IRM,** intermediate remedial measures.

**IRMC,** inter-regulatory risk management council.

**IRN,** International Rivers Network.

**IRPTC,** International Register of Potentially Toxic Chemicals.

**IRR,** Institute of Resource Recovery.

**IRRC,** Investor Responsibility Research Center.

**IRRI,** International Rice Research Institute.

**IS,** industrial source, or interim status.

**ISAR,** International Society for Animal Rights.

**ISCCED,** Independent Sector Coordinating Committee on Environment and Development.

**ISCL,** Interim Status Compliance Letter.

**ISD,** Intermin Status Document.

**ISFMP,** Interstate Fisheries Management Program.

**ISIS,** International Species Inventory System.

**ISLT,** International Snow Leopard Trust.

**ISMAP,** Indirect Source Model for Air Pollution.

**ISNAR,** International Service for National Agricultural Research.

**ISO,** International Organization for Standardization.

**ISS,** interim status standards.

**ITC,** Interagency Testing Committee, or International Trypanotolerance Center.

**ITSDC,** Interagency Toxic Substanes Data Committee.

**ITTO,** International Tropical Timber Organization.

**IUBS,** International Union of Biological Sciences.

**IUCN,** International Union for the Conservation of Nature and Natural Resources (now IUCN—The World Conservation Union).

**IUFRO,** International Union of Forestry Research Organizations.

**IUPOV,** International Union for the Protection of New Varieties of Plants.

**IWC,** International Whaling Commission, International Wildlife Coalition, or instream waste concentration.

**IWLA,** Izaak Walton League of America.

**IWS,** ionizing wet scrubber.

**JCAE,** Joint Committee on Atomic Energy.

**JONSDAP,** Joint North Sea Data Acquisition Project.

**JTU,** Jackson turbidity unit.

**K,** potassium.

**Kd,** coefficient of soil-water adsorption.

**kg,** kilogram.

**Koc,** coefficient of organic carbon partition, or measure of soil absorption.

**Kow,** coefficient of octanol-water partition.

**KW(H),** kilowatt (hour).

**LAEC,** lowest achievable emission rate.

**LAMP,** Lake Acidification Mitigation Project.

**LBRA,** Laboratory of Biochemical Risk Analysis.

**LC,** lethal concentration, or liquid chromatography.

**$LC_{50}$,** lethal concentration for 50 percent of a test population.

**LCD,** local climatological data.

**LCM,** life cycle management.

**LD,** lethal dose.

**$LD_0$ or LDO,** lethal dosage for none of a test population.

**$LD_1$ or LD LO,** lowest dosage lethal to any of a test population.

**$LD_{50}$,** lethal (or low) dose for 50 percent of a test population (medial lethal dose).

**LDC,** London Dumping Convention, or less-developed country.

**L(D)CRS,** Leachate (Detection) Collection and Removal System.

**LDD,** light-duty diesel.

**LDR(TF),** land-disposal restrictions (task force).

**LDS,** leak detection system.

**LDT(V),** light-duty truck (vehicle).

**LEL,** lowest effective level, or lower explosive limit.

**LEPC,** Local Emergency Planning Committee.

**LFL,** lower flammability limit.

**LG,** Laboratory of Genetics.

**LHRH,** luteinizing hormone-releasing hormone.

**LIB,** Laboratory Information Bulletin.

**LIMB,** limestone-injection, multi-stage burner.

**LIRT,** low input reduced tillage cropping systems.

**LISA,** low input and sustainable agriculture.

**LLW or LLRW,** low-level radioactive waste.

**LMB,** Laboratory of Molecular Biophysics.

**LMC,** Laboratory of Molecular Carcinogensis.

**LMEP,** low noise emission product.

**LMFBR,** liquid metal fast breeder reactor.

**LMG,** Laboratory of Molecular Genetics.

**LMIN,** Laboratory of Molecular and Integrative Neuroscience.

**LNG,** liquefied natural gas.

**LOAEL,** lowest observed adverse effect level.

**LOC,** level of concern, or Library of Congress.

**LOEL,** lowest observed effect level.

**LOIS,** loss of interim status.

**LOSC,** Law of the Sea Convention (Convention on the Law of the Sea).

**LOSIS,** Law of the Sea Information System.

**LPG,** liquid petroleum gas.

**LPP,** Laboratory of Pulmonary Pathobiology.

**LRDT,** Laboratory of Reproductive and Developmental Toxicology.

**LRTAP,** Convention on Long-Range Transboundary Air Pollution.

**LSA,** low specific activity.
**LST,** low-solvent technology.
**LTA,** Land Trust Alliance.
**LTBT,** Limited Test Ban Treaty.
**LTD(U),** land treatment demonstration (or unit).
**LUST,** leaking underground storage tank.
**LWCF,** Land and Water Conservation Fund.
**LWR,** light water reactor.

**MAB,** Man in the Biosphere Program, or monoclonal antibody.
**MAC,** maximum allowable concentrations.
**MADCAP,** Model of Advection, Diffusion, and Chemistry for Air Pollution.
**MAER,** maximum allowable emission rate.
**MARC,** Mining and Reclamation Council, or Monitoring and Assessment Research Centre.
**MARPOL,** International Convention for the Prevention of Pollution from Ships.
**MARPRO,** Marine Profile Data base.
**MARSH,** Matching Aid to Restore States Habitat.
**MATC,** maximum acceptable tolerance concentration, or maximum allowable toxicant concentration.
**MBI,** 4,4'-Methylenebis(N,N-dimethylbenzenamine).
**MBOCA,** 4-4'-Methylenebis(2-chlorobenzenamine); or 4,4'-Methylenebis(2-chloroaniline).
**MBT,** mechanical bathythermograph.
**MBTA,** Migratory Bird Treaty Act.
**MC,** methyl chloroform.
**MCA,** monoclonal antibody.
**MCEF,** mixed cellulose ester filter.

**MCL(G),** maximum contaminant level (goal).
**MCP,** Municipal Compliance Plan.
**MCPP,** mecoprop.
**MCRT,** mean cell retention time.
**MCS,** multiple chemical sensitivities.
**MCU,** Mediterranean Coordination Unit.
**MDA,** methylenedianiline.
**MDB,** Multilateral Development Bank.
**MDI,** methylenebis (phenylisocyanate).
**MDL,** method detection limit.
**MEI,** maximum exposed individual.
**MEK,** methyl ethyl ketone.
**MEP,** multiple extraction procedure.
**MEPC,** Marine Environment Protection Committee.
**MERL,** Municipal Environmental Research Laboratory.
**MESA,** Mining Enforcement and Safety Administration.
**MFBI,** major fuel-burning installation.
**MFBS,** marine and freshwater biomedical science.
**MFC,** metal-finishing category.
**MFCMA,** Magnuson Fishery Conservation and Management Act.
**Mg,** magnesium.
**MGD,** million gallons of water per day.
**mg/kg,** milligrams per kilogram.
**mg/$_1$,** milligrams per liter.
**mg/m$^3$,** miligrams of material per cubic meter or air.
**MGP,** Mountain Gorilla Project.
**MH,** man-hours.
**MHD,** magneto-hydrodynamics.
**MIBK,** methyl isobutyl ketone.
**MIC,** methyl isocyanate.

**MICROMORT,** one-in-a-million chance of death from environmental hazard.
**MICU(N),** mobile intensive care unit (nurse).
**MINDAT,** Minerals Data base (of the Law of the Sea).
**MIRCENS,** Microbiological Resource Centers.
**ML,** meteorology laboratory.
**MLD,** minimum (or median) lethal dose (LD$_{50}$).
**ML(V)SS,** mixed liquor (volatile) suspended solids.
**$\mu$/m$^3$,**micrograms per cubic meter.
**MMA,** medical mutual aid.
**mm Hg,** millimeters of mercury.
**MMM,** Mesocale and Microscale Meteorology.
**MMPA,** Marine Mammal Protection Act.
**MMS,** Minerals Management Service.
**MMT,** million metric tons.
**Mn,** manganese.
**MOA,** memorandum of agreement.
**MOBILE,** Mobile Source Emission Model.
**MOP,** Manual of Practice.
**MOS,** margin of safety.
**MOU,** memorandum of understanding.
**MP,** melting point.
**MPC,** Marine Policy Center.
**MPCL(G),** maximum permissible contaminent level (goal).
**MPRSA,** Marine Protection, Research and Sanctuaries Act.
**MPS,** mononuclear phagocyte system.
**MREM,** millirem, or 1/1000 or a REM.
**MRI,** magnetic resonance imaging.
**MS,** mass spectrometry (or spectrograph).
**MSD,** metropolitan sewer district.

**MSDS,** Material Safety Data Sheet.
**MSEE,** major source enforcement effort.
**MSHA,** Mine Safety and Health Administration.
**MSL,** mean sea level.
**MSW,** municipal solid waste.
**MTB,** Materials Transportation Bureau.
**MTBE,** methyl tertiary butyl ether.
**MTD,** maximum tolerated dose.
**MTU,** mobile treatment unit.
**mV,** millivolt.
**MVAPCA,** Motor Vehicle Air Pollution Control Act.
**MVRS,** Marine Vapor Recovery System.
waste, or molecular weight.
**MWC (or MWL),** municipal waste combustor (or leachate).
**Mwe,** megawatts of electricity.

**N or N$_2$,**nitrogen.
**N$_2$O,** nitrous oxide.
**NA,** natural area.
**NAA,** nonattainment areas.
**NAAHE,** National Association for the Advancement of Humane Education.
**NAAL,** National Alliance for Animal Legislation.
**NAAQS,** National Ambient Air Quality Standards.
**NAAS,** National Air Audit System.
**NACA,** National Agricultural Chemicals Association.
**NADB,** National Atmospheric Data Bank.
**NADP,** National Atmospheric Deposition Program.
**NAL,** National Agricultural Library.
**NALMS,** North American Lake Management Society.
**NALS,** National Agricultural Land Study.

**NAMA** (or **NAMS**), National Air Monitoring Audits (or Systems).

**NANCO,** National Association of Noise Control Officials.

**NAPAP,** National Acid Precipitation Assessment Program.

**NAPBN,** National Air Pollution Background Network.

**NAPC,** National Air Pollution Control Administration.

**NAPCTAC,** National Air Pollution and Control Technical Advisory Committee.

**NAR,** National Asbestos Registry

**NARS,** National Asbestos-Contractor Registry System.

**NARSS,** National Agricultural Research System Survey (Philippines).

**NAS,** National Academy of Sciences, or National Audubon Society.

**NASA,** National Aeronautics and Space Administration.

**NASCO,** North Atlantic Salmon Conservation Organization.

**NASN,** National Air Sampling Network.

**NATICH,** National Air Toxics Information Clearinghouse.

**NAVS,** National Anti-Vivisection Society.

**NAWC,** National Association of Water Companies.

**NAWDEX,** National Water Data Exchange.

**NBAR,** non-binding allocation to responsibility.

**NBS,** National Bureau of Standards.

**NCA,** National Coal Association, or Noise Control Act.

**NCAC** (or **NCAF**), National Clean Air Coalition (or Fund).

**NCAMP,** National Coalition Against Misuse of Pesticides.

**NCAP,** Northwest Coalition for Alternatives to Pesticides.

**NCAQ,** National Commission on Air Quality.

**NCAR,** National Center for Atmospheric Research.

**NCASI,** National Council of the Paper Industry for Air and Stream Improvements.

**NCAT,** National Center for Appropriate Technology.

**NCC,** National Climatic Center.

**NCHA,** National Campers and Hikers Association.

**NCHS,** National Center for Health Statistics.

**NCI,** National Cancer Institute.

**NCMC,** National Coalition for Marine Conservation.

**NCP,** National Contingency Plan, or noncompliance (nonconformance) penalties.

**NCR,** noncompliance report.

**NCRIC,** National Chemical Response and Information Center.

**NCRP,** National Council on Radiation Protection (and Measurement).

**NCS,** National Conservation Strategy, or National Compliance Strategy.

**NCV,** nerve-conduction velocity.

**NCVECS,** National Center for Vehicle Emissions Control and Safety.

**NCWQ,** National Commission on Water Quality.

**NDDN,** National Dry Deposition Network.

**NDIR,** nondispersive infrared analysis.

**NDS,** National Dioxin Study, or national disposal site.

**NDWAC,** National Drinking Water Advisory Council.

**NEA,** National Energy Act.

**NEAFC,** North East Atlantic Fisheries Commission.

**NEDA,** National Environmental Development Association.

**NEDRES,** National Environmental Data Referral Service.

**NEDS,** National Emissions Data System.

**NEEC,** National Environmental Enforcement Council.

**NEELS,** National Emergency Equipment Locator System.

**NEHA,** National Environmental Health Organization.

**NEI,** Nature Expeditions International.

**NEIC,** National Enforcement Investigations Center.

**NEL,** no-effect level.

**NEP,** National Energy Plan, or National Estuary Program.

**NEPA,** National Environmental Policy Act.

**NER,** National Emissions Report.

**NEROS,** Northeast Regional Oxidant Study.

**NESCAUM,** Northeast States for Coordinated Air Use Management.

**NESDIS,** National Environmental Satellite, Data, and Information Service.

**NESHAP(S),** National Emission Standards for Hazardous Air Pollutants.

**NETC,** National Emergency Training Center.

**NF,** national forest.

**NFAN,** National Filter Analysis Network.

**NFMA,** National Forest Management Act.

**NFP,** national focal point.

**NFPA,** National Fire Protection Association.

**NFS,** National Forest System.

**NFT(A),** Nitrogen Fixing Tree (Association).

**NFWF,** National Fish and Wildlife Service.

**NGA,** Natural Gas Association.

**NGO,** nongovernmental organization.

**NGPA,** National Gas Policy Act.

**NGWIC,** National Groundwater Information Center.

**NH$_3$,** ammonia.

**NHANES,** National Health and Nutrition Examination Study.

**NHPA,** National Historic Preservation Act.

**NHTSA,** National Highway Traffic Safety Administration.

**NHWP,** Northeast Hazardous Waste Project.

**Ni,** nickel.

**NI,** not indicated.

**NIAE,** National Institute of Agricultural Engineering.

**NIB,** Nordic Investment Bank.

**NICS,** National Institute for Chemical Studies.

**NIEHS,** National Institute of Environmental Health Sciences.

**NIEI,** National Indoor Environmental Institute.

**NIH,** National Institutes of Health.

**NIM,** National Impact Model.

**NIMBY,** not in my backyard.

**NIOSH,** National Institute of Occupation Safety and Health.

**NIPDWR,** National Interim Primary Drinking Water Regulations.

**NIPF,** non-industrial private foresters.

**NIRL,** negligible individual risk level.

**NIS,** noise information system.

**NITEP,** National Incinerator Testing and Evaluation Program.

**NLPGA,** National Liquid Petroleum Gas Association.

**NM,** national monument.

**NMC,** National Meteorological Center.

**NMFS,** National Marine Fisheries Service.

**NMHC,** nonmethane hydrocarbons.

**NMOC,** nonmethane organic compounds.

**NMP,** National Municipal Policy.

**NMPIS,** National Marine Pollution Information System.

**NMR,** nuclear magnetic resonance.

**NNC,** notice of noncompliance.

**NNPSPP,** National Non-Point Source Pollution Program.

**NO,** nitric oxide.

**NO₂,** nitrogen dioxide.

**NO₃,** nitrate.

**NOAA,** National Oceanic and Atmospheric Administration.

**NOAEL,** no observed adverse effect level.

**NOC,** notice of commencement.

**NOD,** notice of deficiency.

**NODC,** National Oceanographic Data Center.

**NOEL,** no observed effects level.

**NOHSCP/NCP,** National Oil and Hazardous Substances Contingency Plan/National Contingency Plan.

**NOI,** not otherwise indexed.

**NON,** notice of noncompliance.

**NOPES,** Non-Occupational Pesticide Exposure Study.

**NOPPO,** National Ocean Pollution Program Office.

**NOPR,** notice of proposed rulemaking.

**NORA,** National Oil Recyclers Association.

**NOS,** National Ocean Survey, or not otherwise specified.

**NOV/C/D,** notice of violation/compliance/demand.

**NOX,** nitrogen oxide.

**NP,** national park.

**NPAA,** Noise Pollution and Abatement Act.

**NPCA,** National Parks and Conservation Association.

**NPDES,** National Pollution Discharge Elimination System.

**NPDWR,** National Primary Drinking Water Requirements.

**NPFSC,** North Pacific Fur Seal Commission.

**NPGS,** National Plant Germplasm System.

**NPIRES,** National Pesticide Information Retrieval System.

**NPL,** National Priorities List.

**NPN,** National Particulate Network.

**NPS,** National Park Service, non-point source, National Permit Strategy, or National Pesticide Survey.

**NPTN,** National Pesticide Telecommunications Network.

**NPUG,** National Prime User Group.

**NRA,** National Recreation Area.

**NRC,** National Research Council, National Response Center, National Recycling Coalition, Nuclear Regulatory Commission, or non-reusable containers.

**NRCA,** National Resource Council of America.

**NRDC,** Natural Resources Defense Council.

**NRED,** Natural Resources and Energy Division.

**NRI,** National Rivers Inventory.

**NRPTC,** national register of potentially toxic chemicals.

**NRRL,** Northern Regional Research Laboratory.

**NRT,** National Response Team.

**NRWA,** National Rural Water Association.

**NS&T,** National Status and Trends.

**NSDWR,** National Secondary Drinking Water Regulations.

**NSF,** National Science Foundation, or National Sanitation Foundation.

**NSPS,** new source performance standards.

**NSR,** new source (pre-construction) review.

**NSS,** National Speleological Society.

**NSSL,** National Seed Storage Laboratory.

**NSWMA,** National Solid Waste Management Association.

**NSWS,** National Surface Water Survey.

**NTA,** nitrolotriacetic acid.

**NTIS,** National Technical Information Service.

**NTP,** National Toxicology Program.

**NTRM,** Nitrogen-Tillage-Residue Management.

**NTS,** Nevada Test Site.

**NWS,** National Water Alliance.

**NWF,** National Wildlife Federation.

**NWOA,** National Woodland Owners Association.

**NWPA,** Nuclear Waste Policy Act.

**NWR,** national wildlife refuge.

**NWRA,** National Wildlife Refuge Association.

**NWS,** National Weather Service.

**O,** oxygen.

**O₃,** ozone.

**OALOS,** Office for Ocean Affairs and the Law of the Sea.

**OALS,** Office of Arid Lands Studies.

**OAQPS,** Office of Air Quality Planning and Standards.

**OAS,** Organization of American States.

**OCA,** Oceans and Coastal Areas, or Office of Consumer Advisor.

**OCD,** Offshore and Coastal Dispersion.

**OCIA,** Organic Crop Improvement Association.

**OCRM,** Ocean and Coastal Resource Managment.

**OCS,** Outer Continental Shelf.

**OCSLA,** Outer Continental Shelf Lands Act.

**ODC,** Overseas Development Council.

**OE,** Office of Energy.

**OECD,** Organisation of Economic Co-Operation and Development.

**OES/E,** Office of the Environment (U.S. Department of) State/Environment, Health and Natural Resources.

**OES/EGC,** Office of the Environment (U.S. Department of) State/Office of Global Change.

**OES/EHC,** Office of the Environment (U.S. Department of) State/Office of Ecology, Health and Conservation.

**OES/ENV,** Office of the Environment (U.S. Department of) State/Office of Environmental Protection.

**OES/N,** Office of the Environment (U.S. Department of) State/Nuclear Energy and Energy Technology Affairs.

**OES/NED,** Office of the Environment (U.S. Department of) State/Office of Export and Import Control.

**OES/NEP,** Office of the Environment (U.S. Department of) State/Office of

Non-Proliferation and Export Policy.

**OES/NTS,** Office of the Environment (U.S. Department of) State/Office of Nuclear Technology and Safeguards.

**OES/O,** Office of the Environment (U.S. Department of) State/Oceans and Fisheries Affairs.

**OES/OFA,** Office of the Environment (U.S. Department of) State/Office of Fisheries Affairs.

**OES/OLP,** Office of the Environment (U.S. Department of) State/Office of Ocean Law and Policy.

**OES/OSP,** Office of the Environment (U.S. Department of) State/Office of Marine Science and Polar Affairs.

**OES/S,** Office of the Environment (U.S. Department of) State/Science and Technology Affairs.

**OES/SAT,** Office of the Environment (U.S. Department of) State/Office of Advanced Technology.

**OES/SCT,** Office of Environment (U.S. Department of) State/Office of Cooperative Science and Technology Programs.

**OFPANA,** Organic Food Producers Association of North America.

**OIA,** Office of International Affairs.

**OICD,** Office of International Cooperation and Development.

**O&M,** operation and maintenance.

**ONAC,** Office of Noise Abatement Control.

**OP,** organophosphates, or organic phosphates.

**OPA,** Office off Public Affairs.

**OPDIN** Ocean Pollution Data and Information Network.

**OPP,** office of pesticide programs.

**ORD,** Office of Research and Development.

**ORMS,** Operational Radiation Monitoring System, or other regulated materials.

**ORNL,** Oak Ridge National Laboratory.

**ORP,** oxidation-reduction potential.

**ORSTOM,** Office de la recherche scientifique et technique outre-mer (Office of Scientific and Technical Research Overseas).

**ORV,** off-road vehicles.

**OSC,** On-Scene Coordinator.

**OSHA,** Occupational Safety and Health Administration (or Act).

**OSM,** Office of Surface Mining.

**OSWER,** Office of Solid Waste and Emergency Response.

**OT,** Office of Transportation.

**OTA,** Office of Technology Assessment.

**OTEC,** ocean thermal energy conversion.

**$O_x$,** oxidants.

**P,** phosphorus.

**PA,** preliminary assessment, or policy analyst.

**PAA,** Priority Abatement Areas.

**PAC,** political action committee.

**PADRE,** Particle Analysis and Data Reduction Program.

**PAH,** polycyclic aromatic hydrocarbon.

**PAHO,** Pan American Health Organization.

**PAI,** performance audit inspection.

**PAIR,** Preliminary Assessment Information Rules.

**PAN,** perozyacetyl nitrate.

**PAN NA,** Pesticides Action Network, North America.

**PAPR,** powered air purifying respirator.

**PAS,** Planning Advisory Service.

**PASA,** Participating Agency Service Agreement.

**PAWS,** Progressive Animal Welfare Society.

**Pb,** lead.

**PBB,** polybrominated biphenyls.

**PBL,** planetary boundary layer.

**PBNA,** phenyl-ß-naphthylamine.

**PBR,** plant breeder's rights.

**PCARRD,** Philippine Council for Agriculture and Resources Research and Development.

**PCB,** polychlorinated biphenyls.

**PCC,** Population Crisis Committee.

**PCDD,** polychlorinated dibenzodioxin.

**PCDF,** polychlorinated dibenzofuran.

**PCE,** pollution control equipment.

**PCEQ,** President's Commission on Environmental Quality.

**pCi/L,** picocuries of radioactivity per liter.

**PCM,** Phase Contrast Microscopy.

**PCNB,** pentachloronitrobenzene.

**PCP,** pentachlorophenyl, or Penta.

**PD,** Policy Determination.

**PDR,** particulate data reduction.

**PEEM,** Panel of Experts on Environmental Management.

**PEL,** permissible (or personal) exposure limit.

**PEPE,** prolonged elevated pollution episode.

**PET,** polyethylene terephthelate.

**PETA,** People for the Ethical Treatment of Animals.

**PF,** potency factor, or protection factor.

**pH,** pHydrion, measuring hydrogen ion concentration.

**PHC,** principal hazardous constituent.

**PHS,** Public Health Service, or prostaglandin H synthase.

**PHSA,** Public Health Service Act.

**PIC,** products of incomplete combustion, public information center, or prior informed consent.

**PIGS,** Pesticides in Groundwater Strategy.

**PIP,** public involvement program, or pesticide information profiles.

**PIRG,** Public Interest Research Group.

**PLIRRA,** Pollution Liability Insurance and Risk Retention Act.

**PM,** particulate matter, or program manager.

**PMEL,** Pacific Marine Environmental Laboratory.

**PMN,** Premanufacture Notice (or Notification).

**PMR,** pollutant mass rate.

**PNA,** polynuclear aromatic hydrocarbons.

**PNRS,** Preliminary Natural Resources Survey.

**PNV,** potential natural vegetation.

**POC,** point of compliance.

**POE,** point of entry (or exposure).

**POGO,** privately owned/government-operated.

**POHC,** principal organic hazardous constituent.

**POI,** point of interception.

**POLREP,** pollution report.

**POM,** particulate (or polycyclic) organic matter.

**POTW,** privately (or publicly) owned treatment works.

**POU,** point of use.

**PPA,** Pesticide Producers Association, or planned program accomplishment.

**ppb,** parts per billion.

**PPC,** personal protective clothing.

**p-PDA,** p-Phenylenediamine, p-Diaminobenzene, or 1,4-Benzenediamine.

**PPE,** personal protective equipment.

**PPIS,** Pesticide Product Information System.

**ppm,** parts per million.

**PPSP,** Power Plant Siting Program.

**ppt,** parts per trillion.

**ppth,** parts per thousand.

**PR,** preliminary review.

**PRACIPA,** Program Andino Cooperativo de Investigación en Papa.

**PRAPAC,** Programme Regional d'Ameliration de la Cuture de Pomme de Terre en Afrique Centrale.

**PRB,** Population Reference Bureau.

**PRECODEPA,** Programa Regional Cooperativa de Papa (Cooperative Regional Potato Program).

**PRMP,** Plutonium Recovery Modification Project.

**PROCIPA,** Program Cooperativo de Investigaciónes en Papa.

**PRP,** potentially responsible party.

**PSA,** public service announcement.

**P&SA,** Packers and Stockyard Administration.

**PS (AM),** point source (ambient monitoring).

**PSD,** prevention of significant deterioration.

**PSI,** Pollutant Standard Index, or pounds (pressures) per square inch.

**PSTN,** Pesticide Safety Team Network.

**PTBBA,** p-tert-butylbenzoic acid.

**PTBT,** p-tert-butyltoluene.

**PTE,** potential to emit.

**PTFE,** polytetrafluoroethylene (Teflon).

**Pu,** plutonium.

**PUC,** public utility commission.

**PUD,** planned unit development.

**PURPA,** Public Utilities Regulatory Policy Act.

**PVC,** polyvinyl chloride.

**PVPA,** Plant Variety Protection Act.

**PWF,** Pacific Whale Foundation.

**PWG,** pathology working group.

**PWS(S),** public water supply (system).

**Q,** one billion (British thermal units).

**qBtu,** quadrillion British thermal units.

**QCA,** Quiet Communities Act.

**R,** Rankine temperature scale, or Roentgen.

**RA,** reasonable alternative, resource allocation, risk analysis, risk assessment, remedial action, regulatory alternatives, regional administrator, or resource assistant.

**RAC,** Radiation Advisory Committee, Regional Asbestos Coordinator, Recycling Advisory Council, or Response Action Coordinator.

**RACT,** reasonably available control technology.

**RAD,** radiation adsorbed dose.

**RAM,** radioactive material.

**RAMP,** Rural Abandoned Mine Program.

**RAMS,** Regional Air Monitoring System.

**RAN,** Rainforest Action Network.

**RAP,** Radon Action Program, Remedial Accomplishment (or Action) Plan, Response Action Plan, or Regional Air Pollution.

**RBC,** rotating biological contactor.

**RBE,** relative biological effectinvess.

**RCC,** Radiation Coordinating Council.

**RCRA,** Resource Conservation and Recovery Act.

**RCRO,** Regional Coordination and Referral Office.

**RCU,** Region Co-ordinating Unit.

**R&D,** research and development.

**RDB,** Red Data Books.

**RDF,** refuse-derived fuel.

**RDMHC,** Regional Disaster Medical/Health Coordination (or Coordinator).

**rDNA,** recombinant DNA.

**RDX,** cyclonite.

**RE,** reportable event, reasonable efforts.

**REA,** Rural Electrification Administration.

**REAP,** Regional Enforcement Activities Plan.

**REE,** rare earth elements.

**REEP,** Review of Environmental Effects of Pollutants.

**REM,** Roentgen equivalent, man; a measurement of radiation for humans.

**RERF,** Radiation Effects Research Foundation.

**RESOLVE,** Center for Environmental Conflict Resolution.

**RFD,** reference dose values.

**RFF,** Resources for the Future.

**RFI,** remedial field investigations.

**RFLP,** restriction fragment length polymorphisms.

**RI,** remedial investigation, or reconnaissance inspection.

**RIA,** regulatory impact analysis (or assessment).

**RIC,** Radon Information Center, or RTP Information Center.

**RI/FS,** remedial investigation/feasibility study.

**RIP,** rolling injection planter.

**RLL,** rapid and large leakage.

**RMCL,** recommended maximum contaminent level.

**RMI,** Rocky Mountain Institute.

**RMIS,** Resources Management Information System.

**RMP,** resource management plan.

**Rn,** radon.

**RNA,** ribonucleic acid, or research natural area.

**RNRF,** Renewable Natural Resources Foundation.

**RO,** reverse osmosis.

**ROD,** record of decision.

**ROG,** reactive organic gases.

**ROMCOE,** Rocky Mountain Center on the Environment.

**ROSCOP,** Report on Oceanographic Cruises and Data Stations.

**ROW,** rights-of-way.

**RP,** respirable particulates, or responsible party.

**RPAR,** Rubuttable Presumption Against Registration (Special Review).

**RPIS,** Regional Plant Introduction Station.

**RPISU,** radon progeny integrating sampling unit.

**RPM,** remedial project manager, or revolutions per minute.

**RPO,** regional planning (or program) officer.

**RQ,** reportable quantity.

**RR,** respiration rate.

**RRC,** regional response center, or Rodale Research Center.

**RRfd,** risk reference dose.

**RRT,** requisite remedial technology, or regional response team.

**RSCC,** Regional Sample Control Center.

**RSP,** respirable suspended particulates.

**RSSA,** Resource Services Support Agreements.
**RT,** regional total.
**RTC,** Rails-to-Trails Conservancy.
**RTCM,** reasonable transportation control measure.
**RTEC(S),** Registry of Toxic Effects of Chemicals (or Chemical Substances).
**RTEX,** a chemical's location number in the Registry of Toxic Effects of Chemicals (RTEC).
**RTP,** Research Triangle Park.
**RUP,** restricted use pesticide.
**RWC,** residential wood combustion.

**S,** sulfur.
**SA,** Sunshine Act.
**S&A,** sampling (or surveillance) and analysis.
**SAARC,** South Asian Association for Regional Cooperation.
**SAB,** Science Advisory Board.
**SAC,** suspended and cancelled pesticides.
**SACA,** Student Action Corps for Animals.
**SACEP,** South Asian Cooperative Environment Programme.
**SAE,** Society of Automotive Engineers.
**SAF,** Society of American Foresters.
**SAFGAR,** Semi-Arid Grain Research and Development.
**SAIIC,** South and Meso American Indian Information Center.
**SANE,** sulfur and nitrogen emissions.
**SAP,** scientific advisory panel.
**SAPL,** Society for Animal Protective Legislation.
**SAPPRAD,** Southeast Asian Program for Potato Research and Development.
**SARA,** Superfund Amendments and Reauthorization Act.
**SASS,** Source Assessment Sampling System.
**SBB,** Statistics and Biomathematics Branch.
**SBI,** sustainable biosphere initiative.
**SBS,** sick building syndrome.
**SC,** Sierra Club.
**SCA,** Student Conservation Association.
**SCAW,** Scientists Center for Animal Welfare.
**SCB,** Society for Conservation Biology.
**SCC,** Source Classification Code.
**SCE,** sister chromatid exchange.
**SCFM,** standard cubic feet per minute.
**SCLDF,** Sierra Club Legal Defense Fund.
**SCMU,** Species Conservation Monitoring Unit.
**SCOPE,** Scientific Committee on Problems of the Environment.
**SCORP,** Statewide Comprehensive Outdoor Recreation Plan.
**SCS,** Soil Conservation Service, or supplementary control strategy (or system).
**SCSA,** Soil Conservation Society of America.
**SCSP,** Storm and Combined Sewer Program.
**SDWA,** Safe Drinking Water Act.
**Se,** selenium.
**SEAM,** Surface, Environment, and Mining.
**SEAS,** Strategic Environmental Assessment System.
**SECC,** Safe Energy Communication Council.
**SECP,** State Energy Conservation Program.

**SEM,** Scanning Electron Microscopy.
**SENSOR,** Sentinel Event Notification Systems for Occupational Risk.
**SER,** Society for Ecological Restoration.
**SERC,** State Emergency Response Commission.
**SERI,** Solar Energy Research Institute.
**SF,** Superfund.
**SHWL,** seasonal high water level.
**SI,** International System of Units, or spark ignition.
**SIC,** Standard Industrial Code.
**SIF,** Social Investment Forum.
**SIL,** speech interference level.
**SIMS,** secondary ion-mass spectometry.
**SIP,** State Implementation Plan.
**SIPI,** Scientists' Institute for Public Information.
**SIS,** Special Isotope Separation.
**SIT,** student-in-training.
**SITE,** Superfund Innovative Technology Evaluation.
**SLAMS,** State/Local Air Monitoring Station.
**SMCRA,** Surface Mining Control and Reclamation Act.
**SMSL,** Soil Microbiol Systems Laboratory.
**SNAAQS,** Secondary National Ambient Air Quality Standards.
**SNAP,** Significant Noncompliance Action Program, or Systems for Nuclear Auxiliary Power.
**SNARL,** suggested no adverse response level.
**SNC,** significant noncompliers.
**SNOTEL,** snow telemetry.
**SNUR,** significant new use rule.
**SO$_2$,** sulfur dioxide.
**SO$_4$,** sulfate.

**SOC,** synthetic organic chemical (or compound).
**SP,** soluble powder.
**SPC,** South Pacific Commission.
**SPCC,** Spill Prevention, Control (or Containment), and Countermeasures Plan.
**SPE,** secondary particulate emissions.
**SPL,** sound pressure level.
**SPLMD,** soil-pore liquid monitoring device.
**SPMS,** special purpose monitoring stations, or strategic planning and management system.
**SPOC,** single point of contact.
**SPREP,** South Pacific Regional Environment Programme.
**SQBE,** small quantity burner exemption.
**SQG,** small quantity generator.
**SRBC,** Susquehanna River Basin Commission.
**SRC,** solvent-refined coal.
**SRO,** state recycling organizations.
**SRS,** Statistical Reporting Service.
**SS,** Superfund surcharge, or settleable (or suspended) solids.
**SSA,** sole-source aquifer.
**SSEIS,** Standard Support and Environmental Impact Statement, or Stationary Source Emissions and Inventory System.
**SSP,** Species Survival Plan.
**SST,** supersonic transport.
**SSURO,** Stop Sale, Use and Removel Order.
**S&T,** science and technology.
**STALAPCO,** State and Local Air Pollution Control Officials.
**STB,** Systemic Toxicology Branch.

**STCC,** Standard Transportation Commodity Code.
**STD,** salinity-temperature-depth.
**STEL,** short-term exposure limit.
**STP,** sewage treatment plant, or standard temperature and pressure.
**Sv,** Sievert, a measure of radiation dose equivalents.
**SV,** sampling visit.
**SWDA,** Solid Waste Disposal Act.
**SWIE,** Southern Waste Information Exchange.
**SWMTEP,** System-Wide Medium-Term Environment Programme.
**SWMU,** Solid Waste Management Unit.
**SWRI,** Sea World Research Institute.

**T½,** half-life.
**TAC,** Technical Advisory Committee.
**TAMS,** Toxic Air Monitoring System.
**TAN,** Technology Alert Network.
**TAPDS,** Toxic Air Pollutant Data System.
**TBT,** tributyltin.
**TC,** target (or toxic) concentration, or technical center.
**TCBO,** trichlorobutylene oxide.
**TCDD,** tetrachlorodibenzo-$p$-dioxin (dioxin).
**TCDF,** tetrachlorodibenzofuran.
**TCE,** trichloroethylene.
**TCLP,** total concentrate (or toxicity characteristic) leachate procedure.
**TCM,** transportation control measures.
**TCP,** Tropical Conservation Program, or trichloropropane.
**TCRI,** Toxic Chemical Release Inventory.
**TCS,** The Coastal Society.

**TD,** toxic dose.
**TDMS,** Toxicology Data Management System.
**TDS,** total dissolved solids.
**T&E,** threatened and endangered.
**TEG,** tetraethylene glycol.
**TEGD,** Technical Enforcement Guidance Document.
**TEM,** Transmission Electron Microscope.
**TEPP,** tetraethyl pyrphosphate.
**TGO,** total gross output.
**THC,** total hydrocarbons.
**THM,** trihalomethane.
**TI,** temporary intermittent, or therapeutic index.
**TIB,** toxicology information brief.
**TIBL,** thermal internal boundary layer.
**TIC,** technical information coordinator, or tentatively identified compounds.
**TIOF,** The International Osprey Foundation.
**TISE,** take it somewhere else (the "Solid Waste Syndrome").
**TITC,** Toxic Substance Control Act Interagency Testing Committee.
**TLD,** thermolyminescent dosimeter (for measuring radiation exposure).
**TLM** or **TL$_{50}$,** median tolerance limit.
**TLV,** threshold limit value.
**TLV-TWA,** threshold limit value—time weighted average.
**TMI,** Three Mile Island.
**TMPRP,** Timber Management Policy Reform Program.
**TMRC,** theoretical maximum residue contribution.
**TNC(I),** The Nature Conservancy (International).
**TNT,** trinitrotoluene.
**TOA,** trace organic analysis.
**TOC,** total organic carbon (or compound).

**TOSCA,** Toxic Substances Control Act.
**TOC,** tetradichlorozylene.
**TPL,** Trust for Public Land.
**TPTH,** triphenyltinhydroxide.
**TPY,** tons per year.
**TRAFFIC,** Trade Records Analysis of Flora and Fauna in Commerce.
**TRC** (or **TRD**), technical review committee (or document).
**TRI,** Toxic Release Inventory, or Tropical Resources Institute.
**TRIP,** Toxic Release Inventory Program.
**TRO,** temporary restraining order.
**TS,** toxic substances.
**TSCA,** Toxic Substances Control Act.
**TSD,** technical support document.
**TSDF,** treatment, storage, and disposal facility.
**TSOC,** totally synthetic organic chemical (or compound).
**TSP,** total suspended particulates.
**TSS,** total suspended solids (nonfilterable), or terminal security system.
**TTHM,** total trihalomethanes.
**TTMA,** Truck Trailer Manufacturers Association.
**TTO,** total toxic organics.
**TVA,** Tennessee Valley Authority.
**TWA,** time-weighted average concentration.
**2,4,5-T,** 2,4,5-trichlorophenoxyacetic acid.
**2,4,5-TP,** Silvex.
**2,4,-D,** 2,4-dichlorophenoxyacetic acid, Dacamine, Esteron, or Weedone.
**TZ,** treatment zone.
**U,** uranium.
**UAA,** United Action for Animals.
**UAQI,** Uniform Air Quality Index.

**UCC,** ultra clean coal.
**UCL,** upper control limit.
**UCS,** Union of Concerned Scientists.
**UFFI,** urea-formaldehyde form insulation.
**UIC,** underground injection control.
**ULV,** ultra-low volume.
**UMTA,** Urban Mass Transit Administration.
**UMTRCA,** Uranium Mill Tailings Radiation Control Act.
**UN,** United Nations.
**UNAC,** United Nations Association of Canada.
**UNCED,** United National Conference on Environment and Development.
**UNCTAD,** United National Conference on Trade and Development.
**UNCTC,** United Nations Centre of Transnational Corporations.
**UNDP,** United Nations Development Programme.
**UNDTCD,** United Nations Department of Technical Cooperation for Development.
**UNEP,** United Nations Environment Programme.
**UNESCO,** United Nations Educational, Scientific, and Cultural Organization.
**UNFPA,** United Nations Fund for Population Activities.
**UNIDO,** United Nations Industrial Development Organization.
**UNITAR,** United Nations Institute for Training and Research.
**UNSCEAR,** United Nations Scientific Committee on the Effects of Atomic Radiation.
**UNSO,** United Nations Sudano-Sahelian Office.
**UPARR,** Urban Park and Recreation Recovery Program.

**USAID,** United States Agency for International Development.

**USBM,** U.S. Bureau of Mines.

**USC,** Unified Soil Classification, or United States Code.

**USDA,** U.S. Department of Agriculture.

**USDOI,** U.S. Department of the Interior.

**USDW,** underground sources of drinking water.

**USEPA,** U.S. Environmental Protection Agency.

**USFS,** U.S. Forest Service.

**USGS,** U.S. Geological Survey.

**USNRC,** U.S. Nuclear Regulatory Commission.

**USPHS,** U.S. Public Health Service.

**UST,** underground storage tank.

**USUNEP,** United States Committee for the United Nations Environment. Program.

**UV,** ultraviolet.

**UZM,** unsaturated zone monitoring.

**VCM,** vinyl chloride monomer.

**VE(O),** visual emissions (observation).

**VIP,** Volunteers in the Park.

**VISTTA,** visibility impairment from sulfur transformation and transport in the atmosphere.

**VITA,** Volunteers in Technical Assistance.

**VMT,** vehicle miles traveled.

**VOC,** volatile organic compounds (or chemicals).

**VP,** vapor pressure.

**VSD,** virtually safe dose.

**VSI,** visual site inspection.

**VSS,** volatile suspended solids.

**WADTF,** Western Atmospheric Deposition Task Force.

**WAOB,** World Agricultural Outlook Board.

**WAP,** Waste Analysis Plan, or Weatherization Assistance Program.

**WARDA,** West Africa Rice Development Association.

**WASWC,** World Association of Soil and Water Conservation.

**WB,** World Bank.

**WCED,** World Commission on Environment and Development.

**WCI,** Wildlife Conservation International.

**WCMC,** World Conservation Monitoring Centre.

**WCS,** World Conservation Strategy.

**WDCS,** Whale and Dolphin Conservation Society.

**WEC,** World Environment Center.

**WED,** World Environment Day.

**WEF,** Water Environment Federation.

**WENDB,** Water Enforcement National Data Base.

**WFC,** World Food Council, United Nations.

**WFCA,** Western Forestry and Conservation Association.

**WFI,** World Forest Institute.

**WFP,** World Food Programme, United Nations.

**WFS,** World Future Society.

**WHEC,** Wildlife Habitat Enhancement Council.

**WHO,** World Health Organization.

**WHOI,** Woods Hole Oceanographic Institution.

**WHWT,** Water and Hazardous Waste Team.

**WICEM,** World Industry Conference on Environmental Management.

**WID,** Women in Development.

**WIPP,** Waste Isolation Pilot Program.

**WL,** working level, or warning letter.

**WLA/TMDL,** Waste Load Allocation/Total Maximum Daily Load.

**WLFA,** Wildlife Legislative Fund of America.

**WLM,** working level month.

**WMI,** Wildlife Management Institute.

**WMO,** World Meteorological Organization.

**WNA,** World Nature Association.

**WPA,** wellhead protection area.

**WPTI,** Wildlife Preservation Trust International.

**WQA,** Water Quality Association.

**WRC,** Water Resources Council.

**WRDA,** Water Resources Development Act.

**WRI,** World Resources Institute.

**WRSIC,** Water Resources Scientific Information Center.

**WSF,** water soluble fraction.

**WSPA,** World Society for the Protection of Animals.

**WSRA,** Wild and Scenic Rivers Act.

**WSSA,** Weed Science Society of America.

**WSTP,** wastewater sewage treatment plant.

**WTMU,** Wildlife Trade Monitoring Unit.

**WTNA,** Wildfowl Trust of North America.

**WWEMA,** Waste and Waterwater Equipment Manufacturers' Association.

**WWF,** World Wildlife Fund, or World Wide Fund for Nature.

**WWTP,** wastewater treatment plant.

**X,** unnamed unit for measuring radiation exposure.

**XBT,** expendable bathythermograph.

**YES,** Youths for Environment and Service.

**Z,** atomic number.

**ZB,** zinc borate.

**Zn,** zinc.

**ZPG,** Zero Population Growth.

**ZRL,** zero risk level.

## The Green Bookshelf

Here is a sampling of recent general books on environmental issues, selected from the flood of books that are published each year on green concerns. They are grouped into several broad categories: Environmental Directories; General Environmental Reference Works; Resource and Action Guides; Environmental Policy, Politics, Theory, and History; Other General Works; and Kid's Green Bookshelf.

### Environmental Directories

*Conservation Directory.* National Wildlife Foundation, annual.

*Your Resource Guide to Environmental Organizations.* John Seredich, ed. Smiling Dolphins Press, 1991.

*The Nature Directory: A Guide to Environmental Organizations.* Susan D. Lanier-Graham. Walker, 1991.

*GAIA: The National Directory of Government and Academic Environmental Agencies.* Terry L. Johnson. Blue Planet, 1991.

*Who Is Who in Service to the Earth: People, Projects,*

*Organizations, Key Words and 41 Visions of a Positive Future.* Hans J. Keller and Daniel Maziarz, eds. VisionLink Education Foundation, 1991. Address: Shelton Cove Road, #184, Waynesville, NC 28786.

*Directory of International Compatible Environmental Data.* Carter Diamondston. Hemisphere, 1990.

*World Directory of Environmental Organizations.* 3rd ed. Thaddeus C. Trzyna and Ilze Gotelli, eds. California Institute of Public Affairs, 1989.

*Directory of National Environmental Organizations.* Available from U.S. Environmental Directories, Box 65156, St. Paul, MN 44165.

### General Environmental Reference Works

*State of the World.* Lester R. Brown et al. Norton, annual.

*World Resources.* World Resources Institute with the United National Environment Programme and the United Nations Development Programme. Oxford University Press, annual.

*Environment.* John Allen, ed. Dushkin, annual.

*Environment Abstracts.* Bowker, annual.

*Green Index, 1991–1992: A State-by-State Report Card on the Nation's Environmental Health.* Institute for Southern Studies Staff. Island Press, 1991.

*The Earth Care Annual.* Russell Wild, ed. Rodale, annual.

*Gaia Atlas of Future Worlds: Challenge and Opportunity in an Age of Change.* Norman Myers. Doubleday, 1991.

*A Dictionary of the Environment: A Practical Guide to Today's Most Important Environmental Issues.* Steve Elsworth. Trafalgar Square, 1991.

*Encyclopedia of Environmental Studies.* William Ashworth. Facts on File, 1990.

*World Wildlife Fund Atlas of the Environment.* Don Hinrichsen, Geoffrey Lean, and Adam Markham. Prentice Hall, 1990.

*The Complete Book of Home Environmental Hazards.* Robert Altman. Facts on File, 1990.

*Encyclopedia of World Problems and Human Potential.* 3rd ed. Bowker, 1990.

*Environmental Bibliography Search Guide.* Environmental Studies Institute Staff, eds. IASB Enviro, 1990.

*A Guide to Gaia: A Survey of the New Science of Our Living Earth.* Michael Allaby. Penguin, 1989.

*The Dictionary of the Environment.* 3rd ed. Michael Allaby. New York University Press, 1989.

*The Earth Report: The Essential Guide in Global Ecological Issues.* Edward Goldsmith and Nicholas Hilyard, eds. Price Stern, 1988.

*Dictionary of Environmental Protection Technology: In English, German, French, Russian.* E. Seidel. Elsevier, 1988.

*Citizen Participation in Environmental Affairs, 1970–1986: A Bibliography.* Frederick Frankena and Joan K. Frankena, eds. AMS Press, 1988.

### Resource and Action Guides

*Fifty Simple Things Businesses Can Do to Save the Earth.* Earthworks Group Staff. Earth Works, 1991

*Save the Earth at Work.* Bennett Information Group Staff. Adams, Inc. (MA), 1991.

*Green Earth Resource Guide.* Cheryl Gorder. Blue Bird, 1991.

*Social and Environmental Change: A Manual for Advocacy and Organizing.* Bunyan Bryant. Caddo Gap Press, 1991.

*This Planet Is MIine: Teaching Environmental Awareness and Appreciation to Children.* Mary Metzger and Cinthya P. Whittaker. Simon & Schuster, 1991.

*The Whole Earth Ecolog: The Best of Environmental Tools and Ideas.* J. Baldwin, ed. Crown, 1990.

*Earth Right: What You Can Do in Your Home, Workplace, and Community to Save Our Environment.* H. Patricia Hynes. Prima, 1990.

*Treating the Earth as If We Plan to Stay: A Resource Guide to Individual Action.* Anita Bash et al. Beyond War Foundation, 1990.

*Green Lifestyle Guide.* Jeremy Rifkin. Henry Holt, 1990.

*Fifty Simple Things You Can Do to Save The Earth.* Earth Works Project Staff. Greenleaf Publications, 1990.

*The Next Step: Fifty More Things You Can Do to Save the Earth.* Earth Works Group Staff. Andrews and McMeel, 1990.

*Design for a Livable Planet: The Eco-Action Guide to Positive Energy.* Jon Naar. HarperCollins, 1990.

*Our Earth, Ourselves: The Action-Oriented Guide to Help You Protect and Preserve Our Environment.* Ruth Caplan and the Staff of Environmental Action. Bantam, 1990.

*Saving the Earth: A Citizen's Guide to Environment Action.* Will Steger and John Bowermaster. Knopf, 1990.

*Ecologue: The Environmental Catalogue and Consumer's Guide for a Safe Earth.* Bruce Anderson. Prentice Hall, 1990.

*Save Our Planet: 750 Everyday Ways You Can Help Clean Up the Earth.* Diane MacEachern. Dell, 1990.

*One Thousand One Ways to Save the Planet.* Bernadette Vallely. Ivy, 1990.

*Two Minutes a Day for a Greener Planet: Quick and Simple Things Americans Can Do to Save the Earth.* Marjorie Lamb. Harper SF, 1990.

*Fifty Simple Things You Can Do to Save the Earth.* Darryl Henriques et al. Ulysses, 1990.

*Call to Action: Handbook for Ecology, Peace and Justice.* Brad Erickson, ed. Sierra Club Books, 1990.

*Clearer, Cleaner, Safer, Greener: A Blueprint for Detoxifying Your Environment.* Gary Null. Villard, 1990.

*The Green Lifestyle Guide: 1001 Ways to Heal the Earth.* Jeremy Rifkin and the Greenhouse Crisis Foundation, ed. Henry Holt, 1990.

*The Global Ecology Handbook: What You Can Do About the Environmental Crisis.* Global Tomorrow Coalition. Beacon, 1990.

*Design for a Livable Planet: How You Can Help Clean Up the Environment.* Jon Naae. HarperCollins, 1990.

*Heloise: Hints for a Healthy Planet.* Heloise. Putnam, 1990.

*Design for a Livable Planet: The Eco-Action Guide to Positive Energy.* Jon Naar. HarperCollins, 1990.

*Embracing the Earth: Choices for Environmentally Sound Living.* D. Mark Harris and Lyn Pusztai. Noble Press, 1990.

*The Healthy Home.* Linda Mason, 1989.

*The Better Community Catalog: A Sourcebook of Ideas, People, and Strategies for Improving the Place Where You Live.* Partners for Livable Places. Acropolis, 1989.

## Environmental Policy, Politics, Theory, and History

*Biosphere Politics: A New Consciousness for a New Century.* Jeremy Rifkin. Crown, 1991.

*At Odds with Progress: Americans and Conservation.* Bret Wallach. University of Arizona Press, 1991.

*Ethics of Environmental Concern.* 2nd ed. Robin Atfield. University of Georgia Press, 1991.

*The Balance of Nature?: Ecological Issues in the Conservation of Species and Communities.* Stuart L. Pimm. University of Chicago Press, 1991.

*Taking Sides: Clashing Views on Controversial Environmental Issues,* 4th ed. Theodore Goldfarb. Dushkin, 1991.

*Environmental Decision Making: A Multidisciplinary Perspective.* Richard A. Chechile et al., eds. Van Nostrand Reinhold, 1991.

*Tomorrow Will Be Too Late: East Meets West on Global Ecology.* Rolf Edberg and Alexei Yablokov. University of Arizona Press, 1991.

*Defending the World: The Politics and Diplomacy of the Environment.* David Adamson. St. Martin, 1991.

*Ecological Economics: Energy, Environment and Society.* Juan Martinez-Alier. Basil Blackwell, 1991.

*A Primer on Environmental Policy Design.* R.W. Hahn. Gordon and Breach, 1991.

*Environmental Science: Sustaining the Earth.* 3rd ed. G. Tyler Miller, Jr. Wadsworth, 1991.

*Ecology, Community and Lifestyle: Outline of an Ecosophy.* Arne Naess. Cambridge University Press, 1990.

*Upstream–Downstream: Issues in Environmental Ethics.* Donald Scherer, ed. Temple University Press, 1990.

*Environmental Disputes: Community Involvement in Conflict Resolution.* James E. Crowfoot and Julia M. Wondolleck. Island Press, 1990.

*Environmental Accidents: Personal Injury and Public Responsibility.* Richard H. Gaskins. Temple University Press, 1990.

*Environmental Science: A Global Concern.* William P. Cunningham and Barbara Saigo. William C. Brown, 1990.

*Between Two Worlds: Science, th Environmental Movement and Policy Choice.* Lynton K. Caldwell. Cambridge University Press, 1990.

*Natural Resource Conservation: An Ecological Approach.* 5th ed. Oliver S. Owen and Daniel D. Chiras. Macmillan, 1990.

*Discordant Harmonies: A New Ecology for the Twenty-First Century.* Daniel B. Botkin. Oxford University Press, 1990.

*International Environmental Diplomacy: The Management and Resolution of Transfrontier Environmental Problems.* John E. Carroll, ed. Cambridge University Press, 1990.

*Global Environmental Issues and International Business: A Manager's Guide to Trends, Risks and Opportunities.* Bradford S. Gentry. BNA, 1990.

*International Environmental Policy: Emergence and Dimensions.* 2nd ed. Lynton K. Caldwell. Duke, 1990.

*Understanding Who Wins: Organizational Behavior and Environmental Politics.* Leah J. Wilds. Garland, 1990.

*Probability Is All We Have: Uncertainties, Delays and Environmental Policy Making.* James K Hammitt. Garland, 1990.

*Beyond the Fray: Reshaping America's Environmental Response.* Daniel D. Chiras. Johnson (Boulder, CO), 1990.

*Endangered Planet: Environmental Policy for the 1990's.* James J. Florio. Pharos, 1990.

*Prosperity Without Pollution: The Prevention Strategy for Industry and Consumers.* Joel S. Hirschhorn and Kirsten U. Oldenburg. Van Nostrand Reinhold, 1990.

*We Speak for Ourselves: Social Justice, Race, and Environment.* Robert Bullard et al. Panos Institute, 1990.

*International Environmental Policy: Emergence and Dimensions.* 2nd ed. Lynton Keith Caldwell. Duke University Press, 1990.

*The Economy of the Earth: Philosophy, Law and the Environment.* Mark Sagoff. Cambridge University Press, 1990.

*Natural Resource Policymaking: A Framework for Developing Countries.* William Ascher and Robert Healy. Duke University Press, 1990.

*Environmental Politics and Policy.* 2nd ed. Walter A. Rosenbaum. Congressional Quarterly, 1990.

*Environmental Policy in the 1990s.* Norman Vig and Michael Kraft. Congressional Quarterly, 1990.

*Audubon Perspectives: The Fight for Survival.* Roger L. Disilvestro. Wiley, 1990.

*The Environment at Risk: Responding to Growing Dangers.* National Issues Forum Staff. Kendall-Hunt, 1990.

*Earth Education . . . a New Beginning.* Steve Van Matre. Institute Earth, 1990.

*Saving the Earth: The History of a Middle Class Millenarian Movement.* Steven M. Gelber and Martin L. Cook, University of California Press, 1990.

*Managing Planet Earth: Perspectives on Population, Ecology and the Law.* Miguel A Santos. Greenwood, 1990.

*Managing Leviathan: Environmental Politics and the Administrative State.* Robert Paehlke and Douglas Torgerson, eds. Broadview, 1990.

*The Rights of Nature: A History of Environmental Ethics.* Roderick Nash. University of Wisconsin Press, 1989.

*Policy Through Impact Assessment: Institutionalized Analysis as a Policy Strategy.* Robert V. Bartlett, ed. Greenwood, 1989.

*The Political Limits of Environmental Regulation: Tracking the Unicorn.* Bruce Yandle. Greenwood, 1989.

*Ecology and History: The Greening of the West since 1880.* Anna Bramwell. Yale University Press, 1989.

*Earth Rising: Ecological Belief in An Age of Science.* David Oates. Oregon State University Press, 1989.

*Social Change, Energy, and Land Ethics.* Bunyan Bryant. Prakken, 1989.

*Our Precious Habitat: Fifteen Years Later.* 3rd ed. Melvin A. Benarde. Wiley, 1989.

*Earth Conference One: Sharing a Vision for Our Planet.* Anuradha Vittachi. Shambhala, 1989.

*Funding Environmental Programs: An Examination of Alternatives.* Evelyn Shields and Mark Miller, eds. National Governors, 1989.

*Environmental Politics and Policy: Theories and Evidence.* James P. Lester, ed. Duke University Press, 1989.

*Ethics and Environmental Responsibility.* Nigel Dower. Gower, 1989.

*Making the World Less Safe: The Unhealthy Trend in Health, Safety and Environmental Regulation.* Richard L. Stroup and John C. Goodman. National Center for Policy, 1989.

*Managing the Environmental Crisis: Incorporating Competing Values in Natural Resource Administration.* Daniel H. Henning and William R. Mangum. Duke University Press, 1989.

*Perspectives in Ecological Theory.* Jonathan Roughgarden et al., eds. Princeton University Press, 1989.

*Crossroads: Environmental Priorities for the Future.* Peter Borrelli, ed. Island Press, 1988.

*The ends of the Earth: Perspectives of Modern Environmental History.* Donald Worster, ed. Cambridge University Press, 1989.

*The Brundtland Challenge and the Cost of Inaction.* Alex Davidson and Michael Dence, eds. Gower, 1988.

*Nothing to Lose but Our Lives: Empowerment to Oppose Industrial Hazards in a Transitional World.* David Bemdo et al., eds. LRIS, 1988.

*Conservation for People: Alternatives for the Future.* David Pitt, ed. Routledge, 1988.

*Environmental Communication and Public Relations Handbook.* E. Bruce Harrison et al. Government Institute, 1988.

*The Cassandra Conference: Resources and the Human Predicament.* Paul R. Enrlich and John P. Holdren, eds. Texas A&M University Press, 1988.

*The Quiet Crisis and the Next Generation.* rev. ed. Stewart L. Udall. Gibbs Smith, 1988.

*Ecology, Meaning, and Religion.* Roy A. Rappaport. North Atlantic, 1988.

*Environmental Protection Policy.* Eckard Rehbinder and Richard Stewart. De Gruyter, 1988.

*Environmental Policy, Assessment and Communication.* David Canter et al. Gower, 1988.

*Environmental and Natural Resource Economics.* 2nd ed. Thomas Tietenberg. Scott Foresman, 1988.

*The Theory of Environmental Policy.* 2nd ed. William J. Baumol and Wallace E. Oates. Cambridge University Press, 1988.

*Environmental Justice.* Peter S. Wenz. State University of New York Press, 1988.

*American Environmental History.* 2nd ed. Joseph M. Petulla. Macmillan, 1988.

*New Ideas in Environmental Education.* Salvano Briceno and David Pitt, eds. Routledge Chapman and Hall, 1988.

## Other General Works

*Leaving Eden: To Protect and Manage the Earth.* E.G. Nisbet. Cambridge University Press, 1991.

*The World Watch Reader: On Global Environmental Issues.* Lester R. Brown, ed. Norton, 1991.

*A Critique for Ecology.* Robert H. Peters. Cambridge University Press, 1991.

*Environment, Resources and Conservation.* Susan Owens and Peter L. Owens. Cambridge University Press, 1991.

*Eco-Bluff Your Way to Greenism.* Paul S. Wachtel and Jeffrey A. McNeely. Bonus, 1991.

*The Environmental Wars: Reports from the Front Lines.* David Day. St. Martin's, 1990; Ballantine, 1991. "An encyclopedia of ecological activism."

*Sustaining Earth: Response to the Environmental Threat.* D.J. Angell et al., eds. St. Martin's, 1991.

*The Global Citizen.* Donella H. Meadows. Islands Press, 1991.

*Earthkeepers: Environmental Perspectives on Hunger, Poverty, and Injustice.* Art Meyer and Jocele Meyer. Herald, 1991.

*A New Earth: How We Can Quickly Heal the Planet, End the Greenhouse Effect, and Save Our Lives.* Larry Ephron. People Future, 1991.

*Raising an Earth Friendly Child: The Keys to Your Child's Happy, Healthy Future.* Debbie J. Tilsworth and Timothy Tilsworth, eds. Raven Press (AK), 1991.

*World on Fire: Saving an Endangered Earth.* George J. Mitchell. Macmillan, 1991.

*The Green Machine: Ecololgy and the Balance of Nature.* Wallace Arthur. Basil Blackwell, 1991.

*Demanding Clean Food and Water: The Fight for a Basic Human Right.* Joan Goldstein. Plenum, 1990.

*Sustaining the Earth.* John Young. Harvard University Press, 1990.

*Preserving the Global Environment: The Challenge of Shared Leadership.* Jessica T. Mathews, ed. Norton, 1990.

*The Environmental Revolution.* Prince Philip. Beekman, 1990.

*Environmental Advocacy: Concepts, Issues and Dilemmas.* Bunyan Bryant. Caddo Gap Press, 1990.

*Mending the Earth: A World for Our Grandchildren.* Paul Rothkrug and Robert Olson, eds. North Atlantic, 1990.

*Project Earth: Preserving the World God Created.* William B. Badke. Multnomah, 1990.

*The Earth Is the Lord's: Handle with Care.* Vicki Hesterman. Accord, 1990.

*Preserving the World Ecology.* Steven Anzovin, ed. H.W. Wilson, 1990.

*One Earth.* Kenneth Brower. Collins SF, 1990.

*Making Peace with the Planet.* Barry Commoner. Pantheon, 1990.

*When the Bough Breaks: Our Children, Our Environment.* Lloyd Timberlake and Laura Thomas. InBook, 1990.

*Natural Resources for the 21st Century.* R. Neil Sampson and Dwight Hair, eds. Island Press, 1990.

*Conservation of Natural Resources.* Gary Klee. Prentice Hall, 1990.

*Natural Resource Economics: Conservation and Exploitation.* Philip A. Neher. Cambridge University Press, 1990.

*Biologic: Environmental Protection by Design.* David Wann. Johnson Books, 1990.

*Reclaiming America: Restoring Nature to Culture.* Richard Cartwright Austin. Creekside Press, 1990. Address: P.O. Box 331, Abingdon, VA 24210.

*Spiritual Ecology: A Guide for Reconnecting with Nature.* Jim Nollman. Bantam, 1990.

*Our Earth, Ourselves.* Ruth Caplan. Bantam, 1990.

*Caring For Planet Earth: The World Around Us.* Hazel Lucas. Lion USA, 1990.

*Out of the Earth: Civilization and the Life of the Soil,* by Daniel Hillel. New York: Free Press/Macmillan, 1990.

*One Earth, One Future: Our Changing Global Environment.* Washington, DC: National Academy Press, 1990.

*In Search of Environmental Excellence: Moving Beyond Blame.* by Bruce Piasecki and Peter Asmus. New York: Simon & Schuster, 1990.

*The Environment: How Shall We Care for the Environment?* New York: Facts On File, 1990.

*Imperiled Planet: Restoring Our Endangered Ecosystems.* Edward Goldsmith et al. MIT Press, 1990.

*Global Ecology: Towards a Science of the Biosphere.* Mitchell B. Rambler et al., eds. Academic, 1989.

*The Nature of the Environment.* Andrew Goudie. Basil Blackwell, 1989.

*Costing the Earth.* Ronald Banks, ed. Schalkenbach, 1989.

*The Nature of Conservation: A Race Against Time.* Getty Conservation Institute Staff and Philip Ward. J.P. Getty Trust, 1989.

*Our Poisoned Planet: Can We Save It?.* Oliver Trager, ed. Facts On File, 1989.

*Ecology and Our Endangered Life-Support Systems.* Eugene P. Odum. Sinauer, 1989.

*Ariadne's Thread: In Search of a Greener Future.* Mary E. Clark. St. Martin's, 1989.

*The End of Nature.* Bill McKibben. Random House, 1989.

*The Fragile Environment.* R.A. Laskey and L.E. Friday, eds. Cambridge University Press, 1989.

*Saving America's Countryside: A Guide to Rural Conservation.* Samuel N. Stokes et al. Johns Hopkins University Press, 1989.

### Kid's Green Bookshelf

*E For Environment: An Annotated Bibliography of Children's Books with Environmental Themes.* Patti Sinclair. Bowker, 1992.

*I Can Help,* by Merry Fleming Thomasson (Thomasson-Grant, 1992). For children ages 2-7.

*Grover's 10 Terrific Ways to Help Our Wonderful World* (Random House, 1992), for children preschool and kindergarten.

*Dinosaurs to the Rescue!: A Guide to Protecting Our Planet,* by Laurie Krasny Brown and Marc Brown (Little, Brown, 1992). For children preschool-grade 3.

*Endangered Plants.* Elaine Landau. Watts, 1992. For children grades 3-5.

*The Berenstain Bears Don't Pollute (Anymore),* by Stan and Jan Berenstain (Random House, 1991), for children preschool-grade 1.

*Teenage Mutant Ninja Turtles ABC's for a Better Planet* (Random House, 1991). For children preschool-grade 3.

*The Big Green Book.* Fred Pearce. Grosset & Dunlap, 1991. For children ages 7-10.

*Environmental Science Projects: A Source Guide* (Gordon Press, 1991).

*The American Wilderness and Its Future: Conservation Versus Use.* Edward F. Dolan. Watts, 1991. For children grades 9-12.

*Earth Action!: A Guide to Saving the Planet.* Debbie Silver and Bernadette Vallely. Farrar, Straus, & Giroux, 1991. For grades 9-12.

*Save the Earth: An Action Handbook for Kids.* Betty Miles. Knopf, 1991. For grades 5 and up.

*How Green Are You?* David Bellamy. Crown, 1991. For grades 1-4.

*The Environmental Detective Kit.* Douglas Herridge and Susan Hughes. HarperCollins, 1991. For grades 3 and up.

*One World.* Michael Foreman. Arcade, 1991. For grades 2-5.

*Protecting Our Planet.* Ava Drutman and Susan Zuckerman. Good Apple, 1991. For grades 4-8.

*What on Earth You Can Do with Kids.* Robyn Spizman and Marianne Garber. Good Apple, 1991. For grades 1-5.

*Protecting Our Planet—Primary Grades.* Ava D. Drutman. Good Apple, 1991. For grades 1-3.

*My First Green Book.* Angela Wilkes. Knopf, 1991. for Grades 2-5.

*The Environment: An Annotated Bibliography.* Diane M. Brown. Salem Press, 1991. For young adults.

*50 Simple Things Kids Can Do to Save the Earth.* by The Earth Works Group. Kansas City, MO: Andrews and McMeel, 1990.

*Good Planets Are Hard to Find: An Environmental Information Guide for Kids.* Roma Dehr and Ronald Bazar. Firefly, 1990. For grades 4 and up.

*Earth Book for Kids: Activities to Help Heal the Environment.* Linda Schwartz. Learning Works, 1990. For grades 3-7.

*Camelot World: A Kid's Guide to How to Save the Planet.* Billy Goodman. Avon, 1990. Juvenile.

*Nature's Great Balancing Act: In Our Own Backyard.* E. Jaediker Norsgaard. Dutton, 1990. For grades 4 and up.

*Taking a Stand Against Pollution:* David E. Newton. Watts, 1990. Juvenile.

*Blue and Beautiful: Planet Earth, Our Home.* UN, 1990.

*Taking a Stand Against Environmental Pollution.* Newton. Watts, 1990. For young adults.

## General Environmental Series for Kids

Wildlife at Risk series. Bookwright/Watts. For children grades K-4. *Gorillas* (1991) and *Elephants* (1990), by Ian Redmond; *Wolves* (1992) and *Pandas* (1991), by Gillian Standring; *Bears* (1991) and *Rhinos* (1991), by Malcolm Penny; and *Monkeys* (1992), by Tess Lemmon; *Seals and Sea Lions* (1992), *Turtles and Tortoises* (1992), and *Whales and Dolphins* (1991), by Vassili Papastavrou.

Look Closer series. Dorling Kindersley, 1992. For children grades 1-4. *River Life, Meadow, Tree Life, Tide Pool, Pond Life, Rainforest, Desert Life,* and *Coral Reef.*

World About Us series. Gloucester Press/Franklin Watts. For children grades 2-4. *Toxic Waste* (1992), by Margaret Spence; *Nuclear Waste* (1992), by Brian Gardiner; *Polluting the Oceans* (1991), *Acid Rain* (1991), *The Greenhouse Effect* (1991), *The Ozone Layer* (1991), *Tropical Rainforest* (1991), and *Traffic Pollution* (1991), by Michael Bright; *Recycling* (1991) and *Vanishing Habitats* (1991), by Tony Hare.

Tell Me About Books series. Random House. For children grades 2-5. *Desert Animals,* by Michael Chinery (1992); *Grassland Animals* (1992), *Ocean Animals* (1992), *Rainforest Animals* (1992), and *The World of Animals* (1991), by Tom Stacy.

Lighter Look Books. Millbrook Press. For children grades 2-6. *Poison! Beware! Be an Expert Poison Spotter* (1991) and *What a Load of Trash! Rescue Your Household Waste* (1991), by Steve Skidmore; *Buy Now, Pay Later!: Smart Shopping Counts* (1992), *Make a Splash!: Care about the Ocean* (1992), and *Down the Drain: Explore Your Plumbing* (1991), by Thompson Yardley; and *Worm's Eye View: Make Your Own Wildlife Refuge* (1991), by Kipchak Johnson.

Extinct series. Philip Steele. Watts. For children grades 4-7. *Extinct Land Animals: And Those in Danger of Extinction* (1992), with titles also on *Underwater Creatures* (1991), *Insects* (1992), *Amphibians* (1992), *Birds* (1991), and *Reptiles* (1991).

Ecology Watch series. Dillon/Macmillan. For children

grades 5-up. *Rivers, Ponds and Lakes* (1992), by Anita Ganeri; *Grasslands* (1992), and *Mountains* (1992), by Alan Collinson; *Towns and Cities* (1992), *Polar Lands* (1992), and *Rainforests* (1991), by Rodney Aldis; *Deserts* (1991) and *Seas and Oceans* (1991), by Clint Twist.

Green Issues series. Gloucester Press. For grades 5-8. *Vanishing Species* (1991), by Miles Barton; *Waste Disposal and Recycling* (1991), by Sue Becklake; and *Food and Farming* (1991), by John Becklake and Sue Becklake.

Environmental America series. Millbrook Press, 1991. For children grades 4-6. *The North Central States, The Northeastern States, The Northwestern States, The South Central States, The Southeastern States,* and *The Southwestern State.*

Earth at Risk. Chelsea House. For grades 9-12. *Global Warming* (1992), by Burkhard Bilger; *Acid Rain* (1991), by Peter Tyson; and *Overpopulation* (1992), *Extinction* (1992), and *Recycling* (1991), by Rebecca Stefoff.

Kids' Environment Series. John Muir. *Rads, Ergs, and Cheeseburgers: The Kid's Guide to Energy and the Environment.* Bill Yanda. For grades 3 and up. *The Kid's Environment Book: What's Awry and Why.* Anne Pedersen. For grades 6 and up.

Environment Alert! Series. For grades 3-4. Gareth Stevens, 1991. *Dying Oceans. Fragile Mountains. Vanishing Rain Forests.* All by Paula Hogan.

Environment Series. Crabtree, 1991. For grades 3-4. *Buried in Garbage. Reducing, Reusing, and Recycling.* Both by Bobbie Kalman

World About Us Series. Watts, 1991. For grades K-4. *Recycling. Vanishing Habitats.* Both by Tony Hare.

Caring for Our Earth Series. Enslow, 1991. For grades 1-4. *Caring for Our Air. Caring for Our Forest. Caring for Our Land. Caring for Our People.* All by Carol Greene.

Contemporary Issues Series. Girl Scouts USA, 1990. *Earth Matters: A Challenge for Environmental Action.* Girl Scouts USA staff.

Opposing Viewpoints Series. Greenhaven. For grades 10 and up. *Global Resources: Opposing Viewpoints* (William Dudley et al., eds, 1991). *The Environmental Crisis: Opposing Viewpoints* (Neal Bernards, ed., 1991). *The Environment: Opposing Viewpoints* (David L. Bender and Bruno Leone, eds., 1990).

Opposing Viewpoints Juniors Series. Greenhaven, 1990. For grades 3-6. *The Environment: Distinguishing Between Fact and Opinion.* William Dudley.

Conserving Our World Series. Steck-Vaughn, 1990. For grades 4-9. *Conserving the Polar Regions.* Barbara James. *Farming and the Environment.* Mark Lambert.